FRIDAY 22 JULY 2016 **NUMBER 61653**
PUBLISHED BY AUTHORITY | ESTABLISHED 1665
WWW.THEGAZETTE.CO.UK

Supplement No. 1
of Thursday 21 July 2016

List of Statutory Publications 2015

Contents

Preliminary Information	2
UK Legislation	4
Public general acts	4
Public general acts - explanatory notes	6
Local acts	7
Measures of the General Synod	7
Other statutory publications	7
Statutory Instruments, by subject heading	8
Statutory Instruments, by number	138
Subsidiary Numbers	157
Scottish Legislation	162
Acts of the Scottish Parliament	162
Acts of the Scottish Parliament - Explanatory notes	162
Other Scottish statutory publications	None listed
Scottish Statutory Instruments, by subject heading	163
Scottish Statutory Instruments, by number	194
Northern Ireland Legislation	199
Acts of the Northern Ireland Assembly	199
Acts of the Northern Ireland Assembly - explanatory notes	199
Other Northern Ireland statutory publications	199
Statutory Rules of Northern Ireland, by subject heading	200
Statutory Rules of Northern Ireland, by number	225
Welsh Assembly Legislation	229
Acts of the National Assembly for Wales	229
Acts of the National Assembly for Wales - Explanatory notes	229
Alphabetical Index	230

Preface

Content and Layout

This list contains details of the statutory publications and accompanying explanatory documents published during the year. It is arranged in three main sections that group the primary and delegated legislation of the United Kingdom, England & Wales, Scotland and Northern Ireland (Statutory Instruments made by the National Assembly for Wales are included within the UK section). Within each section the publications are listed in the same order:

Acts and their Explanatory Notes;

Statutory Instruments or Statutory Rules, arranged under subject headings. Each entry includes, where available or appropriate: the enabling power; the date when the instrument was issued, made and laid and comes into force; a short note of any effect; territorial extent and classification; a note of the relevant EU legislation; pagination; ISBN and price;

A numerical listing of the instruments, with their subject heading. This list also includes any subsidiary numbers in the series: C for commencement orders; L for instruments relating to court fees or procedure in England and Wales; NI for Orders in Council relating only to Northern Ireland; S for instruments relating only to Scotland; W for instruments made by the National Assembly for Wales;

There is a single alphabetical, subject index.

Unpublished Statutory Instruments

Although the majority of Statutory Instruments are formally published, some SIs of limited, local application are not printed but are available online at legislation.gov.uk and are listed in this publication.

Access to Documents

The full text of all legislation and delegated legislation (Statutory Instruments) is available from the The National Archives website, www.legislation.gov.uk on the day of publication. The website contains a complete dataset from 1988 for Acts and 1987 for Statutory Instruments and partial datasets for earlier years.

The full text of the general statutory instruments and statutory rules are also published in the respective annual editions of: Statutory Instruments, Scottish Statutory Instruments, Statutory Instruments made by the National Assembly for Wales and Statutory Rules of Northern Ireland.

Copies of legislation and published delegated legislation can be purchased from:

- . Online
  http://www.tsoshop.co.uk

- Mail, telephone, fax and email
  TSO
  PO Box 29
  Norwich
  NR3 1GN

  Telephone orders and general enquiries (Tel 0333 202 5070 Fax 0333 202 5080).

Copies of non-print instruments unobtainable from The Stationery Office may be obtained from:

The National Archives, Kew, Richmond, Surrey, TW9 4DU (from 1922 onwards – except for the years 1942, 1950, 1951 and up to SI no. 940 of 1952). Please quote repository reference TS37

British Library, Official Publications and Social Sciences Service, 96 Euston Road, London, NW1 2DB (as before, up to 1980)

Belfast Statutory Publications Office, Castle Buildings, Stormont, Belfast, BT4 3SR (non-print Statutory Rules)

Standing Orders

Standing orders can be set up to ensure the receipt of all statutory publications in a particular subject area, without the need to continually scan lists of new publications or place individual orders. The subject categories used can be either broad or very specific. For more information please contact the TSO Standing Orders department on 0333 202 5070, or fax: 0333 202 5080.

Copyright

Legislation from official sources is reproducible freely under waiver of copyright. Full details of which can be found at:
http://www.nationalarchives.gov.uk/doc/open-government-licence/

Most other TSO publications are Crown or Parliamentary copyright. Information about the licensing arrangements for Crown and Parliamentary copyright can be found on The National Archives' website at
http://www.nationalarchives.gov.uk/doc/open-government-licence/.

To find out more about licensing please contact:

Information Policy Team

The National Archives

Kew, Richmond, Surrey

TW9 4DU

psi@nationalarchives.gsi.gov.uk

List of Abbreviations

accord.	accordance	J.	Jersey
art(s).	article(s)	L.	Legal: fees or procedure in courts in E. & W.
c.	chapter	NI.	Northern Ireland
C.	Commencement	para(s).	paragraph(s)
Cl.	Channel Islands	reg(s).	regulation(s)
E.	England	s(s).	section(s)
EC	European Commission	S.	Scotland
EU	European Union	sch(s).	schedule(s)
G.	Guernsey	SI.	Statutory instrument(s)
GB.	Great Britain	SR.	Statutory rule(s) of Northern Ireland
GLA	Greater London Authority	SR & O.	Statutory rules and orders
IOM	Isle of Man	SSI	Scottish Statutory Instrument
		UK.	United Kingdom
		W.	Wales

UK LEGISLATION

Acts

Public General Acts 2006

Commons Act 2006: Elizabeth II. Chapter 26 (correction slip). - 1 sheet: 30 cm. - Correction slip (to ISBN 9780105426066) dated June 2015. - Free

Public General Acts 2013

Finance Act 2013: Chapter 29 (correction slip). - 1 sheet: 30 cm. - Correction slip (to ISBN 9780105429135) dated June 2015. - Free

Marriage (Same Sex Couples) Act 2013: Chapter 30 (correction slip). - 1 sheet: 30 cm. - Correction slip (to ISBN 9780105430131) dated June 2015. - Free

Public General Acts 2014

Anti-Social Behaviour, Crime and Policing Act 2014: Chapter 12 (correction slip). - 1 sheet: 30 cm. - Correction slip (to ISBN 9780105412144) dated July 2015. - Free

Care Act 2014: Chapter 23 (correction slip). - 1 sheet: 30 cm. - Correction slip (to ISBN 9780105423140) dated June 2015. - Free

Immigration Act 2014: Chapter 22 (correction slip). - 1 sheet: 30 cm. - Correction slip (to ISBN 9780105422143) dated June 2015. - Free

Public General Acts 2015

Armed Forces (Service Complaints and Financial Assistance) Act 2015: Chapter 19. - [2], 20p.: 30 cm. - Royal Assent, 26th March 2015. An Act to make provision about service complaints; about financial assistance for the armed forces community. Explanatory notes to assist in the understanding of the Act are available separately as (ISBN 9780105600084). - 978-0-10-540008-0 £6.00

Consumer Rights Act 2015: Chapter 15. - v, [1], 143p.: 30 cm. - Royal Assent, 26th March 2015. An Act to amend the law relating to the rights of consumers and protection of their interests, to make provision about investigatory powers for enforcing the regulation of traders, to make provision about private actions in competition law. Explanatory notes to assist in the understanding of the Act are available separately (ISBN 9780105600046). - 978-0-10-540004-2 £23.75

Control of Horses Act 2015: Chapter 23. - [2], 4, [2]p.: 30 cm. - Royal Assent, 26th March 2015. An Act to make provision for the taking of action in relation to horses which are in public places. Explanatory notes to assist in the understanding of the Act are available separately (ISBN 9780105600121). - 978-0-10-540012-7 £6.00

Corporation Tax (Northern Ireland) Act 2015: Chapter 21. - [1], 87p.: 30 cm. - Royal Assent, 26th March 2015. An Act to make provision for and in connection with the creation of a Northern Ireland rate of corporation tax. Explanatory notes to assist in the understanding of the Act are available separately (ISBN 9780105600107). - 978-0-10-540010-3 £16.00

Counter-Terrorism and Security Act 2015: Chapter 6. - iii, 69p.: 30 cm. - Royal Assent, 12 February 2015. An Act to make provision in relation to terrorism; to make provision about retention of communications data, about information, authority to carry and security in relation to air, sea and rail transport and about reviews by the Special Immigration Appeals Commission against refusals to issue certificates of naturalisation. Explanatory notes to assist in the understanding of the Act are available separately (ISBN 9780105606154). - 978-0-10-540615-0 £14.25

Criminal Justice and Courts Act 2015: Chapter 2. - v, 175p.: 30 cm. - Royal Assent, 12 February 2015. An Act to make provision about how offenders are dealt with before and after conviction; to amend the offence of possession of extreme pornographic images; to make provision about the proceedings and powers of courts and tribunals; to make provision about judicial review. Explanatory notes to assist in the understanding of the Act are available separately (ISBN 9780105602156). With correction slip dated September 2015. - 978-0-10-540215-2 £27.50

Deregulation Act 2015: Chapter 20. - vi, 252p.: 30 cm. - Royal Assent, 26th March 2015. An Act to make provision for the reduction of burdens resulting from legislation for businesses or other organisations or for individuals; make provision for the repeal of legislation which no longer has practical use; make provision about the exercise of regulatory functions. Explanatory notes to assist in the understanding of the Act are available separately (ISBN 9780105600091). - 978-0-10-540009-7 £29.75

European Union (Approvals) Act 2015: Chapter 37. - 8p.: 30 cm. - Royal Assent, 17th December 2015. An Act to make provision approving for the purposes of section 8 of the European Union Act 2011 certain draft decisions under Article 352 of the Treaty on the Functioning of the European Union. Explanatory notes to assist in the understanding of the Act are available separately (ISBN 9780105600268). - 978-0-10-540026-4 £4.25

European Union (Finance) Act 2015: Chapter 32. - [8]p.: 30 cm. - Royal Assent, 21st July 2015. An Act to approve for the purposes of section 7(1) of the European Union Act 2011 the decision of the Council of 26 May 2014 on the system of own resources of the European Union; and to amend the definition of "the Treaties" and "the EU Treaties" in section 1(2) of the European Communities Act 1972 so as to include that decision. Explanatory notes to assist in the understanding of the Act will be available separately as 2015 c.32-EN (ISBN 9780105600213). - 978-0-10-540021-9 £6.00

European Union Referendum Act 2015: Chapter 36. - 66p.: 30 cm. - Royal Assent, 17th December 2015. An Act to make provision for the holding of a referendum in the United Kingdom and Gibraltar on whether the United Kingdom should remain a member of the European Union. Explanatory notes to assist in the understanding of the Act are available separately (ISBN 9780105600251). - 978-0-10-540025-7 £11.00

Finance Act 2015: Chapter 11. - vii, [1], 340p.: 30 cm. - Royal assent, 26 March 2015. An Act to grant certain duties, to alter other duties, and to amend the law relating to the National Debt and the Public Revenue, and to make further provision in connection with finance. Explanatory notes to the Act are available separately (ISBN 9780105600008). - 978-0-10-540000-4 £39.25

Finance (No. 2) Act 2015: Chapter 33. - iv, 239p.: 30 cm. - Royal assent, 18th November 2015. An Act to grant certain duties, to alter other duties, and to amend the law relating to the National Debt and the Public Revenue, and to make further provision in connection with finance. Explanatory notes to the Act are available separately. - 978-0-10-540022-6 £29.75

Health and Social Care (Safety and Quality) Act 2015: Chapter 28. - [2], 12, [2]p.: 30 cm. - Royal Assent, 26th March 2015. An Act to make provision about the safety of health and social care services in England; to make provision about the integration of information relating to users of health and social care services in England; to make provision about the sharing of information relating to an individual for the purposes of providing that individual with health or social care services in England; to make provision for removing individuals convicted of certain offences from the registers kept by the regulatory bodies for health and social care professions; to make provision about the objectives of the regulatory bodies for health and social care professions and the Professional Standards Authority for Health and Social Care; to make provision about the disposal of cases concerning a person's fitness to practise a health of social care profession. Explanatory notes to assist in the understanding of the Act are available separately (ISBN 9780105600176). - 978-0-10-540017-2 £6.00

Health Service Commissioner for England (Complaint Handling) Act 2015: Chapter 29. - [2], 2p.: 30 cm. - Royal Assent, 26th March 2015. An Act to make provision about the handling of complaints by the Health Service Commissioner for England; to require the Commissioner to notify a complainant of the reason for the delay if the investigation of the complaint is not concluded within a twelve month period; to require the Commissioner to lay before Parliament an annual report giving details of how long investigations of complaints have taken to be concluded and progress towards meeting a target of concluding investigations within a twelve month period. Explanatory notes to assist in the understanding of the Act are available separately (ISBN 9780105600183). - 978-0-10-540018-9 £4.25

House of Commons Commission Act 2015: Chapter 24. - [2], 3, [1]p.: 30 cm. - Royal Assent, 26th March 2015. An Act to amend the House of Commons (Administration) Act 1978 so as to make provision about the membership of the House of Commons Commission, so as to confer a new strategic function on the Commission, and so as to make provision about the exercise of functions on behalf of the Commission or its members. Explanatory notes to assist in the understanding of the Act are available separately (ISBN 9780105600138). - 978-0-10-540013-4 £4.25

House of Lords (Expulsion and Suspension) Act 2015: Chapter 14. - [4], 3, [1]p.: 30 cm. - Royal Assent, 26th March 2015. An Act to make provision empowering the House of Lords to expel or suspend members. Explanatory notes to assist in the understanding of the Act will be available separately. - 978-0-10-540003-5 £4.25

Infrastructure Act 2015: Chapter 7. - iv, 130p.: 30 cm. - Royal Assent, 12 February 2015. An Act to make provision for strategic highways companies and the funding of transport services by land; to make provision for the control of invasive non-native species; to make provision about nationally significant infrastructure projects; to make provision about town and country planning; to make provision about the Homes and Communities Agency and Mayoral development corporations; to make provision about the Greater London Authority so far as it exercises functions for the purposes of housing and regeneration; to make provision about Her Majesty's Land Registry and local land charges; to make provision to enable building regulations to provide for off-site carbon abatement measures; to make provision for giving members of communities the right to buy stakes in local renewable electricity generation facilities; to make provision about maximising economic recovery of petroleum in the United Kingdom; to provide for a levy to be charged on holders of certain energy licences; to enable Her Majesty's Revenue and Customs to exercise functions in connection with the Extractive Industries Transparency Initiative; to make provision for underground access to deep-level land for the purposes of exploiting petroleum or deep geothermal energy; to make provision about renewable heat incentives; to make provision about the reimbursement of persons who have paid for electricity connections; to make provision to enable the Public Works Loan Commissioners to be abolished; to make provision about the electronic communications code. Explanatory notes to assist in the understanding of the Act are available separately (ISBN 9780105607151). With correction slip dated June 2015. - 978-0-10-540715-7 £20.75

Insurance Act 2015: Chapter 4. - ii, 17, [1]p.: 30 cm. - Royal Assent, 12 February 2015. An Act to make new provision about insurance contracts; to amend the Third Parties (Rights against Insurers) Act 2010 in relation to the insured persons to whom that Act applies. Explanatory notes to assist in the understanding of the Act are available separately (ISBN 9780105604150). - 978-0-10-540415-6 £6.00

International Development (Official Development Assistance Target) Act 2015: Chapter 12. - [4], 3, [1]p.: 30 cm. - Royal Assent, 26th March 2015. An Act to make provision about the meeting by the United Kingdom of the target for official development assistance (ODA) to constitute 0.7 per cent of gross national income; to make provision for independent verification that ODA is spent efficiently and effectively. Explanatory notes to assist in the understanding of the Act are available separately (ISBN 9780105600015). - 978-0-10-540001-1 £4.25

Local Government (Religious etc. Observances) Act 2015: Chapter 27. - [2], 4, [2]p.: 30 cm. - Royal Assent, 26th March 2015. An Act to make provision about the inclusion at local authority meetings of observances that are, and about powers of local authorities in relation to events that to any extent are, religious or related to a religious or philosophical belief. Explanatory notes to assist in the understanding of the Act are available separately (ISBN 9780105600169). - 978-0-10-540016-5 £6.00

Local Government (Review of Decisions) Act 2015: Chapter 22. - [2], 4p.: 30 cm. - Royal Assent, 26th March 2015. An Act to make provision about the procedure for conducting investigations under Part 3 of the Local Government Act 1974; and to make provision for cases where an authority to which that Part applies takes a decision that affects the holding of an event for a reason relating to public health or safety. Explanatory notes to assist in the understanding of the Act are available separately (ISBN 9780105600114). - 978-0-10-540011-0 £6.00

Lords Spiritual (Women) Act 2015: Chapter 18. - [2], 2p.: 30 cm. - Royal Assent, 26th March 2015. An Act to make time-limited provision for vacancies among the Lords Spiritual to be filled by bishops who are women. Explanatory notes to assist in the understanding of the Act are available separately as (ISBN 9780105600077). - 978-0-10-540007-3 £4.25

Modern Slavery Act 2015: Chapter 30. - iii, [1], 73p.: 30 cm. - Royal Assent, 26th March 2015. An Act to make provision about slavery, servitude and forced or compulsory labour; to make provision about human trafficking; to make provision for an Antislavery Commissioner. Explanatory notes to assist in the understanding of the Act are available separately (ISBN 9780105600190). - 978-0-10-540019-6 £14.25

Mutuals' Deferred Shares Act 2015: Chapter 13. - [4], 3, [1]p.: 30 cm. - Royal Assent, 26th March 2015. An Act to enable the law relating to societies registered and incorporated under the Friendly Societies Act 1992 and certain mutual insurers to be amended to permit or facilitate the issue of deferred shares; and to restrict the voting rights of members who hold such shares. - 978-0-10-540002-8 £4.25

National Insurance Contributions Act 2015: Chapter 5. - ii, 27p.: 30 cm. - Royal Assent, 12 February 2015. An Act to make provision in relation to national insurance contributions. Explanatory notes to assist in the understanding of the Act are available separately (ISBN 9780105605157). - 978-0-10-540515-3 £6.00

National Insurance Contributions (Rate Ceilings) Act 2015: Chapter 35. - 8p.: 30 cm. - Royal Assent, 17th December 2015. An Act to set a ceiling on the main and additional primary percentages, the secondary percentage and the upper earnings limit in relation to Class 1 national insurance contributions. Explanatory notes to assist in the understanding of the Act are available separately (ISBN 9780105600244). - 978-0-10-540024-0 £4.25

Northern Ireland (Welfare Reform) Act 2015: Chapter 34. - [8]p.: 30 cm. - Royal Assent, 25th November 2015. An Act to make provision in connection with social security and child support maintenance in Northern Ireland; to make provision in connection with arrangements under section 1 of the Employment and Training Act (Northern Ireland) 1950. Explanatory notes to assist in the understanding of the Act are available separately (ISBN 9780105600237). - 978-0-10-540023-3 £4.25

Pension Schemes Act 2015: Chapter 8. - vi, 109p.: 30 cm. - Royal Assent, 3rd March 2015. An Act to make provision about pension schemes, including provision designed to encourage arrangements that offer people different levels of certainty in retirement or that involve different ways of sharing or pooling risk and provision designed to give people greater flexibility in accessing benefits and to help them make informed decisions about what to do with benefits. Explanatory notes to assist in the understanding of the Act are available separately (ISBN 9780105608158). With correction slip dated March 2016. - 978-0-10-540815-4 £19.00

Recall of MPs Act 2015: Chapter 25. - ii, 61p.: 30 cm. - Royal Assent, 26th March 2015. An Act to make provision about the recall of members of the House of Commons. Explanatory notes to assist in the understanding of the Act are available separately (ISBN 9780105600145). - 978-0-10-540014-1 £11.00

Self-Build and Custom Housebuilding Act 2015: Chapter 17. - [2], 6p.: 30 cm. - Royal Assent, 26th March 2015. An Act to place a duty on certain public authorities to keep a register of individuals and associations of individuals who wish to acquire serviced plots of land to bring forward self-build and custom housebuilding projects and to place a duty on certain public authorities to have regard to those registers in carrying out planning and other functions. Explanatory notes to assist in the understanding of the Act are available separately (ISBN 9780105600060). - 978-0-10-540006-6 £6.00

Serious Crime Act 2015: Chapter 9. - v, 128p.: 30 cm. - Royal Assent, 3rd March 2015. An Act to amend the Proceeds of Crime Act 2002, the Computer Misuse Act 1990, Part 4 of the Policing and Crime Act 2009, section 1 of the Children and Young Persons Act 1933, the Sexual Offences Act 2003, the Street Offences Act 1959, the Female Genital Mutilation Act 2003, the Prohibition of Female Genital Mutilation (Scotland) Act 2005 and the Terrorism Act 2006; to make provision about involvement in organised crime groups and about serious crime prevention orders; to make provision for the seizure and forfeiture of drug-cutting agents; to make it an offence to possess an item that contains advice or guidance about committing sexual offences against children; to create an offence in relation to controlling or coercive behaviour in intimate or family relationships; to make provision for the prevention or restriction of the use of communication devices by persons detained in custodial institutions; to make provision approving for the purposes of section 8 of the European Union Act 2011 certain draft decisions under Article 352 of the Treaty on the Functioning of the European Union relating to serious crime; to make provision about codes of practice that relate to the exercise and performance, in connection with the prevention or detection of serious crime, of powers and duties in relation to communications. Explanatory notes to assist in the understanding of the Act are available separately (ISBN 9780105609155). With correction slip dated June 2015. - 978-0-10-540915-1 £20.75

Small Business, Enterprise and Employment Act 2015: Chapter 26. - ix, [1], 275p.: 30 cm. - Royal Assent, 26th March 2015. An Act to make provision about improved access to finance for business and individuals; to make provision about regulatory provisions relating to business and certain voluntary and community bodies; to make provision about the exercise of procurement functions by certain public authorities; to make provision for the creation of a Pubs Code and Adjudicator for the regulation of dealings by pub-owning business with their tied pub tenants; to make provision about the regulation of the provision of childcare; to make provision about information relating to the evaluation of education; to make provision about the regulation of companies; to make provision about company filing requirements; to make provision about the disqualification from appointments relating to companies; to make provision about insolvency; to make provision about the law relating to employment. Explanatory notes to assist in the understanding of the Act are available separately (ISBN 9780105600152). - With three correction slips dated September and December 2015, March 2016 respectively. - 978-0-10-540015-8 £32.75

Social Action, Responsibility and Heroism Act 2015: Chapter 3. - [8]p.: 30 cm. - Royal Assent, 12 February 2015. An Act to make provision as to matters to which a court must have regard in determining a claim in negligence or breach of statutory duty. Explanatory notes to assist in the understanding of the Act are available separately (ISBN 9780105603153). - 978-0-10-540315-9 £4.25

Specialist Printing Equipment and Materials (Offences) Act 2015: Chapter 16. - [2], 4p.: 30 cm. - Royal Assent, 26th March 2015. An Act to make provision for an offence in respect of supplies of specialist printing equipment and related materials. Private Members' Bill published 11 September 2014. Explanatory notes to assist in the understanding of the Act are available separately (ISBN 9780105600053). - 978-0-10-540005-9 £6.00

Stamp Duty Land Tax Act 2015: Chapter 1. - [12]p.: 30 cm. - Royal Assent, 12 February 2015. An Act to make provision about stamp duty land tax on residential property transactions. Explanatory notes to assist in the understanding of the Act are available separately (ISBN 9780105601159). - 978-0-10-540115-5 £6.00

Supply and Appropriation (Anticipation and Adjustments) Act 2015: Chapter 10. - [2], 76p.: 30 cm. - Royal Assent, 26th March 2015. An Act to authorise the use of resources for the year ending with 31 March 2015; to authorise both the issue of sums out of the Consolidated Fund and the application of income for that year; and to appropriate the supply authorised for that year by this Act and by the Supply and Appropriation (Anticipation and Adjustments) Act 2014. - 978-0-10-541015-7 £14.25

Supply and Appropriation (Main Estimates) Act 2015: Chapter 31. - [1], 77p.: 30 cm. - Royal Assent, 21st July 2015. An Act to authorise the use of resources for the year ending with 31 March 2016; to authorise both the issue of sums out of the Consolidated Fund and the application of income for that year; and to appropriate the supply authorised for that year by this Act and by the Supply and Appropriation (Anticipation and Adjustments) Act 2015. - 978-0-10-540020-2 £14.25

Public General Acts - Explanatory Notes 2015

Armed Forces (Service Complaints and Financial Assistance) Act 2015: Chapter 19: explanatory notes. - 13, [3]p.: 30 cm. - These notes refer to the Armed Forces (Service Complaints and Financial Assistance) Act 2015 (c.19) (ISBN 9780105400080) which received Royal Assent on 26 March 2015. - 978-0-10-560008-4 £6.00

Consumer Rights Act 2015: Chapter 15: explanatory notes. - 124p.: 30 cm. - These notes refer to the Consumer Rights Act 2015 (c.15) (ISBN 9780105400042) which received Royal Assent on 26th March 2015. With 2 correction slips dated May 2015 & June 2015. - 978-0-10-560004-6 £19.00

Control of Horses Act 2015: Chapter 23: explanatory notes. - [2], 4p.: 30 cm. - These notes refer to the Control of Horses Act 2015 (c.23) (ISBN 9780105400127) which received Royal assent on 26 March 2015. - 978-0-10-560012-1 £4.25

Corporation Tax (Northern Ireland) Act 2015: Chapter 21: explanatory notes. - [1], 20p.: 30 cm. - These notes refer to the Corporation Tax (Northern Ireland) Act 2015 (c.21) (ISBN 9780105400103) which received Royal Assent on 26 March 2015. - 978-0-10-560010-7 £6.00

Counter-Terrorism and Security Act 2015: Chapter 6: explanatory notes. - 38, [1]p.: 30 cm. - These notes refer to the Counter-Terrorism and Security Act 2015 (c.6) (ISBN 9780105406150) which received Royal Assent on 12 February 2015. - 978-0-10-560615-4 £10.00

Criminal Justice and Courts Act 2015: Chapter 2: explanatory notes. - [1], 106p.: 30 cm. - These notes refer to the Criminal Justice and Courts Act 2015 (c.2) (ISBN 9780105402152) which received Royal Assent on 12 February 2015. - 978-0-10-560215-6 £16.50

Deregulation Act 2015: Chapter 20: explanatory notes. - 153p.: 30 cm. - These notes refer to the Deregulation Act 2015 (c.20) (ISBN 9780105400097) which received Royal Assent on 26 March 2015. - 978-0-10-560009-1 £23.25

European Union (Finance) Act 2015: Chapter 32: explanatory notes. - 10p.: 30 cm. - These notes refer to the European Union (Finance) Act 2015 (c. 32) (ISBN 9780105400219) which received Royal Assent on 21 July 2015. - 978-0-10-560021-3 £6.00

Finance Act 2014: Chapter 26: explanatory notes. - 394p.: 30 cm. - These notes refer to the Finance Act 2014 (c. 26) (ISBN 9780105426141) which received Royal assent on 17 July 2014. - 978-0-10-562614-5 £39.25

Finance Act 2015: Chapter 11: explanatory notes. - 254p.: 30 cm. - These notes refer to the Finance Act 2015 (c. 11) (ISBN 9780105400004) which received Royal assent on 26 March 2015. - 978-0-10-560000-8 £29.75

Health and Social Care (Safety and Quality) Act 2015: Chapter 28: explanatory notes. - 12p.: 30 cm. - These notes refer to the Health and Social Care (Safety and Quality) Act 2015 (c.28) (ISBN 9780105400172) which received Royal Assent on 26 March 2015. - 978-0-10-560017-6 £6.00

Health Service Commissioner for England (Complaint Handling) Act 2015: Chapter 29: explanatory notes. - [1], 3p.: 30 cm. - These notes refer to the Health Service Commissioner for England (Complaint Handling) Act 2015 (c.29) (ISBN 9780105400189) which received Royal assent on 26 March 2015. - 978-0-10-560018-3 £4.25

High Speed Rail (Preparation) Act 2013: Chapter 31: explanatory notes. - 8p.: 30 cm. - These notes refer to the High Speed Rail (Preparation) Act 2013 (c. 31) (ISBN 9780105431138) which received Royal assent on 21 November 2013. - 978-0-10-563113-2 £4.25

House of Commons Commission Act 2015: Chapter 24: explanatory notes. - [1], 4p.: 30 cm. - These notes refer to the House of Commons Commission Act 2015 (c.24) (ISBN 9780105400134) which received Royal Assent on 26th March 2015. - 978-0-10-560013-8 £4.25

Infrastructure Act 2015: Chapter 7: explanatory notes. - 50p.: 30 cm. - These notes refer to the Infrastructure Act 2015 (c.7) (ISBN 9780105407157) which received Royal Assent on 12 February 2015. - 978-0-10-560715-1 £10.00

Inheritance and Trustees' Powers Act 2014: Chapter 16: explanatory notes. - 18, [1]p.: 30 cm. - These notes refer to the Intellectual Inheritance and Trustees' Powers Act 2014 (c. 16) (ISBN 9780105416142) which received Royal assent on 14 May 2014. - 978-0-10-561614-6 £5.75

International Development (Official Development Assistance Target) Act 2015: Chapter 12: explanatory notes. - 6p.: 30 cm. - These notes refer to the International Development (Official Development Assistance Target) Act 2015(c. 12) (ISBN 9780105400011) which received Royal assent on 26th March 2015. - 978-0-10-560001-5 £4.25

Local Government (Religious etc. Observances) Act 2015: Chapter 27: explanatory notes. - [1], 3p.: 30 cm. - These notes refer to the Local Government (Religious etc. Observances) Act 2015 (c.27) (ISBN 9780105400165) which received Royal Assent on 26 March 2015. - 978-0-10-560016-9 £6.00

Local Government (Review of Decisions) Act 2015: Chapter 22: explanatory notes. - [1], 4p.: 30 cm. - These notes refer to the Local Government (Review of Decisions) Act 2015 (c.22) (ISBN 9780105400110) which received Royal Assent on 26 March 2015. - 978-0-10-560011-4 £4.25

Lords Spiritual (Women) Act 2015: Chapter 18: explanatory notes. - 5, [3]p.: 30 cm. - These notes refer to the Lords Spiritual (Women) Act 2015 (c.18) (ISBN 9780105400073) which received Royal Assent on 26 March 2015. - 978-0-10-560007-7 £6.00

Modern Slavery Act 2015: Chapter 30: explanatory notes. - 40p.: 30 cm. - These notes refer to the Modern Slavery Act 2015 (c.30) (ISBN 9780105400196) which received Royal Assent on 26th March 2015. - 978-0-10-560019-0 £10.00

National Insurance Contributions Act 2015: Chapter 5: explanatory notes. - 29, [1]p.: 30 cm. - These notes refer to the National Insurance Contributions Act 2015 (c.5) (ISBN 9780105405153) which received Royal Assent on 12 February 2015. - 978-0-10-560515-7 £10.00

Northern Ireland (Welfare Reform) Act 2015: Chapter 34: explanatory notes. - [12]p.: 30 cm. - These notes refer to the Northern Ireland (Welfare Reform) Act 2015 (c.34) (ISBN 9780105400233) which received Royal Assent on 25th November 2015. - 978-0-10-560023-7 £6.00

Pensions Schemes Act 2015: Chapter 8: explanatory notes. - 42p.: 30 cm. - These notes refer to the Pensions Schemes Act 2015 (c.8) (ISBN 9780105408154) which received Royal Assent on 3 March 2015. - 978-0-10-560815-8 £10.00

Recall of MPs Act 2015: Chapter 25: explanatory notes. - [1], 22p.: 30 cm. - These notes refer to the Criminal Justice and Courts Act 2015 (c.25) (ISBN 9780105400141) which received Royal Assent on 26 March 2015. - 978-0-10-560014-5 £6.00

Self-build and Custom Housebuilding Act 2015: Chapter 17: explanatory notes. - [1], 4, [1]p.: 30 cm. - These notes refer to the Self-build and Custom Housebuilding Act 2015 (c. 17) (ISBN 9780105400066) which received Royal assent on 26 March 2015. - 978-0-10-560006-0 £4.25

Serious Crime Act 2015: Chapter 9: explanatory notes. - 94p.: 30 cm. - These notes refer to the Serious Crime Act 2015 (c.9) (ISBN 9780105409151) which received Royal Assent on 3 March 2015. - 978-0-10-560915-5 £16.00

Small Business, Enterprise and Employment Act 2015: Chapter 26: explanatory notes. - 129p.: 30 cm. - These notes refer to the Small Business, Enterprise and Employment Act 2015 (c.26) (ISBN 9780105400158) which received Royal Assent on 26 March 2015. - 978-0-10-560015-2 £20.75

Social Action, Responsibility and Heroism Act 2015: Chapter 3: explanatory notes. - 4p.: 30 cm. - These notes refer to the Social Action, Responsibility and Heroism Act 2015 (c.3) (ISBN 9780105403159) which received Royal Assent on 12 February 2015. - 978-0-10-560315-3 £4.25

Specialist Printing Equipment and Materials (Offences) Act 2015: Chapter 16: explanatory notes. - [1], 4p.: 30 cm. - These notes refer to the Specialist Printing Equipment and Materials (Offences) Act 2015 (c.16) (ISBN 9780105400059) which received Royal Assent on 26 March 2015. - 978-0-10-560005-3 £4.25

Stamp Duty Land Tax Act 2015: Chapter 1: explanatory notes. - [12]p.: 30 cm. - These notes refer to the Stamp Duty Land Tax Act 2015 (c.1) (ISBN 9780105401155) which received Royal Assent on 12 February 2015. - 978-0-10-560115-9 £6.00

Local Acts 2014

Buckinghamshire County Council (Filming on Highways) Act 2014: Chapter ii. - [8]p.: 30 cm. - Royal assent, 17 December 2014. Buckinghamshire County Council (Filming on Highways) Act 2014. An Act to confer powers on Buckinghamshire County Council in relation to filming on highways. - Corrected reprint. - 978-0-10-545798-5 £4.25

Hertfordshire County Council (Filming on Highways) Act 2014: Chapter i. - [8]p.: 30 cm. - Royal assent, 30 January 2014. Hertfordshire County Council (Filming on Highways) Act 2014. An Act to confer powers on Hertfordshire County Council in relation to filming on highways. - Corrected reprint. Please note this Act was originally published on 14th February 2014, this corrected reprint is being issued free of charge to all known recipients of that Act. - 978-0-10-545748-0 £4.25

MEASURES OF THE GENERAL SYNOD

Measures of the General Synod 2015

1 **Care of Churches and Ecclesiastical Jurisdiction (Amendment) Measure 2015**
- [2], 7p.: 30 cm. - Royal Assent, 12 February 2015. A Measure passed by the General Synod of the Church of England to amend the Care of Churches and Ecclesiastical Jurisdiction Measure 1991 and the Ecclesiastical Jurisdiction Measure 1963. - 978-0-10-855765-1 £3.50

2 **Ecclesiastical Property Measure 2015**
- [2], 4p.: 30 cm. - Royal Assent, 12 February 2015. A Measure passed by the General Synod of the Church of England to amend the law relating to certain ecclesiastical land and personal property held for ecclesiastical purposes. - 978-0-10-855766-8 £3.00

3 **Church of England (Pensions) (Amendment) Measure 2015**
- [2], 4p.: 30 cm. - Royal Assent, 12 February 2015. A Measure passed by the General Synod of the Church of England to extend until 31 December 2025 the period within which the Church Commissioners may make capital payments towards the cost of lump sums and pensions due to be paid or payable under certain pension and superannuation schemes. - 978-0-10-855767-5 £3.00

Other statutory publications

Her Majesty's Stationery Office.

Acts of National Assembly for Wales Bound Vol. 2008-2011. - 2 vols (vii, vii, 306, 306; vii, vii, 308-706, 308-706, 707-732 [Tables of effects], 733-778 [Welsh index], 779-823 [English index]: hdbk: 31 cm. - 978-0-11-840550-8 £208.00

Chronological table of the statutes [1235-2014]. - 3v. (xii, 3142p.): hdbk: 25 cm. - 3 vols. not sold separately. Part I Covering the Acts of the Parliaments of England, Great Britain and the United Kingdom from 1235 to the end of 1968; Part II Covering the Acts of the Parliaments of the United Kingdom from 1969 to the end of 1992; Part III Covering the Acts of the Parliaments of the United Kingdom from 1993 to the end of 2014, the Acts of the Parliaments of Scotland from 1424 to 1707, the Acts of the Scottish Parliament from 1999 to the end of 2014, the Acts of the National Assembly for Wales from 2012 to the end of 2014, the Measures of the National Assembly for Wales from 2008 to 2011 and the Church Assembly Measures and General Synod Measures from 1920 to the end of 2014. - 978-0-11-840548-5 £442.50 per set

Statutory instruments made by the National Assembly for Wales 2009. - 3 v. (xxvi, 1-620; iv, 621-1382; iv, 1383-1992p.): hdbk: 31 cm. - 3 vols. not sold separately. Contain: contents of the edition; guide; lists of instruments; text of general WSIs; classified list of local statutory instruments registered during 2009; tables of effects; numerical and issue list 2008, and index. - 978-0-11-840549-2 £250.00

Statutory Instruments

Arranged by Subject Headings

Acquisition of land, England

The Home Loss Payments (Prescribed Amounts) (England) Regulations 2015 No. 2015/1514. - Enabling power: Land Compensation Act 1973, s. 30 (5). - Issued: 20.07.2015. Made: 13.07.2015. Laid: 16.07.2015. Coming into force: 01.10.2015. Effect: S.I. 2014/1966 revoked with savings. Territorial extent & classification: E. General. - 2p.: 30 cm. - 978-0-11-113790-1 £4.25

Acquisition of land, Wales

The Home Loss Payments (Prescribed Amounts) (Wales) Regulations 2015 No. 2015/1878 (W.275). - Enabling power: Land Compensation Act 1973, s. 30 (5). - Issued: 18.11.2015. Made: 09.11.2015. Laid before the National Assembly for Wales: 13.11.2015. Coming into force: 10.12.2015. Effect: S.I. 2008/2845 (W.255) revoked with savings. Territorial extent & classification: W. General. - In English and Welsh. Welsh title: Rheoliadau Taliadau Colli Cartref (Symiau Rhagnodedig) (Cymru) 2015. - 4p.: 30 cm. - 978-0-348-11190-3 £4.25

Aggregates levy

The Aggregates Levy (Northern Ireland Special Tax Credit) Regulations 2015 No. 2015/946. - Enabling power: Finance Act 2001, ss. 30 (1) (2) (3), 30B (6) (7), 30D (7), 45 (2) (5). - Issued: 02.04.2015. Made: 26.03.2015. Laid: 27.03.2015. Coming into force: 01.04.2015. Effect: None. Territorial extent & classification: E/W/S/NI. General. - 4p.: 30 cm. - 978-0-11-113571-6 £4.25

The Aggregates Levy (Registration and Miscellaneous Provisions) (Amendment) Regulations 2015 No. 2015/1487. - Enabling power: Finance Act 2001, ss. 24 (4), 45 (5). - Issued: 15.07.2015. Made: 09.07.2015. Laid: 09.07.2015. Coming into force: 01.08.2015. Effect: S.I. 2001/4027 amended. Territorial extent & classification: E/W/S/NI. General. - 2p.: 30 cm. - 978-0-11-113769-7 £4.25

Agriculture

The Common Agricultural Policy (Amendment) (No. 2) Regulations 2015 No. 2015/1997. - Enabling power: European Communities Act 1972, s. 2 (2), sch. 2, para. 1A. - Issued: 15.12.2015. Made: 07.12.2015. Laid: 09.12.2015. Coming into force: In accord. with reg. 1 (2). Effect: S.I. 2007/75; 2014/3259, 3263 amended. Territorial extent & classification: E/W/S/NI. General. - EC note: These Regulations amend three sets of regulations that implement the CAP of the European Union; With correction slip dated December 2015. - 16p.: 30 cm. - 978-0-11-114178-6 £6.00

The Common Agricultural Policy (Amendment) Regulations 2015 No. 2015/1325. - Enabling power: European Communities Act 1972, s. 2 (2). - Issued: 21.05.2015. Made: 14.05.2015. Laid: 18.05.2015. Coming into force: in accord. with reg. 1. Effect: S.I. 2014/263, 3259 amended. Territorial extent & classification: E/W/S/NI. General. - 4p.: 30 cm. - 978-0-11-113642-3 £4.25

The Organic Products (Amendment) Regulations 2015 No. 2015/1669. - Enabling power: European Communities Act 1972, s. 2 (2) & Finance Act 1973, s. 56 (1). - Issued: 15.09.2015. Made: 08.09.2015. Laid: 10.09.2015. Coming into force: 01.10.2015. Effect: S.I. 2009/842 amended. Territorial extent & classification: E/W/S/NI. General. - 4p.: 30 cm. - 978-0-11-113916-5 £4.25

The Scotland Act 1998 (Functions Exercisable in or as Regards Scotland) Order 2015 No. 2015/211 (S.2). - Enabling power: Scotland Act 1998, s. 30 (3). - Issued: 18.02.2015. Made: 11.02.2015. Coming into force: 28.02.2015. Effect: None. Territorial extent & classification: E/W/S/NI. General. - Supersedes draft S.I. (ISBN 978111121832) issued 21.10.2014. - 4p.: 30 cm. - 978-0-11-112953-1 £4.25

The Single Common Market Organisation (Emergency Aid for Milk Producers) Regulations 2015 No. 2015/1896. - Enabling power: European Communities Act 1972, s. 2 (2). - Issued: 18.11.2015. Made: 10.11.2015. Laid: 12.11.2015. Coming into force: 16.11.2015. Effect: None. Territorial extent & classification: E/W/S/NI. General. - EC note: These Regulations make provision for the implementation of the Commission Delegated Regulation (EU) 2015/1853 providing for temporary exceptional aid to farmers in the livestock sectors. - 12p.: 30 cm. - 978-0-11-114094-9 £6.00

Agriculture, England

The Animal Feed (Composition, Marketing and Use) (England) Regulations 2015 No. 2015/255. - Enabling power: Agriculture Act 1970, ss. 66 (1), 68 (1), 74A (1) 84 & European Communities Act 1972, s. 2 (2). - Issued: 09.03.2015. Made: 25.02.2015. Laid: 05.03.2015. Coming into force: 06.04.2015. Effect: S.I. 2009/3255 amended & S.I. 2010/2503 revoked with savings & 2004/2334; 2007/3007 revoked. Territorial extent & classification: E. General. - 12p.: 30 cm. - 978-0-11-113144-2 £6.00

The Animal Feed (Hygiene, Sampling etc. and Enforcement) (England) Regulations 2015 No. 2015/454. - Enabling power: Agriculture Act 1970, ss. 66 (1), 67 (5), 74A (4), 79 (9), 84. - Issued: 06.03.2015. Made: 25.02.2015. Laid: 05.03.2015. Coming into force: 06.04.2015. Effect: S.I. 2009/3255 amended & S.I. 2009/3255; 2010/2280 partially revoked & S.I. 2005/3280; 2006/3120; 2013/3133 revoked. Territorial extent & classification: E. General. - EC note: These Regulations provide for the continuing execution and enforcement of Regulation (EC) no. 183/2005 laying down requirements for feed hygiene and Commission Regulation (EC) no. 152/2009 laying down the methods of sampling and analysis for the official control of feed and also make provision as to administration generally in relation to feed law, in particular so as to give effect to Regulation (EC) no. 882/2004. - 32p.: 30 cm. - 978-0-11-113141-1 £6.00

The Brucellosis Incentive and Pig Industry Restructuring (Non-Capital Grant) Revocations (England) Scheme 2015 No. 2015/793. - Enabling power: Agriculture Act 1970, s. 106 (1) (10) & Farm and Rural Development Act 1988, s. 1 (1) (2). - Issued: 26.03.2015. Made: 17.03.2015. Laid: 20.03.2015. Coming into force: 01.07.2015. Effect: S.I. 1972/1329; 1975/2211; 1977/1303; 2001/252 revoked. Territorial extent & classification: E. General. - 2p.: 30 cm. - 978-0-11-113416-0 £4.25

The Environment and Rural Affairs (Miscellaneous Revocations) Regulations 2015 No. 2015/639. - Enabling power: European Communities Act 1972, s. 2 (2) & Water Act 1983, sch. 2, para. 8. - Issued: 16.03.2015. Made: 10.03.2015. Laid: 11.03.2015. Coming into force: 01.04.2015. Effect: S.I. 1981/322; 1983/1267; 1994/2349; 1996/3111, 3186; 1997/813; 1999/2197; 2000/3359 2001/3960; 2005/3522; 2010/1085; 2007/1621 revoked. Territorial extent & classification: E/W. General. - 4p.: 30 cm. - 978-0-11-113295-1 £4.25

The Nitrate Pollution Prevention Regulations 2015 No. 2015/668. - Enabling power: European Communities Act 1972, s. 2 (2). - Issued: 18.03.2015. Made: 09.03.2015. Laid: 12.03.2015. Coming into force: 01.05.2015. Effect: S.I. 2010/1159; 2013/1001 partially revoked & S.I. 2008/2349; 2009/3160; 2012/1849; 2013/2619 revoked. Territorial extent & classification: E. General. - EC note: These Regulations continue to implement in England Council Directive 91/676/EEC (concerning the protection of waters against pollution by nitrates from agricultural sources) and Commission Decision 2009/431 granting a derogation pursuant to that Directive. - 36p.: 30 cm. - 978-0-11-113326-2 £10.00

Agriculture, England and Wales

The Milk Marketing Board (England and Wales) (Revocations) Regulations 2015 No. 2015/955. - Enabling power: Agriculture Act 1993, ss. 14 (2) (3), 62 (1) (2), sch. 2, paras 42 (3) (a), 43 (3), 44 (2) (a). - Issued: 02.04.2015. Made: 26.03.2015. Laid: 27.03.2015. Laid before the National Assembly for Wales: 27.03.2015. Coming into force: 01.07.2015. Effect: S.I. 1994/2460, 2759; 2001/3507 revoked. Territorial extent & classification: E/W. General. - 2p.: 30 cm. - 978-0-11-113584-6 £4.25

Agriculture, Wales

The Agricultural Sector (Wales) Act 2014 (Consequential Modification) Order 2015 No. 2015/2001 (W.304). - Enabling power: Agricultural Sector (Wales) Act 2014, s. 16. - Issued: 16.12.2015. Made: 08.12.2015. Coming into force: 09.12.2015. Effect: 1998 c.39 modified. Territorial extent & classification: W. General. - In English and Welsh: Welsh title: Gorchymyn Deddf Sector Amaethyddol (Cymru) 2014 (Addasu Canlyniadol) 2015. - 4p.: 30 cm. - 978-0-348-11203-0 £4.25

The Common Agricultural Policy Basic Payment Scheme (Wales) Regulations 2015 No. 2015/1252 (W.84). - Enabling power: European Communities Act 1972, s. 2 (2), sch. 2, para. 1A. - Issued: 04.06.2015. Made: 22.04.2015. Laid before the National Assembly for Wales: 23.04.2015. Coming into force: 14.05.2015. Effect: S.I. 2010/1892 (W.185); 2012/3093 (W.311) revoked with saving. Territorial extent & classification: W. General. - In English and Welsh. Welsh title: Rheoliadau Cynllun Taliad Sylfaenol a Chynlluniau Cymorth y Polisi Amaethddol Cyffredin (Cymru) 2015. - 16p.: 30 cm. - 978-0-348-11104-0 £6.00

The Nitrate Pollution Prevention (Wales) (Amendment) Regulations 2015 No. 2015/2020 (W.308). - Enabling power: European Communities Act 1972, s. 2 (2). - Issued: 12.01.2016. Made: 11.01.2015. Laid before the National Assembly for Wales: 14.12.2015. Coming into force: 08.01.2016. Effect: S.I. 2013/2506 (W.245) amended. Territorial extent & classification: W. General. - EC note: These Regulations implement in Wales Commission Decision 2013/781/EC granting derogation pursuant to Council Directive 91/676/EEC concerning the protection of waters against pollution by nitrates from agricultural sources. - In English and Welsh. Welsh title: Rheoliadau Atal Llygredd Nitradau (Cymru) (Diwygio) 2015. - 20p.: 30 cm. - 978-0-348-11223-8 £6.00

Animals

The Animals (Scientific Procedures) Act 1986 (Fees) Order 2015 No. 2015/244. - Enabling power: Animals (Scientific Procedures) Act 1986, s. 8. - Issued: 19.02.2015. Made: 10.02.2015. Laid: 16.02.2015. Coming into force: 01.04.2015. Effect: S.I. 2013/509 revoked. Territorial extent & classification: E/W/S. General. - 2p.: 30 cm. - 978-0-11-112986-9 £4.25

Animals, England

The Animal By-Products (Enforcement) (England) (Amendment) Regulations 2015 No. 2015/1980. - Enabling power: European Communities Act 1972, s. 2 (2). - Issued: 11.12.2015. Made: 04.12.2015. Laid: 08.12.2015. Coming into force: 31.12.2015. Effect: S.I. 2013/2952 amended. Territorial extent & classification: E. General. - 4p.: 30 cm. - 978-0-11-114168-7 £4.25

The Environment and Rural Affairs (Miscellaneous Revocations) Regulations 2015 No. 2015/639. - Enabling power: European Communities Act 1972, s. 2 (2) & Water Act 1983, sch. 2, para. 8. - Issued: 16.03.2015. Made: 10.03.2015. Laid: 11.03.2015. Coming into force: 01.04.2015. Effect: S.I. 1981/322; 1983/1267; 1994/2349; 1996/3111, 3186; 1997/813; 1999/2197; 2000/3359 2001/3960; 2005/3522; 2010/1085; 2007/1621 revoked. Territorial extent & classification: E/W. General. - 4p.: 30 cm. - 978-0-11-113295-1 £4.25

The Microchipping of Dogs (England) Regulations 2015 No. 2015/108. - Enabling power: Animal Welfare Act 2006, s. 12. - Issued: 09.02.2015. Made: 02.02.2015. Coming into force: In accord with reg. 1(b). Effect: S.I. 2007/1120, 2010/543 amended. Territorial extent & classification: E. General. - Supersedes draft S.I. (ISBN 9780111125243) issued 16/12/14. - 12p.: 30 cm. - 978-0-11-112859-6 £6.00

Animals, England: Animal health

The Animals, Water and Sea Fisheries (Miscellaneous Revocations) Order 2015 No. 2015/751. - Enabling power: Sea Fisheries (Shellfish) Act 1967, s. 12 & Animal Health Act 1981, ss. 1, 2, 10, 29, 34 (7), 87, 88 (2) & Water Act 1983, sch. 2 paras 3 (2), 10 (2) & Water Act 1989, ss. 4 (1), 83 (1), 85 (1), 86 (1) (2), 95 (1) (2). - Issued: 24.03.2015. Made: 16.03.2015. Laid: 18.03.2015. Coming into force: 01.07.2015. Effect: S.I. 1965/2040; 1974/1555; 1976/919; 1981/677; 1982/459; 1983/159, 1720, 1927; 1989/1530, 1531, 2017, 2018; 2001/2734 revoked. Territorial extent & classification: E/W. General. - 4p.: 30 cm. - 978-0-11-113382-8 £4.25

The Brucellosis (England) Order 2015 No. 2015/364. - Enabling power: Animal Health Act 1981, ss. 1, 6, 7 (1), 15 (4), 28, 32 (2), 34 (7), 35 (3), 87 (2). - Issued: 02.03.2015. Made: 23.02.2015. Coming into force: 01.04.2015. Effect: S.I. 2000/2055; 2008/618 revoked. Territorial extent & classification: E/W but applies to E only. General. - 8p.: 30 cm. - 978-0-11-113054-4 £6.00

The Cattle Identification (Amendment) Regulations 2015 No. 2015/219. - Enabling power: European Communities Act 1972, s. 2 (2). - Issued: 18.02.2015. Made: 12.02.2018. Laid: 13.02.2015. Coming into force: 06.04.2015. Effect: S.I. 2007/529 amended. Territorial extent & classification: E. General. - 2p.: 30 cm. - 978-0-11-112961-6 £4.25

The Specified Diseases (Notification) (Amendment) (England) Order 2015 No. 2015/2023. - Enabling power: Animal Health Act 1981, ss. 1, 88 (2). - Issued: 17.12.2015. Made: 10.12.2015. Coming into force: 18.12.2015. Effect: S.I. 1996/2628 amended. Territorial extent & classification: E. General. - 4p.: 30 cm. - 978-0-11-114198-4 £4.25

The Tuberculosis (Miscellaneous Amendments) (England) Order 2015 No. 2015/1838. - Enabling power: Animal Health Act 1981, ss. 1, 8 (1). - Issued: 04.11.2015. Made: 19.10.2015. Coming into force: 10.11.2015. Effect: S.I. 2012/1379; 2014/2383 amended. Territorial extent & classification: E. General. - 2p.: 30 cm. - 978-0-11-114036-9 £4.25

Animals, England: Destructive animals

The Mink and Coypus (Revocations) (England) Regulations 2015 No. 2015/613. - Enabling power: Destructive Imported Animals Act 1932, s. 2. - Issued: 16.03.2015. Made: 04.03.2015. Coming into force: 06.04.2015. Effect: S.I. 1975/2223; 1982/1883; 1997/2750, 2751 revoked. Territorial extent & classification: E. General. - 4p.: 30 cm. - 978-0-11-113276-0 £4.25

Animals, England: Diseases of animals

The Brucellosis Incentive and Pig Industry Restructuring (Non-Capital Grant) Revocations (England) Scheme 2015 No. 2015/793. - Enabling power: Agriculture Act 1970, s. 106 (1) (10) & Farm and Rural Development Act 1988, s. 1 (1) (2). - Issued: 26.03.2015. Made: 17.03.2015. Laid: 20.03.2015. Coming into force: 01.07.2015. Effect: S.I. 1972/1329; 1975/2211; 1977/1303; 2001/252 revoked. Territorial extent & classification: E. General. - 2p.: 30 cm. - 978-0-11-113416-0 £4.25

Animals, England: Prevention of cruelty

The Spring Traps Approval (Variation) (England) Order 2015 No. 2015/1427. - Enabling power: Pests Act 1954, s. 8 (3) (7). - Issued: 01.07.2015. Made: 22.06.2015. Coming into force: 21.07.2015. Effect: S.I. 2012/13 varied. Territorial extent & classification: E. General. - 4p.: 30 cm. - 978-0-11-113723-9 £4.25

The Welfare of Animals at the Time of Killing (England) Regulations 2015 No. 2015/1782. - Enabling power: European Communities Act 1972 s. 2 (2), sch. 2 para. 1A. - Issued: 19.10.2015. Made: 12.10.2015. Laid: 15.10.2015. Coming into force: 05.11.2015. Effect: 1968 c.27 ; 1974 c.3; 1986 c.14; S.I. 2009/1574; 2013/2216 amended & S.I. 2000/656 partially revoked & S.I. 1995/731; 1999/400; 2000/3352; 2001/3830; 2003/3272; 2006/1200; 2007/402; 2012/501; 2014/2124 (W.208) revoked. Territorial extent & classification: E. General. - 56p.: 30 cm. - 978-0-11-113991-2 £10.00

Animals, England and Wales: Animal health

The Animal Health (Miscellaneous Revocations) (England and Wales) Order 2015 No. 2015/584. - Enabling power: Animal Health Act 1981, ss. 1, 8 (1), 15 (4), 17 (1), 23, 25, 28, 88 (2). - Issued: 12.03.2015. Made: 04.03.2015. Coming into force: 01.04.2015. Effect: S.R. 1925/1178; 1926/42 & S.I. 1982/234; 1985/328, 1542, 1766; 1987/1601; 1989/244 revoked. Territorial extent & classification: E. General. - 4p.: 30 cm. - 978-0-11-113254-8 £4.25

The Water, Animals, Marine Pollution and Environmental Protection (Miscellaneous Revocations) Order 2015 No. 2015/663. - Enabling power: European Communities Act 1972, ss. 2 (2) & Water Industry Act 1991, s. 5 & Environment Act 1995, s. 9 (1) & Fur Farming (Prohibition) Act 2000, s. 5 & Marine and Coastal Access Act 2009, s. 74.- Issued: 17.03.2015. Made: 05.03.2015. Laid: 12.03.2015. Coming into force: 01.07.2015. Effect: S.I. 1989/1152 revoked with saving in England & S.I. 1996/3061; 2001/3749; 2004/1964; 2010/304 revoked. Territorial extent & classification: E/W. General. - 4p.: 30 cm. - 978-0-11-113320-0 £4.25

Animals, Wales

The Sheep and Goats (Records, Identification and Movement) (Wales) Order 2015 No. 2015/1992 (W.302). - Enabling power: Animal Health Act 1981, ss. 1, 8 (1), 83 (2). - Issued: 16.12.2015. Made: 08.12.2015. Laid before the National Assembly for Wales: 11.12.2015. Coming into force: 01.01.2016; 18.01.2016 in accord. with art. 1 (3). Effect: S.I. 2009/3364 (W.296) revoked. Territorial extent & classification: W. General. - In English and Welsh. Welsh title: Gorchymyn Defaid a Geifr (Cofnodion, Adnabod a Symud) (Cymru) 2015. - 28p.: 30 cm. - 978-0-348-11201-6 £6.00

The Zootechnical Standards (Wales) Regulations 2015 No. 2015/1686 (W.218). - Enabling power: European Communities Act 1972, s. 2 (2), sch. 2, para. 1 A. - Issued: 25.09.2015. Made: 14.09.2015. Laid before the National Assembly for Wales: 17.09.2015. Coming into force: 09.10.2015. Effect: S.I. 1992/2370 & 2008/1064 (W.113) revoked. Territorial extent & classification: W. General. - EC note: These Regulations provide for the recognition of organisations which record the pedigree of cattle, sheep, goats and pigs and set out requirements which govern these organisations in relation to the form and content of pedigree records, the form of zootechnical certificates, and methods of recording breeding performance and assessing genetic value for the acceptance of animals for breeding purposes. - In English and Welsh. Welsh title: Rheoliadau Safonau Sootechnegol (Cymru) 2015. - 12p.: 30 cm. - 978-0-348-11153-8 £6.00

Animals, Wales: Animal health

The Tuberculosis (Wales) (Amendment) Order 2015 No. 2015/1773 (W.245). - Enabling power: Animal Health Act 1981, s. 1. - Issued: 15.10.2015. Made: 06.10.2015. Laid before the National Assembly for Wales: 12.10.2015. Coming into force: 02.11.2015. Effect: S.I. 2010/1379 (W.122) amended. Territorial extent & classification: W. General. - In English and Welsh. Welsh title: Gorchymyn Twbercwlosis (Diwygio) (Cymru) 2015. - 4p.: 30 cm. - 978-0-348-11166-8 £4.25

Animals, Wales: Animal welfare

The Microchipping of Dogs (Wales) Regulations 2015 No. 2015/1990 (W.300). - Enabling power: Animal Welfare Act 2006, s. 12. - Issued: 16.12.2015. Made: 03.12.2015. Coming into force: In accord. with reg. 1 (2). Effect: S.I. 2007/1028 (W.95) amended. Territorial extent & classification: W. General. - In English and Welsh. Welsh title: Rheoliadau Microsglodynnu Cwn (Cymru) 2015. - 16p.: 30 cm. - 978-0-348-11202-3 £6.00

Annual tax on enveloped dwellings

The Annual Tax on Enveloped Dwellings Avoidance Schemes (Prescribed Descriptions of Arrangements) (Amendment) Regulations 2015 No. 2015/464. - Enabling power: Finance Act 2004, ss. 306 (1) (a), 317 (2). - Issued: 10.03.2015. Made: 03.03.2015. Laid: 04.03.2015. Coming into force: 01.04.2015. Effect: S.I. 2013/2571 amended. Territorial extent & classification: E/W/S/NI. General. - 2p.: 30 cm. - 978-0-11-113156-5 £4.25

Antarctica

The Antarctic Act 1994 (Isle of Man) (Amendment) Order 2015 No. 2015/1531. - Enabling power: Antarctic Act 1994, ss. 34 (2) (3) & Antarctic Act 2013, s. 18 (2). - Issued: 22.07.2015. Made: 15.07.2015. Coming into force: 01.08.2015. Effect: S.I. 1995/1035 amended. Territorial extent & classification: Isle of Man. General. - 2p.: 30 cm. - 978-0-11-113808-3 £4.25

The Antarctic Act 1994 (Overseas Territories) (Amendment) Order 2015 No. 2015/823. - Enabling power: Foreign Jurisdiction Act 1890 & British Settlements Acts 1887 and 1945 & Antarctic Act 1994, ss. 34 (2) (3) & Antarctic Act 2013, s. 18 (2). - Issued: 26.03.2015. Made: 19.03.2015. Laid: 26.03.2015. Coming into force: 30.07.2015 subject to art. 1 (2). Effect: S.I. 1995/1030 amended. Territorial extent & classification: Anguilla, Bermuda, British Antarctic Territory, Cayman Islands, Falkland Islands, Montserrat, St Helena and Dependencies, South Georgia and the South Sandwich Islands, Turks and Caicos Islands, Virgin Islands. General. - 4p.: 30 cm. - 978-0-11-113456-6 £4.25

The Antarctic (Recognised Assistance Dog) Regulations 2015 No. 2015/126. - Enabling power: Antarctic Act 1994, ss. 8 (5), 32. - Issued: 10.02.2015. Made: 04.02.2015. Laid: 04.02.2015. Coming into force: 06.04.2015. Effect: None. Territorial extent & classification: E/W/S/NI. General. - 2p.: 30 cm. - 978-0-11-112873-2 £4.25

Arms and ammunition

The Firearms Regulations 2015 No. 2015/860. - Enabling power: European Communities Act 1972, s. 2 (2). - Issued: 30.03.2015. Made: 23.03.2015. Laid: 25.03.2015. Coming into force: 16.04.2015. Effect: 1997 c. 5 & S.I. 2004/702 (N.I. 3) amended. Territorial extent & classification: E/W/S/NI. General. - 4p.: 30 cm. - 978-0-11-113482-5 £4.25

The Firearms (Variation of Fees) Order 2015 No. 2015/611. - Enabling power: Firearms Act 1968, s. 43 & Firearms (Amendment) Act 1988, ss. 11 (4), 17 (9). - Issued: 13.03.2015. Made: 09.03.2015. Laid: 12.03.2015. Coming into force: 06.04.2015. Effect: 1968 c. 27; 1988 c. 45 amended. Territorial extent & classification: E/W/S. General. - 4p.: 30 cm. - 978-0-11-113274-6 £4.25

Bank levy

The Bank Levy (Double Taxation Arrangements) (Netherlands)Regulations 2015 No. 2015/344. - Enabling power: Finance Act 2011, s. 66 (8) to (9A). - Issued: 02.03.2015. Made: 23.02.2015. Laid: 24.02.2015. Coming into force: 17.03.2015. Effect: None. Territorial extent & classification: E/W/S/NI. General. - 8p.: 30 cm. - 978-0-11-113033-9 £6.00

The Double Taxation Relief (Bank Levy) (Netherlands) Order 2015 No. 2015/335. - Enabling power: Finance Act 2011, s. 67A, sch. 19. - Issued: 02.03.2015. Made: 23.02.2015. Laid: 24.02.2015. Coming into force: 17.03.2015. Effect: None. Territorial extent & classification: E/W/S/NI. General. - 8p.: 30 cm. - 978-0-11-113032-2 £6.00

Bankruptcy

The Insolvency Act 1986 (Amendment) Order 2015 No. 2015/922. - Enabling power: Insolvency Act 1986, s. 267 (5). - Issued: 31.03.2015. Made: 19.03.2015. Coming into force: 01.10.2015. Effect: 1986 c.45 amended. Territorial extent & classification: E/W. General. - Supersedes draft S.I. (ISBN 9780111127292) issued 21.01.2015. - 2p.: 30 cm. - 978-0-11-113546-4 £4.25

Banks and banking

The Banking Act 2009 (Inter-Bank Payment Systems) (Disclosure and Publication of Specified Information) (Amendment) Regulations 2015 No. 2015/488. - Enabling power: Banking Act 2009, ss. 204 (6), 259 (1). - Issued: 11.03.2015. Made: 04.03.2015. Laid: 05.03.2015. Coming into force: 01.04.2015. Effect: S.I. 2010/828 amended. Territorial extent & classification: E/W/S/NI. General. - 2p.: 30 cm. - 978-0-11-113186-2 £4.25

The Deposit Guarantee Scheme (Amendment) Regulations 2015 No. 2015/1456. - Enabling power: European Communities Act 1972, s. 2 (2). - Issued: 08.07.2015. Made: 02.07.2015. Laid: at 11.00 a.m. 03.07.2015. Coming into force: at 1.00 p.m. 03.07.2015. Effect: S.I. 2015/486 amended. Territorial extent & classification: E/W/S/NI. General. - EC note: These Regulations further implement Directive 2014/49/EU on deposit guarantee schemes (recast) repealing directive 94/19/EC. - 4p.: 30 cm. - 978-0-11-113735-2 £4.25

The Deposit Guarantee Scheme Regulations 2015 No. 2015/486. - Enabling power: European Communities Act 1972, s. 2 (2). - Issued: 10.03.2015. Made: 04.03.2015. Laid: 05.03.2015. Coming into force: In accord. with reg. 1 (2) (3). Effect: 1985 c.66; 1986 c.45; 2000 c.8; S.I. 1989/2405 (N.I.19) amended S.I. 1995/1442 partially revoked. Territorial extent & classification: E/W/S/NI. General. - EC note: These Regulations implement in part Directive 2014/49/EU on deposit guarantee schemes (recast) repealing directive 94/19/EC. - 12p.: 30 cm. - 978-0-11-113183-1 £6.00

The Financial Services (Banking Reform) Act 2013 (Commencement No. 9) (Amendment) Order 2015 No. 2015/2055 (C.128). - Enabling power: Financial Services (Banking Reform) Act 2013, s. 148 (5). Bringing into operation various provisions of the 2013 Act on 07.03.2016. - Issued: 22.12.2015. Made: 16.12.2015. Coming into force: 16.12.2015. Effect: S.I. 2015/490 amended. Territorial extent & classification: E/W/S/NI. General. - 4p.: 30 cm. - 978-0-11-114237-0 £4.25

Betting, gaming and lotteries

The Gaming Machine (Circumstances of Use) (Amendment) Regulations 2015 No. 2015/121. - Enabling power: Gambling Act 2005, ss. 240, 355 (1). - Issued: 10.02.2014. Made: 02.02.2015. Laid: 04.02.2015. Coming into force: 06.04.2015. Effect: S.I. 2007/2319 amended. Territorial extent & classification: E/W/S. General. - 4p.: 30 cm. - 978-0-11-112871-8 £4.25

The Olympic Lottery Distribution Fund (Winding Up) Order 2015 No. 2015/85. - Enabling power: Horserace Betting and Olympic Lottery Act 2004, ss. 28 (1) to (3). - Issued: 04.02.2015. Made: 29.01.2915. Coming into force: 30.01.2015 in accord. with art. 1. Effect: None. Territorial extent & classification: E/W/S/NI. General. - Supersedes draft SI (ISBN 9780111123324) issued 19.11.2014 - 4p.: 30 cm. - 978-0-11-112830-5 £4.25

British nationality

The British Nationality (General) (Amendment No.2) Regulations 2015 No. 2015/681. - Enabling power: British Nationality Act 1981, s. 41 (1) (b) (ba) (bb) (1A) (3). - Issued: 19.03.2015. Made: 11.03.2015. Laid: 16.03.2015. Coming into force: 06.04.2015. Effect: S.I. 2003/548 amended. Territorial extent & classification: E/W/S/N. General. - 8p.: 30 cm. - 978-0-11-113344-6 £4.25

The British Nationality (General) (Amendment) Regulations 2015 No. 2015/738. - Enabling power: British Nationality Act 1981, s. 41 (1) (bza) (1ZB) (1ZC) (1ZD) (3). - Issued: 24.03.2015. Made: 16.03.2015. Coming into force: In accord. with reg. 1 (1). Effect: S.I. 2003/548 amended. Territorial extent & classification: E/W/S/NI. General. - 8p.: 30 cm. - 978-0-11-113386-6 £4.25

The British Nationality (Proof of Paternity) (Amendment) Regulations 2015 No. 2015/1615. - Enabling power: British Nationality Act 1981, s. 50 (9A) (9B). - Issued: 24.08.2015. Made: 17.08.2015. Laid: 20.08.2015. Coming into force: 10.09.2015. Effect: S.I. 2006/1496 amended. Territorial extent & classification: E/W/S/NI. General. - 2p.: 30 cm. - 978-0-11-113870-0 £4.25

The British Nationality (The Gambia) Order 2015 No. 2015/1771. - Enabling power: British Nationality Act 1981, s. 37 (2). - Issued: 15.10.2015. Made: 08.10.2015. Laid: 15.10.2015. Coming into force: 12.11.2015. Effect: 1981 c.61 amended. Territorial extent & classification: E/W/S/NI. General. - 2p.: 30 cm. - 978-0-11-113981-3 £4.25

Broadcasting

The Broadcasting Act 1996 (Renewal of Local Radio Multiplex Licences) Regulations 2015 No. 2015/904. - Enabling power: Broadcasting Act 1990, s. 200 & Broadcasting Act 1996, s. 58A. - Issued: 31.03.2015. Made: 24.03.2015. Coming into force: 06.04.2015. Effect: 1996 c.55 amended. Territorial extent & classification: E/W/S/NI. General. - Supersedes draft S.I. (ISBN 9780111128787) issued 11.02.2015. - 4p.: 30 cm. - 978-0-11-113528-0 £4.25

The Community Radio (Amendment) Order 2015 No. 2015/1000. - Enabling power: Communications Act 2003, ss. 262, 402 (3), sch. 14, para. 11. - Issued: 07.04.2015. Made: 26.03.2015. Coming into force: In accord with art. 1. Effect: S.I. 2004/1944 amended. Territorial extent & classification: E/W/S/NI. General. - Supersedes draft S.I. (ISBN 9780111130681) issued 03/03/15. - 4p.: 30 cm. - 978-0-11-113630-0 £4.25

The Legislative Reform (Further Renewal of Radio Licences) Order 2015 No. 2015/2052. - Enabling power: Legislative and Regulatory Reform Act 2006, s. 1. - Issued: 22.12.2015. Made: 14.12.2015. Coming into force: In accord. with art. 1. Effect: 1990 c.42 amended. Territorial extent & classification: E/W/S/NI. General. - Supersedes draft S.I. (ISBN 9780111134948) issued 31/03/15. - 4p.: 30 cm. - 978-0-11-114233-2 £4.25

Building and buildings, England and Wales

The Building Regulations & c. (Amendment) Regulations 2015 No. 2015/767. - Enabling power: Building Act 1984, ss. 1, 2B (1), (3) (6), 3, 16 (9), 17 (1) (6), 34, 35, 47 (1), (2), (5), 50 (1) (4) (6), 51 (1) (2), 51A (2) (3), 52 (1) (3) (5), 54 (1) (2) (5) (6), sch. 1, paras 1, 4, 4A, 7, 8 (1), 10, sch. 4, paras 2 (1) to (4), 3 (1) (2). - Issued: 02.04.2015. Made: 26.03.2015. Laid: 27.03.2015. Coming into force: In accord. with reg. 1 (4). Effect: S.I. 2010/2214 amended. Territorial extent & classification: E/W. General. - 36p.: 30 cm. - 978-0-11-113598-3 £10.00

The Energy Performance of Buildings (England and Wales) (Amendment) (No. 2) Regulations 2015 No. 2015/1681. - Enabling power: European Communities Act 1972, s. 2 (2). - Issued: 16.09.2015. Made: 10.09.2015. Laid: 15.09.2015. Coming into force: 09.10.2015. Effect: S.I. 2012/3118 amended. Territorial extent & classification: E/W. General. - 4p.: 30 cm. - 978-0-11-113924-0 £4.25

The Energy Performance of Buildings (England and Wales) (Amendment) Regulations 2015 No. 2015/609. - Enabling power: European Communities Act 1972, s. 2 (2). - Issued: 16.03.2015. Made: 09.03.2015. Laid: 11.03.2015. Coming into force: 06.04.2015. Effect: S.I. 2012/3118 amended. Territorial extent & classification: E/W. General. - 8p.: 30 cm. - 978-0-11-113272-2 £4.25

Building and buildings, Wales

The Building (Amendment) (Wales) Regulations 2015 No. 2015/1486 (W.165). - Enabling power: Building Act 1984, ss. 1, 34, sch. 1, paras 1, 2, 4, 4A, 7, 8, 10. - Issued: 22.07.2015. Made: 07.07.2015. Laid before the National Assembly for Wales: 09.07.2015. Coming into force: In accord. with reg. 1 (3). Effect: S.I. 2010/2214 amended. Territorial extent & classification: W. General. - In English and Welsh. Welsh title: Rheoliadau Adeiladu (Diwygio) (Cymru) 2015. - 12p.: 30 cm. - 978-0-348-11123-1 £6.00

Business names

The Company, Limited Liability Partnership and Business (Names and Trading Disclosures) Regulations 2015 No. 2015/17. - Enabling power: Companies Act 2006, ss. 54 (1) (c), 56 (1) (a) (5), 57 (1) (a) (2) (5), 60 (1) (b), 65 (1) (2) (4), 66 (2) (3) (4) (6), 82, 84, 1193 (1) (c), 1195 (1) (a) (5), 1197 (1) (2) (3), 1292 (1) (2), 1294, 1296. - Issued: 15.01.2015. Made: 07.01.2015. Coming into force: 31.01.2015. Effect: 2000 c.38; S.I. 1989/638; 2003/1593; 2009/1803; 2011/245 amended & S.I. 2008/495; 2009/218, 1085, 2404, 2982 revoked. Territorial extent & classification: E/W/S/NI. General. - Supersedes S.I. draft (ISBN 9780111124154) issued 03/12/14. - 28p.: 30 cm. - 978-0-11-112691-2 £6.00

Capital gains tax

The Community Amateur Sports Clubs Regulations 2015 No. 2015/725. - Enabling power: Corporation Tax Act 2010, ss. 659 (2A) (2B) (2C), 660 (5A) (d) (5B) (8) (9) (a) (b) (10) (12), 660A (1) (3) (4) & Finance Act 2013, sch. 21 para. 8 (1) (2) (a) (3). - Issued: 20.03.2015. Made: 16.03.2015. Coming into force: 01.04.2015. Effect: 2010 c.4 amended. Territorial extent & classification: E/W/S/NI. General. - Supersedes draft S.I. (ISBN 9780111127483) issued 22/01/15. - 12p.: 30 cm. - 978-0-11-113362-0 £6.00

The Double Taxation Relief and International Tax Enforcement (Algeria) Order 2015 No. 2015/1888. - Enabling power: Taxation (International and Other Provisions) Act 2010 s. 2 & Finance Act 2006, ss. 173 (1) to (3). - Issued: 18.11.2015. Made: 11.11.2015. Coming into force: 11.11.2015. Effect: None. Territorial extent & classification: E/W/S/NI. General. - Supersedes draft SI (ISBN 9780111138250) issued 23/07/15 - 24p.: 30 cm. - 978-0-11-114086-4 £6.00

The Double Taxation Relief and International Tax Enforcement (Bulgaria) Order 2015 No. 2015/1890. - Enabling power: Taxation (International and Other Provisions) Act 2010, s. 2 & Finance Act 2006, ss. 173 (1) to (3). - Issued: 18.11.2015. Made: 11.11.2015. Coming into force: 11.11.2015. Effect: None. Territorial extent & classification: E/W/S/NI. General. - Supersedes draft SI (ISBN 9780111138236) issued 23/07/15 - 24p.: 30 cm. - 978-0-11-114088-8 £6.00

The Double Taxation Relief and International Tax Enforcement (Croatia) Order 2015 No. 2015/1889. - Enabling power: Taxation (International and Other Provisions) Act 2010, s. 2 & Finance Act 2006, ss. 173(1) to (3). - Issued: 18.11.2015. Made: 11.11.2015. Coming into force: 11.11.2015. Effect: None. Territorial extent & classification: E/W/S/NI. General. - Supersedes draft SI (ISBN 9780111138229) issued 23/07/15 - 24p.: 30 cm. - 978-0-11-114087-1 £6.00

The Double Taxation Relief and International Tax Enforcement (Kosovo) Order 2015 No. 2015/2007. - Enabling power: Taxation (International and Other Provisions) Act 2010 s. 173 (1) to (3). - Issued: 16.12.2015. Made: 09.12.2015. Coming into force: 09.12.2015. Effect: None. Territorial extent & classification: E/W/S/NI. General. - Supersedes draft S.I. (ISBN 9780111140413) issued 06/11/15. - 24p.: 30 cm. - 978-0-11-114187-8 £6.00

The Double Taxation Relief and International Tax Enforcement (Senegal) Order 2015 No. 2015/1892. - Enabling power: Taxation (International and Other Provisions) Act 2010, s. 2 & Finance Act 2006, ss. 173 (1) to (3). - Issued: 18.11.2015. Made: 11.11.2015. Coming into force: 11.11.2015. Effect: None. Territorial extent & classification: E/W/S/NI. General. - Supersedes draft SI (ISBN 9780111138212) issued 23/07/15 - 24p.: 30 cm. - 978-0-11-114090-1 £6.00

The Double Taxation Relief and International Tax Enforcement (Sweden) Order 2015 No. 2015/1891. - Enabling power: Taxation (International and Other Provisions) Act 2010, s. 2 & Finance Act 2006, ss. 173 (1) to (3). - Issued: 18.11.2015. Made: 11.11.2015. Coming into force: 11.11.2015. Effect: None. Territorial extent & classification: E/W/S/NI. General. - Supersedes draft SI (ISBN 9780111138205) issued 23/07/15 - 24p.: 30 cm. - 978-0-11-114089-5 £6.00

The Finance Act 2007, Schedule 26, Paragraphs 4 and 5 (Valuation of Shares) (Appointed Day) Order 2015 No. 2015/635 (C.33). - Enabling power: Finance Act 2007, sch. 26, paras 4 (2), 5 (2). Bringing into operation various provisions of the 2007 Act on 06.04.2015 in accord. with art. 2. - Issued: 16.03.2015. Made: 09.03.2015. Effect: None. Territorial extent & classification: E/W/S/NI. General. - 2p.: 30 cm. - 978-0-11-113291-3 £4.25

The Finance Act 2014 (High Risk Promoters Prescribed Information) Regulations 2015 No. 2015/549. - Enabling power: Finance Act 2014, ss. 249 (3) (10) (11), 253 (2) (4), 257 (2), 259 (9), 260 (7), 261 (2), 268 (1), 282 (4), 283 (1). - Issued: 12.03.2015. Made: 05.03.2015. Laid: 06.03.2015. Coming into force: 27.03.2015. Effect: None. Territorial extent & classification: E/W/S/NI. General. - 16p.: 30 cm. - 978-0-11-113224-1 £6.00

The Finance Act 2014 (Schedule 34 Prescribed Matters) Regulations 2015 No. 2015/131. - Enabling power: Finance Act 2014, s. 283 (1), sch. 34 paras 8 (1) (3), 9 (2). - Issued: 12.02.2015. Made: 06.02.2015. Laid: 09.02.2015. Coming into force: 02.03.2015. Effect: None. Territorial extent & classification: E/W/S/NI. General. - 4p.: 30 cm. - 978-0-11-112898-5 £4.25

The Individual Savings Account (Amendment No. 2) Regulations 2015 No. 2015/869. - Enabling power: Income Tax (Trading and Other Income) Act 2005, s. 694 to 699, 701 & Taxation of Chargeable Gains Act 1992, s. 151. - Issued: 31.03.2015. Made: 24.03.2015. Laid: 25.03.2015. Coming into force: 06.04.2015. Effect: S.I. 1998/1870 amended. Territorial extent & classification: E/W/S/NI. General. - 2p.: 30 cm. - 978-0-11-113492-4 £4.25

The Individual Savings Account (Amendment No. 3) Regulations 2015 No. 2015/941. - Enabling power: Income Tax (Trading and Other Income) Act 2005, ss. 694 to 699, 701 & Taxation of Chargeable Gains Act 1992, s. 151. - Issued: 02.04.2015. Made: 26.03.2015. Laid: 27.03.2015. Coming into force: 06.04.2015. Effect: S.I. 1998/1870 amended. Territorial extent & classification: E/W/S/NI. General. - 2p.: 30 cm. - 978-0-11-113565-5 £4.25

The Individual Savings Account (Amendment No. 4) Regulations 2015 No. 2015/1370. - Enabling power: Income Tax (Trading and Other Income) Act 2005, ss. 694, 695, 695A, 696, 701 (1) (5) & Taxation of Chargeable Gains Act 1992, s. 151 (1) (2). - Issued: 18.06.2015. Made: 10.06.2015. Laid: 10.06.2015. Coming into force: 01.07.2015. Effect: S.I. 1998/1870 amended. Territorial extent & classification: E/W/S/NI. General. - 4p.: 30 cm. - 978-0-11-113666-9 £4.25

The Individual Savings Account (Amendment) Regulations 2015 No. 2015/608. - Enabling power: Income Tax (Trading and Other Income) Act 2005, s. 694 & Taxation of Chargeable Gains Act 1992, s. 151. - Issued: 17.03.2015. Made: 09.03.2015. Laid: 10.03.2015. Coming into force: 06.04.2015. Effect: S.I. 1998/1870 amended. Territorial extent & classification: E/W/S/NI. General. - 2p.: 30 cm. - 978-0-11-113271-5 £4.25

The International Tax Enforcement (Brazil) Order 2015 No. 2015/1887. - Enabling power: Finance Act 2006, ss. 173 (1) to (3). - Issued: 18.11.2015. Made: 11.11.2015. Coming into force: 11.11.2015. Effect: None. Territorial extent & classification: E/W/S/NI. General. - Supersedes draft SI (ISBN 9780111138243) issued 23/07/15 - 12p.: 30 cm. - 978-0-11-114085-7 £6.00

The Market Value of Shares, Securities and Strips Regulations 2015 No. 2015/616. - Enabling power: Taxation of Chargeable Gains Act, s. 272 (3) (4) & Income Tax (Trading and Other Income) Act 2005, s. 450. - Issued: 16.03.2015. Made: 09.03.2015. Laid: 10.03.2015. Coming into force: 06.04.2015. Effect: S.I. 2006/964 amended. Territorial extent & classification: E/W/S/NI. General. - 4p.: 30 cm. - 978-0-11-113279-1 £4.25

The Offshore Asset Moves Penalty (Specified Territories) Regulations 2015 No. 2015/866. - Enabling power: Finance Act 2015, sch. 21, para. 4 (5). - Issued: 02.04.2015. Made: 26.03.2015, at 5.20 pm. Laid: 27.03.2015, at 12.30 pm. Coming into force: 27.03.2015. Effect: None. Territorial extent & classification: Albania, Andorra, Anguilla, Antigua and Barbuda, Argentina, Aruba, Australia, Austria, The Bahamas, Barbados, Belgium, Belize, Bermuda, Brazil, British Virgin Islands, Brunei Darussalam, Bulgaria, Canada, Cayman Islands, Chile, China, Colombia, Costa Rica, Croatia, Curaçao, Cyprus, Czech Republic, Denmark, Dominica, Estonia, Faroe Islands, Finland, France, Germany, Gibraltar, Greece, Greenland, Grenada, Guernsey, Hong Kong, Hungary, Iceland, India, Indonesia, Ireland, Isle of Man, Israel, Italy, Japan, Jersey, Korea (South), Latvia, Liechtenstein, Lithuania, Luxembourg, Macau, Malaysia, Malta, Marshall Islands, Mauritius, Mexico, Monaco, Montserrat, Netherlands (including Bonaire, Sint Eustatius and Saba) New Zealand (not including Tokelau), Niue, Norway, Poland, Portugal, Qatar, Romania, Russia, Saint Kitts and Nevis, Saint Lucia, Saint Vincent and the Grenadines, Samoa, San Marino, Saudi Arabia, Seychelles, Singapore, Sint Maarten, Slovak Republic, Slovenia, South Africa, Spain, Sweden, Switzerland, Trinidad and Tobago, Turkey, Turks and Caicos Islands, United Arab Emirates, United States of America (not including overseas territories and possessions), Uruguay. General. - 2p.: 30 cm. - 978-0-11-113578-5 £4.25

The Taxation of Chargeable Gains (Gilt-edged Securities) Order 2015 No. 2015/1790. - Enabling power: Taxation of Chargeable Gains Act 1992, sch. 9, para. 1. - Issued: 20.10.2015. Made: 12.10.2015. Effect: None. Territorial extent & classification: E/W/S/NI. General. - 2p.: 30 cm. - 978-0-11-113993-6 £4.25

The Taxation of Regulatory Capital Securities (Amendment) Regulations 2015 No. 2015/2056. - Enabling power: Finance Act 2012, s. 221. - Issued: 22.12.2015. Made: 16.12.2015. Coming into force: 01.01.2016. Effect: S.I. 2013/3209 amended. Territorial extent & classification: E/W/S/NI. General. - Supersedes draft S.I. (ISBN 9780111141144) issued 27/11/15. - 8p.: 30 cm. - 978-0-11-114238-7 £4.25

The Unauthorised Unit Trusts (Tax) (Amendment No. 2) Regulations 2015 No. 2015/2053. - Enabling power: Finance Act 2013, s. 217. - Issued: 22.12.2015. Made: 16.12.2015. Laid: 17.12.2015. Coming into force: 07.01.2016. Effect: S.I. 2013/2819 amended. Territorial extent & classification: E/W/S/NI. General. - 2p.: 30 cm. - 978-0-11-114234-9 £4.25

Caribbean and North Atlantic territories

The Virgin Islands Constitution (Amendment) Order 2015 No. 2015/1767. - Enabling power: West Indies Act 1962, ss. 5, 7. - Issued: 15.10.2015. Made: 08.10.2015. Laid: 15.10.2015. Coming into force: 05.11.2015. Effect: S.I. 2007/1678 amended. Territorial extent & classification: Virgin Islands. General. - 2p.: 30 cm. - 978-0-11-113976-9 £4.25

Channel Tunnel

The Channel Tunnel (International Arrangements) (Charging Framework and Transfer of Economic Regulation Functions) Order 2015 No. 2015/785. - Enabling power: Channel Tunnel Act 1987, s. 11. - Issued: 31.03.2015. Made: 24.03.2015. Laid: 26.03.2015. Coming into force: In accord. with art. 1 (2). Effect: S.I. 2008/2366; 2009/20181 revoked. Territorial extent & classification: E/W/S/NI. General. - 12p.: 30 cm. - 978-0-11-113515-0 £6.00

Charities

The Charities Act 2011 (Accounts and Audit) Order 2015 No. 2015/321. - Enabling power: Charities Act 2011, s. 145 (6) (b), 174 (1), 347 (3) (b). - Issued: 26.02.2015. Made: 19.02.2015. Laid: 23.02.2015. Coming into force: 31.03.2015. Effect: 2011 c.25 amended. Territorial extent & classification: E/W. General. - 2p.: 30 cm. - 978-0-11-113019-3 £4.25

The Charities Act 2011 (Group Accounts) Regulations 2015 No. 2015/322. - Enabling power: Charities Act 2011, ss. 139 (2), 176 (1), 347 (3) (b). - Issued: 26.02.2015. Made: 19.02.2015. Laid: 23.02.2015. Coming into force: 31.03.2015. Effect: None. Territorial extent & classification: E/W. General. - 2p.: 30 cm. - 978-0-11-113018-6 £4.25

The Charities (People's Dispensary for Sick Animals) Order 2015 No. 2015/198. - Enabling power: Charities Act 2011, s. 73 (2). - Issued: 17.02.2015. Made: 10.02.2015. Laid: 13.02.2015. Coming into force: 10.03.2015. Effect: 1949 c. xv; 1956 c. lxvii amended. Territorial extent & classification: E/W. General. - 8p.: 30 cm. - 978-0-11-112940-1 £4.25

The Exempt Charities (No. 2) Order 2015 No. 2015/1894. - Enabling power: Charities Act 2011, sch. 3, para. 4 (1) (a). - Issued: 18.11.2015. Made: 11.11.2015. Coming into force: 12.11.2015. Effect: None. Territorial extent & classification: E/W. General. - 2p.: 30 cm. - 978-0-11-114092-5 £4.25

The Exempt Charities Order 2015 No. 2015/210. - Enabling power: Charities Act 2011, sch. 3, para. 4 (1) (a). - Issued: 18.02.2015. Made: 11.02.2015. Coming into force: 12.02.2015. Effect: None. Territorial extent & classification: E/W. General. - 2p.: 30 cm. - 978-0-11-112952-4 £4.25

The Small Charitable Donations Act (Amendment) Order 2015 No. 2015/2027. - Enabling power: Small Charitable Donations Act 2012, s. 14 (1). - Issued: 18.12.2015. Made: 14.12.2015. Coming into force: 06.04.2016. Effect: 2012 c.23 amended. Territorial extent & classification: E/W/S/NI. General. - 2p.: 30 cm. - 978-0-11-114203-5 £4.25

Childcare

The Childcare Payments Act 2014 (Amendment) Regulations 2015 No. 2015/537. - Enabling power: Childcare Payments Act 2014, ss. 19 (7), 69 (2) (4) (b). - Issued: 11.03.2015. Made: 05.03.2015. Laid: 06.03.2015. Coming into force: 01.06.2015. Effect: 2014 c.28 amended. Territorial extent & classification: E/W/S/NI. General. - 2p.: 30 cm. - 978-0-11-113216-6 £4.25

The Childcare Payments (Eligibility) Regulations 2015 No. 2015/448. - Enabling power: Childcare Payments Act 2014, ss 2 (3) (b) to (d), 3 (4) (5), 7 (3), 8 (2), 9 (2) (3), 10 (2) (3) (4), 14, 32 (5), 33 (5), 69 (2) (4). - Issued: 12.03.2015. Made: 04.03.2015. Coming into force: 05.03.2015 in accord. with reg. 1. Effect: None. Territorial extent & classification: E/W/S/NI. - Supersedes draft S.I. (ISBN 9780111127063) issued 16.01.2015. - 16p.: 30 cm. - 978-0-11-113245-6 £6.00

The Childcare Payments Regulations 2015 No. 2015/522. - Enabling power: Childcare Payments Act 2014, ss. 2 (3) (a) (4), 4 (6), 5 (3), 15 (3) (4) (5), 17 (4), 19 (6), 24 (1) (3) (4), 25, 26 (1) (3), 49 (6), 62 (1) (2) (3) (5), 69 (3) (4). - Issued: 11.03.2015. Made: 04.03.2015. Laid: 05.03.2015. Coming into force: 01.06.2015. Effect: None. Territorial extent & classification: E/W/S/NI. General. - 16p.: 30 cm. - 978-0-11-113208-1 £6.00

Children and young persons

The Child Poverty Act 2010 (Extension of Publication Deadline) Order 2015 No. 2015/83. - Enabling power: Child Poverty Act 2010, s. 8B (5). - Issued: 03.02.2015. Made: 23.01.2015. Laid: 30.01.2015. Coming into force: 06.03.2015. Effect: None. Territorial extent & classification: E/W/S/NI. General. - 2p.: 30 cm. - 978-0-11-112826-8 £4.25

The Children and Families Act 2014 (Commencement No. 6) Order 2015 No. 2015/375 (C.20). - Enabling power: Children and Families Act 2014, s. 139 (6) (7). Bringing into operation various provisions of the 2014 Act on 01.04.2015; 01.10.2015, in accord. with arts 2, 3. - Issued: 03.03.2015. Made: 25.02.2015. Effect: None. Territorial extent & classification: E/W/S. General. - 4p.: 30 cm. - 978-0-11-113067-4 £4.25

The Children and Young People (Scotland) Act 2014 (Consequential and Saving Provisions) Order 2015 No. 2015/907. - Enabling power: Scotland Act 1998, ss. 104, 112 (1), 113 (2) (4) (5). - Issued: 30.03.2015. Made: 24.03.2015. Coming into force: In accord. with arts 1 (2) (3) (4). Effect: 1995 c.36 modified. Territorial extent & classification: E/W/NI. General. - Supersedes draft S.I. (ISBN 9780111130087) issued 27/02/15. - 4p.: 30 cm. - 978-0-11-113531-0 £4.25

Children and young persons, England

The Adoption Information and Intermediary Services (Pre-Commencement Adoptions) (Amendment) Regulations 2015 No. 2015/1685. - Enabling power: Adoption and Children Act 2002, ss. 9 (1), 98 (1) (1A) (3), 140 (7) (8), 144 (2). - Issued: 18.09.2015. Made: 11.09.2015. Laid: 15.09.2015. Coming into force: 10.11.2015. Effect: S.I. 2005/890 amended. Territorial extent & classification: E. General. - 4p.: 30 cm. - 978-0-11-113927-1 £4.25

The Care Planning and Fostering (Miscellaneous Amendments) (England) Regulations 2015 No. 2015/495. - Enabling power: Children Act 1989, ss. 22C (11), 23ZA (1) (b) (3) (4), 23E (1B), 23E (2), 25B (2) (a), 26 (1) (2), 31A (3), 104 (4), sch. 2, paras. 12E, 12F, 19B (7). - Issued: 11.03.2015. Made: 04.03.2015. Laid: 06.03.2015. Coming into force: 01.04.2015. Effect: S.I. 2009/395; 2010/959, 2571; 2011/581 amended. Territorial extent & classification: E. General. - 8p.: 30 cm. - 978-0-11-113193-0 £4.25

The Chief Inspector of Education, Children's Services and Skills (No. 2) Order 2015 No. 2015/1377. - Enabling power: Education and Inspections Act 2006, s. 114 (1). - Issued: 17.06.2015. Made: 10.06.2015. Coming into force: 11.06.2015. Effect: None. Territorial extent & classification: E. General. - 4p.: 30 cm. - 978-0-11-113672-0 £4.25

The Childcare (Early Years Register) (Consequential Provisions) Regulations 2015 No. 2015/963. - Enabling power: Small Business, Enterprise and Employment Act 2015, s. 159 (1) (2). - Issued: 02.04.2015. Made: 26.03.2015. Laid: 27.03.2015. Coming into force: In accord. with reg. 1 (1). Effect: S.I. 2008/979 amended. Territorial extent classification: E. General. - 2p.: 30 cm. - 978-0-11-113595-2 £4.25

The Childcare (Miscellaneous Amendments) Regulations 2015 No. 2015/1562. - Enabling power: Childcare Act 2006, ss. 12 (2), 35 (2) (a) (3) (b) (5) (b), 36 (2) (a) (c) (3) (b) (5) (b), 37 (3), 39 (1) (b), 43 (1), 44 (2) (3), 54 (2) (a) (3) (b) (5) (b), 55 (2) (a) (c) (3) (b) (5) (b), 56 (3), 59 (2) to (5), 62 (2) (a), 63 (2) (a) (c), 64 (3), 67 (2) to (5), 69, 74 (2), 83 (1), 83A (1) (b), 85A, 89 (1), 104 (2). - Issued: 28.07.2015. Made: 21.07.2015. Laid: 23.07.2015. Coming into force: In accord. with reg. 1. Effect: S.I. 2007/722, 3490; 2008/974, 975, 976, 1804; 2012/938; 2014/1920 amended. Territorial extent classification: E. General. - 20p.: 30 cm. - 978-0-11-113843-4 £6.00

The Childcare (Provision of Information About Young Children) (England) (Amendment) Regulations 2015 No. 2015/1696. - Enabling power: Childcare Act 2006, ss 99 (1) (2) (b), 104 (2). - Issued: 24.09.2015. Made: 16.09.2015. Laid: 21.09.2015. Coming into force: 01.01.2016. Effect: S.I. 2009/1554 amended. Territorial extent & classification: E. General. - 2p.: 30 cm. - 978-0-11-113936-3 £4.25

The Childcare (Supply and Disclosure of Information) (Amendment) (England) Regulations 2015 No. 2015/357. - Enabling power: Childcare Act 2006, ss. 84 (1) (3), 104 (2). - Issued: 02.03.2015. Made: 23.02.2015. Laid: 26.02.2015. Coming into force: 01.04.2015. Effect: S.I. 2007/722 amended. Territorial extent & classification: E. General. - 4p.: 30 cm. - 978-0-11-113046-9 £4.25

The Children Act 2004 (Joint Area Reviews) Regulations 2015 No. 2015/1792. - Enabling power: Children Act 2004, ss. 20 (8) (a) to (e), (9) (11), 23 (3), 66 (1). - Issued: 21.10.2015. Made: 14.10.2015. Laid: 16.10.2015. Coming into force: 09.11.2015. Effect: S.I. 2005/1972 amended & S.I. 2005/1973 revoked. Territorial extent & classification: E. General. - 8p.: 30 cm. - 978-0-11-113997-4 £6.00

The Children (Secure Accommodation) (Amendment) (England) Regulations 2015 No. 2015/1883. - Enabling power: Children Act 1989 s. 25 (7) (b). - Issued: 17.11.2015. Made: 10.11.2015. Laid: 13.11.2015. Coming into force: 07.12.2015. Effect: S.I. 1991/1505 amended. Territorial extent & classification: E. General. - 2p.: 30 cm. - 978-0-11-114081-9 £4.25

The Children's Homes (England) Regulations 2015 No. 2015/541. - Enabling power: Interpretation Act 1978, s. 14A & Care Standards Act 2000, ss. 1 (4A), 22 (1) (1A) (2) (a) to (d), (f) to (j) (5) (7) (a) to (h) (j), 34 (1), 35 (1), 118 (5). - Issued: 11.03.2015. Made: 04.03.2015. Laid: 06.03.2015. Coming into force: 01.04.2015. Effect: S.I. 2010/2130 amended & S.I. 2001/3967; 2011/583 revoked. Territorial extent & classification: E. General. - 44p.: 30 cm. - 978-0-11-113217-3 £10.00

The Health and Social Care (Miscellaneous Revocations) Regulations 2015 No. 2015/839. - Enabling power: Health and Medicines Act 1988, s. 26 (6) & Care Standards Act 2000, ss. 12 (2), 15 (3), 16 (3), 118 (5) to (7) & Health and Social Care Act 2001, ss. 65 (1) (2) & Tobacco Advertising and Promotion Act 2002, ss. 19 (2), 20 & National Health Service Act, ss. 8, 28, 187, 272 (7) (8), 273, sch. 6, paras 3, 5, 6. - Issued: 27.03.2015. Made: 23.03.2015 Laid: 26.03.2015. Coming into force: 01.07.2015. Effect: S.I. 1974/29; 2003/7, 1415 revoked in relation to England & S.I. 1985/1876; 1989/1893; 1996/512; 2001/3744; 2003/2323; 2005/640 revoked. Territorial extent & classification: E. General. - 4p.: 30 cm. - 978-0-11-113466-5 £4.25

Her Majesty's Chief Inspector of Education, Children's Services and Skills (Fees and Frequency of Inspections) (Children's Homes etc.) Regulations 2015 No. 2015/551. - Enabling power: Children Act 1989, ss. 87D (2), 104 (4) (a) & Care Standards Act 2000, ss. 12 (2), 15 (3), 16 (3), 31 (7), 118 (5) (6) (7) & Education and Inspections Act 2006, ss. 155 (1) (2), 181 (2) (a) (b). - Issued: 11.03.2015. Made: 04.03.2015. Laid: 09.03.2015. Coming into force: 01.04.2015. Effect: S.I. 2007/694; 2009/2724; 2010/617; 2011/553; 2012/511; 2014/670 revoked. Territorial extent & classification: E. General. - 16p.: 30 cm. - 978-0-11-113226-5 £6.00

The Inspector of Education, Children's Services and Skills (No. 3) Order 2015 No. 2015/1525. - Enabling power: Education and Inspections Act 2006, s. 114 (1). - Issued: 22.07.2015. Made: 15.07.2015. Coming into force: 16.07.2015. Effect: None. Territorial extent & classification: E. General. - 2p.: 30 cm. - 978-0-11-113802-1 £4.25

The Inspectors of Education, Children's Services and Skills (No. 4) Order 2015 No. 2015/1762. - Enabling power: Education and Inspections Act 2006, s. 114 (1). - Issued: 15.10.2015. Made: 08.10.2015. Coming into force: 09.10.2015. Effect: None. Territorial extent & classification: E. General. - 2p.: 30 cm. - 978-0-11-113968-4 £4.25

The Inspectors of Education, Children's Services and Skills (No. 5) Order 2015 No. 2015/1895. - Enabling power: Education and Inspections Act 2006, s. 114 (1). - Issued: 18.11.2015. Made: 11.11.2015. Coming into force: 12.11.2015. Effect: None. Territorial extent & classification: E. General. - 2p.: 30 cm. - 978-0-11-114093-2 £4.25

The Inspectors of Education, Children's Services and Skills (No. 6) Order 2015 No. 2015/2010. - Enabling power: Education and Inspections Act 2006, s. 114 (1). - Issued: 16.12.2015. Made: 09.12.2015. Coming into force: 10.12.2015. Effect: None. Territorial extent & classification: E. General. - 2p.: 30 cm. - 978-0-11-114190-8 £4.25

The Inspectors of Education, Children's Services and Skills Order 2015 No. 2015/224. - Enabling power: Education and Inspections Act 2006, s. 114 (1). - Issued: 18.02.2015. Made: 11.02.2015. Coming into force: 12.02.2015. Effect: None. Territorial extent & classification: E. General. - 4p.: 30 cm. - 978-0-11-112963-0 £4.25

The Small Business, Enterprise and Employment Act 2015 (Commencement No. 1) Regulations 2015 No. 2015/1329 (C.75). - Enabling power: Small Business, Enterprise and Employment Act 2015, ss. 161 (2), 164 (1). Bringing into operation various provisions of the 2015 Act on 26.05.2015; 15.06.2015; 01.07.2015; 01.01.2016, in accord. with arts 2 to 6. - Issued: 28.05.2015. Made: 20.05.2015. Effect: None. Territorial extent & classification: E/W/S/NI. General. - 4p.: 30 cm. - 978-0-11-113644-7 £4.25

The Young Carers (Needs Assessments) Regulations 2015 No. 2015/527. - Enabling power: Children Act 1989, s. 17ZB (8). - Issued: 11.03.2015. Made: 04.03.2015. Laid: 06.03.2015. Coming into force: 01.04.2015. Effect: None. Territorial extent & classification: E. General. - 4p.: 30 cm. - 978-0-11-113211-1 £4.25

Children and young persons, Wales

The Adoption Information and Intermediary Services (Pre-Commencement Adoptions) (Wales) (Amendment) Regulations 2015 No. 2015/1802 (W.257). - Enabling power: Adoption and Children Act 2002, ss. 2 (6), 9 (1), 98 (1) (1A) (2) (3), 144 (2). - Issued: 27.10.2015. Made: 16.10.2015. Laid before the National Assembly for Wales: 20.10.2015. Coming into force: 10.11.2015. Effect: S.I. 2005/2701 (W.190) amended. Territorial extent & classification: W. General. - In English and Welsh. Welsh title: Rheoliadau Gwybodaeth Mabwysiadu a Gwasanaethau Cyfryngol (Mabwysiadau Cyngychwyn) (Cymru) (Diwygio) 2015. - 12p.: 30 cm. - 978-0-348-11172-9 £6.00

The Care Leavers (Wales) Regulations 2015 No. 2015/1820 (W.262). - Enabling power: Social Services and Well-being (Wales) Act 2014, ss. 104 (2) (6), 106 (4), 107 (7) (c) (8), 108 (6), 109 (1) (3), 116 (2), 196 (2). - Issued: 02.11.2015. Made: 21.10.2015. Laid before the National Assembly for Wales: 23.10.2015. Coming into force: 06.04.2016. Effect: S.I. 2001/2189 (W.151) revoked. Territorial extent & classification: W. General. - In English and Welsh. Welsh language title: Rheoliadau Ymadawyr Gofal (Cymru) 2015. - 20p.: 30 cm. - 978-0-348-11175-0 £6.00

The Care Planning, Placement and Case Review (Wales) Regulations 2015 No. 2015/1818 (W.261). - Enabling power: Children Act 1989, ss. 31A, 34 (8) & Social Services and Well-being (Wales) Act 2014, ss. 81 (6) (d), 83 (5), 84, 87, 97 (4) (a) (5), 98 (1) (a), 100 (1) (b) (2) (a), 102 (1) (2), 104 (2) (c) (6), 106 (4), 107 (7) (c), 107 (8) (9), 108 (6), 196 (2). - Issued: 04.11.2015. Made: 21.10.2015. Laid before the National Assembly for Wales: 23.10.2015. Coming into force: 06.04.2016. Effect: S.I. 1991/891, 892, 893; 1995/2015 revoked. Territorial extent & classification: W. General. - In English and Welsh. Welsh title: Rheoliadau Cynllunio Gofal, Lleoli ac Adolygu Achosion (Cymru) 2015. - 72p.: 30 cm. - 978-0-348-11178-1 £14.25

The Children and Families Act 2014 (Commencement) (Wales) Order 2015 No. 2015/1808 (W.259) (C.111). - Enabling power: Children and Families Act 2014, s. 139 (2) (b). Bringing into operation various provisions of the 2014 Act on 19.10.2015 in accord. with art. 2. - Issued: 18.11.2015. Made: 16.10.2015. Effect: None. Territorial extent & classification: W. General. - In English and Welsh. Welsh title: Gorchymyn Deddf Plant a Theuluoedd 2014 (Cychwyn) (Cymru) 2015. - 4p.: 30 cm. - 978-0-348-11187-3 £4.25

The Children (Performances and Activities) (Wales) Regulations 2015 No. 2015/1757 (W.242). - Enabling power: Children and Young Persons Act 1933, s. 25 (2) (8) & Children and Young Persons Act 1963, ss. 37 (3) (4) (5) (6), 39 (3) (5). - Issued: 16.10.2015. Made: 07.10.2015. Laid before the National Assembly for Wales: 09.10.2015. Coming into force: 30.10.2015. Effect: S.I. 1968/1728; 1998/1678; WSI 2007/736 revoked in relation to Wales. Territorial extent & classification: W. General. - With correction slip dated November 2015. - In English and Welsh. Welsh title: Rheoliadau Plant (Perfformiadau a Gweithgareddau) (Cymru) 2015. - 24p.: 30 cm. - 978-0-348-11167-5 £6.00

The Children (Secure Accommodation) (Wales) Regulations 2015 No. 2015/1988 (W.298). - Enabling power: Children Act 1989, s. 104 (4) (c), sch. 4, para. 4 (1), sch. 5, para. 7, sch. 6, para. 10 & Care Standards Act 2000, s. 118 (7) & Social Services and Well-being (Wales) Act 2014, ss. 87, 119 (2) (7), 196 (2). - Issued: 05.01.2016. Made: 02.12.2015. Coming into force: 06.04.2016. Effect: S.I. 1991/1505 amended & S.I. 1991/2034; 1992/211; 1995/1398 disapplied in relation to Wales & WSI 2006/2986 (W.276); 2013/663 (W.76) revoked. Territorial extent & classification: W. General. - Partially revoked by W.S.I. 2016/211 (W.84) (ISBN 9780348112740). - In English & Welsh. Welsh title: Rheoliadau Plant (Llety Diogel) (Cymru) 2015. - 16p.: 30 cm. - 978-0-348-11222-1 £6.00

The Visits to Children in Detention (Wales) Regulations 2015 No. 2015/1823 (W.265). - Enabling power: Social Services and Well-being (Wales) Act 2014, ss. 97 (1) (b) (c) (2) (4), 196 (2). - Issued: 18.11.2015. Made: 21.10.2015. Laid before the National Assembly for Wales: 23.10.2015. Coming into force: 06.04.2016. Effect: None. Territorial extent & classification: W. General. - In English and Welsh. Welsh title: Rheoliadau Ymweliadau â Phlant dan Gadwad (Cymru) 2015. - 12p.: 30 cm. - 978-0-348-11189-7 £6.00

Child trust funds

The Child Trust Funds (Amendment No. 2) Regulations 2015 No. 2015/876. - Enabling power: Child Trust Funds Act 2004, ss. 3 (2) (5), 7, 7A (1), 15, 28 (1) to (3). - Issued: 02.04.2015. Made: 26.03.2015. Laid: 27.03.2015. Coming into force: 06.04.2015. Effect: S.I. 2004/1450 amended. Territorial extent & classification: E/W/S/NI. General. - 2p.: 30 cm. - 978-0-11-113594-5 £4.25

The Child Trust Funds (Amendment No. 3) Regulations 2015 No. 2015/1371. - Enabling power: Child Trust Funds Act 2004, ss. 3 (2) (5) (10), 5 (4), 28 (1) to (3). - Issued: 18.06.2015. Made: 10.06.2015. Laid: 10.06.2015. Coming into force: 01.07.2015. Effect: S.I. 2004/1450 amended. Territorial extent & classification: E/W/S/NI. General. - 4p.: 30 cm. - 978-0-11-113667-6 £4.25

The Child Trust Funds (Amendment) Regulations 2015 No. 2015/600. - Enabling power: Child Trust Funds Act 2004, ss. 12 (2), 28 (1). - Issued: 13.03.2015. Made: 09.03.2015. Laid: 10.03.2015. Coming into force: 06.04.2015. Effect: S.I. 2004/1450 amended. Territorial extent & classification: E/W/S/NI. General. - 2p.: 30 cm. - 978-0-11-113265-4 £4.25

Cinemas and films

The Films Co-Production Agreements (Amendment) Order 2015 No. 2015/1886. - Enabling power: Films Act 1985, s. 4 (5). - Issued: 18.11.2015. Made: 11.11.2015. Coming into force: 12.11.2015. Effect: S.I. 1985/960 amended & S.I. 2014/1561 revoked. Territorial extent & classification: E/W/S/NI. General. - 4p.: 30 cm. - 978-0-11-114084-0 £4.25

The Films (Definition of 'British Film') Order 2015 No. 2015/86. - Enabling power: Films Act 1985, sch. 1, para. 10 (2). - Issued: 04.02.2015. Made: 28.01.2015. Coming into force: 29.01.2015. Effect: 1985 c.21 amended. Territorial extent & classification: E/W/S/NI. General. - 8p.: 30 cm. - 978-0-11-112831-2 £6.00

Civil aviation

The Air Navigation (Amendment) Order 2015 No. 2015/1768. - Enabling power: Civil Aviation Act 1982, ss. 60 (1), 60 (2) (b), 61 (1) (a) & European Communities Act 1972 s. 2 (2). - Issued: 15.10.2015. Made: 08.10.2015. Laid: 15.10.2015. Coming into force: 15.11.2015. Effect: S.I. 2009/3015 amended. Territorial extent & classification: E/W/S/NI. General. - EC note: This Order amends the 2009 Order in order to reflect the coming into force in the United Kingdom of Commission Regulation (EU) No 376/2014 of the European Parliament and of the Council of 3rd April 2014 on the reporting, analysis and follow-up of occurrences in civil aviation, amending Regulation (EU) No 996/2010 of the European Parliament and of the Council and repealing Directive 2003/42/EC of the European Parliament and of the Council and Commission Regulations (EC) No 1321/2007 and (EC) No 1330/2007. - 8p.: 30 cm. - 978-0-11-113978-3 £4.25

The Air Navigation (Dangerous Goods) (Amendment) Regulations 2015 No. 2015/970. - Enabling power: S.I. 2009/3015, art. 132 (1). - Issued: 02.04.2015. Made: 26.03.2015. Coming into force: 30.06.2015. Effect: S.I. 2002/2786 amended & S.I. 2012/3054 revoked. Territorial extent & classification: E/W/S/NI. General. - 2p.: 30 cm. - 978-0-11-113604-1 £4.25

The Air Navigation (Isle of Man) Order 2015 No. 2015/870. - Enabling power: Civil Aviation Act 1982, ss. 60, 61. - Issued: 30.03.2015. Made: 19.03.2015. Coming into force: 01.05.2015. Effect: S.I. 2007/1115; 2008/1487 revoked. Territorial extent & classification: IoM. General. - 128p.: 30 cm. - 978-0-11-113493-1 £19.00

The Air Navigation (Overseas Territories) (Amendment) Order 2015 No. 2015/1769. - Enabling power: Civil Aviation Act 1949, ss. 8, 57, 59, 61, 63 (8) & Civil Aviation Act 1982, s. 61. - Issued: 15.10.2015. Made: 08.10.2015. Laid: 15.10.2015. Coming into force: 05.11.2015. Effect: S.I. 2013/2870 amended. Territorial extent & classification: British Overseas with exception of Gibraltar & British Antarctic Territories. General. - 4p.: 30 cm. - 978-0-11-113979-0 £4.25

The Air Navigation (Overseas Territories) (Environmental Standards) Order (Amendment) 2015 No. 2015/236. - Enabling power: Civil Aviation Act 1949, s. 8 (1) (2) (p) & Civil Aviation Act 1982, s. 108 (1). - Issued: 18.02.2015. Made: 11.02.2015. Laid: 18.02.2015. Coming into force: 11.03.2015. Effect: S.I. 2014/2926 amended. Territorial extent & classification: All the British Overseas Territories except Gibraltar. General. - This Statutory Instrument has been printed to correct an error in The Air Navigation (Overseas Territories) (Environmental Standards) Order 2014 (S.I. 2014/2926, ISBN 9780111123065) and is being issued free of charge to all known recipients that Statutory Instrument. - 2p.: 30 cm. - 978-0-11-112976-0 £4.25

The Air Navigation (Restriction of Flying) (Abingdon Air and Country Show) Regulations 2015 No. 2015/261. - Enabling power: S.I. 2009/3015, art. 161. - Issued: 12.02.2015. Made: 27.01.2015. Coming into force: 02.05.2015. Effect: None. Territorial extent & classification: E. Local. - Available at http://www.legislation.gov.uk/uksi/2015/261/contents/made Non-print

The Air Navigation (Restriction of Flying) (Anmer Hall) (Restricted Zone EG R220) Regulations 2015 No. 2015/1735. - Enabling power: S.I. 2009/3015, art. 161. - Issued: 05.10.2015. Made: 29.09.2015. Coming into force: 01.11.2015. Effect: None. Territorial extent & classification: E. Local. - Available at http://www.legislation.gov.uk/uksi/2015/1735/contents/made Non-print

The Air Navigation (Restriction of Flying) (Ascot) Regulations 2015 No. 2015/1364. - Enabling power: S.I. 2009/3015, art. 161. - Issued: 11.06.2015. Made: 08.06.2015. Coming into force: 13.08.2015. Effect: None. Territorial extent & classification: E. Local. - Available at http://www.legislation.gov.uk/uksi/2015/1364/contents/made Non-print

The Air Navigation (Restriction of Flying) (Balado) Regulations 2015 No. 2015/267. - Enabling power: S.I. 2009/3015, art. 161. - Issued: 13.02.2015. Made: 09.02.2015. Coming into force: 09.07.2015. Effect: None. Territorial extent & classification: E. Local. - Revoked by SI 2015/1008 (Non-print) (ISBN 9786666731052). - Available at http://www.legislation.gov.uk/uksi/2015/267/contents/made. Revoked by S.I. 2015/1008 [non-print] Non-print

CIVIL AVIATION

The Air Navigation (Restriction of Flying) (Balado) (Revocation) Regulations 2015 No. 2015/1008. - Enabling power: S.I. 2009/3015, art. 161. - Issued: 02.04.2015. Made: 30.03.2015 at 13.30 hours. Coming into force: With immediate effect. Effect: S.I. 2015/267 revoked. Territorial extent & classification: E. Local. - Available at http://www.legislation.gov.uk/uksi/2015/1008/contents/made Non-print

The Air Navigation (Restriction of Flying) (Bermondsey) Regulations 2015 No. 2015/1007. - Enabling power: S.I. 2009/3015, art. 161. - Issued: 02.04.2015. Made: 24.03.2015 at 10.45 hours. Coming into force: With immediate effect. Effect: None. Territorial extent & classification: E. Local. - Available at http://www.legislation.gov.uk/uksi/2015/1007/contents/made. Revoked by S.I. 2015/1010 [non print] Non-print

The Air Navigation (Restriction of Flying) (Bermondsey) (Revocation) Regulations 2015 No. 2015/1010. - Enabling power: S.I. 2009/3015, art. 161. - Issued: 02.04.2015. Made: 25.03.2015 at 13.32 hours. Coming into force: With immediate effect. Effect: S.I. 2015/1007 revoked. Territorial extent & classification: E. Local. - Available at http://www.legislation.gov.uk/uksi/2015/1010/contents/made Non-print

The Air Navigation (Restriction of Flying) (Bethnal Green) Regulations 2015 No. 2015/1608. - Enabling power: S.I. 2009/3015, art. 161. - Issued: 17.08.2015. Made: 11.08.2014 at 02.00. Coming into force: with immediate effect. Effect: None. Territorial extent & classification: E. Local. - Available at http://www.legislation.gov.uk/uksi/2015/1608/contents/made Non-print

The Air Navigation (Restriction of Flying) (Bethnal Green) (Revocation) Regulations 2015 No. 2015/1611. - Enabling power: S.I. 2009/3015, art. 161. - Issued: 18.08.2015. Made: 11.08.2014 at 05.00 hours. Coming into force: with immediate effect. Effect: S.I. 2015/1608 revoked. Territorial extent & classification: E. Local. - Available at http://www.legislation.gov.uk/uksi/2015/1611/contents/made Non-print

The Air Navigation (Restriction of Flying) (Bournemouth) Regulations 2015 No. 2015/1099. - Enabling power: S.I. 2009/3015, art. 161. - Issued: 17.04.2015. Made: 14.04.2015. Coming into force: 20.08.2015. Effect: None. Territorial extent & classification: E. Local. - Available at http://www.legislation.gov.uk/uksi/2015/1099/contents/made Non-print

The Air Navigation (Restriction of Flying) (Cheltenham Festival) Regulations 2015 No. 2015/259. - Enabling power: S.I. 2009/3015, art. 161. - Issued: 30.01.2015. Made: 20.01.2015. Coming into force: 10.03.2015. Effect: None. Territorial extent & classification: E. Local. - Available at http://www.legislation.gov.uk/uksi/2015/259/contents/made Non-print

The Air Navigation (Restriction of Flying) (Clacton-on-Sea) Regulations 2015 No. 2015/1324. - Enabling power: S.I. 2009/3015, art. 161. - Issued: 18.05.2015. Made: 14.05.2015. Coming into force: 27.08.2015. Effect: None. Territorial extent & classification: E. Local. - Available at http://www.legislation.gov.uk/uksi/2015/1324/contents/made Non-print

The Air Navigation (Restriction of Flying) (Donna Nook) Regulations 2015 No. 2015/1310. - Enabling power: S.I. 2009/3015, art. 161. - Issued: 12.05.2015. Made: 08.05.2015. Coming into force: 14.05.2015. Effect: None. Territorial extent & classification: E. Local. - Available at http://www.legislation.gov.uk/uksi/2015/1310/contents/made Non-print

The Air Navigation (Restriction of Flying) (Dunsfold) Regulations 2015 No. 2015/1098. - Enabling power: S.I. 2009/3015, art. 161. - Issued: 17.04.2015. Made: 14.04.2015. Coming into force: 29.08.2015. Effect: None. Territorial extent & classification: E. Local. - Available at http://www.legislation.gov.uk/uksi/2015/1098/contents/made Non-print

The Air Navigation (Restriction of Flying) (Duxford) Regulations 2015 No. 2015/263. - Enabling power: S.I. 2009/3015, art. 161. - Issued: 12.02.2015. Made: 29.01.2015. Coming into force: 23.05.2015. Effect: None. Territorial extent & classification: E. Local. - Available at http://www.legislation.gov.uk/uksi/2015/263/contents/made Non-print

The Air Navigation (Restriction of Flying) (Eastbourne) Regulations 2015 No. 2015/515. - Enabling power: S.I. 2009/3015, art. 161. - Issued: 26.02.2015. Made: 19.02.2015. Coming into force: 13.08.2015. Effect: None. Territorial extent & classification: E. Local. - Available at http://www.legislation.gov.uk/uksi/2015/515/contents/made Non-print

The Air Navigation (Restriction of Flying) (East Fortune) Regulations 2015 No. 2015/1077. - Enabling power: S.I. 2009/3015, art. 161. - Issued: 02.04.2015. Made: 30.03.2015. Coming into force: 25.07.2015. Effect: None. Territorial extent & classification: E. Local. - Available at http://www.legislation.gov.uk/uksi/2015/1077/contents/made Non-print

The Air Navigation (Restriction of Flying) (Feltwell) (Amendment) Regulations 2015 No. 2015/1845. - Enabling power: S.I. 2009/3015, art. 161. - Issued: 02.10.2015. Made: 23.10.2015 at 17.15 hours. Laid: - Coming into force: With immediate effect. Effect: S.I. 2015/1825 amended. Territorial extent & classification: E. Local. - Available at http://www.legislation.gov.uk/uksi/2015/1845/contents/made Non-print

The Air Navigation (Restriction of Flying) (Feltwell) Regulations 2015 No. 2015/1825. - Enabling power: S.I. 2009/3015, art. 161. - Issued: 27.10.2015. Made: 21.10.2015, at 18.31 hours. Laid: - Coming into force: with immediate effect. Effect: None. Territorial extent & classification: E. Local. - Revoked by S.I. 2015/1847 (Non-Print) (ISBN 9786666734725). - Available at http://www.legislation.gov.uk/uksi/2015/1825/contents/made Non-print

The Air Navigation (Restriction of Flying) (Feltwell) (Revocation) Regulations 2015 No. 2015/1847. - Enabling power: S.I. 2009/3015, art. 161. - Issued: 03.11.2015. Made: 26.10.2015 at 10.35 hours. Laid: - Coming into force: With immediate effect. Effect: S.I. 2015/1825, 1845 revoked. Territorial extent & classification: E. Local. - Available at http://www.legislation.gov.uk/uksi/2015/1847/contents/made Non-print

The Air Navigation (Restriction of Flying) (Glastonbury Festival) Regulations 2015 No. 2015/270. - Enabling power: S.I. 2009/3015, art. 161. - Issued: 12.02.2015. Made: 20.01.2015. Coming into force: 22.06.2015. Effect: None. Territorial extent & classification: E. Local. - Available at http://www.legislation.gov.uk/uksi/2015/270/contents/made Non-print

The Air Navigation (Restriction of Flying) (Guildford) Regulations 2015 No. 2015/1079. - Enabling power: S.I. 2009/3015, art. 161. - Issued: 02.04.2015. Made: 26.03.2015. Coming into force: 27.06.2015. Effect: None. Territorial extent & classification: E. Local. - Available at http://www.legislation.gov.uk/uksi/2015/1079/contents/made Non-print

The Air Navigation (Restriction of Flying) (Her Majesty The Queen's Birthday Flypast) Regulations 2015 No. 2015/1311. - Enabling power: S.I. 2009/3015, art. 161. - Issued: 14.05.2015. Made: 11.05.2015. Coming into force: 09.06.2015. Effect: None. Territorial extent & classification: E. Local. - Available at http://www.legislation.gov.uk/uksi/2015/1311/contents/made Non-print

The Air Navigation (Restriction of Flying) (Hylands Park) Regulations 2015 No. 2015/1323. - Enabling power: S.I. 2009/3015, art. 161. - Issued: 18.05.2015. Made: 14.05.2015. Coming into force: 21.08.2015. Effect: None. Territorial extent & classification: E. Local. - Available at http://www.legislation.gov.uk/uksi/2015/1323/contents/made Non-print

The Air Navigation (Restriction of Flying) (Jet Formation Display Teams) (No. 2) (Amendment) Regulations 2015 No. 2015/1372. - Enabling power: S.I. 2009/3015, art. 161. - Issued: 12.06.2015. Made: 08.06.2015. Coming into force: 05.07.2015. Effect: S.I. 2015/1281 amended. Territorial extent & classification: E. Local. - Available at http://www.legislation.gov.uk/uksi/2015/1372/contents/made Non-print

The Air Navigation (Restriction of Flying) (Jet Formation Display Teams) (No. 2) Regulations 2015 No. 2015/1281. - Enabling power: S.I. 2009/3015, art. 161. - Issued: 06.05.2015. Made: 30.04.2015. Coming into force: 23.05.2015. Effect: None. Territorial extent & classification: E. Local. - Available at http://www.legislation.gov.uk/uksi/2015/1281/contents/made Non-print

The Air Navigation (Restriction of Flying) (Jet Formation Display Teams) (No. 3) (Amendment) Regulations 2015 No. 2015/1676. - Enabling power: S.I. 2009/3015, art. 161. - Issued: 14.09.2015. Made: 14.08.2015. Coming into force: 29.08.2015. Effect: S.I. 2015/1389 amended. Territorial extent & classification: E. Local. - Available at http://www.legislation.gov.uk/uksi/2015/1676/contents/made Non-print

The Air Navigation (Restriction of Flying) (Jet Formation Display Teams) (No. 3) Regulations 2015 No. 2015/1389. - Enabling power: S.I. 2009/3015, art. 161. - Issued: 18.06.2015. Made: 16.06.2015. Coming into force: 29.07.2015. Effect: None. Territorial extent & classification: E. Local. - Available at http://www.legislation.gov.uk/uksi/2015/1389/contents/made Non-print

CIVIL AVIATION

The Air Navigation (Restriction of Flying) (Jet Formation Display Teams) Regulations 2015 No. 2015/257. - Enabling power: S.I. 2009/3015, art. 161. - Issued: 30.01.2015. Made: 26.01.2015. Coming into force: 05.03.2015. Effect: None. Territorial extent & classification: E. Local. - Available at http://www.legislation.gov.uk/uksi/2015/257/contents/made Non-print

The Air Navigation (Restriction of Flying) (Kensworth) Regulations 2015 No. 2015/1343. - Enabling power: S.I. 2009/3015, art. 161. - Issued: 03.06.2015. Made: at 16.50 hours 22.05.2015. Coming into force: with immediate effect. Effect: None. Territorial extent & classification: E. Local. - Available at http://www.legislation.gov.uk/uksi/2015/1343/contents/made Non-print

The Air Navigation (Restriction of Flying) (Kensworth) (Revocation) Regulations 2015 No. 2015/1345. - Enabling power: S.I. 2009/3015, art. 161. - Issued: 03.06.2015. Made: at 18.05 hours 22.05.2015. Coming into force: with immediate effect. Effect: S.I. 2015/1343 revoked. Territorial extent & classification: E. Local. - Available at http://www.legislation.gov.uk/uksi/2015/1345/contents/made Non-print

The Air Navigation (Restriction of Flying) (Manchester) Regulations 2015 No. 2015/1609. - Enabling power: S.I. 2009/3015, art. 161. - Issued: 17.08.2015. Made: 11.08.2015. Coming into force: 03.10.2015. Effect: None. Territorial extent & classification: E. Local. - Available at http://www.legislation.gov.uk/uksi/2015/1609/contents/made Non-print

The Air Navigation (Restriction of Flying) (Northampton Sywell) (Amendment) Regulations 2015 No. 2015/1117. - Enabling power: S.I. 2009/3015, art. 161. - Issued: 20.04.2015. Made: 15.04.2015. Coming into force: 29.05.2015. Effect: S.I. 2015/0264 amended. Territorial extent & classification: E. Local. - Available at http://www.legislation.gov.uk/uksi/2015/1117/contents/made Non-print

The Air Navigation (Restriction of Flying) (Northampton Sywell) (No. 2) Regulations 2015 No. 2015/1074. - Enabling power: S.I. 2009/3015, art. 161. - Issued: 10.03.2015. Made: 03.03.2015. Coming into force: 04.09.2015. Effect: None. Territorial extent & classification: E. Local. - Available at http://www.legislation.gov.uk/uksi/2015/1074/contents/made Non-print

The Air Navigation (Restriction of Flying) (Northampton Sywell) Regulations 2015 No. 2015/264. - Enabling power: S.I. 2009/3015, art. 161. - Issued: 13.02.2015. Made: 09.02.2015. Coming into force: 29.05.2015. Effect: None. Territorial extent & classification: E. Local. - Available at http://www.legislation.gov.uk/uksi/2015/264/contents/made Non-print

The Air Navigation (Restriction of Flying) (Northern Ireland International Air Show) Regulations 2015 No. 2015/1073. - Enabling power: S.I. 2009/3015, art. 161. - Issued: 13.03.2015. Made: 10.03.2015. Coming into force: 05.09.2015. Effect: None. Territorial extent & classification: E. Local. - Available at http://www.legislation.gov.uk/uksi/2015/1073/contents/made Non-print

The Air Navigation (Restriction of Flying) (Oulton Park) Regulations 2015 No. 2015/1356. - Enabling power: S.I. 2009/3015, art. 161. - Issued: 09.06.2015. Made: 04.06.2015. Coming into force: 31.07.2015. Effect: None. Territorial extent & classification: E. Local. - Available at http://www.legislation.gov.uk/uksi/2015/1356/contents/made Non-print

The Air Navigation (Restriction of Flying) (Overton) Regulations 2015 No. 2015/1365. - Enabling power: S.I. 2009/3015, art. 161. - Issued: 11.06.2015. Made: 08.06.2015. Coming into force: 28.08.2015. Effect: None. Territorial extent & classification: E. Local. - Available at http://www.legislation.gov.uk/uksi/2015/1365/contents/made Non-print

The Air Navigation (Restriction of Flying) (Overton) (Revocation) Regulations 2015 No. 2015/1665. - Enabling power: S.I. 2009/3015, art. 161. - Issued: 10.09.2015. Made: 25.08.2015. Coming into force: with immediate effect. Effect: S.I. 2015/1365 revoked. Territorial extent & classification: E. Local. - Available at http://www.legislation.gov.uk/uksi/2015/1665/contents/made Non-print

The Air Navigation (Restriction of Flying) (Portsmouth) Regulations 2015 No. 2015/1355. - Enabling power: S.I. 2009/3015, art. 161. - Issued: 09.06.2015. Made: 04.06.2015. Coming into force: 23.07.2015. Effect: None. Territorial extent & classification: E. Local. - Available at http://www.legislation.gov.uk/uksi/2015/1355/contents/made Non-print

The Air Navigation (Restriction of Flying) (Remembrance Sunday) Regulations 2015 No. 2015/1704. - Enabling power: S.I. 2009/3015, art. 161. - Issued: 25.09.2015. Made: 21.09.2015. Coming into force: 08.11.2015. Effect: None. Territorial extent & classification: E. Local. - Available at http://www.legislation.gov.uk/uksi/2015/1704/contents/made Non-print

The Air Navigation (Restriction of Flying) (RNAS Yeovilton) Regulations 2015 No. 2015/265. - Enabling power: S.I. 2009/3015, art. 161. - Issued: 16.02.2015. Made: 28.01.2015. Coming into force: 10.07.2015. Effect: None. Territorial extent & classification: E. Local. - Available at http://www.legislation.gov.uk/uksi/2015/265/contents/made Non-print

The Air Navigation (Restriction of Flying) (Royal Air Force Cosford) Regulations 2015 No. 2015/510. - Enabling power: S.I. 2009/3015, art. 161. - Issued: 19.02.2015. Made: 10.02.2015. Coming into force: 12.06.2015. Effect: None. Territorial extent & classification: E. Local. - Available at http://www.legislation.gov.uk/uksi/2015/510/contents/made Non-print

The Air Navigation (Restriction of Flying) (Royal International Air Tattoo RAF Fairford) Regulations 2015 No. 2015/1078. - Enabling power: S.I. 2009/3015, art. 161. - Issued: 02.04.2015. Made: 05.03.2015. Coming into force: 15.07.2015. Effect: None. Territorial extent & classification: E. Local. - Available at http://www.legislation.gov.uk/uksi/2015/1078/contents/made Non-print

The Air Navigation (Restriction of Flying) (Royal Naval Air Station Culdrose) Regulations 2015 No. 2015/1312. - Enabling power: S.I. 2009/3015, art. 161. - Issued: 14.05.2015. Made: 11.05.2015. Coming into force: 29.07.2015. Effect: None. Territorial extent & classification: E. Local. - Available at http://www.legislation.gov.uk/uksi/2015/1312/contents/made Non-print

The Air Navigation (Restriction of Flying) (Runnymede) Regulations 2015 No. 2015/1354. - Enabling power: S.I. 2009/3015, art. 161. - Issued: 09.06.2015. Made: 04.06.2015. Coming into force: 15.06.2015. Effect: None. Territorial extent & classification: E. Local. - Available at http://www.legislation.gov.uk/uksi/2015/1354/contents/made Non-print

The Air Navigation (Restriction of Flying) (Sandringham House) (Restricted Zone EG R219) Regulations 2015 No. 2015/1734. - Enabling power: S.I. 2009/3015, art. 161. - Issued: 05.10.2015. Made: 29.09.2015. Coming into force: 01.12.2015. Effect: None. Territorial extent & classification: E. Local. - Available at http://www.legislation.gov.uk/uksi/2015/1734/contents/made Non-print

The Air Navigation (Restriction of Flying) (Scottish Highlands) (Revocation) Regulations 2015 No. 2015/1589. - Enabling power: S.I. 2009/3015, art. 161. - Issued: 06.08.2015. Made: 03.08.2015. Coming into force: 04.08.2015. Effect: S.I. 2008/1239 revoked. Territorial extent & classification: E. Local. - Available at http://www.legislation.gov.uk/uksi/2015/1589/contents/made Non-print

The Air Navigation (Restriction of Flying) (Shoreham-by-Sea) Regulations 2015 No. 2015/1075. - Enabling power: S.I. 2009/3015, art. 161. - Issued: 02.04.2015. Made: 26.03.2015. Coming into force: 22.08.2015. Effect: None. Territorial extent & classification: E. Local. - Available at http://www.legislation.gov.uk/uksi/2015/1075/contents/made Non-print

The Air Navigation (Restriction of Flying) (Shoreham) (No.2) Regulations 2015 No. 2015/1700. - Enabling power: S.I. 2009/3015, art. 161. - Issued: 22.09.2015. Made: 23.08.2015 at 18.30 hours. Coming into force: with immediate effect. Effect: None. Territorial extent & classification: E. Local. - Available at http://www.legislation.gov.uk/uksi/2015/1700/contents/made Non-print

The Air Navigation (Restriction of Flying) (Shoreham) (No.2) (Revocation) Regulations 2015 No. 2015/1722. - Enabling power: S.I. 2009/3015, art. 161. - Issued: 29.09.2015. Made: 01.09.2015 at 16.10 hours. Coming into force: with immediate effect. Effect: S.I. 2015/1700. Territorial extent & classification: E. Local. - Available at http://www.legislation.gov.uk/uksi/2015/1722/contents/made Non-print

CIVIL AVIATION

The Air Navigation (Restriction of Flying) (Shoreham) Regulations 2015 No. 2015/1699. - Enabling power: S.I. 2009/3015, art. 161. - Issued: 22.09.2015. Made: 22.08.2015 at 17.19 hours. Coming into force: with immediate effect. Effect: None. Territorial extent & classification: E. Local. - Available at http://www.legislation.gov.uk/uksi/2015/1699/contents/made Non-print

The Air Navigation (Restriction of Flying) (Shoreham) (Revocation) Regulations 2015 No. 2015/1721. - Enabling power: S.I. 2009/3015, art. 161. - Issued: 29.09.2015. Made: 23.08.2015 at 10.30 hours. Coming into force: with immediate effect. Effect: S.I. 2015/1699 Territorial extent & classification: E. Local. - Available at http://www.legislation.gov.uk/uksi/2015/1721/contents/made Non-print

The Air Navigation (Restriction of Flying) (Silverstone and Turweston) Regulations 2015 No. 2015/511. - Enabling power: S.I. 2009/3015, art. 161. - Issued: 20.02.2015. Made: 13.02.2015. Coming into force: 04.07.2015. Effect: None. Territorial extent & classification: E. Local. - Available at http://www.legislation.gov.uk/uksi/2015/511/contents/made Non-print

The Air Navigation (Restriction of Flying) (Southport) (Amendment) Regulations 2015 No. 2015/1664. - Enabling power: S.I. 2009/3015, art. 161. - Issued: 10.09.2015. Made: 14.08.2015. Coming into force: 19.09.2015. Effect: S.I. 2015/1097 amended. Territorial extent & classification: E. Local. - Available at http://www.legislation.gov.uk/uksi/2015/1664/contents/made Non-print

The Air Navigation (Restriction of Flying) (Southport) Regulations 2015 No. 2015/1097. - Enabling power: S.I. 2009/3015, art. 161. - Issued: 17.04.2015. Made: 14.04.2015. Coming into force: 19.09.2015. Effect: None. Territorial extent & classification: E. Local. - Available at http://www.legislation.gov.uk/uksi/2015/1097/contents/made Non-print

The Air Navigation (Restriction of Flying) (State Opening of Parliament) Regulations 2015 No. 2015/1318. - Enabling power: S.I. 2009/3015, art. 161. - Issued: 01.06.2015. Made: 12.05.2015. Coming into force: 27.05.2015. Effect: None. Territorial extent & classification: E. Local. - Available at http://www.legislation.gov.uk/uksi/2015/1318/contents/made Non-print

The Air Navigation (Restriction of Flying) (Stokes Bay) Regulations 2015 No. 2015/1106. - Enabling power: S.I. 2009/3015, art. 161. - Issued: 17.04.2015. Made: 19.03.2015. Coming into force: 22.03.2015. Effect: None. Territorial extent & classification: E. Local. - Available at http://www.legislation.gov.uk/uksi/2015/1106/contents/made Non-print

The Air Navigation (Restriction of Flying) (Stonehenge) Regulations 2015 No. 2015/266. - Enabling power: S.I. 2009/3015, art. 161. - Issued: 12.02.2015. Made: 20.01.2015. Coming into force: 20.06.2015. Effect: None. Territorial extent & classification: E. Local. - Available at http://www.legislation.gov.uk/uksi/2015/266/contents/made Non-print

The Air Navigation (Restriction of Flying) (Strathallan Castle) Regulations 2015 No. 2015/1118. - Enabling power: S.I. 2009/3015, art. 161. - Issued: 20.04.2015. Made: 15.04.2015. Coming into force: 09.07.2015. Effect: None. Territorial extent & classification: E. Local. - Available at http://www.legislation.gov.uk/uksi/2015/1118/contents/made Non-print

The Air Navigation (Restriction of Flying) (Sunderland) Regulations 2015 No. 2015/514. - Enabling power: S.I. 2009/3015, art. 161. - Issued: 26.02.2015. Made: 19.02.2015. Coming into force: 24.07.2015. Effect: None. Territorial extent & classification: E. Local. - Available at http://www.legislation.gov.uk/uksi/2015/514/contents/made Non-print

The Air Navigation (Restriction of Flying) (The Solent, Hampshire) (Amendment) Regulations 2015 No. 2015/146. - Enabling power: S.I. 2009/3015, art. 161. - Issued: 10.02.2015. Made: 22.01.2015. Coming into force: 22.01.2015. Effect: S.I. 2015/144 amended. Territorial extent & classification: E. Local. - Available at http://www.legislation.gov.uk/uksi/2015/146/contents/made Non-print

The Air Navigation (Restriction of Flying) (The Solent, Hampshire) Regulations 2015 No. 2015/144. - Enabling power: S.I. 2009/3015, art. 161. - Issued: 06.02.2015. Made: 21.01.2015. Coming into force: 21.01.2015 at 16.45 hours. Effect: None. Territorial extent & classification: E. Local. - Available at http://www.legislation.gov.uk/uksi/2015/144/contents/made Non-print

The Air Navigation (Restriction of Flying) (Tonbridge) (Emergency) (No. 2) Regulations 2015 No. 2015/1918. - Enabling power: S.I. 2009/3015, art. 161. - Issued: 18.11.2015. Made: 13.11.2015 at 1705 hrs. Coming into force: with immediate effect. Effect: None. Territorial extent & classification: E. Local. - Revoked by S.I. 2015/1922 (Non-print) (ISBN 9786666734855). - Available at http://www.legislation.gov.uk/uksi/2015/1918/contents/made Non-print

The Air Navigation (Restriction of Flying) (Tonbridge) (Emergency) (No. 2) (Revocation) Regulations 2015 No. 2015/1922. - Enabling power: S.I. 2009/3015, art. 161. - Issued: 19.11.2015. Made: 19.11.2015. Coming into force: With immediate effect. Effect: S.I. 2015/1918 revoked. Territorial extent & classification: E. Local. - Available at http://www.legislation.gov.uk/uksi/2015/1922/contents/made Non-print

The Air Navigation (Restriction of Flying) (Tonbridge) (Emergency) Regulations 2015 No. 2015/1900. - Enabling power: S.I. 2009/3015, art. 161. - Issued: 16.11.2015. Made: 11.11.2015, at 16:00 hours. Coming into force: with immediate effect. Effect: None. Territorial extent & classification: E. Local. - Revoked by S.I. 2015/1903 (Non-print) (ISBN 9786666734787). - Available at http://www.legislation.gov.uk/uksi/2015/1900/contents/made Non-print

The Air Navigation (Restriction of Flying) (Tonbridge) (Emergency) (Revocation) Regulations 2015 No. 2015/1903. - Enabling power: S.I. 2009/3015, art. 161. - Issued: 17.11.2015. Made: 12.11.2015 at 1400 hours. Coming into force: with immediate effect. Effect: S.I. 2015/1900 revoked. Territorial extent & classification: E. Local. - Available at http://www.legislation.gov.uk/uksi/2015/1903/contents/made Non-print

The Air Navigation (Restriction of Flying) (Trooping the Colour) Regulations 2015 No. 2015/1080. - Enabling power: S.I. 2009/3015, art. 161. - Issued: 02.04.2015. Made: 05.03.2015. Coming into force: 13.06.2015. Effect: None. Territorial extent & classification: E. Local. - Available at http://www.legislation.gov.uk/uksi/2015/1080/contents/made Non-print

The Air Navigation (Restriction of Flying) (Wales National Airshow) Regulations 2015 No. 2015/513. - Enabling power: S.I. 2009/3015, art. 161. - Issued: 26.02.2015. Made: 19.02.2015. Coming into force: 11.07.2015. Effect: None. Territorial extent & classification: E. Local. - Available at http://www.legislation.gov.uk/uksi/2015/513/contents/made Non-print

The Air Navigation (Restriction of Flying) (Wales Rally GB) Regulations 2015 No. 2015/1747. - Enabling power: S.I. 2009/3015, art. 161 . - Issued: 07.10.2015. Made: 05.10.2015. Laid: - Coming into force: 13.11.2015. Effect: None. Territorial extent & classification: E. Local. - Available at http://www.legislation.gov.uk/uksi/2015/1747/contents/made Non-print

The Air Navigation (Restriction of Flying) (Weston Park) Regulations 2015 No. 2015/1076. - Enabling power: S.I. 2009/3015, art. 161. - Issued: 12.03.2015. Made: 03.03.2015. Coming into force: 21.08.2015. Effect: None. Territorial extent & classification: E. Local. - Available at http://www.legislation.gov.uk/uksi/2015/1076/contents/made Non-print

The Air Navigation (Restriction of Flying) (Wimbledon) Regulations 2015 No. 2015/269. - Enabling power: S.I. 2009/3015, art. 161. - Issued: 12.02.2015. Made: 22.01.2015. Coming into force: 29.06.2015. Effect: None. Territorial extent & classification: E. Local. - Available at http://www.legislation.gov.uk/uksi/2015/269/contents/made Non-print

The Aviation Security Regulations 1982 (Civil Penalties) Regulations 2015 No. 2015/930. - Enabling power: Aviation Security Act 1982, s. 22A. - Issued: 31.03.2015. Made: 25.03.2015. Coming into force: 16.04.2015. Effect: None. Territorial extent & classification: E/W/S/NI. General. - Supersedes draft S.I. (ISBN 9780111131008) issued 04.03.2015. - 8p.: 30 cm. - 978-0-11-113552-5 £6.00

The International Interests in Aircraft Equipment (Cape Town Convention) Regulations 2015 No. 2015/912. - Enabling power: European Communities Act 1972, s. 2 (2). - Issued: 01.04.2015. Made: 23.03.2015. Laid: 26.03.2015. Coming into force: In accord. with reg. 2. Effect: 1982 c.16 & S.I. 1972/1268; 2001/493, 494; 2009/3015; 2012/3038 amended. Territorial extent & classification: E/W/S/NI. General. - 80p.: 30 cm. - 978-0-11-113536-5 £14.25

The Rules of the Air Regulations 2015 No. 2015/840. - Enabling power: S.I. 2009/3015, art. 160 (1). - Issued: 27.03.2015. Made: 17.03.2015. Coming into force: 30.04.2015. Effect: S.I. 2007/734, 1371; 2008/669; 2009/2169; 2010/841 revoked. Territorial extent & classification: E/W/S/NI. General. - 16p.: 30 cm. - 978-0-11-113467-2 £8.50

Civil partnership

The Proposed Marriages and Civil Partnerships (Conduct of Investigations, etc.) Regulations 2015 No. 2015/397. - Enabling power: Immigration Act 2014, ss. 50 (1) (5) (9) (10), 51 (1) (d) (3) (4) (5), 74 (8) (d). - Issued: 05.03.2015. Made: 26.02.2015. Coming into force: 01.03.2015. Effect: None. Territorial extent & classification: E/W/S/NI. General. - Supersedes draft SI (ISBN 9780111125564) issued 17/12/14 - 12p.: 30 cm. - 978-0-11-113103-9 £6.00

The Proposed Marriages and Civil Partnerships (Meaning of Exempt Persons and Notice) Regulations 2015 No. 2015/122. - Enabling power: Immigration Act 2014, ss. 49 (3) (4), 61 (1) (2), 74 (8) (d). - Issued: 11.02.2015. Made: 02.02.2015. Laid: 05.02.2015. Coming into force: 02.03.2015. Effect: None. Territorial extent & classification: UK [parts E/W only]. General. - 8p.: 30 cm. - 978-0-11-112884-8 £6.00

The Referral and Investigation of Proposed Marriages and Civil Partnerships (Northern Ireland and Miscellaneous Provisions) Order 2015 No. 2015/395. - Enabling power: Immigration Act 2014, ss. 53 (1) (2) (3), 74 (8) (c) (d). - Issued: 06.03.2015. Made: 26.02.2015. Coming into force: 01.03.2015. Effect: 2004 c.19, 33, 2014 c.22 & S.R. 2005/482 & S.I. 2003/413 (N.I. 3) amended. Territorial extent & classification: E/W/S/NI. General. - Supersedes draft S.I. (ISBN 9780111125025) issued 19/12/14. - 24p.: 30 cm. - 978-0-11-113104-6 £6.00

Civil partnership, England and Wales

The Marriage (Authorised Persons) and Civil Partnership (Registration Provisions) (Amendment) Regulations 2015 No. 2015/177. - Enabling power: Marriage Act 1949, s. 74 (1) (a) & Civil Partnership Act 2004, ss. 8 (2), 9E (1), 12 (2), 21 (2), 36 (1) (2) (a) (3), 258 (2). - Issued: 16.02.2015. Made: 05.02.2015. Laid: - Coming into force: 02.03.2015. Effect: S.I. 1952/1869; 2005/3176 amended. Territorial extent & classification: E/W. General. - 16p.: 30 cm. - 978-0-11-112914-2 £6.00

The Proposed Marriages and Civil Partnerships (Waiting Period) Regulations 2015 No. 2015/159. - Enabling power: Marriage Act 1949, ss. 31 (5ED), 74 (3) & Civil Partnership Act 2004, ss. 12(7), 258 (2). - Issued: 13.02.2015. Made: 02.02.2015. Coming into force: 02.03.2015. Effect: None. Territorial extent & classification: E/W. General. - 8p.: 30 cm. - 978-0-11-112900-5 £6.00

The Referral of Proposed Marriages and Civil Partnerships Regulations 2015 No. 2015/123. - Enabling power: Marriage Act 1949, ss. 28D, 28G (2) (3), 28H (5) (c) (7) (10) (b) (c) & Civil Partnership Act 2004, ss. 9B, 9E (2) (3), 12A (5) (c) (7) (9) (b) (c). - Issued: 10.02.2015. Made: 02.02.2015. Laid: 05.02.2015. Coming into force: 02.03.2015. Effect: None. Territorial extent & classification: E/W. General. - 16p.: 30 cm. - 978-0-11-112877-0 £6.00

Civil partnership, Northern Ireland

The Sham Marriage and Civil Partnership (Scotland and Northern Ireland) (Administrative) Regulations 2015 No. 2015/404. - Enabling power: Immigration Act 2014, ss. 54 (2) (3), 74 (8) (d), sch. 5. - Issued: 05.03.2015. Made: 26.02.2015. Laid before the Scottish Parliament: 27.02.2015. Coming into force: 02.03.2015. Effect: None. Territorial extent & classification: S/NI. General. - 24p.: 30 cm. - 978-0-11-113091-9 £6.00

Civil partnership, Scotland

The Referral and Investigation of Proposed Marriages and Civil Partnerships (Scotland) Order 2015 No. 2015/396. - Enabling power: Immigration Act 2014, ss. 53 (1) (2) (3), 74 (8) (c) (d). - Issued: 06.03.2015. Made: 26.02.2015. Coming into force: 01.03.2015. Effect: 1977 c.15; 2004 c.19, c.33; 2014 c.22 amended. Territorial extent & classification: E/W/S/NI. General. - Supersedes draft S.I. (ISBN) issued 17/12/14. - 24p.: 30 cm. - 978-0-11-113105-3 £6.00

The Sham Marriage and Civil Partnership (Scotland and Northern Ireland) (Administrative) Regulations 2015 No. 2015/404. - Enabling power: Immigration Act 2014, ss. 54 (2) (3), 74 (8) (d), sch. 5. - Issued: 05.03.2015. Made: 26.02.2015. Laid before the Scottish Parliament: 27.02.2015. Coming into force: 02.03.2015. Effect: None. Territorial extent & classification: S/NI. General. - 24p.: 30 cm. - 978-0-11-113091-9 £6.00

Clean air, England

The Smoke Control Areas (Exempted Fireplaces) (England) Order 2015 No. 2015/307. - Enabling power: Clean Air Act 1993, s. 21. - Issued: 23.02.2015. Made: 16.02.2015. Laid: 19.02.2015. Coming into force: 06.04.2015. Effect: S.I. S.I. 2001/422; 2003/2328; 2014/2404 revoked & S.I. 1970/615, 1667; 1971/1265; 1972/438, 955; 1973/2166; 1974/762, 855; 1975/1001, 1111; 1978/1609; 1982/1615; 1983/277, 426, 1018; 1984/1649; 1985/864; 1986/638; 1988/2282; 1989/1769; 1990/345, 2457 revoked in relation to England. Territorial extent & classification: E. General. - 152p.: 30 cm. - 978-0-11-112997-5 £23.25

Clean air, Wales

The Smoke Control Areas (Authorised Fuels) (Wales) (Amendment) Regulations 2015 No. 2015/1517 (W.176). - Enabling power: Clean Air Act 1993, s. 20 (6). - Issued: 25.08.2015. Made: 08.07.2015. Laid before the National Assembly for Wales: 15.07.2015. Coming into force: 04.08.2015. Effect: WSI 2014/684 (W.74) revoked. Territorial extent & classification: W. General. - In English and Welsh. Welsh title: Rheoliadau Ardaloedd Rheoli Mwg (Tanwyddau Awdurdodedig) (Cymru) 2015. - 28p.: 30 cm. - 978-0-348-11146-0 £6.00

The Smoke Control Areas (Exempted Fireplaces) (Wales) Order 2015 No. 2015/1513 (W.175). - Enabling power: Clean Air Act 1993, s. 21. - Issued: 28.07.2015. Made: 08.07.2015. Laid before the National Assembly for Wales: 15.07.2015. Coming into force: 11.08.2015. Effect: S.I. 2014/694 (W.75) revoked. Territorial extent & classification: W. General. - In English and Welsh. Welsh title: Gorchymyn Ardaloedd Rheoli Mwg (Lleoedd Tân Esempt) (Cymru) 2015. - 332p.: 30 cm. - 978-0-348-11132-3 £39.25

Climate change

The Carbon Accounting (2013-2017 Budgetary Period) Regulations 2015 No. 2015/775. - Enabling power: Climate Change Act 2008, ss. 26 (2), 27 (3) (4). - Issued: 25.03.2015. Made: 18.03.2015. Laid: 23.03.2015. Coming into force: 24.03.2015. Effect: S.I. 2009/1257 amended. Territorial extent & classification: E/W/S/NI. General. - 6p.: 30 cm. - 978-0-11-113403-0 £4.25

The Greenhouse Gas Emissions Trading Scheme (Amendment) Regulations 2015 No. 2015/1849. - Enabling power: Pollution Prevention and Control Act 1999, ss. 2, 7 (9), sch. 1 & European Communities Act 1972 s. 2 (2). - Issued: 06.11.2015. Made: 01.11.2015. Laid: 04.11.2015. Coming into force: 04.12.2015. Effect: S.I. 2012/3038 amended. Territorial extent & classification: E/W/S/NI. General. - 16p.: 30 cm. - 978-0-11-114045-1 £6.00

Climate change levy

The Climate Change Levy (General) (Amendment) Regulations 2015 No. 2015/947. - Enabling power: Finance Act 2000, sch. 6, paras 22, 24B (3), 24D, 62 (1) (bb), 146 (7). - Issued: 02.04.2015. Made: 26.03.2015. Laid before the House of Commons: 27.03.2015. Coming into force: 01.04.2015. Effect: S.I. 2001/838 amended. Territorial extent & classification: E/W/S. General. - With correction slip dated January 2016. - 4p.: 30 cm. - 978-0-11-113573-0 £4.25

Coast protection, England

The Coast Protection (Variation of Excluded Waters) (England) Regulations 2015 No. 2015/523. - Enabling power: Coast Protection Act 1949, sch. 4, para. 113. - Issued: 11.03.2015. Made: 03.03.2015. Laid: 06.03.2015. Coming into force: 06.04.2015. Effect: 1949 c.74 varied & S.I. 1958/2146; 1965/204; 1975/1365; 1983/1203, 1503; 1992/1549; 1993/1149; 1997/2675 revoked. Territorial extent & classification: E. General. - 8p.: 30 cm. - 978-0-11-113209-8 £4.25

Commons, England

The Bodmin Moor Commons Council Establishment Order 2015 No. 2015/1515. - Enabling power: Commons Act 2006, ss. 26, 29 (3) (4), 30, 31 (1) to (4), 35 (2), 36 (1) (2) (b). - Issued: 20.07.2015. Made: 14.07.2015. Laid: 16.07.2015. Coming into force: 01.09.2015. Effect: 1908 c.34 revoked with saving. Territorial extent & classification: E. General. - 16p.: 30 cm. - 978-0-11-113792-5 £6.00

Community infrastructure levy, England and Wales

The Community Infrastructure Levy (Amendment) Regulations 2015 No. 2015/836. - Enabling power: Planning Act 2008, ss. 205 (1), 218 (2) (4) (a), 220 (3), 222 (1). - Issued: 27.03.2015. Made: 20.03.2015. Coming into force: In accord. with reg. 1. Effect: S.I. 2010/948 amended. Territorial extent & classification: E/W. General. - Supersedes draf S.I. (ISBN 9780111128374) issued 04/02/15. - 4p.: 30 cm. - 978-0-11-113464-1 £4.25

Companies

The Accounting Standards (Prescribed Bodies) (United States of America and Japan) Regulations 2015 No. 2015/1675. - Enabling power: Companies Act 2006, ss. 464 (1) (3), 1292 (1) (a) & Interpretation Act 1978, s. 14A. - Issued: 16.09.2015. Made: 09.09.2015. Coming into force: 01.10.2015. Effect: None. Territorial extent & classification: E/W/S/NI. General. - These regulations cease to have effect on 30th September 2023. - 4p.: 30 cm. - 978-0-11-113921-9 £4.25

The Companies Act 2006 (Amendment of Part 17) Regulations 2015 No. 2015/472. - Enabling power: Companies Act 2006, s. 657. - Issued: 10.03.2015. Made: 03.03.2015. Coming into force: 04.03.2015 in accord. with reg. 2 (1). Effect: 2006 c.46 amended. Territorial extent & classification: E/W/S/NI. General. - Supersedes draft S.I. (ISBN 9780111127353) issued 22.01.2015. - 4p.: 30 cm. - 978-0-11-113166-4 £4.25

The Companies Act 2006 (Amendment of Part 18) Regulations 2015 No. 2015/532. - Enabling power: Companies Act 2006, s. 737. - Issued: 11.03.2015. Made: 02.03.2015. Coming into force: 06.04.2015. Effect: 2006 c. 46 amended. Territorial extent & classification: E/W/S/NI. General. - Supersedes draft SI (ISBN 9780111127094) issued 19/01/15 - 4p.: 30 cm. - 978-0-11-113213-5 £4.25

The Companies and Limited Liability Partnerships (Filing Requirements) Regulations 2015 No. 2015/1695. - Enabling power: European Communities Act 1972, s. 2 (2) & Interpretation Act 1978, s. 14A & Limited Liability Partnerships Act 2000, ss. 15 (a), 17 (3) (a) & Companies Act 2006, ss. 1042, 1043, 1292 (1). - Issued: 24.09.2015. Made: 17.09.2015. Laid: 18.09.2015. Coming into force: 10.10.2015. Effect: S.I. 1989/638; 2004/2326; 2009/1804, 2436, 2437 amended. Territorial extent & classification: E/W/S/NI. General. - 8p.: 30 cm. - 978-0-11-113935-6 £6.00

The Companies (Cross-Border Mergers) (Amendment) Regulations 2015 No. 2015/180. - Enabling power: European Communities Act 1972, s.2 (2). - Issued: 16.02.2015. Made: 09.02.2015. Laid: 12.02.2015. Coming into force: 06.04.2015. Effect: S.I. 2007/2974 amended. Territorial extent & classification: E/W/S/NI. General. - 2p.: 30 cm. - 978-0-11-112917-3 £4.25

The Companies (Disclosure of Address) (Amendment) Regulations 2015 No. 2015/842. - Enabling power: Companies Act 2006, ss. 243 (2). - Issued: 30.03.2015. Made: 23.03.2015. Laid: 24.03.2015. Coming into force: 30.06.2015. Effect: S.I. 2009/214 amended. Territorial extent & classification: E/W/S/NI. General. - 2p.: 30 cm. - 978-0-11-113468-9 £4.25

The Companies (Disclosures of Date of Birth Information) Regulations 2015 No. 2015/1694. - Enabling power: Companies Act 2006, ss. 243 (3), 1087B (2) (3), 1292 (1). - Issued: 23.09.2015. Made: 17.09.2015. Laid: 18.09.2015. Coming into force: 10.10.2015. Effect: None. Territorial extent & classification: E/W/S/NI. General. - 8p.: 30 cm. - 978-0-11-113934-9 £6.00

The Companies, Partnerships and Groups (Accounts and Reports) (No. 2) Regulations 2015 No. 2015/1672. - Enabling power: Companies Act 2006, ss. 396 (3), 473 (2), 1292 (1). - Issued: 16.09.2015. Made: 09.09.2015. Laid: 10.09.2015. Coming into force: 01.10.2015. Effect: S.I. 2008/409, 410; 2015/980 amended. Territorial extent & classification: E/W/S/NI. General. - 4p.: 30 cm. - 978-0-11-113920-2 £4.25

The Companies, Partnerships and Groups (Accounts and Reports) Regulations 2015 No. 2015/980. - Enabling power: European Communities Act 1972, s. 2 (2) & Companies Act 2006, ss. 396 (3), 404 (3), 409 (1) (2), 412 (1) (2), 468 (1) (2), 473 (2), 484, 1292 (1). - Issued: 01.04.2015. Made: 26.03.2015. Coming into force: 06.04.2015. Effect: 2006 c.46; S.I. 2008/373, 409, 410, 569 amended. Territorial extent & classification: E/W/S/NI. General. - Supersedes draft S.I. (ISBN 9780111130230) issued 27/02/15. - 40p.: 30 cm. - 978-0-11-113613-3 £10.00

The Company, Limited Liability Partnership and Business (Names and Trading Disclosures) Regulations 2015 No. 2015/17. - Enabling power: Companies Act 2006, ss. 54 (1) (c), 56 (1) (a) (5), 57 (1) (a) (2) (5), 60 (1) (b), 65 (1) (2) (4), 66 (2) (3) (4) (6), 82, 84, 1193 (1) (c), 1195 (1) (a) (5), 1197 (1) (2) (3), 1292 (1) (2), 1294, 1296. - Issued: 15.01.2015. Made: 07.01.2015. Coming into force: 31.01.2015. Effect: 2000 c.38; S.I. 1989/638; 2003/1593; 2009/1803; 2011/245 amended & S.I. 2008/495; 2009/218, 1085, 2404, 2982 revoked. Territorial extent & classification: E/W/S/NI. General. - Supersedes S.I. draft (ISBN 9780111124154) issued 03/12/14. - 28p.: 30 cm. - 978-0-11-112691-2 £6.00

The Reports on Payments to Governments (Amendment) Regulations 2015 No. 2015/1928. - Enabling power: European Communities Act 1972 s. 2 (2) & Companies Act 2006 ss. 1102 (2) (3). - Issued: 27.11.2015. Made: 23.11.2015. Laid: 25.11.2015. Coming into force: 18.12.2015. Effect: S.I. 2014/3209 amended. Territorial extent & classification: E/W/S/NI. General. - This Statutory Instrument has been made in consequence of defects in S.I. 2014/3209 (ISBN 9780111124604) as is being issued free of charge to all known recipients of that Statutory Instrument. - 8p.: 30 cm. - 978-0-11-114116-8 £4.25

The Small Business, Enterprise and Employment Act 2015 (Commencement No. 1) Regulations 2015 No. 2015/1329 (C.75). - Enabling power: Small Business, Enterprise and Employment Act 2015, ss. 161 (2), 164 (1). Bringing into operation various provisions of the 2015 Act on 26.05.2015; 15.06.2015; 01.07.2015; 01.01.2016, in accord. with arts 2 to 6. - Issued: 28.05.2015. Made: 20.05.2015. Effect: None. Territorial extent & classification: E/W/S/NI. General. - 4p.: 30 cm. - 978-0-11-113644-7 £4.25

The Small Business, Enterprise and Employment Act 2015 (Commencement No. 2 and Transitional Provisions) Regulations 2015 No. 2015/1689 (C.100). - Enabling power: Small Business, Enterprise and Employment Act 2015, ss. 160 (1), 161 (1) (2), 164 (1), 164 (6). Bringing into operation various provisions of the 2015 Act on 01.10.2015; 10.10.2015, in accord. with arts 2 & 4. - Issued: 22.09.2015. Made: 15.09.2015. Effect: None. Territorial extent & classification: E/W/S/NI. General. - 8p.: 30 cm. - 978-0-11-113929-5 £6.00

The Small Business, Enterprise and Employment Act 2015 (Commencement No. 3) Regulations 2015 No. 2015/2029 (C.125). - Enabling power: Small Business, Enterprise and Employment Act 2015, ss. 161 (1) (2), 164(1). Bringing into operation various provisions of the 2015 Act on 01.01.2016, 06.04.2016, 30.06.2016, in accord. with arts. 2 to 5. - Issued: 21.12.2015. Made: 09.12.2015. Effect: None. Territorial extent & classification: E/W/S/NI. General. - 4p.: 30 cm. - 978-0-11-114206-6 £4.25

The Small Business, Enterprise and Employment Act 2015 (Consequential Amendments) (Insolvency and Company Directors Disqualification) Regulations 2015 No. 2015/1651. - Enabling power: Small Business, Enterprise and Employment Act 2015, ss. 159 (1) (2). - Issued: 11.09.2015. Made: 01.09.2015. Laid: 08.09.2015. Coming into force: 01.10.2015. Effect: S.I. 1987/2023; 2003/358 (N.I.); 2009/2471; 2010/184 (N.I.); 2013/1388 amended. Territorial extent & classification: E/W/S. General. - 16p.: 30 cm. - 978-0-11-113901-1 £6.00

Compensation

The Home Loss Payments (Prescribed Amounts) (England) Regulations 2015 No. 2015/1514. - Enabling power: Land Compensation Act 1973, s. 30 (5). - Issued: 20.07.2015. Made: 13.07.2015. Laid: 16.07.2015. Coming into force: 01.10.2015. Effect: S.I. 2014/1966 revoked with savings. Territorial extent & classification: E. General. - 2p.: 30 cm. - 978-0-11-113790-1 £4.25

Competition

The Competition Act 1998 (Competition and Markets Authority's Rules) Order 2014 (correction slip) No. 2014/458 Cor.. - Correction slip (to ISBN 9780111110676) dated December 2014. - 1 sheet: 30 cm. Free

The Competition Act 1998 (Redress Scheme) Regulations 2015 No. 2015/1587. - Enabling power: Competition Act 1998, ss. 49C (8), 71 (3) (b) & Interpretation Act 1978, s. 14A. - Issued: 10.08.2015. Made: 04.08.2015. Laid: 05.08.2015. Coming into force: 01.10.2015. Effect: None. Territorial extent & classification: E/W/S/NI. General. - 4p.: 30 cm. - 978-0-11-113862-5 £4.25

The Competition Appeal Tribunal Rules 2015 No. 2015/1648. - Enabling power: Enterprise Act 2002, s. 15 (1) to (3), sch. 4, part 2 & Communications Act 2003, ss. 192 (3) (4), 193 (1) (2) (b) (3). - Issued: 11.09.2015. Made: 07.09.2015. Laid: 08.09.2015. Coming into force: 01.10.2015. Effect: S.I. 2003/1372 revoked with saving & S.I. 2004/2068 revoked. Territorial extent & classification: E/W/S/NI. General. - 68p.: 30 cm. - 978-0-11-113898-4 £11.00

The Consumer Rights Act 2015 (Commencement No. 1) Order 2015 No. 2015/1333 (C. 76). - Enabling power: Consumer Rights Act 2015, s. 100 (5). Bringing into operation various provisions of the 2015 Act on 27.05.2015., in accord. with art. 2. - Issued: 29.05.2015. Made: 21.05.2015. Effect: None. Territorial extent & classification: E/W/S/NI. General. - 2p.: 30 cm. - 978-0-11-113645-4 £4.25

The Consumer Rights Act 2015 (Commencement No. 2) Order 2015 No. 2015/1584. - Enabling power: Consumer Rights Act 2015, s. 100 (5) (6). Bringing into operation various provisions of the 2015 Act on 03.08.2015., in accord. with art. 3. - Issued: 07.08.2015. Made: 02.08.2015. Effect: None. Territorial extent & classification: E/W/S/NI. General. - 2p.: 30 cm. - 978-0-11-113860-1 £4.25

The Groceries Code Adjudicator (Permitted Maximum Financial Penalty) Order 2015 No. 2015/722. - Enabling power: Groceries Code Adjudicator Act 2013, s. 9 (6). - Issued: 20.03.2015. Made: 16.03.2015. Coming into force: 06.04.2015. Effect: None. Territorial extent & classification: E/W/S/NI. General. - Supersedes draft S.I. (ISBN 9780111128213) issued 03/02/15. - 4p.: 30 cm. - 978-0-11-113360-6 £4.25

The Water Mergers (Miscellaneous Amendments) Regulations 2015 No. 2015/1936. - Enabling power: Water Industry Act 1991, s. 219 (1), sch. 4ZA, para. 1 & Enterprise Act 2002 ss. 121(1) (2) (c) (3) (d), 124 (2). - Issued: 02.12.2015. Made: 24.11.2015. Laid: 26.11.2015. Coming into force: 18.12.2015. Effect: S.I. 2003/1370; S.I. 2004/3202 amended. Territorial extent & classification: E/W/S/NI. General. - 12p.: 30 cm. - 978-0-11-114124-3 £6.00

Constitutional law

The Children and Young People (Scotland) Act 2014 (Consequential and Saving Provisions) Order 2015 No. 2015/907. - Enabling power: Scotland Act 1998, ss. 104, 112 (1), 113 (2) (4) (5). - Issued: 30.03.2015. Made: 24.03.2015. Coming into force: In accord. with arts 1 (2) (3) (4). Effect: 1995 c.36 modified. Territorial extent & classification: E/W/NI. General. - Supersedes draft S.I. (ISBN 9780111130087) issued 27/02/15. - 4p.: 30 cm. - 978-0-11-113531-0 £4.25

The Courts Reform (Scotland) Act 2014 (Consequential Provisions and Modifications) Order 2015 No. 2015/700. - Enabling power: Scotland Act 1998, ss. 104, 112 (1), 113 (2) (3) (5) (7), 114 (1). - Issued: 19.03.2015. Made: 11.03.2015. Coming into force: in accord with art. 1. Effect: 1975 c.25, c.42; 1978 c.30; 1982 c.27; 1991 c.48; 2005 c.4; S.I. 2009/2231 amended; 1926 c.16; 1934 c.56; 1936 c.6; 1971 c.58 partially repealed; and 1898 c.35; 1952 c.12 repealed. Territorial extent & classification: E/W/S/NI. General. - Supersedes draft S.I. (ISBN 9780111126929) issued 19/01/15. - 12p.: 30 cm. - 978-0-11-113349-1 £6.00

The Food (Scotland) Act 2015 (Consequential Provisions) Order 2015 No. 2015/444. - Enabling power: Scotland Act 1998, ss. 104, 112 (1), 113 (5), 114 (1). - Issued: 09.03.2015. Made: 03.03.2015. Laid: 04.03.2015. Coming into force: In accord. with art. 1 (2). Effect: None. Territorial extent & classification: E/W/S/NI. General. - 4p.: 30 cm. - 978-0-11-113132-9 £4.25

The Government of Wales Act 2006 (Amendment) Order 2015 No. 2015/204. - Enabling power: Government of Wales Act 2006, s. 109. - Issued: 18.02.2015. Made: 11.02.2015. Coming into force: 12.02.2015. Effect: 2006 c. 32 amended. Territorial extent & classification: UK but practical application is limited to Wales. General. - Supersedes draft S.I. (ISBN 9780111122921) issued 10.11.2014. - 2p.: 30 cm. - 978-0-11-112946-3 £4.25

The Government of Wales Act 2006 (Designation of Receipts) (Amendment) Order 2015 No. 2015/640. - Enabling power: Government of Wales Act 2006, ss. 120 (3). - Issued: 17.03.2015. Made: 10.03.2015. Laid: 11.03.2015. Coming into force: 02.04.2015. Effect: S.I. 2007/848 amended. Territorial extent & classification: E/W/S/NI. General. - 2p.: 30 cm. - 978-0-11-113296-8 £4.25

The Higher Education (Wales) Act 2015 (Consequential Provision) Order 2015 No. 2015/1353. - Enabling power: Government of Wales Act 2006, ss. 150 (1) (2). - Issued: 11.06.2015. Made: 04.06.2015. Laid: 09.06.2015. Coming into force: 01.09.2015. Effect: None. Territorial extent & classification: E/W. General. - 4p.: 30 cm. - 978-0-11-113660-7 £4.25

The Human Transplantation (Wales) Act 2013 (Consequential Provision) Order 2015 No. 2015/865. - Enabling power: Government of Wales Act 2006, ss. 150 (1) (2), 157 (2). - Issued: 27.03.2015. Made: 23.03.2015. Coming into force: In accord. with art. 1 (2). Effect: 2004 c. 30; S.I. 2012/1501 amended. Territorial extent & classification: E/W/S/NI. General. - Supersedes draft S.I. (ISBN 9780111127544) issued 23/01/15. - 4p.: 30 cm. - 978-0-11-113489-4 £4.25

The National Assembly for Wales (Disqualification) Order 2015 No. 2015/1536. - Enabling power: Government of Wales Act 2006, s. 16 (6). - Issued: 20.12.2010. Made: 15.12.2010. Coming into force: 01.09.2015. Effect: S.I. 2010/2969 revoked. Territorial extent & classification: UK but practical applications limited to Wales. - Welsh title: Gorchymyn Cynulliad Cenedlaethol Cymru (Anghymhwyso). - [16]p.: 30 cm. - 978-0-11-130005-3 £6.00

The Regulatory Reform (Scotland) Act 2014 (Consequential Modifications) Order 2015 No. 2015/374. - Enabling power: Scotland Act 1998, ss. 104, 112 (1), 113 (2) (3) (4) (5). - Issued: 03.03.2015. Made: 25.02.2015. Coming into force: 26.02.2015. Effect: 1974 c.37; 1988 c.48; 1989 c.29; 1990 c.43; 1995 c.25; 2005 c.5; 2009 c.4; 2009 c.23; S.I. 1997/3032 amended. Territorial extent & classification: E/W/S/NI. General. - Supersedes draft S.I. (ISBN 9780111124505) issued 08/12/14. - 8p.: 30 cm. - 978-0-11-113066-7 £6.00

The Reservoirs (Scotland) Act 2011 (Restrictions on Disclosure of Information in relation to National Security etc.) Order 2015 No. 2015/48. - Enabling power: Scotland Act 1998, ss. 104, 112 (1), 113 (2) (3) (5). - Issued: 27.01.2015. Made: 21.01.2015. Coming into force: In accord. with art. 1 (2) (3). Effect: 2010 c.29 amended. Territorial extent & classification: E/W/S/NI. General. - Supersedes draft SI (ISBN 9780111123362) issued 21/11/14. - 8p.: 30 cm. - 978-0-11-112777-3 £6.00

The Scotland Act 1998 (Functions Exercisable in or as Regards Scotland) Order 2015 No. 2015/211 (S.2). - Enabling power: Scotland Act 1998, s. 30 (3). - Issued: 18.02.2015. Made: 11.02.2015. Coming into force: 28.02.2015. Effect: None. Territorial extent & classification: E/W/S/NI. General. - Supersedes draft S.I. (ISBN 978111121832) issued 21.10.2014. - 4p.: 30 cm. - 978-0-11-112953-1 £4.25

The Scotland Act 1998 (Modification of Schedule 5) Order 2015 No. 2015/1379. - Enabling power: Scotland Act 1998, ss. 30 (2). - Issued: 17.06.2015. Made: 10.06.2015. Coming into force: In accord. with art. 1 (2). Effect: 1998 c.46 modified. Territorial extent & classification: E/W/S/NI. General. - Supersedes draft S.I. (ISBN 9780111127926) issued 02/02/15. - 4p.: 30 cm. - 978-0-11-113674-4 £4.25

The Scotland Act 1998 (Modification of Schedules 4 and 5 and Transfer of Functions to the Scottish Ministers etc.) Order 2015 No. 2015/692. - Enabling power: Scotland Act 1998, ss. 30 (2), 63 (1) (3), 113 (3) (4) (5), 124 (2). - Issued: 26.03.2015. Made: 19.03.2015. Coming into force: In accord. with art. 2. Effect: 1983 c.2; 1998 c. 46 modified. Territorial extent & classification: E/W/S/NI. General. - Supersedes draft SI (ISBN 9780111127551) issued 23/01/15 - 4p.: 30 cm. - 978-0-11-113415-3 £4.25

The Scotland Act 1998 (Modification of Schedules 4 and 5) Order 2015 No. 2015/1764. - Enabling power: Scotland Act 1998, ss. 30 (2) (4). - Issued: 15.10.2015. Made: 08.10.2015. Coming into force: In accord. with art. 1 (2). Effect: 1998 c.46 modified. Territorial extent & classification: E/W/S/NI. General. - Supersedes draft SI (ISBN 9780111137147) issued 06/07/15 - 4p.: 30 cm. - 978-0-11-113970-7 £4.25

The Scotland Act 1998 (River Tweed) Amendment Order 2015 No. 2015/203. - Enabling power: Scotland Act 1998, ss. 111, 113 (2) (3) (4) (5) (7). - Issued: 18.02.2015. Made: 11.02.2015. Coming into force: 12.02.2015. Effect: S.I. 2006/2913 amended. Territorial extent & classification: E/W/S. General. - Supersedes draft S.I. (ISBN 9780111121931) issued 21.10.2014. - 4p.: 30 cm. - 978-0-11-112945-6 £4.25

The Scotland Act 1998 (Variation of Borrowing Power) Order 2015 No. 2015/932. - Enabling power: Scotland Act 1998, s. 66 (5). - Issued: 31.03.2015. Made: 24.03.2015. Laid:-. Coming into force: 01.04.2015. Effect: 1998 c.46 amended. Territorial extent & classification: E/W/S/NI. General. - Supersedes draft S.I. (ISBN 9780111125281) issued 16/12/14. - 2p.: 30 cm. - 978-0-11-113554-9 £4.25

The Scotland Act 2012 (Commencement No. 5) Order 2015 No. 2015/682 (C.40). - Enabling power: Scotland Act 2012, s. 44 (5). Bringing into operation various provisions of the 2012 Act on 01.07.2015, in accord. with art. 2. - Issued: 23.03.2015. Made: 17.03.2015. Effect: None. Territorial extent & classification: E/W/S/NI. General. - 2p.: 30 cm. - 978-0-11-113374-3 £4.25

The Scotland Act 2012 (Saving and Consequential Provisions) Order 2015 No. 2015/683. - Enabling power: Scotland Act 2012, s. 42 (1) (2) (4). - Issued: 23.03.2015. Made: 17.03.2015. Laid: 18.03.2015. Coming into force: In accord. with art. 1. Effect: S.I. 1999/1512; 2010/2999 amended. Territorial extent & classification: E/W/S/NI. General. - Partially revoked by SSI 2015/425 (ISBN 9780111030271) in re to S. - 4p.: 30 cm. - 978-0-11-113371-2 £4.25

The Scottish Administration (Offices) Order 2015 No. 2015/200 (S.1). - Enabling power: Scotland Act 1998, s. 126 (8) (b). - Issued: 18.02.2015. Made: 11.02.2015. Laid before Parliament: 16.02.2015. Laid before the Scottish Parliament: 16.02.2015. Coming into force: 01.04.2015. Effect: None. Territorial extent & classification: E/W/S/NI. General. - 2p.: 30 cm. - 978-0-11-112942-5 £4.25

The Scottish Parliament (Regional Returning Officers) (Revocation) Order 2015 No. 2015/743 (S. 3). - Enabling power: Scotland Act 1998, ss. 12 (6), 113 (4). - Issued: 23.03.2015. Made: 17.03.2015. Coming into force: 30.06.2015. Effect: S.I. 2011/576 revoked. Territorial extent & classification: S. General. - 2p.: 30 cm. - 978-0-11-113376-7 £4.25

The Scottish Parliament (Returning Officers Charges) (Revocation) Order 2015 No. 2015/761 (S. 4). - Enabling power: Representation of the People Act 1983, s. 29 (3) (3A) (4C) & S.I. 2010/2999, art. 18. - Issued: 24.03.2015. Made: 17.03.2015. Coming into force: 30.06.2015. Effect: S.I. 2011/1013 revoked with saving. Territorial extent & classification: S. General. - 4p.: 30 cm. - 978-0-11-113392-7 £4.25

Consultant lobbying

The Registration of Consultant Lobbyists (Amendment) (No. 2) Regulations 2015 No. 2015/1998. - Enabling power: Transparency of Lobbying, Non-Party Campaigning and Trade Union Administration Act 2014, s. 22 (2). - Issued: 15.12.2015. Made: 09.12.2015. Laid: 10.12.2015. Coming into force: 01.01.2016. Effect: 2015/379 amended. Territorial extent & classification: E/W/S/NI. General. - 2p.: 30 cm. - 978-0-11-114179-3 £4.25

The Registration of Consultant Lobbyists (Amendment) Regulations 2015 No. 2015/1477. - Enabling power: Transparency of Lobbying, Non-Party Campaigning and Trade Union Administration Act 2014, s. 22 (2). - Issued: 13.07.2015. Made: 02.07.2015. Laid: 09.07.2015. Coming into force: 28.07.2015. Effect: S.I. 2015/379 amended. Territorial extent & classification: E/W/S/NI. General. - This Statutory Instrument has been made in consequence of a defect in S.I. 2015/379 (ISBN 9780111130698) and is being issued free of charge to all known recipients of that Statutory Instrument. - 2p.: 30 cm. - 978-0-11-113757-4 £4.25

The Registration of Consultant Lobbyists Regulations 2015 No. 2015/379. - Enabling power: Transparency of Lobbying, Non-Party Campaigning and Trade Union Administration Act 2014, s. 4 (5), 9 (3), 22 (2), 23 (2) (3), 24 (2). - Issued: 03.03.2015. Made: 24.02.2015. Laid: 26.02.2015. Coming into force: 01.04.2015. Effect: None. Territorial extent & classification: E/W/S/NI. General. - Amended by S.I. 2015/1477 (ISBN 9780111137574) which is being issued free of charge to all known recipients of this SI. - 4p.: 30 cm. - 978-0-11-113069-8 £4.25

The Transparency of Lobbying, Non-Party Campaigning and Trade Union Administration Act 2014 (Commencement No. 3) Order 2015 No. 2015/954 (C.59). - Enabling power: Transparency of Lobbying, Non-Party Campaigning and Trade Union Administration Act 2014, s. 45 (1) (5) (a). Bringing into operation various provisions of the 2014 Act on 01.04.2015, in accord. with art. 2. - Issued: 02.04.2015. Made: 25.03.2015. Effect: None. Territorial extent & classification: E/W/S/NI. General. - 4p.: 30 cm. - 978-0-11-113583-9 £4.25

Consumer protection

The Alternative Dispute Resolution for Consumer Disputes (Amendment) (No. 2) Regulations 2015 No. 2015/1972. - Enabling power: European Communities Act 1972, s. 2 (2). - Issued: 09.12.2015. Made: 02.12.2015. Laid: 07.12.2015. Coming into force: 09.01.2016. Effect: 1973 c.52; 1980 c.58; 1984 c.16; 2010 c.15; S.I. 1989/1339 (N.I. 11); 2015/542 amended. Territorial extent & classification: E/W/S/NI. General. - This Statutory Instrument corrects errors made by S.I. 2015/1392 (ISBN 9780111136874) and is being issued free of charge to all known recipients of that Statutory Instrument. - 4p.: 30 cm. - 978-0-11-114149-6 £4.25

The Alternative Dispute Resolution for Consumer Disputes (Amendment) Regulations 2015 No. 2015/1392. - Enabling power: European Communities Act 1972, s. 2 (2) & Enterprise Act 2002, 210 (9), 212 (3). - Issued: 24.06.2015. Made: 18.06.2015. Laid: 18.06.2015. Coming into force: 09.01.2016 for the purpose of regs 2 (5) (c) (13) (14) (15) (j), 6, 9; for the remainder: 09.07.2015. Effect: 1973 c.52; 1980 c.58; 1984 c.16; 2002 c.40; 2010 c.15; & S.I. 1989/1339 (NI.11); 2003/1374; 2015/542 amended. Territorial extent & classification: E/W/S/NI. General. - This Statutory Instrument has been corrected by S.I. 2015/1972 (ISBN 9780111141496) issued 09.12.2015 and which is being issued free of charge to all known recipients of this SI 2015/1392. - 16p.: 30 cm. - 978-0-11-113687-4 £6.00

The Alternative Dispute Resolution for Consumer Disputes (Competent Authorities and Information) Regulations 2015 No. 2015/542. - Enabling power: European Communities Act 1972, s. 2 (2). - Issued: 20.03.2015. Made: 16.03.2015. Laid: 17.03.2015. Coming into force: for the purpose of Parts 1 to 3: 07.04.2015; for the purpose of Parts 4 & 5: 09.07.2015. Effect: 2000 c.8; 2002 c.40 amended. Territorial extent & classification: E/W/S/NI. General. - 20p.: 30 cm. - 978-0-11-113359-0 £6.00

The Clinical Thermometers (EEC Requirements) (Revocation) Regulations 2015 No. 2015/419. - Enabling power: European Communities Act 1972, s. 2 (2). - Issued: 05.03.2015. Made: 25.02.2015. Laid: 05.03.2015. Coming into force: 01.04.2015. Effect: S.I. 1993/2360 revoked. Territorial extent & classification: E/W/S/NI. General. - 4p.: 30 cm. - 978-0-11-113112-1 £4.25

The Consumer Contracts (Amendment) Regulations 2015 No. 2015/1629. - Enabling power: European Communities Act 1972, s. 2 (2) & Consumer Rights Act 2015, ss. 96 (1) (2). - Issued: 03.09.2015. Made: 27.08.2015. Laid: 28.08.2015. Coming into force: 01.10.2015. Effect: S.I. 2008/1277; 2013/3134 amended. Territorial extent & classification: E/W/S/NI. General. - EC: These Regulations amend the Consumer Contracts (Information, Cancellation and Additional Charges) Regulations 2013 (S.I. 2013/3134), which implement Directive 2011/83/EU on consumer rights, amending Council Directive 93/13/EEC and Directive 1999/44/EC and repealing Council Directive 85/577/EEC and Directive 97/7/EC. - 4p.: 30 cm. - 978-0-11-113877-9 £4.25

The Consumer Rights Act 2015 (Commencement No. 1) Order 2015 No. 2015/1333 (C.76). - Enabling power: Consumer Rights Act 2015, s. 100 (5). Bringing into operation various provisions of the 2015 Act on 27.05.2015., in accord. with art. 2. - Issued: 29.05.2015. Made: 21.05.2015. Effect: None. Territorial extent & classification: E/W/S/NI. General. - 2p.: 30 cm. - 978-0-11-113645-4 £4.25

The Consumer Rights Act 2015 (Commencement No. 3, Transitional Provisions, Savings and Consequential Amendments) Order 2015 No. 2015/1630 (C.94). - Enabling power: Consumer Rights Act 2015, ss. 96 (1) (2), 97 (1), 100 (5) (6). Bringing into operation various provisions of the 2015 Act on 01.10.2015; 06.04.2016, in accord. with arts 3 & 4. - Issued: 02.10.2015. Made: 27.08.2015. Laid: 28.08.2015. Coming into force: 01.10.2015. Effect: 40 SIs & 1 SR amended & 4 SIs partially revoked. Territorial extent & classification: E/W/S/NI. General. - 20p.: 30 cm. - 978-0-11-113878-6 £6.00

The Consumer Rights Act 2015 (Consequential Amendments) Order 2015 No. 2015/1726. - Enabling power: Consumer Rights Act 2015, ss. 96 (1) (2), sch. 5, paras 12 (1) (5). - Issued: 05.05.2015. Made: 29.09.2015. Coming into force: 01.10.2015. Effect: 1967 c.45; 2002 c.40; 2008 c.13; 2015 c.15 amended & S.I. 2013/3134 partially revoked. Territorial extent & classification: E/W/S/NI. General. - Supersedes S.I. draft (ISBN 9780111136881) issued 24/06/15. - 4p.: 30 cm. - 978-0-11-113948-6 £4.25

The Enterprise Act 2002 (Part 8 Community Infringements and Specified UK Laws) (Amendment) Order 2015 No. 2015/1628. - Enabling power: Enterprise Act 2002, s. 212 (3). - Issued: 03.09.2015. Made: 27.08.2015. Laid: 28.08.2015. Coming into force: 01.10.2015. Effect: S.I. 2003/1374 amended. Territorial extent & classification: E/W/S/NI. General. - 4p.: 30 cm. - 978-0-11-113876-2 £4.25

The Enterprise Act 2002 (Part 8 Domestic Infringements) Order 2015 No. 2015/1727. - Enabling power: Enterprise Act 2002, s. 211. - Issued: 05.10.2015. Made: 29.09.2015. Coming into force: 01.10.2015. Effect: None. Territorial extent & classification: E/W/S/NI. General. - Supersedes draft S.I. (ISBN 9780111136898) issued 24/06/15. - 2p.: 30 cm. - 978-0-11-113949-3 £4.25

The Pyrotechnic Articles (Safety) Regulations 2015 No. 2015/1553. - Enabling power: European Communities Act 1972, s. 2 (2), sch. 2, para. 1A. - Issued: 24.07.2015. Made: 19.07.2015. Laid: 21.07.2015. Coming into force: 17.08.2015. Effect: 1875 c.17; 1974 c.37; 1987 c.43; S.I. 2004/1836; S.R. 2002/147 amended & S.I. 2013/1950 revoked with savings. Territorial extent & classification: E/W/S/NI. General. - EC note: These Regulations transpose Directive 2013/29/EU on the harmonisation of the laws of member states relating to the making available on the market of pyrotechnic articles and Commission Implementing Directive 2014/58/EU setting up a system for the traceability of pyrotechnic articles. The Directive repeals and replaces Directive 2007/23/EC. - 60p.: 30 cm. - 978-0-11-113829-8 £10.00

Consumer protection, England

The Consumer Rights Act 2015 (Commencement) (England) Order 2015 No. 2015/965 (C.62). - Enabling power: Consumer Rights Act 2015, s. 100 (3) (a) (5) (6). Bringing into operation various provisions of the 2015 Act on 27.05.2015., in accord. with art. 2. - Issued: 02.04.2015. Made: 26.03.2015. Effect: None. Territorial extent & classification: E/W/S/NI. General. - 2p.: 30 cm. - 978-0-11-113599-0 £4.25

The Consumer Rights Act 2015 (Commencement No. 2 and Transitional Provision) (England) Order 2015 No. 2015/1575 (C.89). - Enabling power: Consumer Rights Act 2015, ss. 97 (1), 100 (3) (a). Bringing into operation various provisions of the 2015 Act on 01.09.2015., in accord. with art. 2. - Issued: 30.07.2015. Made: 22.07.2015. Effect: None. Territorial extent & classification: E. General. - 4p.: 30 cm. - 978-0-11-113855-7 £4.25

The Duty of Letting Agents to Publicise Fees etc. (Exclusion) (England) Regulations 2015 No. 2015/951. - Enabling power: Consumer Rights Act 2015, s. 84 (3). - Issued: 02.04.2015. Made: 26.03.2014. Laid: 27.03.2015. Coming into force: 27.05.2015. Effect: None. Territorial extent & classification: E. General. - 2p.: 30 cm. - 978-0-11-113579-2 £4.25

Consumer protection, England and Wales

The Compensation (Claims Management Services) (Amendment) Regulations 2015 No. 2015/42. - Enabling power: Compensation Act 2006, ss. 9, 15 (1), sch. - Issued: 27.01.2015. Made: 21.01.2015. Coming into force: 28.01.2015. Effect: S.I. 2006/3322 amended. Territorial extent & classification: E/W. General. - 4p.: 30 cm. - 978-0-11-112771-1 £4.25

Consumer protection, Wales

The Consumer Rights Act 2015 (Commencement No. 3) (Wales) Order 2015 No. 2015/1904 (W.276)(C.117). - Enabling power: Consumer Rights Act 2015, s. 100 (3) (b). Bringing various provisions of the 2015 Act into operation on 23.11.2015 in accord. with arts 2, 3. - Issued: 01.12.2015. Made: 11.11.2015. Effect: WSI. 2015/1831 (W.267) (C.115) revoked. Territorial extent & classification: W. General. - In English and Welsh. Welsh title: Gorchymyn Deddf Hawliau Defnyddwyr 2015 (Cychwyn Rhif 3) (Cymru) 2015. - 4p.: 30 cm. - 978-0-348-11193-4 £4.25

Contracts, England and Wales

The Late Payment of Commercial Debts (Amendment) Regulations 2015 No. 2015/1336. - Enabling power: European Communities Act 1972, s. 2 (2). - Issued: 04.06.2015. Made: 27.05.2015. Laid before Parliament: 29.05.2015. Coming into force: 21.06.2015. Effect: 1998 c.20 amended. Territorial extent & classification: E/W/NI. General. - EC note: These Regulations implement requirements of Directive 2011/7/EU of the European Parliament and of the Council of 16th February 2011 on combating late payment in commercial transactions. - 4p.: 30 cm. - 978-0-11-113647-8 £4.25

Contracts, Northern Ireland

The Late Payment of Commercial Debts (Amendment) Regulations 2015 No. 2015/1336. - Enabling power: European Communities Act 1972, s. 2 (2). - Issued: 04.06.2015. Made: 27.05.2015. Laid before Parliament: 29.05.2015. Coming into force: 21.06.2015. Effect: 1998 c.20 amended. Territorial extent & classification: E/W/NI. General. - EC note: These Regulations implement requirements of Directive 2011/7/EU of the European Parliament and of the Council of 16th February 2011 on combating late payment in commercial transactions. - 4p.: 30 cm. - 978-0-11-113647-8 £4.25

Copyright

The Copyright and Performances (Application to Other Countries) (Amendment) Order 2015 No. 2015/216. - Enabling power: Copyright, Designs and Patents Act 1988, ss. 159, 208. - Issued: 18.02.2015. Made: 11.02.2015. Laid: 18.02.2015. Coming into force: 06.04.2015. Effect: S.I. 2013/536 amended. Territorial extent & classification: E/W/S/NI. General. - 4p.: 30 cm. - 978-0-11-112958-6 £4.25

The Copyright (Cayman Islands) Order 2015 No. 2015/795. - Enabling power: Copyright, Designs and Patents Act 1988, s. 157 (2)- Issued: 26.03.2015. Made: 19.03.2015. Coming into force: In accord. with art. 1. Effect: 1988 c.48 modified. Territorial extent & classification: E/W/S/NI. General. - 20p.: 30 cm. - 978-0-11-113419-1 £6.00

The Enterprise and Regulatory Reform Act 2013 (Commencement No. 8 and Saving Provisions) Order 2015 No. 2015/641 (C.36). - Enabling power: Enterprise and Regulatory Reform Act 2013, ss. 100, 103 (3) (4). Bringing into operation various provisions of the 2013 Act on 06.04.2015 in accord. with art. 2. - Issued: 16.03.2015. Made: 10.03.2015. Effect: None. Territorial extent & classification: E/W/S/NI. General. - Revoked by S.I. 2015/1558 (ISBN 9780111138380). - 4p.: 30 cm. - 978-0-11-113297-5 £4.25

The Enterprise and Regulatory Reform Act 2013 (Commencement No. 8 and Saving Provisions) (Revocation) Order 2015 No. 2015/1558. - Enabling power: Enterprise and Regulatory Reform Act 2013, ss. 100, 103 (3) (4). - Issued: 27.07.2015. Made: 20.07.2015. Effect: S.I. 2015/641 (C.36) revoked. Territorial extent & classification: E/W/S/NI. General. - 2p.: 30 cm. - 978-0-11-113838-0 £4.25

Coroners, England

The Coroners and Justice Act 2009 (Alteration of Coroner Areas) Order 2015 No. 2015/658. - Enabling power: Coroners and Justice Act 2009, sch. 2, para. 2. - Issued: 17.03.2015. Made: 04.03.2015. Laid: 12.03.2015. Coming into force: 02.04.2015. Effect: None. Territorial extent & classification: E. General. - 2p.: 30 cm. - 978-0-11-113315-6 £4.25

Coroners, England and Wales

The Coroners and Justice Act 2009 (Alteration of Coroner Areas) (No. 2) Order 2015 No. 2015/1491. - Enabling power: Coroners and Justice Act 2009, sch. 2, para. 2. - Issued: 15.07.2015. Made: 06.07.2015. Laid: 10.07.2015. Coming into force: 01.08.2015. Effect: None. Territorial extent & classification: E/W. General. - 2p.: 30 cm. - 978-0-11-113773-4 £4.25

The Criminal Justice and Courts Act 2015 (Commencement No. 1, Saving and Transitional Provisions) Order 2015 No. 2015/778 (C.44). - Enabling power: Criminal Justice and Courts Act 2015, s. 95 (1) (6). Bringing into operation various provisions of the 2015 Act on 20.03.2015; 13.04.2015, in accord. with arts 2, 3. - Issued: 25.03.2015. Made: 19.03.2015. Effect: None. Territorial extent & classification: E/W/S/NI. General. - 8p.: 30 cm. - 978-0-11-113405-4 £6.00

Corporation tax

The Authorised Investment Funds (Tax) (Amendment) Regulations 2015 No. 2015/485. - Enabling power: Finance (No. 2) Act 2005, ss. 17 (3), 18 (1) (5). - Issued: 10.03.2015. Made: 04.03.2015. Laid: 05.03.2015. Coming into force: 26.03.2015. Effect: S.I. 2006/964 amended. Territorial extent & classification: E/W/S/NI. General. - 4p.: 30 cm. - 978-0-11-113182-4 £4.25

The Capital Allowances Act 2001 (Extension of first-year allowances) (Amendment) Order 2015 No. 2015/60. - Enabling power: Capital Allowances Act 2001, 45D (1A) (7), 45E (1A). - Issued: 30.01.2015. Made: 26.01.2015. Laid: 27.01.2015. Coming into force: 17.02.2015. Effect: 2001 c.2 amended. Territorial extent & classification: E/W/S/NI. General. - 2p.: 30 cm. - 978-0-11-112794-0 £4.25

The Capital Allowances (Designated Assisted Areas) Order 2015 No. 2015/2047. - Enabling power: Capital Allowances Act 2001, s. 45K (2) (a) (3) (4). - Issued: 22.12.2015. Made: 16.12.2015. Laid: 17.12.2015. Coming into force: 07.01.2016. Effect: None. Territorial extent & classification: E/W/S/NI. General. - 4p.: 30 cm. - 978-0-11-114227-1 £4.25

The Capital Allowances (Energy-saving Plant and Machinery) (Amendment) Order 2015 No. 2015/1508. - Enabling power: Capital Allowances Act 2001, ss. 45A (3) (4). - Issued: 17.07.2015. Made: 13.07.2015. Laid: 14.07.2015. Coming into force: 04.08.2015. Effect: S.I. 2001/2541 amended. Territorial extent & classification: E/W/S/NI. General. - 2p.: 30 cm. - 978-0-11-113782-6 £4.25

The Capital Allowances (Environmentally Beneficial Plant and Machinery) (Amendment) Order 2015 No. 2015/1509. - Enabling power: Capital Allowances Act 2001, s. 45H (3) to (5). - Issued: 17.07.2015. Made: 13.07.2015. Laid: 14.07.2015. Coming into force: 04.08.2015. Effect: S.I. 2003/2076 amended. Territorial extent & classification: E/W/S/NI. General. - 2p.: 30 cm. - 978-0-11-113783-3 £4.25

The Community Amateur Sports Clubs Regulations 2015 No. 2015/725. - Enabling power: Corporation Tax Act 2010, ss. 659 (2A) (2B) (2C), 660 (5A) (d) (5B) (8) (9) (a) (b) (10) (12), 660A (1) (3) (4) & Finance Act 2013, sch. 21 para. 8 (1) (2) (a) (3). - Issued: 20.03.2015. Made: 16.03.2015. Coming into force: 01.04.2015. Effect: 2010 c.4 amended. Territorial extent & classification: E/W/S/NI. General. - Supersedes draft S.I. (ISBN 9780111127483) issued 22/01/15. - 12p.: 30 cm. - 978-0-11-113362-0 £6.00

The Cultural Test (Television Programmes) (Amendment) (No. 2) Regulations 2015 No. 2015/1941. - Enabling power: Corporation Tax Act 2009, s. 1216CB (2). - Issued: 03.12.2015. Made: 26.11.2015. Laid: 30.11.2015. Coming into force: 21.12.2015. Effect: S.I. 2013/1831 amended. Territorial extent & classification: E/W/S/NI. General. - 2p.: 30 cm. - 978-0-11-114128-1 £4.25

The Cultural Test (Television Programmes) (Amendment) Regulations 2015 No. 2015/1449. - Enabling power: Corporation Tax Act 2009, ss. 1216CB (2), 1216CC (7). - Issued: 06.07.2015. Made: 29.06.2015. Laid: 01.07.2015. Coming into force: 23.07.2015. Effect: S.I. 2013/1831 amended. Territorial extent & classification: E/W/S/NI. General. - 8p.: 30 cm. - 978-0-11-113731-4 £6.00

The Double Taxation Relief and International Tax Enforcement (Algeria) Order 2015 No. 2015/1888. - Enabling power: Taxation (International and Other Provisions) Act 2010 s. 2 & Finance Act 2006, ss. 173 (1) to (3). - Issued: 18.11.2015. Made: 11.11.2015. Coming into force: 11.11.2015. Effect: None. Territorial extent & classification: E/W/S/NI. General. - Supersedes draft SI (ISBN 9780111138250) issued 23/07/15 - 24p.: 30 cm. - 978-0-11-114086-4 £6.00

The Double Taxation Relief and International Tax Enforcement (Bulgaria) Order 2015 No. 2015/1890. - Enabling power: Taxation (International and Other Provisions) Act 2010, s. 2 & Finance Act 2006, ss. 173 (1) to (3). - Issued: 18.11.2015. Made: 11.11.2015. Coming into force: 11.11.2015. Effect: None. Territorial extent & classification: E/W/S/NI. General. - Supersedes draft SI (ISBN 9780111138236) issued 23/07/15 - 24p.: 30 cm. - 978-0-11-114088-8 £6.00

The Double Taxation Relief and International Tax Enforcement (Croatia) Order 2015 No. 2015/1889. - Enabling power: Taxation (International and Other Provisions) Act 2010, s. 2 & Finance Act 2006, ss. 173(1) to (3). - Issued: 18.11.2015. Made: 11.11.2015. Coming into force: 11.11.2015. Effect: None. Territorial extent & classification: E/W/S/NI. General. - Supersedes draft SI (ISBN 9780111138229) issued 23/07/15 - 24p.: 30 cm. - 978-0-11-114087-1 £6.00

The Double Taxation Relief and International Tax Enforcement (Guernsey) Order 2015 No. 2015/2008. - Enabling power: Taxation (International and Other Provisions) Act 2010, s. 2 & Finance Act 2006 s. 173 (1). - Issued: 16.12.2015. Made: 09.12.2015. Coming into force: 09.12.2015. Effect: None. Territorial extent & classification: E/W/S/NI. General. - Supersedes draft S.I. (ISBN 9780111140291) issued 02/11/15. - 8p.: 30 cm. - 978-0-11-114188-5 £4.25

The Double Taxation Relief and International Tax Enforcement (Jersey) Order 2015 No. 2015/2009. - Enabling power: Taxation (International and Other Provisions) Act 2010, s. 2 & Finance Act 2006, s. 173 (1). - Issued: 16.12.2015. Made: 09.12.2015. Coming into force: 09.12.2015. Effect: None. Territorial extent & classification: E/W/S/NI. General. - Supersedes draft S.I. (ISBN) issued 02/11/15. - 8p.: 30 cm. - 978-0-11-114189-2 £6.00

The Double Taxation Relief and International Tax Enforcement (Kosovo) Order 2015 No. 2015/2007. - Enabling power: Taxation (International and Other Provisions) Act 2010, s. 2 & Finance Act 2006 s. 173 (1) to (3). - Issued: 16.12.2015. Made: 09.12.2015. Coming into force: 09.12.2015. Effect: None. Territorial extent & classification: E/W/S/NI. General. - Supersedes draft S.I. (ISBN 9780111140413) issued 06/11/15. - 24p.: 30 cm. - 978-0-11-114187-8 £6.00

The Double Taxation Relief and International Tax Enforcement (Senegal) Order 2015 No. 2015/1892. - Enabling power: Taxation (International and Other Provisions) Act 2010, s. 2 & Finance Act 2006, ss. 173 (1) to (3). - Issued: 18.11.2015. Made: 11.11.2015. Coming into force: 11.11.2015. Effect: None. Territorial extent & classification: E/W/S/NI. General. - Supersedes draft SI (ISBN 9780111138212) issued 23/07/15 - 24p.: 30 cm. - 978-0-11-114090-1 £6.00

The Double Taxation Relief and International Tax Enforcement (Sweden) Order 2015 No. 2015/1891. - Enabling power: Taxation (International and Other Provisions) Act 2010, s. 2 & Finance Act 2006, ss. 173 (1) to (3). - Issued: 18.11.2015. Made: 11.11.2015. Coming into force: 11.11.2015. Effect: None. Territorial extent & classification: E/W/S/NI. General. - Supersedes draft SI (ISBN 9780111138205) issued 23/07/15 - 24p.: 30 cm. - 978-0-11-114089-5 £6.00

The Exchange Gains and Losses (Bringing into Account Gains or Losses) (Amendment) Regulations 2015 No. 2015/1960. - Enabling power: Taxation of Chargeable Gains Act 1992, s. 151E & Finance Act 2002, sch. 23 para. 26 (5) & Corporation Tax Act 2009 ss. 328 (4), 606 (4). - Issued: 10.12.2015. Made: 03.12.2015. Laid: 07.12.2015. Coming into force: 31.12.2015. Effect: S.I. 2002/1970 amended. Territorial extent & classification: E/W/S/NI. General. - 2p.: 30 cm. - 978-0-11-114155-7 £4.25

The Finance Act 2007, Schedule 26, Paragraphs 4 and 5 (Valuation of Shares) (Appointed Day) Order 2015 No. 2015/635 (C.33). - Enabling power: Finance Act 2007, sch. 26, paras 4 (2), 5 (2). Bringing into operation various provisions of the 2007 Act on 06.04.2015 in accord. with art. 2. - Issued: 16.03.2015. Made: 09.03.2015. Effect: None. Territorial extent & classification: E/W/S/NI. General. - 2p.: 30 cm. - 978-0-11-113291-3 £4.25

The Finance Act 2012, Sections 26 and 30 (Abolition of Relief for Equalisation Reserves) (Specified Day) Order 2015 No. 2015/1999. - Enabling power: Finance Act 2012, ss. 26 (3), 30 (3). - Issued: 15.12.2015. Made: 07.12.2015. Coming into force: 01.01.2016. Effect: None. Territorial extent & classification: E/W/S/NI. General. - 2p.: 30 cm. - 978-0-11-114180-9 £4.25

The Finance Act 2013, Schedule 21 (Appointed Day) Order 2015 No. 2015/674 (C.37). - Enabling power: Finance Act 2013, sch. 21, para. 9 (2) (3) (a). Bringing into operation various provisions of the 2013 Act on 01.04.2010. - Issued: 19.03.2015. Made: 12.03.2015. Effect: None. Territorial extent & classification: E/W/S/NI. General. - 2p.: 30 cm. - 978-0-11-113336-1 £4.25

The Finance Act 2014 (High Risk Promoters Prescribed Information) Regulations 2015 No. 2015/549. - Enabling power: Finance Act 2014, ss. 249 (3) (10) (11), 253 (2) (4), 257 (2), 259 (9), 260 (7), 261 (2), 268 (1), 282 (4), 283 (1). - Issued: 12.03.2015. Made: 05.03.2015. Laid: 06.03.2015. Coming into force: 27.03.2015. Effect: None. Territorial extent & classification: E/W/S/NI. General. - 16p.: 30 cm. - 978-0-11-113224-1 £6.00

The Finance Act 2014 (Schedule 34 Prescribed Matters) Regulations 2015 No. 2015/131. - Enabling power: Finance Act 2014, s. 283 (1), sch. 34 paras 8 (1) (3), 9 (2). - Issued: 12.02.2015. Made: 06.02.2015. Laid: 09.02.2015. Coming into force: 02.03.2015. Effect: None. Territorial extent & classification: E/W/S/NI. General. - 4p.: 30 cm. - 978-0-11-112898-5 £4.25

The Finance Act 2015, Section 29 (Film Tax Relief) (Specified Day) Regulations 2015 No. 2015/1741. - Enabling power: Finance Act 2015 s. 29 (8). - Issued: 08.10.2015. Made: 02.10.2015. Effect: None. Territorial extent & classification: E/W/S/NI. General. - 2p.: 30 cm. - 978-0-11-113957-8 £4.25

The Housing and Regeneration Transfer Schemes (Tax Consequences) Regulations 2015 No. 2015/1540. - Enabling power: Greater London Authority Act 1999, s. 333DC & Housing and Regeneration Act 2008, s. 53B. - Issued: 22.07.2015. Made: 16.07.2015. Laid: 17.07.2015. Coming into force: 07.08.2015. Effect: None. Territorial extent & classification: E. General. - 8p.: 30 cm. - 978-0-11-113814-4 £4.25

The Income Tax (Construction Industry Scheme) (Amendment of Schedule 11 to the Finance Act 2004) Order 2015 No. 2015/789. - Enabling power: Finance Act 2004, sch. 11, para. 13 (1). - Issued: 26.03.2015. Made: 19.03.2015. Coming into force: 06.04.2015. Effect: 2004 c.12 amended. Territorial extent & classification: E/W/S/NI. General. - 4p.: 30 cm. - 978-0-11-113409-2 £4.25

The Income Tax (Construction Industry Scheme) (Amendment) Regulations 2015 No. 2015/429. - Enabling power: Finance Act 2004, ss. 62, 70. - Issued: 06.03.2015. Made: 02.03.2015. Laid: 03.03.2015. Coming into force: 06.04.2015. Effect: S.I. 2005/2045 amended. Territorial extent & classification: E/W/S/NI. General. - 4p.: 30 cm. - 978-0-11-113119-0 £4.25

The Insurance Companies (Amendment to Section 129 of, and Schedule 17 to, the Finance Act 2012) Regulations 2015 No. 2015/1959. - Enabling power: Finance Act 2012, s. 129 (9), sch. 17, para. 37. - Issued: 08.12.2015. Made: 01.12.2015. Laid: 02.12.2015. Coming into force: 31.12.2015. Effect: 2012 c. 14 amended. Territorial extent & classification: E/W/S/NI. General. - 4p.: 30 cm. - 978-0-11-114141-0 £4.25

The International Tax Enforcement (Brazil) Order 2015 No. 2015/1887. - Enabling power: Finance Act 2006, ss. 173 (1) to (3). - Issued: 18.11.2015. Made: 11.11.2015. Coming into force: 11.11.2015. Effect: None. Territorial extent & classification: E/W/S/NI. General. - Supersedes draft SI (ISBN 9780111138243) issued 23/07/15 - 12p.: 30 cm. - 978-0-11-114085-7 £6.00

The Lloyd's Underwriters (Transitional Equalisation Reserves) (Tax) Regulations 2015 No. 2015/1983. - Enabling power: Finance Act 2009, s. 47 & Finance Act 2012, s. 30 (1). - Issued: 14.12.2015. Made: 07.12.2015. Laid: 08.12.2015. Coming into force: 01.01.2016. Effect: 2012 c.14 modified & S.I. 1996/2991; 2009/2039 revoked. Territorial extent & classification: E/W/S/NI. General. - 4p.: 30 cm. - 978-0-11-114171-7 £4.25

The Loan Relationships and Derivative Contracts (Change of Accounting Practice) (Amendment No. 2) Regulations 2015 No. 2015/1962. - Enabling power: Corporation Tax Act 2009, ss. 319, 598. - Issued: 09.12.2015. Made: 03.12.2015. Laid: 07.12.2015. Coming into force: 31.12.2015. Effect: S.I. 2004/3271 amended. Territorial extent & classification: E/W/S/NI. General. - 4p.: 30 cm. - 978-0-11-114151-9 £4.25

The Loan Relationships and Derivative Contracts (Change of Accounting Practice) (Amendment) Regulations 2015 No. 2015/1541. - Enabling power: Corporation Tax Act 2009, ss. 319, 598. - Issued: 23.07.2015. Made: 16.07.2015. Laid: 17.07.2015. Coming into force: 07.08.2015. Effect: S.I. 2004/3271 amended. Territorial extent & classification: E/W/S/NI. General. - 2p.: 30 cm. - 978-0-11-113815-1 £4.25

The Loan Relationships and Derivative Contracts (Disregard and Bringing into Account of Profits and Losses) (Amendment) Regulations 2015 No. 2015/1961. - Enabling power: Corporation Tax Act 2009, ss. 310 (1) (a) (3), 328 (4), 598 (1) (a) (4) (5), 606 (4). - Issued: 10.12.2015. Made: 03.12.2015. Laid: 07.12.2015. Coming into force: 31.12.2015. Effect: S.I. 2004/3256 amended. Territorial extent & classification: E/W/S/NI. General. - 8p.: 30 cm. - 978-0-11-114153-3 £4.25

The Loan Relationships and Derivative Contracts (Exchange Gains and Losses using Fair Value Accounting) (Amendment) Regulations 2015 No. 2015/1963. - Enabling power: Corporation Tax Act 2009, ss. 475 (3), 705 (3). - Issued: 10.12.2015. Made: 03.12.2015. Laid: 07.12.2015. Coming into force: 31.12.2015. Effect: S.I. 2005/3422 amended. Territorial extent & classification: E/W/S/NI. General. - 2p.: 30 cm. - 978-0-11-114152-6 £4.25

The Market Value of Shares, Securities and Strips Regulations 2015 No. 2015/616. - Enabling power: Taxation of Chargeable Gains Act, s. 272 (3) (4) & Income Tax (Trading and Other Income) Act 2005, s. 450. - Issued: 16.03.2015. Made: 09.03.2015. Laid: 10.03.2015. Coming into force: 06.04.2015. Effect: S.I. 2006/964 amended. Territorial extent & classification: E/W/S/NI. General. - 4p.: 30 cm. - 978-0-11-113279-1 £4.25

The Statutory Shared Parental Pay (Miscellaneous Amendments) Regulations 2015 No. 2015/125. - Enabling power: Finance Act 1999, ss. 132, 133 (2) & Income Tax (Earnings and Pensions) Act 2003, s. 684 & Finance Act 2004, ss. 62 (3) (6) (7), 71. - Issued: 10.02.2015. Made: 03.02.2015. Laid: 05.02.2015. Coming into force: In accord. with reg. 1 (2) (3). Effect: S.I. 2002/3047; 2003/2682; 2005/2045 amended. Territorial extent & classification: E/W/S. General. - 4p.: 30 cm. - 978-0-11-112872-5 £4.25

The Taxation of Chargeable Gains (Gilt-edged Securities) Order 2015 No. 2015/1790. - Enabling power: Taxation of Chargeable Gains Act 1992, sch. 9, para. 1. - Issued: 20.10.2015. Made: 12.10.2015. Effect: None. Territorial extent & classification: E/W/S/NI. General. - 2p.: 30 cm. - 978-0-11-113993-6 £4.25

The Taxation of Regulatory Capital Securities (Amendment) Regulations 2015 No. 2015/2056. - Enabling power: Finance Act 2012, s. 221. - Issued: 22.12.2015. Made: 16.12.2015. Coming into force: 01.01.2016. Effect: S.I. 2013/3209 amended. Territorial extent & classification: E/W/S/NI. General. - Supersedes draft S.I. (ISBN 9780111141144) issued 27/11/15. - 8p.: 30 cm. - 978-0-11-114238-7 £4.25

The Tax Treatment of Financing Costs and Income (Change of Accounting Standards: Investment Entities) Regulations 2015 No. 2015/662. - Enabling power: Taxation (International and Other Provisions) Act 2010, s. 353AA. - Issued: 17.03.2015. Made: 11.03.2015. Laid: 12.03.2015. Coming into force: 02.04.2015. Effect: 2010 c.8 amended. Territorial extent & classification: E/W/S/NI. General. - 4p.: 30 cm. - 978-0-11-113319-4 £4.25

The Unauthorised Unit Trusts (Tax) (Amendment No. 2) Regulations 2015 No. 2015/2053. - Enabling power: Finance Act 2013, s. 217. - Issued: 22.12.2015. Made: 16.12.2015. Laid: 17.12.2015. Coming into force: 07.01.2016. Effect: S.I. 2013/2819 amended. Territorial extent & classification: E/W/S/NI. General. - 2p.: 30 cm. - 978-0-11-114234-9 £4.25

Council tax, England

The Council Tax Reduction Schemes (Prescribed Requirements) (England) (Amendment) Regulations 2015 No. 2015/2041. - Enabling power: Local Government Finance Act 1992, ss. 113 (1) (2), sch. 1A, para. 2. - Issued: 22.12.2015. Made: 16.12.2015. Laid: 21.12.2015. Coming into force: 14.01.2016. Effect: S.I. 2012/2885 amended. Territorial extent & classification: E. General. - 8p.: 30 cm. - 978-0-11-114223-3 £4.25

Council tax, Wales

The Council Tax Reduction Schemes (Prescribed Requirements and Default Scheme) (Wales) (Amendment) Regulations 2015 No. 2015/44 (W.3). - Enabling power: Local Government Finance Act 1992, s. 13A (4) (5), sch. 1B, paras 2 to 7. - Issued: 28.01.2015. Made: 20.01.2015. Coming into force: 21.01.2015 in accord. with reg. 1 (2). Effect: S.I. 2013/3029 (W.301), 3035 (W.303) amended. Territorial extent & classification: W. General. - In English and Welsh. Welsh title: Rheoliadau Cynlluniau Gostyngiadau'r Dreth Gyngor (Gofynion Rhagnodedig a'r Cynllun Diofyn) (Cymru) (Diwygio) 2015. - 20p.: 30 cm. - 978-0-348-11040-1 £6.00

Countryside, England

The National Park Authorities (England) Order 2015 No. 2015/770. - Enabling power: Local Government Act 1972, s. 241 & Town and Country Planning Act 1990, s. 4A (1) & Environment Act 1995, ss. 63 (1) (2), 75 (3) to (7), sch. 7, paras 1 (2) (3), 2 (1) to (3). - Issued: 24.03.2015. Made: 16.03.2015. Laid: 19.03.2015. Coming into force: 01.07.2015. Effect: S.I. 1996/1243, 2546; 2009/557; 2014/571 revoked. Territorial extent & classification: E. General. - 12p.: 30 cm. - 978-0-11-113396-5 £6.00

County court, England and Wales

The Civil Procedure (Amendment No. 2) Rules 2015 No. 2015/670 (L. 9). - Enabling power: Civil Procedure Act 1997, s. 2. - Issued: 18.03.2015. Made: 12.03.2015. Laid: 13.03.2015. Coming into force: In accord. with rule 2. Effect: S.I. 1998/3132; 2014/3299 amended. Territorial extent & classification: E/W. General. - 4p.: 30 cm. - 978-0-11-113332-3 £4.25

The Civil Procedure (Amendment No. 3) Rules 2015 No. 2015/877 (L.11). - Enabling power: Civil Procedure Act 1997, s. 2 & Counter-Terrorism and Security Act 2015, sch. 3, paras 2 to 4, 6. - Issued: 31.03.2015. Made: 25.03.2015. Laid: 26.03.2015. Coming into force: 17.04.2015. Effect: S.I. 1998/3132 amended. Territorial extent & classification: E/W. General. - 4p.: 30 cm. - 978-0-11-113500-6 £4.25

The Civil Procedure (Amendment No. 4) Rules 2015 No. 2015/1569 (L.20). - Enabling power: Civil Procedure Act 1997, s. 2. - Issued: 29.07.2015. Made: 22.07.2015. Laid: 24.07.2015. Coming into force: In accord. with rule 1. Effect: S.I. 1998/3132 amended. Territorial extent & classification: E/W. General. - 8p.: 30 cm. - 978-0-11-113850-2 £4.25

The Civil Procedure (Amendment No. 5) Rules 2015 No. 2015/1881 (L.22). - Enabling power: Civil Procedure Act 1997, ss. 1, 2. - Issued: 17.11.2015. Made: 10.11.2015. Laid: 12.11.2015. Coming into force: 03.12.2015 in accord. with rule 2. Effect: SI 1998/3132 amended. Territorial extent & classification: E/W. General. - 2p.: 30 cm. - 978-0-11-114079-6 £4.25

The Civil Procedure (Amendment) Rules 2015 No. 2015/406 (L. 3). - Enabling power: Counter-Terrorism and Security Act 2015, sch. 3 para. 7. - Issued: 31.03.2015. Made: 26.02.2015. Laid: 27.02.2015. Coming into force: In accord. with rule 1. Effect: S.I. 1998/3132 amended. Territorial extent & classification: E/W. General. - Approved by both Houses of Parliament. Supersedes (ISBN 9780111130957) issued 05/03/15. - 16p.: 30 cm. - 978-0-11-130001-5 £6.00

The Civil Procedure (Amendment) Rules 2015 No. 2015/406 (L. 3). - Enabling power: Counter-Terrorism and Security Act 2015, sch. 3 para. 7. - Issued: 05.03.2015. Made: 26.02.2015. Laid: 27.02.2015. Coming into force: In accord. with rule 1. Effect: S.I. 1998/3132 amended. Territorial extent & classification: E/W. General. - For approval by resolution of each House of Parliament within 40 days. Superseded by approved S.I. 2015/406 (L. 3) (ISBN 9780111300015) issued 31/03/15. - 16p.: 30 cm. - 978-0-11-113095-7 £6.00

The Civil Proceedings and Family Proceedings Fees (Amendment) Order 2015 No. 2015/576 (L.7). - Enabling power: Courts Act 2003, ss. 92 (1) (2) & Anti-Social Behaviour, Crime and Policing Act 2014, s. 180 (1). - Issued: 13.03.2015. Made: 05.03.2015. Coming into force: In accord. with art. 1. Effect: S.I. 2008/1053, 1054 amended. Territorial extent & classification: E/W. General. - Supersedes draft S.I. (ISBN 9780111127490) issued 22.01.2015. - 4p.: 30 cm. - 978-0-11-113246-3 £4.25

The Crime and Courts Act 2013 (Commencement No. 14) Order 2015 No. 2015/1837. - Enabling power: Crime and Courts Act 2013 s. 61(2). Bringing into operation various provisions of the 2013 Act on 03.11.2015. - Issued: 04.11.2015. Made: 27.10.2015. Effect: None. Territorial extent & classification: E/W. General. - 8p.: 30 cm. - 978-0-11-114035-2 £4.25

Court martial (appeals)

The Court Martial Appeal Court (Amendment) Rules 2015 No. 2015/1814. - Enabling power: Courts-Martial (Appeals) Act 1968, s. 49. - Issued: 28.10.2015. Made: 21.10.2015. Laid: 23.10.2015. Coming into force: 16.11.2015. Effect: S.I. 2009/2657 amended. Territorial extent & classification: E/W/S/NI. General. - 2p.: 30 cm. - 978-0-11-114012-3 £4.25

Court of Session

The Courts Reform (Scotland) Act 2014 (Consequential Provisions and Modifications) Order 2015 No. 2015/700. - Enabling power: Scotland Act 1998, ss. 104, 112 (1), 113 (2) (3) (5) (7), 114 (1). - Issued: 19.03.2015. Made: 11.03.2015. Coming into force: in accord with art. 1. Effect: 1975 c.25, c.42; 1978 c.30; 1982 c.27; 1991 c.48; 2005 c.4; S.I. 2009/2231 amended; 1926 c.16; 1934 c.56; 1936 c.6; 1971 c.58 partially repealed; and 1898 c.35; 1952 c.12 repealed. Territorial extent & classification: E/W/S/NI. General. - Supersedes draft S.I. (ISBN 9780111126929) issued 19/01/15. - 12p.: 30 cm. - 978-0-11-113349-1 £6.00

Criminal justice

The Criminal Justice (Armed Forces Code of Practice for Victims of Crime) Regulations 2015 No. 2015/1811. - Enabling power: European Communities Act 1972, s. 2 (2). - Issued: 28.10.2015. Made: 21.10.2015. Laid: 23.10.2015. Coming into force: 16.11.2015. Effect: None. Territorial extent & classification: E/W/S/NI. General. - 64p.: 30 cm. - 978-0-11-114009-3 £10.00

Criminal law

The Anti-social Behaviour, Crime and Policing Act 2014 (Commencement No. 8, Saving and Transitional Provisions) Order 2015 No. 2015/373 (C.19). - Enabling power: Anti-social Behaviour, Crime and Policing Act 2014, s. 185 (1) (7). Bringing into operation various provisions of the 2014 Act on 08.03.2015; 23.03.2015; 08.04.2015, in accord. with arts 2, 3, 4, 5. - Issued: 02.03.2015. Made: 24.02.2015. Effect: None. Territorial extent & classification: E/W/S/NI. General. - 8p.: 30 cm. - 978-0-11-113065-0 £6.00

The Belarus (Asset-Freezing) (Amendment) Regulations 2015 No. 2015/1850. - Enabling power: European Communities Act 1972, s. 2 (2). - Issued: 09.11.2015. Made: 03.11.2015. Laid: 03.11.2015. Coming into force: 04.11.2015. Effect: S.I. 2013/164 amended. Territorial extent & classification: E/W/S/NI & Overseas territories. General. - 2p.: 30 cm. - 978-0-11-114046-8 £4.25

The Burundi (European Union Financial Sanctions) Regulations 2015 No. 2015/1740. - Enabling power: European Communities Act 1972, s. 2 (2), sch. 2, para. 1A. - Issued: 08.10.2015. Made: 02.10.2015, at 11.00 am. Laid: 02.10.2015, at 02.00 pm. Coming into force: 02.10.2015, at 3.00 pm. Effect: None. Territorial extent & classification: E/W/S/NI. General. - 11p.: 30 cm. - 978-0-11-113956-1 £6.00

The Crime and Courts Act 2013 (Commencement No. 12) Order 2015 No. 2015/813 (C.48). - Enabling power: Crime and Courts Act 2013, s. 61 (2). Bringing into operation various provisions of the 2013 Act on 20.03.2015; 01.06.2015, in accord. with arts 2, 3. - Issued: 26.03.2015. Made: 19.03.2015. Effect: None. Territorial extent & classification: E/W/S/NI. General. - 8p.: 30 cm. - 978-0-11-113444-3 £6.00

The Criminal Justice and Courts Act 2015 (Commencement No. 1, Saving and Transitional Provisions) Order 2015 No. 2015/778 (C.44). - Enabling power: Criminal Justice and Courts Act 2015, s. 95 (1) (6). Bringing into operation various provisions of the 2015 Act on 20.03.2015; 13.04.2015, in accord. with arts 2, 3. - Issued: 25.03.2015. Made: 19.03.2015. Effect: None. Territorial extent & classification: E/W/S/NI. General. - 8p.: 30 cm. - 978-0-11-113405-4 £6.00

The Criminal Justice and Courts Act 2015 (Commencement No. 2) Order 2015 No. 2015/1463 (C.82). - Enabling power: Criminal Justice and Courts Act 2015, s. 95 (1). Bringing into operation various provisions of the 2015 Act on 17.07.2015, in accord. with arts 2. - Issued: 09.07.2015. Made: 02.07.2015. Effect: None. Territorial extent & classification: E/W. General. - 2p.: 30 cm. - 978-0-11-113743-7 £4.25

The Federal Republic of Yugoslavia (Freezing of Funds) (Revocation) Regulations 2015 No. 2015/81. - Enabling power: European Communities Act 1972, s. 2 (2). - Issued: 03.02.2015. Made: 28.01.2015. Laid: 29.01.2015. Coming into force: 19.02.2015. Effect: S.I. 2001/59, 3087 revoked. Territorial extent & classification: E/W/S/NI. General. - 2p.: 30 cm. - 978-0-11-112824-4 £4.25

The Offender Rehabilitation Act 2014 (Commencement No. 2) Order 2015 No. 2015/40 (C.5). - Enabling power: Offender Rehabilitation Act 2014, s. 22 (1). Bringing into operation various provisions of the 2014 Act on 01.02.2015 in accord. with art. 2. - Issued: 27.01.2015. Made: 20.01.2015. Effect: None. Territorial extent & classification: E/W/S/NI. General. - 4p.: 30 cm. - 978-0-11-112769-8 £4.25

The Offender Rehabilitation Act 2014 (Incidental Provision) Order 2015 No. 2015/774. - Enabling power: Offender Rehabilitation Act 2014, s. 20 (1). - Issued: 24.03.2015. Made: 18.03.2015. Laid: 20.03.2015. Coming into force: 13.04.2015. Effect: None. Territorial extent & classification: E/W/NI. General. - 2p.: 30 cm. - 978-0-11-113400-9 £4.25

The Serious Crime Act 2015 (Commencement No. 1) Regulations 2015 No. 2015/820 (C.52). - Enabling power: Serious Crime Act 2015, s. 88 (6) (c) (e) (8). Bringing into operation various provisions of the 2015 Act on 03.05.2015; 01.06.2015, in accord. with art. 2 & 3. - Issued: 27.03.2015. Made: 19.03.2015. Effect: None. Territorial extent & classification: E/W/S/NI. General. - 4p.: 30 cm. - 978-0-11-113452-8 £4.25

The South Sudan (European Union Financial Sanctions) (No. 2) Regulations 2015 No. 2015/1361. - Enabling power: European Communities Act 1972, s. 2 (2), sch. 2, para. 1A. - Issued: 12.06.2015. Made: 08.06.2015. Laid: 09.06.2015, at 11.30 am. Coming into force: 09.06.2015, at 12.00 pm. Effect: S.I. 2014/1827 revoked with saving. Territorial extent & classification: E/W/S/NI. General. - EC note: These regs make provision relating to the enforcement of Council Regulation 2015/735 concerning restrictive measures in view of the situation in South Sudan. - 12p.: 30 cm. - 978-0-11-113663-8 £6.00

Criminal law, England and Wales

The Coroners and Justice Act 2009 (Commencement No. 17) Order 2015 No. 2015/819 (C.51). - Enabling power: Coroners and Justice Act 2009, s. 182 (5). Bringing into operation various provisions of the 2009 Act on 13.04.2015, in accord. with art. 2. - Issued: 26.03.2015. Made: 19.03.2015. Effect: None. Territorial extent & classification: E/W. General. - 8p.: 30 cm. - 978-0-11-113451-1 £4.25

The Costs in Criminal Cases (General) (Amendment) Regulations 2015 No. 2015/12. - Enabling power: Prosecution of Offences Act 1985, s. 19 (5). - Issued: 14.01.2015. Made: 08.01.2015. Laid: 09.01.2015. Coming into force: 01.02.2015. Effect: S.I. 1986/1335 amended. Territorial extent & classification: E/W. General. - 2p.: 30 cm. - 978-0-11-112682-0 £4.25

The Criminal Justice Act 2003 (Alcohol Abstinence and Monitoring Requirement) (Prescription of Arrangement for Monitoring) (Amendment) Order 2015 No. 2015/1482. - Enabling power: Criminal Justice Act 2003, ss. 212A (6) (7). - Issued: 14.07.2015. Made: 07.07.2015. Laid: 09.07.2015. Coming into force: 30.07.2015. Effect: S.I. 2014/1787 amended. Territorial extent & classification: E/W. General. - 2p.: 30 cm. - 978-0-11-113761-1 £4.25

The Criminal Justice and Courts Act 2015 (Simple Cautions) (Specification of Either-Way Offences) Order 2015 No. 2015/790. - Enabling power: Criminal Justice and Courts Act 2015, ss. 17 (3), 18 (1). - Issued: 25.03.2015. Made: 19.03.2015. Laid: 23.03.2015. Coming into force: 13.04.2015. Effect: None. Territorial extent & classification: E/W. General. - 4p.: 30 cm. - 978-0-11-113410-8 £4.25

The Criminal Justice and Courts Act 2015 (Simple Cautions) (Specification of Police Ranks) Order 2015 No. 2015/830. - Enabling power: Criminal Justice and Courts Act 2015, ss. 17 (5), 18 (1). - Issued: 26.03.2015. Made: 19.03.2015. Coming into force: 13.04.2015. Effect: None. Territorial extent & classification: E/W. General. - 2p.: 30 cm. - 978-0-11-113463-4 £4.25

The Criminal Justice (Sentencing) (Licence Conditions) Order 2015 No. 2015/337. - Enabling power: Criminal Justice Act 2003, ss. 250 (1) (4) (b) (ii), 330 (3). - Issued: 27.02.2015. Made: 15.02.2015. Laid: 24.02.2015. Coming into force: 23.03.2015. Effect: S.I. 2005/648 revoked. Territorial extent & classification: E/W. General. - 4p.: 30 cm. - 978-0-11-113025-4 £4.25

The Criminal Justice (Specified Class B Drugs) Order 2015 No. 2015/9. - Enabling power: Criminal Justice and Court Services Act 2000, s. 70 (1). - Issued: 14.01.2015. Made: 08.01.2015. Laid: 09.01.2015. Coming into force: 01.02.2015. Effect: None. Territorial extent & classification: E/W. General. - 2p.: 30 cm. - 978-0-11-112678-3 £4.25

The Criminal Procedure and Investigations Act 1996 (Code of Practice) Order 2015 No. 2015/861. - Enabling power: Criminal Procedure and Investigations Act 1996, s. 25 (2). - Issued: 30.03.2015. Made: 28.01.2015. Laid: 29.01.2015. Coming into force: In accord with art. 1. Effect: None. Territorial extent & classification: E/W. General. - 2p.: 30 cm. - 978-0-11-113483-2 £4.25

The Domestic Violence, Crime and Victims Act 2004 (Victims' Code of Practice) Order 2015 No. 2015/1817. - Enabling power: Domestic Violence, Crime and Victims Act 2004, s. 33 (7) (8). - Issued: 28.10.2015. Made: 22.10.2015. Laid: 23.10.2015. Coming into force: 16.11.2015. Effect: None. Territorial extent & classification: E/W. General. - 2p.: 30 cm. - 978-0-11-114015-4 £4.25

The Legal Aid, Sentencing and Punishment of Offenders Act 2012 (Alcohol Abstinence and Monitoring Requirements) Piloting (Amendment) Order 2015 No. 2015/1480 (C.86). - Enabling power: Legal Aid, Sentencing and Punishment of Offenders Act 2012, s. 77 (1) (4). Bringing into operation various provisions of the 2012 Act on 30.07.2015. - Issued: 15.07.2015. Made: 07.07.2015. Effect: SI. 2014/1777 amended. Territorial extent & classification: E/W. General. - This Order amends S.I. 2014/1777 C.77 which brought into force s. 76 of the 2012 Act in relation the South London local justice area for a period of 12 months beginning with 31st July 2014. This Order extends the period of time for which s. 76 is in force, in that area, by a period of 6 months. - 4p.: 30 cm. - 978-0-11-113766-6 £4.25

The Legal Aid, Sentencing and Punishment of Offenders Act 2012 (Commencement No. 11) Order 2015 No. 2015/504 (C.28). - Enabling power: Legal Aid, Sentencing and Punishment of Offenders Act 2012, s. 151 (1). Bringing into operation various provisions of the 2012 Act on 12.03.2015, in accord. with art. 2. - Issued: 11.03.2015. Made: 04.03.2015. Effect: None. Territorial extent & classification: E/W. General. - 4p.: 30 cm. - 978-0-11-113202-9 £4.25

The Legal Aid, Sentencing and Punishment of Offenders Act 2012 (Fines on Summary Conviction) Regulations 2015 No. 2015/664. - Enabling power: Legal Aid, Sentencing and Punishment of Offenders Act 2012, ss 85 (5) to (8), (10) (11), 149 (1) (2). - Issued: 18.03.2015. Made: 11.03.2015. Coming into force: 12.03.2015 in accord. with reg. 1 (1). Effect: 86 Acts; 47 SIs; 1996 cviii; NAWM 2010/1 amended. Territorial extent & classification: E/W. General. - Supersedes draft S.I. (ISBN 9780111126127) issued 23.12.2014. - 44p.: 30 cm. - 978-0-11-113322-4 £10.00

The Prosecution of Offences Act 1985 (Criminal Courts Charge) (Amendment) Regulations 2015 No. 2015/1970. - Enabling power: Prosecution of Offences Act 1985, ss. 21C (1), 29. - Issued: 08.12.2015. Made: 02.12.2015. Laid: 03.12.2015. Coming into force: 24.12.2015. Effect: S.I. 2015/796 amended. Territorial extent & classification: E/W. General. - 2p.: 30 cm. - 978-0-11-114147-2 £4.25

The Prosecution of Offences Act 1985 (Criminal Courts Charge) Regulations 2015 No. 2015/796. - Enabling power: Prosecution of Offences Act 1985, ss. 21A (3), 21C (1), 21E (4) (7), 29. - Issued: 26.03.2015. Made: 19.03.2015. Laid: 23.03.2015. Coming into force: 13.04.2015. Effect: None. Territorial extent & classification: E/W. General. - 8p.: 30 cm. - 978-0-11-113420-7 £4.25

The Recovery of Costs (Remand to Youth Detention Accommodation) (Amendment) Regulations 2015 No. 2015/569. - Enabling power: Legal Aid, Sentencing and Punishment of Offenders Act 2012, s. 103 (2) (a) (6). - Issued: 12.03.2015. Made: 05.03.2015. Laid: 11.03.2015. Coming into force: 01.04.2015. Effect: S.I. 2013/507 amended. Territorial extent & classification: E/W. General. - 2p.: 30 cm. - 978-0-11-113237-1 £4.25

The Serious Crime Act 2015 (Commencement No. 3) Regulations 2015 No. 2015/1809 (C.112). - Enabling power: Serious Crime Act 2015, s. 88 (1). Bringing into operation various provisions of the 2015 Act on 31.10.2015; 10.11.2015, in accord. with arts 2 & 3. - Issued: 26.10.2015. Made: 20.10.2015. Effect: None. Territorial extent & classification: E/W. General. - 4p.: 30 cm. - 978-0-11-114006-2 £4.25

The Serious Crime Act 2015 (Commencement No. 4) Regulations 2015 No. 2015/1976 (C.122). - Enabling power: Serious Crime Act 2015, s. 88 (1). Bringing into operation various provisions of the 2015 Act on 29.12.2015. - Issued: 11.12.2015. Made: 04.12.2015. Coming into force: 29.12.2015. Effect: None. Territorial extent & classification: E/W. General. - 4p.: 30 cm. - 978-0-11-114160-1 £4.25

The Serious Crime Act 2015 (Consequential Amendments) Regulations 2015 No. 2015/800. - Enabling power: Serious Crime Act 2015, s. 85 (2) (3) (c). - Issued: 26.03.2015. Made: 19.03.2015. Laid: 23.03.2015. Coming into force: 03.05.2015. Effect: S.I. 2004/1910; 2006/1116; 2007/1174; 2009/1168; 2013/435 amended. Territorial extent & classification: E/W. General. - 4p.: 30 cm. - 978-0-11-113426-9 £4.25

CRIMINAL LAW, NORTHERN IRELAND

The Sexual Offences Act 2003 (Prescribed Police Stations) (No. 2) Regulations 2015 No. 2015/1523. - Enabling power: Sexual Offences Act 2003, s. 87 (1) (a). - Issued: 21.07.2015. Made: 15.07.2015. Laid: 17.07.2015. Coming into force: 14.09.2015. Effect: S.I. 2015/82 revoked. Territorial extent & classification: E/W. General. - This Statutory Instrument has been made in consequence of a defect in SI 2015/82 (ISBN 9780111128251) and is being issued free of charge to all known recipients of that Statutory Instrument. - 24p.: 30 cm. - 978-0-11-113800-7 £6.00

The Sexual Offences Act 2003 (Prescribed Police Stations) Regulations 2015 No. 2015/82. - Enabling power: Sexual Offences Act 2003, s. 87 (1) (a). - Issued: 03.02.2015. Made: 27.01.2015. Laid: 30.01.2015. Coming into force: 25.02.2015. Effect: S.I. 2013/300 revoked. Territorial extent & classification: E/W. General. - Revoked by S.I. 2015/1523 (ISBN 9780111138007). - 24p.: 30 cm. - 978-0-11-112825-1 £6.00

The Youth Justice and Criminal Evidence Act 1999 (Commencement No. 14) (England and Wales) Order 2015 No. 2015/818 (C.50). - Enabling power: Youth Justice and Criminal Evidence Act 1999, s. 68 (3). Bringing into operation various provisions of the 1999 Act on 13.04.2015, in accord. with art. 2. - Issued: 26.03.2015. Made: 19.03.2015. Effect: None. Territorial extent & classification: E/W. General. - 4p.: 30 cm. - 978-0-11-113450-4 £4.25

The Youth Justice Board for England and Wales (Amendment of Functions) Order 2015 No. 2015/79. - Enabling power: Crime and Disorder Act 1998, s. 41 (6) (6A) (b). - Issued: 04.02.2015. Made: 27.01.2015. Coming into force: In accord. with art. 1. Effect: 1998 c. 37; S.I. 2000/1160 amended. Territorial extent & classification: E/W. General. - Supersedes draft SI (ISBN 9780111124031) issued 01.12.14 - 4p.: 30 cm. - 978-0-11-112818-3 £4.25

Criminal law, Northern Ireland

The Justice and Security (Northern Ireland) Act 2007 (Extension of duration of non-jury trial provisions) Order 2015 No. 2015/1572. - Enabling power: Justice and Security (Northern Ireland) Act 2007, s. 9 (2). - Issued: 29.07.2015. Made: 23.07.2015. Coming into force: 24.07.2015. Effect: None. Territorial extent & classification: NI. General. - Supersedes draft SI (ISBN 9780111136560) issued 09/06/15 - 2p.: 30 cm. - 978-0-11-113853-3 £4.25

Criminal procedure, England and Wales

The Criminal Justice and Courts Act 2015 (Commencement No. 1, Saving and Transitional Provisions) Order 2015 No. 2015/778 (C.44). - Enabling power: Criminal Justice and Courts Act 2015, s. 95 (1) (6). Bringing into operation various provisions of the 2015 Act on 20.03.2015; 13.04.2015, in accord. with arts 2, 3. - Issued: 25.03.2015. Made: 19.03.2015. Effect: None. Territorial extent & classification: E/W/S/NI. General. - 8p.: 30 cm. - 978-0-11-113405-4 £6.00

The Criminal Justice and Courts Act 2015 (Commencement No. 3 and Transitional Provisions) Order 2015 No. 2015/1778 (C.108). - Enabling power: Criminal Justice and Courts Act 2015, ss. 95 (1) (6). Bringing into operation various provisions of the 2015 Act on 26.10.2015 according to art. 3. - Issued: 19.10.2015. Made: 12.10.2015. Coming into force: 26.10.2015. Effect: None. Territorial extent & classification: E/W. General. - 4p.: 30 cm. - 978-0-11-113987-5 £4.25

Criminal proceedings, England and Wales

The Criminal Justice and Courts Act 2015 (Commencement No. 1, Saving and Transitional Provisions) Order 2015 No. 2015/778 (C.44). - Enabling power: Criminal Justice and Courts Act 2015, s. 95 (1) (6). Bringing into operation various provisions of the 2015 Act on 20.03.2015; 13.04.2015, in accord. with arts 2, 3. - Issued: 25.03.2015. Made: 19.03.2015. Effect: None. Territorial extent & classification: E/W/S/NI. General. - 8p.: 30 cm. - 978-0-11-113405-4 £6.00

Cultural objects

The Return of Cultural Objects (Amendment) Regulations 2015 No. 2015/1926. - Enabling power: European Communities Act 1972, s. 2 (2). - Issued: 27.11.2015. Made: 19.11.2015. Laid: 23.11.2015. Coming into force: 18.12.2015. Effect: S.I. 1994/501 amended & S.I. 1997/1719; 2001/3972 revoked. Territorial extent & classification: E/W/S/NI. General. - EC note: These Regulations implement Directive 2014/60/EU of the European Parliament. - 4p.: 30 cm. - 978-0-11-114112-0 £4.25

Customs

The Customs (Contravention of a Relevant Rule) (Amendment) Regulations 2015 No. 2015/636. - Enabling power: Finance Act 2003, ss. 24 (3), 26 (1) to (5), (8) (9), 41 (1) & Finance Act 2014, s. 102. - Issued: 16.03.2015. Made: 10.03.2015. Laid: 11.03.2015. Coming into force: 02.04.2015. Effect: S.I. 2003/3113 amended. Territorial extent & classification: E/W/S/NI. General. - 8p.: 30 cm. - 978-0-11-113292-0 £6.00

The Export Control (Amendment) (No. 2) Order 2015 No. 2015/940. - Enabling power: Export Control Act 2002, ss. 1, 4, 5, 7. - Issued: 01.04.2015. Made: 26.03.2015. Laid: 27.03.2015. Coming into force: 17.04.2015. Effect: S.I. 2008/3231 amended. Territorial extent & classification: E/W/S/NI. General. - 4p.: 30 cm. - 978-0-11-113563-1 £4.25

The Export Control (Amendment) Order 2015 No. 2015/351. - Enabling power: Export Control Act 2002, ss. 1, 2, 4, 5, 7. - Issued: 02.03.2015. Made: 23.02.2015. Laid: 25.02.2015. Coming into force: 24.03.2015. Effect: S.I. 2008/3231 amended. Territorial extent & classification: E/W/S/NI. General. - 28p.: 30 cm. - 978-0-11-113039-1 £6.00

The Export Control (Democratic Republic of Congo Sanctions and Miscellaneous Amendments and Revocations) Order 2015 No. 2015/1546. - Enabling power: European Communities Act 1972, s. 2 (2) & Export Control Act 2002, ss. 3, 4, 5, 7. - Issued: 23.07.2015. Made: 15.07.2015. Laid: 20.07.2015. Coming into force: 11.08.2015. Effect: S.I. 2008/3231; 2013/2012; 2014/3258 amended S.I. 2005/1677; 2008/131, 1964; 2009/2969; 2010/364 revoked. Territorial extent & classification: E/W/S/NI. General. - EC note: These regs make provision for the enforcement of certain trade restrictions against the Democratic Republic of Congo specified in Council Regulation (EC) no. 1183/2005 as amended by Council Regulation (EU) 2015/613. - 8p.: 30 cm. - 978-0-11-113827-4 £6.00

The Export Control (Iran Sanctions) (Amendment) Order 2015 No. 2015/1625. - Enabling power: European Communities Act 1972, s. 2 (2) & Export Control Act 2002, ss. 1, 2, 3, 4, 5, 7. - Issued: 01.09.2015. Made: 24.08.2015. Laid: 26.08.2015. Coming into force: 16.09.2015. Effect: S.I. 2012/1243 amended. Territorial extent & classification: E/W/S/NI. General. - EC note: This Order makes provision relating to the enforcement of the trade restrictions imposed on Iran by Council Regulations (EU) No 267/2012, as amended by Council Regulation (EU) 2015/1327. - 2p.: 30 cm. - 978-0-11-113875-5 £4.25

The Export Control (Russia, Crimea and Sevastopol Sanctions) (Amendment) Order 2015 No. 2015/1933. - Enabling power: European Communities Act 1972 s. 2 (2) & Export Control Act 2002 ss. 3, 5, 7. - Issued: 30.11.2015. Made: 23.11.2015. Laid: 25.11.2015. Coming into force: 16.12.2015. Effect: S.I. 2014/2357 amended. Territorial extent & classification: E/W/S/NI. General. - 4p.: 30 cm. - 978-0-11-114119-9 £4.25

The Export Control (Various Amendments) Order 2015 No. 2015/97. - Enabling power: European Communities Act 1972, s. 2 (2) & Export Control Act 2002, ss. 1, 2, 3, 4, 5, 7. - Issued: 06.02.2015. Made: 29.01.2015. Laid: 03.02.2015. Coming into force: 24.02.2015. Effect: S.I. 2013/2012; 2014/2357, 3258 amended. Territorial extent & classification: E/W/S/NI. General. - EC note: This Order makes provision for the enforcement of amended trade restrictions against Russia specified in Council Regulation (EU) no. 1290/2014 which amends Council Regulation (EU) no. 833/2014 concerning restrictive measures in view of Russia's actions destabilising the situation in Ukraine. The Order also provides for the enforcement of new trade and investment restrictions in the Crimea and Sevastopol specified in Council Regulation (EU) no. 1351/2014 which amends Council Regulation (EU) no. 692/2014 concerning restrictive measures in response to the illegal annexation of Crimea and Sevastopol. - 8p.: 30 cm. - 978-0-11-112848-0 £6.00

The Export Control (Yemen Sanctions) Regulations 2015 No. 2015/1586. - Enabling power: European Communities Act 1972, s. 2 (2). - Issued: 10.08.2015. Made: 02.08.2015. Laid: 05.08.2015. Coming into force: 27.08.2015. Effect: S.I. 2008/3231 amended. Territorial extent & classification: E/W/S/NI. General. - EC note: This Order makes provision for the enforcement of certain trade restrictions in view of the situation in Yemen as specified in Council Regulation (EU) no. 1352/2014, as amended by Council Regulation (EU) 2015/878. - 5p.: 30 cm. - 978-0-11-113861-8 £4.25

The Finance Act 2014, Schedule 21 (Commencement) Order 2015 No. 2015/812 (C.47). - Enabling power: Finance Act 2014, sch. 21 para. 10 (2). Bringing into operation various provisions of this Act on 01.04.2015 in accord. with art. 2. - Issued: 26.03.2015. Made: 20.03.2014. Effect: None. Territorial extent & classification: E/W/S/NI. General. - 4p.: 30 cm. - 978-0-11-113441-2 £4.25

Dangerous drugs

The Misuse of Drugs Act 1971 (Amendment) Order 2015 No. 2015/215. - Enabling power: Misuse of Drugs Act 1971, s. 2 (2). - Issued: 18.02.2015. Made: 11.02.2015. Coming into force: In accord. with art. 1. Effect: 1971 c.38 amended. Territorial extent & classification: E/W/S/NI. General. - Supersedes draft S.I. (ISBN 9780111125861) issued 22.12.2014. - 2p.: 30 cm. - 978-0-11-112957-9 £4.25

The Misuse of Drugs Act 1971 (Temporary Class Drug) (No. 2) Order 2015 No. 2015/1396. - Enabling power: Misuse of Drugs Act 1971, ss. 2A (1) (5), 7A (2) (3) (6), 31 (1). - Issued: 25.06.2015. Made: 17.06.2015. Laid: 25.06.2015. Coming into force: 27.06.2015. Effect: None. Territorial extent & classification: E/W/S/NI. General. - For approval by resolution of each House of Parliament within 40 days beginning with the day on which the Order was made, subject to extension for periods of dissolution, prorogation or adjournment of both Houses for more than four days. - 4p.: 30 cm. - 978-0-11-113692-8 £4.25

The Misuse of Drugs Act 1971 (Temporary Class Drug) (No. 2) Order 2015 No. 2015/1396. - Enabling power: Misuse of Drugs Act 1971, ss. 2A (1) (5), 7A (2) (3) (6), 31 (1). - Issued: 10.02.2016. Made: 17.06.2015. Laid: 25.06.2015. Coming into force: 27.06.2015. Effect: None. Territorial extent & classification: E/W/S/NI. General. - Approved. - 4p.: 30 cm. - 978-0-11-130011-4 £4.25

The Misuse of Drugs Act 1971 (Temporary Class Drug) (No. 3) Order 2015 No. 2015/1929. - Enabling power: Misuse of Drugs Act 1971, ss. 2A (1) (5), 7A (2) (3) (6), 31 (1). - Issued: 10.02.2016. Made: 23.11.2015. Laid: 25.11.2015. Coming into force: 27.11.2015. Effect: S.I. 1973/798; 2001/3998; S.R. 1973/179; 2002/1 extended in application. Territorial extent & classification: E/W/S/NI. General. - Approved. - 4p.: 30 cm. - 978-0-11-130010-7 £4.25

The Misuse of Drugs Act 1971 (Temporary Class Drug) (No. 3) Order 2015 No. 2015/1929. - Enabling power: Misuse of Drugs Act 1971, ss. 2A (1) (5), 7A (2) (3) (6), 31 (1). - Issued: 27.11.2015. Made: 23.11.2015. Laid: 25.11.2015. Coming into force: 27.11.2015. Effect: S.I. 1973/798; 2001/3998; S.R. 1973/179; 2002/1 extended in application. Territorial extent & classification: E/W/S/NI. General. - For approval by resolution of each House of Parliament within 40 days beginning with the day on which the Order was made, subject to extension for periods of dissolution, prorogation or adjournment of both Houses for more than four days. - 4p.: 30 cm. - 978-0-11-114117-5 £4.25

The Misuse of Drugs Act 1971 (Temporary Class Drug) Order 2015 No. 2015/1027. - Enabling power: Misuse of Drugs Act 1971, ss. 2A (1) (5), 7A (2) (3) (6), 31 (1). - Issued: 13.04.2015. Made: 02.04.2015. Coming into force: 10.04.2015. Effect: None. Territorial extent & classification: E/W/S/NI. General. - For approval by resolution of each House of Parliament within 40 days beginning with the day on which the Order was made, subject to extension for periods of dissolution, prorogation or adjournment of both Houses for more than four days. With correction slip dated May 2015. - 4p.: 30 cm. - 978-0-11-113635-5 £4.25

The Misuse of Drugs (Amendment) (England, Wales and Scotland) Regulations 2015 No. 2015/231. - Enabling power: Misuse of Drugs Act 1971, ss. 7, 10, 22, 31. - Issued: 19.02.2015. Made: 12.02.2015. Laid: 18.02.2015. Coming into force: 11.03.2015. Effect: S.I. 2001/3998 amended. Territorial extent & classification: E/W/S. General. - 2p.: 30 cm. - 978-0-11-112977-7 £4.25

The Misuse of Drugs (Amendment) (No. 2) (England, Wales and Scotland) Regulations 2015 No. 2015/891. - Enabling power: Misuse of Drugs Act 1971, ss. 7, 10, 22, 31. - Issued: 31.03.2015. Made: 20.03.2015. Laid: 26.03.2015. Coming into force: In accord. with reg. 1. Effect: S.I. 2001/3998 amended. Territorial extent & classification: E/W/S. General. - 8p.: 30 cm. - 978-0-11-113518-1 £6.00

The Misuse of Drugs (Designation) (Amendment) (England, Wales and Scotland) Order 2015 No. 2015/232. - Enabling power: Misuse of Drugs Act 1971, s. 7 (4). - Issued: 19.02.2015. Made: 12.02.2015. Laid: 18.02.2015. Coming into force: 11.03.2015. Effect: S.I. 2001/3997 amended. Territorial extent & classification: E/W/S. General. - Revoked by S.I. 2015/704 (ISBN 9780111133514). - 2p.: 30 cm. - 978-0-11-112978-4 £4.25

The Misuse of Drugs (Designation) (England, Wales and Scotland) Order 2015 No. 2015/704. - Enabling power: Misuse of Drugs Act 1971, s. 7 (4) (5). - Issued: 19.03.2015. Made: 12.03.2015. Laid: 17.03.2015. Coming into force: 31.05.2015. Effect: S.I. 2001/3997; 2005/1652; 2009/3135; 2010/1143, 1800; 2011/447; 2012/1310; 2013/177, 624; 2014/1274, 1376, 3276; 2015/232 revoked. Territorial extent & classification: E/W/S. General. - 8p.: 30 cm. - 978-0-11-113351-4 £6.00

Data protection

The Data Protection Act 1998 (Commencement No. 4) Order 2015 No. 2015/312 (C.16). - Enabling power: Data Protection Act 1998, s. 75 (3). Bringing into operation various provisions of the 1998 Act on 10.03.2015, in accord. with art. 2. - Issued: 26.02.2015. Made: 11.02.2015. Effect: None. Territorial extent & classification: E/W/S/NI. General. - 4p.: 30 cm. - 978-0-11-112999-9 £4.25

The Protection of Freedoms Act 2012 (Commencement No.11) Order 2015 No. 2015/587 (C.30). - Enabling power: Protection of Freedoms Act 2012, s. 120 (1). Bringing into operation various provisions of the 2012 Act on 16.03.2015, in accord. with art. 2. - Issued: 13.03.2015. Made: 04.03.2015. Effect: None. Territorial extent & classification: E/W/S/NI. General. - 4p.: 30 cm. - 978-0-11-113256-2 £4.25

Deep sea mining

The Deep Sea Mining Act 1981 (Isle of Man) Order 2015 No. 2015/2012. - Enabling power: Deep Sea Mining Act 1981, s. 18 (6). - Issued: 16.12.2015. Made: 09.12.2015. Coming into force: 01.01.2016. Effect: 1981 c.53 modified & extended & S.I. 2000/1112 revoked. Territorial extent & classification: E/W/S/NI. General. - 8p.: 30 cm. - 978-0-11-114192-2 £4.25

Defence

The Armed Forces Act (Continuation) Order 2015 No. 2015/1766. - Enabling power: Armed Forces Act 2006, s. 382 (2). - Issued: 15.10.2015. Made: 08.10.2015. Effect: None. Territorial extent & classification: E/W/S/NI. General. - Supersedes draft SI (ISBN 9780111137444) issued 09/07/15. - 2p.: 30 cm. - 978-0-11-113972-1 £4.25

The Armed Forces (Service Complaints and Financial Assistance) Act 2015 (Commencement) Regulations 2015 No. 2015/1957 (C.121). - Enabling power: Armed Forces (Service Complaints and Financial Assistance) Act 2015, s. 7(1). Bringing into operation various provisions of the 2015 Act on 01.01.2016 in accord. with art. 2. - Issued: 10.12.2015. Made: 03.12.2015. Effect: None. Territorial extent & classification: E/W/S/NI. General. - 2p.: 30 cm. - 978-0-11-114156-4 £4.25

The Armed Forces (Service Complaints and Financial Assistance) Act 2015 (Transitional and Savings Provisions) Regulations 2015 No. 2015/1969. - Enabling power: Armed Forces (Service Complaints and Financial Assistance) Act 2015, s. 6. - Issued: 10.12.2015. Made: 03.12.2015. Laid: 07.12.2015. Coming into force: 01.01.2016. Effect: None. Territorial extent & classification: E/W/S/NI. General. - [12]p.: 30 cm. - 978-0-11-114159-5 £6.00

The Armed Forces (Service Complaints Miscellaneous Provisions) Regulations 2015 No. 2015/2064. - Enabling power: Armed Forces Act 2006, s. 340A (4), 340E (1), 340M (6), 340N (4). - Issued: 24.12.2015. Made: 17.12.2015. Coming into force: 01.01.2016. Effect: None. Territorial extent & classification: E/W/S/NI. General. - 8p.: 30 cm. - 978-0-11-114247-9 £6.00

The Armed Forces (Service Complaints Ombudsman Investigations) Regulations 2015 No. 2015/1956. - Enabling power: Armed Forces Act 2006, 340H (4) (8) (11), 340I (2) (5), 340L (5) (7). - Issued: 10.12.2015. Made: 03.12.2015. Laid: 07.12.2015. Coming into force: 01.01.2016. Effect: None. Territorial extent & classification: E/W/S/NI. General. - 8p.: 30 cm. - 978-0-11-114157-1 £6.00

The Armed Forces (Service Complaints) Regulations 2015 No. 2015/1955. - Enabling power: Armed Forces Act 2006, ss. 340B (1) (2) (4), 340C (1) (2), 340D (1) (2) (6), 340F (2), 340G (1) (3), 340M (5). - Issued: 10.12.2015. Made: 03.12.2015. Laid: 07.12.2015. Coming into force: 01.01.2016. Effect: None. Territorial extent & classification: E/W/S/NI. General. - 8p.: 30 cm. - 978-0-11-114158-8 £6.00

The Armed Forces (Service Courts Rules) (Amendment) Rules 2015 No. 2015/1812. - Enabling power: Armed Forces Act 2006, ss. 151, 163, 288. - Issued: 27.10.2015. Made: 20.10.2015. Laid: 23.10.2015. Coming into force: 16.11.2015. Effect: S.I. 2009/1209, 1211, 2041 amended. Territorial extent & classification: E/W/S/NI. General. - 12p.: 30 cm. - 978-0-11-114010-9 £6.00

The Court Martial and Service Civilian Court (Youth Justice and Criminal Evidence Act 1999) (Amendment) Rules 2015 No. 2015/726. - Enabling power: Armed Forces Act 2006, ss. 163, 288 & Youth Justice and Criminal Evidence Act 1999, ss. 65 (1). - Issued: 20.03.2015. Made: 16.03.2015. Laid: 18.03.2015. Coming into force: In accord with rule 1. Effect: S.I. 2009/2100 amended. Territorial extent & classification: E/W/S/NI. General. - 8p.: 30 cm. - 978-0-11-113363-7 £4.25

The Criminal Justice and Courts Act 2015 (Commencement No. 1, Saving and Transitional Provisions) Order 2015 No. 2015/778 (C.44). - Enabling power: Criminal Justice and Courts Act 2015, s. 95 (1) (6). Bringing into operation various provisions of the 2015 Act on 20.03.2015; 13.04.2015, in accord. with arts 2, 3. - Issued: 25.03.2015. Made: 19.03.2015. Effect: None. Territorial extent & classification: E/W/S/NI. General. - 8p.: 30 cm. - 978-0-11-113405-4 £6.00

The Criminal Justice (Armed Forces Code of Practice for Victims of Crime) Regulations 2015 No. 2015/1811. - Enabling power: European Communities Act 1972, s. 2 (2). - Issued: 28.10.2015. Made: 21.10.2015. Laid: 23.10.2015. Coming into force: 16.11.2015. Effect: None. Territorial extent & classification: E/W/S/NI. General. - 64p.: 30 cm. - 978-0-11-114009-3 £10.00

The Defence Reform Act 2014 (Commencement No. 4) Order 2015 No. 2015/791 (C.45). - Enabling power: Defence Reform Act 2014, s. 50 (1) (2). Bringing into operation various provisions of the 2014 Act on 31.03.2015, in accord. with art. 3. - Issued: 25.03.2015. Made: 19.03.2015. Effect: None. Territorial extent & classification: E/W/S/NI. General. - 2p.: 30 cm. - 978-0-11-113412-2 £4.25

The Offender Rehabilitation Act 2014 (Commencement No. 2) Order 2015 No. 2015/40 (C.5). - Enabling power: Offender Rehabilitation Act 2014, s. 22 (1). Bringing into operation various provisions of the 2014 Act on 01.02.2015 in accord. with art. 2. - Issued: 27.01.2015. Made: 20.01.2015. Effect: None. Territorial extent & classification: E/W/S/NI. General. - 4p.: 30 cm. - 978-0-11-112769-8 £4.25

The RAF Brize Norton Byelaws 2015 No. 2015/1467. - Enabling power: Military Lands Act 1892, s. 14 (1). - Issued: 09.07.2015. Made: 18.06.2015. Coming into force: 18.10.2015. Effect: None. Territorial extent & classification: E/W/S/NI. General. - This Statutory Instrument has been substituted with an SI of the same number but new ISBN (9780111300060) and is therefore superseded by the new version. - 16p., col. maps: 30 cm. - 978-0-11-113745-1 £8.50

The RAF Brize Norton Byelaws 2015 No. 2015/1467. - Enabling power: Military Lands Act 1892, s. 14 (1). - Issued: 29.09.2015. Made: 18.06.2015. Coming into force: 18.10.2015. Effect: None. Territorial extent & classification: E/W/S/NI. General. - This Statutory Instrument has been printed in substitution of the SI of the same number and is being issued free of charge to all known recipients of that Statutory Instrument. - 16p., col. maps: 30 cm. - 978-0-11-130006-0 £8.50

The Reserve Forces (Call-out and Recall) (Financial Assistance) (Amendment) Regulations 2015 No. 2015/460. - Enabling power: Reserve Forces Act 1996, ss. 83, 84. - Issued: 09.03.2015. Made: 03.03.2015. Laid: 05.03.2015. Coming into force: 27.03.2015. Effect: S.I. 2005/859 amended. Territorial extent & classification: E/W/S/NI. General. - 8p.: 30 cm. - 978-0-11-113151-0 £4.25

The Sculthorpe Training Area Byelaws 2015 No. 2015/1492. - Enabling power: Military Lands Act 1892, s. 14 (1). - Issued: 15.07.2015. Made: 18.06.2015. Coming into force: 18.10.2015. Effect: None. Territorial extent & classification: E/W/S/NI. General. - 16p., maps (col.): 30 cm. - 978-0-11-113774-1 £8.50

The Summary Appeal Court (Youth Justice and Criminal Evidence Act 1999) Rules 2015 No. 2015/1813. - Enabling power: Armed Forces Act 2006, s. 151 & Youth Justice and Criminal Evidence Act 1999, ss. 37 (5), 38 (6), 65 (1). - Issued: 28.10.2015. Made: 20.10.2015. Laid: 23.10.2015. Coming into force: 16.11.2015. Effect: None. Territorial extent & classification: E/W/S/NI. General. - 12p.: 30 cm. - 978-0-11-114011-6 £6.00

The Youth Justice and Criminal Evidence Act 1999 (Application to Service Courts) (Amendment) (No. 2) Order 2015 No. 2015/1805. - Enabling power: Youth Justice and Criminal Evidence Act 1999, ss. 61 (1) (2). - Issued: 26.10.2015. Made: 19.10.2015. Laid: 21.10.2015. Coming into force: 15.11.2015. Effect: S.I. 2009/2083 amended. Territorial extent & classification: E/W/S/NI. General. - 8p.: 30 cm. - 978-0-11-114002-4 £4.25

The Youth Justice and Criminal Evidence Act 1999 (Application to Service Courts) (Amendment) Order 2015 No. 2015/727. - Enabling power: Youth Justice and Criminal Evidence Act 1999, ss. 61 (2). - Issued: 20.03.2015. Made: 16.03.2015. Laid: 18.03.2015. Coming into force: In accord. with art. 1. Effect: S.I. 2009/2083 amended. Territorial extent & classification: E/W/S/NI. General. - 2p.: 30 cm. - 978-0-11-113364-4 £4.25

Dentists

The General Dental Council (Overseas Registration Examination Regulations) Order of Council 2015 No. 2015/735. - Enabling power: Dentists Act 1984, ss. 16 (4), 52 (1B). - Issued: 23.03.2015. Made: 16.03.2015. Coming into force: 01.05.2015. Effect: S.I. 2007/1884 revoked. Territorial extent & classification: E/W/S/NI. General. - 4p.: 30 cm. - 978-0-11-113370-5 £4.25

Deregulation

The Deregulation Act 2015 (Commencement No. 1 and Transitional and Saving Provisions) (Amendment) Order 2015 No. 2015/1405 (C.78). - Enabling power: Deregulation Act 2015, s. 115 (9). - Issued: 29.06.2015. Made: 22.06.2015. Effect: S.I. 2015/994 (C.69) amended. Territorial extent & classification: E/W/S/NI. General. - This S.I. has been made in consequence of a defect in S.I. 2015/994 (C.69) (ISBN 9780111136256) published on 02/04/15 and is being issued free of charge to all known recipients of that S.I. - 4p.: 30 cm. - 978-0-11-113702-4 £4.25

The Deregulation Act 2015 (Commencement No. 1 and Transitional and Saving Provisions) Order 2015 No. 2015/994 (C.69). - Enabling power: Deregulation Act 2015, s. 115 (7) (9), sch. 1, part. 4. Bringing into operation various provisions of the 2015 Act on 01.04.2015, 06.04.2015; 10.04.2015; 20.04.2015; 26.05.2015; 08.06.2015; 15.06.2015; 15.06.2015; 30.06.2015; 01.07.2015; 01.10.2015, in accord. with arts 2 to 11. - Issued: 02.04.2015. Made: 27.03.2015. Effect: 2009 c.22 amended. Territorial extent & classification: E/W/S/NI. General. - 16p.: 30 cm. - 978-0-11-113625-6 £6.00

The Deregulation Act 2015 (Commencement No. 2 and Transitional Provisions) Order 2015 No. 2015/1402 (C.77). - Enabling power: Deregulation Act 2015, s. 115 (6) (10) (11). Bringing into operation various provisions of the 2015 Act on 29.06.2015, in accord. with art. 2. - Issued: 26.06.2015. Made: 18.06.2015. Effect: 1985 c.61; 1990 c.41, 2007 c.29 amended. Territorial extent & classification: E/W/S/NI. General. - 4p.: 30 cm. - 978-0-11-113699-7 £4.25

The Deregulation Act 2015 (Commencement No. 3 and Transitional and Saving Provisions) Order 2015 No. 2015/1732 (C.105). - Enabling power: Deregulation Act 2015, ss. 104 (1), 115 (7) (9). Bringing into operation various provisions of the 2015 Act on 01.10.2015, 01.01.2016, in accord. with arts 2, 3. - Issued: 05.10.2015. Made: 29.09.2015. Effect: None. Territorial extent & classification: E/W/S/NI. General. - 8p.: 30 cm. - 978-0-11-113954-7 £6.00

The Deregulation Act 2015 (Consequential Amendments) Order 2015 No. 2015/971. - Enabling power: Deregulation Act 2015, s. 112 (1) (2) (5). - Issued: 02.04.2015. Made: 27.03.2015. Laid: 27.03.2015. Coming into force: In accord. with art. 1 (2). Effect: 47 SIs amended & S.I. 2015/551 partially revoked & S.I. 2013/2668 revoked. Territorial extent & classification: E/W/S/NI. General. - 20p.: 30 cm. - 978-0-11-113605-8 £6.00

The Deregulation Act 2015 (Insolvency) (Consequential Amendments and Transitional and Savings Provisions) Order 2015 No. 2015/1641. - Enabling power: Deregulation Act 2015, s. 112 (1) (2) (4). - Issued: 10.09.2015. Made: 01.09.2015. Laid: 04.09.2015. Coming into force: 01.10.2015. Effect: S.I. 1991/724, 2684; 1994/2421; 1996/1527; 2001/1090; 2003/3363; 2004/400; 2005/590; 2007/2157; 2008/386, 2499 (W.217); 2011/2686; 2013/1388; 2014/2839 & S.S.I. 2011/210 amended & S.I. 1984/887; 1986/952 revoked. Territorial extent & classification: E/W/S. General. - 8p.: 30 cm. - 978-0-11-113888-5 £6.00

The Deregulation Act 2015 (Poisons and Explosives Precursors) (Consequential Amendments, Revocations and Transitional Provisions) Order 2015 No. 2015/968. - Enabling power: Deregulation Act 2015, s. 112 (1) (2). - Issued: 02.04.2015. Made: 27.03.2015. Laid: 27.03.2015. Coming into force: In accord. with art. 1 (2) (3). Effect: S.I. 1975/1023; 1979/72; 1999/672; 2000/2853, 3253; 2007/399, 3544; 2009/669; 2010/231; 2013/50 & S.S.I. 2009/183 amended & S.I. 1982/217, 218; 2014/1942 revoked. Territorial extent & classification: E/W/S/NI. General. - 4p.: 30 cm. - 978-0-11-113602-7 £4.25

Designs

The Appointed Person (Designs) Rules 2015 No. 2015/169. - Enabling power: Registered Designs Act 1949, s. 36 & Copyright, Designs and Patents Act 1988, s. 250. - Issued: 13.02.2015. Made: 05.02.2015. Laid: 11.02.2015. Coming into force: 06.04.2015. Effect: None. Territorial extent & classification: E/W/S/NI. General. - 8p.: 30 cm. - 978-0-11-112905-0 £6.00

Devolution, Scotland

The Children and Young People (Scotland) Act 2014 (Consequential and Saving Provisions) Order 2015 No. 2015/907. - Enabling power: Scotland Act 1998, ss. 104, 112 (1), 113 (2) (4) (5). - Issued: 30.03.2015. Made: 24.03.2015. Coming into force: In accord. with arts 1 (2) (3) (4). Effect: 1995 c.36 modified. Territorial extent & classification: E/W/NI. General. - Supersedes draft S.I. (ISBN 9780111130087) issued 27/02/15. - 4p.: 30 cm. - 978-0-11-113531-0 £4.25

The Courts Reform (Scotland) Act 2014 (Consequential Provisions and Modifications) Order 2015 No. 2015/700. - Enabling power: Scotland Act 1998, ss. 104, 112 (1), 113 (2) (3) (5) (7), 114 (1). - Issued: 19.03.2015. Made: 11.03.2015. Coming into force: in accord with art. 1. Effect: 1975 c.25, c.42; 1978 c.30; 1982 c.27; 1991 c.48; 2005 c.4; S.I. 2009/2231 amended; 1926 c.16; 1934 c.56; 1936 c.6; 1971 c.58 partially repealed; and 1898 c.35; 1952 c.12 repealed. Territorial extent & classification: E/W/S/NI. General. - Supersedes draft S.I. (ISBN 9780111126929) issued 19/01/15. - 12p.: 30 cm. - 978-0-11-113349-1 £6.00

The Food (Scotland) Act 2015 (Consequential Provisions) Order 2015 No. 2015/444. - Enabling power: Scotland Act 1998, ss. 104, 112 (1), 113 (5), 114 (1). - Issued: 09.03.2015. Made: 03.03.2015. Laid: 04.03.2015. Coming into force: In accord. with art. 1 (2). Effect: None. Territorial extent & classification: E/W/S/NI. General. - 4p.: 30 cm. - 978-0-11-113132-9 £4.25

The Regulatory Reform (Scotland) Act 2014 (Consequential Modifications) Order 2015 No. 2015/374. - Enabling power: Scotland Act 1998, ss. 104, 112 (1), 113 (2) (3) (4) (5). - Issued: 03.03.2015. Made: 25.02.2015. Coming into force: 26.02.2015. Effect: 1974 c.37; 1988 c.48; 1989 c.29; 1990 c.43; 1995 c.25; 2005 c.5; 2009 c.4; 2009 c.23; S.I. 1997/3032 amended. Territorial extent & classification: E/W/S/NI. General. - Supersedes draft S.I. (ISBN 9780111124505) issued 08/12/14. - 8p.: 30 cm. - 978-0-11-113066-7 £6.00

The Reservoirs (Scotland) Act 2011 (Restrictions on Disclosure of Information in relation to National Security etc.) Order 2015 No. 2015/48. - Enabling power: Scotland Act 1998, ss. 104, 112 (1), 113 (2) (3) (5). - Issued: 27.01.2015. Made: 21.01.2015. Coming into force: In accord. with art. 1 (2) (3). Effect: 2010 c.29 amended. Territorial extent & classification: E/W/S/NI. General. - Supersedes draft SI (ISBN 9780111123362) issued 21/11/14. - 8p.: 30 cm. - 978-0-11-112777-3 £6.00

The Scotland Act 1998 (Functions Exercisable in or as Regards Scotland) Order 2015 No. 2015/211 (S.2). - Enabling power: Scotland Act 1998, s. 30 (3). - Issued: 18.02.2015. Made: 11.02.2015. Coming into force: 28.02.2015. Effect: None. Territorial extent & classification: E/W/S/NI. General. - Supersedes draft S.I. (ISBN 978111121832) issued 21.10.2014. - 4p.: 30 cm. - 978-0-11-112953-1 £4.25

The Scotland Act 1998 (Modification of Schedule 5) Order 2015 No. 2015/1379. - Enabling power: Scotland Act 1998, ss. 30 (2). - Issued: 17.06.2015. Made: 10.06.2015. Coming into force: In accord. with art. 1 (2). Effect: 1998 c.46 modified. Territorial extent & classification: E/W/S/NI. General. - Supersedes draft S.I. (ISBN 9780111127926) issued 02/02/15. - 4p.: 30 cm. - 978-0-11-113674-4 £4.25

The Scotland Act 1998 (Modification of Schedules 4 and 5 and Transfer of Functions to the Scottish Ministers etc.) Order 2015 No. 2015/692. - Enabling power: Scotland Act 1998, ss. 30 (2), 63 (1) (3), 113 (3) (4) (5), 124 (2). - Issued: 26.03.2015. Made: 19.03.2015. Coming into force: In accord. with art. 2. Effect: 1983 c.2; 1998 c. 46 modified. Territorial extent & classification: E/W/S/NI. General. - Supersedes draft SI (ISBN 9780111127551) issued 23/01/15 - 4p.: 30 cm. - 978-0-11-113415-3 £4.25

The Scotland Act 1998 (Modification of Schedules 4 and 5) Order 2015 No. 2015/1764. - Enabling power: Scotland Act 1998, ss. 30 (2) (4). - Issued: 15.10.2015. Made: 08.10.2015. Coming into force: In accord. with art. 1 (2). Effect: 1998 c.46 modified. Territorial extent & classification: E/W/S/NI. General. - Supersedes draft SI 9780111137147) issued 06/07/15 - 4p.: 30 cm. - 978-0-11-113970-7 £4.25

The Scotland Act 1998 (River Tweed) Amendment Order 2015 No. 2015/203. - Enabling power: Scotland Act 1998, ss. 111, 113 (2) (3) (4) (5) (7). - Issued: 18.02.2015. Made: 11.02.2015. Coming into force: 12.02.2015. Effect: S.I. 2006/2913 amended. Territorial extent & classification: E/W/S. General. - Supersedes draft S.I. (ISBN 9780111121931) issued 21.10.2014. - 4p.: 30 cm. - 978-0-11-112945-6 £4.25

The Scotland Act 1998 (Variation of Borrowing Power) Order 2015 No. 2015/932. - Enabling power: Scotland Act 1998, s. 66 (5). - Issued: 31.03.2015. Made: 24.03.2015. Laid:-. Coming into force: 01.04.2015. Effect: 1998 c.46 amended. Territorial extent & classification: E/W/S/NI. General. - Supersedes draft S.I. (ISBN 9780111125281) issued 16/12/14. - 2p.: 30 cm. - 978-0-11-113554-9 £4.25

The Scotland Act 2012 (Commencement No. 5) Order 2015 No. 2015/682 (C.40). - Enabling power: Scotland Act 2012, s. 44 (5). Bringing into operation various provisions of the 2012 Act on 01.07.2015, in accord. with art. 2. - Issued: 23.03.2015. Made: 17.03.2015. Effect: None. Territorial extent & classification: E/W/S/NI. General. - 2p.: 30 cm. - 978-0-11-113374-3 £4.25

The Scotland Act 2012 (Saving and Consequential Provisions) Order 2015 No. 2015/683. - Enabling power: Scotland Act 2012, s. 42 (1) (2) (4). - Issued: 23.03.2015. Made: 17.03.2015. Laid: 18.03.2015. Coming into force: In accord. with art. 1. Effect: S.I. 1999/1512; 2010/2999 amended. Territorial extent & classification: E/W/S/NI. General. - Partially revoked by SSI 2015/425 (ISBN 9780111030271) in re to S. - 4p.: 30 cm. - 978-0-11-113371-2 £4.25

The Scottish Administration (Offices) Order 2015 No. 2015/200 (S.1). - Enabling power: Scotland Act 1998, s. 126 (8) (b). - Issued: 18.02.2015. Made: 11.02.2015. Laid before Parliament: 16.02.2015. Laid before the Scottish Parliament: 16.02.2015. Coming into force: 01.04.2015. Effect: None. Territorial extent & classification: E/W/S/NI. General. - 2p.: 30 cm. - 978-0-11-112942-5 £4.25

The Scottish Parliament (Regional Returning Officers) (Revocation) Order 2015 No. 2015/743 (S. 3). - Enabling power: Scotland Act 1998, ss. 12 (6), 113 (4). - Issued: 23.03.2015. Made: 17.03.2015. Coming into force: 30.06.2015. Effect: S.I. 2011/576 revoked. Territorial extent & classification: S. General. - 2p.: 30 cm. - 978-0-11-113376-7 £4.25

The Scottish Parliament (Returning Officers Charges) (Revocation) Order 2015 No. 2015/761 (S. 4). - Enabling power: Representation of the People Act 1983, s. 29 (3A) (4C) & S.I. 2010/2999, art. 18. - Issued: 24.03.2015. Made: 17.03.2015. Coming into force: 30.06.2015. Effect: S.I. 2011/1013 revoked with saving. Territorial extent & classification: S. General. - 4p.: 30 cm. - 978-0-11-113392-7 £4.25

Devolution, Wales

The Government of Wales Act 2006 (Amendment) Order 2015 No. 2015/204. - Enabling power: Government of Wales Act 2006, s. 109. - Issued: 18.02.2015. Made: 11.02.2015. Coming into force: 12.02.2015. Effect: 2006 c. 32 amended. Territorial extent & classification: UK but practical application is limited to Wales. General. - Supersedes draft S.I. (ISBN 9780111122921) issued 10.11.2014. - 2p.: 30 cm. - 978-0-11-112946-3 £4.25

The Government of Wales Act 2006 (Designation of Receipts) (Amendment) Order 2015 No. 2015/640. - Enabling power: Government of Wales Act 2006, ss. 120 (3). - Issued: 17.03.2015. Made: 10.03.2015. Laid: 11.03.2015. Coming into force: 02.04.2015. Effect: S.I. 2007/848 amended. Territorial extent & classification: E/W/S/NI. General. - 2p.: 30 cm. - 978-0-11-113296-8 £4.25

The Higher Education (Wales) Act 2015 (Consequential Provision) Order 2015 No. 2015/1353. - Enabling power: Government of Wales Act 2006, ss. 150 (1) (2). - Issued: 11.06.2015. Made: 04.06.2015. Laid: 09.06.2015. Coming into force: 01.09.2015. Effect: None. Territorial extent & classification: E/W. General. - 4p.: 30 cm. - 978-0-11-113660-7 £4.25

The Human Transplantation (Wales) Act 2013 (Consequential Provision) Order 2015 No. 2015/865. - Enabling power: Government of Wales Act 2006, ss. 150 (1) (2), 157 (2). - Issued: 27.03.2015. Made: 23.03.2015. Coming into force: In accord. with art. 1 (2). Effect: 2004 c. 30; S.I. 2012/1501 amended. Territorial extent & classification: E/W/S/NI. General. - Supersedes draft S.I. (ISBN 9780111127544) issued 23/01/15. - 4p.: 30 cm. - 978-0-11-113489-4 £4.25

Disabled persons

The Rail Vehicle Accessibility (B2007 Vehicles) Exemption Order 2015 No. 2015/1631. - Enabling power: Equality Act 2010, ss. 183 (1) (2) (4) (b) (5), 207 (1) (4). - Issued: 08.09.2015. Made: 26.08.2015. Laid: 08.09.2015. Coming into force: 30.09.2015. Effect: None. Territorial extent & classification: E/W/S. General. - 4p.: 30 cm. - 978-0-11-113879-3 £4.25

The Rail Vehicle Accessibility (Non-Interoperable Rail System) (London Underground Northern Line 95TS Vehicles) Exemption Order 2015 No. 2015/393. - Enabling power: Equality Act 2010, ss. 183 (1) (2) (4) (b) (5), 207 (1) (4). - Issued: 05.03.2015. Made: 23.02.2015. Laid: 05.03.2015. Coming into force: 27.03.2015. Effect: None. Territorial extent & classification: E/W/S. General. - 8p.: 30 cm. - 978-0-11-113082-7 £6.00

Disclosure of information

The Disclosure of Exporter Information Regulations 2015 No. 2015/2060. - Enabling power: Small Business, Enterprise and Employment Act 2015, s. 10 (1). - Issued: 23.12.2015. Made: 16.12.2015. Coming into force: 17.12.2015. in accord. with reg. 1. Effect: None. Territorial extent & classification: E/W/S/NI. General. - Supersedes draft S.I. (ISBN 9780111141045) issued 23/11/15. - 2p.: 30 cm. - 978-0-11-114242-4 £4.25

Diverted profits tax

The Finance Act 2009, Sections 101 and 102 (Diverted Profits Tax) (Appointed Day) Order 2015 No. 2015/974 (C.63). - Enabling power: Finance Act 2009, s. 104 (3) (4). Bringing into operation various provisions of the 2009 Act on 01.04.2015, in accord. with art. 2. - Issued: 20.04.2015. Made: 26.03.2015. Effect: None. Territorial extent & classification: E/W/S/NI. General. - 2p.: 30 cm. - 978-0-11-113608-9 £4.25

Dogs, England and Wales

The Dangerous Dogs Exemption Schemes (England and Wales) Order 2015 No. 2015/138. - Enabling power: Dangerous Dogs Act 1991, s. 1 (5) (6) (6A) & Dangerous Dogs (Amendment) Act 1997, s. 4 (1) (c). - Issued: 11.02.2015. Made: 04.02.2015. Laid: 10.02.2015. Coming into force: 03.03.2015. Effect: S.I. 1991/1742 revoked with saving & S.I. 1991/1744, 2297, 2636; 2013/1302 revoked. Territorial extent & classification: E. General. - 12p.: 30 cm. - 978-0-11-112889-3 £6.00

Duchy of Lancaster

The Legislative Reform (Duchy of Lancaster) Order 2015 No. 2015/1560. - Issued: 27.07.2015. Made: 20.07.2015. Coming into force: In accord. with art. 1. Effect: 1817 c.97 (57 Geo 3) amended. Territorial extent & classification: E/W/S/NI. General. - Supersedes draft SI (ISBN 9780111136492) issued 04/06/2015. - 2p.: 30 cm. - 978-0-11-113841-0 £4.25

Ecclesiastical law, England

The Care of Churches and Ecclesiastical Jurisdiction (Amendment) Measure 2015 (Commencement, Transitional and Saving Provisions) Order 2015 No. 2015/593. - Enabling power: Care of Churches and Ecclesiastical Jurisdiction (Amendment) Measure 2015, s. 11 (2) (3). Bringing various provisions of the 2015 Measure into operation 01.04.2015, in accord. with art. 2. - Issued: 13.03.2015. Made: 09.03.2015. Laid before Parliament: -. Effect: None. Territorial extent & classification: E. General. - 4p.: 30 cm. - 978-0-11-113262-3 £4.25

The Ecclesiastical Judges, Legal Officers and Others (Fees) Order 2015 No. 2015/1954. - Enabling power: Ecclesiastical Fees Measure 1986, ss. 6 (1) (1A) (2). - Issued: 08.12.2015. Made: 25.11.2015. Laid: 03.12.2015. Coming into force: 01.03.2016. Effect: S.I. 2014/2072 revoked. Territorial extent & classification: E. General. - 12p.: 30 cm. - 978-0-11-114139-7 £6.00

The Ecclesiastical Offices (Terms of Service) (Amendment) Directions 2015 No. 2015/1612. - Enabling power: S.I. 2009/2108, reg. 23 (1). - Issued: 21.08.2015. Made (sealed by the Archbishops' Council): 16.07.2015. Laid: 21.08.2015. Coming into force: 01.12.2015. Effect: S.I. 2010/1923 amended. Territorial extent & classification: E. General. - 2p.: 30 cm. - 978-0-11-113867-0 £4.25

The Ecclesiastical Offices (Terms of Service) (Amendment) Regulations 2015 No. 2015/1654. - Enabling power: Ecclesiastical Offices (Terms of Service) Measure 2009, s. 2. - Issued: 11.09.2015. Made (sealed by the Archbishops' Council): 16.07.2015. Laid: 09.09.2015. Coming into force: 01.11.2015. Effect: S.I. 2009/2108 amended. Territorial extent & classification: E. General. - 4p.: 30 cm. - 978-0-11-113904-2 £4.25

The Ecclesiastical Property (Exceptions from Requirement for Consent to Dealings) Order 2015 No. 2015/1545. - Enabling power: Parochial Church Councils (Powers) Measure 1956, s. 6 (4A), 6A (1) (a) & Incumbents and Churchwardens (Trusts) Measure 1964, s. 5A (1) (2) (a). - Issued: 23.07.2015. Made (sealed in Archbishops' Council): 16.07.2015. Laid: 20.07.2015. Coming into force: 01.10.2015. Effect: None. Territorial extent & classification: E. General. - 4p.: 30 cm. - 978-0-11-113826-7 £4.25

The Ecclesiastical Property Measure 2015 (Commencement) Order 2015 No. 2015/1468. - Enabling power: Ecclesiastical Property Measure 2015, s. 3 (2). Bringing various provisions of the 2015 Measure into operation on 01.07.2015 in accord. with art. 2. - Issued: 09.07.2015. Made: 18.05.2015. Coming into force: 01.07.2015. Effect: None. Territorial extent & classification: E. General. - 2p.: 30 cm. - 978-0-11-113747-5 £4.25

The Faculty Jurisdiction Rules 2015 No. 2015/1568. - Enabling power: Care of Churches and Ecclesiastical Jurisdiction Measure 1991, ss. 14 (7), 15 (4), 18B, 21 (4), 26. - Issued: 28.07.2015. Made: 18.05.2015. Approved by the General Synod: 11.07.2015. Laid: 24.07.2015. Coming into force: 01.01.2016. Effect: S.I. 2013/1916 revoked with savings. Territorial extent & classification: E. General. - 128p.: 30 cm. - 978-0-11-113849-6 £19.00

The Legal Officers (Annual Fees) Order 2015 No. 2015/1613. - Enabling power: Ecclesiastical Fees Measure 1986, s. 5 (1) (2). - Issued: 21.08.2015. Made: 01.06.2015. Laid: 21.08.2015. Coming into force: 01.01.2016. Effect: S.I. 2014/895 revoked. Territorial extent & classification: E. General. - 12p.: 30 cm. - 978-0-11-113868-7 £6.00

Ecclesiastical law, England and Wales

The Grants to the Churches Conservation Trust Order 2015 No. 2015/908. - Enabling power: Redundant Churches and other Religious Buildings Act 1969, s. 1. - Issued: 01.04.2015. Made: 24.03.2015. Coming into force: 01.04.2015. Effect: S.I. 2011/968 revoked. Territorial extent & classification: E/W. General. - Supersedes draft S.I. (ISBN 9780111127001) issued 16.01.2015; Revoked by S.I. 2016/433 (ISBN 9780111142738). - 2p.: 30 cm. - 978-0-11-113532-7 £4.25

Education, England

The Chief Inspector of Education, Children's Services and Skills (No. 2) Order 2015 No. 2015/1377. - Enabling power: Education and Inspections Act 2006, s. 114 (1). - Issued: 17.06.2015. Made: 10.06.2015. Coming into force: 11.06.2015. Effect: None. Territorial extent & classification: E. General. - 4p.: 30 cm. - 978-0-11-113672-0 £4.25

EDUCATION, ENGLAND

The Children and Families Act 2014 (Transitional and Saving Provisions) (Amendment) (No. 2) Order 2015 No. 2015/1619. - Enabling power: Children and Families Act 2014, s. 137 (1). - Issued: 25.08.2015. Made: 18.08.2015. Coming into force: 01.09.2015. Effect: S.I. 2014/2270 amended. Territorial extent & classification: E. General. - 4p.: 30 cm. - 978-0-11-113872-4 £4.25

The Children and Families Act 2014 (Transitional and Saving Provisions) (Amendment) Order 2015 No. 2015/505. - Enabling power: Children and Families Act 2014, s. 137 (1). - Issued: 10.03.2015. Made: 03.03.2015. Coming into force: 01.04.2015. Effect: S.I. 2014/2270 amended. Territorial extent & classification: E. General. - 8p.: 30 cm. - 978-0-11-113203-6 £6.00

The Designation of Rural Primary Schools (England) Order 2015 No. 2015/1748. - Enabling power: Education and Inspections Act 2006, s. 15 (7) (b). - Issued: 09.10.2015. Made: 05.10.2015. Coming into force: 06.10.2015. Effect: S.I. 2014/2650 revoked. Territorial extent & classification: E. Local. - 2p.: 30 cm. - 978-0-11-113961-5 £4.25

The Designation of Schools Having a Religious Character (England) Order 2015 No. 2015/1804. - Enabling power: School Standards and Framework Act 1998, ss. 69 (3), 69 (4). - Issued: 26.10.2015. Made: 13.10.2015. Effect: S.I. 2007/3561 revoked. Territorial extent & classification: E. General. - 4p.: 30 cm. - 978-0-11-114001-7 £4.25

The Designation of Schools Having a Religious Character (Independent Schools) (England) (No. 2) Order 2015 No. 2015/2075. - Enabling power: School Standards and Framework Act 1998, s. 69 (3). - Issued: 30.12.2015. Made: 23.12.2015. Coming into force: 24.12.2015 in accord. with art. 1. Effect: S.I. 2004/72, 354, 1378; 2012/3174 partially revoked. Territorial extent & classification: E. Local. - 4p.: 30 cm. - 978-0-11-114258-5 £4.25

The Designation of Schools Having a Religious Character (Independent Schools) (England) Order 2015 No. 2015/1636. - Enabling power: School Standards and Framework Act 1998, s. 69 (3). - Issued: 04.09.2015. Made: 28.08.2015. Effect: S.I. 2003/3108; 2012/2265 partially revoked. Territorial extent & classification: E. General. - 4p.: 30 cm. - 978-0-11-113881-6 £4.25

The Designation of Schools Having a Religious Character (Independent Schools) (England) (Revocation) (No. 2) Order 2015 No. 2015/1344. - Enabling power: School Standards and Framework Act 1998, s. 69 (3). - Issued: 05.06.2015. Made: 01.06.2015. Effect: S.I. 2010/1174 partially revoked. Territorial extent & classification: E. General. - 2p.: 30 cm. - 978-0-11-113652-2 £4.25

The Designation of Schools Having a Religious Character (Independent Schools) (England) (Revocation) Order 2015 No. 2015/1267. - Enabling power: School Standards and Framework Act 1998, s. 69 (3). - Issued: 27.04.2015. Made: 23.04.2015. Effect: S.I. 2010/1174 partially revoked. Territorial extent & classification: E. Local. - Available at http://www.legislation.gov.uk/uksi/2015/1267/contents/made Non-print

The Designation of Schools Having a Religious Character (Independent Schools) (England) (Revocation) Order 2015 No. 2015/1267. - Enabling power: School Standards and Framework Act 1998, s. 69 (3). - Issued: 16.10.2015. Made: 23.04.2015. Coming into force: 23.04.2015. Effect: S.I. 2010/1174 partially revoked. Territorial extent & classification: E. General. - 2p.: 30 cm. - 978-0-11-130007-7 £4.25

The Diocese of Chester (Educational Endowments) (Backford Church of England School) Order 2015 No. 2015/1577. - Enabling power: Education Act 1996, ss. 554, 556 & Reverter of Sites Act 1987, s. 5. - Issued: 30.07.2015. Made: 28.07.2015. Coming into force: 26.08.2015. Effect: None. Territorial extent & classification: E. Local. - Available at http://www.legislation.gov.uk/uksi/2015/1577/contents/made Non-print

The Diocese of Derby (Educational Endowments) (The Former Edward Revell Endowed Voluntary Controlled Primary School) Order 2015 No. 2015/246. - Enabling power: Education Act 1996, ss. 554, 556. - Issued: 10.02.2015. Made: 05.02.2015. Coming into force: 17.02.2015. Effect: None. Territorial extent & classification: E. Local. - Available at http://www.legislation.gov.uk/uksi/2015/246/contents/made Non-print

The Diocese of Durham (Educational Endowments) (Cleadon Village CE Infants' School) Order 2015 No. 2015/247. - Enabling power: Education Act 1996, ss. 554, 556 & Reverter of Sites Act 1987, s. 5. - Issued: 10.02.2015. Made: 05.02.2015. Coming into force: 17.02.2015. Effect: None. Territorial extent & classification: E. Local. - Available at http://www.legislation.gov.uk/uksi/2015/247/contents/made Non-print

The Diocese of Ely (Educational Endowments) (Fincham Church of England School) Order 2015 No. 2015/831. - Enabling power: Education Act 1996, ss. 555 (2) (3). - Issued: 12.03.2015. Made: 10.03.2015. Coming into force: 23.03.2015. Effect: None. Territorial extent & classification: E. Local - Available at http://www.legislation.gov.uk/uksi/2015/831/contents/madeNon-print

The Diocese of Ely (Educational Endowments) (Shouldham Church of England School) Order 2015 No. 2015/832. - Enabling power: Education Act 1996, ss. 555 (2) (3). - Issued: 12.03.2015. Made: 10.03.2015. Coming into force: 23.03.2015. Effect: None. Territorial extent & classification: E. Local - Available at http://www.legislation.gov.uk/uksi/2015/832/contents/madeNon-print

The Diocese of Guildford (Educational Endowments) (Down Road Church of England School) (Amendment) Order 2015 No. 2015/1799. - Enabling power: Education Act 1996, ss. 554, 556. - Issued: 20.10.2015. Made: 15.10.2015. Coming into force: 04.11.2015. Effect: S.I. 2010/2435 amended. Territorial extent & classification: E. Local. - Available at http://www.legislation.gov.uk/uksi/2015/1799/contents/made Non-print

The Diocese of Lichfield (Educational Endowments) (Bicton Church of England School) Order 2015 No. 2015/1869. - Enabling power: Education Act 1996, ss. 554, 556. - Issued: 10.11.2015. Made: 05.11.2015. Laid: - Coming into force: 25.11.2015. Effect: None. Territorial extent & classification: E. Local. - Available at http://www.legislation.gov.uk/uksi/2015/1869/contents/made Non-print

The Diocese of Newcastle (Educational Endowments) (Craster Church of England School) Order 2015 No. 2015/1800. - Enabling power: Education Act 1996, ss. 554, 556. - Issued: 20.10.2015. Made: 15.10.2015. Coming into force: 05.11.2015. Effect: None. Territorial extent & classification: E. Local. - Available at http://www.legislation.gov.uk/uksi/2015/1800/contents/made Non-print

The Diocese of St Davids (Educational Endowments) (Shouldham Church of England School) (Amendment) Order 2014 No. 2015/1429. - Enabling power: Education Act 1996, ss. 554, 556. - Issued: 30.06.2015. Made: 23.06.2015. Coming into force: 13.07.2015. Effect: S.I. 2015/832 amended. Territorial extent & classification: E. Local. - Available at http://www.legislation.gov.uk/uksi/2015/1429/contents/made Non-print

The Diocese of Worcester (Educational Endowments) (Evesham Church of England First School) Order 2015 No. 2015/833. - Enabling power: Education Act 1996, ss. 555 (2) (3). - Issued: 12.03.2015. Made: 10.03.2015. Coming into force: 24.03.2015. Effect: None. Territorial extent & classification: E. Local. - Available at http://www.legislation.gov.uk/uksi/2015/833/contents/made Non-print

The Education (Designated Institutions) (England) Order 2015 No. 2015/1703. - Enabling power: Education Reform Act 1988, s. 129 (1). - Issued: 29.09.2015. Made: 22.09.2015. Laid: 24.09.2015. Coming into force: 22.10.2015. Effect: None. Territorial extent & classification: E. General. - 2p.: 30 cm. - 978-0-11-113942-4 £4.25

The Education (Destination Information) (Prescribed Activities) (England) Regulations 2015 No. 2015/1564. - Enabling power: Further and Higher Education Act 1992, ss. 49B (3), 89 (4). - Issued: 28.07.2015. Made: 22.07.2015. Laid: 23.07.2015. Coming into force: 01.09.2015. Effect: None. Territorial application & classification: E General. - 2p.: 30 cm. - 978-0-11-113845-8 £4.25

The Education (Information) (Miscellaneous Amendments) (England) Regulations 2015 No. 2015/902. - Enabling power: Education Act 1996, s. 29 (3) (5), 408, 537, 537A, 563, 569 (4) (5). - Issued: 31.03.2015. Made: 25.03.2015. Laid: 27.03.2015. Coming into force: 01.09.2015. Effect: S.I. 2015/1437; 2007/2324; 2008/3093 amended. Territorial extent & classification: E. General. - 8p.: 30 cm. - 978-0-11-113526-6 £4.25

EDUCATION, ENGLAND

The Education (National Curriculum) (Miscellaneous Amendments) (England) Order 2015 No. 2015/900. - Enabling power: Education Act 2002, ss. 87 (3) (a) (c) (7) (10) (11) (12A), 210 (7). - Issued: 31.03.2015. Made: 25.03.2015. Laid: 27.03.2015. Coming into force: 01.09.2015. Effect: S.I. 2003/1038, 1039; 2004/2783; 2013/2232 amended. Territorial extent & classification: E. General. - 8p.: 30 cm. - 978-0-11-113524-2 £6.00

The Education (National Curriculum) (Specified Purpose) (England) Order 2015 No. 2015/901. - Enabling power: Education Act 2002, s. 76 (2) (b). - Issued: 31.03.2015. Made: 25.03.2015. Laid: 27.03.2015. Coming into force: 01.09.2015. Effect: None. Territorial extent & classification: E. General. - 2p.: 30 cm. - 978-0-11-113525-9 £4.25

The Education (Non-Maintained Special Schools) (England) (Amendment) Regulations 2015 No. 2015/387. - Enabling power: Education Act 1996, ss. 342 (2) (4) (5), 569 (4). - Issued: 03.03.2015. Made: 24.02.2015. Laid: 27.02.2015. Coming into force: 20.03.2015. Effect: S.I. 2011/1627 amended. Territorial extent & classification: E. General. - 4p.: 30 cm. - 978-0-11-113074-2 £4.25

The Education (Non-Maintained Special Schools) (England) Regulations 2015 No. 2015/728. - Enabling power: Education Act 1996, ss. 342 (2) (4) (5) (5A), 342A, 342B, 342C, 569 (4). - Issued: 23.03.2015. Made: 16.03.2015. Laid: 18.03.2015. Coming into force: 01.09.2015. Effect: S.I. 2011/1627; 2015/387 revoked. Territorial extent & classification: E. General. - 16p.: 30 cm. - 978-0-11-113365-1 £6.00

The Education (Prescribed Courses of Higher Education) (Information Requirements) (England) Regulations 2015 No. 2015/225. - Enabling power: Further and Higher Education Act 1992, s. 79 (c). - Issued: 18.02.2015. Made: 12.02.2015. Laid: 13.02.2015. Coming into force: 01.04.2015. Effect: S.I. 2014/2179 revoked. Territorial application & classification: E General. - 172p.: 30 cm. - 978-0-11-112965-4 £25.50

The Education (School Inspection) (England) (Amendment) (No. 2) Regulations 2015 No. 2015/1639. - Enabling power: Education Act 2005, ss. 5 (1) (a), 120 (1) (2) (a) (b). - Issued: 09.09.2015. Made: 03.09.2015. Laid: 04.09.2015. Coming into force: 30.09.2015. Effect: S.I. 2005/2038 amended. Territorial extent & classification: E. General. - 4p.: 30 cm. - 978-0-11-113885-4 £4.25

The Education (School Inspection) (England) (Amendment) Regulations 2015 No. 2015/170. - Enabling power: Education Act 2005, ss. 5 (1) (a), 120 (1) (20 (a) (b). - Issued: 13.02.2015. Made: 06.02.2015. Laid: 11.02.2015. Coming into force: 01.09.2015. Effect: S.I. 2005/2038 amended. Territorial extent & classification: E. General. - 4p.: 30 cm. - 978-0-11-112906-7 £4.25

The Education (School Performance Information) (England) (Amendment) Regulations 2015 No. 2015/1566. - Enabling power: Education Act 1996, ss. 408, 537, 537A, 569 (4). - Issued: 29.07.2015. Made: 22.07.2015. Laid: 23.07.2015. Coming into force: 01.09.2015. Effect: S.I. 2007/2324 amended. Territorial extent & classification: E. General. - 4p.: 30 cm. - 978-0-11-113848-9 £4.25

The Education (Student Information) (England) Regulations 2015 No. 2015/1567. - Enabling power: Apprenticeships, Skills, Children and Learning Act 2009, ss. 253A (1), 262 (3). - Issued: 29.07.2015. Made: 22.07.2015. Laid before Parliament: 23.07.2015. Coming into force: 01.09.2015. Effect: None. Territorial extent & classification: E. General. - 12p.: 30 cm. - 978-0-11-113847-2 £6.00

The Education (Student Support) (Amendment) Regulations 2015 No. 2015/1951. - Enabling power: Teaching and Higher Education Act 1998, ss. 22, 42 (6). - Issued: 07.12.2015. Made: 29.11.2015. Laid: 02.12.2015. Coming into force: 23.12.2015. Effect: S.I. 2011/1986 amended. Territorial extent & classification: E. General. - 20p.: 30 cm. - 978-0-11-114135-9 £6.00

The Further Education Loans (Amendment) Regulations 2015 No. 2015/181. - Enabling power: Teaching and Higher Education Act 1998, ss. 22, 42 (6). - Issued: 16.02.2015. Made: 10.02.2015. Laid: 11.02.2015. Coming into force: 30.03.2015. Effect: S.I. 2012/1818 amended. Territorial extent & classification: E. General. - 4p.: 30 cm. - 978-0-11-112918-0 £4.25

The Inspector of Education, Children's Services and Skills (No. 3) Order 2015 No. 2015/1525. - Enabling power: Education and Inspections Act 2006, s. 114 (1). - Issued: 22.07.2015. Made: 15.07.2015. Coming into force: 16.07.2015. Effect: None. Territorial extent & classification: E. General. - 2p.: 30 cm. - 978-0-11-113802-1 £4.25

The Inspectors of Education, Children's Services and Skills (No. 4) Order 2015 No. 2015/1762. - Enabling power: Education and Inspections Act 2006, s. 114 (1). - Issued: 15.10.2015. Made: 08.10.2015. Coming into force: 09.10.2015. Effect: None. Territorial extent & classification: E. General. - 2p.: 30 cm. - 978-0-11-113968-4 £4.25

The Inspectors of Education, Children's Services and Skills (No. 5) Order 2015 No. 2015/1895. - Enabling power: Education and Inspections Act 2006, s. 114 (1). - Issued: 18.11.2015. Made: 11.11.2015. Coming into force: 12.11.2015. Effect: None. Territorial extent & classification: E. General. - 2p.: 30 cm. - 978-0-11-114093-2 £4.25

The Inspectors of Education, Children's Services and Skills (No. 6) Order 2015 No. 2015/2010. - Enabling power: Education and Inspections Act 2006, s. 114 (1). - Issued: 16.12.2015. Made: 09.12.2015. Coming into force: 10.12.2015. Effect: None. Territorial extent & classification: E. General. - 2p.: 30 cm. - 978-0-11-114190-8 £4.25

The Inspectors of Education, Children's Services and Skills Order 2015 No. 2015/224. - Enabling power: Education and Inspections Act 2006, s. 114 (1). - Issued: 18.02.2015. Made: 11.02.2015. Coming into force: 12.02.2015. Effect: None. Territorial extent & classification: E. General. - 4p.: 30 cm. - 978-0-11-112963-0 £4.25

The National College for High Speed Rail (Government) Regulations 2015 No. 2015/1458. - Enabling power: Further and Higher Education Act 1992, ss. 20 (2), 21 (1), sch. 4. - Issued: 08.07.2015. Made: 02.07.2015. Laid: 03.07.2015. Coming into force: 30.07.2015. Effect: None. Territorial extent & classification: E. General. - 20p.: 30 cm. - 978-0-11-113737-6 £6.00

The National College for High Speed Rail (Incorporation) Order 2015 No. 2015/1457. - Enabling power: Further and Higher Education Act 1992, ss. 16 (1) (a) (5), 17 (2) (b). - Issued: 08.07.2015. Made: 02.07.2015. Laid: 03.07.2015. Coming into force: 30.07.2015. Effect: None. Territorial extent & classification: E. General. - 2p.: 30 cm. - 978-0-11-113736-9 £4.25

The School and Early Years Finance (England) Regulations 2015 No. 2015/2033. - Enabling power: School Standards and Framework Act 1998, ss. 45A, 45AA, 47, 47ZA, 47A (4B) (5), 48 (1) (2), 49 (2) (2A), 138 (7), sch. 14, para. 2B & Education Act 2002 s. 24 (3). - Issued: 21.12.2015. Made: 09.12.2015. Laid: 16.12.2015. Coming into force: 07.01.2016. Effect: S.I. 2012/2261 amended & S.I. 2013/3104 revoked. Territorial extent & classification: E. General. - 44p.: 30 cm. - 978-0-11-114210-3 £10.00

The School Governance (Federations) (England) (Amendment) Regulations 2015 No. 2015/1554. - Enabling power: Academies Act 2010, s. 3 (6). - Issued: 24.07.2015. Made: 20.07.2015. Laid: 21.07.2015. Coming into force: 01.09.2015. Effect: S.I. 2012/1035 amended. Territorial extent & classification: E. General. - 2p.: 30 cm. - 978-0-11-113831-1 £4.25

The School Governance (Miscellaneous Amendments) (England) Regulations 2015 No. 2015/883. - Enabling power: Education Act 2002, ss. 19 (3) (d) (i) to (l), 20 (2), 23 (a) to (c), 26 (b), 34 (5) (b) (e) (6) (c), 210 (7) & Education and Inspections Act 2006, ss. 166 (3) (a) to (c) (e) to (g), 181 (2), sch. 6, 19 (2) (c) (3). - Issued: 31.03.2015. Made: 24.03.2015. Laid: 26.03.2015. Coming into force: 01.09.2015. Effect: S.I. 2003/1962; 2007/958, 1321; 2009/2680; 2010/1918; 2012/1034 amended. Territorial extent & classification: E. General. - 12p.: 30 cm. - 978-0-11-113506-8 £6.00

The School Staffing (England) (Amendment) Regulations 2015 No. 2015/887. - Enabling power: School Standards and Framework Act 1998, s. 72 (1) & Education Act 2002, ss. 35 (4) (5), 36 (4) (5). - Issued: 31.03.2015. Made: 24.03.2015. Laid: 26.03.2015. Coming into force: 29.06.2015. Effect: S.I. 2009/2680 amended. Territorial extent & classification: E. General. - 4p.: 30 cm. - 978-0-11-113510-5 £4.25

The Special Educational Needs and Disability (Amendment) Regulations 2015 No. 2015/359. - Enabling power: Children and Families Act 2014, ss. 37 (4), 44 (7), 51 (4), 135 (3). - Issued: 02.03015. Made: 24.02.2015. Laid: 26.02.2015. Coming into force: 23.03.2015. Effect: S.I. 2014/1530 amended. Territorial extent & classification: E. General. - 4p.: 30 cm. - 978-0-11-113048-3 £4.25

The Special Educational Needs and Disability (Detained Persons) Regulations 2015 No. 2015/62. - Enabling power: Children and Families Act 2014, ss 31 (4), 36 (11), 37 (4), 44 (7), 56 (1), 71 (11), 73 (4), 74 (3), 80 (1) , 135 (3). - Issued: 02.02.2015. Made: 26.01.2015. Laid: 28.01.2015. Coming into force: 01.04.2015. Effect: None. Territorial extent & classification: E. General. - 20p.: 30 cm. - 978-0-11-112798-8 £6.00

The Special Educational Needs and Disability (First-tier Tribunal Recommendation Power) (Pilot) Regulations 2015 No. 2015/358. - Enabling power: Children and Families Act 2014, ss. 51 (4) (c), 135 (2) (3). - Issued: 02.03.2015. Made: 24.02.2015. Laid: 26.02.2015. Coming into force: 01.04.2015. Effect: S.I. 2014/1530 modified. Territorial extent & classification: E. General. - 8p.: 30 cm. - 978-0-11-113047-6 £4.25

The Special Educational Needs (Code of Practice) (Appointed Day) Order 2015 No. 2015/893. - Enabling power: Children and Families Act 2014, s. 78 (6). Appointed day for the coming into force of the 'Special Educational Needs and Disability Code of Practice: 0 to 25 years' (a copy of a draft of which was laid before each House of Parliament on 28th January 2015) is 1st April 2015. - Issued: 30.03.2015. Made: 23.03.2015. Coming into force: 01.04.2015. Effect: None. Territorial extent & classification: E. General. - 2p.: 30 cm. - 978-0-11-113520-4 £4.25

Education, England and Wales

The Deregulation Act 2015 (Commencement No. 4) Order 2015 No. 2015/2074 (C.130). - Enabling power: Deregulation Act 2015, s. 115 (7). Bringing into operation various provisions of the 2015 Act on 01.01.2016, in accord. with art. 2. - Issued: 29.12.2015. Made: 22.12.2015. Effect: None. Territorial extent & classification: E/W. General. - 4p.: 30 cm. - 978-0-11-114257-8 £4.25

The Higher Education (Wales) Act 2015 (Consequential Provision) Order 2015 No. 2015/1353. - Enabling power: Government of Wales Act 2006, ss. 150 (1) (2). - Issued: 11.06.2015. Made: 04.06.2015. Laid: 09.06.2015. Coming into force: 01.09.2015. Effect: None. Territorial extent & classification: E/W. General. - 4p.: 30 cm. - 978-0-11-113660-7 £4.25

The School Teachers' Pay and Conditions Order 2015 No. 2015/1582. - Enabling power: Education Act 2002, ss. 122 (1), 123, 124. - Issued: 13.08.2015. Made: 05.08.2015. Laid: 10.08.2015. Coming into force: 01.09.2015. Effect: S.I. 2014/2405 revoked. Territorial extent & classification: E/W. General. - 4p.: 30 cm. - 978-0-11-113864-9 £4.25

The Teachers (Compensation for Redundancy and Premature Retirement) Regulations 2015 No. 2015/601. - Enabling power: Public Service Pensions Act, ss. 1, 3, sch. 3. - Issued: 13.03.2015. Made: 05.03.2015. Laid: 10.03.2015. Coming into force: 01.04.2015. Effect: S.I. 2010/990; 2014/ 424/512 amended. & S.I. 2005/2198; 2006/3122; 2010/1172; 2014/107 partially revoked & S.I. 1997/311; 1998/2256; 1999/608; 2000/664; 2006/2216 revoked. Territorial extent & classification: E/W. General. - 24p.: 30 cm. - 978-0-11-113266-1 £6.00

The Teachers' Pension Scheme (Amendment) Regulations 2015 No. 2015/592. - Enabling power: Public Service Pensions Act 2013, ss. 1 (1) (2) (d) (3) (4), 2, 3 (1) (2) (3) (a), 18 (5) to (9), sch. 2, para. 4 (a), sch. 3, sch. 5, para. 18. - Issued: 13.03.2015. Made: 05.03.2015. Laid: 10.03.2015. Coming into force: 01.04.2015. Effect: S.I. 2014/512 amended. Territorial extent & classification: E/W. General. - This Statutory Instrument has been printed in substitution of the SI of same number (and ISBN) issued 13.03.2015 and is being issued free of charge to all known recipients of that Statutory Instrument. - 8p.: 30 cm. - 978-0-11-113261-6 £4.25

The Teachers' Pension Scheme (Consequential Provisions) Regulations 2015 No. 2015/436. - Enabling power: Public Service Pensions Act 2013, ss. 1 (1) (2) (d), 3 (1) (2) (3) (a) (4). - Issued: 06.03.2015. Made: 25.02.2015. Coming into force: In accord. with reg. 1. Effect: 1993 c.48; 2004 c.12; S.I. 1996/1172, 1847 modified. Territorial extent & classification: E/W. General. - Supersedes draft S.I. (ISBN 9780111125922) issued 22/12/14. - 8p.: 30 cm. - 978-0-11-113124-4 £6.00

The Teachers' Superannuation (Additional Voluntary Contributions) (Amendment) Regulations 2015 No. 2015/594. - Enabling power: Superannuation Act 1972, ss. 9, 12, sch. 3 & Public Service Pensions Act 2013, ss. 1, 3, sch. 3. - Issued: 13.03.2015. Made: 05.03.2015. Laid: 10.03.2015. Coming into force: 01.04.2015. Effect: S.I. 1994/2924 amended. Territorial extent & classification: E/W. General. - 8p.: 30 cm. - 978-0-11-113263-0 £6.00

Education, Wales

The Cancellation of Student Loans for Living Costs Liability (Wales) Regulations 2015 No. 2015/1418 (W.142). - Enabling power: Teaching and Higher Education Act 1998, ss. 22, 42 (6). - Issued: 07.072015. Made: 24.06.2015. Laid before the National Assembly for Wales: 26.06.2015. Coming into force: 01.08.2015. Effect: None. Territorial extent & classification: W. General. - In English and Welsh. Welsh title: Rheoliadau Dileu Atebolrwydd dros Fenthyciadau i Fyfyrwyr at Gostau Byw (Cymru) 2015. - 8p.: 30 cm. - 978-0-348-11118-7 £6.00

The Consumer Rights Act 2015 (Commencement No.1 and Transitional Provision) (Wales) Order 2015 No. 2015/1605 (W.203) (C.93). - Enabling power: Consumer Rights Act 2015, s. 97 (2), 100 (3) (b). Bringing various provisions of the 2015 Act into operation on 01.09.2015 in accord. with art. 2. - Issued: 24.08.2015. Made: 10.08.2015. Effect: None. Territorial extent & classification: W. General. - In English and Welsh. Welsh title: Gorchymyn Deddf Hawliau Defnyddwyr 2015 (Cychwyn Rhif 1 a Darpariaeth Drosiannol) (Cymru) 2015. - 4p.: 30 cm. - 978-0-348-11144-6 £4.25

The Consumer Rights Act 2015 (Commencement No.2) (Wales) Order 2015 No. 2015/1831 (W.267) (C.115). - Enabling power: Consumer Rights Act 2015, s. 100 (3) (b). Bringing various provisions of the 2015 Act into operation on 21.10.2015 in accord. with arts. 2, 3. - Issued: 30.10.2015. Made: 21.10.2015. Effect: None. Territorial extent & classification: W. General. - Revoked by W.S.I. 2015/1904 (ISBN 9780348111934). - In English and Welsh. Welsh title: Gorchymyn Deddf Hawliau Defnyddwyr 2015 (Cychwyn Rhif 2) (Cymru) 2015. - 4p.: 30 cm. - 978-0-348-11177-4 £4.25

The Eastern High School (Change to School Session Times) Order 2015 No. 2015/1227 (W.81). - Enabling power: Education Act 2002, s. 2 (1). - Issued: 05.05.2015. Made: 20.04.2015. Laid before the National Assembly for Wales: 24.04.2015. Coming into force: 01.06.2015. Effect: None. Territorial extent & classification: W. General. - In English and Welsh. Welsh title: Gorchymyn Ysgol Uwchradd y Dwyrain (Newid Amserau Sesiynau Ysgolion) 2015. - 4p.: 30 cm. - 978-0-348-11091-3 £4.25

The Education Act 2002 (Commencement No.15) (Wales) Order 2015 No. 2015/381 (W.40)(C.22). - Enabling power: Education Act 2002, s. 216 (4) (5). Bringing into force various provisions of the 2002 Act on 27.02.2015. - Issued: 13.04.2015. Made: 24.02.2015. Effect: None. Territorial extent & classification: W. General. - In English and Welsh. Welsh title: Gorchymyn Deddf Addysg 2002 (Cychwyn Rhif 15) (Cymru) 2015. - 12p.: 30 cm. - 978-0-348-11065-4 £6.00

The Education (Chief Inspector of Education and Training in Wales) Order 2015 No. 2015/205. - Enabling power: Education Act 2005, s. 19 (1). - Issued: 18.02.2015. Made: 11.02.2015. Coming into force: 12.02.2015. Effect: S.I. 2010/1553 revoked. Territorial extent & classification: W. General. - 2p.: 30 cm. - 978-0-11-112947-0 £4.25

The Education (Induction Arrangements for School Teachers) (Wales) Regulations 2015 No. 2015/484 (W.41). - Enabling power: Education (Wales) Act 2014, ss. 17, 19 (3), 47 (1). - Issued: 13.01.2015. Made: 03.03.2015. Laid before the National Assembly for Wales: 05.03.2015. Coming into force: 01.04.2015. Effect: W.S.I. 2007/2811 (W.238); 2012/724 (W.96) partially revoked & W.S.I. 2005/1818 (W.146); 2012/1675 (W.216) revoked. Territorial extent & classification: W. General. - In English and Welsh. Welsh title: Rheoliadau Addysg (Trefniadau Sefydlu ar gyfer Athrawon Ysgol) (Cymru) 2015. - 28p.: 30 cm. - 978-0-348-11050-0 £6.00

The Education (Inspection of Nursery Education) (Wales) Regulations 2015 No. 2015/1599 (W.198). - Enabling power: School Standards and Framework Act 1998, ss. 122 (1), 138 (7) (8), sch. 26, paras 6B (1) (a), 13B. - Issued: 25.09.2015. Made: 05.08.2015. Laid before the National Assembly for Wales: 10.08.2015. Coming into force: 01.09.2015. Effect: None. Territorial extent & classification: W. General. - In English and Welsh. Welsh title: Rheoliadau Addysg (Arolygu Addysg Feithrin) (Cymru) 2015. - 8p.: 30 cm. - 978-0-348-11156-9 £4.25

The Education (National Curriculum) (Attainment Targets and Programmes of Study) (Wales) (Amendment) Order 2015 No. 2015/1601 (W.200). - Enabling power: Education Act 2002, ss. 108 (3) (a) (b) (5), 210. - Issued: 25.09.2015. Made: 05.08.2015. Laid before the National Assembly for Wales: 11.08.2015. Coming into force: 01.09.2015. Effect: S.I. 2008/1409 (W.146) amended. Territorial extent & classification: W. General. - In English and Welsh. Welsh title: Gorchymyn Addsg (Cwricwlwm Cenedlaethol) (Targedau Cyrhaeddiad a Rhaglenni Astudio) (Cymru) 2015. - 8p.: 30 cm. - 978-0-348-11157-6 £4.25

EDUCATION, WALES

The Education (Pupil Referral Units) (Application of Enactments) (Wales) (Amendment) Regulations 2015 No. 2015/1793 (W.253). - Enabling power: Education Act 1996, s. 569 (4) (5), sch. 1, para. 3. - Issued: 21.10.2015. Made: 12.10.2015. Laid before the National Assembly for Wales: 15.10.2015. Coming into force: 06.11.2015. Effect: WSI 2007/1069 (W.109) amended. Territorial extent & classification: W. General. - In English and Welsh. Welsh title: Rheoliadau Addysg (Unedau Cyfeirio Disgyblion) (Cymhwyso Deddfiadau) (Cymru) (Diwygio) 2015. - 4p.: 30 cm. - 978-0-348-11168-2 £4.25

The Education (Student Support) (Wales) (Amendment) Regulations 2015 No. 2015/1505 (W.173). - Enabling power: Teaching and Higher Education Act 1998, ss. 22, 42 (6). - Issued: 22.07.2015. Made: 08.07.2015. Laid before the National Assembly for Wales: 13.07.2015. Coming into force: 03.08.2015. Effect: S.I. 2015/54 (W.5) amended. Territorial extent & classification: W. General. - In English and Welsh. Welsh title: Rheoliadau Addysg (Cymorth i Fyfyrwyr) (Cymru) (Diwygio) 2015. - 4p.: 30 cm - 978-0-348-11124-8 £4.25

The Education (Student Support) (Wales) Regulations 2015 No. 2015/54 (W.5). - Enabling power: Teaching and Higher Education Act 1998, ss. 22, 42 (6). - Issued: 23.01.2015. Made: 27.01.2015. Laid before the National Assembly for Wales: 28.01.2015. Coming into force: 19.01.2015. Effect: S.I. 2013/3177 (W.316) revoked. Territorial extent & classification: W. General. - In English and Welsh. Welsh title: Rheoliadau Addysg (Cymorth i Fyfyrwyr) (Cymru) 2015. - 250p.: 30 cm. - 978-0-348-11042-5 £29.75

The Education (Wales) Act 2014 (Commencement No. 3 and Saving and Transitional Provisions) Order 2015 No. 2015/29 (W.2) (C.2). - Enabling power: Education (Wales) Act 2014 , s. 50 (4) (5). Bringing into operation various provisions of the 2014 Act on 16.01.2015; 01.04.2015 in accord. with arts 2 and 3. - Issued: 19.02.2015. Made: 13.01.2015. Effect: None. Territorial extent & classification: W. General. - In English and Welsh. Welsh title: Gorchymyn Deddf Addysg (Cymru) 2014 (Cychwyn Rhif 3 a Darpariaethau Arbed a Throsiannol) 2015. - 12p.: 30 cm. - 978-0-348-11043-2 £6.00

The Education (Wales) Act 2014 (Commencement No. 4) Order 2015 No. 2015/1688 (W.220) (C.99). - Enabling power: Education (Wales) Act 2014 , s. 50 (4) (5). Bringing into operation various provisions of the 2014 Act on 01.01.2016 in accord. with art. 2. - Issued: 25.09.2015. Made: 15.09.2015. Effect: None. Territorial extent & classification: W. General. - In English and Welsh. Welsh title: Gorchymyn Deddf Addysg (Cymru) 2014 (Cychwyn Rhif 4) 2015. - 8p.: 30 cm. - 978-0-348-11155-2 £6.00

The Education Workforce Council (Additional Functions and Revocation) (Wales) Order 2015 No. 2015/194 (W.9). - Enabling power: Education (Wales) Act 2014, ss. 5, 47 (1) (2). - Issued: 18.02.2015. Made: 10.02.2015. Coming into force: 01.04.2015. Effect: None. Territorial extent & classification: W. General. - In English and Welsh. Welsh title: Gorchymyn Cyngor y Gweithlu Addysg (Swyddogaethau Ychwanegol a Dirymu) (Cymru) 2015. - 8p.: 30 cm. - 978-0-348-11046-3 £6.00

The Education Workforce Council (Main Functions) (Wales) Regulations 2015 No. 2015/140 (W.8). - Enabling power: Education (Wales) Act 2014, ss. 10 (2) (b), 13, 14, 15, 25, 26 (6), 28, 33, 35 (4), 36 (2), 37 (2), 47 (1), sch. 2, para. 12. - Issued: 04.03.2015. Made: 03.02.2015. Laid before the National Assembly for Wales: 06.02.2015. Coming into force: 01.04.2015. Effect: S.I. 2000/1979 (W.140); 2001/1424 (W.99), 2496 (W.200); 2003/503 (W.71); 2004/1741 (W.180); 2005/69 (W.7); 2006/1343 (W.133); 2009/1350 (W.126), 1353 (W.129, 1354 (W.130), 2161 (W.184); 2010/2710 (W.227); 2011/2908 (W.312); 2012/166 (W.25); 2012/170 (W.29) revoked in relation to Wales. Territorial extent & classification: W. General. - In English and Welsh. Welsh title: Rheoliadau Cyngor y Gweithlu Addysg (Prif Swyddogaethau) (Cymru) 2015. - 54p.: 30 cm. - 978-0-348-11044-9 £10.00

The Education Workforce Council (Registration Fees) (Wales) Regulations 2015 No. 2015/195 (W.10). - Enabling power: Education (Wales) Act 2014, ss. 12, 36, 47 (1) (2). - Issued: 18.02.2015. Made: 10.02.2015. Coming into force: 01.04.2015. Effect: None. Territorial extent & classification: W. General. - Revoked by W.S.I. 2016/27 (W.9) (ISBN 9780348112306). - In English and Welsh. Welsh title: Rheoliadau Cyngor y Gweithlu Addysg (Ffioedd Cofrestru) (Cymru) 2015. - 8p.: 30 cm. - 978-0-348-11047-0 £6.00

The Government of Maintained Schools (Change of Category) (Wales) Regulations 2015 No. 2015/1521 (W.178). - Enabling power: School Standards and Organisation (Wales) Act 2013, s. 97, sch. 4, para. 38. - Issued: 21.07.2015. Made: 14.07.2015. Laid before the National Assembly for Wales: 16.07.2015. Coming into force: 01.09.2015. Effect: None. Territorial extent & classification: W. General. - In English and Welsh. Welsh title: Rheoliadau Llywodraethu Ysgolion a Gynhelir (Newid Categori) (Cymru) 2015. - 8p.: 30 cm. - 978-0-348-11121-7 £4.25

The Higher Education (Amounts) (Wales) Regulations 2015 No. 2015/1496 (W.168). - Enabling power: Higher Education (Wales) Act 2015, ss. 5 (3) (9), 55 (2). - Issued: 17.07.2015. Made: 07.07.2015. Coming into force: 31.07.2015. Effect: None. Territorial extent & classification: W. General. - In English and Welsh. Welsh title: Rheoliadau Addysg Uwch (Symiau) (Cymru) 2015. - 4p.: 30 cm. - 978-0-348-11119-4 £4.25

The Higher Education (Designation of Providers of Higher Education) (Wales) Regulations 2015 No. 2015/1497 (W.169). - Enabling power: Higher Education (Wales) Act 2015, s. 3 (4). - Issued: 17.07.2015. Made: 07.07.2015. Coming into force: 31.07.2015. Effect: None. Territorial extent & classification: W. General. - In English and Welsh. Welsh title: Rheoliadau Addysg Uwch (Dynodi Darparwyr Addysg Uwch) (Cymru) 2015. - 6p.: 30 cm. - 978-0-348-11120-0 £4.25

The Higher Education (Fee and Access Plans) (Notices and Directions) (Wales) Regulations 2015 No. 2015/1485 (W.164). - Enabling power: Higher Education (Wales) Act 2015, ss. 11 (5), 42 (2) (d), 43 (c), 44 (3). - Issued: 22.07.2015. Made: 07.07.2015. Laid before the National Assembly for Wales: 09.07.2015. Coming into force: 31.07.2015. Effect: None. Territorial extent & classification: W. General. - In English and Welsh. Welsh title: Rheoliadau Addysg Uwch (Cynlluniau Ffioedd a Mynediad) (Hysbysiadau a Chyfarwyddydau) (Cymru) 2015. - 8p.: 30 cm. - 978-0-348-11122-4 £6.00

The Higher Education (Fee and Access Plans) (Wales) Regulations 2015 No. 2015/1498 (W.170). - Enabling power: Higher Education (Wales) Act 2015, ss. 2 (4), 6 (1), 7 (3), 8 (1), 9 (1). - Issued: 17.07.2015. Made: 07.07.2015. Coming into force: 31.07.2015. Effect: None. Territorial extent & classification: W. General. - In English and Welsh. Welsh title: Rheoliadau Addysg Uwch (Cynlluniay Ffioedd a Mynediad) (Cymru) 2015. - 8p.: 30 cm. - 978-0-348-11115-6 £6.00

The Higher Education (Qualifying Courses, Qualifying Persons and Supplementary Provision) (Wales) Regulations 2015 No. 2015/1484 (W.163). - Enabling power: Higher Education (Wales) Act 2015, ss. 5 (2) (b), 5 (5) (b), 55 (2), 58 (3). - Issued: 24.07.2015. Made: 07.07.2015. Laid before the National Assembly for Wales: 09.07.2015. Coming into force: 31.07.2015. Effect: None. Territorial extent & classification: W. General. - In English and Welsh. Welsh title: Rheoliadau Addysg Uwch (Cyrsiau Cymhwysol, Personau Cymhwysol a Darpariaeth Atodol) (Cymru) 2015. - 24p.: 30 cm. - 978-0-348-11127-9 £6.00

The Higher Education (Wales) Act 2015 (Commencement No.1 and Saving Provision) Order 2015 No. 2015/1327 (W.122) (C.74). - Enabling power: Higher Education Act 2015, s. 59 (2) (3). Bringing various provisions of the 2015 Act into operation on 20.05.2015, 25.05.2015, 01.08.2015, 01.09.2015, 01.01.2016. - Issued: 26.05.2015. Made: 19.05.2015. Effect: None. Territorial extent & classification: W. General. - In English and Welsh. Welsh title: Gorchymyn Deddf Addysg Uwch (Cymru) 2015 (Cychwyn Rhif 1 a Darpariaeth Arbed) 2015. - 12p.: 30 cm. - 978-0-348-11099-9 £6.00

The Merthyr Tydfil College Limited (Designated Institution in Further Education) Order 2015 No. 2015/1464 (W.158). - Enabling power: Further and Higher Education Act 1992, s. 28. - Issued: 03.08.2015. Made: 01.07.2015. Laid before the National Assembly for Wales: 06.07.2015. Coming into force: 31.07.2015. Effect: None. Territorial extent & classification: W. General. - In English and Welsh. Welsh language title: Gorchymyn Merthyr Tydfil College Limited (Sefydliad Dynodedig mewn Addysg Bellach) Order 2015. - 4p.: 30 cm. - 978-0-348-11136-1 £4.25

The National Curriculum (Desirable Outcomes, Educational Programmes and Baseline and End of Phase Assessment Arrangements for the Foundation Phase) (Wales) Order 2015 No. 2015/1596 (W.195). - Enabling power: Education Act 2002, ss. 108 (2) (3) (5), 210. - Issued: 13.08.2015. Made: 05.08.2015. Laid before the National Assembly for Wales: 10.08.2015. Coming into force: 01.09.2015. Effect: WSI 2014/1996 (W.198) amended & WSI 2011/1948 (W.214) revoked. Territorial extent & classification: W. General. - In English and Welsh. Welsh title: Gorchymyn y Cwricwlwm Cenedlaethol (Deilliannau Dymunol, Rhaglenni Addysg a Threfniadau Asesu Sylfaenol a Diwedd Cyfnod ar gyfer y Cyfnod Sylfaen) (Cymru) 2015. - 8p.: 30 cm. - 978-0-348-11139-2 £6.00

The National Curriculum (Moderation of Assessment Arrangements for the Second and Third Key Stages) (Wales) Order 2015 No. 2015/1309 (W.113). - Enabling power: Education Act 2002, ss. 108 (3) (c) (7), 210. - Issued: 18.05.2015. Made: 06.05.2015. Laid before the National Assembly for Wales: 11.05.2015. Coming into force: 01.09.2015. Effect: None. Territorial extent & classification: W. General. - In English and Welsh. Welsh title: Gorchymyn y Cwricwlwm Cenedlaethol (Cymedroli Trefniadau Asesu ar gyfer yr Ail Gyfnod Allweddol a'r Trydydd Cyfnod Allweddol) (Cymru) 2015. - 8p.: 30 cm. - 978-0-348-11096-8 £6.00

The Qualifications Wales Act 2015 (Commencement No. 1) Order 2015 No. 2015/1591 (W.191)(C.92). - Enabling power: Qualifications Wales Act 2015, s. 602 (2) (3). Bringing into force various provisions of the 2015 Act on 06.08.2015 in accord. with art. 2. - Issued: 13.08.2015. Made: 05.08.2015 at 16.55. Effect: None. Territorial extent & classification: W. General. - In English and Welsh. Welsh title: Gorchymyn Deddf Cymwysterau Cymru 2015 (Cychwyn Rhif 1) 2015. - 4p.: 30 cm. - 978-0-348-11140-8 £4.25

The Qualifications Wales Act 2015 (Commencement No. 2 and Transitional and Saving Provisions) Order 2015 No. 2015/1687 (W.219)(C.98). - Enabling power: Qualifications Wales Act 2015, s. 60 (2) (3). Bringing into force various provisions of the 2015 Act on 21.09.2015 in accord. with art. 2. - Issued: 28.09.2015. Made: 16.09.2015. Effect: None. Territorial extent & classification: W. General. - In English and Welsh. Welsh title: Gorchymyn Deddf Cymwysterau Cymru 2015 (Cychwyn Rhif 2 a Darparaiethau Trtosiannol ac Arbed) 2015. - 20p.: 30 cm. - 978-0-348-11154-5 £6.00

Electricity

The Contracts for Difference (Allocation) (Amendment) Regulations 2015 No. 2015/981. - Enabling power: Energy Act 2013, ss. 6 (1) (6), 12 (1) to (3), 13 (1) to (3), 16, 19. - Issued: 01.04.2015. Made: 26.03.2015. Coming into force: 27.03.2015 in accord. with reg. 1 (1). Effect: S.I. 2014/2011 amended. Territorial extent & classification: E/W/S. General. - Supersedes draft SI (ISBN 9780111130124) issued 25/02/15 - 8p.: 30 cm. - 978-0-11-113616-4 £6.00

The Contracts for Difference (Standard Terms) (Amendment) Regulations 2015 No. 2015/1425. - Enabling power: Energy Act 2013, ss. 6 (1), 11 (3), 14 (2) (a), 19 (1). - Issued: 30.06.2015. Made: 23.06.2015. Laid: 29.06.2015. Coming into force: 20.07.2015. Effect: S.I. 2014/2012 amended. Territorial extent & classification: E/W/S/NI. General. - 4p.: 30 cm. - 978-0-11-113721-5 £4.25

The Electricity and Gas (Market Integrity and Transparency) (Criminal Sanctions) Regulations 2015 No. 2015/979. - Enabling power: European Communities Act 1972, s. 2 (2). - Issued: 01.04.2015. Made: 23.03.2015. Coming into force: In accord. with reg. 1. Effect: S.I. 2013/208 (NI), 1389 amended. Territorial extent & classification: E/W/S/NI. General. - Supersedes draft S.I. (ISBN 9780111127674) issued 26/01/15. EC note: These regs create criminal offences for two sets of prohibitions in Regulation 1227/2011. - 12p.: 30 cm. - 978-0-11-113612-6 £6.00

The Electricity and Gas (Market Integrity and Transparency) (Enforcement etc.) (Amendment) Regulations 2015 No. 2015/862. - Enabling power: European Communities Act 1972, s. 2 (2). - Issued: 30.03.2015. Made: 23.03.2015. Laid: 25.03.2015. Coming into force: 01.07.2015. Effect: 2000 c. 27 & S.I. 2013/1389 amended. Territorial extent & classification: E/W/S/NI. General. - EC note: These regulations give effect to arts 13, 14, & 18 of Regulation (EU) no. 1227/2011 on wholesale energy market integrity and transparency. - 8p.: 30 cm. - 978-0-11-113484-9 £6.00

The Electricity and Gas (Standards of Performance) (Suppliers) Regulations 2015 No. 2015/1544. - Enabling power: Gas Act 1986, ss. 33A, 33AA, 33AB, 33D, 47 & Electricity Act 1989, ss. 39, 39A, 39B, 42A, 60. - Issued: 29.07.2015. Made: 11.07.2015. Coming into force: 01.01.2016. Effect: S.I. 2005/1135; 2008/696; 2015/699 amended. Territorial extent & classification: E/W/S. General. - 20p.: 30 cm. - 978-0-11-113819-9 £6.00

The Electricity Capacity (Amendment) (No. 2) Regulations 2015 No. 2015/1974. - Enabling power: Energy Act 2013, ss. 27, 28, 30, 40 (1). - Issued: 10.12.2015. Made: 03.12.2015. Coming into force: In accord. with reg. 1. Effect: S.I. 2014/2043 amended. Territorial extent & classification: E/W/S. General. - Supersedes draft S.I. (ISBN 9780111133408) issued 18/03/15. - 4p.: 30 cm. - 978-0-11-114154-0 £4.25

The Electricity Capacity (Amendment) Regulations 2015 No. 2015/875. - Enabling power: Energy Act 2013, ss. 27 to 33, 36, 40 (1). - Issued: 27.03.2015. Made: 23.03.2015. Coming into force: In accord. with reg. 1. Effect: S.I. 2014/2043, 3354 amended. Territorial extent & classification: E/W/S. General. - Supersedes draft SI (ISBN 9780111127452) issued 22/01/15 - 12p.: 30 cm. - 978-0-11-113499-3 £6.00

The Electricity (Competitive Tenders for Offshore Transmission Licences) Regulations 2015 No. 2015/1555. - Enabling power: Electricity Act 1989, ss. 6C, 6D, 60. - Issued: 24.07.2015. Made: 11.07.2015. Coming into force: 03.08.2015. Effect: None. Territorial extent & classification: E/W/S. General. - 36p.: 30 cm. - 978-0-11-113832-8 £10.00

The Electricity (Connection Standards of Performance) Regulations 2015 No. 2015/698. - Enabling power: Electricity Act 1989, ss. 39A , 39B, 40B, 60. - Issued: 25.03.2015. Made: 13.03.2015. Coming into force: 01.04.2015. Effect: None. Territorial extent & classification: E/W/S. General. - 28p.: 30 cm. - 978-0-11-113442-9 £6.00

The Electricity (Exemption from the Requirement for a Generation Licence) (Ferrybridge MFE) (England and Wales) Order 2015 No. 2015/100. - Enabling power: Electricity Act 1989, s. 5. - Issued: 06.02.2015. Made: 29.01.2015. Laid: 04.02.2015. Coming into force: 28.02.2015. Effect: None. Territorial extent & classification: E/W. General. - 2p.: 30 cm. - 978-0-11-112852-7 £4.25

The Electricity (Exemption from the Requirement for a Generation Licence) (Galawhistle) Order 2015 No. 2015/2040. - Enabling power: Electricity Act 1989, s. 5. - Issued: 22.12.2015. Made: 15.12.2015. Laid: 18.12.2015. Coming into force: 18.01.2016. Effect: None. Territorial extent & classification: E/W/S. General. - 2p.: 30 cm. - 978-0-11-114222-6 £4.25

The Electricity (Exemption from the Requirement for a Generation Licence) (Moy) Order 2015 No. 2015/1410. - Enabling power: Electricity Act 1989, s. 5. - Issued: 30.06.2015. Made: 23.06.2015. Laid: 26.06.2015. Coming into force: 25.07.2015. Effect: None. Territorial extent & classification: E/W/S. General. - 2p.: 30 cm. - 978-0-11-113707-9 £4.25

The Electricity Market Reform (General) (Amendment) Regulations 2015 No. 2015/718. - Enabling power: Energy Act 2013, ss. 6 (1), 20, sch. 2, paras. 11, 16 (2) (4) (5). - Issued: 20.03.2015. Made: 14.03.2015. Coming into force: In accord. with reg. 1. Effect: S.I. 2014/2013 amended. Territorial extent & classification: E/W/S/NI. General. - Supersedes draft S.I. (ISBN 9780111127339) issued 21/01/15. - 4p.: 30 cm. - 978-0-11-113356-9 £4.25

The Electricity (Standards of Performance) Regulations 2015 No. 2015/699. - Enabling power: Electricity Act 1989, ss. 39A , 39B, 42A, 60. - Issued: 25.03.2015. Made: 13.03.2015. Coming into force: 01.04.2015. Effect: S.I. 2014/631 partially revoked & 2010/698, 2131 revoked. Territorial extent & classification: E/W/S. General. - 28p.: 30 cm. - 978-0-11-113443-6 £6.00

The Electricity Supplier Obligations (Amendment & Excluded Electricity) Regulations 2015 No. 2015/721. - Enabling power: Energy Act 2013, ss. 6 (1) (5) (6), 9 (1) (2) (4) to (8) (10), 17, 19, 20, 21 (1) (3), 22 (1), sch. 2, para. 16 (2). - Issued: 20.03.2015. Made: 14.03.2015. Coming into force: 01.04.2015. Effect: 2014/2014 amended. Territorial extent & classification: E/W/S/NI. General. - 24p.: 30 cm. - 978-0-11-113358-3 £6.00

The Emissions Performance Standard Regulations 2015 No. 2015/933. - Enabling power: Energy Act 2013, ss. 57 (6) to (8), 60, 62 (9), schs. 4 & 5. - Issued: 31.03.2015. Made: -. Coming into force: In accord. with reg. 1 (1). Effect: S.I. 2012/3038 amended. Territorial extent & classification: E/W/S/NI. General. - Supersedes draft S.I. (ISBN 9780111128466) issued 06/02/15. - 16p.: 30 cm. - 978-0-11-113556-3 £6.00

The Enterprise and Regulatory Reform Act 2013 (Amendment) (Gas and Electricity Appeals) Regulations 2015 No. 2015/16. - Enabling power: European Communities Act 1972, s. 2 (2). - Issued: 15.01.2015. Made: 08.01.2015. Laid: 12.01.2015. Coming into force: 06.02.2015. Effect: 2013 c.24 amended. Territorial extent & classification: E/W/S/NI. General. - 8p.: 30 cm. - 978-0-11-112690-5 £4.25

The Feed-in Tariffs (Amendment) (No. 2) Order 2015 No. 2015/1659. - Enabling power: Energy Act 2008, ss. 43 (3) (a), 104 (2). - Issued: 14.09.2015. Made: 08.09.2015. Laid: 09.09.2015. Coming into force: 30.09.2015. Effect: S.I. 2012/2782 amended. Territorial extent & classification: E/W/S. General. - 2p.: 30 cm. - 978-0-11-113910-3 £4.25

The Feed-in Tariffs (Amendment) (No. 3) Order 2015 No. 2015/2045. - Enabling power: Energy Act 2008, ss. 43 (3) (a), 104 (2). - Issued: 22.12.2015. Made: 16.12.2015. Laid: 18.12.2015. Coming into force: 15.01.2016. Effect: S.I. 2012/2782 amended. Territorial extent & classification: E/W/S/NI. General. - 20p.: 30 cm. - 978-0-11-114226-4 £6.00

The Feed-in Tariffs (Amendment) Order 2015 No. 2015/35. - Enabling power: Energy Act 2008, ss. 43 (3) (a), 104 (2). - Issued: 23.01.2015. Made: 15.01.2015. Laid: 19.01.2015. Coming into force: 01.01.2015. Effect: S.I. 2012/2782 amended. Territorial extent & classification: E/W/S. General. - 4p.: 30 cm. - 978-0-11-112753-7 £4.25

The Power Purchase Agreement Scheme (Amendment) Regulations 2015 No. 2015/1412. - Enabling power: Energy Act 2013, s. 51 (1) to (5). - Issued: 30.06.2015. Made: 23.06.2015. Laid: 25.06.2015. Coming into force: In accord. with reg 1 (2) (3). Effect: S.I. 2014/2511 amended. Territorial extent & classification: E/W/S. General- 4p.: 30 cm. - 978-0-11-113710-9 £4.25

The Regulatory Reform (Scotland) Act 2014 (Consequential Modifications) Order 2015 No. 2015/374. - Enabling power: Scotland Act 1998, ss. 104, 112 (1), 113 (2) (3) (4) (5). - Issued: 03.03.2015. Made: 25.02.2015. Coming into force: 26.02.2015. Effect: 1974 c.37; 1988 c.48; 1989 c.29; 1990 c.43; 1995 c.25; 2005 c.5; 2009 c.4; 2009 c.23; S.I. 1997/3032 amended. Territorial extent & classification: E/W/S/NI. General. - Supersedes draft S.I. (ISBN 9780111124505) issued 08/12/14. - 8p.: 30 cm. - 978-0-11-113066-7 £6.00

The Renewables Obligation Closure (Amendment) Order 2015 No. 2015/920. - Enabling power: Electricity Act 1989, ss. 32K, 32LA. - Issued: 02.04.2015. Made: 23.03.2015. Coming into force: In accord. with art. 1. Effect: S.I. 2014/2388 amended. Territorial extent & classification: E/W/S. General. - 8p.: 30 cm. - 978-0-11-113543-3 £6.00

The Warm Home Discount (Miscellaneous Amendments) Regulations 2015 No. 2015/652. - Enabling power: Pensions Act 2008 142, ss 144 (2) (4) & Energy Act 2010, ss 9, 10, 14 (4), 31 (5) (6). - Issued: 16.03.2015. Made: 10.03.2015. Coming into force: 11.03.2015 in accord. with reg. 1. Effect: S.I. 2011/1033, 1830 amended. Territorial extent & classification: E/W/S. - Supersedes draft S.I. (ISBN 9780111126943) issued 15/01/15. - 8p.: 30 cm. - 978-0-11-113310-1 £6.00

Electricity, England and Wales

The Electricity (Exemption from the Requirement for a Generation Licence) (Frodsham) (England and Wales) Order 2015 No. 2015/1409. - Enabling power: Electricity Act 1989, s. 5. - Issued: 07.07.2015. Made: 23.06.2015. Laid: 25.06.2015. Coming into force: 25.07.2015. Effect: None. Territorial extent & classification: E/W. General. - 2p.: 30 cm. - 978-0-11-113706-2 £4.25

The Renewables Obligation Order 2015 No. 2015/1947. - Enabling power: Electricity Act 1989, ss. 32 to 32K, 32LA, 32M & European Communities Act 1972 s. 2 (2). - Issued: 03.12.2015. Made: 26.11.2015. Coming into force: In accord. with art. 1. Effect: S.I. 2014/2388 amended & S.I. 2009/785; 2010/829, 1107; 2011/984; 2013/768; 2014/893 revoked with saving. Territorial extent & classification: E/W/S/NI. General. - Supersedes draft S.I. (ISBN 9780111138359) issued 27.07.2015. - 100p.: 30 cm. - 978-0-11-114132-8 £16.50

Electricity, Wales

The Emissions Performance Standard (Enforcement) (Wales) Regulations 2015 No. 2015/1388 (W.137). - Enabling power: Energy Act 2013, ss. 60, 62 (9), sch. 5. - Issued: 25.06.2015. Made: 15.06.2015. Laid before the National Assembly for Wales: 16.06.2015. Coming into force: 08.07.2015. Effect: S.I. 2012/3038 amended. Territorial extent & classification: W. General. - In English and Welsh. Welsh title: Rheoliadau Safon Perfformiad Allyraidau (Gorfodi) (Cymru) 2015. - 18p.: 30 cm. - 978-0-348-11111-8 £6.00

Electronic communications

The 823-832 MHz and 1785-1805 MHz etc. Frequency Bands (Management) Regulations 2015 No. 2015/1658. - Enabling power: European Communities Act 1972, s. 2 (2). - Issued: 14.09.2015. Made: 07.09.2015. Laid: 09.09.2015. Coming into force: 02.10.2015. Effect: None. Territorial extent & classification: E/W/S/NI. General. - EC note: These Regulations implement in the United Kingdom the Commission Decision 2014/641/EU of 1st September 2014 on harmonised technical conditions for radio spectrum use by wireless audio programme making and special events equipment in the Union. - 2p.: 30 cm. - 978-0-11-113909-7 £4.25

The Data Retention and Investigatory Powers Act 2014 (Commencement) Order 2015 No. 2015/929 (C.57). - Enabling power: Data Retention and Investigatory Powers Act 2014, s. 8 (2). Bringing into operation various provisions of the 2014 Act on 13.04.2015. - Issued: 01.04.2015. Made: 24.03.2015. Effect: None. Territorial extent & classification: UK. General. - 2p.: 30 cm. - 978-0-11-113551-8 £4.25

The Electronic Commerce Directive (Financial Services and Markets) (Amendment) Order 2015 No. 2015/852. - Enabling power: European Communities Act 1972, s. 2 (2). - Issued: 31.03.2015. Made: 23.03.2015. Coming into force: In accord. with art. 1 (2). Effect: S.I. 2001/544; 2002/1775 amended. Territorial extent & classification: E/W/S/NI. General. - Supersedes draft SI (ISBN 9780111125939) issued 22/12/14 - 4p.: 30 cm. - 978-0-11-113475-7 £4.25

The Privacy and Electronic Communications (EC Directive) (Amendment) Regulations 2015 No. 2015/355. - Enabling power: European Communities Act 1972, s. 2 (2). - Issued: 02.03.2015. Made: 24.02.2015. Laid: 25.02.2015. Coming into force: 06.04.2015. Effect: S.I. 2003/2426 amended. Territorial extent & classification: E/W/S/NI. General. - 8p.: 30 cm. - 978-0-11-113043-8 £4.25

The Statutory Shared Parental Pay (Miscellaneous Amendments) Regulations 2015 No. 2015/125. - Enabling power: Finance Act 1999, ss. 132, 133 (2) & Income Tax (Earnings and Pensions) Act 2003, s. 684 & Finance Act 2004, ss. 62 (3) (6) (7), 71. - Issued: 10.02.2015. Made: 03.02.2015. Laid: 05.02.2015. Coming into force: In accord. with reg 1 (2) (3). Effect: S.I. 2002/3047; 2003/2682; 2005/2045 amended. Territorial extent & classification: E/W/S. General. - 4p.: 30 cm. - 978-0-11-112872-5 £4.25

The Wireless Telegraphy (Licence Charges) (Amendment) (No. 2) Regulations 2015 No. 2015/1995. - Enabling power: Wireless Telegraphy Act 2006, ss. 12, 13 (2), 122. - Issued: 15.12.2015. Made: 09.12.2015. Coming into force: 31.12.2015. Effect: S.I. 2011/1128 amended. Territorial extent & classification: E/W/S/NI. General. - 2p.: 30 cm. - 978-0-11-114176-2 £4.25

The Wireless Telegraphy (Licence Charges) (Amendment) Regulations 2015 No. 2015/1334. - Enabling power: Wireless Telegraphy Act 2006, ss. 12, 13 (2), 122 (7). - Issued: 03.06.2015. Made: 27.05.2015. Coming into force: 08.06.2015. Effect: S.I. 2011/1128 amended. Territorial extent & classification: E/W/S/NI. General. - 4p.: 30 cm. - 978-0-11-113646-1 £4.25

The Wireless Telegraphy (Licence Charges for the 900 MHz frequency band and the 1800 MHz frequency band) (Amendment and Further Provisions) Regulations 2015 No. 2015/1709. - Enabling power: Wireless Telegraphy Act 2006, ss. 12, 13 (2), 122 (7). - Issued: 30.09.2015. Made: 23.09.2015. Coming into force: 15.10.2015. Effect: S.I. 2011/1128 amended. Territorial extent & classification: E/W/S/NI. General. - 4p.: 30 cm. - 978-0-11-113943-1 £4.25

The Wireless Telegraphy (Limitation of Number of Grants of Recognised Spectrum Access for Satellite Receive-Only Earth Stations) (Amendment) Order 2015 No. 2015/1398. - Enabling power: Wireless Telegraphy Act 2006, s. 29 (1) to (3). - Issued: 24.06.2015. Made: 18.06.2015. Coming into force: 10.07.2015. Effect: S.I. 2011/2757 amended. Territorial extent & classification: E/W/S/NI. General. - 4p.: 30 cm. - 978-0-11-113694-2 £4.25

The Wireless Telegraphy (Limitation on Number of Licences) (Amendment) Order 2015 No. 2015/999. - Enabling power: Wireless Telegraphy Act 2006, s. 29 (1) to (3). - Issued: 02.04.2015. Made: 27.03.2015. Coming into force: 17.04.2015. Effect: S.I. 2014/774 amended. Territorial extent & classification: E/W/S/NI. General. - 2p.: 30 cm. - 978-0-11-113629-4 £4.25

The Wireless Telegraphy (Mobile Spectrum Trading) (Amendment) Regulations 2015 No. 2015/1339. - Enabling power: Wireless Telegraphy Act 2006, ss. 30 (1) (3), 122 (7). - Issued: 04.06.2015. Made: 29.05.2015. Coming into force: 19.06.2015. Effect: S.I. 2011/1507 amended. Territorial extent & classification: E/W/S/NI. General. - 4p.: 30 cm. - 978-0-11-113651-5 £4.25

The Wireless Telegraphy (Recognised Spectrum Access and Licence) (Spectrum Trading) (Amendment) Regulations 2015 No. 2015/1401. - Enabling power: Wireless Telegraphy Act 2006, ss. 30 (1) to (3), 122 (7). - Issued: 24.06.2015. Made: 18.06.2015. Coming into force: 10.07.2015. Effect: S.I. 2009/17 amended. Territorial extent & classification: E/W/S/NI. General. - 2p.: 30 cm. - 978-0-11-113697-3 £4.25

The Wireless Telegraphy (Recognised Spectrum Access Charges) (Amendment) Regulations 2015 No. 2015/1399. - Enabling power: Wireless Telegraphy Act 2006, ss. 21, 22 (2) (3). - Issued: 24.06.2015. Made: 18.06.2015. Coming into force: 10.07.2015. Effect: S.I. 2007/392 amended. Territorial extent & classification: E/W/S/NI. General. - 4p.: 30 cm. - 978-0-11-113695-9 £4.25

The Wireless Telegraphy (Recognised Spectrum Access for Satellite Receive-Only Earth Stations) (Amendment) Regulations 2015 No. 2015/1397. - Enabling power: Wireless Telegraphy Act 2006, ss. 18 (1) (b), 122 (7), sch. 2. para. 1. - Issued: 24.06.2015. Made: 18.06.2015. Coming into force: 10.07.2015. Effect: S.I. 2011/2763 amended. Territorial extent & classification: E/W/S/NI. General. - 4p.: 30 cm. - 978-0-11-113693-5 £4.25

The Wireless Telegraphy (Register) (Amendment) Regulations 2015 No. 2015/1400. - Enabling power: Wireless Telegraphy Act 2006, ss. 31 (1) (2), 122 (7). - Issued: 24.06.2015. Made: 18.06.2015. Coming into force: 10.07.2015. Effect: S.I. 2012/2186 amended. Territorial extent & classification: E/W/S/NI. General. - 2p.: 30 cm. - 978-0-11-113696-6 £4.25

The Wireless Telegraphy (Spectrum Trading) (Amendment) Regulations 2015 No. 2015/1338. - Enabling power: Wireless Telegraphy Act 2006, ss. 30 (1) (3), 122 (7). - Issued: 04.06.2015. Made: 29.05.2015. Coming into force: 19.06.2015. Effect: S.I. 2012/2187 amended. Territorial extent & classification: E/W/S/NI. General. - 2p.: 30 cm. - 978-0-11-113650-8 £4.25

The Wireless Telegraphy (Ultra-Wideband Equipment) (Exemption) Regulations 2015 No. 2015/591. - Enabling power: Wireless Telegraphy Act 2006, s. 8 (3). - Issued: 13.03.2015. Made: 09.03.2015. Coming into force: 25.03.2015. Effect: S.I. 2009/2517; 2010/2761 revoked. Territorial extent & classification: E/W/S/NI/CI/IoM. General. - EC note: These Regulations give effect to Commission Decision 2014/702/EU on allowing the use of radio spectrum equipment using ultra-wideband technology in a harmonised manner in the Community. - 24p.: 30 cm. - 978-0-11-113260-9 £6.00

The Wireless Telegraphy (White Space Devices) (Exemption) Regulations 2015 No. 2015/2066. - Enabling power: Wireless Telegraphy Act 2006, s. 8 (3). - Issued: 24.12.2015. Made: 18.12.2015. Coming into force: 31.12.2015. Effect: None. Territorial extent & classification: E/W/S/NI. General. - 8p.: 30 cm. - 978-0-11-114249-3 £6.00

Employment

The Gangmasters (Licensing Authority) Regulations 2015 No. 2015/805. - Enabling power: Gangmasters (Licensing) Act 2004, ss. 1 (5), 25 (2). - Issued: 26.03.2015. Made: 19.03.2015. Coming into force: 20.03.2015 in accord. with reg. 1 (1). Effect: S.I. 2005/448 revoked. Territorial extent & classification: E/W/S/NI. General. - Supersedes draft S.I. (ISBN 9780111116159) issued 11.06.2014. - 8p.: 30 cm. - 978-0-11-113431-3 £4.25

The Small Business, Enterprise and Employment Act 2015 (Commencement No. 3) Regulations 2015 No. 2015/2029 (C.125). - Enabling power: Small Business, Enterprise and Employment Act 2015, ss. 161 (1) (2), 164(1). Bringing into operation various provisions of the 2015 Act on 01.01.2016, 06.04.2016, 30.06.2016, in accord. with arts. 2 to 5. - Issued: 21.12.2015. Made: 09.12.2015. Effect: None. Territorial extent & classification: E/W/S/NI. General. - 4p.: 30 cm. - 978-0-11-114206-6 £4.25

Employment and training

The Industrial Training Levy (Construction Industry Training Board) Order 2015 No. 2015/701. - Enabling power: Industrial Training Act 1982, ss. 11 (2), 12 (3) (4). - Issued: 19.03.2015. Made: 10.03.2015. Coming into force: 11.03.2015. Effect: None. Territorial extent & classification: E/W/S. General. - Supersedes draft S.I. (ISBN 9780111127643) issued 26/01/15. - 12p.: 30 cm. - 978-0-11-113350-7 £6.00

The Industrial Training Levy (Engineering Construction Industry Training Board) Order 2015 No. 2015/677. - Enabling power: Industrial Training Act 1982, ss. 11 (2), 12 (3) (4). - Issued: 18.03.2015. Made: 10.03.2015. Coming into force: On the day after the day it is made. Effect: None. Territorial extent & classification: E/W/S. General. - Supersedes draft S.I. (ISBN 9780111127650) issued 26/01/15. - 8p.: 30 cm. - 978-0-11-113339-2 £6.00

Employment and training, England

The Apprenticeships (Modifications to the Specification of Apprenticeship Standards for England) (No. 2) Order 2015 No. 2015/1761. - Enabling power: Apprenticeships, Skills, Children and Learning Act 2009, s. 25 (3). - Issued: 15.10.2015. Made: 08.10.2015. Laid: 09.10.2015. Coming into force: In accord. with art. 1. Effect: None. Territorial extent & classification: E. General. - 2p.: 30 cm. - 978-0-11-113967-7 £4.25

The Apprenticeships (Modifications to the Specification of Apprenticeship Standards for England) Order 2015 No. 2015/303. - Enabling power: Apprenticeships, Skills, Children and Learning Act 2009, s. 25 (3). - Issued: 23.02.2015. Made: 12.02.2015. Laid: 18.02.2015. Coming into force: 06.04.2015. Effect: Brings into effect the modified specification of apprenticeship standards for England, BIS/15/14 (available on www.gov.uk). Territorial extent & classification: E. General. - 2p.: 30 cm. - 978-0-11-112995-1 £4.25

The English Apprenticeships (Consequential Amendments to Primary Legislation) Order 2015 No. 2015/1852. - Enabling power: Deregulation Act 2015, ss. 112 (1) (2). - Issued: 09.11.2015. Made: 03.11.2015. Laid: - Coming into force: In accord. with art. 1. Effect: 1996 c.56; 2008 c.25 amended. Territorial extent & classification: E. General. - Supersedes draft S.I. (ISBN 9780111138366) issued 27/07/15. - 4p.: 30 cm. - 978-0-11-114048-2 £4.25

Employment and training, Wales

The Apprenticeships (Designation of Welsh Certifying Authority) (Amendment) Order 2015 No. 2015/1733 (W.236). - Enabling power: Apprenticeships, Skills, Children and Learning Act 2009, s. 10 (1) (b) (3). - Issued: 07.10.2015. Made: 29.09.2015. Coming into force: 16.10.2015. Effect: S.I. 2013/1191 (W.127) amended. Territorial extent & classification: W. General. - In English and Welsh. Welsh title: Gorchymyn Prentisiaethau (Dynodi Awdurdod Ardystio Cymru) (Diwygio) 2015. - 4p.: 30 cm. - 978-0-348-11159-0 £4.25

Employment tribunals

The Employment Tribunals (Early Conciliation: Exemptions and Rules of Procedure) Regulations 2014 (correction slip) No. 2014/254 Cor.. - Correction slip (to ISBN 9780111109779) dated December 2014. - 1 sheet: 30 cm. Free

Energy

The Domestic Renewable Heat Incentive Scheme (Amendment) Regulations 2015 No. 2015/143. - Enabling power: Energy Act 2008, ss 100 (1) (2), 104 (2). - Issued: 11.02.2015. Made: 04.02.2015. Coming into force: 05.02.2015 in accord. with reg. 1. Effect: S.I. 2014/928 amended. Territorial extent & classification: E/W/S, General. - 8p.: 30 cm. - 978-0-11-112893-0 £6.00

The Energy Act 2011 (Commencement No. 3) Order 2015 No. 2015/880 (C.55). - Enabling power: Energy Act 2011, s. 121 (1). Bringing into operation various provisions of the 2011 Act on 26.03.2015, in accord. with reg. 2. - Issued: 31.03.2015. Made: 25.03.2015. Effect: None. Territorial extent & classification: E/W/S/NI. General. - 4p.: 30 cm. - 978-0-11-113503-7 £4.25

The Energy Act 2013 (Commencement No. 2) Order 2015 No. 2015/614 (C.31). - Enabling power: Energy Act 2013, s. 156 (1). Bringing into operation various provisions of the 2013 Act on 11.03.2015. - Issued: 16.03.2015. Made: 10.03.2015. Effect: None. Territorial extent & classification: E/W/S. General. - 2p.: 30 cm. - 978-0-11-113277-7 £4.25

ENERGY: SUSTAINABLE AND RENEWABLE FUELS

The Energy Act 2013 (Commencement No. 3) Order 2015 No. 2015/817 (C.49). - Enabling power: Energy Act 2013, s. 156 (1). Bringing into operation various provisions of the 2013 Act on 30.04.2015, in accord. with art. 2. - Issued: 26.03.2015. Made: 15.03.2015. Effect: None. Territorial extent & classification: E/W/S. General. - 2p.: 30 cm. - 978-0-11-113449-8 £4.25

The Energy Savings Opportunity Scheme (Amendment) Regulations 2015 No. 2015/1731. - Enabling power: European Communities Act 1972, s. 2 (2). - Issued: 05.10.2015. Made: 29.09.2015. Laid: 02.10.2015. Coming into force: 26.10.2015. Effect: S.I. 2014/1643 amended. Territorial extent & classification: E/W/S/NI. General. - This Statutory Instrument has been made in consequence of defects in S.I. 2014/1643 (ISBN 9780111138892) and is being issued free of charge to all known recipients of that Statutory Instrument. EC note: Implement art. 8 (4) (5) (6) of Directive 2012/27/EU on energy efficiency. - 4p.: 30 cm. - 978-0-11-113953-0 £4.25

The Heat Network (Metering and Billing) (Amendment) Regulations 2015 No. 2015/855. - Enabling power: European Communities Act 1972, s. 2 (2). - Issued: 30.03.2015. Made: 23.03.2015. Laid: 25.03.2015. Coming into force: 20.04.2015. Effect: S.I. 2014/3120 amended. Territorial extent & classification: E/W/S, General. - This Statutory Instrument has been printed to correct errors in S.I. 2014/3120 (ISBN 9780111123980) and is being issued free of charge of all known recipients of that Statutory Instrument. EC note: These Regs amend S.I. 2014/3120 which implemented arts 9 (1) (3), 10, 11 of Directive 2012/27/EU on energy efficiency amending Directives 2009/125/EC and 2010/30/EU. - 4p.: 30 cm. - 978-0-11-113478-8 £4.25

The Infrastructure Act 2015 (Commencement No.1) Regulations 2015 No. 2015/481 (C.26). - Enabling power: Infrastructure Act 2015, s. 57 (1) (b) (4) (a) (7) (c). Bringing into operation various provisions of the 2013 Act on 05.03.2015, 12.04.2015. - Issued: 10.03.2015. Made: 02.03.2015. Effect: None. Territorial extent & classification: E/W/S/NI. General. - 2p.: 30 cm. - 978-0-11-113179-4 £4.25

The Infrastructure Act 2015 (Commencement No. 4) Regulations 2015 No. 2015/1576 (C.90). - Enabling power: Infrastructure Act 2015, s. 57 (7) (c). Bringing into operation various provisions of the 2015 Act on 30.07.2015, in accord. with art. 2. - Issued: 31.07.2015. Made: 21.07.2015. Effect: None. Territorial extent & classification: E/W. General. - 2p.: 30 cm. - 978-0-11-113856-4 £4.25

The Renewable Heat Incentive Scheme (Amendment) (No. 2) Regulations 2015 No. 2015/477. - Enabling power: Energy Act 2008, s. 100 (1) (2) (b). - Issued: 10.03.2015. Made: 04.03.2015. Laid: 04.03.2015. Coming into force: 04.03.2015. Effect: S.I. 2011/2860 amended. Territorial extent & classification: E/W/S. General. - This Statutory Instrument has been made in consequence of a defect in S.I. 2015/197 (ISBN 9780111129395) and is being issued free of charge to all known recipients of that Statutory Instrument. - 2p.: 30 cm. - 978-0-11-113172-5 £4.25

The Renewable Heat Incentive Scheme (Amendment) Regulations 2015 No. 2015/197. - Enabling power: Energy Act 2008, ss. 100 (1) (2), 104 (2). - Issued: 17.02.2015. Made: 11.02.2015. Coming into force: in accord. with reg. 1. Effect: S.I. 2011/2860 amended. Territorial extent & classification: E/W/S. General. - Supersedes S.I. draft (ISBN 9780111124970) issued 15/12/14. A defect in this SI was corrected in S.I. 2015/477 (ISBN 9780111131725) which was issued free of charge to all known recipients of this SI. - 20p.: 30 cm. - 978-0-11-112939-5 £6.00

The Renewable Heat Incentive Scheme and Domestic Renewable Heat Incentive Scheme (Amendment) (No. 2) Regulations 2015 No. 2015/1459. - Enabling power: Energy Act 2008, s. 100 (1) (2), 104 (2). - Issued: 08.07.2015. Made: 30.06.2015. Laid: 06.07.2015. Coming into force: In accord. with reg. 1 (1) (2). Effect: S.I. 2011/2860, 2014/928 amended. Territorial extent & classification: E/W/S. General. - 8p.: 30 cm. - 978-0-11-113738-3 £6.00

The Renewable Heat Incentive Scheme and Domestic Renewable Heat Incentive Scheme (Amendment) Regulations 2015 No. 2015/145. - Enabling power: Energy Act 2008, ss. 100 (1) (2), 104 (2). - Issued: 12.02.2015. Made: 04.02.2015. Coming into force: in accord. with reg. 1 (1) (2). Effect: S.I. 2011/2860; 2014/928 amended. Territorial extent & classification: E/W/S. General. - Supersedes draft S.I. (ISBN 9780111125502) issued 18/12/14. - 20p.: 30 cm. - 978-0-11-112894-7 £6.00

Energy: Sustainable and renewable fuels

The Renewable Transport Fuel Obligations (Amendment) Order 2015 No. 2015/534. - Enabling power: Energy Act 2004, ss. 124 (1) (2), 125A (1) (a), 125B (1) (a), 126 (1) (2) (j) (k), 192 (4) (a) (c). - Issued: 11.03.2015. Made: 04.03.2015. Coming into force: 15.04.2015. Effect: S.I. 2007/3072 amended. Territorial extent & classification: E/W/S/NI. General. - Supersedes draft SI (ISBN 9780111126776) issued 14/01/15 - 4p.: 30 cm. - 978-0-11-113215-9 £4.25

Energy conservation

The Ecodesign for Energy-Related Products and Energy Information (Amendment) Regulations 2015 No. 2015/469. - Enabling power: European Communities Act 1972, s. 2 (2). - Issued: 10.03.2015. Made: 02.03.2015. Laid: 04.03.2015. Coming into force: In accord. with reg. 1. Effect: S.I. 2010/2617; 2011/1524 amended. Territorial extent & classification: UK. General. - EC note: These Regulations partially implement Commission Regulations (EU) no. 548, 1254/2014- 4p.: 30 cm. - 978-0-11-113161-9 £4.25

Energy conservation, England and Wales

The Energy Efficiency (Domestic Private Rented Property) Order 2015 No. 2015/799. - Enabling power: Energy Act 2011, s. 42 (1) (a) (iii). - Issued: 01.04.2015. Made: 26.03.2015. Coming into force: 01.04.2016. Effect: None. Territorial extent & classification: E/W. General. - Supersedes draft SI (ISBN 9780111128343) issued 04/02/15 - 2p.: 30 cm. - 978-0-11-113596-9 £4.25

The Energy Efficiency (Private Rented Property) (England and Wales) Regulations 2015 No. 2015/962. - Enabling power: Energy Act 2011, ss. 43 (1) (4), 44, 45 (1) (2) (4) (5) (a) (b) (d) to (f) (6) (a) to (c), 46 (1) (4), 47, 48 (1) (2) (3) (a) (b) (d), 49 (1) (4), 50, 51 (1) to (3) (4) (a) (b) (d) to (f), (5) (a) (c), 52 (1). - Issued: 01.04.2015. Made: 26.03.2015. Coming into force: In accord. with reg. 1 (2). Effect: None. Territorial extent & classification: E/W. General. - Supersedes draft SI (ISBN 9780111132432) issued 12/03/15 - 32p.: 30 cm. - 978-0-11-113593-8 £10.00

Energy, England

The Smoke and Carbon Monoxide Alarm (England) Regulations 2015 No. 2015/1693. - Enabling power: Energy Act 2013, ss. 150 (1) to (6) (10) & Housing Act 2004, sch. 4, para. 3 (a). - Issued: 23.09.2015. Made: 17.09.2015. Coming into force: In accord. with reg. 1 (1). Effect: 2004 c.34 amended. Territorial extent & classification: E. General. - Supersedes draft S.I. (ISBN 9780111133439) issued 19/03/15. - 12p.: 30 cm. - 978-0-11-113933-2 £6.00

Enforcement

The Enforcement by Deduction from Accounts (Prescribed Information) Regulations 2015 No. 2015/1986. - Enabling power: Finance (No. 2) Act 2015, sch. 8, paras 3 (2), 8 (2) (a) (c) (d) (4) (b), 23 (1). - Issued: 14.12.2015. Made: 08.12.2015. Laid: 09.12.2015. Coming into force: 25.01.2016. Effect: None. Territorial extent & classification: E/W/S/NI. General. - 4p.: 30 cm. - 978-0-11-114174-8 £4.25

Environmental protection

The Agricultural or Forestry Tractors (Emission of Gaseous and Particulate Pollutants) and Tractor etc (EC Type Approval) (Amendment) Regulations 2015 No. 2015/1350. - Enabling power: European Communities Act 1972, s. 2 (2). - Issued: 10.06.2015. Made: 04.06.2015. Laid: 08.06.2015. Coming into force: 30.06.2015. Effect: S.I. 2002/1891; 2005/390 amended. Territorial extent & classification: E/W/S/NI. General. - 4p.: 30 cm. - 978-0-11-113657-7 £4.25

The Batteries and Accumulators (Placing on the Market) (Amendment) Regulations 2015 No. 2015/63. - Enabling power: European Communities Act 1972, s. 2 (2). - Issued: 02.02.2015. Made: 24.01.2015. Laid: 28.01.2015. Coming into force: in accord. with reg. 3 & 4, 01.10.2015; 01.01.2017; 01.07.2015. Effect: S.I. 2008/2164 amended. Territorial extent & classification: E/W/S/NI. General. - 4p.: 30 cm. - 978-0-11-112799-5 £4.25

The Fluorinated Greenhouse Gases Regulations 2015 No. 2015/310. - Enabling power: European Communities Act 1972, s. 2 (2), sch. 2, para. 1A. - Issued: 23.02.2015. Made: 16.02.2015. Laid: 19.02.20. Coming into force: 19.03.2015. Effect: S.I. 2010/1513; 2012/2897; 2013/755 (W.90) amended & S.I. 2009/261 revoked. Territorial extent & classification: GB, including "offshore installations" as defined in Reg. 2, except in relation to importation, where the Regs will also apply in NI. General. - EC note: These Regulations give effect to Regulation No 517/2014 on certain fluorinated greenhouse gases. They also give effect to Commission Regulations 1491/2007; 1497/2007; 1516/2007; 303/2008; 304/2008; 305/2008; 306/2008; 307/2008; 308/2008 and 1191/2014. - 28p.: 30 cm. - 978-0-11-112998-2 £6.00

The Hazardous Waste (Miscellaneous Amendments) Regulations 2015 No. 2015/1360. - Enabling power: European Communities Act 1972, s. 2 (2), sch. 2, para. 1 A & Pollution Prevention and Control Act 1999, s. 2, sch. 1. - Issued: 12.06.2015. Made: 05.06.2015. Laid: 09.06.2015. Coming into force: 01.07.2015. Effect: 1990 c.43 & S.I. 2005/894; 2008/2164, 2841; 2009/890; 2010/675; 2011/988; 2012/811 amended & S.I. 2005/895, 1673 revoked. Territorial extent & classification: E/W/S/NI. General. - With correction slip dated June 2015. - 12p.: 30 cm. - 978-0-11-113662-1 £6.00

The Justification Decision (Generation of Electricity by the UK ABWR Nuclear Reactor) Regulations 2015 No. 2015/209. - Enabling power: European Communities Act 1972, s. 2 (2). - Issued: 17.02.2014. Made: 11.02.2015. Coming into force: 12.02.2015. Effect: None. Territorial extent & classification: E/W/S/NI. General. - Supersedes S.I. draft (ISBN 9780111125045) issued 12/02/15. - 4p.: 30 cm. - 978-0-11-112951-7 £4.25

The Large Combustion Plants (Transitional National Plan) Regulations 2015 No. 2015/1973. - Enabling power: European Communities Act 1972, s. 2 (2). - Issued: 09.12.2015. Made: 02.12.2015. Laid: 04.12.2015. Coming into force: In accord. with reg. 1. Effect: S.I. 2010/675; S.S.I. 2012/360; S.R. 2013/160 amended & S.I. 2007/2325 revoked with savings. Territorial extent & classification: E/W/S/NI. General. - EC note: These Regulations implement Directive 2010/75/EU of the European Parliament and of the Council on industrial emissions (integrated pollution prevention and control) (Recast) in the United Kingdom. - 12p.: 30 cm. - 978-0-11-114150-2 £6.00

The Marine Works (Environmental Impact Assessment) (Amendment) Regulations 2015 No. 2015/446. - Enabling power: European Communities Act 1972, s. 2 (2). - Issued: 09.03.2015. Made: 27.02.2015. Laid: 04.03.2015. Coming into force: 27.03.2015. Effect: S.I. 2007/1518 amended. Territorial extent & classification: E/W/S/NI. General- EC note: These Regulations update references Directive 2011/92/EU on the assessment of the effects of certain public and private projects on the environment. - 4p.: 30 cm. - 978-0-11-113134-3 £4.25

The Nagoya Protocol (Compliance) (Amendment) Regulations 2015 No. 2015/1691. - Enabling power: European Communities Act 1972, s. 2 (2). - Issued: 23.09.2015. Made: 14.09.2015. Laid: 18.09.2015. Coming into force: 11.10.2015. Effect: S.I. 2015/821 amended. Territorial extent & classification: E/W/S/NI. General. - This Statutory Instrument has been made in consequence of a defect in S.I. 2015/821 (ISBN 9780111134535) and is being issued free of charge to all known recipients of that Statutory Instrument. - 2p.: 30 cm. - 978-0-11-113931-8 £6.00

The Nagoya Protocol (Compliance) Regulations 2015 No. 2015/821. - Enabling power: European Communities Act 1972, s. 2 (2). - Issued: 27.03.2015. Made: 17.03.2015. Laid: 23.03.2015. Coming into force: In accord with reg. 1. Effect: None. Territorial extent & classification: E/W/S/NI. General. - 20p.: 30 cm. - 978-0-11-113453-5 £6.00

The Noise Emission in the Environment by Equipment for use Outdoors (Amendment) Regulations 2015 No. 2015/98. - Enabling power: European Communities Act 1972, s. 2 (2). - Issued: 06.02.2015. Made: 29.01.2015. Laid: 03.02.2015. Coming into force: 01.04.2015. Effect: S.I. 2001/1701 amended. Territorial extent & classification: E/W/S/NI. General. - EC note: These Regs relate to the implementation of Directive 2000/14/EC. - 4p.: 30 cm. - 978-0-11-112849-7 £4.25

The Offshore Installations (Offshore Safety Directive) (Safety Case etc.) Regulations 2015 No. 2015/398. - Enabling power: European Communities Act 1972, s. 2 (2) & Health and safety at Work etc Act 1974, ss. 15 (1) (2) (3) (a) (4) (5) (b) (6) (b) (c) (d), 82 (3) (a), sch. 3, paras 1 (1) (c) (2), 8 (1), 9, 14, 15 (1), 16 & Petroleum Act 1987, s. 23 (1) (b) & Offshore safety Act 1992, s. 1 (2). - Issued: 25.03.2015. Made: 19.03.2015. Laid: 23.03.2015. Coming into force: 19.07.2015. Effect: S.I. 1989/971, 1671; 1995/738, 743; 1996/913; 2005/3117; 2013/1471; 2015/363 amended & S.I. 1989/1671; 1993/1823; 1995/743; 1996/913; 2002/3117; 2015/363 partially revoked & S.I. 1972/1542; 1973/1842; 1977/835; 1982/1513; 1987/1331 revoked. Territorial extent & classification: E/W/S. General. - EC note: Implements art. 3 (2) Council Directive 92/91/EEC concerning maximum requirements for improving the safety and health protection of workers in the mineral extracting industries. - 68p.: 30 cm. - 978-0-11-113414-6 £11.00

The Ozone-Depleting Substances Regulations 2015 No. 2015/168. - Enabling power: European Communities Act 1972, s. 2 (2). - Issued: 13.02.2015. Made: 09.02.2015. Laid: 11.02.2015. Coming into force: 07.03.2015. Effect: S.I. 2012/2897; 2013/755 partially revoked & 2009/216; 2011/1543 revoked. Territorial extent & classification: E/W/S. General & NI only in relation to import & export. - 16p.: 30 cm. - 978-0-11-112904-3 £6.00

The Packaging (Essential Requirements) Regulations 2015 No. 2015/1640. - Enabling power: European Communities Act 1972, s. 2 (2). - Issued: 09.09.2015. Made: 01.09.2015. Laid: 04.09.2015. Coming into force: 01.10.2015. Effect: S.I. 2004/693; 2007/3544; 2015 c.15 amended & S.I. 2005/894, 1806 (W.138); 2011/988; 2013/755 (W.90) & S.S.I. 2011/226 & S.R. (N.I.) 2005/300 partially revoked & S.I. 2003/1941; 2004/1188; 2006/1492; 2009/1504; 2013/2212 revoked. Territorial extent & classification: E/W/S/NI. General. - EC note: These Regulations implement articles 9 and 11 of Directive 94/62/EC of the European Parliament and Council on Packaging and Packaging Waste as amended by Directives 2004/12/EC, Commission Decision 2006/340/EC and Decision 2009/292/EC, article 1 and the Annex of Directive 2013/2/EU and article 1 of Directive (EU) 2015/720. - 16p.: 30 cm. - 978-0-11-113887-8 £6.00

The Pollution Prevention and Control (Fees) (Miscellaneous Amendments and Other Provisions) Regulations 2015 No. 2015/1431. - Enabling power: Finance Act 1973, s. 56 (1) (2) & Merchant Shipping Act 1995, s. 302 (1) & Marine and Coastal Access Act 2009, ss. 67 (2) (3) (b), 316 (1) (a). - Issued: 03.07.2015. Made: 25.06.2015. Laid: 30.06.2015. Coming into force: 22.07.2015. Effect: S.I. 1999/360; 2001/1754 amended. Territorial extent & classification: E/W/S/NI. General. - 8p.: 30 cm. - 978-0-11-113726-0 £6.00

The Regulatory Reform (Scotland) Act 2014 (Consequential Modifications) Order 2015 No. 2015/374. - Enabling power: Scotland Act 1998, ss. 104, 112 (1), 113 (2) (3) (4) (5). - Issued: 03.03.2015. Made: 25.02.2015. Coming into force: 26.02.2015. Effect: 1974 c.37; 1988 c.48; 1989 c.29; 1990 c.43; 1995 c.25; 2005 c.5; 2009 c.4; 2009 c.23; S.I. 1997/3032 amended. Territorial extent & classification: E/W/S/NI. General. - Supersedes draft S.I. (ISBN 9780111124505) issued 08/12/14. - 8p.: 30 cm. - 978-0-11-113066-7 £6.00

The Ship Recycling Facilities Regulations 2015 No. 2015/430. - Enabling power: European Communities Act 1972, s. 2 (2) & Health & safety at Work Act 1974, ss. 15 (1) (2) (4) (a), 43 (2), sch. 3, paras. 1 (1) (e) (2), 4 (1). - Issued: 06.03.2015. Made: 23.02.2015. Laid: 03.03.2015. Coming into force: 26.03.2015. Effect: None. Territorial extent & classification: E/W/S. General. - EC note: These Regulations implement certain aspects of Regulation (EU) no. 1257/2013 on ship recycling. - 8p.: 30 cm. - 978-0-11-113120-6 £4.25

The Waste Batteries and Accumulators (Amendment) Regulations 2015 No. 2015/1935. - Enabling power: European Communities Act 1972, s. 2 (2). - Issued: 02.12.2015. Made: 18.11.2015. Laid: 26.11.2015. Coming into force: 01.01.2016. Effect: S.I. 2009/890 amended. Territorial extent & classification: E/W/S/NI. General. - EC note: These Regulations amend S.I. 2009/890, which partially implement Directive 2006/66/EC of the European Parliament and of the Council on batteries and accumulators and waste batteries and accumulators. - 4p.: 30 cm. - 978-0-11-114122-9 £4.25

The Waste Electrical and Electronic Equipment (Amendment) Regulations 2015 No. 2015/1968. - Enabling power: European Communities Act 1972, s. 2 (2). - Issued: 08.12.2015. Made: 01.12.2015. Laid: 03.12.2015. Coming into force: 25.12.2015. Effect: S.I. 2013/3113 amended. Territorial extent & classification: E/W/S/NI. General. - EC note: These Regulations amend the "WEEE regulations", S.I. 2013/3113 which implements Directive 2012/19/EU on waste electrical and electronic equipment. - 8p.: 30 cm. - 978-0-11-114146-5 £6.00

ENVIRONMENTAL PROTECTION, ENGLAND

Environmental protection, England

The Anti-social Behaviour (Designation of the City of London Corporation) Order 2015 No. 2015/858. - Enabling power: Anti-social Behaviour, Crime and Policing Act 2014, ss. 71 (1), 181 (2). - Issued: 30.03.2015. Made: 20.03.2015. Laid: 25.03.2015. Coming into force: 16.04.2015. Effect: S.I. SI 1989/304 amended. Territorial extent & classification: E. General. - 4p.: 30 cm. - 978-0-11-113485-6 £4.25

The Environmental Damage (Prevention and Remediation) (England) (Amendment) Regulations 2015 No. 2015/1391. - Enabling power: European Communities Act 1972, s.2 (2). - Issued: 24.06.2015. Made: 15.06.2015. Laid: 18.06.2015. Coming into force: 19.07.2015. Effect: S.I. 2015/810 amended. Territorial extent & classification: E. General. - This Statutory Instrument has been made in consequence of defects in S.I. 2015/810 (ISBN 9780111134382) and is being issued free of charge to all known recipients of that Statutory Instrument. - 2p.: 30 cm. - 978-0-11-113685-0 £4.25

The Environmental Damage (Prevention and Remediation) (England) Regulations 2015 No. 2015/810. - Enabling power: European Communities Act 1972, s.2 (2). - Issued: 26.03.2015. Made: 19.03.2015. Laid: 23.03.2015. Coming into force: 19.07.2015. Effect: S.I. 2009/153, 3275; 2010/587 revoked. Territorial extent & classification: E. General. - This SI has been corrected by S.I. 2015/1391 (ISBN 9780111136850) which is being issued free of charge to all known recipients of this SI. - 32p.: 30 cm. - 978-0-11-113438-2 £10.00

The Environmental Permitting (England and Wales) (Amendment) (England) Regulations 2015 No. 2015/324. - Enabling power: Pollution Prevention and Control Act 1999, s. 2, sch. 1 & Regulatory Enforcement and Sanctions Act 2008, s. 62. - Issued: 26.02.2015. Made: 16.02.2015. Coming into force: 06.04.2015. Effect: S.I. 2010/675 amended. Territorial extent & classification: E. General. - 8p.: 30 cm. - 978-0-11-113014-8 £4.25

The Environmental Protection (Anglers' Lead Weights) (England) Regulations 2015 No. 2015/815. - Enabling power: Environmental Protection Act 1990, s. 140 (1). - Issued: 27.03.2015. Made: 19.03.2015. Laid: 23.03.2015. Coming into force: 01.07.2015. Effect: S.I. 1986/1922; 1993/49 revoked. Territorial extent & classification: E. General. - 4p.: 30 cm. - 978-0-11-113447-4 £4.25

The Environment and Rural Affairs (Miscellaneous Revocations) Regulations 2015 No. 2015/639. - Enabling power: European Communities Act 1972, s. 2 (2) & Water Act 1983, sch. 2, para. 8. - Issued: 16.03.2015. Made: 10.03.2015. Laid: 11.03.2015. Coming into force: 01.04.2015. Effect: S.I. 1981/322; 1983/1267; 1994/2349; 1996/3111, 3186; 1997/813; 1999/2197; 2000/3359 2001/3960; 2005/3522; 2010/1085; 2007/1621 revoked. Territorial extent & classification: E/W. General. - 4p.: 30 cm. - 978-0-11-113295-1 £4.25

The Household Waste (Fixed Penalty and Penalty Charge) Regulations 2015 No. 2015/969. - Enabling power: Environment Protection Act 1990, s. 46B (3) (4) & London Local Authorities 2007 ss. 20B (4) 95), 20D (2). - Issued: 02.04.2015. Made: 26.03.2015. Laid: 27.03.2015. Coming into force: 15.06.2015. Effect: S.I. 2007/3482 modified. Territorial extent & classification: E. General. - 4p.: 30 cm. - 978-0-11-113603-4 £4.25

The Single Use Carrier Bags Charges (England) Order 2015 No. 2015/776. - Enabling power: Climate Change Act 2008, s. 90 (3) (5), sch. 6 & Regulatory Enforcement and Sanctions Act 2008, s. 4 (4) (a). - Issued: 27.03.2015. Made: 19.03.2015. Coming into force: In accord. with art. 1 (c). Effect: 2008 c.13 amended. Territorial extent & classification: E. General. - Supersedes draft SI (ISBN 9780111127735) issued 28/01/15 - 20p.: 30 cm. - 978-0-11-113498-6 £6.00

The Water, Animals, Marine Pollution and Environmental Protection (Miscellaneous Revocations) Order 2015 No. 2015/663. - Enabling power: European Communities Act 1972, ss. 2 (2) & Water Industry Act 1991, s. 5 & Environment Act 1995, s. 9 (1) & Fur Farming (Prohibition) Act 2000, s. 5 & Marine and Coastal Access Act 2009, s. 74. - Issued: 17.03.2015. Made: 05.03.2015. Laid: 12.03.2015. Coming into force: 01.07.2015. Effect: S.I. 1989/1152 revoked with saving in England & S.I. 1996/3061; 2001/3749; 2004/1964; 2010/304 revoked. Territorial extent & classification: E/W. General. - 4p.: 30 cm. - 978-0-11-113320-0 £4.25

Environmental protection, England and Wales

The Anti-social Behaviour (Authorised Persons) Order 2015 No. 2015/749. - Enabling power: Anti-social Behaviour, Crime and Policing Act 2014, s. 53 (4). - Issued: 23.03.2015. Made: 17.03.2015. Coming into force: In accord. with art. 1. Effect: None. Territorial extent & classification: E/W. General. - Supersedes draft S.I. (ISBN 9780111127131) issued 19/01/15. - 2p.: 30 cm. - 978-0-11-113380-4 £4.25

The Anti-social Behaviour, Crime and Policing Act 2014 (Commencement No. 8, Saving and Transitional Provisions) Order 2015 No. 2015/373 (C.19). - Enabling power: Anti-social Behaviour, Crime and Policing Act 2014, s. 185 (1) (7). Bringing into operation various provisions of the 2014 Act on 08.03.2015; 23.03.2015; 08.04.2015, in accord. with arts 2, 3, 4, 5. - Issued: 02.03.2015. Made: 24.02.2015. Effect: None. Territorial extent & classification: E/W/S/NI. General. - 8p.: 30 cm. - 978-0-11-113065-0 £6.00

The Clean Neighbourhoods and Environment Act 2005 (Commencement No. 6 and Saving) (England and Wales) Order 2015 No. 2015/425 (C.24). - Enabling power: Clean Neighbourhoods and Environment Act 2005, s. 108 (1) (2) (f) (g) (o) (5). Bringing into operation various provisions of the 2005 Act on 03.03.2015; 06.04.2015. - Issued: 09.03.2015. Made: 02.03.2015. Effect: None. Territorial extent & classification: E/W. General. - 8p.: 30 cm. - 978-0-11-113169-5 £6.00

The Control of Waste (Dealing with Seized Property) (England and Wales) Regulations 2015 No. 2015/426. - Enabling power: Control of Pollution (Amendment) Act 1989, ss. 5A (2) to (4), 6 (1) (c) (5) to (7), 8 (2) & Environmental Protection Act 1990, s. 34C (2) to (4). - Issued: 10.03.2015. Made: 03.03.2015. Laid before Parliament & the National Assembly for Wales: 05.03.2015. Coming into force: 06.04.2015. Effect: S.I. 1991/1624 revoked with saving. Territorial extent & classification: E/W. General. - 12p.: 30 cm. - 978-0-11-113174-9 £6.00

The Environmental Permitting (England and Wales) (Amendment) (No. 2) Regulations 2015 No. 2015/934. - Enabling power: Pollution Prevention and Control Act 1999, s. 2, sch. 1. - Issued: 01.04.2015. Made: 26.03.2015. Laid: 27.03.2015. Coming into force: 15.06.2015. Effect: S.I. 2010/675 amended. Territorial extent & classification: E/W. General. - This Statutory Instrument has been made in consequence of a defect in S.I. 2015/918 (ISBN 9780111135402) issued 01.04.2015 and is being issued free of charge to all known recipients of that Statutory Instrument. - 4p.: 30 cm. - 978-0-11-113557-0 £4.25

The Environmental Permitting (England and Wales) (Amendment) (No. 3) Regulations 2015 No. 2015/1756. - Enabling power: Pollution Prevention and Control Act 1999, ss. 2, 7 (9) (a), sch. 1. - Issued: 14.10.2015. Made: 06.10.2015. Laid before Parliament & the National Assembly for Wales: 09.10.2015. Coming into force: 30.10.2015. Effect: S.I. 2010/675 amended. Territorial extent & classification: E/W. General. - 4p.: 30 cm. - 978-0-11-113965-3 £4.25

The Environmental Permitting (England and Wales) (Amendment) Regulations 2015 No. 2015/918. - Enabling power: Pollution Prevention and Control Act 1999, s. 2, sch. 1. - Issued: 30.03.2015. Made: 20.03.2015. Laid before Parliament: -. Coming into force: 21.03.2015 in accord. with reg. 1 (2). Effect: S.I. 2010/675 amended. Territorial extent & classification: E/W. General. - Supersedes draft S.I. (ISBN 9780111126028) issued 22/12/14. - 8p.: 30 cm. - 978-0-11-113540-2 £6.00

The Financial Assistance for Environmental Purposes (England and Wales) Order 2015 No. 2015/479. - Enabling power: Environmental Protection Act 1990, s. 153 (4). - Issued: 10.03.2015. Made: 02.03.2015. Laid: 05.03.2015. Coming into force: 01.04.2015. Effect: 1990 c. 43 amended & S.I. 1991/682; 1992/654; 1993/1062, 1518; 1995/150, 554, 1085, 3099; 1996/505, 1431; 1997/651; 1998/538, 1001, 3234; 2000/207, 2211; 2002/1686, 2021; 2003/714, 2119; 2005/1805; 2006/1735; 2007/1671; 2008/3243; 2009/1506 revoked. Territorial extent & classification: E/W. General. - 4p.: 30 cm. - 978-0-11-113175-6 £4.25

The Pollution Prevention and Control (Designation of Directives) (England and Wales) Order 2015 No. 2015/1352. - Enabling power: Pollution Prevention and Control Act 1999, sch. 1, para. 20 (2) (c). - Issued: 10.06.2015. Made: 04.06.2015. Coming into force: In accordance with art 1 (1). Effect: S.I. 2013/123 partially revoked. Territorial extent & classification: E/W. General. - EC note: This Order designates 2 European directives for the purposes of paragraph 20 (1) (b) of schedule 1 to the Pollution Prevention and Control Act 1999 (c.24). - Partially revoked by S.I. 2016/398 (ISBN 978011114558). - 4p.: 30 cm. - 978-0-11-113659-1 £4.25

The Pollution Prevention and Control (Designation of Energy Efficiency Directive) (England and Wales) Order 2015 No. 2015/816. - Enabling power: Pollution Prevention and Control Act 1999, sch. 1, para. 20 (2) (c). - Issued: 26.03.2015. Made: 19.03.2015. Coming into force: 20.03.2015. Effect: None. Territorial extent & classification: E/W. General. - EC note: This Order designates Directive 2012/27/EU as relevant directives for the purposes of paragraph 20(2)(c) of Schedule 1 to the Pollution Prevention and Control Act 1999. - 4p.: 30 cm. - 978-0-11-113448-1 £4.25

Environmental protection, Wales

The Environmental Damage (Prevention and Remediation) (Amendment) (Wales) Regulations 2015 No. 2015/1394 (W.138). - Enabling power: European Communities Act 1972, s. 2 (2), sch. 2, para. 1A. - Issued: 25.06.2015. Made: 17.06.2015. Laid before the National Assembly for Wales: 19.06.2015. Coming into force: 19.07.2015. Effect: S.I. 2009/995 (W.81). Territorial extent & classification: W. General. - EC note: These Regulations implement Directive 2004/35/EC on environmental liability with regard to the prevention and remedying of environmental damage. - In English and Welsh. Welsh title: Rheoliadau Difrod Amgylcheddol (Atal ac Adfer) (Diwygio) (Cymru) 2015. - 8p.: 30 cm. - 978-0-348-11112-5 £6.00

The Environmental Damage (Prevention and Remediation) (Wales) (Amendment) (No.2) Regulations 2015 No. 2015/1937 (W.291). - Enabling power: European Communities Act 1972, s. 2 (2). - Issued: 03.12.2015. Made: 24.11.2015. Laid before the National Assembly for Wales: 27.11.2015. Coming into force: 18.12.2015. Effect: S.I. 2009/995 (W.81) amended. Territorial extent & classification: W. General. - EC note: These regs continue to implement Directive 2004/35/EC of the European Parliament and of the Council on environmental liability with regard to the prevention and remedying of environmental damage. - In English and Welsh. Welsh title: Rheoliadau Difrod Amgylcheddol (Atal ac Adfer) (Cymru) (Diwygio) (Rhif 2) 2015. - 8p.: 30 cm. - 978-0-348-11195-8 £6.00

The Hazardous Waste (Miscellaneous Amendments) (Wales) Regulations 2015 No. 2015/1417 (W.141). - Enabling power: European Communities Act 1972, s. 2 (2). - Issued: 23.07.2015. Made: 24.06.2015. Laid before the National Assembly for Wales: 26.06.2015. Coming into force: 20.07.2015. Effect: W.S.I. 2004/1490 (W.155); 2005/1806 (W.138); S.I. 2010/675 amended. Territorial extent & classification: W. General. - EC note: The amendments made by these Regulations are necessary in order to: implement Commission Regulation (EU) No 1357/2014 which amends Directive 2008/98/EC; implement Commission Decision 2014/955/EU which amends Commission Decision 2000/532/EC ; recognise the recasting of Directive 2002/96/EC as Directive 2012/19/EU; recognise changes in terminology made by Regulation (EC) No 1272/2008. - In English and Welsh. Welsh title: Rheoliadau Gwastraff Peryglus (Diwygiadau Amrywiol) (Cymru) 2015. - 16p.: 30 cm. - 978-0-348-11133-0 £6.00

European Union

The European Communities (Designation) (No. 2) Order 2015 No. 2015/1530. - Enabling power: European Communities Act 1972, s. 2 (2) & Government of Wales Act 2006, s. 59 (1). - Issued: 22.07.2015. Made: 15.07.2015. Laid: 22.07.2015. Coming into force: 13.08.2015. Effect: S.I. 2013/1445 amended. Territorial extent & classification: E/W/S/NI. General. - 4p.: 30 cm. - 978-0-11-113807-6 £4.25

The European Communities (Designation) (No. 3) Order 2015 No. 2015/1770. - Enabling power: European Communities Act 1972, s. 2 (2). - Issued: 15.10.2015. Made: 08.10.2015. Laid: 15.10.2015. Coming into force: 06.11.2015. Effect: 2000/738 partially revoked. Territorial extent & classification: E/W/S/NI. General. - 4p.: 30 cm. - 978-0-11-113980-6 £4.25

The European Communities (Designation) Order 2015 No. 2015/814. - Enabling power: European Communities Act 1972, s. 2 (2) & Government of Wales Act 2006, s. 59 (1). - Issued: 26.03.20015. Made: 19.03.2015. Laid: 26.03.2015. Coming into force: 17.04.2015. Effect: S.I. 2005/850 partially revoked in accord. with art. 5. Territorial extent & classification: E/W/S/NI. General. - 4p.: 30 cm. - 978-0-11-113445-0 £4.25

The European Grouping of Territorial Cooperation Regulations 2015 No. 2015/1493. - Enabling power: European Communities Act 1972, s. 2 (2). - Issued: 15.07.2015. Made: 08.07.2015. Laid: 10.07.2015. Coming into force: 31.07.2015. Effect: S.I. 2007/1949 revoked with saving & S.I. 2008/728 revoked. Territorial extent & classification: E/W/S/NI. General. - EC note: These Reg (EC) no. 1082/2006 of the European Parliament and of the Council provided for the creation of a new form of body corporate: the European grouping of territorial cooperation. The Regulation has been amended by Reg. (EU) no. 1302/2013. These Regulations revoke and replace the European Grouping of Territorial Cooperation Regulations 2007. - 8p.: 30 cm. - 978-0-11-113775-8 £6.00

The European Union (Definition of Treaties) (Association Agreement) (Georgia) Order 2015 No. 2015/843. - Enabling power: European Communities Act 1972, s. 1 (3). - Issued: 27.03.2015. Made: 19.03.2015. Coming into force: In accord with art. 2. Effect: None. Territorial extent & classification: E/W/S/NI. General. - Supersedes draft S.I. (ISBN 9780111126981) issued 16/01/15. - 2p.: 30 cm. - 978-0-11-113469-6 £4.25

The European Union (Definition of Treaties) (Association Agreement) (Moldova) Order 2015 No. 2015/847. - Enabling power: European Communities Act 1972, s. 1 (3). - Issued: 27.03.2015. Made: 19/03/2015. Coming into force: In accord with art. 2. Effect: None. Territorial extent & classification: E/W/S/NI. General. - Supersedes draft S.I. (ISBN 9780111126868) issued 15/01/15. - 2p.: 30 cm. - 978-0-11-113471-9 £4.25

The European Union (Definition of Treaties) (Association Agreement) (Ukraine) Order 2015 No. 2015/844. - Enabling power: European Communities Act 1972, s. 1 (3). - Issued: 27.03.2015. Made: 19.03.2015. Coming into force: In accord with art. 2. Effect: None. Territorial extent & classification: E/W/S/NI. General. - Supersedes draft S.I. (ISBN 9780111126950) issued 16/01/15. - 2p.: 30 cm. - 978-0-11-113470-2 £4.25

Evidence, England and Wales

The Blood Tests (Evidence of Paternity) (Amendment) Regulations 2015 No. 2015/1834. - Enabling power: Family Law Reform Act 1969, s. 22 (1). - Issued: 05.11.2015. Made: 30.10.2015. Coming into force: 23.11.2015. Effect: S.I. 1971/1861 amended. Territorial extent & classification: E/W. General. - 4p.: 30 cm. - 978-0-11-114039-0 £4.25

The Blood Tests (Evidence of Paternity) (Amendment) (Review) Regulations 2015 No. 2015/2048. - Enabling power: Family Law Reform Act 1969, s. 22 (1). - Issued: 22.12.2015. Made: 14.12.2015. Laid: 17.12.2015. Coming into force: 11.01.2016. Effect: S.I. 2015/1834 amended. Territorial extent & classification: E/W. General. - This S.I. has been printed to correct an error in S.I. 2015/1834 (ISBN 9780111140390) and is being issued free of charge to all known recipients of that S.I. - 2p.: 30 cm. - 978-0-11-114228-8 £4.25

Excise

The Aircraft Operators (Accounts and Records) (Amendment) (No. 2) Regulations 2015 No. 2015/942. - Enabling power: Customs and Excise Management Act 1979, s. 118A (1) (2) & Finance Act 1994, sch. 6, para. 1 (1). - Issued: 02.04.2015. Made: 26.03.2015. Laid: 27.03.2015. Coming into force: 01.05.2015. Effect: S.I. 1994/1737 amended. Territorial extent & classification: E/W/S/NI. General. - 4p.: 30 cm. - 978-0-11-113566-2 £4.25

The Aircraft Operators (Accounts and Records) (Amendment) Regulations 2015 No. 2015/3. - Enabling power: Customs and Excise Management Act 1979, s. 118A (1) (2) & Finance Act 1994, sch. 6, para. 1 (1). - Issued: 12.01.2015. Made: 05.01.2015. Laid: 07.01.2015. Coming into force: 01.04.2015. Effect: S.I. 1994/1737 amended. Territorial extent & classification: E/W/S/NI. General. - 2p.: 30 cm. - 978-0-11-112658-5 £4.25

The Alcoholic Liquor Duties (Alcoholic Ingredients Relief) Regulations 2015 No. 2015/2050. - Enabling power: European Communities Act 1972, s. 2 (2). - Issued: 22.12.2015. Made: 16.12.2015. Laid: 17.12.2015. Coming into force: 01.02.2016. Effect: 1995 c.4 amended. Territorial extent & classification: E/W/S/NI. General. - EC note: These Regulations implement article 27 (1) (c) of Directive 92/83/EEC of 19th October 1992 on the harmonisations of the structures of excise duties on alcohol beverages. - 4p.: 30 cm. - 978-0-11-114230-1 £4.25

The Excise Goods (Aircraft and Ship's Stores) Regulations 2015 No. 2015/368. - Enabling power: Customs and Excise Management Act 1979, ss. 60A, 93 & Finance (No. 2) Act 1992, s. 1. - Issued: 03.03.2015. Made: 24.02.2015. Laid: 26.02.2015. Coming into force: 01.04.2015. Effect: S.I. 1988/809; 1999/1565; 2010/593 amended. Territorial extent & classification: E/W/S/NI. General. - 8p.: 30 cm. - 978-0-11-113060-5 £4.25

The Finance Act 2014, Schedule 21 (Commencement) Order 2015 No. 2015/812 (C.47). - Enabling power: Finance Act 2014, sch. 21 para. 10 (2). - Bringing into operation various provisions of this Act on 01.04.2015 in accord. with art. 2. - Issued: 26.03.2015. Made: 20.03.2014. Effect: None. Territorial extent & classification: E/W/S/NI. General. - 4p.: 30 cm. - 978-0-11-113441-2 £4.25

The Gaming Duty (Amendment) Regulations 2015 No. 2015/1351. - Enabling power: Finance Act 1997, s. 12 (4). - Issued: 10.06.2015. Made: 03.06.2015. Laid: 05.06.2015. Coming into force: 01.10.2015. Effect: S.I. 1997/2196 amended & S.I. 2013/1819 revoked. Territorial extent & classification: E/W/S/NI. General. - 4p.: 30 cm. - 978-0-11-113658-4 £4.25

The Hydrocarbon Oil and Biofuels (Road Fuel in Defined Areas) (Reliefs) (Amendment) Regulations 2015 No. 2015/550. - Enabling power: Hydrocarbon Oil Duties Act 1979, s. 20AA. - Issued: 12.03.2015. Made: 04.03.2015. Laid: 06.03.2015. Coming into force: 01.04.2015. Effect: S.I. 2011/2935 amended. Territorial extent & classification: E/W/S/NI. General. - 4p.: 30 cm. - 978-0-11-113225-8 £4.25

The Hydrocarbon Oil Duties (Reliefs for Electricity Generation) (Amendments for Carbon Price Support) Regulations 2015 No. 2015/943. - Enabling power: Hydrocarbon Oil Duties Act 1979, s. 20AA (1) (a) (2). - Issued: 02.04.2015. Made: 26.03.2015. Laid: 27.03.2015. Coming into force: 01.04.2015. Effect: S.I. 2005/3320 amended. Territorial extent & classification: E/W/S. General. - With correction slip dated August 2015. - 4p.: 30 cm. - 978-0-11-113568-6 £4.25

The Hydrocarbon Oil (Marking and Designated Markers) (Amendment) Regulations 2015 No. 2015/36. - Enabling power: Hydrocarbon Oil Duties Act 1979, s. 24 (1), 24A (3), sch. 4. - Issued: 23.01.2015. Made: 19.01.2015. Laid: 20.01.2015. Coming into force: 01.04.2015. Effect: S.I. 2002/1773 amended. Territorial extent & classification: E/W/S/NI. General. - 4p.: 30 cm. - 978-0-11-112758-2 £4.25

The International Tax Enforcement (Brazil) Order 2015 No. 2015/1887. - Enabling power: Finance Act 2006, ss. 173 (1) to (3). - Issued: 18.11.2015. Made: 11.11.2015. Coming into force: 11.11.2015. Effect: None. Territorial extent & classification: E/W/S/NI. General. - Supersedes draft SI (ISBN 9780111138243) issued 23/07/15 - 12p.: 30 cm. - 978-0-11-114085-7 £6.00

The Revenue Traders (Accounts and Records) (Amendment) Regulations 2015 No. 2015/1650. - Enabling power: Customs and Excise Management Act 1979, s. 118A. - Issued: 11.09.2015. Made: 07.09.2015. Laid: 09.09.2015. Coming into force: 01.10.2015. Effect: S.I. 1992/3150 amended. Territorial extent & classification: E/W/S/NI. General. - 2p.: 30 cm. - 978-0-11-113900-4 £4.25

The Wholesaling of Controlled Liquor (Amendment) Regulations 2015 No. 2015/1921. - Enabling power: Alcoholic Liquor Duties Act 1979, s. 88E. - Issued: 25.11.2015. Made: 18.11.2015. Laid: 20.11.2015. Coming into force: 01.01.2016. Effect: S.I. 2015/1516 amended. Territorial extent & classification: E/W/S/NI. General. - This Statutory Instrument has been made in consequence of a defect in S.I. 2015/1516 (ISBN 9780111137956) and is being issued free of charge to all known recipients of that Statutory Instrument. - 2p.: 30 cm. - 978-0-11-114109-0 £4.25

The Wholesaling of Controlled Liquor Regulations 2015 No. 2015/1516. - Enabling power: Alcoholic Liquor Duties Act 1979, ss.88A (7), 88B (1), 88C (3), 88E, 88I & Finance Act 1999, s.133. - Issued: 21.07.2015. Made: 15.07.2015. Laid: 16.07.2015. Coming into force: 01.10.2015. Effect: None. Territorial extent & classification: E/W/S/NI. General. - 8p.: 30 cm. - 978-0-11-113795-6 £6.00

Extradition

The Anti-social Behaviour, Crime and Policing Act 2014 (Commencement No. 9 and Transitional Provisions) Order 2015 No. 2015/987 (C.66). - Enabling power: Anti-social Behaviour, Crime and Policing Act 2014, s. 185 (1) (7). Bringing into operation various provisions of the 2014 Act on 15.04.2015, in accord. with art. 2. - Issued: 02.04.2015. Made: 25.03.2015. Effect: None. Territorial extent & classification: E/W/S/NI. General. - 8p.: 30 cm. - 978-0-11-113619-5 £6.00

The Extradition Act 2003 (Amendment to Designations and Appeals) Order 2015 No. 2015/992. - Enabling power: Extradition Act 2003, ss. 69 (1), 71 (4), 73 (5), 74 (11) (b), 84 (7), 86 (7), 223 (3) (b) (8) & Anti-social Behaviour, Crime and Policing Act 2014, ss. 181 (2), 182 (6). - Issued: 02.04.2015. Made: 25.03.2015. Coming into force: In accord. with art. 1. Effect: 2003 c.41; S.I. 2003/3334 amended. Territorial extent & classification: E/W/S/NI. General. - Supersedes S.I. draft (ISBN 9780111127322) issued 21/01/15. - 8p.: 30 cm. - 978-0-11-113623-2 £6.00

Family court, England and Wales

The Family Court (Composition and Distribution of Business) (Amendment) Rules 2015 No. 2015/1421 (L.16). - Enabling power: Matrimonial and Family Proceedings Act 1984, ss. 31D (1) (3) & Constitutional Reform Act 2005, sch. 1, part. 1, para 2 (2) (b). - Issued: 02.07.2015. Made: 24.06.2015. Laid: 26.06.2015. Coming into force: 17.07.2015. Effect: S.I. 2014/840 amended. Territorial extent & classification: E/W. General. - 2p.: 30 cm. - 978-0-11-113717-8 £4.25

The Family Procedure (Amendment No. 2) Rules 2015 No. 2015/1420 (L.15). - Enabling power: Civil Jurisdiction and Judgments Act 1982, s. 48 & County Courts Act 1984, s. 110 (4) & Courts Act 2003, ss. 75, 76 & Female Genital Mutilation Act 2003, sch 2, part 1, para. 14 (2). - Issued: 02.07.2015. Made: 24.06.2015. Laid: 26.06.2015. Coming into force: In accord. with rule 1. Effect: S.I. 2010/2955 amended. Territorial extent & classification: E/W. General. - 8p.: 30 cm. - 978-0-11-113716-1 £6.00

The Family Procedure (Amendment No. 3) Rules 2015 No. 2015/1868 (L.21). - Enabling power: Courts Act 2003, ss. 75, 76 & Children and Families Act 2014 s. 10. - Issued: 12.11.2015. Made: 04.11.2015. Laid: 10.11.2015. Coming into force: In accord. with rule 1. Effect: S.I. 2010/2955 amended. Territorial extent & classification: E/W. General. - 4p.: 30 cm. - 978-0-11-114067-3 £4.25

The Family Procedure (Amendment) Rules 2015 No. 2015/913 (L.13). - Enabling power: Civil Jurisdiction and Judgments Act 1982, s. 48 & Courts Act 2003, ss. 75, 76. - Issued: 01.04.2015. Made: 23.03.2015. Laid: 26.03.2015. Coming into force: 01.07.2015. Effect: S.I. 2010/2955 amended. Territorial extent & classification: E/W. General. - 8p.: 30 cm. - 978-0-11-113537-2 £4.25

The Family Proceedings Fees (Amendment No. 2) Order 2015 No. 2015/1419 (L.14). - Enabling power: Courts Act 2003, ss. 92. - Issued: 06.07.2015. Made: 24.06.2015. Laid: 26.06.2015. Coming into force: 17.07.2015. Effect: S.I. 2008/1054 amended. Territorial extent & classification: E/W. General. - 2p.: 30 cm. - 978-0-11-113715-4 £4.25

Family Proceedings Fees (Amendment) Order 2015 No. 2015/687 (L.10). - Enabling power: Courts Act 2003, ss. 92, 108 (6). - Issued: 19.03.2015. Made: 11.03.2015. Laid: 16.03.2015. Coming into force: 06.4.2015. Effect: S.I. 2008/1054, 2013/1407 amended. Territorial extent & classification: E/W. General. - 4p.: 30 cm. - 978-0-11-113346-0 £4.25

The Justices' Clerks and Assistants (Amendment) Rules 2015 No. 2015/890 (L. 12). - Enabling power: Matrimonial and Family Proceedings Act 1984, ss. 31O (1), 31P (1). - Issued: 31.03.2015. Made: 23.03.2015. Laid: 26.03.2015. Coming into force: 01.07.2015. Effect: S.I. 2014/603 amended. Territorial extent & classification: E/W. General. - 2p.: 30 cm. - 978-0-11-113517-4 £4.25

Family law: Child support

The Child Maintenance and Other Payments Act 2008 (Commencement No. 15) Order 2015 No. 2015/176 (C.10). - Enabling power: Child Maintenance and Other Payments Act 2008, s. 62 (3). Bringing into operation various provisions of the 2008 Act on 23.03.2015, in accord. with art. 2. - Issued: 13.02.2015. Made: 09.02.2015. Effect: None. Territorial extent & classification: E/W/S. General. - 8p.: 30 cm. - 978-0-11-112912-8 £4.25

The Child Support (Miscellaneous and Consequential Amendments) Regulations 2015 No. 2015/338. - Enabling power: Child Support Pensions and Social Security Act 2000, ss. 28ZD (1), 34 (1) (b), 41B (3), 49D (2) (c), 51 (1) (2) (i), 52 (4), 54 (1), sch. 1 para. 5 (1) (2). - Issued: 27.02.2015. Made: 19.02.2015. Laid: 26.02.2015. Coming into force: In accord. with reg 1. Effect: S.I. 1999/991 modified & S.I. 1992/1813, 1815, 1816, 1989; 2008/2551; 2012/2677 amended. Territorial extent & classification: E/W/S. General. - 8p.: 30 cm. - 978-0-11-113026-1 £4.25

Family law, England and Wales

The Female Genital Mutilation Protection Order (Relevant Third Party) Regulations 2015 No. 2015/1422. - Enabling power: Female Genital Mutilation Act 2003, sch. 2, part 1, para 2 (7). - Issued: 02.07.2015. Made: 25.06.2015. Laid: 26.06.2015. Coming into force: 17.07.2015. Effect: None. Territorial extent & classification: E/W. General. - 2p.: 30 cm. - 978-0-11-113718-5 £4.25

The Serious Crime Act 2015 (Commencement No. 2) Regulations 2015 No. 2015/1428 (C.80). - Enabling power: Serious Crime Act 2015, s. 88 (1). Bringing into operation various provisions of the 2015 Act on 17.07.2015 in accord. with art. 2. - Issued: 02.07.2015. Made: 25.06.2015. Effect: None. Territorial extent & classification: E/W/NI. General. - 4p.: 30 cm. - 978-0-11-113724-6 £4.25

Family law, Northern Ireland

The Serious Crime Act 2015 (Commencement No. 2) Regulations 2015 No. 2015/1428 (C.80). - Enabling power: Serious Crime Act 2015, s. 88 (1). Bringing into operation various provisions of the 2015 Act on 17.07.2015 in accord. with art. 2. - Issued: 02.07.2015. Made: 25.06.2015. Effect: None. Territorial extent & classification: E/W/NI. General. - 4p.: 30 cm. - 978-0-11-113724-6 £4.25

Family proceedings, England and Wales

The Civil Proceedings and Family Proceedings Fees (Amendment) Order 2015 No. 2015/576 (L.7). - Enabling power: Courts Act 2003, ss. 92 (1) (2) & Anti-Social Behaviour, Crime and Policing Act 2014, s. 180 (1). - Issued: 13.03.2015. Made: 05.03.2015. Coming into force: In accord. with art. 1. Effect: S.I. 2008/1053, 1054 amended. Territorial extent & classification: E/W. General. - Supersedes draft S.I. (ISBN 9780111127490) issued 22.01.2015. - 4p.: 30 cm. - 978-0-11-113246-3 £4.25

The Family Court (Composition and Distribution of Business) (Amendment) Rules 2015 No. 2015/1421 (L.16). - Enabling power: Matrimonial and Family Proceedings Act 1984, ss. 31D (1) (3) & Constitutional Reform Act 2005, sch. 1, part. 1, para 2 (2) (b). - Issued: 02.07.2015. Made: 24.06.2015. Laid: 26.06.2015. Coming into force: 17.07.2015. Effect: S.I. 2014/840 amended. Territorial extent & classification: E/W. General. - 2p.: 30 cm. - 978-0-11-113717-8 £4.25

The Family Procedure (Amendment No. 2) Rules 2015 No. 2015/1420 (L.15). - Enabling power: Civil Jurisdiction and Judgments Act 1982, s. 48 & County Courts Act 1984, s. 110 (4) & Courts Act 2003, ss. 75, 76 & Female Genital Mutilation Act 2003, sch 2, part 1, para. 14 (2). - Issued: 02.07.2015. Made: 24.06.2015. Laid: 26.06.2015. Coming into force: In accord. with rule 1. Effect: S.I. 2010/2955 amended. Territorial extent & classification: E/W. General. - 8p.: 30 cm. - 978-0-11-113716-1 £6.00

The Family Procedure (Amendment No. 3) Rules 2015 No. 2015/1868 (L.21). - Enabling power: Courts Act 2003, ss. 75, 76 & Children and Families Act 2014 s. 10. - Issued: 12.11.2015. Made: 04.11.2015. Laid: 10.11.2015. Coming into force: In accord. with rule 1. Effect: S.I. 2010/2955 amended. Territorial extent & classification: E/W. General. - 4p.: 30 cm. - 978-0-11-114067-3 £4.25

The Family Procedure (Amendment) Rules 2015 No. 2015/913 (L.13). - Enabling power: Civil Jurisdiction and Judgments Act 1982, s. 48 & Courts Act 2003, ss. 75, 76. - Issued: 01.04.2015. Made: 23.03.2015. Laid: 26.03.2015. Coming into force: 01.07.2015. Effect: S.I. 2010/2955 amended. Territorial extent & classification: E/W. General. - 8p.: 30 cm. - 978-0-11-113537-2 £4.25

The Family Proceedings Fees (Amendment No. 2) Order 2015 No. 2015/1419 (L.14). - Enabling power: Courts Act 2003, ss. 92. - Issued: 06.07.2015. Made: 24.06.2015. Laid: 26.06.2015. Coming into force: 17.07.2015. Effect: S.I. 2008/1054 amended. Territorial extent & classification: E/W. General. - 2p.: 30 cm. - 978-0-11-113715-4 £4.25

The Family Proceedings Fees (Amendment) Order 2015 No. 2015/687 (L.10). - Enabling power: Courts Act 2003, ss. 92, 108 (6). - Issued: 19.03.2015. Made: 11.03.2015. Laid: 16.03.2015. Coming into force: 06.4.2015. Effect: S.I. 2008/1054, 2013/1407 amended. Territorial extent & classification: E/W. General. - 4p.: 30 cm. - 978-0-11-113346-0 £4.25

Farriers

The Farriers' Qualifications (European Recognition) Regulations 2015 No. 2015/2072. - Enabling power: European Communities Act 1972, s. 2 (2). - Issued: 29.12.2015. Made: 18.12.2015. Laid: 22.12.2015. Coming into force: 18.01.2016. Effect: 1975 c.35 amended. Territorial extent & classification: E/W/S. General. - EC note: These Regulations amend the Act 1975 c.35 to cross-refer appropriately to the S.I. 2015/2059, which have been made as a result of an amendment to Directive 2005/36/EC of the European Parliament and of the Council on the recognition of professional qualifications. - 2p.: 30 cm. - 978-0-11-114255-4 £4.25

Fees

The Insolvency Practitioners and Insolvency Services Account (Fees) (Amendment) Order 2015 No. 2015/1977. - Enabling power: Insolvency Act 1986, s. 415A. - Issued: 11.12.2015. Made: 02.12.2015. Laid: 07.12.2015. Coming into force: 31.12.2015. Effect: S.I. 2003/3363 amended. Territorial extent & classification: E/W/S. General. - 2p.: 30 cm. - 978-0-11-114161-8 £4.25

Fees and charges

The Global Entry Scheme (Screening Process) (Fees) Regulations 2015 No. 2015/802. - Enabling power: Finance Act 1973, s. 56 (1) (2). - Issued: 26.03.2015. Made: 19.03.2015. Laid: 23.03.2015. Coming into force: 01.07.2015. Effect: None. Territorial extent & classification: E/W/S/NI. General. - 4p.: 30 cm. - 978-0-11-113428-3 £4.25

Fees, England and Wales

The Insolvency Proceedings (Fees) (Amendment) Order 2015 No. 2015/1819. - Enabling power: Insolvency Act 1986, ss. 414, 415. - Issued: 29.10.2015. Made: 22.10.2015. Laid: 23.10.2015. Coming into force: 16.11.2015. Effect: S.I. 2004/593 amended. Territorial extent & classification: E/W. General. - 4p.: 30 cm. - 978-0-11-114016-1 £4.25

Financial services

The Money Laundering (Amendment) Regulations 2015 No. 2015/11. - Enabling power: European Communities Act 1972, s. 2 (2). - Issued: 14.01.2015. Made: 08.01.2015. Laid: 09.01.2015. Coming into force: 06.02.2015. Effect: S.I. 2007/2157 amended. Territorial extent & classification: E/W/S/NI. General. - With correction slip dated December 2015. - 2p.: 30 cm. - 978-0-11-112681-3 £4.25

Financial services and markets

The Bank of England Act 1998 (Macro-prudential Measures) (No.2) Order 2015 No. 2015/905. - Enabling power: Bank of England Act 1998, ss 9I (2), 9L. - Issued: 01.04.2015. Made: 25.30.2015. Coming into force: 01.01.2019, for the purpose of the article 4(b); 06.04.2015, for the remainder. Effect: None. Territorial extent & classification: E/W/S/NI. - Supersedes draft (ISBN 9780111129371) issued 18.02.2015. - 8p.: 30 cm. - 978-0-11-113529-7 £4.25

The Bank of England Act 1998 (Macro-prudential Measures) Order 2015 No. 2015/909. - Enabling power: Bank of England Act 1998, ss 9I (2), 9L. - Issued: 01.04.2015. Made: 25.03.2015. Coming into force: 06.04.2015. Effect: None. Territorial extent & classification: E/W/S/NI. General. - Supersedes draft S.I. (ISBN 9780111129364) issued 18.02.2015. - 8p.: 30 cm. - 978-0-11-113533-4 £4.25

FINANCIAL SERVICES AND MARKETS

The Capital Requirements (Capital Buffers and Macro-prudential Measures) (Amendment) Regulations 2015 No. 2015/19. - Enabling power: European Communities Act 1972, s. 2 (2). - Issued: 19.01.2014. Made: 12.01.2015. Laid: 13.01.2015. Coming into force: In accord. with reg. 1, para. (2) to (4). Effect: S.I. 2014/894 amended. Territorial extent & classification: E/W/S/NI. General. - These regs implement in part the provisions relating to systemic risk buffers Directive 2013/36/EU arts. 133, 134 on access to the activity of credit institutions and the prudential supervision of credit institutions and investment firms. - 12p.: 30 cm. - 978-0-11-112703-2 £6.00

The Electronic Commerce Directive (Financial Services and Markets) (Amendment) Order 2015 No. 2015/612. - Enabling power: European Communities Act 1972, s. 2 (2). - Issued: 31.03.2015. Made: 23.03.2015. Coming into force: In accord. with art. 1 (2). Effect: S.I. 2001/544; 2002/1775 amended. Territorial extent & classification: E/W/S/NI. General. - Supersedes draft SI (ISBN 9780111125939) issued 22/12/14 - 4p.: 30 cm. - 978-0-11-113475-7 £4.25

The European Long-term Investment Funds Regulations 2015 No. 2015/1882. - Enabling power: European Communities Act 1972, s. 2 (2) & Financial Services and Markets Act 2000, ss. 213, (10), 214 (5), 224 (4), 428 (1) (3). - Issued: 17.11.2015. Made: 11.11.2015. Laid: 12.11.2015. Coming into force: 03.12.2015. Effect: 1907 c.24 modified; 2000 c.8 & S.I. 2001/1060, 1783; 2005/1529; 2013/419, 1773 amended. Territorial extent & classification: E/W/S/NI. General. - 8p.: 30 cm. - 978-0-11-114080-2 £6.00

The Financial Markets and Insolvency (Settlement Finality) (Amendment) Regulations 2015 No. 2015/347. - Enabling power: European Communities Act 1972. s. 2 (2). - Issued: 02.03.2015. Made: 23.02.2015. Laid: 24.02.2015. Coming into force: 18.03.2015. Effect: S.I. 1999/2979 amended. Territorial extent & classification: E/W/S/NI. General. - 2p.: 30 cm. - 978-0-11-113035-3 £4.25

The Financial Services and Markets Act 2000 (Banking Reform) (Pensions) Regulations 2015 No. 2015/547. - Enabling power: Financial Services and Markets Act 2000, ss. 142W, 428 (3). - Issued: 11.03.2015. Made: 04.03.2015. Coming into force: In accord. with reg. 1 (2). Effect: None. Territorial extent & classification: E/W/S/NI. General. - Supersedes draft SI (ISBN 9780111127667) issued 26/01/15 - 8p.: 30 cm. - 978-0-11-113222-7 £6.00

The Financial Services and Markets Act 2000 (Collective Investment Schemes) (Amendment) Order 2015 No. 2015/2061. - Enabling power: Financial Services and Markets Act 2000, s. 235 (5). - Issued: 23.12.2015. Made: 17.12.2015. Laid: 18.12.2015. Coming into force: 18.01.2016. Effect: S.I. 2001/1062 amended. Territorial extent & classification: E/W/S/NI. General. - 4p.: 30 cm. - 978-0-11-114246-2 £4.25

The Financial Services and Markets Act 2000 (Collective Investment Schemes) (Amendment) Order 2015 No. 2015/754. - Enabling power: Financial Services and Markets Act 2000, ss. 235 (5), 428 (3). - Issued: 24.03.2015. Made: 17.03.2015. Laid: 18.03.2015. Coming into force: 13.04.2015. Effect: S.I. 2011/1062 amended. Territorial extent & classification: E/W/S/NI. General. - 4p.: 30 cm. - 978-0-11-113383-5 £4.25

The Financial Services and Markets Act 2000 (Exemption) (Amendment) Order 2015 No. 2015/447. - Enabling power: Financial Services and Markets Act 2000, s. 38. - Issued: 09.03.2015. Made: 03.03.2015. Laid: 04.03.2015. Coming into force: 30.03.2015. Effect: S.I. 2001/1201 amended. Territorial extent & classification: E/W/S/NI. General. - 4p.: 30 cm. - 978-0-11-113135-0 £4.25

The Financial Services and Markets Act 2000 (Miscellaneous Provisions) (No. 2) Order 2015 No. 2015/352. - Enabling power: Financial Services and Markets Act 2000, ss. 21 (5) (6), 22 (1) (5), 38, sch. 2 para. 25 (1) (a). - Issued: 02.03.2015. Made: 23.02.2015. Laid: 25.02.2015. Coming into force: 18.03.2015. Effect: S.I. 2001/544, 1201; 2005/1529 amended. Territorial extent & classification: E/W/S/NI. General. - 4p.: 30 cm. - 978-0-11-113040-7 £4.25

The Financial Services and Markets Act 2000 (Miscellaneous Provisions) Order 2015 No. 2015/853. - Enabling power: Financial Services and Markets Act 2000, ss. 21 (5) (9), 22 (1) (1A) (5), 55C. - Issued: 27.03.2015. Made: 23.03.2015. Coming into force: 24.03.2015. Effect: 2008 c.8 & S.I. 2001/544; 2005/1529 amended. Territorial extent & classification: E/W/S/NI. General. - Supersedes draft S.I. (ISBN 9780111128695) issued 09/02/15. - 8p.: 30 cm. - 978-0-11-113476-4 £6.00

The Financial Services and Markets Act 2000 (Misconduct and Appropriate Regulator) Order 2015 No. 2015/1864. - Enabling power: European Communities Act 1972, s. 2 (2) & Financial Services and Markets Act 2000, ss. 204A (7), 428 (3) & Financial Services (Banking Reform) Act 2013, s. 145 (1) & Small Business, Enterprise and Employment Act 2015, s. 28 (2) (a). - Issued: 11.11.2015. Made: 04.11.2015. Laid:-. Coming into force: In accord. with art. 1. Effect: 2000 c.8 amended. Territorial extent & classification: E/W/S/NI. General. - Supersedes draft S.I. (ISBN 9780111139868) 16/10/15. - 4p.: 30 cm. - 978-0-11-114062-8 £4.25

The Financial Services and Markets Act 2000 (Over the Counter Derivatives, Central Counterparties and Trade Repositories) (Amendment) Regulations 2015 No. 2015/348. - Enabling power: European Communities Act 1972, s. 2 (2). - Issued: 02.03.2015. Made: 23.02.2015. Laid: 24.02.2015. Coming into force: 18.03.2015. Effect: S.I. 2013/504 amended. Territorial extent & classification: E/W/S/NI. General. - This S.I. has been made in consequence of a defect in S.I. 2013/504 (ISBN 9780111536131) issued 11/03/13 and is being issued free of charge to all known recipients of that S.I. - 2p.: 30 cm. - 978-0-11-113036-0 £4.25

The Financial Services and Markets Act 2000 (Regulated Activities) (Amendment) (No. 2) Order 2015 No. 2015/731. - Enabling power: Financial Services and Markets Act 2000, ss. 22 (1) (5), 428 (3), sch. 2, para. 25 (1) (a). - Issued: 23.03.2015. Made: 16.03.2015. Coming into force: 06.04.2015. Effect: S.I. 2001/544 amended. Territorial extent & classification: E/W/S/NI. General. - Supersedes draft SI (ISBN 9780111128237) issued 04/02/15. - 4p.: 30 cm. - 978-0-11-113378-1 £4.25

The Financial Services and Markets Act 2000 (Regulated Activities) (Amendment) (No. 3) Order 2015 No. 2015/1863. - Enabling power: Financial Services and Markets Act 2000, sch. 2, para. 26 (2). - Issued: 11.11.2015. Made: 04.11.2015. Coming into force: In accord. with art. 1. Effect: S.I. 2001/544 amended. Territorial extent & classification: E/W/S/NI. General. - Supersedes draft S.I. (ISBN 9780111138373) issued 27/07/15. - 4p.: 30 cm. - 978-0-11-114061-1 £4.25

The Financial Services and Markets Act 2000 (Regulated Activities) (Amendment) Order 2015 No. 2015/369. - Enabling power: Financial Services and Markets Act 2000, ss. 22 (1A) (5), 428 (3), sch. 2, para. 25 & Financial Services Act 2012, s. 93 (4). - Issued: 04.03.2015. Made: 23.02.2015. Coming into force: 01.04.2015. Effect: S.I. 2001/544; 2013/637 amended. Territorial extent & classification: E/W/S/NI. General. - Supersedes draft S.I. (ISBN 9780111127629) issued 26/01/15. - 8p.: 30 cm. - 978-0-11-113061-2 £6.00

The Financial Services and Markets Act 2000 (Regulated Activities) (Amendment) (Pensions Guidance Exclusions) Order 2015 No. 2015/489. - Enabling power: Financial Services and Markets Act 2000, ss. 22 (1) (5), sch. 2, para. 25 (1) (a). - Issued: 11.03.2015. Made: 04.03.2015. Laid: 05.03.2015. Coming into force: 26.03.2015. Effect: S.I. 2001/544 amended. Territorial extent & classification: E/W/S/NI. General. - 4p.: 30 cm. - 978-0-11-113187-9 £4.25

The Financial Services and Markets Act 2000 (Regulated Activities) (Transitional Provisions) Order 2015 No. 2015/732. - Enabling power: Financial Services and Markets Act 2000, s. 426 (1), sch. 2. - Issued: 23.03.2015. Made: 16.03.2015. Laid: 17.03.2015. Coming into force: 06.04.2015. Effect: None. Territorial extent & classification: E/W/S/NI. General. - 2p.: 30 cm. - 978-0-11-113366-8 £4.25

The Financial Services and Markets Act 2000 (Regulation of Auditors and Actuaries) (PRA Specified Powers) Order 2015 No. 2015/61. - Enabling power: Financial Services and Markets Act 2000, s. 345A (1). - Issued: 02.02.2015. Made: 26.01.2015. Laid: 27.01.2015. Coming into force: 20.02.2015. Effect: None. Territorial extent & classification: E/W/S/NI. General. - 2p.: 30 cm. - 978-0-11-112795-7 £4.25

The Financial Services and Markets Act 2000 (Relevant Authorised Persons) Order 2015 No. 2015/1865. - Enabling power: Financial Services and Markets Act 2000, ss. 71A (4), 428 (3) & Financial Services (Banking Reform) Act 2013, s. 146 & Small Business, Enterprise and Employment Act 2015, s. 28 (2) (a). - Issued: 11.11.2015. Made: 04.11.2015. Laid: - Coming into force: 09.11.2015. Effect: 2000 c.8 amended. Territorial extent & classification: E/W/S/NI. General. - Supersedes draft S.I. (ISBN 9780111138168) issued 23/07/15. - 4p.: 30 cm. - 978-0-11-114063-5 £4.25

The Financial Services (Banking Reform) Act 2013 (Commencement (No. 8) and Consequential Provisions) Order 2015 No. 2015/428 (C.25). - Enabling power: Financial Services (Banking Reform) Act 2013, ss. 145, 148 (5). Bringing into operation various provisions of this Act on 26.03.2015, in accord. with art. 2. - Issued: 06.03.2015. Made: 27.02.2015. Laid: 03.03.2015. Effect: 1985 c.6; 2007 asp 3 modified & S.I. 2010/1188 amended. Territorial extent & classification: E/W/S/NI. General. - 8p.: 30 cm. - 978-0-11-113118-3 £6.00

The Financial Services (Banking Reform) Act 2013 (Commencement (No. 9) Order 2015 No. 2015/490 (C.27). - Enabling power: Financial Services (Banking Reform) Act 2013, s. 148 (5). Bringing into operation various provisions of this Act on 07.03.2016, in accord. with art. 2. - Issued: 11.03.2015. Made: 04.03.2015. Effect: None. Territorial extent & classification: E/W/S/NI. General. - 4p.: 30 cm. - 978-0-11-113188-6 £4.25

The Financial Services (Banking Reform) Act 2013 (Transitional and Savings Provisions) (Amendment) Order 2015 No. 2015/1660. - Enabling power: Financial Services (Banking Reform) Act 2013, s. 146. - Issued: 14.09.2015. Made: 08.09.2015. Laid: 09.09.2015. Coming into force: 01.10.2015. Effect: S.I. 2015/492 amended. Territorial extent & classification: E/W/S/NI. General. - 4p.: 30 cm. - 978-0-11-113911-0 £4.25

The Financial Services (Banking Reform) Act 2013 (Transitional and Savings Provisions) Order 2015 No. 2015/492. - Enabling power: Financial Services (Banking Reform) Act 2013, s. 146. - Issued: 11.03.2015. Made: 04.03.2014. Laid: 05.03.2015. Coming into force: 26.03.2015. Effect: None. Territorial extent & classification: E/W/S/NI. General. - 16p.: 30 cm. - 978-0-11-113190-9 £6.00

The Mortgage Credit Directive (Amendment) Order 2015 No. 2015/1557. - Enabling power: European Communities Act, s. 2 (2) & Financial Services and Markets Act 2000, ss. 22 (1). - Issued: 27.07.2015. Made: 20.07.2015. Laid: 21.07.2015. Coming into force: In accord. with art. 1. Effect: S.I. 1983/1553; 2015/910 amended. Territorial extent & classification: E/W/S/NI. General. - 4p.: 30 cm. - 978-0-11-113834-2 £4.25

The Mortgage Credit Directive Order 2015 No. 2015/910. - Enabling power: European Communities Act, s. 2 (2), sch. 2, para. 1A & Financial Services and Markets Act 2000, ss 21 (9) (15), 22 (1) (5), 38, 409, 428 (3). - Issued: 01.04.2015. Made: 25.03.2015. Coming into force: In accord. with art. 1. Effect: 1974 c.39; 2000 c.8 & S.I. 1983/1553; 2001/1201, 1217, 1783, 2188, 2511, 3084; 2004/1481; 2005/1529; 2010/1013, 1014; 2013/1881 amended. Territorial extent & classification: E/W/S/NI. General. - With correction slip dated July 2015. - Supersedes draft S.I. (ISBN 9780111130810) issued 02.02.2015. - EC note: This Order transposes in part Directive 2014/17/EU on credit agreements for consumers relating to residential immovable property and amending Directives 2008/48/EC and 2013/36/EU and Regulation (EU) no. 1093/2010. - 60p.: 30 cm. - 978-0-11-113534-1 £10.00

The Payment Accounts Regulations 2015 No. 2015/2038. - Enabling power: European Communities Act 1972, s. 2 (2). - Issued: 21.12.2015. Made: 15.12.2015. Coming into force: In accord. with reg. 1 (2). Effect: 2008 c.8; S.I. 2001/1420, 2188 modified. Territorial extent & classification: E/W/S/NI. General. - EC note: These Regulations implement Directive 2014/92/EU of the European Parliament and of the Council of 23rd July 2014 on the comparability of fees related to payment accounts, payment account switching and access to payment accounts with basic features. - 36p.: 30 cm. - 978-0-11-114214-1 £10.00

The Payment Card Interchange Fee Regulations 2015 No. 2015/1911. - Enabling power: European Communities Act 1972, s. 2 (2). - Issued: 23.11.2015. Made: 16.11.2015. Laid: 17.11.2015. Coming into force: 09.12.2015. Effect: 2002 c.40; 2013 c.33 & S.I. 2009/209 amended. Territorial extent & classification: E/W/S/NI. General. - 16p.: 30 cm. - 978-0-11-114103-8 £6.00

The Payment Services (Amendment) Regulations 2015 No. 2015/422. - Enabling power: European Communities Act 1972, s. 2 (2). - Issued: 11.03.2015. Made: 04.03.2015. Laid: 05.03.2015. Coming into force: 01.04.2015. Effect: S.I. 2009/209 amended. Territorial extent & classification: E/W/S/NI. General. - 4p.: 30 cm. - 978-0-11-113184-8 £4.25

The Payment to Treasury of Penalties (Enforcement Costs of the Payment Systems Regulator) Order 2015 No. 2015/487. - Enabling power: Financial Services (Banking Reform) Act 2013, sch. 4, para. 10 (4) (b) (5) (b). - Issued: 11.03.2015. Made: 04.03.2015. Laid: 05.03.2015. Coming into force: 01.04.2015. Effect: None. Territorial extent & classification: E/W/S/NI. General. - 4p.: 30 cm. - 978-0-11-113185-5 £4.25

The Small and Medium Sized Business (Credit Information) Regulations 2015 No. 2015/1945. - Enabling power: Small Business, Enterprise and Employment Act 2015 ss. 4, 6 (1) to (8), 7 (1) (2), 28 (2), 161 (2). - Issued: 03.12.2015. Made: 26.11.2015. Coming into force: 01.01.2016. Effect: None. Territorial extent & classification: E/W/S/NI. General. - Supersedes draft S.I. (ISBN 9780111138861) issued 10.09.2015. - 28p.: 30 cm. - 978-0-11-114130-4 £6.00

The Small and Medium Sized Business (Finance Platforms) Regulations 2015 No. 2015/1946. - Enabling power: Small Business, Enterprise and Employment Act 2015, ss. 5, 6 (1) to (4) (9), 7 (1) (2), 28 (2), 161 (2). - Issued: 03.12.2015. Made: 26.11.2015. Coming into force: 01.01.2016. Effect: None. Territorial extent & classification: E/W/S/NI. General. - Supersedes draft S.I. (ISBN 9780111138939) issued 10.09.2015. - 24p.: 30 cm. - 978-0-11-114131-1 £6.00

The Small Business, Enterprise and Employment Act 2015 (Commencement No. 2 and Transitional Provisions) Regulations 2015 No. 2015/1689 (C.100). - Enabling power: Small Business, Enterprise and Employment Act 2015, ss. 160 (1), 161 (1) (2), 164 (1), 164 (6). Bringing into operation various provisions of the 2015 Act on 01.10.2015; 10.10.2015, in accord. with arts 2 & 4. - Issued: 22.09.2015. Made: 15.09.2015. Effect: None. Territorial extent & classification: E/W/S/NI. General. - 8p.: 30 cm. - 978-0-11-113929-5 £6.00

The Solvency 2 Regulations 2015 No. 2015/575. - Enabling power: European Communities Act 1972, s. 2 (2). - Issued: 12.03.2015. Made: 06.03.2015. Laid: 09.03.2015. Coming into force: In accord. with reg. 1. Effect: 9 Acts & 36 SIs amended. Territorial extent & classification: E/W/S/NI. General. - 68p.: 30 cm. - 978-0-11-113244-9 £11.00

The Transparency Regulations 2015 No. 2015/1755. - Enabling power: European Communities Act 1972, s. 2 (2). - Issued: 14.10.2015. Made: 08.10.2015. Laid: 09.10.2015. Coming into force: In accord. 1 (2) (3) (4). Effect: 2000 c.8 amended. Territorial extent & classification: E/W/S/NI. General. - EC note: These Regulations implement in part Directive 2013/50/EU of the European Parliament and of the Council of 22 October 2013 which amends Directive 2004/109/EC of the European Parliament and of the Council of 15 December 2004 on the harmonisation of transparency requirements in relation to information about issuers whose securities are admitted to trading on a regulated market. - 8p.: 30 cm. - 978-0-11-113964-6 £6.00

Fire and rescue services, England

The Dorset and Wiltshire Fire and Rescue Authority (Combination Scheme) Order 2015 No. 2015/435. - Enabling power: Fire and Rescue Services Act 2004, ss. 2, 3, 4, 60 (2). - Issued: 06.03.2015. Made: 02.03.2015. Laid: 04.03.2015. Coming into force: In accord. with art. 1. Effect: S.I. 1996/2916, 2920 revoked. Territorial extent & classification: E. General. - 8p.: 30 cm. - 978-0-11-113123-7 £6.00

The Firefighters' Compensation Scheme and Pension Scheme (England) (Amendment) Order 2015 No. 2015/590. - Enabling power: Fire and Rescue Services Act 2004, ss. 34, 60. - Issued: 13.03.2015. Made: 06.03.2015. Laid: 10.03.2015. Coming into force: In accord. with art. 1. Effect: S.I. 2006/1811, 3432 amended. Territorial extent & classification: E. General. - 20p.: 30 cm. - 978-0-11-113259-3 £6.00

The Firefighters' Pension Scheme (Amendment) (England) Order 2015 No. 2015/579. - Enabling power: Fire Services Act 1947, s. 26 (1) to (5)- Issued: 12.03.2015. Made: 06.03.2015. Laid: 10.03.2015. Coming into force: 01.04.2015. Effect: S.I. 1992/129 amended in relation to England. Territorial extent & classification: E. General. - 4p.: 30 cm. - 978-0-11-113249-4 £4.25

Fire and rescue services, Wales

The Fire and Rescue Authorities (Performance Indicators) (Wales) Order 2015 No. 2015/604 (W.49). - Enabling power: Local Government (Wales) Measure 2009, ss. 8 (1) (a). - Issued: 17.03.2015. Made: 09.03.2015. Laid before the National Assembly for Wales: 10.03.2015. Coming into force: 01.04.2015. Effect: W.S.I. 2011/558 (W.80) revoked. Territorial extent & classification: W. General. - In English and Welsh. Welsh title: Gorchymyn Awdurdodau Tân ac Achub (Dangosyddion Perfformiad) (Cymru) 2015. - 8p.: 30 cm. - 978-0-348-11055-5 £4.25

The Fire and Rescue Services (Appointment of Inspector) (Wales) Order 2015 No. 2015/1524. - Enabling power: Fire and Rescue Services Act 2004, s. 28 (1). - Issued: 22.07.2015. Made: 15.07.2015. Coming into force: In accord. with art. 1. Effect: S.I. 2013/3155 revoked. Territorial extent and classification: W. General. - 2p.: 30 cm. - 978-0-11-113801-4 £4.25

The Fire and Rescue Services (National Framework) (Wales) (Revision) (No. 2) Order 2015 No. 2015/1991 (W.301). - Enabling power: Fire and Rescue Services Act 2004, ss. 21 (6), 62. - Issued: 18.12.2015. Made: 08.12.2015. Laid before the National Assembly for Wales: 09.12.2015. Coming into force: 01.01.2016. Effect: S.I. 2015/1931 (W.289) revoked. Territorial extent & classification: W. General. - In English and Welsh. Welsh title: Gorchymyn Gwasanaethau Tân ac Achub (Fframwaith Cenedlaethol) (Cymru) (Adolygu) (Rhyf 2) 2015. - 4p.: 30 cm. - 978-0-348-11205-4 £4.25

The Fire and Rescue Services (National Framework) (Wales) (Revision) Order 2015 No. 2015/1931 (W.289). - Enabling power: Fire and Rescue Services Act 2004, ss. 21 (6), 62. - Issued: 04.12.2015. Made: 23.11.2015. Laid before the National Assembly for Wales: 24.11.2015. Coming into force: 01.01.2016. Effect: None. Territorial extent & classification: W. General. - Revoked by W.S.I. 2015/1991 (W.301) (ISBN 9780348112054) issued 18/12/15. - Gorchymyn Gwasanaethau Tân ac Achub (Fframwaith Cenedlaethol) (Cymru) (Adolygu) 2015. - 4p.: 30 cm. - 978-0-348-11191-0 £4.25

The Firefighters' Compensation Scheme and Pension Scheme (Wales) (Amendment) Order 2015 No. 2015/1013 (W.69). - Enabling power: Fire and Rescue Services Act 2004, ss. 34, 60, 62. - Issued: 17.04.2015. Made: 30.03.2015. Laid before the National Assembly for Wales: 31.03.2015. Coming into force: In accord with art. 1. Effect: S.I. 2007/1072 (W.110), 1073 (W.111) amended. Territorial extent & classification: W. General. - Gorchymyn Cynllun Digolledu a Chynllun Pensiwn y Diffoddwyr Tân (Cymru) (Diwygio) 2015. - 34p.: 30 cm. - 978-0-348-11069-2 10.00

The Firefighters' Pension (Wales) Scheme (Contributions) (Amendment) Order 2015 No. 2015/1014 (W.70). - Enabling power: Fire Services Act 1947, s. 26 (1). - Issued: 13.04.2015. Made: 30.03.2015. Laid before the National Assembly for Wales: 31.03.2015. Coming into force: 01.04.2015. Effect: S.I. 1992/129 amended in relation to Wales. Territorial extent & classification: W. General. - In English and Welsh. Welsh title: Gorchymyn Cynllun Pensiwn y Dynion Tân (Cymru) (Cyfraniadau) (Diwygio) 2015. - 8p.: 30 cm. - 978-0-348-11066-1 £4.25

Fish farming, England

The Grants for Fishing and Aquaculture Industries Regulations 2015 No. 2015/1711. - Enabling power: European Communities Act 1972, s. 2 (2). - Issued: 01.10.2015. Made: 21.09.2015. Laid: 25.09.2015. Coming into force: 31.10.2015. Effect: S.I. 2007/3284 revoked with saving. Territorial extent & classification: E. General. - EC note: These Regulations supplement Regulation (EU) no. 508/2014 of the European Parliament and of the Council on the European Maritime Fisheries Fund and lay down rules for the implementation of Council Regulation (EU) no. 1303/2013. - 8p.: 30 cm. - 978-0-11-113945-5 £6.00

Food

The Food (Scotland) Act 2015 (Consequential Provisions) Order 2015 No. 2015/444. - Enabling power: Scotland Act 1998, ss. 104, 112 (1), 113 (5), 114 (1). - Issued: 09.03.2015. Made: 03.03.2015. Laid: 04.03.2015. Coming into force: In accord. with art. 1 (2). Effect: None. Territorial extent & classification: E/W/S/NI. General. - 4p.: 30 cm. - 978-0-11-113132-9 £4.25

The Welfare Food (Amendment No. 2) Regulations 2015 No. 2015/1580. - Enabling power: Social Security Act 1988, s. 13 & Social Security Contributions and Benefits Act 1992, s. 175 (3) (4). - Issued: 05.08.2015. Made: 28.07.2015. Laid: 05.08.2015. Coming into force: 01.10.2015. Effect: S.I. 1996/1434 amended. Territorial extent & classification: E/W/S. General. - 2p.: 30 cm. - 978-0-11-113858-8 £4.25

The Welfare Food (Amendment) Regulations 2015 No. 2015/917. - Enabling power: Social Security Act 1988, s. 13 & Social Security Contributions and Benefits Act 1992, s. 175 (3) (4). - Issued: 01.04.2015. Made: 25.03.2015. Laid: 27.03.2015. Coming into force: 01.07.2015. Effect: S.I. 1996/1434 amended. Territorial extent & classification: E/W/S. General. - 2p.: 30 cm. - 978-0-11-113539-6 £4.25

Food, England

The Animals and Animal Products (Examination for Residues and Maximum Residue Limits) (England and Scotland) Regulations 2015 No. 2015/787. - Enabling power: European Communities Act 1972, s. 2 (2). - Issued: 25.03.2015. Made: 18.03.2015. Laid: 20.03.2015. Coming into force: 01.07.2015. Effect: S.I. 2012/2897 partially revoked & S.I. 1997/1729; 2001/3590; 2004/147; 2006/755; 2009/1925; 2013/804 revoked. Territorial extent & classification: E/S. General. - EC note: These Regulations implement Council Directive 96/22/EC concerning the prohibition on the use in stock farming of certain substances having a hormonal or thyrostatic action of beta-agonists and Council Directive 96/23/EC on measures to monitor certain substances and residues thereof in live animals and animal products and provide for the execution of Regulation (EC) no. 470/2009 laying down Community procedures for the establishment of residue limits of pharmacologically active substances in foodstuffs of animal origin and Commission Regulation (EU) no. 371/2010 on pharmacologically active substances and their classification regulating maximum residue limits on foodstuffs of animal origin. - 20p.: 30 cm. - 978-0-11-113407-8 £6.00

The Condensed Milk and Dried Milk (England) Regulations 2015 No. 2015/675. - Enabling power: Food Safety Act 1990, ss. 6 (4), 16 (1), 17 (1), 26 (1) (3), 31 (1), 48 (1) & European Communities Act 1972, sch. 2, para. 1A. - Issued: 19.03.2015. Made: 10.03.2015. Laid: 13.03.2015. Coming into force: 06.04.2015. Effect: S.I. 2003/1596; 2008/85 revoked. Territorial extent & classification: E. General. - 12p.: 30 cm. - 978-0-11-113337-8 £6.00

The Country of Origin of Certain Meats (England) Regulations 2015 No. 2015/518. - Enabling power: Food Safety Act 1990, ss. 6 (4), 16 (1), 17 (1), 26 (1) (2) (3), 31 (1), 48 (1) & European Communities Act 1972, s. 2 (2), sch. 2, para. 1A. - Issued: 11.03.2015. Made: 04.03.2015. Laid: 09.03.2015. Coming into force: 01.04.2015. Effect: 1990 c.16 modified. Territorial extent & classification: E. General. - 8p.: 30 cm. - 978-0-11-113206-7 £6.00

The Honey (England) Regulations 2015 No. 2015/1348. - Enabling power: Food Safety Act 1990, ss. 6 (4), 16 (1) (a) (e), 17 (1), 26 (1) (3), 48 (1). - Issued: 08.06.2015. Made: 30.05.2015. Laid: 03.06.2015. Coming into force: 24.06.2015. Effect: S.I. 1814/1855 amended & S.I. 2003/2243; 2005/1920 revoked. Territorial extent & classification: E. General. - 16p.: 30 cm. - 978-0-11-113654-6 £6.00

Food, Scotland

The Animals and Animal Products (Examination for Residues and Maximum Residue Limits) (England and Scotland) Regulations 2015 No. 2015/787. - Enabling power: European Communities Act 1972, s. 2 (2). - Issued: 25.03.2015. Made: 18.03.2015. Laid: 20.03.2015. Coming into force: 01.07.2015. Effect: S.I. 2012/2897 partially revoked & S.I. 1997/1729; 2001/3590; 2004/147; 2006/755; 2009/1925; 2013/804 revoked. Territorial extent & classification: E/S. General. - EC note: These Regulations implement Council Directive 96/22/EC concerning the prohibition on the use in stock farming of certain substances having a hormonal or thyrostatic action of beta-agonists and Council Directive 96/23/EC on measures to monitor certain substances and residues thereof in live animals and animal products and provide for the execution of Regulation (EC) no. 470/2009 laying down Community procedures for the establishment of residue limits of pharmacologically active substances in foodstuffs of animal origin and Commission Regulation (EU) no. 371/2010 on pharmacologically active substances and their classification regulating maximum residue limits on foodstuffs of animal origin. - 20p.: 30 cm. - 978-0-11-113407-8 £6.00

Food, Wales

The Country of Origin of Certain Meats (Wales) Regulations 2015 No. 2015/1519 (W.177). - Enabling power: European Communities Act 1972, s. 2 (2), sch. 2, para. 1A & Food Safety Act 1990, ss. 6 (4), 16 (1), 17 (1), 26 (1) (2) (3), 31 (1), 48(1). - Issued: 23.07.2015. Made: 13.07.2015. Laid before the National Assembly for Wales: 16.07.2015. Coming into force: 10.08.2015. Effect: None. Territorial extent & classification: W. General. - EC note: These Regulations make provision to enforce, in Wales, certain provisions of Commission Implementing Regulation (EU) No 1337/2013 laying down rules for the application of Regulation (EU) No 1169/2011 of the European Parliament and of the Council as regards the indication of the country of origin or place of provenance for fresh, chilled and frozen meat of swine, sheep, goats and poultry. - In English and Welsh. Welsh language title: Rheoliadau Gwlad Tarddiad Cigoedd Penodol (Cymru) 2015. - 12p.: 30 cm. - 978-0-348-11131-6 £6.00

The Honey (Wales) Regulations 2008 No. 2015/1507 (W.174). - Enabling power: Food Safety Act 1990, ss. 6 (4), 16 (1) (a) (e), 17 (1), 26 (1) (3), 48 (1). - Issued: 24.07.2015. Made: 08.07.2015. Laid before the National Assembly for Wales: 13.07.2015. Coming into force: 03.08.2015. Effect: S.I. 2014/2303 amended & S.I. 2003/3044; 2005/3052; 2008/543 revoked. Territorial extent & classification: W. General. - EC note: These regs implement Council Directive 2001/110/EC relating to honey. - In English and Welsh. Welsh title: Rheoliadau Mêl (Cymru) 2015. - 26p.: 30 cm. - 978-0-348-11128-6 £6.00

The Natural Mineral Water, Spring Water and Bottled Drinking Water (Wales) Regulations 2015 No. 2015/1867 (W.274). - Enabling power: Food Safety Act 1990, ss. 6 (4), 16 (1), 17 (1), 26 (1) (3), 31, 48 (1) & European Communities Act 1972, sch. 2, para. 1A. - Issued: 02.12.2015. Made: 04.11.2015. Laid before the National Assembly for Wales: 06.11.2015. Coming into force: 28.11.2015. Effect: W.S.I. 2010/66 (W.16); 2013/479 (W.55); 2014/2303 (W.227) amended & WSI 2007/3165 (W.276); 2009/1897 (W.170); 2010/748 (W.76); 2011/400 (W.57) revoked. Territorial extent & classification: W. General. - With correction slip dated December 2015. - In English and Welsh. Welsh title: Rheoliadau Dwr Mwynol Naturiol, Dwr Ffynnon a Dwr Yfed wedi'i Botelu (Cymru) 2015. - 84p.: 30 cm. - 978-0-348-11182-8 £11.00

Forestry

The Public Bodies (Abolition of the Home Grown Timber Advisory Committee) Order 2015 No. 2015/475. - Enabling power: Public Bodies Act 2011, ss 1 (1), 6 (1) (5), 35 (2). - Issued: 10.03.2015. Made: 01.03.2015. Coming into force: In accord. with art. 1. Effect: 1967 c.10; 2011 c.24 partially repealed & S.I. 1999/1747 partially revoked. Territorial extent & classification: E/W/S/NI. General. - Supersedes draft S.I. (ISBN 9780111124437) issued 08.12.2014. - 4p.: 30 cm. - 978-0-11-113170-1 £4.25

Freedom of information

The Freedom of Information (Designation as Public Authorities) Order 2015 No. 2015/851. - Enabling power: Freedom of Information Act 2000, s. 5 (1) (a) (2), 7 (5). - Issued: 27.03.2015. Made: 23.03.2015. Coming into force: In accord. with art. 1 (2). Effect: None. Territorial extent & classification: E. General. - Supersedes draft S.I. (ISBN 9780111126844) issued 15/01/15. - 4p.: 30 cm. - 978-0-11-113474-0 £4.25

The Protection of Freedoms Act 2012 (Commencement No.11) Order 2015 No. 2015/587 (C.30). - Enabling power: Protection of Freedoms Act 2012, s. 120 (1). Bringing into operation various provisions of the 2012 Act on 16.03.2015, in accord. with art. 2. - Issued: 13.03.2015. Made: 04.03.2015. Effect: None. Territorial extent & classification: E/W/S/NI. General. - 4p.: 30 cm. - 978-0-11-113256-2 £4.25

Gas

The Electricity and Gas (Market Integrity and Transparency) (Criminal Sanctions) Regulations 2015 No. 2015/979. - Enabling power: European Communities Act 1972, s. 2 (2). - Issued: 01.04.2015. Made: 23.03.2015. Coming into force: In accord. with reg. 1. Effect: S.I. 2013/208 (NI), 1389 amended. Territorial extent & classification: E/W/S/NI. General. - Supersedes draft S.I. (ISBN 9780111127674) issued 26/01/15. EC note: These regs create criminal offences for two sets of prohibitions in Regulation 1227/2011. - 12p.: 30 cm. - 978-0-11-113612-6 £6.00

The Electricity and Gas (Market Integrity and Transparency) (Enforcement etc.) (Amendment) Regulations 2015 No. 2015/862. - Enabling power: European Communities Act 1972, s. 2 (2). - Issued: 30.03.2015. Made: 23.03.2015. Laid: 25.03.2015. Coming into force: 01.07.2015. Effect: 2000 c. 27 & S.I. 2013/1389 amended. Territorial extent & classification: E/W/S. General. - EC note: These regulations give effect to arts 13, 14, & 18 of Regulation (EU) no. 1227/2011 on wholesale energy market integrity and transparency. - 8p.: 30 cm. - 978-0-11-113484-9 £6.00

The Electricity and Gas (Standards of Performance) (Suppliers) Regulations 2015 No. 2015/1544. - Enabling power: Gas Act 1986, ss. 33A, 33AA, 33AB, 33D, 47 & Electricity Act 1989, ss. 39, 39A, 39B, 42A, 60. - Issued: 29.07.2015. Made: 11.07.2015. Coming into force: 01.01.2016. Effect: S.I. 2005/1135; 2008/696; 2015/699 amended. Territorial extent & classification: E/W/S. General. - 20p.: 30 cm. - 978-0-11-113819-9 £6.00

The Enterprise and Regulatory Reform Act 2013 (Amendment) (Gas and Electricity Appeals) Regulations 2015 No. 2015/16. - Enabling power: European Communities Act 1972, s. 2 (2). - Issued: 15.01.2015. Made: 08.01.2015. Laid: 12.01.2015. Coming into force: 06.02.2015. Effect: 2013 c.24 amended. Territorial extent & classification: E/W/S/NI. General. - 8p.: 30 cm. - 978-0-11-112690-5 £4.25

The Gas (Calculation of Thermal Energy) (Amendment) Regulations 2015 No. 2015/953. - Enabling power: Gas Act 1986, s. 12 (1) (3) (4) (5). - Issued: 02.04.2015. Made: 23.03.2015. Coming into force: 01.10.2015. Effect: S.I. 1996/439 amended. Territorial extent & classification: E/W/S. General. - 2p.: 30 cm. - 978-0-11-113582-2 £4.25

The Warm Home Discount (Miscellaneous Amendments) Regulations 2015 No. 2015/652. - Enabling power: Pensions Act 2008 142, ss 144 (2) (4) & Energy Act 2010, ss 9, 10, 14 (4), 31 (5) (6). - Issued: 16.03.2015. Made: 10.03.2015. Coming into force: 11.03.2015 in accord. with reg. 1. Effect: S.I. 2011/1033, 1830 amended. Territorial extent & classification: E/W/S. - Supersedes draft S.I. (ISBN 9780111126943) issued 15/01/15. - 8p.: 30 cm. - 978-0-11-113310-1 £6.00

Government resources and accounts

The Government Resources and Accounts Act 2000 (Estimates and Accounts) (Amendment) Order 2015 No. 2015/2062. - Enabling power: Government Resources and Accounts Act 2000, s. 4A (3) (4). - Issued: 23.12.2015. Made: 17.12.2015. Laid: 18.12.2015. Coming into force: 31.01.2016. Effect: S.I. 2015/632 amended. Territorial extent & classification: E/W/S/NI. General. - 8p.: 30 cm. - 978-0-11-114244-8 £6.00

The Government Resources and Accounts Act 2000 (Estimates and Accounts) Order 2015 No. 2015/632. - Enabling power: Government Resources and Accounts Act 2000, s. 4A (3) (4). - Issued: 17.03.2015. Made: 10.03.2015. Laid: 11.03.2015. Coming into force: 01.04.2015. Effect: None. Territorial extent & classification: E/W/S/NI. General. - 16p.: 30 cm. - 978-0-11-113288-3 £6.00

The Whole of Government Accounts (Designation of Bodies) Order 2015 No. 2015/1655. - Enabling power: Government Resources and Accounts Act 2000, s. 10 (1). - Issued: 14.09.2015. Made: 07.09.2015. Laid: 08.09.2015. Coming into force: 02.10.2015. Effect: None. Territorial extent & classification: E/W/S/NI. General. - 24p.: 30 cm. - 978-0-11-113905-9 £6.00

Government trading funds

The Defence Support Group Trading Fund (Revocation) Order 2015 No. 2015/473. - Enabling power: Government Trading Funds Act 1973, ss. 1, 6 (1). - Issued: 10.03.2015. Made: 03.03.2015. Laid: 06.03.2015. Coming into force: 01.04.2015. Effect: S.I. 2008/563 revoked. Territorial extent & classification: E/W/S/NI. General. - 2p.: 30 cm. - 978-0-11-113167-1 £4.25

The Driver and Vehicle Standards Agency Trading Fund Order 2015 No. 2015/41. - Enabling power: Government Trading Funds Act 1973, ss. 1, 2 (1) (3) (7), 2AA, 2A, 2C, 6 (1). - Issued: 27.01.2015. Made: 12.01.2015. Coming into force: 01.04.2015. Effect: S.I. 1991/773; 1992/471; 1997/668, 873; 2003/942; 2006/623; 2007/468; 2009/469 revoked. Territorial extent & classification: E/W/S. General. - 8p.: 30 cm. - 978-0-11-112770-4 £4.25

Harbours, docks, piers and ferries

The Blyth Harbour Revision Order 2015 No. 2015/1384. - Enabling power: Harbours Act 1964, s. 14 (2) (a). - Issued: 18.06.2015. Made: 05.06.2015. Laid: 12.06.2015. Coming into force: 10.07.2015. Effect: 1986 c.xxi partially repealed. Territorial extent & classification: E. General. - 4p.: 30 cm. - 978-0-11-113679-9 £4.25

The Great Yarmouth Port Authority (Constitution) Harbour Revision Order 2015 No. 2015/1395. - Enabling power: Harbours Act 1964, s. 14 (1) (3). - Issued: 24.06.2015. Made: 12.06.2015. Laid: 19.06.2015. Coming into force: In accord. with art. 1. Effect: 1911 c. xcix partially repealed & S.I. 1989/1737 partially revoked & S.I. 1984/1067 revoked (01.11.2015). Territorial extent & classification: E. Local. - 12p.: 30 cm. - 978-0-11-113691-1 £6.00

The Harbour Directions (Designation of Harbour Authorities) (No. 2) Order 2015 No. 2015/1656. - Enabling power: Harbours Act 1964, s. 40A (4) (b). - Issued: 14.09.2015. Made: 07.09.2015. Laid: 09.09.2015. Coming into force: 01.10.2015. Effect: None. Territorial extent & classification: E/W. General. - 8p.: 30 cm. - 978-0-11-113906-6 £6.00

The Harbour Directions (Designation of Harbour Authorities) Order 2015 No. 2015/573. - Enabling power: Harbours Act 1964, s. 40A (4) (b). - Issued: 12.03.2015. Made: 05.03.2015. Laid: 09.03.2015. Coming into force: 06.04.2015. Effect: None. Territorial extent & classification: E/W. Local. - 4p.: 30 cm. - 978-0-11-113241-8 £4.25

The Littlehampton Harbour Revision Order 2015 No. 2015/1387. - Enabling power: Harbours Act 1964, s. 14 (1) (3). - Issued: 19.06.2015. Made: 12.06.2015. Laid: 15.06.2015. Coming into force: 10.07.2015. Effect: 1927 c. lxvii amended. Territorial extent & classification: E. Local. - With correction slip dated June 2015. - 12p.: 30 cm. - 978-0-11-113682-9 £6.00

The Poole Harbour (Works) Revision Order 2015 No. 2015/1390. - Enabling power: Harbours Act 1964, s. 14 (1) (3). - Issued: 23.06.2015. Made: 12.06.2015. Laid: 19.06.2015. Coming into force: 10.07.2015. Effect: None. Territorial extent & classification: E. Local. - 12p.: 30 cm. - 978-0-11-113684-3 £6.00

The Port of London Authority (Constitution) Harbour Revision Order 2015 No. 2015/2003. - Enabling power: Harbours Act 1964, s. 15 (1). - Issued: 16.12.2015. Made: 09.12.2015. Coming into force: 31.12.2015. Effect: 1968 c.xxxii amended. Territorial extent & classification: E. Local. - 2p.: 30 cm. - 978-0-11-114183-0 £4.25

Health and personal social services, Northern Ireland

The Health Service Medicines (Control of Prices and Supply of Information) (Amendment) Regulations 2015 No. 2015/233. - Enabling power: National Health Service Act 2006, ss. 261 (7), 262 to 265, 266 (1) (a) (2), 272 (7) (8). - Issued: 18.02.2015. Made: 10.02.2015. Laid: 17.02.2015. Coming into force: 09.03.2015. Effect: S.I. 2007/1320; 2008/3258 amended. Territorial extent & classification: E/W/S/NI. General. - 4p.: 30 cm. - 978-0-11-112972-2 £4.25

Health and safety

The Classification, Labelling and Packaging of Chemicals (Amendments to Secondary Legislation) Regulations 2015 No. 2015/21. - Enabling power: European Communities Act 1972, s. 2 (2), sch. 2 para. 1A & Health and Safety at Work etc Act 1974, 15 (1) (2), 80 (1), 82 (3) (a) & Merchant Shipping Act 1995, ss 55 (2), 85 (1), (3) (5) to (7), 86 (1). - Issued: 19.01.2015. Made: 12.01.2015. Laid: 19.01.2015. Coming into force: In accord. with reg. 1 (2) (3). Effect: S.I. 1996/341, 825; 1997/2962; 1998/494, 2411; 1999/3242; 2001/3444; 2002/282, 2676, 2677, 2776; 2005/1541; 2006/456; 2007/3100, 3544; 2008/2852; 2009/669; 2010/330; 2012/632; 2013/1506 amended. Territorial extent & classification: E/W/S/NI. General. - 16p.: 30 cm. - 978-0-11-112708-7 £6.00

The Construction (Design and Management) Regulations 2015 No. 2015/51. - Enabling power: Health and Safety at Work etc. Act 1974, ss 15 (1) (2) (3) (a) (c) 5(a) (8) (9), 80 (1) (2) (c), 82 (3) (a), sch. 3, paras 1 (1) (2), 6 to 12, 14, 15 (1), 16, 18, 20, 21. - Issued: 29.01.2015. Made: 22.01.2015. Laid: 29.01.2015. Coming into force: 06.04.2015. Effect: 1961 c.34; S.I. 1992//3004; 1996/1656; 1997/553; 1998/494, 2306, 2451; 2005/735, 1541; 2006/557; 2008/2852; 2013/1471 amended. Territorial extent & classification: E/W/S. General. - 28p.: 30 cm. - 978-0-11-112781-0 £6.00

The Control of Major Accident Hazards (Amendment) Regulations 2015 No. 2015/1393. - Enabling power: European Communities Act 1972, s. 2 (2) & Health and Safety at Work etc. Act 1974, s. 15 (1). - Issued: 24.06.2015. Made: 18.06.2015. Laid: 19.06.2015. Coming into force: 13.07.2015. Effect: S.I. 2015/483 amended. Territorial extent & classification: E/W/S. General. - This S.I. has been made in consequence of a defect in S.I. 2015/483 (ISBN 9780111131817) published on 09/03/15 and is being issued free of charge to all known recipients of that S.I. - 4p.: 30 cm. - 978-0-11-113690-4 £4.25

The Control of Major Accident Hazards Regulations 2015 No. 2015/483. - Enabling power: Health and Safety at Work etc. Act 1974, ss. 15 (1) (2) (3) (a) (3) (c) (4) (a) (5) (a) (6) (d) (8), 43 (2) (3) (4) (6), 80 (1), 82 (3) (a), sch. 3, paras 1 (1) (2), 15, 16, 20 & European Communities Act 1972, s. 2 (2). - Issued: 09.03.2015. Made: 02.03.2015. Laid: 09.03.2015. Coming into force: 01.06.2015. Effect: S.I. 2005/1541, 2042; 2006/557; 2011/988; 2013/755, 1893; 2014/1637; 2015/363; S.S.I. 2005/494; 2006/458 amended & S.I. 2013/766 partially revoked & S.I. 1999/743; 2005/1088; 2008/1087; 2009/1595; 2014/162 revoked. Territorial extent & classification: E/W/S. General. - This SI has been corrected by S.I. 2015/1393 (ISBN 9780111136904) which is being issued free of charge to all known recipients of this S.I. - 44p.: 30 cm. - 978-0-11-113181-7 £10.00

The Control of Poisons and Explosives Precursors Regulations 2015 No. 2015/966. - Enabling power: Poisons Act 1972, ss. 3A (8), 4A (10), 7 (1), 9B (1), 10 (1). - Issued: 02.04.2015. Made: 27.03.2015. Laid: 27.03.2015. Coming into force: In accord. with reg. 1 (2) and (3). Effect: 1972 c. 66 modified. Territorial extent & classification: E/W/S. General. - 8p.: 30 cm. - 978-0-11-113600-3 £6.00

The Deregulation Act 2015 (Health and Safety at Work) (General Duties of Self-Employed Persons) (Consequential Amendments) Order 2015 No. 2015/1637. - Enabling power: Deregulation Act 2015, s. 112. - Issued: 07.09.2015. Made: 31.08.2015. Laid: 07.09.2015. Coming into force: 01.10.2015. Effect: 1974 c.37; S.I. 1981/917; 1992/2966, 2793; 1998/2306, 2307; 1999/3242; 2002/2677; 2005/735, 1093, 1643; 2013/1471; 2014/1663 amended. Territorial extent & classification: E/W/S. General. - 8p.: 30 cm. - 978-0-11-113882-3 £6.00

The Health and Safety and Nuclear (Fees) Regulations 2015 No. 2015/363. - Enabling power: European Communities Act 1972, s. 2 (2) & Health and Safety at Work etc. Act 1974, ss. 43 (2) (4) (5) (6), 82 (3) (a) & Energy Act 2013, ss. 101 (1) (2) (3), 113 (1) (6) (7). - Issued: 02.03.2015. Made: 23.02.2015. Laid: 02.03.2015. Coming into force: 06.04.2015. Effect: S.I. 2012/1652; 2013/1507 revoked. Territorial extent and classification: E/W/S. General. - Revoked by S.I. 2016/253 (ISBN 9780111144619). - 36p.: 30 cm. - 978-0-11-113053-7 £10.00

The Health and Safety at Work etc. Act 1974 (General Duties of Self-Employed Persons) (Prescribed Undertakings) Regulations 2015 No. 2015/1583. - Enabling power: Health and Safety at Work etc. Act 1974, ss. 3 (2) (2A), 53 (1), 82 (3) (a). - Issued: 07.08.2015. Made: 03.08.2015. Coming into force: 01.10.2015. Effect: None. Territorial extent & classification: E/W/S. General. - Supersedes draft S.I. (ISBN 9780111136980) issued 25/06/15. - 4p.: 30 cm. - 978-0-11-113859-5 £4.25

The Justification Decision (Generation of Electricity by the UK ABWR Nuclear Reactor) Regulations 2015 No. 2015/209. - Enabling power: European Communities Act 1972, s. 2 (2). - Issued: 17.02.2014. Made: 11.02.2015. Coming into force: 12.02.2015. Effect: None. Territorial extent & classification: E/W/S/NI. General. - Supersedes S.I. draft (ISBN 9780111125045) issued 12/02/15. - 4p.: 30 cm. - 978-0-11-112951-7 £4.25

The Offshore Installations (Offshore Safety Directive) (Safety Case etc.) Regulations 2015 No. 2015/398. - Enabling power: European Communities Act 1972, s. 2 (2) & Health and safety at Work etc Act 1974, ss. 15 (1) (2) (3) (a) (4) (5) (b) (6) (b) (c) (d), 82 (3) (a), sch. 3, paras 1 (1) (c) (2), 8 (1), 9, 14, 15 (1), 16 & Petroleum Act 1987, s. 23 (1) (b) & Offshore safety Act 1992, s. 1 (2). - Issued: 25.03.2015. Made: 19.03.2015. Laid: 23.03.2015. Coming into force: 19.07.2015. Effect: S.I. 1989/971, 1671; 1995/738, 743; 1996/913; 2005/3117; 2013/1471; 2015/363 amended & S.I. 1989/1671; 1993/1823; 1995/743; 1996/913; 2002/3117; 2015/363 partially revoked & S.I. 1972/1542; 1973/1842; 1977/835; 1982/1513; 1987/1331 revoked. Territorial extent & classification: E/W/S. General. - EC note: Implements art. 3 (2) Council Directive 92/91/EEC concerning maximum requirements for improving the safety and health protection of workers in the mineral extracting industries. - 68p.: 30 cm. - 978-0-11-113414-6 £11.00

The Pressure Equipment (Amendment) Regulations 2015 No. 2015/399. - Enabling power: European Communities Act 1972, s. 2 (2). - Issued: 05.03.2015. Made: 25.02.2015. Laid: 27.02.2015. Coming into force: 01.06.2015. Effect: S.I. 1999/2001 amended. Territorial extent & classification: E/W/S/NI. General. - 4p.: 30 cm. - 978-0-11-113086-5 £4.25

The Pyrotechnic Articles (Safety) Regulations 2015 No. 2015/1553. - Enabling power: European Communities Act 1972, s. 2 (2), sch. 2, para. 1A. - Issued: 24.07.2015. Made: 19.07.2015. Laid: 21.07.2015. Coming into force: 17.08.2015. Effect: 1875 c.17; 1974 c.37; 1987 c.43; S.I. 2004/1836; S.R. 2002/147 amended & S.I. 2013/1950 revoked with savings. Territorial extent & classification: E/W/S/NI. General. - EC note: These Regulations transpose Directive 2013/29/EU on the harmonisation of the laws of member states relating to the making available on the market of pyrotechnic articles and Commission Implementing Directive 2014/58/EU setting up a system for the traceability of pyrotechnic articles. The Directive repeals and replaces Directive 2007/23/EC. - 60p.: 30 cm. - 978-0-11-113829-8 £10.00

The Railways and Other Guided Transport Systems (Safety) (Amendment) Regulations 2015 No. 2015/1917. - Enabling power: Health and Safety at Work etc. Act 1974, ss. 15 (1) (2), sch. 3, para. 15 (1). - Issued: 24.11.2015. Made: 16.11.2015. Laid: 18.11.2015. Coming into force: 11.12.2015. Effect: S.I. 2006/599 amended. Territorial extent & classification: E/W/S. General. - These Regulations amend S.I. 2006/599 in order to implement Commission Directive 2014/88/EU as regards common safety indicators and common methods of calculating accident costs. - 4p.: 30 cm. - 978-0-11-114108-3 £4.25

The Ship Recycling Facilities Regulations 2015 No. 2015/430. - Enabling power: European Communities Act 1972, s. 2 (2) & Health & safety at Work Act 1974, ss. 15 (1) (2) (4) (a), 43 (2), sch. 3, paras. 1 (1) (e) (2), 4 (1). - Issued: 06.03.2015. Made: 23.02.2015. Laid: 03.03.2015. Coming into force: 26.03.2015. Effect: None. Territorial extent & classification: E/W/S. General. - EC note: These Regulations implement certain aspects of Regulation (EU) no. 1257/2013 on ship recycling. - 8p.: 30 cm. - 978-0-11-113120-6 £4.25

Health care and associated professions

The General Dental Council (Indemnity Arrangements) (Dentists and Dental Care Professionals) Rules Order of Council 2015 No. 2015/1758. - Enabling power: Dentists Act 1984, ss. 26A (4) (5) (6), 36L (4) (5) (6). - Issued: 14.10.2015. Made: 08.10.2015. Laid before Parliament & Scottish Parliament: 12.10.2015. Coming into force: 23.11.2015. Effect: None. Territorial extent & classification: E/W/S/NI. General. - 8p.: 30 cm. - 978-0-11-113966-0 £4.25

The General Dental Council (Overseas Registration Examination Regulations) Order of Council 2015 No. 2015/735. - Enabling power: Dentists Act 1984, ss. 16 (4), 52 (1B). - Issued: 23.03.2015. Made: 16.03.2015. Coming into force: 01.05.2015. Effect: S.I. 2007/1884 revoked. Territorial extent & classification: E/W/S/NI. General. - 4p.: 30 cm. - 978-0-11-113370-5 £4.25

The General Medical Council (Fitness to Practise and Over-arching Objective) and the Professional Standards Authority for Health and Social Care (References to Court) Order 2015 No. 2015/794. - Enabling power: Health Act 1999, ss. 60, 62 (4) (4A), sch. 3. - Issued: 26.03.2015. Made: 19.03.2015. Coming into force: In accord. with art. 1 (2) (3). Effect: 1983 c.54; 2002 c.17 amended. Territorial extent & classification: E/W/S/NI. General. - Supersedes draft SI (ISBN 9780111130056) issued 24/02/15 - 36p.: 30 cm. - 978-0-11-113417-7 £10.00

The Health and Social Care Act 2012 (Commencement No. 9) Order 2015 No. 2015/409 (C.23). - Enabling power: Health and Social Care Act 2012, s. 306. Bringing into operation various provisions of the 2012 Act on 16.03.2015 in accord. with art. 2. - Issued: 05.03.2015. Made: 26.02.2015. Coming into force: -Effect: None. Territorial extent & classification: E/W/S/NI. General. - 8p.: 30 cm. - 978-0-11-113099-5 £6.00

The Health Care and Associated Professions (Knowledge of English) Order 2015 No. 2015/806. - Enabling power: Health Act 1999, ss. 60, 62 (4) (4A), sch. 3. - Issued: 26.03.2015. Made: 19.03.2015. Coming into force: In accord. with art. 1 (2) to (4). Effect: 1984 c.24; S.I. 1976/1213 (NI.22); 2002/253; 2010/231 amended. Territorial extent & classification: E/W/S/NI. General. - Supersedes draft S.I. (ISBN 9780111130070) issued 25.02.2015. - 24p.: 30 cm. - 978-0-11-113432-0 £6.00

The Health Care and Associated Professions (Knowledge of English) Order 2015 (Commencement No. 1) Order of Council 2015 No. 2015/1451. - Enabling power: S.I. 2015/806, art. 1 (3). Bringing into operation various provisions of the 2015 Order on 19.10.2015; 04.01.2016; 18.01.2016; 01.04.2016; 01.06.2016, accord. to arts 2 to 6. - Issued: 07.07.2015. Made: 30.06.2015. Laid: 01.07.2015. Coming into force: 19.10.2015. Effect: None. Territorial extent & classification: E/W/S/NI. General. - 2p.: 30 cm. - 978-0-11-113732-1 £4.25

The Professional Standards Authority for Health and Social Care (Fees) Regulations 2015 No. 2015/400. - Enabling power: National Health Service Reform and Health Care Professions Act 2002, ss. 25A (1) (3) (10) (11), 38 (5) (7). - Issued: 05.03.2015. Made: 26.02.2015. Laid: 27.02.2015. Laid before the Scottish Parliament: 27.02.2015. Coming into force: 01.04.2015. Effect: None. Territorial extent & classification: E/W/S/NI. General. - 4p.: 30 cm. - 978-0-11-113087-2 £4.25

Health care and associated professions: Chiropractors

The General Chiropractic Council (Indemnity Arrangements) Rules Order of Council 2015 No. 2015/1511. - Enabling power: Chiropractors Act 1994, ss. 6 (2) (3), 35 (2), 37 (5) to (7). - Issued: 20.07.2015. Made: 08.07.2015. Coming into force: 16.07.2015. Effect: None. Territorial extent & classification: E/W/S/NI. General. - 4p.: 30 cm. - 978-0-11-113787-1 £4.25

Health care and associated professions: Dentists

The Dentists Act 1984 (Medical Authorities) Order 2015 No. 2015/991. - Enabling power: S.I. 2009/1182, art. 7 (4) (b). - Issued: 02.04.2015. Made: 24.03.2015. Laid:-. Coming into force: 30.03.2015. Effect: None. Territorial extent & classification: E/W/S/NI. General. - 2p.: 30 cm. - 978-0-11-113622-5 £4.25

Health care and associated professions: Doctors

The General Medical Council (Amendments to Miscellaneous Rules and Regulations) Order of Council 2015 No. 2015/1964. - Enabling power: Medical Act 1983, s. 35CC (1), (4) to (7), sch. 1, para. 19B to 19D, 19G, sch. 4, paras 1 (1) (2ZA) (2ZB) (2A) (2B) to (2E) (3) (4) (4B) to (4D), 5A (1) (2ZC) (2ZE), 5C (1) (2), 7A (4) (6) (9). - Issued: 08.12.2015. Made: 01.12.2015. Laid: 02.12.2015. Coming into force: 31.12.2015. Effect: S.I. 2004/2607, 2608, 2609, 2612; 2012/2685 amended. Territorial extent & classification: E/W/S/NI. General. - 36p.: 30 cm. - 978-0-11-114142-7 £10.00

HEALTH CARE AND ASSOCIATED PROFESSIONS: HEALTH PROFESSIONS

The General Medical Council (Constitution of Panels, Tribunals and Investigation Committee) Rules Order of Council 2015 No. 2015/1965. - Enabling power: Medical Act 1983, sch. 1, paras. 19B to 19D, 19G, 23, 23B. - Issued: 08.12.2015. Made: 01.12.2015. Laid: 02.12.2015. Coming into force: 31.12.2015. Effect: S.I. 2004/2611; 2005/402; 2009/2751; 2010/474 revoked. Territorial extent & classification: E/W/S/NI. General. - 8p.: 30 cm. - 978-0-11-114143-4 £6.00

The General Medical Council (Constitution of the Medical Practitioners Tribunal Service) Rules Order of Council 2015 No. 2015/1967. - Enabling power: Medical Act 1983, sch. 1, para. 19F. - Issued: 08.12.2015. Made: 01.12.2015. Laid: 02.12.2015. Coming into force: 31.12.2015. Effect: None. Territorial extent & classification: E/W/S/NI. General. - 12p.: 30 cm. - 978-0-11-114145-8 £6.00

The General Medical Council (Fitness to Practise and Over-arching Objective) and the Professional Standards Authority for Health and Social Care (References to Court) Order 2015 (Commencement No.1 and Transitory Provisions) Order of Council 2015 No. 2015/1579 (C.91). - Enabling power: S.I. 2015/794, art. 1 (3) (5). Bringing into operation various provisions of the 2015 Order on 03.08.2015, in accord. with art. 2. - Issued: 04.08.2015. Made: 29.07.2015. Effect: None. Territorial extent & classification: E/W/S/NI. General. - 4p.: 30 cm. - 978-0-11-113857-1 £4.25

The General Medical Council (Fitness to Practise and Over-arching Objective) and the Professional Standards Authority for Health and Social Care (References to Court) Order 2015 (Commencement No. 2 and Transitional Provisions) Order of Council 2015 No. 2015/1952 (C.120). - Enabling power: S.I. 2015/794, art. 1 (3) (5). Bringing into operation various provisions of the 2015 Order on 31.12.2015. - Issued: 07.12.2015. Made: 01.12.2015. Effect: None. Territorial extent & classification: E/W/S/NI. General. - 4p.: 30 cm. - 978-0-11-114137-3 £4.25

The General Medical Council (Legal Assessors and Legally Qualified Persons) Rules Order of Council 2015 No. 2015/1958. - Enabling power: Medical Act 1983, sch. 4, paras. 1 (4E), 7 (3) (4)- Issued: 08.12.2015. Made: 01.12.2015. Laid: 02.12.2015. Coming into force: 31.12.2015. Effect: S.I. 2004/2625; 2005/896 revoked. Territorial extent & classification: E/W/S/NI. General. - 8p.: 30 cm. - 978-0-11-114140-3 £4.25

The General Medical Council (Licence to Practise and Revalidation) (Amendment) Regulations Order of Council 2015 No. 2015/1375. - Enabling power: Medical Act 1983, ss. 29A (2) to (4), 29B (1) (2) (3), 29D (1) (2), 29J (3), 44C (4) (5). - Issued: 16.06.2015. Made: 09.06.2015. Laid: 12.06.2015. Coming into force: 01.08.2015. Effect: S.I. 2012/2685 amended. Territorial extent & classification: E/W/S/NI. General. - 4p.: 30 cm. - 978-0-11-113670-6 £4.25

The General Medical Council (Maximum Period of Provisional Registration) Regulations Order of Council 2015 No. 2015/92. - Enabling power: Medical Act 1983, s. 31 (1) (4A). - Issued: 05.02.2015. Made: 21.01.2015. Laid: 02.02.2015. Coming into force: 01.04.2015. Effect: None. Territorial extent & classification: E/W/S/NI. General. - 4p.: 30 cm. - 978-0-11-112841-1 £4.25

Health care and associated professions: Health professions

The Health and Care Professions Council (Registration and Fees) (Amendment) (No. 2) Rules Order of Council 2015 No. 2015/1337. - Enabling power: S.I. 2002/254, arts 7 (1) (2), 10 (1), 41 (2). - Issued: 04.06.2015. Made: 28.05.2015. Laid before Parliament: 29.05.2015. Laid before the Scottish Parliament: 29.05.2015. Coming into force: 01.07.2015. Effect: 2003/1572 amended. Territorial extent & classification: E/W/S/NI. General. - 4p.: 30 cm. - 978-0-11-113648-5 £4.25

The Health and Care Professions Council (Registration and Fees) (Amendment) Rules Order of Council 2015 No. 2015/93. - Enabling power: S.I. 2002/254, arts 7 (1) (2), 9 (2), 11A (4) (5) (6), 41 (2). - Issued: 05.02.2015. Made: 21.01.2015. Laid before Parliament: 02.02.2015. Laid before the Scottish Parliament: 02.02.2015. Coming into force: 01.04.2015. Effect: 2003/1572 amended. Territorial extent & classification: E/W/S/NI. General. - 4p.: 30 cm. - 978-0-11-112843-5 £4.25

Health care and associated professions: Nurses and midwives

The Nursing and Midwifery Council (Fitness to Practise) (Education, Registration and Registration Appeals) (Amendment No. 2) Rules Order of Council 2015 No. 2015/1923. - Enabling power: The Nursing and Midwifery Order 2001, arts 7 (1) (2), 9 (2), 26 (3), 28A, 32 (1) (2), 37 (4), 47 (2). - Issued: 25.11.2015. Made: 19.11.2015. Laid: 23.11.2015. Coming into force: 19.01.2016. Effect: S.I. 2004/1761 amended. Territorial extent & classification: E/W/S/NI. General. - 8p.: 30 cm. - 978-0-11-114110-6 £6.00

The Nursing and Midwifery Council (Fitness to Practise) (Education, Registration and Registration Appeals) (Amendment) Rules Order of Council 2015 No. 2015/52. - Enabling power: S.I. 2002/253, arts 7 (1) (2), 9 (1) (2), 10 (1), 12A (4) to (7), 22 (5), 26 (2) to (5), 26A (1), 26B, 26C (1), 37 (4) (5), 47 (2). - Issued: 29.01.2015. Made: 21.01.2015. Laid: 27.01.2015. Coming into force: 09.03.2015. Effect: S.I. 2004/1761, 1767 amended. Territorial extent & classification: E/W/S/NI. General. - 16p.: 30 cm. - 978-0-11-112783-4 £6.00

Health care and associated professions: Osteopaths

The General Osteopathic Council (Constitution) (Amendment) Order 2015 No. 2015/1906. - Enabling power: Osteopaths Act 1993, s. 1 (4), para. 1B (1) (a) (f) (4). - Issued: 19.11.2015. Made: 11.11.2015. Laid: 18.11.2015. Coming into force: 18.12.2015. Effect: S.I. 2009/263 amended. Territorial extent & classification: E/W/S/NI. General. - 2p.: 30 cm. - 978-0-11-114101-4 £4.25

The General Osteopathic Council (Indemnity Arrangements) Rules Order of Council 2015 No. 2015/693. - Enabling power: Osteopaths Act 1993, ss. 6 (2) (3), 35 (2), 37 (5) to (8). - Issued: 19.03.2015. Made: 10.03.2015. Coming into force: 01.05.2015. Effect: None. Territorial extent & classification: E/W/S/NI. General. - 4p.: 30 cm. - 978-0-11-113347-7 £4.25

Health services, England

The Care and Support (Isle of Scilly) Order 2015 No. 2015/642. - Enabling power: National Health Service and Community Care Act 1990, s. 67 (6) & Community Care (Residential Accommodation) Act 1992, s. 2 (5) & Care Act 2014, s. 128 (4). - Issued: 16.03.2015. Made: 10.03.2015. Laid: 11.03.2015. Coming into force: in accord with art. 1. Effect: 2014 c. 23 modified & S.I. 1993/570 amended. Territorial extent & classification: E. General. - 2p.: 30 cm. - 978-0-11-113298-2 £4.25

Health services, England and Wales

The Care Act 2014 (Health Education England and the Health Research Authority) (Consequential Amendments and Revocations) Order 2015 No. 2015/137. - Enabling power: Care Act 2014, s. 123 (1) (2). - Issued: 11.02.2015. Made: 04.02.2015. Laid: 11.02.2015. Coming into force: 01.04.2015. Effect: S.I. 1990/2024; 1995/2800, 2801; 1996/251; 1999/873, 874; 2004/1031; 2005/3361, 3373, 2415, 2531; 2008/1185; 2009/779 (W.67), 1385 (W.141), 3097 (W.270); 2011/2260; 2012/922, 1261; 2013/349; 2014/566 amended & S.I 2013/647, 1197 revoked. Territorial extent & classification: E/W. General. - Partially revoked by SI 2015/559 (ISBN 9780111132296) in re to E. - 8p.: 30 cm. - 978-0-11-112888-6 £6.00

Highways

The Infrastructure Act 2015 (Commencement No.1) Regulations 2015 No. 2015/481 (C.26). - Enabling power: Infrastructure Act 2015, s. 57 (1) (b) (4) (a) (7) (c). Bringing into operation various provisions of the 2013 Act on 05.03.2015, 12.04.2015. - Issued: 10.03.2015. Made: 02.03.2015. Effect: None. Territorial extent & classification: E/W/S/NI. General. - 2p.: 30 cm. - 978-0-11-113179-4 £4.25

Highways, England

The A11 Trunk Road (Fiveways to Thetford Improvement) (Detrunking) 2011 (Amendment) Order 2015 No. 2015/1581. - Enabling power: Highways Act 1980, ss. 10, 12. - Issued: 03.08.2015. Made: 18.03.2015. Coming into force: 25.03.2015. Effect: None. Territorial extent & classification: E. Local. - Available at http://www.legislation.gov.uk/uksi/2015/1581/contents/made Non-print

The Appointment of a Strategic Highways Company Order 2015 No. 2015/376. - Enabling power: Infrastructure Act 2015, ss. 1 (1) (2), 2 (1) to (3). - Issued: 19.03.2015. Made: 10.03.2015. Coming into force: 01.04.2015. Effect: None. Territorial extent & classification: E. General. - This Statutory Instrument has been published in substitution of the SI of the same title which was incorrectly numbered as S.I. 2015/651 and published online in error. - 2p.: 30 cm. - 978-0-11-113345-3 £4.25

The Bournemouth-Swanage Motor Road and Ferry (Revision of Tolls) Order 2015 No. 2015/1105. - Enabling power: Transport Charges &c. (Miscellaneous Provisions Act 1954, s. 6. - Issued: 17.04.2015. Made: 23.02.2015. Coming into force: 02.03.2015. Effect: None. Territorial extent & classification: E. Local. - Available at http://www.legislation.gov.uk/uksi/2015/1105/contents/made Non-print

The Cambridgeshire County Council (A142 Ely Southern Bypass) Bridge Scheme 2015 Confirmation Instrument 2015 No. 2015/1824. - Enabling power: Highways Act 1980, s. 106 (3). - Issued: 28.10.2015. Made: 08.10.2015. Coming into force: In accord. with art. 1. Effect: None. Territorial extent & classification: E. Local. - 8p., map: 30 cm. - 978-0-11-114017-8 £4.25

The Council of the City of Wakefield (Wakefield Eastern Relief Road) Bridge Scheme 2015 Confirmation Instrument 2015 No. 2015/1474. - Enabling power: Highways Act 1980, s. 106 (3). - Issued: 13.07.2015. Made: 11.06.2015. Coming into force: In accord. with art. 1. Effect: None. Territorial extent & classification: E. Local. - 8p., plan: 30 cm. - 978-0-11-113754-3 £4.25

The Delegation of Functions (Strategic Highways Companies) (England) Regulations 2015 No. 2015/378. - Enabling power: Infrastructure Acr 2015, s. 7. - Issued: 09.03.2015. Made: 02.03.2015. Laid: 05.03.2015. Coming into force: 01.04.2015. Effect: None. Territorial extent & classification: E. General. - 10p.: 30 cm. - 978-0-11-113148-0 £6.00

The Infrastructure Act 2015 (Strategic Highways Companies) (Consequential, Transitional and Savings Provisions) Regulations 2015 No. 2015/377. - Enabling power: Infrastructure Act 2015, s. 19. - Issued: 09.03.2015. Made: 02.03.2015. Laid: 05.03.2015. Coming into force: 01.04.2015. Effect: None. Territorial extent & classification: E. General. - Partially revoked by SI 2015/595 (ISBN 9780111134399). - 16p.: 30 cm. - 978-0-11-113146-6 £6.00

The M32 Motorway (Hambrook Interchange to Lower Ashley Road Interchange) and Connecting Roads Scheme 1989 (Variation for Slip Road Crossing) Scheme 2015 No. 2015/1901. - Enabling power: Highways Act 1980, s. 16. - Issued: 19.11.2015. Made: 12.11.2015. Coming into force: 10.12.2015. Effect: None. Territorial extent & classification: E. Local. - 2p.: 30 cm. - 978-0-11-114098-7 £4.25

The Office of Rail Regulation (Change of Name) Regulations 2015 No. 2015/1682. - Enabling power: Transport Safety Act 2003, s. 15A. - Issued: 17.09.2015. Made: 10.09.2015. Laid: 17.09.2015. Coming into force: 16.10.2015. Effect: 1962 c.46; 1967 c.13; 1974 c.37; 1975 c.24; 1983 c.16; 1984 c.12; 1986 c.31, c.46; 1991 c.56, c.57; 1993 c.43; 1994 c.40; 1996 c.61; 1998 c.41; 1999 c.29; 2000 c.27, c.38; 2002 c.40; 2003 c.20; 2005 c.14; 2006 c.51; 2008 c.13. c.18; 2012 c.19; 2013 c.24, c.32; 2015 c.7, c.15 & S.I. 1990/304; 1997/553; 1998/494, 1833; 1999/2244; 2001/2975; 2002/2677; 2005/1093, 1541, 1643, 1992, 3049, 3050, 3207; 2006/557, 598, 599, 1010, 1466; 2007/2657, 3531; 2008/1261; 1597, 1660; 2008/2852; 2009/1348, 2264; 2010/104, 432, 724, 1140, 1504; 2011/2055, 3066; 2012/632, 767, 1128, 2284, 2635; 2013/1471, 1506; 2014/2418; 2015/51, 462, 785, 786 & 2007 asp 8, S.S.I. 2006/456; 2007/570; 2012/345 & 2011 nawm 1 amended. Territorial extent & classification: E/W/S. General. - 20p.: 30 cm. - 978-0-11-113925-7 £6.00

The Severn Bridges Tolls Order 2015 No. 2015/2030. - Enabling power: Severn Bridges Act 1992, s. 9 (1) (2)(b) (3) (b) (4) (6). - Issued: 21.12.2015. Made: 14.12.2015. Coming into force: 01.01.2016. Effect: S.I. 2014/3313 revoked. Territorial extent & classification: E. Local. - 2p.: 30 cm. - 978-0-11-114207-3 £4.25

The Street Works (Qualifications of Supervisors and Operatives) (England) (Amendment) Regulations 2015 No. 2015/384. - Enabling power: New Roads and Street Works Act 1991, s. 67. - Issued: 02.03.2015. Made: 23.02.2015. Laid: 02.03.2015. Coming into force: 06.04.2015. Effect: S.I. 2009/2257 amended. Territorial extent & classification: E. General. - 4p.: 30 cm. - 978-0-11-113072-8 £4.25

The Sunderland City Council (Sunderland Strategic Transport Corridor - New Wear Bridge) Scheme 2014 Confirmation Instrument 2015 No. 2015/31. - Enabling power: Highways Act 1980, s. 106 (3). - Issued: 22.011.2015. Made: 12.01.2015. Coming into force: In accord. with s. 1. Effect: None. Territorial extent & classification: E. Local. - 8p., plans: 30 cm. - 978-0-11-112746-9 £6.00

The Swansea to Manchester Trunk Road (A483) and the Newtown to Aberystwyth Trunk Road (A489) (Newtown Bypass and De-Trunking) Order 2015 No. 2015/2016 (W.305). - Enabling power: Highways Act 1980, ss. 10, 12. - Issued: 15.12.2015. Made: 08.12.2015. Coming into force: 18.12.2015. Effect: None. Territorial extent & classification: W. Local. - Available at http://www.legislation.gov.uk/wsi/2015/2016/contents/made. - In English and Welsh. Welsh title: Gorchymyn Cefnffordd Abertawe i Fanceinion (Yr A483) a Chefnffordd y Drenewydd i Aberystwyth (Yr A489) (Ffordd Osgoi'r Drenewydd a Thynnu Statws Cefnffordd) 2015 Non-print

The Traffic Management Act 2004 (Commencement No. 8) (England) Order 2015 No. 2015/199 (C.13). - Enabling power: Traffic Management Act 2004, s. 99. Bringing into operation various provisions of the 2004 Act on 06.04.2015 in accord. with art. 2. - Issued: 18.02.2015. Made: 09.02.2015. Effect: None. Territorial extent & classification: E. General. - 4p.: 30 cm. - 978-0-11-112941-8 £4.25

The Traffic Management (Borough Council of Calderdale) Permit Scheme Order 2015 No. 2015/328. - Enabling power: Traffic Management Act 2004, ss. 34 (4) (5), 39 (2). - Issued: 23.02.2015. Made: 09.02.2015. Coming into force: 31.03.2015. Effect: None. Territorial extent & classification: E. General. - 116p., figs: 30 cm. - 978-0-11-113020-9 £19.00

The Traffic Management (Brighton and Hove City Council) Permit Scheme Order 2015 No. 2015/90. - Enabling power: Traffic Management Act 2004, ss 34 (4) (5), 39 (2). - Issued: 04.02.2015. Made: 21.01.2015. Coming into force: 30.03.2015. Effect: None. Territorial extent & classification: E. General. - 36p.: 30 cm. - 978-0-11-112839-8 £10.00

The Traffic Management (City of Bradford Metropolitan District)) Permit Scheme Order 2015 No. 2015/330. - Enabling power: Traffic Management Act 2004, ss. 34 (4) (5), 39 (2). - Issued: 23.02.2015. Made: 09.02.2015. Coming into force: 31.03.2015. Effect: None. Territorial extent & classification: E. General. - 116p., figs: 30 cm. - 978-0-11-113022-3 £19.00

The Traffic Management (Council of the City of Wakefield MDC) Permit Scheme Order 2015 No. 2015/293. - Enabling power: Traffic Management Act 2004, ss. 34 (4) (5), 39 (2). - Issued: 23.02.2015. Made: 09.02.2015. Coming into force: 31.03.2015. Effect: None. Territorial extent & classification: E. General. - 120p.: 30 cm. - 978-0-11-112990-6 £19.00

The Traffic Management (Derbyshire County Council) Permit Scheme Order 2015 No. 2015/107. - Enabling power: Traffic Management Act 2004, ss 34 (4) (5), 39 (2). - Issued: 04.02.2015. Made: 21.01.2015. Coming into force: 31.03.2015. Effect: None. Territorial extent & classification: E. General. - 28p.: 30 cm. - 978-0-11-112858-9 £6.00

The Traffic Management (Essex County Council) Permit Scheme Order 2015 No. 2015/37. - Enabling power: Traffic Management Act 2004, ss. 34 (4) (5), 39 (2). - Issued: 23.01.2015. Made: 07.01.2015. Coming into force: 16.03.2015. Effect: None. Territorial extent & classification: E. General. - 108p., fig: 30 cm. - 978-0-11-112759-9 £16.50

The Traffic Management (Knowsley Metropolitan Borough Council) Permit Scheme Order 2015 No. 2015/34. - Enabling power: Traffic Management Act 2004, ss. 34 (4) (5), 39 (2). - Issued: 20.01.2015. Made: 07.01.2015. Coming into force: 02.03.2015. Effect: None. Territorial extent & classification: E. General. - 42p.: 30 cm. - 978-0-11-112752-0 £10.00

The Traffic Management (Lancashire County Council) Permit Scheme Order 2015 No. 2015/38. - Enabling power: Traffic Management Act 2004, ss. 34 (4) (5), 39 (2). - Issued: 23.01.2015. Made: 07.01.2015. Coming into force: 09.03.2015. Effect: None. Territorial extent & classification: E. General. - 36p.: 30 cm. - 978-0-11-112760-5 £10.00

The Traffic Management (Milton Keynes Council) Permit Scheme Order 2015 No. 2015/91. - Enabling power: Traffic Management Act 2004, ss. 34 (4) (5), 39 (2). - Issued: 13.02.2015. Made: 21.01.2015. Coming into force: 30.03.2015. Effect: None. Territorial extent & classification: E. Local. - 36p.: 30 cm. - 978-0-11-112840-4 £10.00

The Traffic Management (Nottingham City Council) Permit Scheme Order 2015 No. 2015/39. - Enabling power: Traffic Management Act 2004, ss 34 (4) (5), 39 (2). - Issued: 23.01.2015. Made: 07.01.2015. Coming into force: 16.03.2015. Effect: None. Territorial extent & classification: E. General. - 80p., fig: 30 cm. - 978-0-11-112761-2 £14.25

The Traffic Management Permit Scheme (England) (Amendment) Regulations 2015 No. 2015/958. - Enabling power: Traffic Management Act 2004, ss. 37 (1) to (4), (7) (8) (12). - Issued: 02.04.2015. Made: 26.03.2015. Laid: 27.03.2015. Coming into force: 30.06.2015. Effect: S.I. 2007/3372 amended. Territorial extent & classification: E. General. - 6p.: 30 cm. - 978-0-11-113587-7 £6.00

The Traffic Management (Southampton City Council) Permit Scheme Order 2015 No. 2015/105. - Enabling power: Traffic Management Act 2004, ss 34 (4) (5), 39 (2). - Issued: 04.02.2015. Made: 21.01.2015. Coming into force: 30.03.2015. Effect: None. Territorial extent & classification: E. General. - 36p., fig: 30 cm. - 978-0-11-112853-4 £10.00

The Whitchurch Bridge (Revision of Tolls) Order 2015 No. 2015/1573. - Enabling power: Transport Charges &c. (Miscellaneous Provisions) Act 1954, s. 6. - Issued: 27.07.2015. Made: 23.07.2015. Coming into force: 30.07.2015. Effect: S.I. 2009/2729 revoked. Territorial extent & classification: E. Local. - Available at http://www.legislation.gov.uk/uksi/2015/1573/contents/made Unpublished

The Whitney-on-Wye Bridge (Revision of Tolls) Order 2015 No. 2015/1404. - Enabling power: Transport Charges & c. (Miscellaneous Provisions) Act 1954. - Issued: 29.06.2015. Made: 22.06.2015. Coming into force: 29.06.2015. Effect: S.I. 2009/2817 revoked. Territorial extent & classification: E. Local. - 2p.: 30 cm. - 978-0-11-113701-7 £4.25

The Worcestershire County Council (Hoobrook Bridge) Scheme 2014 Confirmation Instrument 2015 No. 2015/1124. - Enabling power: Highways Act 1980, s. 106 (3). - Issued: 27.04.2015. Made: 25.03.2015. Coming into force: In accord. with art. 1. Effect: None. Territorial extent & classification: E. Local. - 8p., plans: 30 cm. - 978-0-11-113636-2 £6.00

Housing

The Rent Officers (Housing Benefit and Universal Credit Functions) (Local Housing Allowance Amendments) Order 2015 No. 2015/1753. - Enabling power: Housing Act 1996, ss. 122 (1) (6). - Issued: 13.10.2015. Made: 07.10.2015. Laid: 12.10.2015. Coming into force: 02.11.2015. Effect: S.I. 1997/1984, 1995; 2013/382 amended. Territorial extent & classification: E/W/S. General. - 4p.: 30 cm. - 978-0-11-113962-2 £4.25

Housing, England

The Allocation of Housing (Qualification Criteria for Right to Move) (England) Regulations 2015 No. 2015/967. - Enabling power: Housing Act 1996, ss. 160ZA (8) (b), 172 (4). - Issued: 02.04.2015. Made: 26.03.2015. Laid: 27.03.2015. Coming into force: 20.04.2015. Effect: None. Territorial extent & classification: E. General. - 4p.: 30 cm. - 978-0-11-113601-0 £4.25

The Housing (Right to Buy) (Prescribed Forms) (Amendment) (England) Order 2015 No. 2015/1542. - Enabling power: Housing Act 1985, s. 176 (1) (5). - Issued: 23.07.2015. Made: 16.07.2015. Laid: 20.07.2015. Coming into force: 17.08.2015. Effect: S.I. 1986/2194 amended & S.I. 2005/2876; 2007/784; 2014/1797 revoked with savings. Territorial extent & classification: E. General. - 20p.: 30 cm. - 978-0-11-113817-5 £6.00

The Housing (Tenancy Deposits) (Specified Interest Rate) (Revocation) (England) Order 2015 No. 2015/14. - Enabling power: Housing Act 2004, sch. 10, para. 3 (5) (b). - Issued: 14.01.2015. Made: 05.01.2015. Coming into force: 04.02.2015. Effect: S.I. 2007/798 revoked. Territorial extent & classification: E. General. - 2p.: 30 cm. - 978-0-11-112685-1 £4.25

The Selective Licensing of Houses (Additional Conditions) (England) Order 2015 No. 2015/977. - Enabling power: Housing Act 2004, ss. 80 (7) (8), 250 (2). - Issued: 02.04.2015. Made: 26.03.2015. Coming into force: In accord with art. 1. Effect: None. Territorial extent & classification: E. General. - Supersedes draft SI (ISBN 9780111131435) issued 09/03/15 - 4p.: 30 cm. - 978-0-11-113610-2 £4.25

The Smoke and Carbon Monoxide Alarm (England) Regulations 2015 No. 2015/1693. - Enabling power: Energy Act 2013, ss. 150 (1) to (6) (10) & Housing Act 2004, sch. 4, para. 3 (a). - Issued: 23.09.2015. Made: 17.09.2015. Coming into force: In accord. with reg. 1 (1). Effect: 2004 c.34 amended. Territorial extent & classification: E. General. - Supersedes draft S.I. (ISBN 9780111133439) issued 19/03/15. - 12p.: 30 cm. - 978-0-11-113933-2 £6.00

Housing, England and Wales

The Anti-social Behaviour, Crime and Policing Act 2014 (Commencement No. 8, Saving and Transitional Provisions) Order 2015 No. 2015/373 (C.19). - Enabling power: Anti-social Behaviour, Crime and Policing Act 2014, s. 185 (1) (7). Bringing into operation various provisions of the 2014 Act on 08.03.2015; 23.03.2015; 08.04.2015, in accord. with arts 2, 3, 4, 5. - Issued: 02.03.2015. Made: 24.02.2015. Effect: None. Territorial extent & classification: E/W/S/NI. General. - 8p.: 30 cm. - 978-0-11-113065-0 £6.00

Housing, Wales

The Anti-social Behaviour, Crime and Policing Act 2014 (Consequential Amendments) (Wales) Order 2015 No. 2015/1321 (W.119). - Enabling power: Anti-social Behaviour, Crime and Policing Act 2014, s. 181 (4) (a). - Issued: 18.05.2015. Made: 12.05.2015. Coming into force: 19.05.2015. Effect: 1996 c.52 amended. Territorial extent & classification: W. General. - In English and Welsh. Welsh title: Gorchymyn Deddf Ymddygiad Gwrthgymdeithasol, Troseddu a Phlismona 2014 (Diwygiadau Canlyniadol) (Cymru) 2015. - 4p.: 30 cm. - 978-0-348-11098-2 £4.25

The Code of Practice for Landlords and Agents licensed under Part 1 of the Housing (Wales) Act 2014 (Appointed Date) Order 2015 No. 2015/1932 (W.290). - Enabling power: Housing (Wales) Act 2014, s. 40 (7). Appointing 23.11.2015 as the coming into force date of the 2014 Code of Practice. - Issued: 01.12.2015. Made: 18.11.2015. Effect: None. Territorial extent & classification: W. General. - In English and Welsh: Welsh title: Gorchymyn Cod Ymarfer Landlordiaid ac Asiantau sydd wedi'u trwyddedu o dan Ran 1 o Ddeddf Tai (Cymru) 2014 (Dyddiad Penodedig) 2015. - 4p.: 30 cm. - 978-0-348-11196-5 £4.25

The Consumer Rights Act 2015 (Commencement No. 3) (Wales) Order 2015 No. 2015/1904 (W.276)(C.117). - Enabling power: Consumer Rights Act 2015, s. 100 (3) (b). Bringing various provisions of the 2015 Act into operation on 23.11.2015 in accord. with arts 2, 3. - Issued: 01.12.2015. Made: 11.11.2015. Effect: WSI. 2015/1831 (W.267) (C.115) revoked. Territorial extent & classification: W. General. - In English and Welsh. Welsh title: Gorchymyn Deddf Hawliau Defnyddwyr 2015 (Cychwyn Rhif 3) (Cymru) 2015. - 4p.: 30 cm. - 978-0-348-11193-4 £4.25

The Homelessness (Intentionality) (Specified Categories) (Wales) Order 2015 No. 2015/1265 (W.85). - Enabling power: Housing (Wales) Act 2014, ss. 78 (1), 142 (2). - Issued: 13.05.2015. Made: 21.04.2015. Coming into force: 27.04.2015. Effect: None. Territorial extent & classification: W. General. - In English and Welsh. Welsh title: Rheoliadau Digartrefedd (Bwriadoldeb) (Categorïau Penodedig) (Cymru) 2015. - 8p.: 30 cm. - 978-0-348-11094-4 £6.00

The Homelessness (Review Procedure) (Wales) Regulations 2015 No. 2015/1266 (W.86). - Enabling power: Housing (Wales) Act 2014, ss. 86 (1) (2), 142 (2) (c). - Issued: 13.05.2015. Made: 21.04.2015. Coming into force: 27.04.2015. Effect: S.I. 1996/3122; 1997/631, 2046; 1999/71 revoked in relation to Wales. Territorial extent & classification: W. General. - In English and Welsh. Welsh title: Rheoliadau Digartrefedd (Gweithdrefn Adolygu) (Cymru) 2015. - 8p.: 30 cm. - 978-0-348-11095-1 £6.00

The Homelessness (Suitability of Accommodation) (Wales) Order 2015 No. 2015/1268 (W.87). - Enabling power: Housing (Wales) Act 2014, ss. 59 (3), 142 (2). - Issued: 07.05.2015. Made: 21.04.2015. Coming into force: 27.04.2015. Effect: S.I. 1996/3204; 1997/1741; WSI 2006/650(W.71) revoked with saving. Territorial extent & classification: W. General. - In English and Welsh. Welsh title: Gorchymyn Digartrefedd (Addasrwydd Llety) (Cymru) 2015. - 16p.: 30 cm. - 978-0-348-11090-6 £6.00

The Home Loss Payments (Prescribed Amounts) (Wales) Regulations 2015 No. 2015/1878 (W.275). - Enabling power: Land Compensation Act 1973, s. 30 (5). - Issued: 18.11.2015. Made: 09.11.2015. Laid before the National Assembly for Wales: 13.11.2015. Coming into force: 10.12.2015. Effect: S.I. 2008/2845 (W.255) revoked with savings. Territorial extent & classification: W. General. - In English and Welsh. Welsh title: Rheoliadau Taliadau Colli Cartref (Symiau Rhagnodedig) (Cymru) 2015. - 4p.: 30 cm. - 978-0-348-11190-3 £4.25

The Housing (Right to Buy and Right to Acquire) (Limits on Discount) (Amendment) (Wales) Order 2015 No. 2015/1349 (W.130). - Enabling power: Housing Act 1985, s. 131 (2) & Housing Act 1996, s. 17 (1) (a). - Issued: 26.06.2015. Made: 01.06.2015. Laid before the National Assembly for Wales: 04.06.2015. Coming into force: 14.07.2015. Effect: S.I. 1997/569; 1999/292 amended & S.I. 2003/803 (W.97) revoked. Territorial extent & classification: W. General. - In English and Welsh. Welsh title: Gorchymyn Tai (Hawl i Brynu a Hawl i Gaffael) (Terfynau'r Disgownt) (Diwygio) (Cymru) 2015. - 4p.: 30 cm. - 978-0-348-11116-3 £4.25

The Housing (Right to Buy) (Prescribed Forms) (Wales) (Amendment) Regulations 2015 No. 2015/1795 (W.255). - Enabling power: Housing Act 1985, s. 176 (1) (5). - Issued: 27.10.2015. Made: 12.10.2015. Coming into force: 19.10.2015. Effect: WSI. 2015/1320 (W.118) amended. Territorial extent & classification: W. General. - In English and Welsh. Welsh title: Rheoliadau Tai (Hawl i Brynu) (Ffurflenni Rhagnodedig) (Cymru) (Diwygio) 2015. - 4p.: 30 cm. - 978-0-348-11173-6 £4.25

The Housing (Right to Buy) (Prescribed Forms) (Wales) Regulations 2015 No. 2015/1320 (W.118). - Enabling power: Housing Act 1985, s. 176 (1) (5). - Issued: 12.08.2015. Made: 20.01.2015. Coming into force: 22.01.2015. Effect: S.I. 1986/2194; 1989/239, 240; 1992/1707; 1993/2245, 2246; 1994/2931, 2932; 1996/2652 revoked with savings in relation to Wales. Territorial extent & classification: W. General. - In English and Welsh. Welsh title: Rheoliadau Tai (Hawl i Brynu) (Ffurflenni Rhagnodedig) (Cymru) 2015. - 88p.: 30 cm. - 978-0-348-11097-5 £16.00

The Housing (Wales) Act 2014 (Commencement No. 2) Order 2015 No. 2015/380 (W.39)(C.21). - Enabling power: Housing (Wales) Act 2014, s. 145 (3). Bringing into operation various provisions of the 2014 Act on 25.02.2015, in accord. with art. 2. - Issued: 05.03.2015. Made: 23.02.2015. Effect: None. Territorial extent & classification: W. General. - In English and Welsh. Welsh title: Gorchymyn Deddf Tai (Cymru) 2014 (Cychwyn Rhif 2) 2015. - 8p.: 30 cm. - 978-0-348-11049-4 £6.00

The Housing (Wales) Act 2014 (Commencement No. 3 and Transitory, Transitional and Saving Provisions) Order 2015 No. 2015/1272 (W.88)(C.73). - Enabling power: Housing (Wales) Act 2014, s. 145 (3) (4). Bringing into operation various provisions of the 2014 Act on 27.04.2015; 01.07.2015 in accord. with arts 4, 5, 6, 7, 8. - Issued: 05.05.2015. Made: 21.04.2015. Effect: None. Territorial extent & classification: W. General. - In English and Welsh. Welsh title: Gorchymyn Deddf Tai (Cymru) 2014 (Cychwyn Rhif 3 a Darpariaethau Darfodol a Throsiannol a Darapraiethau Arbed) 2015. - 12p.: 30 cm. - 978-0-348-11089-0 £6.00

The Housing (Wales) Act 2014 (Commencement No. 4) Order 2015 No. 2015/1826 (W.266)(C.114). - Enabling power: Housing (Wales) Act 2014, s. 145 (3). Bringing into operation various provisions of the 2014 Act on 23.11.2015 in accord. with art. 2. - Issued: 29.10.2015. Made: 21.10.2015. Effect: None. Territorial extent & classification: W. General. - In English and Welsh. Welsh title: Gorchymyn Deddf Tai (Cymru) 2014 (Cychwyn Rhif 4) 2015. - 8p.: 30 cm. - 978-0-348-11176-7 £6.00

The Housing (Wales) Act 2014 (Commencement No. 5) Order 2015 No. 2015/2046 (W.310) (C.127). - Enabling power: Housing (Wales) Act 2014, s. 145 (3) (4). Bringing into operation various provisions of the 2014 Act on 16.12.2015; 01.04.2016. - Issued: 22.12.2015. Made: 15.12.2015. Effect: None. Territorial extent & classification: W. General. - In English and Welsh. Welsh title: Gorchymyn Deddf Tai (Cymru) 2014 (Cychwyn Rhif 5) 2015. - 12p.: 30 cm. - 978-0-348-11207-8 £6.00

The Housing (Wales) Act 2014 (Consequential Amendments) Regulations 2015 No. 2015/752 (W.59). - Enabling power: Housing (Wales) Act 2014, s. 144 (1) (2). - Issued: 24.03.2015. Made: 16.03.2015. Laid: 18.03.2015. Coming into force: 27.04.2015. Effect: S.I. 1996/3205 amended. Territorial extent & classification: W. General. - In English and Welsh. Welsh title: Rheoliadau Deddf Tai (Cymru) 2014 (Diwygiadau Canlyniadol) 2015. - 4p.: 30 cm. - 978-0-348-11058-6 £4.25

The Regulation of Private Rented Housing (Designation of Licensing Authority) (Wales) Order 2015 No. 2015/1026 (W.75). - Enabling power: Housing (Wales) Act 2014, s. 3 (1) (a). - Issued: 24.04.2015. Made: 25.03.2015. Coming into force: 01.04.2015. Effect: None. Territorial extent & classification: W. General. - In English and Welsh. Welsh title: Gorhymyn Rheoleiddio Tai Rhent Preifat (Dynodi Awdurdod Trwyddedu) (Cymru) 2015. - 4p.: 30 cm. - 978-0-348-11074-6 £4.25

The Regulation of Private Rented Housing (Information, Periods and Fees for Registration and Licensing) (Wales) Regulations 2015 No. 2015/1368 (W.136). - Enabling power: Housing (Wales) Act 2014, ss. 15 (1) (4), 16 (1) (e), 19 (1) (b) (d), 21 (4), 23 (1) (b), 46, 142 (2). - Issued: 23.06.2015. Made: 07.06.2015. Laid: 12.06.2015. Coming into force: 07.07.2015. Effect: None. Territorial extent & classification: W. General. - In English and Welsh. Welsh title: Rheoliadau Rheoleiddio Tai Rhent Preifat (Gwybodaeth, Cyfnodau a Ffioedd ar gyfer Cofrestru a Thrwyddedu) (Cymru) 2015. - 8p.: 30 cm. - 978-0-348-11109-5 £6.00

The Regulation of Private Rented Housing (Training Requirements) (Wales) Regulations 2015 No. 2015/1366 (W.134). - Enabling power: Housing (Wales) Act 2014, ss. 19 (2) (b) (3), 46, 142. - Issued: 23.06.2015. Made: 02.06.2015. Coming into force: 03.06.2015. Effect: None. Territorial extent & classification: W. General. - In English and Welsh. Welsh title: Rheoliadau Rheoleiddio Tai Rhent Preifat (Gofynion Hyfforddi) (Cymru) 2015. - 12p.: 30 cm. - 978-0-348-11110-1 £6.00

The Residential Property Tribunal Procedures and Fees (Wales) (Amendment) Regulations 2015 No. 2015/1821 (W.263). - Enabling power: Housing Act 2004, s. 250 (2), sch. 13. - Issued: 06.11.2015. Made: 21.10.2015. Laid before the National Assembly for Wales: 04.11.2015. Coming into force: 23.11.2015. Effect: S.I. 2012/531 (W.83) amended. Territorial extent & classification: W. General. - In English and Welsh. Welsh title: Rheoliadau Gweithdrefnau a Ffioedd Tribiwnlys Eiddo Preswyl (Cymru) (Diwygio Rhif 2) 2015. - 8p.: 30 cm. - 978-0-348-11179-8 £6.00

The Small Business, Enterprise and Employment Act 2015 (Commencement No. 1) (Wales) Regulations 2015 No. 2015/1710 (W.225) (C.103). - Enabling power: Small Business, Enterprise and Employment Act 2015, s. 164 (5). Bringing various provisions of the 2015 Act into operation on 01.10.2015 in accord. with art. 2. - Issued: 01.10.2015. Made: 21.09.2015. Effect: None. Territorial extent & classification: W. General. - In English and Welsh. Welsh title: Rheoliadau Deddf Busnesau Bach, Menter a Chyflogaeth 2015 (Cychwyn) (Cymru) 2015. - 4p.: 30 cm. - 978-0-348-11158-3 £4.25

Human fertilisation and embryology

The Human Fertilisation and Embryology (Mitochondrial Donation) Regulations 2015 No. 2015/572. - Enabling power: Human Fertilisation and Embryology Act 1990, ss. 3ZA (5) (6), 31ZA (2) (a), 35A, 45 (1) (3A). - Issued: 12.03.2015. Made: 04.03.15. Coming into force: 29.10.2015. Effect: 1990 c.37; 2008 c.22; S.I. 2004/1511 amended Territorial extent & classification: E/W/S/NI. General. - Supersedes draft S.I. (ISBN 9780111125816) issued 22/12/14. - 8p.: 30 cm. - 978-0-11-113240-1 £6.00

Human tissue, England and Wales

The Human Transplantation (Wales) Act 2013 (Consequential Provision) Order 2015 No. 2015/865. - Enabling power: Government of Wales Act 2006, ss. 150 (1) (2), 157 (2). - Issued: 27.03.2015. Made: 23.03.2015. Coming into force: In accord. with art. 1 (2). Effect: 2004 c. 30; S.I. 2012/1501 amended. Territorial extent & classification: E/W/S/NI. General. - Supersedes draft S.I. (ISBN 9780111127544) issued 23/01/15. - 4p.: 30 cm. - 978-0-11-113489-4 £4.25

Human tissue, Northern Ireland

The Human Transplantation (Wales) Act 2013 (Consequential Provision) Order 2015 No. 2015/865. - Enabling power: Government of Wales Act 2006, ss. 150 (1) (2), 157 (2). - Issued: 27.03.2015. Made: 23.03.2015. Coming into force: In accord. with art. 1 (2). Effect: 2004 c. 30; S.I. 2012/1501 amended. Territorial extent & classification: E/W/S/NI. General. - Supersedes draft S.I. (ISBN 9780111127544) issued 23/01/15. - 4p.: 30 cm. - 978-0-11-113489-4 £4.25

Human tissue, Wales

The Human Transplantation (Appointed Representatives) (Wales) Regulations 2015 No. 2015/1760 (W.244). - Enabling power: Human Transplantation (Wales) Act 2013, ss. 8 (10) (b), 20 (1) (2). - Issued: 15.10.2015. Made: 07.10.2015. Coming into force: 01.12.2015. Effect: None. Territorial extent & classification: W. General. - In English and Welsh. Welsh title: Rheoliadau Trawsblannu Dynol (Cynrychiolwyr Penodedig) (Cymru) 2015. - 4p.: 30 cm. - 978-0-348-11162-0 £4.25

The Human Transplantation (Excluded Relevant Material) (Wales) Regulations 2015 No. 2015/1775 (W.247). - Enabling power: Human Transplantation (Wales) Act 2013, ss. 7 (2), 20 (1) (2). - Issued: 15.10.2015. Made: 07.10.2015. Coming into force: 01.12.2015, at 00.01. Effect: None. Territorial extent & classification: W. General. - In English and Welsh. Welsh title: Rheoliadau Trawsblannu Dynol (Deunydd Perthnasol a Eithrir) (Cymru) 2015. - 4p.: 30 cm. - 978-0-348-11163-7 £4.25

The Human Transplantation (Persons who Lack Capacity to Consent) (Wales) Regulations 2015 No. 2015/1774 (W.246). - Enabling power: Human Transplantation (Wales) Act 2013, ss. 9 (2), 20 (1) (2). - Issued: 15.10.2015. Made: 07.10.2015. Coming into force: 01.12.2015, at 00.01. Effect: None. Territorial extent & classification: W. General. - In English and Welsh. Welsh title: Rheoliadau Trawsblannu Dynol (Personau nad yw'r Galluedd ganddynt i Gydsynio) (Cymru) 2015. - 4p.: 30 cm. - 978-0-348-11164-4 £4.25

The Human Transplantation (Wales) Act 2013 (Commencement) Order 2015 No. 2015/1679 (W.216)(C.96). - Enabling power: Human Transplantation (Wales) Act 2013, ss. 21 (1) (2) (5). Bringing into operation various provisions of the 2013 Act on 12.09.2015; 01.12.2015, in accord with arts 2 & 3. - Issued: 22.09.2015. Made: 09.09.2015. Effect: None. Territorial extent & classification: W. General. - In English and Welsh. Welsh title: Gorchymyn Deddf Trawsblannu Dynol (Cymru) 2013 (Cychwyn) 2015. - 4p.: 30 cm. - 978-0-348-11152-1 £4.25

Immigration

The Asylum Support (Amendment No. 2) Regulations 2015 No. 2015/944. - Enabling power: Immigration and Asylum Act 1999, ss. 95 (12), 166 (3), 167 (1), sch. 8 paras 1, 3 (a). - Issued: 02.04.2015. Made: 26.03.2015. Laid: 27.03.2015. Coming into force: 06.04.2015. Effect: S.I. 2000/704 amended & S.I. 2011/907; 2015/645 revoked. Territorial extent & classification: E/W/S/NI. General. - Revoked by S.I. 2015/944 (ISBN 9780111137765). - 2p.: 30 cm. - 978-0-11-113569-3 £4.25

The Asylum Support (Amendment No. 3) Regulations 2015 No. 2015/1501. - Enabling power: Immigration and Asylum Act 1999, ss. 95 (12), 166 (3), 167 (1), sch. 8 paras 1, 3 (a). - Issued: 16.07.2015. Made: 08.07.2015. Laid: 16.07.2015. Coming into force: 10.08.2015. Effect: S.I. 2015/944 revoked. Territorial extent & classification: E/W/S/NI. General. - 2p.: 30 cm. - 978-0-11-113776-5 £4.25

The Asylum Support (Amendment) Regulations 2015 No. 2015/645. - Enabling power: Immigration and Asylum Act 1999, ss. 95 (12), 166 (3), 167 (1), sch. 8 paras 1, 3 (a). - Issued: 16.03.2015. Made: 05.03.2015. Laid: 12.03.2015. Coming into force: 06.04.2015. Effect: S.I. 2011/907 revoked. Territorial extent & classification: E/W/S/NI. General. - 2p.: 30 cm. - 978-0-11-113303-3 £4.25

The Authority to Carry Scheme (Civil Penalties) Regulations 2015 No. 2015/957. - Enabling power: Counter-Terrorism and Security Act 2015, s. 24. - Issued: 01.04.2015. Made: 24.03.2015. Coming into force: 31.03.2015. Effect: None. Territorial extent & classification: E/W/S/NI. General. - Supersedes draft SI (ISBN 9780111130940) issued 05/03/15. - 8p.: 30 cm. - 978-0-11-113586-0 £4.25

The Channel Tunnel (International Arrangements) and Channel Tunnel (Miscellaneous Provisions) (Amendment) Order 2015 No. 2015/856. - Enabling power: Channel Tunnel Act 1987, s. 11. - Issued: 30.03.2015. Made: 23.03.2015. Laid: 25.03.20154. Coming into force: 16.04.2015. Effect: S.I. 1993/1813; 1997/1405 amended. Territorial extent & classification: E/W/S/NI. General. - 4p.: 30 cm. - 978-0-11-113479-5 £4.25

The Counter-Terrorism and Security Act 2015 (Authority to Carry Scheme) Regulations 2015 No. 2015/997. - Enabling power: Counter-Terrorism Act 2015, s. 23 (1). - Issued: 07.04.2015. Made: 24.03.2015. Coming into force: 31.03.2015. Effect: None. Territorial extent & classification: E/W/S/NI. General. - Supersedes draft SI (ISBN 9780111130933) issued 05/03/15 - 2p.: 30 cm. - 978-0-11-113627-0 £4.25

The Immigration Act 2014 (Commencement No. 4, Transitional and Saving Provisions and Amendment) Order 2015 No. 2015/371 (C.18). - Enabling power: Immigration Act 2014, ss. 73 (1), 75 (3). Bringing into operation various provisions of the 2014 Act on 01.03.2015, 02.03.2015, 06.04.2015 in accord. with arts 2 to 8. - Issued: 04.03.2015. Made: 25.02.2015. Effect: S.I. 2014/2771 amended & S.I. 2014/2928 revoked. Territorial extent & classification: E/W/S/NI. General. - 8p.: 30 cm. - 978-0-11-113073-5 £6.00

The Immigration Act 2014 (Commencement No. 5) Order 2015 No. 2015/874 (C.54). - Enabling power: Immigration Act 2014, ss. 73 (1), 75 (3). Bringing into operation various provisions of the 2014 Act on 06.04.2015, in accord. with art 2. - Issued: 30.03.2015. Made: 23.03.2015. Effect: None. Territorial extent & classification: E/W/S/NI. General. - 4p.: 30 cm. - 978-0-11-113497-9 £4.25

The Immigration and Nationality (Fees) (Amendment) Regulations 2015 No. 2015/1424. - Enabling power: Immigration Act 2014, ss. 68 (1) (10) (12), 69 (1). - Issued: 02.07.2015. Made: 25.06.2015. Laid: 26.06.2015. Coming into force: 27.06.2015 in accord. with reg. 1. Effect: S.I. 2015/768 amended. Territorial extent & classification: E/W/S/NI/CI. General. - This S.I. has been made in consequence of a defect in S.I. 2015/768 (ISBN 9780111133941) published on 24/03/15 and is being issued to all known recipients of that S.I. free of charge. - 4p.: 30 cm. - 978-0-11-113720-8 £4.25

The Immigration and Nationality (Fees) Order 2015 No. 2015/746. - Enabling power: Immigration Act 2014, ss. 68 (1) to (6) (12), 69 (1) (2), 74 (8) (a) (b) (d). - Issued: 23.03.2015. Made: 17.03.2015. Coming into force: In accord. with art. 1. Effect: None. Territorial extent & classification: E/W/S/NI. General. - Supersedes draft S.I. (ISBN 9780111128459) issued 06/02/15. Revoked with saving by S.I. 2016/177 (ISBN 9780111143780). - 8p.: 30 cm. - 978-0-11-113379-8 £6.00

The Immigration and Nationality (Fees) Regulations 2015 No. 2015/768. - Enabling power: Immigration Act 2014, ss. 68 (1) (7) (8) (10) (12), 69 (1) (2), 74 (8) (a) (b) (d). - Issued: 24.03.2015. Made: 18.03.2015. Laid: 19.03.2015. Coming into force: 06.04.2015. Effect: None. Territorial extent & classification: E/W/S/NI/CI. General. - Corrected by S.I. 2015/1424 (ISBN 9780111137208) which issued free of charge to all known recipients of this S.I. - 36p.: 30 cm. - 978-0-11-113394-1 £10.00

The Immigration and Police (Passenger, Crew and Service Information) (Amendment) Order 2015 No. 2015/859. - Enabling power: Immigration Act 1971, sch. 2, paras 27 (2), 27B & Immigration, Asylum and Nationality Act 2006, s. 32. - Issued: 30.03.2015. Made: 19.03.2015. Laid: 25.03.2015. Coming into force: 15.04.2015. Effect: S.I. 2008/5 amended. Territorial extent & classification: E/W/S/NI. General. - 4p.: 30 cm. - 978-0-11-113481-8 £4.25

The Immigration (Appeals) (Consequential Amendments and Saving Provisions) Order 2015 No. 2015/383. - Enabling power: Immigration Act 2014, s. 73 (2) (3), 74 (8). - Issued: 03.03.2015. Made: 25.02.2015. Laid: 26.02.2015. Coming into force: 06.04.2015. Effect: S.I. 2007/3187; 2009/275; 2010/782 amended. Territorial extent & classification: E/W/S/NI. General. - 4p.: 30 cm. - 978-0-11-113071-1 £4.25

The Immigration (Biometric Registration) (Amendment) (No. 2) Regulations 2015 No. 2015/897. - Enabling power: UK Borders Act 2007, ss. 5 (1) (a) (2) (a), 6 (6) (a) (b) (c). - Issued: 01.04.2015. Made: 24.03.2015. Coming into force: In accord. with reg. 1 (2). Effect: S.I. 2008/3048 amended. Territorial extent & classification: E/W/S/NI. - Supersedes draft S.I. (ISBN 9780111125809) issued 22/12/14. - 4p.: 30 cm. - 978-0-11-113559-4 £4.25

The Immigration (Biometric Registration) (Amendment) Regulations 2015 No. 2015/433. - Enabling power: UK Borders Act 2007, ss. 5, 6 (6) (a) (b) (c), 7, 8, 15 (1) (g). - Issued: 09.03.2015. Made: 25.02.2015. Coming into force: In accord. with reg. 1 (1). Effect: S.I. 2008/3048 amended. Territorial extent & classification: E/W/S/NI. General. - Supersedes draft S.I. (ISBN 9780111127513) issued 23/01/15. - 12p.: 30 cm. - 978-0-11-113164-0 £6.00

The Immigration (Biometric Registration) (Civil Penalty Code of Practice) Order 2015 No. 2015/565. - Enabling power: UK Borders Act 2007, ss. 13 (6), 14 (1) (2). Bringing into operation various provisions of the 'Code of practice about sanctions for non-compliance with the biometric registration regulations' on 31.03.2015. - Issued: 12.03.2015. Made: 04.03.2015. Laid: 09.03.2015. Coming into force: 31.03.2015. Effect: None. Territorial extent & classification: E/W/S/NI. General. - 2p.: 30 cm. - 978-0-11-113235-7 £4.25

The Immigration (Biometric Registration) (Objection to Civil Penalty) (Amendment) Order 2015 No. 2015/564. - Enabling power: UK Borders Act 2007, ss. 10, 14 (1) (2) (a). - Issued: 12.03.2015. Made: 04.03.2015. Laid: 09.03.2015. Coming into force: 31.03.2015. Effect: S.I. 2008/2830 amended. Territorial extent & classification: E/W/S/NI. General. - 8p.: 30 cm. - 978-0-11-113233-3 £6.00

The Immigration (Designation of Travel Bans) (Amendment No. 2) Order 2015 No. 2015/1994. - Enabling power: Immigration Act 1971, s. 8B (5). - Issued: 15.12.2015. Made: 07.12.2015. Laid: 10.12.2015. Coming into force: 21.12.2015. Effect: S.I. 2015/388 revoked. Territorial extent & classification: E/W/S/NI. General. - 12p.: 30 cm. - 978-0-11-114175-5 £6.00

The Immigration (Designation of Travel Bans) (Amendment) Order 2015 No. 2015/388. - Enabling power: Immigration Act 1971, s. 8B (5). - Issued: 04.03.2015. Made: 25.02.2015. Laid: 27.02.2015. Coming into force: 06.03.2015. Effect: S.I. 2000/2724 amended & S.I. 2014/1849 revoked. Territorial extent & classification: E/W/S/NI. General. - Revoked by SI 2015/1994 (ISBN 9780111141755). - 12p.: 30 cm. - 978-0-11-113075-9 £6.00

The Immigration (European Economic Area) (Amendment) Regulations 2015 No. 2015/694. - Enabling power: European Communities Act 1972, s. 2 (2) & Nationality, Immigration and Asylum Act 2002, s. 109 & European Union (Croatian Accession and Irish Protocol) Act 2013, s. 4. - Issued: 19.03.2015. Made: 12.03.2015. Laid: 16.03.2015. Coming into force: 06.04.2015. Effect: S.I. 2006/1003; 2013/1460 amended. Territorial extent & classification: E/W/S/NI. General. - 12p.: 30 cm. - 978-0-11-113348-4 £6.00

The Immigration (Exemption from Control) (Amendment) Order 2015 No. 2015/1866. - Enabling power: Immigration Act 1971, s. 8 (2). - Issued: 11.11.2015. Made: 04.11.2015. Laid: 06.11.2015. Coming into force: 28.11.2015. Effect: S.I. 1972/1613 amended. Territorial extent & classification: E/W/S/NI. General. - 4p.: 30 cm. - 978-0-11-114064-2 £4.25

The Immigration (Guernsey) Order 2015 No. 2015/1533. - Enabling power: Immigration Act 2014, s. 76 (6) & Immigration, Asylum and Nationality Act 2006, s. 63 (3). - Issued: 22.07.2015. Made: 15.07.2015. Coming into force: In accord. with art. 1. Effect: 2006 c.13; 2014 c.22 modified. Territorial extent & classification: Guernsey. General. - 4p.: 30 cm. - 978-0-11-113810-6 £4.25

The Immigration (Health Charge) Order 2015 No. 2015/792. - Enabling power: Immigration Act 2014, ss. 38, 74 (8). - Issued: 25.03.2015. Made: 16.03.2015. Coming into force: 06.04.2015. Effect: None. Territorial extent & classification: E/W/S/NI. General. - Supersedes draft SI (ISBN 9780111128473) issued 06/02/15 - 8p.: 30 cm. - 978-0-11-113413-9 £6.00

The Immigration (Isle of Man) (Amendment) Order 2015 No. 2015/1765. - Enabling power: Immigration, Asylum and Nationality Act 2006, s. 63 (3) (3A) & Immigration Act 2014, s. 76 (6). - Issued: 15.10.2015. Made: 08.10.2015. Coming into force: In accord. with art. 1 (2). Effect: 2014 c.22 modified & amended & S.I. 2008/680 amended. Territorial extent & classification: E/W/S/NI. General. - 8p.: 30 cm. - 978-0-11-113971-4 £6.00

The Immigration (Jersey) Order 2015 No. 2015/1532. - Enabling power: Immigration, Asylum and Nationality Act 2006, s. 63 (3) & Immigration Act 2014, s. 76 (6). - Issued: 22.07.2012. Made: 15.07.2015. Coming into force: In accord. with art. 1. Effect: 2006 c. 13; 2014 c.22 modified. Territorial extent & classification: Jersey. General. - 4p.: 30 cm. - 978-0-11-113809-0 £4.25

The Immigration (Leave to Enter and Remain) (Amendment) Order 2015 No. 2015/434. - Enabling power: Immigration Act 1971, ss. 3A (1) (2) (3) (4) (10), 3B (1) (2) (3). - Issued: 09.03.2015. Made: 25.02.2015. Coming into force: In accord. with art. 1 (1). Effect: S.I. 2000/1161 amended. Territorial extent & classification: E/W/S/NI. General. - Supersedes draft S.I. (ISBN 9780111127506) issued 23.01.2015. - 4p.: 30 cm. - 978-0-11-113163-3 £4.25

The Immigration (Passenger Transit Visa) (Amendment) (No. 2) Order 2015 No. 2015/1534. - Enabling power: Immigration and Asylum Act 1999, s. 41. - Issued: 22.07.2015. Made: 15.07.2015. Laid: 20.07.2015. Coming into force: 10.08.2015. Effect: S.I. 2014/2702 amended. Territorial extent & classification: E/W/S/NI. General. - 2p.: 30 cm. - 978-0-11-113811-3 £4.25

The Immigration (Passenger Transit Visa) (Amendment) Order 2015 No. 2015/657. - Enabling power: Immigration and Asylum Act 1999, s. 41. - Issued: 17.03.2015. Made: 10.03.2015. Laid: 16.03.2015. Coming into force: arts 1, 2 (1) and (13) 17.03.2015; remainder 24.04.2015. Effect: S.I. 2014/2702 amended. Territorial extent & classification: E/W/S/NI. General. - 4p.: 30 cm. - 978-0-11-113314-9 £4.25

The Immigration (Provision of Physical Data) (Amendment) Regulations 2015 No. 2015/737. - Enabling power: Nationality, Immigration and Asylum Act 2002, s. 126. - Issued: 24.03.2015. Made: 16.03.2015. Coming into force: In accord. with reg. 1 (1). Effect: S.I. 2006/1743 amended. Territorial extent & classification: E/W/S/NI. General. - Supersedes draft S.I. (ISBN 9780111125878) issued 22/12/14. - 8p.: 30 cm. - 978-0-11-113385-9 £4.25

The Immigration (Variation of Leave) (Revocation) Order 2015 No. 2015/863. - Enabling power: Immigration Act 1971, ss. 3 (3) (a), 4 (1), 32 (1). - Issued: 30.03.2015. Made: 23.03.2015. Coming into force: 20.04.2015. Effect: S.I. 1976/1572; 1989/1005; 1991/980, 1083; 1993/1657; 2000/2445 revoked. Territorial extent & classification: UK. General. - 2p.: 30 cm. - 978-0-11-113487-0 £4.25

The Passenger, Crew and Service Information (Civil Penalties) Regulations 2015 No. 2015/961. - Enabling power: Immigration Act 1971, sch. 2, para. 27BB & Immigration, Asylum and Nationality Act 2006, s. 32B. - Issued: 01.04.2015. Made: 24.03.2015. Coming into force: 31.03.2015. Effect: None. Territorial extent & classification: E/W/S/NI. General. - Supersedes draft SI (ISBN 9780111130971) issued 08/03/15. - 8p.: 30 cm. - 978-0-11-113592-1 £6.00

The Proposed Marriages and Civil Partnerships (Conduct of Investigations, etc.) Regulations 2015 No. 2015/397. - Enabling power: Immigration Act 2014, ss. 50 (1) (5) (9) (10), 51 (1) (d) (3) (4) (5), 74 (8) (d). - Issued: 05.03.2015. Made: 26.02.2015. Coming into force: 01.03.2015. Effect: None. Territorial extent & classification: E/W/S/NI. General. - Supersedes draft SI (ISBN 9780111125564) issued 17/12/14 - 12p.: 30 cm. - 978-0-11-113103-9 £6.00

The Proposed Marriages and Civil Partnerships (Meaning of Exempt Persons and Notice) Regulations 2015 No. 2015/122. - Enabling power: Immigration Act 2014, ss. 49 (3) (4), 61 (1) (2), 74 (8) (d). - Issued: 11.02.2015. Made: 02.02.2015. Laid: 05.02.2015. Coming into force: 02.03.2015. Effect: None. Territorial extent & classification: UK [parts E/W only]. General. - 8p.: 30 cm. - 978-0-11-112884-8 £6.00

The Proposed Marriages and Civil Partnerships (Waiting Period) Regulations 2015 No. 2015/159. - Enabling power: Marriage Act 1949, ss. 31 (5ED), 74 (3) & Civil Partnership Act 2004, ss. 12(7), 258 (2). - Issued: 13.02.2015. Made: 02.02.2015. Coming into force: 02.03.2015. Effect: None. Territorial extent & classification: E/W. General. - 8p.: 30 cm. - 978-0-11-112900-5 £6.00

The Referral and Investigation of Proposed Marriages and Civil Partnerships (Northern Ireland and Miscellaneous Provisions) Order 2015 No. 2015/395. - Enabling power: Immigration Act 2014, ss. 53 (1) (2) (3), 74 (8) (c) (d). - Issued: 06.03.2015. Made: 26.02.2015. Coming into force: 01.03.2015. Effect: 2004 c.19, 33, 2014 c.22 & S.R. 2005/482 & S.I. 2003/413 (N.I. 3) amended. Territorial extent & classification: E/W/S/NI. General. - Supersedes draft S.I. (ISBN9780111125025) issued 19/12/14. - 24p.: 30 cm. - 978-0-11-113104-6 £6.00

The Referral and Investigation of Proposed Marriages and Civil Partnerships (Scotland) Order 2015 No. 2015/396. - Enabling power: Immigration Act 2014, ss. 53 (1) (2) (3), 74 (8) (c) (d). - Issued: 06.03.2015. Made: 26.02.2015. Coming into force: 01.03.2015. Effect: 1977 c.15; 2004 c.19, c.33; 2014 c.22 amended. Territorial extent & classification: E/W/S/NI. General. - Supersedes draft S.I. (ISBN) issued 17/12/14. - 24p.: 30 cm. - 978-0-11-113105-3 £6.00

The Referral of Proposed Marriages and Civil Partnerships Regulations 2015 No. 2015/123. - Enabling power: Marriage Act 1949, ss. 28D, 28G (2) (3), 28H (5) (c) (7) (10) (b) (c) & Civil Partnership Act 2004, ss. 9B, 9E (2) (3), 12A (5) (c) (7) (9) (b) (c). - Issued: 10.02.2015. Made: 02.02.2015. Laid: 05.02.2015. Coming into force: 02.03.2015. Effect: None. Territorial extent & classification: E/W. General. - 16p.: 30 cm. - 978-0-11-112877-0 £6.00

The Sham Marriage and Civil Partnership (Scotland and Northern Ireland) (Administrative) Regulations 2015 No. 2015/404. - Enabling power: Immigration Act 2014, ss. 54 (2) (3), 74 (8) (d), sch. 5. - Issued: 05.03.2015. Made: 26.02.2015. Laid before the Scottish Parliament: 27.02.2015. Coming into force: 02.03.2015. Effect: None. Territorial extent & classification: S/NI. General. - 24p.: 30 cm. - 978-0-11-113091-9 £6.00

The Special Immigration Appeals Commission (Procedure) (Amendment) Rules 2015 No. 2015/867. - Enabling power: Special Immigration Appeals Commission Act 1997, ss. 5, 8. - Issued: 27.03.2015. Made: 23.03.2015. Coming into force: In accord. with rule 1. Effect: S.I. 2003/1034 amended. Territorial extent & classification: E/W/S/NI. General. - Supersedes draft S.I. (ISBN 9780111127162) issued 19/01/15. - 4p.: 30 cm. - 978-0-11-113490-0 £4.25

Income tax

The Capital Allowances Act 2001 (Extension of first-year allowances) (Amendment) Order 2015 No. 2015/60. - Enabling power: Capital Allowances Act 2001, 45D (1A) (7), 45E (1A). - Issued: 30.01.2015. Made: 26.01.2015. Laid: 27.01.2015. Coming into force: 17.02.2015. Effect: 2001 c.2 amended. Territorial extent & classification: E/W/S/NI. General. - 2p.: 30 cm. - 978-0-11-112794-0 £4.25

The Capital Allowances (Energy-saving Plant and Machinery) (Amendment) Order 2015 No. 2015/1508. - Enabling power: Capital Allowances Act 2001, ss. 45A (3) (4). - Issued: 17.07.2015. Made: 13.07.2015. Laid: 14.07.2015. Coming into force: 04.08.2015. Effect: S.I. 2001/2541 amended. Territorial extent & classification: E/W/S/NI. General. - 2p.: 30 cm. - 978-0-11-113782-6 £4.25

The Capital Allowances (Environmentally Beneficial Plant and Machinery) (Amendment) Order 2015 No. 2015/1509. - Enabling power: Capital Allowances Act 2001, s. 45H (3) to (5). - Issued: 17.07.2015. Made: 13.07.2015. Laid: 14.07.2015. Coming into force: 04.08.2015. Effect: S.I. 2003/2076 amended. Territorial extent & classification: E/W/S/NI. General. - 2p.: 30 cm. - 978-0-11-113783-3 £4.25

The Community Amateur Sports Clubs Regulations 2015 No. 2015/725. - Enabling power: Corporation Tax Act 2010, ss. 659 (2A) (2B) (2C), 660 (5A) (d) (5B) (8) (9) (a) (b) (10) (12), 660A (1) (3) (4) & Finance Act 2013, sch. 21 para. 8 (1) (2) (a) (3). - Issued: 20.03.2015. Made: 16.03.2015. Coming into force: 01.04.2015. Effect: 2010 c.4 amended. Territorial extent & classification: E/W/S/NI. General. - Supersedes draft S.I. (ISBN 9780111127483) issued 22/01/15. - 12p.: 30 cm. - 978-0-11-113362-0 £6.00

The Data-gathering Powers (Relevant Data) (Amendment) Regulations 2015 No. 2015/672. - Enabling power: Finance Act 2011, sch. 23, para. 1(3). - Issued: 18.03.2015. Made: 12.03.2015. Laid: 13.03.2015. Coming into force: 06.04.2015. Effect: S.I. 2012/847 amended. Territorial extent & classification: E/W/S/NI. General. - 2p.: 30 cm. - 978-0-11-113334-7 £4.25

The Double Taxation Relief and International Tax Enforcement (Algeria) Order 2015 No. 2015/1888. - Enabling power: Taxation (International and Other Provisions) Act 2010 s. 2 & Finance Act 2006, ss. 173 (1) to (3). - Issued: 18.11.2015. Made: 11.11.2015. Coming into force: 11.11.2015. Effect: None. Territorial extent & classification: E/W/S/NI. General. - Supersedes draft SI (ISBN 9780111138250) issued 23/07/15 - 24p.: 30 cm. - 978-0-11-114086-4 £6.00

The Double Taxation Relief and International Tax Enforcement (Bulgaria) Order 2015 No. 2015/1890. - Enabling power: Taxation (International and Other Provisions) Act 2010, s. 2 & Finance Act 2006, ss. 173 (1) to (3). - Issued: 18.11.2015. Made: 11.11.2015. Coming into force: 11.11.2015. Effect: None. Territorial extent & classification: E/W/S/NI. General. - Supersedes draft SI (ISBN 9780111138236) issued 23/07/15 - 24p.: 30 cm. - 978-0-11-114088-8 £6.00

The Double Taxation Relief and International Tax Enforcement (Croatia) Order 2015 No. 2015/1889. - Enabling power: Taxation (International and Other Provisions) Act 2010, s. 2 & Finance Act 2006, ss. 173(1) to (3). - Issued: 18.11.2015. Made: 11.11.2015. Coming into force: 11.11.2015. Effect: None. Territorial extent & classification: E/W/S/NI. General. - Supersedes draft SI (ISBN 9780111138229) issued 23/07/15 - 24p.: 30 cm. - 978-0-11-114087-1 £6.00

The Double Taxation Relief and International Tax Enforcement (Guernsey) Order 2015 No. 2015/2008. - Enabling power: Taxation (International and Other Provisions) Act 2010, s. 2 & Finance Act 2006 s. 173 (1). - Issued: 16.12.2015. Made: 09.12.2015. Coming into force: 09.12.2015. Effect: None. Territorial extent & classification: E/W/S/NI. General. - Supersedes draft S.I. (ISBN 9780111140291) issued 02/11/15. - 8p.: 30 cm. - 978-0-11-114188-5 £4.25

The Double Taxation Relief and International Tax Enforcement (Jersey) Order 2015 No. 2015/2009. - Enabling power: Taxation (International and Other Provisions) Act 2010, s. 2 & Finance Act 2006, s. 173 (1). - Issued: 16.12.2015. Made: 09.12.2015. Coming into force: 09.12.2015. Effect: None. Territorial extent & classification: E/W/S/NI. General. - Supersedes draft S.I. (ISBN) issued 02/11/15. - 8p.: 30 cm. - 978-0-11-114189-2 £6.00

The Double Taxation Relief and International Tax Enforcement (Kosovo) Order 2015 No. 2015/2007. - Enabling power: Taxation (International and Other Provisions) Act 2010, s. 2 & Finance Act 2006 s. 173 (1) to (3). - Issued: 16.12.2015. Made: 09.12.2015. Coming into force: None. Territorial extent & classification: E/W/S/NI. General. - Supersedes draft S.I. (ISBN 9780111140413) issued 06/11/15. - 24p.: 30 cm. - 978-0-11-114187-8 £6.00

The Double Taxation Relief and International Tax Enforcement (Senegal) Order 2015 No. 2015/1892. - Enabling power: Taxation (International and Other Provisions) Act 2010, s. 2 & Finance Act 2006, ss. 173 (1) to (3). - Issued: 18.11.2015. Made: 11.11.2015. Coming into force: 11.11.2015. Effect: None. Territorial extent & classification: E/W/S/NI. General. - Supersedes draft SI (ISBN 9780111138212) issued 23/07/15 - 24p.: 30 cm. - 978-0-11-114090-1 £6.00

The Double Taxation Relief and International Tax Enforcement (Sweden) Order 2015 No. 2015/1891. - Enabling power: Taxation (International and Other Provisions) Act 2010, s. 2 & Finance Act 2006, ss. 173 (1) to (3). - Issued: 18.11.2015. Made: 11.11.2015. Coming into force: 11.11.2015. Effect: None. Territorial extent & classification: E/W/S/NI. General. - Supersedes draft SI (ISBN 9780111138205) issued 23/07/15 - 24p.: 30 cm. - 978-0-11-114089-5 £6.00

The Finance Act 2004 (Registered Pension Schemes and Annual Allowance Charge) (Amendment) Order 2015 No. 2015/80. - Enabling power: Finance Act 2004, ss 238A, 282 (A1). - Issued: 03.02.2015. Made: 27.01.2015. Coming into force: 28.01.2015. Effect: 2004 c.12 amended. Territorial extent & classification: E/W/S/NI. General. - Supersedes draft S.I. (ISBN 9780111124918) issued 15/12/14. - 16p.: 30 cm. - 978-0-11-112820-6 £6.00

The Finance Act 2007, Schedule 26, Paragraphs 4 and 5 (Valuation of Shares) (Appointed Day) Order 2015 No. 2015/635 (C.33). - Enabling power: Finance Act 2007, sch. 26, paras 4 (2), 5 (2). Bringing into operation various provisions of the 2007 Act on 06.04.2015 in accord. with art. 2. - Issued: 16.03.2015. Made: 09.03.2015. Effect: None. Territorial extent & classification: E/W/S/NI. General. - 2p.: 30 cm. - 978-0-11-113291-3 £4.25

The Finance Act 2012, Sections 26 and 30 (Abolition of Relief for Equalisation Reserves) (Specified Day) Order 2015 No. 2015/1999. - Enabling power: Finance Act 2012, ss. 26 (3), 30 (3). - Issued: 15.12.2015. Made: 07.12.2015. Coming into force: 01.01.2016. Effect: None. Territorial extent & classification: E/W/S/NI. General. - 2p.: 30 cm. - 978-0-11-114180-9 £4.25

The Finance Act 2014 (High Risk Promoters Prescribed Information) Regulations 2015 No. 2015/549. - Enabling power: Finance Act 2014, ss. 249 (3) (10) (11), 253 (2) (4), 257 (2), 259 (9), 260 (7), 261 (2), 268 (1), 282 (4), 283 (1). - Issued: 12.03.2015. Made: 05.03.2015. Laid: 06.03.2015. Coming into force: 27.03.2015. Effect: None. Territorial extent & classification: E/W/S/NI. General. - 16p.: 30 cm. - 978-0-11-113224-1 £6.00

The Finance Act 2014, Schedule 9 (Employment-related Securities etc.) (Consequential etc. Amendments) Regulations 2015 No. 2015/360. - Enabling power: Finance Act 2014, s. 52, sch. 9 paras 49, 50. - Issued: 02.03.2015. Made: 24.02.2015. Laid: 25.02.2015. Coming into force: 06.04.2015. Effect: 2003 c.1 amended. Territorial extent & classification: E/W/S/NI. General. - 2p.: 30 cm. - 978-0-11-113050-6 £4.25

The Finance Act 2014 (Schedule 34 Prescribed Matters) Regulations 2015 No. 2015/131. - Enabling power: Finance Act 2014, s. 283 (1), sch. 34 paras 8 (1) (3), 9 (2). - Issued: 12.02.2015. Made: 06.02.2015. Laid: 09.02.2015. Coming into force: 02.03.2015. Effect: None. Territorial extent & classification: E/W/S/NI. General. - 4p.: 30 cm. - 978-0-11-112898-5 £4.25

The Finance Act 2014, Section 18(2) to (4) (Appointed Day) Order 2015 No. 2015/931 (C.58). - Enabling power: Finance Act 2014, s. 18 (5). Bringing into operation various provisions of this Act on 06.04.15, in accord. with art. 2. - Issued: 01.04.2015. Made: 26.03.2015. Effect: -. Territorial extent & classification: E/W/S/NI. General. - 2p.: 30 cm. - 978-0-11-113553-2 £4.25

The Finance Act 2015 (Paragraphs 10 to 12 of Schedule 6) Regulations 2015 No. 2015/1836. - Enabling power: Finance Act 2015, sch. 6, para. 14. - Issued: 04.11.2015. Made: 27.10.2015. Laid: - Coming into force: 30.11.2015. Effect: None. Territorial extent & classification: E/W/S/NI. General. - 2p.: 30 cm. - 978-0-11-114034-5 £4.25

INCOME TAX

The Finance Act 2015, Section 23 (Appointed Day) Regulations 2015 No. 2015/2035 (C.126). - Enabling power: Finance Act 2015, s. 23 (3). Bringing into operation various provisions of the 2015 Act, in accord. with art. 2 on 01.01.2016. - Issued: 21.12.2015. Made: 15.12.2015. Effect: None. Territorial extent & classification: E/W/S/NI. General. - 2p.: 30 cm. - 978-0-11-114212-7 £4.25

The Income Tax (Approved Expenses) Regulations 2015 No. 2015/1948. - Enabling power: Income Tax (Earnings and Pensions) Act 2003, s. 289A (6) (a) (7). - Issued: 04.12.2015. Made: 27.11.2015. Laid: 30.11.2015. Coming into force: 21.12.2015. Effect: None. Territorial extent & classification: E/W/S/NI. General. - 2p.: 30 cm. - 978-0-11-114133-5 £4.25

The Income Tax (Construction Industry Scheme) (Amendment of Schedule 11 to the Finance Act 2004) Order 2015 No. 2015/789. - Enabling power: Finance Act 2004, sch. 11, para. 13 (1). - Issued: 26.03.2015. Made: 19.03.2015. Coming into force: 06.04.2015. Effect: 2004 c.12 amended. Territorial extent & classification: E/W/S/NI. General. - 4p.: 30 cm. - 978-0-11-113409-2 £4.25

The Income Tax (Construction Industry Scheme) (Amendment) Regulations 2015 No. 2015/429. - Enabling power: Finance Act 2004, ss. 62, 70. - Issued: 06.03.2015. Made: 02.03.2015. Laid: 03.03.2015. Coming into force: 06.04.2015. Effect: S.I. 2005/2045 amended. Territorial extent & classification: E/W/S/NI. General. - 4p.: 30 cm. - 978-0-11-113119-0 £4.25

The Income Tax (Deposit-takers and Building Societies) (Interest Payments) (Amendment) Regulations 2015 No. 2015/653. - Enabling power: Income Tax Act 2007, ss. 852 (1) (2) (4), 871. - Issued: 17.03.2015. Made: 11.03.2015. Laid: 12.03.2015. Coming into force: 06.04.2015. Effect: S.I. 2008/2682 amended. Territorial extent & classification: E/W/S/NI. General. - 4p.: 30 cm. - 978-0-11-113311-8 £4.25

The Income Tax (Limit for Rent-a-Room Relief) Order 2015 No. 2015/1539. - Enabling power: Income Tax (Trading and Other Income) Act 2005, s. 789 (5)- Issued: 22.07.2015. Made: 16.07.2015. Laid before the House of Commons: 17.07.2015. Coming into force: 13.08.2015. Effect: 2005 c.5 amended. Territorial extent & classification: E/W/S/NI. General. - 2p.: 30 cm. - 978-0-11-113813-7 £4.25

The Income Tax (Pay As You Earn) (Amendment No. 2) Regulations 2015 No. 2015/171. - Enabling power: Taxes Management Act 1970, s. 113 (1) & Finance Act 2002, s. 136 & Income Tax (Earnings and Pensions) Act 2003, s. 716B. - Issued: 16.02.2015. Made: 09.02.2015. Laid: 10.02.2015. Coming into force: 06.04.2015. Effect: S.I. 2003/2682 amended. Territorial extent & classification: E/W/S/NI. General. - 8p.: 30 cm. - 978-0-11-112907-4 £4.25

The Income Tax (Pay As You Earn) (Amendment No. 3) Regulations 2015 No. 2015/1667. - Enabling power: Income Tax (Earnings and Pensions) Act 2003, s. 684. - Issued: 15.09.2015. Made: 09.09.2015. Laid: 10.09.2015. Coming into force: 01.10.2015. Effect: S.I. 2003/2682 amended. Territorial extent & classification: E/W/S/NI. General. - 4p.: 30 cm. - 978-0-11-113915-8 £4.25

The Income Tax (Pay As You Earn) (Amendment No. 4) Regulations 2015 No. 2015/1927. - Enabling power: Taxes Management Act 1970, s. 113 (1) & Finance Act 1999, s. 133 (1) & Income Tax (Earnings and Pensions) Act 2003, s. 684 (1) (2). - Issued: 27.11.2015. Made: 23.11.2015. Laid: 23.11.2015. Coming into force: 14.12.2015. Effect: S.I. 2003/2682 amended. Territorial extent & classification: E/W/S/NI. General. - 12p.: 30 cm. - 978-0-11-114113-7 £6.00

The Income Tax (Pay As You Earn) (Amendment) Regulations 2015 No. 2015/2. - Enabling power: Finance Act 1999, s. 133 & Income Tax (Earnings and Pensions) Act 2003, s. 684 (1) (2)- Issued: 12.01.2015. Made: 05.01.2015. Laid: 07.01.2015. Coming into force: 29.01.2015. Effect: S.I. 2003/2682 amended. Territorial extent & classification: E/W/S/NI. General. - 4p.: 30 cm. - 978-0-11-112656-1 £4.25

The Income Tax (Professional Fees) Order 2015 No. 2015/886. - Enabling power: Income Tax (Earnings and Pensions) Act 2003, s. 343 (3) (4). - Issued: 31.03.2015. Made: 24.03.2015. Coming into force: 01.04.2015. Effect: 2003 c.1 amended. Territorial extent & classification: W. General. - 2p.: 30 cm. - 978-0-11-113509-9 £4.25

The Income Tax (Qualifying Child Care) Regulations 2015 No. 2015/346. - Enabling power: Income Tax (Earnings and Pensions) Act 2003, s. 318D (2). - Issued: 02.03.2015. Made: 23.02.2015. Laid: 24.02.2015. Coming into force: 01.04.2015. Effect: 2003 c.1 amended. Territorial extent & classification: E/W/S/NI. General. - 2p.: 30 cm. - 978-0-11-113034-6 £4.25

The Individual Savings Account (Amendment No. 2) Regulations 2015 No. 2015/869. - Enabling power: Income Tax (Trading and Other Income) Act 2005, s. 694 to 699, 701 & Taxation of Chargeable Gains Act 1992, s. 151. - Issued: 31.03.2015. Made: 24.03.2015. Laid: 25.03.2015. Coming into force: 06.04.2015. Effect: S.I. 1998/1870 amended. Territorial extent & classification: E/W/S/NI. General. - 2p.: 30 cm. - 978-0-11-113492-4 £4.25

The Individual Savings Account (Amendment No. 3) Regulations 2015 No. 2015/941. - Enabling power: Income Tax (Trading and Other Income) Act 2005, ss. 694 to 699, 701 & Taxation of Chargeable Gains Act 1992, s. 151. - Issued: 02.04.2015. Made: 26.03.2015. Laid: 27.03.2015. Coming into force: 06.04.2015. Effect: S.I. 1998/1870 amended. Territorial extent & classification: E/W/S/NI. General. - 2p.: 30 cm. - 978-0-11-113565-5 £4.25

The Individual Savings Account (Amendment No. 4) Regulations 2015 No. 2015/1370. - Enabling power: Income Tax (Trading and Other Income) Act 2005, ss. 694, 695, 695A, 696, 701 (1) (5) & Taxation of Chargeable Gains Act 1992, s. 151 (1) (2). - Issued: 18.06.2015. Made: 10.06.2015. Laid: 10.06.2015. Coming into force: 01.07.2015. Effect: S.I. 1998/1870 amended. Territorial extent & classification: E/W/S/NI. General. - 4p.: 30 cm. - 978-0-11-113666-9 £4.25

The Individual Savings Account (Amendment) Regulations 2015 No. 2015/608. - Enabling power: Income Tax (Trading and Other Income) Act 2005, s. 694 & Taxation of Chargeable Gains Act 1992, s. 151. - Issued: 17.03.2015. Made: 09.03.2015. Laid: 10.03.2015. Coming into force: 06.04.2015. Effect: S.I. 1998/1870 amended. Territorial extent & classification: E/W/S/NI. General. - 2p.: 30 cm. - 978-0-11-113271-5 £4.25

The International Tax Enforcement (Brazil) Order 2015 No. 2015/1887. - Enabling power: Finance Act 2006, ss. 173 (1) to (3). - Issued: 18.11.2015. Made: 11.11.2015. Coming into force: 11.11.2015. Effect: None. Territorial extent & classification: E/W/S/NI. General. - Supersedes draft SI (ISBN 9780111138243) issued 23/07/15 - 12p.: 30 cm. - 978-0-11-114085-7 £6.00

The Life Insurance Qualifying Policies (Statement and Reporting Requirements) (Amendment) Regulations 2015 No. 2015/544. - Enabling power: Income and Corporation Taxes Act 1988, sch. 15, para. B3 (7). - Issued: 12.03.2015. Made: 04.03.2015. Laid: 06.03.2015. Coming into force: 26.03.2015. Effect: S.I. 2013/1820 amended. Territorial extent & classification: E/W/S/NI. General. - 2p.: 30 cm. - 978-0-11-113219-7 £4.25

The Lloyd's Underwriters (Transitional Equalisation Reserves) (Tax) Regulations 2015 No. 2015/1983. - Enabling power: Finance Act 2009, s. 47 & Finance Act 2012, s. 30 (1). - Issued: 14.12.2015. Made: 07.12.2015. Laid: 08.12.2015. Coming into force: 01.01.2016. Effect: 2012 c.14 modified & S.I. 1996/2991; 2009/2039 revoked. Territorial extent & classification: E/W/S/NI. General. - 4p.: 30 cm. - 978-0-11-114171-7 £4.25

The Market Value of Shares, Securities and Strips Regulations 2015 No. 2015/616. - Enabling power: Taxation of Chargeable Gains Act, s. 272 (3) (4) & Income Tax (Trading and Other Income) Act 2005, s. 450. - Issued: 16.03.2015. Made: 09.03.2015. Laid: 10.03.2015. Coming into force: 06.04.2015. Effect: S.I. 2006/964 amended. Territorial extent & classification: E/W/S/NI. General. - 4p.: 30 cm. - 978-0-11-113279-1 £4.25

The Offshore Asset Moves Penalty (Specified Territories) Regulations 2015 No. 2015/866. - Enabling power: Finance Act 2015, sch. 21, para. 4 (5). - Issued: 02.04.2015. Made: 26.03.2015, at 5.20 pm. Laid: 27.03.2015, at 12.30 pm. Coming into force: 27.03.2015. Effect: None. Territorial extent & classification: Albania, Andorra, Anguilla, Antigua and Barbuda, Argentina, Aruba, Australia, Austria, The Bahamas, Barbados, Belgium, Belize, Bermuda, Brazil, British Virgin Islands, Brunei Darussalam, Bulgaria, Canada, Cayman Islands, Chile, China, Colombia, Costa Rica, Croatia, Curaçao, Cyprus, Czech Republic, Denmark, Dominica, Estonia, Faroe Islands, Finland, France, Germany, Gibraltar, Greece, Greenland, Grenada, Guernsey, Hong Kong, Hungary, Iceland, India, Indonesia, Ireland, Isle of Man, Israel, Italy, Japan, Jersey, Korea (South), Latvia, Liechtenstein, Lithuania, Luxembourg, Macau, Malaysia, Malta, Marshall Islands, Mauritius, Mexico, Monaco, Montserrat, Netherlands (including Bonaire, Sint Eustatius and Saba) New Zealand (not including Tokelau), Niue, Norway, Poland, Portugal, Qatar, Romania, Russia, Saint Kitts and Nevis, Saint Lucia, Saint Vincent and the Grenadines, Samoa, San Marino, Saudi Arabia, Seychelles, Singapore, Sint Maarten, Slovak Republic, Slovenia, South Africa, Spain, Sweden, Switzerland, Trinidad and Tobago, Turkey, Turks and Caicos Islands, United Arab Emirates, United States of America (not including overseas territories and possessions), Uruguay. General. - 2p.: 30 cm. - 978-0-11-113578-5 £4.25

The Overseas Pension Schemes (Miscellaneous Amendments) Regulations 2015 No. 2015/673. - Enabling power: Finance Act 2004, ss. 150 (8), 169 (4) (4A) (4B), (8), 251 (4). - Issued: 19.03.2015. Made: 12.03.2015. Laid: 13.03.2015. Coming into force: 06.04.2015. Effect: S.I. 2006/206, 208 amended. Territorial extent & classification: E/W/S/NI. General. - 8p.: 30 cm. - 978-0-11-113335-4 £6.00

The Qualifying Private Placement Regulations 2015 No. 2015/2002. - Enabling power: Income Tax Act 2007, s. 888A. - Issued: 15.12.2015. Made: 09.12.2015. Laid: 10.12.2015. Coming into force: 01.01.2016. Effect: None. Territorial extent & classification: E/W/S/NI. General. - 4p.: 30 cm. - 978-0-11-114182-3 £4.25

The Registered Pension Schemes (Audited Accounts)(Specified Persons) (Amendment) Regulations 2015 No. 2015/1518. - Enabling power: Finance Act 2004, ss. 250 (6), 282 (A1). - Issued: 21.07.2015. Made: 15.07.2015. Laid: 16.07.2015. Coming into force: 01.09.2015. Effect: S.I. 2005/3546 amended. Territorial extent & classification: E/W/S/NI. General. - 4p.: 30 cm. - 978-0-11-113797-0 £4.25

The Registered Pension Schemes (Provision of Information) (Amendment No. 2) Regulations 2015 No. 2015/1455. - Enabling power: Finance Act 2004, ss. 251, 282 (A1). - Issued: 21.07.2015. Made: 15.07.2015 at 9.35. a.m. Laid: 16.07.2015. Coming into force: 01.09.2015. Effect: S.I. 2006/567 amended. Territorial extent & classification: E/W/S/NI. General. - 8p.: 30 cm. - 978-0-11-113796-3 £4.25

The Registered Pension Schemes (Provision of Information) (Amendment) Regulations 2015 No. 2015/606. - Enabling power: Finance Act 2004, ss. 251. - Issued: 13.03.2015. Made: 09.03.2015. Laid before the House of Commons: 10.03.2015. Coming into force: 06.04.2015. Effect: S.I. 2006/567 amended. Territorial extent & classification: E/W/S/NI. General. - 8p.: 30 cm. - 978-0-11-113269-2 £4.25

The Registered Pension Schemes (Splitting of Schemes) (Amendment) Regulations 2015 No. 2015/667. - Enabling power: Finance Act 2004, s. 274A. - Issued: 18.03.2015. Made: 12.03.2015. Laid: 12.03.2015. Coming into force: 06.04.2015. Effect: S.I. 2006/569 amended. Territorial extent & classification: E/W/S/NI. General. - 4p.: 30 cm. - 978-0-11-113325-5 £4.25

The Registered Pension Schemes (Transfer of Sums and Assets) (Amendment No. 2) Regulations 2015 No. 2015/1454. - Enabling power: Finance Act 2004, sch. 28, paras 27AA(3) (4), 27FA(3) (4) & Finance Act 2015, sch. 4, para. 3 (4). - Issued: 21.07.2015. Made: 15.07.2015 at 9.30 a.m. Laid: 16.07.2015. Coming into force: 01.09.2015. Effect: S.I. 2006/499 amended. Territorial extent & classification: E/W/S/NI. General. - 4p.: 30 cm. - 978-0-11-113794-9 £4.25

The Registered Pension Schemes (Transfer of Sums and Assets) (Amendment) Regulations 2015 No. 2015/633. - Enabling power: Finance Act 2004, sch. 28, paras. 3 (2B) (2C), 6 (1B) (1C), 17 (3) (4), 20 (1B) (1C), 27C (2) (3), 27H (2) (3). - Issued: 16.03.2015. Made: 10.03.2015. Laid: 11.03.2015. Coming into force: 06.04.2015. Effect: S.I. 2006/499 amended. Territorial extent & classification: E/W/S/NI. General. - 4p.: 30 cm. - 978-0-11-113289-0 £4.25

The Scotland Act 2012, Section 25 (Appointed Years) Order 2015 No. 2015/2000. - Enabling power: Scotland Act 2012, ss. 25 (4), 25 (5). - Issued: 15.12.2015. Made: 08.12.2015. Effect: None. Territorial extent & classification: E/W/S/NI. General. - 2p.: 30 cm. - 978-0-11-114181-6 £4.25

The Scottish Rate of Income Tax (Consequential Amendments) Order 2015 No. 2015/1810. - Enabling power: Scotland Act 1998, s. 80G (1A) (2). - Issued: 28.10.2015. Made: 20.10.2015. Coming into force: In accord. with art. 1. Effect: 2004 c.12; 2005 c.5, c.22; 2007 c.3 & S.I. 2005/3448 amended. Territorial extent & classification: E/W/S/NI. General. - Supersedes draft SI (ISBN 9780111137093) issued 30/06/15. - 8p.: 30 cm. - 978-0-11-114008-6 £6.00

The Statutory Shared Parental Pay (Miscellaneous Amendments) Regulations 2015 No. 2015/125. - Enabling power: Finance Act 1999, ss. 132, 133 (2) & Income Tax (Earnings and Pensions) Act 2003, s. 684 & Finance Act 2004, ss. 62 (3) (6) (7), 71. - Issued: 10.02.2015. Made: 03.02.2015. Laid: 05.02.2015. Coming into force: In accord. with reg. 1 (2) (3). Effect: S.I. 2002/3047; 2003/2682; 2005/2045 amended. Territorial extent & classification: E/W/S. General. - 4p.: 30 cm. - 978-0-11-112872-5 £4.25

The Taxation of Regulatory Capital Securities (Amendment) Regulations 2015 No. 2015/2056. - Enabling power: Finance Act 2012, s. 221. - Issued: 22.12.2015. Made: 16.12.2015. Coming into force: 01.01.2016. Effect: S.I. 2013/3209 amended. Territorial extent & classification: E/W/S/NI. General. - Supersedes draft S.I. (ISBN 9780111141144) issued 27/11/15. - 8p.: 30 cm. - 978-0-11-114238-7 £4.25

The Taxes (Interest Rate) (Amendment) Regulations 2015 No. 2015/411. - Enabling power: Finance Act 1989, s. 178 (1) (2) (s). - Issued: 05.03.2015. Made: 27.02.2015. Laid: 02.03.2015. Coming into force: 06.04.2015. Effect: S.I. 1989/1297 amended. Territorial extent & classification: E/W/S/NI. General. - 2p.: 30 cm. - 978-0-11-113101-5 £4.25

The Tax Relief for Social Investments (Accreditation of Social Impact Contractor) (Amendment) Regulations 2015 No. 2015/2051. - Enabling power: Income Tax Act 2007, ss. 257JE, 257JF. - Issued: 22.12.2015. Made: 16.12.2015. Laid: 17.12.2015. Coming into force: 09.01.2016. Effect: S.I. 2014/3066 amended. Territorial extent & classification: E/W/S/NI. General. - 4p.: 30 cm. - 978-0-11-114231-8 £4.25

The Unauthorised Unit Trusts (Tax) (Amendment No. 2) Regulations 2015 No. 2015/2053. - Enabling power: Finance Act 2013, s. 217. - Issued: 22.12.2015. Made: 16.12.2015. Laid: 17.12.2015. Coming into force: 07.01.2016. Effect: S.I. 2013/2819 amended. Territorial extent & classification: E/W/S/NI. General. - 2p.: 30 cm. - 978-0-11-114234-9 £4.25

The Unauthorised Unit Trusts (Tax) (Amendment) Regulations 2015 No. 2015/463. - Enabling power: Finance Act 2013, s. 217. - Issued: 12.03.2015. Made: 03.03.2015. Laid: 04.03.2015. Coming into force: 06.04.2015. Effect: S.I. 2013/2819 amended. Territorial extent & classification: E/W/S/NI. General. - 2p.: 30 cm. - 978-0-11-113155-8 £4.25

The Van Benefit and Car and Van Fuel Benefit Order 2015 No. 2015/1979. - Enabling power: Income Tax (Earnings and Pensions) Act 2003, ss. 170 (1A) (2) (5) (6). - Issued: 11.12.2015. Made: 07.12.2015. Laid: 08.12.2015. Coming into force: 31.12.2015. Effect: 2003 c.1 amended. Territorial extent & classification: E/W/S/NI. General. - 2p.: 30 cm. - 978-0-11-114167-0 £4.25

The Venture Capital Trust (Winding Up and Mergers) (Tax) (Amendment) Regulations 2015 No. 2015/361. - Enabling power: Income Tax Act 2007, ss. 321 (1), 322 (5A), 324 (1) (e). - Issued: 03.03.2015. Made: 24.02.2015. Laid: 25.02.2015. Coming into force: 19.03.2015. Effect: S.I. 2004/2199 amended. Territorial extent & classification: E/W/S/NI. General. - 2p.: 30 cm. - 978-0-11-113051-3 £4.25

Infrastructure planning

The A160/A180 (Port of Immingham Improvement) Development Consent (Correction) Order 2015 No. 2015/1231. - Enabling power: Planning Act 2008, s. 119, sch. 4. - Issued: 27.04.2015. Made: 21.04.2015. Coming into force: 22.04.2015. Effect: None. Territorial extent & classification: E. General. - This Order corrects errors in the S.I.2015/129 (ISBN 9780111128954) issued 11/02/15. - 4p.: 30 cm. - 978-0-11-113637-9 £4.25

INFRASTRUCTURE PLANNING

The A160/A180 (Port of Immingham Improvement) Development Consent Order 2015 No. 2015/129. - Enabling power: Planning Act 2008, ss 114, 115, 117, 120, 122, sch. 5, part 1, paras 1 to 3, 5 10 to 15, 17, 19, 22, 26, 33, 36, 37. - Issued: 11.02.2015. Made: 04.02.2015. Coming into force: 25.02.2015. Effect: None. Territorial extent & classification: E. General. - 76p.: 30 cm. - 978-0-11-112895-4 £14.25

The Cornwall Council (A30 Temple to Higher Carblake Improvement) (Correction) Order 2015 No. 2015/243. - Enabling power: Planning Act 2008, s. 119, sch. 4. - Issued: 18.02.2015. Made: 12.02.2015. Coming into force: 13.02.2015. Effect: S.I. 2015/147 amended. Territorial extent & classification: E. Local. - This Statutory Instrument has been made in consequence of a defect in S.I. 2015/147 (ISBN 9780111128978) and is being issued free of charge to all known recipients of that Statutory Instrument. - 4p.: 30 cm. - 978-0-11-112985-2 £4.25

The Cornwall Council (A30 Temple to Higher Carblake Improvement) Order 2015 No. 2015/147. - Enabling power: Planning Act 2008, ss. 114, 115, 117, 120, 122, sch. 5 part 1, paras 1 to 3, 10 to 17, 19, 22, 23, 26, 33, 36, 37. - Issued: 12.02.2015. Made: 05.02.2015. Coming into force: 26.02.2015. Effect: None. Territorial extent & classification: E. Local. - 52p.: 30 cm. - 978-0-11-112897-8 £10.00

The Dogger Bank Creyke Beck Offshore Wind Farm (Correction) Order 2015 No. 2015/1742. - Enabling power: Planning Act 2008, sch. 4, para. 1 (4) (8). - Issued: 08.10.2015. Made: 02.10.2015. Laid: -Coming into force: 05.10.2015. Effect: S.I. 2015/318 corrected. Territorial extent & classification: E. Local. - 2p.: 30 cm. - 978-0-11-113958-5 £4.25

The Dogger Bank Creyke Beck Offshore Wind Farm Order 2015 No. 2015/318. - Enabling power: Planning Act 2008, ss. 114, 120. - Issued: 23.02.2015. Made: 17.02.2015. Coming into force: 11.03.2015. Effect: None. Territorial extent & classification: E/W. General. - With correction slip dated January 2016. - 136p.: 30 cm. - 978-0-11-113009-4 £20.75

The Dogger Bank Teesside A and B Offshore Wind Farm Order 2015 No. 2015/1592. - Enabling power: Planning Act 2008, ss. 114, 120. - Issued: 11.08.2015. Made: 04.08.2015. Coming into force: 26.08.2015. Effect: 1981 c.66 amended & 1965 c.56; 1973 c.26 modified. Territorial extent & classification: E. Local. - 152p.: 30 cm. - 978-0-11-113863-2 £23.25

The Ferrybridge Multifuel 2 Power Station Order 2015 No. 2015/1832. - Enabling power: Planning Act 2008, ss. 114, 115, 120. - Issued: 03.11.2015. Made: 28.10.2015. Coming into force: 19.11.2015. Effect: None. Territorial extent & classification: E. Local. - 48p.: 30 cm. - 978-0-11-114031-4 £10.00

The Galloper Wind Farm (Amendment) Order 2015 No. 2015/1460. - Enabling power: Planning Act 2008, s. 153, sch. 6, para. 2. - Issued: 08.07.2015. Made: 02.07.2015. Coming into force: 03.07.2015. Effect: S.I. 2013/1203 amended. Territorial extent & classification: E. Local. - 2p.: 30 cm. - 978-0-11-113740-6 £4.25

The Hinkley Point C (Nuclear Generating Station) (Amendment) Order 2015 No. 2015/1666. - Enabling power: Planning Act 2008, sch. 6. para. 2. - Issued: 15.09.2015. Made: 09.09.2015. Coming into force: 10.09.2015. Effect: S.I. 2013/648 amended. Territorial extent & classification: E/W. General. - 16p.: 30 cm. - 978-0-11-113914-1 £6.00

The Hirwaun Generating Station (Correction) Order 2015 No. 2015/2070. - Enabling power: Planning Act 2008, sch. 4, para. 1 (4) (8). - Issued: 29.12.2015. Made: 21.12.2015. Coming into force: 22.12.2015. Effect: S.I. 2015/1574 amended. Territorial extent & classification: W. Local. - This Order corrects an error identified in the S.I. 2015/1574. - 2p.: 30 cm. - 978-0-11-114253-0 £4.25

The Hirwaun Generating Station Order 2015 No. 2015/1574. - Enabling power: Planning Act 2008, ss. 114, 115, 120. - Issued: 29.07.2015. Made: 23.07.2015. Coming into force: 14.08.2015. Effect: 1965 c.56; 1973 c.26 modified & 1981 c.66 amended. Territorial extent & classification: W. Local. - 72p.: 30 cm. - 978-0-11-113854-0 £14.25

The Hornsea One Offshore Wind Farm (Correction) Order 2015 No. 2015/1280. - Enabling power: Planning Act 2008, sch. 4, paras 1(4) (8). - Issued: 07.05.2015. Made: 30.04.2015. Coming into force: 01.05.2015. Effect: None. Territorial extent & classification: E/W. General. - This Order corrects errors and omissions in the SI. 2014/162 (ISBN 9780111126219) issued 23/12/14. With correction slip dated May 2015. - 4p.: 30 cm. - 978-0-11-113640-9 £4.25

The Infrastructure Act 2015 (Commencement No. 2 and Transitional Provisions) Regulations 2015 No. 2015/758 (C.41). - Enabling power: Infrastructure Act 2015, s. 57 (5) (11). Bringing into operation various provisions of the 2015 Act on 12.04.2015, 14.07.2015, in accord. with arts 2, 3. - Issued: 24.03.2015. Made: 18.03.2015. Effect: None. Territorial extent & classification: E/W/S/NI. General. - 2p.: 30 cm. - 978-0-11-113389-7 £4.25

The Infrastructure Act 2015 (Commencement No. 3) Regulations 2015 No. 2015/1543 (C.88). - Enabling power: Infrastructure Act 2015, s. 57 (2). Bringing into operation various provisions of the 2015 Act on 31.07.2015, in accord. with art. 2. - Issued: 22.07.2015. Made: 15.07.2015. Effect: None. Territorial extent & classification: E/W/S/NI though the part of the Act brought into force by this instrument applies to E only. General. - 2p.: 30 cm. - 978-0-11-113818-2 £4.25

The Infrastructure Planning (Changes to, and Revocation of, Development Consent Orders) (Amendment) Regulations 2015 No. 2015/760. - Enabling power: Planning Act 2008, s. 4, sch. 6, paras 2 (5) (8) (8A), 4 (1) (4) (5A). - Issued: 24.03.2015. Made: 18.03.2015. Laid: 23.03.2015. Coming into force: 14.07.2015. Effect: S.I. 2011/2055 amended. Territorial extent & classification: E/W/S. General. - 8p.: 30 cm. - 978-0-11-113391-0 £6.00

The Infrastructure Planning (Interested Parties and Miscellaneous Prescribed Provisions) Regulations 2015 No. 2015/462. - Enabling power: Planning Act 2008, ss. 88 (3A), 102 (4), 150 (1), 154 (1) (3), 170 (3) (5), 232 (3). - Issued: 09.03.2015. Made: 03.03.2015. Laid: 05.03.2015. Coming into force: 06.04.2015. Effect: S.I. 2012/635, 2732; 2013/522; 2014/469 partially revoked & 2010/102, 105; 2013/520 revoked. Territorial extent & classification: E/W/S. General. - 16p.: 30 cm. - 978-0-11-113154-1 £6.00

The Infrastructure Planning (Radioactive Waste Geological Disposal Facilities) Order 2015 No. 2015/949. - Enabling power: Planning Act 2008, ss. 14 (3) (4), 232 (3). - Issued: 02.04.2015. Made: 26.03.2015. Coming into force: 27.03.2015. Effect: S.I. 2008 c.29 amended. Territorial extent & classification: E. General. - Supersedes draft S.I. (ISBN 9780111126790) issued 14/01/15. - 4p.: 30 cm. - 978-0-11-113576-1 £4.25

The Knottingley Power Plant Order 2015 No. 2015/680. - Enabling power: Planning Act 2008, ss. 114, 115, 120, 147. - Issued: 19.03.2015. Made: 10.03.2015. Coming into force: 01.04.2015. Effect: None. Territorial extent & classification: E/W/S/NI. General. - 60p.: 30 cm. - 978-0-11-113342-2 £10.00

The Lancashire County Council (Torrisholme to the M6 Link (A683 Completion of Heysham to M6 Link Road)) (Amendment) Order 2015 No. 2015/571. - Enabling power: Planning Act 2008, s. 153, sch. 6, para. 2. - Issued: 12.03.2015. Made: 05.03.2015. Coming into force: 26.03.2015. Effect: S.I. 2013/675 amended. Territorial extent & classification: E. General. - 4p.: 30 cm. - 978-0-11-113239-5 £4.25

The Norfolk County Council (Norwich Northern Distributor Road (A1067 to A47(T))) Order 2015 No. 2015/1347. - Enabling power: Planning Act 2008, ss. 114, 115, 117, 120, 122, sch. 5, part 1, paras 1 to 3, 10 to 17, 19, 22, 23, 26, 36, 37. - Issued: 09.06.2015. Made: 02.06.2015. Coming into force: 23.06.2015. Effect: 1965 c.56 modified. Territorial extent & classification: E. General. - 208p.: 30 cm. - 978-0-11-113655-3 £27.50

The North Killingholme (Generating Station) (Correction) Order 2015 No. 2015/1829. - Enabling power: Planning Act 2008, s. 119, sch. 4, para. 1 (4) (8). - Issued: 02.11.2015. Made: 26.10.2015. Laid: - Coming into force: 27.10.2015. Effect: S.I. 2014/2434 corrected. Territorial extent & classification: E/W. Local. - This Order corrects errors and omissions in S.I. 2014/2434 (ISBN 9780111120699) issued 17/09/14. - 2p.: 30 cm. - 978-0-11-114026-0 £4.25

The Northumberland County Council (A1 - South East Northumberland Link Road (Morpeth Northern Bypass)) Development Consent Order 2015 No. 2015/23. - Enabling power: Planning Act 2008, ss 114, 115, 120, 122, sch. 5, part 1, paras 1 to 3, 10 to 17, 19, 26, 33, 36, 37. - Issued: 20.01.2015. Made: 12.01.2015. Coming into force: 02.02.2015. Effect: None. Territorial extent & classification: E. Local. - 50p.: 30 cm. - 978-0-11-112744-5 £10.00

The Planning (Hazardous Substances) Regulations 2015 No. 2015/627. - Enabling power: Planning (Hazardous Substances) Act 1990, ss. 4 (4), 4 (5), 5, 7, 8, 17 (2), 21 (2) (3) (3A), 24 (4), 25, 26A, 28, 30, 40 (1) (4) & European Communities Act 1972, s. 2 (2), sch. 2, para. 1A. - Issued: 25.03.2015. Made: 18.03.2015. Laid: 24.03.2015. Coming into force: 01.06.2015. Effect: S.I 2000/1491; 2006/1466; 2008/580; 2012/767 amended & S.I. 1992/656; 1999/981; 2014/1638 partially revoked & 2006/1282; 2009/1901; 2010/1050 revoked. Territorial extent & classification: E. General. - 50p.: 30 cm. - 978-0-11-113423-8 £10.00

The Port Talbot Steelworks Generating Station Order 2015 No. 2015/1984. - Enabling power: Planning Act 2008, ss. 114, 120. - Issued: 14.12.2015. Made: 08.12.2015. Coming into force: 30.12.2015. Effect: 1965 c.56; 1973 c.26 modified. Territorial extent & classification: E/W/S/NI. Local. - 52p.: 30 cm. - 978-0-11-114172-4 £10.00

The Preesall Underground Gas Storage Facility (Correction) Order 2015 No. 2015/2071. - Enabling power: Planning Act 2008, sch. 4, para. 1 (4) (8). - Issued: 29.12.2015. Made: 21.12.2015. Coming into force: 22.12.2015. Effect: S.I. 2015/1561 amended. Territorial extent & classification: E. Local. - This Order corrects errors and omissions in the S.I. 2015/1561. - 4p.: 30 cm. - 978-0-11-114254-7 £4.25

The Preesall Underground Gas Storage Facility Order 2015 No. 2015/1561. - Enabling power: Planning Act 2008, ss. 103, 114, 115, 120, 122, 123, 142, 149A. - Issued: 29.07.2015. Made: 17.07.2015. Coming into force: 07.08.2015. Effect: 1981 c.66 modified. Territorial extent & classification: E. Local. - 78p.: 30 cm. - 978-0-11-113842-7 £14.25

The Progress Power (Gas Fired Power Station) Order 2015 No. 2015/1570. - Enabling power: Planning Act 2008, ss. 114, 115, 120. - Issued: 29.07.2015. Made: 23.07.2015. Coming into force: 14.08.2015. Effect: 1965 c.56; 1973 c.26; 1997/1160 modified & S.I. 1981 c.66 amended. Territorial extent & classification: E. Local. - 68p.: 30 cm. - 978-0-11-113851-9 £11.00

The Rampion Offshore Wind Farm (Correction) Order 2015 No. 2015/1319. - Enabling power: Planning Act 2008, sch. 4, paras 1(4), 1 (8). - Issued: 19.05.2015. Made: 13.05.2015. Coming into force: 14.05.2015. Effect: None. Territorial extent & classification: E/W. General. - The Order corrects errors and omissions identified in S.I. 2014/1873 (ISBN 9780111118733) issued 24/07/14. - 4p.: 30 cm. - 978-0-11-113641-6 £4.25

The Swansea Bay Tidal Generating Station (Correction) Order 2015 No. 2015/1830. - Enabling power: Planning Act 2008, s. 119, sch. 4, para. 1 (4) (8). - Issued: 02.11.2015. Made: 26.10.2015. Laid: - Coming into force: 27.10.2015. Effect: S.I. 2015/1386 corrected. Territorial extent & classification: W. Local. - This Order corrects errors and omissions in S.I. 2015/1386 (ISBN 9780111136812) issued 18/06/15. - 4p.: 30 cm. - 978-0-11-114027-7 £4.25

The Swansea Bay Tidal Generating Station Order 2015 No. 2015/1386. - Enabling power: Planning Act 2008, ss. 114, 120. - Issued: 18.06.2015. Made: 09.06.2015. Coming into force: 30.06.2015. Effect: None. Territorial extent & classification: W. Local. - 88p.: 30 cm. - 978-0-11-113681-2 £16.00

The Thames Water Utilities Limited (Thames Tideway Tunnel) (Correction) Order 2015 No. 2015/723. - Enabling power: Planning Act 2008, sch. 4, para. 1 (3). - Issued: 20.03.2015. Made: 12.03.2015. Coming into force: 17.03.2015. Effect: 2014/2384 modified. Territorial extent & classification: E/W. Local. - This Order corrects errors and omission in the S.I. 2014/2384 (ISBN 9780111120439) issued 12/09/14. - 12p.: 30 cm. - 978-0-11-113361-3 £6.00

The Walney Extension Offshore Wind Farm (Correction) Order 2015 No. 2015/1270. - Enabling power: Planning Act 2008, s.119, sch. 4. - Issued: 30.04.2015. Made: 24.04.2015. Coming into force: 25.04.2015. Effect: None. Territorial extent & classification: E. Local. - The Order corrects errors and omissions in the SI 2014/2950 (ISBN 9780111123263) issued 17/11/14. - 4p.: 30 cm. - 978-0-11-113638-6 £4.25

The White Moss Landfill Order 2015 No. 2015/1317. - Enabling power: Planning Act 2008, s. 114- Issued: 02.06.2015. Made: 19.05.2015. Coming into force: 09.06.2015. Effect: None Territorial extent & classification: E/W/S/NI. General. - 24p.: 30 cm. - 978-0-11-113643-0 £6.00

The Willington C Gas Pipeline (Correction) Order 2015 No. 2015/1616. - Enabling power: Planning Act 2008, sch. 4, para. 1 (4) (8). - Issued: 24.08.2015. Made: 18.08.2015. Coming into force: 19.08.2015. Effect: S.I. 2014/3328 corrected. Territorial extent & classification: E. Local. - The Order corrects errors and omissions in S.I. 2014/3328 (ISBN 9780111126202) issued 22/12/14. - 4p.: 30 cm. - 978-0-11-113871-7 £4.25

Inheritance tax

The Inheritance Tax (Electronic Communications) Regulations 2015 No. 2015/1378. - Enabling power: Finance Act 1999, s. 132. - Issued: 17.06.2015. Made: 09.06.2015. Laid: 11.06.2015. Coming into force: 06.07.2015. Effect: None. Territorial extent & classification: E/W/S/NI. General. - 8p.: 30 cm. - 978-0-11-113673-7 £4.25

The International Tax Enforcement (Brazil) Order 2015 No. 2015/1887. - Enabling power: Finance Act 2006, ss. 173 (1) to (3). - Issued: 18.11.2015. Made: 11.11.2015. Coming into force: 11.11.2015. Effect: None. Territorial extent & classification: E/W/S/NI. General. - Supersedes draft SI (ISBN 9780111138243) issued 23/07/15 - 12p.: 30 cm. - 978-0-11-114085-7 £6.00

The Offshore Asset Moves Penalty (Specified Territories) Regulations 2015 No. 2015/866. - Enabling power: Finance Act 2015, sch. 21, para. 4 (5). - Issued: 02.04.2015. Made: 26.03.2015, at 5.20 pm. Laid: 27.03.2015, at 12.30 pm. Coming into force: 27.03.2015. Effect: None. Territorial extent & classification: Albania, Andorra, Anguilla, Antigua and Barbuda, Argentina, Aruba, Australia, Austria, The Bahamas, Barbados, Belgium, Belize, Bermuda, Brazil, British Virgin Islands, Brunei Darussalam, Bulgaria, Canada, Cayman Islands, Chile, China, Colombia, Costa Rica, Croatia, Curaçao, Cyprus, Czech Republic, Denmark, Dominica, Estonia, Faroe Islands, Finland, France, Germany, Gibraltar, Greece, Greenland, Grenada, Guernsey, Hong Kong, Hungary, Iceland, India, Indonesia, Ireland, Isle of Man, Israel, Italy, Japan, Jersey, Korea (South), Latvia, Liechtenstein, Lithuania, Luxembourg, Macau, Malaysia, Malta, Marshall Islands, Mauritius, Mexico, Monaco, Montserrat, Netherlands (including Bonaire, Sint Eustatius and Saba) New Zealand (not including Tokelau), Niue, Norway, Poland, Portugal, Qatar, Romania, Russia, Saint Kitts and Nevis, Saint Lucia, Saint Vincent and the Grenadines, Samoa, San Marino, Saudi Arabia, Seychelles, Singapore, Sint Maarten, Slovak Republic, Slovenia, South Africa, Spain, Sweden, Switzerland, Trinidad and Tobago, Turkey, Turks and Caicos Islands, United Arab Emirates, United States of America (not including overseas territories and possessions), Uruguay. General. - 2p.: 30 cm. - 978-0-11-113578-5 £4.25

Insolvency

The Insolvency (Protection of Essential Supplies) Order 2015 No. 2015/989. - Enabling power: Enterprise and Regulatory Reform Act 2013, ss. 92, 93, 94, 95. - Issued: 02.04.2015. Made: 26.03.2015. Coming into force: 01.10.2015. Effect: 1986 c.45; 2009 c.1 & S.I. 1994/2421; 2001/1090; 2011/245 & S.S.I. 2001/128 amended. Territorial extent & classification: E/W/S. General. - Supersedes draft S.I. (ISBN 9780111128992) issued 12/02/15. - 12p.: 30 cm. - 978-0-11-113621-8 £6.00

The Small Business, Enterprise and Employment Act 2015 (Commencement No. 1) Regulations 2015 No. 2015/1329 (C.75). - Enabling power: Small Business, Enterprise and Employment Act 2015, ss. 161 (2), 164 (1). Bringing into operation various provisions of the 2015 Act on 26.05.2015; 15.06.2015; 01.07.2015; 01.01.2016, in accord. with arts 2 to 6. - Issued: 28.05.2015. Made: 20.05.2015. Effect: None. Territorial extent & classification: E/W/S/NI. General. - 4p.: 30 cm. - 978-0-11-113644-7 £4.25

The Small Business, Enterprise and Employment Act 2015 (Commencement No. 2 and Transitional Provisions) Regulations 2015 No. 2015/1689 (C.100). - Enabling power: Small Business, Enterprise and Employment Act 2015, ss. 160 (1), 161 (1) (2), 164 (1), 164 (6). Bringing into operation various provisions of the 2015 Act on 01.10.2015; 10.10.2015, in accord. with arts 2 & 4. - Issued: 22.09.2015. Made: 15.09.2015. Effect: None. Territorial extent & classification: E/W/S/NI. General. - 8p.: 30 cm. - 978-0-11-113929-5 £6.00

The Small Business, Enterprise and Employment Act 2015 (Consequential Amendments) (Insolvency and Company Directors Disqualification) Regulations 2015 No. 2015/1651. - Enabling power: Small Business, Enterprise and Employment Act 2015, ss. 159 (1) (2). - Issued: 11.09.2015. Made: 01.09.2015. Laid: 08.09.2015. Coming into force: 01.10.2015. Effect: S.I. 1987/2023; 2003/358 (N.I.); 2009/2471; 2010/184 (N.I.); 2013/1388 amended. Territorial extent & classification: E/W/S. General. - 16p.: 30 cm. - 978-0-11-113901-1 £6.00

Insolvency: Insolvency practitioners

The Insolvency Practitioners (Amendment) Regulations 2015 No. 2015/391. - Enabling power: Insolvency Act 1986, s. 419 (1) (2) (c) (2) (f). - Issued: 04.03.2015. Made: 25.02.2015. Laid: 27.02.2015. Coming into force: 01.10.2015. Effect: S.I. 2005/524 amended. Territorial extent & classification: E/W/S. General. - 2p.: 30 cm. - 978-0-11-113079-7 £4.25

The Insolvency Practitioners and Insolvency Services Account (Fees) (Amendment) Order 2015 No. 2015/1977. - Enabling power: Insolvency Act 1986, s. 415A. - Issued: 11.12.2015. Made: 02.12.2015. Laid: 07.12.2015. Coming into force: 31.12.2015. Effect: S.I. 2003/3363 amended. Territorial extent & classification: E/W/S. General. - 2p.: 30 cm. - 978-0-11-114161-8 £4.25

The Insolvency Practitioners (Recognised Professional Bodies) (Revocation of Recognition) Order 2015 No. 2015/2067. - Enabling power: Insolvency Act 1986, s. 391N (1). - Issued: 24.12.2015. Made: 16.12.2015. Laid: 22.12.2015. Coming into force: 18.01.2016. Effect: S.I. 1986/1764 amended. Territorial extent & classification: E/W/S/NI. General. - 2p.: 30 cm. - 978-0-11-114250-9 £4.25

Insolvency, England and Wales

The Insolvency Act 1986 (Amendment) Order 2015 No. 2015/922. - Enabling power: Insolvency Act 1986, s. 267 (5). - Issued: 31.03.2015. Made: 19.03.2015. Coming into force: 01.10.2015. Effect: 1986 c.45 amended. Territorial extent & classification: E/W. General. - Supersedes draft S.I. (ISBN 9780111127292) issued 21.01.2015. - 2p.: 30 cm. - 978-0-11-113546-4 £4.25

The Insolvency (Amendment) Rules 2015 No. 2015/443. - Enabling power: Insolvency Act 1986, ss. 411, 412. - Issued: 09.03.2015. Made: 02.03.2015. Laid: 03.03.2015. Coming into force: 06.04.2015, for the purposes of Rules 1 and 13; 01.10.2015, remainder. Effect: S.I. 1986/1925 amended. Territorial extent & classification: E/W. General. - 8p.: 30 cm. - 978-0-11-113131-2 £6.00

The Insolvency Proceedings (Fees) (Amendment) Order 2015 No. 2015/1819. - Enabling power: Insolvency Act 1986, ss. 414, 415. - Issued: 29.10.2015. Made: 22.10.2015. Laid: 23.10.2015. Coming into force: 16.11.2015. Effect: S.I. 2004/593 amended. Territorial extent & classification: E/W. General. - 4p.: 30 cm. - 978-0-11-114016-1 £4.25

Insolvency, England and Wales: Individuals

The Insolvency Proceedings (Monetary Limits) (Amendment) Order 2015 No. 2015/26. - Enabling power: Insolvency Act 1986, s. 418. - Issued: 21.01.2015. Made: 14.01.2015. Laid: 15.01.2015. Coming into force: 01.10.2015. Effect: S.I. 1986/1996 amended. Territorial extent & classification: E/W. General. - 2p.: 30 cm. - 978-0-11-112727-8 £4.25

Insurance

The Flood Reinsurance (Scheme and Scheme Administrator Designation) Regulations 2015 No. 2015/1875. - Enabling power: Water Act 2014 ss. 64 (1) (b), 65 (1) (2). - Issued: 18.11.2015. Made: 10.11.2015. Coming into force: 11.11.2015 in accord. with reg. 1. Effect: None. Territorial extent & classification: E/W/S/NI. General. - Supersedes draft SI (ISBN 9780111137291) issued 06/07/15 - 2p.: 30 cm. - 978-0-11-114099-4 £4.25

The Flood Reinsurance (Scheme Funding and Administration) Regulations 2015 No. 2015/1902. - Enabling power: Water Act 2014, ss. 64 (3) (4), 66 (1) (2) (3) (4), 67 (1) (2) (3) (4) (5) (6) (7) (9), 69 (4), 82 (3) (5) (7), 84 (3) (4). - Issued: 18.11.2015. Made: 10.11.2015. Coming into force: 11.11.2015 in accord. with reg. 1 (b). Effect: None. Territorial extent & classification: E/W/S/NI. General. - Supersedes draft SI (ISBN 9780111137307) issued 06/07/15 - 16p.: 30 cm. - 978-0-11-114100-7 £6.00

Intellectual property

The Intellectual Property Act 2014 (Commencement No. 4) Order 2015 No. 2015/165 (C.9). - Enabling power: Intellectual Property Act 2014, ss. 24 (1) (2). Bringing into operation various provisions of the 2014 Act on 06.04.2015, in accord. with art. 2. - Issued: 13.02.2015. Made: 05.02.2015. Effect: None. Territorial extent & classification: E/W/S/NI. General. - 4p.: 30 cm. - 978-0-11-112903-6 £4.25

International development

The African Development Bank (Further Payments to Capital Stock) Order 2015 No. 2015/1702. - Enabling power: International Development Act 2002, s. 11. - Issued: 29.09.2015. Made: 18.09.2015. Laid: -Coming into force: In accord. with art. 1. Effect: None. Territorial extent & classification: E/W/S/NI. General. - Supersedes draft SI (ISBN 9780111137857) published 20/07/15. - 4p.: 30 cm. - 978-0-11-113941-7 £4.25

The Asian Infrastructure Investment Bank (Initial Capital Contribution) Order 2015 No. 2015/1835. - Enabling power: International Development Act 2002 s. 11. - Issued: 04.11.2015. Made: 27.10.2015. Laid: - Coming into force: 28.10.2015 in accord. with art. 1. Effect: None. Territorial extent & classification: E/W/S/NI. General. - Supersedes draft SI (ISBN 9780111138960) issued 11/09/15 - 2p.: 30 cm. - 978-0-11-114033-8 £4.25

The International Fund for Agricultural Development (Tenth Replenishment) Order 2015 No. 2015/2069. - Enabling power: International Development Act 2002, s. 11. - Issued: 29.12.2015. Made: 17.12.2015. Coming into force: In accord. with art. 1. Effect: None. Territorial extent & classification: E/W/S/NI. General. - Supersedes draft S.I. (ISBN 9780111136867) issued 24/06/15. - 4p.: 30 cm. - 978-0-11-114252-3 £4.25

International immunities and privileges

The Asian Infrastructure Investment Bank (Immunities and Privileges) Order 2015 No. 2015/1884. - Enabling power: International Organisations Act 1968, s. 1. - Issued: 18.11.2015. Made: 11.11.2015. Coming into force: In accord. with art. 1 (2). Effect: None. Territorial extent & classification: E/W/S/NI. General. - Supersedes draft SI (ISBN 9780111139820) issued 19/10/15 - 4p.: 30 cm. - 978-0-11-114082-6 £4.25

Investigatory powers

The Regulation of Investigatory Powers (Acquisition and Disclosure of Communications Data: Code of Practice) Order 2015 No. 2015/927. - Enabling power: Regulation of Investigatory Powers Act 2000, s. 71 (5) (8). - Issued: 01.04.2015. Made: 24.03.2015. Coming into force: 25.03.2015 in accord. with art. 1. Effect: None. Territorial extent & classification: E/W/S/NI. General. - Supersedes draft SI (ISBN 9780111131763) issued 10/03/15 - 2p.: 30 cm. - 978-0-11-113591-4 £4.25

The Regulation of Investigatory Powers (Communications Data) (Amendment) Order 2015 No. 2015/228. - Enabling power: Regulation of Investigatory Powers Act 2000, ss. 22 (2) (h), 25 (1) (g) (3) (4). - Issued: 18.02.2015. Made: 11.02.2015. Coming into force: In accord. with art. 1. Effect: S.I. 2010/480 amended. Territorial extent & classification: E/W/S/NI. General. - Supersedes S.I. draft (ISBN 9780111125083) issued 15/12/14. - 4p.: 30 cm. - 978-0-11-112968-5 £4.25

The Retention of Communications Data (Code of Practice) Order 2015 No. 2015/926. - Enabling power: Regulation of Investigatory Powers Act 2000, s. 71 (5). - Issued: 01.04.2015. Made: 24.03.2015. Coming into force: 25.03.2015 in accord. with art. 1. Effect: None. Territorial extent & classification: E/W/S/NI. General. - Supersedes draft SI (ISBN 9780111131770) issued 10/03/15 - 2p.: 30 cm. - 978-0-11-113590-7 £4.25

The Regulation of Investigatory Powers (Directed Surveillance and Covert Human Intelligence Sources) (Amendment) Order 2015 No. 2015/937. - Enabling power: Regulation of Investigatory Powers Act 2000, ss. 30 (3) (6), 78 (5). - Issued: 01.04.2015. Made: 26.03.2015. Laid: 27.03.2015. Coming into force: 01.10.2015. Effect: S.I. 2010/521 amended. Territorial extent & classification: E/W. General. - 2p.: 30 cm. - 978-0-11-113561-7 £4.25

Judgments

The Civil Jurisdiction and Judgments (Hague Convention on Choice of Court Agreements 2005) Regulations 2015 No. 2015/1644. - Enabling power: European Communities Act 1972, s. 2 (2). - Issued: 10.09.2015. Made: 03.09.2015. Laid: 07.09.2015. Coming into force: 01.10.2015. Effect: S.I. 1982 c.27 & S.I. 1997/302, 2780; 1998/3132 amended. Territorial extent & classification: E/W/S/NI. General. - 10p.: 30 cm. - 978-0-11-113890-8 £6.00

The Civil Jurisdiction and Judgments (Maintenance) and International Recovery of Maintenance (Hague Convention 2007 etc) (Amendment) Order 2015 No. 2015/1489. - Enabling power: European Communities Act 1972, s. 2 (2) & Crime and Courts Act 2013, s. 59. - Issued: 15.07.2015. Made: 06.07.2015. Laid: 10.07.2015. Coming into force: 31.07.2015. Effect: S.I. 2011/1484; 2012/2814 amended. Territorial extent & classification: E/W/S/NI. General. - 4p.: 30 cm. - 978-0-11-113771-0 £4.25

Judicature, Northern Ireland

The Justice and Security (Northern Ireland) Act 2007 (Extension of duration of non-jury trial provisions) Order 2015 No. 2015/1572. - Enabling power: Justice and Security (Northern Ireland) Act 2007, s. 9 (2). - Issued: 29.07.2015. Made: 23.07.2015. Coming into force: 24.07.2015. Effect: None. Territorial extent & classification: NI. General. - Supersedes draft SI (ISBN 9780111136560) issued 09/06/15 - 2p.: 30 cm. - 978-0-11-113853-3 £4.25

Juries, England and Wales

The Criminal Justice and Courts Act 2015 (Commencement No. 1, Saving and Transitional Provisions) Order 2015 No. 2015/778 (C.44). - Enabling power: Criminal Justice and Courts Act 2015, s. 95 (1) (6). Bringing into operation various provisions of the 2015 Act on 20.03.2015; 13.04.2015, in accord. with arts 2, 3. - Issued: 25.03.2015. Made: 19.03.2015. Effect: None. Territorial extent & classification: E/W/S/NI. General. - 8p.: 30 cm. - 978-0-11-113405-4 £6.00

Justice, Northern Ireland

The Justice and Security (Northern Ireland) Act 2007 (Extension of duration of non-jury trial provisions) Order 2015 No. 2015/1572. - Enabling power: Justice and Security (Northern Ireland) Act 2007, s. 9 (2). - Issued: 29.07.2015. Made: 23.07.2015. Coming into force: 24.07.2015. Effect: None. Territorial extent & classification: NI. General. - Supersedes draft SI (ISBN 9780111136560) issued 09/06/15 - 2p.: 30 cm. - 978-0-11-113853-3 £4.25

Justices of the Peace, England and Wales

The Justices' Allowances Regulations 2015 No. 2015/1423. - Enabling power: Courts Act 2003, ss. 15 (8), 109 (4) (5). - Issued: 07.07.2015. Made: 18.06.2015. Laid: 26.06.2015. Coming into force: 01.08.2015. Effect: S.I. 1976/117, 2118 revoked with saving. Territorial extent & classification: E/W. General. - 12p.: 30 cm. - 978-0-11-113719-2 £6.00

The Local Justice Areas (No. 2) Order 2015 No. 2015/1870. - Enabling power: Courts Act 2003, ss. 8 (4), 108 (6). - Issued: 13.11.2015. Made: 06.11.2015. Laid: 10.11.2015. Coming into force: In accord. with art. 1. Effect: S.I. 2005/554 amended. Territorial extent & classification: E/W. General. - 4p.: 30 cm. - 978-0-11-114068-0 £4.25

The Local Justice Areas Order 2015 No. 2015/1506. - Enabling power: Courts Act 2003, ss. 8 (4), 108 (6). - Issued: 17.07.2015. Made: 09.07.2015. Laid: 13.07.2015. Coming into force: In accord. with art. 1. Effect: S.I. 2005/554 amended. Territorial extent & classification: E/W. General. - 4p.: 30 cm. - 978-0-11-113779-6 £4.25

Land drainage, England and Wales

The Lombards Wall to Gravesend Bridge Internal Drainage District Order 2015 No. 2015/1552. - Enabling power: Land Drainage Act 1991, s. 3 (5) (7). - Issued: 24.07.2015. Made: 16.07.2015. Coming into force: 17.07.2015 in accord with art. 1. Effect: None. Territorial extent & classification: E/W. General. - 4p.: 30 cm. - 978-0-11-113828-1 £4.25

The Powysland Internal Drainage District (Abolition) Order 2015 No. 2015/923. - Enabling power: Land Drainage Act 1991, s. 3 (5) (7). - Issued: 01.04.2015. Made: 24.03.2015. Coming into force: 25.03.2015 in accord with art. 1. Effect: None. Territorial extent & classification: E/W. General. - 4p.: 30 cm. - 978-0-11-113547-1 £4.25

Land drainage, Wales

The Lower Wye and Caldicot and Wentlooge Internal Drainage Districts (Abolition) Order 2015 No. 2015/872 (W.65). - Enabling power: Land Drainage Act 1991, s. 3 (5) (7). - Issued: 05.05.2015. Made: 24.03.2015. Coming into force: In accord with art 1. Effect: None. Territorial extent & classification: W. General. - In English & Welsh. Welsh language title: Gorchymyn Ardaloedd Draenio Mewnol Rhannau Isaf Afon Gwy a Chil-y-coed a Gwynllwg (Diddymu) 2015. - 8p.: 30 cm. - 978-0-348-11076-0 £6.00

Land, England

The Homes and Communities Agency (Transfer of Property etc.) Regulations 2015 No. 2015/1471. - Enabling power: Housing and Regeneration Act 2008, ss. 1 (1), 53A (2), 320 (1) (7) (ca). - Issued: 10.07.2015. Made: 02.07.2015. Laid: 08.07.2015. Coming into force: 04.08.2015. Effect: None. Territorial extent & classification: E. General. - 4p.: 30 cm. - 978-0-11-113750-5 £4.25

Landfill tax

The Devolution of Landfill Tax (Consequential, Transitional and Saving Provisions) Order 2015 No. 2015/599. - Enabling power: Scotland Act 2012, ss. 42 (3) (4) (5). - Issued: 13.03.2015. Made: 09.03.2015. Laid: 10.03.2015. Coming into force: 31.03.2015. Effect: S.I. 1996/1527 amended. Territorial extent & classification: E/W/S/NI. General. - 4p.: 30 cm. - 978-0-11-113264-7 £4.25

The Scotland Act 2012, Section 31 (Disapplication of UK Landfill Tax) (Appointed Day) Order 2015 No. 2015/638 (C.35). - Enabling power: Scotland Act 2012, s. 31 (4). Bringing into operation various provisions of the 2012 Act on 01.04.2015, in accord. with art. 2. - Issued: 16.03.2015. Made: 09.03.2015. Effect: None. Territorial extent & classification: E/W/S/NI. General. - 2p.: 30 cm. - 978-0-11-113294-4 £4.25

Landfill tax, England and Wales

The Landfill Tax (Amendment) (No. 2) Regulations 2015 No. 2015/846. - Enabling power: Finance Act 1996, ss. 71 (9), sch. 5, paras. 2, 2A, 2B, 2C, 23. - Issued: 02.04.2015. Made: 26.03.2015. Laid: 27.03.2015. Coming into force: 01.04.2015. Effect: S.I. 1996/1527 amended. Territorial extent & classification: E/W/NI. General. - 4p.: 30 cm. - 978-0-11-113580-8 £4.25

The Landfill Tax (Amendment) (No. 3) Regulations 2015 No. 2015/1453. - Enabling power: Finance Act 1996, s. 71 (9), sch. 5, paras 2, 2A, 2B, 2C. - Issued: 07.07.2015. Made: 01.07.2015. Laid: 01.07.2015. Coming into force: 02.07.2015. Effect: S.I. 1996/1527 amended. Territorial extent & classification: E/W/NI. General. - 2p.: 30 cm. - 978-0-11-113733-8 £4.25

The Landfill Tax (Amendment) Regulations 2015 No. 2015/744. - Enabling power: Finance Act 1996, ss. 51 (1), 53 (1), 53 (4). - Issued: 23.03.2015. Made: 17.03.2015. Laid: 18.03.2015. Coming into force: 01.04.2015. Effect: S.I. 1996/1527 amended. Territorial extent & classification: E/W/NI. General. - 2p.: 30 cm. - 978-0-11-113377-4 £4.25

The Landfill Tax (Qualifying Fines) (No. 2) Order 2015 No. 2015/1385. - Enabling power: Finance Act 1996, ss. 42 (3A) (3B), 63A (2) to (5). - Issued: 18.06.2015. Made: 12.06.2015. Laid: 12.06.2015. Coming into force: 15.06.2015. Effect: None. Territorial extent & classification: E/W/NI. General. - For approval by resolution of the House of Commons within 28 days. Superseded by approved version (ISBN 9780111300022) issued 22.06.2015. - 4p.: 30 cm. - 978-0-11-113680-5 £4.25

The Landfill Tax (Qualifying Fines) (No. 2) Order 2015 No. 2015/1385. - Enabling power: Finance Act 1996, ss. 42 (3A) (3B), 63A (2) to (5). - Issued: 22.06.2015. Made: 12.06.2015. Laid: 12.06.2015. Coming into force: 15.06.2015. Effect: None. Territorial extent & classification: E/W/NI. General. - Approved by the House of Commons. - 4p.: 30 cm. - 978-0-11-130002-2 £4.25

The Landfill Tax (Qualifying Fines) Order 2015 No. 2015/845. - Enabling power: Finance Act 1996, ss. 42 (3A) (3B), 63A (2) to (5). - Issued: 02.04.2015. Made: 26.03.2015. Laid: 27.03.2015. Coming into force: 01.04.2015. Effect: None. Territorial extent & classification: E/W/NI. General. - For approval by resolution of the House of Commons within twenty eight days beginning with the day on which the Order was made. - 4p.: 30 cm. - 978-0-11-113567-9 £4.25

Landfill tax, Northern Ireland

The Landfill Tax (Amendment) (No. 2) Regulations 2015 No. 2015/846. - Enabling power: Finance Act 1996, ss. 71 (9), sch. 5, paras. 2, 2A, 2B, 2C, 23. - Issued: 02.04.2015. Made: 26.03.2015. Laid: 27.03.2015. Coming into force: 01.04.2015. Effect: S.I. 1996/1527 amended. Territorial extent & classification: E/W/NI. General. - 4p.: 30 cm. - 978-0-11-113580-8 £4.25

The Landfill Tax (Amendment) (No. 3) Regulations 2015 No. 2015/1453. - Enabling power: Finance Act 1996, s. 71 (9), sch. 5, paras 2, 2A, 2B, 2C. - Issued: 07.07.2015. Made: 01.07.2015. Laid: 01.07.2015. Coming into force: 02.07.2015. Effect: S.I. 1996/1527 amended. Territorial extent & classification: E/W/NI. General. - 2p.: 30 cm. - 978-0-11-113733-8 £4.25

The Landfill Tax (Amendment) Regulations 2015 No. 2015/744. - Enabling power: Finance Act 1996, ss. 51 (1), 53 (1), 53 (4). - Issued: 23.03.2015. Made: 17.03.2015. Laid: 18.03.2015. Coming into force: 01.04.2015. Effect: S.I. 1996/1527 amended. Territorial extent & classification: E/W/NI. General. - 2p.: 30 cm. - 978-0-11-113377-4 £4.25

The Landfill Tax (Qualifying Fines) (No. 2) Order 2015 No. 2015/1385. - Enabling power: Finance Act 1996, ss. 42 (3A) (3B), 63A (2) to (5). - Issued: 18.06.2015. Made: 12.06.2015. Laid: 12.06.2015. Coming into force: 15.06.2015. Effect: None. Territorial extent & classification: E/W/NI. General. - For approval by resolution of the House of Commons within 28 days. Superseded by approved version (ISBN 9780111300022) issued 22.06.2015. - 4p.: 30 cm. - 978-0-11-113680-5 £4.25

The Landfill Tax (Qualifying Fines) (No. 2) Order 2015 No. 2015/1385. - Enabling power: Finance Act 1996, ss. 42 (3A) (3B), 63A (2) to (5). - Issued: 22.06.2015. Made: 12.06.2015. Laid: 12.06.2015. Coming into force: 15.06.2015. Effect: None. Territorial extent & classification: E/W/NI. General. - Approved by the House of Commons. - 4p.: 30 cm. - 978-0-11-130002-2 £4.25

The Landfill Tax (Qualifying Fines) Order 2015 No. 2015/845. - Enabling power: Finance Act 1996, ss. 42 (3A) (3B), 63A (2) to (5). - Issued: 02.04.2015. Made: 26.03.2015. Laid: 27.03.2015. Coming into force: 01.04.2015. Effect: None. Territorial extent & classification: E/W/NI. General. - For approval by resolution of the House of Commons within twenty eight days beginning with the day on which the Order was made. - 4p.: 30 cm. - 978-0-11-113567-9 £4.25

Landlord and tenant, England

The Agricultural Holdings Act 1986 (Variation of Schedule 8) (England) Order 2015 No. 2015/Un-num. - Enabling power: Agricultural Holdings Act 1986, s. 91 (1). - Issued: 07.12.2015. Made: 24.11.2015. Laid: 02.12.2015. Coming into force: 06.04.2016. Effect: 1986 c.5 amended. Territorial extent & classification: E. General. - Superseded by S.I. 2015/2082 (ISBN 9780111143179) issued 02/02/16. For approval by resolution of each House of Parliament. - 2p.: 30 cm. - 978-0-11-114136-6 £4.25

The Agricultural Holdings Act 1986 (Variation of Schedule 8) (England) Order 2015 No. 2015/2082. - Enabling power: Agricultural Holdings Act 1986, s. 91 (1). - Issued: 02.02.2016. Made: 24.11.2015. Laid: 02.12.2015. Coming into force: 06.04.2016. Effect: 1986 c.5 amended. Territorial extent & classification: E. General. - Approved by both Houses of Parliament. - Supersedes draft SI (ISBN 9780111141366) issued 07/12/15 - 2p.: 30 cm. - 978-0-11-114317-9 £4.25

The Agricultural Holdings (Units of Production) (England) Order 2015 No. 2015/1745. - Enabling power: Agricultural Holdings Act 1986, sch. 6, para. 4. - Issued: 09.10.2015. Made: 01.10.2015. Laid: 07.10.2015. Coming into force: 07.11.2015. Effect: S.I. 2014/2712 revoked. Territorial extent & classification: E. General. - 4p.: 30 cm. - 978-0-11-113960-8 £4.25

The Agriculture (Model Clauses for Fixed Equipment) (England) Regulations 2015 No. 2015/950. - Enabling power: Agricultural Holdings Act 1986, s. 7 (1) (2). - Issued: 02.04.2015. Made: 26.03.2015. Laid: 27.03.2015. Coming into force: 01.10.2015. Effect: S.I. 1959/171; 1973/1473; 1988/281, 282 revoked. Territorial extent & classification: E. General. - 12p.: 30 cm. - 978-0-11-113577-8 £6.00

The Assured Shorthold Tenancy Notices and Prescribed Requirements (England) (Amendment) Regulations 2015 No. 2015/1725. - Enabling power: Housing Act 1988, ss. 21 (8). - Issued: 05.10.2015. Made: 29.09.2015. Laid: 29.09.2015. Coming into force: 30.09.2015. Effect: S.I. 2015/1646 amended. Territorial extent & classification: E. General. - This S.I. has been made in consequence of defects in S.I. 2015/1646 (ISBN 9780111139080) issued 14/09/15 and is being issued free of charge to all known recipients of that S.I. - 8p.: 30 cm. - 978-0-11-113947-9 £4.25

The Assured Shorthold Tenancy Notices and Prescribed Requirements (England) Regulations 2015 No. 2015/1646. - Enabling power: Housing Act 1988, ss. 8 (3), 21 (8), 21 A, 21B. - Issued: 14.09.2015. Made: 07.09.2015. Laid: 09.09.2015. Coming into force: 01.10.2015. Effect: S.I. 2015/620 amended. Territorial extent & classification: E. General. - 8p.: 30 cm. - 978-0-11-113908-0 £6.00

The Assured Tenancies and Agricultural Occupancies (Forms) (England) Regulations 2015 No. 2015/620. - Enabling power: Housing Act 1988, ss. 6 (2) (3), 8 (3), 13 (2) (4), 22 (1), 45 (1) (5), sch. 2 A, paras. 7 (2), 9 (2) (a)- Issued: 16.03.2015. Made: 09.03.2015. Coming into force: 06.04.2015. Effect: S.I. 1997/194 revoked in relation to England with savings & S.I. 2003/260 revoked with savings. Territorial extent & classification: E. General. - 28p.: 30 cm. - 978-0-11-113283-8 £6.00

The Landlord and Tenant (Notices) (Revocations) (England) Regulations 2015 No. 2015/1. - Enabling power: Landlord and Tenant Act 1954, s. 66. - Issued: 09.01.2015. Made: 05.01.2015. Laid: 08.01.2015. Coming into force: 04.02.2015. Effect: S.I. 1957/1157; 1967/1831 revoked. Territorial extent & classification: E. General. - This publication should have been published on 9 January 2015, Daily List 006. - 2p.: 30 cm. - 978-0-11-112655-4 £4.25

The Small Business, Enterprise and Employment Act 2015 (Commencement No. 2 and Transitional Provisions) Regulations 2015 No. 2015/1689 (C.100). - Enabling power: Small Business, Enterprise and Employment Act 2015, ss. 160 (1), 161 (1) (2), 164 (1), 164 (6). Bringing into operation various provisions of the 2015 Act on 01.10.2015; 10.10.2015, in accord. with arts 2 & 4. - Issued: 22.09.2015. Made: 15.09.2015. Effect: None. Territorial extent & classification: E/W/S/NI. General. - 8p.: 30 cm. - 978-0-11-113929-5 £6.00

Landlord and tenant, England: Agricultural holdings

The Agriculture (Calculation of Value for Compensation) (Revocations) (England) Regulations 2015 No. 2015/327. - Enabling power: Agricultural Holdings Act 1986, s. 66 (2). - Issued: 26.02.2015. Made: 15.02.2015. Laid: 23.02.2015. Coming into force: 01.10.2015. Effect: S.I. 1978/809; 1980/751; 1981/822;1983/1475 revoked. Territorial extent & classification: E. General. - 2p.: 30 cm. - 978-0-11-113017-9 £4.25

Landlord and tenant, Wales

The Agricultural Holdings (Units of Production) (Wales) (No. 2) Order 2015 No. 2015/1642 (W.214). - Enabling power: Agricultural Holdings Act 1986, sch. 6, para. 4. - Issued: 15.09.2015. Made: 02.09.2015. Laid before the National Assembly for Wales: 04.09.2015. Coming into force: 28.09.2015. Effect: S.I. 2015/1020 (W.73) revoked. Territorial extent & classification: W. General. - In English and Welsh: Welsh title: Gorchymyn Daliadau Amaethyddol (Unedau Cynhyrchu) (Cymru) (Rhif 2) 2015. - 8p.: 30 cm. - 978-0-348-11148-4 £6.00

The Agricultural Holdings (Units of Production) (Wales) (No. 3) Order 2015 No. 2015/1975 (W.296). - Enabling power: Agricultural Holdings Act 1986, sch. 6, para. 4. - Issued: 14.12.2015. Made: 02.12.2015. Laid before the National Assembly for Wales: 08.12.2015. Coming into force: 30.12.2015. Effect: S.I. 2015/1642 (W.214) amended. Territorial extent & classification: W. General. - In English and Welsh: Welsh title: Gorchymyn Daliadau Amaethyddol (Unedau Cynhyrchu) (Cymru) (Rhif 3) 2015. - 8p.: 30 cm. - 978-0-348-11199-6 £6.00

The Agricultural Holdings (Units of Production) (Wales) Order 2015 No. 2015/1020 (W.73). - Enabling power: Agricultural Holdings Act 1986, sch. 6, para. 4. - Issued: 01.05.2015. Made: 27.03.2015. Laid before the National Assembly for Wales: 31.03.2015. Coming into force: 21.04.2015. Effect: S.I. 2014/41 (W.3) revoked. Territorial extent & classification: W. General. - Revoked by SI 2015/1642 (W.214) (ISBN 9780348111484). - In English and Welsh: Welsh title: Gorchymyn Daliadau Amaethyddol (Unedau Cynhyrchu) (Cymru) 2015. - 8p.: 30 cm. - 978-0-348-11077-7 £6.00

The Small Business, Enterprise and Employment Act 2015 (Commencement No. 1) (Wales) Regulations 2015 No. 2015/1710 (W.225) (C.103). - Enabling power: Small Business, Enterprise and Employment Act 2015, s. 164 (5). Bringing various provisions of the 2015 Act into operation on 01.10.2015 in accord. with art. 2. - Issued: 01.10.2015. Made: 21.09.2015. Effect: None. Territorial extent & classification: W. General. - In English and Welsh. Welsh title: Rheoliadau Deddf Busnesau Bach, Menter a Chyflogaeth 2015 (Cychwyn) (Cymru) 2015. - 4p.: 30 cm. - 978-0-348-11158-3 £4.25

Legal aid and advice, England and Wales

The Civil and Criminal Legal Aid (Amendment) (No. 2) Regulations 2015 No. 2015/1678. - Enabling power: Legal Aid, Sentencing and Punishment of Offenders Act 2012, ss. 2 (3), 12 (2) (3), 23 (1) (2) (8), 25 (3), 27 (6) (c) (e), 30 (2), 41 (1) (2) (3) (b) (c). - Issued: 16.09.2015. Made: 09.09.2015. Laid: 11.09.2015. Coming into force: In accord. with reg. 1. Effect: S.I. 2012/3098; 2013/9, 422, 435, 483, 503, 614, 1369 amended. Territorial extent & classification: E/W. General. - 8p.: 30 cm. - 978-0-11-113923-3 £6.00

The Civil and Criminal Legal Aid (Amendment) Regulations 2015 No. 2015/1416. - Enabling power: Legal Aid, Sentencing and Punishment of Offenders Act 2012, ss. 2 (3), 12 (2), 14 (h), 21 (2) to (4), 23 (1) (6), 41 (1) to (3). - Issued: 30.06.2015. Made: 23.06.2015. Laid: 26.06.2015. Coming into force: In accord. with reg. 1. Effect: S.I. 2012/3098; 2013/9, 422, 435, 480 amended. Territorial extent & classification: E/W. General. - 8p.: 30 cm. - 978-0-11-113713-0 £6.00

The Civil and Criminal Legal Aid (Remuneration) (Amendment) Regulations 2015 No. 2015/325. - Enabling power: Legal Aid, Sentencing and Punishment of Offenders Act 2012, ss. 2 (3), 41 (1) to (3). - Issued: 26.02.2015. Made: 12.02.2015. Laid: 23.02.2015. Coming into force: 23.03.2015. Effect: S.I. 2013/422, 435 amended. Territorial extent & classification: E/W. General. - 8p.: 30 cm. - 978-0-11-113015-5 £4.25

The Civil Legal Aid (Merits Criteria) (Amendment) (No. 2) Regulations 2015 No. 2015/1571. - Enabling power: Legal Aid, Sentencing and Punishment of Offenders Act 2012, ss. 11 (1) (b), 41 (1) (a) (b) (3) (a) (c), sch. 3, para 3 (2). - Issued: 30.12.2015. Made: 23.07.2015. Laid: 24.07.2015. Coming into force: 27.07.2015. Effect: S.I. 2013/104 amended. Territorial extent & classification: E/W. General. - Approved by both Houses of Parliament. - 8p.: 30 cm. - 978-0-11-130009-1 £6.00

The Civil Legal Aid (Merits Criteria) (Amendment) (No. 2) Regulations 2015 No. 2015/1571. - Enabling power: Legal Aid, Sentencing and Punishment of Offenders Act 2012, ss. 11 (1) (b), 41 (1) (a) (3) (a) (c), sch. 3, para. 3 (2). - Issued: 29.07.2015. Made: 23.07.2015. Laid: 24.07.2015. Coming into force: 27.07.2015. Effect: S.I. 2013/104 amended. Territorial extent & classification: E/W. General. - For approval by resolution of each House of Parliament within 120 days beginning with the day on which the Regulations were made, subject to extensions for periods of dissolution, prorogation or adjournment for more than 4 days. - 8p.: 30 cm. - 978-0-11-113852-6 £6.00

The Civil Legal Aid (Merits Criteria) (Amendment) Regulations 2015 No. 2015/1414. - Enabling power: Legal Aid, Sentencing and Punishment of Offenders Act 2012, ss. 11 (1) (b), 41 (1) (a) (b) (2) (b). - Issued: 30.12.2015. Made: 23.06.2015. Laid: 25.06.2015. Coming into force: In accord. with reg. 1. Effect: S.I. 2013/104 amended. Territorial extent & classification: E/W. General. - Approved by both Houses of Parliament. - 4p.: 30 cm. - 978-0-11-130008-4 £4.25

The Civil Legal Aid (Merits Criteria) (Amendment) Regulations 2015 No. 2015/1414. - Enabling power: Legal Aid, Sentencing and Punishment of Offenders Act 2012, ss. 11 (1) (b), 41 (1) (a) (b) (2) (b). - Issued: 06.07.2015. Made: 23.06.2015. Laid: 25.06.2015. Coming into force: In accord. with reg. 1. Effect: S.I. 2013/104 amended. Territorial extent & classification: E/W. General. - For approval by resolution of each House of Parliament within 120 days beginning with the day on which the Regulations were made, subject to extensions for periods of dissolution, prorogation or adjournment for more than 4 days. - 4p.: 30 cm. - 978-0-11-113711-6 £4.25

The Civil Legal Aid (Merits Criteria and Information about Financial Resources) (Amendment) Regulations 2015 No. 2015/2005. - Enabling power: Legal Aid, Sentencing and Punishment of Offenders Act 2012, ss. 11 (1) (b), 22 (3) (f), 41 (1) (a) (b). - Issued: 16.12.2015. Made: 09.12.2015. Coming into force: 10.12.2015 in accord. with reg. 1. Effect: S.I. 2013/104, 628 amended. Territorial extent & classification: E/W. General. - 4p.: 30 cm. - 978-0-11-114185-4 £4.25

The Civil Legal Aid (Remuneration) (Amendment) Regulations 2015 No. 2015/898. - Enabling power: Legal Aid, Sentencing and Punishment of Offenders Act 2012, ss. 2 (3), 41 (1) (3). - Issued: 31.03.2015. Made: 25.03.2015. Laid: 26.03.2015. Coming into force: 27.03.2015. Effect: S.I. 2013/422 amended. Territorial extent & classification: E/W. General. - 8p.: 30 cm. - 978-0-11-113522-8 £6.00

The Crime and Courts Act 2013 (Commencement No. 12) Order 2015 No. 2015/813 (C.48). - Enabling power: Crime and Courts Act 2013, s. 61 (2). Bringing into operation various provisions of the 2013 Act on 20.03.2015; 01.06.2015, in accord. with arts 2, 3. - Issued: 26.03.2015. Made: 19.03.2015. Effect: None. Territorial extent & classification: E/W/S/NI. General. - 8p.: 30 cm. - 978-0-11-113444-3 £6.00

The Criminal Legal Aid (Contribution Orders) (Amendment) Regulations 2015 No. 2015/710. - Enabling power: Legal Aid, Sentencing and Punishment of Offenders Act 2012, ss. 23, 41. - Issued: 20.03.2015. Made: 11.03.2015. Laid: 19.03.2015. Coming into force: 01.06.2015. Effect: S.I. 2013/483 amended. Territorial extent & classification: E/W. General. - 4p.: 30 cm. - 978-0-11-113353-8 £4.25

The Criminal Legal Aid (General) (Amendment) Regulations 2015 No. 2015/326. - Enabling power: Legal Aid, Sentencing and Punishment of Offenders Act 2012, ss. 14 (h), 41 (1) (3). - Issued: 26.02.2015. Made: 12.02.2015. Laid: 23.02.2015. Coming into force: 23.03.2015 Effect: S.I. 2013/9 amended. Territorial extent & classification: E/W. General. - 4p.: 30 cm. - 978-0-11-113016-2 £4.25

The Criminal Legal Aid (Remuneration) (Amendment) Regulations 2015 No. 2015/882. - Enabling power: Legal Aid, Sentencing and Punishment of Offenders Act 2012, ss. 2 (3), 41 (1) to (3). - Issued: 31.03.2015. Made: 24.03.2015. Laid: 26.03.2015. Coming into force: 05.05.2015. Effect: S.I. 2013/435 amended. Territorial extent & classification: E/W. General. - 8p.: 30 cm. - 978-0-11-113505-1 £4.25

The Criminal Legal Aid (Remuneration etc.) (Amendment) (No. 2) Regulations 2015 No. 2015/2049. - Enabling power: Legal Aid, Sentencing and Punishment of Offenders Act 2012, ss. 2 (3), 13 (4) (5), 15 (1) (6) (7) (9), 21 (2), 41 (1) to (3). - Issued: 22.12.2015. Made: 15.12.2015. Laid: 17.12.2015. Coming into force: 10.01.2016. Effect: SI 2015/1369 amended. Territorial extent & classification: E/W. General. - This S.I. corrects an error in S.I. 2015/1369 (ISBN 9780111136645) and is being issued free of charge to all known recipients of that S.I. Revoked by S.I. 2016/313 (ISBN 9780111144893). - 4p.: 30 cm. - 978-0-11-114229-5 £4.25

The Criminal Legal Aid (Remuneration etc.) (Amendment) Regulations 2015 No. 2015/1369. - Enabling power: Legal Aid, Sentencing and Punishment of Offenders Act 2012, ss. 2 (3), 13 (4) (5), 15 (9), 18 (3) (4), 21 (2), 41 (1) to (3). - Issued: 15.06.2015. Made: 09.06.2015. Laid: 10.06.2015. Coming into force: 01.07.2015, 11.01.2016 in accord. with reg. 1. Effect: S.I. 2013/9 , 422, 435, 471 amended. Territorial extent & classification: E/W. General. - Partially revoked by S.I. 2016/313 (ISBN 9780111144893). - 64p.: 30 cm. - 978-0-11-113664-5 £11.00

The Legal Aid, Community Legal Service and Criminal Defence Service (Amendment) Regulations 2015 No. 2015/838. - Enabling power: Access to Justice Act 1999, ss. 7, 10, 17A, 25 (8), sch. 3, paras. 3B, 8 (2) & Legal Aid, Sentencing and Punishment of Offenders Act 2012, ss. 14 (h), 21 (2) (3), 22 (3) (f), 23 (1) (6), 41 (1) (2). - Issued: 27.03.2015. Made: 23.03.2015. Laid: 23.03.2015. Coming into force: In accord. with reg. 1. Effect: S.I. 2000/516; 2001/1437; 2006/2492; 2009/212, 3328; 2013/9, 471, 480, 483, 628 amended. Territorial extent & classification: E/W. General. - Partially revoked by S.I. 2015/1408 (ISBN 9780111137055). - 4p.: 30 cm. - 978-0-11-113465-8 £4.25

The Legal Aid (Information about Financial Resources) (Amendment) Regulations 2015 No. 2015/1408. - Enabling power: Legal Aid, Sentencing and Punishment of Offenders Act 2012, ss. 22 (3) (f), 41 (1) (b) (3) (c). - Issued: 30.06.2015. Made: 23.06.2015. Laid: 25.06.2015. Coming into force: 26.06.2015. Effect: S.I. 2013/628 amended & S.I. 2015/838 partially revoked. Territorial extent & classification: E/W. General. - This S.I. has been made as a consequence of a defect in S.I. 2015/838 (ISBN 9780111134658) published on 27/03/15 and is being issued free of charge to all known recipients of that S.I. - 2p.: 30 cm. - 978-0-11-113705-5 £4.25

Legal aid, England and Wales

The Restraint Orders (Legal Aid Exception and Relevant Legal Aid Payments) Regulations 2015 No. 2015/868. - Enabling power: Proceeds of Crime Act 2002, s. 41 (5A) (10) & Crime and Courts Act 2013, s. 47. - Issued: 27.03.2015. Made: 23.03.2015. Coming into force: In accord. with reg. 1. Effect: 2002 c.29 modified. Territorial extent & classification: E/W. General. - Supersedes draft S.I. (ISBN 9780111128381) issued 05/02/15. - 4p.: 30 cm. - 978-0-11-113491-7 £4.25

Legal services, England and Wales

The Criminal Justice and Courts Act 2015 (Commencement No. 1, Saving and Transitional Provisions) Order 2015 No. 2015/778 (C.44). - Enabling power: Criminal Justice and Courts Act 2015, s. 95 (1) (6). Bringing into operation various provisions of the 2015 Act on 20.03.2015; 13.04.2015, in accord. with arts 2, 3. - Issued: 25.03.2015. Made: 19.03.2015. Effect: None. Territorial extent & classification: E/W/S/NI. General. - 8p.: 30 cm. - 978-0-11-113405-4 £6.00

The Legal Services Act 2007 (The Law Society) (Modification of Functions) Order 2015 No. 2015/401. - Enabling power: Legal Services Act 2007, ss. 69, 204 (3) (4). - Issued: 03.03.2015. Made: 24.02.2015. Coming into force: In accord. with art. 1. Effect: 1974 c.47; 1985 c.61 & S.I. 2000/1119 amended. Territorial extent & classification: E/W. General. - Supersedes draft SI (ISBN 9780111124772) issued 11/12/14 - 12p.: 30 cm. - 978-0-11-113088-9 £6.00

The Legal Services Act 2007 (Warrant)(Approved Regulator) Regulations 2015 No. 2015/935. - Enabling power: Legal Services Act 2007, ss. 42 (6) (7), 48 (6) (7), 204 (3). - Issued: 01.04.2015. Made: 24.03.2015. Coming into force: In accord. with reg. 1 (1). Effect: None. Territorial extent & classification: E/W. General. - Supersedes draft S.I. (9780111127858) issued 30.01.2015. This Statutory Instrument supersedes the draft Legal Services Act 2007 (Warrant) Regulations 2010 which were laid before Parliament and published on 10th February 2010. It is being issued free of charge to all known recipients of that draft Statutory Instrument. - 4p.: 30 cm. - 978-0-11-113558-7 £4.25

The Legal Services Act 2007 (Warrant) (Licensing Authority) Regulations 2015 No. 2015/938. - Enabling power: Legal Services Act 2007, ss. 79 (6) (7), 204 (3). - Issued: 01.04.2015. Made: 24.03.2015. Coming into force: In accord. with reg. 1 (1). Effect: None. Territorial extent & classification: E/W. General. - Supersedes draft S.I. (ISBN 9780111127865) issued 30/01/15. - 4p.: 30 cm. - 978-0-11-113560-0 £4.25

Libraries

The Public Lending Right Scheme 1982 (Commencement of Variation) Order 2015 No. 2015/7. - Enabling power: Public Lending Right Act 1979, s. 3 (7). - Issued: 13.01.2015. Made: 05.01.2015. Laid: 08.01.2015. Coming into force: 03.02.2015. Effect: None. Territorial extent & classification: E/W/S/NI. General. - 2p.: 30 cm. - 978-0-11-112673-8 £4.25

Licences and licensing, England and Wales

The Licensing Act 2003 (Late Night Refreshment) Regulations 2015 No. 2015/1781. - Enabling power: Licensing Act 2003 s. 193, sch. 2, para. 2A (2). - Issued: 19.10.2015. Made: 13.10.2015. Laid: 15.10.2015. Coming into force: 05.11.2015. Effect: None. Territorial extent & classification: E/W. General. - 4p.: 30 cm. - 978-0-11-113990-5 £4.25

Licensing (marine)

The Marine Licensing (Delegation of Functions) (Amendment) Order 2015 No. 2015/1674. - Enabling power: Marine and Coastal Access Act 2009, ss. 98 (1), 99 (2) to (5), 316 (1) (b). - Issued: 16.09.2015. Made: 08.09.2015. Laid: 10.09.2015. Coming into force: 01.10.2015. Effect: S.I. 2011/627 amended. Territorial extent & classification: E/W/S/NI. General. - 4p.: 30 cm. - 978-0-11-113919-6 £4.25

The Marine Works (Environmental Impact Assessment) (Amendment) Regulations 2015 No. 2015/446. - Enabling power: European Communities Act 1972, s. 2 (2). - Issued: 09.03.2015. Made: 27.02.2015. Laid: 04.03.2015. Coming into force: 27.03.2015. Effect: S.I. 2007/1518 amended. Territorial extent & classification: E/W/S/NI. General. - EC note: These Regulations update references Directive 2011/92/EU on the assessment of the effects of certain public and private projects on the environment. - 4p.: 30 cm. - 978-0-11-113134-3 £4.25

The Regulatory Reform (Scotland) Act 2014 (Consequential Modifications) Order 2015 No. 2015/374. - Enabling power: Scotland Act 1998, ss. 104, 112 (1), 113 (2) (3) (4) (5). - Issued: 03.03.2015. Made: 25.02.2015. Coming into force: 26.02.2015. Effect: 1974 c.37; 1988 c.48; 1989 c.29; 1990 c.43; 1995 c.25; 2005 c.5; 2009 c.4; 2009 c.23; S.I. 1997/3032 amended. Territorial extent & classification: E/W/S/NI. General. - Supersedes draft S.I. (ISBN 9780111124505) issued 08/12/14. - 8p.: 30 cm. - 978-0-11-113066-7 £6.00

Limited liability partnerships

The Companies and Limited Liability Partnerships (Filing Requirements) Regulations 2015 No. 2015/1695. - Enabling power: European Communities Act 1972, s. 2 (2) & Interpretation Act 1978, s. 14A & Limited Liability Partnerships Act 2000, ss. 15 (a), 17 (3) (a) & Companies Act 2006, ss. 1042, 1043, 1292 (1). - Issued: 24.09.2015. Made: 17.09.2015. Laid: 18.09.2015. Coming into force: 10.10.2015. Effect: S.I. 1989/638; 2004/2326; 2009/1804, 2436, 2437 amended. Territorial extent & classification: E/W/S/NI. General. - 8p.: 30 cm. - 978-0-11-113935-6 £6.00

The Company, Limited Liability Partnership and Business (Names and Trading Disclosures) Regulations 2015 No. 2015/17. - Enabling power: Companies Act 2006, ss. 54 (1) (c), 56 (1) (a) (5), 57 (1) (a) (2) (5), 60 (1) (b), 65 (1) (2) (4), 66 (2) (3) (4) (6), 82, 84, 1193 (1) (c), 1195 (1) (a) (5), 1197 (1) (2) (3), 1292 (1) (2), 1294, 1296. - Issued: 15.01.2015. Made: 07.01.2015. Coming into force: 31.01.2015. Effect: 2000 c.38; S.I. 1989/638; 2003/1593; 2009/1803; 2011/245 amended & S.I. 2008/495; 2009/218, 1085, 2404, 2982 revoked. Territorial extent & classification: E/W/S/NI. General. - Supersedes S.I. draft (ISBN 9780111124154) issued 03/12/14. - 28p.: 30 cm. - 978-0-11-112691-2 £6.00

Local government, England

The Ashfield (Electoral Changes) Order 2015 No. 2015/112. - Enabling power: Local Democracy, Economic Development and Construction Act 2009, s. 59 (1). - Issued: 09.02.2015. Made: 02.02.2015. Coming into force: In accord. with art. 1 (2). Effect: None. Territorial extent & classification: E. Local. - Supersedes draft S.I. (ISBN 9780111124086) issued 02/12/14. - 4p.: 30 cm. - 978-0-11-112864-0 £4.25

The Borough of Rotherham (Scheme of Elections) Order 2015 No. 2015/884. - Enabling power: Local Government Act 2000, ss. 86 (A1) (3) (4) (7), 87 (1) (3), 105. - Issued: 31.03.2015. Made: 25.03.2015. Laid: 26.03.2015. Coming into force: 24.04.2015. Effect: None. Territorial extent & classification: E. General. - 2p.: 30 cm. - 978-0-11-113507-5 £4.25

The Bristol (Electoral Changes) Order 2015 No. 2015/1871. - Enabling power: Local Democracy, Economic Development and Construction Act 2009, s. 59 (1). - Issued: 13.11.2015. Made: 05.11.2015. Coming into force: In accord. with arts 1 (2) - (4). Effect: None. Territorial extent & classification: E. Local. - Supersedes draft S.I. (ISBN 9780111137802) issued 17/07/15. - 4p.: 30 cm. - 978-0-11-114070-3 £4.25

LOCAL GOVERNMENT, ENGLAND

The Broxtowe (Electoral Changes) Order 2015 No. 2015/72. - Enabling power: Local Democracy, Economic Development and Construction Act 2009, s. 59 (1). - Issued: 03.02.2015. Made: 23.01.2015. Coming into force: In accord. with art. 1 (2). Effect: None. Territorial extent & classification: E. Local. - Supersedes draft SI (ISBN 9780111123522) issued 24/11/14. - 8p.: 30 cm. - 978-0-11-112811-4 £4.25

The Cherwell (Electoral Changes) Order 2015 No. 2015/1872. - Enabling power: Local Democracy, Economic Development and Construction Act 2009, s. 59 (1). - Issued: 13.11.2015. Made: 05.11.2015. Coming into force: In accord. with arts 1 (2) (3). Effect: None. Territorial extent & classification: E. Local. - Supersedes draft S.I. (ISBN 9780111137888) issued 20/07/15. - 8p.: 30 cm. - 978-0-11-114071-0 £6.00

The City of Birmingham (Scheme of Elections) (Amendment) Order 2015 No. 2015/666. - Enabling power: Local Government Act 2000, ss. 86 (A1) (3) (4) (7), 87 (1) (3), 105 (2). - Issued: 18.03.2015. Made: 12.03.2015. Laid: 13.03.2015. Coming into force: 16.04.2015. Effect: S.I. 2014/43 amended. Territorial extent & classification: E. General. - 2p.: 30 cm. - 978-0-11-113324-8 £4.25

The City of Birmingham (Scheme of Elections) Order 2015 No. 2015/43. - Enabling power: Local Government Act 2000, s. 86 (A1) (3) (4) (7), 87 (1) (3). - Issued: 27.01.2015. Made: 21.01.2015. Laid: 22.01.2015. Coming into force: 16.02.2015. Effect: None. Territorial extent & classification: E. General. - 2p.: 30 cm. - 978-0-11-112772-8 £4.25

The Colchester (Electoral Changes) Order 2015 No. 2015/1859. - Enabling power: Local Democracy, Economic Development and Construction Act 2009, s. 59(1)- Issued: 10.11.2015. Made: 03.11.2015. Laid: - Coming into force: In accord. with art. 1 (2). Effect: None. Territorial extent & classification: E. Local. - Supersedes draft S.I. (ISBN 9780111137659) issued 14/07/15 - 4p.: 30 cm. - 978-0-11-114057-4 £4.25

The Community Right to Challenge (Business Improvement Districts) Regulations 2015 No. 2015/582. - Enabling power: Localism Act 2011, ss. 81 (6) (e). - Issued: 12.03.2015. Made: 05.03.2015. Coming into force: 06.03.2015 in accord. with reg. 1. Effect: None. Territorial extent and classification: E. General. - Supersedes S.I. draft (ISBN 9780111127100) issued 19/01/15. - 4p.: 30 cm. - 978-0-11-113252-4 £4.25

The Cotswold (Electoral Changes) Order 2015 No. 2015/113. - Enabling power: Local Democracy, Economic Development and Construction Act 2009, s. 59 (1). - Issued: 09.02.2015. Made: 03.02.2015. Coming into force: In accord. with art. 1 (2). Effect: None. Territorial extent & classification: E. Local. - Supersedes draft S.I. (ISBN 9780111123508) issued 24/11/14. - 8p.: 30 cm. - 978-0-11-112865-7 £6.00

The Council Tax and Non-Domestic Rating (Powers of Entry: Safeguards) (England) Order 2015 No. 2015/982. - Enabling power: Protection of Freedoms Act 2012, ss. 40, 41 (1), 44 (1). - Issued: 02.04.2015. Made: 26.03.2015. Coming into force: 01.10.2015. Effect: 1988 c. 41; 1992 c. 14 amended. Territorial extent & classification: E. General. - Supersedes draft SI (ISBN 9780111130858) issued 04/03/15 - 4p.: 30 cm. - 978-0-11-113617-1 £4.25

The Doncaster (Electoral Changes) Order 2015 No. 2015/114. - Enabling power: Local Democracy, Economic Development and Construction Act 2009, s. 59 (1). - Issued: 09.02.2015. Made: 02.02.2015. Coming into force: In accord. with art. 1 (2). Effect: None. Territorial extent & classification: E. Local. - Supersedes draft S.I. (ISBN 9780111124109) issued 05/12/14. - 4p.: 30 cm. - 978-0-11-112866-4 £4.25

The East Northamptonshire (Electoral Changes) Order 2015 No. 2015/563. - Enabling power: Local Government and Public Involvement in Health Act 2007, s. 92 (3). - Issued: 06.03.2015. Made: 03.03.2015. Coming into force: in accord. with art. 1 (2) (3). Effect: None. Territorial extent & classification: E. Local. - Available at http://www.legislation.gov.uk/uksi/2015/563/contents/made Non-print

The Erewash (Electoral Changes) Order 2015 No. 2015/77. - Enabling power: Local Democracy, Economic Development and Construction Act 2009, s. 59 (1). - Issued: 03.02.2015. Made: 27.01.2015. Coming into force: In accord. with art. 1 (2). Effect: None. Territorial extent & classification: E. Local. - Supersedes draft S.I. (ISBN 9780111123805) issued 01/12/14. - 4p.: 30 cm. - 978-0-11-112816-9 £4.25

The Gloucester (Electoral Changes) Order 2015 No. 2015/2026. - Enabling power: Local Democracy, Economic Development and Construction Act 2009, s. 59 (1). - Issued: 18.12.2015. Made: 11.12.2015. Coming into force: In accord. with art. 1 (2) (3). Effect: None. Territorial extent & classification: E. Local. - 4p.: 30 cm. - 978-0-11-114202-8 £4.25

The Greater Manchester Combined Authority (Amendment) Order 2015 No. 2015/960. - Enabling power: Local Democracy, Economic Development and Construction Act 2009, ss. 104 (1), 114 (1) (2). - Issued: 02.04.2015. Made: 26.03.2015. Coming into force: In accord. with art. 1. Effect: S.I. 2011/908 amended. Territorial extent & classification: E. General. - Supersedes draft S.I. (ISBN 9780111130452) issued 02/03/15. - 8p.: 30 cm. - 978-0-11-113589-1 £4.25

The Hertfordshire (Electoral Changes) Order 2015 No. 2015/1873. - Enabling power: Local Democracy, Economic Development and Construction Act 2009, s. 59 (1). - Issued: 13.11.2015. Made: 05.11.2015. Coming into force: In accord. with art. 1 (2) - (5). Effect: None. Territorial extent & classification: E. Local. - Supersedes draft S.I. (ISBN 9780111137864) issued 20/07/15. - 12p.: 30 cm. - 978-0-11-114072-7 £6.00

The High Peak (Electoral Changes) Order 2015 No. 2015/78. - Enabling power: Local Democracy, Economic Development and Construction Act 2009, s. 59 (1). - Issued: 03.02.2015. Made: 27.01.2015. Coming into force: In accord. with art. 1 (2). Effect: None. Territorial extent & classification: E. Local. - Supersedes draft S.I. (ISBN 9780111123812) issued 01/12/14. - 8p.: 30 cm. - 978-0-11-112817-6 £4.25

The Knowsley (Electoral Changes) Order 2015 No. 2015/2036. - Enabling power: Local Democracy, Economic Development and Construction Act 2009, s. 59 (1). - Issued: 21.12.2015. Made: 11.12.2015. Coming into force: In accord. with art. 1 (2) (3) (4). Effect: None. Territorial extent & classification: E. Local. - Supersedes draft S.I. (ISBN 9780111140215) issued 30/10/15. - 8p.: 30 cm. - 978-0-11-114213-4 £4.25

The Lichfield (Electoral Changes) Order 2015 No. 2015/111. - Enabling power: Local Democracy, Economic Development and Construction Act 2009, s. 59 (1). - Issued: 09.02.2015. Made: 02.02.2015. Coming into force: In accord. with art. 1 (2). Effect: None. Territorial extent & classification: E. Local. - Supersedes draft S.I. (ISBN 9780111124093) issued 02/12/14. - 8p.: 30 cm. - 978-0-11-112863-3 £4.25

The Lincoln (Electoral Changes) Order 2015 No. 2015/1461. - Enabling power: Local Democracy, Economic Development and Construction Act 2009, s. 59 (1). - Issued: 09.07.2015. Made: 29.06.2015. Coming into force: In accord. with art. 1 (2). Effect: None. Territorial extent & classification: E. Local. - Supersedes draft S.I. (ISBN 9780111133880) issued 24/03/15. - 4p.: 30 cm. - 978-0-11-113741-3 £4.25

The Local Authorities (Prohibition of Charging Residents to Deposit Household Waste) Order 2015 No. 2015/973. - Enabling power: Localism Act 2011, ss. 5 (3) (5), 235 (2). - Issued: 02.04.2015. Made: 26.03.2015. Coming into force: In accord with art. 1 (2). Effect: None. Territorial extent & classification: E. General. - Supersedes draft SI (ISBN 9780111130629) issued 03/03/15. - 2p.: 30 cm. - 978-0-11-113607-2 £4.25

The Local Authorities (Standing Orders) (England) (Amendment) Regulations 2015 No. 2015/881. - Enabling power: Local Government and Housing Act 1989, ss. 8, 20, 190. - Issued: 09.04.2015. Made: 25.03.2015. Laid: 25.03.2015. Coming into force: 11.05.2015. Effect: S.I. 2001/3384 amended. Territorial extent & classification: E. General. - 8p.: 30 cm. - 978-0-11-113504-4 £4.25

The Local Government (Electronic Communications) (England) Order 2015 No. 2015/5. - Enabling power: Electronic Communications Act 2000, ss 8, 9. - Issued: 12.01.2015. Made: 06.01.2015. Laid: 07.01.2015. Coming into force: 30.01.2015. Effect: 1972 c.70 amended. Territorial extent & classification: E. General. - 4p.: 30 cm. - 978-0-11-112660-8 £4.25

The Local Government (Prohibition of Charges at Household Waste Recycling Centres) (England) Order 2015 No. 2015/619. - Enabling power: Local Government Act 2003, ss. 94, 123 (1). - Issued: 16.03.2015. Made: 09.03.2015. Laid: 12.03.2015. Coming into force: 06.04.2015. Effect: None. Territorial extent & classification: E. General. - 4p.: 30 cm. - 978-0-11-113282-1 £4.25

The Local Government (Transparency) (Descriptions of Information) (England) Order 2015 No. 2015/471. - Enabling power: Local Government, Planning and Land Act 1980, s. 3 (6). - Issued: 10.03.2015. Made: 07.01.2015. Laid: 12.01.2015. Coming into force: In accord. with art. 1. Effect: None. Territorial extent & classification: E. General. - 2p.: 30 cm. - 978-0-11-113165-7 £4.25

The Local Government (Transparency Requirements) (England) Regulations 2015 No. 2015/480. - Enabling power: Local Government, Planning and Land Act 1980, s. 3 (1) (2) (3) (4). - Issued: 10.03.2015. Made: 03.03.2015. Laid: 05.03.2015. Coming into force: 01.04.2015. Effect: S.I. 2014/2680 revoked. Territorial extent & classification: E. General. - 4p.: 30 cm. - 978-0-11-113178-7 £4.25

The NHS Bodies and Local Authorities Partnership Arrangements (Amendment) Regulations 2015 No. 2015/1940. - Enabling power: National Health Service Act 2006, ss. 75 (1) (2) (3), 272 (7). - Issued: 02.12.2015. Made: 25.11.2015. Laid: 30.11.2015. Coming into force: 01.04.2016. Effect: S.I. 2000/617 amended. Territorial extent & classification: E. General. - 4p.: 30 cm. - 978-0-11-114127-4 £4.25

The Peterborough (Electoral Changes) Order 2015 No. 2015/1858. - Enabling power: Local Democracy, Economic Development and Construction Act 2009, s. 59 (1). - Issued: 09.11.2015. Made: 03.11.2015. Coming into force: In accord. with art. 1 (2). Effect: None. Territorial extent & classification: E. Local. - Supersedes draft SI (ISBN 9780111137673) issued 15/07/15 - 8p.: 30 cm. - 978-0-11-114056-7 £6.00

The Poole (Electoral Changes) Order 2015 No. 2015/73. - Enabling power: Local Democracy, Economic Development and Construction Act 2009, s. 59 (1). - Issued: 03.02.2015. Made: 23.01.2015. Coming into force: In accord. with art. 1 (2). Effect: None. Territorial extent & classification: E. Local. - Supersedes draft SI (ISBN 9780111122853) issued 07/11/14 - 4p.: 30 cm. - 978-0-11-112812-1 £4.25

The Purbeck (Electoral Changes) Order 2015 No. 2015/115. - Enabling power: Local Government and Public Involvement in Health Act 2007, s. 92 (3). - Issued: 09.02.2015. Made: 03.02.15. Coming into force: In accord. with art. 1 (2). Effect: None. Territorial extent & classification: E. - 4p.: 30 cm. - 978-0-11-112867-1 £4.25

The Rochford (Electoral Changes) Order 2015 No. 2015/1860. - Enabling power: Local Democracy, Economic Development and Construction Act 2009, s. 59 (1). - Issued: 10.11.2015. Made: 03.11.2015. Laid: - Coming into force: In accord. with art. 1 (2) - (4). Effect: None. Territorial extent & classification: E. Local. - Supersedes draft S.I. (ISBN 9780111137680) issued 15/07/15 - 8p.: 30 cm. - 978-0-11-114058-1 £6.00

The Rugby (Electoral Changes) Order 2015 No. 2015/120. - Enabling power: Local Government and Public Involvement in Health Act 2007, s. 92 (3). - Issued: 09.02.2015. Made: 03.02.2015. Coming into force: In accord. with art. 1 (2). Effect: None. Territorial extent & classification: E. Local. - 4p.: 30 cm. - 978-0-11-112870-1 £4.25

The Sheffield (Electoral Changes) Order 2015 No. 2015/1861. - Enabling power: Local Democracy, Economic Development and Construction Act 2009, s. 59 (1). - Issued: 10.11.2015. Made: 03.11.2015. Laid: - Coming into force: In accord. with art. 1 (2). Effect: None. Territorial extent & classification: E. Local. - Supersedes draft S.I. (ISBN 9780111137642) issued 14/07/15 - 4p.: 30 cm. - 978-0-11-114059-8 £4.25

The Smaller Authorities (Transparency Requirements) (England) Regulations 2015 No. 2015/494. - Enabling power: Local Government, Planning and Land Act 1980, ss. 3 (1) (2) (3) (4). - Issued: 10.03.2015. Made: 04.03.2015. Laid: 09.03.2015. Coming into force: 01.04.2015. Effect: None. Territorial extent & classification: E. General. - 4p.: 30 cm. - 978-0-11-113192-3 £4.25

The South Bucks (Electoral Changes) Order 2015 No. 2015/75. - Enabling power: Local Democracy, Economic Development and Construction Act 2009, s. 59 (1). - Issued: 03.02.2015. Made: 23.01.2015. Coming into force: In accord. with art. 1 (2). Effect: None. Territorial extent & classification: E. Local. - Supersedes draft S.I. (ISBN 9780111123539) issued 24/11/14. - 8p.: 30 cm. - 978-0-11-112814-5 £4.25

The Stafford (Electoral Changes) Order 2015 No. 2015/69. - Enabling power: Local Democracy, Economic Development and Construction Act 2009, s. 59 (1). - Issued: 03.02.2015. Made: 23.01.2015. Coming into force: In accord. with art. 1 (2). Effect: None. Territorial extent & classification: E. Local. - Supersedes draft SI (ISBN 9780111122846) issued 07/11/14. - 4p.: 30 cm. - 978-0-11-112808-4 £4.25

The Stroud (Electoral Changes) Order 2015 No. 2015/2034. - Enabling power: Local Democracy, Economic Development and Construction Act 2009, s. 59 (1). - Issued: 21.12.2015. Made: 11.12.2015. Coming into force: In accord. with art. 1 (2) (3). Effect: None. Territorial extent & classification: E. Local. - Supersedes draft S.I. (ISBN 9780111140246) issued 30/10/15. - 8p.: 30 cm. - 978-0-11-114211-0 £4.25

The Swindon (Electoral Changes) Order 2015 No. 2015/116. - Enabling power: Local Government and Public Involvement in Health Act 2007, s. 92 (3). - Issued: 09.02.2015. Made: 03.02.2015. Coming into force: In accord. with arts. 1 (2). Effect: None. Territorial extent & classification: E. Local. - 2p.: 30 cm. - 978-0-11-112868-8 £4.25

The Warwickshire (Electoral Changes) Order 2015 No. 2015/1874. - Enabling power: Local Democracy, Economic Development and Construction Act 2009, s. 59 (1). - Issued: 30.11.2015. Made: 05.11.2015. Coming into force: In accord. with art. 1 (2) (3). Effect: None. Territorial extent & classification: E. Local. - Supersedes draft SI (ISBN 9780111137819) issued 17/07/15 - 8p.: 30 cm. - 978-0-11-114073-4 £6.00

The West Devon (Electoral Changes) Order 2015 No. 2015/74. - Enabling power: Local Democracy, Economic Development and Construction Act 2009, s. 59 (1). - Issued: 03.02.2015. Made: 23.01.2015. Coming into force: In accord. with art. 1 (2). Effect: None. Territorial extent & classification: E. Local. - Supersedes draft SI (ISBN 9780111123553) issued 24/11/14 - 4p.: 30 cm. - 978-0-11-112813-8 £4.25

The West Dorset (Electoral Changes) Order 2015 No. 2015/76. - Enabling power: Local Democracy, Economic Development and Construction Act 2009, s. 59 (1). - Issued: 03.02.2015. Made: 27.01.2015. Coming into force: In accord. with art. 1 (2). Effect: None. Territorial extent & classification: E. Local. - Supersedes draft SI (ISBN 9780111123829) issued 01/12/14 - 8p.: 30 cm. - 978-0-11-112815-2 £4.25

The Winchester (Electoral Changes) Order 2015 No. 2015/2063. - Enabling power: Local Democracy, Economic Development and Construction Act 2009 s. 59 (1). - Issued: 23.12.2015. Made: 11.12.2015. Coming into force: In accord. with art. 1 (2) (3) (4). Effect: None. Territorial extent & classification: E. Local. - Supersedes draft SI (ISBN 9780111140208) issued 30/10/15 - 8p.: 30 cm. - 978-0-11-114245-5 £6.00

The Woking (Electoral Changes) Order 2015 No. 2015/1462. - Enabling power: Local Democracy, Economic Development and Construction Act 2009, s. 59 (1). - Issued: 09.07.2015. Made: 29.06.2015. Coming into force: In accord. with art. 1 (2). Effect: None. Territorial extent & classification: E. Local. - Supersedes draft S.I. (ISBN 9780111133873) issued 24/03/15. - 4p.: 30 cm. - 978-0-11-113742-0 £4.25

The Wyre Forest (Electoral Changes) Order 2015 No. 2015/70. - Enabling power: Local Democracy, Economic Development and Construction Act 2009, s. 59 (1). - Issued: 03.02.2015. Made: 23.01.2015. Coming into force: In accord. with art. 1 (2). Effect: None. Territorial extent & classification: E. Local. - Supersedes draft SI (ISBN 9780111123546) issued 24/11/14. - 4p.: 30 cm. - 978-0-11-112810-7 £4.25

Local government, England: Finance

The Transport Levying Bodies (Amendment) Regulations 2015 No. 2015/27. - Enabling power: Local Government Finance Act 1988, ss 74, 143 (1) (2). - Issued: 20.01.2015. Made: 10.01.2015. Laid: 20.01.2015. Coming into force: 16.02.2015. Effect: S.I. 1992/2789 amended. Territorial extent & classification: E. General. - 8p.: 30 cm. - 978-0-11-112728-5 £4.25

Local government, England and Wales

The Accounts and Audit Regulations 2015 No. 2015/234. - Enabling power: Local Audit and Accountability Act 2014, ss. 32, 43 (2). - Issued: 19.02.2015. Made: 12.02.2015. Laid: 17.02.2015. Coming into force: 01.04.2015. Effect: S.I. 2011/3058; 2012/854; 2013/235 partially revoked & S.I. 2011/817 revoked. Territorial extent & classification: E/W. General. - 16p.: 30 cm. - 978-0-11-112974-6 £6.00

LOCAL GOVERNMENT, WALES

The Legislative Reform (Community Governance Reviews) Order 2015 No. 2015/998. - Enabling power: Legislative and Regulatory Reform Act 2006, s. 1. - Issued: 08.04.2015. Made: 26.03.2015. Coming into force: 27.03.2015 in accord. with art. 1. Effect: 2007 c.28 amended. Territorial extent & classification: E/W. General. - Supersedes draft S.I. (ISBN 9780111125120) issued 15.12.2014. - 4p.: 30 cm. - 978-0-11-113628-7 £4.25

The Local Audit and Accountability Act 2014 (Commencement No. 5) Order 2015 No. 2015/179 (C.11). - Enabling power: Local Audit and Accountability Act 2014 s. 49 (1) (5). Bringing into operation various provisions of the 2014 Act on 10.02.2015, in accord. with art. 2. - Issued: 16.02.2015. Made: 09.02.2015. Effect: None. Territorial extent & classification: E/W. General. - 4p.: 30 cm. - 978-0-11-112916-6 £4.25

The Local Audit and Accountability Act 2014 (Commencement No. 6) Order 2015 No. 2015/223 (C.15). - Enabling power: Local Audit and Accountability Act 2014 s. 49 (1) (5). Bringing into operation various provisions of the 2014 Act on 12.02.2015, in accord. with art. 2. - Issued: 18.02.2015. Made: 11.02.2015. Effect: None. Territorial extent & classification: E/W. General. - 4p.: 30 cm. - 978-0-11-112962-3 £4.25

The Local Audit and Accountability Act 2014 (Commencement No. 7, Transitional Provisions and Savings) Order 2015 No. 2015/841 (C.53). - Enabling power: Local Audit and Accountability Act 2014 s. 49 (1) (5) (8). Bringing into operation various provisions of the 2014 Act on 01.04.2015, 01.04.2017. - Issued: 30.03.2015. Made: 23.03.2015. Effect: None. Territorial extent & classification: E/W. General. - 12p.: 30 cm. - 978-0-11-113486-3 £6.00

The Local Audit (Appointing Person) Regulations 2015 No. 2015/192. - Enabling power: Local Audit and Accountability Act 2014, ss. 17 (1) (2) (b) (3) to (10), 43 (2), 46 (1). - Issued: 17.02.2015. Made: 09.02.2015. Coming into force: 10.02.2015 in accord. with reg. 1. Effect: 2001 c.24; 2006 c.41; 2014 c.2 modified. Territorial extent & classification: E/W. General. - Supersedes S.I. draft (ISBN 9780111126134) issued 23/12/14. - 16p.: 30 cm. - 978-0-11-112928-9 £6.00

The Local Audit (Smaller Authorities) Regulations 2015 No. 2015/184. - Enabling power: Local Audit and Accountability Act 2014, ss. 5 (1) to (3) (4) (a) (c) to (g) (5) (a) to (c) (6) to (9), 6 (4), 43 (2), 46 (1). - Issued: 16.02.2015. Made: 09.02.2015. Coming into force: In accord. with reg. 1. Effect: 1968 c.73; 2001 c.24; 2014 c.2 modified. Territorial extent & classification: E/W. General. - Supersedes S.I. draft (ISBN 9780111126103) issued 23/12/14. - 24p.: 30 cm. - 978-0-11-112922-7 £6.00

The Local Authorities (Capital Finance and Accounting) (England) (Amendment) Regulations 2015 No. 2015/341. - Enabling power: Local Government Act 2003, ss. 11, 21 (1), 123. - Issued: 02.03.2015. Made: 17.02.2015. Laid: 25.02.2015. Coming into force: 01.04.2015. Effect: S.I. 2003/3146 amended. Territorial extent & classification: E/W. General. - 12p.: 30 cm. - 978-0-11-113029-2 £6.00

Local government, Wales

The Local Government Byelaws (Wales) Act 2012 (Commencement No. 2), Transitional Provisions and Savings) Order 2015 No. 2015/1025 (W.74) (C.70). - Enabling power: Local Government Byelaws (Wales) Act 2012, s. 22 (2) (3). Bringing various provisions of the 2012 Act into operation on 31.03.2015. - Issued: 29.04.2015. Made: 25.04.2015. Effect: None. Territorial extent & classification: W. General. - In English and Welsh. Welsh title: Gorchymyn Deddf Is-ddeddfau Llywodraeth Leol (Cymru) 2012 (Cychwyn Rhif 2, Darpariaethau Trosiannol ac Arbedion) 2015. - 8p.: 30 cm. - 978-0-348-11070-8 £6.00

The Local Government (Democracy) (Wales) Act 2013 (Commencement No. 2) Order 2015 No. 2015/1182 (W.79) (C.71). - Enabling power: Local Government (Democracy) (Wales) Act 2013, s. 75 (3). Bringing various provisions of the 2013 Act into operation on 01.05.2015, in accord. with art. 2. - Issued: 24.04.2015. Made: 16.04.2015. Effect: None. Territorial extent & classification: W. General. - In English and Welsh. Welsh title: Gorchymyn Deddf Llywodraeth Leol (Democratiaeth) (Cymru) 2013 (Cychwyn Rhif 2) 2015. - 4p.: 30 cm. - 978-0-348-11073-9 £4.25

The Playing Fields (Community Involvement in Disposal Decisions) (Wales) Regulations 2015 No. 2015/1403 (W.139). - Enabling power: Playing Fields (Community Involvement in Disposal Decisions) (Wales) Measure 2010, s. 1. - Issued: 07.07.2015. Made: 22.06.2015. Laid before the National Assembly for Wales: 24.06.2015. Coming into force: 01.10.2015. Effect: None. Territorial extent & classification: W. General. - In English and Welsh. Welsh title: Reholiadau Caeau Chwarae (Ymgysylltiad Cymunedau a Phenderfyniadau Gwaredu) (Cymru) 2015. - 12p.: 30 cm. - 978-0-348-11114-9 £6.00

The Violence against Women, Domestic Abuse and Sexual Violence (Wales) Act 2015 (Commencement No. 1) Order 2015 No. 2015/1680 (W.217) (C.97). - Enabling power: Violence against Women, Domestic Abuse and Sexual Violence (Wales) Act 2015, s. 25 (3). Bringing various provisions of the 2015 Act into operation on 05.10.2015. - Issued: 21.09.2015. Made: 06.09.2015. Effect: None. Territorial extent & classification: W. General. - In English and Welsh. Welsh title: Gorchymyn Deddf Trais yn erbyn Menywod, Cam-drin Domestig a Thrais Rhywiol (Cymru) 2015 (Cychwyn Rhif 1) 2015. - 4p.: 30 cm. - 978-0-348-11149-1 £4.25

The Violence against Women, Domestic Abuse and Sexual Violence (Wales) Act 2015 (Commencement No. 2) Order 2015 No. 2015/2019 (W.307) (C.124). - Enabling power: Violence against Women, Domestic Abuse and Sexual Violence (Wales) Act 2015, s. 25 (3). Bringing various provisions of the 2015 Act into operation on 04.01.2016, in accord. with art. 2. - Issued: 18.12.2015. Made: 10.12.2015. Effect: None. Territorial extent & classification: W. General. - In English and Welsh. Welsh title: Gorchymyn Deddf Trais yn erbyn Menywod, Cam-drin Domestig a Thrais Rhywiol (Cymru) 2015 (Cychwyn Rhif 2) 2015. - 4p.: 30 cm. - 978-0-348-11206-1 £4.25

London government

The Greater London Authority (Consolidated Council Tax Requirement Procedure) Regulations 2015 No. 2015/2032. - Enabling power: Greater London Authority Act 1999, sch. 6, para. 10. - Issued: 21.12.2015. Made: 15.12.2015. Laid: 17.12.2015. Coming into force: 15.01.2016. Effect: 1999 c.29 modified. Territorial extent & classification: Extends E/W/S but applies to E. only. General. - 2p.: 30 cm. - 978-0-11-114209-7 £4.25

The Household Waste (Fixed Penalty and Penalty Charge) Regulations 2015 No. 2015/969. - Enabling power: Environment Protection Act 1990, s. 46B (3) (4) & London Local Authorities 2007 ss. 20B (4) 95), 20D (2). - Issued: 02.04.2015. Made: 26.03.2015. Laid: 27.03.2015. Coming into force: 15.06.2015. Effect: S.I. 2007/3482 modified. Territorial extent & classification: E. General. - 4p.: 30 cm. - 978-0-11-113603-4 £4.25

Magistrates' courts, England and Wales

The Criminal Justice and Courts Act 2015 (Commencement No. 1, Saving and Transitional Provisions) Order 2015 No. 2015/778 (C.44). - Enabling power: Criminal Justice and Courts Act 2015, s. 95 (1) (6). Bringing into operation various provisions of the 2015 Act on 20.03.2015; 13.04.2015, in accord. with arts 2, 3. - Issued: 25.03.2015. Made: 19.03.2015. Effect: None. Territorial extent & classification: E/W/S/NI. General. - 8p.: 30 cm. - 978-0-11-113405-4 £6.00

The Criminal Procedure (Amendment No. 2) Rules 2015 No. 2015/646 (L.8). - Enabling power: Courts Act 2003, s. 69. - Issued: 16.03.2015. Made: 09.03.2015. Laid: 12.03.2015. Coming into force: 06.04.2015. Effect: S.I. 2014/610 amended. Territorial extent and classification: E/W. General. - 12p.: 30 cm. - 978-0-11-113304-0 £6.00

The Criminal Procedure (Amendment) Rules 2015 No. 2015/13 (L.1). - Enabling power: Courts Act 2003, s. 69. - Issued: 15.01.2015. Made: 07.01.2015. Laid: 12.01.2015. Coming into force: 02.02.2015; 06.04.2015, in accord. with rule 2. Effect: S.I. 2014/1610 amended. Territorial extent and classification: E/W. General. - 24p.: 30 cm. - 978-0-11-112683-7 £6.00

The Criminal Procedure Rules 2015 No. 2015/1490 (L.18). - Enabling power: Courts Act 2003, s. 69 & Road Traffic Offenders Act 1988, s. 12 (1) (3) & Criminal Law act 1977, s. 48 & Indictments Act 1915, s. 2 & Administration of Justice (Miscellaneous Provisions) Act 1933, s. 2 (6) & Bail Act 1976, s. 5B (9) & Criminal Justice Act 1967, s. 9 (2A) & Police and Criminal Evidence Act 1984, s. 81 & Criminal Procedure and Investigations Act 1996, ss. 19, 20 (3) & Criminal Justice Act 2003, ss. 30 (1), 132 (4), 174 (4) & Youth Justice and Criminal Evidence Act 1999, ss. 37, 38 & Magistrates' Courts Act 1980, s. 12 (7ZA) & Powers of Criminal Courts (Sentencing) Act 2000, s. 155 (7) & Proceeds of Crime Act 2002, ss. 91, 351 (2), 362 (2), 369 (2), 375 (1) & Senior Courts Act 1981, ss. 19, 52, 66, 67, 73 (2), 74 (2) (3) (4), 87 (4) & Criminal Justice 1988, s. 159 (6) & Terrorism Act 2000, sch. 5, para. 10, sch. 6, para. 4, sch. 6A, para. 5 & Extradition Act 2003, ss. 36A (4), 36B (3), 118A (4), 118B (3). - Issued: 20.07.2015. Made: 03.07.2015. Laid: 20.07.2015. Coming into force: 05.10.2015. Effect: S.I. 2014/1610 revoked. Territorial extent and classification: E/W. General. - 445p.: 30 cm. - 978-0-11-113772-7 £46.25

The Magistrates' Courts (Injunctions: Anti-Social Behaviour) Rules 2015 No. 2015/423 (L.5). - Enabling power: Magistrates' Courts Act 1980, s. 144 & Anti-Social Behaviour, Crime and Policing Act 2014, s. 18 (2) (3). - Issued: 06.03.2015. Made: 25.02.2015. Laid: 03.03.2015. Coming into force: In accord. with rule 1 (2). Effect: None. Territorial extent & classification: E/W. General. - 8p.: 30 cm. - 978-0-11-113115-2 £6.00

The Magistrates' Courts (Injunctions: Gang-related Violence) Rules 2015 No. 2015/421 (L.4). - Enabling power: Magistrates' Courts Act 1980, s. 144 & Policing and Crime Act 2009, s. 48 (4). - Issued: 06.03.2015. Made: 25.02.2015. Laid: 03.03.2015. Coming into force: In accord. with rule 1 (2). Effect: None. Territorial extent & classification: E/W. General. - 8p.: 30 cm. - 978-0-11-113114-5 £6.00

The Magistrates' Courts (Modern Slavery Act 2015) Rules 2015 No. 2015/1478 (L.17). - Enabling power: Magistrates Courts Act 1980, s. 144 & Modern Slavery Act 2015, s. 16 (6), 32. - Issued: 13.07.2015. Made: 07.07.2015. Laid: 10.07.2015. Coming into force: 31.07.2015. Effect: None. Territorial extent & classification: E/W. General. - 4p.: 30 cm. - 978-0-11-113758-1 £4.25

Marine management

The Marine Licensing (Delegation of Functions) (Amendment) Order 2015 No. 2015/1674. - Enabling power: Marine and Coastal Access Act 2009, ss. 98 (1), 99 (2) to (5), 316 (1) (b). - Issued: 16.09.2015. Made: 08.09.2015. Laid: 10.09.2015. Coming into force: 01.10.2015. Effect: S.I. 2011/627 amended. Territorial extent & classification: E/W/S/NI. General. - 4p.: 30 cm. - 978-0-11-113919-6 £4.25

The Marine Works (Environmental Impact Assessment) (Amendment) Regulations 2015 No. 2015/446. - Enabling power: European Communities Act 1972, s. 2 (2). - Issued: 09.03.2015. Made: 27.02.2015. Laid: 04.03.2015. Coming into force: 27.03.2015. Effect: S.I. 2007/1518 amended. Territorial extent & classification: E/W/S/NI. General- EC note: These Regulations update references Directive 2011/92/EU on the assessment of the effects of certain public and private projects on the environment. - 4p.: 30 cm. - 978-0-11-113134-3 £4.25

Marine pollution

The Merchant Shipping (Oil Pollution Preparedness, Response and Co-operation Convention) (Amendment) Regulations 2015 No. 2015/386. - Enabling power: European Communities Act 1972, s. 2 (2). - Issued: 26.03.2015. Made: 19.03.2015. Laid: 23.03.2015. Coming into force: 19.07.2015. Effect: S.I. 1998/1056 amended. Territorial extent & classification: E/W/S. General. - EC note: Amends S.I. 1998/1056 to implement environment requirements of Directive 2013/30/EU. - 12p.: 30 cm. - 978-0-11-113433-7 £6.00

Marine pollution, England

The Water, Animals, Marine Pollution and Environmental Protection (Miscellaneous Revocations) Order 2015 No. 2015/663. - Enabling power: European Communities Act 1972, ss. 2 (2) & Water Industry Act 1991, s. 5 & Environment Act 1995, s. 9 (1) & Fur Farming (Prohibition) Act 2000, s. 5 & Marine and Coastal Access Act 2009, s. 74- Issued: 17.03.2015. Made: 05.03.2015. Laid: 12.03.2015. Coming into force: 01.07.2015. Effect: S.I. 1989/1152 revoked with saving in England & S.I. 1996/3061; 2001/3749; 2004/1964; 2010/304 revoked. Territorial extent & classification: E/W. General. - 4p.: 30 cm. - 978-0-11-113320-0 £4.25

Marriage

The Proposed Marriages and Civil Partnerships (Conduct of Investigations, etc.) Regulations 2015 No. 2015/397. - Enabling power: Immigration Act 2014, ss. 50 (1) (5) (9) (10), 51 (1) (d) (3) (4) (5), 74 (8) (d). - Issued: 05.03.2015. Made: 26.02.2015. Coming into force: 01.03.2015. Effect: None. Territorial extent & classification: E/W/S/NI. General. - Supersedes draft SI (ISBN 9780111125564) issued 17/12/14 - 12p.: 30 cm. - 978-0-11-113103-9 £6.00

The Proposed Marriages and Civil Partnerships (Meaning of Exempt Persons and Notice) Regulations 2015 No. 2015/122. - Enabling power: Immigration Act 2014, ss. 49 (3) (4), 61 (1) (2), 74 (8) (d). - Issued: 11.02.2015. Made: 02.02.2015. Laid: 05.02.2015. Coming into force: 02.03.2015. Effect: None. Territorial extent & classification: UK [parts E/W only]. General. - 8p.: 30 cm. - 978-0-11-112884-8 £6.00

The Referral and Investigation of Proposed Marriages and Civil Partnerships (Northern Ireland and Miscellaneous Provisions) Order 2015 No. 2015/395. - Enabling power: Immigration Act 2014, ss. 53 (1) (2) (3), 74 (8) (c) (d). - Issued: 06.03.2015. Made: 26.02.2015. Coming into force: 01.03.2015. Effect: 2004 c.19, 33, 2014 c.22 & S.R. 2005/482 & S.I. 2003/413 (N.I. 3) amended. Territorial extent & classification: E/W/S/NI. General. - Supersedes draft S.I. (ISBN 9780111125025) issued 19/12/14. - 24p.: 30 cm. - 978-0-11-113104-6 £6.00

Marriage, England and Wales

The Proposed Marriages and Civil Partnerships (Waiting Period) Regulations 2015 No. 2015/159. - Enabling power: Marriage Act 1949, ss. 31 (5ED), 74 (3) & Civil Partnership Act 2004, ss. 12(7), 258 (2). - Issued: 13.02.2015. Made: 02.02.2015. Coming into force: 02.03.2015. Effect: None. Territorial extent & classification: E/W. General. - 8p.: 30 cm. - 978-0-11-112900-5 £6.00

The Referral of Proposed Marriages and Civil Partnerships Regulations 2015 No. 2015/123. - Enabling power: Marriage Act 1949, ss. 28D, 28G (2) (3), 28H (5) (c) (7) (10) (b) (c) & Civil Partnership Act 2004, ss. 9B, 9E (2) (3), 12A (5) (c) (7) (9) (b) (c). - Issued: 10.02.2015. Made: 02.02.2015. Laid: 05.02.2015. Coming into force: 02.03.2015. Effect: None. Territorial extent & classification: E/W. General. - 16p.: 30 cm. - 978-0-11-112877-0 £6.00

Marriage, Northern Ireland

The Sham Marriage and Civil Partnership (Scotland and Northern Ireland) (Administrative) Regulations 2015 No. 2015/404. - Enabling power: Immigration Act 2014, ss. 54 (2) (3), 74 (8) (d), sch. 5. - Issued: 05.03.2015. Made: 26.02.2015. Laid before the Scottish Parliament: 27.02.2015. Coming into force: 02.03.2015. Effect: None. Territorial extent & classification: S/NI. General. - 24p.: 30 cm. - 978-0-11-113091-9 £6.00

Marriage, Scotland

The Referral and Investigation of Proposed Marriages and Civil Partnerships (Scotland) Order 2015 No. 2015/396. - Enabling power: Immigration Act 2014, ss. 53 (1) (2) (3), 74 (8) (c) (d). - Issued: 06.03.2015. Made: 26.02.2015. Coming into force: 01.03.2015. Effect: 1977 c.15; 2004 c.19, c.33; 2014 c.22 amended. Territorial extent & classification: E/W/S/NI. General. - Supersedes draft S.I. (ISBN) issued 17/12/14. - 24p.: 30 cm. - 978-0-11-113105-3 £6.00

MEDICINES

The Sham Marriage and Civil Partnership (Scotland and Northern Ireland) (Administrative) Regulations 2015 No. 2015/404. - Enabling power: Immigration Act 2014, ss. 54 (2) (3), 74 (8) (d), sch. 5. - Issued: 05.03.2015. Made: 26.02.2015. Laid before the Scottish Parliament: 27.02.2015. Coming into force: 02.03.2015. Effect: None. Territorial extent & classification: S/NI. General. - 24p.: 30 cm. - 978-0-11-113091-9 £6.00

Medicines

The Human Medicines (Amendment) (No. 2) Regulations 2015 No. 2015/903. - Enabling power: European Communities Act 1972, s. 2 (2) (5)- Issued: 31.03.2015. Made: 24.03.2015. Laid: 27.03.2015. Coming into force: 01.07.2015. Effect: S.I. 2012/1916 amended. Territorial extent & classification: E/W/S/NI. General. - 4p.: 30 cm. - 978-0-11-113527-3 £4.25

The Human Medicines (Amendment) (No. 3) Regulations 2015 No. 2015/1503. - Enabling power: European Communities Act 1972, s. 2 (2) (5)- Issued: 16.07.2015. Made: 09.07.2015. Laid: 16.07.2015. Coming into force: 01.10.2015. Effect: S.I. 2012/1916 amended. Territorial extent & classification: E/W/S/NI. General. - 4p.: 30 cm. - 978-0-11-113777-2 £4.25

The Human Medicines (Amendment) Regulations 2015 No. 2015/323. - Enabling power: European Communities Act 1972, s. 2 (2) (5)- Issued: 25.02.2015. Made: 17.02.2015. Laid: 25.02.2015. Coming into force: 01.04.2015. Effect: S.I. 2012/1916 amended. Territorial extent & classification: E/W/S/NI. General. - 4p.: 30 cm. - 978-0-11-113013-1 £4.25

Mental capacity, England and Wales

The Court of Protection (Amendment) Rules 2015 No. 2015/548 (L.6). - Enabling power: Mental Capacity Act 2005, ss. 50 (2), 51, 53 (2) (4), 55, 56, 65 (1). - Issued: 11.03.2015. Made: 04.03.2015. Laid: 09.03.2015. Coming into force: In accord. with rule 2. Effect: S.I. 2007/1744 amended. Territorial extent & classification: E/W. General. - [28]p.: 30 cm. - 978-0-11-113223-4 £6.00

The Lasting Powers of Attorney, Enduring Powers of Attorney and Public Guardian (Amendment) Regulations 2015 No. 2015/899. - Enabling power: Mental Capacity Act 2005, ss. 58 (3), 65 (1) (2), sch. 1. - Issued: 31.03.2015. Made: 25.03.2015. Laid: 26.03.2015. Coming into force: 01.07.2015. Effect: S.I. 2007/1253 amended. Territorial extent & classification: E/W. General. - 80p.: 30 cm. - 978-0-11-113523-5 £14.25

Mental health, England and Wales

The Care Act 2014 (Commencement No. 4) Order 2015 No. 2015/993 (C.68). - Enabling power: Care Act 2014, ss. 124, 127 (1) (5). Bringing into operation various provisions of the 2014 Act on 01.04.2015, 06.04.2015, in accord. with arts 2, 4. - Issued: 02.04.2015. Made: 26.03.2015. Effect: None. Territorial extent & classification: E/W/S/NI. General. - 8p.: 30 cm. - 978-0-11-113624-9 £6.00

Merchant shipping

The Merchant Shipping (Code of Safe Working Practices) (Amendments and Revocation) Regulations 2015 No. 2015/1692. - Enabling power: Merchant Shipping Act 1995, ss. 85 (1) (a) (3) (q) (5) (a) (7) (c) (d). - Issued: 23.09.2015. Made: 15.09.2015. Laid: 23.09.2015. Coming into force: 20.10.2015. Effect: S.I. 1997/2962 amended & S.I. 1998/1838 revoked. Territorial extent & classification: E/W/S/NI. General. - 4p.: 30 cm. - 978-0-11-113932-5 £4.25

The Merchant Shipping (Fees) Regulations 2015 No. 2015/315. - Enabling power: Merchant Shipping Act 1995, s. 302- Issued: 24.02.2015. Made: 09.02.2015. Laid: 23.02.2015. Coming into force: 23.03.2015. Effect: S.I. 2006/2055 amended. Territorial extent & classification: E/W/S/NI. General. - 2p.: 30 cm. - 978-0-11-113003-2 £4.25

The Merchant Shipping (Light Dues) (Amendment) Regulations 2015 No. 2015/458. - Enabling power: Merchant Shipping Act 1995, s. 205 (5). - Issued: 09.03.2015. Made: 26.02.2015. Laid: 05.03.2015. Coming into force: 01.04.2015. Effect: S.I. 1997/562 amended. Territorial extent & classification: E/W/S/NI. General. - 2p.: 30 cm. - 978-0-11-113149-7 £4.25

The Merchant Shipping (Oil Pollution) (Jersey) Order 1997 (Revocation) Order 2015 No. 2015/1893. - Enabling power: Merchant Shipping Act 1995, s. 315 (2). - Issued: 18.11.2015. Made: 15.11.2015. Coming into force: In accord. with art. 1. Effect: S.I. 1997/2598 revoked. Territorial extent & classification: E/W/S/NI. General. - 2p.: 30 cm. - 978-0-11-114091-8 £4.25

The Merchant Shipping (United Kingdom Wreck Convention Area) Order 2015 No. 2015/172. - Enabling power: Merchant Shipping Act 1995, ss. 255R. - Issued: 13.02.2015. Made: 05.02.2015. Laid: 13.02.2015. Coming into force: 14.04.2015. Effect: None. Territorial extent & classification: E/W/S/NI. General. - 2p.: 30 cm. - 978-0-11-112908-1 £4.25

The Wreck Removal Convention Act 2011 (Commencement) Order 2015 No. 2015/133 (C.7). - Enabling power: Wreck Removal Convention Act 2011, s. 2. Bringing into operation various provisions of the 2011 Act on 05.02.2015; 14.04.2015. - Issued: 11.02.2015. Made: 28.01.2015. Effect: None. Territorial extent & classification: E/W/S/NI. General. - 2p.: 30 cm. - 978-0-11-112881-7 £4.25

Merchant shipping: Alcohol and drugs

The Merchant Shipping (Alcohol) (Prescribed Limits Amendment) Regulations 2015 No. 2015/1730. - Enabling power: Railways and Transport Safety Act 2003, s. 88 (4). - Issued: 05.10.2015. Made: 28.09.2015. Coming into force: 20.10.2015. Effect: 2003 c.20 amended. Territorial extent & classification: E/W/S/NI. General. - Supersedes draft SI (ISBN 9780111136836) issued 22/06/15. - 4p.: 30 cm. - 978-0-11-113952-3 £4.25

Merchant shipping: Maritime security

The Port Security (Port of Oban) Designation Order 2015 No. 2015/1504. - Enabling power: European Communities Act 1972, s. 2 (2). - Issued: 16.07.2015. Made: 09.07.2015. Laid: 15.07.2015. Coming into force: 05.08.2015. Effect: None. Territorial extent & classification: E/W/S/NI. General. - EC note: This Order is one of a series to implement Directive 2005/65/EC on enhancing port security at individual ports across the UK. The Directive was transposed in relation to the UK as a whole by the Port Security Regulations 2009 (S.I. 2009/2048). - 12p., col. maps: 30 cm. - 978-0-11-113778-9 £8.50

Merchant shipping: Safety

The Merchant Shipping (Boatmasters' Qualifications, Crew and Hours of Work) Regulations 2015 No. 2015/410. - Enabling power: Merchant Shipping Act 1995, ss. 47 (1) (3) to (4B), 85 (1) (3) (5) to (7), 86 (1) (2), 302 (1), 307 (1) & European Communities Act 1972, s. 2 (2). - Issued: 09.03.2015. Made: 26.02.2015. Laid: 04.03.2015. Coming into force: 04.04.2015. Effect: S.I. 2006/2055 amended & S.I. 2006/3223, 3224 revoked. Territorial extent & classification: E/W/S/NI. General. - 32p.: 30 cm. - 978-0-11-113145-9 £6.00

The Merchant Shipping (Miscellaneous Safety) (Revocations) Regulations 2015 No. 2015/68. - Enabling power: Merchant Shipping Act 1995, ss. 85 (1) (3) (5) to (7), 86 (1) (2) (a). - Issued: 04.02.2015. Made: 08.01.2015. Laid: 04.02.2015. Coming into force: 28.02.2015. Effect: S.I. 1965/1046; 1972/531; 1988/1637, 1641 revoked. Territorial extent & classification: E/W/S/NI. General. - Revoked with saving by S.I. 2016/226 (ISBN 9780111144206). - 4p.: 30 cm. - 978-0-11-112807-7 £4.25

The Merchant Shipping (Standards of Training, Certification and Watchkeeping) Regulations 2015 No. 2015/782. - Enabling power: European Communities Act 1972, s. 2 (2) & Merchant Shipping Act 1995, ss. 47 (1) (4A) (4B), 85 (1) (3) (5) to (7), 86 (1) (2), 307 (1). - Issued: 31.03.2015. Made: 23.03.2015. Laid: 26.03.2015. Coming into force: 09.06.2015. Effect: S.I. 1998/1609, 2771 amended & S.I. 1970/294; 1997/1911; 2000/484, 836; 2008/2851 revoked. Territorial extent & classification: E/W/S/NI. General. - EC note: These Regulations implement in part Directive 2012/35/EU. - 32p.: 30 cm. - 978-0-11-113516-7 £6.00

The Merchant Shipping (Survey and Certification) Regulations 2015 No. 2015/508. - Enabling power: Merchant Shipping Act 1995, s. 85 (1) (1B) (3) (5) to (7), 86 (1). - Issued: 11.03.2015. Made: 02.03.2015. Laid: 09.03.2015. Coming into force: 06.03.2015. Effect: S.I. 1995/1210; 1996/2418; 2000/1334 revoked. Territorial extent & classification: E/W/S/NI. General. - 16p.: 30 cm. - 978-0-11-113205-0 £6.00

The Merchant Shipping (Weighing of Goods Vehicles and other Cargo) (Revocations) Regulations 2015 No. 2015/629. - Enabling power: Merchant Shipping Act 1995, ss. 85 (1) (3) (5) (6) (7), 86 (1). - Issued: 16.03.2015. Made: 09.03.2015. Laid: 12.03.2015. Coming into force: 06.04.2015. Effect: S.I. 1988/1275; 1989/270, 568 revoked. Territorial extent & classification: E/W/S/NI. General. - 4p.: 30 cm. - 978-0-11-113286-9 £4.25

Ministers of the Crown

The Chancellor of the Duchy of Lancaster Order 2015 No. 2015/1376. - Enabling power: Ministers of the Crown Act 1975, s. 1. - Issued: 17.06.2015. Made: 10.06.2015. Laid: 11.06.2015. Coming into force: 22.06.2015. Effect: 1983 c.2; 1985 c.50; 1986 c.56; 1990 c.8; 1992 c.14; 1999 c.29; 2000 c.2, c.22, c.41; 2002 c.24; 2003 c.3; 2006 c.22; 2009 c.12; 2011 c.1, c.13; 2013 c.6; 2014 c.4; 2014 c.29; 2015 c.25 & S.I. 2001/341, 497, 1184; 2013/3197; 2014/3178 amended. Territorial extent & classification: E/W/S/NI. General. - 16p.: 30 cm. - 978-0-11-113671-3 £6.00

The Transfer of Functions (Information and Public Records) Order 2015 No. 2015/1897. - Enabling power: Ministers of the Crown Act 1975, ss. 1, 2. - Issued: 18.11.2015. Made: 11.11.2015. Laid: 18.11.2015. Coming into force: 09.12.2015. Effect: 1958 c. 51; 2000 c.36; 2006 c.32; S.I. 2004/3391 amended. Territorial extent & classification: E/W/S/NI. General. - 12p.: 30 cm. - 978-0-11-114095-6 £6.00

The Transfer of Functions (Pensions Guidance) Order 2015 No. 2015/2013. - Enabling power: Ministers of the Crown Act 1975, s. 1. - Issued: 16.12.2015. Made: 09.12.2015. Laid: 16.12.2015. Coming into force: 01.04.2016. Effect: 2000 c.8 amended. Territorial extent & classification: E/W/S/NI. General. - 4p.: 30 cm. - 978-0-11-114193-9 £4.25

The Transfer of Tribunal Functions (Police and Crime Commissioner Elections) Order 2015 No. 2015/1526. - Enabling power: Ministers of Crown Act 1975, s. 1. - Issued: 22.07.2015. Made: 15.07.2015. Laid: 22.07.2015. Coming into force: 12.08.2015. Effect: 2011 c.13; S.I. 2012/1917, 2088 amended. Territorial extent & classification: E/W. General. - 8p.: 30 cm. - 978-0-11-113803-8 £4.25

Modern slavery

The Modern Slavery Act 2015 (Commencement No. 1, Saving and Transitional Provisions) Regulations 2015 No. 2015/1476 (C.85). - Enabling power: Modern Slavery Act 2015. s. 61 (1) (8). Bringing into operation various provisions of this Act on 31.07.2015 in accord. with arts 2 to 7. - Issued: 13.07.2015. Made: 06.07.2015. Effect: None. Territorial extent & classification: E/W/S/NI. General. - 4p: 30 cm. - 978-0-11-113756-7 £4.25

The Modern Slavery Act 2015 (Commencement No. 2) Regulations 2015 No. 2015/1690 (C.101). - Enabling power: Modern Slavery Act 2015. s. 61 (1). Bringing into operation various provisions of this Act on 15.10.2015; 01.11.2015 in accord. with arts 2 & 3. - Issued: 22.09.2015. Made: 16.09.2015. Effect: None. Territorial extent & classification: E/W/S/NI. General. - 2p: 30 cm - 978-0-11-113930-1 £4.25

The Modern Slavery Act 2015 (Commencement No. 3 and Transitional Provision) Regulations 2015 No. 2015/1816 (C.113). - Enabling power: Modern Slavery Act 2015, ss. 61 (1) (8). Bringing into operation various provisions of the 2015 Act on 29.10.15; 31.03.16, according to regs 2 & 3. - Issued: 28.10.2015. Made: 22.10.2015. Effect: None. Territorial extent & classification: E/W/S/NI. General. - 2p.: 30 cm. - 978-0-11-114014-7 £4.25

The Modern Slavery Act 2015 (Transparency in Supply Chains) Regulations 2015 No. 2015/1833. - Enabling power: Modern Slavery Act 2015, ss. 54 (2) (b) (3). - Issued: 03.11.2015. Made: 28.10.2015. Coming into force: 29.10.2015 in accord. with reg. 1. Effect: None. Territorial extent & classification: E/W/S/NI. General. - Supersedes draft SI (ISBN 9780111138847) issued 08/09/15. - 2p.: 30 cm. - 978-0-11-114032-1 £4.25

Modern slavery, England and Wales

The Modern Slavery Act 2015 (Consequential Amendments) Regulations 2015 No. 2015/1472. - Enabling power: Modern Slavery Act 2015. s. 57 (2) (3). - Issued: 10.07.2015. Made: 06.07.2015. Laid: 08.07.2015. Coming into force: 31.07.2015. Effect: S.I. 2006/1116; 2009/37; 1168, 1209; 2041; 2013/349, 554, 817; 2015/102, 790. Territorial extent & classification: E/W. General. - 8p: 30 cm. - 978-0-11-113751-2 £4.25

The Modern Slavery Act 2015 (Duty to Notify) Regulations 2015 No. 2015/1743. - Enabling power: Modern Slavery Act 2015, s. 52 (2). - Issued: 09.10.2015. Made: 01.10.2015. Laid: 09.10.2015. Coming into force: 01.11.2015. Effect: None. Territorial extent & classification: E/W. General. - 4p.: 30 cm. - 978-0-11-113959-2 £4.25

National Crime Agency

The Crime and Courts Act 2013 (National Crime Agency and Proceeds of Crime) (Northern Ireland) Order 2015 No. 2015/798. - Enabling power: Crime and Courts Act 2013, s. 59 (1) (2) (3), sch. 24, paras. 2, 3, 5, 7 (1), sch. 25, paras. 3, 4, 7 (1) (2), 10, 11, 14 (1). - Issued: 26.03.2015. Made: 19.03.2015. Coming into force: 20.03.2015. Effect: 1998 c.32; 2000 c.32; 2002 c.26, 29 S.I. 1989/1341 (N.I. 12) amended. Territorial extent & classification: E/W/S/NI. General. - Supersedes draft S.I. (ISBN 9780111128299) issued 04.02.2015- 12p.: 30 cm. - 978-0-11-113422-1 £6.00

National debt

The National Savings (No. 2) Regulations 2015 No. 2015/624. - Enabling power: National Debt Act 1972, s. 3, 11. - Issued: 19.03.2015. Made: 10.03.2015. Laid: 13.03.2015. Coming into force: 06.04.2015. Effect: S.I. 1998/1449 amended & 64 SIs revoked. Territorial extent & classification: E/W/S/NI/IsleofMan/ChannelIslands. General. - 56p.: 30 cm. - 978-0-11-113321-7 £10.00

The National Savings Regulations 2015 No. 2015/623. - Enabling power: National Savings Bank Act 1971, ss. 2 (1), 3 (2), 4, 6 (1), 7 (2), 8, 9 (1), 15 (3) & Finance Act 1962, s. 33 & Financial Services and Markets Act 2000, ss. 426, 427 & Finance Act 2002, s. 140 (2). - Issued: 18.03.2015. Made: 10.03.2015. Laid: 13.03.2015. Coming into force: 06.04.2015. Effect: 2009 c.10; S.I. 1972/764; 1998/1449 amended & 50 SIs revoked. Territorial extent & classification: E/W/S/NI. General. - 36p.: 30 cm. - 978-0-11-113331-6 £10.00

National election expenditure

The European Parliamentary Elections (Miscellaneous Provisions) (United Kingdom and Gibraltar) Order 2015 No. 2015/1982. - Enabling power: European Parliament (Representation) Act 2003, ss. 12, 13 (3) (4). - Issued: 14.12.2015. Made: 07.12.2015. Laid: - Coming into force: 08.12.2015 in accord. with art. 1 (2). Effect: 2000 c.41 amended. Territorial extent & classification: E/W/S/NI & Gibraltar. General. - Supersedes draft S.I. (ISBN 9780111140048) issued 26/10/15. - 4p.: 30 cm. - 978-0-11-114170-0 £4.25

National Health Service, England

The Care Act 2014 (Commencement No. 4) Order 2015 No. 2015/993 (C.68). - Enabling power: Care Act 2014, ss. 124, 127 (1) (5). Bringing into operation various provisions of the 2014 Act on 01.04.2015, 06.04.2015, in accord. with arts 2, 4. - Issued: 02.04.2015. Made: 26.03.2015. Effect: None. Territorial extent & classification: E/W/S/NI. General. - 8p.: 30 cm. - 978-0-11-113624-9 £6.00

The Care Quality Commission (Membership) (Amendment) Regulations 2015 No. 2015/1479. - Enabling power: Health and Social Care Act 2008, s. 161 (3) (4), sch. 1, para. 3 (3) to (5). - Issued: 14.07.2015. Made: 07.07.2015. Laid: 14.07.2015. Coming into force: 01.09.2015. Effect: S.I. 2008/2252; 2011/2547; 2013/2157 revoked. Territorial extent & classification: E. General. - 12p.: 30 cm. - 978-0-11-113760-4 £6.00

NATIONAL HEALTH SERVICE, ENGLAND

The Delegation of Additional Functions to the NHS Business Services Authority (Awdurdod Gwasanaethau Busnes y GIG) Regulations 2015 No. 2015/127. - Enabling power: National Health Service Act 2006, ss. 7 (1), 273 (4) (b) (zi). - Issued: 11.02.2015. Made: 05.02.2015. Laid: 10.02.2015. Coming into force: 01.04.2015. Effect: None. Territorial extent & classification: E. General. - 4p.: 30 cm. - 978-0-11-112887-9 £4.25

The False or Misleading Information (Specified Care Providers and Specified Information) Regulations 2015 No. 2015/988. - Enabling power: Care Act 2014, s. 92 (1). - Issued: 02.04.2015. Made: 26.03.2015. Coming into force: In accord. with reg. 1. Effect: None. Territorial extent & classification: E. General. - Supersedes draft S.I. (ISBN 9780111129234) issued 16/02/15. - 8p.: 30 cm. - 978-0-11-113620-1 £6.00

The Health and Social Care Act 2008 (Regulated Activities) (Amendment) Regulations 2015 No. 2015/64. - Enabling power: Health and Social Care Act 2008, ss. 20 (1) (3) (5A), 35, 86 (2), 87 (1) (2), 161 (3) (4). - Issued: 02.02.2015. Made: 26.01.2015 Laid: 28.01.2015. Coming into force: 01.04.2015. Effect: S.I. 2014/2936 amended. Territorial extent & classification: E. General. - 8p.: 30 cm. - 978-0-11-112800-8 £6.00

The Health and Social Care Act 2012 (Commencement No. 9) Order 2015 No. 2015/409 (C.23). - Enabling power: Health and Social Care Act 2012, s. 306. Bringing into operation various provisions of the 2012 Act on 16.03.2015 in accord. with art. 2. - Issued: 05.03.2015. Made: 26.02.2015. Coming into force: -Effect: None. Territorial extent & classification: E/W/SNI. General. - 8p.: 30 cm. - 978-0-11-113099-5 £6.00

The Health and Social Care Act 2012 (Consistent Identifier) Regulations 2015 No. 2015/1439. - Enabling power: Health and Social Care Act 2012, s. 251A (1). - Issued: 09.07.2015. Made: 01.07.2015. Laid: 07.07.2015. Coming into force: 01.10.2015. Effect: None. Territorial extent & classification: E. General. - 2p.: 30 cm. - 978-0-11-113739-0 £4.25

The Health and Social Care Act 2012 (Continuity of Information: Interpretation) Regulations 2015 No. 2015/1470. - Enabling power: Health and Social Care Act 2012, s. 251C (3) (4). - Issued: 10.07.2015. Made: 01.07.2015. Laid: 07.07.2015. Coming into force: 01.10.2015. Effect: None. Territorial extent & classification: E. General. - 8p.: 30 cm. - 978-0-11-113749-9 £4.25

The Health and Social Care (Miscellaneous Revocations) Regulations 2015 No. 2015/839. - Enabling power: Health and Medicines Act 1988, s. 26 (6) & Care Standards Act 2000, ss. 12 (2), 15 (3), 16 (3), 118 (5) to (7) & Health and Social Care Act 2001, ss. 65 (1) (2) & Tobacco Advertising and Promotion Act 2002, ss. 19 (2), 20 & National Health Service Act, ss. 8, 28, 187, 272 (7) (8), 273, sch. 6, paras 3, 5, 6. - Issued: 27.03.2015. Made: 23.03.2015 Laid: 26.03.2015. Coming into force: 01.07.2015. Effect: S.I. 1974/29; 2003/7, 1415 revoked in relation to England & S.I. 1985/1876; 1989/1893; 1996/512; 2001/3744; 2003/2323; 2005/640 revoked. Territorial extent & classification: E. General. - 4p.: 30 cm. - 978-0-11-113466-5 £4.25

The Health and Social Care (Safety and Quality) Act 2015 (Commencement No. 1 and Transitory Provision) Regulations 2015 No. 2015/1438 (C.81). - Enabling power: Health and Social Care (Safety and Quality) Act 2015, ss. 6 (4) (5). Bringing into operation various provisions of the 2015 Act on 25.06.2015; 01.10.2015, in accord. with art. 2 & 3. - Issued: 06.07.2015. Made: 24.06.2015. Effect: 2012 c.7 modified. Territorial extent & classification: E. General. - 4p.: 30 cm. - 978-0-11-113728-4 £4.25

The Health Service Commissioner for England (Revocations) Order 2015 No. 2015/822. - Enabling power: Health Service Commissioners Act 1993, s. 2 (5) (b) (6). - Issued: 26.03.2015. Made: 19.03.2015. Laid: 26.03.2015. Coming into force: 01.07.2015. Effect: S.I. 1998/3149; 2006/3332; 2009/883 revoked. Territorial extent & classification: E. General. - 2p.: 30 cm. - 978-0-11-113455-9 £4.25

The Local Audit and Accountability Act 2014 (Independent Trustees) Amendment Order 2015 No. 2015/972. - Enabling power: Local Audit and Accountability Act 2014, s. 2, sch. 13. - Issued: 02.04.2015. Made: 25.03.2015. Effect: 2014 c.2 amended. Territorial extent & classification: E. General. - 2p.: 30 cm. - 978-0-11-113606-5 £4.25

The Local Audit and Accountability Act 2014 (Special Trustees) Amendment Regulations 2015 No. 2015/975. - Enabling power: Local Audit and Accountability Act 2014, s. 2 (3). - Issued: 01.04.2015. Made: 25.03.15. Coming into force: 01.04.2015. Effect: 2014 c.2 amended. Territorial extent & classification: E. General. - Supersedes draft S.I. (ISBN 9780111128503) issued 06/02/15. - 2p.: 30 cm. - 978-0-11-113609-6 £4.25

The Local Audit (Health Service Bodies Auditor Panel and Independence) (England) Regulations 2015 No. 2015/18. - Enabling power: Local Audit and Accountability Act 2014, s. 10 (8), sch. 4, paras 3, 4. - Issued: 16.01.2015. Made: 06.01.2015. Laid: 15.01.2015. Coming into force: 01.04.2015. Effect: None. Territorial extent & classification: E. General. - 8p.: 30 cm. - 978-0-11-112696-7 £4.25

The Local Authorities (Public Health Functions and Entry to Premises by Local Healthwatch Representatives) and Local Authority (Public Health, Health and Wellbeing Boards and Health Scrutiny) (Amendment) Regulations 2015 No. 2015/921. - Enabling power: National Health Service Act 2006, ss. 6C (2), 272 (7) (8), 275. - Issued: 31.03.2015. Made: 23.03.2015. Coming into force: In accord. with reg. 1 (2) (3). Effect: S.I. 2013/218, 351 amended. Territorial extent & classification: E. General. - Supersedes draft S.I. (ISBN 9780111128053) issued 02/02/15. - 8p.: 30 cm. - 978-0-11-113545-7 £4.25

The London North West Healthcare National Health Service Trust (Originating Capital) Order 2015 No. 2015/650. - Enabling power: National Health Service Act 2006, ss. 27, 272 (7), sch. 5, para. 1 (1). - Issued: 16.03.2015. Made: 06.03.2015. Coming into force: 31.03.2015. Effect: None. Territorial extent & classification: E. General. - 2p.: 30 cm. - 978-0-11-113308-8 £4.25

The National Health Service (Amendments to Primary Care Terms of Service relating to the Electronic Prescription Service) Regulations 2015 No. 2015/915. - Enabling power: National Health Service Act 2006, ss. 85, 89 (1) (2) (a) (c) (d), 94 (1) (3) (f), 126, 129, 132, 272(7) (8), sch. 12, paras 3 (1) (3) (c) (f). - Issued: 01.04.2015. Made: 24.03.2015. Laid: 27.03.2015. Coming into force: 01.07.2015. Effect: S.I. 2004/291, 627; 2013/349 amended. Territorial extent & classification: E. General. - Partially revoked by SI 2015/1862 (ISBN 9780111140758) and SI 2015/1879 (ISBN 9780111140765). - 4p.: 30 cm. - 978-0-11-113544-0 £4.25

The National Health Service (Charges for Drugs and Appliances) Regulations 2015 No. 2015/570. - Enabling power: National Health Service Act 2006, ss. 172 (1) (2), 174, 178, 182, 184 (1), 272 (7) (8). - Issued: 11.03.2015. Made: 04.03.2015. Laid: 11.03.2015. Coming into force: 01.04.2015. Effect: 8 SIs amended & 19 SIs partially revoked & 16 SIs revoked. Territorial extent & classification: E. General. - 32p.: 30 cm. - 978-0-11-113238-8 £6.00

The National Health Service (Charges, Payments and Remission of Charges) (Uprating, Miscellaneous Amendments and Transitional Provision) Regulations 2015 No. 2015/417. - Enabling power: National Health Service Act 2006, ss. 115 (1) (2), 116 (2), 176 (1) (2), 179 (1) (3), 180 (1) to (5), 182, 184 (2), 272 (7) (8). - Issued: 05.03.2015. Made: 27.02.2015. Laid: 05.03.2015. Coming into force: 01.04.2015. Effect: S.I. 2003/2382; 2005/3477; 2008/1186; 2013/461 amended. Territorial extent & classification: E. General. - 4p.: 30 cm. - 978-0-11-113110-7 £4.25

The National Health Service (Charges to Overseas Visitors) (Amendment) Regulations 2015 No. 2015/2025. - Enabling power: National Health Service Act 2006, ss. 175, 272 (7) (8). - Issued: 18.12.2015. Made: 14.12.2015. Laid: 17.12.2015. Coming into force: 01.02.2016. Effect: S.I. 2015/238 amended. Territorial extent & classification: E. General. - This S.I. rectifies a defect in S.I. 2015/238 (ISBN 9780111129807) and is being issued free of charge to all known recipients of that S.I. - 8p.: 30 cm. - 978-0-11-114201-1 £4.25

The National Health Service (Charges to Overseas Visitors) Regulations 2015 No. 2015/238. - Enabling power: National Health Service Act 2006, ss. 175, 272 (7) (8). - Issued: 19.02.2015. Made: 05.02.2015. Laid: 16.02.2015. Coming into force: 06.04.2015. Effect: S.I. 2006/1260, 3388; 2013/2269 amended & S.I. 2013/235 partially revoked & S.I. 2011/1556; 2012/1586; 2014/1534 revoked. Territorial extent & classification: E. General. - 24p.: 30 cm. - 978-0-11-112980-7 £6.00

The National Health Service (Clinical Negligence Scheme) Regulations 2015 No. 2015/559. - Enabling power: National Health Service Act 2006, ss. 71, 272 (7) (8). - Issued: 12.03.2015. Made: 04.03.2015. Laid: 11.03.2015. Coming into force: 01.04.2015. Effect: S.I. 2002/2469; 2004/696; 2005/604; 2012/1641; 2014/3090; 2015/137 partially revoked & S.I. 1996/251; 1997/527; 1999/1274; 2000/2341; 2002/1073; 2006/3087; 2013/497; 2014/933 revoked. Territorial extent & classification: E. General. - 20p.: 30 cm. - 978-0-11-113229-6 £6.00

NATIONAL HEALTH SERVICE, ENGLAND AND WALES

The National Health Service Commissioning Board and Clinical Commissioning Groups (Responsibilities and Standing Rules) (Amendment) (No. 2) Regulations 2015 No. 2015/1430. - Enabling power: National Health Service Act 2006, ss. 6E, 272 (7) (8). - Issued: 02.07.2015. Made: 25.06.2015. Laid: 01.07.2015. Coming into force: 01.10.2015. Effect: S.I. 2012/2996 amended. Territorial extent & classification: E. General. - 2p.: 30 cm. - 978-0-11-113725-3 £4.25

The National Health Service Commissioning Board and Clinical Commissioning Groups (Responsibilities and Standing Rules) (Amendment) Regulations 2015 No. 2015/415. - Enabling power: National Health Service Act 2006, ss. 3B (1) (a), (2) (c), (3)(b), 176 (1), (2)(d), 180 (1), (2) (b), (3) (b), (4) (5), 181, 182, 183 (a), 184 (1) (2), 272 (7) (8). - Issued: 05.03.2015. Made: 24.02.2015. Laid: 05.03.2015. Coming into force: 01.04.2015. Effect: S.I. 2012/2996 amended. Territorial extent & classification: E. General. - 4p.: 30 cm. - 978-0-11-113108-4 £4.25

The National Health Service (Exemptions from Charges, Payments and Remission of Charges) (Amendment and Transitional Provision) Regulations 2015 No. 2015/1776. - Enabling power: National Health Service Act 2006, ss. 115 (1) (a), (2) (c), (3)(b), 176 (1), (2)(d), 180 (1), (2) (b), (3) (b), (4) (5), 181, 182, 183 (a), 184 (1) (2), 272 (7) (8). - Issued: 15.10.2015. Made: 01.10.2015. Laid: 15.10.2015. Coming into force: 01.11.2015. Effect: S.I. 2003/2382; 2008/1186; 2013/461 amended. Territorial extent & classification: E. General. - 8p.: 30 cm. - 978-0-11-113984-4 £6.00

The National Health Service (General Medical Services Contracts and Personal Medical Services Agreements) (Amendment) Regulations 2015 No. 2015/196. - Enabling power: National Health Service Act 2006, ss. 85, 89 (1) (2) (a) (c) (d) (h) (3) (a) (c) (6), 90 (1) (2) (a) (3), 94 (1) (3) (f) (g) (7) (8) (c) (9), 272 (7) (8). - Issued: 17.02.2015. Made: 10.02.2015. Laid: 17.02.2015. Coming into force: 01.04.2015. Effect: S.I. 2004/291, 627 amended. Territorial extent & classification: E. General. - Revoked by S.I. 2015/1862 (ISBN 9780111140758). - 20p.: 30 cm. - 978-0-11-112938-8 £6.00

The National Health Service (General Medical Services Contracts) Regulations 2015 No. 2015/1862. - Enabling power: National Health Service Act 2006, ss. 9 (8), 83 (3) (6), 85 (1), 86 (1) (4), 89 (1) (1A) (a) (b) (3), 90 (1) (3), 91(1), 97(6) (8), 187, 272 (2) (8). - Issued: 17.11.2015. Made: 06.11.2015. Laid: 13.11.2015. Coming into force: 07.12.2015. Effect: S.I. 2004/629, 906; 2015/2414; 2009/309; 2010/76; 2012/1631; 2013/335, 349, 350, 500 amended & S.I. 2005/893, 3315; 2008/1514, 1700; 2009/309, 2205, 2230, 2972; 2010/22, 231, 234; 2012/1479, 1916, 2404; 2013/363; 2014/1887; 2015/915 partially revoked & S.I. 2004/291, 433, 865, 2694; 2006/1501; 2007/3491; 2010/578; 2012/970; 2014/465, 2721; 2015/196 revoked Territorial extent & classification: E. General. - 128p.: 30 cm. - 978-0-11-114075-8 £19.00

The National Health Service (Licence Exemptions, etc) Amendment Regulations 2015 No. 2015/190. - Enabling power: Health and Social Care Act 2012, ss. 83 (1) to (3), 150 (1), 304 (9) (10). - Issued: 16.02.2015. Made: 10.02.2015. Laid: 12.02.2015. Coming into force: 01.04.2015. Effect: S.I. 2013/2677 amended. Territorial extent & classification: E. General. - 2p.: 30 cm. - 978-0-11-112926-5 £4.25

The National Health Service (Licensing and Pricing) (Amendment) Regulations 2015 No. 2015/2018. - Enabling power: Health and Social Care Act 2012, ss. 118 (14) (b), 120 (2) (6), 150 (1), 304 (9) (10). - Issued: 16.12.2015. Made: 10.12.2015. Coming into force: 11.12.2015 in accord. with reg. 1. Effect: S.I. 2013/2214 amended. Territorial extent & classification: E. General. - 2p.: 30 cm. - 978-0-11-114196-0 £4.25

The National Health Service (Performers Lists) (England) (Amendment) Regulations 2015 No. 2015/362. - Enabling power: National Health Service Act 2006, ss. 91, 106, 123, 272 (7) (8). - Issued: 03.03.2015. Made: 24.02.2015. Laid: 26.02.2015. Coming into force: 01.04.2015. Effect: S.I. 2013/335 amended. Territorial extent & classification: E. General. - 4p.: 30 cm. - 978-0-11-113052-0 £4.25

The National Health Service (Personal Medical Services Agreements) Regulations 2015 No. 2015/1879. - Enabling power: National Health Service Act 2006, ss. 93 (2), 94 (1) (2) (3) (3A) (a) (6) (7) (8) (9), 272 (7) (8). - Issued: 17.11.2015. Made: 06.11.2015. Laid: 13.11.2015. Coming into force: 07.12.2015. Effect: S.I. 2004/906; 2009/309; 2010/76; 2013/349, 350, 500; 2015/570 amended & S.I. 2005/893, 3315, 3491; 2006/1501; 2008/1514, 1700; 2009/309, 2205, 2230, 2972; 2010/22, 231, 234; 2012/1479, 1916, 2404; 2013/363; 2014/1887; 2015/915 partially revoked & S.I. 2004/627 revoked. Territorial extent & classification: E. General. - 104p.: 30 cm. - 978-0-11-114076-5 £16.50

The National Health Service (Pharmaceutical and Local Pharmaceutical Services) (Amendment and Transitional Provision) Regulations 2015 No. 2015/58. - Enabling power: National Health Service Act 2006, ss 126, 129, 130, 132, 139 (9), 145 (1), 272 (7) (8), sch. 12, para. 2 (2) (b), 3. - Issued: 30.01.2015. Made: 23.01.2015. Laid: 30.01.2015. Coming into force: 01.03.2015. Effect: S.I. 2013/349 amended. Territorial extent & classification: E. General. - 8p.: 30 cm. - 978-0-11-112791-9 £4.25

The National Health Service (Primary Dental Services and General Ophthalmic Services) (Miscellaneous Amendments and Transitional Provision) Regulations 2015 No. 2015/416. - Enabling power: National Health Service Act 2006, ss. 104, 109, 121 (1) (2) (h), 272 (7) (8). - Issued: 05.03.2015. Made: 27.02.2015. Laid: 05.03.2015. Coming into force: In accord. with reg. 1 (2) (3). Effect: S.I. 2005/3361, 3373; 2008/1185 amended. Territorial extent & classification: E. General. - 8p.: 30 cm. - 978-0-11-113109-1 £4.25

The National Health Service (Primary Dental Services) (Miscellaneous Amendments) (No. 2) Regulations 2015 No. 2015/1728. - Enabling power: National Health Service Act 2006, ss. 7 (1), 104, 109, 176, 272 (7) (8), 273 (4). - Issued: 05.10.2015. Made: 28.09.2015. Laid: 05.10.2015. Coming into force: 01.11.2015. Effect: S.I. 2005/3361, 3373, 3477; 2013/469 amended. Territorial extent & classification: E. General. - 20p.: 30 cm. - 978-0-11-113950-9 £6.00

The National Health Service (Revision of NHS Constitution- Guiding Principles) Regulations 2015 No. 2015/1426. - Enabling power: Health Act 2009, s. 4 (4). - Issued: 30.06.2015. Made: 23.06.2015. Laid: 29.06.2015. Coming into force: 27.07.2015. Effect: S.I. 2013/317 partially revoked. Territorial extent & classification: E. General. - 4p.: 30 cm. - 978-0-11-113722-2 £4.25

The National Health Service Trust Development Authority (Amendment) Regulations 2015 No. 2015/1559. - Enabling power: National Health Service Act 2006, ss. 272 (7) (8) (a), sch. 6, para. 5. - Issued: 27.07.2015. Made: 20.07.2015. Laid: 27.07.2015. Coming into force: 05.10.2015. Effect: S.I. 2012/922 amended. Territorial extent & classification: E. General. - 2p.: 30 cm. - 978-0-11-113839-7 £4.25

The NHS Bodies and Local Authorities Partnership Arrangements (Amendment) Regulations 2015 No. 2015/1940. - Enabling power: National Health Service Act 2006, ss. 75 (1) (2) (3), 272 (7). - Issued: 02.12.2015. Made: 25.11.2015. Laid: 30.11.2015. Coming into force: 01.04.2016. Effect: S.I. 2000/617 amended. Territorial extent & classification: E. General. - 4p.: 30 cm. - 978-0-11-114127-4 £4.25

The NHS Foundation Trusts (Trust Funds: Appointment of Trustees) Amendment Order 2015 No. 2015/678. - Enabling power: National Health Service Act 2006, ss. 51 (1) (2), 64 (5) (6), 273 (1). - Issued: 18.03.2015. Made: 11.03.2015. Coming into force: 01.04.2015. Effect: S.I. 2007/1766 amended. Territorial extent & classification: E. General. - 2p.: 30 cm. - 978-0-11-113341-5 £4.25

The Social Security (Information-sharing) (NHS Payments and Remission of Charges etc.) (England) Regulations 2015 No. 2015/124. - Enabling power: Welfare Reform Act 2012, ss. 131 (1) (3) (11) (g), 132 (8), 133 (1) (2). - Issued: 11.02.2015. Made: 04.02.2015. Laid: 10.02.2015. Coming into force: 01.04.2015. Effect: None. Territorial extent & classification: E. General. - 8p.: 30 cm. - 978-0-11-112886-2 £6.00

The West Middlesex University Hospital National Health Service Trust (Dissolution) Order 2015 No. 2015/1621. - Enabling power: National Health Service Act 2006, ss. 25 (1), 272 (7), 273 (1), sch. 4, para. 28. - Issued: 27.08.2015. Made: 19.08.2015. Coming into force: 01.09.2015. Effect: S.I. 1992/2585 revoked. Territorial extent & classification: E. General. - 2p.: 30 cm. - 978-0-11-113873-1 £4.25

National Health Service, England and Wales

The Care Act 2014 (Health Education England and the Health Research Authority) (Consequential Amendments and Revocations) Order 2015 No. 2015/137. - Enabling power: Care Act 2014, s. 123 (1) (2). - Issued: 11.02.2015. Made: 04.02.2015. Laid: 11.02.2015. Coming into force: 01.04.2015. Effect: S.I. 1990/2024; 1995/2800, 2801; 1996/251; 1999/873, 874; 2004/1031; 2005/3361, 3373, 2415, 2531; 2008/1185; 2009/779 (W.67), 1385 (W.141), 3097 (W.270); 2011/2260; 2012/922, 1261; 2013/349; 2014/566 amended & S.I 2013/647, 1197 revoked. Territorial extent & classification: E/W. General. - Partially revoked by SI 2015/559 (ISBN 9780111132296) in re to E. - 8p.: 30 cm. - 978-0-11-112888-6 £6.00

The Health and Social Care (Miscellaneous Revocations etc.) Order 2015 No. 2015/864. - Enabling power: Health Authorities Act 1995, sch. 2, paras 4, 7 (1) (a), 13, 14, 16, 18, 19 , 20 & Health Act 1999, ss. 44, 63 & Health and Social Care Act 2001, ss. 64 (6), 70 (10) & Health and Social Care (Community Health and Standards) Act 2003, ss. 201 (1) & National Health Service Act 2006, ss. 28, 272 (7) (8), 273 (1), 278 (4), sch. 4, para. 22 & Health and Social Care Act 2008, ss. 161 (3) (4), 167 (1) (3). - Issued: 27.03.2015. Made: 23.03.2015 Laid: 26.03.2015. Coming into force: 01.07.2015. Effect: 2 SIs amended & 7 SIs revoked in relation to England & 1 S.I. partially revoked & 14 SIs revoked. Territorial extent & classification: E/W. General. - 4p.: 30 cm. - 978-0-11-113488-7 £4.25

The Health Service Medicines (Control of Prices and Supply of Information) (Amendment) Regulations 2015 No. 2015/233. - Enabling power: National Health Service Act 2006, ss. 261 (7), 262 to 265, 266 (1) (a) (2), 272 (7) (8). - Issued: 18.02.2015. Made: 10.02.2015. Laid: 17.02.2015. Coming into force: 09.03.2015. Effect: S.I. 2007/1320; 2008/3258 amended. Territorial extent & classification: E/W/S/NI. General. - 4p.: 30 cm. - 978-0-11-112972-2 £4.25

The National Health Service (Cross-Border Healthcare) (Amendment) Regulations 2015 No. 2015/139. - Enabling power: European Communities Act 1972, s. 2 (2). - Issued: 11.02.2015. Made: 04.02.2015. Laid: 11.02.2015. Coming into force: 27.03.2015. Effect: S.I. 2013/2269 amended. Territorial extent & classification: E/W. General. - These Regulations amend S.I. 2013/2269 to implement in England and Wales art. 4 of Commission Implementing Directive 2012/52/EU laying down measures to facilitate the recognition of medical prescriptions issued in another member state. - 4p.: 30 cm. - 978-0-11-112890-9 £4.25

The National Health Service Litigation Authority (Amendment) Regulations 2015 No. 2015/1683. - Enabling power: National Health Service Act 2006, ss. 28 (8), 272 (7) (8), sch. 6, para. 5 (a) & National Health Service (Consequential Provisions) Act 2006, s. 4, sch. 2, para. 8. - Issued: 17.09.2015. Made: 11.09.2015. Laid: 17.09.2015. Coming into force: 09.11.2015. Effect: S.I. 1995/2801 amended. Territorial extent & classification: E/W. General. - 2p.: 30 cm. - 978-0-11-113926-4 £4.25

The National Health Service Pension Scheme (Amendment) Regulations 2015 No. 2015/581. - Enabling power: Public Service Pensions Act 2013, ss. 1, 3, 25, sch. 3. - Issued: 12.03.2015. Made: 04.03.2015. Laid: 11.03.2015. Coming into force: 01.04.2015. Effect: None. Territorial extent & classification: E/W. General. - This Statutory Instrument has been made in consequence of defects in S.I. 2015/94 (ISBN 9780111129340) and is being issued free of charge to all known recipients of that S.I. - 4p.: 30 cm. - 978-0-11-113251-7 £4.25

The National Health Service Pension Scheme (Consequential Provisions) Regulations 2015 No. 2015/432. - Enabling power: Public Service Pensions Act 2013, ss. 1 (1) (2) (e), 2 (1), 3 (1) (2) (3) (a) (4). - Issued: 06.03.2015. Made: 25.02.2015. Coming into force: In accord. with reg. 1. Effect: None. Territorial extent & classification: E/W. General. - Supersedes draft S.I. (ISBN 9780111125915) issued 22/12/14. - 8p.: 30 cm. - 978-0-11-113122-0 £6.00

The National Health Service Pension Scheme, Injury Benefits and Additional Voluntary Contributions (Amendment) Regulations 2015 No. 2015/96. - Enabling power: Superannuation Act 1972, ss. 10 (1) (2), 12 91) (20 94), sch. 3. - Issued: 17.02.2015. Made: 05.02.2015. Laid: 12.02.2015. Coming into force: In Accord. with reg. 1. Effect: S.I. 1995/300, 866; 2000/619; 2008/653 amended. Territorial extent & classification: E/W. General. - 36p.: 30 cm. - 978-0-11-112924-1 £10.00

The National Health Service Pension Scheme Regulations 2015 No. 2015/94. - Enabling power: Public Service Pensions Act 2013, ss. 1 (1) (2) (e), 2 to 4, 5 (1) (2) (4), 7 (1) (4), 8 (1) (a) (2) (a), 11 (1), 12 (6) (7), 14, 18 (5) to (7), 25, sch. 2, para. 5 (a), 37 (c)- Issued: 26.02.2015. Made: 05.02.2015. Laid: 12.02.2015. Coming into force: 01.04.2015. Effect: None. Territorial extent & classification: E/W. General. - 176p.: 30 cm. - 978-0-11-112934-0 £25.50

The National Health Service Pension Scheme (Transitional and Consequential Provisions) Regulations 2015 No. 2015/95. - Enabling power: Superannuation Act 1972, ss. 10 (1) (2), sch. 3 & Public Service Pensions Act 2013, ss. 1, 3, 18 (5), sch. 3. - Issued: 13.02.2015. Made: 05.02.2015. Laid: 12.02.2015. Coming into force: 01.04.2015. Effect: S.I. 1995/300; 2008/653 amended. Territorial extent & classification: E/W. General. - 42p.: 30 cm. - 978-0-11-112902-9 £10.00

The Personal Injuries (NHS Charges) (Amounts) Regulations 2015 No. 2015/295. - Enabling power: Health and Social Care (Community Health and Standards) Act 2003, ss. 153 (2) (5) (7) (8) (12), 163 (1), 195 (1) (2). - Issued: 23.02.2015. Made: 12.02.2015. Laid: 20.02.2015. Coming into force: In accord. with reg. 1. Effect: S.I. 2009/316 revoked with saving & S.I. 2007/115; 2008/252; 2009/834; 2010/189; 2011/520; 2012/387; 2013/282; 2014/204 revoked. Territorial extent & classification: E/W. General. - 8p.: 30 cm. - 978-0-11-112991-3 £6.00

National Health Service, Scotland

The Health Service Medicines (Control of Prices and Supply of Information) (Amendment) Regulations 2015 No. 2015/233. - Enabling power: National Health Service Act 2006, ss. 261 (7), 262 to 265, 266 (1) (a) (2), 272 (7) (8). - Issued: 18.02.2015. Made: 10.02.2015. Laid: 17.02.2015. Coming into force: 09.03.2015. Effect: S.I. 2007/1320; 2008/3258 amended. Territorial extent & classification: E/W/S/NI. General. - 4p.: 30 cm. - 978-0-11-112972-2 £4.25

National Health Service, Wales

The Community Health Councils (Constitution, Membership and Procedures) (Wales) (Amendment) Regulations 2015 No. 2015/509 (W.43). - Enabling power: National Health Service (Wales) Act 2006, ss. 12, 19, 187 (1), 203 (9) (10), sch. 2, para. 7 (3), sch. 3, para. 25 (3), sch. 10, paras 2, 2A (2), 3, 4. - Issued: 17.03.2015. Made: 03.03.2015. Laid before the National Assembly for Wales: 06.03.2015. Coming into force: 01.04.2015. Effect: W.S.I. 2010/288 (W.37) amended. Territorial extent & classification: W. General. - In English and Welsh. Rheoliadau Cynghorau Iechyd Cymuned (Cyfansoddiad, Aelodaeth a Gweithdrefnau) (Cymru) (Diwygio) 2015. - 16p.: 30 cm. - 978-0-348-11054-8 £6.00

The Community Health Councils (Establishment, Transfer of Functions and Abolition) (Wales) (Amendment) Order 2015 No. 2015/507 (W.42). - Enabling power: National Health Service (Wales) Act 2006, ss. 182 (2) (3), 203 (9) (10) (a), sch. 10. - Issued: 16.03.2015. Made: 03.03.2015. Laid before the National Assembly for Wales: 06.03.2015. Coming into force: 01.04.2015. Effect: W.S.I. 2010/289 (W.38) amended. Territorial extent & classification: W. General. - In English and Welsh. Gorchymyn Cynghorau Iechyd Cymuned (Sefydlu, Trosglwyddo Swyddogaethau a Diddymu) (Cymru) (Diwygio) 2015. - 8p.: 30 cm. - 978-0-348-11053-1 £6.00

The National Health Service (Dental Charges) (Wales) (Amendment) Regulations 2015 No. 2015/512 (W.44). - Enabling power: National Health Service (Wales) Act 2006, ss. 125, 203 (9) (10). - Issued: 123.03.2015. Made: 03.03.2015. Laid before the National Assembly for Wales: 06.03.2015. Coming into force: 01.04.2015. Effect: S.I. 2006/491 (W.60) amended & WSI 2014/461 (W.54) revoked. Territorial extent & classification: W. General. - In English and Welsh: Rheoliadau'r Gwasanaeth Iechyd Gwladol (Ffioedd Deintyddol) (Cymru) (Diwygio) 2015. - 4p.: 30 cm. - 978-0-348-11052-4 £4.25

The National Health Service (Optical Charges and Payments) (Amendment) (Wales) (No. 2) Regulations 2015 No. 2015/1600 (W.199). - Enabling power: National Health Service (Wales) Act 2006, ss. 71, 76 (9), 128, 129, 203 (9) (10). - Issued: 20.08.2015. Made: 04.08.2015. Laid before the National Assembly for Wales: 10.08.2015. Coming into force: 31.08.2015. Effect: S.I. 1997/818 amended. Territorial extent & classification: W. General. - In English and Welsh. Welsh title: Rheoliadau'r Gwasanaeth Iechyd Gwladol (Ffioedd a Thaliadau Optegol) (Diwygio) (Cymru) (Rhif 2) 2015. - 4p.: 30 cm. - 978-0-348-11143-9 £4.25

The National Health Service (Optical Charges and Payments) (Amendment) (Wales) Regulations 2015 No. 2015/603 (W.48). - Enabling power: National Health Service (Wales) Act 2006, ss. 128, 129, 130, 203 (9) (10). - Issued: 24.04.2015. Made: 07.03.2015. Laid before the National Assembly for Wales: 10.03.2015. Coming into force: 01.04.2015. Effect: S.I. 1997/818 amended. Territorial extent & classification: W. General. - In English and Welsh. Welsh title: Rheoliadau'r Gwasanaeth Iechyd Gwladol (Ffioedd a Thaliadau Optegol) (Diwygio) (Cymru) 2015. - 8p.: 30 cm. - 978-0-348-11072-2 £6.00

The National Health Service (Welfare Reform Consequential Amendments) (Wales) Regulations 2015 No. 2015/631 (W.51). - Enabling power: National Health Service (Wales) Act 2006, ss. 71, 128, 129, 130, 131, 203 (9) (10). - Issued: 03.06.2015. Made: 09.06.2015. Laid before the National Assembly for Wales: 10.03.2015. Coming into force: 01.04.2015. Effect: S.I. 1986/975; 1997/818; 2007/1104 (W.116) amended & S.I. 2014/460 (W.53) revoked. Territorial extent & classification: W. General. - Revoked by SI 2016/97 (W.46) (ISBN 9780348112542). - In English and Welsh. Welsh title: Rheoliadau'r Gwasanaeth Iechyd Gwladol (Diwygiadau Canlyniadol Diwygio Lles) (Cymru) 2015. - 4p.: 30 cm. - 978-0-348-11105-7 £4.25

Nationality

The British Nationality (General) (Amendment No. 3) Regulations 2015 No. 2015/1806. - Enabling power: British Nationality Act 1981, ss. 41 (1) (a), 41 (1) (b) (ba) (1A) (3). - Issued: 26.10.2015. Made: 19.10.2015. Laid: 22.10.2015. Coming into force: 12.11.2015. Effect: S.I. 2003/548 amended. Territorial extent & classification: E/W/S/NI. General. - 4p.: 30 cm. - 978-0-11-114003-1 £4.25

The Immigration and Nationality (Fees) (Amendment) Regulations 2015 No. 2015/1424. - Enabling power: Immigration Act 2014, ss. 68 (1) (10) (12), 69 (1). - Issued: 02.07.2015. Made: 25.06.2015. Laid: 26.06.2015. Coming into force: 27.06.2015 in accord. with reg. 1. Effect: S.I. 2015/768 amended. Territorial extent & classification: E/W/S/NI/CI. General. - This S.I. has been made in consequence of a defect in S.I. 2015/768 (ISBN 9780111133941) published on 24/03/15 and is being issued to all known recipients of that S.I. free of charge. - 4p.: 30 cm. - 978-0-11-113720-8 £4.25

The Immigration and Nationality (Fees) Regulations 2015 No. 2015/768. - Enabling power: Immigration Act 2014, ss. 68 (1) (7) (8) (10) (12), 69 (1) (2), 74 (8) (a) (b) (d). - Issued: 24.03.2015. Made: 18.03.2015. Laid: 19.03.2015. Coming into force: 06.04.2015. Effect: None. Territorial extent & classification: E/W/S/NI/CI. General. - Corrected by S.I. 2015/1424 (ISBN 9780111137208) which issued free of charge to all known recipients of this S.I. - 36p.: 30 cm. - 978-0-11-113394-1 £10.00

Northern Ireland

The Crime and Courts Act 2013 (Consequential Amendments) Order 2015 No. 2015/230. - Enabling power: Crime and Courts Act 2013, s. 58 (4) (j). - Issued: 18.02.2015. Made: 12.02.2015. Coming into force: In accord. with art. 1. Effect: 2002 c.29 amended. Territorial extent & classification: NI. General. - 2p.: 30 cm. - 978-0-11-112969-2 £4.25

The Crime and Courts Act 2013 (National Crime Agency and Proceeds of Crime) (Northern Ireland) Order 2015 No. 2015/798. - Enabling power: Crime and Courts Act 2013, s. 59 (1) (2) (3), sch. 24, paras. 2, 3, 5, 7 (1), sch. 25, paras. 3, 4, 7 (1) (2), 10, 11, 14 (1). - Issued: 26.03.2015. Made: 19.03.2015. Coming into force: 20.03.2015. Effect: 1998 c.32; 2000 c.32; 2002 c.26, 29 S.I. 1989/1341 (N.I. 12) amended. Territorial extent & classification: E/W/S/NI. General. - Supersedes draft S.I. (ISBN 9780111128299) issued 04.02.2015- 12p.: 30 cm. - 978-0-11-113422-1 £6.00

The Local Elections (Forms) (Northern Ireland) Order 2015 No. 2015/566. - Enabling power: Northern Ireland Act 1998, s. 84 (1) (1A). - Issued: 26.03.2015. Made: 19.03.2015. Coming into force: In accord. with reg. 1 (2). Effect: 1962 c.14; 2001 c.7 & S.I. 1985/454; 2013/3156 amended. Territorial extent & classification: NI. General. - Supersedes draft SI (ISBN 9780111126677) issued 13/01/15. - 24p.: 30 cm. - 978-0-11-113418-4 £6.00

The Northern Ireland Assembly (Elections) (Amendment) Order 2015 No. 2015/1610. - Enabling power: Northern Ireland Assembly Act 1998, s. 34 (4) (6). - Issued: 19.08.2015. Made: 29.07.2015. Coming into force: In accord. with art 1 (2). Effect: S.I. 2001/2599 amended. Territorial extent & classification: NI. General. - Supersedes draft S.I. (ISBN 9780111137598) issued 14/07/15. - 4p.: 30 cm. - 978-0-11-113866-3 £4.25

The Northern Ireland Assembly (Elections) (Forms) Order 2015 No. 2015/222. - Enabling power: Northern Ireland Act 1998, ss 34 (4) (6). - Issued: 19.02.2015. Made: 11.02.2015. Coming into force: 12.02.2015 in accord. with art. 1 (2). Effect: S.I. 2001/2599 amended. Territorial extent & classification: NI. General. - Supersedes draft S.I. (ISBN 9780111126684) issued 13.01.2015. - 16p.: 30 cm. - 978-0-11-112973-9 £6.00

The Northern Ireland (Elections) (Amendment) (No. 2) Order 2015 No. 2015/1939. - Enabling power: Representation of the People Act 1983, s.10A (7) & Northern Ireland Act 1998, ss. 34 (4) (6). - Issued: 02.12.2015. Made: 26.11.2015. Laid: 30.11.2015. Effect: S.I. 2001/2599; 2008/1741 amended. Territorial extent & classification: NI. General. - Supersedes draft S.I. (ISBN 9780111140406) issued 05/11/15. - 4p.: 30 cm. - 978-0-11-114126-7 £4.25

Offshore installations

The Offshore Installations (Safety Zones) (No. 2) Order 2015 No. 2015/1406. - Enabling power: Petroleum Act 1987, s. 22. - Issued: 29.06.2015. Made: 23.06.2015. Coming into force: In accord. with art. 1 (2). Effect: S.I. 2015/407 amended. Territorial extent & classification: E/W/S. General. - 4p.: 30 cm. - 978-0-11-113703-1 £4.25

The Offshore Installations (Safety Zones) (No. 3) Order 2015 No. 2015/1673. - Enabling power: Petroleum Act 1987, s. 22. - Issued: 15.09.2015. Made: 09.09.2015. Coming into force: In accord. with art. 1 (2). Effect: S.I. 1997/735; 1998/1660; 2001/2528; 2008/2157 amended. Territorial extent & classification: E/W/S. General. - 4p.: 30 cm. - 978-0-11-113918-9 £4.25

The Offshore Installations (Safety Zones) Order 2015 No. 2015/407. - Enabling power: Petroleum Act 1987, s. 22. - Issued: 04.03.2015. Made: 23.02.2015. Coming into force: In accord. with art. 1 (2). Effect: None. Territorial extent & classification: E/W/S. General. - 4p.: 30 cm. - 978-0-11-113096-4 £4.25

Overseas territories

The Burundi (Sanctions) (Overseas Territories) Order 2015 No. 2015/1898. - Enabling power: Saint Helena Act 1833, s. 112 & British Settlements Act 1887 & British Settlements Act 1945. - Issued: 18.11.2015. Made: 11.11.2015. Laid: 18.11.2015. Coming into force: 10.12.2015. Effect: None. Territorial extent & classification: Anguilla, Bermuda, British Antarctic Territory, British Indian Ocean Territory, Cayman Islands, Falkland Islands, Montserrat, Pitcairn, Henderson, Ducie and Oeno Islands, St. Helena and Dependencies, South Georgia and South Sandwich Islands, The Sovereign Base Areas of Akrotiri and Dhekelia in the Island of Cyprus, Turks and Caicos Islands, Virgin Islands. General. - EC note: This Order gives effect in specified Overseas Territories to sanctions against Burundi adopted by the European Union in Council Decision 2015/1763/CFSP. - 12p.: 30 cm. - 978-0-11-114096-3 £6.00

The Central African Republic (Sanctions) (Overseas Territories) (Amendment) Order 2015 No. 2015/1380. - Enabling power: United Nations Act 1946, s. 1 & St Helena Act 1833, s. 112 & British Settlements Acts 1887 &1945. - Issued: 17.06.2015. Made: 10.06.2015. Laid: 17.06.2015. Coming into force: 08.07.2015. Effect: S.I. 2014/1368 amended. Territorial extent & classification: Anguilla; British Antarctic Territory; British Indian Ocean Territory; Cayman Islands; Falkland Islands; Montserrat; Pitcairn, Henderson, Ducie and Oeno Islands; St Helena, Ascension and Tristan da Cunha; South Georgia and the South Sandwich Islands; the Sovereign Base areas of Akrotiri and Dhekelia in the Island of Cyprus; Turks and Caicos Islands; Virgin Islands. General. - EC note: This Order reflects the implementation of those provisions by the European Union in Council Decision (CFSP) 2015/739 and Council Regulation (EU) 2015/734. - 2p.: 30 cm. - 978-0-11-113675-1 £4.25

The Democratic Republic of the Congo (Sanctions) (Overseas Territories) Order 2015 No. 2015/1382. - Enabling power: United Nations Act 1946, s. 1 & Saint Helena Act 1833, s. 112 & British Settlements Acts 1887 & 1945. - Issued: 17.06.2015. Made: 10.06.2015. Laid: 17.06.2015. Coming into force: 08.07.2015. Effect: S.I. 2003/2627; 2005/1461, 1988; 2012/2750 revoked. Territorial extent & classification: Anguilla, Bermuda, British Antarctic Territory, British Indian Ocean Territory, Cayman Islands, Falkland Islands, Montserrat, Pitcairn, Henderson, Ducie and Oeno Islands, St. Helena and Dependencies, South Georgia and South Sandwich Islands, the Sovereign Base Areas of Akrotiri and Dhekelia in the Island of Cyprus, Turks and Caicos Islands, Virgin Islands. General. - EC note: This Order also reflects the implementation of these sanctions by the European Union in Council Decision 2010/788/CFSP and Council Regulation 1183/2205. - 16p.: 30 cm. - 978-0-11-113677-5 £6.00

OVERSEAS TERRITORIES

The Iran (Restrictive Measures) (Overseas Territories) (Amendment and Suspension) Order 2015 No. 2015/825. - Enabling power: Saint Helena Act 1833, s. 112 & British Settlement Acts 1887 and 1945. - Issued: 26.03.2015. Made: 19.03.2015. Laid: 26.03.2015. Coming into force: 16.04.2015. Effect: S.I. 2012/1756 amended. Territorial extent & classification: Anguilla, British Antarctic Territory, British Indian Ocean Territory, Cayman Islands, Falkland Islands, Montserrat, Pitcairn (including Henderson, Ducie and Oeno Islands), St Helena, Ascension and Tristan da Cunha, South Georgia and the South Sandwich Islands, the Sovereign Base Areas of Akrotiri and Dhekelia, the Turks and Caicos Islands and the Virgin Islands. General. - EC note: Give effect in specified Overseas Territories to sanctions Council Regulation (EU) no. 42/2014 which amends Council Regulation (EU) no. 267/2012. - Revoked by S.I. 2016/371 (ISBN 9780111145401). - 4p.: 30 cm. - 978-0-11-113458-0 £4.25

The Iran (Restrictive Measures) (Overseas Territories) (Amendment) (No. 2) Order 2015 No. 2015/1772. - Enabling power: United Nations Act 1946, s. 1 & Saint Helena Act 1833, s. 112 & British Settlements Act 1887 & British Settlements Act 1945. - Issued: 15.10.2015. Made: 08.10.2015. Laid: 15.10.2015. Coming into force: 05.11.2015. Effect: S.I. 2012/1756 amended. Territorial extent & classification: Anguilla, British Antarctic Territory, British Indian Ocean Territory, Cayman Islands, the Falklands Islands, Montserrat, Pitcairn (including Henderson, Ducoe and Oeno Islands), St Helena, Ascension and Tristan da Cunha, South Georgia and the South Sandwich Islands, the Sovereign Base Areas of Akrotiri and Dhekelia, the Turks and Caicos Islands and the Virgin Islands, Bermuda legislates separately to apply EU sanctions & implemented in Gibraltar by Council Reg. (EU) 267/2012. General. - Revoked by S.I. 2016/371 (ISBN 9780111145401). - 4p.: 30 cm. - 978-0-11-113983-7 £4.25

The Iraq (Sanctions) (Overseas Territories) Order 2015 No. 2015/1383. - Enabling power: United Nations Act 1946, s. 1 & Saint Helena Act 1833, s. 112 & British Settlements Act 1887 and 1945. - Issued: 17.06.2015. Made: 10.06.2015. Laid: 17.06.2015. Coming into force: 08.07.2015. Effect: S.I. 2003/1516; 2004/1983, 2671; 2012/2748 revoked. Territorial extent & classification: Anguilla, Bermuda, British Antarctic Territory, British Indian Ocean Territory, Cayman Islands, Falkland Islands, Montserrat, Pitcairn, Henderson, Ducie and Oeno Islands, St. Helena and Dependencies, South Georgia and South Sandwich Islands, The Sovereign Base Areas of Akrotiri and Dhekelia in the Island of Cyprus, Turks and Caicos Islands, Virgin Islands. General. - EC note: This Order also reflects the implementation of these sanctions by the European Union in Council Common Position 2003/CFSP and Council Regulation 1210/2003. - 16p.: 30 cm. - 978-0-11-113678-2 £6.00

The Liberia (Sanctions) (Overseas Territories) Order 2015 No. 2015/1899. - Enabling power: United Nations Act 1946, s. 1 & Saint Helena Act 1833 s. 112 & British Settlements Act 1945 & British Settlements Act 1887. - Issued: 18.11.2015. Made: 11.11.2015. Laid: 18.11.2015. Coming into force: 10.12.2015. Effect: None. Territorial extent & classification: Anguilla, British Antarctic Territory, British Indian Ocean Territory, Cayman Is., Falkland Is., Montserrat, Pitcairn, Henderson, Ducie & Oeno Is., St Helena, Ascension Island & Tristan da Cunha, South Georgia & South Sandwich Is., the Sovereign Base Areas of Akrotiri & Dhekelia (Cyprus), Turks & Caicos Is., Virgin Is. General. - EC note: This Order gives effect in specified Overseas Territories to sanctions imposed on Liberia by the United Nations Security Council, most recently renewed by resolution 2237 (2015) of 2nd September 2015. This Order also reflects the implementation of these sanctions by the European Union in Council Decision (CFSP) 2015/1782 and Council Regulation (EU) 2015/1776, both adopted on 5th October 2015. Council Regulation (EU) 2015/1776 repealed Council Regulation (EC) No. 872/2004 of 29th April 2004. Council Decision (CFSP) 2015/1782 amended Council Common Position 2008/109/CFSP of 12th February 2008. - 12p.: 30 cm. - 978-0-11-114097-0 £6.00

The Russia, Crimea and Sevastopol (Sanctions) (Overseas Territories) (Amendment) Order 2015 No. 2015/213. - Enabling power: Saint Helena Act 1833, s. 112 & British Settlements Act 1887 & 1945. - Issued: 18.02.2015. Made: 11.02.2015. Laid: 18.02.2015. Coming into force: 11.03.2015. Effect: S.I. 2014/2710 amended. Territorial extent & classification: Anguilla, British Antarctic Territory, British Indian Ocean Territory, Cayman Is., Falkland Is., Montserrat, Pitcairn, Henderson, Ducie & Oeno Is., St Helena, Ascension & Tristan da Cunha, South Georgia & the South Sandwich Is., the Sovereign Base Areas of Akrotiri & Dhekelia (Cyprus), Turks & Caicos Is., Virgin Is. General. - EC note: This Order gives effect in specified Overseas Territories to provisions in Council Decision 2014/872/CFSP which amends certain restrictive measures imposed on Russia by Council Decision 2014/512/CFSP. In addition, this Order gives effect to further sanctions imposed on Crimea and Sevastopol by Council Decision 2014/933/CFSP. - 8p.: 30 cm. - 978-0-11-112955-5 £6.00

The South Sudan (Sanctions) (Overseas Territories) (Amendment) Order 2015 No. 2015/1527. - Enabling power: Saint Helena Act 1833, s. 112 & British Settlements Acts 1887 and 1945. - Issued: 22.07.2015. Made: 15.07.2015. Laid: 22.07.2015. Coming into force: 12.08.2015. Effect: S.I. 2014/2703 amended. Territorial extent & classification: Anguilla, British Antarctic Territory, British Indian Ocean Territory, Cayman Islands, the Falkland Islands, Montserrat, Pitcairn (including Henderson, Ducie and Oeno Islands), St Helena, Ascension and Tristan da Cunha, South Georgia and the South Sandwich Islands, the Sovereign Base Areas of Akrotiri and Dhekelia, the Turks and Caicos Islands and the Virgin Islands. General. - EC note: Article 2 of this Order makes one minor amendment to article 3 (1) of the principle Order to update the definition of the "Council Regulation" to give effect to the repeal of Council Regulation (EU) no. 748/2014 and its replacement by Council Regulation (EU) no. 2015/735 which integrates some of the restrictive measures imposed by UN Security Council resolution 2206 and Council Decision (CFSP) 2015/740. - 2p.: 30 cm. - 978-0-11-113804-5 £4.25

The Syria (Restrictive Measures) (Overseas Territories) (Amendment) (No. 2) Order 2015 No. 2015/1528. - Enabling power: Saint Helena Act 1833, s. 112 & British Settlements Acts 1887, 1945. - Issued: 22.07.2015. Made: 15.07.2015. Laid: 22.07.2015. Coming into force: 13.08.2015. Effect: S.I. 2012/1755 amended. Territorial extent & classification: Anguilla, British Antarctic Territory, British Indian Ocean Territory, Cayman Islands, Falkland Islands, Montserrat, Pitcairn, Henderson, Ducie and Oeno Islands, St. Helena, Ascension & Tristan da Cunha, South Georgia and the South Sandwich Islands, the Sovereign Base Areas of Akrotiri and Dhekelia in the Island of Cyprus, the Turks and Caicos Islands, Virgin Islands. General. - EC note: Gives effect in specified Overseas Territories to sanctions in respect of Syria adopted by the European Union in Council Decision 2013/255/CFSP. - 2p.: 30 cm. - 978-0-11-113805-2 £4.25

The Syria (Restrictive Measures) (Overseas Territories) (Amendment) Order 2015 No. 2015/824. - Enabling power: Saint Helena Act 1833, s. 112 & British Settlements Acts 1887, 1945. - Issued: 26.03.2015. Made: 19.03.2015. Laid: 26.03.2015. Coming into force: 16.04.2015. Effect: S.I. 2012/1755 amended. Territorial extent & classification: Anguilla, British Antarctic Territory, British Indian Ocean Territory, Cayman Islands, Falkland Islands, Montserrat, Pitcairn, Henderson, Ducie and Oeno Islands, St. Helena, Ascension & Tristan da Cunha, South Georgia and South Sandwich Islands, The Sovereign Base Areas of Akrotiri and Dhekelia in the Island of Cyprus, Turks and Caicos Islands, Virgin Islands. General. - EC note: Give effect in specified Overseas Territories to sanctions in respect of Syria adopted by the European Union in Council Regulation (EU) no. 36/2012 & gives effect to changes in Council Regulation (EU) 1323/2014. - 4p.: 30 cm. - 978-0-11-113457-3 £4.25

The Yemen (Sanctions) (Overseas Territories) (No. 2) Order 2015 No. 2015/1381. - Enabling power: United Nations Act 1946, s. 1 & Saint Helena Act 1833, s. 112 & British Settlements Acts 1887 & 1945. - Issued: 17.06.2015. Made: 10.06.2015. Laid: 17.06.2015. Coming into force: 18.06.2015. Effect: None. Territorial extent & classification: Anguilla, British Antarctic Territory, British Indian Ocean Territory, Cayman Is., Falkland Is., Montserrat, Pitcairn, Henderson, Ducie & Oeno Is., St Helena, Ascension & Tristan da Cunha, South Georgia & the South Sandwich Is., the Sovereign Base Areas of Akrotiri & Dhekelia (Cyprus), Turks & Caicos Is., Virgin Is. General. - EC note: This Order also reflects the implementation of these sanctions by the European Union in Council Decision 2014/932/CFSP. - 16p.: 30 cm. - 978-0-11-113676-8 £6.00

The Yemen (Sanctions) (Overseas Territories) Order 2015 No. 2015/218. - Enabling power: United Nations Act 1946, s. 1 & Saint Helena Act 1833, s. 112 & British Settlements Acts 1887 & 1945. - Issued: 18.02.2015. Made: 11.02.2015. Laid: 18.02.2015. Coming into force: 11.03.2015. Effect: None. Territorial extent & classification: Anguilla, British Antarctic Territory, British Indian Ocean Territory, Cayman Is., Falkland Is., Montserrat, Pitcairn, Henderson, Ducie & Oeno Is., St Helena, Ascension & Tristan da Cunha, South Georgia & the South Sandwich Is., the Sovereign Base Areas of Akrotiri & Dhekelia (Cyprus), Turks & Caicos Is., Virgin Is. General. - 16p.: 30 cm. - 978-0-11-112960-9 £6.00

The Zimbabwe (Sanctions) (Overseas Territories) (Amendment and Revocation) Order 2015 No. 2015/826. - Enabling power: St Helena Act 1833, s. 112 & British Settlements Acts 1887 and 1945. - Issued: 26.03.2015. Made: 19.03.2015. Laid: 26.03.2015. Coming into force: 16.04.2015. Effect: S.I. 2012/2753 amended & S.I. 2013/1446 partially revoked. Territorial extent & classification: Anguilla, Bermuda, British Antarctic Territory, British Indian Ocean Territory, Cayman Islands, Falkland Islands, Montserrat, Pitcairn, Henderson, Ducie and Oeno Islands, St. Helena and Dependencies, South Georgia and South Sandwich Islands, The Sovereign Base Areas of Akrotiri and Dhekelia in the Island of Cyprus, Turks and Caicos Islands, Virgin Islands. General. - EC note: This Order gives effect in certain Overseas Territories to the suspension of sanctions in Council Decision 2013/160/CFSP against Zimbabwe, as continued in Council Decision 2015/277/CFSP. - 4p.: 30 cm. - 978-0-11-113459-7 £4.25

Parliamentary Commissioner

The Parliamentary Commissioner Order 2015 No. 2015/214. - Enabling power: Parliamentary Commissioner Act 1967, s. 4 (2). - Issued: 18.02.2015. Made: 11.02.2015. Laid: 18.02.2015. Coming into force: 06.04.2015. Effect: 1967 c. 13 amended. Territorial extent & classification: E/W/S/NI. General. - 2p.: 30 cm. - 978-0-11-112956-2 £4.25

Partnership

The Companies, Partnerships and Groups (Accounts and Reports) Regulations 2015 No. 2015/980. - Enabling power: European Communities Act 1972, s. 2 (2) & Companies Act 2006, ss. 396 (3), 404 (3), 409 (1) (2), 412 (1) (2), 468 (1) (2), 473 (2), 484, 1292 (1). - Issued: 01.04.2015. Made: 26.03.2015. Coming into force: 06.04.2015. Effect: 2006 c.46; S.I. 2008/373, 409, 410, 569 amended. Territorial extent & classification: E/W/S/NI. General. - Supersedes draft S.I. (ISBN 9780111130230) issued 27/02/15. - 40p.: 30 cm. - 978-0-11-113613-3 £10.00

The Reports on Payments to Governments (Amendment) Regulations 2015 No. 2015/1928. - Enabling power: European Communities Act 1972 s. 2 (2) & Companies Act 2006 ss. 1102 (2) (3). - Issued: 27.11.2015. Made: 23.11.2015. Laid: 25.11.2015. Coming into force: 18.12.2015. Effect: S.I. 2014/3209 amended. Territorial extent & classification: E/W/S/NI. General. - This Statutory Instrument has been made in consequence of defects in S.I. 2014/3209 (ISBN 9780111124604) as is being issued free of charge to all known recipients of that Statutory Instrument. - 8p.: 30 cm. - 978-0-11-114116-8 £4.25

Payment scheme

The Childcare Payments Act 2014 (Amendment) Regulations 2015 No. 2015/537. - Enabling power: Childcare Payments Act 2014, ss. 19 (7), 69 (2) (4) (b). - Issued: 11.03.2015. Made: 05.03.2015. Laid: 06.03.2015. Coming into force: 01.06.2015. Effect: 2014 c.28 amended. Territorial extent & classification: E/W/S/NI. General. - 2p.: 30 cm. - 978-0-11-113216-6 £4.25

The Childcare Payments (Eligibility) Regulations 2015 No. 2015/448. - Enabling power: Childcare Payments Act 2014, ss 2 (3) (b) to (d), 3 (4) (5), 7 (3), 8 (2), 9 (2) (3), 10 (2) (3) (4), 14, 32 (5), 33 (5), 69 (2) (4). - Issued: 12.03.2015. Made: 04.03.2015. Coming into force: 05.03.2015 in accord. with reg. 1. Effect: None. Territorial extent & classification: E. - Supersedes draft S.I. (ISBN 9780111127063) issued 16.01.2015. - 16p.: 30 cm. - 978-0-11-113245-6 £6.00

The Childcare Payments Regulations 2015 No. 2015/522. - Enabling power: Childcare Payments Act 2014, ss. 2 (3) (a) (4), 4 (6), 5 (3), 15 (3) (4) (5), 17 (4), 19 (6), 24 (1) (3) (4), 25, 26 (1) (3), 49 (6), 62 (1) (2) (3) (5), 69 (3) (4). - Issued: 11.03.2015. Made: 04.03.2015. Laid: 05.03.2015. Coming into force: 01.06.2015. Effect: None. Territorial extent & classification: E/W/S/NI. General. - 16p.: 30 cm. - 978-0-11-113208-1 £6.00

The Diffuse Mesothelioma Payment Scheme (Amendment) Regulations 2015 No. 2015/367. - Enabling power: Mesothelioma Act 2014, ss. 1, 17 (4). - Issued: 02.03.2015. Made: 23.02.2015. Laid: 27.02.2015. Coming into force: 31.03.2015. Effect: S.I. 2014/916 amended. Territorial extent & classification: E/W/S/NI. General. - 4p.: 30 cm. - 978-0-11-113058-2 £4.25

Pensions

The Armed Forces and Reserve Forces (Compensation Scheme) (Amendment) Order 2015 No. 2015/413. - Enabling power: Armed forces (Pensions and Compensation) Act 2004, s. 1 (2)- Issued: 05.03.2015. Made: 25.02.2015. Laid: 03.03.2015. Coming into force: 06.04.2015. Effect: S.I. 2011/517 amended. Territorial extent & classification: E/W/S/NI. General. - 4p.: 30 cm. - 978-0-11-113106-0 £4.25

The Armed Forces (Enhanced Learning Credit Scheme and Further and Higher Education Commitment Scheme) (Amendment) Order 2015 No. 2015/497. - Enabling power: Armed Forces (Pensions and Compensation) Act 2004, s. 1 (1) (3). - Issued: 10.03.2015. Made: 03.03.2015. Laid: 06.03.2015. Coming into force: 01.04.2015. Effect: S.I. 2012/1796 amended. Territorial extent & classification: E/W/S/NI. General. - 2p.: 30 cm. - 978-0-11-113195-4 £4.25

The Armed Forces (Transitional Provisions) Pensions Regulations 2015 No. 2015/568. - Enabling power: Public Service Pensions Act 2013, ss. 1 (1) (2) (h), 2 (1) (h), 3 (1) to (4), 18 (5). - Issued: 13.03.2015. Made: 03.03.2015. Laid: 09.03.2015. Coming into force: 01.04.2015. Effect: AFPS 1975; FTRS 1997; Reserve Forces Non-Regular Permanent Staff (Pensions & Attributable Benefits Scheme) Regulations 2011; S.I. 2005/437, 438; 2010/832; 2014/2336, 2328 amended. Territorial extent & classification: E/W/S/NI. General. - 120p.: 30 cm. - 978-0-11-113236-4 £19.00

The Automatic Enrolment (Earnings Trigger and Qualifying Earnings Band) Order 2015 No. 2015/468. - Enabling power: Pensions Act 2008, ss. 3 (1) (c), 5 (1) (c), 13 (1) (a) (b). - Issued: 06.03.2015. Made: 02.03.2015. Coming into force: 06.04.2015. Effect: S.I. 2014/623 partially revoked. Territorial extent & classification: E/W/S. General. - Supersedes draft S.I. (ISBN 9780111127124) issued 19/01/15; Partially revoked by S.I. 2016/435 (ISBN 9780111143407). - 4p.: 30 cm. - 978-0-11-113160-2 £4.25

The Funded Public Service Pension Schemes (Reduction of Cash Equivalents) Regulations 2015 No. 2015/892. - Enabling power: Pension Schemes Act 1993, ss. 97C, 182 (2) (3), 183(1). - Issued: 01.04.2015. Made: 25.03.2015. Laid: 26.03.2015. Coming into force: 16.04.2015. Effect: None. Territorial extent & classification: E/W/S. General. - 8p.: 30 cm. - 978-0-11-113519-8 £6.00

The Guaranteed Minimum Pensions Increase Order 2015 No. 2015/470. - Enabling power: Pension Schemes Act 1993, s. 109 (1). - Issued: 09.03.2015. Made: 02.03.2015. Coming into force: 06.04.2015. Effect: None. Territorial extent & classification: E/W/S. General. - Supersedes draft S.I. (ISBN 9780111127049) issued 19/01/15. - 2p.: 30 cm. - 978-0-11-113162-6 £4.25

The Judicial Pensions and Retirement Act 1993 (Addition of Qualifying Judicial Offices) Order 2015 No. 2015/109. - Enabling power: Judicial Pensions and Retirement Act 1993, ss. 1 (8), 30 (1). - Issued: 09.02.2015. Made: 02.02.2015. Laid: 05.02.2015. Coming into force: 02.03.2015. Effect: 1993 c.8 amended. Territorial extent & classification: E/W/S/NI. General. - 2p.: 30 cm. - 978-0-11-112860-2 £4.25

The Judicial Pensions (Miscellaneous) (Amendment) Regulations 2015 No. 2015/533. - Enabling power: Judicial Pensions and Retirement Act 1993, s. 2 (7) (e). - Issued: 11.03.2015. Made: 04.03.2015. Laid: 09.03.2015. Coming into force: 01.04.2015. Effect: S.I. 1995/632 amended. Territorial extent & classification: E/W/S/NI. General. - 4p.: 30 cm. - 978-0-11-113214-2 £4.25

The National Employment Savings Trust (Amendment) Order 2015 No. 2015/178. - Enabling power: Pensions Act 2008, ss. 67 (1) (8), 70 (4), 144 (2) (4). - Issued: 13.02.2015. Made: 09.02.2015. Coming into force: 01.04.2017. Effect: S.I. 2010/917 amended & 2008 c.30 partially repealed. Territorial extent & classification: E/W/S. General. - 4p.: 30 cm. - 978-0-11-112915-9 £4.25

PENSIONS

The Naval, Military and Air Forces Etc. (Disablement and Death) Service Pensions (Amendment) Order 2015 No. 2015/208. - Enabling power: Social Security (Miscellaneous Provisions) Act 1977, ss. 12 (1), 24 (3). - Issued: 18.02.2015. Made: 11.02.2015. Laid: 18.02.2015. Coming into force: 06.04.2015. Effect: S.I. 2006/606 amended. Territorial extent & classification: E/W/S/NI. General. - 12p.: 30 cm. - 978-0-11-112950-0 £6.00

The Occupational and Personal Pension Schemes (Automatic Enrolment) (Amendment) Regulations 2015 No. 2015/501. - Enabling power: Pension Act 2008, ss. 3 (5), 4 (1) (2) (3), 5 (2), 9 (3), 10, 23A (1) (a) (b) (2) (4) (b), 25, 30 (7A), 87A (1) (3) (4), 99, 144 (2) (4). - Issued: 10.03.2015. Made: 04.03.2015. Laid: 09.03.2015. Coming into force: 01.04.2015. Effect: S.I. 2010/772 amended. Territorial extent & classification: E/W/S. General. - 12p.: 30 cm. - 978-0-11-113199-2 £6.00

The Occupational and Personal Pension Schemes (Disclosure of Information) (Amendment) Regulations 2015 No. 2015/482. - Enabling power: Pensions Scheme Act 1993, ss. 113 (1) (3), 181 (1), 182 (2) 93], 183 (1). - Issued: 09.03.2015. Made: 03.03.2015. Laid: 09.03.2015. Coming into force: 06.04.2015. Effect: S.I. 2013/2734 amended. Territorial extent & classification: E/W/S. General. - 12p.: 30 cm. - 978-0-11-113180-0 £6.00

The Occupational and Personal Pension Schemes (Transfer Values) (Amendment and Revocation) Regulations 2015 No. 2015/498. - Enabling power: Pensions Scheme Act 1993, ss. 93 (5) (10) (a) (b), 93A (5), 95 (2) (b) (6A), 97 (1) (2) (a) (b) (3B) (4), 99 (4A) (4B), 101F (6A), 113 (1) (3), 181 (1), 182 (2) (3), 183 (1) & Pensions Act 1995, s. 10 (2) (b) & Pension Schemes Act 2015, ss. 83 (1), 86. - Issued: 10.03.2015. Made: 03.03.2015. Laid: 09.03.2015. Coming into force: 06.04.2015 exc. reg. 14 which comes into force 01.04.2017. Effect: S.I. 1987/1112; 1996/1847; 2010/6 amended & S.I. 2010/6 revoked (01.04.2017). Territorial extent & classification: E/W/S. General. - 8p.: 30 cm. - 978-0-11-113196-1 £6.00

The Occupational Pension Schemes (Charges and Governance) (Amendment) Regulations 2015 No. 2015/889. - Enabling power: Pensions Act 2014, ss. 43 (a), 54 (5), sch. 18, paras 1 (1) (2) (a) (3). - Issued: 31.03.2015. Made: 25.03.2015. Laid: 25.03.2015. Coming into force: 06.04.2015. Effect: S.I. 2015/879 amended. Territorial extent & classification: E/W/S. General. - This Statutory Instrument has been made in consequence of a defect in S.I. 2015/879 (ISBN 9780111135020) and is being issued free of charge to all known recipients of that Statutory Instrument. - 2p.: 30 cm. - 978-0-11-113513-6 £4.25

The Occupational Pension Schemes (Charges and Governance) Regulations 2015 No. 2015/879. - Enabling power: Pension Schemes Act 1993, ss. 113 (1), 181 (1), 182 (2) (3) & Pensions Act 1995, ss. 35 (1) (3) (4), 36 (1) (1A) (a) (9), 68 (2) (e), 124 (1), 174 (2) (3) & Welfare Reform and Pensions Act 1999, ss. 1 (5), 8 (1), 83 (4) (a) & Pensions Act 2004, ss. 60 (2) (h), 259 (1), 315, 318 (1) & Pensions Act 2014, ss. 43, 54 (5) (6), sch. 18, paras. 1 (1) (2) (a) (3) (5), 2 (1) to (3), (5), 6, 7. - Issued: 31.03.2015. Made: 23.03.2015. Coming into force: In accord. with reg. 1. Effect: 2004 c. 35 & S.I. 1996/1715; 2000/1403; 2005/597, 3378; 2006/349, 759 amended. Territorial extent & classification: E/W/S. General. - Supersedes draft SI (ISBN 9780111128329) issued 04/02/15 - 28p.: 30 cm. - 978-0-11-113502-0 £6.00

The Occupational Pension Schemes (Consequential and Miscellaneous Amendments) Regulations 2015 No. 2015/493. - Enabling power: Pensions Scheme Act 1993, ss. 12C (1) (c), 71 (6), 181 (1), 182 (2) (3), 183 (1) & Pensions Act 1995, ss. 67 (3) (b), 68 (2) (e), 91 (5) (c) (iii), 124 (1), 174 (2) (3). - Issued: 09.03.2015. Made: 03.03.2015. Laid: 09.03.2015. Coming into force: 06.04.2015. Effect: S.I. 1991/167; 1996/1172; 1997/785; 2006/759 amended. Territorial extent & classification: E/W/S. General. - 8p.: 30 cm. - 978-0-11-113191-6 £4.25

The Occupational Pension Schemes (Levies) (Amendment) Regulations 2015 No. 2015/84. - Enabling power: Pension Schemes Act 2004, ss 117 (1) (3), 315 (2), 318 (1). - Issued: 04.02.2015. Made: 28.01.2015. Laid: 04.02.2015. Coming into force: In accord. with reg. 1. Effect: S.I. 2005/842 amended & S.I. 2007/994; 2012/539 partially revoked & 2008/910 revoked. Territorial extent & classification: E/W/S. General. - 4p.: 30 cm. - 978-0-11-112827-5 £4.25

The Occupational Pension Schemes (Power to Amend Schemes to Reflect Abolition of Contracting-out) Regulations 2015 No. 2015/118. - Enabling power: Pensions Act 2014, ss. 24 (5), 54 (5) (6), sch. 14 paras 2 (3) (4), 4, 6, 10 (1), 12, 13, 14 (1) (2). - Issued: 04.03.2015. Made: 25.02.2015. Laid: 04.03.2015. Coming into force: 06.04.2015. Effect: None. Territorial extent & classification: E/W/S. General. - 12p.: 30 cm. - 978-0-11-113078-0 £6.00

The Occupational Pension Schemes (Schemes that were Contracted-out) (No. 2) Regulations 2015 No. 2015/1677. - Enabling power: Pensions Schemes Act 1993, ss. 7, 9, 11 (5), 12A (4), 12D, 16 (3) (4), 17 (6), 20 (1) (3), 21 (1) (2), 24C, 25 (2), 34, 36 (6), 37 (1), 37A(1)(c), 50 (1B), 51 (2) (4), 53 (3), 55 (2) (2B) (2C), 56 (2), 57 (1) (2), 61 (7) (11), 155, 156 (2), 181 (1) (2), 182 (2) (3), 183 (1), sch. 2, pt I & Pension Schemes (Northern Ireland) Act 1993, ss. 51 (2) (2B) (2C), 52 (2), 53 (1) (2), 57 (7) (11), 176 (1), 177 (2) to (4), 178 (1), sch. 1, paras 1, 2, 5 & Pensions Act 1995, ss. 92 (6), 174 (3). - Issued: 16.09.2015. Made: 09.09.2015. Laid: 16.09.2015. Coming into force: in accord. with reg. 1 (2). Effect: S.I. 1996/1462 amended & S.I. 1996/1172 amended & partially revoked & S.I. 2015/1452; S.R. 1996/493 partially revoked. Territorial extent & classification: E/W/S except Part 8, which extends to NI. General. - This Statutory Instrument has been made in consequence of a defect in S.I. 2015/1452 (ISBN 9780111137987) issued 21.07.2015 and is being issued free of charge to all known recipients of that Statutory Instrument. - 36p.: 30 cm. - 978-0-11-113922-6 £10.00

The Occupational Pension Schemes (Schemes that were Contracted-out) Regulations 2015 No. 2015/1452. - Enabling power: Pensions Schemes Act 1993, s. 185 (1). - Issued: 21.07.2015. Made: 14.07.2015. Coming into force: in accord. with reg. 1 (2). Effect: S.I. 1996/1462 amended & S.I. 1996/1172 amended & partially revoked & S.R. 1996/493 partially revoked. Territorial extent & classification: E/W/S except Part 8, which extends to NI. General. - 36p.: 30 cm. - 978-0-11-113798-7 £10.00

The Occupational Pensions (Revaluation) Order 2015 No. 2015/1916. - Enabling power: Pension Schemes Act 1993, sch. 3, para. 2 (1). - Issued: 24.11.2015. Made: 17.11.2015. Laid: 24.11.2015. Coming into force: 01.01.2016. Effect: 1993 c.48 amended. Territorial extent & classification: E/W/S. General. - 2p.: 30 cm. - 978-0-11-114107-6 £4.25

The Pension Protection Fund and Occupational Pension Schemes (Levy Ceiling) Order 2015 No. 2015/66. - Enabling power: Pensions Act 2004, ss 178 (1) (6), 315 (2) (5). - Issued: 02.02.2015. Made: 26.01.2015. Laid: 02.02.2015. Coming into force: In accord. with art. 1 (2). Effect: S.I. 2014/10 partially revoked. Territorial extent & classification: E/W/S. General. - Revoked by S.I. 2016/82 (ISBN 9780111143162)- 2p.: 30 cm. - 978-0-11-112802-2 £4.25

The Pensions Act 2004 (Code of Practice) (Governance and Administration of Public Service Pension Schemes) Appointed Day Order 2015 No. 2015/456. - Enabling power: Pensions Act 2004, s. 91 (9). Bringing Code of practice no. 14 into effect on 01.04.2015. - Issued: 09.03.2015. Made: -. Effect: None. Territorial extent & classification: E/W/S. General. - 2p.: 30 cm. - 978-0-11-113147-3 £4.25

The Pensions Act 2011 (Commencement No. 6) Order 2015 No. 2015/676 (C.38). - Enabling power: Pensions Act 2011, s. 38 (4). Bringing into operation various provisions of the 2011 Act on 01.04.2015 in accord. with art. 2. - Issued: 18.03.2015. Made: 12.03.2015. Effect: None. Territorial extent & classification: E/W/S. General. - 2p.: 30 cm. - 978-0-11-113338-5 £4.25

The Pensions Act 2014 (Commencement No. 4) Order 2015 No. 2015/134 (C.8). - Enabling power: Pensions Act 2014, s. 56 (1) (4) (7). Bringing into operation various provisions of the 2014 Act on 05.02.2015; 23.02.2015; 01.10.2015, in accord. with art. 2. - Issued: 11.02.2015. Made: 04.02.2015. Coming to force: -. Effect: None. Territorial extent & classification: E/W/S. General. - 4p.: 30 cm. - 978-0-11-112883-1 £4.25

The Pensions Act 2014 (Commencement No. 5) Order 2015 No. 2015/1475 (C.84). - Enabling power: Pensions Act 2014, s. 56 (1) (4) (7). Bringing into operation various provisions of the 2014 Act on 07.07.2015; 12.10.2015; 06.04.2016 in accord. with arts 3, 4. - Issued: 13.07.2015. Made: 06.07.2015. Coming to force: -. Effect: None. Territorial extent & classification: E/W/S. General. - 4p.: 30 cm. - 978-0-11-113755-0 £4.25

The Pensions Act 2014 (Commencement No. 6) Order 2015 No. 2015/1670 (C.95). - Enabling power: Pensions Act 2014, s. 56 (1) (7). Bringing into operation various provisions of the 2014 Act on 12.10.2015 in accord. with art. 2. - Issued: 15.09.2015. Made: 09.09.2015. Coming to force: -. Effect: None. Territorial extent & classification: E/W/S. General. - 4p.: 30 cm. - 978-0-11-113917-2 £4.25

The Pensions Act 2014 (Commencement No.7) and (Savings) (Amendment) Order 2015 No. 2015/2058 (C.129). - Enabling power: Pensions Act 2014 ss. 56 (1) (4) (7) (8). Bringing into operation various provisions of the 2014 Act on 15.01.2016. - Issued: 23.12.2015. Made: 16.12.2015. Effect: S.I. 2015/1502 amended. Territorial extent & classification: E/W/S/NI. General. - 4p.: 30 cm. - 978-0-11-114240-0 £4.25

The Pensions Act 2014 (Savings) Order 2015 No. 2015/1502. - Enabling power: Pensions Act 2014, s. 56 (8). - Issued: 20.07.2015. Made: 14.07.2015. Coming to force: -. Effect: None. Territorial extent & classification: E/W/S. General- 4p.: 30 cm. - 978-0-11-113791-8 £4.25

The Pension Schemes Act 2015 (Commencement No. 1) Regulations 2015 No. 2015/1851 (C.116). - Enabling power: Pension Schemes Act 2015, s. 89 (4) (b). Bringing into operation various provisions of the 2015 Act on 16.11.2015, in accord. with art. 2. - Issued: 09.11.2015. Made: 02.11.2015. Laid: - Effect: None. Territorial extent & classification: E/W/S. General. - 2p.: 30 cm. - 978-0-11-114047-5 £4.25

The Pension Schemes Act 2015 (Transitional Provisions and Appropriate Independent Advice) Regulations 2015 No. 2015/742. - Enabling power: Pensions Schemes Act 2015, ss. 48 (2) (3) (a) (4) (8), 49, 86, 89 (6). - Issued: 23.03.2015. Made: 17.03.2015. Laid: 17.03.2015. Coming into force: 06.04.2015. Effect: None. Territorial extent & classification: E/W/S. General. - 8p.: 30 cm. - 978-0-11-113375-0 £6.00

The Pensions Increase (Review) Order 2015 No. 2015/671. - Enabling power: Social Security Pensions Act 1975, s. 59 (1) (2) (5) (5ZA). - Issued: 19.03.2015. Made: 12.03.2015. Laid: 13.03.2015. Coming into force: 06.04.2015. Effect: None. Territorial extent & classification: E/W/S/NI. General. - 4p.: 30 cm. - 978-0-11-113333-0 £4.25

The Personal Injuries (Civilians) Scheme (Amendment) Order 2015 No. 2015/555. - Enabling power: Personal Injuries (Emergency Provisions) Act 1939, ss. 1, 2. - Issued: 12.03.2015. Made: 03.03.2015. Laid: 06.03.2015. Coming into force: 06.04.2015. Effect: S.I. 1983/686 amended. Territorial extent & classification: E/W/S/NI. General. - 8p.: 30 cm. - 978-0-11-113228-9 £4.25

The Superannuation (Admission to Schedule 1 to the Superannuation Act 1972) Order 2015 No. 2015/919. - Enabling power: Superannuation Act 1972, s. 1 (5) (8) (a). - Issued: 01.04.2015. Made: 25.03.2015. Laid: 26.03.2015. Coming into force: 16.04.2015. Effect: 1972 c. 11 amended. Territorial extent & classification: UK. General. - 4p.: 30 cm. - 978-0-11-113542-6 £4.25

The Unfunded Public Service Defined Benefits Schemes (Transfers) Regulations 2015 No. 2015/1614. - Enabling power: Pensions Scheme Act 1993, ss. 95 (2A) (d), 95 (5A), 182 (2) (3). - Issued: 20.08.2015. Made: 14.08.2015. Laid: 17.08.2015. Coming into force: In accord. with 1 (2). Effect: None. Territorial extent & classification: E/W/S. General. - 4p.: 30 cm. - 978-0-11-113869-4 £4.25

Pensions, England

The Firefighters' Compensation Scheme and Pension Scheme (England) (Amendment) Order 2015 No. 2015/590. - Enabling power: Fire and Rescue Services Act 2004, ss. 34, 60. - Issued: 13.03.2015. Made: 06.03.2015. Laid: 10.03.2015. Coming into force: In accord. with art. 1. Effect: S.I. 2006/1811, 3432 amended. Territorial extent & classification: E. General. - 20p.: 30 cm. - 978-0-11-113259-3 £6.00

The Firefighters' Pension Scheme (Amendment) (England) Order 2015 No. 2015/579. - Enabling power: Fire Services Act 1947, s. 26 (1) to (5)- Issued: 12.03.2015. Made: 06.03.2015. Laid: 10.03.2015. Coming into force: 01.04.2015. Effect: S.I. 1992/129 amended in relation to England. Territorial extent & classification: E. General. - 4p.: 30 cm. - 978-0-11-113249-4 £4.25

Pensions, England and Wales

The Police Pensions and Police (Injury Benefit) (Amendment) Regulations 2015 No. 2015/2057. - Enabling power: Police Pensions Act 1976, s. 1. - Issued: 23.12.2015. Made: 14.12.2015. Laid: 18.12.2015. Coming into force: 18.01.2016. Effect: S.I. 1987/257; 2006/932 amended. Territorial extent & classification: E/W. General. - 4p.: 30 cm. - 978-0-11-114239-4 £4.25

Pensions, Wales

The Firefighters' Compensation Scheme and Pension Scheme (Wales) (Amendment) Order 2015 No. 2015/1013 (W.69). - Enabling power: Fire and Rescue Services Act 2004, ss. 34, 60, 62. - Issued: 17.04.2015. Made: 30.03.2015. Laid before the National Assembly for Wales: 31.03.2015. Coming into force: In accord with art. 1. Effect: S.I. 2007/1072 (W.110), 1073 (W.111) amended. Territorial extent & classification: W. General. - In English and Welsh. Welsh title: Gorchymyn Cynllun Digolledu a Chynllun Pensiwn y Diffoddwyr Tân (Cymru) (Diwygio) 2015. - 34p.: 30 cm. - 978-0-348-11069-2 10.00

The Firefighters' Pension (Wales) Scheme (Contributions) (Amendment) Order 2015 No. 2015/1014 (W.70). - Enabling power: Fire Services Act 1947, s. 26 (1). - Issued: 13.04.2015. Made: 30.03.2015. Laid before the National Assembly for Wales: 31.03.2015. Coming into force: 01.04.2015. Effect: S.I. 1992/129 amended in relation to Wales. Territorial extent & classification: W. General. - In English and Welsh. Welsh title: Gorchymyn Cynllun Pensiwn y Dynion Tân (Cymru) (Cyfraniadau) (Diwygio) 2015. - 8p.: 30 cm. - 978-0-348-11066-1 £4.25

Pesticides

The Public Bodies (Abolition of the Advisory Committees on Pesticides) Order 2015 No. 2015/978. - Enabling power: Public Bodies Act 2011, ss.1 (1), 6 (1) (5), 35 (2). - Issued: 01.04.2015. Made: 26.03.2015. Coming into force: In accord. with art. 1. Effect: 1967 c.13; 1985 c.48; 1999 c.28; 2000 c.36; 2011 c.24 partially repealed & S.I. 1999/1319, 1747, 1512 partially revoked & S.I. 1985/1516, 1517; S.R. 1987/341, 342 revoked. Territorial extent & classification: E/W/S/NI. General. - Supersedes draft S.I. (ISBN 9780111125656) issued 19/12/14. - 8p.: 30 cm. - 978-0-11-113611-9 £4.25

Petroleum

The Offshore Petroleum Licensing (Offshore Safety Directive) Regulations 2015 No. 2015/385. - Enabling power: European Communities Act 1972, s. 2 (2). - Issued: 26.03.2015. Made: 19.03.2015. Laid: 23.03.2015. Coming into force: 19.07.2015. Effect: None. Territorial extent & classification: GB & outside GB in relevant waters. General. - These Regulations, together with, in particular (a) the Offshore Installations (Prevention of Fire and Explosion, and Emergency Response) Regulations 1995 (SI 1995/743) (as amended by the Offshore Installations (Offshore Safety Directive) (Safety Case etc.) Regulations 2015 (SI 2015/398)); (b) the Merchant Shipping (Oil Pollution Preparedness, Response and Co-operation Convention) Regulations 1998 (SI 1998/1056) (as amended by the Merchant Shipping (Oil Pollution Preparedness, Response and Co-operation Convention) (Amendment) Regulations 2015 (SI 2015/386)); and (c) the Offshore Installations (Offshore Safety Directive) (Safety Case etc.) Regulations 2015 (SI 2015/398), implement Directive 2013/30/EU of the European Parliament and of the Council on safety of offshore oil and gas operations and amending Directive 2004/35/EC. - 12p.: 30 cm. - 978-0-11-113424-5 £6.00

The Oil and Gas Authority (Levy) Regulations 2015 No. 2015/1661. - Enabling power: Infrastructure Act 2015, s. 42 (1), sch. 7, paras 3, 5 to 7. - Issued: 14.09.2015. Made: 08.09.2015. Laid: 09.09.2015. Coming into force: 01.10.2015. Effect: None. Territorial extent & classification: E/W/S. General. - 4p.: 30 cm. - 978-0-11-113912-7 £4.25

The Petroleum Licensing (Applications) Regulations 2015 No. 2015/766. - Enabling power: Petroleum Act 1998, s. 4 (1) (2). - Issued: 24.03.2015. Made: 18.03.2015. Laid: 20.03.2015. Coming into force: 30.07.2015. Effect: None. Territorial extent & classification: E/W/S/NI. General. - 12p.: 30 cm. - 978-0-11-113393-4 £6.00

Pilotage

The Yarmouth (Isle of Wight) Harbour Commissioners (Removal of Pilotage Functions) Order 2015 No. 2015/132. - Enabling power: Pilotage Act 1987, s. 1 (4A). - Issued: 10.02.2015. Made: 29.01.2015. Laid: 06.02.2015. Coming into force: 01.03.2015. Effect: None. Territorial extent & classification: E/W/S/NI. General. - 2p.: 30 cm. - 978-0-11-112879-4 £4.25

Plant health, England

The Plant Health (England) (Amendment) Order 2015 No. 2015/1827. - Enabling power: Plant Health Act 1967, ss. 2, 3 (1) (4) & European communities Act 1972, sch. 2 para. 1A. - Issued: 30.10.2015. Made: 22.10.2015. Laid: 27.10.2015. Coming into force: 20.11.2015. Effect: S.I. 2015/610 amended. Territorial extent & classification: E. General. - EC note: Amends S.I. 2015/610 to implement: Commission implementing Decision (EU) 2015/237; (EU) 2015/749; (EU) 2015/789; (EU) 2015/893. - 8p.: 30 cm. - 978-0-11-114018-5 £6.00

The Plant Health (England) Order 2015 No. 2015/610. - Enabling power: Plant Health Act 1967, ss. 2, 3, 4 (1) & European Communities Act 1972, s. 2 (2)- Issued: 13.03.2015. Made: 04.03.2015. Laid: 10.03.2015. Coming into force: 01.07.2015. Effect: 19 SIs revoked. Territorial extent & classification: E. General. - 144p.: 30 cm. - 978-0-11-113273-9 £20.75

The Plant Health (Export Certification) (England) (Amendment) Order 2015 No. 2015/382. - Enabling power: Plant Health Act 1967, ss. 3 (1), 4A. - Issued: 03.03.2015. Made: 23.02.2015. Laid: 26.02.2015. Coming into force: 06.04.2015. Effect: S.I. 2004/1404 amended. Territorial extent & classification: E. General. - 4p.: 30 cm. - 978-0-11-113070-4 £4.25

The Plant Health (Fees) (England) (Amendment) Regulations 2015 No. 2015/1996. - Enabling power: Finance Act 1973, s. 56 (1). - Issued: 15.12.2015. Made: 08.12.2015. Laid: 10.12.2015. Coming into force: 01.01.2016. Effect: S.I. 2014/601 amended. Territorial extent & classification: E General. - 8p.: 30 cm. - 978-0-11-114177-9 £6.00

The Plant Health (Fees) (Forestry) (England and Scotland) Regulations 2015 No. 2015/350. - Enabling power: European Communities Act 1972, s. 2 (2). - Issued: 02.03.2015. Made: 23.02.2015. Laid: 25.02.2015. Coming into force: 06.04.2015. Effect: S.I. 2006/2697; 2008/702; 2009/2956; 2010/2001; 2014/589 revoked. Territorial extent & classification: E/S. General. - 8p.: 30 cm. - 978-0-11-113038-4 £6.00

The Plant Health (Forestry) (Miscellaneous Revocations) (England) Order 2015 No. 2015/741. - Enabling power: Plant Health Act 1967, ss. 3 (1) (2) (4), 5 (1). - Issued: 23.03.2015. Made: 16.03.2015. Laid: 18.03.2015. Coming into force: 01.07.2015. Effect: S.I. 1974/768; 1984/688; 1992/44 revoked. Territorial extent & classification: E/S. General. - 2p.: 30 cm. - 978-0-11-113373-6 £4.25

Plant health, Scotland

The Plant Health (Fees) (Forestry) (England and Scotland) Regulations 2015 No. 2015/350. - Enabling power: European Communities Act 1972, s. 2 (2). - Issued: 02.03.2015. Made: 23.02.2015. Laid: 25.02.2015. Coming into force: 06.04.2015. Effect: S.I. 2006/2697; 2008/702; 2009/2956; 2010/2001; 2014/589 revoked. Territorial extent & classification: E/S. General. - 8p.: 30 cm. - 978-0-11-113038-4 £6.00

Plant health, Wales

The Plant Health (Forestry) (Amendment) (Wales) Order 2015 No. 2015/1723 (W.235). - Enabling power: Plant Health Act 1967, ss. 2, 3 (1) & European Communities Act 1972, s. sch. 2, para. 1A. - Issued: 20.10.2015. Made: 24.09.2015. Laid before the National Assembly for Wales: 29.09.2015. Coming into force: 20.10.2015. Effect: S.I. 2005/2517 partially revoked/amended. Territorial extent & classification: W. General. - In English and Welsh. Welsh title: Gorchymyn Iechyd Planhigion (Coedwigaeth) (Diwygio) (Cymru) 2015. - 8p.: 30 cm. - 978-0-348-11171-2 £6.00

The Plant Health (Wales) (Amendment) Regulations 2015 No. 2015/777 (W.61). - Enabling power: Finance Act 1973, s. 56 (1). - Issued: 24.04.2015. Made: 17.03.2015. Laid before the National Assembly for Wales: 19.03.2015. Coming into force: 09.04.2015. Effect: S.I. 2014/1792 (W.185) amended. Territorial extent & classification: W. General. - In English & Welsh. Welsh title: Rheoliadau Iechyd Planhigion (Ffioedd) (Cymru) (Diwygio) 2015. - 12p.: 30 cm. - 978-0-348-11075-3 £6.00

Police

The Ministry of Defence Police (Conduct etc.) Regulations 2015 No. 2015/25. - Enabling power: Ministry of Defence Police Act 1987, ss. 3A, 4 (1) to (4), (6), 4A. - Issued: 22.01.2015. Made: 11.01.2015. Laid: 19.01.2015. Coming into force: 23.02.2015. Effect: S.I. 2009/3069 revoked with saving, S.I. 2009/3070; 2012/808 amended. Territorial extent & classification: E/W/S/NI. General. - 52p.: 30 cm. - 978-0-11-112743-8 £10.00

The Passenger, Crew and Service Information (Civil Penalties) Regulations 2015 No. 2015/961. - Enabling power: Immigration Act 1971, sch. 2, para. 27BB & Immigration, Asylum and Nationality Act 2006, s. 32B. - Issued: 01.04.2015. Made: 24.03.2015. Coming into force: 31.03.2015. Effect: None. Territorial extent & classification: E/W/S/NI. General. - Supersedes draft SI (ISBN 9780111130971) issued 08/03/15. - 8p.: 30 cm. - 978-0-11-113592-1 £6.00

Police, England and Wales

The Anti-social Behaviour, Crime and Policing Act 2014 (Commencement No. 8, Saving and Transitional Provisions) Order 2015 No. 2015/373 (C.19). - Enabling power: Anti-social Behaviour, Crime and Policing Act 2014, s. 185 (1) (7). Bringing into operation various provisions of the 2014 Act on 08.03.2015; 23.03.2015; 08.04.2015, in accord. with arts 2, 3, 4, 5. - Issued: 02.03.2015. Made: 24.02.2015. Effect: None. Territorial extent & classification: E/W/S/NI. General. - 8p.: 30 cm. - 978-0-11-113065-0 £6.00

The Independent Police Complaints Commission (Complaints and Misconduct) (Contractors) Regulations 2015 No. 2015/431. - Enabling power: Police Reform Act 2002, ss.12 (8) (9), 23 (2), 105 (4) (5). - Issued: 06.03.2015. Made: 26.02.2015. Laid: 03.03.2015. Coming into force: 08.04.2015. Effect: None. Territorial extent & classification: E/W. General. - 76p.: 30 cm. - 978-0-11-113121-3 £14.25

The Police (Amendment) Regulations 2015 No. 2015/455. - Enabling power: Police Act 1996, ss. 50. - Issued: 06.03.2015. Made: 26.02.2015. Laid: 05.03.2015. Coming into force: 01.04.2015. Effect: S.I. 2003/527 amended. Territorial extent & classification: E/W. General. - 4p.: 30 cm. - 978-0-11-113142-8 £4.25

The Police and Crime Commissioner Elections (Designation of Local Authorities) Order 2015 No. 2015/2028. - Enabling power: Police Reform and Social Responsibility Act 2011, s. 75 (1). - Issued: 18.12.2015. Made: 14.12.2015. Coming into force: 05.05.2016. Effect: S.I. 2012/2084 revoked. Territorial extent & classification: E/W. General. - 4p.: 30 cm. - 978-0-11-114204-2 £4.25

The Police and Crime Commissioner Elections (Designation of Police Area Returning Officers) Order 2015 No. 2015/2031. - Enabling power: Police Reform and Social Responsibility Act 2011, ss. 54 (1) (b), 154 (5) (b). - Issued: 21.12.2015. Made: 14.12.2015. Coming into force: 15.12.2015 in accord. with art. 1 (2). Effect: S.I. 2012/2085 revoked so far as it would relate to an election of a police and crime commissioner the poll for which takes place on or after 1st May 2016. Territorial extent & classification: E/W. General. - 4p.: 30 cm. - 978-0-11-114208-0 £4.25

The Police and Crime Commissioner Elections Order 2015 No. 2015/665. - Enabling power: Police Reform and Social Responsibility Act 2011, ss 58 (1) (a) (2) (e) (5) (5A). - Issued: 18.03.2015. Made: 09.03.2015. Coming into force: 07.05.2015. Effect: None. Territorial extent & classification: E/W. General. - Supersedes draft SI (ISBN 9780111127216) issued 20/01/15 - 4p.: 30 cm. - 978-0-11-113323-1 £4.25

The Police and Criminal Evidence Act 1984 (Codes of Practice) (Revision of Code A) Order 2015 No. 2015/418. - Enabling power: Police and Criminal Evidence Act 1984, s. 67 (5). - Issued: 05.03.2015. Made: 26.02.2015. Coming into force: In accord. with art. 1. Effect: None. Territorial extent & classification: E/W. General. - Supersedes draft S.I. (ISBN 9780111124611) issued 10/12/14. - 2p.: 30 cm. - 978-0-11-113111-4 £4.25

The Police Appeals Tribunals (Amendment) Rules 2015 No. 2015/625. - Enabling power: Police Act 1996, ss. 85. - Issued: 16.03.2015. Made: 09.03.2015. Laid: 12.03.2015. Coming into force: 01.05.2015. Effect: S.I. 2012/2630 amended. Territorial extent & classification: E/W. General. - 4p.: 30 cm. - 978-0-11-113302-6 £4.25

The Police (Conduct) (Amendment) Regulations 2015 No. 2015/626. - Enabling power: Police Act 1996, ss. 50, 51, 84. - Issued: 16.03.2015. Made: 09.03.2015. Laid: 12.03.2015. Coming into force: In accord. with reg. 1. Effect: S.I. 2012/2632 amended. Territorial extent & classification: E/W. General. - 8p.: 30 cm. - 978-0-11-113301-9 £6.00

The Police Federation (Amendment) Regulations 2015 No. 2015/630. - Enabling power: Police Act 1996, s. 60 (1) (2) (3). - Issued: 16.03.2015. Made: 09.03.2015. Laid: 12.03.2015. Coming into force: 02.04.2015. Effect: S.I. 1969/1787 amended. Territorial extent & classification: E/W. General. - 4p.: 30 cm. - 978-0-11-113287-6 £4.25

The Police Pensions and Police (Injury Benefit) (Amendment) Regulations 2015 No. 2015/2057. - Enabling power: Police Pensions Act 1976, s. 1. - Issued: 23.12.2015. Made: 14.12.2015. Laid: 18.12.2015. Coming into force: 18.01.2016. Effect: S.I. 1987/257; 2006/932 amended. Territorial extent & classification: E/W. General. - 4p.: 30 cm. - 978-0-11-114239-4 £4.25

The Police (Promotion) (Amendment) Regulations 2015 No. 2015/453. - Enabling power: Police Act 1996, s. 50. - Issued: 06.03.2015. Made: 26.02.2015. Laid: 05.03.2015. Coming into force: 01.04.2015. Effect: S.I. 1996/1685 amended. Territorial extent & classification: E/W. General. - 4p.: 30 cm. - 978-0-11-113140-4 £4.25

The Protection of Freedoms Act 2012 (Code of Practice for Powers of Entry and Description of Relevant Persons) Order 2015 No. 2015/240. - Enabling power: Protection of Freedoms Act 2012, ss. 48 (2), 51 (5). - Issued: 19.02.2015. Made: 11.02.2015. Coming into force: In accord. with art. 1. Effect: None. Territorial extent & classification: E/W. General. - Supersedes draft S.I. (ISBN 9780111124802) issued 11.12.2014. - 2p.: 30 cm. - 978-0-11-112982-1 £4.25

The Protection of Freedoms Act 2012 (Destruction, Retention and Use of Biometric Data) (Transitional, Transitory and Saving Provisions) (Amendment) Order 2015 No. 2015/1739. - Enabling power: Protection of Freedoms Act 2012, s. 25. - Issued: 08.10.2015. Made: 30.09.2015. Laid: 05.10.2015. Coming into force: 31.10.2015. Effect: S.I. 2013/1813 amended. Territorial extent & classification: E/W. General. - 2p.: 30 cm. - 978-0-11-113955-4 £4.25

The Serious Organised Crime and Police Act 2005 (Commencement No. 15) Order 2015 No. 2015/188 (C.12). - Enabling power: Serious Organised Crime and Police Act 2005, s. 178 (8) (9). Bringing into operation various provisions of the 2005 Act on 09.03.2015, in accord. with art. 2. - Issued: 26.02.2015. Made: 11.02.2015. Effect: None. Territorial extent & classification: E/W. General. - 8p.: 30 cm. - 978-0-11-113000-1 £4.25

The Special Constables (Amendment) Regulations 2015 No. 2015/461. - Enabling power: Police Act 1996, ss. 51. - Issued: 09.03.2015. Made: 27.02.2015. Laid: 05.03.2015. Coming into force: 01.04.2015. Effect: S.I. 1965/536 amended. Territorial extent & classification: E/W. General. - 4p.: 30 cm. - 978-0-11-113152-7 £4.25

Police, Northern Ireland

The Anti-social Behaviour, Crime and Policing Act 2014 (Commencement No. 8, Saving and Transitional Provisions) Order 2015 No. 2015/373 (C.19). - Enabling power: Anti-social Behaviour, Crime and Policing Act 2014, s. 185 (1) (7). Bringing into operation various provisions of the 2014 Act on 08.03.2015; 23.03.2015; 08.04.2015, in accord. with arts 2, 3, 4, 5. - Issued: 02.03.2015. Made: 24.02.2015. Effect: None. Territorial extent & classification: E/W/S/NI. General. - 8p.: 30 cm. - 978-0-11-113065-0 £6.00

Political parties

The European Parliamentary Elections (Miscellaneous Provisions) (United Kingdom and Gibraltar) Order 2015 No. 2015/1982. - Enabling power: European Parliament (Representation) Act 2003, ss. 12, 13 (3) (4). - Issued: 14.12.2015. Made: 07.12.2015. Laid: - Coming into force: 08.12.2015 in accord. with art. 1 (2). Effect: 2000 c.41 amended. Territorial extent & classification: E/W/S/NI & Gibraltar. General. - Supersedes draft S.I. (ISBN 9780111140048) issued 26/10/15. - 4p.: 30 cm. - 978-0-11-114170-0 £4.25

Prevention and suppression of terrorism

The Authority to Carry Scheme (Civil Penalties) Regulations 2015 No. 2015/957. - Enabling power: Counter-Terrorism and Security Act 2015, s. 24. - Issued: 01.04.2015. Made: 24.03.2015. Coming into force: 31.03.2015. Effect: None. Territorial extent & classification: E/W/S/NI. General. - Supersedes draft SI (ISBN 9780111130940) issued 05/03/15. - 8p.: 30 cm. - 978-0-11-113586-0 £4.25

The Counter-Terrorism and Security Act 2015 (Authority to Carry Scheme) Regulations 2015 No. 2015/997. - Enabling power: Counter-Terrorism Act 2015, s. 23 (1). - Issued: 07.04.2015. Made: 24.03.2015. Coming into force: 31.03.2015. Effect: None. Territorial extent & classification: E/W/S/NI. General. - Supersedes draft SI (ISBN 9780111130933) issued 05/03/15 - 2p.: 30 cm. - 978-0-11-113627-0 £4.25

The Counter-Terrorism and Security Act 2015 (Code of Practice for Officers exercising functions under Schedule 1) Regulations 2015 No. 2015/217. - Enabling power: Counter-Terrorism Act 2015, s. 19 (3), sch. 1. - Issued: 31.03.2015. Made: 12.02.2015. Laid: 12.02.2015. Coming into force: 13.02.2015. Effect: None. Territorial extent & classification: E/W/S/NI. General. - Approved by both Houses of Parliament. Supersedes (ISBN 9780111129593) issued 18/02/15. - 2p.: 30 cm. - 978-0-11-130000-8 £4.25

The Counter-Terrorism and Security Act 2015 (Code of Practice for Officers exercising functions under Schedule 1) Regulations 2015 No. 2015/217. - Enabling power: Counter-Terrorism Act 2015, s. 19 (3), sch. 1. - Issued: 18.02.2015. Made: 12.02.2015. Laid: 12.02.2015. Coming into force: 13.02.2015. Effect: None. Territorial extent & classification: E/W/S/NI. General. - For approval by resolution of each House of Parliament within forty days beginning with the day on which the Regulations were made. Superseded by approved S.I. 2015/217 (ISBN 9780111300008) issued 31/03/15. - 2p.: 30 cm. - 978-0-11-112959-3 £4.25

The Counter-Terrorism and Security Act 2015 (Commencement No. 1) Regulations 2015 No. 2015/956 (C.60). - Enabling power: Counter-Terrorism and Security Act 2015, s. 52 (3) (4). Bringing into operation various provisions of the 2015 Act on 31.03.2015; 13.04.2015; 01.07.2015, in accord. with art. 2, 3 and 4. - Issued: 02.04.2015. Made: 26.03.2015. Effect: None. Territorial extent & classification: E/W/S. General. - 4p.: 30 cm. - 978-0-11-113585-3 £4.25

The Counter-Terrorism and Security Act 2015 (Commencement No. 2) Regulations 2015 No. 2015/1698 (C.102). - Enabling power: Counter-Terrorism and Security Act 2015, s. 52 (3) (4). Bringing into operation various provisions of the 2015 Act on 18.09.2015, in accord. with art. 2. - Issued: 24.09.2015. Made: 17.09.2015. Effect: None. Territorial extent & classification: E/W/S. General. - 2p.: 30 cm. - 978-0-11-113938-7 £4.25

The Counter-Terrorism and Security Act 2015 (Commencement No. 3) Regulations 2015 No. 2015/1729 (C.104). - Enabling power: Counter-Terrorism and Security Act 2015, s. 52 (3). Bringing into operation various provisions of the 2015 Act on 01.10.2015, in accord. with art. 2. - Issued: 05.10.2015. Made: 28.09.2015. Effect: None. Territorial extent & classification: E/W/S. General. - 2p.: 30 cm. - 978-0-11-113951-6 £4.25

The Counter-Terrorism and Security Act 2015 (Risk of Being Drawn into Terrorism) (Amendment and Guidance) Regulations 2015 No. 2015/928. - Enabling power: Counter-Terrorism and Security Act 2015, ss. 27 (1) (3), 29 (5), 39 (1) (4). - Issued: 01.04.2015. Made: 24.03.2015. Coming into force: In accord. with reg. 2. Effect: 2015 c.6 amended. Territorial extent & classification: E/W/S. General. - Supersedes draft S.I. (ISBN 9780111133309) issued 18/03/15. - 8p.: 30 cm. - 978-0-11-113550-1 £6.00

The Counter-Terrorism and Security Act 2015 (Risk of Being Drawn into Terrorism) (Guidance) Regulations 2015 No. 2015/1697. - Enabling power: Counter-Terrorism and Security Act 2015, s. 29 (5). - Issued: 24.09.2015. Made: 17.09.2015. Coming into force: 18.09.2015 in accord. with reg. 2. Effect: None. Territorial extent & classification: E/W/S. General. - Supersedes draft SI (ISBN 9780111138120) issued 22/07/15 - 2p.: 30 cm. - 978-0-11-113937-0 £4.25

The Temporary Exclusion Orders (Notices) Regulations 2015 No. 2015/438. - Enabling power: Counter-Terrorism and Security Act 2015, s. 13 (1) (2). - Issued: 06.03.2015. Made: 02.03.2015. Laid: 03.03.2015. Coming into force: 26.03.2015. Effect: None. Territorial extent & classification: E/W/S/NI. General. - 4p.: 30 cm. - 978-0-11-113126-8 £4.25

The Terrorism Act 2000 (Code of Practice for Examining Officers and Review Officers) Order 2015 No. 2015/906. - Enabling power: Terrorism Act 2000, s. 123 (1) (b), sch. 14, para. 7 (3) (4). - Issued: 31.03.2015. Made: 24.03.2015. Coming into force: In accord. with art. 1. Effect: None. Territorial extent & classification: E/W/S/NI. General. - Supersedes draft S.I. (ISBN 9780111130841) issued 04/03/15. - 2p.: 30 cm. - 978-0-11-113530-3 £4.25

The Terrorism Act 2000 (Proscribed Organisations) (Amendment) (No. 2) Order 2015 No. 2015/959. - Enabling power: Terrorism Act 2000, s. 3 (3) (a). - Issued: 02.04.2015. Made: 26.03.2015. Coming into force: In accord. with art. 1. Effect: None. Territorial extent & classification: E/W/S/NI. General. - 2p.: 30 cm. - 978-0-11-113588-4 £4.25

The Terrorism Act 2000 (Proscribed Organisations) (Amendment) Order 2015 No. 2015/55. - Enabling power: Terrorism Act 2000, s. 3 (3) (a). - Issued: 30.01.2015. Made: 22.01.2015. Coming into force: 23.01.2015. Effect: None. Territorial extent & classification: E/W/S/NI. General. - Supersedes draft S.I. (ISBN 9780111127872) issued 22/01/15. - 2p.: 30 cm. - 978-0-11-112787-2 £4.25

The Terrorist Asset-Freezing etc. Act 2010 (Isle of Man) (Revocation) Order 2015 No. 2015/1763. - Enabling power: Terrorist Asset-Freezing etc. Act 2010, s. 54 (1). - Issued: 15.10.2015. Made: 08.10.2015. Coming into force: In accord. with art. 1. Effect: S.I. 2011/749 revoked. Territorial extent & classification: E/W/S/NI. General. - 2p.: 30 cm. - 978-0-11-113969-1 £4.25

Prisons, England and Wales

The Criminal Justice and Courts Act 2015 (Commencement No. 1, Saving and Transitional Provisions) Order 2015 No. 2015/778 (C.44). - Enabling power: Criminal Justice and Courts Act 2015, s. 95 (1) (6). Bringing into operation various provisions of the 2015 Act on 20.03.2015; 13.04.2015, in accord. with arts 2, 3. - Issued: 25.03.2015. Made: 19.03.2015. Effect: None. Territorial extent & classification: E/W/S/NI. General. - 8p.: 30 cm. - 978-0-11-113405-4 £6.00

The Prison and Young Offender Institution (Amendment) Rules 2015 No. 2015/1638. - Enabling power: Prison Act 1952, s. 47 (1). - Issued: 07.09.2015. Made: 27.08.2015. Laid: 03.09.2015. Coming into force: In accord. with rule 1 (2) (3). Effect: S.I. 1999/728; 2000/3371 amended. Territorial extent & classification: E/W. General. - 4p.: 30 cm. - 978-0-11-113883-0 £4.25

The Prisons (Property) Act 2013 (Commencement) Order 2015 No. 2015/771 (C.42). - Issued: 24.03.2015. Made: 05.03.2015. Effect: None. Territorial extent & classification: E/W. General. - Enabling power: Prisons (Property) Act 2013, s. 2 (2). Bringing into operation various provisions of the 2013 Act on 26.03.2015, in accord. with art. 2. - 2p.: 30 cm. - 978-0-11-113397-2 £4.25

Proceeds of crime

The Crime and Courts Act 2013 (National Crime Agency and Proceeds of Crime) (Northern Ireland) Order 2015 No. 2015/798. - Enabling power: Crime and Courts Act 2013, s. 59 (1) (2) (3), sch. 24, paras. 2, 3, 5, 7 (1), sch. 25, paras. 3, 4, 7 (1) (2), 10, 11, 14 (1). - Issued: 26.03.2015. Made: 19.03.2015. Coming into force: 20.03.2015. Effect: 1998 c.32; 2000 c.32; 2002 c.26, 29 S.I. 1989/1341 (N.I. 12) amended. Territorial extent & classification: E/W/S/NI. General. - Supersedes draft S.I. (ISBN 9780111128299) issued 04.02.2015- 12p.: 30 cm. - 978-0-11-113422-1 £6.00

The Policing and Crime Act 2009 (Commencement No. 10, Transitional Provision and Savings) Order 2015 No. 2015/983 (C.64). - Enabling power: Policing and Crime Act 2009, s. 116 (1) (7). Bringing into operation various provisions of the 2009 Act on 01.06.2015, in accord. with art. 2. - Issued: 02.04.2015. Made: 26.03.2015. Effect: None. Territorial extent & classification: E/W/S/NI. General. - 12p.: 30 cm. - 978-0-11-113618-8 £6.00

The Proceeds of Crime Act 2002 (Cash Searches: Code of Practice) (England and Wales and Scotland) Order 2015 No. 2015/705. - Enabling power: Proceeds of Crime Act 2002, ss. 292 (4) (5), 459 (2). - Issued: 19.03.2015. Made: 12.03.2015. Coming into force: 01.06.2015. Effect: None. Territorial extent & classification: E/W/S. General. - Supersedes draft S.I. (ISBN 9780111125786) issued 19.12.2014. Revoked by SI 2016/208 (ISBN 9780111144053) in re to E/W. - 4p.: 30 cm. - 978-0-11-113352-1 £4.25

The Proceeds of Crime Act 2002 (Enforcement in different parts of the United Kingdom) (Amendment) Order 2015 No. 2015/1749. - Enabling power: Proceeds of Crime Act 2002, ss. 443, 459 (2). - Issued: 15.10.2015. Made: 08.10.2015. Laid: 15.10.2015. Coming into force: 30.11.2015. Effect: S.I. 2002/3133 amended. Territorial extent & classification: E/W/S/NI. General. - 8p.: 30 cm. - 978-0-11-113974-5 £6.00

The Proceeds of Crime Act 2002 (External Investigations) (Amendment) Order 2015 No. 2015/1751. - Enabling power: Proceeds of Crime Act 2002 ss. 445, 459 (2). - Issued: 15.10.2015. Made: 08.10.2015. Laid: 15.10.2015. Coming into force: 30.11.2015. Effect: S.I. 2013/2605 amended. Territorial extent & classification: E/W/S/NI. General. - 8p.: 30 cm. - 978-0-11-113975-2 £6.00

The Proceeds of Crime Act 2002 (External Investigations) (Scotland) Order 2015 No. 2015/206. - Enabling power: Proceeds of Crime Act 2002, ss. 445, 459 (2). - Issued: 18.02.2015. Made: 11.02.2015. Laid: 16.02.2015. Coming into force: 16.03.2015. Effect: None. Territorial extent & classification: S. General. - 20p.: 30 cm. - 978-0-11-112948-7 £6.00

The Proceeds of Crime Act 2002 (External Requests and Orders) (Amendment) Order 2015 No. 2015/1750. - Enabling power: Proceeds of Crime Act 2002, ss. 444, 459 (2). - Issued: 15.10.2015. Made: 08.10.2015. Laid: 15.10.2015. Coming into force: 30.11.2015. Effect: S.I. 2005/3181 amended. Territorial extent & classification: E/W/S/NI. General. - 24p.: 30 cm. - 978-0-11-113973-8 £6.00

The Proceeds of Crime Act 2002 (Investigations in different parts of the United Kingdom) (Amendment) Order 2015 No. 2015/925. - Enabling power: Proceeds of Crime Act 2009, s. 112 (3) to (5) & Crime and Courts Act 2013, ss. 58 (12), 59 (1) (2). - Issued: 01.04.2015. Made: 26.03.2015. Laid: 27.03.2015. Coming into force: 01.06.2015. Effect: S.I. 2003/425 amended. Territorial extent & classification: E/W/S/NI. General. - 8p.: 30 cm. - 978-0-11-113549-5 £4.25

The Serious Crime Act 2015 (Commencement No. 1) Regulations 2015 No. 2015/820 (C.52). - Enabling power: Serious Crime Act 2015, s. 88 (6) (c) (e) (8). Bringing into operation various provisions of the 2015 Act on 03.05.2015; 01.06.2015, in accord. with art. 2 & 3. - Issued: 27.03.2015. Made: 19.03.2015. Effect: None. Territorial extent & classification: E/W/S/NI. General. - 4p.: 30 cm. - 978-0-11-113452-8 £4.25

Proceeds of crime, England and Wales

The Administrative Forfeiture of Cash (Forfeiture Notices) (England and Wales) (Amendment) Regulations 2015 No. 2015/1854. - Enabling power: Proceeds of Crime Act 2002, ss. 297A (3) (4), 459 (2) (a). - Issued: 09.11.2015. Made: 29.10.2015. Laid: 05.11.2015. Coming into force: 30.11.2015. Effect: S.I. 2015/857 amended. Territorial extent & classification: E/W. General. - 2p.: 30 cm. - 978-0-11-114052-9 £4.25

The Administrative Forfeiture of Cash (Forfeiture Notices) (England and Wales) Regulations 2015 No. 2015/857. - Enabling power: Proceeds of Crime Act 2002, ss. 297A (3) (4), 459 (2) (a). - Issued: 30.03.2015. Made: 23.03.2015. Laid: 25.03.2015. Coming into force: 01.06.2015. Effect: None. Territorial extent & classification: E/W. General. - 4p.: 30 cm. - 978-0-11-113480-1 £4.25

The Crime and Courts Act 2013 (Commencement No. 12) Order 2015 No. 2015/813 (C.48). - Enabling power: Crime and Courts Act 2013, s. 61 (2). Bringing into operation various provisions of the 2013 Act on 20.03.2015; 01.06.2015, in accord. with arts 2, 3. - Issued: 26.03.2015. Made: 19.03.2015. Effect: None. Territorial extent & classification: E/W/S/NI. General. - 8p.: 30 cm. - 978-0-11-113444-3 £6.00

The Crime and Courts Act 2013 (Commencement No. 13 and Savings) Order 2015 No. 2015/964 (C.61). - Enabling power: Crime and Courts Act 2013, ss. 60 (a), 61 (2). Bringing into operation various provisions of the 2013 Act on 01.06.2015, in accord. with art. 2. - Issued: 02.04.2015. Made: 26.03.2015. Effect: 2002 c.29 amended. Territorial extent & classification: E/W/S/NI. General. - 8p.: 30 cm. - 978-0-11-113597-6 £6.00

The Proceeds of Crime Act 2002 (Appeals under Part 2) (Amendment) Order 2015 No. 2015/1855. - Enabling power: Proceeds of Crime Act 2002, ss. 89 (3), 90 (2), 459 (2). - Issued: 09.11.2015. Made: 29.10.2015. Laid: 05.11.2015. Coming into force: 30.11.2015. Effect: S.I. 2003/82 amended. Territorial extent & classification: E/W. General. - 2p.: 30 cm. - 978-0-11-114053-6 £4.25

The Proceeds of Crime Act 2002 (Application of Police and Criminal Evidence Act 1984) Order 2015 No. 2015/759. - Enabling power: Proceeds of Crime Act 2002, ss. 355 (2), 459 (2). - Issued: 24.03.2015. Made: 16.03.2015. Laid: 19.03.2015. Coming into force: 01.06.2015. Effect: 1984 c.60 modified & S.I. 2003/174 revoked with saving. Territorial extent & classification: E/W. General. - 8p.: 30 cm. - 978-0-11-113390-3 £4.25

The Proceeds of Crime Act 2002 (External Investigations) (Amendment) (No. 2) Order 2015 No. 2015/1752. - Enabling power: Proceeds of Crime Act 2002, ss. 445, 459 (2). - Issued: 15.10.2015. Made: 08.10.2015. Laid: 15.10.2015. Coming into force: 30.11.2015. Effect: S.I. 2014/1893 amended. Territorial extent & classification: E/W/NI. General. - 4p.: 30 cm. - 978-0-11-113977-6 £4.25

The Proceeds of Crime Act 2002 (External Requests and Orders) Order 2005 (England and Wales) (Appeals under Part 2) (Amendment) Order 2015 No. 2015/1856. - Enabling power: Proceeds of Crime Act 2002 (External Requests and Orders) Order 2005, arts 5, 47 (3), 48 (2). - Issued: 09.11.2015. Made: 29.10.2015. Laid: 05.11.2015. Coming into force: 30.11.2015. Effect: S.I. 2012/138 amended. Territorial extent & classification: E/W. General. - 2p.: 30 cm. - 978-0-11-114054-3 £4.25

The Proceeds of Crime Act 2002 (Investigations: Code of Practice) (England and Wales) Order 2015 No. 2015/729. - Enabling power: Proceeds of Crime Act 2002, ss 377 (4) (8), 459 (2). - Issued: 23.03.2015. Made: 12.03.2015. Coming into force: 01.06.2015. Effect: None. Territorial extent & classification: E/W. General. - Supersedes draft SI (ISBN 9780111125823) issued 19/12/14. Revoked by SI 2016/209 (ISBN 9780111144060). - 4p.: 30 cm. - 978-0-11-113367-5 £4.25

The Proceeds of Crime Act 2002 (Investigative Powers of Prosecutors: Code of Practice) (England and Wales) Order 2015 No. 2015/612. - Enabling power: Proceeds of Crime Act 2002, ss. 377A (5) (9), 459 (2). - Issued: 16.03.2015. Made: 09.03.2015. Coming into force: 01.06.2015. Effect: None. Territorial extent & classification: E/W. General. - Supersedes draft S.I. (ISBN 9780111127681) issued 26/01/15. Revoked by SI 2016/222 (ISBN 9780111144145). - 4p.: 30 cm. - 978-0-11-113275-3 £4.25

The Proceeds of Crime Act 2002 (References to Financial Investigators) (England and Wales) Order 2015 No. 2015/1853. - Enabling power: Proceeds of Crime Act 2002, ss. 453, 459 (2). - Issued: 09.11.2015. Made: 29.10.2015. Laid: 05.11.2015. Coming into force: 30.11.2015. Effect: S.I. 2009/975, 2707 revoked. Territorial extent & classification: E/W. General. - 16p.: 30 cm. - 978-0-11-114051-2 £6.00

The Proceeds of Crime Act 2002 (Search, Seizure and Detention of Property: Code of Practice) (England and Wales) Order 2015 No. 2015/730. - Enabling power: Proceeds of Crime Act 2002, s. 47S (4). - Issued: 23.03.2015. Made: 12.03.2015. Coming into force: 01.06.2015. Effect: None. Territorial extent & classification: E/W. General. - Supersedes draft SI (ISBN 9780111125854) issued 19/12/14. Revoked by SI 2016/207 (ISBN 9780111144046). - 4p.: 30 cm. - 978-0-11-113368-2 £4.25

The Restraint Orders (Legal Aid Exception and Relevant Legal Aid Payments) Regulations 2015 No. 2015/868. - Enabling power: Proceeds of Crime Act 2002, s. 41 (5A) (10) & Crime and Courts Act 2013, s. 47. - Issued: 27.03.2015. Made: 23.03.2015. Coming into force: In accord. with reg. 1. Effect: 2002 c.29 modified. Territorial extent & classification: E/W. General. - Supersedes draft S.I. (ISBN 9780111128381) issued 05/02/15. - 4p.: 30 cm. - 978-0-11-113491-7 £4.25

Proceeds of crime, Northern Ireland

The Proceeds of Crime Act 2002 (External Investigations) (Amendment) (No. 2) Order 2015 No. 2015/1752. - Enabling power: Proceeds of Crime Act 2002, ss. 445, 459 (2). - Issued: 15.10.2015. Made: 08.10.2015. Laid: 15.10.2015. Coming into force: 30.11.2015. Effect: S.I. 2014/1893 amended. Territorial extent & classification: E/W/NI. General. - 4p.: 30 cm. - 978-0-11-113977-6 £4.25

Professional qualifications

The European Union (Recognition of Professional Qualifications) Regulations 2015 No. 2015/2059. - Enabling power: European Communities Act 1972, s. 2 (2), sch. 2, para. 1A. - Issued: 30.12.2015. Made: 17.12.2015. Laid: 21.12.2015. Coming into force: 18.01.2016. Effect: S.I. 2000/1119; 2003/1662; 2009/1976, 2999; S.I. 2012/1115 amended & S.I. 2009/1182; 2010/231, 233; 2012/765; 1479 partially revoked & S.I. 2007/2781 revoked with savings & S.I. 2013/732 revoked. Territorial extent & classification: E/W/S/NI. General. - EC note: These Regulations revoke and replace the European Communities (Recognition of Professional Qualifications) Regulations 2007 which implemented in part Council Directive 2005/36/EC (last amended by Directive 2013/55/EU) and Regulation (EU) 1024/2012- 52p.: 30 cm. - 978-0-11-114251-6 £10.00

Public bodies

The Public Bodies (Abolition of the Advisory Committees on Pesticides) Order 2015 No. 2015/978. - Enabling power: Public Bodies Act 2011, ss.1 (1), 6 (1) (5), 35 (2). - Issued: 01.04.2015. Made: 26.03.2015. Coming into force: In accord. with art. 1. Effect: 1967 c.13; 1985 c.48; 1999 c.28; 2000 c.36; 2011 c.24 partially repealed & S.I. 1999/1319, 1747, 1512 partially revoked & S.I. 1985/1516, 1517; S.R. 1987/341, 342 revoked. Territorial extent & classification: E/W/S/NI. General. - Supersedes draft S.I. (ISBN 9780111125656) issued 19/12/14. - 8p.: 30 cm. - 978-0-11-113611-9 £4.25

The Public Bodies (Abolition of the Home Grown Timber Advisory Committee) Order 2015 No. 2015/475. - Enabling power: Public Bodies Act 2011, ss 1 (1), 6 (1) (5), 35 (2). - Issued: 10.03.2015. Made: 01.03.2015. Coming into force: In accord. with art. 1. Effect: 1967 c.10; 2011 c.24 partially repealed & S.I. 1999/1747 partially revoked. Territorial extent & classification: E/W/S/NI. General. - Supersedes draft S.I. (ISBN 9780111124437) issued 08.12.2014. - 4p.: 30 cm. - 978-0-11-113170-1 £4.25

The Public Bodies (Abolition of the Library Advisory Council for England) Order 2015 No. 2015/850. - Enabling power: Public Bodies Act 2011, ss. 1, 6 (1) (5), 35 (2). - Issued: 27.03.2015. Made: 16.03.2015. Coming into force: In accord. with art. 1. Effect: 1964 c. 75; 1967 c. 13; 2000 c. 36 partially repealed & S.I. 1981/207 partially repealed/amended. Territorial extent & classification: E/W/S/NI. General. - Supersedes draft S.I. (ISBN 9780111122860) issued 07/11/14. - 4p.: 30 cm. - 978-0-11-113473-3 £4.25

Public finance and accountability

The Scotland Act 1998 (Variation of Borrowing Power) Order 2015 No. 2015/932. - Enabling power: Scotland Act 1998, s. 66 (5). - Issued: 31.03.2015. Made: 24.03.2015. Laid:-. Coming into force: 01.04.2015. Effect: 1998 c.46 amended. Territorial extent & classification: E/W/S/NI. General. - Supersedes draft S.I. (ISBN 9780111125281) issued 16/12/14. - 2p.: 30 cm. - 978-0-11-113554-9 £4.25

Public health

The Motor Fuel (Composition and Content) (Amendment) Regulations 2015 No. 2015/1796. - Enabling power: Clean Air Act 1993, ss. 30 (1) (3), 31 (1) (3). - Issued: 28.10.2015. Made: 15.10.2015. Laid: 28.10.2015. Coming into force: 18.11.2015. Effect: S.I. 1999/3107 amended. Territorial extent & classification: E/W/S/NI. General. - 4p.: 30 cm. - 978-0-11-113998-1 £4.25

The Standardised Packaging of Tobacco Products Regulations 2015 No. 2015/829. - Enabling power: Children and Families Act 2014, ss. 94, 135 (2) (3) & European Communities Act 1972, s. 2 (2). - Issued: 26.03.2015. Made: 19.03.2015. Coming into force: 20.05.2016. Effect: 1991 c.23; S.I. 1991/2872 (NI.25) amended & S.I. 2002/3041 partially revoked. Territorial extent & classification: E/W/S/NI. General. - Supersedes draft S.I (ISBN 9780111129876) issued 23.02.2015. - 24p.: 30 cm. - 978-0-11-113462-7 £6.00

The Vaccine Damage Payments (Specified Disease) Order 2015 No. 2015/47. - Enabling power: Vaccine Damage Payments Act 1979, ss. 1 (2) (i), 2 (2). - Issued: 27.01.2015. Made: 20.01.2015. Laid: 27.01.2015. Coming into force: 28.02.2015. Effect: 1979 c.17 modified. Territorial extent & classification: E/W/S/NI/IoM. General. - 2p.: 30 cm. - 978-0-11-112776-6 £4.25

Public health, England

The Animal By-Products (Enforcement) (England) (Amendment) Regulations 2015 No. 2015/1980. - Enabling power: European Communities Act 1972, s. 2 (2). - Issued: 11.12.2015. Made: 04.12.2015. Laid: 08.12.2015. Coming into force: 31.12.2015. Effect: S.I. 2013/2952 amended. Territorial extent & classification: E. General. - 4p.: 30 cm. - 978-0-11-114168-7 £4.25

The Care Quality Commission (Membership) (Amendment) Regulations 2015 No. 2015/1479. - Enabling power: Health and Social Care Act 2008, s. 161 (3) (4), sch. 1, para. 3 (3) to (5). - Issued: 14.07.2015. Made: 07.07.2015. Laid: 14.07.2015. Coming into force: 01.09.2015. Effect: S.I. 2008/2252; 2011/2547; 2013/2157 revoked. Territorial extent & classification: E. General. - 12p.: 30 cm. - 978-0-11-113760-4 £6.00

The Control of Noise (Code of Practice for Construction and Open Sites) (England) Order 2015 No. 2015/227. - Enabling power: Control of Pollution Act 1974, s. 71 (1) (b) (2) (3). - Issued: 18.02.2015. Made: 11.02.2015. Laid: 13.02.2015. Coming into force: 06.04.2015. Effect: S.I. 2002/461 revoked. Territorial extent & classification: E. General. - 2p.: 30 cm. - 978-0-11-112967-8 £4.25

The False or Misleading Information (Specified Care Providers and Specified Information) Regulations 2015 No. 2015/988. - Enabling power: Care Act 2014, s. 92 (1). - Issued: 02.04.2015. Made: 26.03.2015. Coming into force: In accord. with reg. 1. Effect: None. Territorial extent & classification: E. General. - Supersedes draft S.I. (ISBN 9780111129234) issued 16/02/15. - 8p.: 30 cm. - 978-0-11-113620-1 £6.00

The Health and Social Care Act 2008 (Regulated Activities) (Amendment) Regulations 2015 No. 2015/64. - Enabling power: Health and Social Care Act 2008, ss. 20 (1) (3) (5A), 35, 86 (2), 87 (1) (2), 161 (3) (4). - Issued: 02.02.2015. Made: 26.01.2015 Laid: 28.01.2015. Coming into force: 01.04.2015. Effect: S.I. 2014/2936 amended. Territorial extent & classification: E. General. - 8p.: 30 cm. - 978-0-11-112800-8 £6.00

The Health and Social Care Act 2012 (Consistent Identifier) Regulations 2015 No. 2015/1439. - Enabling power: Health and Social Care Act 2012, s. 251A (1). - Issued: 09.07.2015. Made: 01.07.2015. Laid: 07.07.2015. Coming into force: 01.10.2015. Effect: None. Territorial extent & classification: E. General. - 2p.: 30 cm. - 978-0-11-113739-0 £4.25

The Health and Social Care Act 2012 (Continuity of Information: Interpretation) Regulations 2015 No. 2015/1470. - Enabling power: Health and Social Care Act 2012, s. 251C (3) (4). - Issued: 10.07.2015. Made: 01.07.2015. Laid: 07.07.2015. Coming into force: 01.10.2015. Effect: None. Territorial extent & classification: E. General. - 8p.: 30 cm. - 978-0-11-113749-9 £4.25

The Health and Social Care (Miscellaneous Revocations etc.) Order 2015 No. 2015/864. - Enabling power: Health Authorities Act 1995, sch. 2, paras 4, 7 (1) (a), 13, 14, 16, 18, 19 , 20 & Health Act 1999, ss. 44, 63 & Health and Social Care Act 2001, ss. 64 (6), 70 (10) & Health and Social Care (Community Health and Standards) Act 2003, ss. 201 (1) & National Health Service Act 2006, ss. 28, 272 (7) (8), 273 (1), 278 (4), sch. 4, para. 22 & Health and Social Care Act 2008, ss. 161 (3) (4), 167 (1) (3). - Issued: 27.03.2015. Made: 23.03.2015 Laid: 26.03.2015. Coming into force: 01.07.2015. Effect: 2 SIs amended & 7 SIs revoked in relation to England & 1 S.I. partially revoked & 14 SIs revoked. Territorial extent & classification: E/W. General. - 4p.: 30 cm. - 978-0-11-113488-7 £4.25

The Health and Social Care (Miscellaneous Revocations) Regulations 2015 No. 2015/839. - Enabling power: Health and Medicines Act 1988, s. 26 (6) & Care Standards Act 2000, ss. 12 (2), 15 (3), 16 (3), 118 (5) to (7) & Health and Social Care Act 2001, ss. 65 (1) (2) & Tobacco Advertising and Promotion Act 2002, ss. 19 (2), 20 & National Health Service Act, ss. 8, 28, 187, 272 (7) (8), 273, sch. 6, paras 3, 5, 6. - Issued: 27.03.2015. Made: 23.03.2015 Laid: 26.03.2015. Coming into force: 01.07.2015. Effect: S.I. 1974/29; 2003/7, 1415 revoked in relation to England & S.I. 1985/1876; 1989/1893; 1996/512; 2001/3744; 2003/2323; 2005/640 revoked. Territorial extent & classification: E. General. - 4p.: 30 cm. - 978-0-11-113466-5 £4.25

The Health and Social Care (Safety and Quality) Act 2015 (Commencement No. 1 and Transitory Provision) Regulations 2015 No. 2015/1438 (C.81). - Enabling power: Health and Social Care (Safety and Quality) Act 2015, ss. 6 (4) (5). Bringing into operation various provisions of the 2015 Act on 25.06.2015; 01.10.2015, in accord. with art. 2 & 3. - Issued: 06.07.2015. Made: 24.06.2015. Effect: 2012 c.7 modified. Territorial extent & classification: E. General. - 4p.: 30 cm. - 978-0-11-113728-4 £4.25

The Local Authorities (Public Health Functions and Entry to Premises by Local Healthwatch Representatives) and Local Authority (Public Health, Health and Wellbeing Boards and Health Scrutiny) (Amendment) Regulations 2015 No. 2015/921. - Enabling power: National Health Service Act 2006, ss. 6C (2), 272 (7) (8), 275. - Issued: 31.03.2015. Made: 23.03.2015. Coming into force: In accord. with reg. 1 (2) (3). Effect: S.I. 2013/218, 351 amended. Territorial extent & classification: E. General. - Supersedes draft S.I. (ISBN 9780111128053) issued 02/02/15. - 8p.: 30 cm. - 978-0-11-113545-7 £4.25

The Proxy Purchasing of Tobacco, Nicotine Products etc. (Fixed Penalty Notice) (England) Regulations 2015 No. 2015/936. - Enabling power: Health Act 2006, sch. 1, para 4. - Issued: 01.04.2015. Made: 26.03.2015. Laid: 27.03.2015. Coming into force: 01.10.2015. Effect: None. Territorial extent & classification: E. General. - 8p.: 30 cm. - 978-0-11-113564-8 £6.00

The Smoke-free (Private Vehicles) Regulations 2015 No. 2015/286. - Enabling power: Health Act 2006, ss. 5, 6 (2) (b), 9 (1A), 10 (1) (2), sch. 1, para 5. - Issued: 23.02.2015. Made: 12.02.2015. Coming into force: 01.10.2015. Effect: None. Territorial extent & classification: E. General. - Supersedes draft S.I. (ISBN 9780111126004) issued 22/12/14. - 4p.: 30 cm. - 978-0-11-112989-0 £4.25

The Smoke-free (Vehicle Operators and Penalty Notices) (Amendment) Regulations 2015 No. 2015/939. - Enabling power: Health Act 2006, s. 8 (3), sch. 1, para. 4. - Issued: 02.04.2015. Made: 26.03.2015. Laid: 27.03.2015. Coming into force: 01.10.2015. Effect: S.I. 2007/760 amended. Territorial extent & classification: E. General. - 12p.: 30 cm. - 978-0-11-113562-4 £6.00

Public health, England: Contamination of food

The Food Protection (Emergency Prohibitions) (Lead in Ducks and Geese) (England) (Revocation) Order 2015 No. 2015/300. - Enabling power: Food and Environment Protection Act 1985, ss. 1 (1) (2) (10), 24 (1) (3). - Issued: 23.02.2015. Made: 12.02.2015. Laid: 23.02.2015. Coming into force: 06.04.2015. Effect: S.I. 1992/2726 revoked. Territorial extent & classification: E. General. - 2p.: 30 cm. - 978-0-11-112992-0 £4.25

Public health, England and Wales

The Nicotine Inhaling Products (Age of Sale and Proxy Purchasing) Regulations 2015 No. 2015/895. - Enabling power: Children and Families Act 2014, ss. 92 (1) (6) (7), 93 (8), 135 (2). - Issued: 01.04.2015. Made: 25.03.2015. Coming into force: In accord with reg. 1. Effect: 2008 c.13 amended. Territorial extent & classification: E/W. General. - Supersedes draft S.I. (ISBN 9780111130568) issued 03/03/15. - 4p.: 30 cm. - 978-0-11-113614-0 £4.25

The Proxy Purchasing of Tobacco, Nicotine Products etc. (Fixed Penalty Amount) Regulations 2015 No. 2015/896. - Enabling power: Health Act 2006, sch. 1, paras 5, 8. - Issued: 01.04.2015. Made: 26.03.2015. Coming into force: 01.10.2015. Effect: None. Territorial extent & classification: E/W. General. - Supersedes draft S.I. (ISBN 9780111130599) issued 03/03/15. - 2p.: 30 cm. - 978-0-11-113615-7 £4.25

Public health, Wales

The Proxy Purchasing of Tobacco, Nicotine Products etc. (Fixed Penalty Notice) (Wales) Regulations 2015 No. 2015/1663 (W.215). - Enabling power: Health Act 2006, sch. 1, para. 4. - Issued: 22.09.2015. Made: 04.09.2015. Laid before the National Assembly for Wales: 10.09.2015. Coming into force: 01.10.2015. Effect: None. Territorial extent & classification: W. General. - In English and Welsh. Welsh title: Rheoliadau Prynu Tybaco, Cynhyrchion Nicotin etc. drwy Ddirprwy (Hysbysiad Cosb Benodedig) (Cymru) 2015. - 12p.: 30 cm. - 978-0-348-11151-4 £6.00

The Smoke-free Premises etc. (Wales) (Amendment) Regulations 2015 No. 2015/1363 (W.133). - Enabling power: Health Act 2006, ss. 5, 8 (3), 9 (1A), 10 (1) (2), sch. para. 4. - Issued: 26.06.2015. Made: 02.06.2015. Coming into force: 01.10.2015. Effect: S.I. 2007/787 (W.68) amended. Territorial extent & classification: W. General. - In English and Welsh. Welsh title: Rheoliadau Mangreoedd etc. Difwg (Cymru) (Diwygio) 2015. - 16p.: 30 cm. - 978-0-348-11107-1 £6.00

Public order, Northern Ireland

The Public Processions (Electronic Communication of Notices) (Northern Ireland) Order 2015 No. 2015/235. - Enabling power: Electronic Communications Act 2000, ss. 8 (1) (2) (a) to (c) (3) (4) (a) to (c) (6) (a), 9 (1) (a) (5) (a) (6) (a) (c). - Issued: 19.02.2015. Made: 12.02.2015. Laid: 17.02.2015. Coming into force: In accord. with art. 1 (2). Effect: 1998 c.2; S.I. 2004/416; 2005/904 amended. Territorial extent & classification: NI. General. - 8p.: 30 cm. - 978-0-11-112975-3 £4.25

Public passenger transport

The Office of Rail Regulation (Change of Name) Regulations 2015 No. 2015/1682. - Enabling power: Transport Safety Act 2003, s. 15A. - Issued: 17.09.2015. Made: 10.09.2015. Laid: 17.09.2015. Coming into force: 16.10.2015. Effect: 1962 c.46; 1967 c.13; 1974 c.37; 1975 c.24; 1983 c.16; 1984 c.12; 1986 c.31, c.46; 1991 c.56, c.57; 1993 c.43; 1994 c.40; 1996 c.61; 1998 c.41; 1999 c.29; 2000 c.27, c.38; 2002 c.40; 2003 c.20; 2005 c.14; 2006 c.51; 2008 c.13. c.18; 2012 c.19; 2013 c.24, c.32; 2015 c.7, c.15 & S.I. 1990/304; 1997/553; 1998/494, 1833; 1999/2244; 2001/2975; 2002/2677; 2005/1093, 1541, 1643, 1992, 3049, 3050, 3207; 2006/557, 598, 599, 1010, 1466; 2007/2657, 3531; 2008/1261; 1597, 1660; 2008/2852; 2009/1348, 2264; 2010/104, 432, 724, 1140, 1504; 2011/2055, 3066; 2012/632, 767, 1128, 2284, 2635; 2013/1471, 1506; 2014/2418; 2015/51, 462, 785, 786 & 2007 asp 8, S.S.I. 2006/456; 2007/570; 2012/345 & 2011 nawm 1 amended. Territorial extent & classification: E/W/S. General. - 20p.: 30 cm. - 978-0-11-113925-7 £6.00

Public passenger transport, England and Wales

The Public Service Vehicles (Conduct of Drivers, Inspectors, Conductors and Passengers) (Amendment) (England and Wales) Regulations 2015 No. 2015/888. - Enabling power: Public Passenger Vehicles Act 1981, ss. 24 (1), 25 (1), 60 (1) (1A). - Issued: 30.03.2015. Made: 24.03.2015. Laid: 26.03.2015. Coming into force: 30.06.2015. Effect: S.I. 1990/1020 amended. Territorial extent & classification: E/W. General. - 8p.: 30 cm. - 978-0-11-113511-2 £4.25

Public procurement

The Public Contracts Regulations 2015 No. 2015/102. - Enabling power: European Communities Act 1972, s. 2 (2). - Issued: 10.02.2015. Made: 04.02.2015. Laid: 05.02.2015. Coming into force: In accord. with reg 1 (2) to (6). Effect: 4 Acts; 11 SIs amended & S.I. 2006/5 revoked with savings. Territorial extent & classification: UK (E/W/NI and sch. 6, para. 19 also applies to S). General. - EC note: These Regulations revoke & replace S.I. 2006//5 and implements for E/W/NI Directive 2014/24/EU on public procurement and repeals directive 2004/18/EC. They also implement for E/W/NI Council Directive 89/665/EEC. - 128p.: 30 cm. - 978-0-11-112880-0 £19.00

Public records

The Public Record Office (Fees) Regulations 2015 No. 2015/2042. - Enabling power: Public Records Act 1958, s. 2 (5). - Issued: 22.12.2015. Made: 15.12.2015. Coming into force: 01.02.2016. Effect: S.I. 2013/3267 revoked. Territorial extent & classification: E/W/S/NI. General. - 4p.: 30 cm. - 978-0-11-114224-0 £4.25

Public sector information

The Re-use of Public Sector Information Regulations 2015 No. 2015/1415. - Enabling power: European Communities Act 1972, s. 2 (2). - Issued: 01.07.2015. Made: 24.06.2015. Laid: 25.06.2015. Coming into force: 18.07.2015. Effect: 2000 c.36 amended & S.I. 2005/1515 revoked with savings. Territorial extent & classification: E/W/S/NI. General. - EC note: These regs implement Directive 2013/37/EU which amends Directive 2003/98/EC. With correction slip dated 13 November 2015. - 16p.: 30 cm. - 978-0-11-113712-3 £6.00

Public service pensions

The Armed Forces Pension (Consequential Provisions) Regulations 2015 No. 2015/390. - Enabling power: Public Service Pensions Act 2013, ss. 1 (1), 2 (h), 2 (1), 3 (1) (2) (3) (a) (4). - Issued: 04.03.2015. Made: 23.02.2015. Coming into force: In accord. with reg. 1. Effect: S.I. 1996/1172 modified. Territorial extent & classification: E/W/S/NI. General. - Supersedes draft S.I. (ISBN 9780111125717) issued 22/12/14. - 8p.: 30 cm. - 978-0-11-113077-3 £6.00

The Armed Forces Pension Scheme and Early Departure Payments Scheme (Amendment) Regulations 2015 No. 2015/466. - Enabling power: Public Service Pensions Act 2013, s. 1 (1). - Issued: 10.03.2015. Made: 03.03.2015. Laid: 05.03.2015. Coming into force: 01.04.2015. Effect: S.I. 2014/2328, 2336 amended. Territorial extent & classification: E/W/S/NI. General. - 8p.: 30 cm. - 978-0-11-113158-9 £6.00

The Judicial Pensions Regulations 2015 No. 2015/182. - Enabling power: Public Service Pensions Act 2013, ss. 1 (1) (2) (b), 2 (1), 3 (1) (2) (3) (a) (3) (c) (4), 4 (3) (6). - Issued: 19.02.2015. Made: 09.02.2015. Coming into force: in accord. with reg. 1 (2) to (4). Effect: 1981 c.20, 1993 c.8, c.48, S.I. 1996/1172, 1847 amended. Territorial extent & classification: E/W/S/NI. General. - Supersedes draft S.I. (ISBN 9780111124895) issued 12.12.2015. - 100p.: 30 cm. - 978-0-11-112919-7 £16.50

The Public Service (Civil Servants and Others) Pensions (Amendment) Regulations 2015 No. 2015/602. - Enabling power: Public Service Pensions Act 2013, ss. 1 (1) (2) (a), 2 (1), 3 (1) (2) (3), sch. 3- Issued: 13.03.2015. Made: 09.03.2015. Laid: 10.03.2015. Coming into force: 01.04.2015. Effect: S.I. 2014/1964 amended. Territorial extent & classification: E/W/S/NI. General. - 12p.: 30 cm. - 978-0-11-113267-8 £6.00

The Public Service (Civil Servants and Others) Pensions (Consequential and Amendment) Regulations 2015 No. 2015/372. - Enabling power: Public Service Pensions Act 2013, ss. 1 (1) (2) (a), 2 (1), 3 (1) (2) (3) (a), 4- Issued: 03.03.2015. Made: 23.02.2015. Coming into force: In accord with reg. 1. Effect: 2014 c.19 amended. Territorial extent & classification: E/W/S/NI. General. - This S.I. is being issued free of charge to all known recipients of S.I. 2014/1964 (ISBN 9780111119259) as Part 5 of this S.I. corrects errors in that S.I. - 12p.: 30 cm. - 978-0-11-113064-3 £6.00

The Public Service Pensions Act 2013 (Commencement No. 6, Saving Provision and Amendment) Order 2015 No. 2015/4 (C.1). - Enabling power: Public Service Pensions Act 2013, s. 41 (2) (3). Bringing into operation various provisions of the 2013 Act on 01.04.2015. - Issued: 12.01.2015. Made: 06.01.2015. Coming into force: in accord. with art. 2. Effect: S.I. 2014/1912 (C.86) amended. Territorial extent & classification: E/W/S/NI. General. - 4p.: 30 cm. - 978-0-11-112659-2 £4.25

The Public Service Pensions Act 2013 (Judicial Offices) (Amendment) Order 2015 No. 2015/1483. - Enabling power: Public Service Pensions Act 2013, sch. 1. para. 2. - Issued: 14.07.2015. Made: 07.07.2015. Laid: 10.07.2015. Coming into force: 01.08.2015. Effect: S.I. 2015/580 amended. Territorial extent & classification: E/W/S/NI. General. - 2p.: 30 cm. - 978-0-11-113763-5 £4.25

The Public Service Pensions Act 2013 (Judicial Offices) Order 2015 No. 2015/580. - Enabling power: Public Service Pensions Act 2013, sch. 1. para. 2. - Issued: 12.03.2015. Made: 05.03.2015. Laid: 10.03.2015. Coming into force: 01.04.2015. Effect: None. Territorial extent & classification: E/W and non-devolved offices in Scotland and Northern Ireland. General. - 8p.: 30 cm. - 978-0-11-113250-0 £4.25

Public service pensions, England

The Firefighters' Pension Scheme (Amendment) (Governance) Regulations 2015 No. 2015/465. - Enabling power: Public Service Pensions Act 2013, ss. 1, 3, 7 (2), 12 (6), 12 (7), sch. 3. - Issued: 10.03.2015. Made: 03.03.2015. Laid: 05.03.2015. Coming into force: 01.04.2015. Effect: S.I. 2014/2848 amended. Territorial extent & classification: E. General. - 8p.: 30 cm. - 978-0-11-113157-2 £4.25

The Firefighters' Pension Scheme (England) (Amendment) Regulations 2015 No. 2015/871. - Enabling power: Public Service Pensions Act 2013, ss. 1 (1) (2), 2 (1), 3 (1) (2) (3) (a), sch. 2, para. 6 (a), sch. 3. - Issued: 31.03.2015. Made: 24.03.2015. Laid: 25.03.2015. Coming into force: 01.04.2015. Effect: S.I. 2014/2848 amended. Territorial extent & classification: E. General. - This Statutory Instrument has been made in consequence of defects in S.I. 2015/589 (ISBN 9780111132586) issued 13/03/15 and is being issued free of charge to all known recipients of that Statutory Instrument. - 2p.: 30 cm. - 978-0-11-113495-5 £4.25

The Firefighters' Pension Scheme (England) (Consequential Provisions) Regulations 2015 No. 2015/319. - Enabling power: Public Service Pensions Act 2013, ss. 1 (1) (2) (f), 2 (1), 3 (1) (2) (3) (a) (4). - Issued: 25.02.2015. Made: 15.02.2015. Coming into force: In accord. with reg. 1. Effect: 1993 48; S.I. 1996/1172, 1847 modified. Territorial extent & classification: E. General. - 8p.: 30 cm. - 978-0-11-113010-0 £6.00

PUBLIC SERVICE PENSIONS, ENGLAND AND WALES

The Firefighters' Pension Scheme (England) (Transitional and Consequential Provisions) Regulations 2015 No. 2015/589. - Enabling power: Public Service Pensions Act 2013, ss. 1 (1) (2), 2 (1), 3 (1) (2) (3) (a) (c) (6) (7), 18 (5) (6), sch. 2, para. 6 (a), sch. 3, sch. 7, paras. 1 (2) (ii), 2 (2) (ii), 5 (1). - Issued: 13.03.2015. Made: 06.03.2015. Laid: 10.03.2015. Coming into force: 01.04.2015. Effect: S.I. 1992/129; 2006/3432; 2014/2848 amended. Territorial extent & classification: E. General. - 28p.: 30 cm. - 978-0-11-113258-6 £6.00

Public service pensions, England and Wales

The Local Government Pension Scheme (Amendment) (Governance) Regulations 2015 No. 2015/57. - Enabling power: Public Service Pensions Act 2013, ss 1, 3, 5 (7), 7 (2), 12 (6) (7), sch. 3. - Issued: 30.01.2015. Made: 26.01.2015. Laid: 28.01.2015. Coming into force: In accord. with reg. 1 (3). Effect: S.I. 2013/2356 amended. Territorial extent & classification: E/W. General. - 12p.: 30 cm. - 978-0-11-112790-2 £6.00

The Local Government Pension Scheme (Amendment) Regulations 2015 No. 2015/755. - Enabling power: Public Service Pensions Act 2013, ss. 1, 3, sch. 3. - Issued: 24.03.2015. Made: 17.03.2015. Laid: 19.03.2015. Coming into force: 11.04.2015. Effect: S.I. 2013/2356; 2014/525. Territorial extent & classification: E/W. General. - 12p.: 30 cm. - 978-0-11-113384-2 £6.00

The National Health Service Pension Scheme (Amendment) Regulations 2015 No. 2015/581. - Enabling power: Public Service Pensions Act 2013, ss. 1, 3, 25, sch. 3. - Issued: 12.03.2015. Made: 04.03.2015. Laid: 11.03.2015. Coming into force: 01.04.2015. Effect: None. Territorial extent & classification: E/W. General. - This Statutory Instrument has been made in consequence of defects in S.I. 2015/94 (ISBN 9780111129340) and is being issued free of charge to all known recipients of that S.I. - 4p.: 30 cm. - 978-0-11-113251-7 £4.25

The National Health Service Pension Scheme (Consequential Provisions) Regulations 2015 No. 2015/432. - Enabling power: Public Service Pensions Act 2013, ss. 1 (1) (2) (e), 2 (1), 3 (1) (2) (3) (a) (4). - Issued: 06.03.2015. Made: 25.02.2015. Coming into force: In accord. with reg. 1. Effect: None. Territorial extent & classification: E/W. General. - Supersedes draft S.I. (ISBN 9780111125915) issued 22/12/14. - 8p.: 30 cm. - 978-0-11-113122-0 £6.00

The National Health Service Pension Scheme Regulations 2015 No. 2015/94. - Enabling power: Public Service Pensions Act 2013, ss. 1 (1) (2) (e), 2 to 4, 5 (1) (2) (4), 7 (1) (4), 8 (1) (a) (2) (a), 11 (1), 12 (6) (7), 14, 18 (5) to (7), 25, sch. 2, para. 5 (a), 37 (c)- Issued: 26.02.2015. Made: 05.02.2015. Laid: 12.02.2015. Coming into force: 01.04.2015. Effect: None. Territorial extent & classification: E/W. General. - 176p.: 30 cm. - 978-0-11-112934-0 £25.50

The National Health Service Pension Scheme (Transitional and Consequential Provisions) Regulations 2015 No. 2015/95. - Enabling power: Superannuation Act 1972, ss. 10 (1) (2), sch. 3 & Public Service Pensions Act 2013, ss. 1, 3, 18 (5), sch. 3. - Issued: 13.02.2015. Made: 05.02.2015. Laid: 12.02.2015. Coming into force: 01.04.2015. Effect: S.I. 1995/300; 2008/653 amended. Territorial extent & classification: E/W. General. - 42p.: 30 cm. - 978-0-11-112902-9 £10.00

The Police Pensions (Consequential Provisions) Regulations 2015 No. 2015/370. - Enabling power: Public Service Pensions Act 2013, ss. 1 (1) (2) (g), 2 (1), 3 (1) (2) (3) (a) (4). - Issued: 03.03.2015. Made: 23.02.2015. Coming into force: In accord. with reg. 1. Effect: S.I. 1996/1172 modified. Territorial extent & classification: E/W. General. - Supersedes draft S.I. (ISBN 9780111125908) issued 22/12/14. - 8p.: 30 cm. - 978-0-11-113063-6 £6.00

The Police Pensions Regulations 2015 No. 2015/445. - Enabling power: Public Service Pensions Act 2013, ss. 1 (1) (2) (g), 2 (1), 3 (1) (2) (3) (a) (c), 4 (3) (5), sch. 2, para. 7, sch. 3, sch. 7, para. 1 (2) (ii), 2 (2) (ii), 5 (i). - Issued: 09.03.2015. Made: 27.02.2015. Laid: 05.03.2015. Coming into force: 01.04.2015. Effect: None. Territorial extent & classification: E/W. General. - 136p.: 30 cm. - 978-0-11-113133-6 £20.75

The Public Service Pensions Revaluation Order 2015 No. 2015/769. - Enabling power: Public Service Pensions Act 2013, ss. 9 (2) (3) (4) (b). - Issued: 25.03.2015. Made: 18.03.2015. Laid: 19.03.2015. Coming into force: 11.04.2015. Effect: None. Territorial extent & classification: E/W/S/NI. General. - 2p.: 30 cm. - 978-0-11-113395-8 £4.25

The Teachers' Pension Scheme (Amendment) Regulations 2015 No. 2015/592. - Enabling power: Public Service Pensions Act 2013, ss. 1 (1) (2) (d) (3) (4), 2, 3 (1) (2) (3) (a), 18 (5) to (9), sch. 2, para. 4 (a), sch. 3, sch. 5, para. 18. - Issued: 13.03.2015. Made: 05.03.2015. Laid: 10.03.2015. Coming into force: 01.04.2015. Effect: S.I. 2014/512 amended. Territorial extent & classification: E/W. General. - This Statutory Instrument has been printed in substitution of the SI of same number (and ISBN) issued 13.03.2015 and is being issued free of charge to all known recipients of that Statutory Instrument. - 8p.: 30 cm. - 978-0-11-113261-6 £4.25

The Teachers' Pension Scheme (Consequential Provisions) Regulations 2015 No. 2015/436. - Enabling power: Public Service Pensions Act 2013, ss. 1 (1) (2) (d), 3 (1) (2) (3) (a) (4). - Issued: 06.03.2015. Made: 25.02.2015. Coming into force: In accord. with reg. 1. Effect: 1993 c.48; 2004 c.12; S.I. 1996/1172, 1847 modified. Territorial extent & classification: E/W. General. - Supersedes draft S.I. (ISBN 9780111125922) issued 22/12/14. - 8p.: 30 cm. - 978-0-11-113124-4 £6.00

Public service pensions, Wales

The Firefighters' Pension Scheme (Wales) (Consequential Provisions) Regulations 2015 No. 2015/848 (W.63). - Enabling power: Public Service Pensions Act 2013, ss. 1 (1) (2) (f), 2 (1), 3 (1) (2) (3)(a) (4), sch. 2, para. 6 (b). - Issued: 30.03.2015. Made: 17.03.2015. Coming into force: In accord. with reg. 1. Effect: S.I. 1996/1847 modified. Territorial extent & classification: W. General. - In English and Welsh. Welsh title: Rheoliadau Cynllun Pensiwn y Diffoddwyr Tân (Cymru) (Darpariaethau Canlyniadol) 2015. - 16p.: 30 cm. - 978-0-348-11062-3 £6.00

The Firefighters' Pension Scheme (Wales) Regulations 2015 No. 2015/622 (W.50). - Enabling power: Public Service Pensions Act 2013, ss. 1 (1) (2) (f), 2 (1), 3 (1) (2) (3)(a) (c), 4 (5) (6), 12 (6) (7), 18 (5), (5A) (6) (7), sch. 2, para. 6 (b), sch. 3, sch. 5, paras 20, 21. - Issued: 31.03.2015. Made: 09.03.2015. Laid before the National Assembly for Wales: 10.03.2015. Coming into force: 01.04.2015. Effect: None. Territorial extent & classification: W. General. - In English and Welsh. Welsh title: Rheoliadau Cynllun Pensiwn y Diffoddwyr Tân (Cymru) 2015. - 158p.: 30 cm. - 978-0-348-11061-6 £23.25

The Firefighters' Pension Scheme (Wales) (Transitional and Consequential Provisions) Regulations 2015 No. 2015/1016 (W.71). - Enabling power: Public Service Pensions Act 2013, ss. 1 (1) (2), 2 (1), 3 (1) (2) (3) (a) (c) (6) (7), 18 (5) (6), sch. 2, para. 6 (b), sch. 3, paras 1 (2) (ii), 2 (2) (ii), 5 (1), sch. 7. - Issued: 16.04.2015. Made: 31.03.2015. Laid before the National Assembly for Wales: 31.03.2015. Coming into force: 01.04.2015. Effect: S.I. 1992/129; 2007/1072 (W.110); 2015/622 (W.50) amended. Territorial extent & classification: W. General. - In English and Welsh. Welsh title: Rheoliadau Cynllun Pensiwn y Diffoddwyr Tân (Cymru) (Darpariaethau Trosiannol a Chanlyniadol) 2015. - 56p.: 30 cm. - 978-0-348-11068-5 £10.00

Railways

The Railways (Interoperability) (Amendment) Regulations 2015 No. 2015/2022. - Enabling power: Transport Act 2000, s. 247. - Issued: 17.12.2015. Made: 10.12.2015. Laid: 17.12.2015. Coming into force: 08.01.2016. Effect: S.I. 2011/3066 amended. Territorial extent & classification: E/W/S/NI. General. - EC note: These Regulations amend S.I. 2011/3066 in order to implement Commission Directive 2014/106/EU of 5 December 2014 amending Annexes V and VI to Directive 2008/57/EC of the European Parliament and of the Council on the interoperability of the rail system within the Community. - 4p.: 30 cm. - 978-0-11-114197-7 £4.25

Rating and valuation, England

The Council Tax and Non-Domestic Rating (Demand Notices) (England) (Amendment) Regulations 2015 No. 2015/427. - Enabling power: Local Government Finance Act 1988, s. 143 (1), sch. 9, paras 1, 2 (2) (ga). - Issued: 06.03.2015. Made: 27.02.2015. Laid: 03.03.2015. Coming into force: 01.04.2015. Effect: S.I. 2003/2613 amended. Territorial extent & classification: E. General. - 12p.: 30 cm. - 978-0-11-113117-6 £6.00

The Council Tax and Non-Domestic Rating (Powers of Entry: Safeguards) (England) Order 2015 No. 2015/982. - Enabling power: Protection of Freedoms Act 2012, ss. 40, 41 (1), 44 (1). - Issued: 02.04.2015. Made: 26.03.2015. Coming into force: 01.10.2015. Effect: 1988 c. 41; 1992 c. 14 amended. Territorial extent & classification: E. General. - Supersedes draft SI (ISBN 9780111130858) issued 04/03/15 - 4p.: 30 cm. - 978-0-11-113617-1 £4.25

The Local Government Finance Act 1988 (Non-Domestic Rating Multipliers) (England) Order 2015 No. 2015/135. - Enabling power: Local Government Finance Act 1988, sch. 7, para. 5 (3). - Issued: 11.02.2015. Made: 07.01.2015. Laid: 07.01.2015. Coming into force: In accord. with art. 1. Effect: None. Territorial extent & classification: E. General. - Approved by the House of Commons. Supersedes version laid before the House for approval (ISBN 9780111126646), published on 13.01.2015. - 2p.: 30 cm. - 978-0-11-112885-5 £4.25

The Non-Domestic Rating (Alteration of Lists and Appeals) (England) (Amendment) Regulations 2015 No. 2015/424. - Enabling power: Local Government Finance Act 1988, ss. 55 (2) (6), 143 (1). - Issued: 06.03.2015. Made: 27.02.2015. Laid: 03.03.2015. Coming into force: 28.03.2015. Effect: S.I. 2009/2268 amended. Territorial extent & classification: E. General. - 4p.: 30 cm. - 978-0-11-113116-9 £4.25

The Non-Domestic Rating (Designated Area) Regulations 2015 No. 2015/353. - Enabling power: Local Government Finance Act 1988, sch. 7B, para. 39. - Issued: 02.03.2015. Made: 24.02.2015. Laid: 25.02.2015. Coming into force: 18.03.2015. Effect: None. Territorial extent & classification: E. General. - 4p.: 30 cm. - 978-0-11-113041-4 £4.25

The Non-Domestic Rating (Levy and Safety Net) (Amendment) (No. 2) Regulations 2015 No. 2015/2039. - Enabling power: Local Government Finance Act 1988, ss. 143 (1), 143 (2), sch. 7B, paras 22, 25, 37 (1) (2). - Issued: 21.12.2015. Made: 15.12.2015. Coming into force: 16.12.2015 in accord. with reg. 1. Effect: S.I. 2013/737 amended. Territorial extent & classification: E. General. - 2p.: 30 cm. - 978-0-11-114215-8 £4.25

The Non-Domestic Rating (Levy and Safety Net) (Amendment) Regulations 2015 No. 2015/617. - Enabling power: Local Government Finance Act 1988, s. 143 (1) (2), sch. 7B, paras. 22, 25, 28. - Issued: 16.03.2015. Made: 09.03.2015. Coming into force: In accord. with reg. 1. Effect: S.I. 2013/737 amended. Territorial extent & classification: E. General. - Supersedes draft S.I. (ISBN 9780111127179) issued 20/01/15. - 8p.: 30 cm. - 978-0-11-113280-7 £6.00

The Non-Domestic Rating (Northern Line Extension) Regulations 2015 No. 2015/354. - Enabling power: Local Government Finance Act 1988, sch. 7B, para. 39. - Issued: 02.03.2015. Made: 24.02.2015. Laid: 25.02.2015. Coming into force: 18.03.2015. Effect: None. Territorial extent & classification: E. General. - 8p.: 30 cm. - 978-0-11-113042-1 £6.00

The Non-Domestic Rating (Shale Oil and Gas and Miscellaneous Amendments) Regulations 2015 No. 2015/628. - Enabling power: Local Government Finance Act 1988, ss. 97 (2A) (2B), 99, 143 (1), sch. 7B, paras 6 (3) (4), 7 (2), 8 (1) (2), 9 (5) (6), 10 (1) (2) (d), 11 (1) (3), 33 (1) (6), 40, 41, 42. - Issued: 16.03.2015. Made: 09.03.2015. Coming into force: In accord. with reg. 1. Effect: S.I. 2013/106, 452 amended. Territorial extent & classification: E. General. - Supersedes draft S.I. (ISBN 9780111127797) issued 29/01/15. - 16p.: 30 cm. - 978-0-11-113285-2 £6.00

The Non-Domestic Rating (Small Business Rate Relief) (England) (Amendment) Order 2015 No. 2015/106. - Enabling power: Local Government Finance Act 1988, ss 44 (9) (a), 143 (1). - Issued: 06.02.2015. Made: 02.02.2015. Laid: 04.02.2015. Coming into force: 02.03.2015. Effect: S.I. 2012/148 amended. Territorial extent & classification: E. General. - 2p.: 30 cm. - 978-0-11-112857-2 £4.25

Rating and valuation, Wales

The Council Tax (Exceptions to Higher Amounts) (Wales) Regulations 2015 No. 2015/2068 (W.311). - Enabling power: Local Government Finance Act 1992, s. 12A (4) (5), 12B (5) (6). - Issued: 05.01.2016. Made: 21.12.2015. Laid before the National Assembly for Wales: 22.12.2015. Coming into force: 31.01.2016. Effect: None. Territorial extent & classification: W. General. - In English & Welsh: Welsh title: Rheoliadau'r Dreth Gyngor (Eithriadau rhag Symiau Uwch) (Cymru) 2015. - 12p.: 30 cm. - 978-0-348-11208-5 £6.00

The Non-Domestic Rating Contributions (Wales) (Amendment) Regulations 2015 No. 2015/1905 (W.277). - Enabling power: Local Government Finance Act 1988, s. 60, sch. 8, paras 4, 6. - Issued: 01.12.2015. Made: 11.11.2015. Laid before the National Assembly for Wales: 30.11.2015. Coming into force: 31.12.2015. Effect: S.I. 1992/3238 amended. Territorial extent & classification: W. General. - In English and Welsh: Welsh title: Rheoliadau Cyfraniadau Ardrethu Annomestig (Cymru) (Diwygio) 2015. - 4p.: 30 cm. - 978-0-348-11192-7 £4.25

The Non-Domestic Rating (Demand Notices) (Wales) (Amendment) Regulations 2015 No. 2015/655 (W.52). - Enabling power: Local Government Finance Act 1988, ss. 62, 146 (6), sch. 9, paras 1, 2 (2) & Welsh Language Act 1993, s. 26 (3). - Issued: 27.03.2015. Made: 09.03.2015. Laid before the National Assembly for Wales: 11.03.2015. Coming into force: 01.04.2015. Effect: S.I. 1993/252 amended. Territorial extent & classification: W. General. - In English and Welsh: Welsh title: Rheoliadau Ardrethu Annomestig (Hysbysiadau Galw am Dalu) (Cymru) (Diwygio) 2015. - 4p.: 30 cm. - 978-0-348-11059-3 £4.25

The Non-Domestic Rating (Miscellaneous Provisions) (Amendment) (Wales) Regulations 2015 No. 2015/1759 (W.243). - Enabling power: Local Government Finance Act 1988, s. 143 (1), sch. 6, para. 2 (8). - Issued: 15.10.2015. Made: 08.10.2015. Laid before the National Assembly for Wales: 09.10.2015. Coming into force: 31.10.2015. Effect: S.I. 1989/2303 amended. Territorial extent & classification: W. General. - In English and Welsh: Welsh title: Rheoliadau Ardrethu Annomestig (Darpariaethau Amrywiol) (Diwygio) (Cymru) 2015. - 4p.: 30 cm. - 978-0-348-11165-1 £4.25

The Non-Domestic Rating (Small Business Relief) (Wales) Order 2015 No. 2015/229 (W.11). - Enabling power: Local Government Finance Act 1988, ss. 43 (4B) (b), 44 (9), 143 (1), 146 (6). - Issued: 19.02.2015. Made: 11.02.2015. Laid before the National Assembly for Wales: 13.02.2015. Coming into force: 09.03.2015. Effect: S.I. 2008/2770(W.246); 2010/273(W.36), 2223(W.195); 2011/995(W.148); 2012/465(W.76); 2013/371(W.44); 2014/372(W.40) revoked with savings. Territorial extent & classification: W. General. - In English and Welsh: Welsh title: Gorchymyn Ardrethu Annomestig (Rhyddhad Ardrethi i Fusnesau Bach) (Cymru) (Diwygio) 2015. - 16p.: 30 cm. - 978-0-348-11048-7 £6.00

The Non-Domestic Rating (Waterways) (Wales) Regulations 2015 No. 2015/539 (W.46). - Enabling power: Local Government Finance Act 1988, ss. 64 (3), 65 (4), 143 (1) (2). - Issued: 13.03.2015. Made: 04.03.2015. Laid before the National Assembly for Wales: 06.03.2015. Coming into force: 01.04.2015. Effect: None. Territorial extent & classification: W. General. - In English and Welsh: Welsh title: Rheoliadau Ardrethu Annomestig (Dyfrffyrdd) (Cymru) 2015. - 4p.: 30 cm. - 978-0-348-11051-7 £4.25

Registration of births, deaths, marriages, etc., England and Wales

The Gender Recognition Register (Marriage and Civil Partnership) Regulations 2015 No. 2015/50. - Enabling power: Gender Recognition Act 2004, ss 11A (1) (2), sch. 3. - Issued: 28.01.2015. Made: 22.01.2015. Coming into force: 06.02.2015. Effect: None. Territorial extent & classification: E/W. General. - 10p.: 30 cm. - 978-0-11-112780-3 £6.00

The Marriage (Authorised Persons) and Civil Partnership (Registration Provisions) (Amendment) Regulations 2015 No. 2015/177. - Enabling power: Marriage Act 1949, s. 74 (1) (a) & Civil Partnership Act 2004, ss. 8 (2), 9E (1), 12 (2), 21 (2), 36 (1) (2) (a) (3), 258 (2). - Issued: 16.02.2015. Made: 05.02.2015. Laid: - Coming into force: 02.03.2015. Effect: S.I. 1952/1869; 2005/3176 amended. Territorial extent & classification: E/W. General. - 16p.: 30 cm. - 978-0-11-112914-2 £6.00

The Registration of Births, Deaths and Marriages and Registration of Civil Partnerships (Fees) (Amendment) Order 2015 No. 2015/117. - Enabling power: Public Expenditure and Receipts Act 1968, ss. 5 (1) (2), sch. 3, para. 1 & Civil Partnership Act 2004, ss. 34(1), 258(2). - Issued: 10.02.2015. Made: 02.02.2015. Laid: 05.02.2015. Coming into force: 02.03.2015. Effect: S.I. 2010/441; 2014/1789 amended. Territorial extent & classification: E/W. General. - 4p.: 30 cm. - 978-0-11-112875-6 £4.25

REGULATORY REFORM

The Registration of Marriages Regulations 2015 No. 2015/207. - Enabling power: Marriage Act 1949, ss. 27 (1), 27A (3) (4) (7), 27B (2) (b), 28G (1) (3), 31 (2) (5) (5D), 35 (1), 55 (1), 57 (2), 74 (1) (b) (3), 76 (5) & Marriage (Registrar General's Licence) Act 1970, ss. 2 (1), 7, 18 & Registration Service Act 1953, s. 20 (a). - Issued: 18.02.2015. Made: 05.02.2015. Coming into force: 02.03.2015. Effect: S.I. 2005/3177 partially revoked & S.I. 1986/1442; 1997/2204; 1999/1621; 2005/155; 2009/2806; 2011/1172 revoked. Territorial extent & classification: E/W. General. - Superseded by S.I. same number (ISBN 9780111300039) issued 29/06/15. - 48p.: 30 cm. - 978-0-11-112949-4 £10.00

The Registration of Marriages Regulations 2015 No. 2015/207. - Enabling power: Marriage Act 1949, ss. 27 (1), 27A (3) (4) (7), 27B (2) (b), 28G (1) (3), 31 (2) (5) (5D), 35 (1), 55 (1), 57 (2), 74 (1) (b) (3), 76 (5) & Marriage (Registrar General's Licence) Act 1970, ss. 2 (1), 7, 18 & Registration Service Act 1953, s. 20 (a). - Issued: 29.06.2015. Made: 05.02.2015. Coming into force: 02.03.2015. Effect: S.I. 2005/3177 partially revoked & S.I. 1986/1442; 1997/2204; 1999/1621; 2005/155; 2009/2806; 2011/1172 revoked. Territorial extent & classification: E/W. General. - This S.I. has been printed in substitution of the S.I. of the same number (ISBN 9780111129494) published 18/02/15 and is being issued free of charge to all known recipients of that S.I. - 48p.: 30 cm. - 978-0-11-130003-9 £10.00

Regulatory reform

The Legislative Reform (Further Renewal of Radio Licences) Order 2015 No. 2015/2052. - Enabling power: Legislative and Regulatory Reform Act 2006, s. 1. - Issued: 22.12.2015. Made: 14.12.2015. Coming into force: In accord. with art. 1. Effect: 1990 c.42 amended. Territorial extent & classification: E/W/S/NI. General. - Supersedes draft S.I. (ISBN 9780111134948) issued 31/03/15. - 4p.: 30 cm. - 978-0-11-114233-2 £4.25

The Small Business, Enterprise and Employment Act 2015 (Commencement No. 1) Regulations 2015 No. 2015/1329 (C.75). - Enabling power: Small Business, Enterprise and Employment Act 2015, ss. 161 (2), 164 (1). Bringing into operation various provisions of the 2015 Act on 26.05.2015; 15.06.2015; 01.07.2015; 01.01.2016, in accord. with arts 2 to 6. - Issued: 28.05.2015. Made: 20.05.2015. Effect: None. Territorial extent & classification: E/W/S/NI. General. - 4p.: 30 cm. - 978-0-11-113644-7 £4.25

Regulatory reform, England and Wales

The Legislative Reform (Community Governance Reviews) Order 2015 No. 2015/998. - Enabling power: Legislative and Regulatory Reform Act 2006, s. 1. - Issued: 08.04.2015. Made: 26.03.2015. Coming into force: 27.03.2015 in accord. with art. 1. Effect: 2007 c.28 amended. Territorial extent & classification: E/W. General. - Supersedes draft S.I. (ISBN 9780111125120) issued 15.12.2014. - 4p.: 30 cm. - 978-0-11-113628-7 £4.25

Rehabilitation of offenders, England and Wales

The Rehabilitation of Offenders Act 1974 (Exceptions) Order 1975 (Amendment) (England and Wales) Order 2015 No. 2015/317. - Enabling power: Rehabilitation of Offenders Act 1974, ss. 4 (4), 7 (4), 10 (1), sch. 2, paras. 4, 6 (4). - Issued: 24.02.2015. Made: 17.02.2015. Coming into force: In accord. with art. 1 (2). Effect: S.I. 1975/1023 amended. Territorial extent & classification: E/W. General. - 4p.: 30 cm. - 978-0-11-113006-3 £4.25

Representation of the people

The Election Judges Rota Rules 2015 No. 2015/329 (L.2). - Enabling power: Senior Courts Act 1981, s. 142 (1). - Issued: 26.02.2015. Made: 18.02.2015. Laid: 23.02.2015. Coming into force: 20.03.2015. Effect: None. Territorial extent & classification: E/W. General. - 4p.: 30 cm. - 978-0-11-113021-6 £4.25

The Elections (Policy Development Grants Scheme) (Amendment) (No. 2) Order 2015 No. 2015/302. - Enabling power: Political Parties, Elections and Referendums Act 2000, s.12. - Issued: 23.02.2015. Made: 16.02.2015. Laid: 18.02.2015. Coming into force: 01.03.2015, arts 1, 2; 02.03.2015, remainder. Effect: S.I. 2006/602 amended & S.I. 2015/128 amended. Territorial extent & classification: E/W/S/NI. General. - This Order supersedes S.I. 2015/128 (ISBN 9780111128763) and is being issued free of charge to all known recipients of that Statutory Instrument. - 4p.: 30 cm. - 978-0-11-112994-4 £4.25

The Elections (Policy Development Grants Scheme) (Amendment) Order 2015 No. 2015/128. - Enabling power: Political Parties, Elections and Referendums Act 2000, s.12. - Issued: 10.02.2015. Made: 04.02.2014. Laid: 05.02.2015 Coming into force: 02.03.2014. Effect: S.I. 2006/602 amended. Territorial extent & classification: E/W/S/NI. General. - 4p.: 30 cm. - 978-0-11-112876-3 £4.25

The Electoral Registration and Administration Act 2013 (Transitional Provisions) Order 2015 No. 2015/1520. - Enabling power: Electoral Registration and Administration Act 2013, s. 13 (2), 25 (1), sch. 5, para. 28 (1). - Issued: 21.07.2015. Made: 15.07.2015. Laid: 16.07.2015. Coming into force: 06.08.2015 in accord. with art. 1. Effect: None. Territorial extent & classification: E/W/S. General. - 2p.: 30 cm. - 978-0-11-113799-4 £4.25

The European Parliamentary Elections (Amendment) Regulations 2015 No. 2015/459. - Enabling power: European Parliamentary Elections Act 2002, s. 7 (1). - Issued: 06.03.2015. Made: 02.03.2015. Coming into force: 03.03.2015. Effect: S.I. 2004/293 amended. Territorial extent & classification: E/W/S consequential amendments relating to the ERA Act also extend to Gibraltar. - Supersedes draft SI (ISBN 9780111126516) issued 08/01/15 - 4p.: 30 cm. - 978-0-11-113150-3 £4.25

The European Parliamentary Elections (Miscellaneous Provisions) (United Kingdom and Gibraltar) Order 2015 No. 2015/1982. - Enabling power: European Parliament (Representation) Act 2003, ss. 12, 13 (3) (4). - Issued: 14.12.2015. Made: 07.12.2015. Laid: - Coming into force: 08.12.2015 in accord. with art. 1 (2). Effect: 2000 c.41 amended. Territorial extent & classification: E/W/S/NI & Gibraltar. General. - Supersedes draft S.I. (ISBN 9780111140048) issued 26/10/15. - 4p.: 30 cm. - 978-0-11-114170-0 £4.25

The Northern Ireland Assembly (Elections) (Amendment) Order 2015 No. 2015/1610. - Enabling power: Northern Ireland Assembly Act 1998, s. 34 (4) (6). - Issued: 19.08.2015. Made: 29.07.2015. Coming into force: In accord. with art 1 (2). Effect: S.I. 2001/2599 amended. Territorial extent & classification: NI. General. - Supersedes draft S.I. (ISBN 9780111137598) issued 14/07/15. - 4p.: 30 cm. - 978-0-11-113866-3 £4.25

The Northern Ireland (Elections) (Amendment) (No. 2) Order 2015 No. 2015/1939. - Enabling power: Representation of the People Act 1983, s.10A (7) & Northern Ireland Act 1998, ss. 34 (4) (6). - Issued: 02.12.2015. Made: 26.11.2015. Coming into force: 30.11.2015. Effect: S.I. 2001/2599; 2008/1741 amended. Territorial extent & classification: NI. General. - Supersedes draft S.I. (ISBN 9780111140406) issued 05/11/15. - 4p.: 30 cm. - 978-0-11-114126-7 £4.25

The Parliamentary Elections (Returning Officers' Charges) Order 2015 No. 2015/476. - Enabling power: Representation of the People Act 1983, s. 29 (3) (3A) (4C). - Issued: 10.03.2015. Made: 26.02.2015. Coming into force: 27.02.2015 in accord. with art. 1 (1). Effect: S.I. 2010/830 revoked. Territorial extent & classification: E/W/S/NI. General. - 32p.: 30 cm. - 978-0-11-113171-8 £10.00

The Representation of the People (Ballot Paper) Regulations 2015 No. 2015/656. - Enabling power: Representation of the People Act 1983, s. 201 (3), sch. 1, rule 19 (4). - Issued: 17.03.2015. Made: 09.03.2015. Coming into force: In accord. with reg. 1 (1). Effect: 1983 c.2 amended. Territorial extent & classification: E/W/S/NI. General. - Supersedes draft S.I. (ISBN 9780111126998) issued 16/01/15. - 8p.: 30 cm. - 978-0-11-113313-2 £6.00

The Scottish Parliament (Regional Returning Officers) (Revocation) Order 2015 No. 2015/743 (S. 3). - Enabling power: Scotland Act 1998, ss. 12 (6), 113 (4). - Issued: 23.03.2015. Made: 17.03.2015. Coming into force: 30.06.2015. Effect: S.I. 2011/576 revoked. Territorial extent & classification: S. General. - 2p.: 30 cm. - 978-0-11-113376-7 £4.25

The Scottish Parliament (Returning Officers Charges) (Revocation) Order 2015 No. 2015/761 (S. 4). - Enabling power: Representation of the People Act 1983, s. 29 (3) (3A) (4C) & S.I. 2010/2999, art. 18. - Issued: 24.03.2015. Made: 17.03.2015. Coming into force: 30.06.2015. Effect: S.I. 2011/1013 revoked with saving. Territorial extent & classification: S. General. - 4p.: 30 cm. - 978-0-11-113392-7 £4.25

Representation of the people, England and Wales

The Local Elections (Parishes and Communities) (England and Wales) (Amendment) Rules 2015 No. 2015/104. - Enabling power: Representation of the People Act 1983, s. 36 (1) (2). - Issued: 06.02.2015. Made: 30.01.2015. Laid: 04.02.2015. Coming into force: In accord. with rule 1 (2). Effect: S.I. 2006/3305 amended. Territorial extent & classification: E/W. General. - 12p.: 30 cm. - 978-0-11-112854-1 £6.00

The Local Elections (Principal Areas) (England and Wales) (Amendment) Rules 2015 No. 2015/103. - Enabling power: Representation of the People Act 1983, s. 36 (1) (2). - Issued: 06.02.2015. Made: 30.01.2015. Laid: 04.02.2015. Coming into force: In accord. with rule 1 (2). Effect: S.I. 2006/3304 amended. Territorial extent & classification: E/W. General. - 12p.: 30 cm. - 978-0-11-112856-5 £6.00

The Representation of the People (Combination of Polls) (England and Wales) Regulations 2015 No. 2015/654. - Enabling power: Representation of the People Act 1985, s. 15 (5) & Local Government Act 2000, ss. 9HE (1) (a) (2) (d) (3) (a) (b), 9MG (2) to (4), 44 (1) (a) (2) (d) (3) (a). - Issued: 17.03.2015. Made: 09.03.2015. Coming into force: 07.05.2015. Effect: S.I. 2004/294 amended. Territorial extent & classification: E/W. General. - Supersedes draft S.I. (ISBN 9780111127209) issued 20/01/15. - 4p.: 30 cm. - 978-0-11-113312-5 £4.25

The Representation of the People (England and Wales) (Amendment) (No. 2) Regulations 2015 No. 2015/1971. - Enabling power: Representation of the People Act 1983, ss. 10ZC (3), 10ZD (3), 53 (1) (3), sch. 2 paras 1, 1A, 1B, 2, 3ZA. - Issued: 09.12.2015. Made: 02.12.2015. Coming into force: 03.12.2015 in accord. with reg. 1. Effect: S.I. 2001/341 amended. Territorial extent & classification: E/W. General. - Supersedes draft SI (ISBN 9780111139448) issued 12/10/15 - 8p.: 30 cm. - 978-0-11-114148-9 £4.25

The Representation of the People (England and Wales) (Amendment) Regulations 2015 No. 2015/467. - Enabling power: Representation of the People Act 1983, ss. 9D (3) (4), 10ZC (3), 10ZD (3), 53 (1) (3), sch. 2, paras. 1, 1A, 1B, 3ZA. - Issued: 06.03.2015. Made: 02.03.2015. Coming into force: In accord. with reg. 1. Effect: S.I. 2001/341 amended. Territorial extent & classification: E/W. General. - Supersedes draft S.I. (ISBN 9780111126714) issued 13/01/15. - 4p.: 30 cm. - 978-0-11-113159-6 £4.25

Representation of the people, Northern Ireland

The European Parliamentary Elections (Forms) (Northern Ireland) Regulations 2015 No. 2015/220. - Enabling power: European Parliamentary Elections Act 2002, s. 7 (1) (4) (4A). - Issued: 18.02.2015. Made: 11.02.2015. Coming into force: In accord. with art. 1 (2). Effect: S.I. 2004/1267 amended. Territorial extent & classification: NI. General. - Supersedes draft S.I. (ISBN 97801111266530) issued 13/01/15. - 20p.: 30 cm. - 978-0-11-112970-8 £6.00

The Parliamentary Elections (Forms) (Northern Ireland) Regulations 2015 No. 2015/221. - Enabling power: Representation of the People Act 1983, ss. 53 (1) (c), 201 (1) (3), sch. 1, rules 24 (1) (c) (3), 28 (3) (3 A), 32 (3) & Representation of the People Act 1985, s. 15 (5). - Issued: 19.02.2015. Made: 11.02.2015. Coming into force: 12.02.2015 in accord. with reg. 1 (2). Effect: S.I. 2008/1741 amended. Territorial extent & classification: NI. General. - Supersedes S.I. draft (ISBN 97801111266600 issued 13/01/15. - 16p.: 30 cm. - 978-0-11-112971-5 £6.00

The Parliamentary Elections (Returning Officer's Charges) (Northern Ireland) Order 2015 No. 2015/885. - Enabling power: Representation of the People Act 1983, s. 29 (3) (4C). - Issued: 31.03.2014. Made: 20.03.2015. Coming into force: In accord. with art. 1 (1). Effect: S.I. 2010/869 revoked. Territorial extent & classification: NI. General. - 4p.: 30 cm. - 978-0-11-113508-2 £4.25

Representation of the people, Scotland

The Representation of the People (Scotland) (Amendment) (No. 2) Regulations 2015 No. 2015/1966. - Enabling power: Representation of the People Act 1983, ss. 10ZC (3), 10ZD (3), 53 (1) (3), sch. 2, paras 1A, 3ZA. - Issued: 08.12.2015. Made: 01.12.2015. Coming into force: In accord. with reg. 1. Effect: S.I. 2001/497 amended. Territorial extent & classification: S. General. - Supersedes draft SI (ISBN 9780111139394) issued 16/10/15 - 8p.: 30 cm. - 978-0-11-114144-1 £4.25

The Representation of the People (Scotland) (Amendment) Regulations 2015 No. 2015/450. - Enabling power: Representation of the People Act 1983, ss. 9D (3) (4), 10ZC (3), 10ZD (3), 53 (1) (3), sch. 2 paras. 1, 1A, 1B, 3ZA, 12. - Issued: 09.03.2015. Made: 03.03.2015. Coming into force: In accord with reg. 1. Effect: S.I. 2001/497 amended. Territorial extent & classification: S. General. - Supersedes draft SI (ISBN 9780111126578) issued 12/01/15 - 4p.: 30 cm. - 978-0-11-113137-4 £4.25

Representation of the people, Wales

The Parliamentary Elections (Welsh Forms) (Amendment) Order 2015 No. 2015/803. - Enabling power: Welsh Language Act 1993, s. 26 (2). - Issued: 26.03.2015. Made: 19.03.2015. Laid: 23.03.2015. Coming into force: 20.03.2015 in accord. with art. 1 (2). Effect: S.I. 2007/1014 amended. Territorial extent & classification: W. General. - In English and Welsh. - 24p.: 30 cm. - 978-0-11-113429-0 £6.00

Revenue and customs

The Taxes, etc. (Fees for Payment by Internet) (Amendment) Regulations 2015 No. 2015/1777. - Enabling power: Finance Act 2008, ss. 136 (1) to(3). - Issued: 16.10.2015. Made: 09.10.2015. Laid: 12.10.2015. Coming into force: 02.11.2015. Effect: S.I. 2011/711 amended. Territorial extent & classification: E/W/S/NI. General. - Revoked by S.I. 2016/333 (ISBN 9780111145081). - 2p.: 30 cm. - 978-0-11-113985-1 £4.25

Revenue and customs, England and Wales

The Police and Criminal Evidence Act 1984 (Application to Revenue and Customs) Order 2015 No. 2015/1783. - Enabling power: Police and Criminal Evidence Act 1984 ss. 114 (2) (3). - Issued: 20.10.2015. Made: 13.10.2015. Laid: 14.10.2015. Coming into force: 04.11.2015. Effect: 1984 c. 60 modified & S.I. 2007/3175; 2010/360; 2014/788 revoked. Territorial extent & classification: E/W. General. - 16p.: 30 cm. - 978-0-11-113994-3 £6.00

Rights in performances

The Copyright and Performances (Application to Other Countries) (Amendment) Order 2015 No. 2015/216. - Enabling power: Copyright, Designs and Patents Act 1988, ss. 159, 208. - Issued: 18.02.2015. Made: 11.02.2015. Laid: 18.02.2015. Coming into force: 06.04.2015. Effect: S.I. 2013/536 amended. Territorial extent & classification: E/W/S/NI. General. - 4p.: 30 cm. - 978-0-11-112958-6 £4.25

Rights of the subject, England and Wales: Powers of entry

The Protection of Freedoms Act 2012 (Code of Practice for Powers of Entry and Description of Relevant Persons) Order 2015 No. 2015/240. - Enabling power: Protection of Freedoms Act 2012, ss. 48 (2), 51 (5). - Issued: 19.02.2015. Made: 11.02.2015. Coming into force: In accord. with art. 1. Effect: None. Territorial extent & classification: E/W. General. - Supersedes draft S.I. (ISBN 9780111124802) issued 11.12.2014. - 2p.: 30 cm. - 978-0-11-112982-1 £4.25

River, England: Salmon and freshwater fisheries

The Keeping and Introduction of Fish (England and River Esk Catchment Area) Regulations 2015 No. 2015/10. - Enabling power: Marine Coastal Access Act 2009, s. 316 (6). - Issued: 14.01.2015. Made: 07.01.2015. Coming into force: 19.01.2015. Effect: 1975 c.51 amended. Territorial extent & classification: E/S. General. - Supersedes S.I. draft (ISBN 9780111123072) issued 12/11/14. - 12p.: 30 cm. - 978-0-11-112680-6 £6.00

River, England and Wales

The Scotland Act 1998 (River Tweed) Amendment Order 2015 No. 2015/203. - Enabling power: Scotland Act 1998, ss. 111, 113 (2) (3) (4) (5) (7). - Issued: 18.02.2015. Made: 11.02.2015. Coming into force: 12.02.2015. Effect: S.I. 2006/2913 amended. Territorial extent & classification: E/W/S. General. - Supersedes draft S.I. (ISBN 9780111121931) issued 21.10.2014. - 4p.: 30 cm. - 978-0-11-112945-6 £4.25

River, Scotland

The Scotland Act 1998 (River Tweed) Amendment Order 2015 No. 2015/203. - Enabling power: Scotland Act 1998, ss. 111, 113 (2) (3) (4) (5) (7). - Issued: 18.02.2015. Made: 11.02.2015. Coming into force: 12.02.2015. Effect: S.I. 2006/2913 amended. Territorial extent & classification: E/W/S. General. - Supersedes draft S.I. (ISBN 9780111121931) issued 21.10.2014. - 4p.: 30 cm. - 978-0-11-112945-6 £4.25

River, Scotland: Salmon and freshwater fisheries

The Keeping and Introduction of Fish (England and River Esk Catchment Area) Regulations 2015 No. 2015/10. - Enabling power: Marine Coastal Access Act 2009, s. 316 (6). - Issued: 14.01.2015. Made: 07.01.2015. Coming into force: 19.01.2015. Effect: 1975 c.51 amended. Territorial extent & classification: E/S. General. - Supersedes S.I. draft (ISBN 9780111123072) issued 12/11/14. - 12p.: 30 cm. - 978-0-11-112680-6 £6.00

River, Wales

The Prohibition of Keeping or Release of Live Fish (Specified Species) (Wales) Order 2015 No. 2015/88 (W.7). - Enabling power: European Communities Act 1972, ss. 1 (1), 2 (2). - Issued: 18.02.2015. Made: 28.01.2015. Laid before the National Assembly for Wales: 02.02.2015. Coming into force: 27.02.2015. Effect: S.I. 1998/2409; 2003/416 (W.60) revoked & S.I. 2011/2292 partially revoked. Territorial extent & classification: W. General. - In English and Welsh. Welsh title: Gorchymyn Gwahardd Cadw new Ollwng Pysgod Byw (Rhywogaethau Penodedig) (Cymru) 2015. - 12p.: 30 cm. - 978-0-348-11041-8 £6.00

Road traffic

The A14 Trunk Road (Rothwell, Northamptonshire) (Temporary Prohibition of Traffic) Order 2015 No. 2015/685. - Enabling power: Road Traffic Regulation Act 1984, s. 14 (1) (a). - Issued: 11.02.2015. Made: 23.01.2015. Coming into force: 30.01.2015. Effect: None. Territorial extent & classification: E. Local. - Available at http://www.legislation.gov.uk/uksi/2015/685/contents/made Non-print

The Agricultural or Forestry Tractors (Emission of Gaseous and Particulate Pollutants) and Tractor etc (EC Type Approval) (Amendment) Regulations 2015 No. 2015/1350. - Enabling power: European Communities Act 1972, s. 2 (2). - Issued: 10.06.2015. Made: 04.06.2015. Laid: 08.06.2015. Coming into force: 30.06.2015. Effect: S.I. 2002/1891; 2005/390 amended. Territorial extent & classification: E/W/S/NI. General. - 4p.: 30 cm. - 978-0-11-113657-7 £4.25

The Crime and Courts Act 2013 (Consequential Amendments) (No.2) Order 2015 No. 2015/733. - Enabling power: Crime and Courts Act 2013, s. 59. - Issued: 23.03.2015. Made: 16.03.2015. Coming into force: In accord with art. 1. Effect: 1988 c.53 amended. Territorial extent & classification: E/W/S. General. - Supersedes draft SI (ISBN 9780111127308) issued 21/01/15 - 4p.: 30 cm. - 978-0-11-113369-9 £4.25

The Electrically Assisted Pedal Cycles (Amendment) Regulations 2015 No. 2015/24. - Enabling power: Road Traffic Regulation Act 1984, s. 140 (1) (c) & Road Traffic Act 1988, s. 189 (1) (c). - Issued: 09.03.2015. Made: 12.01.2015. Laid: 16.01.2015. Coming into force: 06.04.2015. Effect: S.I. 1983/1168 amended. Territorial extent & classification: E/W/S. General. - Approved version of SI of same title and ISBN issued 20.01.2015. - 4p.: 30 cm. - 978-0-11-112723-0 £4.25

The Motor Cars (Driving Instruction) (Amendment) Regulations 2015 No. 2015/952. - Enabling power: Road Traffic Act 1988, ss. 123 (2), 125 (2D) (3) (5) (a) (ii), 129 (1C) (5) (5ZA), 132 (1) (2) (a), 133A (2) (6), 133B (2A), 134 (a), 141. - Issued: 02.04.2015. Made: 26.03.2015. Laid: 27.03.2015. Coming into force: 08.06.2015. Effect: S.I. 2005/1902 amended. Territorial extent & classification: E/W/S. General. - 8p.: 30 cm. - 978-0-11-113581-5 £6.00

The Motor Vehicles (Driving Licences) (Amendment) (No. 2) Regulations 2015 No. 2015/412. - Enabling power: Road Traffic Act 1988, ss 105 (1) (2) (c) (3) & European Communities Act 1972, s. 2 (2). - Issued: 04.03.2015. Made: 25.02.2015. Laid: 04.03.2015. Coming into force: 26.03.2015. Effect: S.I. 1999/2864 amended. Territorial extent & classification: E/W/S. General. - Revoked by SI 2015/719 (ISBN 9780111133576). - 4p.: 30 cm. - 978-0-11-113102-2 £4.25

The Motor Vehicles (Driving Licences) (Amendment) (No. 3) Regulations 2015 No. 2015/719. - Enabling power: Road Traffic Act 1988, ss. 105 (1) (2) (c) (3) & European Communities Act 1972, s. 2 (2). - Issued: 20.03.2015. Made: 16.03.2015. Laid: 20.03.2015. Coming into force: In accord. with reg. 1. Effect: S.I. 2015/412 revoked (25.03.2015). Territorial extent & classification: E/W/S. General. - This Statutory Instrument has been made in consequence of defects in S.I. 2015/412 (ISBN 9780111131022) published 04/03/15 and is being issued free of charge to all known recipients of that statutory instrument. - 4p.: 30 cm. - 978-0-11-113357-6 £4.25

The Motor Vehicles (Driving Licences) (Amendment) (No. 4) Regulations 2015 No. 2015/1797. - Enabling power: Road Traffic Act 1988, ss. 89 (2A) (3) (6) (c), 105 (1) (2) (a) (ee) (3), 108 (1). - Issued: 22.10.2015. Made: 15.10.2015. Laid: 22.10.2015. Coming into force: 31.12.2015. Effect: S.I. 1999/2684 amended. Territorial extent & classification: E/W/S. General. - 8p.: 30 cm. - 978-0-11-113999-8 £4.25

The Motor Vehicles (Driving Licences) (Amendment) Regulations 2015 No. 2015/15. - Enabling power: Road Traffic Act 1988, ss 97 (1) (a), 105 (1) (2) (a) (4). - Issued: 15.01.2015. Made: 07.01.2015. Laid: 13.01.2015. Coming into force: 04.02.2015. Effect: S.I. 1999/2864 amended. Territorial extent & classification: E/W/S. General. - 2p.: 30 cm. - 978-0-11-112689-9 £4.25

The Motor Vehicles (Insurance Requirements) (Immobilisation, Removal and Disposal) (Amendment) Regulations 2015 No. 2015/854. - Enabling power: Road Traffic Act 1988, ss. 144D (1), 160 (1), sch. 2A. - Issued: 27.03.2015. Made: 23.03.2015. Laid: 25.03.2015. Coming into force: 30.06.2015. Effect: 2011/1120 amended. Territorial extent & classification: E/W/S. General. - This Statutory Instrument has been made in consequence of defects in S.I. 2011/1120 (ISBN 9780111510711) issued 20/04/11 and is being issued free of charge to all known recipients of that Statutory Instrument. - 4p.: 30 cm. - 978-0-11-113477-1 £4.25

The Motor Vehicles (Wearing of Seat Belts) (Amendment) (No. 2) Regulations 2015 No. 2015/574. - Enabling power: Road Traffic Act 1988, s. 15 (3) (5). - Issued: 12.03.2015. Made: 04.03.2015. Coming into force: 01.04.2015. Effect: S.I. 1993/176 amended. Territorial extent & classification: E/W/S. General. - 2p.: 30 cm. - 978-0-11-113242-5 £4.25

The Motor Vehicles (Wearing of Seat Belts) (Amendment) Regulations 2015 No. 2015/242. - Enabling power: Road Traffic Act 1988, s. 14 (1) (2). - Issued: 19.02.2015. Made: 10.02.2015. Coming into force: 03.03.2015. Effect: S.I. 1993/176 amended. Territorial extent & classification: E/W/S. General. - Supersedes draft S.I. (ISBN 9780111124567) issued 10.12.2014. - 2p.: 30 cm. - 978-0-11-112984-5 £4.25

The Motor Vehicles (Wearing of Seat Belts by Children in Front Seats) (Amendment) Regulations 2015 No. 2015/402. - Enabling power: Road Traffic Act 1988, s. 15 (1) (5). - Issued: 05.03.2015. Made: 26.02.2015. Laid: 02.03.2015. Coming into force: 27.03.2015. Effect: S.I. 1993/31 amended. Territorial extent & classification: E/W/S. General. - EC note: These Regs implement requirements of Council Directive 2014/37/EU. - 4p.: 30 cm. - 978-0-11-113089-6 £4.25

The Passenger and Goods Vehicles (Recording Equipment) (Downloading of Data) Regulations 2015 No. 2015/502. - Enabling power: Transport Act 1968, s. 95 (1). - Issued: 10.03.2015. Made: 03.03.2015. Coming into force: 06.04.2015. Effect: 1968 c.73 amended. Territorial extent & classification: E/W/S. General. - Supersedes draft SI (ISBN 9780111126622) issued 13/01/15. - 4p.: 30 cm. - 978-0-11-113200-5 £4.25

The Pedal Cycles (Construction and Use) (Amendment) Regulations 2015 No. 2015/474. - Enabling power: Road Traffic Act 1988, s. 81 (1) (2) (4) (5). - Issued: 10.03.2015. Made: 03.03.2015. Laid: 05.03.2015. Coming into force: 06.04.2015. Effect: S.I. 1983/1176 amended. Territorial extent & classification: E/W/S. General. - 4p.: 30 cm. - 978-0-11-113168-8 £4.25

The Rehabilitation Courses (Relevant Drink Offences) (Amendment) Regulations 2015 No. 2015/366. - Enabling power: Road Traffic Offenders Act 1988, ss. 34B (3) (10), 34BA (5), 34C (4). - Issued: 02.03.2015. Made: 23.02.2015. Laid: 27.02.2015. Coming into force: 06.04.2015. Effect: S.I. 2012/2939. Territorial extent & classification: E/S. General. - This S.I. has been made in consequence of defects in S.I. 2012/2939 (ISBN 9780111531228) issued 30/11/12 and is being issued free of charge to all known recipients of that S.I. - 8p.: 30 cm. - 978-0-11-113057-5 £6.00

The Retention and Sale of Registration Marks Regulations 2015 No. 2015/193. - Enabling power: Vehicle Excise and Registration Act 1994, ss. 26, 27, 57 (2). - Issued: 17.02.2015. Made: 10.02.2015. Laid: 16.02.2015. Coming into force: 09.03.2015. Effect: S.I. 1993/987; 1995/2880 amended. Territorial extent & classification: E/W/S/NI. General. - 12p.: 30 cm. - 978-0-11-112933-3 £6.00

The Road Safety Act 2006 (Commencement No. 11 and Transitional Provisions) Order 2015 No. 2015/560 (C.29). - Enabling power: Road Safety Act 2006, s. 61 (1) (2) (6). Bringing into operation various provisions of the 2006 Act on 08.06.2015, in accord. with art. 2. - Issued: 12.03.2015. Made: 03.03.2015. Effect: None. Territorial extent & classification: E/W/S. General. - 8p.: 30 cm. - 978-0-11-113230-2 £6.00

The Road Safety Act 2006 (Consequential Amendments) Order 2015 No. 2015/583. - Enabling power: Road Safety Act 2006, s. 60. - Issued: 12.03.2015. Made: 03.03.15. Coming into force: 08.06.2015. Effect: 7 Acts & 10 SIs amended & 1991 c.40; 1995 c.13, c.40; 2003 c.32; 2012 c.10; S.I. 1996/1974 partially revoked/repealed. Territorial extent & classification: E/W/S/NI. General. - Supersedes draft S.I. (ISBN 9780111127315) issued 21/01/15. - 12p.: 30 cm. - 978-0-11-113253-1 £6.00

The Road Traffic Offenders Act 1988 and Motor Vehicles (Driving Licences) (Amendment) Regulations 2015 No. 2015/2004. - Enabling power: Road Traffic Act 1988, ss. 89 (3) (a) (3) (ba), 105 (1) (2) (a) (3) & European Communities Act 1972, s. 2 (2). - Issued: 15.12.2015. Made: 07.12.2015. Laid: 11.12.2015. Coming into force: 04.01.2016. Effect: 1988 c.53 & S.I. 1999/2864 amended. Territorial extent & classification: E/W/S. General. - EC note: These Regulations make further provision to implement Directive 2006/126/EC of the European Parliament and of the Council of 20 December 2006 on driving licences. - 4p.: 30 cm. - 978-0-11-114184-7 £4.25

The Road Vehicles (Construction and Use) (Amendment) Regulations 2015 No. 2015/142. - Enabling power: Road Traffic Act 1988, s. 41 (1) (2) (5). - Issued: 12.02.2015. Made: 04.02.2015. Laid: 10.02.2015. Coming into force: 09.03.2015. Effect: S.I. 1986/1078 amended. Territorial extent & classification: E/W/S. General. - 8p.: 30 cm. - 978-0-11-112892-3 £6.00

The Road Vehicles (Registration and Licensing) (Amendment) (No. 2) Regulations 2015 No. 2015/1657. - Enabling power: Vehicle Excise and Registration Act 1994, ss. 22 (1) (2), 22A (2) (a), 57, 59 (2) (a). - Issued: 14.09.2015. Made: 07.09.2015. Laid: 09.09.2015. Coming into force: 01.10.2015. Effect: S.I. 2002/2742 amended. Territorial extent & classification: E/W/S/NI. General. - 8p.: 30 cm. - 978-0-11-113907-3 £6.00

The Road Vehicles (Registration and Licensing) (Amendment) Regulations 2015 No. 2015/403. - Enabling power: Vehicle Excise and Registration Act 1994, ss. 22 (1) (2), 57, 59 (2) (a). - Issued: 05.03.2015. Made: 24.02.2015. Laid: 02.03.2015. Coming into force: 23.03.2015. Effect: S.I. 2002/2742 amended. Territorial extent & classification: E/W/S/NI. General. - 8p.: 30 cm. - 978-0-11-113090-2 £6.00

The Vehicle Drivers (Certificates of Professional Competence) (Amendment) Regulations 2015 No. 2015/2024. - Enabling power: European Communities Act 1972, s. 2 (2). - Issued: 18.12.2015. Made: 10.12.2015. Laid: 17.12.2015. Coming into force: 25.01.2016. Effect: S.I. 2007/605 amended. Territorial extent & classification: E/W/S/NI. General. - 4p.: 30 cm. - 978-0-11-114200-4 £4.25

Road traffic: Special roads

The M3 Motorway (Junctions 2 to 4a) (Variable Speed Limits) Regulations 2015 No. 2015/241. - Enabling power: Road Traffic Regulation Act 1984, s. 17 (2) (3). - Issued: 19.02.2015. Made: 13.02.2015. Laid: 19.02.2015. Coming into force: 08.04.2015. Effect: S.I. 2009/1421 amended. Territorial extent & classification: W. Local - 978-0-11-112983-8 £4.25

Road traffic: Speed limits

The A43 Trunk Road (Ardley, Oxfordshire) (50 Miles Per Hour Speed Limit and Derestriction) Order 2015 No. 2015/1224. - Enabling power: Road Traffic Regulation Act 1984, s. 82 (2), 83 (1), 84 (1) (a) (2), 122A, sch. 9, para. 27 (1). - Issued: 24.03.2015. Made: 12.03.2015. Coming into force: 26.03.2015. Effect: S.I. 1993/1917; 2007/342 revoked. Territorial extent & classification: E. Local. - Available at http://www.legislation.gov.uk/uksi/2015/1224/contents/made Non-print

The A49 Trunk Road (The Grove, Craven Arms, Shropshire) (40 Miles Per Hour Speed Limit) Order 2015 No. 2015/1178. - Enabling power: Road Traffic Regulation Act 1984, ss. 84 (1) (a) (2). - Issued: 24.03.2015. Made: 20.02.2015. Coming into force: 06.03.2015. Effect: None. Territorial extent & classification: E. Local. - Available at http://www.legislation.gov.uk/uksi/2015/1178/contents/made Non-print

The A57 Trunk Road (Denton Roundabout)(40 Miles Per Hour Speed Limit) Order 2015 No. 2015/1084. - Enabling power: Road Traffic Regulation Act 1984, ss. 84 (1) (a) (2), 122A. - Issued: 16.04.2015. Made: 09.02.2015. Coming into force: 16.02.2015. Effect: None. Territorial extent & classification: E. Local. - Available at http://www.legislation.gov.uk/uksi/2015/1084/contents/made Non-print

The A453 and A50 Trunk Roads (M1 Junction 24, Kegworth, Leicestershire) (40 and 50 Miles Per Hour Speed Limit and Derestriction) Order 2015 No. 2015/1072. - Enabling power: Road Traffic Regulation Act 1984, s. 82 (2), 83 (1), 84 (1) (a) (2), 122A, sch. 9, para. 27 (1). - Issued: 18.02.2015. Made: 05.02.2015. Coming into force: 19.02.2015. Effect: S.I. 1998/378, 1144 revoked. Territorial extent & classification: E. Local. - Available at http://www.legislation.gov.uk/uksi/2015/1072/contents/made Non-print

Road traffic: Traffic regulation

The A1 and A1(M) Trunk Road (Newark-on-Trent to South of Doncaster) (Temporary Restriction and Prohibition of Traffic) Order 2015 No. 2015/1199. - Enabling power: Road Traffic Regulation Act 1984, s. 14 (1) (a). - Issued: 25.03.2015. Made: 06.03.2015. Coming into force: 13.03.2015. Effect: S.I. 2014/1242 revoked. Territorial extent & classification: E. Local. - Available at http://www.legislation.gov.uk/uksi/2015/1199/contents/made Non-print

The A1(M) and M1 Motorways (A1(M) Junctions 1 and 5, M1 Junctions 1 - 6) (Temporary Restriction and Prohibition of Traffic) Order 2015 No. 2015/1308. - Enabling power: Road Traffic Regulation Act 1984, s. 14 (1) (a). - Issued: 11.05.2015. Made: 16.03.2015. Coming into force: 05.04.2015. Effect: None. Territorial extent & classification: E. Local. - Available at http://www.legislation.gov.uk/uksi/2015/1308/contents/made Non-print

ROAD TRAFFIC: TRAFFIC REGULATION

The A1(M) Motorway (Junction 4 to North of Junction 6) (Temporary Restriction and Prohibition of Traffic) Order 2015 No. 2015/1104. - Enabling power: Road Traffic Regulation Act 1984, s. 14 (1) (a) (7), sch. 9, para. 27 (1) & S.I. 1982/1163, reg. 16 (2). - Issued: 03.03.2015. Made: 16.02.2015. Coming into force: 23.02.2015. Effect: S.I. 2014/2972 revoked. Territorial extent & classification: E. Local. - Available at http://www.legislation.gov.uk/uksi/2015/1104/contents/made Non-print

The A1(M) Motorway (Junction 35 and Junction 37) (Temporary Prohibition of Traffic) Order 2015 No. 2015/745. - Enabling power: Road Traffic Regulation Act 1984, s. 14 (1) (a). - Issued: 03.02.2015. Made: 22.01.2015. Coming into force: 01.02.2015. Effect: None. Territorial extent & classification: E. Local. - Available at http://www.legislation.gov.uk/uksi/2015/745/contents/made Non-print

The A1(M) Motorway (Junction 35 to Junction 37) (Temporary Prohibition of Traffic) Order 2015 No. 2015/1034. - Enabling power: Road Traffic Regulation Act 1984, s. 14 (1) (a). - Issued: 10.02.2015. Made: 29.01.2015. Coming into force: 08.02.2015. Effect: None. Territorial extent & classification: E. Local. - Available at http://www.legislation.gov.uk/uksi/2015/1034/contents/made Non-print

The A1(M) Motorway (Junction 38) (Temporary Prohibition of Traffic) Order 2015 No. 2015/1160. - Enabling power: Road Traffic Regulation Act 1984, s. 14 (1) (a). - Issued: 16.03.2015. Made: 26.02.2015. Coming into force: 08.03.2015. Effect: None. Territorial extent & classification: E. Local. - Available at http://www.legislation.gov.uk/uksi/2015/1160/contents/made Non-print

The A1(M) Motorway (Junction 44) (Temporary Prohibition of Traffic) (No.2) Order 2015 No. 2015/1276. - Enabling power: Road Traffic Regulation Act 1984, s. 14 (1) (a). - Issued: 30.04.2015. Made: 26.03.2015. Coming into force: 06.04.2015. Effect: None. Territorial extent & classification: E. Local. - Available at http://www.legislation.gov.uk/uksi/2015/1276/contents/made Non-print

The A1(M) Motorway (Junction 44) (Temporary Prohibition of Traffic) Order 2015 No. 2015/1151. - Enabling power: Road Traffic Regulation Act 1984, s. 14 (1) (a). - Issued: 06.03.2015. Made: 19.02.2015. Coming into force: 01.03.2015. Effect: None. Territorial extent & classification: E. Local. - Available at http://www.legislation.gov.uk/uksi/2015/1151/contents/made Non-print

The A1(M) Motorway (Junction 56 to Junction 65) (Temporary Restriction and Prohibition of Traffic) Order 2015 No. 2015/148. - Enabling power: Road Traffic Regulation Act 1984, s. 14 (1) (a) & S.I. 1982/1163, reg. 16 (2). - Issued: 28.01.2015. Made: 08.01.2015. Coming into force: 11.01.2015. Effect: None. Territorial extent & classification: E. Local. - Available at http://www.legislation.gov.uk/uksi/2015/148/contents/made Non-print

The A1(M) Motorway (Junction 58 to Junction 59) (Temporary Restriction and Prohibition of Traffic) Order 2015 No. 2015/762. - Enabling power: Road Traffic Regulation Act 1984, s. 14 (1) (a). - Issued: 04.02.2015. Made: 21.01.2015. Coming into force: 01.02.2015. Effect: None. Territorial extent & classification: E. Local. - Available at http://www.legislation.gov.uk/uksi/2015/762/contents/made Non-print

The A1(M) Motorway (Junctions 1 - 3) (Temporary Restriction and Prohibition of Traffic) Order 2015 No. 2015/1051. - Enabling power: Road Traffic Regulation Act 1984, s. 14 (1) (a) (7). - Issued: 03.02.2015. Made: 26.01.2015. Coming into force: 14.02.2015. Effect: None. Territorial extent & classification: E. Local. - Available at http://www.legislation.gov.uk/uksi/2015/1051/contents/made Non-print

The A1 Trunk Road and the A1(M) Motorway (Junctions 1, 3 and 4, Northbound Slip Roads) (Temporary Prohibition of Traffic) Order 2015 No. 2015/1259. - Enabling power: Road Traffic Regulation Act 1984 s. 14 (1) (a). - Issued: 26.03.2015. Made: 23.03.2015. Coming into force: 16.04.2015. Effect: None. Territorial extent & classification: E. Local. - Available at http://www.legislation.gov.uk/uksi/2015/1259/contents/made Non-print

The A1 Trunk Road (Barnsdale Bar to Redhouse Interchange) (Temporary Prohibition of Traffic) Order 2015 No. 2015/1060. - Enabling power: Road Traffic Regulation Act 1984, s. 14 (1) (a). - Issued: 18.02.2015. Made: 05.02.2015. Coming into force: 15.02.2015. Effect: None. Territorial extent & classification: E. Local. - Available at http://www.legislation.gov.uk/uksi/2015/1060/contents/made Non-print

The A1 Trunk Road (Biggleswade, Bedfordshire) (Temporary Restriction and Prohibition of Traffic) Order 2015 No. 2015/156. - Enabling power: Road Traffic Regulation Act 1984, s. 14 (1) (a). - Issued: 28.01.2015. Made: 12.01.2015. Coming into force: 19.01.2015. Effect: None. Territorial extent & classification: E. Local. - Available at http://www.legislation.gov.uk/uksi/2015/156/contents/made Non-print

The A1 Trunk Road (Coddington, Nottinghamshire) (Temporary Prohibition of Traffic) Order 2015 No. 2015/1158. - Enabling power: Road Traffic Regulation Act 1984, s. 14 (1) (a). - Issued: 11.03.2015. Made: 24.02.2015. Coming into force: 03.03.2015. Effect: None. Territorial extent & classification: E. Local. - Available at http://www.legislation.gov.uk/uksi/2015/1158/contents/made Non-print

The A1 Trunk Road (Denton Burn Interchange) (Temporary Prohibition of Traffic) Order 2015 No. 2015/1248. - Enabling power: Road Traffic Regulation Act 1984, s. 14 (1) (a). - Issued: 24.04.2015. Made: 26.02.2015. Coming into force: 08.03.2015. Effect: None. Territorial extent & classification: E. Local. - Available at http://www.legislation.gov.uk/uksi/2015/1248/contents/made Non-print

The A1 Trunk Road (Derwenthaugh to Eighton Lodge) (Temporary Restriction and Prohibition of Traffic) Order 2014 Amendment Order 2015 No. 2015/684. - Enabling power: Road Traffic Regulation Act 1984, ss. 14 (1) (a), 15 (2). - Issued: 02.02.2015. Made: 22.01.2015. Coming into force: 30.01.2015. Effect: None. Territorial extent & classification: E. Local. - Available at http://www.legislation.gov.uk/uksi/2015/684/contents/made Non-print

The A1 Trunk Road (Detchant Lodge to Cragmill Road) (Temporary Restriction and Prohibition of Traffic) Order 2015 No. 2015/1220. - Enabling power: Road Traffic Regulation Act 1984, s. 14 (1) (a). - Issued: 24.03.2015. Made: 12.03.2015. Coming into force: 21.03.2015. Effect: None. Territorial extent & classification: E. Local. - Available at http://www.legislation.gov.uk/uksi/2015/1220/contents/made Non-print

The A1 Trunk Road (Duns Road Junction to East Ord Roundabout) (Temporary Restriction and Prohibition of Traffic) Order 2015 No. 2015/1245. - Enabling power: Road Traffic Regulation Act 1984, s. 14 (1) (a). - Issued: 24.04.2015. Made: 19.02.2015. Coming into force: 01.05.2015. Effect: None. Territorial extent & classification: E. Local. - Available at http://www.legislation.gov.uk/uksi/2015/1245/contents/made Non-print

The A1 Trunk Road (Fletton Parkway Interchange, City of Peterborough) Southbound Exit Slip Road (Temporary Prohibition of Traffic) Order 2015 No. 2015/155. - Enabling power: Road Traffic Regulation Act 1984, s. 14 (1) (a). - Issued: 28.01.2015. Made: 12.01.2015. Coming into force: 19.01.2015. Effect: None. Territorial extent & classification: E. Local. - Available at http://www.legislation.gov.uk/uksi/2015/155/contents/made Non-print

The A1 Trunk Road (Gosforth Park Northbound Layby) (Prohibition of Waiting) Order 2015 No. 2015/764. - Enabling power: Road Traffic Regulation Act 1984, s. 1 (1), 2 (1) (2). - Issued: 30.01.2015. Made: 19.01.2015. Coming into force: 02.02.2015. Effect: None. Territorial extent & classification: E. Local. - Available at http://www.legislation.gov.uk/uksi/2015/764/contents/made Non-print

The A1 Trunk Road (Hitchcroft to Denwick) (Temporary Restriction and Prohibition of Traffic) Order 2015 No. 2015/757. - Enabling power: Road Traffic Regulation Act 1984, s. 14 (1) (a) (7). - Issued: 03.02.2015. Made: 22.01.2015. Coming into force: 01.02.2015. Effect: None. Territorial extent & classification: E. Local. - Available at http://www.legislation.gov.uk/uksi/2015/757/contents/made Non-print

The A1 Trunk Road (Laybys between Westerhope and Kenton Bar) (Temporary Prohibition of Traffic) Order 2015 No. 2015/1185. - Enabling power: Road Traffic Regulation Act 1984, ss. 14 (1) (a). - Issued: 20.03.2015. Made: 05.03.2015. Coming into force: 15.03.2015. Effect: None. Territorial extent & classification: E. Local. - Available at http://www.legislation.gov.uk/uksi/2015/1185/contents/made Non-print

The A1 Trunk Road (North Brunton to Seaton Burn) (Temporary Restriction and Prohibition of Traffic) Order 2015 No. 2015/756. - Enabling power: Road Traffic Regulation Act 1984, s. 14 (1) (a). - Issued: 03.02.2015. Made: 22.01.2015. Coming into force: 01.02.2015. Effect: None. Territorial extent & classification: E. Local. - Available at http://www.legislation.gov.uk/uksi/2015/756/contents/made Non-print

ROAD TRAFFIC: TRAFFIC REGULATION

The A1 Trunk Road (Ranby, Nottinghamshire) (Temporary Prohibition of Traffic) Order 2015 No. 2015/1168. - Enabling power: Road Traffic Regulation Act 1984, s. 14 (1) (a). - Issued: 25.03.2015. Made: 02.03.2015. Coming into force: 09.03.2015. Effect: None. Territorial extent & classification: E. Local. - Available at http://www.legislation.gov.uk/uksi/2015/1168/contents/made Non-print

The A1 Trunk Road (Shotton Interchange to Clifton Interchange) (Temporary Restriction and Prohibition of Traffic) Order 2015 No. 2015/1114. - Enabling power: Road Traffic Regulation Act 1984, s. 14 (1) (a). - Issued: 24.02.2015. Made: 12.02.2015. Coming into force: 25.02.2015. Effect: None. Territorial extent & classification: E. Local. - Available at http://www.legislation.gov.uk/uksi/2015/1114/contents/made Non-print

The A1 Trunk Road (Shotton Interchange to Highfields Roundabout) (Temporary Restriction and Prohibition of Traffic) Order 2015 No. 2015/1021. - Enabling power: Road Traffic Regulation Act 1984, s. 14 (1) (a). - Issued: 12.02.2015. Made: 29.01.2015. Coming into force: 07.02.2015. Effect: None. Territorial extent & classification: E. Local. - Available at http://www.legislation.gov.uk/uksi/2015/1021/contents/made Non-print

The A2 Trunk Road (Dover Road, A260 - A2050) (Temporary Prohibition of Traffic) Order 2015 No. 2015/529. - Enabling power: Road Traffic Regulation Act 1984, s. 14 (1) (a). - Issued: 25.02.2015. Made: 16.02.2015. Coming into force: 09.03.2015. Effect: None. Territorial extent & classification: E. Local. - Available at http://www.legislation.gov.uk/uksi/2015/529/contents/made Non-print

The A3 Trunk Road (Hawkley Road - Ham Barn Roundabout (Footpath/Cycle track)) (Temporary Prohibition of Traffic) Order 2015 No. 2015/1179. - Enabling power: Road Traffic Regulation Act 1984, s. 14 (1) (a). - Issued: 11.03.2015. Made: 16.02.2015. Coming into force: 07.03.2015. Effect: None. Territorial extent & classification: E. Local. - Available at http://www.legislation.gov.uk/uksi/2015/1179/contents/made Non-print

The A3 Trunk Road (Queen Elizabeth Country Park, Lay-by Closure) (Temporary Prohibition of Traffic) Order 2015 No. 2015/1128. - Enabling power: Road Traffic Regulation Act 1984, s. 14 (1) (a). - Issued: 23.02.2015. Made: 09.02.2015. Coming into force: 28.02.2015. Effect: None. Territorial extent & classification: E. Local. - Available at http://www.legislation.gov.uk/uksi/2015/1128/contents/made Non-print

The A4 Trunk Road (Crowley Way, Avonmouth) and the M5 Motorway (Junction 18 'U' and 'W' Loops) (Temporary Prohibition of Traffic) Order 2015 No. 2015/1113. - Enabling power: Road Traffic Regulation Act 1984, s. 14 (1) (a). - Issued: 04.03.2015. Made: 19.02.2015. Coming into force: 24.02.2015. Effect: None. Territorial extent & classification: E. Local. - Available at http://www.legislation.gov.uk/uksi/2015/1113/contents/made Non-print

The A5 Trunk Road (A505 Dunstable, Central Bedfordshire to Flamstead, Hertfordshire) (Temporary Restriction and Prohibition of Traffic) No. 2015/332. - Enabling power: Road Traffic Regulation Act 1984, s. 14 (1) (a). - Issued: 02.02.2015. Made: 19.01.2015. Coming into force: 26.01.2015. Effect: None. Territorial extent & classification: E. Local. - Available at http://www.legislation.gov.uk/uksi/2015/332/contents/made Non-print

The A5 Trunk Road (Crick, Northamptonshire) (Temporary Restriction and Prohibition of Traffic) Order 2015 No. 2015/1176. - Enabling power: Road Traffic Regulation Act 1984, s. 14 (1) (a). - Issued: 13.03.2015. Made: 23.02.2015. Coming into force: 02.03.2015. Effect: None. Territorial extent & classification: E. Local. - Available at http://www.legislation.gov.uk/uksi/2015/1176/contents/made Non-print

The A5 Trunk Road (Hinckley, Leicestershire) (Temporary Prohibition of Traffic) Order 2015 No. 2015/1095. - Enabling power: Road Traffic Regulation Act 1984, s. 14 (1) (a). - Issued: 25.02.2015. Made: 16.02.2015. Coming into force: 23.02.2015. Effect: None. Territorial extent & classification: E. Local. - Available at http://www.legislation.gov.uk/uksi/2015/1095/contents/made Non-print

The A5 Trunk Road (Muckley Corner, Staffordshire) (Temporary Prohibition of Traffic) Order 2015 No. 2015/1202. - Enabling power: Road Traffic Regulation Act 1984, s. 14 (1) (a). - Issued: 20.04.2015. Made: 16.03.2015. Coming into force: 23.03.2015. Effect: None. Territorial extent & classification: E. Local. - Available at http://www.legislation.gov.uk/uksi/2015/1202/contents/made Non-print

The A5 Trunk Road (North Dunstable, Bedfordshire) (Temporary Restriction and Prohibition of Traffic) Order 2015 No. 2015/1236. - Enabling power: Road Traffic Regulation Act 1984, s. 14 (1) (a). - Issued: 26.03.2015. Made: 23.03.2015. Coming into force: 30.03.2015. Effect: None. Territorial extent & classification: E. Local. - Available at http://www.legislation.gov.uk/uksi/2015/1236/contents/made Non-print

The A5 Trunk Road (Wolfshead to Queen's Head, Shropshire) (Temporary Prohibition of Traffic) Order 2015 No. 2015/277. - Enabling power: Road Traffic Regulation Act 1984, s. 14 (1) (a). - Issued: 02.02.2015. Made: 19.01.2015. Coming into force: 26.01.2015. Effect: None. Territorial extent & classification: E. Local. - Available at http://www.legislation.gov.uk/uksi/2015/277/contents/made Non-print

The A11 Trunk Road (B1085 Red Lodge Interchange (South), Suffolk) and the A14 Trunk Road (West of Waterhall Interchange Junction 38), Cambridgeshire (Temporary 50 Miles Per Hour Speed Restriction) Order 2015 No. 2015/1041. - Enabling power: Road Traffic Regulation Act 1984, s. 14 (1) (a). - Issued: 12.02.2015. Made: 02.02.2015. Coming into force: 09.02.2015. Effect: None. Territorial extent & classification: E. Local. - Available at http://www.legislation.gov.uk/uksi/2015/1041/contents/made Non-print

The A11 Trunk Road (Fulbourn, Cambridgeshire) Exit Slip Roads (Temporary Prohibition of Traffic) Order 2015 No. 2015/160. - Enabling power: Road Traffic Regulation Act 1984, s. 14 (1) (a). - Issued: 28.01.2015. Made: 12.01.2015. Coming into force: 19.01.2015. Effect: None. Territorial extent & classification: E. Local. - Available at http://www.legislation.gov.uk/uksi/2015/160/contents/made Non-print

The A12 Trunk Road (Bascule Bridge, Lowestoft, Suffolk) (Temporary Prohibition of Traffic and Pedestrians) Order 2015 No. 2015/1123. - Enabling power: Road Traffic Regulation Act 1984, s. 14 (1) (a). - Issued: 20.04.2015. Made: 16.02.2015. Coming into force: 23.02.2015. Effect: None. Territorial extent & classification: E. Local. - Available at http://www.legislation.gov.uk/uksi/2015/1123/contents/made Non-print

The A12 Trunk Road (Junction 11 Brook Street Interchange to Junction 15 Webbs Farm Interchange) Essex (Temporary Restriction and Prohibition of Traffic) Order 2014 Variation Order 2015 No. 2015/1274. - Enabling power: Road Traffic Regulation Act 1984, s. 14 (1) (a). sch. 9, para. 27 (1). - Issued: 29.04.2015. Made: 20.03.2015. Coming into force: 27.03.2015. Effect: None. Territorial extent & classification: E. Local. - Available at http://www.legislation.gov.uk/uksi/2015/1274/contents/made Non-print

The A12 Trunk Road (Junction 12 Marylands Interchange to Junction 14 Furze Hill Interchange, Essex) (Temporary Restriction and Prohibition of Traffic) Order 2015 No. 2015/1069. - Enabling power: Road Traffic Regulation Act 1984, s. 14 (1) (a). - Issued: 24.02.2015. Made: 09.02.2015. Coming into force: 16.02.2015. Effect: None. Territorial extent & classification: E. Local. - Available at http://www.legislation.gov.uk/uksi/2015/1069/contents/made Non-print

The A12 Trunk Road (Junction 16 Stock Road Interchange, Galleywood, Chelmsford, Essex) Exit Slip Roads (Temporary Prohibition of Traffic) Order 2015 No. 2015/1102. - Enabling power: Road Traffic Regulation Act 1984, s. 14 (1) (a). - Issued: 03.03.2015. Made: 16.02.2015. Coming into force: 23.02.2015. Effect: None. Territorial extent & classification: E. Local. - Available at http://www.legislation.gov.uk/uksi/2015/1102/contents/made Non-print

The A12 Trunk Road (Junction 21 Witham South to Junction 24 Kelvedon North, Braintree) Essex (Temporary Prohibition of Traffic) Order 2015 No. 2015/1195. - Enabling power: Road Traffic Regulation Act 1984, s. 14 (1) (a). - Issued: 19.03.2015. Made: 02.03.2015. Coming into force: 09.03.2015. Effect: S.I. 2014/3447 amended. Territorial extent & classification: E. Local. - Available at http://www.legislation.gov.uk/uksi/2015/1195/contents/made Non-print

ROAD TRAFFIC: TRAFFIC REGULATION

The A12 Trunk Road (Marks Tey, Colchester, Essex) (Temporary Restriction and Prohibition of Traffic) Order 2015 No. 2015/765. - Enabling power: Road Traffic Regulation Act 1984, s. 14 (1) (a). - Issued: 06.02.2015. Made: 26.01.2015. Coming into force: 02.02.2015. Effect: None. Territorial extent & classification: E. Local. - Available at http://www.legislation.gov.uk/uksi/2015/765/contents/made Non-print

The A12 Trunk Road (Old London Road, Marks Tey, Essex) (Prohibition and Restriction of Waiting) Order 2015 No. 2015/1243. - Enabling power: Road Traffic Regulation Act 1984, s. 1 (1), 2 (1) (2), 4 (1) (2). - Issued: 24.04.2015. Made: 13.02.2015. Coming into force: 27.02.2015. Effect: None. Territorial extent & classification: E. Local. - Available at http://www.legislation.gov.uk/uksi/2015/1243/contents/made Non-print

The A13 Trunk Road (Wennington Interchange - Stifford Interchange) (Temporary Restriction and Prohibition of Traffic) Order 2015 No. 2015/250. - Enabling power: Road Traffic Regulation Act 1984, s. 14 (1) (a). - Issued: 16.02.2015. Made: 05.01.2015. Coming into force: 24.01.2015. Effect: None. Territorial extent & classification: E. Local. - Available at http://www.legislation.gov.uk/uksi/2015/250/contents/made Non-print

The A14 Trunk Road (Junction 16 Catworth to Junction 24 Godmanchester) and the A1(M) Motorway (Junction 14 to Junction 16) Cambridgeshire (Temporary Restriction and Prohibition of Traffic) Order 2015 No. 2015/835. - Enabling power: Road Traffic Regulation Act 1984, s. 14 (1) (a). - Issued: 06.02.2015. Made: 26.01.2015. Coming into force: 02.02.2015. Effect: None. Territorial extent & classification: E. Local. - Available at http://www.legislation.gov.uk/uksi/2015/835/contents/made Non-print

The A14 Trunk Road (Junction 47 Woolpit Interchange, Suffolk) Slip Roads (Temporary Prohibition of Traffic) Order 2015 No. 2015/158. - Enabling power: Road Traffic Regulation Act 1984, s. 14 (1) (a). - Issued: 28.01.2015. Made: 12.01.2015. Coming into force: 19.01.2015. Effect: None. Territorial extent & classification: E. Local. - Available at http://www.legislation.gov.uk/uksi/2015/158/contents/made Non-print

The A14 Trunk Road (Junction 49 Tot Hill to Junction 58 Levington) Suffolk (Temporary Restriction and Prohibition of Traffic) Order 2015 No. 2015/834. - Enabling power: Road Traffic Regulation Act 1984, s. 14 (1) (a) (7). - Issued: 06.02.2015. Made: 26.01.2015. Coming into force: 02.02.2015. Effect: None. Territorial extent & classification: E. Local. - Available at http://www.legislation.gov.uk/uksi/2015/834/contents/made Non-print

The A14 Trunk Road (Kettering to Thrapston, Northamptonshire) (Temporary Restriction and Prohibition of Traffic) Order 2015 No. 2015/1177. - Enabling power: Road Traffic Regulation Act 1984, s. 14 (1) (a). - Issued: 13.03.2015. Made: 24.02.2015. Coming into force: 03.03.2015. Effect: None. Territorial extent & classification: E. Local. - Available at http://www.legislation.gov.uk/uksi/2015/1177/contents/made Non-print

The A19 Trunk Road and the A66 Trunk Road (Stockton Road Interchange) (Temporary Prohibition of Traffic) Order 2015 No. 2015/736. - Enabling power: Road Traffic Regulation Act 1984, s. 14 (1) (a). - Issued: 02.02.2015. Made: 22.01.2015. Coming into force: 01.02.2015. Effect: None. Territorial extent & classification: E. Local. - Available at http://www.legislation.gov.uk/uksi/2015/736/contents/made Non-print

The A19 Trunk Road (Howden Interchange to Coast Road Interchange) (Temporary Prohibition of Traffic) Order 2015 No. 2015/1071. - Enabling power: Road Traffic Regulation Act 1984, s. 14 (1) (a). - Issued: 18.02.2015. Made: 05.02.2015. Coming into force: 18.02.2015. Effect: None. Territorial extent & classification: E. Local. - Available at http://www.legislation.gov.uk/uksi/2015/1071/contents/made Non-print

The A19 Trunk Road (Osmotherley) (Temporary Prohibition of Traffic) Order 2015 No. 2015/1091. - Enabling power: Road Traffic Regulation Act 1984, s. 14 (1) (a). - Issued: 24.02.2015. Made: 12.02.2015. Coming into force: 22.02.2015. Effect: None. Territorial extent & classification: E. Local. - Available at http://www.legislation.gov.uk/uksi/2015/1091/contents/made Non-print

The A19 Trunk Road (Seaton Burn Interchange to Howdon Interchange) (Temporary Prohibition of Traffic) Order 2015 No. 2015/1005. - Enabling power: Road Traffic Regulation Act 1984, s. 14 (1) (a). - Issued: 13.02.2015. Made: 29.01.2015. Coming into force: 05.02.2015. Effect: None. Territorial extent & classification: E. Local. - Available at http://www.legislation.gov.uk/uksi/2015/1005/contents/made Non-print

The A19 Trunk Road (Silverlink Interchange to Holystone Interchange) (Temporary Restriction and Prohibition of Traffic) Order 2015 No. 2015/252. - Enabling power: Road Traffic Regulation Act 1984, s. 14 (1) (a). - Issued: 29.01.2014. Made: 15.01.2015. Coming into force: 25.01.2015. Effect: None. Territorial extent & classification: E. Local. - Available at http://www.legislation.gov.uk/uksi/2015/252/contents/made Non-print

The A21 Trunk Road (Pembury Road, Near Tonbridge) (Temporary Restriction and Prohibition of Traffic) Order 2015 No. 2015/1226. - Enabling power: Road Traffic Regulation Act 1984, s. 14 (1) (a), 15 (2), sch. 9, para. 27 (1). - Issued: 23.03.2015. Made: 09.03.2015. Coming into force: 28.03.2015. Effect: None. Territorial extent & classification: E. Local. - Available at http://www.legislation.gov.uk/uksi/2015/1226/contents/made Non-print

The A27, M27 and A3(M) Motorways (A27 Harts Farm Way Junction - M27 Junction 12) (Temporary Prohibition of Traffic) Order 2015 No. 2015/1244. - Enabling power: Road Traffic Regulation Act 1984, s. 14 (1) (a). - Issued: 24.04.2015. Made: 09.02.2015. Coming into force: 28.02.2015. Effect: None. Territorial extent & classification: E. Local. - Available at http://www.legislation.gov.uk/uksi/2015/1244/contents/made Non-print

The A27 Trunk Road (Holmbush Interchange - Hangleton Interchange, Southwick Tunnel) (Temporary Prohibition of Traffic) Order 2015 No. 2015/702. - Enabling power: Road Traffic Regulation Act 1984, s. 14 (1) (a). - Issued: 28018.2015. Made: 12.01.2015. Coming into force: 31.01.2015. Effect: None. Territorial extent & classification: E. Local. - Available at http://www.legislation.gov.uk/uksi/2015/702/contents/made Non-print

The A27 Trunk Road (Holmbush Interchange to Hangleton) (Temporary Prohibition of Traffic) Order 2015 No. 2015/1212. - Enabling power: Road Traffic Regulation Act 1984, s. 14 (1) (a). - Issued: 23.03.2015. Made: 09.03.2015. Coming into force: 01.04.2015. Effect: None. Territorial extent & classification: E. Local. - Available at http://www.legislation.gov.uk/uksi/2015/1212/contents/made Non-print

The A30 Trunk Road (Bodmin) (Temporary Restriction and Prohibition of Traffic) Order 2015 No. 2015/1122. - Enabling power: Road Traffic Regulation Act 1984, s. 14 (1) (a). - Issued: 06.03.2015. Made: 24.02.2015. Coming into force: 27.02.2015. Effect: None. Territorial extent & classification: E. Local. - Available at http://www.legislation.gov.uk/uksi/2015/1122/contents/made Non-print

The A30 Trunk Road (Bolventor, Cornwall) (Temporary Restriction and Prohibition of Traffic) Order 2015 No. 2015/149. - Enabling power: Road Traffic Regulation Act 1984, s. 14 (1) (a). - Issued: 28.01.2015. Made: 06.01.2015. Coming into force: 13.01.2015. Effect: None. Territorial extent & classification: E. Local. - Available at http://www.legislation.gov.uk/uksi/2015/149/contents/made Non-print

The A30 Trunk Road (Lifton to Sourton Cross) (Temporary Restriction and Prohibition of Traffic) Order 2015 No. 2015/1023. - Enabling power: Road Traffic Regulation Act 1984, s. 14 (1) (a). - Issued: 17.02.2015. Made: 04.02.2015. Coming into force: 07.02.2015. Effect: None. Territorial extent & classification: E. Local. - Available at http://www.legislation.gov.uk/uksi/2015/1023/contents/made Non-print

The A30 Trunk Road (M5 Junction 31 to Alphington) (Temporary Restriction and Prohibition of Traffic) Order 2015 No. 2015/1203. - Enabling power: Road Traffic Regulation Act 1984, s. 14 (1) (a). - Issued: 23.03.2015. Made: 10.03.2015. Coming into force: 14.03.2015. Effect: None. Territorial extent & classification: E. Local. - Available at http://www.legislation.gov.uk/uksi/2015/1203/contents/made Non-print

The A30 Trunk Road (M25 Junction 13, Link Road) (Temporary Prohibition of Traffic) Order 2015 No. 2015/1214. - Enabling power: Road Traffic Regulation Act 1984, s. 14 (1) (a). - Issued: 23.03.2015. Made: 09.03.2015. Coming into force: 02.04.2015. Effect: None. Territorial extent & classification: E. Local. - Available at http://www.legislation.gov.uk/uksi/2015/1214/contents/made Non-print

The A30 Trunk Road (Tavistock Road Junction, Launceston) (Temporary Prohibition of Traffic) Order 2015 No. 2015/1129. - Enabling power: Road Traffic Regulation Act 1984, s. 14 (1) (a). - Issued: 06.03.2015. Made: 24.02.2015. Coming into force: 28.02.2015. Effect: None. Territorial extent & classification: E. Local. - Available at http://www.legislation.gov.uk/uksi/2015/1129/contents/made Non-print

ROAD TRAFFIC: TRAFFIC REGULATION

The A30 Trunk Road (Whiddon Down to Tongue End Cross) (Temporary Restriction and Prohibition of Traffic) Order 2015 No. 2015/153. - Enabling power: Road Traffic Regulation Act 1984, s. 14 (1) (a). - Issued: 28.01.2015. Made: 14.01.2015. Coming into force: 17.01.2015. Effect: None. Territorial extent & classification: E. Local. - Available at http://www.legislation.gov.uk/uksi/2015/153/contents/made Non-print

The A31 Trunk Road (Cadnam - Verwood Interchange) (Temporary Restriction and Prohibition of Traffic) Order 2015 No. 2015/556. - Enabling power: Road Traffic Regulation Act 1984, s. 14 (1) (a). - Issued: 24.02.2015. Made: 09.02.2015. Coming into force: 05.03.2015. Effect: None. Territorial extent & classification: Local. - Available at http://www.legislation.gov.uk/uksi/2015/556/contents/made Non-print

The A31 Trunk Road (Near Ringwood) (Temporary Prohibition of Traffic) Order 2015 No. 2015/1206. - Enabling power: Road Traffic Regulation Act 1984, s. 14 (1) (a). - Issued: 20.03.2015. Made: 09.03.2015. Coming into force: 28.03.2015. Effect: None. Territorial extent & classification: E. Local. - Available at http://www.legislation.gov.uk/uksi/2015/1206/contents/made Non-print

The A31 Trunk Road (Palmersford Roundabout - Canford Bottom Roundabout) (Temporary Prohibition of Traffic) Order 2015 No. 2015/1017. - Enabling power: Road Traffic Regulation Act 1984, s. 14 (1) (a). - Issued: 30.01.2015. Made: 19.01.2015. Coming into force: 07.02.2015. Effect: None. Territorial extent & classification: E. Local. - Available at http://www.legislation.gov.uk/uksi/2015/1017/contents/made Non-print

The A31 Trunk Road (Rufus Stone Road) (Temporary Prohibition of Traffic) Order 2015 No. 2015/260. - Enabling power: Road Traffic Regulation Act 1984, s. 14 (1) (a). - Issued: 13.02.2015. Made: 02.02.2015. Coming into force: 23.02.2015. Effect: None. Territorial extent & classification: E. Local. - Available at http://www.legislation.gov.uk/uksi/2015/260/contents/made Non-print

The A31 Trunk Road (Verwood Interchange - Bere Regis Roundabout) (Temporary Restriction and Prohibition of Traffic) Order 2015 No. 2015/528. - Enabling power: Road Traffic Regulation Act 1984, s. 14 (1) (a). - Issued: 28.02.2015. Made: 16.02.2015. Coming into force: 12.03.2015. Effect: None. Territorial extent & classification: E. Local. - Available at http://www.legislation.gov.uk/uksi/2015/528/contents/made Non-print

The A34 Trunk Road (East Ilsley Interchange - Abingdon North Interchange) (Temporary Restriction and Prohibition of Traffic) (Amendment) Order 2015 No. 2015/1087. - Enabling power: Road Traffic Regulation Act 1984, s. 14 (1) (a). - Issued: 17.04.2015. Made: 17.02.2015. Coming into force: 20.02.2015. Effect: S.I. 2014/3434 amended. Territorial extent & classification: E. Local. - Available at http://www.legislation.gov.uk/uksi/2015/1087/contents/made Non-print

The A34 Trunk Road (Hinksey Hill Interchange- A44 Peartree Interchange) (Temporary Prohibition of Traffic) Order 2015 No. 2015/1054. - Enabling power: Road Traffic Regulation Act 1984, s. 14 (1) (a). - Issued: 04.02.2015. Made: 26.01.2015. Coming into force: 14.02.2015. Effect: None. Territorial extent & classification: E. Local. - Available at http://www.legislation.gov.uk/uksi/2015/1054/contents/made Non-print

The A34 Trunk Road (M4 Junction 13 - Milton Interchange) (Temporary Restriction and Prohibition of Traffic) Order 2015 No. 2015/1225. - Enabling power: Road Traffic Regulation Act 1984, s. 14 (1) (a). - Issued: 20.03.2015. Made: 09.03.2015. Coming into force: 28.03.2015. Effect: None. Territorial extent & classification: E. Local. - Available at http://www.legislation.gov.uk/uksi/2015/1225/contents/made Non-print

The A34 Trunk Road (M40 Junction 9 - West Ilsley) (Temporary Restriction and Prohibition of Traffic) Order 2015 No. 2015/1258. - Enabling power: Road Traffic Regulation Act 1984, s. 14 (1) (a). - Issued: 26.03.2015. Made: 23.03.2015. Coming into force: 16.04.2015. Effect: None. Territorial extent & classification: E. Local. - Available at http://www.legislation.gov.uk/uksi/2015/1258/contents/made Non-print

The A34 Trunk Road (Milton Interchange - Chieveley Interchange) (Temporary Prohibition of Traffic) Order 2015 No. 2015/1055. - Enabling power: Road Traffic Regulation Act 1984, s. 14 (1) (a). - Issued: 04.02.2015. Made: 26.01.2015. Coming into force: 14.02.2015. Effect: None. Territorial extent & classification: E. Local. - Available at http://www.legislation.gov.uk/uksi/2015/1055/contents/made Non-print

The A34 Trunk Road (Near Oxford) (Temporary Prohibition of Traffic) Order 2015 No. 2015/1211. - Enabling power: Road Traffic Regulation Act 1984, s. 14 (1) (a). - Issued: 20.03.2015. Made: 09.03.2015. Coming into force: 28.03.2015. Effect: None. Territorial extent & classification: Local. - Available at http://www.legislation.gov.uk/uksi/2015/1211/contents/made Non-print

The A34 Trunk Road (Tufton Interchange, Slip Roads) (Temporary Prohibition of Traffic) Order 2015 No. 2015/1304. - Enabling power: Road Traffic Regulation Act 1984, s. 14 (1) (a). - Issued: 08.05.2015. Made: 09.03.2015. Coming into force: 28.03.2015. Effect: None. Territorial extent & classification: E. Local. - Available at http://www.legislation.gov.uk/uksi/2015/1304/contents/made Non-print

The A35 Trunk Road (Bere Regis to Puddletown, Dorset) (Temporary Prohibition of Traffic) Order 2015 No. 2015/1089. - Enabling power: Road Traffic Regulation Act 1984, s. 14 (1) (a). - Issued: 03.03.2015. Made: 18.02.2015. Coming into force: 21.02.2015. Effect: None. Territorial extent & classification: E. Local. - Available at http://www.legislation.gov.uk/uksi/2015/1089/contents/made Non-print

The A36 Trunk Road (Claverton to Dundas) (Temporary Restriction and Prohibition of Traffic) Order 2015 No. 2015/1121. - Enabling power: Road Traffic Regulation Act 1984, s. 14 (1) (a). - Issued: 06.03.2015. Made: 24.02.2015. Coming into force: 27.02.2015. Effect: None. Territorial extent & classification: E. Local. - Available at http://www.legislation.gov.uk/uksi/2015/1121/contents/made Non-print

The A36 Trunk Road (South Newton, Near Salisbury) (Temporary Restriction of Traffic) Order 2015 No. 2015/709. - Enabling power: Road Traffic Regulation Act 1984, s. 14 (1) (a). - Issued: 04.02.2015. Made: 27.01.2015. Coming into force: 31.01.2015. Effect: None. Territorial extent & classification: E. Local. - Available at http://www.legislation.gov.uk/uksi/2015/709/contents/made Non-print

The A38 and A50 Trunk Roads (Willington, Derbyshire) (Temporary Prohibition of Traffic) Order 2015 No. 2015/1162. - Enabling power: Road Traffic Regulation Act 1984, s. 14 (1) (a). - Issued: 13.03.2015. Made: 26.02.2015. Coming into force: 03.03.2015. Effect: None. Territorial extent & classification: E. Local. - Available at http://www.legislation.gov.uk/uksi/2015/1162/contents/made Non-print

The A38 Trunk Road (Alfreton, Derbyshire) (Temporary Prohibition of Traffic) Order 2015 No. 2015/161. - Enabling power: Road Traffic Regulation Act 1984, s. 14 (1) (a). - Issued: 29.01.2015. Made: 12.01.2015. Coming into force: 19.01.2015. Effect: None. Territorial extent & classification: E. Local. - Available at http://www.legislation.gov.uk/uksi/2015/161/contents/made Non-print

The A38 Trunk Road (Chudleigh Station and Lower Dean Junctions, Devon) (Temporary Prohibition of Traffic) Order 2015 No. 2015/1130. - Enabling power: Road Traffic Regulation Act 1984, s. 14 (1) (a). - Issued: 13.03.2015. Made: 25.02.2015. Coming into force: 28.02.2015. Effect: None. Territorial extent & classification: E. Local. - Available at http://www.legislation.gov.uk/uksi/2015/1130/contents/made Non-print

The A38 Trunk Road (Hilliard's Cross, Staffordshire) (Temporary Prohibition of Traffic) Order 2015 No. 2015/248. - Enabling power: Road Traffic Regulation Act 1984, s. 14 (1) (a). - Issued: 17.02.2015. Made: 05.01.2015. Coming into force: 12.01.2015. Effect: None. Territorial extent & classification: E. Local. - Available at http://www.legislation.gov.uk/uksi/2015/248/contents/made Non-print

The A38 Trunk Road (Largin Wood, Near Dobwalls) (Temporary Prohibition of Traffic) Order 2015 No. 2015/1125. - Enabling power: Road Traffic Regulation Act 1984, s. 14 (1) (a). - Issued: 09.03.2015. Made: 24.02.2015. Coming into force: 27.02.2015. Effect: None. Territorial extent & classification: E. Local. - Available at http://www.legislation.gov.uk/uksi/2015/1125/contents/made Non-print

ROAD TRAFFIC: TRAFFIC REGULATION

The A38 Trunk Road (Little Eaton, Derbyshire) (Temporary Prohibition of Traffic) Order 2015 No. 2015/1187. - Enabling power: Road Traffic Regulation Act 1984, s. 14 (1) (a). - Issued: 25.03.2015. Made: 09.03.2015. Coming into force: 16.03.2015. Effect: None. Territorial extent & classification: E. Local. - Available at http://www.legislation.gov.uk/uksi/2015/1187/contents/made Non-print

The A38 Trunk Road (South Normanton, Derbyshire) (Temporary Prohibition of Traffic) Order 2015 No. 2015/1126. - Enabling power: Road Traffic Regulation Act 1984, s. 14 (1) (a). - Issued: 11.03.2015. Made: 20.02.2015. Coming into force: 27.02.2015. Effect: None. Territorial extent & classification: E. Local. - Available at http://www.legislation.gov.uk/uksi/2015/1126/contents/made Non-print

The A40 Trunk Road (Denham Court Drive, Denham) (Temporary Prohibition of Traffic) Order 2015 No. 2015/1204. - Enabling power: Road Traffic Regulation Act 1984, s. 14 (1) (b). - Issued: 18.03.2015. Made: 02.03.2015. Coming into force: 24.03.2015. Effect: None. Territorial extent & classification: E. Local. - Available at http://www.legislation.gov.uk/uksi/2015/1204/contents/made Non-print

The A40 Trunk Road (Elmbridge Court Roundabout to Arle Court Roundabout, Gloucestershire) (Temporary Prohibition of Traffic) Order 2015 No. 2015/1049. - Enabling power: Road Traffic Regulation Act 1984, s. 14 (1) (a). - Issued: 18.02.2015. Made: 04.02.2015. Coming into force: 10.02.2015. Effect: None. Territorial extent & classification: E. Local. - Available at http://www.legislation.gov.uk/uksi/2015/1049/contents/made Non-print

The A40 Trunk Road (Huntley to Highnam) (Temporary Prohibition of Traffic) Order 2015 No. 2015/1247. - Enabling power: Road Traffic Regulation Act 1984, s. 14 (1) (a). - Issued: 27.04.2015. Made: 27.02.2015. Coming into force: 07.03.2015. Effect: None. Territorial extent & classification: E. Local. - Available at http://www.legislation.gov.uk/uksi/2015/1247/contents/made Non-print

The A40 Trunk Road (Over Roundabout, Gloucestershire) (Temporary Prohibition of Traffic) Order 2015 No. 2015/1184. - Enabling power: Road Traffic Regulation Act 1984, s. 14 (1) (a). - Issued: 20.03.2015. Made: 09.03.2015. Coming into force: 14.03.2015. Effect: None. Territorial extent & classification: E. Local. - Available at http://www.legislation.gov.uk/uksi/2015/1184/contents/made Non-print

The A41 Trunk Road (Chester Road) Northbound and Southbound Carriageways (Temporary Prohibition of Traffic) Order 2015 No. 2015/530. - Enabling power: Road Traffic Regulation Act 1984, s. 14 (1) (a). - Issued: 09.03.2015. Made: 19.02.2015. Coming into force: 08.03.2015. Effect: None. Territorial extent & classification: E. Local. - Available at http://www.legislation.gov.uk/uksi/2015/530/contents/made Non-print

The A42 Trunk Road (A42 to M1 Junction 23a, Leicestershire) (Temporary Restriction and Prohibition of Traffic) Order 2015 No. 2015/1127. - Enabling power: Road Traffic Regulation Act 1984, s. 14 (1) (a). - Issued: 13.03.2015. Made: 20.02.2015. Coming into force: 27.02.2015. Effect: None. Territorial extent & classification: E. Local. - Available at http://www.legislation.gov.uk/uksi/2015/1127/contents/made Non-print

The A43 Trunk Road and M40 Motorway (M40 Junction 10, Oxfordshire) (Temporary Restriction and Prohibition of Traffic) Order 2015 No. 2015/1009. - Enabling power: Road Traffic Regulation Act 1984, s. 14 (1) (a), sch. 9, para. 27 (1). - Issued: 17.02.2015. Made: 30.01.2015. Coming into force: 06.02.2015. Effect: S.I. 2014/2478 revoked. Territorial extent & classification: E. Local. - Available at http://www.legislation.gov.uk/uksi/2015/1009/contents/made Non-print

The A43 Trunk Road (Ardley, Oxfordshire) (Temporary Prohibition of Traffic) Order 2015 No. 2015/1205. - Enabling power: Road Traffic Regulation Act 1984, s. 14 (1) (b). - Issued: 20.04.2015. Made: 20.03.2015. Coming into force: 27.03.2015. Effect: None. Territorial extent & classification: E. Local. - Available at http://www.legislation.gov.uk/uksi/2015/1205/contents/made Non-print

The A43 Trunk Road (Evenley, Northamptonshire) (Temporary Prohibition of Traffic) Order 2015 No. 2015/1070. - Enabling power: Road Traffic Regulation Act 1984, s. 14 (1) (a). - Issued: 02.04.2015. Made: 10.02.2015. Coming into force: 17.02.2015. Effect: None. Territorial extent & classification: E. Local. - Available at http://www.legislation.gov.uk/uksi/2015/1070/contents/made Non-print

The A43 Trunk Road (Evenley, Northamptonshire) (Temporary Prohibition of Traffic) Order 2015 No. 2015/1024. - Enabling power: Road Traffic Regulation Act 1984, s. 14 (1) (a). - Issued: 09.03.2015. Made: 10.02.2015. Coming into force: 17.02.2015. Effect: None. Territorial extent & classification: E. Local. - Available at http://www.legislation.gov.uk/uksi/2015/1024/contents/made Non-print

The A43 Trunk Road (Whitfield, Northamptonshire) (Temporary Restriction and Prohibition of Traffic) Order 2015 No. 2015/1116. - Enabling power: Road Traffic Regulation Act 1984, s. 14 (1) (a). - Issued: 04.03.2015. Made: 18.02.2015. Coming into force: 25.02.2015. Effect: None. Territorial extent & classification: E. Local. - Available at http://www.legislation.gov.uk/uksi/2015/1116/contents/made Non-print

The A45 Trunk Road (Earls Barton, Northamptonshire) (Temporary Restriction and Prohibition of Traffic) Order 2015 No. 2015/289. - Enabling power: Road Traffic Regulation Act 1984, s. 14 (1) (a). - Issued: 02.02.2015. Made: 19.01.2015. Coming into force: 26.01.2015. Effect: None. Territorial extent & classification: E. Local. - Available at http://www.legislation.gov.uk/uksi/2015/289/contents/made Non-print

The A45 Trunk Road (Little Irchester, Near Wellingborough, Northamptonshire) (Temporary Restriction and Prohibition of Traffic) Order 2015 No. 2015/1100. - Enabling power: Road Traffic Regulation Act 1984, s. 14 (1) (a). - Issued: 26.02.2015. Made: 16.02.2015. Coming into force: 23.02.2015. Effect: None. Territorial extent & classification: E. Local. - Available at http://www.legislation.gov.uk/uksi/2015/1100/contents/made Non-print

The A45 Trunk Road (Wellingborough, Northamptonshire) (Temporary Restriction and Prohibition of Traffic) Order 2015 No. 2015/1002. - Enabling power: Road Traffic Regulation Act 1984, s. 14 (1) (a). - Issued: 25.03.2015. Made: 26.01.2015. Coming into force: 02.02.2015. Effect: None. Territorial extent & classification: E. Local. - Available at http://www.legislation.gov.uk/uksi/2015/1002/contents/made Non-print

The A45 Trunk Road (Wilby - Great Billing, Northamptonshire) (Temporary Prohibition of Traffic) Order 2015 No. 2015/1011. - Enabling power: Road Traffic Regulation Act 1984, s. 14 (1) (a). - Issued: 17.02.2015. Made: 30.01.2015. Coming into force: 06.02.2015. Effect: None. Territorial extent & classification: E. Local. - Available at http://www.legislation.gov.uk/uksi/2015/1011/contents/made Non-print

The A45 Trunk Road (Wilby - Great Billing, Northamptonshire) (Temporary Restriction and Prohibition of Traffic) Order 2015 No. 2015/1219. - Enabling power: Road Traffic Regulation Act 1984, s. 14 (1) (a). - Issued: 25.03.2015. Made: 09.03.2015. Coming into force: 16.03.2015. Effect: None. Territorial extent & classification: E. Local. - Available at http://www.legislation.gov.uk/uksi/2015/1219/contents/made Non-print

The A45 Trunk Road (Wootton - Great Billing, Northamptonshire) (Temporary Restriction and Prohibition of Traffic) (No.2) Order 2015 No. 2015/1022. - Enabling power: Road Traffic Regulation Act 1984, s. 14 (1) (a). - Issued: 17.02.2015. Made: 30.01.2015. Coming into force: 07.02.2015. Effect: The A45 Trunk Road (Wootton - Great Billing, Northamptonshire) (Temporary Restriction and Prohibition of Traffic) Order 2015 revoked. Territorial extent & classification: E. Local. - Available at http://www.legislation.gov.uk/uksi/2015/1022/contents/made Non-print

The A45 Trunk Road (Wootton, Northamptonshire) (Temporary Prohibition of Traffic) Order 2015 No. 2015/331. - Enabling power: Road Traffic Regulation Act 1984, s. 14 (1) (a). - Issued: 24.02.2015. Made: 05.01.2015. Coming into force: 12.01.2015. Effect: None. Territorial extent & classification: E. Local. - Available at http://www.legislation.gov.uk/uksi/2015/331/contents/made Non-print

The A46 Trunk Road (Glenfield, Leicestershire) (Temporary Restriction and Prohibition of Traffic) Order 2015 No. 2015/1082. - Enabling power: Road Traffic Regulation Act 1984, s. 14 (1) (a). - Issued: 25.02.2015. Made: 13.02.2015. Coming into force: 20.02.2015. Effect: None. Territorial extent & classification: E. Local. - Available at http://www.legislation.gov.uk/uksi/2015/1082/contents/made Non-print

The A46 Trunk Road (Syston to North of Six Hills, Leicestershire) (Temporary Prohibition of Traffic) Order 2015 No. 2015/1046. - Enabling power: Road Traffic Regulation Act 1984, s. 14 (1) (a). - Issued: 14.04.2015. Made: 02.02.2015. Coming into force: 09.02.2015. Effect: None. Territorial extent & classification: E. Local. - Available at http://www.legislation.gov.uk/uksi/2015/1046/contents/made Non-print

ROAD TRAFFIC: TRAFFIC REGULATION

The A46 Trunk Road (Warwick, Warwickshire) (Temporary Prohibition of Traffic) Order 2015 No. 2015/150. - Enabling power: Road Traffic Regulation Act 1984, s. 14 (1) (a). - Issued: 29.01.2015. Made: 09.01.2015. Coming into force: 16.01.2015. Effect: None. Territorial extent & classification: E. Local. - Available at http://www.legislation.gov.uk/uksi/2015/150/contents/made Non-print

The A46 Trunk Road (Widmerpool) (Temporary Restriction and Prohibition of Traffic) Order 2015 No. 2015/1175. - Enabling power: Road Traffic Regulation Act 1984, s. 14 (1) (a). - Issued: 11.03.2015. Made: 23.02.2015. Coming into force: 02.03.2015. Effect: None. Territorial extent & classification: E. Local. - Available at http://www.legislation.gov.uk/uksi/2015/1175/contents/made Non-print

The A47 Trunk Road (Guyhirn Roundabout to Churchill Road Roundabout, Wisbech, Cambridgeshire) (Temporary Prohibition of Traffic) Order 2015 No. 2015/1103. - Enabling power: Road Traffic Regulation Act 1984, s. 14 (1) (a). - Issued: 03.03.2015. Made: 16.02.2015. Coming into force: 23.02.2015. Effect: None. Territorial extent & classification: E. Local. - Available at http://www.legislation.gov.uk/uksi/2015/1103/contents/made Non-print

The A47 Trunk Road (Junction 15 Nene Parkway Interchange to Eye Road Roundabout) City of Peterborough (Temporary Restriction of Traffic and Prohibition of Traffic and Pedestrians) Order 2015 No. 2015/1278. - Enabling power: Road Traffic Regulation Act 1984, s. 14 (1) (a), sch. 9, para. 27 (1). - Issued: 30.04.2015. Made: 02.03.2015. Coming into force: 09.03.2015. Effect: S.I. 2015/334 revoked. Territorial extent & classification: E. Local. - Available at http://www.legislation.gov.uk/uksi/2015/1278/contents/made Non-print

The A47 Trunk Road (Soke Parkway, Junction 15 Nene Parkway Interchange to Junction 20 Paston Parkway Interchange, City of Peterborough) (Temporary Restriction and Prohibition of Traffic) Order 2015 No. 2015/334. - Enabling power: Road Traffic Regulation Act 1984, s. 14 (1) (a). - Issued: 02.02.2015. Made: 19.01.2015. Coming into force: 26.01.2015. Effect: None. Territorial extent & classification: E. Local. - Revoked by SI 2015/1278 (Non-print) (ISBN 9786666733582). - Available at http://www.legislation.gov.uk/uksi/2015/334/contents/made Non-print

The A47 Trunk Road (Toftwood Interchange to Longwater Interchange, Norfolk) (Temporary Prohibition of Traffic) Order 2015 No. 2015/586. - Enabling power: Road Traffic Regulation Act 1984, s. 14 (1) (a). - Issued: 02.02.20115. Made: 19.01.2015. Coming into force: 26.01.2015. Effect: None. Territorial extent & classification: E. Local. - Available at http://www.legislation.gov.uk/uksi/2015/586/contents/made Non-print

The A47 Trunk Road (Trowse Interchange to Brundall, Norfolk) (Temporary Restriction and Prohibition of Traffic and Pedestrians) Order 2015 No. 2015/1003. - Enabling power: Road Traffic Regulation Act 1984, s. 14 (1) (a), sch. 9, para. 27 (1). - Issued: 02.04.2015. Made: 26.01.2015. Coming into force: 02.02.2015. Effect: None. Territorial extent & classification: E. Local. - Available at http://www.legislation.gov.uk/uksi/2015/1003/contents/made Non-print

The A50 Trunk Road (Blythe Bridge to Uttoxeter, Staffordshire) (Temporary Restriction and Prohibition of Traffic) Order 2015 No. 2015/1083. - Enabling power: Road Traffic Regulation Act 1984, s. 14 (1) (a). - Issued: 26.02.2015. Made: 13.02.2015. Coming into force: 20.02.2015. Effect: None. Territorial extent & classification: E. Local. - Available at http://www.legislation.gov.uk/uksi/2015/1083/contents/made Non-print

The A50 Trunk Road (Foston to Etwall, Derbyshire) (Temporary Prohibition of Traffic) Order 2015 No. 2015/679. - Enabling power: Road Traffic Regulation Act 1984, s. 14 (1) (a). - Issued: 11.02.2015. Made: 19.01.2015. Coming into force: 26.01.2015. Effect: None. Territorial extent & classification: E. Local. - Available at http://www.legislation.gov.uk/uksi/2015/679/contents/made Non-print

The A50 Trunk Road (Hilton to Findern, Derbyshire) (Temporary Prohibition of Traffic) Order 2015 No. 2015/557. - Enabling power: Road Traffic Regulation Act 1984, s. 14 (1) (a). - Issued: 10.03.2015. Made: 23.02.2015. Coming into force: 02.03.2015. Effect: None. Territorial extent & classification: E. Local. - Available at http://www.legislation.gov.uk/uksi/2015/557/contents/made Non-print

The A50 Trunk Road (Meir Tunnel, Stoke-On-Trent) (Temporary Prohibition of Traffic) Order 2015 No. 2015/1119. - Enabling power: Road Traffic Regulation Act 1984, s. 14 (1) (a). - Issued: 13.03.2015. Made: 18.02.2015. Coming into force: 25.02.2015. Effect: None. Territorial extent & classification: E. Local. - Available at http://www.legislation.gov.uk/uksi/2015/1119/contents/made Non-print

The A50 Trunk Road (Sudbury - Foston, Derbyshire) (Temporary Restriction and Prohibition of Traffic) Order 2015 No. 2015/1111. - Enabling power: Road Traffic Regulation Act 1984, s. 14 (1) (a). - Issued: 03.03.2015. Made: 17.02.2015. Coming into force: 24.02.2015. Effect: None. Territorial extent & classification: E. Local. - Available at http://www.legislation.gov.uk/uksi/2015/1111/contents/made Non-print

The A50 Trunk Road (Uttoxeter to Sudbury) (Temporary Prohibition of Traffic) Order 2015 No. 2015/1198. - Enabling power: Road Traffic Regulation Act 1984, s. 14 (1) (a). - Issued: 25.03.2015. Made: 09.03.2015. Coming into force: 16.03.2015. Effect: None. Territorial extent & classification: E. Local. - Available at http://www.legislation.gov.uk/uksi/2015/1198/contents/made Non-print

The A52 and A1 Trunk Roads (Barrowby, Lincolnshire) (Temporary Prohibition of Traffic) Order 2015 No. 2015/1165. - Enabling power: Road Traffic Regulation Act 1984, s. 14 (1) (a). - Issued: 25.03.2015. Made: 02.03.2015. Coming into force: 09.03.2015. Effect: None. Territorial extent & classification: E. Local. - Available at http://www.legislation.gov.uk/uksi/2015/1165/contents/made Non-print

The A52 Trunk Road (Aslockton, Nottinghamshire) (Temporary Restriction of Traffic) Order 2015 No. 2015/696. - Enabling power: Road Traffic Regulation Act 1984, s. 14 (1) (a). - Issued: 11.02.2015. Made: 23.01.2015. Coming into force: 30.01.2015. Effect: None. Territorial extent & classification: E. Local. - Available at http://www.legislation.gov.uk/uksi/2015/696/contents/made Non-print

The A52 Trunk Road (Bingham to Barrowby) (Temporary Prohibition of Traffic) Order 2015 No. 2015/1101. - Enabling power: Road Traffic Regulation Act 1984, s. 14 (1) (a). - Issued: 26.02.2015. Made: 16.02.2015. Coming into force: 23.02.2015. Effect: None. Territorial extent & classification: E. Local. - Available at http://www.legislation.gov.uk/uksi/2015/1101/contents/made Non-print

The A52 Trunk Road (Clifton Boulevard, Nottingham) (Temporary Prohibition of Traffic) Order 2015 No. 2015/1246. - Enabling power: Road Traffic Regulation Act 1984, s. 14 (1) (a). - Issued: 24.04.2015. Made: 24.02.2015. Coming into force: 03.03.2015. Effect: None. Territorial extent & classification: E. Local. - Available at http://www.legislation.gov.uk/uksi/2015/1246/contents/made Non-print

The A57 Trunk Road (Denton Roundabout)(24 Hour Clearway and One-Way Traffic) Order 2015 No. 2015/1085. - Enabling power: Road Traffic Regulation Act 1984, ss.1 (1) (2) (1) (2), 122A. - Issued: 16.04.2015. Made: 09.02.2015. Coming into force: 16.02.2015. Effect: None. Territorial extent & classification: E. Local. - Available at http://www.legislation.gov.uk/uksi/2015/1085/contents/made Non-print

The A57 Trunk Road (Hattersley Roundabout) (Temporary Restriction and Prohibition of Traffic) Order 2015 No. 2015/1092. - Enabling power: Road Traffic Regulation Act 1984, s. 14 (1) (a). - Issued: 24.02.2015. Made: 12.02.2015. Coming into force: 22.02.2015. Effect: None. Territorial extent & classification: E. Local. - Available at http://www.legislation.gov.uk/uksi/2015/1092/contents/made Non-print

The A61 Trunk Road and the A616 Trunk Road (Westwood Roundabout to Wortley Interchange) (Temporary Prohibition of Traffic) Order 2015 No. 2015/1058. - Enabling power: Road Traffic Regulation Act 1984, s. 14 (1) (a). - Issued: 18.02.2015. Made: 05.02.2015. Coming into force: 15.02.2015. Effect: None. Territorial extent & classification: E. Local. - Available at http://www.legislation.gov.uk/uksi/2015/1058/contents/made Non-print

The A63 Trunk Road (Castle Street) (Temporary Prohibition of Traffic) Order 2015 No. 2015/708. - Enabling power: Road Traffic Regulation Act 1984, s. 14 (1) (a). - Issued: 03.02.2015. Made: 22.01.2015. Coming into force: 31.01.2015. Effect: None. Territorial extent & classification: E. Local. - Available at http://www.legislation.gov.uk/uksi/2015/708/contents/made Non-print

ROAD TRAFFIC: TRAFFIC REGULATION

The A63 Trunk Road (Clive Sullivan Way to Garrison Road Roundabout) (Temporary Prohibition of Traffic) Order 2015 No. 2015/1047. - Enabling power: Road Traffic Regulation Act 1984, s. 14 (1) (a). - Issued: 10.04.2015. Made: 29.01.2015. Coming into force: 10.02.2015. Effect: None. Territorial extent & classification: E. Local. - Available at http://www.legislation.gov.uk/uksi/2015/1047/contents/made Non-print

The A63 Trunk Road (Western Interchange to Brighton Street Interchange) (Temporary Prohibition of Traffic) Order 2015 No. 2015/164. - Enabling power: Road Traffic Regulation Act 1984, s. 14 (1) (a). - Issued: 28.01.2015. Made: 08.01.2015. Coming into force: 20.01.2015. Effect: None. Territorial extent & classification: E. Local. - Available at http://www.legislation.gov.uk/uksi/2015/164/contents/made Non-print

The A63 Trunk Road (Western Interchange to Priory Way Interchange) (Temporary Prohibition of Traffic) Order No. 2015/1170. - Enabling power: Road Traffic Regulation Act 1984, s. 14 (1) (a). - Issued: 20.03.2015. Made: 05.03.2015. Coming into force: 15.03.2015. Effect: None. Territorial extent & classification: E. Local. - Available at http://www.legislation.gov.uk/uksi/2015/1170/contents/made Non-print

The A64 Trunk Road (Crambeck to Musley Bank Interchange) (Temporary Restriction and Prohibition of Traffic) Order 2015 No. 2015/1145. - Enabling power: Road Traffic Regulation Act 1984, s. 14 (1) (a). - Issued: 05.03.2015. Made: 19.02.2015. Coming into force: 01.03.2015. Effect: None. Territorial extent & classification: E. Local. - Available at http://www.legislation.gov.uk/uksi/2015/1145/contents/made Non-print

The A64 Trunk Road (Ganton) (Temporary Restriction and Prohibition of Traffic) Order 2015 No. 2015/724. - Enabling power: Road Traffic Regulation Act 1984, s. 14 (1) (a). - Issued: 02.02.2015. Made: 22.01.2015. Coming into force: 01.02.2015. Effect: None. Territorial extent & classification: E. Local. - Available at http://www.legislation.gov.uk/uksi/2015/724/contents/made Non-print

The A64 Trunk Road (Hopgrove) (Temporary Prohibition of Traffic) Order 2015 No. 2015/1090. - Enabling power: Road Traffic Regulation Act 1984, s. 14 (1) (a). - Issued: 18.02.2015. Made: 05.02.2015. Coming into force: 22.02.2015. Effect: None. Territorial extent & classification: E. Local. - Available at http://www.legislation.gov.uk/uksi/2015/1090/contents/made Non-print

The A64 Trunk Road (Shepherdfields Lane, Whitwell-on-the-Hill) (Temporary Prohibition of Traffic) Order 2015 No. 2015/1241. - Enabling power: Road Traffic Regulation Act 1984, s. 14 (1) (a). - Issued: 30.03.2015. Made: 26.03.2015. Coming into force: 06.04.2015. Effect: None. Territorial extent & classification: E. Local. - Available at http://www.legislation.gov.uk/uksi/2015/1241/contents/made Non-print

The A64 Trunk Road (Tadcaster Bar to Headley Bar) (Temporary Prohibition of Traffic) Order 2015 No. 2015/1207. - Enabling power: Road Traffic Regulation Act 1984, s. 14 (1) (a). - Issued: 26.03.2015. Made: 19.03.2015. Coming into force: 26.03.2015. Effect: None. Territorial extent & classification: E. Local. - Available at http://www.legislation.gov.uk/uksi/2015/1207/contents/made Non-print

The A64 Trunk Road (Tadcaster Ings to Askham Bryan) (Temporary Restriction and Prohibition of Traffic) Order 2015 No. 2015/1193. - Enabling power: Road Traffic Regulation Act 1984, s. 14 (1) (a). - Issued: 13.03.2015. Made: 26.02.2015. Coming into force: 08.03.2015. Effect: None. Territorial extent & classification: E. Local. - Available at http://www.legislation.gov.uk/uksi/2015/1193/contents/made Non-print

The A66 and A595 Trunk Roads (Cockermouth Business Park Drainage Scheme) (Temporary Prohibition and Restriction of Traffic) Order 2015 No. 2015/1137. - Enabling power: Road Traffic Regulation Act 1984, s. 14 (1) (a). - Issued: 04.03.2015. Made: 12.02.2015. Coming into force: 01.03.2015. Effect: None. Territorial extent & classification: E. Local. - Available at http://www.legislation.gov.uk/uksi/2015/1137/contents/made Non-print

The A66 Trunk Road (Barras Junction to Bluegrass Resurfacing) (Temporary Prohibition and Restriction of Traffic) Order 2015 No. 2015/1156. - Enabling power: Road Traffic Regulation Act 1984, s. 14 (1) (a). - Issued: 18.03.2015. Made: 26.02.2015. Coming into force: 01.03.2015. Effect: None. Territorial extent & classification: E. Local. - Available at http://www.legislation.gov.uk/uksi/2015/1156/contents/made Non-print

The A66 Trunk Road (Bassenthwaite Lake) (Temporary Prohibition and Restriction of Traffic) Order 2015 No. 2015/1063. - Enabling power: Road Traffic Regulation Act 1984, s. 14 (1) (a). - Issued: 03.03.2015. Made: 29.01.2015. Coming into force: 15.02.2015. Effect: None. Territorial extent & classification: E. Local. - Available at http://www.legislation.gov.uk/uksi/2015/1063/contents/made Non-print

The A66 Trunk Road (Boathouse Lane Interchange to Thornaby Road Interchange) (Temporary Prohibition of Traffic) Order 2015 No. 2015/1140. - Enabling power: Road Traffic Regulation Act 1984, s. 14 (1) (a). - Issued: 05.03.2015. Made: 19.02.2015. Coming into force: 01.03.2015. Effect: None. Territorial extent & classification: E. Local. - Available at http://www.legislation.gov.uk/uksi/2015/1140/contents/made Non-print

The A66 Trunk Road (Briery Bridge to Storms Farm Underpass) (Temporary Prohibition and Restriction of Traffic) Order 2015 No. 2015/1255. - Enabling power: Road Traffic Regulation Act 1984, s. 14 (1) (a). - Issued: 01.04.2015. Made: 26.03.2015. Coming into force: 12.04.2015. Effect: None. Territorial extent & classification: E. Local. - Available at http://www.legislation.gov.uk/uksi/2015/1255/contents/made Non-print

The A66 Trunk Road (Dubwath to Thornthwaite) (Temporary Restriction and Prohibition of Traffic) Order 2015 No. 2015/715. - Enabling power: Road Traffic Regulation Act 1984, s. 14 (1) (a). - Issued: 29.01.2015. Made: 15.01.2015. Coming into force: 01.02.2015. Effect: None. Territorial extent & classification: E. Local. - Available at http://www.legislation.gov.uk/uksi/2015/715/contents/made Non-print

The A66 Trunk Road (Haversheaf Access Road to Whinfell Park Access Road) (Temporary Restriction of Traffic) Order 2015 No. 2015/1135. - Enabling power: Road Traffic Regulation Act 1984, s. 14 (1) (a). - Issued: 25.02.2015. Made: 13.02.2015. Coming into force: 01.03.2015. Effect: None. Territorial extent & classification: E. Local. - Available at http://www.legislation.gov.uk/uksi/2015/1135/contents/made Non-print

The A66 Trunk Road (Kemplay to Temple Sowerby) (Temporary Prohibition and Restriction of Traffic) Order 2015 No. 2015/1067. - Enabling power: Road Traffic Regulation Act 1984, s. 14 (1) (a). - Issued: 04.03.2015. Made: 12.02.2015. Coming into force: 15.02.2015. Effect: None. Territorial extent & classification: E. Local. - Available at http://www.legislation.gov.uk/uksi/2015/1067/contents/made Non-print

The A66 Trunk Road (Little Burdon Roundabout to Yarm Road Interchange) (Temporary 50 Miles Per Hour Speed Restriction) Order 2015 No. 2015/1136. - Enabling power: Road Traffic Regulation Act 1984, s. 14 (1) (a). - Issued: 26.02.2015. Made: 19.02.2015. Coming into force: 01.03.2015. Effect: None. Territorial extent & classification: E. Local. - Available at http://www.legislation.gov.uk/uksi/2015/1136/contents/made Non-print

The A66 Trunk Road (Rokeby Park to Greta Bridge) (Temporary Restriction and Prohibition of Traffic) Order 2015 No. 2015/1194. - Enabling power: Road Traffic Regulation Act 1984, s. 14 (1) (a). - Issued: 16.03.2015. Made: 26.02.2015. Coming into force: 09.03.2015. Effect: None. Territorial extent & classification: E. Local. - Available at http://www.legislation.gov.uk/uksi/2015/1194/contents/made Non-print

The A66 Trunk Road (Scotch Corner Interchange) (Temporary Restriction and Prohibition of Traffic) Order 2015 No. 2015/268. - Enabling power: Road Traffic Regulation Act 1984, s. 14 (1) (a). - Issued: 18.02.2015. Made: 05.02.2015. Coming into force: 22.02.2015. Effect: None. Territorial extent & classification: E. Local. - Available at http://www.legislation.gov.uk/uksi/2015/268/contents/made Non-print

The A66 Trunk Road (Stainmore Layby) (Temporary Prohibition and Restriction of Traffic) Order 2015 No. 2015/1139. - Enabling power: Road Traffic Regulation Act 1984, s. 14 (1) (a). - Issued: 04.03.2015. Made: 12.02.2015. Coming into force: 01.03.2015. Effect: None. Territorial extent & classification: E. Local. - Available at http://www.legislation.gov.uk/uksi/2015/1139/contents/made Non-print

The A69 Trunk Road (Denton Burn Interchange to Rose Hill Interchange) (Temporary Restriction and Prohibition of Traffic) Order 2015 No. 2015/1238. - Enabling power: Road Traffic Regulation Act 1984, s. 14 (1) (a). - Issued: 26.03.2015. Made: 19.03.2015. Coming into force: 31.03.2015. Effect: None. Territorial extent & classification: E. Local. - Available at http://www.legislation.gov.uk/uksi/2015/1238/contents/made Non-print

The A160 Trunk Road (Brocklesby Interchange to Eastfield Road Junction) (Temporary Restriction and Prohibition of Traffic) Order 2015 No. 2015/1232. - Enabling power: Road Traffic Regulation Act 1984, s. 14 (1) (a). - Issued: 26.03.2015. Made: 19.03.2015. Coming into force: 29.03.2015. Effect: None. Territorial extent & classification: E. Local. - Available at http://www.legislation.gov.uk/uksi/2015/1232/contents/made Non-print

The A162 Trunk Road (Ferrybridge) (Temporary Prohibition of Traffic) Order 2015 No. 2015/1142. - Enabling power: Road Traffic Regulation Act 1984, s. 14 (1) (a). - Issued: 05.03.2015. Made: 19.02.2015. Coming into force: 01.03.2015. Effect: None. Territorial extent & classification: E. Local. - Available at http://www.legislation.gov.uk/uksi/2015/1142/contents/made Non-print

The A168 Trunk Road (Dishforth Interchange) (Temporary Restriction and Prohibition of Traffic) Order 2015 No. 2015/553. - Enabling power: Road Traffic Regulation Act 1984, s. 14 (1) (a) & S.I. 1982/1163 reg. 16 (2). - Issued: 04.03.2015. Made: 19.02.2015. Coming into force: 08.03.2015. Effect: None. Territorial extent & classification: E. Local. - Available at http://www.legislation.gov.uk/uksi/2015/553/contents/made Non-print

The A180 Trunk Road (Barnetby Interchange to Pyewipe Roundabout) (Temporary Prohibition of Traffic) Order 2015 No. 2015/1152. - Enabling power: Road Traffic Regulation Act 1984, s. 14 (1) (a). - Issued: 05.03.2015. Made: 19.02.2015. Coming into force: 01.03.2015. Effect: None. Territorial extent & classification: E. Local. - Available at http://www.legislation.gov.uk/uksi/2015/1152/contents/made Non-print

The A259 Trunk Road (A268 Fishmarket Road - Mill Lane) (Temporary Prohibition of Traffic) Order 2015 No. 2015/536. - Enabling power: Road Traffic Regulation Act 1984, s. 14 (1) (a). - Issued: 25.02.2015. Made: 16.02.2015. Coming into force: 07.03.2015. Effect: None. Territorial extent & classification: E. Local. - Available at http://www.legislation.gov.uk/uksi/2015/536/contents/made Non-print

The A259 Trunk Road (Guestling Green) (Temporary Restriction and Prohibition of Traffic) Order 2015 No. 2015/1052. - Enabling power: Road Traffic Regulation Act 1984, s. 14 (1) (a). - Issued: 03.02.2015. Made: 26.01.2015. Coming into force: 14.02.2015. Effect: None. Territorial extent & classification: E. Local. - Available at http://www.legislation.gov.uk/uksi/2015/1052/contents/made Non-print

The A259 Trunk Road (King Offa Way) (Temporary Prohibition of Traffic) Order 2015 No. 2015/703. - Enabling power: Road Traffic Regulation Act 1984, s. 14 (1) (a). - Issued: 28.01.2015. Made: 12.01.2015. Coming into force: 31.01.2015. Effect: None. Territorial extent & classification: E. Local. - Available at http://www.legislation.gov.uk/uksi/2015/703/contents/made Non-print

The A303 Trunk Road and A36 Trunk Road (Deptford Junction Slip Roads) (Temporary Prohibition of Traffic) Order 2015 No. 2015/1115. - Enabling power: Road Traffic Regulation Act 1984, s. 14 (1) (a). - Issued: 03.03.2015. Made: 18.02.2015. Coming into force: 25.02.2015. Effect: None. Territorial extent & classification: E. Local. - Available at http://www.legislation.gov.uk/uksi/2015/1115/contents/made Non-print

The A303 Trunk Road (Countess Roundabout to Parkhouse Junction, Wiltshire) (Temporary Prohibition of Traffic) Order 2015 No. 2015/251. - Enabling power: Road Traffic Regulation Act 1984, s. 14 (1) (a). - Issued: 02.02.2015. Made: 21.01.2015. Coming into force: 24.01.2015. Effect: None. Territorial extent & classification: E. Local. - Available at http://www.legislation.gov.uk/uksi/2015/251/contents/made Non-print

The A303 Trunk Road (Laverstoke Lane, Slip Road) (Temporary Prohibition of Traffic) Order 2015 No. 2015/1086. - Enabling power: Road Traffic Regulation Act 1984, s. 14 (1) (a). - Issued: 13.02.2015. Made: 02.02.2015. Coming into force: 21.02.2015. Effect: None. Territorial extent & classification: E. Local. - Available at http://www.legislation.gov.uk/uksi/2015/1086/contents/made Non-print

The A303 Trunk Road (Parkhouse Interchange - Longparish Interchange) (Temporary Prohibition of Traffic) Order 2015 No. 2015/554. - Enabling power: Road Traffic Regulation Act 1984, s. 14 (1) (a). - Issued: 25.02.2015. Made: 16.02.2015. Coming into force: 07.03.2015. Effect: None. Territorial extent & classification: E. Local. - Available at http://www.legislation.gov.uk/uksi/2015/554/contents/made Non-print

The A303 Trunk Road (Picket Twenty Interchange - Hundred Acre Interchange) (Temporary Prohibition of Traffic) Order 2015 No. 2015/1235. - Enabling power: Road Traffic Regulation Act 1984, s. 14 (1) (a). - Issued: 23.03.2015. Made: 09.03.2015. Coming into force: 30.03.2015. Effect: None. Territorial extent & classification: E. Local. - Available at http://www.legislation.gov.uk/uksi/2015/1235/contents/made Non-print

The A421 Trunk Road (Bedford Southern Bypass, Elstow, Bedfordshire) Eastbound (Lay-by)(Prohibition of Waiting) Order 2015 No. 2015/1218. - Enabling power: Road Traffic Regulation Act 1984, s. 1 (1), 2 (1) (2), 4 (1) (2). - Issued: 18.03.2015. Made: 02.03.2015. Coming into force: 16.03.2015. Effect: None. Territorial extent & classification: E. Local. - Available at http://www.legislation.gov.uk/uksi/2015/1218/contents/made Non-print

The A446 and A452 Trunk Roads (Solihull and Warwickshire) (Temporary Prohibition of Traffic) Order 2015 No. 2015/695. - Enabling power: Road Traffic Regulation Act 1984, s. 14 (1) (a). - Issued: 11.02.2015. Made: 23.01.2015. Coming into force: 30.01.2015. Effect: None. Territorial extent & classification: E. Local. - Available at http://www.legislation.gov.uk/uksi/2015/695/contents/made Non-print

The A449 Trunk Road (Coven, Staffordshire) (Temporary Prohibition of Traffic) Order 2015 No. 2015/686. - Enabling power: Road Traffic Regulation Act 1984, s. 14 (1) (a). - Issued: 11.02.2015. Made: 23.01.2015. Coming into force: 30.01.2015. Effect: None. Territorial extent & classification: E. Local. - Available at http://www.legislation.gov.uk/uksi/2015/686/contents/made Non-print

The A500 Trunk Road (Sideway, Stoke-On-Trent) (Temporary Prohibition of Traffic) Order 2015 No. 2015/558. - Enabling power: Road Traffic Regulation Act 1984, s. 14 (1) (a). - Issued: 09.03.2015. Made: 23.02.2015. Coming into force: 02.03.2015. Effect: None. Territorial extent & classification: E. Local. - Available at http://www.legislation.gov.uk/uksi/2015/558/contents/made Non-print

The A500 Trunk Road (Stoke-On-Trent) (Temporary Prohibition of Traffic) Order 2015 No. 2015/1167. - Enabling power: Road Traffic Regulation Act 1984, s. 14 (1) (a). - Issued: 25.03.2015. Made: 02.03.2015. Coming into force: 09.03.2015. Effect: None. Territorial extent & classification: E. Local. - Available at http://www.legislation.gov.uk/uksi/2015/1167/contents/made Non-print

The A550 Trunk Road (Welsh Road) (Temporary Prohibition of Traffic) Order 2015 No. 2015/1154. - Enabling power: Road Traffic Regulation Act 1984, s. 14 (1) (a). - Issued: 19.03.2015. Made: 25.02.2015. Coming into force: 01.03.2015. Effect: None. Territorial extent & classification: E. Local. - Available at http://www.legislation.gov.uk/uksi/2015/1154/contents/made Non-print

The A590 Trunk Road (Brettargh Holt) and the M6 Motorway (Junction 36) (Temporary Prohibition and Restriction of Traffic) Order 2015 No. 2015/1120. - Enabling power: Road Traffic Regulation Act 1984, s. 14 (1) (a). - Issued: 04.03.2015. Made: 18.02.2015. Coming into force: 26.02.2015. Effect: None. Territorial extent & classification: E. Local. - Available at http://www.legislation.gov.uk/uksi/2015/1120/contents/made Non-print

The A590 Trunk Road (Greenodd to Barrow End) (Temporary Prohibition and Restriction of Traffic) Order 2015 No. 2015/1065. - Enabling power: Road Traffic Regulation Act 1984, s. 14 (1) (a). - Issued: 03.03.2015. Made: 11.02.2015. Coming into force: 15.02.2015. Effect: None. Territorial extent & classification: E. Local. - Available at http://www.legislation.gov.uk/uksi/2015/1065/contents/made Non-print

The A590 Trunk Road (Newby Bridge) (Temporary Restriction and Prohibition of Traffic) Order 2015 No. 2015/714. - Enabling power: Road Traffic Regulation Act 1984, s. 14 (1) (a). - Issued: 29.01.2015. Made: 15.01.2015. Coming into force: 01.02.2015. Effect: None. Territorial extent & classification: E. Local. - Available at http://www.legislation.gov.uk/uksi/2015/714/contents/made Non-print

The A595 Trunk Road (Bigrigg to Moor Row) (Temporary Restriction and Prohibition of Traffic) Order 2015 No. 2015/1064. - Enabling power: Road Traffic Regulation Act 1984, s. 14 (1) (a). - Issued: 03.03.2015. Made: 28.01.2015. Coming into force: 15.02.2015. Effect: None. Territorial extent & classification: E. Local. - Available at http://www.legislation.gov.uk/uksi/2015/1064/contents/made Non-print

ROAD TRAFFIC: TRAFFIC REGULATION

The A616 Trunk Road and the A61 Trunk Road (Flouch Roundabout to Tankersley Roundabout) (Temporary Restriction and Prohibition of Traffic) Order 2015 No. 2015/1208. - Enabling power: Road Traffic Regulation Act 1984, s. 14 (1) (a). - Issued: 20.03.2015. Made: 05.03.2015. Coming into force: 15.03.2015. Effect: None. Territorial extent & classification: E. Local. - Available at http://www.legislation.gov.uk/uksi/2015/1208/contents/made Non-print

The A631 Trunk Road (Tinsley Viaduct) (Temporary Prohibition of Traffic) Order 2015 No. 2015/1161. - Enabling power: Road Traffic Regulation Act 1984, s. 14 (1) (a). - Issued: 16.03.2015. Made: 26.02.2015. Coming into force: 08.03.2015. Effect: None. Territorial extent & classification: E. Local. - Available at http://www.legislation.gov.uk/uksi/2015/1161/contents/made Non-print

The A696 Trunk Road (Kenton Bar Interchange to Prestwick Road End Roundabout) (Temporary Restriction and Prohibition of Traffic) Order 2015 No. 2015/1057. - Enabling power: Road Traffic Regulation Act 1984, s. 14 (1) (a). - Issued: 18.02.2015. Made: 05.02.2015. Coming into force: 15.02.2015. Effect: None. Territorial extent & classification: E. Local. - Available at http://www.legislation.gov.uk/uksi/2015/1057/contents/made Non-print

The A5005 Trunk Road (Longton, Stoke-On-Trent) (Temporary Prohibition of Traffic) Order 2015 No. 2015/273. - Enabling power: Road Traffic Regulation Act 1984, s. 14 (1) (a). - Issued: 02.02.2015. Made: 19.01.2015. Coming into force: 26.01.2015. Effect: None. Territorial extent & classification: E. Local. - Available at http://www.legislation.gov.uk/uksi/2015/273/contents/made Non-print

The A5036 Trunk Road (Princess Way/Church Road Roundabout) (Prohibition of Left and Right Turns and One Way Traffic) Order 2015 No. 2015/1328. - Enabling power: Road Traffic Regulation Act 1984, ss. 1 (1), 2 (1) (2), 122A. - Issued: 26.05.2015. Made: 25.03.2015. Coming into force: 31.03.2015. Effect: None. Territorial extent & classification: E. Local. - Available at http://www.legislation.gov.uk/uksi/2015/1328/contents/made Non-print

The A5148 and A38 Trunk Roads (Lichfield, Staffordshire) (Temporary Prohibition of Traffic) Order 2015 No. 2015/1166. - Enabling power: Road Traffic Regulation Act 1984, s. 14 (1) (a). - Issued: 25.03.2015. Made: 02.03.2015. Coming into force: 09.03.2015. Effect: None. Territorial extent & classification: E. Local. - Available at http://www.legislation.gov.uk/uksi/2015/1166/contents/made Non-print

The M1 Motorway and A52 Trunk Road (M1 Junctions 23a - 25) (Temporary Restriction and Prohibition of Traffic) Order 2015 No. 2015/275. - Enabling power: Road Traffic Regulation Act 1984, s. 14 (1) (a) & S.I. 1982/1163, reg. 16 (2). - Issued: 02.02.2014. Made: 19.01.2014. Coming into force: 26.01.2015. Effect: None. Territorial extent & classification: E. Local. - Available at http://www.legislation.gov.uk/uksi/2015/275/contents/made Non-print

The M1 Motorway (Junction 31 to Junction 36) (Temporary Restriction and Prohibition of Traffic) Order 2015 No. 2015/1035. - Enabling power: Road Traffic Regulation Act 1984, s. 14 (1) (a) & S.I. 1982/1163, reg. 16 (2). - Issued: 11.02.2015. Made: 29.01.2015. Coming into force: 08.02.2015. Effect: None. Territorial extent & classification: E. Local. - Available at http://www.legislation.gov.uk/uksi/2015/1035/contents/made Non-print

The M1 Motorway (Junction 36 to Junction 37) (Temporary Restriction and Prohibition of Traffic) Order 2015 No. 2015/1036. - Enabling power: Road Traffic Regulation Act 1984, s. 14 (1) (a) & S.I. 1982/1163, reg. 16 (2). - Issued: 11.02.2015. Made: 29.01.2015. Coming into force: 08.02.2015. Effect: None. Territorial extent & classification: E. Local. - Available at http://www.legislation.gov.uk/uksi/2015/1036/contents/made Non-print

The M1 Motorway (Junction 38) (Temporary Prohibition of Traffic) Order 2015 No. 2015/1061. - Enabling power: Road Traffic Regulation Act 1984, s. 14 (1) (a). - Issued: 18.02.2015. Made: 05.02.2015. Coming into force: 15.02.2015. Effect: None. Territorial extent & classification: E. Local. - Available at http://www.legislation.gov.uk/uksi/2015/1061/contents/made Non-print

The M1 Motorway (Junction 39 to Junction 42) (Temporary Restriction and Prohibition of Traffic) Order 2013 Amendment Order 2015 No. 2015/1181. - Enabling power: Road Traffic Regulation Act 1984, s. 14 (1) (a) (15) (2) & S.I. 1982/1163, reg. 16 (2). - Issued: 13.03.2015. Made: 26.02.2015. Coming into force: 07.03.2015. Effect: S.I.2013/970 amended. Territorial extent & classification: E. Local. - Available at http://www.legislation.gov.uk/uksi/2015/1181/contents/made Non-print

The M1 Motorway (Junction 42 to Junction 44) (Temporary Prohibition of Traffic) Order 2015 No. 2015/1149. - Enabling power: Road Traffic Regulation Act 1984, s. 14 (1) (a). - Issued: 05.03.2015. Made: 19.02.2015. Coming into force: 01.03.2015. Effect: None. Territorial extent & classification: E. Local. - Available at http://www.legislation.gov.uk/uksi/2015/1149/contents/made Non-print

The M1 Motorway (Junction 45 to Junction 47) (Temporary Prohibition of Traffic) Order 2015 No. 2015/1147. - Enabling power: Road Traffic Regulation Act 1984, s. 14 (1) (a). - Issued: 06.03.2015. Made: 19.02.2015. Coming into force: 01.03.2015. Effect: None. Territorial extent & classification: E. Local. - Available at http://www.legislation.gov.uk/uksi/2015/1147/contents/made Non-print

The M1 Motorway (Junction 46) (Temporary Restriction and Prohibition of Traffic) Order 2015 No. 2015/1146. - Enabling power: Road Traffic Regulation Act 1984, s. 14 (1) (a). - Issued: 05.03.2015. Made: 19.02.2015. Coming into force: 01.03.2015. Effect: None. Territorial extent & classification: E. Local. - Available at http://www.legislation.gov.uk/uksi/2015/1146/contents/made Non-print

The M1 Motorway (Junction 46 to Junction 47) (Temporary Prohibition of Traffic) Order 2015 No. 2015/1171. - Enabling power: Road Traffic Regulation Act 1984, s. 14 (1) (a). - Issued: 20.03.2015. Made: 05.03.2015. Coming into force: 15.03.2015. Effect: None. Territorial extent & classification: E. Local. - Available at http://www.legislation.gov.uk/uksi/2015/1171/contents/made Non-print

The M1 Motorway (Junctions 1 - 4, Slip Roads) (Temporary Prohibition of Traffic) Order 2015 No. 2015/516. - Enabling power: Road Traffic Regulation Act 1984, s. 14 (1) (a). - Issued: 24.02.2015. Made: 09.02.2015. Coming into force: 01.04.2015. Effect: None. Territorial extent & classification: E. Local. - Available at http://www.legislation.gov.uk/uksi/2015/516/contents/made Non-print

The M1 Motorway (Junctions 2 - 4) (Temporary Restriction and Prohibition of Traffic) Order 2015 No. 2015/1053. - Enabling power: Road Traffic Regulation Act 1984, s. 14 (1) (a) (7). - Issued: 03.02.2015. Made: 26.01.2015. Coming into force: 14.02.2015. Effect: None. Territorial extent & classification: E. Local. - Available at http://www.legislation.gov.uk/uksi/2015/1053/contents/made Non-print

The M1 Motorway (Junctions 20 to 21, Leicestershire) (Temporary Restriction of Traffic) Order 2015 No. 2015/1096. - Enabling power: Road Traffic Regulation Act 1984, s. 14 (1) (a). - Issued: 26.02.2015. Made: 16.02.2015. Coming into force: 23.02.2015. Effect: None. Territorial extent & classification: E. Local. - Available at http://www.legislation.gov.uk/uksi/2015/1096/contents/made Non-print

The M2 Motorway and the A2 Trunk Road (Junctions 1 - 4, Slip Roads) (Temporary Prohibition of Traffic) Order 2015 No. 2015/1257. - Enabling power: Road Traffic Regulation Act 1984, s. 14 (1) (a). - Issued: 19.03.2015. Made: 02.03.2015. Coming into force: 16.04.2015. Effect: None. Territorial extent & classification: E. Local. - Available at http://www.legislation.gov.uk/uksi/2015/1257/contents/made Non-print

The M2 Motorway (Junctions 1 - 2) (Temporary Prohibition of Traffic) Order 2015 No. 2015/1062. - Enabling power: Road Traffic Regulation Act 1984, s. 14 (1) (a). - Issued: 15.04.2015. Made: 12.01.2015. Coming into force: 31.01.2015. Effect: None. Territorial extent & classification: E. Local. - Available at http://www.legislation.gov.uk/uksi/2015/1062/contents/made Non-print

The M2 Motorway (Junctions 5 - 7, Slip Roads) (Temporary Prohibition of Traffic) Order 2015 No. 2015/1262. - Enabling power: Road Traffic Regulation Act 1984, s. 14 (1) (a). - Issued: 26.03.2015. Made: 23.03.2015. Coming into force: 16.04.2015. Effect: None. Territorial extent & classification: E. Local. - Available at http://www.legislation.gov.uk/uksi/2015/1262/contents/made Non-print

The M3 and M27 Motorways (M3 Junctions 9 - 14, M27 Junction 4) (Temporary Prohibition of Traffic) Order 2015 No. 2015/1015. - Enabling power: Road Traffic Regulation Act 1984, s. 14 (1) (a). - Issued: 29.01.2015. Made: 19.01.2015. Coming into force: 07.02.2015. Effect: None. Territorial extent & classification: E. Local. - Available at http://www.legislation.gov.uk/uksi/2015/1015/contents/made Non-print

ROAD TRAFFIC: TRAFFIC REGULATION

The M3 and the M25 Motorways (M3 Junctions 1 - 5) (Temporary Restriction and Prohibition of Traffic) (Amendment) Order 2015 No. 2015/49. - Enabling power: Road Traffic Regulation Act 1984, s. 14 (1) (a). - Issued: 26.01.2015. Made: 16.01.2015. Coming into force: 19.01.2015. Effect: None. Territorial extent & classification: E. Local. - Available at http://www.legislation.gov.uk/uksi/2015/49/contents/made Non-print

The M3 Motorway (Junction 4 - Kitsmead Lane, Carriageways) (Temporary Restriction of Traffic) Order 2015 No. 2015/1056. - Enabling power: Road Traffic Regulation Act 1984, s. 14 (1) (a). - Issued: 30.01.2015. Made: 19.01.2015. Coming into force: 15.02.2015. Effect: None. Territorial extent & classification: E. Local. - Available at http://www.legislation.gov.uk/uksi/2015/1056/contents/made Non-print

The M3 Motorway (Junctions 5 - 9) (Temporary Restriction and Prohibition of Traffic) Order 2015 No. 2015/520. - Enabling power: Road Traffic Regulation Act 1984, s. 14 (1) (a). - Issued: 06.03.2015. Made: 23.02.2015. Coming into force: 14.03.2015. Effect: None. Territorial extent & classification: E. Local. - Available at http://www.legislation.gov.uk/uksi/2015/520/contents/made Non-print

The M4 Motorway (Junction 3) (Temporary Prohibition of Traffic) Order 2015 No. 2015/535. - Enabling power: Road Traffic Regulation Act 1984, s. 14 (1) (a). - Issued: 25.02.2015. Made: 16.02.2015. Coming into force: 07.03.2015. Effect: None. Territorial extent & classification: E. Local. - Available at http://www.legislation.gov.uk/uksi/2015/535/contents/made Non-print

The M4 Motorway (Junctions 1 - 3) (Temporary Prohibition of Traffic) Order 2015 No. 2015/1275. - Enabling power: Road Traffic Regulation Act 1984, s. 14 (1) (a). - Issued: 29.04.2015. Made: 09.03.2015. Coming into force: 01.04.2015. Effect: None. Territorial extent & classification: E. Local. - Available at http://www.legislation.gov.uk/uksi/2015/1275/contents/made Non-print

The M4 Motorway (Junctions 3 - 5) (Temporary Prohibition of Traffic) Order 2015 No. 2015/1251. - Enabling power: Road Traffic Regulation Act 1984, s. 14 (1) (a) (7). - Issued: 24.03.2015. Made: 16.03.2015. Coming into force: 07.04.2015. Effect: None. Territorial extent & classification: E. Local. - Available at http://www.legislation.gov.uk/uksi/2015/1251/contents/made Non-print

The M4 Motorway (Junctions 5 -15) (Temporary Prohibition of Traffic) Order 2015 No. 2015/526. - Enabling power: Road Traffic Regulation Act 1984, s. 14 (1) (a) (7). - Issued: 06.03.2015. Made: 23.02.2015. Coming into force: 14.03.2015. Effect: None. Territorial extent & classification: E. Local. - Available at http://www.legislation.gov.uk/uksi/2015/526/contents/made Non-print

The M4 Motorway (Junctions 11 - 12) (Temporary Restriction and Prohibition of Traffic) Order 2015 No. 2015/1239. - Enabling power: Road Traffic Regulation Act 1984, s. 14 (1) (a). - Issued: 24.03.2015. Made: 16.03.2015. Coming into force: 05.04.2015. Effect: None. Territorial extent & classification: E. Local. - Available at http://www.legislation.gov.uk/uksi/2015/1239/contents/made Non-print

The M4 Motorway (Junctions 15-16) (Temporary Restriction and Prohibition of Traffic) Order 2015 No. 2015/713. - Enabling power: Road Traffic Regulation Act 1984, ss. 14 (1) (a) & S.I. 1982/1163, reg. 16 (2). - Issued: 09.02.2015. Made: 28.01.2015. Coming into force: 31.01.2015. Effect: None. Territorial extent & classification: E. Local. - Available at http://www.legislation.gov.uk/uksi/2015/713/contents/made Non-print

The M4 Motorway (Slip Roads at Junction 34 (Miskin), Vale of Glamorgan & Rhondda Cynon Taf) (Temporary Prohibition of Vehicles) Order 2015 No. 2015/1322 (W.120). - Enabling power: Road Traffic Regulation Act 1984, s. 14 (1) (4). - Issued: 19.05.2015. Made: 14.05.2015. Coming into force: 19.05.2015. Effect: None. Territorial extent & classification: E. Local. - Available at http://www.legislation.gov.uk/uksi/2015/1322/contents/made Non-print

The M5 and M42 Motorways (M5 Junctions 4a - 6) (Temporary Restriction and Prohibition of Traffic) Order 2015 No. 2015/1223. - Enabling power: Road Traffic Regulation Act 1984, s. 14 (1) (a), 15 (2) & S.I. 1982/1163, reg. 16 (2). - Issued: 20.04.2015. Made: 18.03.2015. Coming into force: 25.03.2015. Effect: None. Territorial extent & classification: E. Local. - Available at http://www.legislation.gov.uk/uksi/2015/1223/contents/made Non-print

The M5 Motorway (Junction 1, Sandwell) (Temporary Prohibition of Traffic) Order 2015 No. 2015/1250. - Enabling power: Road Traffic Regulation Act 1984, s. 14 (1) (a). - Issued: 27.04.2015. Made: 09.03.2015. Coming into force: 16.03.2015. Effect: None. Territorial extent & classification: E. Local. - Available at http://www.legislation.gov.uk/uksi/2015/1250/contents/made Non-print

The M5 Motorway (Junction 5 - Junction 4A) (Temporary Prohibition of Traffic) Order 2015 No. 2015/1201. - Enabling power: Road Traffic Regulation Act 1984, s. 14 (1) (a). - Issued: 20.04.2015. Made: 16.03.2015. Coming into force: 23.03.2015. Effect: None. Territorial extent & classification: E. Local. - Available at http://www.legislation.gov.uk/uksi/2015/1201/contents/made Non-print

The M5 Motorway (Junction 5, Worcestershire) (Temporary Prohibition of Traffic) Order 2015 No. 2015/288. - Enabling power: Road Traffic Regulation Act 1984, s. 14 (1) (a). - Issued: 02.02.2015. Made: 19.01.2014. Coming into force: 26.01.2015. Effect: None. Territorial extent & classification: E. Local. - Available at http://www.legislation.gov.uk/uksi/2015/288/contents/made Non-print

The M5 Motorway (Junction 15) and M4 Motorway (Junction 20) (Almondsbury Interchange Slip Roads) (Temporary Prohibition of Traffic) Order 2015 No. 2015/1222. - Enabling power: Road Traffic Regulation Act 1984, s. 14 (1) (a). - Issued: 26.03.2015. Made: 18.03.2015. Coming into force: 25.03.2015. Effect: None. Territorial extent & classification: E. Local. - Available at http://www.legislation.gov.uk/uksi/2015/1222/contents/made Non-print

The M5 Motorway (Junction 18 'Y' Loop Slip Road) (Temporary Prohibition of Traffic) Order 2015 No. 2015/1273. - Enabling power: Road Traffic Regulation Act 1984, s. 14 (1) (a). - Issued: 29.04.2015. Made: 06.03.2015. Coming into force: 14.03.2015. Effect: None. Territorial extent & classification: E. Local. - Available at http://www.legislation.gov.uk/uksi/2015/1273/contents/made Non-print

The M5 Motorway (Junction 29) (Temporary Restriction and Prohibition of Traffic) Order 2015 No. 2015/1192. - Enabling power: Road Traffic Regulation Act 1984, s. 14 (1) (a) & S.I. 1982/1163, reg. 16 (2). - Issued: 18.03.2015. Made: 03.03.2015. Coming into force: 07.03.2015. Effect: None. Territorial extent & classification: E. Local. - Available at http://www.legislation.gov.uk/uksi/2015/1192/contents/made Non-print

The M5 Motorway (Junctions 1-2, Sandwell) (Temporary Prohibition of Traffic) Order 2015 No. 2015/984. - Enabling power: Road Traffic Regulation Act 1984, s. 14 (1) (a). - Issued: 16.02.2015. Made: 26.01.2015. Coming into force: 02.02.2015. Effect: None. Territorial extent & classification: E. Local. - Available at http://www.legislation.gov.uk/uksi/2015/984/contents/made Non-print

The M5 Motorway (Junctions 2 to 1, Sandwell) (Temporary Prohibition of Traffic) Order 2015 No. 2015/1112. - Enabling power: Road Traffic Regulation Act 1984, s. 14 (1) (a). - Issued: 03.03.2015. Made: 17.02.2015. Coming into force: 24.02.2015. Effect: None. Territorial extent & classification: E. Local. - Available at http://www.legislation.gov.uk/uksi/2015/1112/contents/made Non-print

The M5 Motorway (Junctions 9-11A) (Temporary Restriction and Prohibition of Traffic) Order 2015 No. 2015/1088. - Enabling power: Road Traffic Regulation Act 1984, s. 14 (1) (a) & S.I. 1982/1163, reg. 16 (2). - Issued: 26.02.2015. Made: 17.02.2015. Coming into force: 21.02.2015. Effect: None. Territorial extent & classification: E. Local. - Available at http://www.legislation.gov.uk/uksi/2015/1088/contents/made Non-print

The M5 Motorway (Junctions 11-14) (Temporary Restriction and Prohibition of Traffic) Order 2015 No. 2015/152. - Enabling power: Road Traffic Regulation Act 1984, s. 14 (1) (a) & S.I. 1982/1163 reg. 16 (2). - Issued: 28.01.2015. Made: 14.01.2015. Coming into force: 17.01.2015. Effect: None. Territorial extent & classification: E. Local. - Available at http://www.legislation.gov.uk/uksi/2015/152/contents/made Non-print

ROAD TRAFFIC: TRAFFIC REGULATION

The M5 Motorway (Junctions 18-17) (Temporary Restriction and Prohibition of Traffic) Order 2015 No. 2015/1196. - Enabling power: Road Traffic Regulation Act 1984, s. 14 (1) (a) & S.I. 1982/1163, reg. 16 (2). - Issued: 23.03.2015. Made: 10.03.2015. Coming into force: 13.03.2015. Effect: None. Territorial extent & classification: E. Local. - Available at http://www.legislation.gov.uk/uksi/2015/1196/contents/made Non-print

The M5 Motorway (Junctions 21-25) (Temporary Restriction and Prohibition of Traffic) Order 2015 No. 2015/1050. - Enabling power: Road Traffic Regulation Act 1984, s. 14 (1) (a) & S.I. 1982/1163, reg. 16 (2). - Issued: 23.02.2015. Made: 09.02.2015. Coming into force: 13.02.2015. Effect: None. Territorial extent & classification: E. Local. - Available at http://www.legislation.gov.uk/uksi/2015/1050/contents/made Non-print

The M5 Motorway (Junctions 27-30) (Temporary Restriction and Prohibition of Traffic) Order 2015 No. 2015/151. - Enabling power: Road Traffic Regulation Act 1984, s. 14 (1) (a) & S.I. 1982/1163 reg. 16 (2). - Issued: 28.01.2015. Made: 14.01.2015. Coming into force: 17.01.2015. Effect: None. Territorial extent & classification: E. Local. - Available at http://www.legislation.gov.uk/uksi/2015/151/contents/made Non-print

The M6 and M5 Motorways (M6 Junction 7 to 10) (Temporary Prohibition of Traffic) Order 2015 No. 2015/1042. - Enabling power: Road Traffic Regulation Act 1984, s. 14 (1) (a). - Issued: 17.02.2015. Made: 02.02.2015. Coming into force: 09.02.2015. Effect: None. Territorial extent & classification: E. Local. - Available at http://www.legislation.gov.uk/uksi/2015/1042/contents/made Non-print

The M6 and M42 Motorways (M6 Junction 3a to 4, Warwickshire) (Temporary Prohibition of Traffic) Order 2015 No. 2015/1004. - Enabling power: Road Traffic Regulation Act 1984, s. 14 (1) (a). - Issued: 16.02.2015. Made: 27.01.2015. Coming into force: 03.02.2015. Effect: None. Territorial extent & classification: E. Local. - Available at http://www.legislation.gov.uk/uksi/2015/1004/contents/made Non-print

The M6 and M42 Motorways (M6 Junction 4a) (Link Roads) (Temporary Restriction and Prohibition of Traffic) Order 2015 No. 2015/697. - Enabling power: Road Traffic Regulation Act 1984, s. 14 (1) (a). - Issued: 16.02.2015. Made: 23.01.2015. Coming into force: 30.01.2015. Effect: None. Territorial extent & classification: E. Local. - Available at http://www.legislation.gov.uk/uksi/2015/697/contents/made Non-print

The M6 and M69 Motorways (M6 Junction 2) (Temporary Prohibition of Traffic) Order 2015 No. 2015/1043. - Enabling power: Road Traffic Regulation Act 1984, s. 14 (1) (a). - Issued: 17.02.2015. Made: 02.02.2015. Coming into force: 09.02.2015. Effect: None. Territorial extent & classification: E. Local. - Available at http://www.legislation.gov.uk/uksi/2015/1043/contents/made Non-print

The M6 Motorway (Junction 3, Warwickshire) (Temporary Prohibition of Traffic) Order 2015 No. 2015/1048. - Enabling power: Road Traffic Regulation Act 1984, s. 14 (1) (a). - Issued: 17.02.2015. Made: 03.02.2014. Coming into force: 10.02.2015. Effect: None. Territorial extent & classification: E. Local. - Available at http://www.legislation.gov.uk/uksi/2015/1048/contents/made Non-print

The M6 Motorway (Junction 4 - 4a) (Temporary Prohibition of Traffic) Order 2015 No. 2015/837. - Enabling power: Road Traffic Regulation Act 1984, s. 14 (1) (a). - Issued: 16.02.2015. Made: 26.01.2015. Coming into force: 02.02.2015. Effect: None. Territorial extent & classification: E. Local. - Available at http://www.legislation.gov.uk/uksi/2015/837/contents/made Non-print

The M6 Motorway (Junction 6, Birmingham) (Link Road) (Temporary Prohibition of Traffic) Order 2015 No. 2015/287. - Enabling power: Road Traffic Regulation Act 1984, s. 14 (1) (a). - Issued: 02.02.2014. Made: 19.01.2014. Coming into force: 26.01.2015. Effect: None. Territorial extent & classification: E. Local. - Available at http://www.legislation.gov.uk/uksi/2015/287/contents/made Non-print

The M6 Motorway (Junction 16, Staffordshire) (Temporary Prohibition of Traffic) Order 2015 No. 2015/163. - Enabling power: Road Traffic Regulation Act 1984, s. 14 (1) (a). - Issued: 29.01.2015. Made: 12.01.2015. Coming into force: 19.01.2015. Effect: None. Territorial extent & classification: E. Local. - Available at http://www.legislation.gov.uk/uksi/2015/163/contents/made Non-print

The M6 Motorway (Junction 17 Northbound and Southbound Exit and Entry Slip Roads) (Temporary Prohibition of Traffic) Order 2015 No. 2015/166. - Enabling power: Road Traffic Regulation Act 1984, s. 14 (1) (a). - Issued: 02.02.2015. Made: 20.01.2015. Coming into force: 22.01.2015. Effect: None. Territorial extent & classification: E. Local. - Available at http://www.legislation.gov.uk/uksi/2015/166/contents/made Non-print

The M6 Motorway (Junction 18 Southbound Entry Slip Road) (Temporary Prohibition of Traffic) Order 2015 No. 2015/1040. - Enabling power: Road Traffic Regulation Act 1984, s. 14 (1) (a). - Issued: 13.04.2015. Made: 20.01.2015. Coming into force: 08.02.2015. Effect: None. Territorial extent & classification: E. Local. - Available at http://www.legislation.gov.uk/uksi/2015/1040/contents/made Non-print

The M6 Motorway (Junction 29 Northbound Exit Slip Road and Junction 29 Roundabout) (Temporary Prohibition of Traffic) Order 2015 No. 2015/1132. - Enabling power: Road Traffic Regulation Act 1984, s. 14 (1) (a). - Issued: 18.03.2015. Made: 26.02.2015. Coming into force: 28.02.2015. Effect: None. Territorial extent & classification: E. Local. - Available at http://www.legislation.gov.uk/uksi/2015/1132/contents/made Non-print

The M6 Motorway (Junction 36-38 Northbound Carriageway and Slip Roads) (Temporary Restriction of Traffic) Order 2015 No. 2015/763. - Enabling power: Road Traffic Regulation Act 1984, s. 14 (1) (a). - Issued: 29.01.2015. Made: 14.01.2015. Coming into force: 02.02.2015. Effect: None. Territorial extent & classification: E. Local. - Available at http://www.legislation.gov.uk/uksi/2015/763/contents/made Non-print

The M6 Motorway (Junction 37-39 Northbound and Southbound Carriageways and Slip Roads) (Temporary Prohibition and Restriction of Traffic) Order 2015 No. 2015/1044. - Enabling power: Road Traffic Regulation Act 1984, s. 14 (1) (a) & S.I. 1982/1163, reg. 16 (2). - Issued: 14.04.2015. Made: 21.01.2015. Coming into force: 08.02.2015. Effect: None. Territorial extent & classification: E. Local. - Available at http://www.legislation.gov.uk/uksi/2015/1044/contents/made Non-print

The M6 Motorway (Junction 38-36 Southbound Carriageway and Slip Roads) (Temporary Restriction of Traffic) Order 2015 No. 2015/986. - Enabling power: Road Traffic Regulation Act 1984, s. 14 (1) (a). - Issued: 03.03.2015. Made: 28.01.2015. Coming into force: 02.02.2015. Effect: None. Territorial extent & classification: E. Local. - Available at http://www.legislation.gov.uk/uksi/2015/986/contents/made Non-print

The M6 Motorway (Junctions 1-2, Warwickshire) (Temporary Restriction and Prohibition of Traffic) Order 2015 No. 2015/976. - Enabling power: Road Traffic Regulation Act 1984, s. 14 (1) (a). - Issued: 16.02.2015. Made: 26.01.2015. Coming into force: 02.02.2015. Effect: None. Territorial extent & classification: E. Local. - Available at http://www.legislation.gov.uk/uksi/2015/976/contents/made Non-print

The M6 Motorway (Junctions 2 to 3, Coventry and Warwickshire) (Temporary Prohibition of Traffic) Order 2015 No. 2015/1242. - Enabling power: Road Traffic Regulation Act 1984, s. 14 (1) (a). - Issued: 20.04.2015. Made: 30.03.2015. Coming into force: 06.04.2015. Effect: None. Territorial extent & classification: E. Local. - Available at http://www.legislation.gov.uk/uksi/2015/1242/contents/made Non-print

The M6 Motorway (Junctions 2 to 3) (Temporary Prohibition of Traffic) Order 2015 No. 2015/1189. - Enabling power: Road Traffic Regulation Act 1984, s. 14 (1) (a). - Issued: 25.03.2015. Made: 09.03.2015. Coming into force: 16.03.2015. Effect: None. Territorial extent & classification: E. Local. - Available at http://www.legislation.gov.uk/uksi/2015/1189/contents/made Non-print

The M6 Motorway (Junctions 4 to 3, Warwickshire) (Temporary Prohibition of Traffic) Order 2015 No. 2015/1190. - Enabling power: Road Traffic Regulation Act 1984, s. 14 (1) (a). - Issued: 25.03.2015. Made: 09.03.2015. Coming into force: 16.03.2015. Effect: None. Territorial extent & classification: E. Local. - Available at http://www.legislation.gov.uk/uksi/2015/1190/contents/made Non-print

The M6 Motorway (Junctions 10 to 8, Walsall) (Temporary Restriction and Prohibition of Traffic) Order 2015 No. 2015/1173. - Enabling power: Road Traffic Regulation Act 1984, s. 14 (1) (a). - Issued: 11.03.2015. Made: 23.02.2015. Coming into force: 02.03.2015. Effect: None. Territorial extent & classification: E. Local. - Available at http://www.legislation.gov.uk/uksi/2015/1173/contents/made Non-print

The M6 Motorway (Junctions 15 to 13) (Temporary Prohibition of Traffic) Order 2015 No. 2015/1197. - Enabling power: Road Traffic Regulation Act 1984, s. 14 (1) (a). - Issued: 25.03.2015. Made: 09.03.2015. Coming into force: 16.03.2015. Effect: None. Territorial extent & classification: E. Local. - Available at http://www.legislation.gov.uk/uksi/2015/1197/contents/made Non-print

ROAD TRAFFIC: TRAFFIC REGULATION

The M6 Motorway (Junctions 16-18 Northbound and Southbound Carriageways and Slip Roads) and Sandbach Area (Temporary Prohibition and Restriction of Traffic) Order 2015 No. 2015/167. - Enabling power: Road Traffic Regulation Act 1984, s. 14 (1) (a) & S.I. 1982/1163, reg. 16(2). - Issued: 23.01.2015. Made: 06.01.2015. Coming into force: 23.01.2015. Effect: None. Territorial extent & classification: E. Local. - Available at http://www.legislation.gov.uk/uksi/2015/167/contents/made Non-print

The M6 Motorway (Junctions 19-20A Northbound and Southbound Carriageways, Link and Slip Roads), the M56 and Knutsford Service Area (Temporary Prohibition and Restriction of Traffic) Order 2015 No. 2015/1093. - Enabling power: Road Traffic Regulation Act 1984, s. 14 (1) (a) & S.I. 1982/1163, reg. 16 (2). - Issued: 04.03.2015. Made: 18.02.2015. Coming into force: 22.02.2015. Effect: None. Territorial extent & classification: E. Local. - Available at http://www.legislation.gov.uk/uksi/2015/1093/contents/made Non-print

The M6 Motorway (Junctions 26-28 Northbound Carriageway and Slip Roads) (Temporary Prohibition and Restriction of Traffic) Order 2015 No. 2015/1037. - Enabling power: Road Traffic Regulation Act 1984, s. 14 (1) (a) & S.I. 1982/1163, reg. 16 (2). - Issued: 03.03.2015. Made: 05.02.2015. Coming into force: 08.02.2015. Effect: None. Territorial extent & classification: E. Local. - Available at http://www.legislation.gov.uk/uksi/2015/1037/contents/made Non-print

The M6 Motorway (Junctions 37-38 Northbound Exit and Entry Slip Roads) (Temporary Prohibition of Traffic) Order 2015 No. 2015/1186. - Enabling power: Road Traffic Regulation Act 1984, s. 14 (1) (a). - Issued: 26.03.2015. Made: 11.03.2015. Coming into force: 15.03.2015. Effect: None. Territorial extent & classification: E. Local. - Available at http://www.legislation.gov.uk/uksi/2015/1186/contents/made Non-print

The M6 Motorway (Junctions 39-41 Northbound and Southbound Carriageways and Slip Roads) (Temporary Restriction of Traffic) Order 2015 No. 2015/1029. - Enabling power: Road Traffic Regulation Act 1984, s. 14 (1) (a). - Issued: 09.04.2015. Made: 15.01.2015. Coming into force: 02.02.2015. Effect: None. Territorial extent & classification: E. Local. - Available at http://www.legislation.gov.uk/uksi/2015/1029/contents/made Non-print

The M6 Motorway (Junctions 39-41 Northbound and Southbound Exit and Entry Slip Roads) (Temporary Prohibition of Traffic) Order 2015 No. 2015/1216. - Enabling power: Road Traffic Regulation Act 1984, s. 14 (1) (a). - Issued: 26.03.2015. Made: 13.03.2015. Coming into force: 15.03.2015. Effect: None. Territorial extent & classification: E. Local. - Available at http://www.legislation.gov.uk/uksi/2015/1216/contents/made Non-print

The M6 Motorway (Junctions 41-42 Northbound Carriageway) (Temporary Restriction of Traffic) Order 2015 No. 2015/1138. - Enabling power: Road Traffic Regulation Act 1984, s. 14 (1) (a). - Issued: 04.03.2015. Made: 12.02.2015. Coming into force: 01.03.2015. Effect: None. Territorial extent & classification: E. Local. - Available at http://www.legislation.gov.uk/uksi/2015/1138/contents/made Non-print

The M6 Toll Motorway (Hammerwich to Weeford) (Staffordshire) (Temporary Restriction and Prohibition of Traffic) Order 2015 No. 2015/1668. - Enabling power: Road Traffic Regulation Act 1984, s. 14 (1) (a) & S.I. 1982/1163, reg. 16 (2). - Issued: 11.09.2015. Made: 14.08.2015. Coming into force: 21.08.2015. Effect: None. Territorial extent & classification: E. Local. - Available at http://www.legislation.gov.uk/uksi/2015/1668/contents/made Non-print

The M6 Toll Motorway (Junctions T5 and T6, Staffordshire) (Slip Roads)(Temporary Prohibition of Traffic) Order 2015 No. 2015/2081. - Enabling power: Road Traffic Regulation Act 1984 s. 14 (1) (a). - Issued: 28.01.2016. Made: 31.12.2015. Coming into force: 07.01.2016. Effect: None. Territorial extent & classification: E. Local. - Available at http://www.legislation.gov.uk/uksi/2015/2081/contents/made Non-print

The M11 Motorway (Junction 8) and the A120 Trunk Road (Birchanger Roundabout to Priory Wood Roundabout) Essex (Temporary Restriction and Prohibition of Traffic) Order 2015 No. 2015/333. - Enabling power: Road Traffic Regulation Act 1984, s. 14 (1) (a). - Issued: 02.02.2014. Made: 19.01.2015. Coming into force: 26.01.2015. Effect: None. Territorial extent & classification: E. Local. - Available at http://www.legislation.gov.uk/uksi/2015/333/contents/made Non-print

The M18 Motorway and A1(M) Motorway (Wadworth) (Temporary Prohibition of Traffic) Order 2015 No. 2015/739. - Enabling power: Road Traffic Regulation Act 1984, s. 14 (1) (a). - Issued: 02.02.2015. Made: 22.01.2015. Coming into force: 01.02.2015. Effect: None. Territorial extent & classification: E. Local. - Available at http://www.legislation.gov.uk/uksi/2015/739/contents/made Non-print

The M18 Motorway (Junction 1 to Junction 6) (Temporary Restriction and Prohibition of Traffic) Order 2015 No. 2015/1033. - Enabling power: Road Traffic Regulation Act 1984, s. 14 (1) (a) & S.I. 1982/1163, reg. 16 (2). - Issued: 11.02.2015. Made: 29.01.2015. Coming into force: 08.02.2015. Effect: None. Territorial extent & classification: E. Local. - Available at http://www.legislation.gov.uk/uksi/2015/1033/contents/made Non-print

The M18 Motorway (Junction 3 to Junction 4) (Temporary Restriction and Prohibition of Traffic) Order 2015 No. 2015/1141. - Enabling power: Road Traffic Regulation Act 1984, s. 14 (1) (a) & S.I. 1982/1163, reg. 16 (2). - Issued: 05.03.2015. Made: 19.02.2015. Coming into force: 01.03.2015. Effect: None. Territorial extent & classification: E. Local. - Available at http://www.legislation.gov.uk/uksi/2015/1141/contents/made Non-print

The M18 Motorway (Junction 4 to Junction 5) (Temporary Prohibition of Traffic) Order 2015 No. 2015/154. - Enabling power: Road Traffic Regulation Act 1984, s. 14 (1) (a). - Issued: 28.01.2015. Made: 08.01.2015. Coming into force: 18.01.2015. Effect: None. Territorial extent & classification: E. Local. - Available at http://www.legislation.gov.uk/uksi/2015/154/contents/made Non-print

The M20 Motorway and the A20 Trunk Road (Junctions 9 - 13, Slip Roads) (Temporary Prohibition of Traffic) Order 2015 No. 2015/1261. - Enabling power: Road Traffic Regulation Act 1984, s. 14 (1) (a). - Issued: 26.03.2015. Made: 23.03.2015. Coming into force: 16.04.2015. Effect: None. Territorial extent & classification: E. Local. - Available at http://www.legislation.gov.uk/uksi/2015/1261/contents/made Non-print

The M20 Motorway (Junctions 4 - 8) (Temporary Prohibition of Traffic) Order 2015 No. 2015/1213. - Enabling power: Road Traffic Regulation Act 1984, s. 14 (1) (a). - Issued: 23.03.2015. Made: 09.03.2015. Coming into force: 02.04.2015. Effect: None. Territorial extent & classification: E. Local. - Available at http://www.legislation.gov.uk/uksi/2015/1213/contents/made Non-print

The M25 and the M26 Motorways (Junctions 4 and 5) (Temporary Prohibition of Traffic) Order 2015 No. 2015/1269. - Enabling power: Road Traffic Regulation Act 1984, s. 14 (1) (a). - Issued: 01.04.2015. Made: 30.03.2015. Coming into force: 23.04.2015. Effect: None. Territorial extent & classification: E. Local. - Available at http://www.legislation.gov.uk/uksi/2015/1269/contents/made Non-print

The M25 Motorway and the A2 and A282 Trunk Roads (Junctions 1B - 5) (Temporary Prohibition of Traffic) Order 2015 No. 2015/519. - Enabling power: Road Traffic Regulation Act 1984, s. 14 (1) (a). - Issued: 06.03.2015. Made: 23.02.2015. Coming into force: 22.03.2015. Effect: None. Territorial extent & classification: E. Local. - Available at http://www.legislation.gov.uk/uksi/2015/519/contents/made Non-print

The M25 Motorway and the A2 and the A282 Trunk Roads (Junction 2) (Temporary Prohibition of Traffic) Order 2015 No. 2015/1264. - Enabling power: Road Traffic Regulation Act 1984, s. 14 (1) (a). - Issued: 01.04.2015. Made: 30.03.2015. Coming into force: 21.04.2015. Effect: None. Territorial extent & classification: E. Local. - Available at http://www.legislation.gov.uk/uksi/2015/1264/contents/made Non-print

ROAD TRAFFIC: TRAFFIC REGULATION

The M25 Motorway and the A40 Trunk Road (M25 Junctions 19, 22 and 23 and Denham Roundabout) (Temporary Prohibition of Traffic) Order 2015 No. 2015/1260. - Enabling power: Road Traffic Regulation Act 1984, s. 14 (1) (a). - Issued: 26.03.2015. Made: 23.03.2015. Coming into force: 16.04.2015. Effect: None. Territorial extent & classification: E. Local. - Available at http://www.legislation.gov.uk/uksi/2015/1260/contents/made Non-print

The M25 Motorway and the A282 Trunk Road (Junctions 30 - 31) (Temporary Prohibition of Traffic) Order 2015 No. 2015/1254. - Enabling power: Road Traffic Regulation Act 1984, s. 14 (1) (a). - Issued: 26.03.2015. Made: 23.03.2015. Coming into force: 11.04.2015. Effect: None. Territorial extent & classification: E. Local. - Available at http://www.legislation.gov.uk/uksi/2015/1254/contents/made Non-print

The M25 Motorway (Junction 7) (Temporary Prohibition of Traffic) Order 2015 No. 2015/1134. - Enabling power: Road Traffic Regulation Act 1984, s. 14 (1) (a). - Issued: 21.04.2015. Made: 09.02.2015. Coming into force: 28.02.2015. Effect: None. Territorial extent & classification: E. Local. - Available at http://www.legislation.gov.uk/uksi/2015/1134/contents/made Non-print

The M25 Motorway (Junctions 10 - 11) (Temporary Restriction of Traffic) Order 2015 No. 2015/56. - Enabling power: Road Traffic Regulation Act 1984, ss 14 (1) (a) (7). - Issued: 28.01.2015. Made: 05.01.2015. Coming into force: 24.01.2015. Effect: None. Territorial extent & classification: E. Local. - Available at http://www.legislation.gov.uk/uksi/2015/56/contents/made Non-print

The M25 Motorway (Junctions 16 - 17) (Temporary Prohibition of Traffic) Order 2015 No. 2015/1030. - Enabling power: Road Traffic Regulation Act 1984, s. 14 (1) (a). - Issued: 07.04.2015. Made: 19.01.2015. Coming into force: 07.02.2015. Effect: None. Territorial extent & classification: E. Local. - Available at http://www.legislation.gov.uk/uksi/2015/1030/contents/made Non-print

The M25 Motorway (Junctions 19 - 21A) (Temporary Restriction and Prohibition of Traffic) (No. 2) Order 2015 No. 2015/1307. - Enabling power: Road Traffic Regulation Act 1984, s. 14 (1) (a). - Issued: 11.05.2015. Made: 23.03.2015. Coming into force: 11.04.2015. Effect: S.I. 2015/1110 revoked. Territorial extent & classification: E. Local. - Available at http://www.legislation.gov.uk/uksi/2015/1307/contents/made Non-print

The M25 Motorway (Junctions 19 - 21A) (Temporary Restriction and Prohibition of Traffic) Order 2015 No. 2015/1110. - Enabling power: Road Traffic Regulation Act 1984, s. 14 (1) (a). - Issued: 20.04.2015. Made: 05.01.2015. Coming into force: 27.01.2015. Effect: None. Territorial extent & classification: E. Local. - Revoked by SI 2015/1307 (Non-print) (ISBN 9786666733629). - Available at http://www.legislation.gov.uk/uksi/2015/1110/contents/made Non-print

The M25 Motorway (Junctions 28 - 29) (Temporary Prohibition of Traffic) Order 2015 No. 2015/1253. - Enabling power: Road Traffic Regulation Act 1984, s. 14 (1) (a). - Issued: 26.03.2015. Made: 23.03.2015. Coming into force: 11.04.2015. Effect: None. Territorial extent & classification: E. Local. - Available at http://www.legislation.gov.uk/uksi/2015/1253/contents/made Non-print

The M25 Motorway, the M4 Motorway and the M40 Motorway (M25 Junctions 15 and 16) (Temporary Restriction and Prohibition of Traffic) Order 2015 No. 2015/1019. - Enabling power: Road Traffic Regulation Act 1984, s. 14 (1) (a). - Issued: 30.01.2015. Made: 19.01.2015. Coming into force: 07.02.2015. Effect: None. Territorial extent & classification: E. Local. - Available at http://www.legislation.gov.uk/uksi/2015/1019/contents/made Non-print

The M27 and M275 Motorways (M27 Junction 11 - A27 Hilsea Interchange) (Temporary Prohibition of Traffic) Order 2015 No. 2015/538. - Enabling power: Road Traffic Regulation Act 1984, s. 14 (1) (a). - Issued: 25.02.2015. Made: 16.02.2015. Coming into force: 07.03.2015. Effect: None. Territorial extent & classification: E. Local. - Available at http://www.legislation.gov.uk/uksi/2015/538/contents/made Non-print

The M27 Motorway (Junction 10) (Temporary Prohibition of Traffic) Order 2015 No. 2015/525. - Enabling power: Road Traffic Regulation Act 1984, s. 14 (1) (a). - Issued: 06.03.2015. Made: 23.02.2015. Coming into force: 14.03.2015. Effect: None. Territorial extent & classification: E. Local. - Available at http://www.legislation.gov.uk/uksi/2015/525/contents/made Non-print

The M32 Motorway (Junction 1) (Temporary Prohibition of Traffic) Order 2015 No. 2015/1249. - Enabling power: Road Traffic Regulation Act 1984, s. 14 (1) (a). - Issued: 27.04.2015. Made: 06.03.2015. Coming into force: 14.03.2015. Effect: None. Territorial extent & classification: E. Local. - Available at http://www.legislation.gov.uk/uksi/2015/1249/contents/made Non-print

The M40 Motorway (Junction 12) Slip Roads (Temporary Prohibition of Traffic) Order 2015 No. 2015/279. - Enabling power: Road Traffic Regulation Act 1984, s. 14 (1) (a). - Issued: 02.02.2014. Made: 19.01.2014. Coming into force: 26.01.2015. Effect: None. Territorial extent & classification: E. Local. - Available at http://www.legislation.gov.uk/uksi/2015/279/contents/made Non-print

The M40 Motorway (Junctions 1 to 5) (Temporary Prohibition of Traffic) Order 2015 No. 2015/1157. - Enabling power: Road Traffic Regulation Act 1984, s. 14 (1) (a). - Issued: 12.03.2015. Made: 23.02.2015. Coming into force: 02.03.2015. Effect: None. Territorial extent & classification: E. Local. - Available at http://www.legislation.gov.uk/uksi/2015/1157/contents/made Non-print

The M40 Motorway (Junctions 6 to 9) (Temporary Prohibition of Traffic) Order 2015 No. 2015/1279. - Enabling power: Road Traffic Regulation Act 1984, s. 14 (1) (a). - Issued: 01.05.2015. Made: 23.02.2015. Coming into force: 02.03.2015. Effect: None. Territorial extent & classification: E. Local. - Available at http://www.legislation.gov.uk/uksi/2015/1279/contents/made Non-print

The M40 Motorway (Junctions 10 to 11) Slip Roads (Temporary Prohibition of Traffic) Order 2015 No. 2015/1107. - Enabling power: Road Traffic Regulation Act 1984, s. 14 (1) (a). - Issued: 03.03.2015. Made: 16.02.2015. Coming into force: 23.02.2015. Effect: None. Territorial extent & classification: E. Local. - Available at http://www.legislation.gov.uk/uksi/2015/1107/contents/made Non-print

The M40 Motorway (Junctions 13 to 15) Slip Roads (Temporary Prohibition of Traffic) Order 2015 No. 2015/1108. - Enabling power: Road Traffic Regulation Act 1984, s. 14 (1) (a). - Issued: 03.03.2015. Made: 16.02.2015. Coming into force: 23.02.2015. Effect: None. Territorial extent & classification: E. Local. - Available at http://www.legislation.gov.uk/uksi/2015/1108/contents/made Non-print

The M42 and M6 Toll Motorways (Coleshill to Water Orton, Warwickshire) (Temporary Prohibition of Traffic) Order 2015 No. 2015/1671. - Enabling power: Road Traffic Regulation Act 1984, s. 14 (1) (a). - Issued: 11.09.2015. Made: 07.09.2015. Coming into force: 18.09.2015. Effect: None. Territorial extent & classification: E. Local. - Available at http://www.legislation.gov.uk/uksi/2015/1671/contents/made Non-print

The M42 and M40 Motorways (M42 Junctions 1 to 4) (Temporary Prohibition of Traffic) Order 2015 No. 2015/1215. - Enabling power: Road Traffic Regulation Act 1984, s. 14 (1) (a). - Issued: 20.04.2015. Made: 27.03.2015. Coming into force: 03.04.2015. Effect: None. Territorial extent & classification: E. Local. - Available at http://www.legislation.gov.uk/uksi/2015/1215/contents/made Non-print

The M42 Motorway (Junction 6) (Slip Road) (Temporary Prohibition of Traffic) Order 2015 No. 2015/1164. - Enabling power: Road Traffic Regulation Act 1984, s. 14 (1) (a). - Issued: 25.03.2015. Made: 02.03.2015. Coming into force: 09.03.2015. Effect: None. Territorial extent & classification: E. Local. - Available at http://www.legislation.gov.uk/uksi/2015/1164/contents/made Non-print

The M42 Motorway (Junction 9, Warwickshire) (Temporary Prohibition of Traffic) Order 2015 No. 2015/1169. - Enabling power: Road Traffic Regulation Act 1984, s. 14 (1) (a). - Issued: 25.03.2015. Made: 02.03.2015. Coming into force: 09.03.2015. Effect: None. Territorial extent & classification: E. Local. - Available at http://www.legislation.gov.uk/uksi/2015/1169/contents/made Non-print

The M42 Motorway (Junctions 5 to 4, Solihull) (Temporary Prohibition of Traffic) Order 2015 No. 2015/1191. - Enabling power: Road Traffic Regulation Act 1984, s. 14 (1) (a). - Issued: 25.03.2015. Made: 09.03.2015. Coming into force: 16.03.2015. Effect: None. Territorial extent & classification: E. Local. - Available at http://www.legislation.gov.uk/uksi/2015/1191/contents/made Non-print

ROAD TRAFFIC: TRAFFIC REGULATION

The M42 Motorway (Junctions 11 to 10) (Temporary Prohibition of Traffic) Order 2015 No. 2015/1163. - Enabling power: Road Traffic Regulation Act 1984, s. 14 (1) (a). - Issued: 25.03.2015. Made: 02.03.2015. Coming into force: 09.03.2015. Effect: None. Territorial extent & classification: E. Local. - Available at http://www.legislation.gov.uk/uksi/2015/1163/contents/made Non-print

The M45 Motorway (Thurlaston to M1) (Temporary Restriction and Prohibition of Traffic) Order 2015 No. 2015/245. - Enabling power: Road Traffic Regulation Act 1984, s. 14 (1) (a). - Issued: 12.02.2014. Made: 05.01.2014. Coming into force: 12.01.2015. Effect: None. Territorial extent & classification: E. Local. - Available at http://www.legislation.gov.uk/uksi/2015/245/contents/made Non-print

The M48 Motorway (Junctions 1-2) (Severn Bridge High Winds) (Temporary Restriction and Prohibition of Traffic) Order 2015 No. 2015/1228. - Enabling power: Road Traffic Regulation Act 1984, s. 14 (1) (b). - Issued: 26.03.2015. Made: 24.03.2015. Coming into force: 28.03.2015. Effect: None. Territorial extent & classification: E. Local. - Available at http://www.legislation.gov.uk/uksi/2015/1228/contents/made Non-print

The M50 Motorway (Junction 1 - Junction 4) (Temporary Restriction and Prohibition of Traffic) Order 2015 No. 2015/1237. - Enabling power: Road Traffic Regulation Act 1984, s. 14 (1) (a). - Issued: 20.04.2015. Made: 23.03.2015. Coming into force: 30.03.2015. Effect: None. Territorial extent & classification: E. Local. - Available at http://www.legislation.gov.uk/uksi/2015/1237/contents/made Non-print

The M53 Motorway (Junction 5 Southbound Carriageway and the Northbound and Southbound Slip Roads) (Temporary Prohibition of Traffic) Order 2015 No. 2015/253. - Enabling power: Road Traffic Regulation Act 1984, s. 14 (1) (a). - Issued: 02.02.2015. Made: 07.01.2014. Coming into force: 25.01.2015. Effect: None. Territorial extent & classification: E. Local. - Available at http://www.legislation.gov.uk/uksi/2015/253/contents/made Non-print

The M53 Motorway (Junctions 1-4 Northbound and Southbound Carriageways and Slip Roads) (Moreton Spur) (Temporary Prohibition and Restriction of Traffic) Order 2015 No. 2015/1006. - Enabling power: Road Traffic Regulation Act 1984, s. 14 (1) (a) & S.I. 1982/1163, reg. 16 (2). - Issued: 03.03.2015. Made: 21.01.2015. Coming into force: 05.02.2015. Effect: None. Territorial extent & classification: E. Local. - Available at http://www.legislation.gov.uk/uksi/2015/1006/contents/made Non-print

The M53 Motorway (Junctions 4-3 Northbound Carriageway and Slip Roads) (Temporary Prohibition of Traffic) Order 2015 No. 2015/1031. - Enabling power: Road Traffic Regulation Act 1984, s. 14 (1) (a). - Issued: 03.02.2015. Made: 21.01.2015. Coming into force: 08.02.2015. Effect: None. Territorial extent & classification: E. Local. - Available at http://www.legislation.gov.uk/uksi/2015/1031/contents/made Non-print

The M54 Motorway (Junction 2 to 3) (Temporary Prohibition of Traffic) Order 2015 No. 2015/1188. - Enabling power: Road Traffic Regulation Act 1984, s. 14 (1) (a). - Issued: 25.03.2015. Made: 09.03.2015. Coming into force: 16.03.2015. Effect: None. Territorial extent & classification: E. Local. - Available at http://www.legislation.gov.uk/uksi/2015/1188/contents/made Non-print

The M55 Motorway (Junctions 4-1 Eastbound Carriageway and Slip Roads) (Temporary Prohibition and Restriction of Traffic) Order 2015 No. 2015/1131. - Enabling power: Road Traffic Regulation Act 1984, s. 14 (1) (a). - Issued: 18.03.2015. Made: 26.02.2015. Coming into force: 28.02.2015. Effect: None. Territorial extent & classification: E. Local. - Available at http://www.legislation.gov.uk/uksi/2015/1131/contents/made Non-print

The M56 Motorway (Junction 5 Westbound Entry Slip Road) (Temporary Prohibition of Traffic) Order 2015 No. 2015/254. - Enabling power: Road Traffic Regulation Act 1984, s. 14 (1) (a). - Issued: 28.01.2015. Made: 07.01.2015. Coming into force: 26.01.2015. Effect: None. Territorial extent & classification: E. Local. - Available at http://www.legislation.gov.uk/uksi/2015/254/contents/made Non-print

The M56 Motorway (Junctions 1-3 Eastbound and Westbound Carriageways and Slip Roads) and the M60 Motorway (Temporary Prohibition of Traffic) Order 2015 No. 2015/1221. - Enabling power: Road Traffic Regulation Act 1984, s. 14 (1) (a). - Issued: 26.03.2015. Made: 17.03.2015. Coming into force: 22.03.2015. Effect: None. Territorial extent & classification: E. Local. - Available at http://www.legislation.gov.uk/uksi/2015/1221/contents/made Non-print

The M56 Motorway (Junctions 9-7 Westbound and Eastbound Carriageways and Slip Road) and the M6 Motorway (Temporary Prohibition of Traffic) Order 2015 No. 2015/1012. - Enabling power: Road Traffic Regulation Act 1984, s. 14 (1) (a). - Issued: 18.03.2015. Made: 21.01.2015. Coming into force: 06.02.2015. Effect: None. Territorial extent & classification: E. Local. - Available at http://www.legislation.gov.uk/uksi/2015/1012/contents/made Non-print

The M57 Motorway (Junctions 1-2 Northbound Carriageway, Northbound and Southbound Slip and Link Roads) and M62 (Temporary Prohibition of Traffic) Order 2015 No. 2015/1039. - Enabling power: Road Traffic Regulation Act 1984, s. 14 (1) (a). - Issued: 13.04.2015. Made: 21.01.2015. Coming into force: 08.02.2015. Effect: None. Territorial extent & classification: E. Local. - Available at http://www.legislation.gov.uk/uksi/2015/1039/contents/made Non-print

The M60, M61, M62, M66 and M602 Motorways (Manchester Smart Motorway Scheme) (Temporary Prohibition and Restriction of Traffic) Order 2015 No. 2015/136. - Enabling power: Road Traffic Regulation Act 1984, ss. 14 (1) (a), 15 (2), sch. 9, para. 27 (1) & Motorways Traffic (England and Wales) Regulations 1982, reg. 16 (2). - Issued: 05.02.2015. Made: 20.01.2015. Coming into force: 22.01.2015. Effect: S.I. 2014/2052 revoked. Territorial extent & classification: E. Local. - Available at http://www.legislation.gov.uk/uksi/2015/136/contents/made Non-print

The M60 Motorway (Junction 7 Clockwise Exit and Anticlockwise Entry Slip Roads) (Greater Manchester Marathon) (Temporary Prohibition of Traffic) Order 2015 No. 2015/1263. - Enabling power: Road Traffic Regulation Act 1984, s. 16A (2) (a). - Issued: 13.04.2015. Made: 31.03.2015. Coming into force: 18.04.2015. Effect: None. Territorial extent & classification: E. Local. - Available at http://www.legislation.gov.uk/uksi/2015/1263/contents/made Non-print

The M60 Motorway (Junctions 25-1 Clockwise and Anticlockwise Carriageways and Slip Roads) (Temporary Prohibition of Traffic) Order 2015 No. 2015/1133. - Enabling power: Road Traffic Regulation Act 1984, s. 14 (1) (a). - Issued: 18.03.2015. Made: 24.02.2015. Coming into force: 28.02.2015. Effect: None. Territorial extent & classification: E. Local. - Available at http://www.legislation.gov.uk/uksi/2015/1133/contents/made Non-print

The M61 Motorway (Junction 5 Southbound Exit Slip Road) (Temporary Prohibition of Traffic) Order 2015 No. 2015/1038. - Enabling power: Road Traffic Regulation Act 1984, s. 14 (1) (a). - Issued: 13.04.2015. Made: 21.01.2015. Coming into force: 08.02.2015. Effect: None. Territorial extent & classification: E. Local. - Available at http://www.legislation.gov.uk/uksi/2015/1038/contents/made Non-print

The M62 Motorway (Junction 8 Westbound Entry Slip Road) (Temporary Prohibition of Traffic) Order 2015 No. 2015/1256. - Enabling power: Road Traffic Regulation Act 1984, s. 14 (1) (a). - Issued: 01.04.2015. Made: 25.03.2015. Coming into force: 12.04.2015. Effect: None. Territorial extent & classification: E. Local. - Available at http://www.legislation.gov.uk/uksi/2015/1256/contents/made Non-print

The M62 Motorway (Junction 23 to Junction 24) (Temporary Prohibition of Traffic) Order 2015 No. 2015/1068. - Enabling power: Road Traffic Regulation Act 1984, s. 14 (1) (a). - Issued: 18.02.2015. Made: 05.02.2015. Coming into force: 16.02.2015. Effect: None. Territorial extent & classification: E. Local. - Available at http://www.legislation.gov.uk/uksi/2015/1068/contents/made Non-print

The M62 Motorway (Junction 25 to Junction 26) (Temporary Prohibition of Traffic) Order 2015 No. 2015/1148. - Enabling power: Road Traffic Regulation Act 1984, s. 14 (1) (a). - Issued: 05.03.2015. Made: 19.02.2015. Coming into force: 01.03.2015. Effect: None. Territorial extent & classification: E. Local. - Available at http://www.legislation.gov.uk/uksi/2015/1148/contents/made Non-print

ROAD TRAFFIC: TRAFFIC REGULATION

The M62 Motorway (Junction 25 to Junction 30) (Temporary Restriction and Prohibition of Traffic) Order 2011 (Revocation) Order 2015 No. 2015/249. - Enabling power: Road Traffic Regulation Act 1984, ss. 14 (1) (a) (7), 15 (2). - Issued: 03.02.2015. Made: 15.01.2015. Coming into force: 23.01.201. Effect: None. Territorial extent & classification: Local. - Available at http://www.legislation.gov.uk/uksi/2015/249/contents/made Non-print

The M62 Motorway (Junction 29) (Temporary Prohibition of Traffic) Order 2015 No. 2015/1159. - Enabling power: Road Traffic Regulation Act 1984, s. 14 (1) (a). - Issued: 13.03.2015. Made: 26.02.2015. Coming into force: 08.03.2015. Effect: None. Territorial extent & classification: E. Local. - Available at http://www.legislation.gov.uk/uksi/2015/1159/contents/made Non-print

The M62 Motorway (Junction 34 to Junction 33) (Temporary Restriction and Prohibition of Traffic) Order 2015 No. 2015/1622. - Enabling power: Road Traffic Regulation Act 1984, s. 14 (1) (a) & S.I. 1982/1163, reg. 16 (2). - Issued: 26.08.2015. Made: 29.01.2015. Coming into force: 08.02.2015. Effect: None. Territorial extent & classification: E. Local. - Available at http://www.legislation.gov.uk/uksi/2015/1622/contents/made Non-print

The M62 Motorway (Junction 34 to Junction 38) (Temporary Prohibition of Traffic) Order 2015 No. 2015/1143. - Enabling power: Road Traffic Regulation Act 1984, s. 14 (1) (a). - Issued: 05.03.2015. Made: 19.02.2015. Coming into force: 01.03.2015. Effect: None. Territorial extent & classification: E. Local. - Available at http://www.legislation.gov.uk/uksi/2015/1143/contents/made Non-print

The M62 Motorway (Junction 37) (Temporary Prohibition of Traffic) Order 2015 No. 2015/1081. - Enabling power: Road Traffic Regulation Act 1984, s. 14 (1) (a). - Issued: 24.02.2015. Made: 12.02.2015. Coming into force: 20.02.2015. Effect: None. Territorial extent & classification: E. Local. - Available at http://www.legislation.gov.uk/uksi/2015/1081/contents/made Non-print

The M62 Motorway (Junctions 11-12 Eastbound and Westbound Carriageways) (Temporary Prohibition and Restriction of Traffic) Order 2015 No. 2015/1172. - Enabling power: Road Traffic Regulation Act 1984, s. 14 (1) (a). - Issued: 19.03.2015. Made: 25.02.2015. Coming into force: 01.03.2015. Effect: None. Territorial extent & classification: E. Local. - Available at http://www.legislation.gov.uk/uksi/2015/1172/contents/made Non-print

The M65 Motorway (Junctions 5-6 Eastbound and Westbound Carriageways and Slip Roads) (Temporary Prohibition of Traffic) Order 2015 No. 2015/1032. - Enabling power: Road Traffic Regulation Act 1984, s. 14 (1) (a). - Issued: 03.02.2015. Made: 20.01.2015. Coming into force: 08.02.2015. Effect: None. Territorial extent & classification: E. Local. - Available at http://www.legislation.gov.uk/uksi/2015/1032/contents/made Non-print

The M69 and M6 Motorways (M69 Junction 1 to M6 Junction 2) (Temporary Prohibition of Traffic) Order 2015 No. 2015/1066. - Enabling power: Road Traffic Regulation Act 1984, s. 14 (1) (a). - Issued: 16.04.2015. Made: 19.01.2015. Coming into force: 26.01.2015. Effect: None. Territorial extent & classification: E. Local. - Available at http://www.legislation.gov.uk/uksi/2015/1066/contents/made Non-print

The M180 Motorway (Junction 2) (Temporary Prohibition of Traffic) Order 2015 No. 2015/734. - Enabling power: Road Traffic Regulation Act 1984, s. 14 (1) (a). - Issued: 02.02.2015. Made: 22.01.2015. Coming into force: 01.02.2015. Effect: None. Territorial extent & classification: E. Local. - Available at http://www.legislation.gov.uk/uksi/2015/734/contents/made Non-print

The M180 Motorway (Junction 2 to Junction 5) (Temporary Prohibition of Traffic) Order 2015 No. 2015/1144. - Enabling power: Road Traffic Regulation Act 1984, s. 14 (1) (a). - Issued: 05.03.2015. Made: 19.02.2015. Coming into force: 01.03.2015. Effect: None. Territorial extent & classification: E. Local. - Available at http://www.legislation.gov.uk/uksi/2015/1144/contents/made Non-print

The M180 Motorway (Junction 4 to Junction 3) (Temporary Prohibition of Traffic) Order 2015 No. 2015/1155. - Enabling power: Road Traffic Regulation Act 1984, s. 14 (1) (a). - Issued: 06.03.2015. Made: 19.02.2015. Coming into force: 02.03.2015. Effect: None. Territorial extent & classification: E. Local. - Available at http://www.legislation.gov.uk/uksi/2015/1155/contents/made Non-print

The M180 Motorway (Junction 4 to Junction 5) (Temporary Restriction and Prohibition of Traffic) Order 2015 No. 2015/1271. - Enabling power: Road Traffic Regulation Act 1984, s. 14 (1) (a) & S.I. 1982/1163, reg. 16 (2). - Issued: 28.04.2015. Made: 12.02.2015. Coming into force: 22.02.2015. Effect: None. Territorial extent & classification: E. Local. - Available at http://www.legislation.gov.uk/uksi/2015/1271/contents/made Non-print

The M181 Motorway (Midmoor to Frodingham) (Temporary Restriction and Prohibition of Traffic) Order 2015 No. 2015/707. - Enabling power: Road Traffic Regulation Act 1984, s. 14 (1) (a). - Issued: 02.02.2015. Made: 22.01.2015. Coming into force: 31.01.2015. Effect: None. Territorial extent & classification: E. Local. - Available at http://www.legislation.gov.uk/uksi/2015/707/contents/made Non-print

The M621 Motorway (Gildersome Interchange) (Temporary Restriction and Prohibition of Traffic) Order 2015 No. 2015/1233. - Enabling power: Road Traffic Regulation Act 1984, s. 14 (1) (a) & S.I. 1982/1163, reg. 16 (2). - Issued: 26.03.2015. Made: 19.03.2015. Coming into force: 29.03.2015. Effect: None. Territorial extent & classification: E. Local. - Available at http://www.legislation.gov.uk/uksi/2015/1233/contents/made Non-print

The M621 Motorway (Junction 1) (Temporary Restriction and Prohibition of Traffic) Order 2015 No. 2015/1094. - Enabling power: Road Traffic Regulation Act 1984, s. 14 (1) (a) & S.I. 1982/1163, reg. 16 (2). - Issued: 25.02.2015. Made: 12.02.2015. Coming into force: 23.02.2015. Effect: None. Territorial extent & classification: E. Local. - Available at http://www.legislation.gov.uk/uksi/2015/1094/contents/made Non-print

The M621 Motorway (Junction 2A to Junction 3) (Temporary Prohibition of Traffic) Order 2015 No. 2015/1045. - Enabling power: Road Traffic Regulation Act 1984, s. 14 (1) (a). - Issued: 11.02.2015. Made: 29.01.2015. Coming into force: 10.02.2015. Effect: None. Territorial extent & classification: E. Local. - Available at http://www.legislation.gov.uk/uksi/2015/1045/contents/made Non-print

The Old Great North Road Trunk Road (Darrington) (Temporary Prohibition of Traffic) Order 2015 No. 2015/1200. - Enabling power: Road Traffic Regulation Act 1984, s. 14 (1) (a). - Issued: 20.03.2015. Made: 05.03.2015. Coming into force: 19.03.2015. Effect: None. Territorial extent & classification: E. Local. - Available at http://www.legislation.gov.uk/uksi/2015/1200/contents/made Non-print

The A11 Trunk Road (Snetterton to Thetford, Norfolk) Southbound (Temporary Prohibition of Traffic) Order 2015 No. 2015/157. - Enabling power: Road Traffic Regulation Act 1984, s. 14 (1) (a). - Issued: 28.01.2015. Made: 12.01.2015. Coming into force: 19.01.2015. Effect: None. Territorial extent & classification: E. Local. - Available at http://www.legislation.gov.uk/uksi/2015/157/contents/made Non-print

The A19 Trunk Road (Seaton Lane Interchange) (Temporary Prohibition of Traffic) Order 2015 No. 2015/1059. - Enabling power: Road Traffic Regulation Act 1984, s. 14 (1) (a). - Issued: 18.02.2015. Made: 05.02.2015. Coming into force: 15.02.2015. Effect: None. Territorial extent & classification: E. Local. - Available at http://www.legislation.gov.uk/uksi/2015/1059/contents/made Non-print

The A36 Trunk Road (South Newton, Near Salisbury) (Temporary Restriction of Traffic) (No.2) Order 2015 No. 2015/1183. - Enabling power: Road Traffic Regulation Act 1984, s. 14 (1) (a). - Issued: 18.03.2015. Made: 03.03.2015. Coming into force: 07.03.2015. Effect: None. Territorial extent & classification: E. Local. - Available at http://www.legislation.gov.uk/uksi/2015/1183/contents/made Non-print

The A303 Trunk Road (M3 Junction 8 - Bullington Cross Interchange) (Temporary Prohibition of Traffic) Order 2015 No. 2015/1234. - Enabling power: Road Traffic Regulation Act 1984, s. 14 (1) (a). - Issued: 23.03.2015. Made: 09.03.2015. Coming into force: 30.03.2015. Effect: None. Territorial extent & classification: E. Local. - Available at http://www.legislation.gov.uk/uksi/2015/1234/contents/made Non-print

The A585 Trunk Road (Windy Harbour Junction) (Temporary Prohibition of Traffic) Order 2015 No. 2015/1153. - Enabling power: Road Traffic Regulation Act 1984, s. 14 (1) (a). - Issued: 18.03.2015. Made: 26.02.2015. Coming into force: 01.03.2015. Effect: None. Territorial extent & classification: E. Local. - Available at http://www.legislation.gov.uk/uksi/2015/1153/contents/made Non-print

The M5 Motorway (Junctions 14-13) (Temporary Restriction and Prohibition of Traffic) Order 2015 No. 2015/711. - Enabling power: Road Traffic Regulation Act 1984, s. 14 (1) (a) & S.I. 1982/1163, reg. 16 (2). - Issued: 05.02.2015. Made: 27.01.2015. Coming into force: 31.01.2015. Effect: None. Territorial extent & classification: E. Local. - Available at http://www.legislation.gov.uk/uksi/2015/711/contents/made Non-print

The M5 Motorway (Junctions 18-22) (Temporary Restriction and Prohibition of Traffic) Order 2015 No. 2015/712. - Enabling power: Road Traffic Regulation Act 1984, s. 14 (1) (a) & S.I. 1982/1163, reg. 16 (2). - Issued: 06.02.2015. Made: 28.01.2015. Coming into force: 31.01.2015. Effect: None. Territorial extent & classification: E. Local. - Available at http://www.legislation.gov.uk/uksi/2015/712/contents/made Non-print

The M6 and M42 Motorways (M6 Junction 4a, Warwickshire) (Link Road) (Temporary Prohibition of Traffic) Order 2015 No. 2015/1174. - Enabling power: Road Traffic Regulation Act 1984, s. 14 (1) (a). - Issued: 11.03.2015. Made: 23.02.2015. Coming into force: 02.03.2015. Effect: None. Territorial extent & classification: E. Local. - Available at http://www.legislation.gov.uk/uksi/2015/1174/contents/made Non-print

The M6 Motorway (Junctions 32-33 Northbound and Southbound Carriageways) (Temporary Restriction of Traffic) Order 2015 No. 2015/1209. - Enabling power: Road Traffic Regulation Act 1984, s. 14 (1) (a) & S.I. 1982/1163, reg. 16 (2). - Issued: 25.03.2015. Made: 13.03.2015. Coming into force: 15.03.2015. Effect: None. Territorial extent & classification: E. Local. - Available at http://www.legislation.gov.uk/uksi/2015/1209/contents/made Non-print

The M6 Motorway (Junctions 43-45 Northbound and Southbound Carriageways and Slip Roads) and Todhills Services (Temporary Prohibition and Restriction of Traffic) Order 2015 No. 2015/1210. - Enabling power: Road Traffic Regulation Act 1984, s. 14 (1) (a). - Issued: 26.03.2015. Made: 13.03.2015. Coming into force: 15.03.2015. Effect: None. Territorial extent & classification: E. Local. - Available at http://www.legislation.gov.uk/uksi/2015/1210/contents/made Non-print

The M56 Motorway (Junction 7 Eastbound Exit Slip Road) (Temporary Prohibition of Traffic) Order 2015 No. 2015/1240. - Enabling power: Road Traffic Regulation Act 1984, s. 14 (1) (a). - Issued: 24.03.2015. Made: 17.03.2015. Coming into force: 06.04.2015. Effect: None. Territorial extent & classification: S. Local. - Available at: http://www.legislation.gov.uk/uksi/2015/1240/contents/made Non-print

The M62 Motorway (Junction 27) (Temporary Prohibition of Traffic) Order 2015 No. 2015/1150. - Enabling power: Road Traffic Regulation Act 1984, s. 14 (1) (a). - Issued: 06.03.2015. Made: 19.02.2015. Coming into force: 01.03.2015. Effect: None. Territorial extent & classification: E. Local. - Available at http://www.legislation.gov.uk/uksi/2015/1150/contents/made Non-print

Road traffic, England

The Civil Enforcement of Parking Contraventions (England) General (Amendment No. 2) Regulations 2015 No. 2015/1001. - Enabling power: Traffic Management Act 2004, ss. 78, 78A, 89. - Issued: 08.04.2015. Made: 27.03.2015. Coming into force: 01.04.2015. Effect: S.I. 2007/3482, 3483 amended. Territorial extent & classification: E. General. - 4p.: 30 cm. - 978-0-11-113632-4 £4.25

The Civil Enforcement of Parking Contraventions (England) General (Amendment) Regulations 2015 No. 2015/561. - Enabling power: Traffic Management Act 2004, ss. 72, 73 (3), 89. - Issued: 12.03.2015. Made: 05.03.2015. Laid: 06.03.2015. Coming into force: 06.04.2015. Effect: S.I. 2007/3483 amended. Territorial extent & classification: E. General. - 2p.: 30 cm. - 978-0-11-113231-9 £4.25

The M275 and M27 Motorway (Speed Limit and Bus Lane) Regulations 2015 No. 2015/405. - Enabling power: Road Traffic Regulation Act 1984, s. 17 (2) (3). - Issued: 05.03.2015. Made: 25.02.2015. Laid: 02.03.2015. Coming into force: 14.04.2015. Effect: S.I. 2014/790 revoked. Territorial extent & classification: E. Local. - This Statutory Instrument ha been made in consequence of a defect in S.I. 2014/790 (ISBN 9780111112618) published 27/03/14 and is being issued free of charge to all known recipients of that Statutory Instruments. - 4p.: 30 cm. - 978-0-11-113092-6 £4.25

The Use of Invalid Carriages on Highways (Amendment) (England and Scotland) Regulations 2015 No. 2015/59. - Enabling power: Chronically Sick and Disabled Persons Act 1970, s. 20 (1) (2) (3). - Issued: 02.02.2015. Made: 23.01.2015. Laid: 02.02.2015. Coming into force: 09.03.2015. Effect: S.I. 1988/2268 amended. Territorial extent & classification: E/S. General. - With correction slip dated February 2015. - 4p.: 30 cm. - 978-0-11-112793-3 £4.25

Road traffic, England: Special roads

The M1 Motorway (Junctions 28 to 35a) (Variable Speed Limits) Regulations 2015 No. 2015/1701. - Enabling power: Road Traffic Regulation Act 1984, s. 17 (2) (3). - Issued: 28.09.2015. Made: 18.09.2015. Laid: 25.09.2015. Coming into force: 20.10.2015. Effect: None. Territorial extent & classification: E. General. - 4p.: 30 cm. - 978-0-11-113940-0 £4.25

The M1 Motorway (Junctions 39 to 42) (Variable Speed Limits) Regulations 2015 No. 2015/408. - Enabling power: Road Traffic Regulation Act 1984, s. 17 (2) (3). - Issued: 05.03.2015. Made: 23.02.2015. Laid: 05.03.2015. Coming into force: 08.04.2015. Effect: None. Territorial extent & classification: E. Local. - 4p.: 30 cm. - 978-0-11-113098-8 £4.25

The M6 Motorway (Junctions 10a to 13)(Variable Speed Limits) Regulations 2015 No. 2015/8. - Enabling power: Road Traffic Regulation Act 1984, s. 17 (2) (3). - Issued: 14.01.2015. Made: 07.01.2015. Laid: 12.01.2015. Coming into force: 09.02.2015. Effect: None. Territorial extent & classification: E. Local. - 8p.: 30 cm. - 978-0-11-112675-2 £4.25

Road traffic, England and Wales

The Drug Driving (Specified Limits) (England and Wales) (Amendment) Regulations 2015 No. 2015/911. - Enabling power: Road Traffic Act 1988, s. 5A. - Issued: 27.03.2015. Made: 23.03.2015. Coming into force: -14.04.2015. Effect: 2014/2868 amended. Territorial extent & classification: E/W. General. - Supersedes draft S.I. (ISBN 9780111128824) issued 11.02.2015. - 2p.: 30 cm. - 978-0-11-113535-8 £4.25

The Motor Vehicles (Variation of Speed Limits for Naval, Military and Air Force Vehicles) (England and Wales) Regulations 2015 No. 2015/1653. - Enabling power: Road Traffic Regulation Act 1984, s. 130 (3). - Issued: 11.09.2015. Made: 07.09.2015. Laid: 09.09.2015. Coming into force: 01.10.2015. Effect: 1984 c.27 amended. Territorial extent & classification: E/W. General. - 4p.: 30 cm. - 978-0-11-113903-5 £4.25

Road traffic, England and Wales: Special roads

The Motorways Traffic (England and Wales) (Amendment) (England) Regulations 2015 No. 2015/392. - Enabling power: Road Traffic Regulation Act 1984, s. 17 (2) (3). - Issued: 04.03.2015. Made: 24.02.2015. Laid: 04.03.2015. Coming into force: 06.04.2015. Effect: S.I. 1982/1163 amended. Territorial extent & classification: E/W. General. - 2p.: 30 cm. - 978-0-11-113080-3 £4.25

Road traffic, Scotland

The Use of Invalid Carriages on Highways (Amendment) (England and Scotland) Regulations 2015 No. 2015/59. - Enabling power: Chronically Sick and Disabled Persons Act 1970, s. 20 (1) (2) (3). - Issued: 02.02.2015. Made: 23.01.2015. Laid: 02.02.2015. Coming into force: 09.03.2015. Effect: S.I. 1988/2268 amended. Territorial extent & classification: E/S. General. - 4p.: 30 cm. - With correction slip dated February 2015 - 978-0-11-112793-3 £4.25

Road traffic, Wales

The Cycle Racing on Highways (Amendment) (Wales) Regulations 2015 No. 2015/706 (W.57). - Enabling power: Road Traffic Act 1988, s. 31 (2) (3). - Issued: 24.03.2015. Made: 10.03.2015. Laid before the National Assembly for Wales: 16.03.2015. Coming into force: 07.04.2015. Effect: S.I. 1960/250 amended. Territorial extent & classification: W. General. - In English and Welsh. Welsh title: Rheoliadau Rasio Beiciau ar Briffyrdd (Diwygio) (Cymru) 2015. - 8p.: 30 cm. - 978-0-348-11056-2 £4.25

The M4 Motorway (West of Junction 23A (Magor) to East of Junction 29 (Castleton)) (Variable Speed Limits) Regulations 2015 No. 2015/1018 (W.72). - Enabling power: Road Traffic Act 1984, s. 17 (2) (3). - Issued: 14.04.2015. Made: 30.03.2015. Laid before the National Assembly for Wales: 31.03.2015. Coming into force: 21.04.2015. Effect: S.I. 2011/94 (W.19) revoked. Territorial extent & classification: W. General. - In English and Welsh. Welsh language title: Rheoliadau Trafford yr M4 (Man i'r Gorllewin o Gyffordd 23A (Magwyr) i Fan i'r Dwyrain o Gyffordd 29 (Cas-bach)) (Terfyn Cyflymder Amrywiadwy) 2015. - 12p.: 30 cm. - 978-0-348-11067-8 £6.00

The Use of Invalid Carriages on Highways (Amendment) (Wales) Regulations 2015 No. 2015/779 (W.62). - Enabling power: Chronically Sick and Disabled Persons Act 1970, s. 20. - Issued: . 30.03.2015. Made: 18.03.2015. Laid before the National Assembly for Wales: 19.03.2015. Coming into force: 09.04.2015. Effect: S.I. 1988/2268 amended. Territorial extent & classification: W. General. - In English and Welsh. Welsh title: Rheoliadau Defnyddio Cerbydau Pobl Anabl ar Briffyrdd (Diwygio) (Cymru) 2015. - 4p.: 30 cm. - 978-0-348-11060-9 £4.25

Road traffic, Wales: Speed limits

The A40 Trunk Road (Llangynnwr Roundabout to Pensarn Roundabout and Pensarn Roundabout to West of Pont Lesneven Roundabout, Carmarthenshire) and The A48 Trunk Road (South East of Pensarn Roundabout, Carmarthenshire) (40 and 50 MPH Speed Limits and De-restriction) Order 2015 No. 2015/1446 (W.154). - Enabling power: Road Traffic Regulation Act 1984, ss. 82 (2), 84 (1) (2), 124, sch. 9, para. 27. - Issued: 03.07.2015. Made: 23.06.2015. Coming into force: 25.06.2015. Effect: S.I. 2000/249 (W.4); 2009/3420 (W.302) revoked. Territorial extent & classification: W. Local. - Available at http://www.legislation.gov.uk/wsi/2015/1446/contents/made. - In English and Welsh. Welsh title: Gorchymyn Cefnffordd yr A40 (Cylchfan Llangynnwr i Gylchfan Pen-sarn a Chylchfan Pen-sarn i Fan i'r Gorllewin o Gylchfan Pont Lesneven, Sir Gaerfyrddin) a Chefnffordd yr A48 (I'r De-ddwyrain o Gylchfan Pen-sarn, Sir Gaerfyrddin) (Terfynau Cyflymder 40 a 50 MYA a Chodi Cyfyngiadau) 2015 Non-print

The A55 Trunk Road (Junction 8, Pant Lodge Interchange, Isle of Anglesey to Junction 9, Treborth Interchange, Gwynedd) (50 MPH Speed Limit) Order 2015 No. 2015/304 (W.34). - Enabling power: Road Traffic Regulation Act 1984, ss. 84 (1) (2), 124, sch. 9, para. 27. - Issued: 24.02.2015. Made: 27.01.2015. Coming into force: 29.01.2015. Effect: S.I. 1983/1772 revoked. Territorial extent & classification: W. Local. - Available at http://www.legislation.gov.uk/wsi/2015/304/contents/made. - In English and Welsh. Welsh title: Gorchymyn Cefnffordd yr A55 (Cyffordd 8, Cyfnewidfa Pant Lodge, Ynys Môn i Gyffordd 9, Cyfnewidfa Treborth, Gwynedd) (Terfyn Cyflymder 50 MYA) 2015 Non-print

The A470 Trunk Road (Northbound Link Road at Coryton Interchange, Cardiff) (40 mph Speed Limit) Order 2015 No. 2015/1444 (W.152). - Enabling power: Road Traffic Regulation Act 1984, s. 84 (1) (2). - Issued: 03.07.2015. Made: 11.06.2015. Coming into force: 15.06.2015. Effect: None. Territorial extent & classification: W. Local. - Available at http://www.legislation.gov.uk/wsi/2015/1444/contents/made. - In English and Welsh. Welsh title: Gorchymyn Cefnffordd yr A470 (Ffordd Gyswllt Tua'r Gogledd yng Nghyfnewidfa Coryton, Caerdydd) (Terfyn Cyflymder 40 mya) 2015 Non-print

The Trunk Road (A40) (Monmouth Road, Abergavenny, Gwent) (40 MPH Speed Limit) Order 1991 (Revocation) Order 2015 No. 2015/1708 (W.224). - Enabling power: Road Traffic Regulation Act 1984, s. 84 (1) (2), 124, sch. 9, para. 27. - Issued: 28.09.2015. Made: 27.08.2015. Coming into force: 28.08.2015. Effect: S.I. 1991/1591 revoked. Territorial extent & classification: W. Local. - Available at http://www.legislation.gov.uk/wsi/2015/1708/contents/made. - In English and Welsh. Welsh title: Gorchymyn (Dirymu) Gorchymyn Cefnffordd (yr A40) (Ffordd Trefynwy, y Fenni, Gwent) (Terfyn Cyflymder 40 MYA) 1991 2015 Non-print

Road traffic, Wales: Traffic regulation

The A5 and A470 Trunk Roads (Waterloo Bridge, Near Betws-y-Coed, Conwy) (Temporary Traffic Restrictions and No Overtaking) Order 2015 No. 2015/294 (W.29). - Enabling power: Road Traffic Regulation Act 1984, s. 14 (1) (4). - Issued: 23.02.2015. Made: 26.01.2015. Coming into force: 02.02.2015. Effect: None. Territorial extent & classification: W. Local. - Available at http://www.legislation.gov.uk/wsi/2015/294/contents/made. - In English and Welsh. Welsh title: Gorchymyn Cefnffyrdd yr A5 a'r A470 (Pont Waterloo, ger Betws-y-coed, Conwy) (Cyfyngiadau Traffig Dros Dro a Dim Goddiweddyd) 2015 Non-print

The A5 Trunk Road (Bethesda, Gwynedd) (Prohibition and Restriction of Waiting) Order 2013 (Variation) Order 2015 No. 2015/1950 (W.295). - Enabling power: Road Traffic Regulation Act 1984, s. 1 (1), 2 (1) (2), 4 (2), 124, sch. 9, para. 27. - Issued: 03.12.2015. Made: 30.11.2015. Coming into force: 01.12.2015. Effect: WSI 2013/791 (W.95) varied. Territorial extent & classification: W. Local. - Available at http://www.legislation.gov.uk/wsi/2015/1950/contents/made. - In English and Welsh. Welsh title: Gorchymyn Gorchymyn Cefnffordd yr A5 (Bethesda, Gwynedd) (Gwahardd Aros a Chyfyngu ar Aros) 2013 (Amrywio) 2015 Non-print

The A5 Trunk Road (Capel Curig to Betws-y-Coed, Conwy County Borough) (Temporary Speed Restrictions and No Overtaking) Order 2015 No. 2015/272 (W.16). - Enabling power: Road Traffic Regulation Act 1984, ss. 14 (1) (4) & S.I. 1999/672 art. 2, sch. 1, sch. 11, para. 30. - Issued: 19.02.2015. Made: 05.01.2015. Coming into force: 12.01.2015. Effect: None. Territorial extent & classification: W. Local. - Available at http://www.legislation.gov.uk/wsi/2015/272/contents/made. - In English and Welsh. Welsh title: Gorchymyn Cefnffordd yr A5 (Capel Curig i Fetws-y-coed, Bwrdeistref Sirol Conwy) (Cyfyngiadau Cyflymder a Dim Goddiweddyd Dros Dro) 2015 Non-print

The A5 Trunk Road (Cerrigydrudion West Junction, Conwy County Borough) (Temporary Speed Restrictions & No Overtaking) Order 2015 No. 2015/2077 (W.313). - Enabling power: Road Traffic Regulation Act 1984, s. 14 (1) (4) (7). - Issued: 06.01.2016. Made: 29.12.2015. Coming into force: 04.01.2016. Effect: None. Territorial extent & classification: W. Local. - Available at http://www.legislation.gov.uk/wsi/2015/2077/contents/made. - In English and Welsh. Welsh title: Gorchymyn Cefnffordd yr A5 (Cyffordd Gorllewin Cerrigydrudion, Bwrdeistref Sirol Conwy) (Cyfyngiadau Cyflymder Dros Dro a Dim Goddiweddyd) 2015 Non-print

The A5 Trunk Road (Chirk Bypass, Wrexham County Borough) (Temporary Prohibition of Vehicles & Cyclists) Order 2015 No. 2015/1294 (W.101). - Enabling power: Road Traffic Regulation Act 1984, s. 14 (1) (4). - Issued: 11.05.2015. Made: 27.03.2015. Coming into force: 01.04.2015. Effect: None. Territorial extent & classification: W. Local. - Available at http://www.legislation.gov.uk/wsi/2015/1294/contents/made. - In English and Welsh. Welsh title: Gorchymyn Cefnffordd yr A5 (Ffordd Osgoi'r Waun, Bwrdeistref Sirol Wrecsam) (Gwahardd Cerbydau a Beicwyr dros Dro) 2015 Non-print

The A5 Trunk Road (Coed y Gloddfa, Conwy) (Temporary Traffic Restrictions and Prohibitions) Order 2015 No. 2015/282 (W.22). - Enabling power: Road Traffic Regulation Act 1984, ss. 14 (1) (4) & S.I. 1999/672 art. 2, sch. 1, sch. 11, para. 30. - Issued: 19.02.2015. Made: 06.01.2015. Coming into force: 12.01.2015. Effect: None. Territorial extent & classification: W. Local. - Available at http://www.legislation.gov.uk/wsi/2015/282/contents/made. - In English and Welsh. Welsh title: Gorchymyn Cefnffordd yr A5 (Coed y Gloddfa, Conwy) (Cyfyngiadau a Gwaharddiadau Traffig Dros Dro) 2015 Non-print

The A5 Trunk Road (Conwy/Gwynedd Border to Capel Curig, Conwy County Borough) (Temporary Speed Restrictions and No Overtaking) Order 2015 No. 2015/276 (W.18). - Enabling power: Road Traffic Regulation Act 1984, ss. 14 (1) (4) & S.I. 1999/672 art. 2, sch. 1, sch. 11, para. 30. - Issued: 19.02.2015. Made: 05.01.2015. Coming into force: 12.01.2015. Effect: None. Territorial extent & classification: W. Local. - Available at http://www.legislation.gov.uk/wsi/2015/276/contents/made. - In English and Welsh. Welsh title: Gorchymyn Cefnffordd yr A5 (Ffin Conwy/Gwynedd i Gapel Curig, Bwrdeistref Sirol Conwy) (Cyfyngiadau Cyflymder Dros Dro a Dim Goddiweddyd) 2015 Non-print

ROAD TRAFFIC, WALES: TRAFFIC REGULATION

The A5 Trunk Road (Corwen, Denbighshire) (Various Waiting Restrictions) Order 2015 No. 2015/1925 (W.288). - Enabling power: Road Traffic Regulation Act 1984, ss. 1 (1), 2 (1) (2), 4 (2), 124, sch. 9, para. 27. - Issued: 24.11.2015. Made: 29.10.2015. Coming into force: 30.10.2015. Effect: S.I. 1995/2564 revoked. Territorial extent & classification: W. Local. - Available at http://www.legislation.gov.uk/wsi/2015/1925/contents/made. - In English and Welsh. Welsh title: Gorchymyn Cefnffordd yr A5 (Corwen, Sir Ddinbych) (Amrywiol Gyfyngiadau ar Aros) 2015 Non-print

The A5 Trunk Road (Gwern Gof Isaf, Ogwen, West of Capel Curig, Conwy) (Temporary Prohibition of Vehicles) Order 2015 No. 2015/1298 (W.105). - Enabling power: Road Traffic Regulation Act 1984, s. 16A. - Issued: 11.05.2015. Made: 07.04.2015. Coming into force: 14.04.2015. Effect: None. Territorial extent & classification: W. Local. - Available at http://www.legislation.gov.uk/wsi/2015/1298/contents/made. - In English and Welsh. Welsh title: Gorchymyn Cefnffordd yr A5 (Gwern Gof Isaf, Ogwen, Man i'r Gorllewin o Gapel Curig, Conwy) (Gwahardd Cerbydau Dros Dro) 2015 Non-print

The A5 Trunk Road (Holyhead Road, Betws-y-Coed, Conwy County Borough) (Temporary Prohibition of Vehicles) Order 2015 No. 2015/1715 (W.229). - Enabling power: Road Traffic Regulation Act 1984, s. 16A. - Issued: 29.09.2015. Made: 08.09.2015. Coming into force: 12.09.2015. Effect: None. Territorial extent & classification: W. Local. - http://www.legislation.gov.uk/wsi/2015/1715/contents/made. - In English and Welsh. Welsh title: Gorchymyn Cefnffordd yr A5 (Ffordd Caergybi, Betws-y-coed, Bwrdeistref Sirol Conwy) (Gwahardd Cerbydau Dros Dro) 2015 Non-print

The A5 Trunk Road (Llangollen, Denbighshire) (Temporary Traffic Prohibitions & Restrictions) (No.2) Order 2015 No. 2015/1313 (W.114). - Enabling power: Road Traffic Regulation Act 1984, s. 14 (1) (4). - Issued: 14.05.2015. Made: 07.05.2015. Coming into force: 13.05.2015. Effect: None. Territorial extent & classification: W. Local. - Available at http://www.legislation.gov.uk/wsi/2015/1313/contents/made. - In English and Welsh. Welsh title: Gorchymyn Cefnffordd yr A5 (Llangollen, Sir Ddinbych) (Gwaharddiadau a Chyfyngiadau Traffig Dros Dro) (Rhif 2) 2015 Non-print

The A5 Trunk Road (Llangollen, Denbighshire) (Temporary Traffic Prohibitions & Restrictions) Order 2015 No. 2015/290 (W.26). - Enabling power: Road Traffic Regulation Act 1984, ss. 14 (1) (4). - Issued: 23.02.2015. Made: 12.01.2015. Coming into force: 19.01.2015. Effect: None. Territorial extent & classification: W. Local. - Available at http://www.legislation.gov.uk/wsi/2015/290/contents/made. - In English and Welsh. Welsh title: Gorchymyn Cefnffordd yr A5 (Llangollen, Sir Ddinbych) (Gwaharddiadau a Chyfyngiadau Traffig Dros Dro) 2015 Non-print

The A5 Trunk Road (North of Penmachno, Conwy County Borough) (Temporary Speed Restrictions & No Overtaking) Order 2015 No. 2015/299 (W.33). - Enabling power: Road Traffic Regulation Act 1984, s. 14 (1) (4). - Issued: 24.02.2015. Made: 26.01.2015. Coming into force: 02.02.2015. Effect: None. Territorial extent & classification: W. Local. - Available at http://www.legislation.gov.uk/wsi/2015/299/contents/made. - In English and Welsh. Welsh title: Gorchymyn Cefnffordd yr A5 (Man i'r Gogledd o Benmachno, Bwrdeistref Sirol Conwy) (Cyfyngiadau Cyflymder a Dim Goddiweddyd Dros Dro) 2015 Non-print

The A5 Trunk Road (Pentre Du, Betws-y-Coed, Conwy County Borough) (Temporary 40 mph Speed Limit) Order 2015 No. 2015/1627 (W.210). - Enabling power: Road Traffic Regulation Act 1984, s. 14 (1) (4). - Issued: 28.08.2015. Made: 25.08.2015. Coming into force: 01.09.2015. Effect: None. Territorial extent & classification: W. Local. - http://www.legislation.gov.uk/wsi/2015/1627/contents/made. - In English and Welsh. Welsh title: Gorchymyn Cefnffordd yr A5 (Pentre Du, Betws-y-coed, Bwrdeistref Sirol Conwy) (Terfyn Cyflymder 40 mya Dros Dro) 2015 Non-print

The A5 Trunk Road (Tregarth, Gwynedd) (Temporary Traffic Restrictions and No Overtaking) Order 2015 No. 2015/308 (W.36). - Enabling power: Road Traffic Regulation Act 1984, s. 14 (1) (4). - Issued: 24.02.2015. Made: 05.01.2015. Coming into force: 12.01.2015. Effect: None. Territorial extent & classification: W. Local. - Available at http://www.legislation.gov.uk/wsi/2015/308/contents/made. - In English and Welsh. Welsh title: Gorchymyn Cefnffordd yr A5 (Tre-garth, Gwynedd) (Cyfyngiadau Traffig Dros Dro a Dim Goddiweddyd) 2015 Non-print

The A5 Trunk Road (Ty'n y Maes, South of Bethesda, Gwynedd) (Temporary 30 MPH Speed Limit) Order 2015 No. 2015/1720 (W.234). - Enabling power: Road Traffic Regulation Act 1984, s. 14 (1) (4). - Issued: 30.09.2015. Made: 21.09.2015. Coming into force: 25.09.2015. Effect: None. Territorial extent & classification: W. Local. - Available at http://www.legislation.gov.uk/wsi/2015/1720/contents/made. - In English and Welsh. Welsh title: Gorchymyn Cefnffordd yr A5 (Ty'n-y-maes, Man i'r De o Fethesda, Gwynedd) (Terfyn Cyflymder 30 MYA Dros Dro) 2015 Non-print

The A40 and A487 Trunk Roads (Fishguard, Pembrokeshire) (Temporary Traffic Prohibitions and Restriction) Order 2015 No. 2015/1789 (W.252). - Enabling power: Road Traffic Regulation Act 1984, ss. 14 (1) (4). - Issued: 16.10.2015. Made: 08.10.2015. Coming into force: 18.10.2015. Effect: None. Territorial extent & classification: W. Local. - Available at http://www.legislation.gov.uk/wsi/2015/1789/contents/made. - In English and Welsh. Welsh title: Gorchymyn Cefnffyrdd yr A40 a'r A487 (Abergwaun, Sir Benfro) (Gwaharddiadau a Chyfyngiad Traffig Dros Dro) 2015 Non-print

The A40 Trunk Road and Link Road (Travellers' Rest, Carmarthenshire) (Temporary 30 MPH Speed Limit) Order 2015 No. 2015/1340 (W.127). - Enabling power: Road Traffic Regulation Act 1984, s. 14 (1) (4). - Issued: 03.06.2015. Made: 21.05.2015. Coming into force: 01.06.2015. Effect: None. Territorial extent & classification: W. Local. - Available at http://www.legislation.gov.uk/wsi/2015/1340/contents/made. - In English and Welsh. Welsh title: Gorchymyn Cefnffordd yr A40 (Cylchfan Dixton, Trefynwy i'r Ffin rhwng Cymru a Lloegr, Sir Fynwy) (Gwaharddiadau a Chyfyngiad Traffig Dros Dro) 2015 Non-print

The A40 Trunk Road and Link Road (Travellers' Rest Junction, Carmarthenshire) (Temporary Prohibition of Vehicles and 30 MPH Speed Limit) Order 2015 No. 2015/2079 (W.315). - Enabling power: Road Traffic Regulation Act 1984, s. 14 (1) (4) (7). - Issued: 08.01.2016. Made: 29.12.2015. Coming into force: 04.01.2016. Effect: None. Territorial extent & classification: W. Local. - Available at http://www.legislation.gov.uk/wsi/2015/2079/contents/made. - In English and Welsh. Welsh title: Gorchymyn Cefnffordd yr A40 a'r Ffordd Gyswllt (Cyffordd Travellers' Rest, Sir Gaerfyrddin) (Gwahardd Cerbydau a Therfyn Cyflymder 30 MYA Dros Dro) 2015 Non-print

The A40 Trunk Road (Chapel Farm Over-Bridge, Near Monmouth, Monmouthshire) (Temporary Prohibition of Vehicles) Order 2015 No. 2015/1316 (W.117). - Enabling power: Road Traffic Regulation Act 1984, s. 14 (1) (4). - Issued: 18.05.2015. Made: 12.05.2015. Coming into force: 18.05.2015. Effect: None. Territorial extent & classification: W. Local. - Available at http://www.legislation.gov.uk/wsi/2015/1316/contents/made. - In English and Welsh. Welsh title: Gorchymyn Cefnffordd yr A40 (Trosbont Chapel Farm, Ger Trefynwy, Sir Fynwy) (Gwahardd Cerbydau Dros Dro) 2015 Non-print

The A40 Trunk Road (Dixton Roundabout, Monmouth to the Wales/England Border, Monmouthshire) (Temporary Traffic Prohibitions & Restriction) Order 2015 No. 2015/1341 (W.128). - Enabling power: Road Traffic Regulation Act 1984, s. 14 (1) (4). - Issued: 03.06.2015. Made: 21.05.2015. Coming into force: 28.05.2015. Effect: None. Territorial extent & classification: W. Local. - Available at http://www.legislation.gov.uk/wsi/2015/1341/contents/made. - In English and Welsh. Welsh title: Gorchymyn Cefnffordd yr A40 (Cylchfan Dixton, Trefynwy i'r Ffin rhwng Cymru a Lloegr, Sir Fynwy) (Gwaharddiadau a Chyfyngiad Traffig Dros Dro) 2015 Non-print

The A40 Trunk Road (Haverfordwest to Fishguard, Pembrokeshire) (Temporary Speed Restrictions & No Overtaking) Order 2015 No. 2015/1913 (W.282). - Enabling power: Road Traffic Regulation Act 1984, s. 14 (1) (4) (7). - Issued: 20.11.2015. Made: 12.10.2015. Coming into force: 19.10.2015. Effect: None Territorial extent & classification: W. Local. - Available at http://www.legislation.gov.uk/uksi/2015/1913/contents/made. - In English and Welsh. Welsh title: Gorchymyn Cefnffordd yr A40 (Hwlffordd i Abergwaun, Sir Benfro) (Cyfyngiadau Cyflymder Dros Dro a Dim Goddiweddyd) 2015 Non-print

ROAD TRAFFIC, WALES: TRAFFIC REGULATION

The A40 Trunk Road (Llandovery Level Crossing, Llandovery, Carmarthenshire) (Temporary Prohibition of Vehicles) Order 2015 No. 2015/1300 (W.107). - Enabling power: Road Traffic Regulation Act 1984, s. 14 (1) (4). - Issued: 11.05.2015. Made: 07.04.2015. Coming into force: 13.04.2015. Effect: None. Territorial extent & classification: W. Local. - Available at http://www.legislation.gov.uk/wsi/2015/1300/contents/made. - In English and Welsh. Welsh title: Gorchymyn Cefnffordd yr A40 (Croesfan Reilffordd Llanymddyfri, Llanymddyfri, Sir Gaerfyrddin) (Gwahardd Cerbydau Dros Dro) 2015 Non-print

The A40 Trunk Road (Llangadog to Llandovery, Carmarthenshire) (Temporary Traffic Prohibitions & Restrictions) Order 2015 No. 2015/1593 (W.192). - Enabling power: Road Traffic Regulation Act 1984, ss. 14 (1) (4) (7), 124, sch. 9, para. 27. - Issued: 11.08.2015. Made: 27.07.2015. Coming into force: 01.08.2015. Effect: S.I. 2014/2659 (W.264) revoked. Territorial extent & classification: W. Local. - Available at http://www.legislation.gov.uk/wsi/2015/1593/contents/made. - In English and Welsh. Welsh title: Gorchymyn Cefnffordd yr A40 (Llangadog i Lanymddyfri, Sir Gaerfyrddin) (Gwaharddiadau a Chyfyngiadau Traffig Dros Dro) 2015 Non-print

The A40 Trunk Road (Nantarwenlliw to Pontargothi, Carmarthenshire) (Temporary Speed Restrictions & No Overtaking) Order 2015 No. 2015/1714 (W.228). - Enabling power: Road Traffic Regulation Act 1984, s. 14 (1) (4). - Issued: 29.09.2015. Made: 07.09.2015. Coming into force: 14.09.2015. Effect: None. Territorial extent & classification: W. Local. - Available at http://www.legislation.gov.uk/wsi/2015/1714/contents/made. - In English and Welsh. Welsh title: Gorchymyn Cefnffordd yr A40 (Nantarwenlliw i Bontargothi, Sir Gaerfyrddin) (Cyfyngiadau Cyflymder Dros Dro a Dim Goddiweddyd) 2015 Non-print

The A40 Trunk Road (Nantgaredig to White Mill, Carmarthenshire) (Temporary 40 mph Speed Limit) Order 2015 No. 2015/1590 (W.190). - Enabling power: Road Traffic Regulation Act 1984, s. 14 (1) (4). - Issued: 07.08.2015. Made: 24.07.2015. Coming into force: 29.07.2015. Effect: None. Territorial extent & classification: W. Local. - Available at http://www.legislation.gov.uk/wsi/2015/1590/contents/made. - In English and Welsh. Welsh title: Gorchymyn Cefnffordd yr A40 (Nantgaredig i White Mill, Sir Gaerfyrddin) (Terfyn Cyflymder 40 mya Dros Dro) 2015 Non-print

The A40 Trunk Road (Park Road, Abergavenny, Monmouthshire) (Temporary Closure of Footway) Order 2015 No. 2015/1942 (W.292). - Enabling power: Road Traffic Regulation Act 1984, s. 14 (1) (4). - Issued: 01.12.2015. Made: 12.11.2015. Coming into force: 16.11.2015. Effect: None. Territorial extent & classification: W. Local. - Available at http://www.legislation.gov.uk/wsi/2015/1942/contents/made. - In English and Welsh. Welsh title: Gorchymyn Cefnffordd yr A40 (Heol y Parc, Y Fenni, Sir Fynwy) (Cau Troetffordd Dros Dro) 2015 Non-print

The A40 Trunk Road (Pensarn Roundabout, Carmarthen to Llandovery, Carmarthenshire) (Temporary Prohibition of Vehicles) Order 2015 No. 2015/1943 (W.293). - Enabling power: Road Traffic Regulation Act 1984, s. 14 (1) (4). - Issued: 01.12.2015. Made: 16.11.2015. Coming into force: 23.11.2015. Effect: None. Territorial extent & classification: W. Local. - Available at http://www.legislation.gov.uk/wsi/2015/1943/contents/made. - In English and Welsh. Welsh title: Gorchymyn Cefnffordd yr A40 (Cylchfan Pen-sarn, Caerfyrddin i Lanymddyfri, Sir Gaerfyrddin) (Gwahardd Cerbydau Dros Dro) 2015 Non-print

The A40 Trunk Road (Raglan Interchange to Monmouth, Monmouthshire) (Temporary Traffic Prohibitions & Restriction) Order 2015 No. 2015/1440 (W.148). - Enabling power: Road Traffic Regulation Act 1984, s. 14 (1) (4) (7). - Issued: 03.07.2015. Made: 01.06.2015. Coming into force: 07.06.2015. Effect: None. Territorial extent & classification: W. Local. - Available at http://www.legislation.gov.uk/wsi/2015/1440/contents/made. - In English and Welsh. Welsh title: Gorchymyn Cefnffordd yr A40 (Cyfnewidfa Rhaglan i Drefynwy, Sir Fynwy) (Gwaharddiadau a Chyfyngiad Traffig Dros Dro) 2015 Non-print

The A40 Trunk Road (St Clears Roundabout, Carmarthenshire to Haverfordwest, Pembrokeshire) (Temporary Speed Restrictions & No Overtaking) Order 2015 No. 2015/1910 (W.281). - Enabling power: Road Traffic Regulation Act 1984, s. 14 (1) (4) (7). - Issued: 18.11.2015. Made: 12.10.2015. Coming into force: 19.10.2015. Effect: None. Territorial extent & classification: W. Local. - Available at http://www.legislation.gov.uk/wsi/2015/1910/contents/made. - In English and Welsh. Welsh title: Gorchymyn Cefnffordd yr A40 (Cylchfan Sanclêr, Sir Gaerfyrddin i Hwlffordd, Sir Benfro) (Cyfyngiadau Cyflymder Dros Dro a Dim Goddiweddyd) 2015 Non-print

The A40 Trunk Road (Westbound Slip Roads at Johnstown, Carmarthenshire) (Temporary Prohibition of Vehicles) Order 2015 No. 2015/1299 (W.106). - Enabling power: Road Traffic Regulation Act 1984, s. 14 (1) (4). - Issued: 11.05.2015. Made: 07.04.2015. Coming into force: 13.04.2015. Effect: None. Territorial extent & classification: W. Local. - Available at http://www.legislation.gov.uk/wsi/2015/1299/contents/made. - In English and Welsh. Welsh title: Gorchymyn Cefnffordd yr A40 (Y Ffyrdd Ymuno ac Ymadael tua'r Gorllewin yn Nhre Ioan, Sir Gaerfyrddin) (Gwahardd Cerbydau Dros Dro) 2015 Non-print

The A44 Trunk Road (Capel Bangor to Blaengeuffordd, Ceredigion) (Temporary 40 mph and Part-time 20 mph Speed Limits) Order 2015 No. 2015/1434 (W.144). - Enabling power: Road Traffic Regulation Act 1984, s. 14 (1) (4) (7). - Issued: 02.07.2015. Made: 29.05.2015. Coming into force: 05.06.2015. Effect: None. Territorial extent & classification: W. Local. - Available at http://www.legislation.gov.uk/wsi/2015/1434/contents/made. - In English and Welsh. Welsh title: Gorchymyn Cefnffordd yr A44 (Capel Bangor i Flaengeuffordd, Ceredigion) (Terfynau Cyflymder 40 mya Dros Dro ac 20 mya Rhan-amser) 2015 Non-print

The A44 Trunk Road (East of Ponterwyd, Ceredigion) (Temporary Speed Restrictions & No Overtaking) Order 2015 No. 2015/1290 (W.97). - Enabling power: Road Traffic Regulation Act 1984, s. 14 (1) (4) (7). - Issued: 12.05.2015. Made: 26.03.2015. Coming into force: 01.04.2015. Effect: None. Territorial extent & classification: W. Local. - Available at http://www.legislation.gov.uk/wsi/2015/1290/contents/made. - In English and Welsh. Welsh title: Gorchymyn Cefnffordd yr A44 (Man i'r Dwyrain o Bonterwyd, Ceredigion) (Cyfyngiadau Traffig Dros Dro a Dim Goddiweddyd) 2015 Non-print

The A44 Trunk Road (Llywernog, West of Ponterwyd, Ceredigion) (Temporary Speed Restrictions & No Overtaking) Order 2015 No. 2015/1289 (W.96). - Enabling power: Road Traffic Regulation Act 1984, s. 14 (1) (4). - Issued: 12.05.2015. Made: 26.03.2015. Coming into force: 01.04.2015. Effect: None. Territorial extent & classification: W. Local. - Available at http://www.legislation.gov.uk/wsi/2015/1289/contents/made. - In English and Welsh. Welsh title: Gorchymyn Cefnffordd yr A44 (Llywernog, i'r Gorllewin o Bonterwyd, Ceredigion) (Cyfyngiadau Cyflymder Dros Dro a Dim Goddiweddyd) 2015 Non-print

The A44 Trunk Road (West of Llangurig, Powys) (Temporary Traffic Restrictions & Prohibitions) Order 2015 No. 2015/1944 (W.294). - Enabling power: Road Traffic Regulation Act 1984, s. 14 (1) (4). - Issued: 01.12.2015. Made: 16.11.2015. Coming into force: 23.11.2015. Effect: None. Territorial extent & classification: W. Local. - Available at http://www.legislation.gov.uk/wsi/2015/1944/contents/made. - In English and Welsh. Welsh title: Gorchymyn Cefnffordd yr A44 (Man i'r Gorllewin o Langurig, Powys) (Cyfyngiadau a Gwaharddiadau Traffig Dros Dro) 2015 Non-print

The A48 and A40 Trunk Roads (St Clears to Cross Hands, Carmarthenshire) (Temporary Traffic Restrictions and Prohibitions) Order 2015 No. 2015/309 (W.37). - Enabling power: Road Traffic Regulation Act 1984, s. 14 (1) (4). - Issued: 24.02.2015. Made: 16.02.2015. Coming into force: 23.02.2015. Effect: None. Territorial extent & classification: W. Local. - Available at http://www.legislation.gov.uk/wsi/2015/309/contents/made. - In English and Welsh. Welsh title: Gorchymyn Cefnffyrdd yr A48 a'r A40 (Sanclêr i Cross Hands, Sir Gaerfyrddin) (Cyfyngiadau a Gwaharddiadau Traffig Dros Dro) 2015 Non-print

The A48 Trunk Road (Cross Hands Roundabout to Pont Abraham Roundabout, Carmarthenshire) (Temporary Traffic Restrictions and Prohibitions) Order 2015 No. 2015/1706 (W.222). - Enabling power: Road Traffic Regulation Act 1984, s. 14 (1) (4) (7). - Issued: 28.09.2015. Made: 03.09.2015. Coming into force: 14.09.2015. Effect: None. Territorial extent & classification: W. Local. - Available at http://www.legislation.gov.uk/wsi/2015/1706/contents/made. - In English and Welsh. Welsh title: Gorchymyn Cefnffordd yr A48 (Cylchfan Cross Hands i Gylchfan Pont Abraham, Sir Gaerfyrddin) (Cyfyngiadau a Gwaharddiadau Traffig Dros Dro) 2015 Non-print

The A48 Trunk Road (Cross Hands Roundabout to South-East of Pensarn Roundabout) and the A40 Trunk Road (Pensarn Roundabout to St Clears Roundabout, Carmarthenshire) (Temporary Traffic Restrictions and Prohibitions) Order 2015 No. 2015/1707 (W.223). - Enabling power: Road Traffic Regulation Act 1984, s. 14 (1) (4). - Issued: 28.09.2015. Made: 03.09.2015. Coming into force: 14.09.2015. Effect: None. Territorial extent & classification: W. Local. - Available at http://www.legislation.gov.uk/wsi/2015/1707/contents/made. - In English and Welsh. Welsh title: Gorchymyn Cefnffordd yr A48 (Cylchfan Cross Hands i Fan i'r De-ddwyrain o Gylchfan Pen-sarn) a Chefnffordd yr A40 (Cylchfan Pen-sarn i Gylchfan Sanclêr, Sir Gaerfyrddin) (Cyfyngiadau a Gwaharddiadau Traffig Dros Dro) 2015 Non-print

The A48 Trunk Road (Wye Bridge, Chepstow, Monmouthshire) (Temporary 30 MPH Speed Limit) Order 2015 No. 2015/1547 (W.182). - Enabling power: Road Traffic Regulation Act 1984, s. 14 (1) (4) (7). - Issued: 21.07.2015. Made: 07.07.2015. Coming into force: 12.07.2015. Effect: None. Territorial extent & classification: W. Local. - Available at http://www.legislation.gov.uk/wsi/2015/1547/contents/made. - In English and Welsh. Welsh title: Gorchymyn Cefnffordd yr A48 (Pont Afon Gwy, Cas-gwent, Sir Fynwy) (Terfyn Cyflymder 30 MYA Dros Dro) 2015 Non-print

The A55 Trunk Road (Eastbound Slip Roads at Junction 17 (Conwy Morfa), Conwy County Borough) (Temporary Prohibition of Vehicles) Order 2015 No. 2015/280 (W.20). - Enabling power: Road Traffic Regulation Act 1984, ss. 14 (1) (4) & S.I. 1999/672 art. 2, sch. 1, sch. 11, para. 30. - Issued: 19.02.2015. Made: 05.01.2015. Coming into force: 12.01.2015. Effect: None. Territorial extent & classification: W. Local. - Available at http://www.legislation.gov.uk/wsi/2015/280/contents/made. - In English and Welsh. Welsh title: Gorchymyn Cefnffordd yr A55 (Ffyrdd Ymuno ac Ymadael tua'r Dwyrain wrth Gyffordd 17 (Morfa Conwy), Bwrdeistref Sirol Conwy) (Gwahardd Cerbydau Dros Dro) 2015 Non-print

The A55 Trunk Road (Junction 1, Kingsland Roundabout, Holyhead, Isle of Anglesey to east of Junction 11, Llys y Gwynt Interchange, Bangor, Gwynedd) (Temporary Prohibition of Vehicles & 40 MPH Speed Limit) Order 2015 No. 2015/691 (W.56). - Enabling power: Road Traffic Regulation Act 1984, s. 14 (1) (4) (7). - Issued: 17.03.2015. Made: 10.03.2015. Coming into force: 16.03.2015. Effect: None. Territorial extent & classification: W. Local. - Available at http://www.legislation.gov.uk/wsi/2015/691/contents/made. - In English and Welsh. Welsh title: Gorchymyn Cefnffordd yr A55 (Cyffordd 1, Cylchfan Kingsland, Caergybi, Ynys Môn i Fan i'r Dwyrain o Gyffordd 11, Cyfnewidfa Llys y Gwynt, Bangor, Gwynedd) (Gwahardd Cerbydau a Therfyn Cyflymder o 40 mya Dros Dro) 2015 Non-print

The A55 Trunk Road (Junction 8, Pant Lodge Interchange, Isle of Anglesey to Junction 9, Treborth Interchange, Gwynedd) (Britannia Bridge High Winds) (Temporary Prohibition of Vehicles and Cyclists) Order 2015 No. 2015/1713 (W.227). - Enabling power: Road Traffic Regulation Act 1984, s. 14 (1) (4). - Issued: 02.10.2015. Made: 08.09.2015. Coming into force: 14.09.2015. Effect: None. Territorial extent & classification: W. Local. - Available at http://www.legislation.gov.uk/wsi/2015/1713/contents/made. - In English and Welsh. Welsh title:Gorchymyn Cefnffordd yr A55 (Cyffordd 8, Cyfnewidfa Pant Lodge, Ynys Môn i Gyffordd 9, Cyfnewidfa Treborth, Gwynedd) (Gwyntoedd Cryfion ar Bont Britannia) (Gwahardd Cerbydau a Beicwyr Dros Dro) 2015 Non-print

The A55 Trunk Road (Junction 11 (Llys y Gwynt Interchange), Bangor, Gwynedd to Junction 36a (Broughton), Flintshire) and The A494 Trunk Road (Ewloe Interchange, Flintshire to the Wales/England Border) (Temporary Prohibition of Vehicles, Cyclists & Pedestrians) Order 2015 No. 2015/1291 (W.98). - Enabling power: Road Traffic Regulation Act 1984, s. 14 (1) (4). - Issued: 12.05.2015. Made: 30.03.2015. Coming into force: 01.04.2015. Effect: None. Territorial extent & classification: W. Local. - Available at http://www.legislation.gov.uk/wsi/2015/1291/contents/made. - Gorchymyn Cefnffordd yr A55 (Cyffordd 11 (Cyfnewidfa Llys y Gwynt), Bangor, Gwynedd i Gyffordd 36a (Brychdyn), Sir y Fflint) a Chefnffordd yr A494 (Cyfnewidfa Ewlo, Sir y Fflint i Ffin Cymru/Lloegr) (Gwahardd Cerbydau, Beicwyr a Cherddwyr Dros Dro) 2015 Non-print

The A55 Trunk Road (Junction 11 (Llys y Gwynt Interchange), Bangor, Gwynedd to the Wales/England Border) and The A494/A550 Trunk Road (Ewloe Interchange, Flintshire) (Temporary 40 mph Speed Limit & Prohibition of Vehicles) Order 2015 No. 2015/1283 (W.90). - Enabling power: Road Traffic Regulation Act 1984, s. 14 (1) (4) (7). - Issued: 12.05.2015. Made: 25.03.2015. Coming into force: 01.04.2015. Effect: None. Territorial extent & classification: W. Local. - Available at http://www.legislation.gov.uk/wsi/2015/1283/contents/made. - In English and Welsh. Welsh title: Gorchymyn Cefnffordd yr A55 (Cyffordd 11 (Cyfnewidfa Llys y Gwynt), Bangor, Gwynedd i Ffin Cymru/Lloegr) a Chefnffordd yr A494/A550 (Cyfnewidfa Ewloe, Sir y Fflint) (Terfyn Cyflymder 40 mya a Gwahardd Cerbydau Dros Dro) 2015 Non-print

The A55 Trunk Road (Junction 11 (Llys y Gwynt Interchange) to Junction 14 (Madryn Interchange), Gwynedd) (Temporary Prohibition of Vehicles, Cyclists and Pedestrians) Order 2015 No. 2015/1606 (W.204). - Enabling power: Road Traffic Regulation Act 1984, s. 14 (1) (4). - Issued: 17.08.2015. Made: 11.08.2015. Coming into force: 17.08.2015. Effect: None. Territorial extent & classification: W. Local. - Available at http://www.legislation.gov.uk/wsi/2015/1606/contents/made. - Welsh title: Gorchymyn Cefnffordd yr A55 (Cyffordd 11 (Cyfnewidfa Llys y Gwynt) i Gyffordd 14 (Cyfnewidfa Madryn), Gwynedd) (Gwahardd Cerbydau, Beicwyr a Cherddwyr Dros Dro) 2015 Non-print

The A55 Trunk Road (Junction 11, Llys y Gwynt, Llandygai, Gwynedd) (Temporary Prohibition of Vehicles, Cyclists and Pedestrians) Order 2015 No. 2015/297 (W.31). - Enabling power: Road Traffic Regulation Act 1984, s. 14 (1) (4). - Issued: 23.02.2015. Made: 26.01.2015. Coming into force: 01.02.2015. Effect: None. Territorial extent & classification: W. Local. - Available at http://www.legislation.gov.uk/wsi/2015/297/contents/made. - In English and Welsh. Welsh title: Gorchymyn Cefnffordd yr A55 (Cyffordd 11, Llys y Gwynt, Llandygái, Gwynedd) (Gwahardd Cerbydau, Beicwyr a Cherddwyr Dros Dro) 2015 Non-print

The A55 Trunk Road (Junction 11 (Llys y Gwynt) to Junction 14 (Madryn Interchange), Gwynedd) (Temporary Traffic Prohibitions & Restriction) Order 2015 No. 2015/262 (W.14). - Enabling power: Road Traffic Regulation Act 1984, ss. 14 (1) (4) & S.I. 1999/672 art. 2, sch. 1, sch. 11, para. 30. - Issued: 19.02.2015. Made: 05.01.2015. Coming into force: 12.01.2015. Effect: None. Territorial extent & classification: W. Local. - Available at http://www.legislation.gov.uk/wsi/2015/262/contents/made. - In English and Welsh. Welsh title: Gorchymyn Cefnffordd yr A55 (Cyffordd 11 (Llys y Gwynt) i Gyffordd 14 (Cyfnewidfa Madryn), Gwynedd) (Gwaharddiadau a Chyfyngiad Traffig Dros Dro) 2015 Non-print

The A55 Trunk Road (Junction 14, Madryn Interchange, Gwynedd to Junction 15, Llanfairfechan Roundabout, Conwy) (Temporary Prohibition of Vehicles, Cyclists and Pedestrians) Order 2015 No. 2015/291 (W.27). - Enabling power: Road Traffic Regulation Act 1984, s. 14 (1) (4). - Issued: 23.02.2015. Made: 19.01.2015. Coming into force: 26.01.2015. Effect: None. Territorial extent & classification: E. Local. - Available at http://www.legislation.gov.uk/wsi/2015/291/contents/made. - In English and Welsh. Welsh title: Gorchymyn Cefnffordd yr A55 (Cyffordd 14, Cyfnewidfa Madryn, Gwynedd i Gyffordd 15, Cylchfan Llanfairfechan, Conwy) (Gwahardd Cerbydau, Beicwyr a Cherddwyr Dros Dro) 2015 Non-print

The A55 Trunk Road (Junction 17 (Conwy Morfa) to Junction 19 (Glan Conwy), Conwy County Borough) (Temporary Prohibition of Vehicles & 40 mph Speed Limit) Order 2015 No. 2015/688 (W.53). - Enabling power: Road Traffic Regulation Act 1984, s. 14 (1) (4). - Issued: 17.03.2015. Made: 09.03.2015. Coming into force: 15.03.2015. Effect: None. Territorial extent & classification: W. Local. - Available at http://www.legislation.gov.uk/wsi/2015/688/contents/made. - In English and Welsh. Welsh title: Gorchymyn Cefnffordd yr A55 (Cyffordd 17 (Morfa Conwy) i Gyffordd 19 (Llansanffraid Glan Conwy), Bwrdeistref Sirol Conwy) (Gwahardd Cerbydau a Therfyn Cyflymder o 40 mya Dros Dro) 2015 Non-print

ROAD TRAFFIC, WALES: TRAFFIC REGULATION

The A55 Trunk Road (Junction 19 (Llandudno Junction) to Junction 22 (Old Colwyn), Conwy County Borough) (Temporary Traffic Prohibitions & Restriction) Order 2015 No. 2015/689 (W.54). - Enabling power: Road Traffic Regulation Act 1984, s. 14 (1) (4) (7). - Issued: 17.03.2015. Made: 09.03.2015. Coming into force: 15.03.2015. Effect: None. Territorial extent & classification: W. Local. - Available at http://www.legislation.gov.uk/wsi/2015/689/contents/made. - In English and Welsh. Welsh title: Gorchymyn Cefnffordd yr A55 (Cyffordd 19 (Cyffordd Llandudno) i Gyffordd 22 (Hen Golwyn), Bwrdeistref Sirol Conwy) (Gwaharddiadau a Chyfyngiad Traffig Dros Dro) 2015 Non-print

The A55 Trunk Road (Junction 22 (Old Colwyn) to Junction 23 (Llanddulas), Conwy County Borough) (Temporary Traffic Prohibitions & Restriction) Order 2015 No. 2015/690 (W.55). - Enabling power: Road Traffic Regulation Act 1984, s. 14 (1) (4) (7). - Issued: 17.03.2015. Made: 09.03.2015. Coming into force: 15.03.2015. Effect: None. Territorial extent & classification: W. Local. - Available at http://www.legislation.gov.uk/wsi/2015/690/contents/made. - In English and Welsh. Welsh title: Gorchymyn Cefnffordd yr A55 (Cyffordd 22 (Hen Golwyn) i Gyffordd 23 (Llanddulas), Bwrdeistref Sirol Conwy) (Gwaharddiadau a Chyfyngiad Traffig Dros Dro) 2015 Non-print

The A55 Trunk Road (Junction 23, Llanddulas to Junction 22, Old Colwyn, Conwy) (Temporary Prohibition of Vehicles) Order 2015 No. 2015/849 (W.64). - Enabling power: Road Traffic Regulation Act 1984, s. 14 (1) (4) (7). - Issued: 26.03.2015. Made: 23.03.2015. Coming into force: 30.03.2015. Effect: None. Territorial extent & classification: W. Local. - Available at http://www.legislation.gov.uk/wsi/2015/849/contents/made. - In English and Welsh. Welsh title: Gorchymyn Cefnffordd yr A55 (Cyffordd 23, Llanddulas i Gyffordd 22, Hen Golwyn, Conwy) (Gwahardd Cerbydau Dros Dro) 2015 Non-print

The A55 Trunk Road (Junction 27, Talardy Interchange, Denbighshire, Eastbound On Slip Road) (Temporary Prohibition of Vehicles, Cyclists and Pedestrians) Order 2015 No. 2015/281 (W.21). - Enabling power: Road Traffic Regulation Act 1984, ss. 14 (1) (4) & S.I. 1999/672 art. 2, sch. 1, sch. 11, para. 30. - Issued: 19.02.2015. Made: 05.01.2015. Coming into force: 11.01.2015. Effect: None. Territorial extent & classification: W. Local. - Available at http://www.legislation.gov.uk/wsi/2015/281/contents/made. - In English and Welsh. Welsh title: Gorchymyn Cefnffordd yr A55 (Cyffordd 27, Cyfnewidfa Talardy, Sir Ddinbych, Slipffordd Ymuno Tua'r Dwyrain) (Gwahardd Cerbydau, Beicwyr a Cherddwyr Dros Dro) 2015 Non-print

The A55 Trunk Road (Junction 31 (Caerwys) to Junction 32 (Dolphin Junction), Flintshire) (Temporary 40 mph Speed Limit & Prohibition of Vehicles) Order 2015 No. 2015/517 (W.45). - Enabling power: Road Traffic Regulation Act 1984, s. 14 (1) (4). - Issued: 09.03.2015. Made: 02.03.2015. Coming into force: 07.03.2015. Effect: None. Territorial extent & classification: W. Local. - Available at http://www.legislation.gov.uk/wsi/2015/517/contents/made. - In English and Welsh. Welsh title: Gorchymyn Cefnffordd yr A55 (Cyffordd 31 (Caerwys) i Gyffordd 32 (Cyffordd Dolphin), Sir y Fflint) (Terfyn Cyflymder 40 mya a Gwahardd Cerbydau Dros Dro) 2015 Non-print

The A55 Trunk Road (Junction 32 (Dolphin Junction) to Junction 34 (Ewloe Interchange), Flintshire) (Temporary Traffic Prohibitions & Restriction) Order 2015 No. 2015/1712 (W.226). - Enabling power: Road Traffic Regulation Act 1984, s. 14 (1) (4). - Issued: 02.10.2015. Made: 07.09.2015. Coming into force: 10.09.2015. Effect: None. Territorial extent & classification: W. Local. - Available at http://www.legislation.gov.uk/wsi/2015/1712/contents/made. - In English and Welsh. Welsh title: Gorchymyn Cefnffordd yr A55 (Cyffordd 32 (Cyffordd Dolphin) i Gyffordd 34 (Cyfnewidfa Ewloe), Sir y Fflint) (Gwaharddiadau a Chyfyngiad Traffig Dros Dro) 2015 Non-print

The A55 Trunk Road (Junction 36, Warren Interchange to Junction 36A, Broughton, Flintshire) (Temporary Prohibition of Vehicles, Cyclists and Pedestrians) Order 2015 No. 2015/1617 (W.205). - Enabling power: Road Traffic Regulation Act 1984, s. 14 (1) (4). - Issued: 21.08.2015. Made: 14.08.2015. Coming into force: 18.08.2015. Effect: None. Territorial extent & classification: W. Local. - Available at http://www.legislation.gov.uk/wsi/2015/1617/contents/made. - In English and Welsh. Welsh title: Gorchymyn Cefnffordd yr A55 (Cyffordd 36, Cyfnewidfa Warren i Gyffordd 36A, Brychdyn, Sir y Fflint) (Gwahardd Cerbydau, Beicwyr a Cherddwyr Dros Dro) 2015 Non-print

The A55 Trunk Road (Penmaenbach Tunnel, Conwy County Borough) (Temporary Traffic Prohibitions & Restrictions) Order 2015 No. 2015/1229 (W.82). - Enabling power: Road Traffic Regulation Act 1984, ss. 14 (1) (4) (7). - Issued: 24.04.2015. Made: 25.03.2015. Coming into force: 01.04.2015. Effect: S.I. 1989/1958; 1990/328, 1586; 1994/3088; 2004/2876 suspended in accord. with art. 8. Territorial extent & classification: W. Local. - Available at http://www.legislation.gov.uk/wsi/2015/1229/contents/made. - In English and Welsh. Welsh title: Gorchymyn Cefnffordd yr A494 (Ffordd Osgoi'r Wyddgrug, Sir y Fflint) (Gwahardd Cerbydau a Beicwyr Dros Dro) Non-print

The A55 Trunk Road (Pen-y-clip Tunnel, Conwy County Borough) (Temporary Traffic Prohibitions & Restriction) Order 2015 No. 2015/2080 (W.316). - Enabling power: Road Traffic Regulation Act 1984, s. 14 (1) (4) (7). - Issued: 08.01.2016. Made: 29.12.2016. Coming into force: 05.01.2016. Effect: None. Territorial extent & classification: W. Local. - Available at http://www.legislation.gov.uk/wsi/2015/2080/contents/made. - In English and Welsh. Welsh title: Gorchymyn Cefnffordd yr A55 (Twnnel Pen-y-clip, Bwrdeistref Sirol Conwy) (Gwaharddiadau a Chyfyngiad Traffig Dros Dro) 2015 Non-print

The A55 Trunk Road (Slip Roads at Junction 6 (Nant Turnpike Interchange), Isle of Anglesey) (Temporary Prohibition of Vehicles) Order 2015 No. 2015/1717 (W.231). - Enabling power: Road Traffic Regulation Act 1984, s. 14 (1) (4). - Issued: 30.09.2015. Made: 14.09.2015. Coming into force: 21.09.2015. Effect: None. Territorial extent & classification: W. Local. - Available at http://www.legislation.gov.uk/wsi/2015/1717/contents/made. - In English and Welsh. Welsh title: Gorchymyn Cefnffordd yr A55 (Ffyrdd Ymuno ac Ymadael wrth Gyffordd 6 (Cyfnewidfa Tyrpeg Nant), Ynys Môn) (Gwahardd Cerbydau Dros Dro) 2015 Non-print

The A55 Trunk Road (Slip Roads at Junction 20, Brompton Avenue and Junction 21, Victoria Avenue, Conwy) (Temporary Prohibition of Vehicles, Cyclists and Pedestrians) Order 2015 No. 2015/45 (W.4). - Enabling power: Road Traffic Regulation Act 1984, ss. 14 (1) (4). - Issued: 27.01.2015. Made: 05.01.2015. Coming into force: 11.01.2015. Effect: None. Territorial extent & classification: W. Local. - Available at http://www.legislation.gov.uk/wsi/2015/45/contents/made. - In English and Welsh. Welsh title: Gorchymyn Cefnffordd yr A55 (Ffyrdd Ymuno wrth Gyffordd 20, Brompton Avenue a Chyffordd 21, Victoria Avenue, Conwy) (Gwahardd Cerbydau, Beicwyr a Cherddwyr Dros Dro) 2015 Non-print

The A55 Trunk Road (Westbound Exit Slip Road at Junction 20 (Princes Drive), Colwyn Bay, Conwy) (Temporary Prohibition of Vehicles, Cyclists and Pedestrians) Order 2015 No. 2015/71 (W.6). - Enabling power: Road Traffic Regulation Act 1984, ss 14 (1) (4). - Issued: 30.01.2015. Made: 05.01.2015. Coming into force: 11.01.2015. Effect: None. Territorial extent & classification: W. Local. - Available at http://www.legislation.gov.uk/wsi/2015/71/contents/made. - In English and Welsh. Welsh title: Gorchymyn Cefnffordd yr A55 (Ffordd Ymadael Tua'r Gorllewin wrth Gyffordd 20 (Rhodfa'r Tywysog), Bae Colwyn, Conwy) (Gwahardd Cerbydau, Beicwyr a Cherddwyr Dros Dro) 2015 Non-print

The A55 Trunk Road (Westbound Slip Roads at Junction 17 (Conwy Morfa), Conwy County Borough) (Temporary Prohibition of Vehicles) Order 2015 No. 2015/292 (W.28). - Enabling power: Road Traffic Regulation Act 1984, ss. 14 (1) (4). - Issued: 23.02.2015. Made: 21.01.2015. Coming into force: 28.01.2015. Effect: None. Territorial extent & classification: W. Local. - Available at http://www.legislation.gov.uk/wsi/2015/292/contents/made. - In English and Welsh. Welsh title: Gorchymyn Cefnffordd yr A55 (Ffyrdd Ymuno ac Ymadael tua'r Gorllewin wrth Gyffordd 17 (Morfa Conwy), Bwrdeistref Sirol Conwy) (Gwahardd Cerbydau Dros Dro) 2015 Non-print

The A55 Trunk Road (West of Penmaenbach Tunnel to Junction 15a, Red Gables, Penmaenmawr, Conwy) (Temporary Traffic Prohibitions & Restrictions) Order 2015 No. 2015/1719 (W.233). - Enabling power: Road Traffic Regulation Act 1984, s. 14 (1) (4) (7). - Issued: 30.09.2015. Made: 21.09.2015. Coming into force: 28.09.2015. Effect: S.I. 1989/1958; 2004/2876 suspended. Territorial extent & classification: W. Local. - Available at http://www.legislation.gov.uk/wsi/2015/1719/contents/made. - In English and Welsh. Welsh title: Gorchymyn Cefnffordd yr A55 (Man i'r Gorllewin o Dwnnel Penmaen-bach i Gyffordd 15a, Red Gables, Penmaen-mawr, Conwy) (Gwaharddiadau a Chyfyngiadau Traffig Dros Dro) 2015 Non-print

The A458 Trunk Road (Buttington Level Crossing, Buttington Cross, Powys) (Temporary Prohibition of Vehicles) Order 2015 No. 2015/1303 (W.110). - Enabling power: Road Traffic Regulation Act 1984, s. 14 (1) (4). - Issued: 11.05.2015. Made: 27.04.2015. Coming into force: 02.05.2015. Effect: None. Territorial extent & classification: W. Local. - Available at http://www.legislation.gov.uk/wsi/2015/1303/contents/made. - In English and Welsh. Welsh title: Gorchymyn Cefnffordd yr A458 (Croesfan Reilffordd Buttington, Buttington Cross, Powys) (Gwahardd Cerbydau Dros Dro) 2015 Non-print

The A458 Trunk Road (Church Street, Welshpool, Powys) (Temporary Prohibition of Vehicles & Cyclists) Order 2015 No. 2015/1314 (W.115). - Enabling power: Road Traffic Regulation Act 1984, s. 14 (1) (4). - Issued: 14.05.2015. Made: 11.05.2015. Coming into force: 18.05.2015. Effect: None. Territorial extent & classification: W. Local. - Available at http://www.legislation.gov.uk/wsi/2015/1314/contents/made. - In English and Welsh. Welsh title: Gorchymyn Cefnffordd yr A458 (Church Street, Y Trallwng, Powys) (Gwahardd Cerbydau a Beicwyr Dros Dro) 2015 Non-print

The A458 Trunk Road (Neuadd Bridge to Llangadfan, Powys) (Temporary Traffic Prohibitions and Restrictions) Order 2015 No. 2015/271 (W.15). - Enabling power: Road Traffic Regulation Act 1984, ss. 14 (1) (4) & S.I. 1999/672 art. 2, sch. 1, sch. 11, para. 30. - Issued: 19.02.2015. Made: 05.01.2015. Coming into force: 12.01.2015. Effect: None. Territorial extent & classification: W. Local. - Available at http://www.legislation.gov.uk/wsi/2015/271/contents/made. - In English and Welsh. Welsh title: Gorchymyn Cefnffordd yr A458 (Pont Neuadd i Langadfan, Powys) (Gwaharddiadau a Chyfyngiadau Traffig Dros Dro) 2015 Non-print

The A458 Trunk Road (Pont Nant-yr-ehedydd, East of Mallwyd, Gwynedd) (Temporary Traffic Prohibitions & Restrictions) Order 2015 No. 2015/278 (W.19). - Enabling power: Road Traffic Regulation Act 1984, ss. 14 (1) (4) & S.I. 1999/672 art. 2, sch. 1, sch. 11, para. 30. - Issued: 19.02.2015. Made: 05.01.2015. Coming into force: 12.01.2015. Effect: None. Territorial extent & classification: W. Local. - Available at http://www.legislation.gov.uk/wsi/2015/278/contents/made. - In English and Welsh. Welsh title: Gorchymyn Cefnffordd yr A458 (Pont Nant yr Ehedydd, Man i'r Dwyrain o Fallwyd, Gwynedd) (Gwaharddiadau a Chyfyngiadau Traffig Dros Dro) 2015 Non-print

The A465 Trunk Road (Dowlais, Merthyr Tydfil to Ebbw Vale West Junction, Blaenau Gwent) (Temporary Speed Restrictions & No Overtaking) Order 2015 No. 2015/1618 (W.206). - Enabling power: Road Traffic Regulation Act 1984, s. 14 (1) (4). - Issued: 21.08.2015. Made: 17.08.2015. Coming into force: 24.08.2015. Effect: None. Territorial extent & classification: W. Local. - Available at http://www.legislation.gov.uk/wsi/2015/1618/contents/made. - In English and Welsh. Welsh title: Gorchymyn Cefnffordd yr A465 (Dowlais, Merthyr Tudful i Gyffordd Gorllewin Glynebwy, Blaenau Gwent) (Cyfyngiadau Cyflymder Dros Dro a Dim Goddiweddyd) 2015 Non-print

The A465 Trunk Road (Ebbw Vale West Junction, Blaenau Gwent to Hardwick Roundabout, Monmouthshire) (Temporary Traffic Prohibitions and Restrictions) Order 2015 No. 2015/1315 (W.116). - Enabling power: Road Traffic Regulation Act 1984, s. 14 (1) (4). - Issued: 14.05.2015. Made: 01.05.2015. Coming into force: 07.05.2015. Effect: None. Territorial extent & classification: W. Local. - Available at http://www.legislation.gov.uk/wsi/2015/1315/contents/made. - In English and Welsh. Welsh title: Gorchymyn Cefnffordd yr A465 (Cyffordd Gorllewin Glynebwy, Blaenau Gwent i Gylchfan Hardwick, Sir Fynwy) (Gwaharddiadau a Chyfyngiadau Traffig Dros Dro) 2015 Non-print

The A465 Trunk Road (Llangua to Hardwick Roundabout, Monmouthshire) (Temporary Speed Restrictions & No Overtaking) Order 2015 No. 2015/1588 (W.189). - Enabling power: Road Traffic Regulation Act 1984, s. 14 (1) (4). - Issued: 07.08.2015. Made: 29.07.2015. Coming into force: 10.08.2015. Effect: None. Territorial extent & classification: W. Local. - Available at http://www.legislation.gov.uk/wsi/2015/1588/contents/made. - In English and Welsh. Welsh title: Gorchymyn Cefnffordd yr A465 (Llangiwa i Gylchfan Hardwick, Sir Fynwy) (Cyfyngiadau Cyflymder Dros Dro a Dim Goddiweddyd) 2015 Non-print

The A465 Trunk Road & M4 Motorway (Neath Interchange to Llandarcy Interchange, Neath Port Talbot) (Temporary Traffic Prohibition & Restrictions) Order 2015 No. 2015/1633 (W.212). - Enabling power: Road Traffic Regulation Act 1984, s. 14 (1) (4) (7). - Issued: 01.09.2015. Made: 25.08.2015. Coming into force: 01.09.2015. Effect: None. Territorial extent & classification: W. Local. - Available at http://www.legislation.gov.uk/wsi/2015/1633/contents/made. - In English and Welsh. Welsh title: Gorchymyn Cefnffordd yr A465 a Thraffordd yr M4 (Cyfnewidfa Castell-nedd i Gyfnewidfa Llandarcy, Castell-nedd Port Talbot) (Gwaharddiad a Chyfyngiadau Traffig Dros Dro) 2015 Non-print

The A465 Trunk Road (Princetown, Caerphilly County Borough to Brynmawr Roundabout, Blaenau Gwent) (Temporary Prohibitions & Restrictions) Order 2015 No. 2015/1445 (W.153). - Enabling power: Road Traffic Regulation Act 1984, s. 14 (1) (4). - Issued: 03.07.2015. Made: 18.06.2015. Coming into force: 24.06.2015. Effect: None. Territorial extent & classification: W. Local. - Available at http://www.legislation.gov.uk/wsi/2015/1445/contents/made. - In English and Welsh. Welsh title: Gorchymyn Cefnffordd yr A465 (Princetown, Bwrdeistref Sirol Caerffili i Gylchfan Bryn-mawr, Blaenau Gwent) (Gwaharddiadau a Chyfyngiadau Traffig Dros Dro) 2015 Non-print

The A465 Trunk Road (Slip Roads at Neath Interchange, Neath Port Talbot) (Temporary Prohibition of Vehicles) Order 2015 No. 2015/1705 (W.221). - Enabling power: Road Traffic Regulation Act 1984, s. 14 (1) (4). - Issued: 28.09.2015. Made: 01.09.2015. Coming into force: 07.09.2015. Effect: NoneTerritorial extent & classification: W. Local. - Available at http://www.legislation.gov.uk/wsi/2015/1705/contents/made. - In English and Welsh. Welsh title: Gorchymyn Cefnffordd yr A465 (Ffyrdd Ymuno ac Ymadael yng Nghyfnewidfa Castell-nedd, Castell-nedd Port Talbot) (Gwahardd Cerbydau Dros Dro) 2015 Non-print

The A465 Trunk Road (Westbound Off-Slip Road, Llanfoist Interchange, Monmouthshire) (Temporary Prohibition of Vehicles) Order 2015 No. 2015/1620 (W.207). - Enabling power: Road Traffic Regulation Act 1984, s. 14 (1) (4). - Issued: 24.08.2015. Made: 18.08.2015. Coming into force: 01.09.2015. Effect: None. Territorial extent & classification: W. Local. - Available at http://www.legislation.gov.uk/wsi/2015/1620/contents/made. - In English and Welsh. Welsh title: Gorchymyn Cefnffordd yr A465 (Ffordd Ymadael Tua'r Gorllewin, Cyfnewidfa Llan-ffwyst, Sir Fynwy) (Gwahardd Cerbydau Dros Dro) 2015 Non-print

The A470, A40, A479 & A483 Trunk Roads (Coryton, Cardiff to Llanddewi, Powys) (Temporary Prohibition of Vehicles) Order 2015 No. 2015/1914 (W.283). - Enabling power: Road Traffic Regulation Act 1984, s. 14 (1) (4). - Issued: 20.11.2015. Made: 10.11.2015. Coming into force: 18.11.2015. Effect: None. Territorial extent & classification: W. Local. - Available at http://www.legislation.gov.uk/wsi/2015/1914/contents/made. - In English and Welsh. Welsh title: Gorchymyn Cefnffyrdd yr A470, yr A40, yr A479 a'r A483 (Coryton, Caerdydd i Landdewi, Powys) (Gwahardd Cerbydau Dros Dro) 2015 Non-print

The A470 & A479 Trunk Roads (Llyswen, Powys) (Temporary 30 mph Speed Limit) Order 2015 No. 2015/1604 (W.202). - Enabling power: Road Traffic Regulation Act 1984, ss. 14 (1) (4). - Issued: 14.08.2015. Made: 10.08.2015. Coming into force: 13.08.2015. Effect: None. Territorial extent & classification: W. Local. - Available at http://www.legislation.gov.uk/wsi/2015/1604/contents/made. - In English and Welsh. Welsh title: Gorchymyn Cefnffyrdd yr A470 a'r A479 (Llys-wen, Powys) (Terfyn Cyflymder 30 mya Dros Dro) 2015 Non-print

The A470 Trunk Road (Blaenau Ffestiniog, Gwynedd) (Temporary Prohibition of Vehicles) Order 2015 No. 2015/1306 (W.112). - Enabling power: Road Traffic Regulation Act 1984, s. 16A. - Issued: 12.05.2015. Made: 14.04.2015. Coming into force: 18.04.2015. Effect: None. Territorial extent & classification: W. Local. - Available at http://www.legislation.gov.uk/wsi/2015/1306/contents/made. - In English and Welsh. Welsh title: Gorchymyn Cefnffordd yr A470 (Blaenau Ffestiniog, Gwynedd) (Gwahardd Cerbydau Dros Dro) 2015 Non-print

ROAD TRAFFIC, WALES: TRAFFIC REGULATION

The A470 Trunk Road (Bodnant, Conwy County Borough) (Temporary Speed Restrictions & No Overtaking) Order 2015 No. 2015/1450 (W.157). - Enabling power: Road Traffic Regulation Act 1984, s. 14 (1) (4). - Issued: 26.08.2015. Made: 30.06.2015. Coming into force: 06.07.2015. Effect: None. Territorial extent & classification: W. Local. - This Welsh Statutory Instrument has been published in substitution of the WSI of the same title to replace the previous version of that Welsh Statutory Instrument which was numbered incorrectly as (W.158). This number should read (W.157). - Available at http://www.legislation.gov.uk/wsi/2015/1450/contents/made. - In English and Welsh. Welsh title: Gorchymyn Cefnffordd yr A470 (Bodnant, Bwrdeistref Sirol Conwy) (Cyfyngiadau Cyflymder Dros Dro a Dim Goddiweddyd) 2015 Non-print

The A470 Trunk Road (East of Gellilydan, Gwynedd) (Temporary Speed Restrictions & No Overtaking) Order 2015 No. 2015/1594 (W.193). - Enabling power: Road Traffic Regulation Act 1984, ss. 14 (1) (4). - Issued: 11.08.2015. Made: 29.07.2015. Coming into force: 03.08.2015. Effect: None. Territorial extent & classification: W. Local. - Available at http://www.legislation.gov.uk/wsi/2015/1594/contents/made. - In English and Welsh. Welsh title: Gorchymyn Cefnffordd yr A470 (Man i'r Dwyrain o Gellilydan, Gwynedd) (Cyfyngiadau Cyflymder Dros Dro a Dim Goddiweddyd) 2015 Non-print

The A470 Trunk Road (Ganllwyd, Gwynedd) (Temporary Part-time 20 mph Speed Limit) Order 2015 No. 2015/1435 (W.145). - Enabling power: Road Traffic Regulation Act 1984, s. 14 (1) (4). - Issued: 02.07.2015. Made: 29.05.2015. Coming into force: 05.06.2015. Effect: None. Territorial extent & classification: W. Local. - Available at http://www.legislation.gov.uk/wsi/2015/1435/contents/made. - In English and Welsh. Welsh title: Gorchymyn Cefnffordd yr A470 (Y Ganllwyd, Gwynedd) (Terfyn Cyflymder 20 mya Rhan-amser Dros Dro) 2015 Non-print

The A470 Trunk Road (Llanelltyd, Gwynedd) (Temporary Speed Restrictions & No Overtaking) Order 2015 No. 2015/1602 (W.201). - Enabling power: Road Traffic Regulation Act 1984, s. 14 (1) (4). - Issued: 12.08.2015. Made: 28.07.2015. Coming into force: 03.08.2015. Effect: None. Territorial extent & classification: W. Local. - Available at http://www.legislation.gov.uk/wsi/2015/1602/contents/made. - In English and Welsh. Welsh title: Gorchymyn Cefnffordd yr A470 (Llanelltud, Gwynedd) (Cyfyngiadau Cyflymder Dros Dro a Dim Goddiweddyd) 2015 Non-print

The A470 Trunk Road (Moat Lane Level Crossing, Caersws, Powys) (Temporary Prohibition of Vehicles) Order 2015 No. 2015/1448 (W.156). - Enabling power: Road Traffic Regulation Act 1984, s. 14 (1) (4). - Issued: 03.07.2015. Made: 19.06.2015. Coming into force: 27.06.2015. Effect: None. Territorial extent & classification: W. Local. - Available at http://www.legislation.gov.uk/wsi/2015/1448/contents/made. - In English and Welsh. Welsh title: Gorchymyn Cefnffordd yr A470 (Croesfan Reilffordd Moat Lane, Caersws, Powys) (Gwahardd Cerbydau Dros Dro) 2015 Non-print

The A470 Trunk Road (Newbridge-on-Wye, Powys) (Temporary Part-time 20 mph Speed Limit) Order 2015 No. 2015/1437 (W.147). - Enabling power: Road Traffic Regulation Act 1984, s. 14 (1) (4) (7). - Issued: 03.07.2015. Made: 29.05.2015. Coming into force: 05.06.2015. Effect: None. Territorial extent & classification: W. Local. - Available at http://www.legislation.gov.uk/wsi/2015/1437/contents/made. - In English and Welsh. Welsh title: Gorchymyn Cefnffordd yr A470 (Pontnewydd ar Wy, Powys) (Terfyn Cyflymder 20 mya Rhan-amser Dros Dro) 2015 Non-print

The A470 Trunk Road (Northbound Link Road, Coryton Interchange, Cardiff) (Clearway, Prohibition of Left and Right Hand Turns and Prohibition of Pedestrians) Order 2015 No. 2015/1538 (W.181). - Enabling power: Road Traffic Regulation Act 1984, ss. 1 (1), 2 (1), 2 (2) (3). - Issued: 20.07.2015. Made: 13.07.2015. Coming into force: 15.07.2015. Effect: None. Territorial extent & classification: W. Local. - Available at http://www.legislation.gov.uk/wsi/2015/1538/contents/made. - In English and Welsh. Welsh title: Gorchymyn Cefnffordd yr A470 (Ffordd Gyswllt Tua'r Gogledd, Cyfnewidfa Coryton, Caerdydd) (Clirffordd, Gwahardd Troi i'r Chwith a Throi i'r Dde a Gwahardd Cerddwyr) 2015 Non-print

The A470 Trunk Road (South of Carno, Powys) (Temporary Traffic Prohibitions and Restrictions) Order 2015 No. 2015/258 (W.13). - Enabling power: Road Traffic Regulation Act 1984, ss. 14 (1) (4) & S.I. 1999/672 art. 2, sch. 1, sch. 11, para. 30. - Issued: 19.02.2015. Made: 05.01.2015. Coming into force: 12.01.2015. Effect: None. Territorial extent & classification: W. Local. - Available at http://www.legislation.gov.uk/wsi/2015/258/contents/made. - In English and Welsh. Welsh title: Gorchymyn Cefnffordd yr A470 (Man i'r De o Garno, Powys) (Gwaharddiadau a Chyfyngiadau Traffig Dros Dro) 2015 Non-print

The A470 Trunk Road (Tal-y-Cafn, Conwy County Borough) (Temporary Speed Restrictions & No Overtaking) Order 2015 No. 2015/1746 (W.241). - Enabling power: Road Traffic Regulation Act 1984, ss. 14 (1) (4), 124, sch. 9, para. 27. - Issued: 07.10.2015. Made: 05.10.2015. Coming into force: 12.10.2015. Effect: S.I. 2015/1450 (W.158) revoked. Territorial extent & classification: W. Local. - Available at http://www.legislation.gov.uk/wsi/2015/1746/contents/made. - In English and Welsh. Welsh title: Gorchymyn Cefnffordd yr A470 (Tal-y-Cafn, Bwrdeistref Sirol Conwy) (Cyfyngiadau Cyflymder Dros Dro a Dim Goddiweddyd) 2015 Non-print

The A477 Trunk Road (Carew Roundabout, East of Milton to Waterloo Roundabout, Pembroke Dock, Pembrokeshire) (Temporary Speed Restrictions & No Overtaking) Order 2015 No. 2015/1907 (W.278). - Enabling power: Road Traffic Regulation Act 1984, s. 14 (1) (4). - Issued: 18.11.2015. Made: 02.11.2015. Coming into force: 09.11.2015. Effect: None. Territorial extent & classification: W. Local. - Available at http://www.legislation.gov.uk/wsi/2015/1907/contents/made. - In English and Welsh. Welsh title: Gorchymyn Cefnffordd yr A477 (Cylchfan Caeriw, Man i'r Dwyrain o Milton i Gylchfan Waterloo, Doc Penfro, Sir Benfro) (Cyfyngiadau Cyflymder Dros Dro a Dim Goddiweddyd) 2015 Non-print

The A477 Trunk Road (East Williamston to Amroth Road, East of Kilgetty, Pembrokeshire) (Temporary Speed Restrictions & No Overtaking) Order 2015 No. 2015/1908 (W.279). - Enabling power: Road Traffic Regulation Act 1984, s. 14 (1) (4) (7). - Issued: 18.11.2015. Made: 02.11.2015. Coming into force: 09.11.2015. Effect: None. Territorial extent & classification: W. Local. - Available at http://www.legislation.gov.uk/wsi/2015/1908/contents/made. - In English and Welsh. Welsh title: Gorchymyn Cefnffordd yr A477 (East Williamston i Amroth Road, i'r Dwyrain o Gilgeti, Sir Benfro) (Cyfyngiadau Cyflymder Dros Dro a Dim Goddiweddyd) 2015 Non-print

The A477 Trunk Road (Old Amroth Road Junction, Pembrokeshire to East of Llanteg, Carmarthenshire) (Temporary Traffic Restrictions and No Overtaking) Order 2015 No. 2015/1473 (W.161). - Enabling power: Road Traffic Regulation Act 1984, s. 14 (1) (4) (7). - Issued: 09.07.2015. Made: 06.07.2015. Coming into force: 13.07.2015. Effect: None. Territorial extent & classification: W. Local. - Available at http://www.legislation.gov.uk/wsi/2015/1473/contents/made. - In English and Welsh. Welsh title: Gorchymyn Cefnffordd yr A477 (Cyffordd Old Amroth Road, Sir Benfro i Fan i'r Dwyrain o Lan-teg, Sir Gaerfyrddin) (Cyfyngiadau Traffig Dros Dro a Dim Goddiweddyd) 2015 Non-print

The A477 Trunk Road (St Clears, Carmarthenshire to Pembroke Dock, Pembrokeshire), the A40 Trunk Road (Penblewin Roundabout to Haverfordwest and Haverfordwest to Fishguard, Pembrokeshire) and the A4076 Trunk Road (Haverfordwest to Milford Haven, Pembrokeshire) (Temporary Prohibition of Vehicles) Order 2015 No. 2015/1295 (W.102). - Enabling power: Road Traffic Regulation Act 1984, s. 14 (1) (4). - Issued: 11.05.2015. Made: 02.04.2015. Coming into force: 13.04.2015. Effect: None. Territorial extent & classification: W. Local. - Available at http://www.legislation.gov.uk/wsi/2015/1295/contents/made. - In English and Welsh. Welsh title: Gorchymyn Cefnffordd yr A477 (Sanclêr, Sir Gaerfyrddin i Ddoc Penfro, Sir Benfro), Cefnffordd yr A40 (Cylchfan Penblewin i Hwlffordd a Hwlffordd i Abergwaun, Sir Benfro) a Chefnffordd yr A4076 (Hwlffordd i Aberdaugleddau, Sir Benfro) (Gwahardd Cerbydau Dros Dro) 2015 Non-print

The A477 Trunk Road (Westbound and Eastbound Lay-bys, West of Llanddowror, Carmarthenshire) (Prohibition of Entry Points) Order 2015 No. 2015/1301 (W.108). - Enabling power: Road Traffic Regulation Act 1984, ss. 1 (1), 2 (1) (2). - Issued: 11.05.2015. Made: 14.04.2015. Coming into force: 16.04.2015. Effect: None. Territorial extent & classification: W. Local. - Available at http://www.legislation.gov.uk/wsi/2015/1301/contents/made. - In English and Welsh. Welsh title: Gorchymyn Cefnffordd yr A477 (Cilfannau tua'r Gorllewin a thua'r Dwyrain, Man i'r Gorllewin o Landdowror, Sir Gaerfyrddin) (Mannau Gwahardd Mynediad) 2015 Non-print

ROAD TRAFFIC, WALES: TRAFFIC REGULATION

The A477 Trunk Road (West of Milton, Pembrokeshire) (Temporary Speed Restrictions & No Overtaking) Order 2015 No. 2015/285 (W.25). - Enabling power: Road Traffic Regulation Act 1984, ss. 14 (1) (4) & S.I. 1999/672 art. 2, sch. 1, sch. 11, para. 30. - Issued: 19.02.2015. Made: 12.01.2015. Coming into force: 19.01.2015. Effect: None. Territorial extent & classification: W. Local. - Available at http://www.legislation.gov.uk/wsi/2015/285/contents/made. - In English and Welsh. Welsh title: Gorchymyn Cefnffordd yr A477 (Man i'r Gorllewin o Milton, Sir Benfro) (Cyfyngiadau Cyflymder Dros Dro a Dim Goddiweddyd) 2015 Non-print

The A479 Trunk Road (Tretower to Cwmdu and Cwmdu to Lower Genffordd, Powys) (Temporary 50 MPH Speed Limit) Order 2015 No. 2015/296 (W.30). - Enabling power: Road Traffic Regulation Act 1984, s. 14 (1) (4). - Issued: 23.02.2015. Made: 26.01.2015. Coming into force: 01.02.2015. Effect: None. Territorial extent & classification: W. Local. - Available at http://www.legislation.gov.uk/wsi/2015/296/contents/made. - In English and Welsh. Welsh title: Gorchymyn Cefnffordd yr A479 (Tretwr i Gwmdu a Chwmdu i Lower Genffordd, Powys) (Terfyn Cyflymder 50 MYA Dros Dro) 2015 Non-print

The A483 & A40 Trunk Roads (Llandovery, Carmarthenshire) (Temporary Traffic Prohibitions & Restrictions) Order 2015 No. 2015/1548 (W.183). - Enabling power: Road Traffic Regulation Act 1984, s. 14 (1) (4) (7). - Issued: 21.07.2015. Made: 13.07.2015. Coming into force: 20.07.2015. Effect: S.I. 1991/2156; 1992/1340 suspended. Territorial extent & classification: W. Local. - Available at http://www.legislation.gov.uk/wsi/2015/1548/contents/made. - In English and Welsh. Welsh title: Gorchymyn Cefnffyrdd yr A483 a'r A40 (Llanymddyfri, Sir Gaerfyrddin) (Gwaharddiadau a Chyfyngiadau Traffig Dros Dro) 2015 Non-print

The A483 Trunk Road (Ammanford, Carmarthenshire) (Temporary 10 MPH Speed Limit and No Overtaking) Order 2015 No. 2015/284 (W.24). - Enabling power: Road Traffic Regulation Act 1984, ss. 14 (1) (4) & S.I. 1999/672 art. 2, sch. 1, sch. 11, para. 30. - Issued: 19.02.2015. Made: 12.01.2015. Coming into force: 19.01.2015. Effect: None. Territorial extent & classification: W. Local. - Available at http://www.legislation.gov.uk/wsi/2015/284/contents/made. - In English and Welsh. Welsh title: Gorchymyn Cefnffordd yr A483 (Rhydaman, Sir Gaerfyrddin) (Terfyn Cyflymder o 10 MYA Dros Dro a Dim Goddiweddyd) 2015 Non-print

The A483 Trunk Road (Ffairfach Level Crossing, Ffairfach, Carmarthenshire) (Temporary Prohibition of Vehicles) Order 2015 No. 2015/1302 (W.109). - Enabling power: Road Traffic Regulation Act 1984, s. 14 (1) (4). - Issued: 11.05.2015. Made: 17.04.2015. Coming into force: 23.04.2015. Effect: None. Territorial extent & classification: W. Local. - Available at http://www.legislation.gov.uk/wsi/2015/1302/contents/made. - In English and Welsh. Welsh title: Gorchymyn Cefnffordd yr A483 (Croesfan Reilffordd Ffair-fach, Ffair-fach, Sir Gaerfyrddin) (Gwahardd Cerbydau Dros Dro) 2015 Non-print

The A483 Trunk Road (Junction 1, Ruabon Interchange to the Wales/England Border, Wrexham County Borough) (Temporary Traffic Prohibitions and 40 MPH Speed Limit) Order 2015 No. 2015/1109 (W.77). - Enabling power: Road Traffic Regulation Act 1984, ss. 14 (1) (4) (7) & S.I. 1999/672 art. 2, sch. 1, sch. 11, para. 30. - Issued: 21.04.2015. Made: 24.03.2015. Coming into force: 01.04.2015. Effect: None. Territorial extent & classification: W. Local. - Available at http://www.legislation.gov.uk/wsi/2015/1109/contents/made. - In English and Welsh. Welsh title: Gorchymyn Cefnffordd yr A483 (Cyffordd 1, Cyfnewidfa Rhiwabon i'r Ffin rhwng Cymru a Lloegr, Bwrdeistref Sirol Wrecsam) (Gwaharddiadau Traffig Dros Dro a Therfyn Cyflymder 40 MYA) 2015 Non-print

The A483 Trunk Road (Junction 5 (Mold Road Interchange) to Junction 6 (Gresford Interchange), Wrexham County Borough) (Temporary Prohibition of Vehicles) Order 2015 No. 2015/306 (W.35). - Enabling power: Road Traffic Regulation Act 1984, s. 14 (1) (4). - Issued: 24.02.2015. Made: 02.02.2015. Coming into force: 09.02.2015. Effect: None. Territorial extent & classification: W. Local. - Available at http://www.legislation.gov.uk/wsi/2015/306/contents/made. - In English and Welsh. Welsh title: Gorchymyn Cefnffordd yr A483 (Cyffordd 5 (Cyfnewidfa Ffordd yr Wyddgrug) i Gyffordd 6 (Cyfnewidfa Gressffordd), Bwrdeistref Sirol Wrecsam) (Gwahardd Cerbydau Dros Dro) 2015 Non-print

The A483 Trunk Road (Llanelwedd Church in Wales Primary School, Llanelwedd, Powys) (Temporary 30mph and Part-time 20mph Speed Limits) Order 2015 No. 2015/1342 (W.129). - Enabling power: Road Traffic Regulation Act 1984, s. 14 (1) (4) (7). - Issued: 03.06.2015. Made: 27.05.2015. Coming into force: 01.06.2015. Effect: None. Territorial extent & classification: W. Local. - Available at http://www.legislation.gov.uk/wsi/2015/1342/contents/made. - In English and Welsh. Welsh title: Gorchymyn Cefnffordd yr A483 (Ysgol yr Eglwys yng Nghymru Llanelwedd, Llanelwedd, Powys) (Terfynau Cyflymder 30mya Dros Dro ac 20mya Rhan-amser) 2015 Non-print

The A483 Trunk Road (Newbridge Bypass, Wrexham County Borough) (Temporary Prohibition of Vehicles) Order 2015 No. 2015/1282 (W.89). - Enabling power: Road Traffic Regulation Act 1984, ss. 14 (1) (4). - Issued: 12.05.2015. Made: 25.03.2015. Coming into force: 01.04.2015. Effect: None. Territorial extent & classification: W. Local. - Available at http://www.legislation.gov.uk/wsi/2015/1282/contents/made. - In English and Welsh. Welsh title: Gorchymyn Cefnffordd yr A483 (Ffordd Osgoi Newbridge, Bwrdeistref Sirol Wrecsam) (Gwahardd Cerbydau Dros Dro) 2015 Non-print

The A483 Trunk Road (Newtown to Welshpool, Powys) (Temporary Traffic Prohibitions & Restrictions) Order 2015 No. 2015/274 (W.17). - Enabling power: Road Traffic Regulation Act 1984, ss. 14 (1) (4) & S.I. 1999/672 art. 2, sch. 1, sch. 11, para. 30. - Issued: 19.02.2015. Made: 05.01.2015. Coming into force: 12.01.2015. Effect: None. Territorial extent & classification: W. Local. - Available at http://www.legislation.gov.uk/wsi/2015/274/contents/made. - In English and Welsh. Welsh title: Gorchymyn Cefnffordd yr A483 (Y Drenewydd i'r Trallwng, Powys) (Gwaharddiadau a Chyfyngiadau Traffig Dros Dro) 2015 Non-print

The A483 Trunk Road (North of Llanbadarn Fynydd, Powys) (Temporary Prohibition of Vehicles) Order 2015 No. 2015/1718 (W.232). - Enabling power: Road Traffic Regulation Act 1984, s. 14 (1) (4). - Issued: 30.09.2015. Made: 21.09.2015. Coming into force: 28.09.2015. Effect: None. Territorial extent & classification: W. Local. - Available at http://www.legislation.gov.uk/wsi/2015/1718/contents/made. - In English and Welsh. Welsh title: Gorchymyn Cefnffordd yr A483 (Man i'r Gogledd o Lanbadarn Fynydd, Powys) (Gwahardd Cerbydau Dros Dro) 2015 Non-print

The A483 Trunk Road (Pool Road, Newtown, Powys) (Temporary Prohibition of Vehicles) Order 2015 No. 2015/1549 (W.184). - Enabling power: Road Traffic Regulation Act 1984, s. 14 (1) (4). - Issued: 21.07.2015. Made: 13.07.2015. Coming into force: 19.07.2015. Effect: None. Territorial extent & classification: W. Local. - Available at http://www.legislation.gov.uk/wsi/2015/1549/contents/made. - In English and Welsh. Welsh title: Gorchymyn Cefnffordd yr A483 (Pool Road, Y Drenewydd, Powys) (Gwahardd Cerbydau Dros Dro) 2015 Non-print

The A483 Trunk Road (Sarnybryncaled Roundabout, Near Welshpool, Powys) (Temporary Prohibition of Waiting) Order 2015 No. 2015/1441 (W.149). - Enabling power: Road Traffic Regulation Act 1984, s. 14 (1) (4). - Issued: 03.07.2015. Made: 08.06.2015. Coming into force: 14.06.2015. Effect: None. Territorial extent & classification: W. Local. - Available at http://www.legislation.gov.uk/wsi/2015/1441/contents/made. - In English and Welsh. Welsh title: Gorchymyn Cefnffordd yr A483 (Cylchfan Sarn y Bryn Caled, ger y Trallwng, Powys) (Gwahardd Aros Dros Dro) 2015 Non-print

The A487 Trunk Road (Bontnewydd, Gwynedd) (Temporary Part-time 20 mph Speed Limit) Order 2015 No. 2015/1436 (W.146). - Enabling power: Road Traffic Regulation Act 1984, s. 14 (1) (4). - Issued: 02.07.2015. Made: 29.05.2015. Coming into force: 05.06.2015. Effect: None. Territorial extent & classification: W. Local. - Available at http://www.legislation.gov.uk/wsi/2015/1436/contents/made. - In English and Welsh. Welsh title: Gorchymyn Cefnffordd yr A487 (Y Bontnewydd, Gwynedd) (Terfyn Cyflymder 20 mya Rhan-amser Dros Dro) 2015 Non-print

The A487 Trunk Road (Brynhoffnant, Ceredigion) (Temporary Traffic Restrictions & No Overtaking) Order 2015 No. 2015/1284 (W.91). - Enabling power: Road Traffic Regulation Act 1984, s. 14 (1) (4) (7). - Issued: 12.05.2015. Made: 26.03.2015. Coming into force: 01.04.2015. Effect: None. Territorial extent & classification: W. Local. - Available at http://www.legislation.gov.uk/wsi/2015/1284/contents/made. - In English and Welsh. Welsh title: Gorchymyn Cefnffordd yr A487 (Brynhoffnant, Ceredigion) (Cyfyngiadau Traffig Dros Dro a Dim Goddiweddyd) 2015 Non-print

ROAD TRAFFIC, WALES: TRAFFIC REGULATION

The A487 Trunk Road (Llanarth, Ceredigion) (Temporary 40 mph, 30 mph & Part-time 20 mph Speed Limits) Order 2015 No. 2015/1433 (W.143). - Enabling power: Road Traffic Regulation Act 1984, s. 14 (1) (4) (7). - Issued: 02.07.2015. Made: 29.05.2015. Coming into force: 05.06.2015. Effect: None. Territorial extent & classification: W. Local. - Available at http://www.legislation.gov.uk/wsi/2015/1433/contents/made. - In English and Welsh. Welsh title: Gorchymyn Cefnffordd yr A487 (Llannarth, Ceredigion) (Terfynau Cyflymder 40 mya a 30 mya Dros Dro ac 20 mya Rhan-amser) 2015 Non-print

The A487 Trunk Road (Llanarth to Castell Pigyn, Ceredigion) (Temporary Speed Restrictions & No Overtaking) Order 2015 No. 2015/1993 (W.303). - Enabling power: Road Traffic Regulation Act 1984, s. 14 (1) (4) (7). - Issued: 11.12.2015. Made: 03.12.2015. Coming into force: 09.12.2015. Effect: None. Territorial extent & classification: W. Local. - Available at http://www.legislation.gov.uk/wsi/2015/1993/contents/made. - In English and Welsh. Welsh title: Gorchymyn Cefnffordd yr A487 (Llannarth i Gastell Pigyn, Ceredigion) (Cyfyngiadau Cyflymder Dros Dro a Dim Goddiweddyd) 2015 Non-print

The A487 Trunk Road (Llanfarian to Rhydyfelin, Ceredigion) (Temporary Traffic Restrictions & No Overtaking) Order 2015 No. 2015/1287 (W.94). - Enabling power: Road Traffic Regulation Act 1984, s. 14 (1) (4) (7). - Issued: 12.05.2015. Made: 26.03.2015. Coming into force: 01.04.2015. Effect: None. Territorial extent & classification: W. Local. - Available at http://www.legislation.gov.uk/wsi/2015/1287/contents/made. - In English and Welsh. Welsh title: Gorchymyn Cefnffordd yr A487 (Llanfarian i Rydyfelin, Ceredigion) (Cyfyngiadau Traffig Dros Dro a Dim Goddiweddyd) 2015 Non-print

The A487 Trunk Road (Llanon, Ceredigion) (Temporary Traffic Restrictions & No Overtaking) Order 2015 No. 2015/1285 (W.92). - Enabling power: Road Traffic Regulation Act 1984, s. 14 (1) (4) (7). - Issued: 12.05.2015. Made: 26.03.2015. Coming into force: 01.04.2015. Effect: None. Territorial extent & classification: W. Local. - Available at http://www.legislation.gov.uk/wsi/2015/1285/contents/made. - In English and Welsh. Welsh title: Gorchymyn Cefnffordd yr A487 (Llan-non, Ceredigion) (Cyfyngiadau Traffig Dros Dro a Dim Goddiweddyd) 2015 Non-print

The A487 Trunk Road (Newport, Pembrokeshire) (Temporary Prohibition of Vehicles) Order 2015 No. 2015/1788 (W.251). - Enabling power: Road Traffic Regulation Act 1984, ss. 14 (1) (4). - Issued: 16.10.2015. Made: 08.10.2015. Coming into force: 18.10.2015. Effect: None. Territorial extent & classification: W. Local. - Available at http://www.legislation.gov.uk/wsi/2015/1788/contents/made. - In English and Welsh. Welsh title: Gorchymyn Cefnffordd yr A487 (Trefdraeth, Sir Benfro) (Gwahardd Cerbydau Dros Dro) 2015 Non-print

The A487 Trunk Road (North East of Cardigan to Penparc, Ceredigion) (Temporary Speed Restrictions & No Overtaking) Order 2015 No. 2015/1293 (W.100). - Enabling power: Road Traffic Regulation Act 1984, ss. 14 (1) (4) (7). - Issued: 12.05.2015. Made: 27.03.2015. Coming into force: 02.04.2015. Effect: None. Territorial extent & classification: W. Local. - Available at http://www.legislation.gov.uk/wsi/2015/1293/contents/made. - In English and Welsh. Welsh title: Gorchymyn Cefnffordd yr A487 (Man i'r Gogledd-ddwyrain o Aberteifi hyd at Benparc, Ceredigion) (Cyfyngiadau Cyflymder Dros Dro a Dim Goddiweddyd) 2015 Non-print

The A487 Trunk Road (North of Comins Coch to Bow Street, Ceredigion) (Temporary Speed Restrictions & No Overtaking) Order 2015 No. 2015/1288 (W.95). - Enabling power: Road Traffic Regulation Act 1984, s. 14 (1) (4) (7). - Issued: 12.05.2015. Made: 26.03.2015. Coming into force: 01.04.2015. Effect: None. Territorial extent & classification: W. Local. - Available at http://www.legislation.gov.uk/wsi/2015/1288/contents/made. - In English and Welsh. Welsh title: Gorchymyn Cefnffordd yr A487 (I'r Gogledd o Gomins Coch i Bow Street, Ceredigion) (Cyfyngiadau Cyflymder a Dim Goddiweddyd Dros Dro) 2015 Non-print

The A487 Trunk Road (North Parade, Aberystwyth, Ceredigion) (Temporary Prohibition of Vehicles) Order 2015 No. 2015/1738 (W.239). - Enabling power: Road Traffic Regulation Act 1984, s. 14 (1) (4). - Issued: 05.10.2015. Made: 25.06.2015. Coming into force: 05.10.2015. Effect: None. Territorial extent & classification: W. Local. - Available at http://www.legislation.gov.uk/wsi/2015/1738/contents/made. - In English and Welsh. Welsh title: Gorchymyn Cefnffordd yr A487 (Rhodfa'r Gogledd, Aberystwyth, Ceredigion) (Gwahardd Cerbydau Dros Dro) 2015 Non-print

The A487 Trunk Road (Penmorfa to Bryncir, Gwynedd) (Temporary Traffic Restrictions & No Overtaking) Order 2015 No. 2015/1292 (W.99). - Enabling power: Road Traffic Regulation Act 1984, ss. 14 (1) (4). - Issued: 12.05.2015. Made: 31.03.2015. Coming into force: 06.04.2015. Effect: None. Territorial extent & classification: W. Local. - Available at http://www.legislation.gov.uk/wsi/2015/1292/contents/made. - In English and Welsh. Welsh title: Gorchymyn Cefnffordd yr A487 (Penmorfa i Fryncir, Gwynedd) (Cyfyngiadau Traffig Dros Dro a Dim Goddiweddyd) 2015 Non-print

The A487 Trunk Road (Talybont, Ceredigion) (Temporary Traffic Restrictions & No Overtaking) Order 2015 No. 2015/1286 (W.93). - Enabling power: Road Traffic Regulation Act 1984, s. 14 (1) (4) (7). - Issued: 12.05.2015. Made: 26.03.2015. Coming into force: 01.04.2015. Effect: None. Territorial extent & classification: W. Local. - Available at http://www.legislation.gov.uk/wsi/2015/1286/contents/made. - In English and Welsh. Welsh title: Gorchymyn Cefnffordd yr A487 (Tal-y-bont, Ceredigion) (Cyfyngiadau Traffig Dros Dro a Dim Goddiweddyd) 2015 Non-print

The A487 Trunk Road (Temple Bar, Pembrokeshire to Pembrokeshire / Ceredigion Boundary) (Temporary Speed Restrictions and No Overtaking) Order 2015 No. 2015/1787 (W.250). - Enabling power: Road Traffic Regulation Act 1984, ss. 14 (1) (4). - Issued: 16.10.2015. Made: 08.10.2015. Coming into force: 19.10.2015. Effect: None. Territorial extent & classification: W. Local. - Available at http://www.legislation.gov.uk/wsi/2015/1787/contents/made. - In English and Welsh. Welsh title: Gorchymyn Cefnffordd yr A487 (Temple Bar, Sir Benfro i'r Ffin Rhwng Sir Benfro a Cheredigion) (Cyfyngiadau Cyflymder Dros Dro a Dim Goddiweddyd) 2015 Non-print

The A487 Trunk Road (Y Felinheli Bypass, Gwynedd) (Temporary Traffic Prohibitions & Restrictions) Order 2015 No. 2015/1481 (W.162). - Enabling power: Road Traffic Regulation Act 1984, s. 14 (1) (4). - Issued: 16.07.2015. Made: 25.06.2015. Coming into force: 01.07.2015. Effect: None. Territorial extent & classification: W. Local. - Available at http://www.legislation.gov.uk/wsi/2015/1481/contents/made. - In English and Welsh. Welsh title: Gorchymyn Cefnffordd yr A487 (Ffordd Osgoi'r Felinheli, Gwynedd) (Gwaharddiadau a Chyfyngiadau Traffig Dros Dro) 2015 Non-print

The A487 Trunk Road (Ysgol Tal y Bont, Ceredigion) (Temporary Part-time 20 mph Speed Limit) Order 2015 No. 2015/1442 (W.150). - Enabling power: Road Traffic Regulation Act 1984, s. 14 (1) (4). - Issued: 03.07.2015. Made: 08.06.2015. Coming into force: 11.06.2015. Effect: None. Territorial extent & classification: W. Local. - Available at http://www.legislation.gov.uk/wsi/2015/1442/contents/made. - In English and Welsh. Welsh title: Gorchymyn Cefnffordd yr A487 (Ysgol Tal-y-bont, Ceredigion) (Terfyn Cyflymder 20 mya Rhan-amser Dros Dro) 2015 Non-print

The A494/A550 Trunk Road (Deeside Park Interchange, Flintshire) (Temporary Prohibition of Vehicles) (No. 2) Order 2015 No. 2015/1550 (W.185). - Enabling power: Road Traffic Regulation Act 1984, s. 14 (1) (4), 124, sch. 9, para. 27. - Issued: 21.07.2015. Made: 14.07.2015. Coming into force: 20.07.2015. Effect: S.I. 2015/256 (W.12) revoked. Territorial extent & classification: W. Local. - Available at http://www.legislation.gov.uk/wsi/2015/1550/contents/made. - Welsh title: Gorchymyn Cefnffordd yr A494/ A550 (Cyfnewidfa Parc Glannau Dyfrdwy, Sir y Fflint) (Gwahardd Cerbydau Dros Dro) (Rhif 2) 2015 Non-print

The A494/A550 Trunk Road (Deeside Park Interchange, Flintshire) (Temporary Prohibition of Vehicles) Order 2015 No. 2015/256 (W.12). - Enabling power: Road Traffic Regulation Act 1984, s. 14 (1) (4) & S.I. 1999/672 art. 2, sch. 1, sch. 11, para. 30. - Issued: 19.02.2015. Made: 05.01.2015. Coming into force: 12.01.2015. Effect: None. Territorial extent & classification: W. Local. - Available at http://www.legislation.gov.uk/wsi/2015/256/contents/made. - In English and Welsh. Welsh title: Gorchymyn Cefnffordd yr A494/A550 (Cyfnewidfa Parc Glannau Dyfrdwy, Sir y Fflint) (Gwahardd Cerbydau Dros Dro) 2015 Non-print

ROAD TRAFFIC, WALES: TRAFFIC REGULATION

The A494 Trunk Road (Bala, Gwynedd) (Temporary Prohibition of Vehicles) Order 2015 No. 2015/1737 (W.238). - Enabling power: Road Traffic Regulation Act 1984, s. 16A. - Issued: 05.10.2015. Made: 01.09.2015. Coming into force: 06.09.2015. Effect: None. Territorial extent & classification: W. Local. - Available at http://www.legislation.gov.uk/wsi/2015/1737/contents/made. - Welsh title: Gorchymyn Cefnffordd yr A494 (Y Bala, Gwynedd) (Gwahardd Cerbydau Dros Dro) 2015 Non-print

The A494 Trunk Road (Drome Corner Interchange, Flintshire to the Wales/England Border) (Temporary Prohibition of Vehicles) Order 2015 No. 2015/311 (W.38). - Enabling power: Road Traffic Regulation Act 1984, ss. 14 (1) (4). - Issued: 20.02.2015. Made: 18.02.2015. Coming into force: 23.02.2015. Effect: None. Territorial extent & classification: W. Local. - Available at http://www.legislation.gov.uk/wsi/2015/311/contents/made. - In English and Welsh. Welsh title: Gorchymyn Cefnffordd yr A494 (Cyfnewidfa Drome Corner, Sir y Fflint i'r Ffin rhwng Cymru a Lloegr) (Gwahardd Cerbydau Dros Dro) 2015 Non-print

The A494 Trunk Road (Gwyddelwern, Denbighshire) (Temporary 40 mph Speed Limit) Order 2015 No. 2015/1447 (W.155). - Enabling power: Road Traffic Regulation Act 1984, s. 14 (1) (4). - Issued: 03.07.2015. Made: 25.06.2015. Coming into force: 01.07.2015. Effect: None. Territorial extent & classification: W. Local. - Available at http://www.legislation.gov.uk/wsi/2015/1447/contents/made. - In English and Welsh. Welsh title: Gorchymyn Cefnffordd yr A494 (Gwyddelwern, Sir Ddinbych) (Terfyn Cyflymder 40 mya Dros Dro) 2015 Non-print

The A494 Trunk Road (Llanbedr Dyffryn Clwyd, Denbighshire) (Temporary Speed Restrictions & No Overtaking) Order 2015 No. 2015/298 (W.32). - Enabling power: Road Traffic Regulation Act 1984, s. 14 (1) (4). - Issued: 24.02.2015. Made: 26.01.2015. Coming into force: 02.02.2015. Effect: None. Territorial extent & classification: W. Local. - Available at http://www.legislation.gov.uk/wsi/2015/298/contents/made. - In English and Welsh. Welsh title: Gorchymyn Cefnffordd yr A494 (Llanbedr Dyffryn Clwyd, Sir Ddinbych) (Cyfyngiadau Cyflymder a Dim Goddiweddyd Dros Dro) 2015 Non-print

The A494 Trunk Road (Mold Bypass, Flintshire) (Temporary Prohibition of Vehicles & Cyclists) Order 2015 No. 2015/1230 (W.83). - Enabling power: Road Traffic Regulation Act 1984, ss. 14 (1) (4). - Issued: 24.04.2015. Made: 25.03.2015. Coming into force: 01.04.2015. Effect: None. Territorial extent & classification: W. Local. - Available at http://www.legislation.gov.uk/wsi/2015/1230/contents/made. - In English and Welsh. Welsh title: Gorchymyn Cefnffordd yr A494 (Ffordd Osgoi'r Wyddgrug, Sir y Fflint) (Gwahardd Cerbydau a Beicwyr Dros Dro) 2015 Non-print

The A494 Trunk Road (Slip Roads at Queensferry Interchange, Flintshire) (Temporary Prohibition of Large Vehicles and 30 MPH Speed Limit) Order 2015 No. 2015/1624 (W.208). - Enabling power: Road Traffic Regulation Act 1984, s. 14 (1) (4) (7). - Issued: 26.08.2015. Made: 20.08.2015. Coming into force: 01.09.2015. Effect: None. Territorial extent & classification: W. Local. - Available at http://www.legislation.gov.uk/wsi/2015/1624/contents/made. - Welsh title: Gorchymyn Cefnffordd yr A494 (Ffyrdd Ymadael wrth Gyfnewidfa Queensferry, Sir y Fflint) (Gwahardd Cerbydau Mawr Dros Dro a Therfyn Cyflymder 30 MYA) 2015 Non-print

The A494 Trunk Road (Wernfechan, Ruthin, Denbighshire) (Prohibition of Waiting) Order 2015 No. 2015/2017 (W.306). - Enabling power: Road Traffic Regulation Act 1984, ss. 1 (1), 2 (1) (2), 4 (2), 124, sch. 9, para. 27. - Issued: 15.12.2015. Made: 04.12.2015. Coming into force: 10.12.2015. Effect: S.I. 1986/1548 revoked. Territorial extent & classification: W. Local. - Available at http://www.legislation.gov.uk/wsi/2015/2017/contents/made. - In English and Welsh. Welsh title: Gorchymyn Cefnffordd yr A494 (Wern Fechan, Rhuthun, Sir Ddinbych) (Gwahardd Aros) 2015 Non-print

The A494 Trunk Road (Ysgol O. M. Edwards, Llanuwchllyn, Gwynedd) (Temporary Part-time 20mph Speed Limit) Order 2015 No. 2015/1443 (W.151). - Enabling power: Road Traffic Regulation Act 1984, s. 14 (1) (4) (7). - Issued: 03.07.2015. Made: 08.06.2015. Coming into force: 11.06.2015. Effect: None. Territorial extent & classification: W. Local. - Available at http://www.legislation.gov.uk/wsi/2015/1443/contents/made. - Welsh title: Gorchymyn Cefnffordd yr A494 (Ysgol O. M. Edwards, Llanuwchllyn, Gwynedd) (Terfyn Cyflymder 20mya Rhan-amser Dros Dro) 2015 Non-print

The A4042 Trunk Road (Cwmbran Roundabout to Pontypool Roundabout, Torfaen) (Temporary Prohibition of Vehicles, Cyclists and Pedestrians) Order 2015 No. 2015/540 (W.47). - Enabling power: Road Traffic Regulation Act 1984, s. 14 (1) (4). - Issued: 09.03.2015. Made: 24.02.2015. Coming into force: 01.03.2015. Effect: None. Territorial extent & classification: W. Local. - Available at http://www.legislation.gov.uk/wsi/2015/540/contents/made. - In English and Welsh. Welsh title: Gorchymyn Cefnffordd yr A4042 (Cylchfan Cwmbrân i Gylchfan Pont-y-pwl, Torfaen) (Gwahardd Cerbydau, Beicwyr a Cherddwyr Dros Dro) 2015 Non-print

The A4042 Trunk Road (Llanellen to Hardwick Gyratory, Abergavenny, Monmouthshire) (Temporary Traffic Prohibitions & Restrictions) Order 2015 No. 2015/1626 (W.209). - Enabling power: Road Traffic Regulation Act 1984, s. 14 (1) (4). - Issued: 28.08.2015. Made: 25.08.2015. Coming into force: 01.09.2015. Effect: None. Territorial extent & classification: W. Local. - Available at http://www.legislation.gov.uk/wsi/2015/1626/contents/made. - In English and Welsh. Welsh title: Gorchymyn Cefnffordd yr A4042 (Llanelen i System Gylchu Hardwick, y Fenni, Sir Fynwy) (Gwaharddiadau a Chyfyngiadau Traffig Dros Dro) 2015 Non-print

The A4042 Trunk Road (Westbound Link Road, Caerleon Roundabout to Grove Park Roundabout, Newport) (Temporary Prohibition of Vehicles) Order 2015 No. 2015/1585 (W.188). - Enabling power: Road Traffic Regulation Act 1984, s. 14 (1) (4). - Issued: 07.08.2015. Made: 28.07.2015. Coming into force: 05.08.2015. Effect: None. Territorial extent & classification: W. Local. - Available at http://www.legislation.gov.uk/wsi/2015/1585/contents/made. - In English and Welsh. Welsh title: Gorchymyn Cefnffordd yr A4042 (Ffordd Gyswllt Tua'r Gorllewin, Cylchfan Caerllion i Gylchfan Grove Park, Casnewydd) (Gwahardd Cerbydau Dros Dro) 2015 Non-print

The A4076 Trunk Road (Freemans Way, Haverfordwest, Pembrokeshire) (Temporary Prohibition of Vehicles) Order 2015 No. 2015/1297 (W.104). - Enabling power: Road Traffic Regulation Act 1984, s. 14 (1) (4). - Issued: 11.05.2015. Made: 02.04.2015. Coming into force: 13.04.2015. Effect: None. Territorial extent & classification: W. Local. - Available at http://www.legislation.gov.uk/wsi/2015/1297/contents/made. - In English and Welsh. Welsh title: Gorchymyn Cefnffordd yr A4076 (Freemans Way, Hwlffordd, Sir Benfro) (Gwahardd Cerbydau Dros Dro) 2015 Non-print

The A4232 Trunk Road (Culverhouse Cross, Cardiff) (Temporary Prohibition of Vehicles) Order 2015 No. 2015/1716 (W.230). - Enabling power: Road Traffic Regulation Act 1984, s. 14 (1) (4). - Issued: 29.09.2015. Made: 09.09.2015. Coming into force: 14.09.2015. Effect: None. Territorial extent & classification: W. Local. - Available at http://www.legislation.gov.uk/wsi/2015/1716/contents/made. - In English and Welsh. Welsh title: Gorchymyn Cefnffordd yr A4232 (Croes Cwrlwys, Caerdydd) (Gwahardd Cerbydau Dros Dro) 2015 Non-print

The A4810 Steelworks Access Road (Queen's Way, Llanwern, Newport) (Temporary Prohibition of Vehicles) Order 2015 No. 2015/1326 (W.121). - Enabling power: Road Traffic Regulation Act 1984, s. 14 (1) (4). - Issued: 21.05.2015. Made: 05.05.2015. Coming into force: 09.05.2015. Effect: None. Territorial extent & classification: W. Local. - Available at http://www.legislation.gov.uk/wsi/2015/1326/contents/made. - In English and Welsh. Welsh title: Gorchymyn Ffordd Fynediad Gwaith Dur yr A4810 (Queen's Way, Llan-wern, Casnewydd) (Gwahardd Cerbydau Dros Dro) 2015 Non-print

The M4 Motorway (Junction 23a (Magor), Monmouthshire to Junction 28 (Tredegar Park), Newport) (Temporary Prohibition of Vehicles) Order 2015 No. 2015/1632 (W.211). - Enabling power: Road Traffic Regulation Act 1984, s. 14 (1) (4). - Issued: 01.09.2015. Made: 25.08.2015. Coming into force: 01.09.2015. Effect: None. Territorial extent & classification: W. Local. - Available at http://www.legislation.gov.uk/wsi/2015/1632/contents/made. - In English and Welsh. Welsh title: Gorchymyn Traffordd yr M4 (Cyffordd 23a (Magwyr), Sir Fynwy i Gyffordd 28 (Parc Tredegar), Casnewydd) (Gwahardd Cerbydau Dros Dro) 2015 Non-print

The M4 Motorway (Junction 23, Rogiet to the Wales/England Border, Monmouthshire) (Temporary Prohibition of Vehicles) Order 2015 No. 2015/1296 (W.103). - Enabling power: Road Traffic Regulation Act 1984, s. 14 (1) (4). - Issued: 11.05.2015. Made: 02.04.2015. Coming into force: 11.04.2015. Effect: None. Territorial extent & classification: W. Local. - Available at http://www.legislation.gov.uk/wsi/2015/1296/contents/made. - In English and Welsh. Welsh title: Gorchymyn Traffordd yr M4 (Cyffordd 23, Rogiet i Ffin Cymru/Lloegr, Sir Fynwy) (Gwahardd Cerbydau Dros Dro) 2015 Non-print

The M4 Motorway (Junction 24 (Coldra) to Junction 28 (Tredegar Park), Newport) (Temporary Prohibition of Vehicles & 40 mph Speed Limit) Order 2015 No. 2015/2078 (W.314). - Enabling power: Road Traffic Regulation Act 1984, s. 14 (1) (4) (7). - Issued: 06.01.2016. Made: 29.12.2015. Coming into force: 04.01.2016. Effect: None. Territorial extent & classification: W. Local. - Available at http://www.legislation.gov.uk/wsi/2015/2078/contents/made. - In English and Welsh. Welsh title: Gorchymyn Traffordd yr M4 (Cyffordd 24 (Y Coldra) i Gyffordd 28 (Parc Tredegar), Casnewydd) (Gwahardd Cerbydau a Therfyn Cyflymder 40 mya Dros Dro) 2015 Non-print

The M4 Motorway (Junction 32 (Coryton), Cardiff) and The A470 Trunk Road (Coryton Interchange, Cardiff to Abercynon Roundabout, Rhondda Cynon Taf) (Temporary Prohibition of Vehicles and Speed Restrictions) Order 2015 No. 2015/283 (W.23). - Enabling power: Road Traffic Regulation Act 1984, s. 14 (1) (4) (7) & S.I. 1999/672 art. 2, sch. 1, sch. 11, para. 30. - Issued: 19.02.2015. Made: 06.01.2015. Coming into force: 12.01.2015. Effect: None. Territorial extent & classification: W. Local. - Available at http://www.legislation.gov.uk/wsi/2015/283/contents/made. - In English and Welsh. Welsh title: Gorchymyn Traffordd yr M4 (Cyffordd 32 (Coryton), Caerdydd) a Chefnffordd yr A470 (Cyfnewidfa Coryton, Caerdydd i Gylchfan Abercynon, Rhondda Cynon Taf) (Gwahardd Cerbydau Dros Dro a Chyfyngiadau Cyflymder Dros Dro) 2015 Non-print

The M4 Motorway (Junction 32 (Coryton) to Junction 33 (Capel Llanilltern), Cardiff) (Temporary Traffic Prohibition & Restrictions) Order 2015 No. 2015/1634 (W.213). - Enabling power: Road Traffic Regulation Act 1984, s. 14 (1) (4) (7). - Issued: 01.09.2015. Made: 25.08.2015. Coming into force: 01.09.2015. Effect: None. Territorial extent & classification: W. Local. - Available at http://www.legislation.gov.uk/wsi/2015/1634/contents/made. - In English and Welsh. Welsh title: Gorchymyn Traffordd yr M4 (Cyffordd 32 (Coryton) i Gyffordd 33 (Capel Llanilltern), Caerdydd) (Gwahardiad a Chyfyngiadau Traffig Dros Dro) 2015 Non-print

The M4 Motorway (Junction 33 (Capel Llanilltern Interchange)) & The A4232 Trunk Road (Capel Llanilltern to Culverhouse Cross, Cardiff) (Temporary Traffic Prohibitions & Restrictions) Order 2015 No. 2015/1595 (W.194). - Enabling power: Road Traffic Regulation Act 1984, s. 14 (1) (4) (7). - Issued: 11.08.2015. Made: 30.07.2015. Coming into force: 03.08.2015. Effect: None. Territorial extent & classification: W. Local. - Available at http://www.legislation.gov.uk/wsi/2015/1595/contents/made. - In English and Welsh. Welsh title: Gorchymyn Traffordd yr M4 (Cyffordd 33 (Cyfnewidfa Capel Llanilltern)) a Chefnffordd yr A4232 (Capel Llanilltern i Groes Cwrlwys, Caerdydd) (Gwahardiadau a Chyfyngiadau Traffig Dros Dro) 2015 Non-print

The M4 Motorway (Junction 37, Pyle, Bridgend County Borough to Junction 39, Groes, Neath Port Talbot) (Temporary Prohibition of Vehicles) Order 2015 No. 2015/1551 (W.186). - Enabling power: Road Traffic Regulation Act 1984, s. 14 (1) (4). - Issued: 23.07.2015. Made: 14.07.2015. Coming into force: 20.07.2015. Effect: None. Territorial extent & classification: W. Local. - Available at http://www.legislation.gov.uk/wsi/2015/1551/contents/made. - In English and Welsh. Welsh title: Gorchymyn Traffordd yr M4 (Cyffordd 37, Y Pîl, Bwrdeistref Sirol Pen-y-bont ar Ogwr i Gyffordd 39, Y Groes, Castell-nedd Port Talbot) (Gwahardd Cerbydau Dros Dro) 2015 Non-print

The M4 Motorway (Junction 42, Earlswood, Neath Port Talbot to West of Junction 44, Lonlas, Swansea) (Temporary 50 MPH Speed Limit, Prohibitions and Trafficking of Hard Shoulder) Order 2015 No. 2015/753 (W.60). - Enabling power: Road Traffic Regulation Act 1984, s. 14 (1) (4) (7). - Issued: 20.03.2015. Made: 13.03.2015. Coming into force: 23.03.2015. Effect: None. Territorial extent & classification: W. Local. - Available at http://www.legislation.gov.uk/wsi/2015/753/contents/made. - In English and Welsh. Welsh title: Gorchymyn Traffordd yr M4 (Cyffordd 42, Earlswood, Castell-nedd Port Talbot i Bwynt i'r Gorllewin o Gyffordd 44, Lôn-las, Abertawe) (Cyfyngiad Cyflymder 50 mya, Gwaharddiadau a Chaniatáu Traffig ar y Llain Galed Dros Dro) 2015 Non-print

The M4 Motorway (Junction 42 (Earlswood) to Junction 43 (Llandarcy), Neath Port Talbot) & The A465 Trunk Road (Llandarcy, Neath Port Talbot to Hirwaun, Rhondda Cynon Taf) (Temporary Prohibition of Vehicles) Order 2015 No. 2015/1909 (W.280). - Enabling power: Road Traffic Regulation Act 1984, s. 14 (1) (4). - Issued: 18.11.2015. Made: 02.11.2015. Coming into force: 09.11.2015. Effect: None. Territorial extent & classification: W. Local. - Available at http://www.legislation.gov.uk/wsi/2015/1909/contents/made. - In English and Welsh. Welsh title: Gorchymyn Traffordd yr M4 (Cyffordd 42 (Earlswood) i Gyffordd 43 (Llandarcy), Castell-nedd Port Talbot) a Chefnffordd yr A465 (Llandarcy, Castell-nedd Port Talbot i Hirwaun, Rhondda Cynon Taf) (Gwahardd Cerbydau Dros Dro) 2015 Non-print

The M4 Motorway (Slip Roads at Junction 46 (Llangyfelach), Swansea) (Temporary Prohibition of Vehicles) Order 2015 No. 2015/1535 (W.180). - Enabling power: Road Traffic Regulation Act 1984, s. 14 (1) (4). - Issued: 20.07.2015. Made: 27.05.2015. Coming into force: 01.06.2015. Effect: None. Territorial extent & classification: W. Local. - Available at http://www.legislation.gov.uk/wsi/2015/1535/contents/made. - In English and Welsh. Welsh title: Gorchymyn Traffordd yr M4 (Ffyrdd Ymuno ac Ymadael wrth Gyffordd 46 (Llangyfelach), Abertawe) (Gwahardd Cerbydau Dros Dro) 2015 Non-print

The M4 Motorway (Slip Roads between Junction 23a (Magor), Monmouthshire and Junction 28 (Tredegar Park), Newport) (Temporary Prohibition of Vehicles) Order 2015 No. 2015/1915 (W.284). - Enabling power: Road Traffic Regulation Act 1984, s. 14 (1) (4). - Issued: 20.11.2015. Made: 01.10.2015. Coming into force: 04.10.2015. Effect: None. Territorial extent & classification: W. Local. - Available at http://www.legislation.gov.uk/wsi/2015/1915/contents/made. - In English and Welsh. Welsh title: Gorchymyn Traffordd yr M4 (Slipffyrdd rhwng Cyffordd 23a (Magwyr), Sir Fynwy a Chyffordd 28 (Parc Tredegar), Casnewydd) (Gwahardd Cerbydau Dros Dro) 2015 Non-print

The M4 Motorway (Slip Roads between Junction 38 (Margam) and Junction 43 (Llandarcy), Neath Port Talbot) (Temporary Prohibition of Vehicles) Order 2015 No. 2015/2037 (W.309). - Enabling power: Road Traffic Regulation Act 1984, s. 14 (1) (4). - Issued: 18.12.2015. Made: 10.12.2015. Coming into force: 16.12.2015. Effect: None. Territorial extent & classification: W. Local. - Available at http://www.legislation.gov.uk/wsi/2015/2037/contents/made. - In English and Welsh. Welsh title: Gorchymyn Traffordd yr M4 (Slipffyrdd rhwng Cyffordd 38 (Margam) a Chyffordd 43 (Llandarsi), Castell-nedd Port Talbot) (Gwahardd Cerbydau Dros Dro) 2015 Non-print

Salmon and freshwater Wales

The Prohibition of Keeping or Release of Live Fish (Specified Species) (Wales) Order 2015 No. 2015/88 (W.7). - Enabling power: European Communities Act 1972, ss. 1 (1), 2 (2). - Issued: 18.02.2015. Made: 28.01.2015. Laid before the National Assembly for Wales: 02.02.2015. Coming into force: 27.02.2015. Effect: S.I. 1998/2409; 2003/416 (W.60) revoked & S.I. 2011/2292 partially revoked. Territorial extent & classification: W. General. - In English and Welsh. Welsh title: Gorchymyn Gwahardd Cadw new Ollwng Pysgod Byw (Rhywogaethau Penodedig) (Cymru) 2015. - 12p.: 30 cm. - 978-0-348-11041-8 £6.00

Sea fisheries, England

The Undersized Bass (Revocation) (England) Order 2015 No. 2015/1791. - Enabling power: Sea Fish (Conservation) Act 1967 ss. 1 (1) (2) (3) (6), 3 (1) (2), 15 (3), 20 (1). - Issued: 20.10.2015. Made: 12.10.2015. Laid: 16.10.2015. Coming into force: 11.11.2015. Effect: S.I. 1989/1285; S.I. 2007/857 revoked in relation to England. Territorial extent & classification: E. General. - 2p.: 30 cm. - 978-0-11-113996-7 £4.25

Sea fisheries, England: Boats and methods of fishing

The Fishing Boats Designation (England) Order 2015 No. 2015/648. - Enabling power: Fishery Limits Act 1967, s. 2 (1) (4), 6 (2) & Interpretation Act 1978, s. 14A. - Issued: 17.03.2015. Made: 13.03.2015. Coming into force: 01.07.2015. Effect: S.I. 1965/1241, 1448, 1569; 1970/318; 1983/253; 1986/382; 1992/3108; 1996/248, 1035; 1997/1630 revoked. Territorial extent & classification: E. General. - 16p.: 30 cm. - 978-0-11-113306-4 £6.00

The Salmon and Migratory Trout (Prohibition of Fishing and Landing) (England) Order 2015 No. 2015/441. - Enabling power: Sea Fish (Conservation) Act 1967, ss. 5 (1) (2), 6 (1) (2) (3). - Issued: 09.03.2015. Made: 27.02.2015. Laid: 03.03.2015. Coming into force: 25.03.2015. Effect: S.I. 1972/1966; 1973/188, 189, 207, 210; 1975/639, 844; 1983/58, 59, 60 revoked. Territorial extent & classification: E. General. - 8p.: 30 cm. - 978-0-11-113129-9 £6.00

Sea fisheries, England: Conservation of sea fish

The Sea Fish Licensing (England) Order 2015 No. 2015/647. - Enabling power: Sea Fish (Conservation) Act 1967, ss. 4 (1) (2), 15 (3), 20 (1) & Interpretation Act 1987, s. 14A & Scotland Act 1998, ss. 105, 112, 113. - Issued: 16.03.2015. Made: 09.03.2015. Laid: 13.03.2015. Coming into force: 01.07.2015. Effect: S.I. 1999/1820 partially revoked & S.I. 1992/2633; 1993/188, 2291 revoked. Territorial extent & classification: E. General. - 8p.: 30 cm. - 978-0-11-113305-7 £4.25

Sea fisheries, England: Fishery limits

The Fishing Boats Designation (England) Order 2015 No. 2015/648. - Enabling power: Fishery Limits Act 1967, s. 2 (1) (4), 6 (2) & Interpretation Act 1978, s. 14A. - Issued: 17.03.2015. Made: 13.03.2015. Coming into force: 01.07.2015. Effect: S.I. 1965/1241, 1448, 1569; 1970/318; 1983/253; 1986/382; 1992/3108; 1996/248, 1035; 1997/1630 revoked. Territorial extent & classification: E. General. - 16p.: 30 cm. - 978-0-11-113306-4 £6.00

Sea fisheries, England: Landing and sale of sea fish

The Salmon and Migratory Trout (Prohibition of Fishing and Landing) (England) Order 2015 No. 2015/441. - Enabling power: Sea Fish (Conservation) Act 1967, ss. 5 (1) (2), 6 (1) (2) (3). - Issued: 09.03.2015. Made: 27.02.2015. Laid: 03.03.2015. Coming into force: 25.03.2015. Effect: S.I. 1972/1966; 1973/188, 189, 207, 210; 1975/639, 844; 1983/58, 59, 60 revoked. Territorial extent & classification: E. General. - 8p.: 30 cm. - 978-0-11-113129-9 £6.00

Sea fisheries, England: Sea fish industry

The Grants for Fishing and Aquaculture Industries Regulations 2015 No. 2015/1711. - Enabling power: European Communities Act 1972, s. 2 (2). - Issued: 01.10.2015. Made: 21.09.2015. Laid: 25.09.2015. Coming into force: 31.10.2015. Effect: S.I. 2007/3284 revoked with saving. Territorial extent & classification: E. General. - EC note: These Regulations supplement Regulation (EU) no. 508/2014 of the European Parliament and of the Council on the European Maritime Fisheries Fund and lay down rules for the implementation of Council Regulation (EU) no. 1303/2013. - 8p.: 30 cm. - 978-0-11-113945-5 £6.00

Sea fisheries, England: Shellfish

The Animals, Water and Sea Fisheries (Miscellaneous Revocations) Order 2015 No. 2015/751. - Enabling power: Sea Fisheries (Shellfish) Act 1967, s. 12 & Animal Health Act 1981, ss. 1, 2, 10, 29, 34 (7), 87, 88 (2) & Water Act 1983, sch. 2 paras 3 (2), 10 (2) & Water Act 1989, ss. 4 (1), 83 (1), 85 (1), 86 (1) (2), 95 (1) (2). - Issued: 24.03.2015. Made: 16.03.2015. Laid: 18.03.2015. Coming into force: 01.07.2015. Effect: S.I. 1965/2040; 1974/1555; 1976/919; 1981/677; 1982/459; 1983/159, 1720, 1927; 1989/1530, 1531, 2017, 2018; 2001/2734 revoked. Territorial extent & classification: E/W. General. - 4p.: 30 cm. - 978-0-11-113382-8 £4.25

The Poole Harbour Fishery Order 2015 No. 2015/1346. - Enabling power: Sea Fisheries (Shellfish) Act 1967, s. 1 (2). - Issued: 05.06.2015. Made: 28.05.2015. Laid: 02.06.2015. Coming into force: 01.07.2015. Effect: S.I. 1985/847 revoked. Territorial extent & classification: E. General. - 4p.: 30 cm. - 978-0-11-113653-9 £4.25

Sea fisheries, England and Wales

The Sea Fishing (Enforcement and Miscellaneous Provisions) Order 2015 No. 2015/191. - Enabling power: Fisheries Act 1981, s. 30 (2). - Issued: 17.02.2015. Made: 08.02.2015. Laid: 12.02.2015. Laid before the National Assembly for Wales: 12.02.2015. Coming into force: 06.03.2015. Effect: S.I. 2005/1605; 2007/1842; 2008/691 amended & 57 SIs revoked & 7 partially revoked. Territorial extent & classification: E/W/part NI. General. - 12p.: 30 cm. - 978-0-11-112927-2 £6.00

Sea fisheries, Northern Ireland

The Sea Fishing (Enforcement and Miscellaneous Provisions) Order 2015 No. 2015/191. - Enabling power: Fisheries Act 1981, s. 30 (2). - Issued: 17.02.2015. Made: 08.02.2015. Laid: 12.02.2015. Laid before the National Assembly for Wales: 12.02.2015. Coming into force: 06.03.2015. Effect: S.I. 2005/1605; 2007/1842; 2008/691 amended & 57 SIs revoked & 7 partially revoked. Territorial extent & classification: E/W/part NI. General. - 12p.: 30 cm. - 978-0-11-112927-2 £6.00

Sea fisheries, Wales: Conservation of sea fish

The Specified Crustaceans (Prohibition on Fishing, Landing, Sale and Carriage) (Wales) Order 2015 No. 2015/2076 (W.312). - Enabling power: Sea Fish (Conservation) Act 1967, ss.1 (1) (2) (3) (4) (6), 5 (1) (2), 6 (1) (3), 20 (1) & Marine and Coastal Access Act 2009, ss. 189 (1), 316 (1). - Issued: 08.01.2016. Made: 23.12.2015. Laid before the National Assembly for Wales: 30.12.2015. Coming into force: 01.02.2016. Effect: Byelaw 19 of the North Sea Fisheries Committee & S.I. 2010/630 (C.42) amended & S.I. 1986/497; 1989/2443; 1993/1178; 2002/676 (W.73), 1897 (W.198) & Byelaw 3, 5, 6, 7, 46 of the former South Wales Sea Fisheries Committee; Byelaw 29, 31 of the former North Western and North Wales Sea Fisheries Committee revoked in relation to Wales & S.I. 2000/874 revoked in relation the area of the Welsh zone that lies beyond Wales & S.I. 1989/919 revoked in relation to Wales and the Welsh zone. Territorial extent & classification: W. General. - In English and Welsh: Gorchymyn Cramenogion Penodedig (Gwahardd eu Pysgota) (eu Glanio, eu Gwerthu a'u Cludo) (Cymru) 2015. - 20p.: 30 cm. - 978-0-348-11224-5 £6.00

Seeds, England

The Seed Potatoes (England) Regulations 2015 No. 2015/1953. - Enabling power: Plant Varieties and Seeds Act 1964, ss. 16(1) to (5), 36. - Issued: 07.12.2015. Made: 30.11.2015. Laid: 02.12.2015. Coming into force: 01.01.2016. Effect: 1964 c.14 modified & S.I. 2001/3510 amended & S.I. 2006/1161; 2008/560; 2009/2342; 2010/1511 revoked. Territorial extent & classification: E. General. - 32p.: 30 cm. - 978-0-11-114138-0 £6.00

Senior courts of England and Wales

The Civil Procedure (Amendment No. 2) Rules 2015 No. 2015/670 (L. 9). - Enabling power: Civil Procedure Act 1997, s. 2. - Issued: 18.03.2015. Made: 12.03.2015. Laid: 13.03.2015. Coming into force: In accord. with rule 2. Effect: S.I. 1998/3132; 2014/3299 amended. Territorial extent & classification: E/W. General. - 4p.: 30 cm. - 978-0-11-113332-3 £4.25

The Civil Procedure (Amendment No. 3) Rules 2015 No. 2015/877 (L.11). - Enabling power: Civil Procedure Act 1997, s. 2 & Counter-Terrorism and Security Act 2015, sch. 3, paras 2 to 4, 6. - Issued: 31.03.2015. Made: 25.03.2015. Laid: 26.03.2015. Coming into force: 17.04.2015. Effect: S.I. 1998/3132 amended. Territorial extent & classification: E/W. General. - 4p.: 30 cm. - 978-0-11-113500-6 £4.25

The Civil Procedure (Amendment No. 4) Rules 2015 No. 2015/1569 (L.20). - Enabling power: Civil Procedure Act 1997, s. 2. - Issued: 29.07.2015. Made: 22.07.2015. Laid: 24.07.2015. Coming into force: In accord. with rule 1. Effect: S.I. 1998/3132 amended. Territorial extent & classification: E/W. General. - 8p.: 30 cm. - 978-0-11-113850-2 £4.25

The Civil Procedure (Amendment No. 5) Rules 2015 No. 2015/1881 (L.22). - Enabling power: Civil Procedure Act 1997, ss. 1, 2. - Issued: 17.11.2015. Made: 10.11.2015. Laid: 12.11.2015. Coming into force: 03.12.2015 in accord. with rule 2. Effect: SI 1998/3132 amended. Territorial extent & classification: E/W. General. - 2p.: 30 cm. - 978-0-11-114079-6 £4.25

The Civil Procedure (Amendment) Rules 2015 No. 2015/406 (L. 3). - Enabling power: Counter-Terrorism and Security Act 2015, sch. 3 para. 7. - Issued: 31.03.2015. Made: 26.02.2015. Laid: 27.02.2015. Coming into force: In accord. with rule 1. Effect: S.I. 1998/3132 amended. Territorial extent & classification: E/W. General. - Approved by both Houses of Parliament. Supersedes (ISBN 9780111130957) issued 05/03/15. - 16p.: 30 cm. - 978-0-11-130001-5 £6.00

The Civil Procedure (Amendment) Rules 2015 No. 2015/406 (L. 3). - Enabling power: Counter-Terrorism and Security Act 2015, sch. 3 para. 7. - Issued: 05.03.2015. Made: 26.02.2015. Laid: 27.02.2015. Coming into force: In accord. with rule 1. Effect: S.I. 1998/3132 amended. Territorial extent & classification: E/W. General. - For approval by resolution of each House of Parliament within 40 days. Superseded by approved S.I. 2015/406 (L. 3) (ISBN 9780111300015) issued 31/03/15. - 16p.: 30 cm. - 978-0-11-113095-7 £6.00

The Civil Proceedings and Family Proceedings Fees (Amendment) Order 2015 No. 2015/576 (L.7). - Enabling power: Courts Act 2003, ss. 92 (1) (2) & Anti-Social Behaviour, Crime and Policing Act 2014, s. 180 (1). - Issued: 13.03.2015. Made: 05.03.2015. Coming into force: In accord. with art. 1. Effect: S.I. 2008/1053, 1054 amended. Territorial extent & classification: E/W. General. - Supersedes draft S.I. (ISBN 9780111127490) issued 22.01.2015. - 4p.: 30 cm. - 978-0-11-113246-3 £4.25

The Crime and Courts Act 2013 (Commencement No. 14) Order 2015 No. 2015/1837. - Enabling power: Crime and Courts Act 2013 s. 61(2). Bringing into operation various provisions of the 2013 Act on 03.11.2015. - Issued: 04.11.2015. Made: 27.10.2015. Effect: None. Territorial extent & classification: E/W. General. - 8p.: 30 cm. - 978-0-11-114035-2 £4.25

The Criminal Justice and Courts Act 2015 (Commencement No. 1, Saving and Transitional Provisions) Order 2015 No. 2015/778 (C.44). - Enabling power: Criminal Justice and Courts Act 2015, s. 95 (1) (6). Bringing into operation various provisions of the 2015 Act on 20.03.2015; 13.04.2015, in accord. with arts 2, 3. - Issued: 25.03.2015. Made: 19.03.2015. Effect: None. Territorial extent & classification: E/W/S/NI. General. - 8p.: 30 cm. - 978-0-11-113405-4 £6.00

The Criminal Procedure (Amendment No. 2) Rules 2015 No. 2015/646 (L.8). - Enabling power: Courts Act 2003, s. 69. - Issued: 16.03.2015. Made: 09.03.2015. Laid: 12.03.2015. Coming into force: 06.04.2015. Effect: S.I. 2014/610 amended. Territorial extent and classification: E/W. General. - 12p.: 30 cm. - 978-0-11-113304-0 £6.00

The Criminal Procedure (Amendment) Rules 2015 No. 2015/13 (L.1). - Enabling power: Courts Act 2003, s. 69. - Issued: 15.01.2015. Made: 07.01.2015. Laid: 12.01.2015. Coming into force: 02.02.2015; 06.04.2015, in accord. with rule 2. Effect: S.I. 2014/1610 amended. Territorial extent and classification: E/W. General. - 24p.: 30 cm. - 978-0-11-112683-7 £6.00

The Criminal Procedure Rules 2015 No. 2015/1490 (L.18). - Enabling power: Courts Act 2003, s. 69 & Road Traffic Offenders Act 1988, s. 12 (1) (3) & Criminal Law act 1977, s. 48 & Indictments Act 1915, s. 2 & Administration of Justice (Miscellaneous Provisions) Act 1933, s. 2 (6) & Bail Act 1976, s. 5B (9) & Criminal Justice Act 1967, s. 9 (2A) & Police and Criminal Evidence Act 1984, s. 81 & Criminal Procedure and Investigations Act 1996, ss. 19, 20 (3) & Criminal Justice Act 2003, ss. 30 (1), 132 (4), 174 (4) & Youth Justice and Criminal Evidence Act 1999, ss. 37, 38 & Magistrates' Courts Act 1980, s. 12 (7ZA) & Powers of Criminal Courts (Sentencing) Act 2000, s. 155 (7) & Proceeds of Crime Act 2002, ss. 91, 351 (2), 362 (2), 369 (2), 375 (1) & Senior Courts Act 1981, ss. 19, 52, 66, 67, 73 (2), 74 (2) (3) (4), 87 (4) & Criminal Justice 1988, s. 159 (6) & Terrorism Act 2000, sch. 5, para. 10, sch. 6, para. 4, sch. 6A, para. 5 & Extradition Act 2003, ss. 36A (4), 36B (3), 118A (4), 118B (3). - Issued: 20.07.2015. Made: 03.07.2015. Laid: 20.07.2015. Coming into force: 05.10.2015. Effect: S.I. 2014/1610 revoked. Territorial extent and classification: E/W. General. - 445p.: 30 cm. - 978-0-11-113772-7 £46.25

The Election Judges Rota Rules 2015 No. 2015/329 (L.2). - Enabling power: Senior Courts Act 1981, s. 142 (1). - Issued: 26.02.2015. Made: 18.02.2015. Laid: 23.02.2015. Coming into force: 20.03.2015. Effect: None. Territorial extent & classification: E/W. General. - 4p.: 30 cm. - 978-0-11-113021-6 £4.25

The Family Procedure (Amendment No. 2) Rules 2015 No. 2015/1420 (L.15). - Enabling power: Civil Jurisdiction and Judgments Act 1982, s. 48 & County Courts Act 1984, s. 110 (4) & Courts Act 2003, ss. 75, 76 & Female Genital Mutilation Act 2003, sch 2, part 1, para. 14 (2). - Issued: 02.07.2015. Made: 24.06.2015. Laid: 26.06.2015. Coming into force: In accord. with rule 1. Effect: S.I. 2010/2955 amended. Territorial extent & classification: E/W. General. - 8p.: 30 cm. - 978-0-11-113716-1 £6.00

The Family Procedure (Amendment No. 3) Rules 2015 No. 2015/1868 (L.21). - Enabling power: Courts Act 2003, ss. 75, 76 & Children and Families Act 2014 s. 10. - Issued: 12.11.2015. Made: 04.11.2015. Laid: 10.11.2015. Coming into force: In accord. with rule 1. Effect: S.I. 2010/2955 amended. Territorial extent & classification: E/W. General. - 4p.: 30 cm. - 978-0-11-114067-3 £4.25

The Family Procedure (Amendment) Rules 2015 No. 2015/913 (L.13). - Enabling power: Civil Jurisdiction and Judgments Act 1982, s. 48 & Courts Act 2003, ss. 75, 76. - Issued: 01.04.2015. Made: 23.03.2015. Laid: 26.03.2015. Coming into force: 01.07.2015. Effect: S.I. 2010/2955 amended. Territorial extent & classification: E/W. General. - 8p.: 30 cm. - 978-0-11-113537-2 £4.25

The Family Proceedings Fees (Amendment No. 2) Order 2015 No. 2015/1419 (L.14). - Enabling power: Courts Act 2003, ss. 92. - Issued: 06.07.2015. Made: 24.06.2015. Laid: 26.06.2015. Coming into force: 17.07.2015. Effect: S.I. 2008/1054 amended. Territorial extent & classification: E/W. General. - 2p.: 30 cm. - 978-0-11-113715-4 £4.25

Family Proceedings Fees (Amendment) Order 2015 No. 2015/687 (L.10). - Enabling power: Courts Act 2003, ss. 92, 108 (6). - Issued: 19.03.2015. Made: 11.03.2015. Laid: 16.03.2015. Coming into force: 06.4.2015. Effect: S.I. 2008/1054, 2013/1407 amended. Territorial extent & classification: E/W. General. - 4p.: 30 cm. - 978-0-11-113346-0 £4.25

The Maximum Number of Judges Order 2015 No. 2015/1885. - Enabling power: Senior Courts Act 1981, s. 2 (4). - Issued: 18.11.2015. Made: 11.11.2015. Coming into force: 12.11.2015 in accord. with art. 1. Effect: 1981 c. 54 amended. Territorial extent & classification: E/W. General. - Supersedes draft SI (ISBN 9780111138922) issued 10/09/15 - 2p.: 30 cm. - 978-0-11-114083-3 £4.25

Serious crime prevention orders

The Serious Crime Act 2015 (Commencement No. 1) Regulations 2015 No. 2015/820 (C.52). - Enabling power: Serious Crime Act 2015, s. 88 (6) (c) (e) (8). Bringing into operation various provisions of the 2015 Act on 03.05.2015; 01.06.2015, in accord. with art. 2 & 3. - Issued: 27.03.2015. Made: 19.03.2015. Effect: None. Territorial extent & classification: E/W/S/NI. General. - 4p.: 30 cm. - 978-0-11-113452-8 £4.25

Sheriff Court

The Courts Reform (Scotland) Act 2014 (Consequential Provisions and Modifications) Order 2015 No. 2015/700. - Enabling power: Scotland Act 1998, ss. 104, 112 (1), 113 (2) (3) (5) (7), 114 (1). - Issued: 19.03.2015. Made: 11.03.2015. Coming into force: in accord with art. 1. Effect: 1975 c.25, c.42; 1978 c.30; 1982 c.27; 1991 c.48; 2005 c.4; S.I. 2009/2231 amended; 1926 c.16; 1934 c.56; 1936 c.6; 1971 c.58 partially repealed; and 1898 c.35; 1952 c.12 repealed. Territorial extent & classification: E/W/S/NI. General. - Supersedes draft S.I. (ISBN 9780111126929) issued 19/01/15. - 12p.: 30 cm. - 978-0-11-113349-1 £6.00

Social care

The Care Act 2014 (Commencement No. 4) Order 2015 No. 2015/993 (C.68). - Enabling power: Care Act 2014, ss. 124, 127 (1) (5). Bringing into operation various provisions of the 2014 Act on 01.04.2015, 06.04.2015, in accord. with arts 2, 4. - Issued: 02.04.2015. Made: 26.03.2015. Effect: None. Territorial extent & classification: E/W/S/NI. General. - 8p.: 30 cm. - 978-0-11-113624-9 £6.00

The Care and Support (Business Failure) Regulations 2015 No. 2015/301. - Enabling power: Care Act 2014, ss. 52 (12), 125 (7) (8). - Issued: 23.02.2015. Made: 11.02.2015. Coming into force: In accord with reg. 1 (2) (3). Effect: None. Territorial extent & classification: E/W/S/NI. General. - Supersedes draft S.I. (ISBN 9780111124161) issued 03/12/14. - 4p.: 30 cm. - 978-0-11-112993-7 £4.25

The Care and Support (Miscellaneous Amendments) Regulations 2015 No. 2015/644. - Enabling power: Care Act 2014, ss. 14 (5) (7), 17 (11) (12), 33 (1) (2), 34 (1) (7), 39 (1) (8), 75 (7), 125 (7) (8), sch. 1, paras 1 (6) (7), 2 (9) (10), 4 (5) (6). - Issued: 16.03.2015. Made: 10.03.2015. Laid: 11.03.2015. Coming into force: in accord with reg. 1 (2). Effect: S.I. 2014/2671, 2672, 2828, 2839, 2871 amended. Territorial extent & classification: E/W except for the amendment to S.I. General. 2014/2839 which extend to UK. - 4p.: 30 cm. - 978-0-11-113300-2 £4.25

Social care, England

The Adoption Information and Intermediary Services (Pre-Commencement Adoptions) (Amendment) Regulations 2015 No. 2015/1685. - Enabling power: Adoption and Children Act 2002, ss. 9 (1), 98 (1) (1A) (3), 140 (7) (8), 144 (2). - Issued: 18.09.2015. Made: 11.09.2015. Laid: 15.09.2015. Coming into force: 10.11.2015. Effect: S.I. 2005/890 amended. Territorial extent & classification: E. General. - 4p.: 30 cm. - 978-0-11-113927-1 £4.25

The Care Act 2014 (Consequential Amendments) (Secondary Legislation) Order 2015 No. 2015/643. - Enabling power: Care Act 2014, ss. 123 (1) (2), 125 (7) (8). - Issued: 16.03.2015. Made: 10.03.2015. Laid: 11.03.2015. Coming into force: In accord. with art. 1 (2). Effect: 48 Sis amended & S.I. 2014/829 partially revoked & S.I. 2003/2276, 2277 revoked. Territorial extent & classification: E. General. - 20p.: 30 cm. - 978-0-11-113299-9 £6.00

The Care Act 2014 (Transitional Provision) Order 2015 No. 2015/995. - Enabling power: Care Act 2014, ss. 124, 125 (7). - Issued: 02.04.2015. Made: 26.03.2015. Coming into force: In accord. with art. 1 (1). Effect: None. Territorial extent & classification: E. General. - 4p.: 30 cm. - 978-0-11-113626-3 £4.25

The Care and Support (Children's Carers) Regulations 2015 No. 2015/305. - Enabling power: Care Act 2014, ss. 62 (2), 125 (7) (8). - Issued: 23.02.2015. Made: 11.02.2015. Coming into force: In accord with reg. 1 (1). Effect: 2014 c.23 modified. Territorial extent & classification: E. General. - Supersedes draft SI (ISBN 9780111124178) issued 03/12/14. - 8p.: 30 cm. - 978-0-11-112996-8 £4.25

The Care and Support (Eligibility Criteria) Regulations 2015 No. 2015/313. - Enabling power: Care Act 2014, ss. 13 (7) (8), 125 (7) (8). - Issued: 23.02.2015. Made: 11.02.2015. Coming into force: in accord with reg. 1. Effect: None. Territorial extent & classification: E. General. - Supersedes draft S.I. (ISBN 9780111124185) issued 03/12/14. - 4p.: 30 cm. - 978-0-11-113001-8 £4.25

The Care and Support (Isle of Scilly) Order 2015 No. 2015/642. - Enabling power: National Health Service and Community Care Act 1990, s. 67 (6) & Community Care (Residential Accommodation) Act 1992, s. 2 (5) & Care Act 2014, s. 128 (4). - Issued: 16.03.2015. Made: 10.03.2015. Laid: 11.03.2015. Coming into force: in accord with art. 1. Effect: 2014 c. 23 modified & S.I. 1993/570 amended. Territorial extent & classification: E. General. - 2p.: 30 cm. - 978-0-11-113298-2 £4.25

The Care and Support (Market Oversight Criteria) Regulations 2015 No. 2015/314. - Enabling power: Care Act 2014, ss. 53 (1), 125 (7) (8). - Issued: 23.02.2015. Made: 11.02.2015. Coming into force: in accord with reg. 1 (1). Effect: None. Territorial extent & classification: E. General. - Supersedes draft S.I. (ISBN 9780111124192) issued 03/12/14 - 4p.: 30 cm. - 978-0-11-113002-5 £4.25

The Care Quality Commission (Membership) (Amendment) Regulations 2015 No. 2015/1479. - Enabling power: Health and Social Care Act 2008, s. 161 (3) (4), sch. 1, para. 3 (3) to (5). - Issued: 14.07.2015. Made: 07.07.2015. Laid: 14.07.2015. Coming into force: 01.09.2015. Effect: S.I. 2008/2252; 2011/2547; 2013/2157 revoked. Territorial extent & classification: E. General. - 12p.: 30 cm. - 978-0-11-113760-4 £6.00

The Children's Homes (England) Regulations 2015 No. 2015/541. - Enabling power: Interpretation Act 1978, s. 14A & Care Standards Act 2000, ss. 1 (4A), 22 (1) (1A) (2) (a) to (d), (f) to (j) (5) (7) (a) to (h) (j), 34 (1), 35 (1), 118 (5). - Issued: 11.03.2015. Made: 04.03.2015. Laid: 06.03.2015. Coming into force: 01.04.2015. Effect: S.I. 2010/2130 amended & S.I. 2001/3967; 2011/583 revoked. Territorial extent & classification: E. General. - 44p.: 30 cm. - 978-0-11-113217-3 £10.00

The Health and Social Care Act 2008 (Regulated Activities) (Amendment) Regulations 2015 No. 2015/64. - Enabling power: Health and Social Care Act 2008, ss. 20 (1) (3) (5A), 35, 86 (2), 87 (1) (2), 161 (3) (4). - Issued: 02.02.2015. Made: 26.01.2015 Laid: 28.01.2015. Coming into force: 01.04.2015. Effect: S.I. 2014/2936 amended. Territorial extent & classification: E. General. - 8p.: 30 cm. - 978-0-11-112800-8 £6.00

The Health and Social Care Act 2012 (Consistent Identifier) Regulations 2015 No. 2015/1439. - Enabling power: Health and Social Care Act 2012, s. 251A (1). - Issued: 09.07.2015. Made: 01.07.2015. Laid: 07.07.2015. Coming into force: 01.10.2015. Effect: None. Territorial extent & classification: E. General. - 2p.: 30 cm. - 978-0-11-113739-0 £4.25

The Health and Social Care Act 2012 (Continuity of Information: Interpretation) Regulations 2015 No. 2015/1470. - Enabling power: Health and Social Care Act 2012, s. 251C (3) (4). - Issued: 10.07.2015. Made: 01.07.2015. Laid: 07.07.2015. Coming into force: 01.10.2015. Effect: None. Territorial extent & classification: E. General. - 8p.: 30 cm. - 978-0-11-113749-9 £4.25

The Health and Social Care (Miscellaneous Revocations) Regulations 2015 No. 2015/839. - Enabling power: Health and Medicines Act 1988, s. 26 (6) & Care Standards Act 2000, ss. 12 (2), 15 (3), 16 (3), 118 (5) to (7) & Health and Social Care Act 2001, ss. 65 (1) (2) & Tobacco Advertising and Promotion Act 2002, ss. 19 (2), 20 & National Health Service Act, ss. 8, 28, 187, 272 (7) (8), 273, sch. 6, paras 3, 5, 6. - Issued: 27.03.2015. Made: 23.03.2015 Laid: 26.03.2015. Coming into force: 01.07.2015. Effect: S.I. 1974/29; 2003/7, 1415 revoked in relation to England & S.I. 1985/1876; 1989/1893; 1996/512; 2001/3744; 2003/2323; 2005/640 revoked. Territorial extent & classification: E. General. - 4p.: 30 cm. - 978-0-11-113466-5 £4.25

The Health and Social Care (Safety and Quality) Act 2015 (Commencement No. 1 and Transitory Provision) Regulations 2015 No. 2015/1438 (C.81). - Enabling power: Health and Social Care (Safety and Quality) Act 2015, ss. 6 (4) (5). Bringing into operation various provisions of the 2015 Act on 25.06.2015; 01.10.2015, in accord. with art. 2 & 3. - Issued: 06.07.2015. Made: 24.06.2015. Effect: 2012 c.7 modified. Territorial extent & classification: E. General. - 4p.: 30 cm. - 978-0-11-113728-4 £4.25

The Local Authorities (Public Health Functions and Entry to Premises by Local Healthwatch Representatives) and Local Authority (Public Health, Health and Wellbeing Boards and Health Scrutiny) (Amendment) Regulations 2015 No. 2015/921. - Enabling power: National Health Service Act 2006, ss. 6C (2), 272 (7) (8), 275. - Issued: 31.03.2015. Made: 23.03.2015. Coming into force: In accord. with reg. 1 (2) (3). Effect: S.I. 2013/218, 351 amended. Territorial extent & classification: E. General. - Supersedes draft S.I. (ISBN 9780111128053) issued 02/02/15. - 8p.: 30 cm. - 978-0-11-113545-7 £4.25

Social care, England and Wales

The Care Act 2014 (Health Education England and the Health Research Authority) (Consequential Amendments and Revocations) Order 2015 No. 2015/137. - Enabling power: Care Act 2014, s. 123 (1) (2). - Issued: 11.02.2015. Made: 04.02.2015. Laid: 11.02.2015. Coming into force: 01.04.2015. Effect: S.I. 1990/2024; 1995/2800, 2801; 1996/251; 1999/873, 874; 2004/1031; 2005/3361, 3373, 2415, 2531; 2008/1185; 2009/779 (W.67), 1385 (W.141), 3097 (W.270); 2011/2260; 2012/922, 1261; 2013/349; 2014/566 amended & S.I 2013/647, 1197 revoked. Territorial extent & classification: E/W. General. - Partially revoked by SI 2015/559 (ISBN 9780111132296) in relation to E. - 8p.: 30 cm. - 978-0-11-112888-6 £6.00

Social care, Wales

The Adult Protection and Support Orders (Authorised Officer) (Wales) Regulations 2015 No. 2015/1465 (W.159). - Enabling power: Social Services and Well-being (Wales) Act 2014, s. 127 (9). - Issued: 03.08.2015. Made: 01.07.2015. Coming into force: 06.04.2016. Effect: None. Territorial extent & classification: W. General. - In English and Welsh: Welsh title: Rheoliadau Gorchmynion Amddiffyn a Chynorthwyo Oedolion (Swyddog Awdurdodedig) (Cymru) 2015. - 4p.: 30 cm. - 978-0-348-11134-7 £4.25

The Care and Support (Assessment) (Wales) Regulations 2015 No. 2015/1305 (W.111). - Enabling power: Social Services and Well-being (Wales) Act 2014, s. 30. - Issued: 10.08.2015. Made: 06.05.2015. Laid before the National Assembly for Wales: 08.05.2015. Coming into force: 06.04.2016. Effect: None. Territorial extent & classification: W. General. - In English & Welsh. Welsh title: Rheoliadau Gofal a Chymorth (Asesu) (Cymru) 2015. - 8p.: 30 cm. - 978-0-348-11138-5 £4.25

SOCIAL CARE, WALES

The Care and Support (Business Failure) (Wales) Regulations 2015 No. 2015/1920 (W.286). - Enabling power: Social Services and Well-being (Wales) Act 2014, ss. 191 (7), 196 (2). - Issued: 07.12.2015. Made: 18.11.2015. Laid before the National Assembly for Wales: 20.11.2015. Coming into force: 06.04.2016. Effect: None. Territorial extent & classification: W. General. - In English & Welsh. Welsh title: Rheoliadau Gofal a Chymorth (Methiant Busnes) (Cymru) 2015. - 8p.: 30 cm. - 978-0-348-11198-9 £6.00

The Care and Support (Care Planning) (Wales) Regulations 2015 No. 2015/1335 (W.126). - Enabling power: Social Services and Well-being (Wales) Act 2014, ss. 54 (5) (6), 55, 126 (3). - Issued: 04.06.2015. Made: 21.05.2015. Laid before the National Assembly for Wales: 01.06.2015. Coming into force: 06.04.2016. Effect: None. Territorial extent & classification: W. General. - In English and Welsh. Welsh title: Rheoliadau Gofal a Chymorth (Cynllunio Gofal) (Cymru) 2015. - 12p.: 30 cm. - 978-0-348-11102-6 £6.00

The Care and Support (Charging) (Wales) Regulations 2015 No. 2015/1843 (W.271). - Enabling power: Social Services and Well-being (Wales) Act 2014, ss. 50, 52, 53 (3), 61, 62, 66, 67, 69, 196 (2). - Issued: 05.01.2016. Made: 27.10.2015. Laid before the National Assembly for Wales: 03.11.2015. Coming into force: 06.04.2016. Effect: None. Territorial extent & classification: W. General. - In English & Welsh. Welsh title: Rheoliadau Gofal a Chymorth (Gosod Ffioedd) (Cymru) 2015. - 24p.: 30 cm. - 978-0-348-11219-1 £6.00

The Care and Support (Choice of Accommodation) (Wales) Regulations 2015 No. 2015/1840 (W.268). - Enabling power: Social Services and Well-being (Wales) Act 2014, ss. 57, 196 (2) (c). - Issued: 18.11.2015. Made: 27.10.2015. Laid before the National Assembly for Wales: 03.11.2015. Coming into force: 06.04.2016. Effect: None. Territorial extent & classification: W. General. - In English and Welsh. Welsh title: Rheoliadau Gofal a Chymorth (Dewis o Lety) (Cymru) 2015. - 8p.: 30 cm. - 978-0-348-11188-0 £6.00

The Care and Support (Deferred Payment) (Wales) Regulations 2015 No. 2015/1841 (W.269). - Enabling power: Social Services and Well-being (Wales) Act 2014, s. 68, 196 (2). - Issued: 10.11.2015. Made: 27.10.2015. Laid before the National Assembly for Wales: 03.11.2015. Coming into force: 06.04.2016. Effect: None. Territorial extent & classification: W. General. - In English & Welsh. Welsh title: Rheoliadau Gofal a Chymorth (Taliadau Gohiriedig) (Cymru) 2015. - 12p.: 30 cm. - 978-0-348-11180-4 £6.00

The Care and Support (Direct Payments) (Wales) Regulations 2015 No. 2015/1815 (W.260). - Enabling power: Social Services and Well-being (Wales) Act 2014, ss. 50, 51, 52, 53, 196 (2). - Issued: 16.11.2015. Made: 21.10.2015. Laid before the National Assembly for Wales: 03.11.2015. Coming into force: 06.04.2016. Effect: 1983 c.20 modified. Territorial extent & classification: W. General. - In English & Welsh. Welsh title: Rheoliadau Gofal a Chymorth (Taliadau Uniongyrchol) (Cymru) 2015. - 20p.: 30 cm. - 978-0-348-11183-5 £6.00

The Care and Support (Disputes about Ordinary Residence, etc.) (Wales) Regulations 2015 No. 2015/1494 (W.166). - Enabling power: Social Services and Well-being (Wales) Act 2014, s. 195 (2). - Issued: 22.07.2015. Made: 07.07.2015. Laid before the National Assembly for Wales: 10.07.2015. Coming into force: 06.04.2016. Effect: None. Territorial extent & classification: W. General. - In English & Welsh. Welsh title: Rheoliadau Gofal a Chymorth (Anghydfodau ynghylch Preswylfa Arferol, etc.) (Cymru) 2015. - 12p.: 30 cm. - 978-0-348-11126-2 £6.00

The Care and Support (Eligibility) (Wales) Regulations 2015 No. 2015/1578 (W.187). - Enabling power: Social Services and Well-being (Wales) Act 2014, ss. 32 (3) (4) (5). - Issued: 03.08.2015. Made: 24.07.2015. Coming into force: 06.04.2016. Effect: None. Territorial extent & classification: W. General. - In English and Welsh. Welsh title: Rheoliadau Gofal a Chymorth (Cymhwystra) (Cymru) 2015. - 10p.: 30 cm. - 978-0-348-11137-8 £6.00

The Care and Support (Financial Assessment) (Wales) Regulations 2015 No. 2015/1844 (W.272). - Enabling power: Social Services and Well-being (Wales) Act 2014, ss. 50 (1), 52 (1), 53 (3), 64 (1), 65, 196 (2). - Issued: 16.11.2015. Made: 27.10.2015. Laid before the National Assembly for Wales: 03.11.2015. Coming into force: 06.04.2016. Effect: None. Territorial extent & classification: W. General. - In English & Welsh. Welsh title: Rheoliadau Gofal a Chymorth (Asesiad Ariannol) (Cymru) 2015. - 38p.: 30 cm. - 978-0-348-11185-9 £10.00

The Care and Support (Ordinary Residence) (Specified Accommodation) (Wales) Regulations 2015 No. 2015/1499 (W.171). - Enabling power: Social Services and Well-being (Wales) Act 2014, s. 194 (1). - Issued: 19.08.2015. Made: 07.07.2015. Laid before the National Assembly for Wales: 10.07.2015. Coming into force: 06.04.2016. Effect: None. Territorial extent & classification: W. General. - In English and Welsh. Welsh title: Rheoliadau Gofal a Chymorth (Preswylfa) (Llety Penodedig) (Cymru) 2015. - 4p.: 30 cm. - 978-0-348-11145-3 £4.25

The Care and Support (Partnership Arrangements for Population Assessments) (Wales) Regulations 2015 No. 2015/1495 (W.167). - Enabling power: Social Services and Well-being (Wales) Act 2014, s. 166 (1) (3) (4). - Issued: 22.07.2015. Made: 08.07.2015. Coming into force: 06.04.2016. Effect: None. Territorial extent & classification: W. General. - In English & Welsh. Welsh title: Rheoliadau Gofal a Chymorth (Trefniadau Partneriaeth ar gyfer Asesiadau Poblogaeth) (Cymru) 2015. - 8p.: 30 cm. - 978-0-348-11125-5 £6.00

The Care and Support (Population Assessment) (Wales) Regulations 2015 No. 2015/1367 (W.135). - Enabling power: Social Services and Well-being (Wales) Act 2014, ss. 14 (1) (2), 198 (1). - Issued: 24.06.2015. Made: 05.06.2015. Laid before the National Assembly for Wales: 12.06.2015. Coming into force: 06.04.2016. Effect: None. Territorial extent & classification: W. General. - In English and Welsh. Welsh title: Rheoliadau Gofal a Chymorth (Asesiadau Poblogaeth) (Cymru) 2015. - 4p.: 30 cm. - 978-0-348-11108-8 £4.25

The Care and Support (Provision of Health Services) (Wales) Regulations 2015 No. 2015/1919 (W.285). - Enabling power: Social Services and Well-being (Wales) Act 2014, ss. 47 (6) (a), 47 (8) (a), 196 (2). - Issued: 07.12.2015. Made: 18.11.2015. Laid before the National Assembly for Wales: 20.11.2015. Coming into force: 06.04.2016. Effect: None. Territorial extent & classification: W. General. - In English & Welsh. Welsh title: Rheoliadau Gofal a Chymorth (Darparu Gwasanaethau Iechyd) (Cymru) 2015. - 8p.: 30 cm. - 978-0-348-11197-2 £4.25

The Care and Support (Review of Charging Decisions and Determinations) (Wales) Regulations 2015 No. 2015/1842 (W.270). - Enabling power: Social Services and Well-being (Wales) Act 2014, ss. 50, 51, 52, 53 (3), 67 (2), 70 (8) (a), 73, 196 (2). - Issued: 16.11.2015. Made: 27.10.2015. Laid before the National Assembly for Wales: 03.11.2015. Coming into force: 06.04.2016. Effect: WSI 2011/964 (W.138) revoked. Territorial extent & classification: W. General. - In English & Welsh. Welsh title: Rheoliadau Gofal a Chymorth (Adolygu Penderfyniadau a Dyfarniadau Gosod Ffi) (Cymru) 2015. - 16p.: 30 cm. - 978-0-348-11184-2 £6.00

The Children (Secure Accommodation) (Wales) Regulations 2015 No. 2015/1988 (W.298). - Enabling power: Children Act 1989, s. 104 (4) (c), sch. 4, para. 4 (1), sch. 5, para. 7, sch. 6, para. 10 & Care Standards Act 2000, s. 118 (7) & Social Services and Well-being (Wales) Act 2014, ss. 87, 119 (2) (7), 196 (2). - Issued: 05.01.2016. Made: 02.12.2015. Coming into force: 06.04.2016. Effect: S.I. 1991/1505 amended & S.I. 1991/2034; 1992/211; 1995/1398 disapplied in relation to Wales & WSI 2006/2986 (W.276); 2013/663 (W.76) revoked. Territorial extent & classification: W. General. - Partially revoked by W.S.I. 2016/211 (W.84) (ISBN 9780348112740). - In English & Welsh. Welsh title: Rheoliadau Plant (Llety Diogel) (Cymru) 2015. - 16p.: 30 cm. - 978-0-348-11222-1 £6.00

The National Assistance (Sums for Personal Requirements) and Social Care Charges (Wales) (Miscellaneous Amendments) Regulations 2015 No. 2015/720 (W.58). - Enabling power: National Assistance Act 1948, s. 22 (4) & Social Care Charges (Wales) Measure 2010, ss. 2 (2), 7 (2), 12 (2), 17 (2). - Issued: 24.03.2015. Made: 13.03.2015. Laid before the National Assembly for Wales: 16.03.2015. Coming into force: 06.04.2015. Effect: S.I. 2011/962 (W.136), 963 (W.137), S.I. 2014/666 (W.73) partially revoked. Territorial extent & classification: W. General. - Revoked by W.S.I. 2016/211 (W.84) (ISBN 9780348112740). - In English & Welsh. Welsh title: Rheoliadau Cymorth Gwladol (Symiau at Anghenion Personol) a Ffioedd Gofal Cymdeithasol (Cymru) (Diwygiadau Amrywiol) 2015. - 8p.: 30 cm. - 978-0-348-11057-9 £4.25

The National Independent Safeguarding Board (Wales) (No. 2) Regulations 2015 No. 2015/1803 (W.258). - Enabling power: Social Services and Well-being (Wales) Act 2014, ss. 133 (1) (2). - Issued: 16.11.2015. Made: 30.10.2015. Laid before the National Assembly for Wales: 03.11.2015. Coming into force: 25.11.2015. Effect: WSI. 2015/1358 (W.132) revoked. Territorial extent & classification: W. General. - In English and Welsh. Welsh title: Rheoliadau'r Bwrdd Diogelu Annibynnol Cenedlaethol (Cymru) (Rhif 2) 2015. - 8p.: 30 cm. - 978-0-348-11186-6 £6.00

The National Independent Safeguarding Board (Wales) Regulations 2015 No. 2015/1358 (W.132). - Enabling power: Social Services and Well-being (Wales) Act 2014, ss. 133 (1) (2). - Issued: 15.06.2015. Made: 04.06.2015. Laid before the National Assembly for Wales: 09.06.2015. Coming into force: 01.10.2016. Effect: None. Territorial extent & classification: W. General. - Revoked by W.S.I. 2015/1803 (ISBN 9780348111866). - In English and Welsh. Welsh title: Rheoliadau'r Bwrdd Diogelu Anibynnol Cenedlaethol (Cymru) 2015. - 8p.: 30 cm. - 978-0-348-11106-4 £4.25

The Partnership Arrangements (Wales) Regulations 2015 No. 2015/1989 (W.299). - Enabling power: Social Services and Well-being (Wales) Act 2014, s. 166 (1) (b), (2) to (5), 167 (3), 168 (1) (2). - Issued: 17.12.2015. Made: 02.12.2015. Coming into force: In accord. with reg. 1 (2). Effect: None. Territorial extent & classification: W. General. - In English & Welsh. Welsh title: Rheoliadau Trefniadau Partneriaeth (Cymru) 2015. - 20p.: 30 cm. - 978-0-348-11204-7 £6.00

The Safeguarding Boards (Functions and Procedures) (Wales) Regulations 2015 No. 2015/1466 (W.160). - Enabling power: Social Services and Well-being (Wales) Act 2014, s. 135 (4). - Issued: 03.08.2015. Made: 01.07.2015. Coming into force: 06.04.2016. Effect: None. Territorial extent & classification: W. General. - In English and Welsh. Welsh title: Rheoliadau Bwrddau Diogelu (Swyddogaethau a Gweithdrefnau) (Cymru) 2015. - 12p.: 30 cm. - 978-0-348-11135-4 £6.00

The Safeguarding Boards (General) (Wales) Regulations 2015 No. 2015/1357 (W.131). - Enabling power: Social Services and Well-being (Wales) Act 2014, ss. 134 (1) (3), 136 (3). - Issued: 26.06.2015. Made: 04.06.2015. Laid before the National Assembly for Wales: 09.06.2015. Coming into force: 06.04.2016. Effect: None. Territorial extent & classification: W. General. - In English and Welsh. Welsh title: Rheoliadau Bwrddau Diogelu (Cyffredinol) (Cymru) 2015. - 8p.: 30 cm. - 978-0-348-11117-0 £6.00

The Social Services and Well-being (Wales) Act 2014 (Commencement No. 2) Order 2015 No. 2015/1744 (W.240) (C.107). - Enabling power: Social Services and Well-being (Wales) Act 2014, s. 199 (2). Bringing into operation various provisions of the 2014 Act on 21.10.2015, in accord. with art. 2. - Issued: 13.10.2015. Made: 25.09.2015. Effect: None. Territorial extent & classification: W. General. - In English and Welsh. Welsh title: Gorchymyn Deddf Gwasanaethau Cymdeithasol a Llesiant (Cymru) 2014 (Cychwyn Rhif 2) 2015. - 4p.: 30 cm. - 978-0-348-11161-3 £4.25

The Social Services and Well-being (Wales) Act 2014 (Social Enterprise, Co-operative and Third Sector) (Wales) Regulations 2015 No. 2015/1500 (W.172). - Enabling power: Social Services and Well-being (Wales) Act 2014, s. 16 (3). - Issued: 23.07.2015. Made: 08.07.2015. Coming into force: 06.04.2016. Effect: None. Territorial extent & classification: W. General. - In English and Welsh. Welsh title: Rheoliadau Deddf Gwasanaethau Cymdeithasol a Llesiant (Cymru) 2014 (Mentrau Cymdeithasol, Cydweithredol a Thrydydd Sector) (Cymru) 2015. - 8p.: 30 cm. - 978-0-348-11130-9 £6.00

Social security

The Child Benefit and Tax Credits Up-rating Order 2015 No. 2015/567. - Enabling power: Welfare Benefits Up-rating Act 2013, ss. 1 (1) (2) (3) (7), 2 (1) (2) (3) & Social Security Administration (Northern Ireland) Act 1992, s. 132 (1). - Issued: 12.03.2015. Made: 05.03.2015. Coming into force: 06.04.2015. Effect: S.I. 2002/2005, 2007; 2006/965 amended. Territorial extent & classification: E/W/S/NI. General. - 4p.: 30 cm. - 978-0-11-113234-0 £4.25

The Child Benefit (General) (Amendment) Regulations 2015 No. 2015/1512. - Enabling power: Social Security Contributions and Benefits Act 1992, s. 142 (2) (b), 175 (1) (1A) (3) & Social Security Contributions and Benefits (Northern Ireland) Act 1992, s. 138 (2) (b), 171 (1) (3). - Issued: 20.07.2015. Made: 14.07.2015. Laid: 15.07.2015. Coming into force: 31.08.2015. Effect: S.I. 2006/223 amended. Territorial extent & classification: E/W/S/NI. General. - 2p.: 30 cm. - 978-0-11-113789-5 £4.25

The Employment Allowance (Care and Support Workers) Regulations 2015 No. 2015/578. - Enabling power: National Insurance Contributions Act 2014, s. 5 (1) (b). - Issued: 12.03.2015. Made: 04.03.2015. Coming into force: 06.04.2015. Effect: 2014 c.7 amended. Territorial extent & classification: E/W/S/NI. General. - Supersedes draft S.I. (ISBN 9780111127407) issued 22.01.2015. - 2p.: 30 cm. - 978-0-11-113248-7 £4.25

The Employment and Support Allowance (Repeat Assessments and Pending Appeal Awards) (Amendment) Regulations 2015 No. 2015/437. - Enabling power: Social Security Administration Act 1992, ss. 1 (1), 189 (1) (4), 191 & Welfare Reform Act 2007, ss. 8 (1) (5) (6), 22, 25 (2) (3) (5), 29 sch. 2, para. 1, sch. 4, pars. 1, 7, 8. - Issued: 06.03.2015. Made: 02.03.2015. Laid: 05.03.2015. Coming into force: 30.03.2015. Effect: S.I. 1987/1968; 2008/794; 2010/1907; 2013/379, 380. Territorial extent & classification: E/W/S. General. - 8p.: 30 cm. - 978-0-11-113125-1 £6.00

The Guardian's Allowance Up-rating Order 2015 No. 2015/439. - Enabling power: Social Security Administration Act 1992, ss. 150 (9) (10) (a) (i), 189 (4). - Issued: 09.03.2015. Made: 02.03.2015. Coming into force: 06.04.2015. Effect: 1992 c. 4 amended. Territorial extent & classification: E/W/S. General. - Supersedes draft SI (ISBN 9780111534366) issued on 12.02.2013. - 2p.: 30 cm. - 978-0-11-113127-5 £4.25

The Guardian's Allowance Up-rating Regulations 2015 No. 2015/545. - Enabling power: Social Security Contributions and Benefits Act 1992, ss. 113 (1), 175 (1) (3) (4) & Social Security Administration Act 1992, ss. 155 (3), 189 (1) (4) (5), 190, 191 & Social Security Contributions and Benefits (Northern Ireland) Act 1992, ss. 113 (1), 171 (1) (3) (4) & Social Security Administration (Northern Ireland) Act 1992, ss. 135 (3), 165 (1) (4) (5), 167 (1). - Issued: 12.03.2015. Made: 05.03.2015. Laid: 06.03.2015. Coming into force: 06.04.2015. Effect: None. Territorial extent & classification: E/W/S. General. - 4p.: 30 cm. - 978-0-11-113220-3 £4.25

The Housing Benefit (Abolition of the Family Premium and date of claim) (Amendment) Regulations 2015 No. 2015/1857. - Enabling power: Social Security Contributions and Benefits Act 1992, ss. 123 (1) (d), 135 (1), 136 (1) (3) (5), 137 (1), 175 (1) (3) (4) & Social Security Administration Act 1992, ss. 5 (1) (b), 189 (1), 191. - Issued: 09.11.2015. Made: 03.11.2015. Laid: 09.11.2015. Coming into force: 01.04.2016, for the purposes of reg.1; 01.05.2016, for all other purposes. Effect: S.I. 2006/213 amended. Territorial extent & classification: E/W/S. General. - 4p.: 30 cm. - 978-0-11-114055-0 £4.25

The Housing Benefit and Housing Benefit (Persons who have attained the qualifying age for state pension credit) (Income from earnings) (Amendment) Regulations 2015 No. 2015/6. - Enabling power: Social Security, Contributions and Benefits Act 1992, ss 136 (3) (4), 136A (3), 137 (1). - Issued: 12.01.2015. Made: 06.01.2015. Laid: 12.01.2015. Coming into force: 09.02.2015. Effect: S.I. 2006/213; 214 amended. Territorial extent & classification: E/W/S. General. - 4p.: 30 cm. - 978-0-11-112661-5 £4.25

The Income-related Benefits (Subsidy to Authorities) Amendment Order 2015 No. 2015/1784. - Enabling power: Social Security Administration Act 1992, ss. 140B (1) (3) (4) (4A), 140F (2), 189 (1) (4) (5) (7). - Issued: 19.10.2015. Made: 12.10.2015. Laid: 19.10.2015. Coming into force: 09.11.2015. Effect: S.I. 1998/562 amended. Territorial extent & classification: E/W/S. General. - 24p.: 30 cm. - 978-0-11-113992-9 £6.00

The Jobseeker's Allowance (Extended Period of Sickness) Amendment Regulations 2015 No. 2015/339. - Enabling power: Social Security Contributions and Benefits Act 1992, ss. 171D, 175 (3) to (5) & Jobseekers Act 1995, ss. 6 (4), 7 (4), 6F (1), 35 (1), 36 (2) (4) & Social Security Act 1998, ss. 9 (1), 10 (6), 79 (1), 84 & Welfare Reform Act 2007, s. 24 (1) (2), sch. 2, para. 1 & Welfare Reform Act 2012, sch. 6, para. 1 (1). - Issued: 27.02.2015. Made: 23.02.2015. Laid: 25.02.2015. Coming into force: 30.03.2015. Effect: S.I. 1996/207; 1999/991; 2008/794; 2013/378, 379, 381; 2014/1230 amended. Territorial extent & classification: E/W/S. General. - 12p.: 30 cm. - 978-0-11-113027-8 £6.00

The Mesothelioma Lump Sum Payments (Conditions and Amounts) (Amendment) Regulations 2015 No. 2015/500. - Enabling power: Child Maintenance and Other Payments Act 2008, ss 46 (3), 53 (1) (2) (b). - Issued: 10.03.2015. Made: 03.03.2015. Coming into force: 01.04.2015. Effect: S.I. 2008/1963 amended. Territorial extent & classification: E/W/S. General. - Supersedes draft SI (ISBN 9780111126707) issued 14/01/15- 4p.: 30 cm. - 978-0-11-113198-5 £4.25

The National Insurance Contributions (Application of Part 7 of the Finance Act 2004) (Amendment) Regulations 2015 No. 2015/531. - Enabling power: Social Security Administration Act 1992, ss. 132A (1), 189 (4) (5). - Issued: 11.03.2015. Made: 05.03.2015. Laid: 06.03.2015. Coming into force: 12.04.2015. Effect: S.I. 2012/1868 amended. Territorial extent & classification: E/W/S/NI. General. - 8p.: 30 cm. - 978-0-11-113212-8 £4.25

SOCIAL SECURITY

The Pensions Act 2014 (Consequential, Supplementary and Incidental Amendments) Order 2015 No. 2015/1985. - Enabling power: Pensions Act 2014, ss. 53, 54 (5). - Issued: 11.12.2015. Made: 07.12.2015. Laid: 11.12.2015. Coming into force: In accord. with art. 1 (2). Effect: S.I. 1975/173, 563; 1979/597, 642, 676; 1982/1408; 1987/1967, 1968; 1988/35, 664; 1989/306, 364; 1992/1815; 1995/866; 1996/207, 2890; 1999/991; 2001/155, 1002, 1004, 1085, 3252; 2002/1792, 2006; 2005/453, 3061; 2006/213, 214; 2007/1398; 2008/794; 2009/212; 2010/426, 2132, 2133; 2012/2677, 2885, 2886; 2013/383, 384, 628; 2014/3229; 2015/173 & S.S.I. 2012/303, 319 amended. Territorial extent & classification: E/W/S/NI. General. - 28p.: 30 cm. - 978-0-11-114173-1 £6.00

The Pneumoconiosis etc. (Workers' Compensation) (Payment of Claims) (Amendment) Regulations 2015 No. 2015/503. - Enabling power: Pneumoconiosis etc. (Workers' Compensation) Act 1979, ss 1 (1) (2) (4), 7 (1) (2). - Issued: 10.03.2015. Made: 03.03.2015. Coming into force: 01.04.2015. Effect: S.I. 1988/668 amended. Territorial extent & classification: E/W/S. General. - Supersedes draft SI (ISBN 9780111126721) issued 14/01/15 - 8p.: 30 cm. - 978-0-11-113201-2 £6.00

The Social Fund (Budgeting Loans) (Applications and Miscellaneous Provisions) Regulations 2015 No. 2015/1411. - Enabling power: Social Security Administration Act 1992, ss. 12, 189 (1) (4) (5) (6). - Issued: 30.06.2015. Made: 23.06.2015. Laid: 30.06.2015. Coming into force: 22.07.2015. Effect: S.I. 2008/2265; 2009/3033 revoked. Territorial extent & classification: E/W/S. General. - 4p.: 30 cm. - 978-0-11-113708-6 £4.25

The Social Fund Cold Weather Payments (General) Amendment (No.2) Regulations 2015 No. 2015/1662. - Enabling power: Social Security Contributions and Benefits Act 1992, ss. 138 (2), 175 (1) (3) (5). - Issued: 14.09.2015. Made: 07.09.2015. Laid: 14.09.2015. Coming into force: 01.11.2015. Effect: S.I. 1988/1724 amended. Territorial extent & classification: E/W/S. General. - 8p.: 30 cm. - 978-0-11-113913-4 £6.00

The Social Fund Cold Weather Payments (General) Amendment Regulations 2015 No. 2015/183. - Enabling power: Social Security Contributions and Benefits Act 1992, ss. 138 (2) (4), 175 (1) (3). - Issued: 16.02.2015. Made: 09.02.2015. Laid: 12.02.2015. Coming into force: 23.03.2015. Effect: S.I. 1988/1724 amended. Territorial extent & classification: E/W/S. General. - 2p.: 30 cm. - 978-0-11-112921-0 £4.25

The Social Security and Tax Credits (Miscellaneous Amendments) Regulations 2015 No. 2015/175. - Enabling power: Social Security Contributions and Benefits Act 1992, ss. 3 (2), 175 (3) (4) & Social Security Contributions and Benefits (Northern Ireland) Act 1992, ss. 3 (2), 171 (3) (4) & Tax Credits Act 2002, s. 7 (6). - Issued: 16.02.2015. Made: 09.02.2005. Laid: 10.02.2015. Coming into force: In accord. with reg. 1 (2) & (3). Effect: S.I. 2001/1004; 2002/2006 amended. Territorial extent & classification: E/W/S/NI. General. - 8p.: 30 cm. - 978-0-11-112911-1 £4.25

The Social Security (Application of Reciprocal Agreements with Australia, Canada and New Zealand) (EEA States and Switzerland) Regulations 2015 No. 2015/349. - Enabling power: European Communities Act 1972, s. 2 (2). - Issued: 27.02.2015. Made: 23.02.2015. Laid: 25.02.2015. Coming into force: 01.04.2015. Effect: S.I. 1983/1894; 1992/1312; 1995/2699 modified. Territorial extent & classification: E/W/S/NI. General. - 4p.: 30 cm. - 978-0-11-113037-7 £4.25

The Social Security Benefit (Computation of Earnings) (Amendment) Regulations 2015 No. 2015/784. - Enabling power: Social Security Contributions and Benefits Act 1992, ss. 3 (2) (3), 175 (1), (1A) (3) (4). - Issued: 25.03.2015. Made: 19.03.2015. Laid: 20.03.2015. Coming into force: 01.07.2015. Effect: S.I. 1996/2745 amended. Territorial extent & classification: E/W/S. General. - 4p.: 30 cm. - 978-0-11-113406-1 £4.25

The Social Security Benefits Up-rating Order 2015 No. 2015/457. - Enabling power: Social Security Administration Act 1992, ss. 150, 150A, 151, 189 (1) (4) (5). - Issued: 10.03.2015. Made: -. Coming into force: In accord. with art. 1. Effect: 1965 c.21; 1992 c.4; 1993 c.48 & 15 SIs amended & S.I. 2014/516 revoked (05.05.2015). Territorial extent & classification: E/W/S. General. - Supersedes draft SI (ISBN 9780111127148) issued 19/01/15- 48p.: 30 cm. - 978-0-11-113204-3 £10.00

The Social Security Benefits Up-rating Regulations 2015 No. 2015/496. - Enabling power: Social Security Contributions and Benefits Act 1992, ss. 90, 113 (1), 122 (1), 175 (1) (3) & Social Security Administration Act 1992, ss. 5 (1) (p), 155 (3), 189 (1) (4), 191. - Issued: 10.03.2015. Made: 04.03.2015. Laid: 09.03.2015. Coming into force: 06.04.2015. Effect: S.I. 1977/343; 1987/1968 amended & S.I. 2014/618 revoked. Territorial extent & classification: E/W/S. General. - Partially revoked by S.I. 2016/246 (ISBN 9780111144435). - 4p.: 30 cm. - 978-0-11-113194-7 £4.25

The Social Security (Contributions) (Amendment) Regulations 2015 No. 2015/543. - Enabling power: Social Security Contributions and Benefits Act 1992, ss. 3 (2) (3), 175 (3) & Social Security Contributions and Benefits (Northern Ireland) Act 1992, ss. 3 (2) (3), 171 (3) (10). - Issued: 12.03.2015. Made: 05.03.2015. Laid: 06.03.2015. Coming into force: 06.04.2015. Effect: S.I. 2001/1004 amended. Territorial extent & classification: E/W/S/NI. General. - 2p.: 30 cm. - 978-0-11-113218-0 £4.25

The Social Security Contributions (Amendments in Consequence of Part 4 of the Finance Act 2014) Regulations 2015 No. 2015/521. - Enabling power: Social Security Contributions and Benefits Act 1992, ss. 175 (4), sch. 1, paras. 6 (1) (2) & Social Security Contributions and Benefits (Northern Ireland) Act 1992, s. 171 (4), sch. 1, para. 6 (1) (2) & Social Security Contributions (Transfer of Functions, etc.) Act 1999, ss. 13, 25 (2) & S.I. 1999/671, arts 12, 23 (7). - Issued: 11.03.2015. Made: 05.03.2015. Laid: 05.03.2015. Coming into force: 12.04.2015. Effect: S.I. 1999/1027; 2001/1004 amended. Territorial extent & classification: E/W/S/NI. General. - 4p.: 30 cm. - 978-0-11-113207-4 £4.25

The Social Security Contributions (Decisions and Appeals) (Amendment) Regulations 2015 No. 2015/174. - Enabling power: Social Security Contributions (Transfer of Functions, etc.) Act 1999, ss. 9, 11, 13, 25 (3) (5) & S.I. 1999/671, arts. 8, 10, 12, 23 (5) (7). - Issued: 16.02.2015. Made: 09.02.2015. Laid: 11.02.2015. Coming into force: In accord. with reg. 1 (2) & (3). Effect: S.I. 1999/1027 amended. Territorial extent & classification: E/W/S/NI. General. - This Statutory Instrument has been printed in substitution of the SI of the same number and is being issued free of charge to all known recipients of that Statutory Instrument. - 4p.: 30 cm. - 978-0-11-112910-4 £4.25

The Social Security (Contributions) (Limited Liability Partnership) (Amendment) Regulations 2015 No. 2015/607. - Enabling power: Social Security Contributions and Benefits Act 1992, ss. 2 (2) (b) (2A), 122 (2), 175 (3) & Social Security Contributions and Benefits (Northern Ireland) Act 1992, ss. 2 (2) (b) (2A), 121 (2), 171 (3). - Issued: 17.03.2015. Made: 09.03.2015. Laid: 10.03.2015. Coming into force: 06.04.2015. Effect: S.I. 2014/3159 amended. Territorial extent & classification: E/W/S/NI. General. - 4p.: 30 cm. - 978-0-11-113270-8 £4.25

The Social Security (Contributions) (Limits and Thresholds) (Amendment) Regulations 2015 No. 2015/577. - Enabling power: Social Security Contributions and Benefits Act 1992, ss. 5 (1) (4) to (6), 9A (7) (8), 175 (3) & Social Security Contributions and Benefits (Northern Ireland) Act 1992, ss. 5 (1) (4) to (6), 9A (7) (8), 171 (3) (10). - Issued: 12.03.2015. Made: 04.03.2015. Coming into force: 06.04.2015. Effect: S.I. 2001/1004 amended. Territorial extent & classification: E/W/S/NI. General. - Supersedes draft S.I. (ISBN 9780111127377) issued 21/01/14. - 4p.: 30 cm. - 978-0-11-113247-0 £4.25

The Social Security (Contributions) (Republic of Chile) Order 2015 No. 2015/828. - Enabling power: Social Security Administration Act 1992, s. 179 (1) (a) (2). - Issued: 26.03.2015. Made: 19.03.2015. Coming into force: 01.06.2015. Effect: 1992 c.2, c.4; S.I. 1999/671 modified. Territorial extent & classification: E/W/S/NI. General. - 16p.: 30 cm. - 978-0-11-113461-0 £6.00

The Social Security (Contributions) (Re-rating and National Insurance Funds Payments) Order 2015 No. 2015/588. - Enabling power: Social Security Administration Act 1992, ss 141 (4) (5), 142 (2) (3) & Social Security Administration (Northern Ireland) Act 1992, s. 129 & Social Security Act 1993, ss 2 (2) (3) & S.I. 1993/592 (N.I. 2), art. 4. - Issued: 13.03.2015. Made: 04.03.2015. Coming into force: 06.04.2015. Effect: 1992 c.4, 7 amended. Territorial extent & classification: E/W/S/NI. General. - Supersedes draft S.I. (ISBN 9780111127391) issued 22.01.2015. - 4p.: 30 cm. - 978-0-11-113257-9 £4.25

The Social Security (Crediting and Treatment of Contributions, and National Insurance Numbers) (Amendment) Regulations 2015 No. 2015/1828. - Enabling power: Social Security Administration Act 1992, ss. 182C (1), 189 (1) (4). - Issued: 02.11.2015. Made: 26.10.2015. Laid: 02.11.2015. Coming into force: 30.11.2015. Effect: S.I. 2001/769 amended. Territorial extent & classification: E/W/S. General. - 2p.: 30 cm. - 978-0-11-114019-2 £4.25

SOCIAL SECURITY

The Social Security (Fees Payable by Qualifying Lenders) (Amendment) Regulations 2015 No. 2015/343. - Enabling power: Social Security Administration Act 1992, ss. 15A (2) (b), 189 (1) (4). - Issued: 27.02.2015. Made: 23.02.2015. Laid: 27.02.2015. Coming into force: 01.04.2015. Effect: S.I. 1987/1968; 2013/380 amended. Territorial extent & classification: E/W/S. General. - 4p.: 30 cm. - 978-0-11-113031-5 £4.25

The Social Security (Housing Costs Amendments) Regulations 2015 No. 2015/1647. - Enabling power: Social Security Contributions and Benefits Act 1992, ss. 123 (1) (a), 135 (1), 137 (1), 175 (1) (3) (4); Jobseekers Act 1995, ss. 4 (5), 35 (1), 36 (2) (4) & Welfare Reform Act 2007, ss. 4 (2) (a), 24 (1), 25 (2) (3) (5) & Welfare Reform Act 2012, ss. 11 (4) (5) (b), 40, 42 (1) (2) (3), sch. 6, para. 1. - Issued: 11.09.2015. Made: 07.09.2015. Laid: 10.09.2015. Coming into force: 01.04.2016. Effect: S.I. 1987/1967; 1996/207; 2008/794; 2013/376; 2014/1230 amended & S.I. 2008/3195 revoked with savings. Territorial extent & classification: E/W/S. General. - 8p.: 30 cm. - 978-0-11-113897-7 £4.25

The Social Security (Industrial Injuries) (Prescribed Diseases) Amendment Regulations 2015 No. 2015/87. - Enabling power: Social Security Contributions and Benefits Act 1992, ss 108 (2), 109 (2), 122 (1), 175 (1) (3) to (5), sch. 6, para. 2. - Issued: 05.02.2015. Made: 29.01.2015. Laid: 05.02.2015. Coming into force: 16.03.2015. Effect: S.I. 1985/967 amended. Territorial extent & classification: E/W/S. General. - 4p.: 30 cm. - 978-0-11-112833-6 £4.25

The Social Security (Information-sharing in relation to Welfare Services etc.) (Amendment) Regulations 2015 No. 2015/46. - Enabling power: Welfare Reform Act 2012, ss. 131 (1) (3) (11), 133 (1) (2). - Issued: 27.01.2015. Made: 21.01.2015. Laid: 23.01.2015. Coming into force: 13.02.2015. Effect: S.I. 2012/1483 amended. Territorial extent & classification: E/W/S. General. - 8p.: 30 cm. - 978-0-11-112775-9 £4.25

The Social Security (Invalid Care Allowance) (Amendment) Regulations 2015 No. 2015/162. - Enabling power: Social Security Contributions and Benefits Act 1992, ss. 70 (8), 175 (1). - Issued: 13.02.2015. Made: 08.02.2015. Laid: 12.02.2015. Coming into force: 06.04.2015. Effect: S.I. 1976/409 amended. Territorial extent & classification: E/W/S. General. - 2p.: 30 cm. - 978-0-11-112901-2 £4.25

The Social Security (Maternity Allowance) (Earnings) (Amendment) Regulations 2015 No. 2015/342. - Enabling power: Social Security Contributions and Benefits Act 1992, ss. 35A (4) (5), 175 (1) (3) (4). - Issued: 27.02.2015. Made: 23.02.2015. Laid: 26.02.2015. Coming into force: 06.04.2015. Effect: S.I. 2000/688 amended. Territorial extent & classification: E/W/S. General. - 2p.: 30 cm. - 978-0-11-113030-8 £4.25

The Social Security (Members of the Reserve Forces) (Amendment) Regulations 2015 No. 2015/389. - Enabling power: Social Security Contributions and Benefits Act 1992, ss. 136 (3) (4) (5) (b), 137 (1), 175 (3) (4) & Jobseekers Act 1995, ss. 6 (4), 7 (4), 12 (1) to (3) (4) (5), 35 (1), 36 (2) (4) & Welfare Reform Act 2007, ss. 17 (1) (2) (3) (b), 24 (1), 25 (2) (3) (5). - Issued: 03.03.2015. Made: 23.02.2015. Laid: 02.03.2015. Coming into force: 06.04.2015. Effect: S.I. 1987/1967; 1996/207; 2008/794; 2013/378 amended. Territorial extent & classification: E/W/S. General. - 8p.: 30 cm. - 978-0-11-113076-6 £6.00

The Social Security (Miscellaneous Amendments No. 2) Regulations 2015 No. 2015/478. - Enabling power: Social Security Contributions and Benefits Act 1992, ss. 1(6) (7), 2 (2) (b) (2A), 3 (2) (3), 12 (6), 13 (1) (7), 19 (3) (5A), 119, 175 (3) (4), sch. 1, paras 7B, 7BB, 8 (1)(q) (1A) & Social Security Contributions and Benefits (Northern Ireland) Act 1992, ss. 1(6) (7), 2 (2) (b) (2A), 3 (2) (3), 12 (6), 13 (1) (7), 19 (3) (5A), 119, 171 (3) (4), sch. 1, paras 7B, 7BB, 8 (1) (q) (1A) & National Insurance Contributions Act 2015, s. 3. - Issued: 10.03.2015. Made: 03.03.2015. Laid: 04.03.2015. Coming into force: In accord. with reg. 1. Effect: S.I. 1978/1689; 1987/1967; 1992/1815; 1996/207, 2745; 2001/155, 1004; 2004/770; 2006/213, 214; 2008/607, 794; 2009/600; 2012/821; 2013/376, 378, 379; S.R. 1978/401; 1996/520 amended & S.I. 2007/2520; 2008/3099 revoked. Territorial extent & classification: E/W/S. General. - 16p.: 30 cm. - 978-0-11-113173-2 £6.00

The Social Security (Miscellaneous Amendments) Regulations 2015 No. 2015/67. - Enabling power: Social Security Administration Act 1992, ss 182C (1), 189 (4) & Social Security Contributions and Benefits Act 1992, 35 (3), 35B (11), 136 (3) (5), 136A, 137 (1), 138 (2) (4), 175 (1) (3) (4) & Jobseekers Act 1995, ss 12 (1) (4), 35 (1), 36 (2) (4) & State Pension Credit Act 2002, ss 15 (3) (6), 17 (1), 19 (1) & Welfare Reform Act 2007, ss 17 (1) (3), 24 (1), 25 (2) (3) (5) (a) & Welfare Reform Act 2012, ss 8 (3), 40, 42 (1) (2) (3) (a), sch. 1, para. 4 (1) (b) (3) (a). - Issued: 03.02.2015. Made: 26.01.2015. Laid: 02.02.2015. Coming into force: 23.02.2015. Effect: S.I. 1987/416; 2000/729; 2001/769; 2006/213 amended. Territorial extent & classification: E/W/S. General. - 8p.: 30 cm. - 978-0-11-112806-0 £4.25

The Social Security (Overpayments and Recovery) Amendment Regulations 2015 No. 2015/499. - Enabling power: Social Security Administration Act 1992, ss. 71 (8) (9A) (9C), 71ZA, 71ZD, 75 (8) (10), 78 (3C) (3E), 189 (1) (4) (6), 191. - Issued: 10.03.2015. Made: 04.03.2015. Laid: 06.03.2015. Coming into force: 06.04.2015. Effect: S.I. 1988/664; 2013/384 amended. Territorial extent & classification: E/W/S. General. - 8p.: 30 cm. - 978-0-11-113197-8 £4.25

The Social Security (Penalty as Alternative to Prosecution) (Maximum Amount) Order 2015 No. 2015/202. - Enabling power: Social Security Administration Act 1992, s. 115A (3B) (b), 189 (4). - Issued: 17.02.2015. Made: 10.02.2015 Coming into force: 01.04.2015. Effect: 1992 c.5 amended. Territorial extent & classification: E/W/S/NI. General. - Supersedes S.I. draft (ISBN 9780111124246) issued 08/12/14. - 2p.: 30 cm. - 978-0-11-112944-9 £4.25

The Social Security Pensions (Flat Rate Accrual Amount) Order 2015 No. 2015/185. - Enabling power: Social Security Administration Act 1992, ss. 148AA (3) to (6), 189 (1) (4) (5). - Issued: 17.02.2015. Made: 09.02.2015. Laid: 16.02.2015. Coming into force: 06.04.2015. Effect: None. Territorial extent & classification: E/W/S. General. - 2p.: 30 cm. - 978-0-11-112930-2 £4.25

The Social Security Pensions (Low Earnings Threshold) Order 2015 No. 2015/186. - Enabling power: Social Security Administration Act 1992, s. 148A (3) to (5), 189 (1) (4) (5). - Issued: 17.02.2015. Made: 09.02.2015. Laid: 16.02.2015. Coming into force: 06.04.2015. Effect: None. Territorial extent & classification: E/W/S. General. - 2p.: 30 cm. - 978-0-11-112931-9 £4.25

The Social Security Revaluation of Earnings Factors Order 2015 No. 2015/187. - Enabling power: Social Security Administration Act 1992, ss. 148 (3) (4), 189 (1) (4) (5). - Issued: 17.02.2015. Made: 09.02.2015. Laid: 16.02.2015. Coming into force: 06.04.2015. Effect: None. Territorial extent & classification: E/W/S. General. - 4p.: 30 cm. - 978-0-11-112932-6 £4.25

The Social Security (Traineeships and Qualifying Young Persons) Amendment Regulations 2015 No. 2015/336. - Jobseekers Act 1995, ss. 6 (4), 7 (4), 17A, 35 (1), 36 (2) (a) (4) (a), sch. 1, para. 14 (b) & Welfare Reform Act 2012, ss. 4 (6) (b), 42 (2) (3). - Issued: 27.02.2015. Made: 23.02.2014. Laid: 27.02.2015. Coming into force: 27.03.2015. Effect: S.I. 1996/207 amended. Territorial extent & classification: E/W/S. General- 4p.: 30 cm. - 978-0-11-113024-7 £4.25

The State Pension Credit (Amendment) Regulations 2015 No. 2015/1529. - Enabling power: Social Security Contributions and Benefits Act 1992, s. 175 (3) & State Pension Credit Act 2002, ss. 3Z, 9 (5), 17 (1) & Pensions Act 2014, s. 28 (3). - Issued: 20.07.2015. Made: 13.07.2015. Laid: 20.07.2015. Coming into force: 06.04.2016. Effect: S.I. 2002/1792 amended. Territorial extent & classification: E/W/S. General. - 4p.: 30 cm. - 978-0-11-113806-9 £4.25

The State Pension Regulations 2015 No. 2015/173. - Enabling power: Social Security Contributions and Benefits Act 1992, ss. 55A (6), 175 (4) & Welfare Reform and Pensions Act 1999, ss. 23 (1) (a), (b) (ii) (c) (i) (2). 48 (1) (f) (ii), 49 (4) (4A) & Pensions Act 2014, ss. 2 (3), 4 (2), 8 (3) (7) (8), 16 (1) (6), 17 (4) (5), 18 (1), 19 (1) (3), 22 (1), 54 (5) (6), sch. 8, para. 4, sch. 10, para. 4. - Issued: 13.02.2015. Made: 09.02.2015. Coming into force: 06.04.2016. Effect: S.I. 2000/2914, 1051. Territorial extent & classification: E/W/S. General. - 16p.: 30 cm. - 978-0-11-112909-8 £6.00

SOCIAL SECURITY, ENGLAND

The Universal Credit and Miscellaneous Amendments Regulations 2015 No. 2015/1754. - Enabling power: Social Security Administration Act 1992 ss. 1 (1), 5 (1) (p) (r) & Social Security Contributions and Benefits Act 1992 ss. 70 (7), 135 (1) (5) (6), 137 (1), 175 (1), 175 (3) & Jobseekers Act 1995 ss. 4 (5), 35 (1), 36 (2) & State Pension Credit Act 2002 ss. 2(3) (b), 2 (7), 17 (1), 19 (1) & Welfare Reform Act 2007 ss. 4(2), 24 (1), 25 (2), 25 (3) & Welfare Reform Act 2012 ss. 6 (1) (c) (3), 7 (3), 8 (3), 9 (2), 10 (2) (3), 11 (4), 12 (1) (3) (4), 19 (2) (d) (3) (b) (4), 22 (2), 24 (1) (a), 26 (8) (a) (c), 27 (9) (a) (c), 28 (2) (f), 32 (1) (2) (4), 37 (4), 42 (2) (3) sch. 1 paras 3 (2), 4 (1) (3) (a) (4). - Issued: 14.10.2015. Made: 07.10.2015. Laid: 14.10.2015. Coming into force: In accord. with reg. 1. Effect: 1992 c.4; S.I. 1976/409; 1987/1967; 1996/207; 2002/1792; 2006/213, 214; 2008/794; 2013/376, 380, 383; 2014/2887; 2015/89, 345 amended. Territorial extent & classification: E/W/S. General. - 16p.: 30 cm. - 978-0-11-113963-9 £6.00

The Universal Credit (EEA Jobseekers) Amendment Regulations 2015 No. 2015/546. - Enabling power: Welfare Reform Act 2012, ss. 4 (5) (a), 42 (2) (3), sch. 1, para. 7. - Issued: 12.03.2015. Made: 05.03.2015. Laid: 09.03.2015. Coming into force: 10.06.2015. Effect: S.I. 2013/376 amended/partially revoked. Territorial extent & classification: E/W/S. General. - 4p.: 30 cm. - 978-0-11-113221-0 £4.25

The Universal Credit (Surpluses and Self-employed Losses) (Digital Service) Amendment Regulations 2015 No. 2015/345. - Enabling power: Welfare Reform Act 2012, s. 42 (2) (3), sch. 1 para. 4 (1) (3) (a) (4). - Issued: 02.03.2015. Made: 23.02.2015. Laid: 26.02.2015. Coming into force: 06.04.2016. Effect: S.I. 2013/376 amended. Territorial extent & classification: E/W/S. General. - 8p.: 30 cm. - 978-0-11-113049-0 £6.00

The Universal Credit (Transitional Provisions) (Amendment) Regulations 2015 No. 2015/1780. - Enabling power: Welfare Reform Act 2012, s. 42 (2), sch. 6 para. 1 (1). - Issued: 19.10.2015. Made: 12.10.2015. Laid: 19.10.2015. Coming into force: 16.11.2015. Effect: S.I. 2014/1230 amended. Territorial extent & classification: E/W/S. General. - 4p.: 30 cm. - 978-0-11-113989-9 £4.25

The Universal Credit (Waiting Days) (Amendment) Regulations 2015 No. 2015/1362. - Enabling power: Welfare Reform Act 2012, ss. 6 (1) (c) (3), 7 (3) (a), 32, 42 (2), sch. 6, para. 1 (1). - Issued: 16.06.2015. Made: 09.06.2015. Laid: 11.06.2015. Coming into force: 03.08.2015. Effect: S.I. 2013/376 amended. Territorial extent & classification: E/W/S. General. - 4p.: 30 cm. - 978-0-11-113665-2 £4.25

The Universal Credit (Work Allowance) Amendment Regulations 2015 No. 2015/1649. - Enabling power: Welfare Reform Act 2012, ss. 8 (3) (a), 40, 42 (1) (2) (6). - Issued: 11.09.2015. Made: 07.09.2015. Laid: 10.09.2015. Coming into force: 11.04.2016 Effect: S.I. 2013/376 amended. Territorial extent & classification: E/W/S. General. - 4p.: 30 cm. - 978-0-11-113899-1 £4.25

The Universal Credit (Work-related Requirements) In Work Pilot Scheme and Amendment Regulations 2015 No. 2015/89. - Enabling power: Welfare Reform Act 2012, ss. 18 (5), 22 (2), 41 (1) (a) (2) (b) (4), 42 (2) (3). - Issued: 04.02.2015. Made: 29.01.2015. Coming into force: In accord. with reg. 1. Effect: S.I. 2013/376 amended. Territorial extent & classification: E/W/S. General. - Supersedes draft SI (ISBN 9780111123836) issued 01.12.2014. - 8p.: 30 cm. - 978-0-11-112836-7 £4.25

The Welfare Benefits Up-Rating Order 2015 No. 2015/30. - Enabling power: Welfare Benefits Uprating Act 2013, s. 1. - Issued: 21.01.2015. Made: 14.01.2015. Coming into force: In accord. with art. 1. Effect: 1992 c. 4; 1986/1960; 1987/1967; 1996/207; 2002/2818; 2008/794; 2013/378, 379; 2014/3051 amended & S.I. 2014/147 revoked. Territorial extent & classification: E/W/S. General. - 20p.: 30 cm. - 978-0-11-112736-0 £6.00

The Welfare Reform Act 2012 (Commencement No. 9, 11, 13, 14, 16, 17 and 19 and Transitional and Transitory Provisions (Amendment)) Order 2015 No. 2015/32 (C.3). - Enabling power: Welfare Reform Act 2012, s. 150 (3) (4) (a) (b) (i). Bringing into operation various provisions of the 2012 Act on in accord. with art. 3. - Issued: 23.01.2015. Made: 19.01.2014. Effect: S.I. 2013/983 (C.41), 1511 (C.60), 2567 (C.107), 2846 (C.114); 2014/209 (C.7), 1583 (c. 61), 2321 (C.99) amended. Territorial extent & classification: E/W/S. General. - 16p.: 30 cm. - 978-0-11-112756-8 £6.00

The Welfare Reform Act 2012 (Commencement No. 21 and Transitional and Transitory Provisions) Order 2015 No. 2015/33 (C.4). - Enabling power: Welfare Reform Act 2012, s. 150 (3) (4) (a) (b) (i) (c). Bringing into operation various provisions of the 2012 Act in accord. with arts 3, 4. - Issued: 23.01.2015. Made: 19.01.2015. Effect: None. Territorial extent & classification: E/W/S. General. - 16p.: 30 cm. - 978-0-11-112757-5 £6.00

The Welfare Reform Act 2012 (Commencement No. 22 and Transitional and Transitory Provisions Order 2015 No. 2015/101 (C.6). - Enabling power: Welfare Reform Act 2012, s. 150 (3) (4) (a) (b) (i) (c). Bringing into operation various provisions of the 2012 Act in accord. with art. 3. - Issued: 16.02.2015. Made: 10.02.2015. Effect: S.I. 2014/2887 modified. Territorial extent & classification: E/W/S. General. - Partially revoked by S.I. 2015/1537 (C.87) (ISBN 9780111138304). - 20p.: 30 cm. - 978-0-11-112913-5 £6.00

The Welfare Reform Act 2012 (Commencement No. 23 and Transitional and Transitory Provisions) (Amendment) Order 2015 No. 2015/740 (C.39). - Enabling power: Welfare Reform Act 2012, s. 150 (3) (4) (a) (b) (i) (c). Bringing into operation various provisions of the 2012 Act in accord. with art. 2. - Issued: 23.03.2015. Made: 17.03.2015. Effect: S.I. 2015/634 (C.32) amended. Territorial extent & classification: E/W/S. General. - This Statutory Instrument has been made in consequence of a defect in S.I. 2015/634 (C.32) and is being issued free of charge to all known recipients of that Statutory Instrument. - 2p.: 30 cm. - 978-0-11-113372-9 £4.25

The Welfare Reform Act 2012 (Commencement No. 23 and Transitional and Transitory Provisions) Order 2015 No. 2015/634 (C.32). - Enabling power: Welfare Reform Act 2012, s. 150 (3) (4) (a) (b) (i) (c). Bringing into operation various provisions of the 2012 Act in accord. with art. 3. - Issued: 16.03.2015. Made: 10.03.2015. Effect: S.I. 2013/983 (C.41); 2015/33 (C.4) amended & S.I. 2014/2887; 2015/345 modified. Territorial extent & classification: E/W/S. General. - Partially revoked by S.I. 2015/1930 (ISBN 9780111141182). - 20p.: 30 cm. - 978-0-11-113290-6 £6.00

The Welfare Reform Act 2012 (Commencement No. 24 and Transitional and Transitory Provisions and Commencement No. 9 and Transitional and Transitory Provisions (Amendment)) Order 2015 No. 2015/1537 (C.87). - Enabling power: Welfare Reform Act 2012, s. 150 (3) (4) (a) (b) (i) (c). Bringing into operation various provisions of the 2012 Act in accord. with para. 3. - Issued: 24.07.2015. Made: 20.07.2015. Effect: S.I. 2013/983 C.41; 2014/2887; 2015/345 amended & S.I. 2015/101 C.6 partially revoked. Territorial extent & classification: E/W/S. General. - Partially revoked by S.I. 2015/1930 (ISBN 9780111141182). - 24p.: 30 cm. - 978-0-11-113830-4 £6.00

The Welfare Reform Act 2012 (Commencement No. 25 and Transitional and Transitory Provisions) Order 2015 No. 2015/1930 (C.118). - Enabling power: Welfare Reform Act 2012, ss. 150 (3) (4) (a) (b) (i) (c). Bringing into operation various provisions of the 2012 Act. - Issued: 30.11.2015. Made: 23.11.2015. Effect: S.I. 2015/634 (C.32), 1537 (C.87) modified/partially revoked. Territorial extent & classification: E/W/S. General. - 16p.: 30 cm. - 978-0-11-114118-2 £6.00

The Welfare Reform (Northern Ireland) Order 2015 No. 2015/2006 (NI.1). - Enabling power: Northern Ireland (Welfare Reform) Act 2015, s. 1. - Issued: 16.12.2015. Made: 09.12.2015. Coming into force: In accord. with art. 2. Effect: 9 Acts & 8 SIs amended & 21 Acts & 16 SIs partially repealed. Territorial extent & classification: NI except amendments, repeals & revocation have the same extent as the provision to which they relate. General. - Supersedes draft S.I. (ISBN 9780111141236) issued 02/12/15. - 132p.: 30 cm. - 978-0-11-114186-1 £20.75

Social security, England

The Social Security (Information-sharing) (NHS Payments and Remission of Charges etc.) (England) Regulations 2015 No. 2015/124. - Enabling power: Welfare Reform Act 2012, ss. 131 (1) (3) (11) (g), 132 (8), 133 (1) (2). - Issued: 11.02.2015. Made: 04.02.2015. Laid: 10.02.2015. Coming into force: 01.04.2015. Effect: None. Territorial extent & classification: E. General. - 8p.: 30 cm. - 978-0-11-112886-2 £6.00

Social security, Northern Ireland

The Guardian's Allowance Up-rating (Northern Ireland) Order 2015 No. 2015/440. - Enabling power: Northern Ireland Administration Act 1992, ss. 132 (1), 165 (4). - Issued: 09.03.2015. Made: 02.03.2015. Coming into force: 06.04.2015. Effect: 1992 c.7 amended. Territorial extent & classification: NI. General. - 2p.: 30 cm. - 978-0-11-113128-2 £4.25

The Social Security Benefit (Computation of Earnings) (Amendment) (Northern Ireland) Regulations 2015 No. 2015/811. - Enabling power: Social Security Contributions and Benefits (Northern Ireland) Act 1992, ss. 3 (2) (3), 171 (3) (4) (10). - Issued: 26.03.2015. Made: 20.03.2015. Laid: 23.03.2015. Coming into force: 01.07.2015. Effect: S.R. 1996/520 amended. Territorial extent & classification: NI. General. - 4p.: 30 cm. - 978-0-11-113440-5 £4.25

Social services

The Care Act 2014 and Children and Families Act 2014 (Consequential Amendments) Order 2015 No. 2015/914. - Enabling power: Care Act 2014. ss. 123 (1) (2), 125 (7) (8) & Children and Families Act 2014, ss 135 (3), 136 (1) (2). - Issued: 07.04.2015. Made: 26.03.2015. Coming into force: In accord. with art. 1 (2). Effect: 39 Acts amended. Territorial extent & classification: E/W/S/NI. General. - Supersedes draft S.I. (ISBN 9780111128626) issued 09/02/15. - 24p.: 30 cm. - 978-0-11-113631-7 £6.00

Sports grounds and sporting events

The Safety of Sports Grounds (Designation) (Amendment) Order 2015 No. 2015/1556. - Enabling power: Safety of Sports Grounds Act 1975, ss. 1 (1), 18 (2). - Issued: 24.07.2015. Made: 17.07.2015. Laid: 21.07.2015. Coming into force: 01.10.2015. Effect: S.I. 2015/661 amended & S.I. 2015/1374 revoked. Territorial extent & classification: E/W/S. General. - 4p.: 30 cm. - 978-0-11-113833-5 £4.25

Sports grounds and sporting events, England and Wales

The Football Spectators (Corresponding Offences) (Revocation) Order 2015 No. 2015/212. - Enabling power: Football Spectators Act 1989, ss. 22 (1). - Issued: 18.02.2015. Made: 11.02.2015. Laid: 18.02.2015. Coming into force: 11.03.2015. Effect: S.I. 1990/992, 993; 1992/708, 1724; 1996/1634, 1635; 1998/1266; 2000/1108, 1109 revoked. Territorial extent & classification: E/W. General. - 2p.: 30 cm. - 978-0-11-112954-8 £4.25

The Safety of Sports Grounds (Designation) (Amendment) (No.2) Order 2015 No. 2015/1807. - Enabling power: Safety of Sports Grounds Act 1975, ss. 1 (1), 18 (2). - Issued: 26.10.2015. Made: 20.10.2015. Laid: 21.10.2015. Coming into force: 15.11.2015. Effect: S.I. 2015/661 amended. Territorial extent & classification: E/W. General. - 2p.: 30 cm. - 978-0-11-114005-5 £4.25

The Safety of Sports Grounds (Designation) (No. 2) Order 2015 No. 2015/1374. - Enabling power: Safety of Sports Grounds Act 1975, s. 1 (1). - Issued: 16.06.2015. Made: 08.06.2015. Laid: 11.06.2015. Coming into force: 03.08.2015. Effect: None. Territorial extent & classification: E/W. General. - Revoked by SI 2015/1556 (ISBN 9780111138335). - 2p.: 30 cm. - 978-0-11-113669-0 £4.25

The Safety of Sports Grounds (Designation) Order 2015 No. 2015/661. - Enabling power: Safety of Sports Grounds Act 1975, s. 1 (1), 18 (2). - Issued: 17.03.2015. Made: 10.03.2015. Laid: 12.03.2015. Coming into force: 01.10.2015. Effect: 51 SIs revoked. Territorial extent & classification: E/W. General. - 12p.: 30 cm. - 978-0-11-113318-7 £6.00

Stamp duty

The Stamp Duty and Stamp Duty Reserve Tax (Investment Exchanges and Clearing Houses) (Revocation) Regulations 2015 No. 2015/1779. - Enabling power: Finance Act 1991, ss. 116, 117. - Issued: 19.10.2015. Made: 12.10.2015. Laid: 13.10.2015. Coming into force: 10.11.2015. Effect: S.I. 2009/1828; 2011/667 revoked. Territorial extent & classification: E/W/S/NI. General. - 2p.: 30 cm. - 978-0-11-113988-2 £4.25

The Taxation of Regulatory Capital Securities (Amendment) Regulations 2015 No. 2015/2056. - Enabling power: Finance Act 2012, s. 221. - Issued: 22.12.2015. Made: 16.12.2015. Coming into force: 01.01.2016. Effect: S.I. 2013/3209 amended. Territorial extent & classification: E/W/S/NI. General. - Supersedes draft S.I. (ISBN 9780111141144) issued 27/11/15. - 8p.: 30 cm. - 978-0-11-114238-7 £4.25

Stamp duty land tax

The Scotland Act 2012, Section 29 (Disapplication of UK Stamp Duty Land Tax) (Appointed Day) Order 2015 No. 2015/637 (C.34). - Enabling power: Scotland Act 2012, s. 29 (4). Bringing into operation various provisions of the 2012 Act on 01.04.2015, in accord. with art. 2. - Issued: 16.03.2015. Made: 09.03.2015. Effect: None. Territorial extent & classification: E/W/S/NI. General. - 2p.: 30 cm. - 978-0-11-113293-7 £4.25

Stamp duty reserve tax

The Stamp Duty and Stamp Duty Reserve Tax (Investment Exchanges and Clearing Houses) (Revocation) Regulations 2015 No. 2015/1779. - Enabling power: Finance Act 1991, ss. 116, 117. - Issued: 19.10.2015. Made: 12.10.2015. Laid: 13.10.2015. Coming into force: 10.11.2015. Effect: S.I. 2009/1828; 2011/667 revoked. Territorial extent & classification: E/W/S/NI. General. - 2p.: 30 cm. - 978-0-11-113988-2 £4.25

The Taxation of Regulatory Capital Securities (Amendment) Regulations 2015 No. 2015/2056. - Enabling power: Finance Act 2012, s. 221. - Issued: 22.12.2015. Made: 16.12.2015. Coming into force: 01.01.2016. Effect: S.I. 2013/3209 amended. Territorial extent & classification: E/W/S/NI. General. - Supersedes draft S.I. (ISBN 9780111141144) issued 27/11/15. - 8p.: 30 cm. - 978-0-11-114238-7 £4.25

Statistics Board

The Statistics and Registration Service Act 2007 (Disclosure of Revenue Information) Regulations 2015 No. 2015/1277. - Enabling power: Statistics and Registration Service Act 2007, s. 47 (1). - Issued: 05.05.2015. Made: 25.03.2015. Coming into force: 26.03.2015. Effect: None. Territorial extent & classification: E/W/S/NI. General. - Supersedes draft S.I. (ISBN 9780111128749) issued 10/02/15. - 4p.: 30 cm. - 978-0-11-113639-3 £4.25

Succession

The Succession to the Crown Act 2013 (Commencement) Order 2015 No. 2015/894 (C.56). - Enabling power: Succession to the Crown Act 2013, s. 5 (2). Bringing into operation various provisions of the 2013 Act on 26.03.2015. - Issued: 01.04.2015. Made: 24.03.2015. Effect: None. Territorial extent & classification: E/W/S/NI. General. - 2p.: 30 cm. - 978-0-11-113521-1 £4.25

Supreme Court of the United Kingdom

The Crime and Courts Act 2013 (Commencement No. 14) Order 2015 No. 2015/1837. - Enabling power: Crime and Courts Act 2013 s. 61(2). Bringing into operation various provisions of the 2013 Act on 03.11.2015. - Issued: 04.11.2015. Made: 27.10.2015. Effect: None. Territorial extent & classification: E/W. General. - 8p.: 30 cm. - 978-0-11-114035-2 £4.25

The Criminal Justice and Courts Act 2015 (Commencement No. 1, Saving and Transitional Provisions) Order 2015 No. 2015/778 (C.44). - Enabling power: Criminal Justice and Courts Act 2015, s. 95 (1) (6). Bringing into operation various provisions of the 2015 Act on 20.03.2015; 13.04.2015, in accord. with arts 2, 3. - Issued: 25.03.2015. Made: 19.03.2015. Effect: None. Territorial extent & classification: E/W/S/NI. General. - 8p.: 30 cm. - 978-0-11-113405-4 £6.00

Tax credits

The Child Benefit and Tax Credits Up-rating Order 2015 No. 2015/567. - Enabling power: Welfare Benefits Up-rating Act 2013, ss. 1 (1) (2) (3) (7), 2 (1) (2) (3) & Social Security Administration (Northern Ireland) Act 1992, s. 132 (1). - Issued: 12.03.2015. Made: 05.03.2015. Coming into force: 06.04.2015. Effect: S.I. 2002/2005, 2007; 2006/965 amended. Territorial extent & classification: E/W/S/NI. General. - 4p.: 30 cm. - 978-0-11-113234-0 £4.25

The Social Security and Tax Credits (Miscellaneous Amendments) Regulations 2015 No. 2015/175. - Enabling power: Social Security Contributions and Benefits Act 1992, ss. 3 (2), 175 (3) (4) & Social Security Contributions and Benefits (Northern Ireland) Act 1992, ss. 3 (2), 171 (3) (4) & Tax Credits Act 2002, s. 7 (6). - Issued: 16.02.2015. Made: 09.02.2005. Laid: 10.02.2015. Coming into force: In accord. with reg. 1 (2) & (3). Effect: S.I. 2001/1004; 2002/2006 amended. Territorial extent & classification: E/W/S/NI. General. - 8p.: 30 cm. - 978-0-11-112911-1 £4.25

The Tax Credits (Claims and Notifications) (Amendment) Regulations 2015 No. 2015/669. - Enabling power: Tax Credits Act 2002, ss. 4 (1) (b), 65 (2) (7) (9), 67. - Issued: 18.03.2015. Made: 12.03.2015. Laid: 12.03.2015. Coming into force: 06.04.2015. Effect: S.I. 2002/2014; 2003/653 amended. Territorial extent & classification: E/W/S/NI. General. - 4p.: 30 cm. - 978-0-11-113328-6 £4.25

The Tax Credits Up-rating Regulations 2015 No. 2015/451. - Enabling power: Tax Credits Act 2002, ss. 7 (1) (a) (3), 9, 11, 13, 65 (1) 67. - Issued: 09.03.2015. Made: 02.03.2015. Coming into force: 06.04.2015. Effect: S.I. 2002/2005, 2007, 2008 amended. Territorial extent & classification: E/W/S/NI. General. - 4p.: 30 cm. - 978-0-11-113138-1 £4.25

The Working Tax Credit (Entitlement and Maximum Rate) (Amendment) Regulations 2015 No. 2015/605. - Enabling power: Tax Credits Act 2002, ss. 10 (2) (3) (d), 65 (1) (7) (9), 67. - Issued: 13.03.2015. Made: 09.03.2015. Laid: 10.03.2015. Coming into force: 06.04.2015. Effect: S.I. 2002/2005 amended. Territorial extent & classification: E/W/S/NI. General. - 2p.: 30 cm. - 978-0-11-113268-5 £4.25

Tax credits, Northern Ireland

The Tax Credits (Appeals) Regulations (Northern Ireland) (Amendment) Order 2015 No. 2015/452. - Enabling power: Finance Act 2008, s. 124 (1) (6) (7). - Issued: 09.03.2015. Made: 02.03.2015. Laid: .-. Coming into force: In accord. with art. 1. Effect: S.R. 2002/403 amended. Territorial extent & classification: NI. General. - Supersedes draft SI (ISBN 9780111127254) issued 21/01/15 - 2p.: 30 cm. - 978-0-11-113139-8 £4.25

Taxes

The Double Taxation Relief and International Tax Enforcement (Canada) Order 2015 No. 2015/2011. - Enabling power: Taxation (International and Other Provisions) Act 2010, s. 2 & Finance Act 2006, s. 173 (1) to (3). - Issued: 16.12.2015. Made: 09.12.2015. Coming into force: 09.12.2015. Effect: None. Territorial extent & classification: E/W/S/NI. General. - Supersedes draft S.I. (ISBN 9780111140253) issued 02/11/15. - 12p.: 30 cm. - 978-0-11-114191-5 £6.00

The International Tax Compliance (Amendment) Regulations 2015 No. 2015/1839. - Enabling power: Finance Act 2013, ss. 222 (1) (2) (3). - Issued: 04.11.2015. Made: 29.10.2015. Laid: 30.10.2015. Coming into force: 20.11.2015. Effect: S.I. 2015/878 amended. Territorial extent & classification: E/W/S/NI. General. - With correction slip dated 10 November 2015. - 4p.: 30 cm. - 978-0-11-114037-6 £4.25

The International Tax Compliance (Crown Dependencies and Gibraltar) (Amendment) Regulations 2015 No. 2015/873. - Enabling power: Finance Act 2002, s. 136 & Finance Act 2013, ss. 222 (1) (2) (3). - Issued: 31.03.2014. Made: 24.03.2015. Laid: 25.03.2015. Coming into force: 15.04.2015. Effect: S.I. 2014/520 amended. Territorial extent & classification: E/W/S/NI. General. - 4p.: 30 cm. - 978-0-11-113496-2 £4.25

The International Tax Compliance Regulations 2015 No. 2015/878. - Enabling power: Finance Act 2013, ss. 222 (1) (2) (3). - Issued: 31.03.2015. Made: 24.03.2015. Laid: 25.03.2015. Coming into force: 15.04.2015. Effect: None. Territorial extent & classification: E/W/S/NI. General. - 16p.: 30 cm. - 978-0-11-113501-3 £6.00

The International Tax Enforcement (Macao) Order 2015 No. 2015/801. - Enabling power: Finance Act 2006, s. 173 (1) to (3). - Issued: 26.03.2015. Made: 19.03.2015. Coming into force: 19.03.2015. Effect: None. Territorial extent & classification: E/W/S/NI. General. - Supersedes draft S.I. (ISBN 9780111127421) issued 22.01.2015. - 12p.: 30 cm. - 978-0-11-113427-6 £6.00

The International Tax Enforcement (Monaco) Order 2015 No. 2015/804. - Enabling power: Finance Act 2006, s. 173 (1) to (3). - Issued: 26.03.2015. Made: 19.03.2015. Coming into force: 19.03.2015. Effect: None. Territorial extent & classification: E/W/S/NI. General. - Supersedes draft S.I. (ISBN 9780111127414) issued 22.01.2015. - 12p.: 30 cm. - 978-0-11-113430-6 £6.00

The Promoters of Tax Avoidance Schemes (Prescribed Circumstances under Section 35) Regulations 2015 No. 2015/130. - Enabling power: Finance Act 2014, ss. 235 (6) (7), 283 (1). - Issued: 12.02.2015. Made: 06.02.2015. Laid: 09.02.2015. Coming into force: 02.03.2015. Effect: None. Territorial extent & classification: E/W/S/NI. General. - 4p.: 30 cm. - 978-0-11-112896-1 £4.25

The Tax Avoidance Schemes (Information) (Amendment) Regulations 2015 No. 2015/948. - Enabling power: Finance Act 2004, ss. 312 (2) (5), 312A (2), 312A (2A), 312A (5), 313 (1) (3) (6), 313ZC (5), 313C (1A) (3) (a), 317 (2), 318 (1). - Issued: 02.04.2015. Made: 26.03.2015. Laid: 27.03.2015. Coming into force: 16.04.2015. Effect: S.I. 2012/1836 amended. Territorial extent & classification: E/W/S/NI. General. - 4p.: 30 cm. - 978-0-11-113574-7 £4.25

The Tax Avoidance Schemes (Promoters and Prescribed Circumstances) (Amendment) Regulations 2015 No. 2015/945. - Enabling power: Finance Act 2004, ss. 307 (5), 318 (1). - Issued: 02.04.2015. Made: 26.03.2015. Laid: 27.03.2015. Coming into force: 17.04.2015. Effect: S.I. 2004/1865 amended. Territorial extent & classification: E/W/S/NI. General. - 2p.: 30 cm. - 978-0-11-113570-9 £4.25

Taxes: Tonnage tax

The Tonnage Tax (Training Requirement) (Amendment) (No. 2) Regulations 2015 No. 2015/1607. - Enabling power: Finance Act 2000, sch. 22, paras 29, 31, 36. - Issued: 20.08.2015. Made: 11.08.2015. Laid: 20.08.2015. Coming into force: 01.10.2015. Effect: S.I. 2000/2129 amended & S.I. 2014/2394 revoked. Territorial extent & classification: E/W/S/NI. General. - 2p.: 30 cm. - 978-0-11-113865-6 £4.25

The Tonnage Tax (Training Requirement) (Amendment) Regulations 2015 No. 2015/788. - Enabling power: Finance Act 2000, sch. 22, paras. 24, 27 to 29, 31, 36. - Issued: 25.03.2015. Made: 18.03.2015. Laid: 23.03.2015. Coming into force: 01.10.2015. Effect: S.I. 2000/2129 amended. Territorial extent & classification: E/W/S/NI. General. - 4p.: 30 cm. - 978-0-11-113408-5 £4.25

Terms and conditions of employment

The Code of Practice (Disciplinary and Grievance Procedures) Order 2015 No. 2015/649. - Issued: 16.03.2015. Made: 10.03.2015. Coming into force: 10.03.2015. Effect: None. Territorial extent & classification: E/W/S. General. - 2p.: 30 cm. - 978-0-11-113307-1 £4.25

The Employment Rights (Increase of Limits) Order 2015 No. 2015/226. - Enabling power: Employment Relations Act 1999, s. 34. - Issued: 18.02.2015. Made: 11.02.2015. Laid: 13.02.2015. Coming into force: 06.04.2015. Effect: S.I. 2014/382 revoked. Territorial extent & classification: E/W/S. General. - Revoked by S.I. 2016/288 (ISBN 9780111144633). - 8p.: 30 cm. - 978-0-11-112966-1 £4.25

The Employment Tribunals Act 1996 (Application of Conciliation Provisions) Order 2015 No. 2015/2054. - Enabling power: Employment Tribunals Act 1996, s. 18 (8) (9). - Issued: 23.12.2015. Made: 15.12.2015. Laid: 17.12.2015. Coming into force: 11.01.2016. Effect: 1996 c.17 & S.I. 2015/2021 amended. Territorial extent & classification: E/W/S. General. - 4p.: 30 cm. - 978-0-11-114235-6 £4.25

The Exclusivity Terms in Zero Hours Contracts (Redress) Regulations 2015 No. 2015/2021. - Enabling power: Employment Rights Act 1996, ss. 27B (1) (5), 209 (1). - Issued: 21.12.2015. Made: 14.12.2015. Coming into force: In accord. with reg. 1. Effect: None. Territorial extent & classification: E/W/S. General. - Supersedes draft SI (ISBN 9780111139950) issued 20/10/15 - 4p.: 30 cm. - 978-0-11-114205-9 £4.25

The National Minimum Wage (Amendment) Regulations 2015 No. 2015/1724. - Enabling power: National Minimum Wage Act 1998, ss. 1 (3), 2, 3, 51. - Issued: 02.10.2015. Made: 27.09.2015. Coming into force: 01.10.2015. Effect: S.I. 2015/621 amended. Territorial extent & classification: E/W/S/NI. General. - 2p.: 30 cm. - 978-0-11-113946-2 £4.25

The National Minimum Wage Regulations 2015 No. 2015/621. - Enabling power: National Minimum Wage Act 1998, ss. 1 (3) (4), 2, 3, 9, 51 (1) (b). - Issued: 16.03.2015. Made: 09.03.2015. Coming into force: 06.04.2015. Effect: 6 SIs partially revoked & 22 SIs revoked. Territorial extent & classification: E/W/S/NI. General. - Supersedes draft S.I. (ISBN 9780111127964) issued 02/02/15. - 32p.: 30 cm. - 978-0-11-113284-5 £6.00

The Protected Disclosures (Extension of Meaning of Worker) Order 2015 No. 2015/491. - Enabling power: Employment Rights Act 1996, s. 43K (4). - Issued: 09.03.2015. Made: 25.02.2015. Coming into force: 06.04.2015. Effect: 1996 c.18 amended. Territorial extent & classification: E/W/S. General. - Supersedes draft SI (ISBN 9780111127018) issued 16/01/15 - 2p.: 30 cm. - 978-0-11-113189-3 £4.25

The Public Interest Disclosure (Prescribed Persons) (Amendment) (No. 2) Order 2015 No. 2015/1981. - Enabling power: Employment Rights Act 1996, s. 43F. - Issued: 11.12.2015. Made: 07.12.2015. Laid: 09.12.2015. Coming into force: 01.02.2016. Effect: S.I. 2014/2418 amended. Territorial extent & classification: E/W/S. General. - 8p.: 30 cm. - 978-0-11-114169-4 £4.25

The Public Interest Disclosure (Prescribed Persons) (Amendment) Order 2015 No. 2015/1407. - Enabling power: Employment Rights Act 1996, ss. 43F. - Issued: 29.06.2015. Made: 23.06.2015. Laid: 26.06.2015. Coming into force: 21.07.2015. Effect: S.I. 2014/2418 amended. Territorial extent & classification: E/W/S. General. - 4p.: 30 cm. - 978-0-11-113704-8 £4.25

The Redundancy Payments (Continuity of Employment in Local Government, etc) (Modification) (Amendment) Order 2015 No. 2015/916. - Enabling power: Employment Rights Act 1996, ss. 209 (1) (b), 236. - Issued: 01.04.2015. Made: 25.03.2015. Laid: 27.03.2015. Coming into force: 01.07.2015. Effect: S.I. 1999/2277 amended. Territorial extent & classification: E/W/S. General. - 2p.: 30 cm. - 978-0-11-113538-9 £4.25

The Shared Parental Leave and Leave Curtailment (Amendment) Regulations 2015 No. 2015/552. - Enabling power: Employment Rights Act 1996, ss. 75A (2) (2A) (b), 75B (2) (3) (aa), 75D (1) (a), 75E (1) (4), 75F (1) (a) (4) (9) (10) (12) (a), 75G (1) (4), 75H (1) (a) (9) (10) (12) (a). - Issued: 11.03.2015. Made: 05.03.2015. Coming into force: 05.04.2015. Effect: S.I. 2014/3050 amended. Territorial extent & classification: E/W/S. General. - Supersedes draft SI (ISBN 9780111127025) issued 16/01/15 - 4p.: 30 cm. - 978-0-11-113227-2 £4.25

The Small Business, Enterprise and Employment Act 2015 (Commencement No. 1) Regulations 2015 No. 2015/1329 (C.75). - Enabling power: Small Business, Enterprise and Employment Act 2015, ss. 161 (2), 164 (1). Bringing into operation various provisions of the 2015 Act on 26.05.2015; 15.06.2015; 01.07.2015; 01.01.2016, in accord. with arts 2 to 6. - Issued: 28.05.2015. Made: 20.05.2015. Effect: None. Territorial extent & classification: E/W/S/NI. General. - 4p.: 30 cm. - 978-0-11-113644-7 £4.25

The Social Security Contributions and Benefits Act 1992 (Application of Parts 12ZA, 12ZB and 12ZC to Parental Order Cases) Regulations 2014 (correction slip) No. 2014/2866 cor. - Correction slip (to ISBN 9780111122532) dated January 2015. - 1 sheet: 30 cm. Free

The Statutory Paternity Pay, Statutory Adoption Pay and Statutory Shared Parental Pay (Amendment) Regulations 2015 No. 2015/2065. - Enabling power: Social Security Contributions and Benefits Act 1992, 171ZJ (1) (5), 171ZS (1) (5), 171ZZ4 (1) (5). - Issued: 24.12.2015. Made: 17.12.2015. Laid: 22.12.2015. Coming into force: 01.02.2016. Effect: S.I. 2002/2822; 2014/3051 amended. Territorial extent & classification: E/W/S. General. - 4p.: 30 cm. - 978-0-11-114248-6 £4.25

The Statutory Shared Parental Pay (General) (Amendment) Regulations 2015 No. 2015/189. - Enabling power: Social Security Contributions and Benefits Act 1992, ss. 171ZU (2) (b) (ii) (4) (c) (ii), 171ZV (2) (e) (4) (c) (ii) (4) (f), 171ZW (1) (c) & Social Security Administration Act 1992, s. 5 (1) (p). - Issued: 17.02.2015. Made: 09.02.2015. Laid: 12.02.2015. Coming into force: 08.03.2015. Effect: S.I. 2014/3051 amended. Territorial extent & classification: E/W/S. General. - This Statutory Instrument has been made in consequence of defects in S.I. 2014/3051(ISBN 9780111123898) published 28/11/14 and is being issued free of charge to all known recipients of that Statutory Instrument. - 2p.: 30 cm. - 978-0-11-112925-8 £4.25

The Welfare Benefits Up-Rating Order 2015 No. 2015/30. - Enabling power: Welfare Benefits Uprating Act 2013, s. 1. - Issued: 21.01.2015. Made: 14.01.2015. Coming into force: In accord. with art. 1. Effect: 1992 c. 4; 1986/1960; 1987/1967; 1996/207; 2002/2818; 2008/794; 2013/378, 379; 2014/3051 amended & S.I. 2014/147 revoked. Territorial extent & classification: E/W/S. General. - 20p.: 30 cm. - 978-0-11-112736-0 £6.00

Territorial sea

The Territorial Sea Act 1987 (Guernsey) (Amendment) Order 2015 No. 2015/827. - Enabling power: Territorial Sea Act 1987, s. 4 (4). - Issued: 26.3.2015. Made: 19.03.2015. Coming into force: 09.04.2015. Effect: S.I. 2014/1105 amended. Territorial extent & classification: Guernsey. General. - This Statutory Instrument has been printed to correct a defect in S.I. 2014/1105 (ISBN 9780111114377) and is being issued free of charge to all known recipients of that Statutory Instrument. - 2p.: 30 cm. - 978-0-11-113460-3 £4.25

Torts, England and Wales

The Social, Responsibility and Heroism Act 2015 (Commencement and Transitional Provision) Regulations 2015 No. 2015/808 (C.46). - Enabling power: Social Action, Responsibility and Heroism Act 2015, s. 5 (2) (3). Bringing into operation various provisions of the 2015 Act on 13.04.2015 in accord. with art 2. - Issued: 25.03.2015. Made: 19.03.2015. Coming to force: -. Effect: None. Territorial extent & classification: E/W. General. - 2p.: 30 cm. - 978-0-11-113435-1 £4.25

Town and country planning, England

The Neighbourhood Planning (General) (Amendment) Regulations 2015 No. 2015/20. - Enabling power: Town and Country Planning Act 1990, ss 61G, 61I, 333 (2A), sch. 4B, para. 1 & Planning and Compulsory Purchase Act 2004, ss 38A, 122. - Issued: 16.01.2015. Made: 12.01.2015. Laid: 14.01.2015. Coming into force: 09.02.2015. Effect: S.I. 2012/637 amended. Territorial extent & classification: E. General. - 4p.: 30 cm. - 978-0-11-112705-6 £4.25

The Planning (Hazardous Substances) (Amendment) Regulations 2015 No. 2015/1359. - Enabling power: Planning (Hazardous Substances) Act 1990, s. 5. - Issued: 12.06.2015. Made: 08.06.2015. Laid: 09.06.2015. Coming into force: 10.06.2015. Effect: S.I 2015/627 amended. Territorial extent & classification: E. General. - This S.I. has been made in consequence of defects in S.I. 2015/627 (ISBN 9780111134238) published on 25/03/15 and is being issued free of charge to all known recipients of that S.I. - 2p.: 30 cm. - 978-0-11-113661-4 £4.25

The Planning (Hazardous Substances) Regulations 2015 No. 2015/627. - Enabling power: Planning (Hazardous Substances) Act 1990, ss. 4 (4), 4 (5), 5, 7, 8, 17 (2), 21 (2) (3) (3A), 24 (4), 25, 26A, 28, 30, 40 (1) (4) & European Communities Act 1972, s. 2 (2), sch. 2, para. 1A. - Issued: 25.03.2015. Made: 18.03.2015. Laid: 24.03.2015. Coming into force: 01.06.2015. Effect: S.I 2000/1491; 2006/1466; 2008/580; 2012/767 amended & S.I. 1992/656; 1999/981; 2014/1638 partially revoked & 2006/1282; 2009/1901; 2010/1050 revoked. Territorial extent & classification: E. General. - 50p.: 30 cm. - 978-0-11-113423-8 £10.00

The Planning (Listed Buildings and Conservation Areas) (Amendment) (England) Regulations 2015 No. 2015/809. - Enabling power: Planning (Listed Buildings and Conservation Areas) Act 1990, ss. 67 (1), 73 (1), 82, 93. - Issued: 25.03.2015. Made: 18.03.2015. Laid: 24.03.2015. Coming into force: 15.04.2015. Effect: S.I. 1990/1519 amended. Territorial extent & classification: E. General. - 4p.: 30 cm. - 978-0-11-113436-8 £4.25

The Town and Country Planning (Compensation) (England) Regulations 2015 No. 2015/598. - Enabling power: Town and Country Planning Act 1990, s. 108 (2A) (3C) (3E) (5) (6). - Issued: 26.03.2015. Made: 18.03.2015. Laid: 24.03.2015. Coming into force: 15.04.2015. Effect: S.I. 2013/1102; 2014/565 revoked. Territorial extent & classification: E. General. - 4p.: 30 cm. - 978-0-11-113437-5 £4.25

TOWN AND COUNTRY PLANNING, ENGLAND AND WALES

The Town and Country Planning (Development Management Procedure) (England) Order 2015 No. 2015/595. - Enabling power: Town and Country Planning Act 1990, ss. 55 (2A) (2B), 59, 61 (1), 61A (5), 61W, 62, 65, 69, 71, 74, 74A, 77 (4), 78, 79 (4), 188, 193, 196 (4), 293A, 333 (4) (7), sch. 1, paras 5, 6, 7 (7), 8 (6), sch.1, 4A & Planning and Compulsory Purchase Act 2004, ss. 54, 88, 122 (3). - Issued: 25.03.2015. Made: 18.03.2015. Laid: 24.03.2015. Coming into force: 15.04.2015. Effect: S.I. 2011/1824; 2013/235, 2879, 2932, 3194; 2014/469, 564, 1532; 2015/377 partially revoked & S.I. 2010/2184; 2012/636, 2274, 3109; 2013/1238, 2136 revoked. Territorial extent & classification: E. General. - 72p.: 30 cm. - 978-0-11-113439-9 £14.25

The Town and Country Planning (Environmental Impact Assessment) (Amendment) Regulations 2015 No. 2015/660. - Enabling power: European Communities Act 1972, s. 2 (2). - Issued: 17.03.2015. Made: 11.03.2015. Laid: 12.03.2015. Coming into force: 06.04.2015. Effect: S.I. 2011/1824 amended. Territorial extent & classification: E. General. - 4p.: 30 cm. - 978-0-11-113317-0 £4.25

The Town and Country Planning General (Amendment) (England) Regulations 2015 No. 2015/807. - Enabling power: Town and Country Planning Act 1990, ss. 316 (1) (3), 333 (1) (2A). - Issued: 25.03.2015. Made: 18.03.2015. Laid: 24.03.2015. Coming into force: 15.04.2015. Effect: S.I. 1992/1492 amended. Territorial extent & classification: E. General. - 4p.: 30 cm. - 978-0-11-113434-4 £4.25

The Town and Country Planning (General Permitted Development) (Amendment) (England) Order 2015 No. 2015/659. - Enabling power: Town and Country Planning Act 1990, ss. 59, 60, 61, 333 (7). - Issued: 17.03.2015. Made: 11.03.2015. Laid: 12.03.2015. Coming into force: 06.04.2015. Effect: S.I. 1995/418 amended. Territorial extent & classification: E. General. - Revoked by SI 2015/596 (ISBN 9780111134467). - 12p.: 30 cm. - 978-0-11-113316-3 £6.00

The Town and Country Planning (General Permitted Development) (England) Order 2015 No. 2015/596. - Enabling power: Town and Country Planning Act 1990, ss. 59, 60, 61, 74, 333 (7) & Coal Industry Act 1994, s. 54. - Issued: 26.03.2015. Made: 18.03.2015. Laid: 24.03.2015. Coming into force: 15.04.2015. Effect: 23 S.Is revoked in relation to England. Territorial extent & classification: E. General. - 164p.: 30 cm. - 978-0-11-113446-7 £23.25

The Town and Country Planning (Operation Stack) Special Development Order 2015 No. 2015/1635. - Enabling power: Town and Country Planning Act 1990, ss. 59, 60. - Issued: 04.09.2015. Made: 28.08.2015. Laid: 01.09.2015. Coming into force: 02.09.2015. Effect: None. Territorial extent & classification: E. General. - 4p., 1 col. map: 30 cm. - 978-0-11-113880-9 £5.25

The Town and Country Planning (Section 62A Applications) (Procedure and Consequential Amendments) (Amendment) Order 2015 No. 2015/797. - Enabling power: Town and Country Planning Act 1990, s. 76C (3). - Issued: 26.03.2015. Made: 18.03.2015. Laid: 24.03.2015. Coming into force: 15.04.2015. Effect: S.I. 2013/2140 amended. Territorial extent & classification: E. General. - 4p.: 30 cm. - 978-0-11-113421-4 £4.25

The Town and Country Planning (Use Classes) (Amendment) (England) Order 2015 No. 2015/597. - Enabling power: Town and Country Planning Act 1990, ss. 55 (2) (f), 333 (7). - Issued: 25.03.2015. Made: 18.03.2015. Laid: 24.03.2015. Coming into force: 15.04.2015. Effect: S.I. 1987/764 amended. Territorial extent & classification: E. General. - 4p.: 30 cm. - 978-0-11-113411-5 £4.25

Town and country planning, England and Wales

The Criminal Justice and Courts Act 2015 (Commencement No. 3 and Transitional Provisions) Order 2015 No. 2015/1778 (C.108). - Enabling power: Criminal Justice and Courts Act 2015, ss. 95 (1) (6). Bringing into operation various provisions of the 2015 Act on 26.10.2015 according to art. 3. - Issued: 19.10.2015. Made: 12.10.2015. Coming into force: 26.10.2015. Effect: None. Territorial extent & classification: E/W. General. - 4p.: 30 cm. - 978-0-11-113987-5 £4.25

Town and country planning, Wales

The Planning and Compulsory Purchase Act 2004 (Commencement No. 14 and Saving) Order 2015 No. 2015/340 (C.17). - Enabling power: Planning and Compulsory Purchase Act 2004, ss. 121 (1) (2), 122 (3). Bringing into operation various provisions of the 2004 Act on 22.06.2015 (in relation to Wales), in accord. with art. 2. - Issued: 27.02.2015. Made: 23.02.2015. Effect: None. Territorial extent & classification: W. General. - 8p.: 30 cm. - 978-0-11-113028-5 £6.00

The Planning (Hazardous Substances) (Wales) Regulations 2015 No. 2015/1597 (W.196). - Enabling power: Planning (Hazardous Substances) Act 1990, ss. 4, 5, 7, 8, 17, 21, 21B, 24, 25, 26A, 28, 30, 40 & Welsh Language Act 1993, s. 26 & European Communities Act 1972, ss. 2 (2), sch. 2, para. 1A. - Issued: 18.09.2015. Made: 03.08.2015. Laid before the National Assembly for Wales: 07.08.2015. Coming into force: 04.09.2015. Effect: S.I. 2005/2839 (W.203); 2012/801 (W.110) amended & S.I. 2006/1282 partially revoked in relation to Wales & S.I. 1992/656; 1999/981 revoked in relation to Wales & S.I. 2010/450 (W.48); 2014/375 (W.43), 2777 (W.283) revoked. Territorial extent & classification: W. General. - EC note: These Regulations implement the land-use aspects of Directive 2012/18/EU of the European Parliament and the Council on the control of major accident hazards involving dangerous substances. - In English and Welsh. Welsh title: Rheoliadau Cynllunio (Sylweddau Peryglus)(Cymru) 2015. - 86p.: 30 cm. - 978-0-348-11150-7 £16.00

The Planning (Listed Buildings and Conservation Areas) (Wales) (Amendment) Regulations 2015 No. 2015/1332 (W.125). - Enabling power: Planning (Listed Buildings and Conservation Areas) Act 1990, ss. 20, 20A, 21, 93. - Issued: 04.06.2015. Made: 20.05.2015. Laid before the National Assembly for Wales: 22.05.2015. Coming into force: 22.06.2015. Effect: W.S.I. 2012/793 (W.108) amended. Territorial extent & classification: W. General. - In English and Welsh. Welsh title: Rheoliadau Cynllunio (Adeiladau Rhestredig ac Ardaloedd Cadwraeth) (Cymru) (Diwygio) 2015. - 4p.: 30 cm. - 978-0-348-11103-3 £4.25

The Planning (Wales) Act 2015 (Commencement No. 1) Order 2015 No. 2015/1736 (W.237)(C.106). - Enabling power: Planning (Wales) Act 2015, s. 584 (4) (b). Bringing into operation various provisions of the 2015 Act on 05.10.2015, in accord. with art. 2. - Issued: 07.10.2015. Made: 29.09.2015. Effect: None. Territorial extent & classification: W. General. - In English and Welsh. Welsh title: Gorchymyn Deddf Cynllunio (Cymru) 2015 (Cychwyn Rhif 1) 2015. - 4p.: 30 cm. - 978-0-348-11160-6 £4.25

The Planning (Wales) Act 2015 (Commencement No. 2 and Transitional and Saving Provisions) Order 2015 No. 2015/1987 (W.297)(C.123). - Enabling power: Planning (Wales) Act 2015, s. 58 (4). Bringing into operation various provisions of the 2015 Act on 04.01.2016; 16.03.2016; 01.04.2016, in accord. with arts 2 to 5. - Issued: 11.12.2015. Made: 02.12.2015. Effect: None. Territorial extent & classification: W. General. - In English and Welsh. Welsh title: Gorchymyn Deddf Cynllunio (Cymru) 2015 (Cychwyn Rhif 2 a Darpariaethau Trosiannol as Arbed) 2015. - 4p.: 30 cm. - 978-0-348-11200-9 £4.25

The Town and Country Planning (Determination of Appeals by Appointed Persons) (Prescribed Classes) (Wales) Regulations 2015 No. 2015/1822 (W.264). - Enabling power: Town and Country Planning Act 1990, s. 333, sch. 6, para. 1 & Planning (Listed Buildings and Conservation Areas) Act 1990, s. 93, sch. 3, para. 1 & Planning (Hazardous Substances) Act 1990, s. 40, para. 1. - Issued: 13.11.2015. Made: 20.10.2015. Laid before the National Assembly for Wales: 26.10.2015. Coming into force: 16.12.2015. Effect: S.I. 1997/420 revoked with saving. Territorial extent & classification: W. General. - In English and Welsh. Welsh language title: Rheoliadau Cynllunio Gwlad a Thref (Penderfynu ar Apelau gan Bersonau Penodedig) (Dosbarthau Rhagnodedig) (Cymru) 2015. - 8p.: 30 cm. - 978-0-348-11181-1 £6.00

The Town and Country Planning (Development Management Procedure) (Wales) (Amendment) Order 2015 No. 2015/1330 (W.123). - Enabling power: Town and Country Planning Act 1990, ss. 55, 65, 69, 71, 78, 78A, 333. - Issued: 04.06.2015. Made: 20.05.2015. Laid before the National Assembly for Wales: 22.05.2015. Coming into force: 22.06.2015. Effect: W.S.I. 2012/801 (W.110) amended. Territorial extent & classification: W. General. - In English and Welsh. Welsh language title: Gorchymyn Cynllunio Gwlad a Thref (Gweithdrefn Rheoli Datblygu) (Cymru) (Diwygio) 2015. - 16p.: 30 cm. - 978-0-348-11101-9 £6.00

The Town and Country Planning (Fees for Applications, Deemed Applications and Site Visits) (Wales) Regulations 2015 No. 2015/1522 (W.179). - Enabling power: Town and Country Planning Act 1990, ss. 303, 333 (2A). - Issued: 13.08.2015. Made: 06.07.2015. Coming into force: 01.10.2015. Effect: S.I. 1989/193; 1990/2473; 1991/2735; 1992/1817, 3052; 1993/3170; 1997/37; WSI 2002/1876 (W.185); 2006/1052 (W.108); 2009/851 (W.76); 2014/1761 (W.176) revoked in so far as they apply to Wales with savings. Territorial extent & classification: W. General. - In English and Welsh. Welsh language title: Rheoliadau Cynllunio Gwlad a Thref (Ffioedd am Geisiadau, Ceisiadau Tybiedig ac Ymweliadau Safle) (Cymru) 2015. - 44p.: 30 cm. - 978-0-348-11141-5 £10.00

The Town and Country Planning (Local Development Plan) (Wales) (Amendment) Regulations 2015 No. 2015/1598 (W.197). - Enabling power: Planning and Compulsory Purchase Act 2004, ss. 62, 63, 69, 77, 122. - Issued: 07.03.2016. Made: 03.08.2015. Laid before the National Assembly for Wales: 07.08.2015. Coming into force: 28.08.2015. Effect: S.I. 2005/2839 (W.203) amended. Territorial extent & classification: W. General. - This Statutory Instrument has been printed in substitution of the SI of same number (and ISBN, issued 01.09.2015) and is being issued free of charge to all known recipients of that Statutory Instrument. - In English and Welsh. Rheoliadau Cynllunio Gwlad a Thref (Cynllun Datblygu Lleol) (Cymru) (Diwygio) 2015. - 20p.: 30 cm. - 978-0-348-11277-1 £6.00

The Town and Country Planning (Local Development Plan) (Wales) (Amendment) Regulations 2015 No. 2015/1598 (W.197). - Enabling power: Planning and Compulsory Purchase Act 2004, ss. 62, 63, 69, 77, 122. - Issued: 01.09.2015. Made: 03.08.2015. Laid before the National Assembly for Wales: 07.08.2015. Coming into force: 28.08.2015. Effect: S.I. 2005/2839 (W.203) amended. Territorial extent & classification: W. General. - In English and Welsh. Rheoliadau Cynllunio Gwlad a Thref (Cynllun Datblygu Lleol) (Cymru) (Diwygio) 2015. - 20p.: 30 cm. - 978-0-348-11147-7 £6.00

The Town and Country Planning (Power to Override Easements and Applications by Statutory Undertakers) (Wales) Order 2015 No. 2015/1794 (W.254). - Enabling power: Planning Act 2008, s. 203. - Issued: 27.10.2015. Made: 13.10.2015. Coming into force: 14.10.2015 in accord. with art 1 (2). Effect: 1980 c.65; 1981 c.64; 1988 c.50; 1990 c.8 amended. Territorial extent & classification: W. General. - In English and Welsh. Welsh language title: Gorchymyn Cynllunio Gwlad a Thref (P.er i Drechu Hawddfreintiau a Cheisiadau gan Ymgymerwyr Statudol) (Cymru) 2015. - 4p.: 30 cm. - 978-0-348-11174-3 £4.25

The Town and Country Planning (Referrals and Appeals) (Written Representations Procedure) (Wales) Regulations 2015 No. 2015/1331 (W.124). - Enabling power: Town and Country Planning Act 1990, ss. 323, 333 & Planning (Listed Buildings and Conservation Areas) Act 1990, ss. 89 (1), 93. - Issued: 05.06.2015. Made: 20.05.2015. Laid before the National Assembly for Wales: 22.05.2015. Coming into force: 22.06.2015. Effect: S.I. 2003/390 (W.52) revoked with savings. Territorial extent & classification: W. General. - In English and Welsh. Welsh language title: Rheoliadau Cynllunio Gwlad a Thref (Atgyfeiriadau ac Apelau) (Gweithdrefn Sylwadau Ysgrifenedig) (Cymru) 2015. - 20p.: 30 cm. - 978-0-348-11100-2 £6.00

Trade unions

The Membership Audit Certificate (Qualified Independent Person) (Specified Conditions) Order 2015 No. 2015/716. - Enabling power: Trade Union and Labour Relations (Consolidation) Act 1992, ss. 24ZB (3) (a). - Issued: 20.03.2015. Made: 16.03.2015. Laid: 16.03.2015. Coming into force: 06.04.2015. Effect: None. Territorial extent & classification: E/W/S. General. - 4p.: 30 cm. - 978-0-11-113354-5 £4.25

The Transparency of Lobbying, Non-Party Campaigning and Trade Union Administration Act 2014 (Commencement No. 2 and Transitional Provision) Order 2015 No. 2015/717. - Enabling power: Transparency of Lobbying, Non-Party Campaigning and Trade Union Administration Act 2014, s. 45 (1) (c) (2). Bringing into operation various provisions of the 2014 Act on 06.04.2015; 01.06.2016, in accord. with arts 3 & 4. - Issued: 20.03.2015. Made: 16.03.2015. Effect: None. Territorial extent & classification: E/W/S/NI. General. - 4p.: 30 cm. - 978-0-11-113355-2 £4.25

Transport

The Counter-Terrorism and Security Act 2015 (Commencement No. 3) Regulations 2015 No. 2015/1729 (C.104). - Enabling power: Counter-Terrorism and Security Act 2015, s. 52 (3). Bringing into operation various provisions of the 2015 Act on 01.10.2015, in accord. with art. 2. - Issued: 05.10.2015. Made: 28.09.2015. Effect: None. Territorial extent & classification: E/W/S. General. - 2p.: 30 cm. - 978-0-11-113951-6 £4.25

The Greater Manchester (Light Rapid Transit System) (Exemptions) (Amendment) Order 2015 No. 2015/1877. - Enabling power: Railways Act 1993, ss. 7 (1) (2) (9), 16B (1) (2) (3) (5), 20 (1) (2) (8), 24 (1) (2) (8), 143 (3), 151 (5) & Railways Act 2005, ss. 25 (7), 38 (1). - Issued: 16.11.2015. Made: 10.11.2015. Laid: 13.11.2015. Coming into force: 06.12.2015. Effect: S.I. 2013/339 amended. Territorial extent & classification: E. General. - 8p., 1 col. map: 30 cm. - 978-0-11-114074-1 £5.25

The Rail Vehicle Accessibility (B2007 Vehicles) Exemption Order 2015 No. 2015/1631. - Enabling power: Equality Act 2010, ss. 183 (1) (2) (4) (b) (5), 207 (1) (4). - Issued: 08.09.2015. Made: 26.08.2015. Laid: 08.09.2015. Coming into force: 30.09.2015. Effect: None. Territorial extent & classification: E/W/S. General. - 4p.: 30 cm. - 978-0-11-113879-3 £4.25

The Rail Vehicle Accessibility (Non-Interoperable Rail System) (London Underground Northern Line 95TS Vehicles) Exemption Order 2015 No. 2015/393. - Enabling power: Equality Act 2010, ss. 183 (1) (2) (4) (b) (5), 207 (1) (4). - Issued: 05.03.2015. Made: 23.02.2015. Laid: 05.03.2015. Coming into force: 27.03.2015. Effect: None. Territorial extent & classification: E/W/S. General. - 8p.: 30 cm. - 978-0-11-113082-7 £6.00

The Railways Infrastructure (Access and Management) (Amendment) Regulations 2015 No. 2015/786. - Enabling power: European Communities Act 1972, s. 2 (2). - Issued: 31.03.2015. Made: 24.03.2015. Laid: 26.03.2015. Coming into force: In accord. with reg. 1 (2). Effect: S.I. 2005/3049 amended. Territorial extent & classification: E/W/S/NI. General. - EC note: Following the repeal of "the 2005 Regulations", (S.I. 2005/3049) these Regulations implement in respect of the Channel Tunnel Directives 91/440/EEC and 2001/14/EC. - 8p.: 30 cm. - 978-0-11-113514-3 £4.25

The Railways (Interoperability) (Amendment) Regulations 2015 No. 2015/2022. - Enabling power: Transport Act 2000, s. 247. - Issued: 17.12.2015. Made: 10.12.2015. Laid: 17.12.2015. Coming into force: 08.01.2016. Effect: S.I. 2011/3066 amended. Territorial extent & classification: E/W/S/NI. General. - EC note: These Regulations amend S.I. 2011/3066 in order to implement Commission Directive 2014/106/EU of 5 December 2014 amending Annexes V and VI to Directive 2008/57/EC of the European Parliament and of the Council on the interoperability of the rail system within the Community. - 4p.: 30 cm. - 978-0-11-114197-7 £4.25

The Railways (North and East London Lines) Exemption Order 2015 No. 2015/237. - Enabling power: Railways Act 1993, s. 24 (1) (2). - Issued: 18.02.2015. Made: 11.02.2015. Laid: 18.02.2015. Coming into force: 31.05.2015. Effect: None. Territorial extent & classification: E/W/S. General. - 4p.: 30 cm. - 978-0-11-112979-1 £4.25

The Train Driving Licences and Certificates (Amendment) Regulations 2015 No. 2015/1798. - Enabling power: European Communities Act 1972, s. 2 (2). - Issued: 22.10.2015. Made: 15.10.2015. Laid: 21.10.2015. Coming into force: In accord. with reg. 1. Effect: S.I. 2010/724 amended. Territorial extent & classification: E/W/S. General. - 8p.: 30 cm. - 978-0-11-114000-0 £4.25

Transport: Sustainable and renewable fuels

The Renewable Transport Fuel Obligations (Amendment) Order 2015 No. 2015/534. - Enabling power: Energy Act 2004, ss. 124 (1) (2), 125A (1) (a), 125B (1) (a), 126 (1) (2) (j) (k), 192 (4) (a) (c). - Issued: 11.03.2015. Made: 04.03.2015. Coming into force: 15.04.2015. Effect: S.I. 2007/3072 amended. Territorial extent & classification: E/W/S/NI. General. - Supersedes draft SI (ISBN 9780111126776) issued 14/01/15 - 4p.: 30 cm. - 978-0-11-113215-9 £4.25

Transport and works, England

The Crossrail (Plumstead Sidings) Order 2015 No. 2015/781. - Enabling power: Transport and Works Act 1992, ss. 1, 5, sch. 1, paras. 1 to 5, 7, 8, 10, 11, 15 to 17 & Crossrail Act 2008, s. 48. - Issued: 09.04.2015. Made: 31.03.2015. Coming into force: 21.04.2015. Effect: None. Territorial extent & classification: E. General. - 20p.: 30 cm. - 978-0-11-113633-1 £6.00

The Ecclesbourne Valley Railway Order 2015 No. 2015/1652. - Enabling power: Transport and Works Act 1992, ss. 1, 5, sch. 1, paras 1, 8, 15, 17. - Issued: 11.09.2015. Made: 07.09.2015. Coming into force: 28.09.2015. Effect: S.I. 1996/2660 partially revoked. Territorial extent & classification: E. Local. - 8p.: 30 cm. - 978-0-11-113902-8 £6.00

The London Underground (Bank Station Capacity Upgrade) Order 2015 No. 2015/2044. - Enabling power: Transport and Works Act 1992 ss. 1, 5, , sch. 1, paras 1 to 5, 7, 8, 10, 11, 15 to 17. - Issued: 30.12.2015. Made: 22.12.2015. Coming into force: 12.01.2016. Effect: None. Territorial extent & classification: E. Local. - 60p.: 30 cm. - 978-0-11-114259-2 £10.00

The Network Rail (Blackthorn and Piddington) (Land Acquisition) Order 2015 No. 2015/1684. - Enabling power: Transport and Works Act 1992, ss. 1, 5, sch. 1, paras 3 to 5, 7, 11, 16. - Issued: 21.09.2015. Made: 09.09.2015. Coming into force: 30.09.2015. Effect: None. Territorial extent & classification: E.Local. - 16p.: 30 cm. - 978-0-11-113928-8 £6.00

The Network Rail (Ordsall Chord) Order 2015 No. 2015/780. - Enabling power: Transport and Works Act 1992, ss. 1, 3, 5, sch. 1, paras 1 to 5, 7, 8, 10, 11, 16. - Issued: 14.04.2015. Made: 31.03.2015. Coming into force: 21.04.2015. Effect: None. Territorial extent & classification: E. Local - 56p.: 30 cm. - 978-0-11-113634-8 £10.00

The Network Rail (Tinsley Chord) Order 2015 No. 2015/1876. - Enabling power: Transport and Works Act 1992, ss. 1, 5, sch. 1, paras 1 to 4, 7 to 12, 16. - Issued: 03.12.2015. Made: 25.11.2015. Coming into force: 16.12.2015. Effect: None. Territorial extent & classification: E. Local. - 36p.: 30 cm. - 978-0-11-114129-8 £10.00

Transport, England

The Crossrail (Plumstead Sidings) Order 2015 No. 2015/781. - Enabling power: Transport and Works Act 1992, ss. 1, 5, sch. 1, paras. 1 to 5, 7, 8, 10, 11, 15 to 17 & Crossrail Act 2008, s. 48. - Issued: 09.04.2015. Made: 31.03.2015. Coming into force: 21.04.2015. Effect: None. Territorial extent & classification: E. General. - 20p.: 30 cm. - 978-0-11-113633-1 £6.00

The Ecclesbourne Valley Railway Order 2015 No. 2015/1652. - Enabling power: Transport and Works Act 1992, ss. 1, 5, sch. 1, paras 1, 8, 15, 17. - Issued: 11.09.2015. Made: 07.09.2015. Coming into force: 28.09.2015. Effect: S.I. 1996/2660 partially revoked. Territorial extent & classification: E. Local. - 8p.: 30 cm. - 978-0-11-113902-8 £6.00

The Greater Manchester Combined Authority (Amendment) Order 2015 No. 2015/960. - Enabling power: Local Democracy, Economic Development and Construction Act 2009, ss. 104 (1), 114 (1) (2). - Issued: 02.04.2015. Made: 26.03.2015. Coming into force: In accord. with art. 1. Effect: S.I. 2011/908 amended. Territorial extent & classification: E. General. - Supersedes draft S.I. (ISBN 9780111130452) issued 02/03/15. - 8p.: 30 cm. - 978-0-11-113589-1 £4.25

The London Underground (Bank Station Capacity Upgrade) Order 2015 No. 2015/2044. - Enabling power: Transport and Works Act 1992 ss. 1, 5, , sch. 1, paras 1 to 5, 7, 8, 10, 11, 15 to 17. - Issued: 30.12.2015. Made: 22.12.2015. Coming into force: 12.01.2016. Effect: None. Territorial extent & classification: E. Local. - 60p.: 30 cm. - 978-0-11-114259-2 £10.00

The Network Rail (Blackthorn and Piddington) (Land Acquisition) Order 2015 No. 2015/1684. - Enabling power: Transport and Works Act 1992, ss. 1, 5, sch. 1, paras 3 to 5, 7, 11, 16. - Issued: 21.09.2015. Made: 09.09.2015. Coming into force: 30.09.2015. Effect: None. Territorial extent & classification: E.Local. - 16p.: 30 cm. - 978-0-11-113928-8 £6.00

The Network Rail (Ordsall Chord) Order 2015 No. 2015/780. - Enabling power: Transport and Works Act 1992, ss. 1, 3, 5, sch. 1, paras 1 to 5, 7, 8, 10, 11, 16. - Issued: 14.04.2015. Made: 31.03.2015. Coming into force: 21.04.2015. Effect: None. Territorial extent & classification: E. Local - 56p.: 30 cm. - 978-0-11-113634-8 £10.00

The Network Rail (Tinsley Chord) Order 2015 No. 2015/1876. - Enabling power: Transport and Works Act 1992, ss. 1, 5, sch. 1, paras 1 to 4, 7 to 12, 16. - Issued: 03.12.2015. Made: 25.11.2015. Coming into force: 16.12.2015. Effect: None. Territorial extent & classification: E. Local. - 36p.: 30 cm. - 978-0-11-114129-8 £10.00

The Railways (Crossrail Services) Exemption Order 2015 No. 2015/239. - Enabling power: Railways Act 1193, s. 24 (1) (2). - Issued: 19.02.2015. Made: 11.02.2015. Laid: 18.02.2015. Coming into force: 31.05.2015. Effect: None. Territorial extent & classification: GB but applies only to E. General. - 4p.: 30 cm. - 978-0-11-112981-4 £4.25

Tribunals and inquiries

The Employment Tribunals and the Employment Appeal Tribunal Fees (Amendment) Order 2015 No. 2015/414. - Enabling power: Tribunals, Courts and Enforcement Act 2007, ss. 42 (1) (d) (2), 49 (3). - Issued: 05.03.2015. Made: 26.02.2015. Laid: 03.03.2015. Coming into force: 25.03.2015. Effect: S.I. 2013/1893. Territorial extent & classification: E/W/S. General. - 4p.: 30 cm. - 978-0-11-113107-7 £4.25

The First-tier Tribunal and Upper Tribunal (Chambers) (Amendment) Order 2015 No. 2015/1563. - Enabling power: Tribunals, Courts and Enforcement Act 2007, s. 7 (9). - Issued: 28.07.2015. Made: 20.07.2015. Laid: 22.07.2015. Coming into force: 01.10.2015. Effect: S.I. 2010/2655 amended. Territorial extent & classification: E/W/S/NI. General. - 2p.: 30 cm. - 978-0-11-113844-1 £4.25

The Section 16 Enterprise Act 2002 Regulations 2015 No. 2015/1643. - Enabling power: Enterprise Act 2002, s. 16 (1) (a). - Issued: 10.09.2015. Made: 03.09.2015. Laid: 07.09.2015. Coming into force: 01.10.2015. Effect: None. Territorial extent & classification: E/W/S/NI. General. - 2p.: 30 cm. - 978-0-11-113889-2 £4.25

The Tribunal Procedure (Amendment) Rules 2015 No. 2015/1510 (L.19). - Enabling power: Tribunals, Courts and Enforcement Act 2007, s. 22, sch. 5. - Issued: 17.07.2015. Made: 08.07.2015. Laid: 15.07.2015. Coming into force: 21.08.2015. Effect: S.I. 2008/2685, 2698, 2699 amended. Territorial extent & classification: E/W/S/NI. General. - 12p.: 30 cm. - 978-0-11-113784-0 £6.00

Tribunals and inquiries, England

The Town and Country Planning (Hearings and Inquiries Procedures) (England) (Amendment and Revocation) Rules 2015 No. 2015/316. - Enabling power: Tribunals and Inquiries Act 1992, s. 9. - Issued: 24.02.2015. Made: 18.02.2015. Laid: 23.02.2015. Coming into force: 06.04.2015. Effect: S.I. 2000/1624, 1625, 1626 amended & S.I. 1992/2038; 2006/1282; 2008/2931; 2009/455; 2011/1824 revoked with saving & S.I. 1986/420; 2002/1223; 2005/2115 revoked. Territorial extent & classification: E. General. - 8p.: 30 cm. - 978-0-11-113004-9 £6.00

Tribunals and inquiries, England and Wales

The Transfer of Tribunal Functions (Transport Tribunal) Order 2015 No. 2015/65. - Enabling power: Tribunals, Courts and Enforcement Act 2007, ss 30 (1) (b) (4), 38. - Issued: 02.02.2015. Made: 26.01.2015. Coming into force: In accord. with art. 1. Effect: S.I. 2000/3226. Territorial extent & classification: E/W. General. - 4p.: 30 cm. - 978-0-11-112801-5 £4.25

United Nations

The United Nations Sanctions (Miscellaneous Amendments) Order 2015 No. 2015/2014. - Enabling power: United Nations Act 1946, s. 1. - Issued: 16.12.2015. Made: 09.12.2015. Laid: 16.12.2015. Coming into force: 25.01.2016. Effect S.I. 2002/2628; 2004/348; 2009/1749 amended. Territorial extent & classification: E/W/S/NI. General. - 4p.: 30 cm. - 978-0-11-114194-6 £4.25

Urban development, England

The Ebbsfleet Development Corporation (Area and Constitution) Order 2015 No. 2015/747. - Enabling power: Local Government, Planning and Land Act 1980, ss. 134 (1), 135 (1), 135 (4), sch. 26, para. 1. - Issued: 02.04.2015. Made: 26.03.2015. Laid: 27.03.2015. Coming into force: 20.04.2015. Effect: None. Territorial extent & classification: E. General. - 4p., plan: 30 cm. - 978-0-11-113572-3 £5.25

The Ebbsfleet Development Corporation (Planning Functions) Order 2015 No. 2015/748. - Enabling power: Local Government, Planning and Land Act 1980, ss. 149 (1) (3) (11) (13). - Issued: 02.04.2015. Made: 26.03.2015. Laid: 27.03.2015. Coming into force: 01.07.2015. Effect: 1990 c.9 modified. Territorial extent & classification: E. General. - 8p.: 30 cm. - 978-0-11-113575-4 £6.00

The Old Oak and Park Royal Development Corporation (Establishment) Order 2015 No. 2015/53. - Enabling power: Localism Act 2011, s. 198. - Issued: 30.01.2015. Made: 23.01.2015. Laid: 27.01.2015. Coming into force: 01.04.2015. Effect: None. Territorial extent & classification: E. General. - 2p.: 30 cm. - 978-0-11-112784-1 £4.25

The Old Oak and Park Royal Development Corporation (Planning Functions) Order 2015 No. 2015/442. - Enabling power: Localism Act 2011, ss. 198 (2) (c), 235 (2). - Issued: 09.03.2015. Made: 02.03.2015. Laid: 04.03.2015. Coming into force: 01.04.2015. Effect: 1990 c.8, c.9 modified. Territorial extent & classification: E. General. - 8p.: 30 cm. - 978-0-11-113130-5 £6.00

Value added tax

The International Tax Enforcement (Brazil) Order 2015 No. 2015/1887. - Enabling power: Finance Act 2006, ss. 173 (1) to (3). - Issued: 18.11.2015. Made: 11.11.2015. Coming into force: 11.11.2015. Effect: None. Territorial extent & classification: E/W/S/NI. General. - Supersedes draft SI (ISBN 9780111138243) issued 23/07/15 - 12p.: 30 cm. - 978-0-11-114085-7 £6.00

The Value Added Tax (Amendment) Regulations 2015 No. 2015/1978. - Enabling power: Value Added Tax Act 1994, ss. 25 (1), 26 (1) (3) (4). - Issued: 11.12.2015. Made: 07.12.2015. Laid: 09.12.2015. Coming into force: 01.01.2016. Effect: S.I. 1995/2518 amended. Territorial extent & classification: E/W/S/NI. General. - 4p.: 30 cm. - 978-0-11-114165-6 £4.25

The Value Added Tax (Caravans) Order 2015 No. 2015/1949. - Enabling power: Value Added Tax Act 1994, s. 30 (4). - Issued: 04.12.2015. Made: 30.11.2015. Laid: 01.12.2015. Coming into force: 02.12.2015. Effect: 1994 c. 23 amended. Territorial extent & classification: E/W/S/NI. General. - 2p.: 30 cm. - 978-0-11-114134-2 £4.25

The Value Added Tax (Increase of Registration Limits) Order 2015 No. 2015/750. - Enabling power: Value Added Tax Act 1994, sch. 1, para. 15, sch. 3, para. 9. - Issued: 23.03.2015. Made: 17.03.2015. Laid: 18.03.2015. Coming into force: 01.04.2015. Effect: 1994 c.23 amended. Territorial extent & classification: E/W/S/NI. General. - 2p.: 30 cm. - 978-0-11-113381-1 £4.25

The Value Added Tax (Refund of Tax to the London Legacy Development Corporation) Order 2015 No. 2015/449. - Enabling power: Value Added Tax Act 1994, s. 33 (3) (k). - Issued: 09.03.2015. Made: 03.03.2015. Laid: 04.03.2015. Coming into force: 01.04.2015. Effect: None. Territorial extent & classification: E/W/S/NI. General. - 2p.: 30 cm. - 978-0-11-113136-7 £4.25

The Value Added Tax (Small Non-Commercial Consignments) Relief (Amendment) Order 2015 No. 2015/2015. - Enabling power: Value Added Tax Act 1994, s. 37 (1). - Issued: 16.12.2015. Made: 10.12.2015. Laid: 11.12.2015. Coming into force: 01.01.2016. Effect: S.I. 1986/939 amended. Territorial extent & classification: E/W/S/NI. General. - 2p.: 30 cm. - 978-0-11-114195-3 £4.25

Veterinary surgeons

The Veterinary Surgeons (Exemptions) Order 2015 No. 2015/772. - Enabling power: Veterinary Surgeons Act 1966, s. 19 (4) (e) (6). - Issued: 25.03.2015. Made: 17.03.2015. Laid: 19.03.2015. Coming into force: 01.07.2015. Effect: S.I. 1962/2557; 1973/308; 1982/1627; 1983/6; 1988/1090; 1990/2217 revoked. Territorial extent & classification: E/W/S/NI. General. - 4p.: 30 cm. - 978-0-11-113398-9 £4.25

The Veterinary Surgeons' Qualifications (European Recognition and Knowledge of Language) Regulations 2015 No. 2015/2073. - Enabling power: European Communities Act 1972, s. 2 (2), sch. 2, para. 1A. - Issued: 29.12.2015. Made: 18.12.2015. Laid: 22.12.2015. Coming into force: 18.01.2016. Effect: 1966 c.36 amended. Territorial extent & classification: E/W/S/NI. General. - EC note: These Regulations amend the Veterinary Surgeons Act 1966 (c.36) in order to implement an amendment to Directive 2005/36/EC on the recognition of professional qualifications which requires professionals benefitting from mutual recognition of qualifications to have sufficient language skills to practice their profession in another member State and enables member States to impose controls in respect of language skills if there is reason suspect they are inadequate. - 8p.: 30 cm. - 978-0-11-114256-1 £6.00

Water, England

The Nitrate Pollution Prevention Regulations 2015 No. 2015/668. - Enabling power: European Communities Act 1972, s. 2 (2). - Issued: 18.03.2015. Made: 09.03.2015. Laid: 12.03.2015. Coming into force: 01.05.2015. Effect: S.I. 2010/1159; 2013/1001 partially revoked & S.I. 2008/2349; 2009/3160; 2012/1849; 2013/2619 revoked. Territorial extent & classification: E. General. - EC note: These Regulations continue to implement in England Council Directive 91/676/EEC (concerning the protection of waters against pollution by nitrates from agricultural sources) and Commission Decision 2009/431 granting a derogation pursuant to that Directive. - 36p.: 30 cm. - 978-0-11-113326-2 £10.00

Water, England and Wales

The Animals, Water and Sea Fisheries (Miscellaneous Revocations) Order 2015 No. 2015/751. - Enabling power: Sea Fisheries (Shellfish) Act 1967, s. 12 & Animal Health Act 1981, ss. 1, 2, 10, 29, 34 (7), 87, 88 (2) & Water Act 1983, sch. 2 paras 3 (2), 10 (2) & Water Act 1989, ss. 4 (1), 83 (1), 85 (1), 86 (1) (2), 95 (1) (2). - Issued: 24.03.2015. Made: 16.03.2015. Laid: 18.03.2015. Coming into force: 01.07.2015. Effect: S.I. 1965/2040; 1974/1555; 1976/919; 1981/677; 1982/459; 1983/159, 1720, 1927; 1989/1530, 1531, 2017, 2018; 2001/2734 revoked. Territorial extent & classification: E/W. General. - 4p.: 30 cm. - 978-0-11-113382-8 £4.25

The Environment and Rural Affairs (Miscellaneous Revocations) Regulations 2015 No. 2015/639. - Enabling power: European Communities Act 1972, s. 2 (2) & Water Act 1983, sch. 2, para. 8. - Issued: 16.03.2015. Made: 10.03.2015. Laid: 11.03.2015. Coming into force: 01.04.2015. Effect: S.I. 1981/322; 1983/1267; 1994/2349; 1996/3111, 3186; 1997/813; 1999/2197; 2000/3359 2001/3960; 2005/3522; 2010/1085; 2007/1621 revoked. Territorial extent & classification: E/W. General. - 4p.: 30 cm. - 978-0-11-113295-1 £4.25

The Water, Animals, Marine Pollution and Environmental Protection (Miscellaneous Revocations) Order 2015 No. 2015/663. - Enabling power: European Communities Act 1972, ss. 2 (2) & Water Industry Act 1991, s. 5 & Environment Act 1995, s. 9 (1) & Fur Farming (Prohibition) Act 2000, s. 5 & Marine and Coastal Access Act 2009, s. 74. - Issued: 17.03.2015. Made: 05.03.2015. Laid: 12.03.2015. Coming into force: 01.07.2015. Effect: S.I. 1989/1152 revoked with saving in England & S.I. 1996/3061; 2001/3749; 2004/1964; 2010/304 revoked. Territorial extent & classification: E/W. General. - 4p.: 30 cm. - 978-0-11-113320-0 £4.25

Water industry, England

The Anglian Water Parks Byelaws (Extension) (Revocation) Order 2015 No. 2015/924. - Enabling power: Water Industry Act 1991, s. 157 (5). - Issued: 31.03.2015. Made: 19.03.2015. Coming into force: 01.07.2015. Effect: S.I. 2003/757; 2004/1106 revoked. Territorial extent & classification: E. Local. - 2p.: 30 cm. - 978-0-11-113548-8 £4.25

Water industry, England and Wales

The Water Act 2014 (Commencement No. 3 and Transitional Provisions) Order 2015 No. 2015/773 (C.43). - Enabling power: Water Act 2014, ss. 91 (1) (3) (4), 94 (3). Bringing into operation various provisions of the 2014 Act on 06.04.2015; 01.09.2015, in accord. with arts 2, 3. - Issued: 25.03.2015. Made: 16.03.2015. Effect: None. Territorial extent & classification: E/W. General. - 6p.: 30 cm. - 978-0-11-113399-6 £4.25

The Water Act 2014 (Commencement No. 4 and Transitional Provisions) Order 2015 No. 2015/1469 (C.83). - Enabling power: Water Act 2014, ss. 9 (1) (4), 94 (3). Bringing into operation various provisions of the 2014 Act on 15.07.2015; 01.09.2015; 01.11.2015, in accord. with arts 2, 3, 4. - Issued: 10.07.2015. Made: 01.07.2015. Effect: None. Territorial extent & classification: E/W. General. - 8p.: 30 cm. - 978-0-11-113748-2 £4.25

The Water Act 2014 (Commencement No. 5 and Transitional Provisions) Order 2015 No. 2015/1938 (C.119). - Enabling power: Water Act 2014, ss. 91 (1), 94 (3). Bringing into operation various provisions of the 2014 Act on 18.12.2015; 01.01.2016 in accord. to arts 2 & 3. - Issued: 02.12.2015. Made: 24.11.2015. Effect: None. Territorial extent & classification: E/W. General. - 8p.: 30 cm. - 978-0-11-114125-0 £6.00

The Water Industry (Charges) (Vulnerable Groups) (Consolidation) Regulations 2015 No. 2015/365. - Enabling power: Water Industry Act 1991, ss. 143A, 213 (2). - Issued: 03.03.2015. Made: 23.02.2015. Laid: 26.02.2015. Coming into force: 01.04.2015 in accord with reg. 1 (1). Effect: S.I. 1999/3441; 2000/519; 2003/552; 2005/59 revoked. Territorial extent & classification: E/W. General. - 8p.: 30 cm. - 978-0-11-113055-1 £6.00

The Water Industry (Specified Infrastructure Projects) (English Undertakers) (Amendment) Regulations 2015 No. 2015/22. - Enabling power: Water Industry Act 1991, ss 36A, 213 (2) (d) (dd). - Issued: 16.01.2015. Made: 09.01.2015. Coming into force: In accord. with reg. 1 (1). Effect: S.I. 2013/1582 amended. Territorial extent & classification: Applies to the provision of infrastructure for use by any undertaker whose area is wholly or mainly in England and forms part of the law of E/W. General. - Supersedes draft SI (ISBN 9780111123232) issued 17/11/14. - 4p.: 30 cm. - 978-0-11-112711-7 £4.25

The Water Mergers (Miscellaneous Amendments) Regulations 2015 No. 2015/1936. - Enabling power: Water Industry Act 1991, s. 219 (1), sch. 4ZA, para. 1 & Enterprise Act 2002 ss. 121(1) (2) (c) (3) (d), 124 (2). - Issued: 02.12.2015. Made: 24.11.2015. Laid: 26.11.2015. Coming into force: 18.12.2015. Effect: S.I. 2003/1370; S.I. 2004/3202 amended. Territorial extent & classification: E/W/S/NI. General. - 12p.: 30 cm. - 978-0-11-114124-3 £6.00

Water resources, England and Wales

The Surface Waters and Water Resources (Miscellaneous Revocations) Regulations 2015 No. 2015/524. - Enabling power: Water Industry Act 1991, s. 92 & Water Resources Act 1991, ss. 50, 82, 102, 116, 219 (2)- Issued: 12.03.2015. Made: 03.03.2015. Laid: 06.03.2015. Laid before the National Assembly for Wales: 06.03.2015. Coming into force: 06.04.2015. Effect: S.I. 1969/976; 1989/2286; 1992/337; 1994/1057; 1996/3001; 1997/1331, 2560; 1998/389; 2003/1053; 2009/1264 revoked. Territorial extent & classification: E/W. General. - 4p.: 30 cm. - 978-0-11-113210-4 £4.25

The Water Environment (Water Framework Directive) (England and Wales) (Amendment) Regulations 2015 No. 2015/1623. - Enabling power: European Communities Act 1972, s. 2 (2). - Issued: 02.09.2015. Made: 24.08.2015. Laid before Parliament & the National Assembly for Wales: 24.08.2015. Coming into force: 14.09.2015. Effect: S.I. 2003/3242 amended. Territorial extent & classification: E/W. General. - EC note: This instrument amends certain provisions of the Water Environment (Water Framework Directive) (England and Wales) Regulations 2003 to transpose aspects of Directive 2013/39/EU. - 8p.: 30 cm. - 978-0-11-113874-8 £6.00

Water supply

The Reservoirs (Scotland) Act 2011 (Restrictions on Disclosure of Information in relation to National Security etc.) Order 2015 No. 2015/48. - Enabling power: Scotland Act 1998, ss. 104, 112 (1), 113 (2) (3) (5). - Issued: 27.01.2015. Made: 21.01.2015. Coming into force: In accord. with art. 1 (2) (3). Effect: 2010 c.29 amended. Territorial extent & classification: E/W/S/NI. General. - Supersedes draft SI (ISBN 9780111123362) issued 21/11/14. - 8p.: 30 cm. - 978-0-11-112777-3 £6.00

Water, Wales

The Nitrate Pollution Prevention (Wales) (Amendment) Regulations 2015 No. 2015/2020 (W.308). - Enabling power: European Communities Act 1972, s. 2 (2). - Issued: 12.01.2016. Made: 11.01.2015. Laid before the National Assembly for Wales: 14.12.2015. Coming into force: 08.01.2016. Effect: S.I. 2013/2506 (W.245) amended. Territorial extent & classification: W. General. - EC note: These Regulations implement in Wales Commission Decision 2013/781/EC granting derogation pursuant to Council Directive 91/676/EEC concerning the protection of waters against pollution by nitrates from agricultural sources. - In English and Welsh. Welsh title: Rheoliadau Atal Llygredd Nitradau (Cymru) (Diwygio) 2015. - 20p.: 30 cm. - 978-0-348-11223-8 £6.00

The Water Act 2014 (Commencement No. 1 and Transitional Provision) (Wales) Order 2015 No. 2015/1786 (W.249)(C.110). - Enabling power: Water Act 2014 , ss. 91 (3), 94 (3). Bringing into operation various provisions of the 2014 Act on 01.11.2015, in accord. with art. 2. - Issued: 21.10.2015. Made: 07.10.2015. Effect: None. Territorial extent & classification: W. General. - In English and Welsh. Welsh title: Gorchymyn Deddf Dwr 2014 (Cychwyn Rhif 1 a Darpariaeth Drosiannol) (Cymru) 2015. - 8p.: 30 cm. - 978-0-348-11170-5 £4.25

Weights and measures

The Clinical Thermometers (EEC Requirements) (Revocation) Regulations 2015 No. 2015/419. - Enabling power: European Communities Act 1972, s. 2 (2). - Issued: 05.03.2015. Made: 25.02.2015. Laid: 05.03.2015. Coming into force: 01.04.2015. Effect: S.I. 1993/2360 revoked. Territorial extent & classification: E/W/S/NI. General. - 4p.: 30 cm. - 978-0-11-113112-1 £4.25

The Weights and Measures (Revocations) Regulations 2015 No. 2015/356. - Enabling power: European Communities Act 1972, s. 2 (2) & Weights and Measures Act 1985, ss. 10 (1), 11 (1) (4), 15 (1) (2), 86 (1), 94 (1). - Issued: 02.03.2015. Made: 22.02.2015. Laid: 25.02.2015. Coming into force: 25.03.2015, for Part 1 of the Schedule.; 01.12.2015, for remaining purposes. Effect: S.I. 1983/530; 1985/306; 1994/1851; 2000/932, 3236; 2001/85; 2003/214; 2006/659; 2009/3045 partially revoked & S.I. 1975/655; 1976/406; 1977/1753; 1979/132; 1988/120, 186, 296, 1128; 1993/2060; 2008/1267 revoked. Territorial extent & classification: E/W/S/NI. General. - 4p.: 30 cm. - 978-0-11-113044-5 £4.25

Well-being, Wales

The Well-being of Future Generations (Wales) Act 2015 (Commencement) Order 2015 No. 2015/1785 (W.248) (C.109). - Enabling power: Well-being of Future Generations (Wales) Act 2015, s. 56 (2). Bringing into operation various provisions of the 2015 Act on 16.10.2015, in accord. with art. 2. - Issued: 21.10.2015. Made: 30.09.2015. Effect: None. Territorial extent & classification: W. General. - In English and Welsh. Welsh title: Gorchymyn Deddf Llesiant Cenedlaethau'r Dyfodol (Cymru) 2015 (Cychwyn) 2015. - 4p.: 30 cm. - 978-0-348-11169-9 £4.25

The Well-being of Future Generations (Wales) Act 2015 (Consequential Provisions) Regulations 2015 No. 2015/1924 (W.287). - Enabling power: Well-being of Future Generations (Wales) Act 2015, s. 53 (1). - Issued: 05.01.2016. Made: 17.11.2015. Coming into force: 23.11.2015. Effect: 2015 anaw 2 modified. Territorial extent & classification: W. General. - In English and Welsh. Welsh title: Rheoliadau Deddf Llesiant Cenedlaethau'r Dyfodol (Cymru) 2015 (Darpariaethau Canlyniadol) 2015. - 4p.: 30 cm. - 978-0-348-11221-4 £4.25

The Well-being of Future Generations (Wales) Act 2015 (Registrable Interests) Regulations 2015 No. 2015/1846 (W.273). - Enabling power: Well-being of Future Generations (Wales) Act 2015, sch. 2, para. 13 (2) (a). - Issued: 05.01.2016. Made: 29.10.2015. Laid before the National Assembly for Wales: 02.11.2015. Coming into force: 23.11.2015. Effect: None. Territorial extent & classification: W. General. - In English and Welsh. Welsh title: Rheoliadau Deddf Llesiant Cenedlaethau'r Dyfodol (Cymru) 2015 (Buddiannau Cofrestradwy) 2015. - 4p.: 30 cm. - 978-0-348-11220-7 £4.25

Welsh language

The Welsh Language Standards (No. 1) Regulations 2015 No. 2015/996 (W.68). - Enabling power: Welsh Language (Wales) Measure 2011, ss. 26, 27, 39, 150 (5). - Issued: 01.05.2015. Made: 24.03.2015. Coming into force: 31.03.2015. Effect: None Territorial extent & classification: W. General. - In English and Welsh: Welsh title: Rheoliadau Safonau'r Gymraeg (Rhif 1) 2015. - 72p.: 30 cm. - 978-0-348-11078-4 £14.25

The Welsh Language (Wales) Measure 2011 (Commencement No. 8) Order 2015 No. 2015/985 (W.66)(C.65). - Enabling power: Welsh Language (Wales) Measure 2011, s. 156 (2). Bringing into force various provisions of the 2011 Measure on 25.03.2015, at 16.00, in accord. with art. 2. - Issued: 07.04.2015. Made: 25.03.2015. Effect: None. Territorial extent & classification: W. General. - In English and Welsh. Welsh title: Gorchymyn Mesur y Gymraeg (Cymru) 2011 (Cychwyn Rhif 8) 2015. - 8p.: 30 cm. - 978-0-348-11063-0 £4.25

The Welsh Language (Wales) Measure 2011 (Commencement No. 9) Order 2015 No. 2015/1217 (W.80)(C.72). - Enabling power: Welsh Language (Wales) Measure 2011, s. 156 (2). Bringing into force various provisions of the 2011 Measure on 30.04.2015. - Issued: 11.05.2015. Made: 20.04.2015. Effect: None. Territorial extent & classification: W. General. - In English and Welsh. Welsh title: Gorchymyn Mesur y Gymraeg (Cymru) 2011 (Cychwyn Rhif 9) 2015. - 6p.: 30 cm. - 978-0-348-11093-7 £4.25

The Welsh Language (Wales) Measure 2011 (Commencement No. 10) Order 2015 No. 2015/1413 (W.140)(C.79). - Enabling power: Welsh Language (Wales) Measure 2011, s. 156 (2). Bringing into force various provisions of the 2011 Measure on 06.07.2015, 07.07.2015 in accord. with arts 2, 3. - Issued: 09.07.2015. Made: 23.06.2015. Effect: None. Territorial extent & classification: W. General. - In English and Welsh. Welsh title: Gorchymyn Mesur y Gymraeg (Cymru) 2011 (Cychwyn Rhif 10) 2015. - 8p.: 30 cm. - 978-0-348-11113-2 £6.00

Welsh language standards

The Welsh Language Standards (No. 1) Regulations 2015 No. 2015/996 (W.68). - Enabling power: Welsh Language (Wales) Measure 2011, ss. 26, 27, 39, 150 (5). - Issued: 01.05.2015. Made: 24.03.2015. Coming into force: 31.03.2015. Effect: None Territorial extent & classification: W. General. - In English and Welsh: Welsh title: Rheoliadau Safonau'r Gymraeg (Rhif 1) 2015. - 72p.: 30 cm. - 978-0-348-11078-4 £14.25

Welsh language, Wales

The Welsh Language Tribunal Rules 2015 No. 2015/1028 (W.76). - Enabling power: Welsh Language (Wales) Measure 2011, s. 123 (1). - Issued: 07.05.2015. Made: 08.04.2015. Laid before the National Assembly for Wales: 09.04.2015. Coming into force: 30.04.2015. Effect: None. Territorial extent & classification: W. General. - In English and Welsh. Welsh title: Rheolau Tribiwnlys y Gymraeg 2015. - 48p.: 30 cm. - 978-0-348-11092-0 £10.00

Wildlife, England

The Infrastructure Act 2015 (Commencement No.1) Regulations 2015 No. 2015/481 (C.26). - Enabling power: Infrastructure Act 2015, s. 57 (1) (b) (4) (a) (7) (c). Bringing into operation various provisions of the 2013 Act on 05.03.2015, 12.04.2015. - Issued: 10.03.2015. Made: 02.03.2015. Effect: None. Territorial extent & classification: E/W/S/NI. General. - 2p.: 30 cm. - 978-0-11-113179-4 £4.25

The Wildlife and Countryside (Registration, Ringing and Marking of Certain Captive Birds) (England) Regulations 2015 No. 2015/618. - Enabling power: Wildlife and Countryside Act 1981, s. 7 (1) (2). - Issued: 16.03.2015. Made: 05.03.2015. Laid: 11.03.2015. Coming into force: 01.07.2015. Effect: S.I. 1982/1221; 1991/478; 1994/1152; 2004/640; 2008/2357 revoked in relation to England. Territorial extent & classification: E. General. - With correction slip dated January 2016. - 8p.: 30 cm. - 978-0-11-113281-4 £4.25

Wildlife, Wales

The Infrastructure Act 2015 (Commencement) (Wales) Regulations 2015 No. 2015/990 (W.67)(C.67). - Enabling power: Infrastructure Act 2015, s. 57 (4) (b). Bringing into force various provisions of the 2015 Act on 12.04.2015 in accord. with art. 2. - Issued: 13.04.2015. Made: 24.03.2015. Effect: None. Territorial extent & classification: W. General. - In English and Welsh. Welsh title: Rheoliadau Deddf Seilwaith 2015 (Cychwyn) (Cymru) 2015. - 4p.: 30 cm. - 978-0-348-11064-7 £4.25

The Wildlife and Countryside Act 1981 (Variation of Schedule 9) (Wales) Order 2015 No. 2015/1180 (W.78). - Enabling power: Wildlife and Countryside Act 1981, s. 22 (5) (a). - Issued: 23.04.2015. Made: 16.04.2015. Laid before the National Assembly for Wales: 20.04.2015. Coming into force: 11.05.2015. Effect: 1981 c. 69 varied in relation to Wales. Territorial extent & classification: W. General. - In English and Welsh. Welsh title: Gorchymyn Deddf Bywyd Gwyllt a Chefn Gwlad 1981 (Amrywio Atodlen 9) (Cymru) 2015. - 4p.: 30 cm. - 978-0-348-11071-5 £4.25

Young offender institutions, England and Wales

The Prison and Young Offender Institution (Amendment) Rules 2015 No. 2015/1638. - Enabling power: Prison Act 1952, s. 47 (1). - Issued: 07.09.2015. Made: 27.08.2015. Laid: 03.09.2015. Coming into force: In accord. with rule 1 (2) (3). Effect: S.I. 1999/728; 2000/3371 amended. Territorial extent & classification: E/W. General. - 4p.: 30 cm. - 978-0-11-113883-0 £4.25

Youth courts and offenders, England and Wales

The Criminal Justice and Courts Act 2015 (Commencement No. 1, Saving and Transitional Provisions) Order 2015 No. 2015/778 (C.44). - Enabling power: Criminal Justice and Courts Act 2015, s. 95 (1) (6). Bringing into operation various provisions of the 2015 Act on 20.03.2015; 13.04.2015, in accord. with arts 2, 3. - Issued: 25.03.2015. Made: 19.03.2015. Effect: None. Territorial extent & classification: E/W/S/NI. General. - 8p.: 30 cm. - 978-0-11-113405-4 £6.00

Statutory Instruments

Arranged by Number

Statutory instruments 2015

1		Landlord and tenant, England
2		Income tax
3		Excise
4 (C.1)		Public service pensions
5		Local government, England
6		Social security
7		Libraries
8		Road traffic, England
9		Criminal law, England and Wales
10		River, England
		River, Scotland
11		Financial services
12		Criminal law, England and Wales
13 (L.1)		Senior courts of England and Wales
		Magistrates' courts, England and Wales
14		Housing, England
15		Road traffic
16		Gas
		Electricity
17		Companies
		Limited liability partnerships
		Business names
18		National Health Service, England
19		Financial services and markets
20		Town and country planning, England
21		Health and safety
22		Water industry, England and Wales
23		Infrastructure planning
24		Road traffic
25		Police
26		Insolvency, England and Wales
27		Local government, England
28 (W.1)		Withdrawn
29 (W.2) (C.2)		Education, Wales
30		Social security
		Terms and conditions of employment
31		Highways, England
32 (C.3)		Social security
33 (C.4)		Social security
34		Highways, England
35		Electricity
36		Excise
37		Highways, England
38		Highways, England
39		Highways, England
40 (C.5)		Criminal law
		Defence
41		Government trading funds
42		Consumer protection, England and Wales
43		Local government, England
44 (W.3)		Council tax, Wales
45 (W.4)		Road traffic, Wales
46		Social security
47		Public health
48		Constitutional law
		Devolution, Scotland
		Water supply
49		Road traffic
50		Registration of births, deaths, marriages, etc., England & Wales
51		Health and safety
52		Health care and associated professions
53		Urban development, England
54 (W.5)		Education, Wales
55		Prevention and suppression of terrorism
56		Road traffic
57		Public service pensions, England and Wales
58		National Health Service, England
59		Road traffic, England
		Road traffic, Scotland
60		Income tax
		Corporation tax
61		Financial services and markets
62		Education, England
63		Environmental protection
64		National Health Service, England
		Social care, England
		Public health, England
65		Tribunals and inquiries, England and Wales
66		Pensions
67		Social security
68		Merchant shipping
69		Local government, England
70		Local government, England
71 (W.6)		Road traffic, Wales
72		Local government, England
73		Local government, England
74		Local government, England
75		Local government, England
76		Local government, England
77		Local government, England
78		Local government, England
79		Criminal law, England and Wales
80		Income tax
81		Criminal law
82		Criminal law, England and Wales
83		Children and young persons
84		Pensions
85		Betting, gaming and lotteries
86		Cinemas and films
87		Social security
88 (W.7)		River, Wales
		Salmon and freshwater Wales
89		Social security
90		Highways, England
91		Highways, England
92		Health care and associated professions
93		Health care and associated professions
94		Public service pensions, England and Wales
		National Health Service, England and Wales
95		National Health Service, England and Wales
		Public service pensions, England and Wales
96		National Health Service, England and Wales
97		Customs
98		Environmental protection
99		Withdrawn
100		Electricity
101 (C.6)		Social security
102		Public procurement
103		Representation of the people, England and Wales
104		

	Representation of the people, England and Wales	155	Road traffic
105	Highways, England	156	Road traffic
106	Rating and valuation, England	157	Road traffic
107	Highways, England	158	Road traffic
108	Animals, England	159	Marriage, England and Wales
109	Pensions		Civil partnership, England and Wales
110	Withdrawn		Immigration
111	Local government, England	160	Road traffic
112	Local government, England	161	Road traffic
113	Local government, England	162	Social security
114	Local government, England	163	Road traffic
115	Local government, England	164	Road traffic
116	Local government, England	165 (C.9)	Intellectual property
117	Registration of births, deaths, marriages, etc., England and Wales	166	Road traffic
		167	Road traffic
118	Pensions	168	Environmental protection
119	Withdrawn	169	Designs
120	Local government, England	170	Education, England
121	Betting, gaming and lotteries	171	Income tax
122	Marriage	172	Merchant shipping
	Civil partnership	173	Social security
	Immigration	174	Social security
123	Marriage, England and Wales	175	Tax credits
	Civil partnership, England and Wales		Social security
	Immigration	176 (C.10)	Family law
124	Social security, England	177	Registration of births, deaths, marriages, etc., England and Wales
	National Health Service, England		
125	Income tax		Civil partnership, England and Wales
	Corporation tax	178	Pensions
	Electronic communications	179 (C.11)	Local government, England and Wales
126	Antarctica	180	Companies
127	National Health Service, England	181	Education, England
128	Representation of the people	182	Public service pensions
129	Infrastructure planning	183	Social security
130	Taxes	184	Local government, England and Wales
131	Income tax	185	Social security
	Capital gains tax	186	Social security
	Corporation tax	187	Social security
132	Pilotage	188 (C.12)	Police, England and Wales
133 (C.7)	Merchant shipping	189	Terms and conditions of employment
134 (C.8)	Pensions	190	National Health Service, England
135	Rating and valuation, England	191	Sea fisheries, England and Wales
136	Road traffic		Sea fisheries, Northern Ireland
137	National Health Service, England and Wales	192	Local government, England and Wales
	Social care, England and Wales	193	Road traffic
	Health services, England and Wales	194 (W.9)	Education, Wales
138	Dogs, England and Wales	195 (W.10)	Education, Wales
139	National Health Service, England and Wales	196	National Health Service, England
140 (W.8)	Education, Wales	197	Energy
141	Withdrawn	198	Charities
142	Road traffic	199 (C.13)	Highways, England
143	Energy	200 (S.1)	Constitutional law
144	Civil aviation		Devolution, Scotland
145	Energy	201	Withdrawn
146	Civil aviation	202	Social security
147	Infrastructure planning	203	Constitutional law
148	Road traffic		Devolution, Scotland
149	Road traffic		River, Scotland
150	Road traffic		River, England and Wales
151	Road traffic	204	Constitutional law
152	Road traffic		Devolution, Wales
153	Road traffic	205	Education, Wales
154	Road traffic	206	Proceeds of crime
		207	

	Registration of births, deaths, marriages, etc., England and Wales	258 (W.13)	Road traffic, Wales
208	Pensions	259	Civil aviation
209	Health and safety	260	Road traffic
	Environmental protection	261	Civil aviation
210	Charities	262 (W.14)	Road traffic, Wales
211 (S.2)	Constitutional law	263	Civil aviation
	Devolution, Scotland	264	Civil aviation
	Agriculture	265	Civil aviation
212	Sports grounds and sporting events, England and Wales	266	Civil aviation
		267	Civil aviation
213	Overseas territories	268	Road traffic
214	Parliamentary Commissioner	269	Civil aviation
215	Dangerous drugs	270	Civil aviation
216	Copyright	271 (W.15)	Road traffic, Wales
	Rights in performances	272 (W.16)	Road traffic, Wales
217	Prevention and suppression of terrorismPrevention and suppression of terrorism	273	Road traffic
		274 (W.17)	Road traffic, Wales
		275	Road traffic
218	Overseas territories	276 (W.18)	Road traffic, Wales
219	Animals, England	277	Road traffic
220	Representation of the people, Northern Ireland	278 (W.19)	Road traffic, Wales
		279	Road traffic
221	Representation of the people, Northern Ireland	280 (W.20)	Road traffic, Wales
		281 (W.21)	Road traffic, Wales
222	Northern Ireland	282 (W.22)	Road traffic, Wales
223 (C.15)	Local government, England and Wales	283 (W.23)	Road traffic, Wales
224	Education, England	284 (W.24)	Road traffic, Wales
	Children and young persons, England	285 (W.25)	Road traffic, Wales
225	Education, England	286	Public health, England
226	Terms and conditions of employment	287	Road traffic
227	Public health, England	288	Road traffic
228	Investigatory powers	289	Road traffic
229 (W.11)	Rating and valuation, Wales	290 (W.26)	Road traffic, Wales
230	Northern Ireland	291 (W.27)	Road traffic, Wales
231	Dangerous drugs	292 (W.28)	Road traffic, Wales
232	Dangerous drugs	293	Highways, England
233	National Health Service, England and Wales	294 (W.29)	Road traffic, Wales
	National Health Service, Scotland	295	National Health Service, England and Wales
	Health and personal social services, Northern Ireland	296 (W.30)	Road traffic, Wales
234	Local government, England and Wales	297 (W.31)	Road traffic, Wales
235	Public order, Northern Ireland	298 (W.32)	Road traffic, Wales
236	Civil aviation	299 (W.33)	Road traffic, Wales
237	Transport	300	Public health, England
238	National Health Service, England	301	Social care
239	Transport, England	302	Representation of the people
240	Police, England and Wales	303	Employment and training, England
	Rights of the subject, England and Wales	304 (W.34)	Road traffic, Wales
241	Road traffic	305	Social care, England
242	Road traffic	306 (W.35)	Road traffic, Wales
243	Infrastructure planning	307	Clean air, England
244	Animals	308 (W.36)	Road traffic, Wales
245	Road traffic	309 (W.37)	Road traffic, Wales
246	Education, England	310	Environmental protection
247	Education, England	311 (W.38)	Road traffic, Wales
248	Road traffic	312 (C.16)	Data protection
249	Road traffic	313	Social care, England
250	Road traffic	314	Social care, England
251	Road traffic	315	Merchant shipping
252	Road traffic	316	Tribunals and inquiries, England
253	Road traffic	317	Rehabilitation of offenders, England and Wales
254	Road traffic		
255	Agriculture, England	318	Infrastructure planning
256 (W.12)	Road traffic, Wales	319	Public service pensions, England
257	Civil aviation		

320	Withdrawn	
321	Charities	
322	Charities	
323	Medicines	
324	Environmental protection, England	
325	Legal aid and advice, England and Wales	
326	Legal aid and advice, England and Wales	
327	Landlord and tenant, England	
328	Highways, England	
329 (L.2)	Representation of the people Senior courts of England and Wales	
330	Highways, England	
331	Road traffic	
332	Road traffic	
333	Road traffic	
334	Road traffic	
335	Bank levy	
336	Social security	
337	Criminal law, England and Wales	
338	Family law	
339	Social security	
340 (C.17)	Town and country planning, Wales	
341	Local government, England and Wales	
342	Social security	
343	Social security	
344	Bank levy	
345	Social security	
346	Income tax	
347	Financial services and markets	
348	Financial services and markets	
349	Social security	
350	Plant health, England Plant health, Scotland	
351	Customs	
352	Financial services and markets	
353	Rating and valuation, England	
354	Rating and valuation, England	
355	Electronic communications	
356	Weights and measures	
357	Children and young persons, England	
358	Education, England	
359	Education, England	
360	Income tax	
361	Income tax	
362	National Health Service, England	
363	Health and safety	
364	Animals, England	
365	Water industry, England and Wales	
366	Road traffic	
367	Payment scheme	
368	Excise	
369	Financial services and markets	
370	Public service pensions, England and Wales	
371 (C.18)	Immigration	
372	Public service pensions	
373 (C.19)	Criminal law Environmental protection, England and Wales Housing, England and Wales Police, England and Wales Police, Northern Ireland	
374	Constitutional law Devolution, Scotland Licensing (marine) Electricity Environmental protection	
375 (C.20)	Children and young persons	
376	Highways, England	
377	Highways, England	
378	Highways, England	
379	Consultant lobbying	
380 (W.39)(C.21)	Housing, Wales	
381 (W.40)(C.22)	Education, Wales	
382	Plant health, England	
383	Immigration	
384	Highways, England	
385	Petroleum	
386	Marine pollution	
387	Education, England	
388	Immigration	
389	Social security	
390	Public service pensions	
391	Insolvency	
392	Road traffic, England and Wales	
393	Disabled persons Transport	
394	Withdrawn	
395	Marriage Civil partnership Immigration	
396	Marriage, Scotland Civil partnership, Scotland Immigration	
397	Marriage Civil partnership Immigration	
398	Health and safety Environmental protection	
399	Health and safety	
400	Health care and associated professions	
401	Legal services, England and Wales	
402	Road traffic	
403	Road traffic	
404	Marriage, Scotland Marriage, Northern Ireland Civil partnership, Scotland Civil partnership, Northern Ireland Immigration	
405	Road traffic, England	
406 (L. 3)	Senior courts of England and Wales County court, England and WalesSenior courts of England and Wales County court, England and Wales	
407	Offshore installations	
408	Road traffic, England	
409 (C.23)	Health care and associated professions National Health Service, England	
410	Merchant shipping	
411	Income tax	
412	Road traffic	
413	Pensions	
414	Tribunals and inquiries	
415	National Health Service, England	
416	National Health Service, England	
417	National Health Service, England	
418	Police, England and Wales	
419	Consumer protection Weights and measures	

420	Withdrawn	474	Road traffic
421 (L.4)	Magistrates' courts, England and Wales	475	Public bodies
422	Financial services and markets		Forestry
423 (L.5)	Magistrates' courts, England and Wales	476	Representation of the people
424	Rating and valuation, England	477	Energy
425 (C.24)	Environmental protection, England and Wales	478	Social security
426	Environmental protection, England and Wales	479	Environmental protection, England and Wales
427	Rating and valuation, England	480	Local government, England
428 (C.25)	Financial services and markets	481 (C.26)	Highways
429	Income tax		Wildlife, England
	Corporation tax		Energy
430	Environmental protection	482	Pensions
	Health and safety	483	Health and safety
431	Police, England and Wales	484 (W.41)	Education, Wales
432	Public service pensions, England and Wales	485	Corporation tax
	National Health Service, England and Wales	486	Banks and banking
433	Immigration	487	Financial services and markets
434	Immigration	488	Banks and banking
435	Fire and rescue services, England	489	Financial services and markets
436	Education, England and Wales	490 (C.27)	Financial services and markets
	Public service pensions, England and Wales	491	Terms and conditions of employment
437	Social security	492	Financial services and markets
438	Prevention and suppression of terrorism	493	Pensions
439	Social security	494	Local government, England
440	Social security, Northern Ireland	495	Children and young persons, England
441	Sea fisheries, England	496	Social security
442	Urban development, England	497	Pensions
443	Insolvency, England and Wales	498	Pensions
444	Constitutional law	499	Social security
	Devolution, Scotland	500	Social security
	Food	501	Pensions
445	Public service pensions, England and Wales	502	Road traffic
446	Environmental protection	503	Social security
	Licensing (marine)	504 (C.28)	Criminal law, England and Wales
	Marine management	505	Education, England
447	Financial services and markets	506	Withdrawn
448	Childcare	507 (W.42)	National Health Service, Wales
	Payment scheme	508	Merchant shipping
449	Value added tax	509 (W.43)	National Health Service, Wales
450	Representation of the people, Scotland	510	Civil aviation
451	Tax credits	511	Civil aviation
452	Tax credits, Northern Ireland	512 (W.44)	National Health Service, Wales
453	Police, England and Wales	513	Civil aviation
454	Agriculture, England	514	Civil aviation
455	Police, England and Wales	515	Civil aviation
456	Pensions	516	Road traffic
457	Social security	517 (W.45)	Road traffic, Wales
458	Merchant shipping	518	Food, England
459	Representation of the people	519	Road traffic
460	Defence	520	Road traffic
461	Police, England and Wales	521	Social security
462	Infrastructure planning	522	Childcare
463	Income tax		Payment scheme
464	Annual tax on enveloped dwellings	523	Coast protection, England
465	Public service pensions, England	524	Water resources, England and Wales
466	Public service pensions	525	Road traffic
467	Representation of the people, England and Wales	526	Road traffic
468	Pensions	527	Children and young persons, England
469	Energy conservation	528	Road traffic
470	Pensions	529	Road traffic
471	Local government, England	530	Road traffic
472	Companies	531	Social security
473	Government trading funds	532	Companies

533	Pensions	586	Road traffic
534	Transport	587 (C.30)	Data protection
	Energy		Freedom of information
535	Road traffic	588	Social security
536	Road traffic	589	Public service pensions, England
537	Childcare	590	Fire and rescue services, England
	Payment scheme		Pensions, England
538	Road traffic	591	Electronic communications
539 (W.46)	Rating and valuation, Wales	592	Public service pensions, England and Wales
540 (W.47)	Road traffic, Wales		Education, England and Wales
541	Social care, England	593	Ecclesiastical law, England
	Children and young persons, England	594	Education, England and Wales
542	Consumer protection	595	Town and country planning, England
543	Social security	596	Town and country planning, England
544	Income tax	597	Town and country planning, England
545	Social security	598	Town and country planning, England
546	Social security	599	Landfill tax
547	Financial services and markets	600	Child trust funds
548 (L.6)	Mental capacity, England and Wales	601	Education, England and Wales
549	Income tax	602	Public service pensions
	Corporation tax	603 (W.48)	National Health Service, Wales
	Capital gains tax	604 (W.49)	Fire and rescue services, Wales
550	Excise	605	Tax credits
551	Children and young persons, England	606	Income tax
552	Terms and conditions of employment	607	Social security
553	Road traffic	608	Income tax
554	Road traffic		Capital gains tax
555	Pensions	609	Building and buildings, England and Wales
556	Road traffic	610	Plant health, England
557	Road traffic	611	Arms and ammunition
558	Road traffic	612	Proceeds of crime, England and Wales
559	National Health Service, England	613	Animals, England
560 (C.29)	Road traffic	614 (C.31)	Energy
561	Road traffic, England	615	Withdrawn
562	Withdrawn	616	Capital gains tax
563	Local government, England		Corporation tax
564	Immigration		Income tax
565	Immigration	617	Rating and valuation, England
566	Northern Ireland	618	Wildlife, England
567	Social security	619	Local government, England
	Tax credits	620	Landlord and tenant, England
568	Pensions	621	Terms and conditions of employment
569	Criminal law, England and Wales	622 (W.50)	Public service pensions, Wales
570	National Health Service, England	623	National debt
571	Infrastructure planning	624	National debt
572	Human fertilisation and embryology	625	Police, England and Wales
573	Harbours, docks, piers and ferries	626	Police, England and Wales
574	Road traffic	627	Town and country planning, England
575	Financial services and markets		Infrastructure planning
576 (L.7)	Senior courts of England and Wales	628	Rating and valuation, England
	County court, England and Wales	629	Merchant shipping
	Family proceedings, England and Wales	630	Police, England and Wales
577	Social security	631 (W.51)	National Health Service, Wales
578	Social security	632	Government resources and accounts
579	Fire and rescue services, England	633	Income tax
	Pensions, England	634 (C.32)	Social security
580	Public service pensions	635 (C.33)	Capital gains tax
581	Public service pensions, England and Wales		Corporation tax
	National Health Service, England and Wales		Income tax
582	Local government, England	636	Customs
583	Road traffic	637 (C.34)	Stamp duty land tax
584	Animals, England and Wales	638 (C.35)	Landfill tax
585	Withdrawn	639	Environmental protection, England

	Animals, England		Family court, England and Wales
	Agriculture, England	688 (W.53)	Road traffic, Wales
	Water, England and Wales	689 (W.54)	Road traffic, Wales
640	Constitutional law	690 (W.55)	Road traffic, Wales
	Devolution, Wales	691 (W.56)	Road traffic, Wales
641 (C.36)	Copyright	692	Constitutional law
642	Health services, England		Devolution, Scotland
	Social care, England	693	Health care and associated professions
643	Social care, England	694	Immigration
644	Social care	695	Road traffic
645	Immigration	696	Road traffic
646 (L.8)	Senior courts of England and Wales	697	Road traffic
	Magistrates' courts, England and Wales	698	Electricity
647	Sea fisheries, England	699	Electricity
648	Sea fisheries, England	700	Constitutional law
649	Terms and conditions of employment		Devolution, Scotland
650	National Health Service, England		Court of Session
651	Withdrawn		Sheriff Court
652	Electricity	701	Employment and training
	Gas	702	Road traffic
653	Income tax	703	Road traffic
654	Representation of the people, England and Wales	704	Dangerous drugs
		705	Proceeds of crime
655 (W.52)	Rating and valuation, Wales	706 (W.57)	Road traffic, Wales
656	Representation of the people	707	Road traffic
657	Immigration	708	Road traffic
658	Coroners, England	709	Road traffic
659	Town and country planning, England	710	Legal aid and advice, England and Wales
660	Town and country planning, England	711	Road traffic
661	Sports grounds and sporting events, England and Wales	712	Road traffic
		713	Road traffic
662	Corporation tax	714	Road traffic
663	Water, England and Wales	715	Road traffic
	Animals, England and Wales	716	Trade unions
	Marine pollution, England	717	Trade unions
	Environmental protection, England	718	Electricity
664	Criminal law, England and Wales	719	Road traffic
665	Police, England and Wales	720 (W.58)	Social care, Wales
666	Local government, England	721	Electricity
667	Income tax	722	Competition
668	Agriculture, England	723	Infrastructure planning
	Water, England	724	Road traffic
669	Tax credits	725	Capital gains tax
670 (L. 9)	Senior courts of England and Wales		Corporation tax
	County court, England and Wales		Income tax
671	Pensions	726	Defence
672	Income tax	727	Defence
673	Income tax	728	Education, England
674 (C.37)	Corporation tax	729	Proceeds of crime, England and Wales
675	Food, England	730	Proceeds of crime, England and Wales
676 (C.38)	Pensions	731	Financial services and markets
677	Employment and training	732	Financial services and markets
678	National Health Service, England	733	Road traffic
679	Road traffic	734	Road traffic
680	Infrastructure planning	735	Health care and associated professions
681	British nationality		Dentists
682 (C.40)	Constitutional law	736	Road traffic
	Devolution, Scotland	737	Immigration
683	Constitutional law	738	British nationality
	Devolution, Scotland	739	Road traffic
684	Road traffic	740 (C.39)	Social security
685	Road traffic	741	Plant health, England
686	Road traffic	742	Pensions
687 (L.10)	Senior courts of England and Wales		
	Family proceedings, England and Wales		

743 (S. 3)	Constitutional law Devolution, Scotland Representation of the people	786	Transport
		787	Food, England Food, Scotland
744	Landfill tax, England and Wales Landfill tax, Northern Ireland	788	Taxes
		789	Income tax Corporation tax
745	Road traffic	790	Criminal law, England and Wales
746	Immigration	791 (C.45)	Defence
747	Urban development, England	792	Immigration
748	Urban development, England	793	Agriculture, England Animals, England
749	Environmental protection, England and Wales	794	Health care and associated professions
750	Value added tax	795	Copyright
751	Animals, England Water, England and Wales Sea fisheries, England	796	Criminal law, England and Wales
		797	Town and country planning, England
752 (W.59)	Housing, Wales	798	National Crime Agency Proceeds of crime Northern Ireland
753 (W.60)	Road traffic, Wales		
754	Financial services and markets		
755	Public service pensions, England and Wales	799	Energy conservation, England and Wales
756	Road traffic	800	Criminal law, England and Wales
757	Road traffic	801	Taxes
758 (C.41)	Infrastructure planning	802	Fees and charges
759	Proceeds of crime, England and Wales	803	Representation of the people, Wales
760	Infrastructure planning	804	Taxes
761 (S. 4)	Constitutional law Devolution, Scotland Representation of the people	805	Employment
		806	Health care and associated professions
762	Road traffic	807	Town and country planning, England
763	Road traffic	808 (C.46)	Torts, England and Wales
764	Road traffic	809	Town and country planning, England
765	Road traffic	810	Environmental protection, England
766	Petroleum	811	Social security, Northern Ireland
767	Building and buildings, England and Wales	812 (C.47)	Customs Excise
768	Immigration Nationality	813 (C.48)	Proceeds of crime, England and Wales Legal aid and advice, England and Wales Criminal law
769	Public service pensions, England and Wales		
770	Countryside, England		
771 (C.42)	Prisons, England and Wales	814	European Union
772	Veterinary surgeons	815	Environmental protection, England
773 (C.43)	Water industry, England and Wales	816	Environmental protection, England and Wales
774	Criminal law	817 (C.49)	Energy
775	Climate change	818 (C.50)	Criminal law, England and Wales
776	Environmental protection, England	819 (C.51)	Criminal law, England and Wales
777 (W.61)	Plant health, Wales	820 (C.52)	Criminal law Proceeds of crime Serious crime prevention orders
778 (C.44)	Criminal law Criminal procedure, England and Wales Criminal proceedings, England and Wales Prisons, England and Wales Legal services, England and Wales Juries, England and Wales Coroners, England and Wales Defence Supreme Court of the United Kingdom Senior courts of England and Wales Magistrates' courts, England and Wales Youth courts and offenders, England and Wales		
		821	Environmental protection
		822	National Health Service, England
		823	Antarctica
		824	Overseas territories
		825	Overseas territories
		826	Overseas territories
		827	Territorial sea
		828	Social security
		829	Public health
		830	Criminal law, England and Wales
779 (W.62)	Road traffic, Wales	831	Education, England
780	Transport and works, England Transport, England	832	Education, England
		833	Education, England
781	Transport and works, England Transport, England	834	Road traffic
		835	Road traffic
782	Merchant shipping	836	Community infrastructure levy, England and Wales
783	Withdrawn		
784	Social security	837	Road traffic
785	Channel Tunnel	838	Legal aid and advice, England and Wales

Number	Subject
839	National Health Service, England
	Social care, England
	Public health, England
	Children and young persons, England
840	Civil aviation
841 (C.53)	Local government, England and Wales
842	Companies
843	European Union
844	European Union
845	Landfill tax, England and Wales
	Landfill tax, Northern Ireland
846	Landfill tax, England and Wales
	Landfill tax, Northern Ireland
847	European Union
848 (W.63)	Public service pensions, Wales
849 (W.64)	Road traffic, Wales
850	Public bodies
851	Freedom of information
852	Financial services and markets
	Electronic communications
853	Financial services and markets
854	Road traffic
855	Energy
856	Immigration
857	Proceeds of crime, England and Wales
858	Environmental protection, England
859	Immigration
860	Arms and ammunition
861	Criminal law, England and Wales
862	Electricity
	Gas
863	Immigration
864	National Health Service, England and Wales
	Public health, England
865	Constitutional law
	Devolution, Wales
	Human tissue, England and Wales
	Human tissue, Northern Ireland
866	Capital gains tax
	Income tax
	Inheritance tax
867	Immigration
868	Proceeds of crime, England and Wales
	Legal aid, England and Wales
869	Income tax
	Capital gains tax
870	Civil aviation
871	Public service pensions, England
872 (W.65)	Land drainage, Wales
873	Taxes
874 (C.54)	Immigration
875	Electricity
876	Child trust funds
877 (L.11)	Senior courts of England and Wales
	County court, England and Wales
878	Taxes
879	Pensions
880 (C.55)	Energy
881	Local government, England
882	Legal aid and advice, England and Wales
883	Education, England
884	Local government, England
885	Representation of the people, Northern Ireland
886	Income tax
887	Education, England
888	Public passenger transport, England and Wales
889	Pensions
890 (L. 12)	Family court, England and Wales
891	Dangerous drugs
892	Pensions
893	Education, England
894 (C.56)	Succession
895	Public health, England and Wales
896	Public health, England and Wales
897	Immigration
898	Legal aid and advice, England and Wales
899	Mental capacity, England and Wales
900	Education, England
901	Education, England
902	Education, England
903	Medicines
904	Broadcasting
905	Financial services and markets
906	Prevention and suppression of terrorism
907	Constitutional law
	Devolution, Scotland
	Children and young persons
908	Ecclesiastical law, England and Wales
909	Financial services and markets
910	Financial services and markets
911	Road traffic, England and Wales
912	Civil aviation
913 (L.13)	Family proceedings, England and Wales
	Senior courts of England and Wales
	Family court, England and Wales
914	Social services
915	National Health Service, England
916	Terms and conditions of employment
917	Food
918	Environmental protection, England and Wales
919	Pensions
920	Electricity
921	National Health Service, England
	Social care, England
	Public health, England
922	Insolvency, England and Wales
	Bankruptcy
923	Land drainage, England and Wales
924	Water industry, England
925	Proceeds of crime
926	Investigatory powers
927	Investigatory powers
928	Prevention and suppression of terrorism
929 (C.57)	Electronic communications
930	Civil aviation
931 (C.58)	Income tax
932	Constitutional law
	Devolution, Scotland
	Public finance and accountability
933	Electricity
934	Environmental protection, England and Wales
935	Legal services, England and Wales
936	Public health, England
937	Investigatory powers
938	Legal services, England and Wales
939	Public health, England

940	Customs	993 (C.68)	Mental health, England and Wales
941	Income tax		National Health Service, England
	Capital gains tax		Social care
942	Excise	994 (C.69)	Deregulation
943	Excise	995	Social care, England
944	Immigration	996 (W.68)	Welsh language
945	Taxes		Welsh language standards
946	Aggregates levy	997	Immigration
947	Climate change levy		Prevention and suppression of terrorism
948	Taxes	998	Regulatory reform, England and Wales
949	Infrastructure planning		Local government, England and Wales
950	Landlord and tenant, England	999	Electronic communications
951	Consumer protection, England	1000	Broadcasting
952	Road traffic	1001	Road traffic, England
953	Gas	1002	Road traffic
954 (C.59)	Consultant lobbying	1003	Road traffic
955	Agriculture, England and Wales	1004	Road traffic
956 (C.60)	Prevention and suppression of terrorism	1005	Road traffic
957	Immigration	1006	Road traffic
	Prevention and suppression of terrorism	1007	Civil aviation
958	Highways, England	1008	Civil aviation
959	Prevention and suppression of terrorism	1009	Road traffic
960	Local government, England	1010	Civil aviation
	Transport, England	1011	Road traffic
961	Immigration	1012	Road traffic
	Police	1013 (W.69)	Fire and rescue services, Wales
962	Energy conservation, England and Wales		Pensions, Wales
963	Children and young persons, England	1014 (W.70)	Fire and rescue services, Wales
964 (C.61)	Proceeds of crime, England and Wales		Pensions, Wales
965 (C.62)	Consumer protection, England	1015	Road traffic
966	Health and safety	1016 (W.71)	Public service pensions, Wales
967	Housing, England	1017	Road traffic
968	Deregulation	1018 (W.72)	Road traffic, Wales
969	London government	1019	Road traffic
	Environmental protection, England	1020 (W.73)	Landlord and tenant, Wales
970	Civil aviation	1021	Road traffic
971	Deregulation	1022	Road traffic
972	National Health Service, England	1023	Road traffic
973	Local government, England	1024	Road traffic
974 (C.63)	Diverted profits tax	1025 (W.74) (C.70)	Local government, Wales
975	National Health Service, England	1026 (W.75)	Housing, Wales
976	Road traffic	1027	Dangerous drugs
977	Housing, England	1028 (W.76)	Welsh language, Wales
978	Pesticides	1029	Road traffic
	Public bodies	1030	Road traffic
979	Electricity	1031	Road traffic
	Gas	1032	Road traffic
980	Companies	1033	Road traffic
	Partnership	1034	Road traffic
981	Electricity	1035	Road traffic
982	Local government, England	1036	Road traffic
	Rating and valuation, England	1037	Road traffic
983 (C.64)	Proceeds of crime	1038	Road traffic
984	Road traffic	1039	Road traffic
985 (W.66)(C.65)	Welsh language	1040	Road traffic
986	Road traffic	1041	Road traffic
987 (C.66)	Extradition	1042	Road traffic
988	Public health, England	1043	Road traffic
	National Health Service, England	1044	Road traffic
989	Insolvency	1045	Road traffic
990 (W.67)(C.67)	Wildlife, Wales	1046	Road traffic
991	Health care and associated professions	1047	Road traffic
992	Extradition	1048	Road traffic

1049	Road traffic	1111	Road traffic
1050	Road traffic	1112	Road traffic
1051	Road traffic	1113	Road traffic
1052	Road traffic	1114	Road traffic
1053	Road traffic	1115	Road traffic
1054	Road traffic	1116	Road traffic
1055	Road traffic	1117	Civil aviation
1056	Road traffic	1118	Civil aviation
1057	Road traffic	1119	Road traffic
1058	Road traffic	1120	Road traffic
1059	Road traffic	1121	Road traffic
1060	Road traffic	1122	Road traffic
1061	Road traffic	1123	Road traffic
1062	Road traffic	1124	Highways, England
1063	Road traffic	1125	Road traffic
1064	Road traffic	1126	Road traffic
1065	Road traffic	1127	Road traffic
1066	Road traffic	1128	Road traffic
1067	Road traffic	1129	Road traffic
1068	Road traffic	1130	Road traffic
1069	Road traffic	1131	Road traffic
1070	Road traffic	1132	Road traffic
1071	Road traffic	1133	Road traffic
1072	Road traffic	1134	Road traffic
1073	Civil aviation	1135	Road traffic
1074	Civil aviation	1136	Road traffic
1075	Civil aviation	1137	Road traffic
1076	Civil aviation	1138	Road traffic
1077	Civil aviation	1139	Road traffic
1078	Civil aviation	1140	Road traffic
1079	Civil aviation	1141	Road traffic
1080	Civil aviation	1142	Road traffic
1081	Road traffic	1143	Road traffic
1082	Road traffic	1144	Road traffic
1083	Road traffic	1145	Road traffic
1084	Road traffic	1146	Road traffic
1085	Road traffic	1147	Road traffic
1086	Road traffic	1148	Road traffic
1087	Road traffic	1149	Road traffic
1088	Road traffic	1150	Road traffic
1089	Road traffic	1151	Road traffic
1090	Road traffic	1152	Road traffic
1091	Road traffic	1153	Road traffic
1092	Road traffic	1154	Road traffic
1093	Road traffic	1155	Road traffic
1094	Road traffic	1156	Road traffic
1095	Road traffic	1157	Road traffic
1096	Road traffic	1158	Road traffic
1097	Civil aviation	1159	Road traffic
1098	Civil aviation	1160	Road traffic
1099	Civil aviation	1161	Road traffic
1100	Road traffic	1162	Road traffic
1101	Road traffic	1163	Road traffic
1102	Road traffic	1164	Road traffic
1103	Road traffic	1165	Road traffic
1104	Road traffic	1166	Road traffic
1105	Highways, England	1167	Road traffic
1106	Civil aviation	1168	Road traffic
1107	Road traffic	1169	Road traffic
1108	Road traffic	1170	Road traffic
1109 (W.77)	Road traffic, Wales	1171	Road traffic
1110	Road traffic	1172	Road traffic

1173	Road traffic	1235	Road traffic
1174	Road traffic	1236	Road traffic
1175	Road traffic	1237	Road traffic
1176	Road traffic	1238	Road traffic
1177	Road traffic	1239	Road traffic
1178	Road traffic	1240	Road traffic
1179	Road traffic	1241	Road traffic
1180 (W.78)	Wildlife, Wales	1242	Road traffic
1181	Road traffic	1243	Road traffic
1182 (W.79) (C.71)	Local government, Wales	1244	Road traffic
1183	Road traffic	1245	Road traffic
1184	Road traffic	1246	Road traffic
1185	Road traffic	1247	Road traffic
1186	Road traffic	1248	Road traffic
1187	Road traffic	1249	Road traffic
1188	Road traffic	1250	Road traffic
1189	Road traffic	1251	Road traffic
1190	Road traffic	1252 (W.84)	Agriculture, Wales
1191	Road traffic	1253	Road traffic
1192	Road traffic	1254	Road traffic
1193	Road traffic	1255	Road traffic
1194	Road traffic	1256	Road traffic
1195	Road traffic	1257	Road traffic
1196	Road traffic	1258	Road traffic
1197	Road traffic	1259	Road traffic
1198	Road traffic	1260	Road traffic
1199	Road traffic	1261	Road traffic
1200	Road traffic	1262	Road traffic
1201	Road traffic	1263	Road traffic
1202	Road traffic	1264	Road traffic
1203	Road traffic	1265 (W.85)	Housing, Wales
1204	Road traffic	1266 (W.86)	Housing, Wales
1205	Road traffic	1267	Education, EnglandEducation, England
1206	Road traffic	1268 (W.87)	Housing, Wales
1207	Road traffic	1269	Road traffic
1208	Road traffic	1270	Infrastructure planning
1209	Road traffic	1271	Road traffic
1210	Road traffic	1272 (W.88)(C.73)	Housing, Wales
1211	Road traffic	1273	Road traffic
1212	Road traffic	1274	Road traffic
1213	Road traffic	1275	Road traffic
1214	Road traffic	1276	Road traffic
1215	Road traffic	1277	Statistics Board
1216	Road traffic	1278	Road traffic
1217 (W.80)(C.72)	Welsh language	1279	Road traffic
1218	Road traffic	1280	Infrastructure planning
1219	Road traffic	1281	Civil aviation
1220	Road traffic	1282 (W.89)	Road traffic, Wales
1221	Road traffic	1283 (W.90)	Road traffic, Wales
1222	Road traffic	1284 (W.91)	Road traffic, Wales
1223	Road traffic	1285 (W.92)	Road traffic, Wales
1224	Road traffic	1286 (W.93)	Road traffic, Wales
1225	Road traffic	1287 (W.94)	Road traffic, Wales
1226	Road traffic	1288 (W.95)	Road traffic, Wales
1227 (W.81)	Education, Wales	1289 (W.96)	Road traffic, Wales
1228	Road traffic	1290 (W.97)	Road traffic, Wales
1229 (W.82)	Road traffic, Wales	1291 (W.98)	Road traffic, Wales
1230 (W.83)	Road traffic, Wales	1292 (W.99)	Road traffic, Wales
1231	Infrastructure planning	1293 (W.100)	Road traffic, Wales
1232	Road traffic	1294 (W.101)	Road traffic, Wales
1233	Road traffic	1295 (W.102)	Road traffic, Wales
1234	Road traffic	1296 (W.103)	Road traffic, Wales

Number	Subject
1297 (W.104)	Road traffic, Wales
1298 (W.105)	Road traffic, Wales
1299 (W.106)	Road traffic, Wales
1300 (W.107)	Road traffic, Wales
1301 (W.108)	Road traffic, Wales
1302 (W.109)	Road traffic, Wales
1303 (W.110)	Road traffic, Wales
1304	Road traffic
1305 (W.111)	Social care, Wales
1306 (W.112)	Road traffic, Wales
1307	Road traffic
1308	Road traffic
1309 (W.113)	Education, Wales
1310	Civil aviation
1311	Civil aviation
1312	Civil aviation
1313 (W.114)	Road traffic, Wales
1314 (W.115)	Road traffic, Wales
1315 (W.116)	Road traffic, Wales
1316 (W.117)	Road traffic, Wales
1317	Infrastructure planning
1318	Civil aviation
1319	Infrastructure planning
1320 (W.118)	Housing, Wales
1321 (W.119)	Housing, Wales
1322 (W.120)	Road traffic
1323	Civil aviation
1324	Civil aviation
1325	Agriculture
1326 (W.121)	Road traffic, Wales
1327 (W.122) (C.74)	Education, Wales
1328	Road traffic
1329 (C.75)	Children and young persons, England
	Companies
	Insolvency
	Regulatory reform
	Terms and conditions of employment
1330 (W.123)	Town and country planning, Wales
1331 (W.124)	Town and country planning, Wales
1332 (W.125)	Town and country planning, Wales
1333 (C.76)	Consumer protection
	Competition
1334	Electronic communications
1335 (W.126)	Social care, Wales
1336	Contracts, England and Wales
	Contracts, Northern Ireland
1337	Health care and associated professions
1338	Electronic communications
1339	Electronic communications
1340 (W.127)	Road traffic, Wales
1341 (W.128)	Road traffic, Wales
1342 (W.129)	Road traffic, Wales
1343	Civil aviation
1344	Education, England
1345	Civil aviation
1346	Sea fisheries, England
1347	Infrastructure planning
1348	Food, England
1349 (W.130)	Housing, Wales
1350	Environmental protection
	Road traffic
1351	Excise
1352	Environmental protection, England and Wales
1353	Constitutional law
	Devolution, Wales
	Education, England and Wales
1354	Civil aviation
1355	Civil aviation
1356	Civil aviation
1357 (W.131)	Social care, Wales
1358 (W.132)	Social care, Wales
1359	Town and country planning, England
1360	Environmental protection
1361	Criminal law
1362	Social security
1363 (W.133)	Public health, Wales
1364	Civil aviation
1365	Civil aviation
1366 (W.134)	Housing, Wales
1367 (W.135)	Social care, Wales
1368 (W.136)	Housing, Wales
1369	Legal aid and advice, England and Wales
1370	Income tax
	Capital gains tax
1371	Child trust funds
1372	Civil aviation
1373	Withdrawn
1374	Sports grounds and sporting events, England and Wales
1375	Health care and associated professions
1376	Ministers of the Crown
1377	Education, England
	Children and young persons, England
1378	Inheritance tax
1379	Constitutional law
	Devolution, Scotland
1380	Overseas territories
1381	Overseas territories
1382	Overseas territories
1383	Overseas territories
1384	Harbours, docks, piers and ferries
1385	Landfill tax, England and Wales
	Landfill tax, Northern IrelandLandfill tax, England and Wales
	Landfill tax, Northern Ireland
1386	Infrastructure planning
1387	Harbours, docks, piers and ferries
1388 (W.137)	Electricity, Wales
1389	Civil aviation
1390	Harbours, docks, piers and ferries
1391	Environmental protection, England
1392	Consumer protection
1393	Health and safety
1394 (W.138)	Environmental protection, Wales
1395	Harbours, docks, piers and ferries
1396	Dangerous drugsDangerous drugs
1397	Electronic communications
1398	Electronic communications
1399	Electronic communications
1400	Electronic communications
1401	Electronic communications
1402 (C.77)	Deregulation
1403 (W.139)	Local government, Wales
1404	Highways, England
1405 (C.78)	Deregulation
1406	Offshore installations
1407	Terms and conditions of employment

1408	Legal aid and advice, England and Wales	1458	Education, England
1409	Electricity, England and Wales	1459	Energy
1410	Electricity	1460	Infrastructure planning
1411	Social security	1461	Local government, England
1412	Electricity	1462	Local government, England
1413 (W.140)(C.79)	Welsh language	1463 (C.82)	Criminal law
1414	Legal aid and advice, England and WalesLegal aid and advice, England and Wales	1464 (W.158)	Education, Wales
		1465 (W.159)	Social care, Wales
1415	Public sector information	1466 (W.160)	Social care, Wales
1416	Legal aid and advice, England and Wales	1467	DefenceDefence
1417 (W.141)	Environmental protection, Wales	1468	Ecclesiastical law, England
1418 (W.142)	Education, Wales	1469 (C.83)	Water industry, England and Wales
1419 (L.14)	Senior courts of England and Wales Family court, England and Wales Family proceedings, England and Wales	1470	National Health Service, England Social care, England Public health, England
1420 (L.15)	Senior courts of England and Wales Family court, England and Wales Family proceedings, England and Wales	1471	Land, England
		1472	Modern slavery, England and Wales
		1473 (W.161)	Road traffic, Wales
1421 (L.16)	Family proceedings, England and Wales Family court, England and Wales	1474	Highways, England
		1475 (C.84)	Pensions
1422	Family law, England and Wales	1476 (C.85)	Modern slavery
1423	Justices of the Peace, England and Wales	1477	Consultant lobbying
1424	Immigration Nationality	1478 (L.17)	Magistrates' courts, England and Wales
		1479	National Health Service, England Social care, England Public health, England
1425	Electricity		
1426	National Health Service, England		
1427	Animals, England	1480 (C.86)	Criminal law, England and Wales
1428 (C.80)	Family law, England and Wales Family law, Northern Ireland	1481 (W.162)	Road traffic, Wales
		1482	Criminal law, England and Wales
1429	Education, England	1483	Public service pensions
1430	National Health Service, England	1484 (W.163)	Education, Wales
1431	Environmental protection	1485 (W.164)	Education, Wales
1432	Withdrawn	1486 (W.165)	Building and buildings, Wales
1433 (W.143)	Road traffic, Wales	1487	Aggregates levy
1434 (W.144)	Road traffic, Wales	1488	Withdrawn
1435 (W.145)	Road traffic, Wales	1489	Judgments
1436 (W.146)	Road traffic, Wales	1490 (L.18)	Senior courts of England and Wales Magistrates' courts, England and Wales
1437 (W.147)	Road traffic, Wales		
1438 (C.81)	National Health Service, England Social care, England Public health, England	1491	Coroners, England and Wales
		1492	Defence
		1493	European Union
1439	National Health Service, England Social care, England Public health, England	1494 (W.166)	Social care, Wales
		1495 (W.167)	Social care, Wales
		1496 (W.168)	Education, Wales
1440 (W.148)	Road traffic, Wales	1497 (W.169)	Education, Wales
1441 (W.149)	Road traffic, Wales	1498 (W.170)	Education, Wales
1442 (W.150)	Road traffic, Wales	1499 (W.171)	Social care, Wales
1443 (W.151)	Road traffic, Wales	1500 (W.172)	Social care, Wales
1444 (W.152)	Road traffic, Wales	1501	Immigration
1445 (W.153)	Road traffic, Wales	1502	Pensions
1446 (W.154)	Road traffic, Wales	1503	Medicines
1447 (W.155)	Road traffic, Wales	1504	Merchant shipping
1448 (W.156)	Road traffic, Wales	1505 (W.173)	Education, Wales
1449	Corporation tax	1506	Justices of the Peace, England and Wales
1450 (W.157)	Road traffic, Wales	1507 (W.174)	Food, Wales
1451	Health care and associated professions	1508	Income tax Corporation tax
1452	Pensions		
1453	Landfill tax, England and Wales	1509	Income tax Corporation tax
1454	Landfill tax, Northern Ireland Income tax		
		1510 (L.19)	Tribunals and inquiries
1455	Income tax	1511	Health care and associated professions
1456	Banks and banking	1512	Social security
1457	Education, England	1513 (W.175)	Clean air, Wales

1514	Acquisition of land, England
	Compensation
1515	Commons, England
1516	Excise
1517 (W.176)	Clean air, Wales
1518	Income tax
1519 (W.177)	Food, Wales
1520	Representation of the people
1521 (W.178)	Education, Wales
1522 (W.179)	Town and country planning, Wales
1523	Criminal law, England and Wales
1524	Fire and rescue services, Wales
1525	Education, England
	Children and young persons, England
1526	Ministers of the Crown
1527	Overseas territories
1528	Overseas territories
1529	Social security
1530	European Union
1531	Antarctica
1532	Immigration
1533	Immigration
1534	Immigration
1535 (W.180)	Road traffic, Wales
1536	Constitutional law
1537 (C.87)	Social security
1538 (W.181)	Road traffic, Wales
1539	Income tax
1540	Corporation tax
1541	Corporation tax
1542	Housing, England
1543 (C.88)	Infrastructure planning
1544	Electricity
	Gas
1545	Ecclesiastical law, England
1546	Customs
1547 (W.182)	Road traffic, Wales
1548 (W.183)	Road traffic, Wales
1549 (W.184)	Road traffic, Wales
1550 (W.185)	Road traffic, Wales
1551 (W.186)	Road traffic, Wales
1552	Land drainage, England and Wales
1553	Consumer protection
	Health and safety
1554	Education, England
1555	Electricity
1556	Sports grounds and sporting events
1557	Financial services and markets
1558	Copyright
1559	National Health Service, England
1560	Duchy of Lancaster
1561	Infrastructure planning
1562	Children and young persons, England
1563	Tribunals and inquiries
1564	Education, England
1565	Withdrawn
1566	Education, England
1567	Education, England
1568	Ecclesiastical law, England
1569 (L.20)	Senior courts of England and Wales
	County court, England and Wales
1570	Infrastructure planning
1571	
	Legal aid and advice, England and WalesLegal aid and advice, England and Wales
1572	Criminal law, Northern Ireland
	Judicature, Northern Ireland
	Justice, Northern Ireland
1573	Highways, England
1574	Infrastructure planning
1575 (C.89)	Consumer protection, England
1576 (C.90)	Energy
1577	Education, England
1578 (W.187)	Social care, Wales
1579 (C.91)	Health care and associated professions
1580	Food
1581	Highways, England
1582	Education, England and Wales
1583	Health and safety
1584	Competition
1585 (W.188)	Road traffic, Wales
1586	Customs
1587	Competition
1588 (W.189)	Road traffic, Wales
1589	Civil aviation
1590 (W.190)	Road traffic, Wales
1591 (W.191)(C.92)	Education, Wales
1592	Infrastructure planning
1593 (W.192)	Road traffic, Wales
1594 (W.193)	Road traffic, Wales
1595 (W.194)	Road traffic, Wales
1596 (W.195)	Education, Wales
1597 (W.196)	Town and country planning, Wales
1598 (W.197)	Town and country planning, WalesTown and country planning, Wales
1599 (W.198)	Education, Wales
1600 (W.199)	National Health Service, Wales
1601 (W.200)	Education, Wales
1602 (W.201)	Road traffic, Wales
1603	Withdrawn
1604 (W.202)	Road traffic, Wales
1605 (W.203) (C.93)	Education, Wales
1606 (W.204)	Road traffic, Wales
1607	Taxes
1608	Civil aviation
1609	Civil aviation
1610	Northern Ireland
	Representation of the people
1611	Civil aviation
1612	Ecclesiastical law, England
1613	Ecclesiastical law, England
1614	Pensions
1615	British nationality
1616	Infrastructure planning
1617 (W.205)	Road traffic, Wales
1618 (W.206)	Road traffic, Wales
1619	Education, England
1620 (W.207)	Road traffic, Wales
1621	National Health Service, England
1622	Road traffic
1623	Water resources, England and Wales
1624 (W.208)	Road traffic, Wales
1625	Customs
1626 (W.209)	Road traffic, Wales
1627 (W.210)	Road traffic, Wales
1628	Consumer protection

1629	Consumer protection		Transport, England
1630 (C.94)	Consumer protection	1685	Social care, England
1631	Disabled persons		Children and young persons, England
	Transport	1686 (W.218)	Animals, Wales
1632 (W.211)	Road traffic, Wales	1687 (W.219)(C.98)	Education, Wales
1633 (W.212)	Road traffic, Wales	1688 (W.220) (C.99)	Education, Wales
1634 (W.213)	Road traffic, Wales	1689 (C.100)	Companies
1635	Town and country planning, England		Insolvency
1636	Education, England		Financial services and markets
1637	Health and safety		Landlord and tenant, England
1638	Prisons, England and Wales	1690 (C.101)	Modern slavery
	Young offender institutions, England and Wales	1691	Environmental protection
		1692	Merchant shipping
1639	Education, England	1693	Energy, England
1640	Environmental protection		Housing, England
1641	Deregulation	1694	Companies
1642 (W.214)	Landlord and tenant, Wales	1695	Companies
1643	Tribunals and inquiries		Limited liability partnerships
1644	Judgments	1696	Children and young persons, England
1645	Withdrawn	1697	Prevention and suppression of terrorism
1646	Landlord and tenant, England	1698 (C.102)	Prevention and suppression of terrorism
1647	Social security	1699	Civil aviation
1648	Competition	1700	Civil aviation
1649	Social security	1701	Road traffic, England
1650	Excise	1702	International development
1651	Insolvency	1703	Education, England
	Companies	1704	Civil aviation
1652	Transport and works, England	1705 (W.221)	Road traffic, Wales
	Transport, England	1706 (W.222)	Road traffic, Wales
1653	Road traffic, England and Wales	1707 (W.223)	Road traffic, Wales
1654	Ecclesiastical law, England	1708 (W.224)	Road traffic, Wales
1655	Government resources and accounts	1709	Electronic communications
1656	Harbours, docks, piers and ferries	1710 (W.225) (C.103)	Housing, Wales
1657	Road traffic		Landlord and tenant, Wales
1658	Electronic communications	1711	Sea fisheries, England
1659	Electricity		Fish farming, England
1660	Financial services and markets	1712 (W.226)	Road traffic, Wales
1661	Petroleum	1713 (W.227)	Road traffic, Wales
1662	Social security	1714 (W.228)	Road traffic, Wales
1663 (W.215)	Public health, Wales	1715 (W.229)	Road traffic, Wales
1664	Civil aviation	1716 (W.230)	Road traffic, Wales
1665	Civil aviation	1717 (W.231)	Road traffic, Wales
1666	Infrastructure planning	1718 (W.232)	Road traffic, Wales
1667	Income tax	1719 (W.233)	Road traffic, Wales
1668	Road traffic	1720 (W.234)	Road traffic, Wales
1669	Agriculture	1721	Civil aviation
1670 (C.95)	Pensions	1722	Civil aviation
1671	Road traffic	1723 (W.235)	Plant health, Wales
1672	Companies	1724	Terms and conditions of employment
1673	Offshore installations	1725	Landlord and tenant, England
1674	Licensing (marine)	1726	Consumer protection
	Marine management	1727	Consumer protection
1675	Companies	1728	National Health Service, England
1676	Civil aviation	1729 (C.104)	Prevention and suppression of terrorism
1677	Pensions		Transport
1678	Legal aid and advice, England and Wales	1730	Merchant shipping
1679 (W.216)(C.96)	Human tissue, Wales	1731	Energy
1680 (W.217) (C.97)	Local government, Wales	1732 (C.105)	Deregulation
1681	Building and buildings, England and Wales	1733 (W.236)	Employment and training, Wales
1682	Public passenger transport	1734	Civil aviation
	Highways, England	1735	Civil aviation
1683	National Health Service, England and Wales	1736 (W.237)(C.106)	Town and country planning, Wales
1684	Transport and works, England	1737 (W.238)	Road traffic, Wales

Number	Subject
1738 (W.239)	Road traffic, Wales
1739	Police, England and Wales
1740	Criminal law
1741	Corporation tax
1742	Infrastructure planning
1743	Modern slavery, England and Wales
1744 (W.240) (C.107)	Social care, Wales
1745	Landlord and tenant, England
1746 (W.241)	Road traffic, Wales
1747	Civil aviation
1748	Education, England
1749	Proceeds of crime
1750	Proceeds of crime
1751	Proceeds of crime
1752	Proceeds of crime, England and Wales
	Proceeds of crime, Northern Ireland
1753	Housing
1754	Social security
1755	Financial services and markets
1756	Environmental protection, England and Wales
1757 (W.242)	Children and young persons, Wales
1758	Health care and associated professions
1759 (W.243)	Rating and valuation, Wales
1760 (W.244)	Human tissue, Wales
1761	Employment and training, England
1762	Education, England
	Children and young persons, England
1763	Prevention and suppression of terrorism
1764	Constitutional law
	Devolution, Scotland
1765	Immigration
1766	Defence
1767	Caribbean and North Atlantic territories
1768	Civil aviation
1769	Civil aviation
1770	European Union
1771	British nationality
1772	Overseas territories
1773 (W.245)	Animals, Wales
1774 (W.246)	Human tissue, Wales
1775 (W.247)	Human tissue, Wales
1776	National Health Service, England
1777	Revenue and customs
1778 (C.108)	Criminal procedure, England and Wales
	Town and country planning, England and Wales
1779	Stamp duty
	Stamp duty reserve tax
1780	Social security
1781	Licences and licensing, England and Wales
1782	Animals, England
1783	Revenue and customs, England and Wales
1784	Social security
1785 (W.248) (C.109)	Well-being, Wales
1786 (W.249)(C.110)	Water, Wales
1787 (W.250)	Road traffic, Wales
1788 (W.251)	Road traffic, Wales
1789 (W.252)	Road traffic, Wales
1790	Capital gains tax
	Corporation tax
1791	Sea fisheries, England
1792	Children and young persons, England
1793 (W.253)	Education, Wales
1794 (W.254)	Town and country planning, Wales
1795 (W.255)	Housing, Wales
1796	Public health
1797	Road traffic
1798	Transport
1799	Education, England
1800	Education, England
1801	Withdrawn
1802 (W.257)	Children and young persons, Wales
1803 (W.258)	Social care, Wales
1804	Education, England
1805	Defence
1806	Nationality
1807	Sports grounds and sporting events, England and Wales
1808 (W.259) (C.111)	Children and young persons, Wales
1809 (C.112)	Criminal law, England and Wales
1810	Income tax
1811	Criminal justice
	Defence
1812	Defence
1813	Defence
1814	Court martial (appeals)
1815 (W.260)	Social care, Wales
1816 (C.113)	Modern slavery
1817	Criminal law, England and Wales
1818 (W.261)	Children and young persons, Wales
1819	Insolvency, England and Wales
	Fees, England and Wales
1820 (W.262)	Children and young persons, Wales
1821 (W.263)	Housing, Wales
1822 (W.264)	Town and country planning, Wales
1823 (W.265)	Children and young persons, Wales
1824	Highways, England
1825	Civil aviation
1826 (W.266)(C.114)	Housing, Wales
1827	Plant health, England
1828	Social security
1829	Infrastructure planning
1830	Infrastructure planning
1831 (W.267) (C.115)	Education, Wales
1832	Infrastructure planning
1833	Modern slavery
1834	Evidence, England and Wales
1835	International development
1836	Income tax
1837	County court, England and Wales
	Senior courts of England and Wales
	Supreme Court of the United Kingdom
1838	Animals, England
1839	Taxes
1840 (W.268)	Social care, Wales
1841 (W.269)	Social care, Wales
1842 (W.270)	Social care, Wales
1843 (W.271)	Social care, Wales
1844 (W.272)	Social care, Wales
1845	Civil aviation
1846 (W.273)	Well-being, Wales
1847	Civil aviation
1848	Withdrawn
1849	Climate change
1850	Criminal law
1851 (C.116)	Pensions

1852	Employment and training, England		Children and young persons, England
1853	Proceeds of crime, England and Wales	1896	Agriculture
1854	Proceeds of crime, England and Wales	1897	Ministers of the Crown
1855	Proceeds of crime, England and Wales	1898	Overseas territories
1856	Proceeds of crime, England and Wales	1899	Overseas territories
1857	Social security	1900	Civil aviation
1858	Local government, England	1901	Highways, England
1859	Local government, England	1902	Insurance
1860	Local government, England	1903	Civil aviation
1861	Local government, England	1904 (W.276)(C.117)	Housing, Wales
1862	National Health Service, England		Consumer protection, Wales
1863	Financial services and markets	1905 (W.277)	Rating and valuation, Wales
1864	Financial services and markets	1906	Health care and associated professions
1865	Financial services and markets	1907 (W.278)	Road traffic, Wales
1866	Immigration	1908 (W.279)	Road traffic, Wales
1867 (W.274)	Food, Wales	1909 (W.280)	Road traffic, Wales
1868 (L.21)	Family proceedings, England and Wales	1910 (W.281)	Road traffic, Wales
	Senior courts of England and Wales	1911	Financial services and markets
	Family court, England and Wales	1912	Withdrawn
1869	Education, England	1913 (W.282)	Road traffic, Wales
1870	Justices of the Peace, England and Wales	1914 (W.283)	Road traffic, Wales
1871	Local government, England	1915 (W.284)	Road traffic, Wales
1872	Local government, England	1916	Pensions
1873	Local government, England	1917	Health and safety
1874	Local government, England	1918	Civil aviation
1875	Insurance	1919 (W.285)	Social care, Wales
1876	Transport and works, England	1920 (W.286)	Social care, Wales
	Transport, England	1921	Excise
1877	Transport	1922	Civil aviation
1878 (W.275)	Housing, Wales	1923	Health care and associated professions
	Acquisition of land, Wales	1924 (W.287)	Well-being, Wales
1879	National Health Service, England	1925 (W.288)	Road traffic, Wales
1880	Withdrawn	1926	Cultural objects
1881 (L.22)	Senior courts of England and Wales	1927	Income tax
	County court, England and Wales	1928	Companies
1882	Financial services and markets		Partnership
1883	Children and young persons, England	1929	Dangerous drugsDangerous drugs
1884	International immunities and privileges	1930 (C.118)	Social security
1885	Senior courts of England and Wales	1931 (W.289)	Fire and rescue services, Wales
1886	Cinemas and films	1932 (W.290)	Housing, Wales
1887	Capital gains tax	1933	Customs
	Corporation tax	1934	Withdrawn
	Excise	1935	Environmental protection
	Income tax	1936	Competition
	Inheritance tax		Water industry, England and Wales
	Value added tax	1937 (W.291)	Environmental protection, Wales
1888	Capital gains tax	1938 (C.119)	Water industry, England and Wales
	Corporation tax	1939	Northern Ireland
	Income tax		Representation of the people
1889	Capital gains tax	1940	National Health Service, England
	Corporation tax		Local government, England
	Income tax	1941	Corporation tax
1890	Capital gains tax	1942 (W.292)	Road traffic, Wales
	Corporation tax	1943 (W.293)	Road traffic, Wales
	Income tax	1944 (W.294)	Road traffic, Wales
1891	Capital gains tax	1945	Financial services and markets
	Corporation tax	1946	Financial services and markets
	Income tax	1947	Electricity, England and Wales
1892	Capital gains tax	1948	Income tax
	Corporation tax	1949	Value added tax
	Income tax	1950 (W.295)	Road traffic, Wales
1893	Merchant shipping	1951	Education, England
1894	Charities	1952 (C.120)	Health care and associated professions
1895	Education, England		

Number	Subject
1953	Seeds, England
1954	Ecclesiastical law, England
1955	Defence
1956	Defence
1957 (C.121)	Defence
1958	Health care and associated professions
1959	Corporation tax
1960	Corporation tax
1961	Corporation tax
1962	Corporation tax
1963	Corporation tax
1964	Health care and associated professions
1965	Health care and associated professions
1966	Representation of the people, Scotland
1967	Health care and associated professions
1968	Environmental protection
1969	Defence
1970	Criminal law, England and Wales
1971	Representation of the people, England and Wales
1972	Consumer protection
1973	Environmental protection
1974	Electricity
1975 (W.296)	Landlord and tenant, Wales
1976 (C.122)	Criminal law, England and Wales
1977	Insolvency
	Fees
1978	Value added tax
1979	Income tax
1980	Animals, England
	Public health, England
1981	Terms and conditions of employment
1982	National election expenditure
	Political parties
	Representation of the people
1983	Corporation tax
	Income tax
1984	Infrastructure planning
1985	Social security
1986	Enforcement
1987 (W.297)(C.123)	Town and country planning, Wales
1988 (W.298)	Social care, Wales
	Children and young persons, Wales
1989 (W.299)	Social care, Wales
1990 (W.300)	Animals, Wales
1991 (W.301)	Fire and rescue services, Wales
1992 (W.302)	Animals, Wales
1993 (W.303)	Road traffic, Wales
1994	Immigration
1995	Electronic communications
1996	Plant health, England
1997	Agriculture
1998	Consultant lobbying
1999	Corporation tax
	Income tax
2000	Income tax
2001 (W.304)	Agriculture, Wales
2002	Income tax
2003	Harbours, docks, piers and ferries
2004	Road traffic
2005	Legal aid and advice, England and Wales
2006 (NI.1)	Social security
2007	Capital gains tax
	Corporation tax
	Income tax
2008	Corporation tax
	Income tax
2009	Corporation tax
	Income tax
2010	Education, England
	Children and young persons, England
2011	Taxes
2012	Deep sea mining
2013	Ministers of the Crown
2014	United Nations
2015	Value added tax
2016 (W.305)	Highways, Wales
2017 (W.306)	Road traffic, Wales
2018	National Health Service, England
2019 (W.307) (C.124)	Local government, Wales
2020 (W.308)	Agriculture, Wales
	Water, Wales
2021	Terms and conditions of employment
2022	Transport
	Railways
2023	Animals, England
2024	Road traffic
2025	National Health Service, England
2026	Local government, England
2027	Charities
2028	Police, England and Wales
2029 (C.125)	Companies
	Employment
2030	Highways, England
2031	Police, England and Wales
2032	London government
2033	Education, England
2034	Local government, England
2035 (C.126)	Income tax
2036	Local government, England
2037 (W.309)	Road traffic, Wales
2038	Financial services and markets
2039	Rating and valuation, England
2040	Electricity
2041	Council tax, England
2042	Public records
2043	Withdrawn
2044	Transport and works, England
	Transport, England
2045	Electricity
2046 (W.310) (C.127)	Housing, Wales
2047	Corporation tax
2048	Evidence, England and Wales
2049	Legal aid and advice, England and Wales
2050	Excise
2051	Income tax
2052	Regulatory reform
	Broadcasting
2053	Capital gains tax
	Corporation tax
	Income tax
2054	Terms and conditions of employment
2055 (C.128)	Banks and banking
2056	Capital gains tax
	Corporation tax
	Income tax
	Stamp duty
	Stamp duty reserve tax

2057	Police, England and Wales	560 (C.29)
	Pensions, England and Wales	587 (C.30)
2058 (C.129)	Pensions	614 (C.31)
2059	Professional qualifications	634 (C.32)
2060	Disclosure of information	635 (C.33)
2061	Financial services and markets	637 (C.34)
2062	Government resources and accounts	638 (C.35)
2063	Local government, England	641 (C.36)
2064	Defence	674 (C.37)
2065	Terms and conditions of employment	676 (C.38)
2066	Electronic communications	682 (C.40)
2067	Insolvency	740 (C.39)
2068 (W.311)	Rating and valuation, Wales	758 (C.41)
2069	International development	771 (C.42)
2070	Infrastructure planning	773 (C.43)
2071	Infrastructure planning	778 (C.44)
2072	Farriers	791 (C.45)
2073	Veterinary surgeons	808 (C.46)
2074 (C.130)	Education, England and Wales	812 (C.47)
2075	Education, England	813 (C.48)
2076 (W.312)	Sea fisheries, Wales	817 (C.49)
2077 (W.313)	Road traffic, Wales	818 (C.50)
2078 (W.314)	Road traffic, Wales	819 (C.51)
2079 (W.315)	Road traffic, Wales	820 (C.52)
2080 (W.316)	Road traffic, Wales	841 (C.53)
2081	Road traffic	874 (C.54)
2082	Landlord and tenant, England	880 (C.55)

Subsidiary Numbers

Commencement orders (bring an act or part of an act into operation) 2015

4 (C.1)
29 (W.2) (C.2)
32 (C.3)
33 (C.4)
40 (C.5)
101 (C.6)
133 (C.7)
134 (C.8)
165 (C.9)
176 (C.10)
179 (C.11)
188 (C.12)
199 (C.13)
223 (C.15)
312 (C.16)
340 (C.17)
371 (C.18)
373 (C.19)
375 (C.20)
380 (W.39)(C.21)
381 (W.40)(C.22)
409 (C.23)
425 (C.24)
428 (C.25)
481 (C.26)
490 (C.27)
504 (C.28)

894 (C.56)
929 (C.57)
931 (C.58)
954 (C.59)
956 (C.60)
964 (C.61)
965 (C.62)
974 (C.63)
983 (C.64)
985 (W.66)(C.65)
987 (C.66)
990 (W.67)(C.67)
993 (C.68)
994 (C.69)
1025 (W.74) (C.70)
1182 (W.79) (C.71)
1217 (W.80)(C.72)
1272 (W.88)(C.73)
1327 (W.122) (C.74)
1329 (C.75)
1333 (C.76)
1402 (C.77)
1405 (C.78)
1413 (W.140)(C.79)
1428 (C.80)
1438 (C.81)
1463 (C.82)
1469 (C.83)
1475 (C.84)
1476 (C.85)
1480 (C.86)
1537 (C.87)
1543 (C.88)
1575 (C.89)
1576 (C.90)
1579 (C.91)
1591 (W.191)(C.92)
1605 (W.203)(C.93)

1630 (C.94)
1670 (C.95)
1679 (W.216)(C.96)
1680 (W.217)(C.97)
1687 (W.219)(C.98)
1688 (W.220)(C.99)
1689 (C.100)
1690 (C.101)
1698 (C.102)
1710 (W.225) (C.103)
1729 (C.104)
1732 (C.105)
1736 (W.237)(C.106)
1744 (W.240)(C.107)
1778 (C.108)
1785 (W.248)(C.109)
1786 (W.249)(C.110)
1808 (W.259)(C.111)
1809 (C.112)
1816 (C.113)
1826 (W.266)(C.114)
1831 (W.267)(C.115)
1851 (C.116)
1904 (W.276)(C.117)
1930 (C.118)
1938 (C.119)
1952 (C.120)
1957 (C.121)
1976 (C.122)
1987 (W.297)(C.123)
2019 (W.307) (C.124)
2029 (C.125)
2035 (C.126)
2046 (W.310) (C.127)
2055 (C.128)
2058 (C.129)
2074 (C.130)

Instruments relating to fees or procedure in courts in England and Wales 2015

13 (L.1)
329 (L.2)
406 (L.3)
406 (L.3)
421 (L.4)
423 (L.5)
548 (L.6)
576 (L.7)
646 (L.8)
670 (L.9)
687 (L.10)
877 (L.11)
890 (L.12)
913 (L.13)
1419 (L.14)
1420 (L.15)
1421 (L.16)
1478 (L.17)
1490 (L.18)
1510 (L.19)
1569 (L.20)
1868 (L.21)
1881 (L.22)

Certain orders in Council relating to Northern Ireland 2015

2006 (NI.1)

Instruments that extend only to Scotland 2015

200 (S.1)
211 (S.2)
743 (S.3)
761 (S.4)

Instruments that extend only to Wales 2015

28 (W.1) Withdrawn
29 (W.2) (C.2)
44 (W.3)
45 (W.4)
54 (W.5)
71 (W.6)
88 (W.7)
140 (W.8)
194 (W.9)
195 (W.10)
229 (W.11)
256 (W.12)
258 (W.13)
262 (W.14)
271 (W.15)
272 (W.16)
274 (W.17)
276 (W.18)
278 (W.19)
280 (W.20)
281 (W.21)
282 (W.22)
283 (W.23)
284 (W.24)
285 (W.25)
290 (W.26)
291 (W.27)
292 (W.28)
294 (W.29)
296 (W.30)
297 (W.31)
298 (W.32)
299 (W.33)
304 (W.34)
306 (W.35)
308 (W.36)
309 (W.37)
311 (W.38)
380 (W.39)(C.21)
381 (W.40)(C.22)
484 (W.41)
507 (W.42)
509 (W.43)
512 (W.44)
517 (W.45)
539 (W.46)
540 (W.47)
603 (W.48)
604 (W.49)
622 (W.50)

631 (W.51)
655 (W.52)
688 (W.53)
689 (W.54)
690 (W.55)
691 (W.56)
706 (W.57)
720 (W.58)
752 (W.59)
753 (W.60)
777 (W.61)
779 (W.62)
848 (W.63)
849 (W.64)
872 (W.65)
985 (W.66)(C.65)
990 (W.67)(C.67)
996 (W.68)
1013 (W.69)
1014 (W.70)
1016 (W.71)
1018 (W.72)
1020 (W.73)
1025 (W.74) (C.70)
1026 (W.75)
1028 (W.76)
1109 (W.77)
1180 (W.78)
1182 (W.79) (C.71)
1217 (W.80)(C.72)
1227 (W.81)
1229 (W.82)
1230 (W.83)
1252 (W.84)
1265 (W.85)
1266 (W.86)
1268 (W.87)
1272 (W.88)(C.73)
1282 (W.89)
1283 (W.90)
1284 (W.91)
1285 (W.92)
1286 (W.93)
1287 (W.94)
1288 (W.95)
1289 (W.96)
1290 (W.97)
1291 (W.98)
1292 (W.99)
1293 (W.100)
1294 (W.101)
1295 (W.102)
1296 (W.103)
1297 (W.104)
1298 (W.105)
1299 (W.106)
1300 (W.107)
1301 (W.108)
1302 (W.109)
1303 (W.110)
1305 (W.111)
1306 (W.112)
1309 (W.113)
1313 (W.114)
1314 (W.115)

1315 (W.116)
1316 (W.117)
1320 (W.118)
1321 (W.119)
1322 (W.120)
1326 (W.121)
1327 (W.122) (C.74)
1330 (W.123)
1331 (W.124)
1332 (W.125)
1335 (W.126)
1340 (W.127)
1341 (W.128)
1342 (W.129)
1349 (W.130)
1357 (W.131)
1358 (W.132)
1363 (W.133)
1366 (W.134)
1367 (W.135)
1368 (W.136)
1388 (W.137)
1394 (W.138)
1403 (W.139)
1413 (W.140)(C.79)
1417 (W.141)
1418 (W.142)
1433 (W.143)
1434 (W.144)
1435 (W.145)
1436 (W.146)
1437 (W.147)
1440 (W.148)
1441 (W.149)
1442 (W.150)
1443 (W.151)
1444 (W.152)
1445 (W.153)
1446 (W.154)
1447 (W.155)
1448 (W.156)
1450 (W.157)
1464 (W.158)
1465 (W.159)
1466 (W.160)
1473 (W.161)
1481 (W.162)
1484 (W.163)
1485 (W.164)
1486 (W.165)
1494 (W.166)
1495 (W.167)
1496 (W.168)
1497 (W.169)
1498 (W.170)
1499 (W.171)
1500 (W.172)
1505 (W.173)
1507 (W.174)
1513 (W.175)
1517 (W.176)
1519 (W.177)
1521 (W.178)
1522 (W.179)
1535 (W.180)

1538 (W.181)	1773 (W.245)
1547 (W.182)	1774 (W.246)
1548 (W.183)	1775 (W.247)
1549 (W.184)	1785 (W.248) (C.109)
1550 (W.185)	1786 (W.249)(C.110)
1551 (W.186)	1787 (W.250)
1578 (W.187)	1788 (W.251)
1585 (W.188)	1789 (W.252)
1588 (W.189)	1793 (W.253)
1590 (W.190)	1794 (W.254)
1591 (W.191)(C.92)	1795 (W.255)
1593 (W.192)	1801 (W.256) Withdrawn
1594 (W.193)	1802 (W.257)
1595 (W.194)	1803 (W.258)
1596 (W.195)	1808 (W.259) (C.111)
1597 (W.196)	1815 (W.260)
1598 (W.197)	1818 (W.261)
1598 (W.197)	1820 (W.262)
1599 (W.198)	1821 (W.263)
1600 (W.199)	1822 (W.264)
1601 (W.200)	1823 (W.265)
1602 (W.201)	1826 (W.266)(C.114)
1604 (W.202)	1831 (W.267) (C.115)
1605 (W.203) (C.93)	1840 (W.268)
1606 (W.204)	1841 (W.269)
1617 (W.205)	1842 (W.270)
1618 (W.206)	1843 (W.271)
1620 (W.207)	1844 (W.272)
1624 (W.208)	1846 (W.273)
1626 (W.209)	1867 (W.274)
1627 (W.210)	1878 (W.275)
1632 (W.211)	1904 (W.276)(C.117)
1633 (W.212)	1905 (W.277)
1634 (W.213)	1907 (W.278)
1642 (W.214)	1908 (W.279)
1663 (W.215)	1909 (W.280)
1679 (W.216)(C.96)	1910 (W.281)
1680 (W.217) (C.97)	1913 (W.282)
1686 (W.218)	1914 (W.283)
1687 (W.219)(C.98)	1915 (W.284)
1688 (W.220) (C.99)	1919 (W.285)
1705 (W.221)	1920 (W.286)
1706 (W.222)	1924 (W.287)
1707 (W.223)	1925 (W.288)
1708 (W.224)	1931 (W.289)
1710 (W.225) (C.103)	1932 (W.290)
1712 (W.226)	1937 (W.291)
1713 (W.227)	1942 (W.292)
1714 (W.228)	1943 (W.293)
1715 (W.229)	1944 (W.294)
1716 (W.230)	1950 (W.295)
1717 (W.231)	1975 (W.296)
1718 (W.232)	1987 (W.297)(C.123)
1719 (W.233)	1988 (W.298)
1720 (W.234)	1989 (W.299)
1723 (W.235)	1990 (W.300)
1733 (W.236)	1991 (W.301)
1736 (W.237)(C.106)	1992 (W.302)
1737 (W.238)	1993 (W.303)
1738 (W.239)	2001 (W.304)
1744 (W.240) (C.107)	2016 (W.305)
1746 (W.241)	2017 (W.306)
1757 (W.242)	2019 (W.307) (C.124)
1759 (W.243)	2020 (W.308)
1760 (W.244)	2037 (W.309)

2046 (W.310) (C.127)
2068 (W.311)
2076 (W.312)
2077 (W.313)

2078 (W.314)
2079 (W.315)
2080 (W.316)

SCOTTISH LEGISLATION

Acts of the Scottish Parliament

Acts of the Scottish Parliament 2014

Bankruptcy and Debt Advice (Scotland) Act 2014: 2014 asp 11 (correction slip). - 1 sheet: 30 cm. - Correction slip (to ISBN 9780105902218) dated September 2015. - Free

Housing (Scotland) Act 2014: 2014 asp 14. - iv, 84p.: 30 cm. - Royal assent, 1 August 2014. An Act of the Scottish Parliament to make provision about housing, including provision about the abolition of the right to buy, social housing, the law affecting private housing, the regulation of letting agents and the licensing of sites for mobile homes. Explanatory notes to assist in the understanding of the Act are available separately (ISBN 9780105902300). Corrected reprint of publication of same title issued 08.08.2015 sent free of charge to all known recipients of the original. - 978-0-10-590228-7 £16.00

Acts of the Scottish Parliament 2015

Air Weapons and Licensing (Scotland) Act 2015: 2015 asp 10. - iv, 72p.: 30 cm. - Royal assent, 4h August 2015. An Act of the Scottish Parliament to make provision for the licensing and regulation of air weapons; to amend the Licensing (Scotland) Act 2005; to amend and extend the licensing provisions of the Civic Government (Scotland) Act 1982. Explanatory notes have been produced to assist in the understanding of this Act and are available separately (ISBN 9780105902720). - 978-0-10-590256-0 £14.25

British Sign Language (Scotland) Act 2015: 2015 asp 11. - [12]p.: 30 cm. - Royal assent, 22nd October 2015. An Act of the Scottish Parliament to promote the use of British Sign Language including by making provision for the preparation and publication of national plans in relation to British Sign Language and by requiring certain authorities to prepare and publish their own British Sign Language plans in connection with the exercise of their functions; and to provide for the manner in which such plans are to be prepared and for their review and updating. Explanatory notes to assist in the understanding of the Act are available separately (ISBN 9780105902607). - 978-0-10-590259-1 £6.00

Budget (Scotland) Act 2015: 2015 asp 2. - [12]p.: 30 cm. - Royal assent, 11 March 2015. An Act of the Scottish Parliament to make provision, for financial year 2015/16, for the use of resources by the Scottish Administration and certain bodies whose expenditure is payable out of the Scottish Consolidated Fund, for the maximum amounts of borrowing by certain statutory bodies and for authorising the payment of sums out of the Fund; to make provision, for financial year 2016/17, for authorising the payment of sums out of the Fund on a temporary basis. - 978-0-10-590243-0 £6.00

Community Charge Debt (Scotland) Act 2015:2015 asp 3. - [8]p.: 30 cm. - Royal assent, 25th March 2015. An Act of the Scottish Parliament to extinguish various liabilities arising by virtue of the Abolition of Domestic Rates, etc. (Scotland) Act 1987. - 978-0-10-590244-7 £4.25

Community Empowerment (Scotland) Act 2015: 2015 asp 6. - vi, 127p.: 30 cm. - Royal assent, 24th July 2015. An Act of the Scottish Parliament to make provision about national outcomes; to confer functions on certain persons in relation to services provided by, and assets of, certain public bodies; to amend Parts 2 and 3 of the Land Reform (Scotland) Act 2003; to enable certain bodies to buy abandoned, neglected or detrimental land; to amend section 7C of the Forestry Act 1967; to enable the Scottish Ministers to make provision about supporters' involvement in and ownership of football clubs; to make provision for registers of common good property and about disposal and use of such property; to restate and amend the law on allotments; to enable participation in decision-making by specified persons having public functions; to enable local authorities to reduce or remit non-domestic rates. Explanatory notes have been prepared by the Scottish Government in order to assist the reader of the Act and are published separately as (ISBN 9780105902584). - 978-0-10-590251-5 £20.75

Food (Scotland) Act 2015: 2015 asp 1. - iii, 34p.: 30 cm. - Royal assent, 13th January 2015. An Act of the Scottish Parliament to establish Food Standards Scotland and make provision as to its functions; to amend the law in relation to food; to enable provision to be made in relation animal feeding stuffs; to make provision for administrative sanctions in relation to offences under the law in relation to food. Explanatory notes to assist in the understanding of the Act are available separately (ISBN 9780105902669). - 978-0-10-590242-3 £10.00

Harbours (Scotland) Act 2015: 2015 asp 13. - [2], 2, [4]p.: 30 cm. - Royal assent, 2nd December 2015. An Act of the Scottish Parliament to repeal sections 10 to 12 of the Ports Act 1991 and amend Schedules 3 and 4 to the Harbours Act 1964. Explanatory notes to assist in the understanding of the Act are available separately (ISBN 9780105902690). - 978-0-10-590263-8 £4.25

Human Trafficking and Exploitation (Scotland) Act 2015: 2015 asp 12. - iii, 32p.: 30 cm. - Royal assent, 4th November 2015. An Act of the Scottish Parliament to make provision about human trafficking and slavery, servitude and forced or compulsory labour, including provision about offences and sentencing, provision for victim support and provision to reduce activity related to offences. Explanatory notes to assist in the understanding of the Act are available separately (ISBN 9780105902621). - 978-0-10-590261-4 £10.00

Legal Writings (Counterparts and Delivery) (Scotland) Act 2015: 2015 asp 4. - [4], 4, [4]p.: 30 cm. - Royal assent, 1st April 2015. An Act of the Scottish Parliament to make provision about execution of documents in counterpart and the delivery by electronic means of traditional documents. Explanatory notes to assist in the understanding of this Act are available separately (ISBN 9780105902508). - 978-0-10-590245-4 £6.00

Mental Health (Scotland) Act 2015: 2015 asp 9. - iii, [1], 41, [3]p.: 30 cm. - Royal assent, 4th August 2015. An Act of the Scottish Parliament to amend the Mental Health (Care and Treatment) (Scotland) Act 2003 in various respects; to make provision about mental health disposals in criminal cases; to make provision as to the rights of victims of crime committed by mentally-disordered persons. Explanatory notes to assist in the understanding of the Act are available separately (ISBN 9780105902737). - 978-0-10-590255-3 £10.00

Prisoners (Control of Release) (Scotland) Act 2015: 2015 asp 8. - [2], 2, [4]p.: 30 cm. - Royal assent, 4th August 2015. An Act of the Scottish Parliament to amend the rules as to automatic early release of long-term prisoners from prison on licence and to allow prisoners serving all but very short sentences to be released from prison on a particular day suitable for their re-integration into the community. Explanatory notes to assist in the understanding of the Act are available separately (ISBN 9780105902577). - 978-0-10-590254-6 £4.25

Scottish Elections (Reduction of Voting Age) Act 2015: 2015 asp 7. - ii, 13p.: 30 cm. - Royal assent, 24th July 2015. An Act of the Scottish Parliament to reduce the voting age to 16 at elections for membership of the Scottish Parliament and local government elections. - 978-0-10-590252-2 £6.00

Welfare Funds (Scotland) Act 2015: 2015 asp 5. - [4], 7, [1]p.: 30 cm. - Royal assent, 8 April 2015. An Act of the Scottish Parliament to make provision about the maintenance of welfare funds and to provide for them to be used to help certain individuals. Explanatory notes to assist in the understanding of the Act are available separately (ISBN 9780105902485). - 978-0-10-590247-8 £6.00

Acts of the Scottish Parliament - Explanatory notes 2013

Land and Buildings Transaction Tax (Scotland) Act 2013 (asp 11): 2015 asp. - 64p.: 30 cm. - Land and Buildings Transaction Tax (Scotland) Act 2013 (asp 11) (ISBN 9780105902027) which received Royal assent on 31 July 2013. - 978-0-10-590246-1 £11.00

Acts of the Scottish Parliament - Explanatory notes 2014

Bankruptcy and Debt Advice (Scotland) Act 2014 (asp 11): 2015 asp. - 26p.: 30 cm. - These notes relate to the Bankruptcy and Debt Advice (Scotland) Act 2014 (asp 11) (ISBN 9780105902218) which received Royal assent on 29 April 2015. - 978-0-10-590249-2 £6.00

Revenue Scotland and Tax Powers Act 2014 (asp 16): 2015 asp. - 65p.: 30 cm. - These notes relate to the Revenue Scotland and Tax Powers Act 2014 (asp 16) (ISBN 9780105902355) which received Royal Assent on 24 September 2014. - 978-0-10-590253-9 £11.00

Acts of the Scottish Parliament - Explanatory notes 2015

Air Weapons and Licensing (Scotland) Act 2015 (asp 10): 2015 asp. - 51p.: 30 cm. - These notes relate to the Air Weapons and Licensing (Scotland) Act 2015 (asp 10) (ISBN 9780105902560) which received Royal Assent on 4 August 2015. - 978-0-10-590272-0 £10.00

British Sign Language (Scotland) Act 2015 (asp 11): 2015 asp. - [12]p.: 30 cm. - These notes relate to the British Sign Language (Scotland) Act 2015 (asp 11) (ISBN 9780105902591) which received Royal Assent on 22 October 2015. - 978-0-10-590260-7 £6.00

Community Empowerment (Scotland) Act 2015 (asp 6): 2015 asp. - 70p.: 30 cm. - These notes relate to the Community Empowerment (Scotland) Act 2015 (asp 6) (ISBN 9780105902584) which received Royal Assent on 24 July 2015. - 978-0-10-590258-4 £14.25

Food (Scotland) Act 2015 (asp 1): 2015 asp. - 14, [1]p.: 30 cm. - These notes relate to the Food (Scotland) Act 2015 (asp 1) (ISBN 9780105902423) which received Royal Assent on 13th January 2015. - 978-0-10-590266-9 £6.00

Harbours (Scotland) Act 2015 (asp 13): 2015 asp. - [8]p.: 30 cm. - These notes relate to the Harbours (Scotland) Act 2015 (asp 13) (ISBN 9780105902638) which received Royal Assent on 2nd December 2015. - 978-0-10-590269-0 £4.25

Human Trafficking and Exploitation (Scotland) Act 2015 (asp 12): 2015 asp. - 24p.: 30 cm. - These notes relate to the Human Trafficking and Exploitation (Scotland) Act 2015 (asp 12) (ISBN 9780105902614) which received Royal Assent on 4 November 2015. - 978-0-10-590262-1 £6.00

Legal Writings (Counterparts and Delivery) (Scotland) Act 2015 (asp 4): 2015 asp. - 9p.: 30 cm. - These notes relate to the Legal Writings (Counterparts and Delivery) (Scotland) Act 2015 (asp 4) (ISBN 9780105902454) which received Royal Assent on 1 April 2015. - 978-0-10-590250-8 £6.00

Mental Health (Scotland) Act 2015 (asp 9): 2015 asp. - 36p.: 30 cm. - These notes relate to the Mental Health (Scotland) Act 2015 (asp 9) (ISBN 9780105902553) which received Royal assent on 4th August 2015. - 978-0-10-590273-7 £10.00

National Galleries of Scotland 2015 (asp 6): 2015 asp. - [8]p.: 30 cm. - These notes relate to the National Galleries of Scotland Act 2016 (asp 6) (ISBN 9780105902751) which received Royal assent on 23 February 2016. - 978-0-10-590276-8 £4.25

Prisoners (Control of Release) (Scotland) Act 2015 (asp 8): 2015 asp. - [12]p.: 30 cm. - These notes relate to the Prisoners (Control of Release) (Scotland) Act 2015 (asp 8) (ISBN 9780105902546) which received Royal Assent on 4th August 2015. - 978-0-10-590257-7 £6.00

Welfare Funds (Scotland) Act 2015 (asp 5): 2015 asp. - [16]p.: 30 cm. - These notes relate to the Welfare Funds (Scotland) Act 2015 (asp 5) (ISBN 9780105902478) which received Royal assent on 8 April 2015. - 978-0-10-590248-5 £6.00

Scottish Statutory Instruments

By Subject Heading

Adults with incapacity

The Adults with Incapacity (Public Guardian's Fees) (Scotland) Regulations 2015 No. 2015/260. - Enabling power: Adults with Incapacity (Scotland) Act 2000, ss. 7 (2), 86 (2). - Issued: 22.06.2015. Made: 15.06.2015. Laid before the Scottish Parliament: 17.06.2015. Coming into force: In accord. with reg. 1. Effect: S.S.I. 2002/131; 2007/320; 2008/52, 238; 2012/289 revoked (22.09.2015). Territorial extent & classification: S. General - 16p.: 30 cm. - 978-0-11-102840-7 £6.00

Agriculture

The Common Agricultural Policy (Direct Payments etc.) (Scotland) Amendment Regulations 2015 No. 2015/215. - Enabling power: European Communities Act 1972, s. 2 (2). - Issued: 02.06.2015. Made: 26.05.2015. Laid before the Scottish Parliament: 28.05.2015. Coming into force: In accord with reg. 1. Effect: S.S.I. 2014/325; 2015/58 amended. Territorial extent & classification: S. General. - EC note: These Regulations amend the Common Agricultural Policy (Direct Payments etc.) (Scotland) Regulations 2015 ("the principal Regulations"), which make provision in Scotland for the administration of Regulation (EU) no. 1307/2013 and other associated EU regulations as referred to in regulation 2 (1) of the principal Regulations. - 12p.: 30 cm. - 978-0-11-102798-1 £6.00

The Common Agricultural Policy (Direct Payments etc.) (Scotland) Regulations 2015 No. 2015/58. - Enabling power: European Communities Act 1972, s. 2 (2), sch. 2, para. 1A. - Issued: 19.02.2015. Made: 13.02.2015. Laid before the Scottish Parliament: 13.02.2015. Coming into force: 16.03.2015. Effect: S.S.I. 2009/376; 2014/325 amended & S.S.I. 2011/416; 2013/265 revoked with savings & S.S.I. 2008/184; 2009/391 revoked. Territorial extent & classification: S. General. - EC note: These regs make provision in Scotland for the administration of Regulation (EU) 1307/2013 establishing rules for direct payments to farmers under support schemes within the framework of the common agricultural policy, as amended by Regulation (EU) 1310/2013 and other associated regulations. Partially revoked by SSI 2015/194 (ISBN 9780111027790). - 20p.: 30 cm. - 978-0-11-102639-7 £6.00

The Common Agricultural Policy Non-IACS Support Schemes (Appeals) (Scotland) Amendment Regulations 2015 No. 2015/167. - Enabling power: European Communities Act 1972, s. 2 (2), sch. 2, para. 1A. - Issued: 13.04.2015. Made: 02.04.2015. Laid before the Scottish Parliament: 08.04.2015. Coming into force: 25.05.2015. Effect: S.S.I. 2004/278 amended. Territorial extent & classification: S. General. - 16p.: 30 cm. - 978-0-11-102753-0 £6.00

The Less Favoured Area Support Scheme (Scotland) Amendment Regulations 2015 No. 2015/185. - Enabling power: European Communities Act 1972, s. 2 (2), sch. 2, para 1A. - Issued: 06.05.2015. Made: 29.04.2015. Laid before the Scottish Parliament: 01.05.2015. Coming into force: 09.06.2015. Effect: S.S.I. 2010/273 amended. Territorial extent & classification: S. General. - 12p.: 30 cm. - 978-0-11-102770-7 £6.00

The Rural Development (Scotland) Regulations 2015 No. 2015/192. - Enabling power: European Communities Act 1972, s. 2 (2). - Issued: 19.05.2015. Made: 12.05.2015. Laid before the Scottish Parliament: 14.05.2015. Coming into force: 12.06.2015. Effect: S.S.I. 2008/64, 66, 100, 135, 159, 162, 233; 2009/1, 155, 233, 335, 411; 2010/87; 2011/85, 106, 260; 2012/182, 307; 2013/309 revoked with saving. Territorial extent & classification: S. General. - 20p.: 30 cm. - 978-0-11-102778-3 £6.00

The Rural Payments (Appeals) (Scotland) Regulations 2015 No. 2015/194. - Enabling power: European Communities Act 1972, s. 2 (2), sch. 2, para. 1A. - Issued: 20.05.2015. Made: 12.05.2015. Laid before the Scottish Parliament: 14.05.2015. Coming into force: 12.06.2015. Effect: S.S.I. 2010/273; 2014/7, 325; 2015/58 partially revoked & S.S.I. 2009/376; 2012/143 revoked with savings. Territorial extent & classification: S. General. - EC note: These Regulations provide for the review of certain decisions of the Scottish Ministers in relation to payment of certain agricultural subsidies and other rural payments. - 12p.: 30 cm. - 978-0-11-102779-0 £6.00

Ancient monuments

The Historic Environment Scotland Act 2014 (Ancillary Provision) Order 2015 No. 2015/271. - Enabling power: Historic Environment Act 2014, s. 27 (1) & Regulatory Reform (Scotland) Act 2014, s. 7. - Issued: 30.06.2015. Made: 24.06.2015. Coming into force: 01.10.2015. Effect: 1984 (C.54); 2003 asp 2, asp 8; 2005 asp 15; 2006 asp 1; 2014 asp 3, asp 12 modified. Territorial extent & classification: S. General. - Supersedes draft S.I. (ISBN 9780111027837) issued 21.05.2015. - 4p.: 30 cm. - 978-0-11-102851-3 £4.25

The Historic Environment Scotland Act 2014 (Commencement No. 2) Order 2015 No. 2015/31 (C.6). - Enabling power: Historic Environment Act 2014, s. 31 (2). Bringing into operation various provisions of the 2014 Act on 27.02.2015 in accord. with art. 2. - Issued: 04.02.2015. Made: 28.01.2015. Laid before the Scottish Parliament: 30.01.2015. Effect: None. Territorial extent & classification: S. General. - 4p.: 30 cm. - 978-0-11-102606-9 £4.25

The Historic Environment Scotland Act 2014 (Commencement No. 3) Order 2015 No. 2015/196 (C.31). - Enabling power: Historic Environment Act 2014, s. 31 (2). Bringing into operation various provisions of the 2014 Act on 01.10.2015 in accord. with art. 2. - Issued: 20.05.2015. Made: 13.05.2015. Laid before the Scottish Parliament: 15.05.2015. Coming into force: 01.10.2015. Effect: None. Territorial extent & classification: S. General. - 4p.: 30 cm. - 978-0-11-102780-6 £4.25

The Historic Environment Scotland Act 2014 (Saving, Transitional and Consequential Provisions) Order 2015 No. 2015/239. - Enabling power: Title Conditions (Scotland) Act 2003, s. 38 (4) & Historic Environment Scotland Act 2014, s. 27. - Issued: 09.06.2015. Made: 02.06.2015. Laid before the Scottish Parliament: 04.06.2015. Coming into force: 01.10.2015. Effect: S.I. 1996/1507 & S.S.I. 2003/453; 2007/570; 2011/146 amended. Territorial extent & classification: S. General. - 12p.: 30 cm. - 978-0-11-102822-3 £6.00

The Historic Environment Scotland (First Planning Period) Order 2015 No. 2015/238. - Enabling power: Historic Environment Scotland Act 2014, s. 9 (7) (a). - Issued: 09.06.2015. Made: 02.06.2015. Laid before the Scottish Parliament: 04.06.2015. Coming into force: 01.10.2015. Effect: None. Territorial extent & classification: S. General. - 2p.: 30 cm. - 978-0-11-102821-6 £4.25

The Scheduled Monument Consent Procedure (Scotland) Regulations 2015 No. 2015/229. - Enabling power: Ancient Monuments and Archaeological Areas Act 1979, ss. 2 (11), 3A (2), 3C, 60, sch. 1, paras 1, 2 (2) (2A) (3), 3 (2), 11 (3) (a). - Issued: 09.06.2015. Made: 02.06.2015. Laid before the Scottish Parliament: 04.06.2015. Coming into force: 01.10.2015. Effect: S.S.I. 2011/375 revoked with saving. Territorial extent & classification: S. General. - 12p.: 30 cm. - 978-0-11-102812-4 £6.00

The Scheduled Monuments and Listed Buildings (Miscellaneous Amendments) (Scotland) Regulations 2015 No. 2015/328. - Enabling power: Ancient Monuments and Archaeological Areas Act 1979, ss. 1 (6), 4D, 9CB & Planning (Listed Buildings and Conservation Areas) (Scotland) Act 1997, ss. 1A, 9 (3), 23 (2), 82 & Transport and Works (Scotland) Act 2007, ss. 14, 28. - Issued: 15.09.2015. Made: 09.09.2015. Laid before the Scottish Parliament: 11.09.2015. Coming into force: 10.10.2015. Effect: S.S.I. 2007/569; 2015/230, 231, 241, 243 amended. Territorial extent & classification: S. General. - 8p.: 30 cm. - 978-0-11-102935-0 £4.25

The Scheduled Monuments (Appeals) (Scotland) Regulations 2015 No. 2015/231. - Enabling power: Ancient Monuments and Archaeological Areas Act 1979, ss.1E, 3C, 4B (3), 4D, 9C (3A), 9CB, 23B. - Issued: 09.06.2015. Made: 02.06.2015. Laid before the Scottish Parliament: 04.06.2015. Coming into force: 01.10.2015. Effect: None. Territorial extent & classification: S. General. - 24p.: 30 cm. - 978-0-11-102814-8 £6.00

The Scheduled Monuments (Determination of Appeals by Appointed Persons) (Prescribed Classes) (Scotland) Regulations 2015 No. 2015/232. - Enabling power: Ancient Monuments and Archaeological Areas Act 1979, sch. 1A, para. 2. - Issued: 09.06.2015. Made: 02.06.2015. Laid before the Scottish Parliament: 04.06.2015. Coming into force: 01.10.2015. Effect: None. Territorial extent & classification: S. General. - 4p.: 30 cm. - 978-0-11-102815-5 £4.25

The Scheduled Monuments(Notification and Publication) (Scotland) Regulations 2015 No. 2015/230. - Enabling power: Ancient Monuments and Archaeological Areas Act 1979, ss.1 (6), 1B. - Issued: 09.06.2015. Made: 02.06.2015. Laid before the Scottish Parliament: 04.06.2015. Coming into force: 01.10.2015. Effect: None. Territorial extent & classification: S. General. - 4p.: 30 cm. - 978-0-11-102813-1 £4.25

Animals

The Trade in Animals and Related Products (Scotland) Amendment Regulations 2015 No. 2015/401. - Enabling power: European Communities Act 1972, s. 2 (2), sch. 2, para. 1A. - Issued: 26.11.2015. Made: 19.11.2015. Laid before the Scottish Parliament: 23.11.2015. Coming into force: 08.01.2016. Effect: S.S.I. 2015/177 amended. Territorial extent & classification: S. General. - 4p.: 30 cm. - 978-0-11-103004-2 £4.25

The Welfare of Animals at the Time of Killing (Scotland) Amendment Regulations 2015 No. 2015/161. - Enabling power: European Communities Act 1972, s. 2 (2). - Issued: 10.04.2015. Made: 01.04.2015. Laid before the Scottish Parliament: 07.04.2015. Coming into force: 19.05.2015. Effect: S.S.I. 2012/321 amended. Territorial extent & classification: S. General. - 4p.: 30 cm. - 978-0-11-102749-3 £4.25

Animals: Animal health

The Animal By-Products (Miscellaneous Amendments) (Scotland) Regulations 2015 No. 2015/393. - Enabling power: European Communities Act 1972, s. 2 (2). - Issued: 24.11.2015. Made: 18.11.2015. Laid before the Scottish Parliament: 20.11.2015. Coming into force: 01.01.2016. Effect: S.S.I. 2005/653; 2013/307 amended. Territorial extent & classification: S. General. - 4p.: 30 cm. - 978-0-11-102994-7 £4.25

The Bovine Viral Diarrhoea (Scotland) Amendment Order 2015 No. 2015/186. - Enabling power: Animal Health Act 1981, ss. 1, 8 (1), 83 (2). - Issued: 07.05.2015. Made: 29.04.2015. Laid before the Scottish Parliament: 01.05.2015. Coming into force: 01.06.2015. Effect: S.S.I. 2013/3 amended & S.S.I. 2013/21, 337, 363 partially revoked. Territorial extent & classification: S. General. - 12p.: 30 cm. - 978-0-11-102771-4 £6.00

The Tuberculosis in Specified Animals (Scotland) Order 2015 No. 2015/327. - Enabling power: Animal Health Act 1981, ss. 1, 7 (1), 8 (1), 15 (4), 25, 32 (3), 34 (7), 83 (2), 83A (6), 87 (2). - Issued: 15.09.2015. Made: 08.09.2015. Laid before the Scottish Parliament: 10.09.2015. Coming into force: 09.10.2015. Effect: S.S.I. 2013/173 amended & S.I. 1989/878, 1316; 1993/2010 revoked in so far as they apply in relation to Scotland. Territorial extent & classification: S. General. - 12p.: 30 cm. - 978-0-11-102934-3 £6.00

Aquaculture

The Alien and Locally Absent Species in Aquaculture (Scotland) Regulations 2015 No. 2015/103. - Enabling power: European Communities Act 1972, s. 2 (2), sch. 2, para. 1A. - Issued: 10.03.2015. Made: 03.03.2015. Laid before the Scottish Parliament: 05.03.2015. Coming into force: 03.04.2015. Effect: None. Territorial extent & classification: S. General. - 16p.: 30 cm. - 978-0-11-102694-6 £6.00

The European Maritime and Fisheries Fund (Grants) (Scotland) Regulations 2015 No. 2015/359. - Enabling power: European Communities Act 1972, s. 2 (2), sch. 2, para. 1A. - Issued: 03.11.2015. Made: 27.10.2015. Laid before the Scottish Parliament: 29.10.2015. Coming into force: 30.11.2015. Effect: S.S.I. 2007/307; 2010/323; 2012/166 revoked with savings. Territorial extent & classification: S. General. - 12p.: 30 cm. - 978-0-11-102962-6 £6.00

The Trade in Animals and Related Products (Scotland) Amendment Regulations 2015 No. 2015/401. - Enabling power: European Communities Act 1972, s. 2 (2), sch. 2, para. 1A. - Issued: 26.11.2015. Made: 19.11.2015. Laid before the Scottish Parliament: 23.11.2015. Coming into force: 08.01.2016. Effect: S.S.I. 2015/177 amended. Territorial extent & classification: S. General. - 4p.: 30 cm. - 978-0-11-103004-2 £4.25

Arms and ammunition

The Air Weapons and Licensing (Scotland) Act 2015 (Commencement No. 1) Order 2015 No. 2015/382 (C.48). - Enabling power: Air Weapons and Licensing (Scotland) Act 2015, s. 88 (2). Bringing into operation various provisions of the 2015 Act on 01.12.15 in accord. with art. 2. - Issued: 18.11.2015. Made: 11.11.2015. Laid before the Scottish Parliament: 13.11.2015. Coming into force: 01.12.2015. Effect: None. Territorial extent & classification: S. General. - 4p.: 30 cm. - 978-0-11-102984-8 £4.25

Bankruptcy

The Bankruptcy and Debt Advice (Scotland) Act 2014 (Commencement No. 2, Savings and Transitionals) Amendment Order 2015 No. 2015/54 (C.10). - Enabling power: Bankruptcy and Debt Advice (Scotland) Act 2014, s. 57 (2) (3). Bringing into operation various provisions of the 2014 Act on 01.04.2015, in accord. with art. 1. - Issued: 12.02.2015. Made: 05.02.2015. Laid before the Scottish Parliament: 09.02.2015. Coming into force: 01.04.2015. Effect: S.S.I. 2014/261 amended. Territorial extent & classification: S. General. - 4p.: 30 cm. - 978-0-11-102637-3 £4.25

The Bankruptcy (Miscellaneous Amendments) (Scotland) Regulations 2015 No. 2015/80. - Enabling power: Bankruptcy (Scotland) Act 1985, ss. 1A (1) (b) (5), 2 (8), 5 (2ZA) (a) (ii) (2D) (6A) 6 (7), 7 (1) (d), 11 (1), 19 (2), 22 (2) (a) (6), 23 (1) (a), 32 (9A), 40 (3B), 43A (2), 43B (1), 45 (3) (a), 49 (3), 51 (7) (a), 54 (2), 54A (2), 54C (2), 54D (2) (a) (c), 54E (2) (5), 69, 69A, 71C, 72 (1A), 72A, 73 (1), sch. 3 paras 5 (1) (6). - Issued: 04.03.2015. Made: 25.02.2015. Laid before the Scottish Parliament: 27.02.2015. Coming into force: 01.04.2015. Effect: S.I. 2014/225, 226, 227 amended. Territorial extent & classification: S. General. - 64p.: 30 cm. - 978-0-11-102672-4 £11.00

The Common Financial Tool etc. (Scotland) Amendment Regulations 2015 No. 2015/149. - Enabling power: Bankruptcy (Scotland) Act 1985, ss. 5D, 71C, 72 (1A), sch. 5, para. 5 & Debt Arrangement and Attachment Act (Scotland) Act 2002, s. 7 (2) (bd). - Issued: 01.04.2015. Made: 25.03.2015. Coming into force: 01.04.2015. Effect: S.S.I. 2014/290 amended. Territorial extent & classification: S. General. - Supersedes draft SI (ISBN 9780111026533) issued 25/02/15 - 8p.: 30 cm. - 978-0-11-102735-6 £6.00

Building and buildings

The Building (Scotland) Amendment Regulations 2015 No. 2015/218. - Enabling power: Building (Scotland) Act 2003, ss. 1, 54 (2). - Issued: 02.06.2015. Made: 27.05.2015. Laid before the Scottish Parliament: 29.05.2015. Coming into force: In accord. with reg. 1 (2) (3). Effect: S.S.I. 2004/406 amended. Territorial extent & classification: S. General. - 4p.: 30 cm. - 978-0-11-102801-8 £4.25

The Energy Performance of Buildings (Scotland) Amendment Regulations 2015 No. 2015/386. - Enabling power: European Communities Act 1972, s. 2(2) & Energy Act 2011, ss. 10, 75. - Issued: 23.11.2015. Made: 16.11.2015. Laid before the Scottish Parliament: 18.11.2015. Coming into force: 19.12.2015. Effect: S.S.I. 2008/309 amended. Territorial extent & classification: S. General. - 4p.: 30 cm. - 978-0-11-102989-3 £4.25

Charities

The Charity Test (Specified Bodies) and the Protection of Charities Assets (Exemption) (Scotland) Amendment Order 2015 No. 2015/148. - Enabling power: Charities and Trustee Investment (Scotland) Act 2005, s. 7 (5), 19 (8) (9). - Issued: 31.03.2015. Made: 25.03.2015. Coming into force: 01.04.2015. Effect: S.S.I. 2006/219, 220 amended. Territorial extent & classification: S. General. - 2p.: 30 cm. - 978-0-11-102734-9 £4.25

Children and young persons

The Aftercare (Eligible Needs) (Scotland) Order 2015 No. 2015/156. - Enabling power: Children (Scotland) Act 1995, s. 29 (8). - Issued: 09.04.2015. Made: 31.03.2015. Coming into force: 01.04.2015. Effect: None. Territorial extent & classification: S. General. - Supersedes draft SI (ISBN 9780111026601) issued 25/02/15 - 2p.: 30 cm. - 978-0-11-102743-1 £4.25

The Children and Young People (Scotland) Act 2014 (Commencement No. 7) Order 2015 No. 2015/61 (C.12). - Enabling power: Children and Young People (Scotland) Act 2014, s. 102 (3). Bringing into operation various provisions of the 2014 Act on 01.04.2015, 15.06.2015 in accord. with art. 2. - Issued: 23.02.2015. Made: 17.02.2015. Laid before the Scottish Parliament: 19.02.2015. Coming into force: 01.04.2015. Effect: None. Territorial extent & classification: S. General. - 8p.: 30 cm. - 978-0-11-102643-4 £4.25

The Children and Young People (Scotland) Act 2014 (Commencement No. 8 and Saving Provision) Order 2015 No. 2015/104 (C.20). - Enabling power: Children and Young People (Scotland) Act 2014, s. 102 (3) (4). Bringing into operation various provisions of the 2014 Act on 30.03.2015, in accord. with art. 2. - Issued: 11.03.2015. Made: 05.03.2015. Laid before the Scottish Parliament: 06.03.2015. Coming into force: 30.03.2015. Effect: None. Territorial extent & classification: S. General. - 8p.: 30 cm. - 978-0-11-102697-7 £4.25

The Children and Young People (Scotland) Act 2014 (Commencement No. 9 and Saving Provision) Order 2015 No. 2015/317 (C.38). - Enabling power: Children and Young People (Scotland) Act 2014, s. 102 (3) (4). Bringing into operation various provisions of the 2014 Act on 30.09.2015, in accord. with art. 2. - Issued: 08.09.2015. Made: 01.09.2015. Laid before the Scottish Parliament: 03.09.2015. Coming into force: 30.09.2015. Effect: None. Territorial extent & classification: S. General. - 8p.: 30 cm. - 978-0-11-102921-3 £6.00

The Children and Young People (Scotland) Act 2014 (Commencement No. 10 and Saving Provision) Order 2015 No. 2015/406 (C.51). - Enabling power: Children and Young People (Scotland) Act 2014, ss. 102 (3) (4). Bringing into operation various provisions of the 2014 Act on 05.01.2016, 01.02.2016, 01.04.2016, in accord. with art. 3- Issued: 07.12.2015. Made: 01.12.2015. Laid before the Scottish Parliament: 03.12.2015. Coming into force: 05.01.2016. Effect: None. Territorial extent & classification: S. General. - 8p.: 30 cm. - 978-0-11-103013-4 £6.00

The Children's Hearings (Scotland) Act 2011 (Rules of Procedure in Children's Hearings) Amendment Rules 2015 No. 2015/21. - Enabling power: Children's Hearing (Scotland) Act 2011, ss. 177, 195. - Issued: 29.01.2015. Made: 22.01.2015. Coming into force: 26.01.2015. Effect: S.S.I. 2013/194 amended. Territorial extent & classification: S. General. - For approval by resolution of the Scottish Parliament. Supersedes draft S.S.I. (ISBN 9780111025246) issued 02/12/14. - 8p.: 30 cm. - 978-0-11-102600-7 £6.00

The Continuing Care (Scotland) Order 2015 No. 2015/158. - Enabling power: Children (Scotland) Act 1995, ss. 26A (2) (b) (6) (9) (a). - Issued: 09.04.2015. Made: 31.03.2015. Coming into force: 01.04.2015. Effect: None. Territorial extent & classification: S. General. - Supersedes draft SI (ISBN 9780111026618) issued 25/02/15. - 8p.: 30 cm. - 978-0-11-102745-5 £4.25

The Police Act 1997 and the Protection of Vulnerable Groups (Scotland) Act 2007 Remedial (No. 2) Order 2015 No. 2015/423. - Enabling power: Convention Rights (Compliance) (Scotland) Act 2001, ss. 12 (1) (3), 14 (5) (a). - Issued: 17.12.2015. Made: 10.12.2015. Coming into force: 08.02.2016. Effect: 1997 c.50 & 2007 asp 14 & S.S.I. 2010/167 amended & S.I. 2015/330 revoked. Territorial extent & classification: S. General. - For approval by resolution of the Scottish Parliament within 120 days beginning with 9th September 2015. - 44p.: 30 cm. - 978-0-11-103024-0 £10.00

The Police Act 1997 and the Protection of Vulnerable Groups (Scotland) Act 2007 Remedial Order 2015 No. 2015/330. - Enabling power: Convention Rights (Compliance) (Scotland) Act 2001, s. 12 (1) (3). - Issued: 16.09.2015. Made: 09.09.2015. Coming into force: 10.09.2015. Effect: 1972 c. 50; 2007 asp 14, S.S.I. 2010/167 amended. Territorial extent & classification: S. General. - Revoked by S.S.I. 2015/423 (ISBN 9780111030240). - 36p.: 30 cm. - 978-0-11-102937-4 £10.00

The Protection of Vulnerable Groups (Scotland) Act 2007 (Fees for Scheme Membership and Disclosure Requests) Amendment Regulations 2015 No. 2015/223. - Enabling power: Protection of Vulnerable Groups (Scotland) Act 2007, ss. 70 (1) (2). - Issued: 03.06.2015. Made: 27.05.2015. Laid before the Scottish Parliament: 29.05.2015. Coming into force: 01.07.2015. Effect: S.S.I. 2010/167 amended. Territorial extent & classification: S. General. - 4p.: 30 cm. - 978-0-11-102805-6 £4.25

The Secure Accommodation (Scotland) Amendment Regulations 2015 No. 2015/20. - Enabling power: Children's Hearing (Scotland) Act 2011, ss 152, 195. - Issued: 29.01.2015. Made: 22.01.2015. Coming into force: 26.01.2015. Effect: S.S.I. 2013/205 amended. Territorial extent & classification: S. - Supersedes draft S.S.I. (ISBN 9780111025253) issued 02.12.14. - 2p.: 30 cm. - 978-0-11-102599-4 £4.25

The Support and Assistance of Young People Leaving Care (Scotland) Amendment Regulations 2015 No. 2015/62. - Enabling power: Regulation of Care (Scotland) Act 2001, s. 73 (2) (a) (c) (d) (3). - Issued: 23.02.2015. Made: 17.02.2015. Laid before the Scottish Parliament: 19.02.2015. Coming into force: 01.04.2015. Effect: S.S.I. 2003/608 amended. Territorial extent & classification: S. General. - 4p.: 30 cm. - 978-0-11-102645-8 £4.25

Civil partnership

The Marriage and Civil Partnership (Scotland) Act 2014 (Commencement No. 4 and Savings Provisions) Order 2015 No. 2015/14 (C.3). - Enabling power: Marriage and Civil Partnership (Scotland) Act 2014, s. 36 (2) (3). - Issued: 27.01.2015. Made: 20.01.2015. Laid before the Scottish Parliament: 22.01.2015. Coming into force: 01.03.2015. Effect: None. Territorial extent & classification: S. General. - 8p.: 30 cm. - 978-0-11-102593-2 £4.25

The Qualifying Civil Partnership Modification (Scotland) Order 2015 No. 2015/371. - Enabling power: Marriage and Civil Partnership (Scotland) Act 2014, ss. 9 (1) (2), 11 (5) (6). - Issued: 05.11.2015. Made: 30.10.2015. Coming into force: 31.10.2015. Effect: 1977 c.15, 2014 asp 5 modified. Territorial extent & classification: S. General. - 4p.: 30 cm. - 978-0-11-102970-1 £4.25

Climate change

The Carbon Accounting Scheme (Scotland) Amendment Regulations 2015 No. 2015/189. - Enabling power: Climate Change (Scotland) Act 2009, ss. 13 (5), 20 (1), 96 (2) (a) & European Communities Act 1972, sch. 2, para. 1A. - Issued: 13.05.2015. Made: 06.05.2015. Laid before the Scottish Parliament: 08.05.2015. Coming into force: 08.06.2015. Effect: S.S.I. 2010/216 amended. Territorial extent & classification: S. General. - 4p.: 30 cm. - 978-0-11-102774-5 £4.25

The Climate Change (Additional Greenhouse Gas) (Scotland) Order 2015 No. 2015/197. - Enabling power: Climate Change (Scotland) Act 2009, ss. 10 (2) (a), 12 (3), 96 (3). - Issued: 21.05.2015. Made: 15.05.2015. Coming into force: 16.05.2015. Effect: 2009 asp. 12 modified. Territorial extent & classification: S. General. - Supersedes draft S.S.I. (ISBN 9780111027394) issued 02/04/15. - 4p.: 30 cm. - 978-0-11-102784-4 £4.25

The Climate Change (Duties of Public Bodies: Reporting Requirements) (Scotland) Order 2015 No. 2015/347. - Enabling power: Climate Change (Scotland) Act 2009, ss. 46 (1), 96 (2) (a). - Issued: 13.10.2015. Made: 06.10.2015. Laid before the Scottish Parliament: 08.10.2015. Coming into force: 23.11.2015. Effect: None. Territorial extent & classification: S. General. - 36p.: 30 cm. - 978-0-11-102954-1 £10.00

Community empowerment

The Community Empowerment (Scotland) Act 2015 (Commencement No. 2) Order 2015 No. 2015/358 (C.44). - Enabling power: Community Empowerment (Scotland) Act 2015, s. 145 (2). Bringing into operation various provisions of the 2015 Act on 13.11.2015, in accord. with arts 1 & 2. - Issued: 03.11.2015. Made: 27.10.2015. Laid before the Scottish Parliament: 29.10.2015. Coming into force: 13.11.2015. Effect: None. Territorial extent & classification: S. General. - 8p.: 30 cm. - 978-0-11-102961-9 £6.00

The Community Empowerment (Scotland) Act 2015 (Commencement No. 3 and Savings) Order 2015 No. 2015/399 (C.50). - Enabling power: Community Empowerment (Scotland) Act 2015, ss. 145 (2) (3). Bringing into operation various provisions of the 2015 Act on 15.04.2016, in accord. with art. 2. - Issued: 26.11.2015. Made: 19.11.2015. Laid before the Scottish Parliament: 23.11.2015. Coming into force: 15.04.2016. Effect: None. Territorial extent & classification: S. General. - 8p.: 30 cm. - 978-0-11-102999-2 £6.00

Constitutional law

The Scottish Parliament (Disqualification) Order 2015 No. 2015/350. - Enabling power: Scotland Act 1998, ss. 15 (1) (2). - Issued: 15.10.2015. Made: 08.10.2015. Coming into force: 09.10.2015. Effect: S.I. 2010/2476 revoked. Territorial extent & classification: S. General. - Supersedes draft SI (ISBN 9780111028582) issued 04/08/15 - 24p.: 30 cm. - 978-0-11-102957-2 £6.00

The Scottish Parliament (Elections etc.) Order 2015 No. 2015/425. - Enabling power: Scotland Act 1998, ss. 12 (1), 113 (2) (4) (5). - Issued: 21.12.2015. Made: 15.12.2015. Coming into force: 16.12.2015 in accord. with art. 1 (1). Effect: S.I. 2010/2999; 2011/2085; 2012/1479; 2015/683 partially revoked with savings. Territorial extent & classification: S. General. - 220p.: 30 cm. - 978-0-11-103027-1 £27.50

The Tweed Regulation Amendment Order 2015 No. 2015/11. - Enabling power: S.I. 2006/2913, arts 36, 54. - Issued: 26.01.2015. Made: 19.01.2015. Laid before the Scottish Parliament: 20.01.2015. Coming into force: 31.01.2015. Effect: S.S.I. 2007/19 amended. Territorial extent & classification: S. General. - 4p.: 30 cm. - 978-0-11-102590-1 £4.25

Contracts

The Late Payment of Commercial Debts (Scotland) Regulations 2015 No. 2015/226. - Enabling power: European Communities Act 1972, s. 2 (2). - Issued: 04.06.2015. Made: 28.05.2015. Laid before the Scottish Parliament: 29.05.2015. Coming into force: 27.06.2015. Effect: 1998 c.20 amended. Territorial extent and classification: S. General. - EC note: Implements Directive 2011/7/EU on combating late payment in commercial transactions. - 4p.: 30 cm. - 978-0-11-102808-7 £4.25

The Legal Writings (Counterparts and Delivery) (Scotland) Act 2015 (Commencement) Order 2015 No. 2015/242 (C.33). - Enabling power: Legal Writings (Counterparts and Delivery) (Scotland) Act 2015, s. 6 (2). Bringing into operation various provisions of the 2015 Act on 01.07.2015. - Issued: 09.06.2015. Made: 03.06.2015. Laid before the Scottish Parliament: 05.06.2015. Coming into force: 01.07.2015. Effect: None. Territorial extent & classification: S. General. - 2p.: 30 cm. - 978-0-11-102825-4 £4.25

Council tax

The Council Tax Reduction (Scotland) Amendment Regulations 2015 No. 2015/46. - Enabling power: Local Government Finance Act 1992, ss. 80, 113 (1), sch. 2, para. 1. - Issued: 10.02.2015. Made: 03.02.2015. Laid before the Scottish Parliament: 05.02.2015. Coming into force: 01.04.2015. Effect: S.S.I. 2012/303, 319 amended. Territorial extent & classification: S. General. - 12p.: 30 cm. - 978-0-11-102625-0 £6.00

Court of Session

Act of Sederunt (Ordinary Cause Rules 1993 Amendment and Miscellaneous Amendments) 2015 No. 2015/296. - Enabling power: Courts Reform (Scotland) Act 2014, ss. 103 (1), 104 (1). - Issued: 07.08.2015. Made: 31.07.2015. Laid before the Scottish Parliament: 03.08.2015. Coming into force: 21.09.2015. Effect: 1993/1956; 2015/227, 228 amended. Territorial extent & classification: S. General. - This S.S.I. has been made to correct errors in S.S.I. 2015/227 (ISBN 9780111028094) and S.S.I. 2015/228 (ISBN 9780111028117) and is being issued free of charge to all known recipients of those instruments. - 4p.: 30 cm. - 978-0-11-102860-5 £4.25

Act of Sederunt (Rules of the Court of Session 1994 Amendment) (No. 3) (Courts Reform (Scotland) Act 2014) 2015 No. 2015/228. - Enabling power: Courts Reform (Scotland) Act 2014, ss. 39 (7), 103 (1). - Issued: 09.06.2015. Made: 02.06.2015. Laid before the Scottish Parliament: 04.06.2015. Coming into force: 22.09.2015. Effect: S.I. 1994/1443 amended. Territorial extent & classification: S. General. - 20p.: 30 cm. - 978-0-11-102811-7 £6.00

Act of Sederunt (Rules of the Court of Session 1994 Amendment) (No. 4) (Protective Expenses Orders) 2015 No. 2015/408. - Enabling power: Courts Reform (Scotland) Act 2014, s. 103 (1). - Issued: 08.12.2015. Made: 02.12.2015. Laid before the Scottish Parliament: 04.12.2015. Coming into force: 11.01.2016. Effect: S.I. 1994/1443 amended. Territorial extent & classification: S. General. - 8p.: 30 cm. - 978-0-11-103014-1 £4.25

Act of Sederunt (Rules of the Court of Session 1994 and Fees of Solicitors in the Sheriff Court Amendment) (Courts Reform (Scotland) Act 2014) 2015 No. 2015/246. - Enabling power: Courts Reform (Scotland) Act 2014, ss. 105 (1), 106 (1). - Issued: 10.06.2015. Made: 04.06.2015. Laid before the Scottish Parliament: 08.06.2015. Coming into force: 22.09.2015. Effect: S.I. 1993/3080; 1994/1443 amended. Territorial extent & classification: S. General. - 8p.: 30 cm. - 978-0-11-102829-2 £4.25

Act of Sederunt (Rules of the Court of Session 1994 and Ordinary Cause Rules 1993 Amendment) (Child Welfare Reporters) 2015 No. 2015/312. - Enabling power: Courts Reform (Scotland) Act 2014, ss. 103 (1), 104 (1). - Issued: 02.09.2015. Made: 26.08.2015. Laid before the Scottish Parliament: 28.08.2015. Coming into force: 26.10.2015. Effect: S.I. 1993/1956; 1994/1443 amended. Territorial extent & classification: S. General. - 12p.: 30 cm. - 978-0-11-102915-2 £6.00

Act of Sederunt (Rules of the Court of Session 1994 and Sheriff Court Rules Amendment) (No. 2) (Personal Injury and Remits) 2015 No. 2015/227. - Enabling power: Courts Reform (Scotland) Act 2014, ss. 103 (1), 104 (1). - Issued: 08.06.2015. Made: 02.06.2015. Laid before the Scottish Parliament: 04.06.2015. Coming into force: 22.09.2015. Effect: S.I. 1993/1956; 1994/1443 amended. Territorial extent & classification: S. General. - 56p.: 30 cm. - 978-0-11-102809-4 £10.00

Act of Sederunt (Rules of the Court of Session 1994 and Sheriff Court Rules Amendment) (No. 3) (Miscellaneous) 2015 No. 2015/283. - Enabling power: Revenue Scotland and Tax Powers Act 2014, s. 225 & Courts Reform (Scotland) Act 2014, ss. 103 (1), 104 (1). - Issued: 13.07.2015. Made: 07.07.2015. Laid before the Scottish Parliament: 09.07.2015. Coming into force: 07.08.2015. Effect: S.I. 1993/1956; 1994/1443; S.S.I. 1997/291; 2002/132, 133, 560; 1999/929 amended. Territorial extent & classification: S. General. - 12p.: 30 cm. - 978-0-11-102854-4 £6.00

Act of Sederunt (Rules of the Court of Session Amendment No. 2) (Regulatory Reform (Scotland) Act 2014) 2015 No. 2015/35. - Enabling power: Court of Session Act 1988, s. 5. - Issued: 04.02.2015. Made: 29.01.2015. Laid before the Scottish Parliament: 30.01.2015. Coming into force: 26.02.2015. Effect: S.I. 1994/1443 amended. Territorial extent & classification: S. General. - 8p.: 30 cm. - 978-0-11-102610-6 £4.25

Act of Sederunt (Rules of the Court of Session Amendment) (Regulation (EU) No. 1215/2012) 2015 No. 2015/26. - Enabling power: Civil Jurisdiction and Judgments Act 1982, s. 48 & Court of Session Act 1988, s. 5 & European Communities Act 1972, sch. 2, para. 1A. - Issued: 03.02.2015. Made: 27.01.2015. Laid before the Scottish Parliament: 28.01.2015. Coming into force: 07.02.2015. Effect: S.I. 1994/1443 amended. Territorial extent & classification: S. General. - 16p.: 30 cm. - 978-0-11-102602-1 £6.00

Act of Sederunt (Rules of the Court of Session and Sheriff Court Bankruptcy Rules Amendment) (Bankruptcy and Debt Advice (Scotland) Act 2014) 2015 No. 2015/119. - Enabling power: Sheriff Courts (Scotland) Act 1971, s. 32 & Court of Session Act 1988, s. 5. - Issued: 24.03.2015. Made: 18.03.2015. Laid before the Scottish Parliament: 19.03.2015. Coming into force: 01.04.2015. Effect: S.I. 1994/1443; 2008/119 amended. Territorial extent & classification: S. General. - 8p.: 30 cm. - 978-0-11-102710-3 £6.00

Act of Sederunt (Rules of the Court of Session and Sheriff Court Rules Amendment No. 3) (Reporting Restrictions) 2015 No. 2015/85. - Enabling power: Sheriff Courts (Scotland) Act 1971, s. 32 & Court of Session Act 1988, s. 5. - Issued: 04.03.2015. Made: 26.02.2015. Laid before the Scottish Parliament: 02.03.2015. Coming into force: 01.04.2015. Effect: 1907 c.51 & S.I. 1994/1443; S.S.I. 1999/929 amended. Territorial extent & classification: S. General. - 8p.: 30 cm. - 978-0-11-102677-9 £6.00

Act of Sederunt (Rules of the Court of Session, Sheriff Appeal Court Rules and Sheriff Court Rules Amendment) (Sheriff Appeal Court) 2015 No. 2015/419. - Enabling power: Courts Reform (Scotland) Act 2014, ss. 103 (1), 104 (1). - Issued: 15.12.2015. Made: 08.12.2015. Laid before the Scottish Parliament: 10.12.2015. Coming into force: In accord. with para. 1 (2) (3). Effect: S.I. 1976/1606; 1986/2297; 1988/2013; 1993/1956, 3128; 1994/1443; 1997/291; 1999/929, 1347; & S.S.I. 2002/132, 133, 560; 2008/119; 2009/284, 382; 2011/388; 2015/227, 356 amended. Territorial extent & classification: S. General. - 20p.: 30 cm. - 978-0-11-103019-6 £6.00

The Court of Session etc. Fees Order 2015 No. 2015/261. - Enabling power: Courts Reform (Scotland) Act 2014, ss. 107 (1) (2). - Issued: 22.06.2015. Made: 15.06.2015. Laid before the Scottish Parliament: 17.06.2015. Coming into force: In accord. with art. 1. Effect: S.S.I. 2013/137 partially revoked & S.I. 1997/688; 1999/755 & S.S.I. 2002/270; 2007/319; 2008/236; 2009/88; 2012/290; 2012/322 revoked (22.09.2015). Territorial extent & classification: S. General. - 28p.: 30 cm. - 978-0-11-102841-4 £6.00

The Courts Reform (Scotland) Act 2014 (Commencement No. 2, Transitional and Saving Provisions) Order 2015 No. 2015/77 (C.17). - Enabling power: Courts Reform (Scotland) Act 2014, s. 138 (2) (3). Bringing into operation various provisions of the 2014 Act on 12.03.2015. - Issued: 02.03.2015. Made: 24.02.2015. Laid before the Scottish Parliament: 26.02.2015. Coming into force: In accord with art. 1. Effect: None. Territorial extent & classification: S. General. - 8p.: 30 cm. - 978-0-11-102667-0 £6.00

The Courts Reform (Scotland) Act 2014 (Commencement No. 3, Transitional and Saving Provisions) Order 2015 No. 2015/247 (C.35). - Enabling power: Courts Reform (Scotland) Act 2014, s. 138 (2) (3). Bringing into operation various provisions of the 2014 Act on 22.09.2015. - Issued: 10.06.2015. Made: 04.06.2015. Laid before the Scottish Parliament: 08.06.2015. Coming into force: 22.09.2015. Effect: None. Territorial extent & classification: S. General. - 12p.: 30 cm. - 978-0-11-102830-8 £6.00

The Courts Reform (Scotland) Act 2014 (Commencement No. 5, Transitional and Saving Provisions) Order 2015 No. 2015/378 (C.47). - Enabling power: Courts Reform (Scotland) Act 2014, s. 138 (2) (3). Bringing into operation various provisions of the 2014 Act on 01.01.2016, in accord. with art. 2. - Issued: 11.11.2015. Made: 04.11.2015. Laid before the Scottish Parliament: 06.11.2015. Coming into force: 01.01.2016. Effect: S.S.I. 2015/247 amended. Territorial extent & classification: S. General. - 8p.: 30 cm. - 978-0-11-102975-6 £6.00

The Courts Reform (Scotland) Act 2014 (Consequential and Supplemental Provisions) Order 2015 No. 2015/402. - Enabling power: Courts Reform (Scotland) Act 2014, s. 137. - Issued: 02.12.2015. Made: 26.11.2015. Coming into force: 01.01.2016. Effect: 1893 c.44; 1973 c.65; 1995 c.46; 2000 asp 7; 2004 asp 8; 2006 asp 16; 2011 asp 1 & S.S.I. 2003/179; 2012/335 modified. Territorial extent & classification: S. General. - Supersedes draft S.S.I. (ISBN 9780111029589) issued 15/10/15. - 8p.: 30 cm. - 978-0-11-103008-0 £4.25

The Courts Reform (Scotland) Act 2014 (Consequential Provisions No. 2) Order 2015 No. 2015/338. - Enabling power: Courts Reform (Scotland) Act 2014, s. 137. - Issued: 24.09.2015. Made: 16.09.2015. Coming into force: 22.09.2015. Effect: 1981 c.22; 1988 c.36, 53; 1991 c.65; 1995 c.43, 46; 2002 asp 6; asp 10; 2003 c.42; 2006 asp 10; asp 11, 2006 c.45; 2010 asp 9, asp 13; 2011 c.23; 2015 c.6 & S.S.I. 2000/301; 2001/315; 2007/504, 505, 507; 2013/6; 2014/337; 2015/77 modified. Territorial extent & classification: S. General. - Supersedes draft SI (ISBN 9780111028346) issued 12/06/15 - 16p.: 30 cm. - 978-0-11-102944-2 £6.00

The Courts Reform (Scotland) Act 2014 (Consequential Provisions) Order 2015 No. 2015/150. - Enabling power: Courts Reform (Scotland) Act 2014, s. 137. - Issued: 01.04.2015. Made: 24.03.2015. Coming into force: 01.04.2015. Effect: 1966 c.19; 1968 c.59; 1972 c.59; 1986 c.45; 1995 c.46; 1999 c.22; 2004 asp 8; 2005 c.12; 2007 asp 3; S.S.I. 2013/50 modified. Territorial extent & classification: S. General. - Supersedes draft SI (ISBN 9780111026663) issued 27/02/15 - 4p.: 30 cm. - 978-0-11-102736-3 £4.25

Criminal law

The Air Weapons and Licensing (Scotland) Act 2015 (Commencement No. 1) Order 2015 No. 2015/382 (C.48). - Enabling power: Air Weapons and Licensing (Scotland) Act 2015, s. 88 (2). Bringing into operation various provisions of the 2015 Act on 01.12.15 in accord. with art. 2. - Issued: 18.11.2015. Made: 11.11.2015. Laid before the Scottish Parliament: 13.11.2015. Coming into force: 01.12.2015. Effect: None. Territorial extent & classification: S. General. - 4p.: 30 cm. - 978-0-11-102984-8 £4.25

The Criminal Justice and Licensing (Scotland) Act 2010 (Commencement No. 12) Order 2015 No. 2015/177 (C.28). - Enabling power: Criminal Justice and Licensing (Scotland) Act 2010, s. 206 (1). Bringing into operation various provisions of the 2010 Act on 07.05.2015. - Issued: 28.04.2015. Made: 21.04.2015. Laid before the Scottish Parliament: 23.04.2015. Coming into force: 07.05.2015. Effect: None. Territorial extent & classification: S. General. - 8p.: 30 cm. - 978-0-11-102761-5 £4.25

CRIMINAL PROCEDURE

The Criminal Justice and Licensing (Scotland) Act 2010 (Commencement No. 13) and the Courts Reform (Scotland) Act 2014 (Commencement No. 4) Order 2015 No. 2015/336 (C.41). - Enabling power: Criminal Justice and Licensing (Scotland) Act 2010, s. 206 (1) & Courts Reform (Scotland) Act 2014, s. 138 (2). Bringing into operation various provisions of both Acts on 19.10.2015, in accord. with arts 1 & 2. - Issued: 23.09.2015. Made: 16.09.2015. Laid before the Scottish Parliament: 18.09.2015. Coming into force: 19.10.2015. Effect: None. Territorial extent & classification: S. General. - 8p.: 30 cm. - 978-0-11-102943-5 £6.00

The Management of Offenders etc. (Scotland) Act 2005 (Commencement No. 8) Order 2015 No. 2015/429 (C.57). - Enabling power: Management of Offenders etc. (Scotland) Act 2005, ss. 24 (2) (3). Bringing into operation various provisions of the 2015 on 31.03.2016, in accord. with art. 2. - Issued: 22.12.2015. Made: 15.12.2015. Laid before the Scottish Parliament: 17.12.2015. Coming into force: 31.03.2016. Effect: None. Territorial extent & classification: S. General. - 4p.: 30 cm. - 978-0-11-103029-5 £4.25

The Management of Offenders etc. (Scotland) Act 2005 (Specification of Persons) Amendment Order 2015 No. 2015/431. - Enabling power: Management of Offenders etc. (Scotland) Act 2005, s. 10 (3). - Issued: 22.12.2015. Made: 15.12.2015. Laid before the Scottish Parliament: 17.12.2015. Coming into force: 31.03.2016. Effect: S.S.I. 2007/92 amended. Territorial extent & classification: S. General. - 2p.: 30 cm. - 978-0-11-103031-8 £4.25

The Victims and Witnesses (Scotland) Act 2014 (Commencement No. 4 and Transitional Provisions) Order 2015 No. 2015/200 (C.32). - Enabling power: Victims and Witnesses (Scotland) Act 2014, s. 34 (2) (3). Bringing into operation various provisions of the 2014 Act on 01.07.2015. - Issued: 27.05.2015. Made: 19.05.2015. Laid before the Scottish Parliament: 21.05.2015. Effect: None. Territorial extent & classification: S. General. - 4p.: 30 cm. - 978-0-11-102786-8 £4.25

The Victims' Rights (Scotland) Regulations 2015 No. 2015/444. - Enabling power: European Communities Act 1972, s. 2 (2). - Issued: 23.12.2015. Made: 17.12.2015. Coming into force: In accord. with reg. 1. Effect: 2014 asp 1 amended. Territorial extent & classification: S. General. - EC note: These Regulations implement, in part, Directive 2012/29/EU of the European Parliament and of the Council establishing minimum standards on the rights, support and protection of victims of crime. Supersedes draft SI (ISBN 9780111030004) issued 26/11/15 - 24p.: 30 cm. - 978-0-11-103043-1 £6.00

Criminal procedure

The European Protection Order (Scotland) Regulations 2015 No. 2015/107. - Enabling power: European Communities Act 1972, s. 2 (2). - Issued: 17.03.2015. Made: 10.03.2015. Coming into force: 11.03.2015. Effect: 1995 c.46 amended. Territorial extent & classification: S. General. - Supersedes draft S.S.I. (ISBN 9780111026274) issued 10/02/15. - 8p.: 30 cm. - 978-0-11-102701-1 £6.00

The Vulnerable Witnesses (Scotland) Act 2004 (Commencement No. 8) Order 2015 No. 2015/244 (C.34). - Enabling power: Vulnerable Witnesses (Scotland) Act 2004. s. 25. Bringing into operation various provisions of the 2004 Act on 01.07.2015. - Issued: 10.06.2015. Made: 03.06.2015. Laid before the Scottish Parliament: 05.06.2015. Coming into force: 01.07.2015. Effect: None. Territorial extent & classification: S. General. - 4p.: 30 cm. - 978-0-11-102827-8 £4.25

Criminal procedure: Evidence

The Justice of the Peace Courts (Special Measures) (Scotland) Order 2015 No. 2015/447. - Enabling power: Criminal Procedure (Scotland) Act 1995, s. 288G. - Issued: 24.12.2015. Made: 17.12.2015. Coming into force: In accord. with art. 1. Effect: None. Territorial extent & classification: S. General. - Supersedes draft S.S.I. (ISBN 9780111029879) issued 20/11/15. - 4p.: 30 cm. - 978-0-11-103045-5 £4.25

Crofters, cottars and small landholders

The Crofting Counties Agricultural Grants (Scotland) Variation Scheme 2015 No. 2015/105. - Enabling power: Crofters (Scotland) Act 1993, ss. 42 (1) (1A) (2) (3), 46 (4) & European Communities Act 1972, s. 2 (2), sch. 2, para. 1A. - Issued: 11.03.2015. Made: 04.03.2015. Laid before the Scottish Parliament: 06.03.2015. Coming into force: 06.04.2015. Effect: S.S.I. 2006/24 amended. Territorial extent & classification: S. General. - 8p.: 30 cm. - 978-0-11-102699-1 £6.00

Debt

The Bankruptcy and Debt Advice (Scotland) Act 2014 (Commencement No. 2, Savings and Transitionals) Amendment Order 2015 No. 2015/54 (C.10). - Enabling power: Bankruptcy and Debt Advice (Scotland) Act 2014, s. 57 (2) (3). Bringing into operation various provisions of the 2014 Act on 01.04.2015, in accord. with art. 1. - Issued: 12.02.2015. Made: 05.02.2015. Laid before the Scottish Parliament: 09.02.2015. Coming into force: 01.04.2015. Effect: S.S.I. 2014/261 amended. Territorial extent & classification: S. General. - 4p.: 30 cm. - 978-0-11-102637-3 £4.25

The Common Financial Tool etc. (Scotland) Amendment Regulations 2015 No. 2015/149. - Enabling power: Bankruptcy (Scotland) Act 1985, ss. 5D, 71C, 72 (1A), sch. 5, para. 5 & Debt Arrangement and Attachment Act (Scotland) Act 2002, s. 7 (2) (bd). - Issued: 01.04.2015. Made: 25.03.2015. Coming into force: 01.04.2015. Effect: S.S.I. 2014/290 amended. Territorial extent & classification: S. General. - Supersedes draft SI (ISBN 9780111026533) issued 25/02/15 - 8p.: 30 cm. - 978-0-11-102735-6 £6.00

The Debt Arrangement Scheme (Scotland) Amendment Regulations 2015 No. 2015/216. - Enabling power: Debt Arrangement and Attachment (Scotland) Act 2002, ss. 7 (1) (2) (b) (bc) (ii) (c) (d), (3), 62 (2). - Issued: 02.06.2015. Made: 27.05.2015. Laid before the Scottish Parliament: 29.05.2015. Coming into force: 27.06.2015. Effect: S.S.I. 2011/141 amended. Territorial extent & classification: S. General. - 4p.: 30 cm. - 978-0-11-102799-8 £4.25

Devolution, Scotland

The Scottish Parliament (Disqualification) Order 2015 No. 2015/350. - Enabling power: Scotland Act 1998, ss. 15 (1) (2). - Issued: 15.10.2015. Made: 08.10.2015. Coming into force: 09.10.2015. Effect: S.I. 2010/2476 revoked. Territorial extent & classification: S. General. - Supersedes draft SI (ISBN 9780111028582) issued 04/08/15 - 24p.: 30 cm. - 978-0-11-102957-2 £6.00

The Tweed Regulation Amendment Order 2015 No. 2015/11. - Enabling power: S.I. 2006/2913, arts 36, 54. - Issued: 26.01.2015. Made: 19.01.2015. Laid before the Scottish Parliament: 20.01.2015. Coming into force: 31.01.2015. Effect: S.S.I. 2007/19 amended. Territorial extent & classification: S. General. - 4p.: 30 cm. - 978-0-11-102590-1 £4.25

Education

The Children and Young People (Scotland) Act 2014 (Commencement No. 8 and Saving Provision) Order 2015 No. 2015/104 (C.20). - Enabling power: Children and Young People (Scotland) Act 2014, s. 102 (3) (4). Bringing into operation various provisions of the 2014 Act on 30.03.2015, in accord. with art. 2. - Issued: 11.03.2015. Made: 05.03.2015. Laid before the Scottish Parliament: 06.03.2015. Coming into force: 30.03.2015. Effect: None. Territorial extent & classification: S. General. - 8p.: 30 cm. - 978-0-11-102697-7 £4.25

The Education (Assisted Places) (Scotland) Revocation Regulations 2015 No. 2015/318. - Enabling power: Education (Scotland) Act 1980, ss. 75A (9) (10), 75B & European Communities Act 1972, s. 2 (2). - Issued: 08.09.2015. Made: 01.09.2015. Laid before the Scottish Parliament: 03.09.2015. Coming into force: 08.10.2015. Effect: S.S.I. 2013/177 partially revoked & S.S.I. 2001/222; 2002/249; 2003/281; 2004/239; 2005/270; 2006/317; 2007/114; 2008/213 revoked. Territorial extent & classification: S. General. - 4p.: 30 cm. - 978-0-11-102922-0 £4.25

The Education (School Lunches) (Scotland) Regulations 2015 No. 2015/269. - Enabling power: Education (Scotland) Act 1980, s. 53 (3) (c). - Issued: 25.06.2015. Made: 16.06.2015 Coming into force: 01.08.2015. Effect: None. Territorial extent & classification: S. General. - Supersedes draft S.S.I. (ISBN 9780111027769) issued 18/05/15. - 4p.: 30 cm. - 978-0-11-102848-3 £4.25

The Education (Student Support) (Miscellaneous Amendments) (Scotland) Regulations 2015 No. 2015/212. - Enabling power: Education (Scotland) Act 1980, ss. 73 (f), 73B, 74 (1). - Issued: 02.06.2015. Made: 26.05.2015. Laid before the Scottish Parliament: 28.05.2015. Coming into force: 01.08.2015. Effect: S.S.I. 2006/333; 2007/154 amended. Territorial extent & classification: S. General. - 4p.: 30 cm. - 978-0-11-102795-0 £4.25

The Glasgow Clyde College (Removal and Appointment of Board Members) (Scotland) Order 2015 No. 2015/348. - Enabling power: Further and Higher Education (Scotland) Act 1992 s. 24 (2). - Issued: 14.10.2015. Made: 08.10.2015. Laid before the Scottish Parliament: 08.10.2015. Coming into force: 08.10.2015 at 9.15 am. Effect: None. Territorial extent & classification: S. General. - 4p.: 30 cm. - 978-0-11-102955-8 £4.25

The Post-16 Education (Scotland) Act 2013 (Commencement No. 6) Order 2015 No. 2015/82 (C.18). - Enabling power: Post-16 Education (Scotland) Act 2013, s. 23 (2). Bringing into operation various provisions of this Act on 31.03.2015 in accord. with art. 2. - Issued: 04.03.2015. Made: 25.02.2015. Laid before the Scottish Parliament: 27.02.2015. Effect: None. Territorial extent & classification: S. General. - 4p.: 30 cm. - 978-0-11-102674-8 £4.25

The Post-16 Education (Scotland) Act 2013 (Modification of Legislation) Order 2015 No. 2015/153. - Enabling power: Charities and Trustee Investment (Scotland) Act 2005, ss. 7 (5), 19 (8) (9) & Further and Higher Education (Scotland) Act 2005, s. 34 (2), sch. 2B, para. 18 (1) & Post-16 Education (Scotland) Act 2013, s. 22 (1). - Issued: 02.04.2015. Made: 26.03.2015. Coming into force: 31.03.2015. Effect: 1980 c.44; 1992 c.37; 2005 asp 6; 2007 asp 14; 2009 asp 9; S.S.I. 2003/176; 2005/325; 2006/218, 220, 401; 2007/105, 152; 2008/162, 268; 2010/181; 2011/215, 389, 455; 2013/73, 84 modified. Territorial extent & classification: S. General. - Supersedes draft SI (ISBN 9780111026656) issued 26/02/15. - 12p.: 30 cm. - 978-0-11-102740-0 £6.00

The Provision of Early Learning and Childcare (Specified Children) (Scotland) Amendment Order 2015 No. 2015/268. - Enabling power: Children and Young People (Scotland) Act 2014, ss. 47 (2) (c) (ii), 99 (1). - Issued: 24.06.2015. Made: 16.06.2015. Coming into force: 01.08.2015. Effect: S.S.I. 2014/196 amended. Territorial extent & classification: S. General. - Supersedes draft S.S.I. (ISBN 9780111027646) issued 05/05/15. - 4p.: 30 cm. - 978-0-11-102847-6 £4.25

The Queen Margaret University, Edinburgh (Scotland) Amendment Order of Council 2015 No. 2015/305. - Enabling power: Further and Higher Education (Scotland) Act 1992, ss. 45, 60. - Issued: 26.08.2015. Made: 19.08.2015. Laid before the Scottish Parliament: 21.08.2015. Coming into force: 28.09.2015. Effect: S.S.I. 2007/116 amended. Territorial extent & classification: S. General. - 4p.: 30 cm. - 978-0-11-102914-5 £4.25

The St Mary's Music School (Aided Places) (Scotland) Regulations 2015 No. 2015/248. - Enabling power: Education (Scotland) Act 1980, ss. 73 (f), 74 (1). - Issued: 10.06.2015. Made: 04.06.2015. Laid before the Scottish Parliament: 05.06.2015. Coming into force: 01.08.2015. Effect: S.S.I. 2001/223; 2002/248; 2003/280; 2004/238; 2005/269; 2006/318; 2007/115; 2008/214; 2009/181; 2014/143 revoked. Territorial extent & classification: S. General. - 24p.: 30 cm. - 978-0-11-102831-5 £6.00

The University of the West of Scotland (Amendment of the University of Paisley (Scotland) Order of Council 1993) Order of Council 2015 No. 2015/209. - Enabling power: Further and Higher Education (Scotland) Act 1992, ss. 45, 60. - Issued: 02.06.2015. Made: 26.05.2015. Laid before the Scottish Parliament: 28.05.2015. Coming into force: 26.05.2015. Effect: S.S.I. 1993/558 amended. Territorial extent & classification: S. General. - 4p.: 30 cm. - 978-0-11-102792-9 £4.25

Electricity

The Renewables Obligation (Scotland) Amendment Order 2015 No. 2015/384. - Enabling power: Electricity Act 1989, ss. 32 (1), 32B (1), 32C (1) to (6), 32D (1) (2), 32J (3), 32K (1) (3) & European Communities Act 1972 s. 2 (2) sch. 2 para. 1A. - Issued: 18.11.2015. Made: 10.11.2015. Coming into force: 01.12.2015. Effect: S.S.I. 2009/140 amended. Territorial extent & classification: S. General. - Supersedes draft SI (ISBN 9780111029473) issued 24/09/15 - 24p.: 30 cm. - 978-0-11-102986-2 £6.00

Energy

The Energy Performance of Buildings (Scotland) Amendment Regulations 2015 No. 2015/386. - Enabling power: European Communities Act 1972, s. 2(2) & Energy Act 2011, ss. 10, 75. - Issued: 23.11.2015. Made: 16.11.2015. Laid before the Scottish Parliament: 18.11.2015. Coming into force: 19.12.2015. Effect: S.S.I. 2008/309 amended. Territorial extent & classification: S. General. - 4p.: 30 cm. - 978-0-11-102989-3 £4.25

Enforcement

The Diligence against Earnings (Variation) (Scotland) Regulations 2015 No. 2015/370. - Enabling power: Debtors (Scotland) Act 1987, ss. 49 (7) (a), 53 (3), 63 (6). - Issued: 05.11.2015. Made: 29.10.2015. Laid before the Scottish Parliament: 02.11.2015. Coming into force: 06.04.2016. Effect: 1987 c.18 varied. Territorial extent & classification: S. General. - 4p.: 30 cm. - 978-0-11-102969-5 £4.25

The Environmental Regulation (Enforcement Measures) (Scotland) Order 2015 No. 2015/383. - Enabling power: Regulatory Reform (Scotland) Act 2014, ss. 20 to 32, 53, 58 (1), 59 & Courts Reform (Scotland) Act 2014, s. 107. - Issued: 18.11.2015. Made: 11.11.2015. Coming into force: 12.11.2015. Effect: 1993 c. 45; S.I. 1996/680 amended. Territorial extent & classification: S. General. - Supersedes draft SI (ISBN 9780111029466) issued 24/09/15 - 40p.: 30 cm. - 978-0-11-102985-5 £10.00

Environmental protection

The Aquaculture and Fisheries (Scotland) Act 2007 (Fixed Penalty Notices) Order 2015 No. 2015/113. - Enabling power: Aquaculture and Fisheries (Scotland) Act 2007, ss. 26 (5), 27 (1) (3), 29 (2) (b), 43 (1) (b). - Issued: 18.03.2015. Made: 11.03.2015. Laid before the Scottish Parliament: 13.03.2015. Coming into force: 27.04.2015. Effect: S.S.I. 2008/101; 2011/60 revoked. Territorial extent & classification: S. General. - 4p.: 30 cm. - 978-0-11-102705-9 £4.25

The Environment Act 1995 (Commencement No. 24) (Scotland) Order 2015 No. 2015/73 (C.15). - Enabling power: Environment Act 1995, s. 125 (3). Bringing into operation various provisions of the 1995 Act on 01.04.2015, in accord. with art. 2. - Issued: 25.02.2015. Made: 18.02.2015. Laid before the Scottish Parliament: 20.02.2015. Effect: None. Territorial extent & classification: S. General. - 8p.: 30 cm. - 978-0-11-102657-1 £4.25

The Environmental Liability (Scotland) Amendment Regulations 2015 No. 2015/214. - Enabling power: European Communities Act 1972, s. 2 (2), sch. 2, para. 1A. - Issued: 02.06.2015. Made: 26.05.2015. Laid before the Scottish Parliament: 28.05.2015. Coming into force: 19.07.2015. Effect: S.S.I. 2009/266 amended. Territorial extent & classification: S. General. - EC note; These Regulations implement Article 38 of Directive 2013/30/EU of the European Parliament and of the Council on the safety of offshore oil and gas operations which amends Directive 2004/35/EC. - 4p.: 30 cm. - 978-0-11-102797-4 £4.25

The Environmental Protection Act 1990 (Commencement No. 20) (Scotland) Order 2015 No. 2015/72 (C.14). - Enabling power: Environment Protection Act 1990, s. 164 (3). Bringing into operation various provisions of the 1990 Act on 01.04.2015, in accord. with art. 2. - Issued: 25.02.2015. Made: 18.02.2015. Laid before the Scottish Parliament: 20.02.2015. Effect: None. Territorial extent & classification: S. General. - 12p.: 30 cm. - 978-0-11-102656-4 £6.00

The Environmental Regulation (Enforcement Measures) (Scotland) Order 2015 No. 2015/383. - Enabling power: Regulatory Reform (Scotland) Act 2014, ss. 20 to 32, 53, 58 (1), 59 & Courts Reform (Scotland) Act 2014, s. 107. - Issued: 18.11.2015. Made: 11.11.2015. Coming into force: 12.11.2015. Effect: 1993 c. 45; S.I. 1996/680 amended. Territorial extent & classification: S. General. - Supersedes draft SI (ISBN 9780111029466) issued 24/09/15 - 40p.: 30 cm. - 978-0-11-102985-5 £10.00

The Financial Assistance for Environmental Purposes (Scotland) Order 2015 No. 2015/210. - Enabling power: Environmental Protection Act 1990, s. 153 (4). - Issued: 02.06.2015. Made: 26.05.2015. Laid before the Scottish Parliament: 28.05.2015. Coming into force: 27.06.2015. Effect: 1990 c. 43 varied. Territorial extent & classification: S. General. - 2p.: 30 cm. - 978-0-11-102793-6 £4.25

The Pollution Prevention and Control Act 1999 (Commencement No. 3) (Scotland) Order 2015 No. 2015/74 (C.16). - Enabling power: Pollution Prevention and Control Act 1999, s. 7 (3). Bringing into operation in Scotland various provisions of the 1999 Act on 01.04.2015, in accord. with art. 2. - Issued: 25.02.2015. Made: 18.02.2015. Laid: 20.02.2015. Effect: None. Territorial extent & classification: S. General. - 4p.: 30 cm. - 978-0-11-102658-8 £4.25

The Pollution Prevention and Control Act 1999 (Commencement No. 4 and Amendment) (Scotland) Order 2015 No. 2015/139 (C.27). - Enabling power: Pollution Prevention and Control Act 1999, s. 7 (3). Bringing into operation in Scotland various provisions of the 1999 Act on 31.03.2015, 01.04.2015, in accord. with art. 1. - Issued: 31.03.2015. Made: 23.03.2015. Laid: 25.03.2015. Effect: None. Territorial extent & classification: S. General. - This Scottish Statutory Instrument has been made in consequence of defects in S.S.I. 2015/74 (ISBN 9780111026588) and is being issued free of charge to all known recipients of that instrument. - 4p.: 30 cm. - 978-0-11-102726-4 £4.25

The Regulatory Reform (Scotland) Act 2014 (Commencement No. 2 and Transitional Provision) Order 2015 No. 2015/52 (C.9). - Enabling power: Regulatory Reform (Scotland) Act 2014, s. 61 (2) (3). Bringing into operation various provisions of the Act on 26.02.2015; 01.10.2015, in accord. with art. 2. - Issued: 11.02.2015. Made: 04.02.2015. Laid before the Scottish Parliament: 06.02.2015. Effect: None. Territorial extent & classification: S. General. - 4p.: 30 cm. - 978-0-11-102632-8 £4.25

The Scottish Marine Regions Order 2015 No. 2015/193. - Enabling power: Marine (Scotland) Act 2010, s. 5 (5). - Issued: 19.05.2015. Made: 12.05.15. Coming into force: 13.05.2015. Effect: None. Territorial extent & classification: S. General. - Supersedes draft S.S.I. (ISBN 9780111027004) issued 13/03/15. - 24p., map: 30 cm. - 978-0-11-102777-6 £6.00

The Single Use Carrier Bags Charge (Fixed Penalty Notices and Amendment) (Scotland) Regulations 2015 No. 2015/159. - Enabling power: Climate Change (Scotland) Act 2009, ss. 88, 88A (3) (4), 96 (2), sch. 1A, paras 3, 4. - Issued: 09.04.2015. Made: 31.03.2015. Coming into force: 01.04.2015. Effect: S.S.I. 2014/161 amended. Territorial extent & classification: S. General. - Supersedes S.S.I. draft (ISBN 9780111026717) issued 02/03/15. - 4p.: 30 cm. - 978-0-11-102746-2 £4.25

The South Arran Marine Conservation 2014 (Urgent Continuation) Order 2015 No. 2015/303. - Enabling power: Marine (Scotland) Act 2010, s. 86 (6). - Issued: 21.08.2015. Made: 17.08.2015. Laid before the Scottish Parliament: 17.08.2015. Coming into force: 28.09.2015. Effect: None. Territorial extent & classification: S. General. - 4p: 30 cm. - 978-0-11-102913-8 £4.25

The South Arran Marine Conservation Order 2015 No. 2015/437. - Enabling power: Inshore Fishing (Scotland) Act 1984, ss. 1, 2A & Marine (Scotland) Act 2010, ss. 85 (1) (a) (2) (4), 86 (1) (3), 88 (1) (2) (6), 92 (1) (5). - Issued: 23.12.2015. Made: 16.12.2015. Laid before the Scottish Parliament: 18.12.2015. Coming into force: 08.02.2016. Effect: SSI 2008/317; 2014/260, 297, 303 revoked. Territorial extent & classification: S. General. - 16p., map: 30 cm. - 978-0-11-103040-0 £6.00

The Waste (Meaning of Hazardous Waste and European Waste Catalogue) (Miscellaneous Amendments) (Scotland) Regulations 2015 No. 2015/188. - Enabling power: European Communities Act 1972, s. 2 (2), sch. 2, para. 1A. - Issued: 11.05.2015. Made: 05.05.2015. Laid before the Scottish Parliament: 07.05.2015. Coming into force: 08.06.2015. Effect: 1990 c.43 & S.I. 1996/972 & S.S.I. 2003/235; 2005/157; 2007/251; 2009/140; 2010/60; 2011/139, 204, 228; 2012/360 amended. Territorial extent & classification: S. General. - 6p.: 30 cm. - 978-0-11-102773-8 £4.25

The Waste (Meaning of Recovery) (Miscellaneous Amendments) (Scotland) Order 2015 No. 2015/438. - Enabling power: European Communities Act 1972, s. 2 (2) & Marine and Coastal Access Act 2009, s. 74. - Issued: 23.12.2015. Made: 16.12.2015. Laid before the Scottish Parliament: 18.12.2015. Coming into force: 01.07.2016. Effect: S.I. 1996/972; S.S.I. 2003/593; 2007/251; 2011/57, 204, 228; 2012/360 amended Territorial extent & classification: S. General. - EC note: This Order amends various enactments to effect changes as a consequence of the amendment of Annex II to Directive 2008/98/EC on waste and repealing Directives "the Waste Directive" by Commission Directive (EU) 2015/1127. - 4p.: 30 cm. - 978-0-11-103041-7 £4.25

The Waste (Recyclate Quality) (Scotland) Regulations 2015 No. 2015/101. - Enabling power: Environment Protection Act 1990, s. 35 (6) & Pollution Prevention and Control Act 1999, s. 2, sch.1. - Issued: 10.03.2015. Made: 03.03.2015. Laid before the Scottish Parliament: 03.03.2015. Coming into force: 01.04.2015. Effect: S.S.I. 2011/228; 2012/360 amended. Territorial extent & classification: S. General. - 4p.: 30 cm. - 978-0-11-102690-8 £4.25

The Water Environment and Water Services (Scotland) Act 2003 (Modification of Part 1) Regulations 2015 No. 2015/270. - Enabling power: Water Environment and Water Services (Scotland) Act 2003, ss. 25, 36 (2). - Issued: 29.06.2015. Made: 22.06.2015. Coming into force: 14.09.2015. Effect: 2003 asp 3 modified & S.S.I. 2009/420 partially revoked. Territorial extent and classification: S. General. - Supersedes draft S.S.I. (ISBN 9780111027820) issued 20/05/15. - 4p.: 30 cm. - 978-0-11-102850-6 £4.25

The Water Environment (Relevant Enactments and Designation of Responsible Authorities and Functions) (Scotland) Amendment Order 2015 No. 2015/323. - Enabling power: Water Environment and Water Services (Scotland) Act 2003, s. 2 (8). - Issued: 11.09.2015. Made: 07.09.2015. Laid before the Scottish Parliament: 09.09.2015. Coming into force: 10.10.2015. Effect: S.S.I. 2011/368 amended. Territorial extent & classification: S. General. - 4p.: 30 cm. - 978-0-11-102927-5 £4.25

The Water Environment (River Basin Management Planning etc.) (Miscellaneous Amendments) (Scotland) Regulations 2015 No. 2015/211. - Enabling power: Water Environment and Water Services (Scotland) Act 2003, ss. 8 (5), 9 (4) to (6), 10 (2) (b), 19 (1), 36 (2) (3) & European Communities Act 1972, s. 2 (2), sch. 2, para. 1A. - Issued: 02.06.2015. Made: 26.05.2015. Laid before the Scottish Parliament: 28.05.2015. Coming into force: In accord. with art. 1(2) (3). Effect: S.S.I. 2011/209; 2013/323 amended & S.S.I. 2009/420 revoked. Territorial extent & classification: S. General. - EC note: Regulation 2 amends Parts 1 and 2 of the 2013 Regulations to take account of amendments made to Directive 2000/60/EC as last amended by Commission Directive 2014/101/EU. - 8p.: 30 cm. - 978-0-11-102794-3 £6.00

The Wester Ross Marine Conservation Order 2015 No. 2015/302. - Enabling power: Marine (Scotland) Act 2010, ss. 85 (1) (a) (2) (4), 86 (1) (3), 88 (1) (2). - Issued: 21.08.2015. Made: 17.08.2015. Laid before the Scottish Parliament: 17.08.2015. Coming into force: 18.08.2015. Effect: None. Territorial extent & classification: S. General. - Revoked by SSI 2016/88 (ISBN 9780111031544). - 4p.: 30 cm. - 978-0-11-102912-1 £4.25

Equality

The Equality Act 2010 (Specific Duties) (Scotland) Amendment Regulations 2015 No. 2015/254. - Enabling power: Equality Act 2010, ss. 153 (3), 155 (1) (c) (2), 207 (4). - Issued: 18.06.2015. Made: 10.06.2015. Coming into force: 11.06.2015. Effect: S.S.I. 2012/162 amended. Territorial extent & classification: S. General. - Supersedes draft S.S.I. (ISBN 9780111027561) issued 24/04/15. - 4p.: 30 cm. - 978-0-11-102838-4 £4.25

Equal opportunities

The Equality Act 2010 (Specification of Public Authorities) (Scotland) Order 2015 No. 2015/83. - Enabling power: Equality Act 2010, s. 151 (3). - Issued: 03.03.2015. Made: 24.02.2015. Coming into force: 01.04.2015. Effect: 2010 c.15 amended. Territorial extent & classification: S. General. - Supersedes draft S.I. (ISBN 9780111025772) issued 13/01/15. - 4p.: 30 cm. - 978-0-11-102675-5 £4.25

Fire services

The Firefighters' Compensation Scheme and Pension Scheme (Amendment) (Scotland) Order 2015 No. 2015/143. - Enabling power: Fire and Rescue Services Act 2004, ss. 34, 60. - Issued: 31.03.2015. Made: 24.03.2015. Laid: 26.03.2015. Coming into force: In accord. with art. 1. Effect: S.S.I. 2006/338; 2007/199 amended. Territorial extent & classification: S. General. - 20p.: 30 cm. - 978-0-11-102730-1 £6.00

The Firemen's Pension Scheme (Amendment No. 2) (Scotland) Order 2015 No. 2015/173. - Enabling power: Fire Services Act 1947, s. 26 (1) to (5) & Superannuation Act 1972, ss. 12, 16. - Issued: 27.04.2015. Made: 21.04.2015. Laid before the Scottish Parliament: 21.04.2015. Coming into force: 20.05.2015. Effect: S.I. 1992/129 amended. Territorial extent & classification: S. General. - 4p.: 30 cm. - 978-0-11-102758-5 £4.25

The Firemen's Pension Scheme (Amendment) (Scotland) Order 2015 No. 2015/140. - Enabling power: Fire Services Act 1947, s. 26 (1) to (5) & Superannuation Act 1972, ss. 12, 16. - Issued: 31.03.2015. Made: 24.03.2015. Laid before the Scottish Parliament: 26.03.2015. Coming into force: 01.04.2015. Effect: S.I. 1992/129 amended in relation to Scotland. Territorial extent & classification: S. General. - 8p.: 30 cm. - 978-0-11-102727-1 £4.25

Fish farming

The Aquaculture and Fisheries (Scotland) Act 2007 (Fixed Penalty Notices) Order 2015 No. 2015/113. - Enabling power: Aquaculture and Fisheries (Scotland) Act 2007, ss. 26 (5), 27 (1) (3), 29 (2) (b), 43 (1) (b). - Issued: 18.03.2015. Made: 11.03.2015. Laid before the Scottish Parliament: 13.03.2015. Coming into force: 27.04.2015. Effect: S.S.I. 2008/101; 2011/60 revoked. Territorial extent & classification: S. General. - 4p.: 30 cm. - 978-0-11-102705-9 £4.25

The European Maritime and Fisheries Fund (Grants) (Scotland) Regulations 2015 No. 2015/359. - Enabling power: European Communities Act 1972, s. 2 (2), sch. 2, para. 1A. - Issued: 03.11.2015. Made: 27.10.2015. Laid before the Scottish Parliament: 29.10.2015. Coming into force: 30.11.2015. Effect: S.S.I. 2007/307; 2010/323; 2012/166 revoked with savings. Territorial extent & classification: S. General. - 12p.: 30 cm. - 978-0-11-102962-6 £6.00

The Trade in Animals and Related Products (Scotland) Amendment Regulations 2015 No. 2015/401. - Enabling power: European Communities Act 1972, s. 2 (2), sch. 2, para. 1A. - Issued: 26.11.2015. Made: 19.11.2015. Laid before the Scottish Parliament: 23.11.2015. Coming into force: 08.01.2016. Effect: S.S.I. 2015/177 amended. Territorial extent & classification: S. General. - 4p.: 30 cm. - 978-0-11-103004-2 £4.25

Flood risk management

The Reservoirs (Panels of Reservoir Engineers: Sections under which Members may be Appointed) (Scotland) Order 2015 No. 2015/92. - Enabling power: Reservoirs (Scotland) Act 2011, ss. 27 (a), 114 (2) (b). - Issued: 05.03.2015. Made: 26.02.2015. Laid before the Scottish Parliament: 02.03.2015. Coming into force: 01.04.2015. Effect: None. Territorial extent & classification: S. General. - 4p.: 30 cm. - 978-0-11-102683-0 £4.25

The Reservoirs (Scotland) Act 2011 (Commencement No. 2) Order 2015 No. 2015/43 (C.7). - Enabling power: Reservoirs (Scotland) Act 2011, s. 116 (1). Bringing into operation various provisions of the 2011 Act on 20.02.2015, in accord. with art. 2. - Issued: 09.02.2015. Made: 03.02.2015. Laid before the Scottish Parliament: 05.02.2015. Effect: None. Territorial extent & classification: S. General. - 4p.: 30 cm. - 978-0-11-102617-5 £4.25

The Reservoirs (Scotland) Act 2011 (Commencement No. 3 and Transitional Provisions) Order 2015 No. 2015/63 (C.13). - Enabling power: Reservoirs (Scotland) Act 2011, ss. 114 (2) (a), 116 (1). Bringing into operation various provisions of the 2011 Act on 01.04.2015, in accord. with art. 2. - Issued: 23.02.2015. Made: 17.02.2015. Laid before the Scottish Parliament: 19.02.2015. Effect: None. Territorial extent & classification: S. General. - 8p.: 30 cm. - 978-0-11-102648-9 £4.25

The Reservoirs (Scotland) Act 2011 (Commencement No. 4) Order 2015 No. 2015/314 (C.37). - Enabling power: Reservoirs (Scotland) Act 2011, ss. 116 (1). Bringing into operation various provisions of the 2011 Act on 01.10.2015, in accord. with art. 2. - Issued: 07.09.2015. Made: 01.09.2015. Laid before the Scottish Parliament: 02.09.2015. Coming into force: 01.10.2015. Effect: None. Territorial extent & classification: S. General. - 8p.: 30 cm. - 978-0-11-102919-0 £4.25

The Reservoirs (Scotland) Amendment Regulations 2015 No. 2015/315. - Enabling power: Reservoirs (Scotland) Act 2011, ss. 2 (3) (a), 9 (3) (a), 14 (1) (3) (4), 23 (8), 24 (7), 114 (2) (b). - Issued: 07.09.2015. Made: 01.09.2015. Laid before the Scottish Parliament: 02.09.2015. Coming into force: 01.10.2015. Effect: S.S.I. 2015/90 amended. Territorial extent & classification: S. General. - Revoked by SSI 2016/43 (ISBN 9780111031087) in relation to S. - 4p.: 30 cm. - 978-0-11-102920-6 £4.25

The Reservoirs (Scotland) Regulations 2015 No. 2015/90. - Enabling power: Reservoirs (Scotland) Act 2011, ss. 1 (6), 2 (3), 9 (3) (a), 10 (2), 14 (1) (3) (4), 28 (7) (8), 30 (2), 114 (2) (b)- Issued: 05.03.2015. Made: 26.02.2015. Laid before the Scottish Parliament: 02.03.2015. Coming into force: 01.04.2015. Effect: None. Territorial extent & classification: S. General. - Revoked by SSI 2016/43 (ISBN 9780111031087). - 16p.: 30 cm. - 978-0-11-102682-3 £6.00

Food

The Fish Labelling (Scotland) Amendment Regulations 2015 No. 2015/48. - Enabling power: Food Safety Act 1990, ss. 16 (1), 17 (2), 26 (1) (a) (3), 48 (1) & European Communities Act 1972, sch. 2, para 1A. - Issued: 10.02.2015. Made: 03.02.2015. Laid before the Scottish Parliament: 05.02.2015. Coming into force: 15.03.2015. Effect: S.S.I. 2013/256 amended. Territorial extent & classification: S. General. - These Regulations enforce in Scotland, the consumer requirements of Chapter 2 of title 1 of Council Regulation (EC) no. 104/2000 on the common organisation of the markets in fishery and aquaculture products and Commission Regulation (EC) no. 104/2000 as regards informing consumers about fishery and aquaculture products. They also enforce the traceability requirements of Council Regulation (EC) no. 1224/2009 establishing a Community control system for ensuring compliance with the rules of the Common Fisheries Policy and Commission implementation of Council Regulation (EC) no. 1224/2009 establishing a Community control system for ensuring compliance with the rules of the Common Fisheries Policy. - 4p.: 30 cm. - 978-0-11-102628-1 £4.25

The Food Information (Miscellaneous Amendments) (Scotland) Regulations 2015 No. 2015/410. - Enabling power: Food Safety Act 1990, ss. 6 (4), 15A (b), 16(1), 17, 18, 26, 45, 48 (1), sch. 1, paras 1, 4 (b) & European Communities Act 1972, s. 2 (2), sch. 2, para. 1A. - Issued: 09.12.2015. Made: 02.12.2015. Laid before the Scottish Parliament: 04.12.2015. Coming into force: 19.01.2016. Effect: S.S.I. 2014/312 amended. Territorial extent & classification: S. General. - 8p.: 30 cm. - 978-0-11-103016-5 £4.25

The Food (Scotland) Act 2015 (Commencement) Order 2015 No. 2015/99 (C.19). - Enabling power: Food (Scotland) Act 2015. Bringing into operation various provisions of the 2015 Act on 01.04.2015. - Issued: 10.03.2015. Made: 03.03.2015. Laid before the Scottish Parliament: 03.03.2015. Effect: None. Territorial extent & classification: S. General. - 2p.: 30 cm. - 978-0-11-102695-3 £4.25

The Food (Scotland) Act 2015 (Consequential and Transitional Provisions) Order 2015 No. 2015/100. - Enabling power: Food (Scotland) Act 2015, s. 61 (a) (b). - Issued: 10.03.2015. Made: 03.03.2015. Laid: 03.03.2015. Coming into force: 01.04.2015. Effect: 37 SIs amended. Territorial extent & classification: S. General. - 8p.: 30 cm. - 978-0-11-102693-9 £6.00

The Food (Scotland) Act 2015 (Consequential Provisions) (No. 2) Order 2015 No. 2015/433. - Enabling power: Food (Scotland) Act 2015 s. 61 (a). - Issued: 23.12.2015. Made: 16.12.2015. Laid before the Scottish Parliament: 18.12.2015. Coming into force: 05.02.2016. Effect: S.I. 2004/3279 modified. Territorial extent & classification: S. General. - 2p.: 30 cm. - 978-0-11-103036-3 £4.25

The Honey (Scotland) Regulations 2015 No. 2015/208. - Enabling power: Food Safety Act 1990, ss. 6 (4), 16 (1) (a) (e), 17 (1), 26 (1) (3), 48 (1). - Issued: 28.05.2015. Made: 21.05.2015. Laid before the Scottish Parliament: 26.05.2015. Coming into force: 24.06.2015. Effect: S.S.I. 2014/312 amended & S.S.I. 2003/569; 2005/307 revoked. Territorial extent and classification: S. General. - 12p.: 30 cm. - 978-0-11-102791-2 £6.00

The Natural Mineral Water, Spring Water and Bottled Drinking Water (Scotland) Amendment Regulations 2015 No. 2015/363. - Enabling power: Food Safety Act 1990, ss. 6 (4), 16 (1), 17 (1), 26 (1) (a) (3), 48 (1). - Issued: 04.11.2015. Made: 28.10.2015. Laid before the Scottish Parliament: 30.10.2015. Coming into force: 28.11.2015. Effect: S.S.I. 2007/483 amended. Territorial extent & classification: S. General. - 12p.: 30 cm. - 978-0-11-102965-7 £6.00

Harbours, docks, piers and ferries

The Caledonian Maritime Assets (Brodick) Harbour Revision Order 2015 No. 2015/6. - Enabling power: Harbours Act 1964, s. 14 (1) (2A) (3). - Issued: 19.01.2015. Made: 13.01.2015. Coming into force: 14.01.2015. Effect: 1920 c.lviii; 1938 c.lxv; 1951 c.vi repealed. Territorial extent & classification: S. General. - 28p., 1 map: 30 cm. - 978-0-11-102581-9 £6.00

The Lerwick Harbour Revision Order 2015 No. 2015/4. - Enabling power: Harbours Act 1964, s. 14 (1) (2) (2A). - Issued: 15.01.2015. Made: 09.01.2015. Coming into force: 10.01.2015. Effect: 1975 c.xxv amended. Territorial extent & classification: S. General. - 12p.: 30 cm. - 978-0-11-102579-6 £6.00

The Peterhead Port Authority Harbour Revision Order 2015 No. 2015/298. - Enabling power: Harbours Act 1964, s. 14 (1) (3). - Issued: 10.08.2015. Made: 04.08.2015. Coming into force: 05.08.2015. Effect: None. Territorial extent & classification: S. Local. - 16p.: 30 cm. - 978-0-11-102861-2 £6.00

High Court of Justiciary

Act of Adjournal (Criminal Procedure Rules 1996 Amendment) (No. 3) (Miscellaneous) 2015 No. 2015/201. - Enabling power: Criminal Procedure (Scotland) Act 1995, s. 305. - Issued: 27.05.2015. Made: 20.05.2015. Laid before the Scottish Parliament: 22.05.2015. Coming into force: 08.06.2015. Effect: S.I. 1996/513 amended. Territorial extent & classification: S. General. - 8p.: 30 cm. - 978-0-11-102787-5 £6.00

Act of Adjournal (Criminal Procedure Rules 1996 Amendment) (No. 4) (Sheriff Appeal Court) 2015 No. 2015/245. - Enabling power: Criminal Procedure (Scotland) Act 1995, s. 305. - Issued: 10.06.2015. Made: 04.06.2015. Laid before the Scottish Parliament: 08.06.2015. Coming into force: 22.09.2015. Effect: S.I. 1996/513 amended. Territorial extent & classification: S. General. - 28p.: 30 cm. - 978-0-11-102828-5 £6.00

Act of Adjournal (Criminal Procedure Rules 1996 Amendment) (No. 5) (Request for Final Decision and Reasons) 2015 No. 2015/375. - Enabling power: Criminal Procedure (Scotland) Act 1995 s. 305. - Issued: 06.11.2015. Made: 02.11.2015. Laid before the Scottish Parliament: 04.11.2015. Coming into force: 02.12.2015. Effect: S.I. 1996/513 amended. Territorial extent & classification: S. General. - 4p.: 30 cm. - 978-0-11-102971-8 £4.25

Act of Adjournal (Criminal Procedure Rules 1996 Amendment) (No. 6) (Special Measures in the Justice of the Peace Court) 2015 No. 2015/443. - Enabling power: Criminal Procedure (Scotland) Act, 1995 s. 305. - Issued: 23.12.2015. Made: 17.12.2015. Laid before the Scottish Parliament: 18.12.2015. Coming into force: 23.12.2015. Effect: S.I. 1996/513 amended. Territorial extent & classification: S. General. - 8p.: 30 cm. - 978-0-11-103042-4 £4.25

Act of Adjournal (Criminal Procedure Rules 1996 and Act of Adjournal (Criminal Procedure Rules 1996 Amendment) (No. 4) (Sheriff Appeal Court) 2015 Amendment) (Miscellaneous) 2015 No. 2015/295. - Enabling power: Criminal Procedure (Scotland) Act 1995, s. 305. - Issued: 06.08.2015. Made: 31.08.2015. Laid before the Scottish Parliament: 03.08.2015. Coming into force: 01.09.2015. Effect: S.I. 1996/513; 2015/245 amended. Territorial extent & classification: S. General. - 16p.: 30 cm. - 978-0-11-102859-9 £6.00

Act of Adjournal (Criminal Procedure Rules Amendment No. 2) (European Protection Orders) 2015 No. 2015/121. - Enabling power: Criminal Procedure (Scotland) Act 1995, s. 305. - Issued: 24.03.2015. Made: 18.03.2015. Laid before the Scottish Parliament: 19.03.2015. Coming into force: 01.04.2015. Effect: S.I. 1996/513 amended. Territorial extent & classification: S. General. - 24p.: 30 cm. - 978-0-11-102712-7 £6.00

Act of Adjournal (Criminal Procedure Rules Amendment) (Reporting Restrictions) 2015 No. 2015/84. - Enabling power: Criminal Procedure (Scotland) Act 1995, s. 305. - Issued: 04.03.2015. Made: 26.02.2015. Laid before the Scottish Parliament: 02.03.2015. Coming into force: 01.04.2015. Effect: S.I. 1996/513 amended. Territorial extent & classification: S. General. - 8p.: 30 cm. - 978-0-11-102676-2 £6.00

The Courts Reform (Scotland) Act 2014 (Commencement No. 3, Transitional and Saving Provisions) Order 2015 No. 2015/247 (C.35). - Enabling power: Courts Reform (Scotland) Act 2014, s. 138 (2) (3). Bringing into operation various provisions of the 2014 Act on 22.09.2015. - Issued: 10.06.2015. Made: 04.06.2015. Laid before the Scottish Parliament: 08.06.2015. Coming into force: 22.09.2015. Effect: None. Territorial extent & classification: S. General. - 12p.: 30 cm. - 978-0-11-102830-8 £6.00

The Courts Reform (Scotland) Act 2014 (Consequential Provisions No. 2) Order 2015 No. 2015/338. - Enabling power: Courts Reform (Scotland) Act 2014, s. 137. - Issued: 24.09.2015. Made: 18.09.2015. Coming into force: 22.09.2015. Effect: 1981 c.22; 1988 c.36, 53; 1991 c.65; 1995 c.43, 46; 2002 asp 6; asp 10; 2003 c.42; 2006 asp 10; asp 11, 2006 c.45; 2010 asp 9, asp 13; 2011 c.23; 2015 c.6 & S.S.I. 2000/301; 2001/315; 2007/504, 505, 507; 2013/6; 2014/337; 2015/77 modified. Territorial extent & classification: S. General. - Supersedes draft SI (ISBN 9780111028346) issued 12/06/15 - 16p.: 30 cm. - 978-0-11-102944-2 £6.00

The Criminal Justice and Licensing (Scotland) Act 2010 (Commencement No. 13) and the Courts Reform (Scotland) Act 2014 (Commencement No. 4) Order 2015 No. 2015/336 (C.41). - Enabling power: Criminal Justice and Licensing (Scotland) Act 2010, s. 206 (1) & Courts Reform (Scotland) Act 2014, s. 138 (2). Bringing into operation various provisions of both Acts on 19.10.2015, in accord. with arts 1 & 2. - Issued: 23.09.2015. Made: 16.09.2015. Laid before the Scottish Parliament: 18.09.2015. Coming into force: 19.10.2015. Effect: None. Territorial extent & classification: S. General. - 8p.: 30 cm. - 978-0-11-102943-5 £6.00

The High Court of Justiciary Fees Order 2015 No. 2015/262. - Enabling power: Courts Reform (Scotland) Act 2014, ss. 107 (1) (2). - Issued: 22.06.2015. Made: 15.06.2015. Laid before the Scottish Parliament: 17.06.2015. Coming into force: In accord. with art. 1. Effect: S.S.I. 2013/137 partially revoked & S.I. 1984/252, 1985/825; 1986/449; 1987/772; 1988/798; 1989/258; 1990/470; 1991/331; 1992/412; 1993/426; 1994/3266; 1996/516; 1999/753; 2007/321; 2008/237; 2009/87; 2012/291 revoked (22.09.2015). Territorial extent & classification: S. General. - 8p.: 30 cm. - 978-0-11-102842-1 £6.00

Housing

The Enhanced Enforcement Areas Scheme (Scotland) Regulations 2015 No. 2015/252. - Enabling power: Housing (Scotland) Act 2014, ss. 28 (1), 101 (1). - Issued: 16.06.2015. Made: 09.06.2015. Coming into force: 10.06.2015. Effect: S.S.I. 2010/168 amended. Territorial extent & classification: S. General. - Supersedes draft S.S.I. (ISBN 9780111027486) issued 09/04/15. - 8p.: 30 cm. - 978-0-11-102837-7 £4.25

The Housing (Scotland) Act 2006 (Repayment Charge and Discharge) Amendment Order 2015 No. 2015/144. - Enabling power: Housing (Scotland) Act 2006, s. 174 & Housing (Scotland) Act 2014, s. 102. - Issued: 01.04.2015. Made: 25.03.2015. Laid before the Scottish Parliament: 27.03.2015. Coming into force: 11.05.2015. Effect: S.S.I. 2007/419 amended. Territorial extent & classification: S. General. - 4p.: 30 cm. - 978-0-11-102731-8 £4.25

The Housing (Scotland) Act 2014 (Commencement No. 2) Order 2015 No. 2015/122 (C.26). - Enabling power: Housing (Scotland) Act 2014, s. 104 (3). Bringing into operation various provisions of the 2014 Act on 01.04.2015, in accord. with art. 2. - Issued: 24.03.2015. Made: 18.03.2015. Laid before the Scottish Parliament: 20.03.2015. Coming into force: 01.04.2015. Effect: None. Territorial extent & classification: S. General. - 4p.: 30 cm. - 978-0-11-102713-4 £4.25

The Housing (Scotland) Act 2014 (Commencement No. 3 and Transitional Provisions) Order 2015 No. 2015/272 (C.36). - Enabling power: Housing (Scotland) Act 2014, s. 104 (3) (5). Bringing into operation various provisions of the 2014 Act on 13.07.2015; 31.08.2015; 01.12.2015, in accord. with art. 2. - Issued: 30.06.2015. Made: 24.06.2015. Laid before the Scottish Parliament: 26.06.2015. Coming into force: 13.07.2015. Effect: None. Territorial extent & classification: S. General. - 8p.: 30 cm. - 978-0-11-102852-0 £4.25

The Housing (Scotland) Act 2014 (Commencement No. 4 and Amendment) Order 2015 No. 2015/349 (C.43). - Enabling power: Housing (Scotland) Act 2014, s. 104 (3). Bringing into operation various provisions of the 2014 Act on 01.12.15, 01.04.16, 01.06.16 in accord. with the sch. - Issued: 15.10.2015. Made: 08.10.2015. Laid before the Scottish Parliament: 12.10.2015. Coming into force: 30.11.2015. Effect: S.S.I. 2015/272 amended. Territorial extent & classification: S. General. - 4p.: 30 cm. - 978-0-11-102956-5 £4.25

The Housing (Scotland) Act 2014 (Commencement No. 5 and Consequential Provision) Order 2015 No. 2015/430 (C.58). - Enabling power: Housing (Scotland) Act 2014, s. 102. Bringing into operation various provisions of the 2014 Act on 02.02.2016, in accord. with art. 2. - Issued: 22.12.2015. Made: 15.12.2015. Laid before the Scottish Parliament: 17.12.2015. Coming into force: 02.02.2016. Effect: S.S.I. 2013/20 amended. Territorial extent & classification: S. General. - 24p.: 30 cm. - 978-0-11-103030-1 £6.00

The Private Rented Housing Panel (Landlord Applications) (Scotland) Regulations 2015 No. 2015/403. - Enabling power: Housing (Scotland) Act 2006, ss. 28B (1), 28C (11). - Issued: 02.12.2015. Made: 26.11.2015. Coming into force: 01.12.2015. Effect: None. Territorial extent & classification: S. General. - Supersedes draft S.S.I. (ISBN 9780111029497) issued 28/09/15. - 8p.: 30 cm. - 978-0-11-103009-7 £4.25

The Private Rented Housing Panel (Tenant and Third Party Applications) (Scotland) Regulations 2015 No. 2015/369. - Enabling power: Housing (Scotland) Act 2006, sch. 2, para. 8. - Issued: 05.11.2015. Made: 29.10.2015. Laid before the Scottish Parliament: 02.11.2015. Coming into force: 01.12.2015. Effect: S.S.I. 2007/173 revoked with saving. Territorial extent & classification: S. General. - 12p.: 30 cm. - 978-0-11-102968-8 £6.00

The Private Rented Housing (Scotland) Act 2011 (Commencement No. 7) Order 2015 No. 2015/326 (C.39). - Enabling power: Private Rented Housing (Scotland) Act 2011, s. 41 (3). Bringing into operation various provisions of the 2011 Act on 22.09.2015, in accord. with art. 2. - Issued: 15.09.2015. Made: 08.09.2015. Laid before the Scottish Parliament: 09.09.2015. Coming into force: 22.09.2015. Effect: None. Territorial extent & classification: S. General. - 4p.: 30 cm. - 978-0-11-102931-2 £4.25

Insolvency

The Bankruptcy and Debt Advice (Scotland) Act 2014 (Commencement No. 2, Savings and Transitionals) Amendment Order 2015 No. 2015/54 (C.10). - Enabling power: Bankruptcy and Debt Advice (Scotland) Act 2014, s. 57 (2) (3). Bringing into operation various provisions of the 2014 Act on 01.04.2015, in accord. with art. 1. - Issued: 12.02.2015. Made: 05.02.2015. Laid before the Scottish Parliament: 09.02.2015. Coming into force: 01.04.2015. Effect: S.S.I. 2014/261 amended. Territorial extent & classification: S. General. - 4p.: 30 cm. - 978-0-11-102637-3 £4.25

The Bankruptcy (Miscellaneous Amendments) (Scotland) Regulations 2015 No. 2015/80. - Enabling power: Bankruptcy (Scotland) Act 1985, ss. 1A (1) (b) (5), 2 (8), 5 (2ZA) (a) (ii) (2D) (6A), 6 (7), 7 (1) (d), 11 (1), 19 (2), 22 (2) (a) (6), 23 (1) (a), 32 (9A), 40 (3B), 43A (2), 43B (1), 45 (3) (a), 49 (3), 51 (7) (a), 54 (2), 54A (2), 54C (2), 54D (2) (a) (c), 54E (2) (5), 69, 69A, 71C, 72 (1A), 72A, 73 (1), sch. 3 paras 5 (1) (6). - Issued: 04.03.2015. Made: 25.02.2015. Laid before the Scottish Parliament: 27.02.2015. Coming into force: 01.04.2015. Effect: S.I. 2014/225, 226, 227 amended. Territorial extent & classification: S. General. - 64p.: 30 cm. - 978-0-11-102672-4 £11.00

The Common Financial Tool etc. (Scotland) Amendment Regulations 2015 No. 2015/149. - Enabling power: Bankruptcy (Scotland) Act 1985, ss. 5D, 71C, 72 (1A), sch. 5, para. 5 & Debt Arrangement and Attachment Act (Scotland) Act 2002, s. 7 (2) (bd). - Issued: 01.04.2015. Made: 25.03.2015. Coming into force: 01.04.2015. Effect: S.S.I. 2014/290 amended. Territorial extent & classification: S. General. - Supersedes draft SI (ISBN 9780111026533) issued 25/02/15 - 8p.: 30 cm. - 978-0-11-102735-6 £6.00

International immunities and privileges

The International Organisations (Immunities and Privileges) (Scotland) Amendment Order 2015 No. 2015/421. - Enabling power: International Organisations Act 1968, s. 1 (2). - Issued: 16.12.2015. Made: 09.12.2015. Coming into force: In accord. with art. 1. Effect: S.S.I. 2009/44 amended. Territorial extent & classification: S. General. - 8p.: 30 cm. - 978-0-11-103021-9 £4.25

Investigatory powers

The Regulation of Investigatory Powers (Covert Human Intelligence Sources - Code of Practice) (Scotland) Order 2015 No. 2015/33. - Enabling power: Regulation of Investigatory Powers (Scotland) Act 2000, s. 24 (5). - Issued: 03.02.2015. Made: 27.01.2015. Coming into force: 02.02.2015. Effect: S.S.I. 2003/181 revoked. Territorial extent & classification: S. General. - Supersedes draft S.S.I. (ISBN 9780111026083) issued 12/12/14. - 4p.: 30 cm. - 978-0-11-102608-3 £4.25

The Regulation of Investigatory Powers (Covert Surveillance and Property Interference - Code of Practice) (Scotland) Order 2015 No. 2015/34. - Enabling power: Regulation of Investigatory Powers (Scotland) Act 2000, s. 24 (5). - Issued: 03.02.2015. Made: 27.01.2015. Coming into force: 02.02.2015. Effect: S.S.I. 2003/183 revoked. Territorial extent & classification: S. General. - Supersedes draft S.S.I. (ISBN 9780111025475) issued 12/12/14. - 4p.: 30 cm. - 978-0-11-102609-0 £4.25

The Regulation of Investigatory Powers (Modification of Authorisation Provisions: Legal Consultations) (Scotland) Order 2015 No. 2015/32. - Enabling power: Regulation of Investigatory Powers (Scotland) Act 2000, s. 27 (1) (b). - Issued: 03.02.2015. Made: 27.01.2015. Coming into force: 02.02.2015. Effect: None. Territorial extent & classification: S. General. - Supersedes draft S.S.I. (ISBN 9780111025390) issued 09/12/14. - 4p.: 30 cm. - 978-0-11-102607-6 £4.25

Judgments

The Civil Jurisdiction and Judgments (Amendment) (Scotland) Regulations 2015 No. 2015/1. - Enabling power: European Communities Act 1972, s. 2 (2). - Issued: 13.01.2015. Made: 07.01.2015. Laid before the Scottish Parliament: 09.01.2015. Coming into force: 07.02.2015. Effect: None. Territorial extent & classification: S. General. - 4p.: 30 cm. - 978-0-11-102576-5 £4.25

Judicial appointments and discipline

Act of Sederunt (Fitness for Judicial Office Tribunal Rules) 2015 No. 2015/120. - Enabling power: Judiciary and Courts (Scotland) Act 2008 s. 37 (5) & Courts Reform (Scotland) Act 2014, s. 23 (5). -
 Issued: 24.03.2015. Made: 18.03.2015. Laid before the Scottish Parliament: 19.03.2015. Coming into force: 01.04.2015. Effect: S.S.I. 2014/102 revoked. Territorial extent & classification: S. General. - 8p.: 30 cm. - 978-0-11-102711-0 £6.00

The Courts Reform (Scotland) Act 2014 (Commencement No. 2, Transitional and Saving Provisions) Order 2015 No. 2015/77 (C.17). - Enabling power: Courts Reform (Scotland) Act 2014, s. 138 (2) (3). Bringing into operation various provisions of the 2014 Act on 12.03.2015. - Issued: 02.03.2015. Made: 24.02.2015. Laid before the Scottish Parliament: 26.02.2015. Coming into force: In accord with art. 1. Effect: None. Territorial extent & classification: S. General. - 8p.: 30 cm. - 978-0-11-102667-0 £6.00

The Courts Reform (Scotland) Act 2014 (Consequential Provisions) Order 2015 No. 2015/150. - Enabling power: Courts Reform (Scotland) Act 2014, s. 137. - Issued: 01.04.2015. Made: 24.03.2015. Coming into force: 01.04.2015. Effect: 1966 c.19; 1968 c.59; 1972 c.59; 1986 c.45; 1995 c.46; 1999 c.22; 2004 asp 8; 2005 c.12; 2007 asp 3; S.S.I. 2013/50 modified. Territorial extent & classification: S. General. - Supersedes draft SI (ISBN 9780111026663) issued 27/02/15 - 4p.: 30 cm. - 978-0-11-102736-3 £4.25

Justice of the Peace Court

Act of Adjournal (Criminal Procedure Rules 1996 Amendment) (No. 3) (Miscellaneous) 2015 No. 2015/201. - Enabling power: Criminal Procedure (Scotland) Act 1995, s. 305. - Issued: 27.05.2015. Made: 20.05.2015. Laid before the Scottish Parliament: 22.05.2015. Coming into force: 08.06.2015. Effect: S.I. 1996/513 amended. Territorial extent & classification: S. General. - 8p.: 30 cm. - 978-0-11-102787-5 £6.00

Act of Adjournal (Criminal Procedure Rules 1996 Amendment) (No. 4) (Sheriff Appeal Court) 2015 No. 2015/245. - Enabling power: Criminal Procedure (Scotland) Act 1995, s. 305. - Issued: 10.06.2015. Made: 04.06.2015. Laid before the Scottish Parliament: 08.06.2015. Coming into force: 22.09.2015. Effect: S.I. 1996/513 amended. Territorial extent & classification: S. General. - 28p.: 30 cm. - 978-0-11-102828-5 £6.00

Act of Adjournal (Criminal Procedure Rules 1996 Amendment) (No. 5) (Request for Final Decision and Reasons) 2015 No. 2015/375. - Enabling power: Criminal Procedure (Scotland) Act 1995 s. 305. - Issued: 06.11.2015. Made: 02.11.2015. Laid before the Scottish Parliament: 04.11.2015. Coming into force: 02.12.2015. Effect: S.I. 1996/513 amended. Territorial extent & classification: S. General. - 4p.: 30 cm. - 978-0-11-102971-8 £4.25

Act of Adjournal (Criminal Procedure Rules 1996 Amendment) (No. 6) (Special Measures in the Justice of the Peace Court) 2015 No. 2015/443. - Enabling power: Criminal Procedure (Scotland) Act, 1995 s. 305. - Issued: 23.12.2015. Made: 17.12.2015. Laid before the Scottish Parliament: 18.12.2015. Coming into force: 23.12.2015. Effect: S.I. 1996/513 amended. Territorial extent & classification: S. General. - 8p.: 30 cm. - 978-0-11-103042-4 £4.25

Act of Adjournal (Criminal Procedure Rules Amendment No. 2) (European Protection Orders) 2015 No. 2015/121. - Enabling power: Criminal Procedure (Scotland) Act 1995, s. 305. - Issued: 24.03.2015. Made: 18.03.2015. Laid before the Scottish Parliament: 19.03.2015. Coming into force: 01.04.2015. Effect: S.I. 1996/513 amended. Territorial extent & classification: S. General. - 24p.: 30 cm. - 978-0-11-102712-7 £6.00

Act of Adjournal (Criminal Procedure Rules Amendment) (Reporting Restrictions) 2015 No. 2015/84. - Enabling power: Criminal Procedure (Scotland) Act 1995, s. 305. - Issued: 04.03.2015. Made: 26.02.2015. Laid before the Scottish Parliament: 02.03.2015. Coming into force: 01.04.2015. Effect: S.I. 1996/513 amended. Territorial extent & classification: S. General. - 8p.: 30 cm. - 978-0-11-102676-2 £6.00

The Courts Reform (Scotland) Act 2014 (Commencement No. 3, Transitional and Saving Provisions) Order 2015 No. 2015/247 (C.35). - Enabling power: Courts Reform (Scotland) Act 2014, s. 138 (2) (3). Bringing into operation various provisions of the 2014 Act on 22.09.2015. - Issued: 10.06.2015. Made: 04.06.2015. Laid before the Scottish Parliament: 08.06.2015. Coming into force: 22.09.2015. Effect: None. Territorial extent & classification: S. General. - 12p.: 30 cm. - 978-0-11-102830-8 £6.00

The Courts Reform (Scotland) Act 2014 (Consequential Provisions No. 2) Order 2015 No. 2015/338. - Enabling power: Courts Reform (Scotland) Act 2014, s. 137. - Issued: 24.09.2015. Made: 18.09.2015. Coming into force: 22.09.2015. Effect: 1981 c.22; 1988 c.36, 53; 1991 c.65; 1995 c.43, 46; 2002 asp 6; asp 10; 2003 c.42; 2006 asp 10; asp 11, 2006 c.45; 2010 asp 9, asp 13; 2011 c.23; 2015 c.6 & S.S.I. 2000/301; 2001/315; 2007/504, 505, 507; 2013/6; 2014/337; 2015/77 modified. Territorial extent & classification: S. General. - Supersedes draft SI (ISBN 9780111028346) issued 12/06/15 - 16p.: 30 cm. - 978-0-11-102944-2 £6.00

The Justice of the Peace Courts Fees (Scotland) Order 2015 No. 2015/263. - Enabling power: Courts Reform (Scotland) Act 2014, ss. 107 (1) (2). - Issued: 22.06.2015. Made: 15.06.2015. Laid before the Scottish Parliament: 17.06.2015. Coming into force: In accord. with art. 1. Effect: S.S.I. 2013/137 partially revoked & S.S.I. 2012/292 revoked (22.09.2015). Territorial extent & classification: S. General. - 8p.: 30 cm. - 978-0-11-102843-8 £6.00

Land and buildings transaction tax

The Land and Buildings Transaction Tax (Addition and Modification of Reliefs) (Scotland) Order 2015 No. 2015/93. - Enabling power: Land and Buildings Transaction Tax (Scotland) Act 2013, s. 27 (3). - Issued: 04.03.2015. Made: 25.02.2015. Coming into force: 01.04.2015. Effect: 2013 asp 11 amended. Territorial extent & classification: S. General. - Supersedes draft SI (ISBN 9780111025758) issued 30/12/14 - 8p.: 30 cm. - 978-0-11-102684-7 £4.25

The Land and Buildings Transaction Tax (Scotland) Act 2013 (Commencement No. 2) Order 2015 No. 2015/108 (C.21). - Enabling power: Land and Buildings Transaction Tax (Scotland) Act 2013, s. 70 (2). Bringing into operation various provisions of the 2013 Act on 01.04.2015, in accord. with art. 2. - Issued: 17.03.2015. Made: 11.03.2015. Laid before the Scottish Parliament: 13.03.2015. Coming into force: 01.04.2015. Effect: None. Territorial extent & classification: S. General. - 2p.: 30 cm. - 978-0-11-102702-8 £4.25

The Land and Buildings Transaction Tax (Sub-sale Development Relief and Multiple Dwellings Relief) (Scotland) Order 2015 No. 2015/123. - Enabling power: Land and Buildings Transaction Tax (Scotland) Act 2013, ss. 27 (3) (a) (b) (4), 68 (1). - Issued: 25.03.2015. Made: 17.03.2015. Coming into force: 01.04.2015. Effect: 2013 asp 11 amended. Territorial extent & classification: S. General. - Supersedes draft SI (ISBN 9780111026014) issued 29/01/15 - 8p.: 30 cm. - 978-0-11-102716-5 £6.00

The Land and Buildings Transaction Tax (Tax Rates and Tax Bands) (Scotland) Order 2015 No. 2015/126. - Enabling power: Land and Buildings Transaction Tax (Scotland) Act 2013, s. 24 (1), sch. 19, para. 3. - Issued: 25.03.2015. Made: 17.03.2015. Coming into force: 01.04.2015. Effect: None. Territorial extent & classification: S. General. - 4p.: 30 cm. - 978-0-11-102717-2 £4.25.

The Land and Buildings Transaction Tax (Transitional Provisions) (Scotland) Amendment Order 2015 No. 2015/71. - Enabling power: Land and Buildings Transaction Tax (Scotland) Act 2013, s. 67 (1). - Issued: 25.02.2015. Made: 18.02.2015. Laid before the Scottish Parliament: 20.02.2015. Coming into force: 01.04.2015. Effect: S.S.I. 2014/377 amended. Territorial extent & classification: S. General. - 2p.: 30 cm. - 978-0-11-102655-7 £4.25

The Land and Buildings Transaction Tax (Open-ended Investment Companies) (Scotland) Regulations 2015 No. 2015/322. - Enabling power: Land and Buildings Transaction Tax (Scotland) Act 2013, s. 46. - Issued: 11.09.2015. Made: 04.09.2015. Laid before the Scottish Parliament: 07.09.2015. Coming into force: 06.10.2015. Effect: None. Territorial extent & classification: S. General. - 4p.: 30 cm. - 978-0-11-102926-8 £4.25

Landfill tax

The Landfill Tax (Scotland) Act 2014 (Commencement No. 2) Order 2015 No. 2015/17 (C.4). - Enabling power: Landfill Tax (Scotland) Act 2014, s. 43 (2). Bringing into operation various provisions of the 2014 Act on 16.02.2015. - Issued: 29.01.2015. Made: 22.01.2015. Laid before the Scottish Parliament: 26.01.2015. Effect: None. Territorial extent & classification: S. General. - 4p.: 30 cm. - 978-0-11-102596-3 £4.25

The Landfill Tax (Scotland) Act 2014 (Commencement No. 3 and Transitional Provisions) Order 2015 No. 2015/109 (C.22). - Enabling power: Landfill Tax (Scotland) Act 2014, s. 43 (2) (3). Bringing into operation various provisions of the 2014 Act on 01.04.2015, in accord. with art. 2. - Issued: 17.03.2015. Made: 11.03.2015. Laid before the Scottish Parliament: 13.03.2015. Effect: None. Territorial extent & classification: S. General. - 4p.: 30 cm. - 978-0-11-102703-5 £4.25

The Scottish Landfill Tax (Administration) Amendment Regulations 2015 No. 2015/152. - Enabling power: Landfill Tax (Scotland) Act 2014, ss. 15 (1), 18, 19, 20, 25. - Issued: 01.04.2015. Made: 25.03.2015. Coming into force: 01.04.2015. Effect: S.S.I. 2013/3 amended. Territorial extent & classification: S. General. - Supersedes draft SI (ISBN 9780111026526) issued 24/02/15 - 4p.: 30 cm. - 978-0-11-102738-7 £4.25

The Scottish Landfill Tax (Administration) Regulations 2015 No. 2015/3. - Enabling power: Landfill Tax (Scotland) Act 2014, ss 15, 18, 19, 20, 22 (9), 23, 25, 30, 32, 37 (1) (4) to (7). - Issued: 14.01.2015. Made: 08.01.2015. Laid before the Scottish Parliament: 09.01.2015. Coming into force: in accord. with reg. 1. Effect: None. Territorial extent & classification: S. General. - 28p.: 30 cm. - 978-0-11-102578-9 £6.00

The Scottish Landfill Tax (Exemption Certificates) Order 2015 No. 2015/151. - Enabling power: Landfill Tax (Scotland) Act 2014, ss. 11 (1) (2). - Issued: 01.04.2015. Made: 25.03.2015. Coming into force: 01.04.2015. Effect: None. Territorial extent & classification: S. General. - Supersedes draft SI (ISBN 9780111026694) issued 02/03/15 - 4p.: 30 cm. - 978-0-11-102737-0 £4.25

The Scottish Landfill Tax (Qualifying Material) Order 2015 No. 2015/45. - Enabling power: Landfill Tax (Scotland) Act 2014, ss. 13 (4), 14 (7). - Issued: 10.02.2015. Made: 03.02.2015. Laid before the Scottish Parliament: 05.02.2015. Coming into force: 01.04.2015. Effect: None. Territorial extent & classification: S. General. - For approval by resolution of the Scottish Parliament within 28 days with the day on which the Order was made, not taking into account periods of dissolution or recess for more than 4 days. - 8p.: 30 cm. - 978-0-11-102624-3 £4.25

The Scottish Landfill Tax (Qualifying Material) Order 2015 No. 2015/45. - Enabling power: Landfill Tax (Scotland) Act 2014, ss. 13 (4), 14 (7). - Issued: 24.07.2015. Made: 03.02.2015. Laid before the Scottish Parliament: 05.02.2015. Coming into force: 01.04.2015. Effect: None. Territorial extent & classification: S. General. - Approved by Scottish Parliament. - 8p.: 30 cm. - 978-0-11-102856-8 £4.25

The Scottish Landfill Tax (Standard Rate and Lower Rate) Order 2015 No. 2015/127. - Enabling power: Landfill Tax (Scotland) Act 2014, s. 13 (2) (5)- Issued: 25.03.2015. Made: 17.03.2015. Coming into force: 01.04.2015. Effect: None. Territorial extent & classification: S. General. - Supersedes draft S.S.I. (ISBN 9780111026342) issued 11/02/15; Revoked by SSI 2016/64 (ISBN 9780111031605). - For approval by resolution of the Scottish Parliament. - 2p.: 30 cm. - 978-0-11-102718-9 £4.25

Land reform

The Community Empowerment (Scotland) Act 2015 (Commencement No. 2) Order 2015 No. 2015/358 (C.44). - Enabling power: Community Empowerment (Scotland) Act 2015, s. 145 (2). Bringing into operation various provisions of the 2015 Act on 13.11.2015, in accord. with arts 1 & 2. - Issued: 03.11.2015. Made: 27.10.2015. Laid before the Scottish Parliament: 29.10.2015. Coming into force: 13.11.2015. Effect: None. Territorial extent & classification: S. General. - 8p.: 30 cm. - 978-0-11-102961-9 £6.00

The Community Empowerment (Scotland) Act 2015 (Commencement No. 3 and Savings) Order 2015 No. 2015/399 (C.50). - Enabling power: Community Empowerment (Scotland) Act 2015, ss. 145 (2) (3). Bringing into operation various provisions of the 2015 Act on 15.04.2016, in accord. with art. 2. - Issued: 26.11.2015. Made: 19.11.2015. Laid before the Scottish Parliament: 23.11.2015. Coming into force: 15.04.2016. Effect: None. Territorial extent & classification: S. General. - 8p.: 30 cm. - 978-0-11-102999-2 £6.00

The Community Right to Buy (Scotland) Regulations 2015 No. 2015/400. - Enabling power: Land Reform (Scotland) Act 2003, ss. 34 (5), 36 (2) (f), 37 (1) (2) (4) (b) (4A) (18) (b), 39 (7) (c), 41 (3) (b), 48 (1) (2), 49 (2), 51A (2) (6), 51B (2) (3) (4), 52 (1) (3) (7), 63 (5), 98 (3). - Issued: 26.11.2015. Made: 19.11.2015. Laid before the Scottish Parliament: 23.11.2015. Coming into force: 15.04.2016. Effect: S.S.I. 2004/228, 229, 231; 2009/156 revoked. Territorial extent & classification: S. General. - 64p.: 30 cm. - 978-0-11-103001-1 £11.00

Lands Tribunal

The Lands Tribunal for Scotland Amendment (Fees) Rules 2015 No. 2015/199. - Enabling power: Lands Tribunal Act 1949, s. 3 (6) (12) (e). - Issued: 27.05.2015. Made: 19.05.2015. Laid before the Scottish Parliament: 21.05.2015. Coming into force: 30.06.2015. Effect: S.I. 1971/218 amended. Territorial extent & classification: S. General. - 2p.: 30 cm. - 978-0-11-102785-1 £4.25

Legal aid and advice

The Advice and Assistance (Assistance by Way of Representation) (Scotland) Amendment (No. 2) Regulations 2015 No. 2015/155. - Enabling power: Legal Aid (Scotland) Act 1986, s. 9. - Issued: 08.04.2015. Made: 31.03.2015. Coming into force: 01.04.2015. Effect: S.S.I. 2003/179 amended. Territorial extent & classification: S. General. - Supersedes draft S.I. (ISBN 9780111026540) issued 25/02/15. - 4p.: 30 cm. - 978-0-11-102742-4 £4.25

The Advice and Assistance (Assistance by Way of Representation) (Scotland) Amendment (No. 3) Regulations 2015 No. 2015/279. - Enabling power: Legal Aid (Scotland) Act 1986, s. 9. - Issued: 02.07.2015. Made: 25.06.2015. Coming into force: 26.06.2015. Effect: S.S.I. 2003/179 amended. Territorial extent & classification: S. General. - Supersedes draft S.S.I. (ISBN 9780111028391) issued 18/06/15. - 2p.: 30 cm. - 978-0-11-102853-7 £4.25

The Advice and Assistance (Assistance by Way of Representation) (Scotland) Amendment Regulations 2015 No. 2015/13. - Enabling power: Legal Aid (Scotland) Act 1986, s. 9. - Issued: 27.01.2015. Made: 20.01.2015. Coming into force: 26.01.2015. Effect: S.S.I. 2003/179 amended. Territorial extent & classification: S. General. - Supersedes draft SI (ISBN 9780111025222) issued 02/12/14. - 4p.: 30 cm. - 978-0-11-102592-5 £4.25

The Civil Legal Aid (Scotland) (Miscellaneous Amendments) Regulations 2015 No. 2015/380. - Enabling power: Legal Aid (Scotland) Act 1986, ss. 33 (2) (a) (3), 36 (1) (2) (a) (c). - Issued: 12.11.2015. Made: 05.11.2015. Laid before the Scottish Parliament: 09.11.2015. Coming into force: 01.01.2016. Effect: S.I. 1989/1490 & S.S.I. 2002/494 amended. Territorial extent & classification: S. General. - 8p.: 30 cm. - 978-0-11-102980-0 £4.25

The Legal Aid (Miscellaneous Amendments) (Scotland) Regulations 2015 No. 2015/337. - Enabling power: Legal Aid (Scotland) Act 1986, ss. 33 (2) (3) (3A), 36 (2) (c). - Issued: 24.09.2015. Made: 17.09.2015. Laid before the Scottish Parliament: 17.09.2015. Coming into force: 22.09.2015. Effect: S.I. 1989/1490, 1491; 1996/2555; 1999/491 amended. Territorial extent & classification: S. General. - 8p.: 30 cm. - 978-0-11-102945-9 £4.25

Licences and licensing

The Air Weapons and Licensing (Scotland) Act 2015 (Commencement No. 1) Order 2015 No. 2015/382 (C.48). - Enabling power: Air Weapons and Licensing (Scotland) Act 2015, s. 88 (2). Bringing into operation various provisions of the 2015 Act on 01.12.15 in accord. with art. 2. - Issued: 18.11.2015. Made: 11.11.2015. Laid before the Scottish Parliament: 13.11.2015. Coming into force: 01.12.2015. Effect: None. Territorial extent & classification: S. General. - 4p.: 30 cm. - 978-0-11-102984-8 £4.25

Licensing (liquor)

The Air Weapons and Licensing (Scotland) Act 2015 (Commencement No. 1) Order 2015 No. 2015/382 (C.48). - Enabling power: Air Weapons and Licensing (Scotland) Act 2015, s. 88 (2). Bringing into operation various provisions of the 2015 Act on 01.12.15 in accord. with art. 2. - Issued: 18.11.2015. Made: 11.11.2015. Laid before the Scottish Parliament: 13.11.2015. Coming into force: 01.12.2015. Effect: None. Territorial extent & classification: S. General. - 4p.: 30 cm. - 978-0-11-102984-8 £4.25

Licensing (marine)

The Aquaculture and Fisheries (Scotland) Act 2007 (Fixed Penalty Notices) Order 2015 No. 2015/113. - Enabling power: Aquaculture and Fisheries (Scotland) Act 2007, ss. 26 (5), 27 (1) (3), 29 (2) (b), 43 (1) (b). - Issued: 18.03.2015. Made: 11.03.2015. Laid before the Scottish Parliament: 13.03.2015. Coming into force: 27.04.2015. Effect: S.S.I. 2008/101; 2011/60 revoked. Territorial extent & classification: S. General. - 4p.: 30 cm. - 978-0-11-102705-9 £4.25

Local government

The Community Empowerment (Scotland) Act 2015 (Commencement No. 2) Order 2015 No. 2015/358 (C.44). - Enabling power: Community Empowerment (Scotland) Act 2015, s. 145 (2). Bringing into operation various provisions of the 2015 Act on 13.11.2015, in accord. with arts 1 & 2. - Issued: 03.11.2015. Made: 27.10.2015. Laid before the Scottish Parliament: 29.10.2015. Coming into force: 13.11.2015. Effect: None. Territorial extent & classification: S. General. - 8p.: 30 cm. - 978-0-11-102961-9 £6.00

The Local Governance (Scotland) Act 2004 (Remuneration and Severance Payments) Amendment Regulations 2015 No. 2015/7. - Enabling power: Local Governance (Scotland) Act 2004, ss. 11, 12, 16 (2). - Issued: 21.01.2015. Made: 14.01.2015. Laid before the Scottish Parliament: 16.01.2015. Coming into force: 01.04.2015. Effect: S.S.I. 2007/183 amended & S.S.I. 2006/471 revoked. Territorial extent & classification: S. General. - 4p.: 30 cm. - 978-0-11-102586-4 £4.25

The Local Government Finance Act 1992 (Commencement No. 11) Order 2015 No. 2015/59 (C.11). - Enabling power: Local Government Finance Act 1992, s. 119 (2). Bringing into operation various provisions of the 1992 Act In accord. with art. 1 (1). - Issued: 23.02.2015. Made: 17.02.2015. Laid before the Scottish Parliament: 18.02.2015. Effect: None. Territorial extent & classification: S. General. - 4p.: 30 cm. - 978-0-11-102641-0 £4.25

The Local Government Finance (Scotland) Amendment Order 2015 No. 2015/125. - Enabling power: Local Government Finance Act 1992, sch. 12, paras. 1, 9 (4). - Issued: 25.03.2015. Made: 17.03.2015. Coming into force: 18.03.2015. Effect: S.S.I. 2015/56 amended. Territorial extent & classification: S. General. - Supersedes draft SI (ISBN 9780111026984) issued 11/03/15 - 8p.: 30 cm. - 978-0-11-102715-8 £4.25

The Local Government Finance (Scotland) Order 2015 No. 2015/56. - Enabling power: Local Government Finance Act 1992, sch. 12, para. 1, 9 (4). - Issued: 17.02.2015. Made: 10.02.2015. Coming into force: 11.02.2015. Effect: S.S.I. 2014/36 partially revoked. Territorial extent & classification: S. General. - Supersedes draft S.S.I. (ISBN 9780111025949) issued 27/01/15; Partially revoked S.S.I. (ISBN 9780111031933). - 8p.: 30 cm. - 978-0-11-102638-0 £4.25

Marine management

The South Arran Marine Conservation 2014 (Urgent Continuation) Order 2015 No. 2015/303. - Enabling power: Marine (Scotland) Act 2010, s. 86 (6). - Issued: 21.08.2015. Made: 17.08.2015. Laid before the Scottish Parliament: 17.08.2015. Coming into force: 28.09.2015. Effect: None. Territorial extent & classification: S. General. - 4p.: 30 cm. - 978-0-11-102913-8 £4.25

The South Arran Marine Conservation Order 2015 No. 2015/437. - Enabling power: Inshore Fishing (Scotland) Act 1984, ss. 1, 2A & Marine (Scotland) Act 2010, ss. 85 (1) (a) (2) (4), 86 (1) (3), 88 (1) (2) (6), 92 (1) (5). - Issued: 23.12.2015. Made: 16.12.2015. Laid before the Scottish Parliament: 18.12.2015. Coming into force: 08.02.2016. Effect: SSI 2008/317; 2014/260, 297, 303 revoked. Territorial extent & classification: S. General. - 16p., map: 30 cm. - 978-0-11-103040-0 £6.00

The Wester Ross Marine Conservation Order 2015 No. 2015/302. - Enabling power: Marine (Scotland) Act 2010, ss. 85 (1) (a) (2) (4), 86 (1) (3), 88 (1) (2). - Issued: 21.08.2015. Made: 17.08.2015. Laid before the Scottish Parliament: 17.08.2015. Coming into force: 18.08.2015. Effect: None. Territorial extent & classification: S. General. - Revoked by SSI 2016/88 (ISBN 9780111031544). - 4p.: 30 cm. - 978-0-11-102912-1 £4.25

Marriage

The Marriage and Civil Partnership (Scotland) Act 2014 (Commencement No. 4 and Savings Provisions) Order 2015 No. 2015/14 (C.3). - Enabling power: Marriage and Civil Partnership (Scotland) Act 2014, s. 36 (2) (3). - Issued: 27.01.2015. Made: 20.01.2015. Laid before the Scottish Parliament: 22.01.2015. Coming into force: 01.03.2015. Effect: None. Territorial extent & classification: S. General. - 8p.: 30 cm. - 978-0-11-102593-2 £4.25

The Marriage (Prescription of Forms) (Scotland) Amendment Regulations 2015 No. 2015/313. - Enabling power: Marriage (Scotland) Act 1977, ss. 3 (1). - Issued: 04.09.2015. Made: 28.08.2015. Laid before the Scottish Parliament: 31.08.2015. Coming into force: In accord. with reg. 1. Effect: S.I. 1997/2349 amended. Territorial extent & classification: S. General. - 6p.: 30 cm. - 978-0-11-102916-9 £4.25

The Qualifying Civil Partnership Modification (Scotland) Order 2015 No. 2015/371. - Enabling power: Marriage and Civil Partnership (Scotland) Act 2014, ss. 9 (1) (2), 11 (5) (6). - Issued: 05.11.2015. Made: 30.10.2015. Coming into force: 31.10.2015. Effect: 1977 c.15, 2014 asp 5 modified. Territorial extent & classification: S. General. - 4p.: 30 cm. - 978-0-11-102970-1 £4.25

Mental health

The Mental Health (Detention in Conditions of Excessive Security) (Scotland) Regulations 2015 No. 2015/364. - Enabling power: Mental Health (Care and Treatment) (Scotland) Act 2003, s. 271A. - Issued: 04.11.2015. Made: 29.10.2015. Coming into force: 16.11.2015. Effect: 2003 asp 13 amended. Territorial extent & classification: S. General. - Supersedes draft S.I. (ISBN 9780111029183) issued 07/09/15. - 4p.: 30 cm. - 978-0-11-102966-4 £4.25

The Mental Health (Scotland) Act 2015 (Commencement No. 1, Transitional and Saving Provisions) Order 2015 No. 2015/361 (C.46). - Enabling power: Mental Health (Scotland) Act 2015, s. 61(2) (3). Bringing into operation various provisions of the 2015 Act on 16.11.2015, in accord. with art. 2. - Issued: 04.11.2015. Made: 29.10.2015. Laid before the Scottish Parliament: 02.11.2015. Coming into force: 16.11.2015. Effect: None. Territorial extent & classification: S. General. - 4p.: 30 cm. - 978-0-11-102964-0 £4.25

The Mental Health (Scotland) Act 2015 (Commencement No. 2) Order 2015 No. 2015/417 (C.54). - Enabling power: Mental Health (Scotland) Act 2015, s. 61 (2). Bringing into operation various provisions of the 2015 Act on 24.12.2015, in accordance with art. 2. - Issued: 15.12.2015. Made: 08.12.2015. Laid before the Scottish Parliament: 09.12.2015. Coming into force: 24.12.2015. Effect: None. Territorial extent & classification: S. General. - 2p.: 30 cm. - 978-0-11-103018-9 £4.25

The Mental Health Tribunal for Scotland (Practice and Procedure) (No. 2) Amendment Rules 2015 No. 2015/334. - Enabling power: Mental Health (Care and Treatment) (Scotland) Act 2003, ss. 21 (4), 326, sch. 2, para. 10. - Issued: 21.09.2015. Made: 15.09.2015. Laid before the Scottish Parliament: 17.09.2015. Coming into force: 16.11.2015. Effect: S.S.I. 2005/519 amended. Territorial extent & classification: S. General. - 8p.: 30 cm. - 978-0-11-102941-1 £4.25

National assistance services

The National Assistance (Assessment of Resources) Amendment (Scotland) Regulations 2015 No. 2015/64. - Enabling power: National Assistance Act 1948, s. 22 (5). - Issued: 24.02.2015. Made: 17.02.2015. Laid before the Scottish Parliament: 19.02.2015. Coming into force: 06.04.2015. Effect: S.I. 1992/2977 amended & S.S.I. 2014/38 revoked. Territorial extent & classification: S. General. - Revoked with saving by S.S.I. 2016/25 (ISBN 9780111030745). - 4p.: 30 cm. - 978-0-11-102649-6 £4.25

The National Assistance (Sums for Personal Requirements) (Scotland) Regulations 2015 No. 2015/65. - Enabling power: National Assistance Act 1948, s. 22 (4). - Issued: 24.02.2015. Made: 17.02.2015. Laid before the Scottish Parliament: 19.02.2015. Coming into force: 06.04.2015. Effect: S.S.I. 2014/39 revoked. Territorial extent & classification: S. General. - 4p.: 30 cm. - 978-0-11-102650-2 £4.25

National Health Service

The Community Care and Health (Scotland) Act 2002 (Commencement No. 4) Order 2015 No. 2015/179 (C.29). - Enabling power: Community Care and Health (Scotland) Act 2002, s. 27 (2) (3). Bringing into operation various provisions of the 2002 Act on 11.05.2015. & 24.06.2015, in accord. with art. 2 (1) (2). - Issued: 28.04.2015. Made: 21.04.2015. Coming into force: 11.05.2015-. Effect: None. Territorial extent & classification: S. General. - 4p.: 30 cm. - 978-0-11-102762-2 £4.25

The National Health Service (Clinical Negligence and Other Risks Indemnity Scheme) (Scotland) Amendment Regulations 2015 No. 2015/102. - Enabling power: National Health Service (Scotland) Act 1978, ss. 85B, 105 (7). - Issued: 10.03.2015. Made: 03.03.2015. Laid before the Scottish Parliament: 05.03.2015. Coming into force: 03.04.2015. Effect: S.S.I. 2000/54 amended. Territorial extent & classification: S. General. - 8p.: 30 cm. - 978-0-11-102692-2 £4.25

The National Health Service (Cross-Border Health Care) (Scotland) (Amendment) Regulations 2015 No. 2015/91. - Enabling power: European Communities Act 1972, s. 2 (2). - Issued: 06.03.2015. Made: 27.02.2015. Laid before the Scottish Parliament: 02.03.2015. Coming into force: 31.03.2015. Effect: S.S.I. 2013/292 amended. Territorial extent & classification: S. General. - 4p.: 30 cm. - 978-0-11-102685-4 £.4.25

The National Health Service (Free Prescriptions and Charges for Drugs and Appliances) (Scotland) Amendment Regulations 2015 No. 2015/160. - Enabling power: National Health Service (Scotland) Act 1978, ss. 69 (1), 105 (7). - Issued: 09.04.2015. Made: 31.03.2015. Laid before the Scottish Parliament: 02.04.2015. Coming into force: 17.05.2015. Effect: S.S.I. 2011/55 amended. Territorial extent & classification: S. General. - 4p.: 30 cm. - 978-0-11-102747-9 £4.25

The National Health Service (Optical Charges and Payments and General Ophthalmic Services) (Scotland) Amendment Regulations 2015 No. 2015/219. - Enabling power: National Health Service (Scotland) Act 1978, ss. 26, 34, 105 (7), 106 (a). - Issued: 02.06.2015. Made: 27.05.2015. Laid before the Scottish Parliament: 29.05.2015. Coming into force: 01.07.2015. Effect: S.I. 1998/642 & S.S.I. 2006/135 amended. Territorial extent & classification: S. General. - 4p.: 30 cm. - 978-0-11-102802-5 £4.25

The National Health Service (Optical Charges and Payments) (Scotland) Amendment Regulations 2015 No. 2015/86. - Enabling power: National Health Service (Scotland) Act 1978, ss. 70 (1), 73 (a), 74 (a), 105 (7), 108 (1), sch. 11, paras. 2, 2A. - Issued: 05.03.2015. Made: 26.02.2015. Laid before the Scottish Parliament: 02.03.2015. Coming into force: 01.04.2015. Effect: S.I. 1998/642 amended. Territorial extent & classification: S. General. - 6p.: 30 cm. - 978-0-11-102678-6 £4.25

The National Health Service (Payments and Remission of Charges) (Miscellaneous Amendments) (Scotland) Regulations 2015 No. 2015/333. - Enabling power: National Health Service (Scotland) Act 1978, ss. 75A, 105 (7), sch. 11, para. 2A. - Issued: 21.09.2015. Made: 15.09.2015. Laid before the Scottish Parliament: 17.09.2015. Coming into force: 01.11.2015. Effect: S.I. 1998/642 & S.S.I. 2003/460; 2015/219 amended. Territorial extent & classification: S. General. - 8p.: 30 cm. - 978-0-11-102940-4 £6.00

The National Health Service Superannuation Scheme (Miscellaneous Amendments) (Scotland) Regulations 2015 No. 2015/96. - Enabling power: Superannuation Act 1972, s. 10 (1) (2), 12 (1) (2) (4), 24, sch. 3. - Issued: 09.03.2015. Made: 02.03.2015. Laid before the Scottish Parliament: 03.03.2015. Coming into force: 01.04.2015. Effect: S.I. 1998/1451, 1594 & S.S.I 2003/344; 2011/117; 2013/174 amended. Territorial extent & classification: S. General. - 36p.: 30 cm. - 978-0-11-102687-8 £10.00

The Personal Injuries (NHS Charges) (Amounts) (Scotland) Amendment Regulations 2015 No. 2015/81. - Enabling power: Health and Social Care (Community Health and Standards) Act 2003, ss. 153 (2) (5), 168, 195 (1) (2). - Issued: 04.03.2015. Made: 25.02.2015. Laid before the Scottish Parliament: 27.02.2015. Coming into force: 01.04.2015. Effect: S.S.I. 2006/588 amended. Territorial extent & classification: S. General. - 4p.: 30 cm. - 978-0-11-102673-1 £4.25

Pensions

The Firefighters' Compensation Scheme and Pension Scheme (Amendment) (Scotland) Order 2015 No. 2015/143. - Enabling power: Fire and Rescue Services Act 2004, ss. 34, 60. - Issued: 31.03.2015. Made: 24.03.2015. Laid: 26.03.2015. Coming into force: In accord. with art. 1. Effect: S.S.I. 2006/338; 2007/199 amended. Territorial extent & classification: S. General. - 20p.: 30 cm. - 978-0-11-102730-1 £6.00

The Firemen's Pension Scheme (Amendment No. 2) (Scotland) Order 2015 No. 2015/173. - Enabling power: Fire Services Act 1947, s. 26 (1) to (5) & Superannuation Act 1972, ss. 12, 16. - Issued: 27.04.2015. Made: 21.04.2015. Laid before the Scottish Parliament: 21.04.2015. Coming into force: 20.05.2015. Effect: S.I. 1992/129 amended. Territorial extent & classification: S. General. - 4p.: 30 cm. - 978-0-11-102758-5 £4.25

The Firemen's Pension Scheme (Amendment) (Scotland) Order 2015 No. 2015/140. - Enabling power: Fire Services Act 1947, s. 26 (1) to (5) & Superannuation Act 1972, ss. 12, 16. - Issued: 31.03.2015. Made: 24.03.2015. Laid before the Scottish Parliament: 26.03.2015. Coming into force: 01.04.2015. Effect: S.I. 1992/129 amended in relation to Scotland. Territorial extent & classification: S. General. - 8p.: 30 cm. - 978-0-11-102727-1 £4.25

The Police Pensions (Amendment) (Scotland) Regulations 2015 No. 2015/174. - Enabling power: Police Pensions Act 1976, s. 1. - Issued: 27.04.2015. Made: 21.04.2015. Laid before the Scottish Parliament: 21.04.2015. Coming into force: 20.05.2015. Effect: S.I. 1987/257 amended. Territorial extent & classification: S. General. - 4p.: 30 cm. - 978-0-11-102759-2 £4.25

The Teachers' Superannuation (Scotland) Amendment Regulations 2015 No. 2015/98. - Enabling power: Superannuation Act 1972, ss. 9, 12, sch. 3. - Issued: 09.03.2015. Made: 02.03.2015. Laid before the Scottish Parliament: 03.03.2015. Coming into force: 01.04.2015. Effect: S.S.I. 2005/393 amended. Territorial extent & classification: S. General. - 24p.: 30 cm. - 978-0-11-102689-2 £6.00

Plant health

The Plant Health (Import Inspection Fees) (Scotland) Amendment Regulations 2015 No. 2015/392. - Enabling power: Finance Act 1973, s. 56 (1) (2). - Issued: 24.11.2015. Made: 18.11.2015. Laid before the Scottish Parliament: 20.11.2015. Coming into force: 01.01.2016. Effect: S.S.I. 2014/338 amended. Territorial extent & classification: S. General. - 8p.: 30 cm. - 978-0-11-102993-0 £6.00

The Plant Health (Scotland) Amendment Order 2015 No. 2015/10. - Enabling power: Plant Health Act 1967, ss. 2, 3, 4 (1) & Agriculture (Miscellaneous Provisions) Act 1972, s. 20. - Issued: 22.01.2015. Made: 15.01.2015. Laid before the Scottish Parliament: 19.01.2015. Coming into force: 26.02.2015. Effect: S.S.I. 2005/613 amended & S.S.I. 2006/474; 2008/350; 2009/153; 2012/266, 326; 2013/366 partially revoked. Territorial extent & classification: S. General. - EC note: Transposes and implements certain EU legislation: DEC 2012/270/EU; 2014/679/EU; DEC 2012/697/EU; 2014/78/EU; 2014/83/EU; 2014/422/EU; 2014/497/EU; 2014/690/EU; Partially revoked by SSI 2016/83 (ISBN 9780111031469). - 28p.: 30 cm. - 978-0-11-102589-5 £6.00

Police

The Police Act 1997 and the Protection of Vulnerable Groups (Scotland) Act 2007 Remedial (No. 2) Order 2015 No. 2015/423. - Enabling power: Convention Rights (Compliance) (Scotland) Act 2001, ss. 12 (1) (3), 14 (5) (a). - Issued: 17.12.2015. Made: 10.12.2015. Coming into force: 08.02.2016. Effect: 1997 c.50 & 2007 asp 14 & S.S.I. 2010/167 amended & S.I. 2015/330 revoked. Territorial extent & classification: S. General. - For approval by resolution of the Scottish Parliament within 120 days beginning with 9th September 2015. - 44p.: 30 cm. - 978-0-11-103024-0 £10.00

The Police Act 1997 and the Protection of Vulnerable Groups (Scotland) Act 2007 Remedial Order 2015 No. 2015/330. - Enabling power: Convention Rights (Compliance) (Scotland) Act 2001, s. 12 (1) (3). - Issued: 16.09.2015. Made: 09.09.2015. Coming into force: 10.09.2015. Effect: 1972 c. 50; 2007 asp 14, S.S.I. 2010/167 amended. Territorial extent & classification: S. General. - Revoked by S.S.I. 2015/423 (ISBN 9780111030240). - 36p.: 30 cm. - 978-0-11-102937-4 £10.00

Prisons

The Discontinuance of Legalised Police Cells (Scotland) Rules 2015 No. 2015/324. - Enabling power: Prisons (Scotland) Act 1989, ss. 14, 39. - Issued: 11.09.2015. Made: 07.09.2015. Laid before the Scottish Parliament: 09.09.2015. Coming into force: 08.10.2015. Effect: S.R. & O. 1882; 1888 p.182; 1893 p.477, p.479 & S.S.I. 2009/380 revoked. Territorial extent & classification: S. General. - 4p.: 30 cm. - 978-0-11-102928-2 £4.25

The Prisoners (Control of Release) (Scotland) Act 2015 (Commencement) Order 2015 No. 2015/409 (C.52). - Enabling power: Prisoners (Control of Release) (Scotland) Act 2015, ss. 3 (2) (3). Bringing into operation various provisions of 2015 Act on 01.02.16, in accord. with art. 2. - Issued: 09.12.2015. Made: 03.12.2015. Laid before the Scottish Parliament: 07.12.2015. Coming into force: 01.02.2016. Effect: 1993 c.9 amended. Territorial extent & classification: S. General. - 2p.: 30 cm. - 978-0-11-103015-8 £4.25

Proceeds of crime

The Proceeds of Crime Act 2002 (Cash Searches: Constables in Scotland: Code of Practice) Order 2015 No. 2015/220. - Enabling power: Proceeds of Crime Act 2002, s. 293 (4). - Issued: 02.06.2015. Made: 26.05.2015. Coming into force: 01.06.2015. Effect: S.S.I. 2009/246 revoked. Territorial extent & classification: S. General. - Supersedes draft S.S.I. (ISBN 9780111027578) issued 24.04.2015. - 4p.: 30 cm. - 978-0-11-102803-2 £4.25

The Proceeds of Crime Act 2002 (Disclosure of Information to and by Lord Advocate and Scottish Ministers) Amendment Order 2015 No. 2015/124. - Enabling power: Proceeds of Crime Act 2002, ss. 439 (6), 441 (9). - Issued: 25.03.2015. Made: 17.03.2015. Coming into force: 18.03.2015. Effect: S.S.I. 2003/93 amended. Territorial extent & classification: S. General. - 4p.: 30 cm. - 978-0-11-102714-1 £4.25

Property factors

The Property Factors (Registration) (Scotland) Amendment Regulations 2015 No. 2015/217. - Enabling power: Property Factors (Scotland) Act 2011, ss. 3 (4), 30 (2). - Issued: 02.06.2015. Made: 27.05.2015. Laid before the Scottish Parliament: 29.05.2015. Coming into force: 01.07.2015. Effect: S.S.I. 2012/181 amended. Territorial extent & classification: S. General. - 2p.: 30 cm. - 978-0-11-102800-1 £4.25

Protection of vulnerable adults

The Police Act 1997 and the Protection of Vulnerable Groups (Scotland) Act 2007 Remedial (No. 2) Order 2015 No. 2015/423. - Enabling power: Convention Rights (Compliance) (Scotland) Act 2001, ss. 12 (1) (3), 14 (5) (a). - Issued: 17.12.2015. Made: 10.12.2015. Coming into force: 08.02.2016. Effect: 1997 c.50 & 2007 asp 14 & S.S.I. 2010/167 amended & S.I. 2015/330 revoked. Territorial extent & classification: S. General. - For approval by resolution of the Scottish Parliament within 120 days beginning with 9th September 2015. - 44p.: 30 cm. - 978-0-11-103024-0 £10.00

The Police Act 1997 and the Protection of Vulnerable Groups (Scotland) Act 2007 Remedial Order 2015 No. 2015/330. - Enabling power: Convention Rights (Compliance) (Scotland) Act 2001, s. 12 (1) (3). - Issued: 16.09.2015. Made: 09.09.2015. Coming into force: 10.09.2015. Effect: 1972 c. 50; 2007 asp 14, S.S.I. 2010/167 amended. Territorial extent & classification: S. General. - Revoked by S.S.I. 2015/423 (ISBN 9780111030240). - 36p.: 30 cm. - 978-0-11-102937-4 £10.00

The Protection of Vulnerable Groups (Scotland) Act 2007 (Fees for Scheme Membership and Disclosure Requests) Amendment Regulations 2015 No. 2015/223. - Enabling power: Protection of Vulnerable Groups (Scotland) Act 2007, ss. 70 (1) (2). - Issued: 03.06.2015. Made: 27.05.2015. Laid before the Scottish Parliament: 29.05.2015. Coming into force: 01.07.2015. Effect: S.S.I. 2010/167 amended. Territorial extent & classification: S. General. - 4p.: 30 cm. - 978-0-11-102805-6 £4.25

Public finance and accountability

The Budget (Scotland) Act 2014 Amendment Order 2015 No. 2015/138. - Enabling power: Budget (Scotland) Act 2014, s. 7 (1). - Issued: 27.03.2015. Made: 19.03.2015. Coming into force: 20.03.2015. Effect: 2014 asp 6 amended. Territorial extent & classification: S. General. - Supersedes draft S.S.I. (ISBN 9780111026366) issued 11/02/15. - 4p.: 30 cm. - 978-0-11-102725-7 £4.25

The Budget (Scotland) Act 2015 Amendment Regulations 2015 No. 2015/434. - Enabling power: Budget (Scotland) Act 2015 s. 7 (1). - Issued: 23.12.2015. Made: 16.12.2015. Coming into force: 17.12.2015. Effect: 2015 asp 2 amended. Territorial extent & classification: S. General. - 4p.: 30 cm. - 978-0-11-103037-0 £4.25

Public health

The Certification of Death (Scotland) Act 2011 (Authorisation of Cremation - Death Outwith Scotland) Regulations 2015 No. 2015/162. - Enabling power: Certification of Death (Scotland) Act 2011, s. 18 (4) & Registration of Births, Deaths and Marriages (Scotland) Act 1965, s. 27A (2). - Issued: 10.04.2015. Made: 02.04.2015. Laid before the Scottish Parliament: 02.04.2015. Coming into force: 13.05.2015. Effect: None. Territorial extent & classification: S. General. - 8p.: 30 cm. - 978-0-11-102750-9 £6.00

The Certification of Death (Scotland) Act 2011 (Commencement No. 2) Order 2015 No. 2015/115 (C.24). - Enabling power: Certification of Death (Scotland) Act 2011, s. 32 (3) (4) (b). Bringing into operation various provisions of the 2011 Act on 25.03.2015, 13.05.2015, in accord. with arts 2 & 3. - Issued: 18.03.2015. Made: 11.03.2015. Laid before the Scottish Parliament: 13.03.2015. Coming into force: 25.03.2015. Effect: None. Territorial extent & classification: S. General. - 4p.: 30 cm. - 978-0-11-102706-6 £4.25

The Certification of Death (Scotland) Act 2011 (Consequential Provisions) Order 2015 No. 2015/164. - Enabling power: Certification of Death (Scotland) Act 2011, s. 28. - Issued: 10.04.2015. Made: 02.04.2015. Laid before the Scottish Parliament: 02.04.2015. Coming into force: 13.05.2015. Effect: S.I. 1935/247 amended. Territorial extent & classification: S. General. - 4p.: 30 cm. - 978-0-11-102751-6 £4.25

The Certification of Death (Scotland) Act 2011 (Post-Mortem Examinations - Death Outwith United Kingdom) Regulations 2015 No. 2015/165. - Enabling power: Certification of Death (Scotland) Act 2011, s. 19 (4). - Issued: 13.04.2015. Made: 02.04.2015. Laid before the Scottish Parliament: 02.04.2015. Coming into force: 13.05.2015. Effect: None. Territorial extent & classification: S. General. - 8p.: 30 cm. - 978-0-11-102755-4 £6.00

The Public Bodies (Joint Working) (Integration Joint Board Establishment) (Scotland) Amendment (No. 2) Order 2015 No. 2015/266. - Enabling power: Public Bodies (Joint Working) (Scotland) Act 2014, s. 9 (2). - Issued: 23.06.2015. Made: 17.06.2015. Laid before the Scottish Parliament: 19.06.2015. Coming into force: 21.09.2015. Effect: S.S.I. 2015/88 amended. Territorial extent & classification: S. General. - 4p.: 30 cm. - 978-0-11-102846-9 £4.25

The Public Bodies (Joint Working) (Integration Joint Board Establishment) (Scotland) Amendment (No. 3) Order 2015 No. 2015/321. - Enabling power: Public Bodies (Joint Working) (Scotland) Act 2014, s. 9 (2). - Issued: 08.09.2015. Made: 02.09.2015. Laid before the Scottish Parliament: 04.09.2015. Coming into force: 03.10.2015. Effect: S.S.I. 2015/88 amended. Territorial extent & classification: S. General. - 4p.: 30 cm. - 978-0-11-102925-1 £4.25

The Public Bodies (Joint Working) (Integration Joint Board Establishment) (Scotland) Amendment Order 2015 No. 2015/222. - Enabling power: Public Bodies (Joint Working) (Scotland) Act 2014, s. 9 (2). - Issued: 03.06.2015. Made: 27.05.2015. Laid before the Scottish Parliament: 29.05.2015. Coming into force: 27.06.2015. Effect: S.S.I. 2015/88 amended. Territorial extent & classification: S. General. - 4p.: 30 cm. - 978-0-11-102804-9 £4.25

The Public Bodies (Joint Working) (Integration Joint Board Establishment) (Scotland) Order 2015 No. 2015/88. - Enabling power: Public Bodies (Joint Working) (Scotland) Act 2014, s. 9 (2). - Issued: 05.03.2015. Made: 26.02.2015. Laid before the Scottish Parliament: 02.03.2015. Coming into force: 01.04.2015. Effect: None. Territorial extent & classification: S. General. - 4p.: 30 cm. - 978-0-11-102680-9 £4.25

The Public Bodies (Joint Working) (Integration Joint Boards and Integration Joint Monitoring Committees) (Amendment) (Scotland) Order 2015 No. 2015/66. - Enabling power: Public Bodies (Joint Working) (Scotland) Act 2014, ss. 12, 17, 69 (1). - Issued: 24.02.2015. Made: 17.02.2015. Laid before the Scottish Parliament: 19.02.2015. Coming into force: 20.03.2015. Effect: S.S.I. 2014/281, 285 amended. Territorial extent & classification: S. General. - This SSI has been printed to correct errors in S.S.I. 2014/281 (ISBN 9780111024713) and S.S.I. 2014/285 (ISBN 9780111024751) and is being issued free of charge to all known recipients of those instruments. - 4p.: 30 cm. - 978-0-11-102651-9 £4.25

The Public Bodies (Joint Working) (Integration Joint Boards and Integration Joint Monitoring Committees) (Scotland) Amendment (No. 2) Order 2015 No. 2015/432. - Enabling power: Public Bodies (Joint Working) (Scotland) Act 2014, ss. 12, 17, 69 (1). - Issued: 22.12.2015. Made: 15.12.2015. Laid before the Scottish Parliament: 17.12.2015. Coming into force: 01.02.2016. Effect: S.S.I. 2014/281, 285 amended. Territorial extent & classification: S. General. - 4p.: 30 cm. - 978-0-11-103032-5 £4.25

The Public Bodies (Joint Working) (Scotland) Act 2014 (Commencement No. 2) Amendment Order 2015 No. 2015/44 (C.8). - Enabling power: Public Bodies (Joint Working) (Scotland) Act 2014, s. 72 (2). Bringing into operation various provisions of the 2014 Act on 25.02.2015 in accord. with art. 2. - Issued: 10.02.2015. Made: 03.02.2015. Laid before the Scottish Parliament: 05.02.2015. Coming into force: 25.02.2015 Effect: S.S.I. 2014/231 amended. Territorial extent & classification: S. General. - 4p.: 30 cm. - 978-0-11-102623-6 £4.25

The Public Bodies (Joint Working) (Scotland) Act 2014 (Consequential Modifications and Saving) Order 2015 No. 2015/157. - Enabling power: Public Bodies (Joint Working) Scotland Act 2014, s. 70. - Issued: 09.04.2015. Made: 31.03.2015. Coming into force: 01.04.2015. Effect: 1968 c.49; 1978 c.29; 1995 c.46; 2000 asp 4, asp 7; 2003 asp 1, asp 13; 2008 asp 5; 2009 c.24; 2010 asp 8; 2011 asp 12; 2013 asp 1; 2014 asp 8; S.S.I. 2005/325; 2006/63, 484 amended. Territorial extent & classification: S. General. - Supersedes draft SI (ISBN 9780111026960) issued 10/03/15 - 12p.: 30 cm. - 978-0-11-102744-8 £6.00

Public passenger transport

The Public Service Vehicles (Registration of Local Services) (Scotland) Amendment Regulations 2015 No. 2015/420. - Enabling power: Transport Act 1985, s. 6 (2) (a) (3) (a) (8) (a) (9) & Public Passenger Vehicles Act 1981, ss. 60 (1) (1A) (2). - Issued: 15.12.2015. Made: 09.12.2015. Laid before the Scottish Parliament: 11.12.2015. Coming into force: 31.01.2016. Effect: S.S.I. 2001/219 amended. Territorial extent & classification: S. General. - 4p.: 30 cm. - 978-0-11-103020-2 £4.25

Public procurement

The Procurement Reform (Scotland) Act 2014 (Commencement No. 1) Order 2015 No. 2015/331 (C.40). - Enabling power: Procurement Reform (Scotland) Act 2014, s. 45 (2). Bringing various provisions of the 2015 Act into operation on 28.09.2015, in accord. with art. 1. - Issued: 17.10.2015. Made: 11.09.2015. Laid before the Scottish Parliament: 14.09.2015. Coming into force: 28.09.2015. Effect: None. Territorial extent & classification: S. General. - 2p.: 30 cm. - 978-0-11-102938-1 £4.25

The Procurement Reform (Scotland) Act 2014 (Commencement No. 2) Order 2015 No. 2015/411 (C.53). - Enabling power: Procurement Reform (Scotland) Act 2014, s. 45(2). Bringing into operation various provisions of the 2014 Act on 11.01.2016. - Issued: 10.12.2015. Made: 03.12.2015. Laid before the Scottish Parliament: 07.12.2015. Coming into force: 11.01.2016. Effect: None. Territorial extent & classification: S. General. - 2p.: 30 cm. - 978-0-11-103017-2 £4.25

The Public Contracts (Scotland) Regulations 2015 No. 2015/446. - Enabling power: European Communities Act 1972, s. 2 (2), sch. 2, para. 1A. - Issued: 30.12.2015. Made: 16.12.2015. Laid before the Scottish Parliament: 18.12.2015. Coming into force: In accord. with reg. 1. Effect: 1998 c.20; 2014 asp. 12; 2015 c.26 & S.S.I. 2008/170; 2010/390; 2012/89, 162; 2013/50; S.I. 2011/1848; 2013/3220; 2014/1643 amended & S.S.I. 2012/88 revoked. Territorial extent & classification: S. General. - Superseded by S.I. 2016/47 (ISBN 9780111031124) issued 02/02/16. EC note: Part 2 implements for Scotland Directive 2014/24/EU on public procurement and repealing Directive 2004/18/EC. - 116p.: 30 cm. - 978-0-11-103044-8 £19.00

Public records

The Public Records (Scotland) Act 2011 (Authorities) Amendment Order 2015 No. 2015/335. - Enabling power: Public Records (Scotland) Act 2011, s. 2 (2). - Issued: 22.09.2015. Made: 16.09.2015. Coming into force: 17.09.2015. Effect: 2011 asp 12 amended. Territorial extent & classification: S. General. - Supersedes Draft S.S.I. (ISBN 9780111028360) issued 16/06/15. - 4p.: 30 cm. - 978-0-11-102942-8 £4.25

Public service pensions

The Firefighters' Pension Scheme (Consequential Provisions) (Scotland) Regulations 2015 No. 2015/117. - Enabling power: Public Service Pensions Act 2013, s. 1 (1) (2) (f), 2 (1), 3 (1) (2) (3) (a) (4). - Issued: 19.03.2015. Made: 11.03.2015. Coming into force: In accord. with reg. 1. Effect: None. Territorial extent & classification: S. General. - Supersedes draft S.S.I. (ISBN 9780111025833) issued 20.01.15. - 8p.: 30 cm. - 978-0-11-102708-0 £6.00

The Firefighters' Pension Schemes (Amendment) (Scotland) Regulations 2015 No. 2015/141. - Enabling power: Public Service Pensions Act 2013, ss. 1 (1) (2) (f), sch. 2. para. 6 (c). - Issued: 31.03.2015. Made: 24.03.2015. Laid before the Scottish Parliament: 26.03.2015. Coming into force: 01.04.2015. Effect: S.S.I. 1992/129; 2007/199; 2015/19 amended. Territorial extent & classification: S. General. - 36p.: 30 cm. - 978-0-11-102728-8 £10.00

The Firefighters' Pension Scheme (Scotland) Regulations 2015 No. 2015/19. - Enabling power: Public Service Pensions Act 2013, ss 1 (1) (2) (f), sch. 2. para. 6 (c). - Issued: 29.01.2015. Made: 22.01.2015. Laid before the Scottish Parliament: 26.01.2015. Coming into force: 01.04.2015. Effect: None. Territorial extent & classification: S. General. - 96p.: 30 cm. - 978-0-11-102598-7 £16.00

The Local Government Pension Scheme (Governance) (Scotland) Regulations 2015 No. 2015/60. - Enabling power: Public Services Pensions Act 2013, ss. 1, 2, 5, 7, sch. 2, para. 3 (b). - Issued: 23.02.2015. Made: 17.02.2015. Laid before the Scottish Parliament: 19.02.2015. Coming into force: 01.04.2015. Effect: None. Territorial extent & classification: S. General. - 8p.: 30 cm. - 978-0-11-102642-7 £6.00

The Local Government Pension Scheme (Scotland) Amendment (No. 2) Regulations 2015 No. 2015/448. - Enabling power: Superannuation Act 1972 ss. 7, 12, sch. 3 & Public Service Pensions Act 2013, s. 1. - Issued: 30.12.2015. Made: 17.12.2015. Laid before the Scottish Parliament: 21.12.2015. Coming into force: 02.02.2016. Effect: S.I. 1998/366 & S.S.I. 2008/229, 230; 2014/164, 233; 2015/87 amended. Territorial extent & classification: S. General. - 16p.: 30 cm. - 978-0-11-103047-9 £6.00

The Local Government Pension Scheme (Scotland) Amendment Regulations 2015 No. 2015/87. - Enabling power: Public Services Pensions Act 2013, s. 1. - Issued: 05.03.2015. Made: 26.02.2015. Laid before the Scottish Parliament: 02.03.2015. Coming into force: 01.04.2015. Effect: S.S.I. 2014/164, 233 amended. Territorial extent & classification: S. General. - 20p.: 30 cm. - 978-0-11-102679-3 £6.00

The National Health Service Pension Scheme (Consequential Provisions) (Scotland) Regulations 2015 No. 2015/145. - Enabling power: Public Service Pensions Act 2013, ss. 1 (1) (2) (e), 2 (1), 3 (1) (2) (3) (a) (4). - Issued: 31.03.2015. Made: 23.03.2015. Coming into force: In accord. with reg. 1. Effect: None. Territorial extent & classification: S. General. - Supersedes draft S.S.I. (ISBN 9780111025840) issued 20/01/15. - 12p.: 30 cm. - 978-0-11-102732-5 £6.00

The National Health Service Pension Scheme (Scotland) Regulations 2015 No. 2015/94. - Enabling power: Public Service Pensions Act 2013, ss. 1 (1) (2) (e), sch. 2, para 5 (b). - Issued: 13.03.2015. Made: 02.03.2015. Laid before the Scottish Parliament: 03.03.2015. Coming into force: 01.04.2015. Effect: None. Territorial extent & classification: S. General. - 152p.: 30 cm. - 978-0-11-102691-5 £23.25

The National Health Service Pension Scheme (Transitional and Consequential Provisions) (Scotland) Regulations 2015 No. 2015/95. - Enabling power: Superannuation Act 1972, ss.1, 3, 18, & Public Service Pensions Act 2013, sch. 3. - Issued: 09.03.2015. Made: 02.03.2015. Laid before the Scottish Parliament: 03.03.2015. Coming into force: 01.04.2015. Effect: S.S.I. 2011/117; 2013/179 amended. Territorial extent & classification: S. General. - 44p.: 30 cm. - 978-0-11-102686-1 £10.00

The Police Pension Scheme (Scotland) Amendment Regulations 2015 No. 2015/325. - Enabling power: Police Service Pensions Act 2013, ss. 1 (1) (2) (g), sch. 2, para. 7 (b). - Issued: 14.09.2015. Made: 08.09.2015. Laid before the Scottish Parliament: 10.09.2015. Coming into force: 01.11.2015. Effect: S.S.I. 2015/142 amended. Territorial extent & classification: S. General. - This S.S.I. corrects errors in S.S.I. 2015/142 (ISBN 9780111027295) and is being issued free of charge to all known recipients of that S.S.I. - 4p.: 30 cm. - 978-0-11-102930-5 £4.25

The Police Pension Scheme (Scotland) Regulations 2015 No. 2015/142. - Enabling power: Police Service Pensions Act 2013, ss. 1 (1) (2) (g), sch. 2, para. 7 (b). - Issued: 31.03.2015. Made: 24.03.2015. Laid before the Scottish Parliament: 26.03.2015. Coming into force: 01.04.2015. Effect: None. Territorial extent & classification: S. General. - 132p.: 30 cm. - 978-0-11-102729-5 £20.75

The Police Pensions (Consequential Provisions) (Scotland) Regulations 2015 No. 2015/118. - Enabling power: Police Service Pensions Act 2013, ss. 1 (1) (2) (g), 2 (1), 3 (1) (2) (3) (a) (4). - Issued: 19.03.2015. Made: 11.03.2015. Coming into force: In accord. with reg. 1. Effect: None. Territorial extent & classification: S. General. - Supersedes draft S.S.I. (ISBN 9780111025826) 20.01.2015. - 8p.: 30 cm. - 978-0-11-102709-7 £6.00

The Teachers' Pension Scheme (Consequential Provisions) (Scotland) Regulations 2015 No. 2015/146. - Enabling power: Public Service Pensions Act 2013, s. 1 (1) (2) (d), 2 (1), 3 (1), (2) (3) (a) (4). - Issued: 31.03.2015. Made: 23.03.2015. Coming into force: In accord. with reg. 1. Effect: None. Territorial extent & classification: S. General. - Supersedes draft S.S.I. (ISBN 9780111025857) issued 20/01/15. - 12p.: 30 cm. - 978-0-11-102733-2 £6.00

The Teachers' Pension Scheme (Scotland) (Amendment) Regulations 2015 No. 2015/97. - Enabling power: Public Service Pensions Act 2013, s. 1 (1) (2) (d), sch. 2, para. 4 (b). - Issued: 09.03.2015. Made: 02.03.2015. Laid before the Scottish Parliament: 03.03.2015. Coming into force: 01.04.2015. Effect: S.S.I. 2014/292 amended. Territorial extent & classification: S. General. - 12p.: 30 cm. - 978-0-11-102688-5 £6.00

Public services reform

The Public Services Reform (Inspection and Monitoring of Prisons) (Scotland) Order 2015 No. 2015/39. - Enabling power: Public Services Reform (Scotland) Act 2010, ss 14, 15. - Issued: 05.02.2015. Made: 28.01.2015. Coming into force: 31.08.2015. Effect: 1994 c.33; 2010 asp 8; 2011/331; S.S.I. 2010/168; 2013/50 amended & 1980 c.55; 2011 asp 12 partially repealed/amended & 1993 c.9, 1994 c.39; 1996 c.18; 1997 c.48; 2005 asp 14; partially repealed & S.I. 1999/1820 partially revoked & 1981/1388 revoked. Territorial extent & classification: S. General. - Supersedes draft S.S.I. (ISBN 9780111025208) issued 28/11/14. - 16p.: 30 cm. - 978-0-11-102615-1 £6.00

The Public Services Reform (Scotland) Act 2010 (Part 2 Extension) Order 2015 No. 2015/234. - Enabling power: Public Services Reform (Scotland) Act 2010, s. 134 (4). - Issued: 09.06.2015. Made: 03.06.2015. Coming into force: 04.06.2015. Effect: None. Territorial extent & classification: S. General. - Supersedes draft S.S.I. (ISBN 9780111027653) issued 05/05/15. - 2p.: 30 cm. - 978-0-11-102817-9 £4.25

Rating and valuation

The Community Empowerment (Scotland) Act 2015 (Commencement No. 1) Order 2015 No. 2015/344 (C.42). - Enabling power: Community Empowerment (Scotland) Act 2015, s. 145 (2). Bringing into operation various provisions of the 2015 Act on 31.10.2015, in accord. with art.2. - Issued: 30.09.2015. Made: 24.09.2015. Laid before the Scottish Parliament: 25.09.2015. Effect: None. Territorial extent & classification: S. General. - 2p.: 30 cm. - 978-0-11-102950-3 £4.25

The Non-Domestic Rate (Scotland) Order 2015 No. 2015/47. - Enabling power: Local Government (Scotland) Act 1975, ss. 7B (1), 37 (1). - Issued: 10.02.2015. Made: 03.02.2015. Laid before the Scottish Parliament: 05.02.2015. Coming into force: 01.04.2015. Effect: None. Territorial extent & classification: S. General. - 2p.: 30 cm. - 978-0-11-102626-7 £4.25

The Non-Domestic Rates (Levying) (Scotland) Amendment Regulations 2015 No. 2015/49. - Enabling power: Local Government etc. (Scotland) Act 1994, s. 153. - Issued: 10.02.2015. Made: 03.02.2015. Laid before the Scottish Parliament: 05.02.2015. Coming into force: 01.04.2015. Effect: S.S.I. 2014/30 amended & S.S.I. 2012/29 revoked with savings. Territorial extent & classification: S. General. - Revoked with saving by SSI 2016/114 (ISBN 9780111031728). - 4p.: 30 cm. - 978-0-11-102629-8 £4.25

The Non-Domestic Rating (Valuation of Utilities) (Scotland) Amendment Order 2015 No. 2015/50. - Enabling power: Valuation and Rating (Scotland) Act 1956, s. 6A (1) (aa) (1B). - Issued: 10.02.2015. Made: 03.02.2015. Laid before the Scottish Parliament: 05.02.2015. Coming into force: 01.04.2015. Effect: S.S.I. 2005/127 amended. Territorial extent & classification: S. General. - 4p.: 30 cm. - 978-0-11-102630-4 £4.25

The Valuation Timetable (Scotland) Amendment Order 2015 No. 2015/51. - Enabling power: Valuation and Rating (Scotland) Act 1956, ss. 13 (1), 42. - Issued: 10.02.2015. Made: 03.02.2015. Laid before the Scottish Parliament: 05.02.2015. Coming into force: 01.04.2015. Effect: S.I. 1995/164 amended. Territorial extent & classification: S. General. - 2p.: 30 cm. - 978-0-11-102631-1 £4.25

Registers and records

The Registers of Scotland (Voluntary Registration, Amendment of Fees, etc.) Order 2015 No. 2015/265. - Enabling power: Land Registration etc. (Scotland) Act 2012, ss. 27 (6), 48 (2), 110 (1) (2), 116 (1). - Issued: 23.06.2015. Made: 16.06.2015. Coming into force: arts 2, 3 and 4 (5) 01.04.2016; remainder 30.06.2015. Effect: S.S.I. 2014/188 amended & 2012 asp 5 partially repealed. Territorial extent & classification: S. General. - Supersedes draft S.S.I. (ISBN 9780111027813) issued on 20.05.2015. - 4p.: 30 cm. - 978-0-11-102845-2 £4.25

Registration of births, deaths and marriages, etc.

The Certification of Death (Scotland) Act 2011 (Application for Review) Regulations 2015 No. 2015/163. - Enabling power: Certification of Death (Scotland) Act 2011, s. 4 (8). - Issued: 13.04.2015. Made: 02.04.2015. Laid before the Scottish Parliament: 02.04.2015. Coming into force: 13.05.2015. Effect: None. Territorial extent & classification: S. General. - 8p.: 30 cm. - 978-0-11-102754-7 £4.25

The Registration of Births, Deaths and Marriages (Scotland) Act 1965 (Prohibition on Disposal of a Body without Authorisation) Regulations 2015 No. 2015/166. - Enabling power: Registration of Births, Deaths and Marriages (Scotland) Act 1965, s. 27A (2). - Issued: 10.04.2015. Made: 02.04.2015. Laid before the Scottish Parliament: 02.04.2015. Coming into force: 13.05.2015. Effect: None. Territorial extent & classification: S. General. - 8p.: 30 cm. - 978-0-11-102752-3 £6.00

The Registration of Births, Still-births, Deaths and Marriages (Prescription of Forms) (Scotland) Amendment Regulations 2015 No. 2015/180. - Enabling power: Registration of Births, Deaths and Marriages (Scotland) Act 1965, ss. 21 (2), 21 (4), 27 (1), 54 (1) (b). - Issued: 29.04.2015. Made: 22.04.2015. Laid before the Scottish Parliament: 24.04.2015. Coming into force: 13.05.2015. Effect: S.I. 1997/2348 amended. Territorial extent & classification: S. General. - 8p.: 30 cm. - 978-0-11-102763-9 £6.00

Regulatory reform

The Historic Environment Scotland Act 2014 (Ancillary Provision) Order 2015 No. 2015/271. - Enabling power: Historic Environment Act 2014, s. 27 (1) & Regulatory Reform (Scotland) Act 2014, s. 7. - Issued: 30.06.2015. Made: 24.06.2015. Coming into force: 01.10.2015. Effect: 1984 (C.54); 2003 asp 2, asp 8; 2005 asp 15; 2006 asp 1; 2014 asp 3, asp 12 modified. Territorial extent & classification: S. General. - Supersedes draft S.I. (ISBN 9780111027837) issued 21.05.2015. - 4p.: 30 cm. - 978-0-11-102851-3 £4.25

The Regulatory Reform (Scotland) Act 2014 (Commencement No. 2 and Transitional Provision) Order 2015 No. 2015/52 (C.9). - Enabling power: Regulatory Reform (Scotland) Act 2014, s. 61 (2) (3). Bringing into operation various provisions of the Act on 26.02.2015; 01.10.2015, in accord. with art. 2. - Issued: 11.02.2015. Made: 04.02.2015. Laid before the Scottish Parliament: 06.02.2015. Effect: None. Territorial extent & classification: S. General. - 4p.: 30 cm. - 978-0-11-102632-8 £4.25

Rehabilitation of offenders

The Rehabilitation of Offenders Act 1974 (Exclusions and Exceptions) (Scotland) Amendment Order 2015 No. 2015/329. - Enabling power: Rehabilitation of Offenders Act 1974, s. 4 (4), 7 (4), 10 (1). - Issued: 16.09.2015. Made: 09.09.2015. Coming into force: 10.09.2015. Effect: S.S.I. 2013/50 amended. Territorial extent & classification: S. General. - Supersedes draft S.S.I. (ISBN 9780111029329) issued 15.09.2015. - 28p.: 30 cm. - 978-0-11-102936-7 £6.00

Representation of the people

The Scottish Independence Referendum (Chief Counting Officer and Counting Officer Charges and Expenses) Order 2015 No. 2015/368. - Enabling power: Scottish Independence Referendum Act 2013, ss. 9 (3) (4). - Issued: 05.11.2015. Made: 29.10.2015. Laid before the Scottish Parliament: 02.11.2015. Coming into force: 30.11.2015. Effect: S.S.I. 2014/101 revoked. Territorial extent & classification: S. General. - 8p.: 30 cm. - 978-0-11-102967-1 £4.25

The Scottish Parliament (Elections etc.) Order 2015 No. 2015/425. - Enabling power: Scotland Act 1998, ss. 12 (1), 113 (2) (4) (5). - Issued: 21.12.2015. Made: 15.12.2015. Coming into force: 16.12.2015 in accord. with art. 1 (1). Effect: S.I. 2010/2999; 2011/2085; 2012/1479; 2015/683 partially revoked with savings. Territorial extent & classification: S. General. - 220p.: 30 cm. - 978-0-11-103027-1 £27.50

River, England and Wales

The Tweed Regulation Amendment Order 2015 No. 2015/11. - Enabling power: S.I. 2006/2913, arts 36, 54. - Issued: 26.01.2015. Made: 19.01.2015. Laid before the Scottish Parliament: 20.01.2015. Coming into force: 31.01.2015. Effect: S.S.I. 2007/19 amended. Territorial extent & classification: S. General. - 4p.: 30 cm. - 978-0-11-102590-1 £4.25

River, Scotland

The Tweed Regulation Amendment Order 2015 No. 2015/11. - Enabling power: S.I. 2006/2913, arts 36, 54. - Issued: 26.01.2015. Made: 19.01.2015. Laid before the Scottish Parliament: 20.01.2015. Coming into force: 31.01.2015. Effect: S.S.I. 2007/19 amended. Territorial extent & classification: S. General. - 4p.: 30 cm. - 978-0-11-102590-1 £4.25

Roads and bridges

The A82 Trunk Road (Camusnagual Ferry to Fort William), The A830 Trunk Road (Caledonian Canal Swing Bridge) (Redetermination of Means of Exercise of Public Right of Passage) Order 2015 No. 2015/15. - Enabling power: Roads (Scotland) Act 1984, ss. 2 (1), 152 (2). - Issued: 22.01.2015. Made: 20.01.2015. Coming into force: 02.02.2015. Effect: None. Territorial extent & classification: S. Local. - Available at http://www.legislation.gov.uk/ssi/2015/15/contents/made Non-print

The A737/A738 Trunk Road (Dalry Bypass) (Side Roads) Order 2015 No. 2015/412. - Enabling power: Roads (Scotland) Act 1984, ss. 12 (1) (5), 70 (1). - Issued: 07.12.2015. Made: 02.12.2015. Coming into force: 16.12.2015. Effect: None. Territorial extent & classification: S. Local. - Available at http://www.legislation.gov.uk/ssi/2015/412/contents/made Non-print

The A737/A738 Trunk Road (Dalry Bypass) (Trunking and Detrunking) Order 2015 No. 2015/413. - Enabling power: Roads (Scotland) Act 1984, ss. 5 (2) (6). - Issued: 07.12.2015. Made: 02.12.2015. Coming into force: 16.12.2015. Effect: None. Territorial extent & classification: S. Local. - Available at http://www.legislation.gov.uk/ssi/2015/413/contents/made Non-print

The A737/A738 Trunk Road (The Den, Dalry) (Side Roads) Order 2015 No. 2015/414. - Enabling power: Roads (Scotland) Act 1984, ss. 12 (1) (5), 70 (1). - Issued: 07.12.2015. Made: 02.12.2015. Coming into force: 16.12.2015. Effect: None. Territorial extent & classification: S. Local. - Available at http://www.legislation.gov.uk/ssi/2015/414/contents/made Non-print

The A737/A738 Trunk Road (The Den, Dalry) (Trunking and Detrunking) Order 2015 No. 2015/415. - Enabling power: Roads (Scotland) Act 1984 ss. 5 (2) (6). - Issued: 02.12.2015. Made: 02.12.2015. Coming into force: 16.12.2015. Effect: None. Territorial extent & classification: S. Local. - Available at http://www.legislation.gov.uk/ssi/2015/415/contents/made Non-print

The Fochabers Cycle Track (Redetermination of Means of Exercise of Public Right of Passage) Order 2015 No. 2015/221. - Enabling power: Roads of Scotland Act 1984, ss. 2 (1), 152 (2). - Issued: 02.06.2015. Made: 27.06.2015. Coming into force: 02.06.2015. Effect: None. Territorial extent & classification: S. Local. - Available at http://www.legislation.gov.uk/ssi/2015/221/contents/made Non-print

The Forth Road Bridge Act 2013 (Commencement) Order 2015 No. 2015/190 (C.30). - Enabling power: Forth Road Bridge Act 2013, s. 7(2). Bringing various provisions of the 2013 Act into operation on 01.06.2015. - Issued: 13.05.2015. Made: 06.05.2015. Laid before the Scottish Parliament: 08.05.2015. Coming into force: 01.06.2015. Effect: None. Territorial extent & classification: S. General. - 2p.: 30 cm. - 978-0-11-102775-2 £4.25

The Scottish Road Works Register (Prescribed Fees) Regulations 2015 No. 2015/89. - Enabling power: New Roads and Street Works Act 1991, ss. 112A (4), 163 (1). - Issued: 05.03.2015. Made: 26.02.2015. Laid before the Scottish Parliament: 02.03.2015. Coming into force: 01.04.2015. Effect: S.S.I. 2014/58 revoked. Territorial extent & classification: S. General. - 4p.: 30 cm. - 978-0-11-102681-6 £4.25

Roads and bridges: Special roads

The M80 (Castlecary Interchange) Special Road Scheme 2015 No. 2015/257. - Enabling power: Roads (Scotland) Act 1984, ss. 7. 8 (2), 10 (1). - Issued: 16.06.2015. Made: 12.06.2015. Coming into force: 22.06.2015. Effect: None. Territorial extent & classification: S. Local. - Available at: http://www.legislation.gov.uk/ssi/2015/257/contents/made Non-print

The M80 (Castlecary Interchange) Special Road (Transfer and Side Road) Order 2015 No. 2015/258. - Enabling power: Roads (Scotland) Act 1984, ss. 9 (1) (b) (c). - Issued: 16.06.2015. Made: 12.06.2015. Coming into force: 22.06.2015. Effect: None. Territorial extent & classification: S. Local. - Available at: http://www.legislation.gov.uk/ssi/2015/258/contents/made Non-print

Road traffic

The A9 Trunk Road (Kincraig to Dalraddy Dualling) (Temporary Prohibition of Traffic and Overtaking) Order 2015 No. 2015/343. - Enabling power: Road Traffic Regulation Act 1984, ss. 2 (1) (2), 4 (1), 14 (1) (a) (4), 15 (2). - Issued: 24.09.2015. Made: 23.09.2015. Coming into force: 02.10.2015. Effect: None. Territorial extent & classification: S. Local. - Available at: http://www.legislation.gov.uk/ssi/2015/343/contents/made Non-print

The A96 Trunk Road (Moss Street, Keith) (Temporary Prohibition On Use of Road) Order 2015 No. 2015/294. - Enabling power: Road Traffic Regulation Act 1984, ss. 2 (1) (2), 4 (1), 16A. - Issued: 31.07.2015. Made: 30.07.2015. Coming into force: 09.08.2015. Effect: None. Territorial extent & classification: S. Local. - Available at: http://www.legislation.gov.uk/ssi/2015/294/contents/made Non-print

The Disabled Persons (Badges for Motor Vehicles) (Scotland) Amendment Regulations 2015 No. 2015/9. - Enabling power: Chronically Sick and Disabled Persons Act 1970, s. 21 & Disabled Persons' Parking Badges (Scotland) Act 2014, s. 6 (1). - Issued: 21.01.2015. Made: 14.01.2015. Laid before the Scottish Parliament: 16.01.2015. Coming into force: 30.03.2015. Effect: S.S.I. 2000/59 amended. Territorial extent & classification: S. General. - 4p.: 30 cm. - 978-0-11-102588-8 £4.25

The Disabled Persons' Parking Badges (Scotland) Act 2014 (Commencement) Order 2015 No. 2015/8 (C.1). - Enabling power: Disabled Persons' Parking Badges (Scotland) Act 2014, s. 7 (2). Bringing into operation various provisions of the 2014 Act on 30.03.2015. - Issued: 21.01.2015. Made: 14.01.2015. Laid before the Scottish Parliament: 16.01.2015. Coming into force: 30.03.2015. Effect: None. Territorial extent & classification: S. General. - 2p.: 30 cm. - 978-0-11-102587-1 £4.25

Road traffic: Speed limits

The A68 Trunk Road (St Boswells) (50mph Speed Limit) Order 2015 No. 2015/345. - Enabling power: Road Traffic Regulation Act 1984, ss. 84 (1) (a). - Issued: 28.09.2015. Made: 25.09.2015. Coming into force: 05.10.2015. Effect: None. Territorial extent & classification: S. Local. - Available at http://www.legislation.gov.uk/ssi/2015/345/contents/made Non-print

The A77 Trunk Road (Girvan) (30mph Speed Limit) Order 2015 No. 2015/203. - Enabling power: Road Traffic Regulation Act 1984, s. 84 (1) (a), 124 (1) (d), sch. 9, para. 27. - Issued: 21.05.2015. Made: 20.05.2015. Coming into force: 28.05.2015. Effect: S.I. 2011/213 revoked. Territorial extent & classification: S. Local. - Available at http://www.legislation.gov.uk/ssi/2015/203/contents/made Non-print

ROAD TRAFFIC: TRAFFIC REGULATION

The A77 Trunk Road (Maybole) (30mph, 20mph and Part-time 20mph Speed Limit) Order 2015 No. 2015/332. - Enabling power: Road Traffic Regulation Act 1984, ss. 82 (2) (a) (b), 83 (1), 84 (1) (a) (c), 124 (1) (d), sch. 9, para. 27. - Issued: 14.09.2015. Made: 11.09.2015. Coming into force: 21.09.2015. Effect: S.S.I. 2005/377; 2007/18 revoked. Territorial extent & classification: S. Local. - Available at: http://www.legislation.gov.uk/ssi/2015/332/contents/made Non-print

The A84 Trunk Road (Balquhidder Station) (50mph Speed Limit) Order 2015 No. 2015/427. - Enabling power: Road Traffic Regulation Act 1984, s. 84 (1) (a). - Issued: 17.12.2015. Made: 09.12.2015. Coming into force: 18.12.2015. Effect: None. Territorial extent & classification: S. Local. - Revoked by S.S.I. 2016/1 (Non-print) (ISBN 9786666735029) issued 06/01/16. - Available at http://www.legislation.gov.uk/ssi/2015/427/contents/made Non-print

The A85 Trunk Road (Lochearnhead to Lix Toll) (50mph Speed Limit) Order 2015 No. 2015/365. - Enabling power: Road Traffic Regulation Act 1984, s. 84 (1) (a). - Issued: 30.10.2015. Made: 29.10.2015. Laid before the Scottish Parliament: - Coming into force: 09.11.2015. Effect: None. Territorial extent & classification: S. Local. - Available at http://www.legislation.gov.uk/ssi/2015/365/contents/made Non-print

The A90 Trunk Road (Longhaven) (50mph Speed Limit) (Part-time 20mph Speed Limit) Order 2015 No. 2015/251. - Enabling power: Road Traffic Regulation Act 1984, ss. 84 (1) (a) (c), 124 (1) (d), sch. 9, para. 27. - Issued: 10.06.2015. Made: 09.06.2015. Coming into force: 17.06.2015. Effect: S.S.I. 2007/83 revoked. Territorial extent & classification: S. Local. - Available at http://www.legislation.gov.uk/ssi/2015/251/contents/made Non-print

The A701 Trunk Road (Amisfield) (50mph Speed Limit) Order 2015 No. 2015/311. - Enabling power: Road Traffic Regulation Act 1984, s. 84 (1) (a). - Issued: 26.08.2015. Made: 25.08.2015. Coming into force: 01.09.2015. Effect: None. Territorial extent & classification: S. Local. - Available at http://www.legislation.gov.uk/ssi/2015/311/contents/made Non-print

The A830 Trunk Road (Blar Mhor and Lochaber High School) (30mph, 40mph and Part-time 20mph Speed Limit) Order 2015 No. 2015/301. - Enabling power: Road Traffic Regulation Act 1984, ss. 84 (1) (a) (c), 124 (1) (d), sch. 9, para. 27. - Issued: 17.08.2015. Made: 13.08.2015. Coming into force: 22.08.2015. Effect: S.S.I. 2006/22 revoked. Territorial extent & classification: S. Local. - Available at: http://www.legislation.gov.uk/ssi/2015/301/contents/made Non-print

The M90/A90 Trunk Road (Kingsway, Dundee) (50mph and 40mph Speed Limit) Order 2015 No. 2015/41. - Enabling power: Road Traffic Regulation Act 1984, s. 84 (1) (a), 124 (1) (d), sch. 9, para. 27. - Issued: 02.02.2015. Made: 30.01.2015. Coming into force: 09.02.2015. Effect: None. Territorial extent & classification: S. Local. - Available at http://www.legislation.gov.uk/ssi/2015/41/contents/made Non-print

The M90/A90 Trunk Road (Maconochie Road, Fraserburgh) (30mph Speed Limit) No. 2015/267. - Enabling power: Road Traffic Regulation Act 1984, ss. 84 (1) (a), 124 (1) (d), sch. 9 para. 27. - Issued: 19.06.2015. Made: 17.06.2015. Coming into force: 24.06.2015. Effect: S.S.I. 1992/1269 revoked. Territorial extent & classification: S. Local. - Available at http://www.legislation.gov.uk/ssi/2015/267/contents/made Non-print

Road traffic: Traffic regulation

The A1 Trunk Road (Gladsmuir Junction to Oaktree Junction) (Temporary Prohibition on Use of Road) (No. 2) Order 2015 No. 2015/373. - Enabling power: Roads (Scotland) Act 1984, s. 62 (1). - Issued: 02.11.2015. Made: 30.10.2015. Laid before the Scottish Parliament: - Coming into force: 01.11.2015. Effect: None. Territorial extent & classification: S. Local. - Available at http://www.legislation.gov.uk/ssi/2015/373/contents/made Non-print

The A1 Trunk Road (Gladsmuir Junction to Oaktree Junction) (Temporary Prohibition on Use of Road) Order 2015 No. 2015/278. - Enabling power: Road Traffic Regulation Act 1984, s. 62 (1). - Issued: 26.06.2015. Made: 24.06.2015. Coming into force: 05.07.2015. Effect: None. Territorial extent & classification: S. Local. - Available at http://www.legislation.gov.uk/ssi/2015/278/contents/made Non-print

The A9 Trunk Road (Kincraig to Dalraddy Dualling) (Temporary 40mph Speed Restriction) Order 2015 No. 2015/300. - Enabling power: Road Traffic Regulation Act 1984, ss. 2 (1) (2), 4 (1), 14 (1) (a) (4), 15 (2). - Issued: 12.08.2015. Made: 10.08.2015. Coming into force: 14.08.2015. Effect: None. Territorial extent & classification: S. Local. - Available at http://www.legislation.gov.uk/ssi/2015/300/contents/made Non-print

The A9 Trunk Road (Kincraig to Dalraddy Dualling) (Temporary Prohibitions of Traffic and Overtaking and Temporary Speed Restriction) (No. 2) Order 2015 No. 2015/55. - Enabling power: Road Traffic Regulation Act 1984, ss. 2 (1) (2), 4 (1), 14 (1) (a) (4). - Issued: 11.02.2014. Made: 09.02.2015. Coming into force: 16.02.2015. Effect: None. Territorial extent & classification: S. Local. - Available at: http://www.legislation.gov.uk/ssi/2015/55/contents/made Non-print

The A9 Trunk Road (Kincraig to Dalraddy Dualling) (Temporary Prohibitions of Traffic and Overtaking and Temporary Speed Restriction) Order 2015 No. 2015/27. - Enabling power: Road Traffic Regulation Act 1984, ss. 2 (1) (2), 4 (1), 14 (1) (a) (4). - Issued: 27.01.2015. Made: 26.01.2015. Coming into force: 02.02.2015. Effect: None. Territorial extent & classification: S. Local. - Available at http://www.legislation.gov.uk/ssi/2015/27/contents/made Non-print

The A68 Trunk Road (Edinburgh Road, Jedburgh) (Temporary Prohibition on Waiting and 30mph Speed Limit) Order 2015 No. 2015/253. - Enabling power: Road Traffic Regulation Act 1984, ss. 2 (1) (2), 4 (1), 14 (1) (b) (4). - Issued: 12.06.2015. Made: 11.06.2015. Coming into force: 20.06.2015. Effect: None. Territorial extent & classification: S. Local. - Available at http://www.legislation.gov.uk/ssi/2015/253/contents/made Non-print

The A68 Trunk Road (Fordel Junction, Dalkeith) (Redetermination of Means of Exercise of Public Right of Passage) Order 2015 No. 2015/198. - Enabling power: Road Traffic Regulation Act 1984, ss. 2(1), 152 (2). - Issued: 18.05.2015. Made: 15.05.2015. Coming into force: 25.05.2015. Effect: None. Territorial extent & classification: S. Local. - Available at http://www.legislation.gov.uk/ssi/2015/198/contents/made Non-print

The A68 Trunk Road (Lauder) (Temporary Prohibition On Use Of Road) Order 2015 No. 2015/407. - Enabling power: Road Traffic Regulation Act 1984, ss. 2 (1) (2), 4 (1), 16A. - Issued: 02.12.2015. Made: 01.12.2015. Coming into force: 12.12.2015. Effect: None. Territorial extent & classification: S. Local. - Available at http://www.legislation.gov.uk/ssi/2015/407/contents/made Non-print

The A75 Trunk Road (London Road, Stranraer) (Temporary Prohibition on Use of Road) Order 2015 No. 2015/449. - Enabling power: Road Traffic Regulation Act 1984, ss. 2 (1) (2), 4 (1), 14 (1) (b) (4). - Issued: 22.12.2015. Made: 21.12.2015. Coming into force: 10.01.2016. Effect: None. Territorial extent & classification: S. Local. - Available at: http://www.legislation.gov.uk/ssi/2015/449/contents/made Non-print

The A77 Trunk Road (Dalrymple Street, Girvan) (Temporary Prohibition On Use of Road) Order 2015 No. 2015/385. - Enabling power: Road Traffic Regulation Act 1984, ss. 2 (1) (2), 4 (1), 16A. - Issued: 16.11.2015. Made: 11.11.2015. Coming into force: 22.11.2015. Effect: None. Territorial extent & classification: S. General. - Available at http://www.legislation.gov.uk/ssi/2015/385/contents/made Non-print

The A78 Trunk Road (Branchton Footbridge) (Temporary Prohibition on Use of Road) Order 2015 No. 2015/287. - Enabling power: Road Traffic Regulation Act 1984, ss. 2 (3), 4 (1), 14 (1) (a) (4). - Issued: 16.07.2015. Made: 15.07.2015. Coming into force: 27.07.2015. Effect: None. Territorial extent & classification: S. Local Non-print

The A78 Trunk Road (Gallowgate Street, Largs) (Temporary Traffic Restrictions) Order 2015 No. 2015/372. - Enabling power: Road Traffic Regulation Act 1984, ss. 2 (1) (2), 4 (1), 14 (1) (a) (4) (7). - Issued: 02.11.2015. Made: 29.10.2015. Laid before the Scottish Parliament: - Coming into force: 09.11.2015. Effect: None. Territorial extent & classification: S. Local. - Available at http://www.legislation.gov.uk/ssi/2015/372/contents/made Non-print

The A82 Trunk Road (Glen Etive) (Temporary Prohibition of Traffic) Order 2015 No. 2015/450. - Enabling power: Roads (Scotland) Act 1984 s. 62 (1). - Issued: 23.12.2015. Made: 22.12.2015. Coming into force: 08.01.2016. Effect: None. Territorial extent & classification: S. Local. - Available at http://www.legislation.gov.uk/ssi/2015/450/contents/made Non-print

The A82 Trunk Road (Laggan Swing Bridge) (Temporary Width Restriction) Order 2015 No. 2015/2. - Enabling power: Road Traffic Regulation Act 1984, ss. 2 (1) (2), 4 (1), 14 (1) (a) (4). - Issued: 08.01.2015. Made: 07.01.2015. Coming into force: 12.01.2015. Effect: None. Territorial extent & classification: S. Local. - Available at http://www.legislation.gov.uk/ssi/2015/2/contents/made Non-print

ROAD TRAFFIC: TRAFFIC REGULATION

The A82 Trunk Road (Pulpit Rock Improvement) (Temporary Prohibition of Traffic and Overtaking and Speed Restriction) Order 2015 No. 2015/191. - Enabling power: Road Traffic Regulation Act 1984, ss. 2 (1) (2), 4 (1), 14 (1) (a) (4). - Issued: 13.05.2015. Made: 08.05.2015. Coming into force: 11.05.2015. Effect: None. Territorial extent & classification: S. Local. - Available at http://www.legislation.gov.uk/ssi/2015/191/contents/made Non-print

The A83 Trunk Road (Campbeltown Raft Race) (Temporary Prohibition On Use of Road) Order 2015 No. 2015/273. - Enabling power: Road Traffic Regulation Act 1984, ss. 2 (1) (2), 4 (1), 16A. - Issued: 25.06.2015. Made: 24.06.2015. Coming into force: 04.07.2015. Effect: None. Territorial extent & classification: S. Local. - Available at: http://www.legislation.gov.uk/ssi/2015/273/contents/made Non-print

The A83 Trunk Road (Inveraray) (Temporary Prohibition On Use of Road) Order 2015 No. 2015/178. - Enabling power: Road Traffic Regulation Act 1984, ss. 2 (1) (2), 4 (1), 16A. - Issued: 23.04.2015. Made: 22.04.2015. Coming into force: 03.05.2015. Effect: None. Territorial extent & classification: S. Local. - Available at: http://www.legislation.gov.uk/ssi/2015/178/contents/made Non-print

The A83 Trunk Road (Poltalloch Street and Lochnell Street, Lochgilphead) (Temporary Prohibition On Use of Road) Order 2015 No. 2015/367. - Enabling power: Road Traffic Regulation Act 1984, ss. 2 (1) (2), 4(1), 16A. - Issued: 30.10.2015. Made: 29.10.2015. Laid before the Scottish Parliament: - Coming into force: 08.11.2015. Effect: None. Territorial extent & classification: S. Local. - Available at http://www.legislation.gov.uk/ssi/2015/367/contents/made Non-print

The A83 Trunk Road (Poltalloch Street, Lochgilphead) (Temporary Prohibition On Use of Road) (No. 2) Order 2015 No. 2015/366. - Enabling power: Road Traffic Regulation Act 1984, ss. 2 (1) (2), 4(1), 16A. - Issued: 30.10.2015. Made: 29.10.2015. Laid before the Scottish Parliament: - Coming into force: 07.11.2015. Effect: None. Territorial extent & classification: S. Local. - Available at http://www.legislation.gov.uk/ssi/2015/366/contents/made Non-print

The A83 Trunk Road (Poltalloch Street, Lochgilphead) (Temporary Prohibition On Use of Road) Order 2015 No. 2015/256. - Enabling power: Road Traffic Regulation Act 1984, ss. 2 (1) (2), 4 (1), 16A. - Issued: 15.06.2015. Made: 12.06.2015. Coming into force: 20.06.2015. Effect: None. Territorial extent & classification: S. Local. - Available at: http://www.legislation.gov.uk/ssi/2015/256/contents/made Non-print

The A83 Trunk Road (Tarbert) (Temporary Prohibition on Waiting, Loading and Unloading) Order 2015 No. 2015/112. - Enabling power: Road Traffic Regulation Act 1984, ss. 2 (1) (2), 4 (1), 14 (1) (a) (4). - Issued: 12.03.2015. Made: 11.03.2015. Coming into force: 22.03.2015. Effect: None. Territorial extent & classification: S. Local. - Available at: http://www.legislation.gov.uk/ssi/2015/112/contents/made Non-print

The A83 Trunk Road (Tarbert to Campbeltown) (Temporary Prohibition On Use of Road) Order 2015 No. 2015/255. - Enabling power: Road Traffic Regulation Act 1984, ss. 2 (1) (2), 4 (1), 16A. - Issued: 15.06.2015. Made: 11.06.2015. Coming into force: 27.06.2015. Effect: None. Territorial extent & classification: S. Local. - Available at: http://www.legislation.gov.uk/ssi/2015/255/contents/made Non-print

The A84 Trunk Road (Callander) (Temporary Prohibition On Use of Road) Order 2015 No. 2015/362. - Enabling power: Road Traffic Regulation Act 1984, ss. 2 (1) (2), 4 (1), 16A. - Issued: 30.10.2015. Made: 29.10.2015. Laid before the Scottish Parliament: - Coming into force: 08.11.2015. Effect: None. Territorial extent & classification: S. Local. - Available at http://www.legislation.gov.uk/ssi/2015/362/contents/made Non-print

The A85 Trunk Road (Drummond Street, Comrie) (Temporary Prohibition on Use of Road) Order 2015 No. 2015/280. - Enabling power: Road Traffic Regulation Act 1984, ss. 2 (1) (2), 4 (1) 16A. - Issued: 01.07.2015. Made: 26.06.2015. Coming into force: 04.07.2015. Effect: None. Territorial extent & classification: S. Local. - Available at: http://www.legislation.gov.uk/ssi/2015/280/contents/made Non-print

The A85 Trunk Road (Laggan Park to Bridge Street, Comrie) (Temporary Prohibition on Use of Road) Order 2015 No. 2015/293. - Enabling power: Road Traffic Regulation Act 1984, ss. 2 (1) (2), 4 (1) 16A. - Issued: 31.07.2015. Made: 30.07.2015. Coming into force: 08.08.2015. Effect: None. Territorial extent & classification: S. Local. - Available at: http://www.legislation.gov.uk/ssi/2015/293/contents/made Non-print

The A85 Trunk Road (Perth Road to James Square, Crieff) (Temporary Prohibition on Use of Road) Order 2015 No. 2015/299. - Enabling power: Road Traffic Regulation Act 1984, ss. 2 (1) (2), 4 (1), 16A. - Issued: 10.08.2015. Made: 06.08.2015. Coming into force: 16.08.2015. Effect: None. Territorial extent & classification: S. Local. - Available at: http://www.legislation.gov.uk/ssi/2015/299/contents/made Non-print

The A90 and A96 Trunk Roads (Aberdeen Western Peripheral Route/Balmedie to Tipperty) (Stonehaven Bypass, Portlethen, Murcar to South Ellon and Blackburn to Bucksburn) (Temporary Prohibition of Traffic, Specified Turns, Overtaking and Speed Restrictions) Order 2015 No. 2015/310. - Enabling power: Road Traffic Regulation Act 1984, ss. 2 (1) (2) (3), 14 (1) (a) (4), 15 (2). - Issued: 21.08.2015. Made: 19.08.2015. Coming into force: 02.09.2015. Effect: S.I. 2015/281 revoked. Territorial extent & classification: S. Local. - Available at http://www.legislation.gov.uk/ssi/2015/310/contents/made Non-print

The A90 Trunk Road (Northbound Slip Road from B980 Castlandhill Road) (Temporary Prohibition on Use of Road) Order 2015 No. 2015/292. - Enabling power: Road Traffic Regulation Act 1984, ss. 2 (1) (2), 4 (1), 14 (1) (a) (4). - Issued: 29.07.2015. Made: 28.07.2015. Coming into force: 07.08.2015. Effect: None. Territorial extent & classification: S. Local. - Available at http://www.legislation.gov.uk/ssi/2015/292/contents/made Non-print

The A90 Trunk Road (Northbound Slip Road from B980 Castlandhill Road) (Temporary Prohibition on Use of Road) Order 2015 No. 2015/285. - Enabling power: Road Traffic Regulation Act 1984, ss. 2 (1) (2), 4 (1), 14 (1) (a) (4). - Issued: 13.07.2015. Made: 10.07.2015. Coming into force: 24.07.2015. Effect: None. Territorial extent & classification: S. Local. - Available at http://www.legislation.gov.uk/ssi/2015/285/contents/made Non-print

The A90 Trunk Road (Northbound Slip Road from B980 Castlandhill Road) (Temporary Speed Restrictions) Order 2015 No. 2015/284. - Enabling power: Road Traffic Regulation Act 1984, ss. 2 (1) (2), 4 (1), 14 (1) (a) (4). - Issued: 13.07.2015. Made: 10.07.2015. Coming into force: 29.07.2015. Effect: None. Territorial extent & classification: S. Local. - Available at http://www.legislation.gov.uk/ssi/2015/284/contents/made Non-print

The A96 Trunk Road (Aberdeen Western Peripheral Route, Blackburn to Bucksburn) (Temporary Prohibition of Traffic, Specified Turns, Overtaking and Speed Restrictions) Order 2015 No. 2015/281. - Enabling power: Road Traffic Regulation Act 1984, ss. 2 (1) (2) (3), 4 (1), 14(1) (a) (4). - Issued: 06.07.2015. Made: 02.07.2015. Coming into force: 06.07.2015. Effect: None. Territorial extent & classification: S. Local. - Available at: http://www.legislation.gov.uk/ssi/2015/281/contents/made Non-print

The A96 Trunk Road (Auchmill Road) (Temporary Prohibition of Specified Turns) Order 2015 No. 2015/42. - Enabling power: Road Traffic Regulation Act 1984, ss. 2 (1) (2), 4 (1), 14 (1) (a) (4). - Issued: 03.02.2015. Made: 02.02.2015. Coming into force: 16.02.2015. Effect: None. Territorial extent & classification: S. Local. - Available at: http://www.legislation.gov.uk/ssi/2015/42/contents/made Non-print

The A96 Trunk Road (Church Road, Keith) (Temporary Prohibition on Use of Road) Order 2015 No. 2015/374. - Enabling power: Road Traffic Regulation Act 1984, ss. 2 (1) (2), 4 (1), 16A. - Issued: 02.11.2015. Made: 28.10.2015. Laid before the Scottish Parliament: - Coming into force: 08.11.2015. Effect: None. Territorial extent & classification: S. Local. - Available at http://www.legislation.gov.uk/ssi/2015/374/contents/made Non-print

The A96 Trunk Road (High Street, Elgin) (Temporary Prohibition on Use of Road) Order 2015 No. 2015/316. - Enabling power: Road Traffic Regulation Act 1984, ss. 2 (1) (2), 4 (1), 14 (1) (a) (4). - Issued: 02.09.2015. Made: 01.09.2015. Coming into force: 14.09.2015. Effect: None. Territorial extent & classification: S. Local. - Available at: http://www.legislation.gov.uk/ssi/2015/316/contents/made Non-print

The A96 Trunk Road (Inveramsay Bridge Improvement) (Temporary Prohibitions on Traffic, Overtaking and Temporary Speed Restriction) (No. 2) Order 2015 No. 2015/416. - Enabling power: Road Traffic Regulation Act 1984, ss. 2 (1) (2), 4 (1), 14 (1) (a) (4), 124 (1) (d), sch. 9, para. 27. - Issued: 08.12.2015. Made: 07.12.2015. Coming into force: 20.12.2015. Effect: S.I. 2015/111 revoked. Territorial extent & classification: S. Local. - Available at http://www.legislation.gov.uk/ssi/2015/416/contents/made Non-print

ROAD TRAFFIC: TRAFFIC REGULATION

The A96 Trunk Road (Inveramsay Bridge Improvement) (Temporary Prohibitions on Traffic, Overtaking and Temporary Speed Restriction) Order 2015 No. 2015/111. - Enabling power: Road Traffic Regulation Act 1984, ss. 2 (1) (2), 4 (1), 14 (1) (a) (4), 15 (2). - Issued: 11.03.2015. Made: 09.03.2015. Coming into force: 16.03.2015. Effect: None. Territorial extent & classification: S. Local. - Revoked by SSI 2015/416 (Non-print) (ISBN 9786666734916). - Available at:
http://www.legislation.gov.uk/ssi/2015/111/contents/made Non-print

The A702 Trunk Road (Biggar) (Temporary Prohibition On Use of Road) Order 2015 No. 2015/445. - Enabling power: Road Traffic Regulation Act 1984, ss. 2 (1) (2), 4 (1), 16A. - Issued: 21.12.2015. Made: 17.12.2015. Coming into force: 31.12.2015. Effect: None. Territorial extent & classification: S. Local. - Available at
http://www.legislation.gov.uk/ssi/2015/445/contents/made Non-print

The A737/A738 Trunk Road (Lochwinnoch) (Temporary 30mph and 20mph Speed Restriction) Order 2015 No. 2015/195. - Enabling power: Road Traffic Regulation Act 1984, ss. 2 (1) (2), 4 (1) (b) (4). - Issued: 13.05.2015. Made: 12.05.2015. Coming into force: 19.05.2015. Effect: None. Territorial extent & classification: S. Local. - Available at:
http://www.legislation.gov.uk/ssi/2015/195/contents/made Non-print

The A972 and A90 Trunk Roads (Kingsway Junction) (Temporary Prohibition of Specified Turn) Order 2015 No. 2015/76. - Enabling power: Road Traffic Regulation Act 1984, ss. 2 (1) (2), 4 (1), 14 (1) (a) (4). - Issued: 24.02.2015. Made: 23.02.2015. Coming into force: 05.03.2015. Effect: None. Territorial extent & classification: S. Local. - Available at http://www.legislation.gov.uk/ssi/2015/76/contents/made Non-print

The A985 Trunk Road (Kincardine Bridge) (Temporary Bus Lane) Order 2015 No. 2015/75. - Enabling power: Road Traffic Regulation Act 1984, ss. 2 (1) (2), 4 (1), 14 (1) (a) (4). - Issued: 23.02.2015. Made: 19.02.2015. Coming into force: 27.02.2015. Effect: None. Territorial extent & classification: S. Local. - Available at:
http://www.legislation.gov.uk/ssi/2015/75/contents/made Non-print

The A985 Trunk Road (Longannet Roundabout to Cairneyhill Roundabout) (Temporary Prohibition on Use of Road) No. 2 Order 2015 No. 2015/426. - Enabling power: Road Traffic Regulation Act 1984, ss. 2 (1) (2), 4 (1), 14 (1) (a) (4), 124 (1) (d), sch. 9, para. 27. - Issued: 17.12.2015. Made: 11.12.2015. Coming into force: 16.12.2015. Effect: S.S.I. 2015/418 revoked. Territorial extent & classification: S. Local. - Available at
http://www.legislation.gov.uk/ssi/2015/426/contents/made Non-print

The A985 Trunk Road (Longannet Roundabout to Cairneyhill Roundabout) (Temporary Prohibition on Use of Road) Order 2015 No. 2015/418. - Enabling power: Road Traffic Regulation Act 1984, ss. 2 (1) (2), 4(1), 14 (1) (a) (4). - Issued: 10.12.2015. Made: 09.12.2015. Coming into force: 12.12.2015. Effect: None. Territorial extent & classification: S. Local. - Revoked by SSI 2015/426 (Non-print) (ISBN 9786666734930). - Available at
http://www.legislation.gov.uk/ssi/2015/418/contents/made Non-print

The M8/A8 Trunk Road (Junction 4) (Temporary Weight Restriction) Order 2015 No. 2015/57. - Enabling power: Roads (Scotland) Act 1984, ss. 2 (1) (2), 4 (1), 14 (1) (a) (4). - Issued: 16.02.2015. Made: 13.02.2015. Coming into force: 20.02.2015. Effect: None. Territorial extent & classification: S. Local. - Available at:
http://www.legislation.gov.uk/ssi/2015/57/contents/made Non-print

The M8, M74 and A725 Trunk Roads (Newhouse, Raith, Daldowie and Easterhouse to Bargeddie) (Temporary Prohibition on Use of Road and Temporary 30mph Speed Limit) Order 2015 No. 2015/147. - Enabling power: Road Traffic Regulation Act 1984, ss. 2 (1) (2), 4 (1), 14 (1) (a) (4). - Issued: 27.03.2015. Made: 23.03.2015. Coming into force: 27.03.2015. Effect: None. Territorial extent & classification: S. Local. - Available at:
http://www.legislation.gov.uk/ssi/2015/147/contents/made Non-print

The M8, M74 and A725 Trunk Roads (Newhouse, Raith, Daldowie and Easterhouse to Bargeddie) (Temporary Prohibition on Use of Road) (No. 2) Order 2015 No. 2015/106. - Enabling power: Road Traffic Regulation Act 1984, ss. 2 (1) (2), 4 (1), 14 (1) (a) (4), 15 (8) (a). - Issued: 06.03.2015. Made: 05.03.2015. Coming into force: 18.03.2015. Effect: None. Territorial extent & classification: S. Local. - Available at:
http://www.legislation.gov.uk/ssi/2015/106/contents/made Non-print

The M8, M74 and A725 Trunk Roads (Newhouse, Raith, Daldowie and Easterhouse to Bargeddie) (Temporary Prohibition on Use of Road) Order 2015 No. 2015/40. - Enabling power: Road Traffic Regulation Act 1984, ss 2 (1) (2), 4 (1), 14 (1) (a) (4). - Issued: 02.02.2015. Made: 29.01.2015. Coming into force: 06.02.2015. Effect: None. Territorial extent & classification: S. Local. - Available at: http://www.legislation.gov.uk/ssi/2015/40/contents/made Non-print

The M8 (Newhouse to Easterhouse) M73 (Maryville to Mollinsburn) M74 (Daldowie to Hamilton) A725 (Raith to Shawhead) Trunk Roads (Temporary Prohibitions of Traffic and Overtaking and Temporary Speed Restrictions) Order 2015 No. 2015/169. - Enabling power: Road Traffic Regulation Act 1984, ss. 2 (1) (2), 4 (1), 14 (1) (a) (4), 15 (2). - Issued: 09.04.2015. Made: 07.04.2015. Coming into force: 10.04.2015. Effect: None. Territorial extent & classification: S. Local. - Available at: http://www.legislation.gov.uk/ssi/2015/169/contents/made Non-print

The M9/A9 Trunk Road (Crubenmore and Etteridge) (Temporary Prohibition of Specified Turns) Order 2015 No. 2015/357. - Enabling power: Road Traffic Regulation Act 1984, ss. 2 (1) (2), 4 (1), 14 (1) (a) (4). - Issued: 26.10.2015. Made: 22.10.2015. Laid before the Scottish Parliament: - Coming into force: 02.11.2015. Effect: None. Territorial extent & classification: S. Local. - Available at
http://www.legislation.gov.uk/ssi/2015/357/contents/made Non-print

The M9/A9 Trunk Road (Munlochy Junction) (Temporary Prohibition of Specified Turns) (No. 2) Order 2015 No. 2015/114. - Enabling power: Road Traffic Regulation Act 1984, ss. 2 (1) (2), 4 (1), 14 (1) (a) (4). - Issued: 13.03.2015. Made: 11.03.2015. Coming into force: 16.03.2015. Effect: None. Territorial extent & classification: S. Local. - Available at http://www.legislation.gov.uk/ssi/2015/114/contents/made Non-print

The M9/A9 Trunk Road (Munlochy Junction) (Temporary Prohibition of Specified Turns) Order 2015 No. 2015/78. - Enabling power: Road Traffic Regulation Act 1984, ss. 2 (1) (2), 4 (1), 14 (1) (a) (4). - Issued: 25.02.2015. Made: 24.02.2015. Coming into force: 01.03.2015. Effect: None. Territorial extent & classification: S. Local. - Available at http://www.legislation.gov.uk/ssi/2015/78/contents/made Non-print

The M9/A9 Trunk Road (T in the Park Event) (Temporary Prohibition of Waiting and Specified Turns and Temporary 50mph Speed Restriction) No. 2015/259. - Enabling power: Road Traffic Regulation Act 1984, ss. 2 (1) (2), 4 (1), 14 (1) (b) (4). - Issued: 16.06.2015. Made: 12.06.2015. Coming into force: 22.06.2015. Effect: None. Territorial extent & classification: S. Local. - Available at
http://www.legislation.gov.uk/ssi/2015/259/contents/made Non-print

The M74 Trunk Road (Polmadie) (Temporary Prohibition on Traffic, Overtaking and Temporary Speed Limit) (No. 2) Order 2015 No. 2015/282. - Enabling power: Road Traffic Regulation Act 1984, ss. 2 (1) (2), 4 (1), 14 (1) (a) (4). - Issued: 06.07.2015. Made: 02.07.2015. Coming into force: 12.07.2015. Effect: None. Territorial extent & classification: S. Local. - Available at:
http://www.legislation.gov.uk/ssi/2015/282/contents/made Non-print

The M74 Trunk Road (Polmadie) (Temporary Prohibition on Traffic, Overtaking and Temporary Speed Limit) Order 2015 No. 2015/168. - Enabling power: Road Traffic Regulation Act 1984, ss. 2 (1) (2), 4 (1), 14 (1) (a) (4). - Issued: 10.04.2015. Made: 08.04.2015. Coming into force: 19.04.2015. Effect: None. Territorial extent & classification: S. Local. - Available at: http://www.legislation.gov.uk/ssi/2015/168/contents/made Non-print

The M90/A90 Trunk Road (A937 Marykirk Junction) (Temporary Prohibition of Specified Turns) Order 2015 No. 2015/304. - Enabling power: Road Traffic Regulation Act 1984, ss. 2 (1) (2), 4 (1), 14 (1) (a) (4). - Issued: 19.08.2015. Made: 17.08.2015. Coming into force: 21.08.2015. Effect: None. Territorial extent & classification: S. Local. - Available at: http://www.legislation.gov.uk/ssi/2015/304/contents/made Non-print

The North East Scotland Trunk Roads (Temporary Prohibitions of Traffic and Overtaking and Temporary Speed Restrictions) (No. 1) Order 2015 No. 2015/25. - Enabling power: Road Traffic Regulation Act 1984, ss 2 (1) (2), 4 (1), 14 (1) (a) (4). - Issued: 26.01.2015. Made: 21.01.2015. Coming into force: 01.02.2015. Effect: None. Territorial extent & classification: E. Local. - Available at:
http://www.legislation.gov.uk/ssi/2015/25/contents/made Non-print

ROAD TRAFFIC: TRAFFIC REGULATION

The North East Scotland Trunk Roads (Temporary Prohibitions of Traffic and Overtaking and Temporary Speed Restrictions) (No. 2) Order 2015 No. 2015/69. - Enabling power: Road Traffic Regulation Act 1984, ss. 2 (1) (2), 4 (1), 14 (1) (a) (4). - Issued: 19.02.2015. Made: 16.02.2015. Coming into force: 01.03.2015. Effect: None. Territorial extent & classification: E. Local. - Available at: http://www.legislation.gov.uk/ssi/2015/69/contents/made Non-print

The North East Scotland Trunk Roads (Temporary Prohibitions of Traffic and Overtaking and Temporary Speed Restrictions) (No. 3) Order 2015 No. 2015/137. - Enabling power: Road Traffic Regulation Act 1984, ss. 2 (1) (2), 4 (1), 14 (1) (a) (4). - Issued: 23.03.2015. Made: 18.03.2015. Coming into force: 01.04.2015. Effect: None. Territorial extent & classification: E. Local. - Available at: http://www.legislation.gov.uk/ssi/2015/137/contents/made Non-print

The North East Scotland Trunk Roads (Temporary Prohibitions of Traffic and Overtaking and Temporary Speed Restrictions) (No. 4) Order 2015 No. 2015/175. - Enabling power: Road Traffic Regulation Act 1984, ss. 2 (1) (2), 4 (1), 14 (1) (a) (4). - Issued: 22.04.2015. Made: 16.04.2015. Coming into force: 01.05.2015. Effect: None. Territorial extent & classification: S. Local. - Available at: http://www.legislation.gov.uk/ssi/2015/175/contents/made Non-print

The North East Scotland Trunk Roads (Temporary Prohibitions of Traffic and Overtaking and Temporary Speed Restrictions) (No. 5) Order 2015 No. 2015/207. - Enabling power: Road Traffic Regulation Act 1984, ss. 2 (1) (2), 4 (1), 14 (1) (a) (4). - Issued: 21.05.2015. Made: 18.05.2015. Coming into force: 01.06.2015. Effect: None. Territorial extent & classification: E. Local. - Available at: http://www.legislation.gov.uk/ssi/2015/207/contents/made Non-print

The North East Scotland Trunk Roads (Temporary Prohibitions of Traffic and Overtaking and Temporary Speed Restrictions) (No. 6) Order 2015 No. 2015/277. - Enabling power: Road Traffic Regulation Act 1984, ss. 2 (1) (2), 4 (1), 14 (1) (a) (4). - Issued: 25.06.2015. Made: 19.06.2015. Coming into force: 01.07.2015. Effect: None. Territorial extent & classification: S. Local. - Available at: http://www.legislation.gov.uk/ssi/2015/277/contents/made Non-print

The North East Scotland Trunk Roads (Temporary Prohibitions of Traffic and Overtaking and Temporary Speed Restrictions) (No. 7) Order 2015 No. 2015/291. - Enabling power: Road Traffic Regulation Act 1984, ss. 2 (1) (2), 4 (1), 14 (1) (a) (4). - Issued: 29.07.2015. Made: 23.07.2015. Coming into force: 01.08.2015. Effect: None. Territorial extent & classification: S. Local. - Available at: http://www.legislation.gov.uk/ssi/2015/291/contents/made Non-print

The North East Scotland Trunk Roads (Temporary Prohibitions of Traffic and Overtaking and Temporary Speed Restrictions) (No. 8) Order 2015 No. 2015/308. - Enabling power: Road Traffic Regulation Act 1984, ss. 2 (1) (2), 4 (1), 14 (1) (a) (4). - Issued: 21.08.2015. Made: 19.08.2015. Coming into force: 01.09.2015. Effect: None. Territorial extent & classification: S. Local. - Available at: http://www.legislation.gov.uk/ssi/2015/308/contents/made Non-print

The North East Scotland Trunk Roads (Temporary Prohibitions of Traffic and Overtaking and Temporary Speed Restrictions) (No. 9) Order 2015 No. 2015/341. - Enabling power: Road Traffic Regulation Act 1984, ss. 2 (1) (2), 4 (1), 14 (1) (a) (4). - Issued: 23.09.2015. Made: 21.09.2015. Coming into force: 01.10.2015. Effect: None. Territorial extent & classification: E. Local. - Available at: http://www.legislation.gov.uk/ssi/2015/341/contents/made Non-print

The North East Scotland Trunk Roads (Temporary Prohibitions of Traffic and Overtaking and Temporary Speed Restrictions) (No. 10) Order 2015 No. 2015/353. - Enabling power: Road Traffic Regulation Act 1984, ss. 2 (1) (2), 4 (1), 14 (1) (a) (4). - Issued: 21.10.2015. Made: 19.10.2015. Laid before the Scottish Parliament: - Coming into force: 01.11.2015. Effect: None. Territorial extent & classification: S. Local. - Available at http://www.legislation.gov.uk/ssi/2015/353/contents/made Non-print

The North East Scotland Trunk Roads (Temporary Prohibitions of Traffic and Overtaking and Temporary Speed Restrictions) (No. 11) Order 2015 No. 2015/394. - Enabling power: Road Traffic Regulation Act 1984, ss. 2 (1) (2), 4 (1), 14 (1) (a) (4). - Issued: 20.11.2015. Made: 17.11.2015. Coming into force: 01.12.2015. Effect: None. Territorial extent & classification: S. Local. - Available at http://www.legislation.gov.uk/ssi/2015/394/contents/made Non-print

The North East Scotland Trunk Roads (Temporary Prohibitions of Traffic and Overtaking and Temporary Speed Restrictions) (No. 12) Order 2015 No. 2015/442. - Enabling power: Road Traffic Regulation Act 1984, ss. 2 (1) (2), 4 (1), 14 (1) (a) (4). - Issued: 18.12.2015. Made: 17.12.2015. Coming into force: 01.01.2016. Effect: None. Territorial extent & classification: S. Local. - Available at http://www.legislation.gov.uk/ssi/2015/442/contents/made Non-print

The North West Scotland Trunk Roads (Temporary Prohibitions of Traffic and Overtaking and Temporary Speed Restrictions) (No. 1) Order 2015 No. 2015/24. - Enabling power: Road Traffic Regulation Act 1984, ss 2 (1) (2), 4 (1), 14 (1) (a) (4). - Issued: 26.01.2015. Made: 21.01.2015. Coming into force: 01.02.2015. Effect: None. Territorial extent & classification: S. Local. - Available at: http://www.legislation.gov.uk/ssi/2015/24/contents/made Non-print

The North West Scotland Trunk Roads (Temporary Prohibitions of Traffic and Overtaking and Temporary Speed Restrictions) (No. 2) Order 2015 No. 2015/70. - Enabling power: Road Traffic Regulation Act 1984, ss. 2 (1) (2), 4 (1), 14 (1) (a) (4). - Issued: 19.02.2015. Made: 16.02.2015. Coming into force: 01.03.2015. Effect: None. Territorial extent & classification: S. Local. - Available at: http://www.legislation.gov.uk/ssi/2015/70/contents/made Non-print

The North West Scotland Trunk Roads (Temporary Prohibitions of Traffic and Overtaking and Temporary Speed Restrictions) (No. 3) Order 2015 No. 2015/136. - Enabling power: Road Traffic Regulation Act 1984, ss. 2 (1) (2), 4 (1), 14 (1) (a) (4). - Issued: 23.03.2015. Made: 18.03.2015. Coming into force: 01.04.2015. Effect: None. Territorial extent & classification: S. Local. - Available at: http://www.legislation.gov.uk/ssi/2015/136/contents/made Non-print

The North West Scotland Trunk Roads (Temporary Prohibitions of Traffic and Overtaking and Temporary Speed Restrictions) (No. 4) Order 2015 No. 2015/172. - Enabling power: Road Traffic Regulation Act 1984, ss. 2 (1) (2), 4 (1), 14 (1) (a) (4). - Issued: 22.04.2015. Made: 16.04.2015. Coming into force: 01.05.2015. Effect: None. Territorial extent & classification: S. Local. - Available at: http://www.legislation.gov.uk/ssi/2015/172/contents/made Non-print

The North West Scotland Trunk Roads (Temporary Prohibitions of Traffic and Overtaking and Temporary Speed Restrictions) (No. 5) Order 2015 No. 2015/206. - Enabling power: Road Traffic Regulation Act 1984, ss. 2 (1) (2), 4 (1), 14 (1) (a) (4). - Issued: 21.05.2015. Made: 18.05.2015. Coming into force: 01.06.2015. Effect: None. Territorial extent & classification: S. Local. - Available at: http://www.legislation.gov.uk/ssi/2015/206/contents/made Non-print

The North West Scotland Trunk Roads (Temporary Prohibitions of Traffic and Overtaking and Temporary Speed Restrictions) (No. 6) Order 2015 No. 2015/276. - Enabling power: Road Traffic Regulation Act 1984, ss. 2 (1) (2), 4 (1), 14 (1) (a) (4). - Issued: 25.06.2015. Made: 19.06.2015. Coming into force: 01.07.2015. Effect: None. Territorial extent & classification: S. Local. - Available at: http://www.legislation.gov.uk/ssi/2015/276/contents/made Non-print

The North West Scotland Trunk Roads (Temporary Prohibitions of Traffic and Overtaking and Temporary Speed Restrictions) (No. 7) Order 2015 No. 2015/290. - Enabling power: Road Traffic Regulation Act 1984, ss. 2 (1) (2), 4 (1), 14 (1) (a) (4). - Issued: 29.07.2015. Made: 23.07.2015. Coming into force: 01.08.2015. Effect: None. Territorial extent & classification: S. Local. - Available at: http://www.legislation.gov.uk/ssi/2015/290/contents/made Non-print

The North West Scotland Trunk Roads (Temporary Prohibitions of Traffic and Overtaking and Temporary Speed Restrictions) (No. 8) Order 2015 No. 2015/307. - Enabling power: Road Traffic Regulation Act 1984, ss. 2 (1) (2), 4 (1), 14 (1) (a) (4). - Issued: 21.08.2015. Made: 19.08.2015. Coming into force: 01.09.2015. Effect: None. Territorial extent & classification: S. Local. - Available at: http://www.legislation.gov.uk/ssi/2015/307/contents/made Non-print

The North West Scotland Trunk Roads (Temporary Prohibitions of Traffic and Overtaking and Temporary Speed Restrictions) (No. 9) Order 2015 No. 2015/342. - Enabling power: Road Traffic Regulation Act 1984, ss. 2 (1) (2), 4 (1), 14 (1) (a) (4). - Issued: 23.09.2015. Made: 21.09.2015. Coming into force: 01.10.2015. Effect: None. Territorial extent & classification: S. Local. - Available at: http://www.legislation.gov.uk/ssi/2015/342/contents/made Non-print

The North West Scotland Trunk Roads (Temporary Prohibitions of Traffic and Overtaking and Temporary Speed Restrictions) (No. 10) Order 2015 No. 2015/355. - Enabling power: Road Traffic Regulation Act 1984, ss. 2 (1) (2), 4 (1), 14 (1) (a) (4). - Issued: 22.10.2015. Made: 19.10.2015. Laid before the Scottish Parliament: - Coming into force: 01.11.2015. Effect: None. Territorial extent & classification: S. Local. - Available at http://www.legislation.gov.uk/ssi/2015/355/contents/made Non-print

The North West Scotland Trunk Roads (Temporary Prohibitions of Traffic and Overtaking and Temporary Speed Restrictions) (No. 11) Order 2015 No. 2015/390. - Enabling power: Road Traffic Regulation Act 1984, ss. 2 (1) (2), 4 (1), 14 (1) (a) (4). - Issued: 19.11.2015. Made: 17.11.2015. Coming into force: 01.12.2015. Effect: None. Territorial extent & classification: S. Local. - Available at http://www.legislation.gov.uk/ssi/2015/390/contents/made Non-print

ROAD TRAFFIC: TRAFFIC REGULATION

The North West Scotland Trunk Roads (Temporary Prohibitions of Traffic and Overtaking and Temporary Speed Restrictions) (No. 12) Order 2015 No. 2015/441. - Enabling power: Road Traffic Regulation Act 1984, ss. 2 (1) (2), 4 (1), 14 (1) (a) (4). - Issued: 18.12.2015. Made: 17.12.2015. Coming into force: 01.01.2016. Effect: None. Territorial extent & classification: S. Local. - Available at http://www.legislation.gov.uk/ssi/2015/441/contents/made Non-print

The South East Scotland Trunk Roads (Temporary Prohibitions of Traffic and Overtaking and Temporary Speed Restrictions) (No. 1) Order 2015 No. 2015/23. - Enabling power: Road Traffic Regulation Act 1984, ss 2 (1) (2), 4 (1), 14 (1) (a) (4). - Issued: 26.01.2015. Made: 21.01.2015. Coming into force: 01.02.2015. Effect: None. Territorial extent & classification: S. Local. - Available at: http://www.legislation.gov.uk/ssi/2015/23/contents/made Non-print

The South East Scotland Trunk Roads (Temporary Prohibitions of Traffic and Overtaking and Temporary Speed Restrictions) (No. 2) Order 2015 No. 2015/68. - Enabling power: Road Traffic Regulation Act 1984, ss. 2 (1) (2), 4 (1), 14 (1) (a) (4). - Issued: 19.02.2015. Made: 16.02.2015. Coming into force: 01.03.2015. Effect: None. Territorial extent & classification: S. Local. - Available at: http://www.legislation.gov.uk/ssi/2015/68/contents/made Non-print

The South East Scotland Trunk Roads (Temporary Prohibitions of Traffic and Overtaking and Temporary Speed Restrictions) (No. 3) Order 2015 No. 2015/135. - Enabling power: Road Traffic Regulation Act 1984, ss. 2 (1) (2), 4 (1), 14 (1) (a) (4). - Issued: 23.03.2015. Made: 18.03.2015. Coming into force: 01.04.2015. Effect: None. Territorial extent & classification: S. Local. - Available at: http://www.legislation.gov.uk/ssi/2015/135/contents/made Non-print

The South East Scotland Trunk Roads (Temporary Prohibitions of Traffic and Overtaking and Temporary Speed Restrictions) (No. 4) Order 2015 No. 2015/171. - Enabling power: Road Traffic Regulation Act 1984, ss. 2 (1) (2), 4 (1), 14 (1) (a) (4). - Issued: 22.04.2015. Made: 16.04.2015. Coming into force: 01.05.2015. Effect: None. Territorial extent & classification: S. Local. - Available at: http://www.legislation.gov.uk/ssi/2015/171/contents/made Non-print

The South East Scotland Trunk Roads (Temporary Prohibitions of Traffic and Overtaking and Temporary Speed Restrictions) (No. 5) Order 2015 No. 2015/205. - Enabling power: Road Traffic Regulation Act 1984, ss. 2 (1) (2), 4 (1), 14 (1) (a) (4). - Issued: 21.05.2015. Made: 18.05.2015. Coming into force: 01.06.2015. Effect: None. Territorial extent & classification: S. Local. - Available at: http://www.legislation.gov.uk/ssi/2015/205/contents/made Non-print

The South East Scotland Trunk Roads (Temporary Prohibitions of Traffic and Overtaking and Temporary Speed Restrictions) (No. 6) Order 2015 No. 2015/275. - Enabling power: Road Traffic Regulation Act 1984, ss. 2 (1) (2), 4 (1), 14 (1) (a) (4). - Issued: 25.06.2015. Made: 19.06.2015. Coming into force: 01.07.2015. Effect: None. Territorial extent & classification: S. Local. - Available at: http://www.legislation.gov.uk/ssi/2015/275/contents/made Non-print

The South East Scotland Trunk Roads (Temporary Prohibitions of Traffic and Overtaking and Temporary Speed Restrictions) (No. 7) Order 2015 No. 2015/289. - Enabling power: Road Traffic Regulation Act 1984, ss. 2 (1) (2), 4 (1), 14 (1) (a) (4). - Issued: 28.07.2015. Made: 23.07.2015. Coming into force: 01.08.2015. Effect: None. Territorial extent & classification: S. Local. - Available at: http://www.legislation.gov.uk/ssi/2015/289/contents/made Non-print

The South East Scotland Trunk Roads (Temporary Prohibitions of Traffic and Overtaking and Temporary Speed Restrictions) (No. 8) Order 2015 No. 2015/309. - Enabling power: Road Traffic Regulation Act 1984, ss. 2 (1) (2), 4 (1), 14 (1) (a) (4). - Issued: 21.08.2015. Made: 19.08.2015. Coming into force: 01.09.2015. Effect: None. Territorial extent & classification: S. Local. - Available at: http://www.legislation.gov.uk/ssi/2015/309/contents/made Non-print

The South East Scotland Trunk Roads (Temporary Prohibitions of Traffic and Overtaking and Temporary Speed Restrictions) (No. 9) Order 2015 No. 2015/339. - Enabling power: Road Traffic Regulation Act 1984, ss. 2 (1) (2), 4 (1), 14 (1) (a) (4). - Issued: 23.09.2015. Made: 21.09.2015. Coming into force: 01.10.2015. Effect: None. Territorial extent & classification: S. Local. - Available at: http://www.legislation.gov.uk/ssi/2015/339/contents/made Non-print

The South East Scotland Trunk Roads (Temporary Prohibitions of Traffic and Overtaking and Temporary Speed Restrictions) (No. 10) Order 2015 No. 2015/354. - Enabling power: Road Traffic Regulation Act 1984, ss. 2 (1) (2), 4 (1), 14 (1) (a) (4). - Issued: 22.10.2015. Made: 19.10.2015. Laid before the Scottish Parliament: - Coming into force: 01.11.2015. Effect: None. Territorial extent & classification: S. Local. - Available at http://www.legislation.gov.uk/ssi/2015/354/contents/made Non-print

The South East Scotland Trunk Roads (Temporary Prohibitions of Traffic and Overtaking and Temporary Speed Restrictions) (No. 11) Order 2015 No. 2015/389. - Enabling power: Road Traffic Regulation Act 1984, ss. 2 (1) (2), 4 (1), 14 (1) (a) (4). - Issued: 19.11.2015. Made: 17.11.2015. Coming into force: 01.12.2015. Effect: None. Territorial extent & classification: S. Local. - Available at http://www.legislation.gov.uk/ssi/2015/389/contents/made Non-print

The South East Scotland Trunk Roads (Temporary Prohibitions of Traffic and Overtaking and Temporary Speed Restrictions) (No. 12) Order 2015 No. 2015/440. - Enabling power: Road Traffic Regulation Act 1984, ss. 2 (1) (2), 4 (1), 14 (1) (a) (4). - Issued: 18.12.2015. Made: 17.12.2015. Coming into force: 01.01.2016. Effect: None. Territorial extent & classification: S. Local. - Available at http://www.legislation.gov.uk/ssi/2015/440/contents/made Non-print

The South West Scotland Trunk Roads (Temporary Prohibitions of Traffic and Overtaking and Temporary Speed Restrictions) (No. 1) Order 2015 No. 2015/22. - Enabling power: Road Traffic Regulation Act 1984, ss 2 (1) (2), 4 (1), 14 (1) (a) (4). - Issued: 26.01.2015. Made: 21.01.2015. Coming into force: 01.02.2015. Effect: None. Territorial extent & classification: S. Local. - Available at: http://www.legislation.gov.uk/ssi/2015/22/contents/made Non-print

The South West Scotland Trunk Roads (Temporary Prohibitions of Traffic and Overtaking and Temporary Speed Restrictions) (No. 2) Order 2015 No. 2015/67. - Enabling power: Road Traffic Regulation Act 1984, ss. 2 (1) (2), 4 (1), 14 (1) (a) (4), 124 (1) (d), sch. 9, para. 27. - Issued: 19.02.2015. Made: 16.02.2015. Coming into force: 01.03.2015. Effect: None. Territorial extent & classification: S. Local. - Available at: http://www.legislation.gov.uk/ssi/2015/67/contents/made Non-print

The South West Scotland Trunk Roads (Temporary Prohibitions of Traffic and Overtaking and Temporary Speed Restrictions) (No. 3) Order 2015 No. 2015/134. - Enabling power: Road Traffic Regulation Act 1984, ss. 2 (1) (2), 4 (1), 14 (1) (a) (4). - Issued: 23.01.2015. Made: 18.03.2015. Coming into force: 01.04.2015. Effect: None. Territorial extent & classification: S. Local. - Available at: http://www.legislation.gov.uk/ssi/2015/134/contents/made Non-print

The South West Scotland Trunk Roads (Temporary Prohibitions of Traffic and Overtaking and Temporary Speed Restrictions) (No. 4) Order 2015 No. 2015/170. - Enabling power: Road Traffic Regulation Act 1984, ss. 2 (1) (2), 4 (1), 14 (1) (a) (4). - Issued: 22.04.2015. Made: 16.04.2015. Coming into force: 01.05.2015. Effect: None. Territorial extent & classification: S. Local. - Available at: http://www.legislation.gov.uk/ssi/2014/170/contents/made Non-print

The South West Scotland Trunk Roads (Temporary Prohibitions of Traffic and Overtaking and Temporary Speed Restrictions) (No. 5) Order 2015 No. 2015/204. - Enabling power: Road Traffic Regulation Act 1984, ss. 2 (1) (2), 4 (1), 14 (1) (a) (4). - Issued: 21.05.2015. Made: 18.05.2015. Coming into force: 01.06.2015. Effect: None. Territorial extent & classification: S. Local. - Available at: http://www.legislation.gov.uk/ssi/2015/204/contents/made Non-print

The South West Scotland Trunk Roads (Temporary Prohibitions of Traffic and Overtaking and Temporary Speed Restrictions) (No. 6) Order 2015 No. 2015/274. - Enabling power: Road Traffic Regulation Act 1984, ss. 2 (1) (2), 4 (1), 14 (1) (a) (4). - Issued: 25.06.2015. Made: 19.06.2015. Coming into force: 01.07.2015. Effect: None. Territorial extent & classification: S. Local. - Available at: http://www.legislation.gov.uk/ssi/2015/274/contents/made Non-print

The South West Scotland Trunk Roads (Temporary Prohibitions of Traffic and Overtaking and Temporary Speed Restrictions) (No. 7) Order 2015 No. 2015/288. - Enabling power: Road Traffic Regulation Act 1984, ss. 2 (1) (2), 4 (1), 14 (1) (a) (4). - Issued: 28.07.2015. Made: 23.07.2015. Coming into force: 01.08.2015. Effect: None. Territorial extent & classification: S. Local. - Available at: http://www.legislation.gov.uk/ssi/2015/288/contents/made Non-print

The South West Scotland Trunk Roads (Temporary Prohibitions of Traffic and Overtaking and Temporary Speed Restrictions) (No. 8) Order 2015 No. 2015/306. - Enabling power: Road Traffic Regulation Act 1984, ss. 2 (1) (2), 4 (1), 14 (1) (a) (4). - Issued: 21.08.2015. Made: 19.08.2015. Coming into force: 01.09.2015. Effect: None. Territorial extent & classification: S. Local. - Available at: http://www.legislation.gov.uk/ssi/2015/306/contents/made Non-print

The South West Scotland Trunk Roads (Temporary Prohibitions of Traffic and Overtaking and Temporary Speed Restrictions) (No. 9) Order 2015 No. 2015/340. - Enabling power: Road Traffic Regulation Act 1984, ss. 2 (1) (2), 4 (1), 14 (1) (a) (4). - Issued: 23.09.2015. Made: 21.09.2015. Coming into force: 01.10.2015. Effect: None. Territorial extent & classification: S. Local. - Available at: http://www.legislation.gov.uk/ssi/2015/340/contents/made Non-print

The South West Scotland Trunk Roads (Temporary Prohibitions of Traffic and Overtaking and Temporary Speed Restrictions) (No. 10) Order 2015 No. 2015/352. - Enabling power: Road Traffic Regulation Act 1984, ss. 2 (1) (2), 4 (1), 14 (1) (a) (4). - Issued: 21.10.2015. Made: 19.10.2015. Laid before the Scottish. Territorial extent & classification: S. Local. - Available at http://www.legislation.gov.uk/ssi/2015/352/contents/made Non-print

The South West Scotland Trunk Roads (Temporary Prohibitions of Traffic and Overtaking and Temporary Speed Restrictions) (No. 11) Order 2015 No. 2015/391. - Enabling power: Road Traffic Regulation Act 1984, ss. 2(1) (2), 4 (1), 14 (1) (a) (4). - Issued: 19.11.2015. Made: 17.11.2015. Coming into force: 01.12.2015. Effect: None. Territorial extent & classification: S. Local. - Available at http://www.legislation.gov.uk/ssi/2015/391/contents/made Non-print

The South West Scotland Trunk Roads (Temporary Prohibitions of Traffic and Overtaking and Temporary Speed Restrictions) (No. 12) Order 2015 No. 2015/439. - Enabling power: Road Traffic Regulation Act 1984, ss. 2 (1) (2), 4 (1), 14 (1) (a) (4). - Issued: 18.12.2015. Made: 17.12.2015. Coming into force: 01.01.2016. Effect: None. Territorial extent & classification: S. Local. - Available at http://www.legislation.gov.uk/ssi/2015/439/contents/made Non-print

Scottish Courts and Tribunals Service

The Criminal Justice and Licensing (Scotland) Act 2010 (Supplementary Provision) Order 2015 No. 2015/388. - Enabling power: Criminal Justice and Licensing (Scotland) Act 2010, s. 204. - Issued: 23.11.2015. Made: 17.11.2015. Coming into force: 28.11.2015. Effect: 2010 asp 13 amended. Territorial extent & classification: S. General. - 4p.: 30 cm. - 978-0-11-102992-3 £4.25

The Scottish Courts and Tribunals Service (Administrative Support) (Specified Persons) Regulations 2015 No. 2015/224. - Enabling power: Judiciary and Courts (Scotland) Act 2008, s. 62 (1) (h). - Issued: 03.06.2015. Made: 27.05.2015. Laid before the Scottish Parliament: 29.05.2015. Coming into force: 27.06.2015. None. Territorial extent & classification: S. General. - 2p.: 30 cm. - 978-0-11-102806-3 £4.25

The Scottish Sentencing Council (Procedure for Appointment of Members) Regulations 2015 No. 2015/225. - Enabling power: Criminal Justice and Licensing (Scotland) Act 2010, sch. 1, paras 2 (3) (4). - Issued: 03.06.2015. Made: 27.05.2015. Laid before the Scottish Parliament: 29.05.2015. Coming into force: 27.06.2015. Effect: None. Territorial extent & classification: S. General. - 4p.: 30 cm. - 978-0-11-102807-0 £4.25

Scottish Court Service

The Courts Reform (Scotland) Act 2014 (Commencement No. 1) Order 2015 No. 2015/12 (C.2). - Enabling power: Courts Reform (Scotland) Act 2014, s. 138 (2). Bringing into operation various provisions of the 2014 Act on 02.02.2015. - Issued: 27.01.2015. Made: 20.01.2015. Laid before the Scottish Parliament: 21.01.2015. Effect: None. Territorial extent & classification: S. General. - 4p.: 30 cm. - 978-0-11-102591-8 £4.25

The Courts Reform (Scotland) Act 2014 (Commencement No. 2, Transitional and Saving Provisions) Order 2015 No. 2015/77 (C.17). - Enabling power: Courts Reform (Scotland) Act 2014, s. 138 (2) (3). Bringing into operation various provisions of the 2014 Act on 12.03.2015. - Issued: 02.03.2015. Made: 24.02.2015. Laid before the Scottish Parliament: 26.02.2015. Coming into force: In accord with art. 1. Effect: None. Territorial extent & classification: S. General. - 8p.: 30 cm. - 978-0-11-102667-0 £6.00

The Scottish Courts and Tribunals Service (Procedure for Appointment of Members) Regulations 2015 No. 2015/53. - Enabling power: Judiciary and Courts (Scotland) Act 2008, sch. 3, para. 3 (2) (3). - Issued: 11.02.2015. Made: 04.02.2015. Laid before the Scottish Parliament: 06.02.2015. Coming into force: 16.03.2015. Effect: S.S.I. 2009/303 revoked. Territorial extent & classification: S. General. - 4p.: 30 cm. - 978-0-11-102633-5 £4.25

Scottish Land Court

The Courts Reform (Scotland) Act 2014 (Commencement No. 3, Transitional and Saving Provisions) Order 2015 No. 2015/247 (C.35). - Enabling power: Courts Reform (Scotland) Act 2014, s. 138 (2) (3). Bringing into operation various provisions of the 2014 Act on 22.09.2015. - Issued: 10.06.2015. Made: 04.06.2015. Laid before the Scottish Parliament: 08.06.2015. Coming into force: 22.09.2015. Effect: None. Territorial extent & classification: S. General. - 12p.: 30 cm. - 978-0-11-102830-8 £6.00

Scottish Public Services Ombudsman

The Scottish Public Services Ombudsman Act 2002 Amendment Order 2015 No. 2015/286. - Enabling power: Scottish Public Services Ombudsman Act 2002, s. 3 (2) (c). - Issued: 22.07.2015. Made: 15.07.2015. Coming into force: 16.07.2015. Effect: 2002 asp 11 amended. Territorial extent & classification: S. General. - Supersedes draft SI (ISBN 9780111027899) issued 28/05/15 - 2p.: 30 cm. - 978-0-11-102855-1 £4.25

Sea fisheries

The Aquaculture and Fisheries (Scotland) Act 2007 (Fixed Penalty Notices) Order 2015 No. 2015/113. - Enabling power: Aquaculture and Fisheries (Scotland) Act 2007, ss. 26 (5), 27 (1) (3), 29 (2) (b), 43 (1) (b). - Issued: 18.03.2015. Made: 11.03.2015. Laid before the Scottish Parliament: 13.03.2015. Coming into force: 27.04.2015. Effect: S.S.I. 2008/101; 2011/60 revoked. Territorial extent & classification: S. General. - 4p.: 30 cm. - 978-0-11-102705-9 £4.25

The European Maritime and Fisheries Fund (Grants) (Scotland) Regulations 2015 No. 2015/359. - Enabling power: European Communities Act 1972, s. 2 (2), sch. 2, para. 1A. - Issued: 03.11.2015. Made: 27.10.2015. Laid before the Scottish Parliament: 29.10.2015. Coming into force: 30.11.2015. Effect: S.S.I. 2007/307; 2010/323; 2012/166 revoked with savings. Territorial extent & classification: S. General. - 12p.: 30 cm. - 978-0-11-102962-6 £6.00

The Inshore Fishing (Prohibited Methods of Fishing) (Luce Bay) Order 2015 No. 2015/436. - Enabling power: Inshore Fishing (Scotland) Act 1984, ss. 1, 2A. - Issued: 23.12.2015. Made: 16.12.2015. Laid before the Scottish Parliament: 18.12.2015. Coming into force: 08.02.2016. Effect: S.S.I. 2004/276 partially revoked. Territorial extent & classification: S. General. - 8p., map: 30 cm. - 978-0-11-103039-4 £6.00

The Inshore Fishing (Prohibition of Fishing and Fishing Methods) (Scotland) Order 2015 No. 2015/435. - Enabling power: Inshore Fishing (Scotland) Act 1984, ss. 1, 2A. - Issued: 23.12.2015. Made: 16.12.2015. Laid before the Scottish Parliament: 18.12.2015. Coming into force: 08.02.2016. Effect: SSI 2004/276 partially revoked & SSI 2007/185 revoked. Territorial extent & classification: S. General. - 32p.: 30 cm. - 978-0-11-103038-7 £6.00

The Sea Fishing (EU Control Measures) (Scotland) Order 2015 No. 2015/320. - Enabling power: Fisheries Act 1981, s. 30 (2) & European Communities Act 1972, s. 2 (2), sch. 2, para. 1A. - Issued: 09.09.2015. Made: 02.09.2015. Laid before the Scottish Parliament: 04.09.2015. Coming into force: 05.10.2015. Effect: S.S.I. 2004/498; 2007/39; 2010/238, 334; 2012/63; 2013/189 & S.I. 2007/1842 amended & S.S.I. 2011/59 partially revoked & S.I. 1970/318; 1993/2015 & S.S.I. 2004/392; 2005/286, 438; 2006/284, 505; 2008/102, 156; 2009/413 revoked with savings. Territorial extent & classification: S. General. - 32p.: 30 cm. - 978-0-11-102924-4 £6.00

Sea fisheries: Conservation of sea fish

The Outer Hebrides (Landing of Crabs and Lobsters) Order 2015 No. 2015/183. - Enabling power: Sea Fish (Conservation) Act 1967, ss. 1 (1) (4) (6), 6 (1) (3), 20 (1). - Issued: 06.05.2015. Made: 28.04.2015. Laid: 30.04.2015. Coming into force: 29.05.2015. Effect: S.I. 1989/19 & S.S.I. 2000/197, 228 amended. Territorial extent & classification: S. General. - 12p.: 30 cm. - 978-0-11-102767-7 £6.00

Sea fisheries: Shellfish

The Little Loch Broom Scallops Several Fishery Order 2015 No. 2015/28. - Enabling power: Sea Fisheries (Shellfish) Act 1967, ss 1, 7 (4) (a) (iii). - Issued: 03.02.2015. Made: 27.01.2015. Laid: 29.01.2015. Coming into force: 09.03.2015. Effect: None. Territorial extent & classification: S. General. - [8]p., col. map: 30 cm. - 978-0-11-102603-8 £8.50

The Loch Ewe, Isle of Ewe, Wester Ross, Scallops Several Fishery Order 2015 No. 2015/30. - Enabling power: Sea Fisheries (Shellfish) Act 1967, ss 1, 7 (4) (a) (iii). - Issued: 03.02.2015. Made: 27.01.2015. Laid: 29.01.2015. Coming into force: 09.03.2015. Effect: S.I. 1997/830 & S.S.I. 2002/185 revoked. Territorial extent & classification: S. General. - [8]p., col. map: 30 cm. - 978-0-11-102605-2 £8.50

Seeds

The Seed Potatoes (Fees) (Scotland) Regulations 2015 No. 2015/396. - Enabling power: Plant Varieties and Seeds Act 1964, ss. 16 (1) (1A) (e) (5) (a), 36. - Issued: 25.11.2015. Made: 19.11.2015. Laid before the Scottish Parliament: 20.11.2015. Coming into force: 01.01.2016. Effect: S.S.I. 2009/306; 2011/414 revoked. Territorial extent & classification: S. General. - 4p.: 30 cm. - 978-0-11-102998-5 £4.25

The Seed Potatoes (Scotland) Regulations 2015 No. 2015/395. - Enabling power: Plant Varieties and Seeds Act 1964, ss. 16 (1) (1A) (2) (3) (4) (5) (5A), 36 & European Communities Act 1972, s. 2(2). - Issued: 25.11.2015. Made: 19.11.2015. Laid before the Scottish Parliament: 20.11.2015. Coming into force: 01.01.2016. Effect: S.I. 2001/3510 partially revoked & SSI 2000/201; 2005/280; 2007/418; 2009/226; 2010/71 revoked. Territorial extent & classification: S. General. - EC note: These Regulations revoke and replace the Seed Potatoes (Scotland) Regulations 2000. The Regulations transpose and give effect to the requirements of Council Directive 2002/56/EC on the marketing of seed potatoes as last amended by Commission Implementing Decision 2014/367/EU. The Regulations also transpose and give effect to Commission Implementing Directive 2013/63/EU amending Annexes I and II to Council Directive 2002/56/EC as regards minimum conditions to be satisfied by seed potatoes and lots of seed potatoes and to other Commission Implementing Directives and Decisions. - 48p.: 30 cm. - 978-0-11-102997-8 £10.00

Shellfish

The Aquaculture and Fisheries (Scotland) Act 2007 (Fixed Penalty Notices) Order 2015 No. 2015/113. - Enabling power: Aquaculture and Fisheries (Scotland) Act 2007, ss. 26 (5), 27 (1) (3), 29 (2) (b), 43 (1) (b). - Issued: 18.03.2015. Made: 11.03.2015. Laid before the Scottish Parliament: 13.03.2015. Coming into force: 27.04.2015. Effect: S.S.I. 2008/101; 2011/60 revoked. Territorial extent & classification: S. General. - 4p.: 30 cm. - 978-0-11-102705-9 £4.25

Sheriff Appeal Court

Act of Adjournal (Criminal Procedure Rules 1996 Amendment) (No. 4) (Sheriff Appeal Court) 2015 No. 2015/245. - Enabling power: Criminal Procedure (Scotland) Act 1995, s. 305. - Issued: 10.06.2015. Made: 04.06.2015. Laid before the Scottish Parliament: 08.06.2015. Coming into force: 22.09.2015. Effect: S.I. 1996/513 amended. Territorial extent & classification: S. General. - 28p.: 30 cm. - 978-0-11-102828-5 £6.00

Act of Adjournal (Criminal Procedure Rules 1996 and Act of Adjournal (Criminal Procedure Rules 1996 Amendment) (No. 4) (Sheriff Appeal Court) 2015 Amendment) (Miscellaneous) 2015 No. 2015/295. - Enabling power: Criminal Procedure (Scotland) Act 1995, s. 305. - Issued: 06.08.2015. Made: 31.08.2015. Laid before the Scottish Parliament: 03.08.2015. Coming into force: 01.09.2015. Effect: S.I. 1996/513; 2015/245 amended. Territorial extent & classification: S. General. - 16p.: 30 cm. - 978-0-11-102859-9 £6.00

Act of Sederunt (Fees of Solicitors in the Sheriff Appeal Court) 2015 No. 2015/387. - Enabling power: Courts Reform (Scotland) Act 2014, s. 106 (1). - Issued: 23.11.2015. Made: 17.11.2015. Laid before the Scottish Parliament: 18.11.2015. Coming into force: 01.01.2016. Effect: None. Territorial extent & classification: S. General. - 16p.: 30 cm. - 978-0-11-102990-9 £6.00

Act of Sederunt (Rules of the Court of Session, Sheriff Appeal Court Rules and Sheriff Court Rules Amendment) (Sheriff Appeal Court) 2015 No. 2015/419. - Enabling power: Courts Reform (Scotland) Act 2014, ss. 103 (1), 104 (1). - Issued: 15.12.2015. Made: 08.12.2015. Laid before the Scottish Parliament: 10.12.2015. Coming into force: In accord. with para. 1 (2) (3). Effect: S.I. 1976/1606; 1986/2297; 1988/2013; 1993/1956, 3128; 1994/1443; 1997/291; 1999/929, 1347; & S.S.I. 2002/132, 133, 560; 2008/119; 2009/284, 382; 2011/388; 2015/227, 356 amended. Territorial extent & classification: S. General. - 20p.: 30 cm. - 978-0-11-103019-6 £6.00

Act of Sederunt (Sheriff Appeal Court Rules) 2015 No. 2015/356. - Enabling power: Scottish Commission for Human Rights Act 2006, s. 14 (7) & Courts Reform (Scotland) Act 2014, s. 104. - Issued: 28.10.2015. Made: 21.10.2015. Laid before the Scottish Parliament: 23.10.2015. Coming into force: 01.01.2016. Effect: None. Territorial extent & classification: S. General. - 104p.: 30 cm. - 978-0-11-102960-2 £16.50

The Courts Reform (Scotland) Act 2014 (Commencement No. 3, Transitional and Saving Provisions) Order 2015 No. 2015/247 (C.35). - Enabling power: Courts Reform (Scotland) Act 2014, s. 138 (2) (3). Bringing into operation various provisions of the 2014 Act on 22.09.2015. - Issued: 10.06.2015. Made: 04.06.2015. Laid before the Scottish Parliament: 08.06.2015. Coming into force: 22.09.2015. Effect: None. Territorial extent & classification: S. General. - 12p.: 30 cm. - 978-0-11-102830-8 £6.00

The Courts Reform (Scotland) Act 2014 (Commencement No. 5, Transitional and Saving Provisions) Order 2015 No. 2015/378 (C.47). - Enabling power: Courts Reform (Scotland) Act 2014, s. 138 (2) (3). Bringing into operation various provisions of the 2014 Act on 01.01.2016, in accord. with art. 2. - Issued: 11.11.2015. Made: 04.11.2015. Laid before the Scottish Parliament: 06.11.2015. Coming into force: 01.01.2016. Effect: S.S.I. 2015/247 amended. Territorial extent & classification: S. General. - 8p.: 30 cm. - 978-0-11-102975-6 £6.00

The Courts Reform (Scotland) Act 2014 (Consequential and Supplemental Provisions) Order 2015 No. 2015/402. - Enabling power: Courts Reform (Scotland) Act 2014, s. 137. - Issued: 02.12.2015. Made: 26.11.2015. Coming into force: 01.01.2016. Effect: 1893 c.44; 1973 c.65; 1995 c.46; 2000 asp 7; 2004 asp 8; 2006 asp 16; 2011 asp 1 & S.S.I. 2003/179; 2012/335 modified. Territorial extent & classification: S. General. - Supersedes draft S.S.I. (ISBN 9780111029589) issued 15/10/15. - 8p.: 30 cm. - 978-0-11-103008-0 £4.25

The Courts Reform (Scotland) Act 2014 (Consequential Provisions No. 2) Order 2015 No. 2015/338. - Enabling power: Courts Reform (Scotland) Act 2014, s. 137. - Issued: 24.09.2015. Made: 18.09.2015. Coming into force: 22.09.2015. Effect: 1981 c.22; 1988 c.36, 53; 1991 c.65; 1995 c.43, 46; 2002 asp 6; asp 10; 2003 c.42; 2006 asp 10; asp 11, 2006 c.45; 2010 asp 9, asp 13; 2011 c.23; 2015 c.6 & S.S.I. 2000/301; 2001/315; 2007/504, 505, 507; 2013/6; 2014/337; 2015/77 modified. Territorial extent & classification: S. General. - Supersedes draft SI (ISBN 9780111028346) issued 12/06/15 - 16p.: 30 cm. - 978-0-11-102944-2 £6.00

The Criminal Justice and Licensing (Scotland) Act 2010 (Commencement No. 13) and the Courts Reform (Scotland) Act 2014 (Commencement No. 4) Order 2015 No. 2015/336 (C.41). - Enabling power: Criminal Justice and Licensing (Scotland) Act 2010, s. 206 (1) & Courts Reform (Scotland) Act 2014, s. 138 (2). Bringing into operation various provisions of both Acts on 19.10.2015, in accord. with arts 1 & 2. - Issued: 23.09.2015. Made: 16.09.2015. Laid before the Scottish Parliament: 18.09.2015. Coming into force: 19.10.2015. Effect: None. Territorial extent & classification: S. General. - 8p.: 30 cm. - 978-0-11-102943-5 £6.00

The Litigants in Person (Costs and Expenses) (Sheriff Appeal Court) Order 2015 No. 2015/398. - Enabling power: Litigants in Person (Costs and Expenses) Act 1975, s. 1 (2) (c). - Issued: 25.11.2015. Made: 19.11.2015. Laid before the Scottish Parliament: 20.11.2015. Coming into force: 01.01.2016. Effect: None. Territorial extent & classification: S. General. - 2p.: 30 cm. - 978-0-11-102996-1 £4.25

The Sheriff Appeal Court Fees Order 2015 No. 2015/379. - Enabling power: Courts Reform (Scotland) Act 2014, s. 107 (1) (2). - Issued: 11.11.2015. Made: 04.11.2015. Laid before the Scottish Parliament: 06.11.2015. Coming into force: In accord. with art. 1. Effect: None. Territorial extent & classification: S. General. - 12p.: 30 cm. - 978-0-11-102976-3 £6.00

Sheriff Court

Act of Adjournal (Criminal Procedure Rules 1996 Amendment) (No. 3) (Miscellaneous) 2015 No. 2015/201. - Enabling power: Criminal Procedure (Scotland) Act 1995, s. 305. - Issued: 27.05.2015. Made: 20.05.2015. Laid before the Scottish Parliament: 22.05.2015. Coming into force: 08.06.2015. Effect: S.I. 1996/513 amended. Territorial extent & classification: S. General. - 8p.: 30 cm. - 978-0-11-102787-5 £6.00

Act of Adjournal (Criminal Procedure Rules 1996 Amendment) (No. 4) (Sheriff Appeal Court) 2015 No. 2015/245. - Enabling power: Criminal Procedure (Scotland) Act 1995, s. 305. - Issued: 10.06.2015. Made: 04.06.2015. Laid before the Scottish Parliament: 08.06.2015. Coming into force: 22.09.2015. Effect: S.I. 1996/513 amended. Territorial extent & classification: S. General. - 28p.: 30 cm. - 978-0-11-102828-5 £6.00

Act of Adjournal (Criminal Procedure Rules 1996 Amendment) (No. 5) (Request for Final Decision and Reasons) 2015 No. 2015/375. - Enabling power: Criminal Procedure (Scotland) Act 1995 s. 305. - Issued: 06.11.2015. Made: 02.11.2015. Laid before the Scottish Parliament: 04.11.2015. Coming into force: 02.12.2015. Effect: S.I. 1996/513 amended. Territorial extent & classification: S. General. - 4p.: 30 cm. - 978-0-11-102971-8 £4.25

Act of Adjournal (Criminal Procedure Rules 1996 Amendment) (No. 6) (Special Measures in the Justice of the Peace Court) 2015 No. 2015/443. - Enabling power: Criminal Procedure (Scotland) Act, 1995 s. 305. - Issued: 23.12.2015. Made: 17.12.2015. Laid before the Scottish Parliament: 18.12.2015. Coming into force: 23.12.2015. Effect: S.I. 1996/513 amended. Territorial extent & classification: S. General. - 8p.: 30 cm. - 978-0-11-103042-4 £4.25

Act of Adjournal (Criminal Procedure Rules 1996 and Act of Adjournal (Criminal Procedure Rules 1996 Amendment) (No. 4) (Sheriff Appeal Court) 2015 Amendment) (Miscellaneous) 2015 No. 2015/295. - Enabling power: Criminal Procedure (Scotland) Act 1995, s. 305. - Issued: 06.08.2015. Made: 31.08.2015. Laid before the Scottish Parliament: 03.08.2015. Coming into force: 01.09.2015. Effect: S.I. 1996/513; 2015/245 amended. Territorial extent & classification: S. General. - 16p.: 30 cm. - 978-0-11-102859-9 £6.00

Act of Adjournal (Criminal Procedure Rules Amendment No. 2) (European Protection Orders) 2015 No. 2015/121. - Enabling power: Criminal Procedure (Scotland) Act 1995, s. 305. - Issued: 24.03.2015. Made: 18.03.2015. Laid before the Scottish Parliament: 19.03.2015. Coming into force: 01.04.2015. Effect: S.I. 1996/513 amended. Territorial extent & classification: S. General. - 24p.: 30 cm. - 978-0-11-102712-7 £6.00

Act of Adjournal (Criminal Procedure Rules Amendment) (Reporting Restrictions) 2015 No. 2015/84. - Enabling power: Criminal Procedure (Scotland) Act 1995, s. 305. - Issued: 04.03.2015. Made: 26.02.2015. Laid before the Scottish Parliament: 02.03.2015. Coming into force: 01.04.2015. Effect: S.I. 1996/513 amended. Territorial extent & classification: S. General. - 8p.: 30 cm. - 978-0-11-102676-2 £6.00

Act of Sederunt (Child Support Rules Amendment) (Miscellaneous) 2015 No. 2015/351. - Enabling power: Debtors (Scotland) Act 1987, s. 90 (4) & Courts Reform (Scotland) Act 2014, s. 104 (1). - Issued: 22.10.2015. Made: 16.10.2015. Laid before the Scottish Parliament: 20.10.2015. Coming into force: 21.12.2015. Effect: S.I. 1993/920 amended. Territorial extent & classification: S. General. - 24p.: 30 cm. - 978-0-11-102959-6 £6.00

Act of Sederunt (Ordinary Cause Rules 1993 Amendment and Miscellaneous Amendments) 2015 No. 2015/296. - Enabling power: Courts Reform (Scotland) Act 2014, ss. 103 (1), 104 (1). - Issued: 07.08.2015. Made: 31.07.2015. Laid before the Scottish Parliament: 03.08.2015. Coming into force: 21.09.2015. Effect: 1993/1956; 2015/227, 228 amended. Territorial extent & classification: S. General. - This S.S.I. has been made to correct errors in S.S.I. 2015/227 (ISBN 9780111028094) and S.S.I. 2015/228 (ISBN 9780111028117) and is being issued free of charge to all known recipients of those instruments. - 4p.: 30 cm. - 978-0-11-102860-5 £4.25

Act of Sederunt (Ordinary Cause Rules Amendment) (Proving the Tenor and Reduction) 2015 No. 2015/176. - Enabling power: Courts Reform (Scotland) Act 2014, s. 104. - Issued: 27.04.2015. Made: 21.04.2015. Laid before the Scottish Parliament: 23.04.2015. Coming into force: 25.05.2015. Effect: 1907 c.51 amended. Territorial extent & classification: S. General. - 8p.: 30 cm. - 978-0-11-102760-8 £4.25

Act of Sederunt (Rules of the Court of Session 1994 and Fees of Solicitors in the Sheriff Court Amendment) (Courts Reform (Scotland) Act 2014) 2015 No. 2015/246. - Enabling power: Courts Reform (Scotland) Act 2014, ss. 105 (1), 106 (1). - Issued: 10.06.2015. Made: 04.06.2015. Laid before the Scottish Parliament: 08.06.2015. Coming into force: 22.09.2015. Effect: S.I. 1993/3080; 1994/1443 amended. Territorial extent & classification: S. General. - 8p.: 30 cm. - 978-0-11-102829-2 £4.25

Act of Sederunt (Rules of the Court of Session 1994 and Ordinary Cause Rules 1993 Amendment) (Child Welfare Reporters) 2015 No. 2015/312. - Enabling power: Courts Reform (Scotland) Act 2014, ss. 103 (1), 104 (1). - Issued: 02.09.2015. Made: 26.08.2015. Laid before the Scottish Parliament: 28.08.2015. Coming into force: 26.10.2015. Effect: S.I. 1993/1956; 1994/1443 amended. Territorial extent & classification: S. General. - 12p.: 30 cm. - 978-0-11-102915-2 £6.00

Act of Sederunt (Rules of the Court of Session 1994 and Sheriff Court Rules Amendment) (No. 2) (Personal Injury and Remits) 2015 No. 2015/227. - Enabling power: Courts Reform (Scotland) Act 2014, ss. 103 (1), 104 (1). - Issued: 08.06.2015. Made: 02.06.2015. Laid before the Scottish Parliament: 04.06.2015. Coming into force: 22.09.2015. Effect: S.I. 1993/1956; 1994/1443 amended. Territorial extent & classification: S. General. - 56p.: 30 cm. - 978-0-11-102809-4 £10.00

Act of Sederunt (Rules of the Court of Session 1994 and Sheriff Court Rules Amendment) (No. 3) (Miscellaneous) 2015 No. 2015/283. - Enabling power: Revenue Scotland and Tax Powers Act 2014, s. 225 & Courts Reform (Scotland) Act 2014, ss. 103 (1), 104 (1). - Issued: 13.07.2015. Made: 07.07.2015. Laid before the Scottish Parliament: 09.07.2015. Coming into force: 07.08.2015. Effect: S.I. 1993/1956; 1994/1443; S.S.I. 1997/291; 2002/132, 133, 560; 1999/929 amended. Territorial extent & classification: S. General. - 12p.: 30 cm. - 978-0-11-102854-4 £6.00

Act of Sederunt (Rules of the Court of Session and Sheriff Court Bankruptcy Rules Amendment) (Bankruptcy and Debt Advice (Scotland) Act 2014) 2015 No. 2015/119. - Enabling power: Sheriff Courts (Scotland) Act 1971, s. 32 & Court of Session Act 1988, s. 5. - Issued: 24.03.2015. Made: 18.03.2015. Laid before the Scottish Parliament: 19.03.2015. Coming into force: 01.04.2015. Effect: S.I. 1994/1443; 2008/119 amended. Territorial extent & classification: S. General. - 8p.: 30 cm. - 978-0-11-102710-3 £6.00

Act of Sederunt (Rules of the Court of Session and Sheriff Court Rules Amendment No. 3) (Reporting Restrictions) 2015 No. 2015/85. - Enabling power: Sheriff Courts (Scotland) Act 1971, s. 32 & Court of Session Act 1988, s. 5. - Issued: 04.03.2015. Made: 26.02.2015. Laid before the Scottish Parliament: 02.03.2015. Coming into force: 01.04.2015. Effect: 1907 c.51 & S.I. 1994/1443; S.S.I. 1999/929 amended. Territorial extent & classification: S. General. - 8p.: 30 cm. - 978-0-11-102677-9 £6.00

Act of Sederunt (Rules of the Court of Session, Sheriff Appeal Court Rules and Sheriff Court Rules Amendment) (Sheriff Appeal Court) 2015 No. 2015/419. - Enabling power: Courts Reform (Scotland) Act 2014, ss. 103 (1), 104 (1). - Issued: 15.12.2015. Made: 08.12.2015. Laid before the Scottish Parliament: 10.12.2015. Coming into force: In accord. with para. 1 (2) (3). Effect: S.I. 1976/1606; 1986/2297; 1988/2013; 1993/1956, 3128; 1994/1443; 1997/291; 1999/929, 1347; & S.S.I. 2002/132, 133, 560; 2008/119; 2009/284, 382; 2011/388; 2015/227, 356 amended. Territorial extent & classification: S. General. - 20p.: 30 cm. - 978-0-11-103019-6 £6.00

Act of Sederunt (Sheriff Court Adoption Rules Amendment) 2015 No. 2015/5. - Enabling power: Sheriff Courts (Scotland) Act 1971, s. 32 & Adoption and Children (Scotland) Act 2007, ss 104, 114. - Issued: 16.01.2015. Made: 12.01.2015. Laid before the Scottish Parliament: 14.01.2015. Coming into force: 26.01.2015. Effect: S.S.I. 2009/284 amended. Territorial extent & classification: S. General. - 4p.: 30 cm. - 978-0-11-102580-2 £4.25

Act of Sederunt (Sheriff Court Rules Amendment) (Miscellaneous) 2015 No. 2015/424. - Enabling power: Courts Reform (Scotland) Act 2014, s. 104 (1). - Issued: 17.12.2015. Made: 11.12.2015. Laid before the Scottish Parliament: 15.12.2015. Coming into force: 01.02.2016. Effect: S.I. 1993/1956; 1997/291 amended. Territorial extent & classification: S. General. - 12p.: 30 cm. - 978-0-11-103025-7 £6.00

The All-Scotland Sheriff Court (Sheriff Personal Injury Court) Order 2015 No. 2015/213. - Enabling power: Courts Reform (Scotland) Act 2014, ss. 41 (1), 133 (1) & S.I. 2015/7010, art. 5. - Issued: 02.06.2015. Made: 26.05.2015. Laid before the Scottish Parliament: 28.05.2015. Coming into force: 22.09.2015. Effect: None. Territorial extent & classification: S. General. - 4p.: 30 cm. - 978-0-11-102796-7 £4.25

SOCIAL CARE

The Courts Reform (Scotland) Act 2014 (Commencement No. 2, Transitional and Saving Provisions) Order 2015 No. 2015/77 (C.17). - Enabling power: Courts Reform (Scotland) Act 2014, s. 138 (2) (3). Bringing into operation various provisions of the 2014 Act on 12.03.2015. - Issued: 02.03.2015. Made: 24.02.2015. Laid before the Scottish Parliament: 26.02.2015. Coming into force: In accord with art. 1. Effect: None. Territorial extent & classification: S. General. - 8p.: 30 cm. - 978-0-11-102667-0 £6.00

The Courts Reform (Scotland) Act 2014 (Commencement No. 3, Transitional and Saving Provisions) Order 2015 No. 2015/247 (C.35). - Enabling power: Courts Reform (Scotland) Act 2014, s. 138 (2) (3). Bringing into operation various provisions of the 2014 Act on 22.09.2015. - Issued: 10.06.2015. Made: 04.06.2015. Laid before the Scottish Parliament: 08.06.2015. Coming into force: 22.09.2015. Effect: None. Territorial extent & classification: S. General. - 12p.: 30 cm. - 978-0-11-102830-8 £6.00

The Courts Reform (Scotland) Act 2014 (Commencement No. 5, Transitional and Saving Provisions) Order 2015 No. 2015/378 (C.47). - Enabling power: Courts Reform (Scotland) Act 2014, s. 138 (2) (3). Bringing into operation various provisions of the 2014 Act on 01.01.2016, in accord. with art. 2. - Issued: 11.11.2015. Made: 04.11.2015. Laid before the Scottish Parliament: 06.11.2015. Coming into force: 01.01.2016. Effect: S.S.I. 2015/247 amended. Territorial extent & classification: S. General. - 8p.: 30 cm. - 978-0-11-102975-6 £6.00

The Courts Reform (Scotland) Act 2014 (Consequential and Supplemental Provisions) Order 2015 No. 2015/402. - Enabling power: Courts Reform (Scotland) Act 2014, s. 137. - Issued: 02.12.2015. Made: 26.11.2015. Coming into force: 01.01.2016. Effect: 1893 c.44; 1973 c.65; 1995 c.46; 2000 asp 7; 2004 asp 8; 2006 asp 16; 2011 asp 1 & S.S.I. 2003/179; 2012/335 modified. Territorial extent & classification: S. General. - Supersedes draft S.S.I. (ISBN 9780111029589) issued 15/10/15. - 8p.: 30 cm. - 978-0-11-103008-0 £4.25

The Courts Reform (Scotland) Act 2014 (Consequential Provisions No. 2) Order 2015 No. 2015/338. - Enabling power: Courts Reform (Scotland) Act 2014, s. 137. - Issued: 24.09.2015. Made: 18.09.2015. Coming into force: 22.09.2015. Effect: 1981 c.22; 1988 c.36, 53; 1991 c.65; 1995 c.43, 46; 2002 asp 6; asp 10; 2003 c.42; 2006 asp 10; asp 11, 2006 c.45; 2010 asp 9, asp 13; 2011 c.23; 2015 c.6 & S.S.I. 2000/301; 2001/315; 2007/504, 505, 507; 2013/6; 2014/337; 2015/77 modified. Territorial extent & classification: S. General. - Supersedes draft SI (ISBN 9780111028346) issued 12/06/15 - 16p.: 30 cm. - 978-0-11-102944-2 £6.00

The Courts Reform (Scotland) Act 2014 (Consequential Provisions) Order 2015 No. 2015/150. - Enabling power: Courts Reform (Scotland) Act 2014, s. 137. - Issued: 01.04.2015. Made: 24.03.2015. Coming into force: 01.04.2015. Effect: 1966 c.19; 1968 c.59; 1972 c.59; 1986 c.45; 1995 c.46; 1999 c.22; 2004 asp 8; 2005 c.12; 2007 asp 3; S.S.I. 2013/50 modified. Territorial extent & classification: S. General. - Supersedes draft SI (ISBN 9780111026663) issued 27/02/15 - 4p.: 30 cm. - 978-0-11-102736-3 £4.25

The Sheriff Court Fees Order 2015 No. 2015/264. - Enabling power: Courts Reform (Scotland) Act 2014, ss. 107 (1) (2). - Issued: 22.06.2015. Made: 15.06.2015. Laid before the Scottish Parliament: 17.06.2015. Coming into force: In accord. with art. 1. Effect: S.S.I. 2013/137 partially revoked & S.I. 1997/687; 1999/754 & S.S.I. 2002/269; 2003/97; 2005/445; 2007/318; 2008/239; 2009/89; 2012/293 revoked (22.09.2015). Territorial extent & classification: S. General. - 28p.: 30 cm. - 978-0-11-102844-5 £6.00

Social care

The Community Care (Personal Care and Nursing Care) (Scotland) Amendment Regulations 2015 No. 2015/154. - Enabling power: Community Care and Health (Scotland) Act 2002, ss. 1 (2) (a), 2, 23 (4). - Issued: 02.04.2015. Made: 26.03.2015. Coming into force: 01.04.2015. Effect: S.S.I. 2002/303 amended & S.S.I. 2014/91 revoked. Territorial extent & classification: S. General. - 4p.: 30 cm. - 978-0-11-102741-7 £4.25

The Community Care (Provision of Residential Accommodation Outwith Scotland) (Scotland) Regulations 2015 No. 2015/202. - Enabling power: Community Care and Health (Scotland) Act 2002, ss. 5(1), 23 (4). - Issued: 27.05.2015. Made: 20.05.2015. Laid before the Scottish Parliament: 26.05.2015. Coming into force: 24.06.2015. Effect: None. Territorial extent & classification: S. General. - 4p.: 30 cm. - 978-0-11-102788-2 £4.25

The Public Bodies (Joint Working) (Integration Joint Board Establishment) (Scotland) Amendment (No. 2) Order 2015 No. 2015/266. - Enabling power: Public Bodies (Joint Working) (Scotland) Act 2014, s. 9 (2). - Issued: 23.06.2015. Made: 17.06.2015. Laid before the Scottish Parliament: 19.06.2015. Coming into force: 21.09.2015. Effect: S.S.I. 2015/88 amended. Territorial extent & classification: S. General. - 4p.: 30 cm. - 978-0-11-102846-9 £4.25

The Public Bodies (Joint Working) (Integration Joint Board Establishment) (Scotland) Amendment (No. 3) Order 2015 No. 2015/321. - Enabling power: Public Bodies (Joint Working) (Scotland) Act 2014, s. 9 (2). - Issued: 08.09.2015. Made: 02.09.2015. Laid before the Scottish Parliament: 04.09.2015. Coming into force: 03.10.2015. Effect: S.S.I. 2015/88 amended. Territorial extent & classification: S. General. - 4p.: 30 cm. - 978-0-11-102925-1 £4.25

The Public Bodies (Joint Working) (Integration Joint Board Establishment) (Scotland) Amendment Order 2015 No. 2015/222. - Enabling power: Public Bodies (Joint Working) (Scotland) Act 2014, s. 9 (2). - Issued: 03.06.2015. Made: 27.05.2015. Laid before the Scottish Parliament: 29.05.2015. Coming into force: 27.06.2015. Effect: S.S.I. 2015/88 amended. Territorial extent & classification: S. General. - 4p.: 30 cm. - 978-0-11-102804-9 £4.25

The Public Bodies (Joint Working) (Integration Joint Board Establishment) (Scotland) Order 2015 No. 2015/88. - Enabling power: Public Bodies (Joint Working) (Scotland) Act 2014, s. 9 (2). - Issued: 05.03.2015. Made: 26.02.2015. Laid before the Scottish Parliament: 02.03.2015. Coming into force: 01.04.2015. Effect: None. Territorial extent & classification: S. General. - 4p.: 30 cm. - 978-0-11-102680-9 £4.25

The Public Bodies (Joint Working) (Integration Joint Boards and Integration Joint Monitoring Committees) (Amendment) (Scotland) Order 2015 No. 2015/66. - Enabling power: Public Bodies (Joint Working) (Scotland) Act 2014, ss. 12, 17, 69 (1). - Issued: 24.02.2015. Made: 17.02.2015. Laid before the Scottish Parliament: 19.02.2015. Coming into force: 20.03.2015. Effect: S.S.I. 2014/281, 285 amended. Territorial extent & classification: S. General. - This SSI has been printed to correct errors in S.S.I. 2014/281 (ISBN 9780111024713) and S.S.I. 2014/285 (ISBN 9780111024751) and is being issued free of charge to all known recipients of those instruments. - 4p.: 30 cm. - 978-0-11-102651-9 £4.25

The Public Bodies (Joint Working) (Integration Joint Boards and Integration Joint Monitoring Committees) (Scotland) Amendment (No. 2) Order 2015 No. 2015/432. - Enabling power: Public Bodies (Joint Working) (Scotland) Act 2014, ss. 12, 17, 69 (1). - Issued: 22.12.2015. Made: 15.12.2015. Laid before the Scottish Parliament: 17.12.2015. Coming into force: 01.02.2016. Effect: S.S.I. 2014/281, 285 amended. Territorial extent & classification: S. General. - 4p.: 30 cm. - 978-0-11-103032-5 £4.25

The Public Bodies (Joint Working) (Scotland) Act 2014 (Commencement No. 2) Amendment Order 2015 No. 2015/44 (C.8). - Enabling power: Public Bodies (Joint Working) (Scotland) Act 2014, s. 72 (2). Bringing into operation various provisions of the 2014 Act on 25.02.2015 in accord. with art. 2. - Issued: 10.02.2015. Made: 03.02.2015. Laid before the Scottish Parliament: 05.02.2015. Coming into force: 25.02.2015 Effect: S.S.I. 2014/231 amended. Territorial extent & classification: S. General. - 4p.: 30 cm. - 978-0-11-102623-6 £4.25

The Public Bodies (Joint Working) (Scotland) Act 2014 (Consequential Modifications and Saving) Order 2015 No. 2015/157. - Enabling power: Public Bodies (Joint Working) Scotland Act 2014, s. 70. - Issued: 09.04.2015. Made: 31.03.2015. Coming into force: 01.04.2015. Effect: 1968 c.49; 1978 c.29; 1995 c.46; 2000 asp 4, asp 7; 2003 asp 1, asp 13; 2008 asp 5; 2009 c.24; 2010 asp 8; 2011 asp 12; 2013 asp 1; 2014 asp 8; S.S.I. 2005/325; 2006/63, 484 amended. Territorial extent & classification: S. General. - Supersedes draft SI (ISBN 9780111026960) issued 10/03/15 - 12p.: 30 cm. - 978-0-11-102744-8 £6.00

The Self-directed Support (Direct Payments) (Scotland) Amendment Regulations 2015 No. 2015/319. - Enabling power: Social Care (Self-directed Support) (Scotland) Act 2013, ss. 15, 22 (1). - Issued: 08.09.2015. Made: 02.09.2015. Laid before the Scottish Parliament: 03.09.2015. Coming into force: 02.10.2015. Effect: S.S.I. 2014/25 amended. Territorial extent & classification: S. General. - 4p.: 30 cm. - 978-0-11-102923-7 £4.25

Social security

The Welfare Funds (Scotland) Act 2015 (Commencement) Order 2015 No. 2015/428 (C.56). - Enabling power: Welfare Funds (Scotland) Act 2015, s. 14 (2). Bringing into operation various provisions of the 2015 Act on 01.02.2016; 01.04.2016, in accord. with art. 2. - Issued: 22.12.2015. Made: 15.12.2015. Laid before the Scottish Parliament: 17.12.2015. Coming into force: 01.02.2016. Effect: None Territorial extent & classification: S. General. - 2p.: 30 cm. - 978-0-11-103028-8 £4.25

Supreme Court of the United Kingdom

The Courts Reform (Scotland) Act 2014 (Commencement No. 3, Transitional and Saving Provisions) Order 2015 No. 2015/247 (C.35). - Enabling power: Courts Reform (Scotland) Act 2014, s. 138 (2) (3). Bringing into operation various provisions of the 2014 Act on 22.09.2015. - Issued: 10.06.2015. Made: 04.06.2015. Laid before the Scottish Parliament: 08.06.2015. Coming into force: 22.09.2015. Effect: None. Territorial extent & classification: S. General. - 12p.: 30 cm. - 978-0-11-102830-8 £6.00

The Courts Reform (Scotland) Act 2014 (Consequential Provisions No. 2) Order 2015 No. 2015/338. - Enabling power: Courts Reform (Scotland) Act 2014, s. 137. - Issued: 24.09.2015. Made: 18.09.2015. Coming into force: 22.09.2015. Effect: 1981 c.22; 1988 c.36, 53; 1991 c.65; 1995 c.43, 46; 2002 asp 6; asp 10; 2003 c.42; 2006 asp 10; asp 11, 2006 c.45; 2010 asp 9, asp 13; 2011 c.23; 2015 c.6 & S.S.I. 2000/301; 2001/315; 2007/504, 505, 507; 2013/6; 2014/337; 2015/77 modified. Territorial extent & classification: S. General. - Supersedes draft SI (ISBN 9780111028346) issued 12/06/15 - 16p.: 30 cm. - 978-0-11-102944-2 £6.00

Taxes

The Revenue Scotland and Tax Powers Act 2014 (Commencement No. 3) Order 2015 No. 2015/18 (C.5). - Enabling power: Revenue Scotland and Tax Powers Act 2014, s. 260 (2). Bringing into operation various provisions of the 2014 Act on 16.02.2015, 24.02.2015. - Issued: 29.01.2015. Made: 22.01.2015. Laid before the Scottish Parliament: 26.01.2015. Effect: None. Territorial extent & classification: S. General. - 8p.: 30 cm. - 978-0-11-102597-0 £6.00

The Revenue Scotland and Tax Powers Act 2014 (Commencement No. 4) Order 2015 No. 2015/110 (C.23). - Enabling power: Revenue Scotland and Tax Powers Act 2014, s. 260 (2). Bringing into operation various provisions of the 2014 Act on 01.04.2015, in accord. with art. 2. - Issued: 17.03.2015. Made: 11.03.2015. Laid before the Scottish Parliament: 13.03.2015. Coming into force: 01.04.2015. Effect: None. Territorial extent & classification: S. General. - 4p.: 30 cm. - 978-0-11-102704-2 £4.25

The Revenue Scotland and Tax Powers Act (Fees for Payment) Regulations 2015 No. 2015/36. - Enabling power: Revenue Scotland and Tax Powers Act 2014, s. 222. - Issued: 05.02.2015. Made: 29.01.2015. Laid before the Scottish Parliament: 02.02.2015. Coming into force: 01.04.2015. Effect: None. Territorial extent & classification: S. General. - 4p.: 30 cm. - 978-0-11-102611-3 £4.25

The Revenue Scotland and Tax Powers Act (Interest on Unpaid Tax and Interest Rates in General) Regulations 2015 No. 2015/128. - Enabling power: Revenue Scotland and Tax Powers Act 2014, ss. 217 (2), 220 (1). - Issued: 25.03.2015. Made: 17.03.2015. Coming into force: 01.04.2015. Effect: None. Territorial extent & classification: S. General. - 4p.: 30 cm. - 978-0-11-102719-6 £4.25

The Revenue Scotland and Tax Powers Act (Involved Third Party) Order 2015 No. 2015/37. - Enabling power: Revenue Scotland and Tax Powers Act 2014, s. 142 (3). - Issued: 05.02.2015. Made: 29.01.2015. Laid before the Scottish Parliament: 02.02.2015. Coming into force: 01.04.2015. Effect: None. Territorial extent & classification: S. General. - 2p.: 30 cm. - 978-0-11-102612-0 £4.25

The Revenue Scotland and Tax Powers Act (Postponement of Tax Pending a Review or Appeal) Regulations 2015 No. 2015/129. - Enabling power: Revenue Scotland and Tax Powers Act 2014, s. 245 (2). - Issued: 25.03.2015. Made: 17.03.2015. Coming into force: 01.04.2015. Effect: None. Territorial extent & classification: S. General. - Supersedes draft S.S.I. (ISBN 9780111026205) issued 09/02/15. - 4p.: 30 cm. - 978-0-11-102720-2 £4.25

The Revenue Scotland and Tax Powers Act (Privileged Communications) Regulations 2015 No. 2015/38. - Enabling power: Revenue Scotland and Tax Powers Act 2014, s. 138 (3). - Issued: 05.02.2015. Made: 29.01.2015. Laid before the Scottish Parliament: 02.02.2015. Coming into force: 01.04.2015. Effect: None. Territorial extent & classification: S. General. - 8p.: 30 cm. - 978-0-11-102613-7 £4.25

The Revenue Scotland and Tax Powers Act (Record Keeping) Regulations 2015 No. 2015/130. - Enabling power: Revenue Scotland and Tax Powers Act 2014, ss. 74 (9) to (11), 81, sch. 3, paras. 3 (3) to (5). - Issued: 25.03.2015. Made: -. Coming into force: 01.04.2015. Effect: None. Territorial extent & classification: S. General. - Supersedes Draft S.S.I. (ISBN 9780111026465) issued 23/02/15. - 4p.: 30 cm. - 978-0-11-102721-9 £4.25

The Revenue Scotland and Tax Powers Act (Reimbursement Arrangements) Regulations 2015 No. 2015/131. - Enabling power: Revenue Scotland and Tax Powers Act 2014, ss. 111, 112. - Issued: 25.03.2015. Made: 17.03.2015. Coming into force: 01.04.2015. Effect: None. Territorial extent & classification: S. General. - Supersedes draft S.S.I. (ISBN 9780111026441) issued 23/02/15. - 4p.: 30 cm. - 978-0-11-102722-6 £4.25

The Revenue Scotland (First Planning Period) Order 2015 No. 2015/16. - Enabling power: Revenue Scotland and Tax Powers Act 2014, s. 11 (7) (a). - Issued: 29.01.2015. Made: 22.01.2015. Laid before the Scottish Parliament: 26.01.2015. Coming into force: 01.04.2015. Effect: None. Territorial extent & classification: S. General. - Revoked by SSI 2014/325 (ISBN 9780111025161). - 2p.: 30 cm. - 978-0-11-102595-6 £4.25

Title conditions

The Historic Environment Scotland Act 2014 (Saving, Transitional and Consequential Provisions) Order 2015 No. 2015/239. - Enabling power: Title Conditions (Scotland) Act 2003, s. 38 (4) & Historic Environment Scotland Act 2014, s. 27. - Issued: 09.06.2015. Made: 02.06.2015. Laid before the Scottish Parliament: 04.06.2015. Coming into force: 01.10.2015. Effect: S.I. 1996/1507 & S.S.I. 2003/453; 2007/570; 2011/146 amended. Territorial extent & classification: S. General. - 12p.: 30 cm. - 978-0-11-102822-3 £6.00

Town and country planning

The Historic Environment Scotland Act 2014 (Saving, Transitional and Consequential Provisions) Order 2015 No. 2015/239. - Enabling power: Title Conditions (Scotland) Act 2003, s. 38 (4) & Historic Environment Scotland Act 2014, s. 27. - Issued: 09.06.2015. Made: 02.06.2015. Laid before the Scottish Parliament: 04.06.2015. Coming into force: 01.10.2015. Effect: S.I. 1996/1507 & S.S.I. 2003/453; 2007/570; 2011/146 amended. Territorial extent & classification: S. General. - 12p.: 30 cm. - 978-0-11-102822-3 £6.00

The Listed Buildings (Notification and Publication) (Scotland) Regulations 2015 No. 2015/241. - Enabling power: Planning (Listed Buildings and Conservation Areas) (Scotland) Act 1997, s. 1A. - Issued: 09.06.2015. Made: 02.06.2015. Laid before the Scottish Parliament: 04.06.2015. Coming into force: 01.10.2015 Effect: None. Territorial extent & classification: S. General. - 4p.: 30 cm. - 978-0-11-102824-7 £4.25

The Planning (Listed Building Consent and Conservation Area Consent Procedure) (Scotland) Regulations 2015 No. 2015/243. - Enabling power: Planning (Listed Buildings and Conservation Areas) (Scotland) Act 1997, ss. 9 (3) to (6), 10, 17, 23 (2), 25 (2), 26 (2), 28 (1), 41D (5), 41I, 66 (3), 82. - Issued: 10.06.2015. Made: 02.06.2015. Laid before the Scottish Parliament: 04.06.2015. Coming into force: 01.10.2015. Effect: S.S.I. 2013/156 amended & S.S.I. 2011/376 partially revoked & S.I. 1987/1529 & S.S.I. 2006/266 revoked with saving. Territorial extent & classification: S. General. - 16p.: 30 cm. - 978-0-11-102826-1 £6.00

The Planning (Listed Buildings and Conservation Areas) (Urgent Works to Crown Land) (Scotland) Regulations 2015 No. 2015/240. - Enabling power: Planning (Listed Buildings and Conservation Areas) (Scotland) Act 1997, ss. 73B (8) (10). - Issued: 09.06.2015. Made: 02.06.2015. Laid before the Scottish Parliament: 04.06.2015. Coming into force: 01.10.2015. Effect: None. Territorial extent & classification: S. General. - 4p.: 30 cm. - 978-0-11-102823-0 £4.25

TRANSPORT

The Scheduled Monuments and Listed Buildings (Miscellaneous Amendments) (Scotland) Regulations 2015 No. 2015/328. - Enabling power: Ancient Monuments and Archaeological Areas Act 1979, ss. 1 (6), 4D, 9CB & Planning (Listed Buildings and Conservation Areas) (Scotland) Act 1997, ss. 1A, 9 (3), 23 (2), 82 & Transport and Works (Scotland) Act 2007, ss. 14, 28. - Issued: 15.09.2015. Made: 09.09.2015. Laid before the Scottish Parliament: 11.09.2015. Coming into force: 10.10.2015. Effect: S.S.I. 2007/569; 2015/230, 231, 241, 243 amended. Territorial extent & classification: S. General. - 8p.: 30 cm. - 978-0-11-102935-0 £4.25

The Town and Country Planning (Appeals) (Scotland) Amendment Order 2015 No. 2015/233. - Enabling power: Town and Country Planning (Scotland) Act 1997, ss. 267, 275, 275A & Planning (Listed Buildings and Conservation Areas) (Scotland) Act 1997, s. 5D. - Issued: 09.06.2015. Made: 02.06.2015. Laid before the Scottish Parliament: 04.06.2015. Coming into force: 01.10.2015. Effect: S.S.I. 2013/156 amended. Territorial extent & classification: S. General. - 8p.: 30 cm. - 978-0-11-102816-2 £4.25

The Town and Country Planning (Determination of Appeals by Appointed Persons) (Prescribed Classes) (Scotland) Amendment Regulations 2015 No. 2015/236. - Enabling power: Planning (Listed Building and Conservation Areas) (Scotland) Act 1997, sch. 3, para. 1. - Issued: 09.06.2015. Made: 02.06.2015. Laid before the Scottish Parliament: 04.06.2015. Coming into force: 01.10.2015. Effect: S.S.I. 2010/467 amended. Territorial extent & classification: S. General. - 2p.: 30 cm. - 978-0-11-102819-3 £4.25

The Town and Country Planning (General Permitted Development) (Scotland) Amendment Order 2015 No. 2015/235. - Enabling power: Town and Country Planning (Scotland) Act 1997, ss. 30, 31, 275. - Issued: 09.06.2015. Made: 02.06.2015. Laid before the Scottish Parliament: 04.06.2015. Coming into force: 01.10.2015. Effect: S.I. 1992/223 & S.S.I. 2006/270 amended. Territorial extent & classification: S. General. - 4p.: 30 cm. - 978-0-11-102818-6 £4.25

The Town and Country Planning (Hazardous Substances) (Scotland) Regulations 2015 No. 2015/181. - Enabling power: European Communities Act 1972, s. 2 (2), sch. 2, para. 1A & Town and Country Planning (Scotland) Act 1997, ss. 252 (1), 267 (1) & Planning (Hazardous Substances) (Scotland) Act 1997, ss. 2 (4) (5), 3, 5, 6 (1), 15 (2), 16 (7), 19 (2) (3), 22 (4) (b), 23 (1) (3), 27 (1), 30 (1), 39 (1). - Issued: 06.05.2015. Made: 28.04.2015. Laid before the Scottish Parliament: 30.04.2015. Coming into force: 01.06.2015. Effect: S.S.I. 2007/570; 2008/426; 2013/155 amended & S.S.I. 2000/179; 2003/1; 2005/344; 2006/270; 2009/378; 2013/119 & S.I. 1996/252; 2014/469 partially revoked & S.S.I. 2010/171; 2014/51 & S.I. 1993/323 revoked. Territorial extent & classification: S. General. - 64p.: 30 cm. - 978-0-11-102768-4 £11.00

The Town and Country Planning (Historic Environment Scotland) Amendment Regulations 2015 No. 2015/237. - Enabling power: European Communities Act 1972, s. 2 (2) & Town and Country Planning (Scotland) Act 1997, ss. 23D, 30, 32, 40, 43, 275. - Issued: 09.06.2015. Made: 02.06.2015. Laid before the Scottish Parliament: 04.06.2015. Coming into force: 01.10.2015. Effect: S.S.I. 1999/1; 2008/426; 2011/139; 2013/155 amended. Territorial extent & classification: S. General. - 8p.: 30 cm. - 978-0-11-102820-9 £4.25

The Town and Country Planning (Miscellaneous Amendments) (Scotland) Regulations 2015 No. 2015/249. - Enabling power: European Communities Act 1972, s. 2 (2) & Town and Country Planning (Scotland) Act 1997, 32, 40, 43A (10), 75A, 75E, 267, 275, 275A. - Issued: 10.06.2015. Made: 04.06.2015. Laid before the Scottish Parliament: 08.06.2015. Coming into force: 14.09.2015. Effect: S.I. 1994/2716 & S.S.I. 2010/432, 433; 2011/139; 2013/155, 156, 157 amended. Territorial extent & classification: S. General. - 8p.: 30 cm. - 978-0-11-102832-2 £6.00

Transport

The National Bus Travel Concession Scheme for Older and Disabled Persons (Scotland) Amendment Order 2015 No. 2015/133. - Enabling power: Transport (Scotland) Act 2005, ss. 40 (1) (3) (4), 52 (4). - Issued: 25.03.2015. Made: 17.03.2015. Coming into force: 01.04.2015. Effect: S.S.I. 2006/107 amended. Territorial extent & classification: S. General. - Supersedes draft S.S.I. (ISBN 9780111026403) issued 20/02/15. - 4p.: 30 cm. - 978-0-11-102724-0 £4.25

Transport and works

The Scheduled Monuments and Listed Buildings (Miscellaneous Amendments) (Scotland) Regulations 2015 No. 2015/328. - Enabling power: Ancient Monuments and Archaeological Areas Act 1979, ss. 1 (6), 4D, 9CB & Planning (Listed Buildings and Conservation Areas) (Scotland) Act 1997, ss. 1A, 9 (3), 23 (2), 82 & Transport and Works (Scotland) Act 2007, ss. 14, 28. - Issued: 15.09.2015. Made: 09.09.2015. Laid before the Scottish Parliament: 11.09.2015. Coming into force: 10.10.2015. Effect: S.S.I. 2007/569; 2015/230, 231, 241, 243 amended. Territorial extent & classification: S. General. - 8p.: 30 cm. - 978-0-11-102935-0 £4.25

Tribunals and inquiries

The Courts Reform (Scotland) Act 2014 (Commencement No. 1) Order 2015 No. 2015/12 (C.2). - Enabling power: Courts Reform (Scotland) Act 2014, s. 138 (2). Bringing into operation various provisions of the 2014 Act on 02.02.2015. - Issued: 27.01.2015. Made: 20.01.2015. Laid before the Scottish Parliament: 21.01.2015. Effect: None. Territorial extent & classification: S. General. - 4p.: 30 cm. - 978-0-11-102591-8 £4.25

The Scottish Tax Tribunals (Conduct and Fitness Assessment Tribunal) Rules 2015 No. 2015/187. - Enabling power: Revenue Scotland and Tax Powers Act 2014, sch. 2, paras 22, 23, 32 (1). - Issued: 07.05.2015. Made: 29.04.2015. Laid before the Scottish Parliament: 01.05.2015. Coming into force: 01.06.2015. Effect: None. Territorial extent & classification: S. General. - 16p.: 30 cm. - 978-0-11-102772-1 £6.00

The Scottish Tax Tribunals (Time Limits and Rules of Procedure) Regulations 2015 No. 2015/184. - Enabling power: Revenue Scotland and Tax Powers Act 2014, ss. 39, 51, 52, 53, 54, 55, 56, 249. - Issued: 06.05.2015. Made: 29.04.2015. Laid before the Scottish Parliament: 01.05.2015. Coming into force: 01.06.2015. Effect: None. Territorial extent & classification: S. General. - 40p.: 30 cm. - 978-0-11-102769-1 £10.00

The Scottish Tax Tribunals (Voting and Offences etc.) Regulations 2015 No. 2015/132. - Enabling power: Revenue Scotland and Tax Powers Act 2014, ss. 32, 50 (1). - Issued: 25.03.2015. Made: 17.03.2015. Coming into force: 01.04.2015. Effect: None. Territorial extent & classification: S. General. - Supersedes draft S.S.I. (ISBN 9780111026182) issued 09/02/15. - 4p.: 30 cm. - 978-0-11-102723-3 £4.25

The Scottish Tribunals (Administrative Support for Listed Tribunals) Order 2015 No. 2015/405. - Enabling power: Courts Reform (Scotland) Act 2014, sch. 4, para. 3 (5). - Issued: 02.12.2015. Made: 26.11.2015. Coming into force: 01.12.2015. Effect: 2014 asp 18 amended. Territorial extent & classification: S. General. - Supersedes draft S.S.I. (ISBN 9780111029534) issued 06/10/15. - 2p.: 30 cm. - 978-0-11-103011-0 £4.25

The Scottish Tribunals (Eligibility for Appointment) Regulations 2015 No. 2015/381. - Enabling power: Tribunals (Scotland) Act 2014, ss. 32 (1) (3), sch. 3, paras 1 (2), 5 (2), 6, 7 (1), sch. 5, paras 5 (2), 6, 7 (1). - Issued: 12.11.2015. Made: 05.11.2015. Laid before the Scottish Parliament: 09.11.2015. Coming into force: 01.01.2016. Effect: None. Territorial extent & classification: S. General. - 4p.: 30 cm. - 978-0-11-102981-7 £4.25

The Scottish Tribunals (Listed Tribunals) Regulations 2015 No. 2015/404. - Enabling power: Tribunals (Scotland) Act 2014, s. 27, (2). - Issued: 02.12.2015. Made: 26.11.2015. Coming into force: 01.12.2015. Effect: 2014 asp 10 amended. Territorial extent & classification: S. General. - 4p.: 30 cm. - 978-0-11-103010-3 £4.25

The Town and Country Planning (Hazardous Substances Inquiry Session Procedure) (Scotland) Amendment Rules 2015 No. 2015/250. - Enabling power: Tribunals and Inquiries Act 1992, s. 9. - Issued: 10.06.2015. Made: 04.06.2015. Laid before the Scottish Parliament: 08.06.2015. Coming into force: 14.09.2015. Effect: S.S.I. 2015/182 amended. Territorial extent & classification: S. General. - This S.S.I. has been printed to correct errors in S.S.I. 2015/182 (ISBN 9780111027660) published on 06/05/15 and is being issued free of charge to all known recipients of that instrument. - 2p.: 30 cm. - 978-0-11-102833-9 £4.25

The Town and Country Planning (Hazardous Substances Inquiry Session Procedure) (Scotland) Rules 2015 No. 2015/182. - Enabling power: Tribunals and Inquiries Act 1992, s. 9. - Issued: 06.05.2015. Made: 28.04.2015. Laid before the Scottish Parliament: 30.04.2015. Coming into force: 01.06.2015. Effect: S.I. 1997/750, 796, amended. Territorial extent & classification: S. General. - 12p.: 30 cm. - 978-0-11-102766-0 £6.00

The Tribunals (Scotland) Act 2014 (Commencement No. 2) Order 2015 No. 2015/116 (C.25). - Enabling power: Tribunals (Scotland) Act 2014, s. 83 (2). Bringing into operation various provisions of the 2014 Act on 01.04.2015, in accord. with art. 2. - Issued: 18.03.2015. Made: 11.03.2015. Laid before the Scottish Parliament: 13.03.2015. Coming into force: 01.04.2015. Effect: None. Territorial extent & classification: S. General. - 2p.: 30 cm. - 978-0-11-102707-3 £4.25

The Tribunals (Scotland) Act 2014 (Commencement No. 3) Order 2015 No. 2015/422 (C.55). - Enabling power: Tribunals (Scotland) Act 2014, s. 83 (2). Bringing into operation various provisions of the Act 2014 on 08.01.2016, in accordance with art. 2. - Issued: 16.12.2015. Made: 09.12.2015. Laid before the Scottish Parliament: 11.12.2015. Effect: None. Territorial extent & classification: S. General. - 4p.: 30 cm. - 978-0-11-103022-6 £4.25

Water

The Designation of Nitrate Vulnerable Zones (Scotland) Regulations 2015 No. 2015/376. - Enabling power: European Communities Act 1972, s. 2 (2). - Issued: 10.11.2015. Made: 03.11.2015. Laid before the Scottish Parliament: 05.11.2015. Coming into force: 01.01.2016. Effect: S.I. 1996/1564 amended & S.S.I. 2014/373 revoked. Territorial extent & classification: S. General. - 4p.: 30 cm. - 978-0-11-102973-2 £4.25

The Water Environment (River Basin Management Planning etc.) (Miscellaneous Amendments) (Scotland) Regulations 2015 No. 2015/211. - Enabling power: Water Environment and Water Services (Scotland) Act 2003, ss. 8 (5), 9 (4) to (6), 10 (2) (b), 19 (1), 36 (2) (3) & European Communities Act 1972, s. 2 (2), sch. 2, para. 1A. - Issued: 02.06.2015. Made: 26.05.2015. Laid before the Scottish Parliament: 28.05.2015. Coming into force: In accord. with art. 1(2) (3). Effect: S.S.I. 2011/209; 2013/323 amended & S.S.I. 2009/420 revoked. Territorial extent & classification: S. General. - EC note: Regulation 2 amends Parts 1 and 2 of the 2013 Regulations to take account of amendments made to Directive 2000/60/EC as last amended by Commission Directive 2014/101/EU. - 8p.: 30 cm. - 978-0-11-102794-3 £6.00

Water industry

The Water Act 2014 (Commencement No. 1) (Scotland) Order 2015 No. 2015/360 (C.45). - Enabling power: Water Act 2014, s. 94 (3) (6), sch. 12. Bringing into operation various provisions of the 2014 Act on 20.11.2015, in accord. with art. 2. - Issued: 04.11.2015. Made: 28.10.2015. Laid before the Scottish Parliament: 30.10.2015. Coming into force: 20.11.2015. Effect: None. Territorial extent & classification: S. General. - 4p.: 30 cm. - 978-0-11-102963-3 £4.25

Water supply

The Local Government Finance Act 1992 (Commencement No. 11) Order 2015 No. 2015/59 (C.11). - Enabling power: Local Government Finance Act 1992, s. 119 (2). Bringing into operation various provisions of the 1992 Act In accord. with art. 1 (1). - Issued: 23.02.2015. Made: 17.02.2015. Laid before the Scottish Parliament: 18.02.2015. Effect: None. Territorial extent & classification: S. General. - 4p.: 30 cm. - 978-0-11-102641-0 £4.25

The Private and Public Water Supplies (Miscellaneous Amendments) (Scotland) Regulations 2015 No. 2015/346. - Enabling power: Water (Scotland) Act 1980, ss. 76B, 76F (5) to (8), 76J, 101 (1) (1A) & European Communities Act 1972, s. 2 (2). - Issued: 05.10.2015. Made: 29.09.2015. Laid before the Scottish Parliament: 01.10.2015. Coming into force: 28.11.2015. Effect: S.S.I. 2006/209; 2014/364 amended. Territorial extent & classification: S. General. - EC note: These Regulations implement Council Directive 2013/51/Euratom laying down requirements for the protection of the health of the general public with regard to radioactive substances in water intended for human consumption. - 20p.: 30 cm. - 978-0-11-102951-0 £6.00

The Provision of Water and Sewerage Services (Reasonable Cost) (Scotland) Regulations 2015 No. 2015/79. - Enabling power: Sewerage (Scotland) Act 1968, s. 1 (3C) (3D) & Water (Scotland) Act 1980, s. 6 (2D) (2E). - Issued: 03.03.2015. Made: 24.02.2015. Laid before the Scottish Parliament: 26.02.2015. Coming into force: 01.04.2015. Effect: S.S.I. 2011/119 revoked. Territorial extent & classification: S. General. - 8p.: 30 cm. - 978-0-11-102668-7 £6.00

The Reservoirs (Panels of Reservoir Engineers: Sections under which Members may be Appointed) (Scotland) Order 2015 No. 2015/92. - Enabling power: Reservoirs (Scotland) Act 2011, ss. 27 (a), 114 (2) (b). - Issued: 05.03.2015. Made: 26.02.2015. Laid before the Scottish Parliament: 02.03.2015. Coming into force: 01.04.2015. Effect: None. Territorial extent & classification: S. General. - 4p.: 30 cm. - 978-0-11-102683-0 £4.25

The Reservoirs (Scotland) Act 2011 (Commencement No. 2) Order 2015 No. 2015/43 (C.7). - Enabling power: Reservoirs (Scotland) Act 2011, s. 116 (1). Bringing into operation various provisions of the 2011 Act on 20.02.2015, in accord. with art. 2. - Issued: 09.02.2015. Made: 03.02.2015. Laid before the Scottish Parliament: 05.02.2015. Effect: None. Territorial extent & classification: S. General. - 4p.: 30 cm. - 978-0-11-102617-5 £4.25

The Reservoirs (Scotland) Act 2011 (Commencement No. 3 and Transitional Provisions) Order 2015 No. 2015/63 (C.13). - Enabling power: Reservoirs (Scotland) Act 2011, ss. 114 (2) (a), 116 (1). Bringing into operation various provisions of the 2011 Act on 01.04.2015, in accord. with art. 2. - Issued: 23.02.2015. Made: 17.02.2015. Laid before the Scottish Parliament: 19.02.2015. Effect: None. Territorial extent & classification: S. General. - 8p.: 30 cm. - 978-0-11-102648-9 £4.25

The Reservoirs (Scotland) Act 2011 (Commencement No. 4) Order 2015 No. 2015/314 (C.37). - Enabling power: Reservoirs (Scotland) Act 2011, ss. 116 (1). Bringing into operation various provisions of the 2011 Act on 01.10.2015, in accord. with art. 2. - Issued: 07.09.2015. Made: 01.09.2015. Laid before the Scottish Parliament: 02.09.2015. Coming into force: 01.10.2015. Effect: None. Territorial extent & classification: S. General. - 8p.: 30 cm. - 978-0-11-102919-0 £4.25

The Reservoirs (Scotland) Amendment Regulations 2015 No. 2015/315. - Enabling power: Reservoirs (Scotland) Act 2011, ss. 2 (3) (a), 9 (3) (a), 14 (1) (3) (4), 23 (8), 24 (7), 114 (2) (b). - Issued: 07.09.2015. Made: 01.09.2015. Laid before the Scottish Parliament: 02.09.2015. Coming into force: 01.10.2015. Effect: S.S.I. 2015/90 amended. Territorial extent & classification: S. General. - Revoked by SSI 2016/43 (ISBN 9780111031087) in re to S. - 4p.: 30 cm. - 978-0-11-102920-6 £4.25

The Reservoirs (Scotland) Regulations 2015 No. 2015/90. - Enabling power: Reservoirs (Scotland) Act 2011, ss. 1 (6), 2 (3), 9 (3) (a), 10 (2), 14 (1) (3) (4), 28 (7) (8), 30 (2), 114 (2) (b)- Issued: 05.03.2015. Made: 26.02.2015. Laid before the Scottish Parliament: 02.03.2015. Coming into force: 01.04.2015. Effect: None. Territorial extent & classification: S. General. - Revoked by SSI 2016/43 (ISBN 9780111031087). - 16p.: 30 cm. - 978-0-11-102682-3 £6.00

Wildlife

The Snares (Training) (Scotland) Order 2015 No. 2015/377. - Enabling power: Wildlife and Countryside Act 1981, s. 11A (8) (a) (i). - Issued: 09.11.2015. Made: 03.11.2015. Laid before the Scottish Parliament: 05.11.2015. Coming into force: 01.01.2016. Effect: S.S.I. 2012/161 revoked. Territorial extent & classification: S. General. - 4p.: 30 cm. - 978-0-11-102974-9 £4.25

Scottish Statutory Instruments

Arranged by Number

Scottish statutory instruments 2015

1	Judgments
2	Road traffic
3	Landfill tax
4	Harbours, docks, piers and ferries
5	Sheriff Court
6	Harbours, docks, piers and ferries
7	Local government
8 (C.1)	Road traffic
9	Road traffic
10	Plant health
11	Constitutional law
	Devolution, Scotland
	River, Scotland
	River, England and Wales
12 (C.2)	Scottish Court Service
	Tribunals and inquiries
13	Legal aid and advice
14 (C.3)	Civil partnership
	Marriage
15	Roads and bridges
16	Taxes
17 (C.4)	Landfill tax
18 (C.5)	Taxes
19	Public service pensions
20	Children and young persons
21	Children and young persons
22	Road traffic
23	Road traffic
24	Road traffic
25	Road traffic
26	Court of Session
27	Road traffic
28	Sea fisheries
29	Withdrawn
30	Sea fisheries
31 (C.6)	Ancient monuments
32	Investigatory powers
33	Investigatory powers
34	Investigatory powers
35	Court of Session
36	Taxes
37	Taxes
38	Taxes
39	Public services reform
40	Road traffic
41	Road traffic
42	Road traffic
43 (C.7)	Flood risk management
	Water supply
44 (C.8)	Public health
	Social care
45	Landfill taxLandfill tax
46	Council tax
47	Rating and valuation
48	Food
49	Rating and valuation
50	Rating and valuation
51	Rating and valuation
52 (C.9)	Regulatory reform
	Environmental protection
53	Scottish Court Service
54 (C.10)	Insolvency
	Bankruptcy
	Debt
55	Road traffic
56	Local government
57	Road traffic
58	Agriculture
59 (C.11)	Local government
	Water supply
60	Public service pensions
61 (C.12)	Children and young persons
62	Children and young persons
63 (C.13)	Flood risk management
	Water supply
64	National assistance services
65	National assistance services
66	Public health
	Social care
67	Road traffic
68	Road traffic
69	Road traffic
70	Road traffic
71	Land and buildings transaction tax
72 (C.14)	Environmental protection
73 (C.15)	Environmental protection
74 (C.16)	Environmental protection
75	Road traffic
76	Road traffic
77 (C.17)	Scottish Court Service
	Court of Session
	Judicial appointments and discipline
	Sheriff Court
78	Road traffic
79	Water supply
80	Insolvency
	Bankruptcy
81	National Health Service
82 (C.18)	Education
83	Equal opportunities
84	High Court of Justiciary
	Sheriff Court
	Justice of the Peace Court
85	Court of Session
	Sheriff Court
86	National Health Service
87	Public service pensions
88	Public health
	Social care
89	Roads and bridges
90	Flood risk management
	Water supply
91	National Health Service
92	Flood risk management
	Water supply
93	Land and buildings transaction tax
94	Public service pensions
95	Public service pensions
96	National Health Service
97	Public service pensions
98	Pensions

99 (C.19)	Food	150	Court of Session
100	Food		Judicial appointments and discipline
101	Environmental protection		Sheriff Court
102	National Health Service	151	Landfill tax
103	Aquaculture	152	Landfill tax
104 (C.20)	Children and young persons	153	Education
	Education	154	Social care
105	Crofters, cottars and small landholders	155	Legal aid and advice
106	Road traffic	156	Children and young persons
107	Criminal procedure	157	Public health
108 (C.21)	Land and buildings transaction tax		Social care
109 (C.22)	Landfill tax	158	Children and young persons
110 (C.23)	Taxes	159	Environmental protection
111	Road traffic	160	National Health Service
112	Road traffic	161	Animals
113	Environmental protection	162	Public health
	Fish farming	163	Registration of births, deaths and marriages, etc.
	Licensing (marine)		
	Sea fisheries	164	Public health
	Shellfish	165	Public health
114	Road traffic	166	Registration of births, deaths and marriages, etc.
115 (C.24)	Public health		
116 (C.25)	Tribunals and inquiries	167	Agriculture
117	Public service pensions	168	Road traffic
118	Public service pensions	169	Road traffic
119	Court of Session	170	Road traffic
	Sheriff Court	171	Road traffic
120	Judicial appointments and discipline	172	Road traffic
121	High Court of Justiciary	173	Fire services
	Sheriff Court		Pensions
	Justice of the Peace Court	174	Pensions
122 (C.26)	Housing	175	Road traffic
123	Land and buildings transaction tax	176	Sheriff Court
124	Proceeds of crime	177 (C.28)	Criminal law
125	Local government	178	Road traffic
126	Land and buildings transaction tax	179 (C.29)	National Health Service
127	Landfill tax	180	Registration of births, deaths and marriages, etc.
128	Taxes		
129	Taxes	181	Town and country planning
130	Taxes	182	Tribunals and inquiries
131	Taxes	183	Sea fisheries
132	Tribunals and inquiries	184	Tribunals and inquiries
133	Transport	185	Agriculture
134	Road traffic	186	Animals
135	Road traffic	187	Tribunals and inquiries
136	Road traffic	188	Environmental protection
137	Road traffic	189	Climate change
138	Public finance and accountability	190 (C.30)	Roads and bridges
139 (C.27)	Environmental protection	191	Road traffic
140	Fire services	192	Agriculture
	Pensions	193	Environmental protection
141	Public service pensions	194	Agriculture
142	Public service pensions	195	Road traffic
143	Fire services	196 (C.31)	Ancient monuments
	Pensions	197	Climate change
144	Housing	198	Road traffic
145	Public service pensions	199	Lands Tribunal
146	Public service pensions	200 (C.32)	Criminal law
147	Road traffic	201	High Court of Justiciary
148	Charities		Sheriff Court
149	Insolvency		Justice of the Peace Court
	Bankruptcy	202	Social care
	Debt	203	Road traffic
		204	Road traffic

205	Road traffic
206	Road traffic
207	Road traffic
208	Food
209	Education
210	Environmental protection
211	Environmental protection
	Water
212	Education
213	Sheriff Court
214	Environmental protection
215	Agriculture
216	Debt
217	Property factors
218	Building and buildings
219	National Health Service
220	Proceeds of crime
221	Roads and bridges
222	Public health
	Social care
223	Children and young persons
	Protection of vulnerable adults
224	Scottish Courts and Tribunals Service
225	Scottish Courts and Tribunals service
226	Contracts
227	Court of Session
	Sheriff Court
228	Court of Session
229	Ancient monuments
230	Ancient monuments
231	Ancient monuments
232	Ancient monuments
233	Town and country planning
234	Public services reform
235	Town and country planning
236	Town and country planning
237	Town and country planning
238	Ancient monuments
239	Ancient monuments
	Town and country planning
	Title conditions
240	Town and country planning
241	Town and country planning
242 (C.33)	Contracts
243	Town and country planning
244 (C.34)	Criminal procedure
245	High Court of Justiciary
	Sheriff Appeal Court
	Sheriff Court
	Justice of the Peace Court
246	Court of Session
	Sheriff Court
247 (C.35)	Supreme Court of the United Kingdom
	Court of Session
	High Court of Justiciary
	Scottish Land Court
	Sheriff Appeal Court
	Sheriff Court
	Justice of the Peace Court
248	Education
249	Town and country planning
250	Tribunals and inquiries
251	Road traffic
252	Housing

253	Road traffic
254	Equality
255	Road traffic
256	Road traffic
257	Roads and bridges
258	Roads and bridges
259	Road traffic
260	Adults with incapacity
261	Court of Session
262	High Court of Justiciary
263	Justice of the Peace Court
264	Sheriff Court
265	Registers and records
266	Public health
	Social care
267	Road traffic
268	Education
269	Education
270	Environmental protection
271	Ancient monuments
	Regulatory reform
272 (C.36)	Housing
273	Road traffic
274	Road traffic
275	Road traffic
276	Road traffic
277	Road traffic
278	Road traffic
279	Legal aid and advice
280	Road traffic
281	Road traffic
282	Road traffic
283	Court of Session
	Sheriff Court
284	Road traffic
285	Road traffic
286	Scottish Public Services Ombudsman
287	Road traffic
288	Road traffic
289	Road traffic
290	Road traffic
291	Road traffic
292	Road traffic
293	Road traffic
294	Road traffic
295	High Court of Justiciary
	Sheriff Appeal Court
	Sheriff Court
296	Court of Session
	Sheriff Court
297	Withdrawn
298	Harbours, docks, piers and ferries
299	Road traffic
300	Road traffic
301	Road traffic
302	Environmental protection
	Marine management
303	Environmental protection
	Marine management
304	Road traffic
305	Education
306	Road traffic
307	Road traffic

308	Road traffic	356	Sheriff Appeal Court
309	Road traffic	357	Road traffic
310	Road traffic	358 (C.44)	Community empowerment
311	Road traffic		Land reform
312	Court of Session		Local government
	Sheriff Court	359	Aquaculture
313	Marriage		Fish farming
314 (C.37)	Flood risk management		Sea fisheries
	Water supply	360 (C.45)	Water industry
315	Flood risk management	361 (C.46)	Mental health
	Water supply	362	Road traffic
316	Road traffic	363	Food
317 (C.38)	Children and young persons	364	Mental health
318	Education	365	Road traffic
319	Social care	366	Road traffic
320	Sea fisheries	367	Road traffic
321	Public health	368	Representation of the people
	Social care	369	Housing
322	Land and buildings transaction tax	370	Enforcement
323	Environmental protection	371	Marriage
324	Prisons		Civil partnership
325	Public service pensions	372	Road traffic
326 (C.39)	Housing	373	Road traffic
327	Animals	374	Road traffic
328	Ancient monuments	375	High Court of Justiciary
	Town and country planning		Sheriff Court
	Transport and works		Justice of the Peace Court
329	Rehabilitation of offenders	376	Water
330	Police	377	Wildlife
	Children and young persons	378 (C.47)	Court of Session
	Protection of vulnerable adults		Sheriff Appeal Court
331 (C.40)	Public procurement		Sheriff Court
332	Road traffic	379	Sheriff Appeal Court
333	National Health Service	380	Legal aid and advice
334	Mental health	381	Tribunals and inquiries
335	Public records	382 (C.48)	Arms and ammunition
336 (C.41)	Criminal law		Criminal law
	High Court of Justiciary		Licences and licensing
	Sheriff Appeal Court		Licensing (liquor)
337	Legal aid and advice	383	Environmental protection
338	Supreme Court of the United Kingdom		Enforcement
	Court of Session	384	Electricity
	High Court of Justiciary	385	Road traffic
	Sheriff Appeal Court	386	Energy
	Sheriff Court		Building and buildings
	Justice of the Peace Court	387	Sheriff Appeal Court
339	Road traffic	388	Scottish Courts and Tribunals Service
340	Road traffic	389	Road traffic
341	Road traffic	390	Road traffic
342	Road traffic	391	Road traffic
343	Road traffic	392	Plant health
344 (C.42)	Rating and valuation	393	Animals
345	Road traffic	394	Road traffic
346	Water supply	395	Seeds
347	Climate change	396	Seeds
348	Education	397 (C.49)	Withdrawn
349 (C.43)	Housing	398	Sheriff Appeal Court
350	Constitutional law	399 (C.50)	Community empowerment
	Devolution, Scotland		Land reform
351	Sheriff Court	400	Land reform
352	Road traffic	401	Animals
353	Road traffic		Aquaculture
354	Road traffic		Fish farming
355	Road traffic	402	Court of Session

	Sheriff Appeal Court	12 (C.2)
	Sheriff Court	14 (C.3)
403	Housing	17 (C.4)
404	Tribunals and inquiries	18 (C.5)
405	Tribunals and inquiries	31 (C.6)
406 (C.51)	Children and young persons	43 (C.7)
407	Road traffic	44 (C.8)
408	Court of Session	52 (C.9)
409 (C.52)	Prisons	54 (C.10)
410	Food	59 (C.11)
411 (C.53)	Public procurement	61 (C.12)
412	Roads and bridges	63 (C.13)
413	Roads and bridges	72 (C.14)
414	Roads and bridges	73 (C.15)
415	Roads and bridges	74 (C.16)
416	Road traffic	77 (C.17)
417 (C.54)	Mental health	82 (C.18)
418	Road traffic	99 (C.19)
419	Court of Session	104 (C.20)
	Sheriff Appeal Court	108 (C.21)
	Sheriff Court	109 (C.22)
420	Public passenger transport	110 (C.23)
421	International immunities and privileges	115 (C.24)
		116 (C.25)
422 (C.55)	Tribunals and inquiries	122 (C.26)
423	Police	139 (C.27)
	Children and young persons	177 (C.28)
	Protection of vulnerable adults	179 (C.29)
424	Sheriff Court	190 (C.30)
425	Constitutional law	196 (C.31)
	Representation of the people	200 (C.32)
426	Road traffic	242 (C.33)
427	Road traffic	244 (C.34)
428 (C.56)	Social security	247 (C.35)
429 (C.57)	Criminal law	272 (C.36)
430 (C.58)	Housing	314 (C.37)
431	Criminal law	317 (C.38)
432	Public health	326 (C.39)
	Social care	331 (C.40)
433	Food	336 (C.41)
434	Public finance and accountability	344 (C.42)
435	Sea fisheries	349 (C.43)
436	Sea fisheries	358 (C.44)
437	Environmental protection	360 (C.45)
	Marine management	361 (C.46)
438	Environmental protection	378 (C.47)
439	Road traffic	382 (C.48)
440	Road traffic	397 (C.49) Withdrawn
441	Road traffic	399 (C.50)
442	Road traffic	406 (C.51)
443	High Court of Justiciary	409 (C.52)
	Sheriff Court	411 (C.53)
	Justice of the Peace Court	417 (C.54)
444	Criminal law	422 (C.55)
445	Road traffic	428 (C.56)
446	Public procurement	429 (C.57)
447	Criminal procedure	430 (C.58)
448	Public service pensions	
449	Road traffic	
450	Road traffic	

List of Scottish Commencement Orders 2015

8 (C.1)

NORTHERN IRELAND LEGISLATION

Acts of the Northern Ireland Assembly

Acts of the Northern Ireland Assembly 2015

Budget Act (Northern Ireland) 2015: Chapter 4. - [4], 51, [1]p.: 30 cm. - Royal assent, 12 March 2015. An Act to authorise the issue out of the Consolidated Fund of certain sums for the service of the year ending 31st March 2015 and 2016; to appropriate those sums for specified purposes; to authorise the Department of Finance and Personnel to borrow on the credit of the appropriated sums; to authorise the use for the public service of certain resources for the year ending 31st March 2015 and 2016; and to revise certain accruing resources in the year ending 31st March 2015. Explanatory notes to the Act are available separately (ISBN 9780105961628). - 978-0-10-595157-5 £10.00

Budget (No. 2) Act (Northern Ireland) 2015: Chapter 7. - [1], 29p.: 30 cm. - Royal assent, 24th July 2015. An Act to authorise the issue out of the Consolidated Fund of certain sums for the service of the year ending 31st March 2016; to appropriate those sums for specified purposes; to authorise the Department of Finance and Personnel to borrow on the credit of the appropriated sums; to authorise the use for the public service of certain resources (including accruing resources) for the year ending 31st March 2016; and to repeal certain spent provisions. Explanatory notes to the Act are available separately (ISBN 9780105962090). - 978-0-10-595160-5 £10.00

Children's Services Co-operation Act (Northern Ireland) 2015: Chapter 10. - [12]p.: 30 cm. - Royal assent, 9th December 2015. An Act to require co-operation among certain public authorities and other persons in order to contribute to the well-being of children and young persons; to require the adoption of a children and young persons strategy. - 978-0-10-595163-6 £6.00

Human Trafficking and Exploitation (Criminal Justice and Support for Victims) Act (Northern Ireland) 2015: Chapter 2. - [48]p.: 30 cm. - Royal assent, 13 January 2015. An Act to make provision about human trafficking, slavery and other forms of exploitation, including measures to prevent and combat such exploitation and to provide support for victims of such exploitation. - 978-0-10-595155-1 £10.00

Justice Act (Northern Ireland) 2015: Chapter 9. - vi, 152p.: 30 cm. - Royal assent, 24th July 2015. An Act to provide for a single jurisdiction for county courts and magistrates' courts; to amend the law on committal for trial; to provide for prosecutorial fines; to make provision in relation to victims and witnesses in criminal proceedings and investigations; to amend the law on criminal records and live links; to provide for violent offences prevention orders; to make other amendments relating to the administration of civil and criminal justice. Explanatory notes to assist in the understanding of the Act are available separately (ISBN 9780105962106). - 978-0-10-595162-9 £23.25

Off-street Parking (Functions of District Councils) Act (Northern Ireland) 2015: Chapter 3. - [2], 5, [1]p.: 30 cm. - Royal assent, 12th March 2015. An Act to transfer to district councils certain functions in relation to off-street parking places. Explanatory Notes to the Act are published separately (ISBN 9780105961635). - 978-0-10-595156-8 £6.00

Ombudsman and Commissioner for Complaints (Amendment) Act (Northern Ireland) 2015: Chapter 6. - [8]p.: 30 cm. - Royal Assent, 20th July 2015. An Act to extend the maximum period for which an acting Assembly Ombudsman for Northern Ireland and an acting Northern Ireland Commissioner for Complaints may hold office. - 978-0-10-595159-9 £4.25

Pensions Act (Northern Ireland) 2015: Chapter 5. - iv, 102p.: 30 cm. - Royal Assent, 23 June 2015. An Act to make provision about pensions and about benefits payable in connection with bereavement. Explanatory notes to the Act are available separately (ISBN 9780105961642). - 978-0-10-595158-2 £16.50

Reservoirs Act (Northern Ireland) 2015: Chapter 8. - vi, 79p.: 30 cm. - Royal assent, 24th July 2015. An Act to Make provision about the regulation of the management, construction and alteration of certain reservoirs, in particular in relation to their safety to collect and store water. Explanatory notes to assist in the understanding of the Act are available separately (ISBN 9780105962113). - 978-0-10-595161-2 £16.00

Work and Families Act (Northern Ireland) 2015: Chapter 1. - [70]p.: 30 cm. - Royal assent, 8 January 2015. An Act to make provision about shared rights to leave from work and statutory pay in connection with caring for children; time off work to accompany to ante-natal appointments or to attend adoption appointments; to make provision about the right to request flexible working. - 978-0-10-595154-4 £14.25

Acts of the Northern Ireland Assembly - Explanatory and financial memorandum 2015

Budget Act (Northern Ireland) 2015: Chapter 4; explanatory notes. - [6]p.: 30 cm. - These Notes refer to the Budget Act (Northern Ireland) 2015 (c. 4) (ISBN 9780105951575) which received Royal Assent on 12 March 2015. - 978-0-10-596162-8 £6.00

Budget (No. 2) Act (Northern Ireland) 2015: Chapter 7; explanatory notes. - [8]p.: 30 cm. - These Notes refer to the Budget (No. 2) Act (Northern Ireland) 2015 (c. 7) (ISBN 9780105951605) which received Royal Assent on 24th July 2015. - 978-0-10-596209-0 £4.25

Human Trafficking and Exploitation (Criminal Justice and Support for Victims) Act (Northern Ireland) 2015: Chapter 2; explanatory notes. - 21, [1]p.: 30 cm. - These Notes refer to the Human Trafficking and Exploitation (Criminal Justice and Support for Victims) Act (Northern Ireland) 2015 (c. 2) which received Royal Assent on 13 January 2015. - 978-0-10-596160-4 £6.00

Justice Act (Northern Ireland) 2015: Chapter 9; explanatory notes. - [36]p.: 30 cm. - These Notes refer to the Justice Act (Northern Ireland) 2015 (c. 9) (ISBN 9780105951629) which received Royal Assent on 24th July 2015. - 978-0-10-596210-6 £10.00

Off-street Parking (Functions of District Councils) Act (Northern Ireland) 2015: Chapter 3; explanatory notes. - [2], 3, [3]p.: 30 cm. - These Notes refer to the Off-street Parking (Functions of District Councils) Act (Northern Ireland) 2015 (c. 3) (ISBN 9780105951568) which received Royal Assent on 12 March 2015. - 978-0-10-596163-5 £4.25

Pensions Act (Northern Ireland) 2015: Chapter 5; explanatory notes. - 30p.: 30 cm. - These Notes refer to the Pensions Act (Northern Ireland) 2015 (c. 5) (ISBN 9780105951582) which received Royal Assent on 23 June 2015. - 978-0-10-596164-2 £6.00

Reservoirs Act (Northern Ireland) 2015: Chapter 8; explanatory notes. - 37p.: 30 cm. - These Notes refer to the Reservoirs Act (Northern Ireland) 2015 (c. 8) (ISBN 9780105951612) which received Royal Assent on 24th July 2015. - 978-0-10-596211-3 £10.00

Work and Families Act (Northern Ireland) 2015: Chapter 1; explanatory notes. - 32p.: 30 cm. - These notes refer to the Work and Families Act (Northern Ireland) 2015 (c.1) which received Royal Assent on 8th January 2015. - 978-0-10-596161-1 £10.00

Other statutory publications

Statutory Publications Office.

Chronological table of statutory rules Northern Ireland: covering the legislation to 31 December 2014. - 11th ed. - ca. 982 pages: looseleaf with binder holes: 30 cm. - Supersedes 10th edition (ISBN 9780337099366). - 978-0-337-09985-4 £138.00

ACCESS TO JUSTICE

Chronological table of the statutes Northern Ireland: covering the legislation to 31 December 2013. - 40th ed. - x, 762p.: looseleaf with binder holes: 30 cm. - 978-0-337-09967-0 £132.00

Chronological table of the statutes Northern Ireland: covering the legislation to 31 December 2014. - 41st ed. - x, 771, [1]p.: looseleaf with binder holes: 30 cm. - 978-0-337-09915-1 £110.00

Northern Ireland statutes 2014: [binder]. - 1 binder: 31 cm. - 978-0-337-09977-9 £25.00 + VAT

The statutes revised: Northern Ireland. - Cumulative supplement vols A-D (1537 - 1920) to 31 December 2014. - 2nd ed. - x, 70p.: looseleaf with binder holes: 30 cm. - The material held in the main updated Statutes revised has been integrated into the UK Statute Law Database, available online at http://www.legislation.gov.uk. However, pre-1921 legislation published in vols A to D and amended since is not currently covered by the Statute Law Database, so printed supplements will continue to be issued for amendments made to that legislation. - 978-0-337-09916-8 £12.00

Title page and index to Northern Ireland statutes volume 2014. - 14p.: looseleaf with binder holes: 30 cm. - A binder for the 2014 statutes is also available (ISBN 9780337099779). - 978-0-337-09978-6 £5.75

Statutory Rules of Northern Ireland

By Subject Heading

Access to justice

The Access to Justice (2003 Order) (Commencement No. 7, Transitional Provisions and Savings) Order (Northern Ireland) 2015 No. 2015/194 (C.13). - Enabling power: S.I. 2003/435 (N.I. 10), arts 1 (2), 48 (1). Bringing into operation various provisions of the 2003 Order on 01.04.2015. - Issued: 13.04.2015. Made: 26.03.2015. Coming into operation: 01.04.2015. Effect: None. Territorial extent & classification: NI. General. - 8p: 30 cm. - 978-0-337-99765-5 £6.00

The Access to Justice (2003 Order) (Commencement No. 8) Order (Northern Ireland) 2015 No. 2015/237 (C.17). - Enabling power: S.I. 2003/435 (N.I. 10), arts 1 (2), 48 (1). Bringing into operation various provisions of the 2003 Order on 01.05.2015. - Issued: 06.05.2015. Made: 30.04.2015. Coming into operation: 01.05.2015. Effect: None. Territorial extent & classification: NI. General. - 8p: 30 cm. - 978-0-337-99789-1 £6.00

The Civil Legal Services (Appeal) Regulations (Northern Ireland) 2015 No. 2015/197. - Enabling power: S.I. 2003/435 (N.I. 10), art. 20A. - Issued: 14.04.2015. Made: 26.03.2015. Coming into operation: 01.04.2015. Effect: None. Territorial extent & classification: NI. General. - Supersedes draft S.R. (ISBN 9780337995774) issued 29/01/15. - 12p.: 30 cm. - 978-0-337-99768-6 £6.00

The Civil Legal Services (Cost Protection) Regulations (Northern Ireland) 2015 No. 2015/199. - Enabling power: S.I. 2003/435 (N.I. 10), arts. 18 (1), 20 (1) (2) (b). - Issued: 14.04.2015. Made: 26.03.2015. Coming into operation: 01.04.2015. Effect: None. Territorial extent & classification: NI. General. - Supersedes draft S.R. 2015/199 (ISBN 9780337995743) issued 29/01/15. - 4p.: 30 cm. - 978-0-337-99770-9 £4.25

The Civil Legal Services (Costs) Regulations (Northern Ireland) 2015 No. 2015/198. - Enabling power: S.I. 2003/435 (N.I. 10), arts. 18 (2), 20 (1) (2) (a) (b) (c) (e) (g), 34 (1) (6) (7). - Issued: 14.04.2015. Made: 26.03.2015. Coming into operation: 01.04.2015. Effect: S.R. 1965/217; 1981/366 partially revoked & S.R. 1965/235 revoked. Territorial extent & classification: NI. General. - 12p.: 30 cm. - 978-0-337-99769-3 £6.00

The Civil Legal Services (Disclosure of Information) Regulations (Northern Ireland) 2015 No. 2015/202. - Enabling power: S.I, 2003/435, arts 32 (1), 34 (1). - Issued: 15.04.2015. Made: 26.03.2015. Coming into operation: 01.04.2015. Effect: None. Territorial extent & classification: NI. General. - Supersedes draft S.R. (ISBN 9780337995767) issued 29/01/15. - 4p.: 30 cm. - 978-0-337-99773-0 £4.25

The Civil Legal Services (Financial) Regulations (Northern Ireland) 2015 No. 2015/196. - Enabling power: S.I. 2003/435 (N.I. 10), arts 13, 17 (1) (2) (b) (5) (6). - Issued: 14.04.2015. Made: 31.03.2015. Coming into operation: 01.04.2015. Effect: S.R. 1965/217; 1981/366 partially revoked & S.R. 1981/189 revoked. Territorial extent & classification: NI. General. - 28p.: 30 cm. - 978-0-337-99767-9 £6.00

The Civil Legal Services (General) Regulations (Northern Ireland) 2015 No. 2015/195. - Enabling power: S.I. 2003/435 (N.I. 10), arts 12 (3), 13, 14 (6), 15, 34 (1). - Issued: 13.04.2015. Made: 31.03.2015. Coming into operation: 01.04.2015. Effect: S.R. 1965/217; 1981/366 partially revoked. Territorial extent & classification: NI. General. - 28p.: 30 cm. - 978-0-337-99766-2 £6.00

The Civil Legal Services (Remuneration) Regulations (Northern Ireland) 2015 No. 2015/201. - Enabling power: S.I. 2003/435 (N.I. 10), arts. 12 (3), 47. - Issued: 15.04.2015. Made: 31.03.2015. Coming into operation: 01.04.2015. Effect: S.R. 1965/217; 1981/366 partially revoked & S.R. 1981/179, 365 revoked. Territorial extent & classification: NI. General. - 38p.: 30 cm. - 978-0-337-99772-3 £10.00

The Civil Legal Services (Statutory Charge) Order (Northern Ireland) 2015 No. 2015/200. - Enabling power: S.I. 2003/435 (N.I. 10), arts. 17 (7) (8). - Issued: 15.04.2015. Made: 26.03.2015. Coming into operation: 01.04.2015. Effect: S.R. 1965/217; 1981/366 partially revoked. Territorial extent & classification: NI. General. - 12p.: 30 cm. - 978-0-337-99771-6 £6.00

Agriculture

The Agriculture (Student fees) (Amendment) Regulations (Northern Ireland) 2015 No. 2015/135. - Enabling power: Agriculture Act (Northern Ireland) 1949, s. 5A (1) (2). - Issued: 11.03.2015. Made: 06.03.2015. Coming into operation: 01.09.2014. Effect: S.R. 2007/54 amended. Territorial extent & classification: NI. General. - 2p: 30 cm. - 978-0-337-99670-2 £4.25

The Common Agricultural Policy Basic Payment and Support Schemes Regulations (Northern Ireland) 2015 No. 2015/191. - Enabling power: European Communities Act 1972, s. 2 (2). - Issued: 01.04.2015. Made: 27.03.2015. Coming into operation: 30.04.2015. Effect: S.R. 2010/161 revoked with saving. Territorial extent & classification: NI. General. - EC note: These Regulations make provision in Northern Ireland for the administration of Regulation (EU) no. 1307/2013 establishing rules for direct payments to farmers under support schemes within the framework of the common agricultural policy. - 8p.: 30 cm. - 978-0-337-99753-2 £6.00

The Common Agricultural Policy (Control and Enforcement) Regulations (Northern Ireland) 2015 No. 2015/192. - Enabling power: European Communities Act 1972, s. 2 (2). - Issued: 01.04.2015. Made: 27.03.2015. Coming into operation: 30.04.2015. Effect: None. Territorial extent & classification: NI. General. - EC note: These Regulations make provision for the implementation in Northern Ireland of the European Regulations (as defined in schedule 1) relating to the administration of the common agricultural policy of the European Union. - With correction slip dated June 2015. - 8p.: 30 cm. - 978-0-337-99756-3 £6.00

The Common Agricultural Policy Direct Payments and Support Schemes (Cross Compliance) (Amendment) Regulations (Northern Ireland) 2015 No. 2015/286. - Enabling power: European Communities Act 1972, s. 2 (2). - Issued: 06.07.2015. Made: 25.06.2015. Coming into operation: 01.08.2015. Effect: S.R. 2014/291 amended. Territorial extent & classification: NI. General. - EC note: In Northern Ireland these Regulations supplement and make provision for the administration and enforcement of Regulation (EU) No. 1306/2013 , Commission Delegated Regulation (EU) No 640/2014 and Commission Implementing Regulation (EU) No 809/2014 in relation to cross compliance under the revised system of direct support schemes under the Common Agricultural Policy which came into force on 1st January 2015. - 4p.: 30 cm. - 978-0-337-99837-9 £4.25

The Common Agricultural Policy (Review of Decisions) Regulations (Northern Ireland) 2015 No. 2015/318. - Enabling power: European Communities Act 1972, s. 2 (2). - Issued: 23.07.2015. Made: 31.07.2015. Coming into operation: 07.08.2015. Effect: None. Territorial extent & classification: NI. General. - With correction slip dated July 2015. - 4p.: 30 cm. - 978-0-337-99853-9 £4.25

NORTHERN IRELAND LEGISLATION

Acts of the Northern Ireland Assembly

Acts of the Northern Ireland Assembly 2015

Budget Act (Northern Ireland) 2015: Chapter 4. - [4], 51, [1]p.: 30 cm. - Royal assent, 12 March 2015. An Act to authorise the issue out of the Consolidated Fund of certain sums for the service of the year ending 31st March 2015 and 2016; to appropriate those sums for specified purposes; to authorise the Department of Finance and Personnel to borrow on the credit of the appropriated sums; to authorise the use for the public service of certain resources for the year ending 31st March 2015 and 2016; and to revise certain accruing resources in the year ending 31st March 2015. Explanatory notes to the Act are available separately (ISBN 9780105961628). - 978-0-10-595157-5 £10.00

Budget (No. 2) Act (Northern Ireland) 2015: Chapter 7. - [1], 29p.: 30 cm. - Royal assent, 24th July 2015. An Act to authorise the issue out of the Consolidated Fund of certain sums for the service of the year ending 31st March 2016; to appropriate those sums for specified purposes; to authorise the Department of Finance and Personnel to borrow on the credit of the appropriated sums; to authorise the use for the public service of certain resources (including accruing resources) for the year ending 31st March 2016; and to repeal certain spent provisions. Explanatory notes to the Act are available separately (ISBN 9780105962090). - 978-0-10-595160-5 £10.00

Children's Services Co-operation Act (Northern Ireland) 2015: Chapter 10. - [12]p.: 30 cm. - Royal assent, 9th December 2015. An Act to require co-operation among certain public authorities and other persons in order to contribute to the well-being of children and young persons; to require the adoption of a children and young persons strategy. - 978-0-10-595163-6 £6.00

Human Trafficking and Exploitation (Criminal Justice and Support for Victims) Act (Northern Ireland) 2015: Chapter 2. - [48]p.: 30 cm. - Royal assent, 13 January 2015. An Act to make provision about human trafficking, slavery and other forms of exploitation, including measures to prevent and combat such exploitation and to provide support for victims of such exploitation. - 978-0-10-595155-1 £10.00

Justice Act (Northern Ireland) 2015: Chapter 9. - vi, 152p.: 30 cm. - Royal assent, 24th July 2015. An Act to provide for a single jurisdiction for county courts and magistrates' courts; to amend the law on committal for trial; to provide for prosecutorial fines; to make provision in relation to victims and witnesses in criminal proceedings and investigations; to amend the law on criminal records and live links; to provide for violent offences prevention orders; to make other amendments relating to the administration of civil and criminal justice. Explanatory notes to assist in the understanding of the Act are available separately (ISBN 9780105962106). - 978-0-10-595162-9 £23.25

Off-street Parking (Functions of District Councils) Act (Northern Ireland) 2015: Chapter 3. - [2], 5, [1]p.: 30 cm. - Royal assent, 12th March 2015. An Act to transfer to district councils certain functions in relation to off-street parking places. Explanatory Notes to the Act are published separately (ISBN 9780105961635). - 978-0-10-595156-8 £6.00

Ombudsman and Commissioner for Complaints (Amendment) Act (Northern Ireland) 2015: Chapter 6. - [8]p.: 30 cm. - Royal Assent, 20th July 2015. An Act to extend the maximum period for which an acting Assembly Ombudsman for Northern Ireland and an acting Northern Ireland Commissioner for Complaints may hold office. - 978-0-10-595159-9 £4.25

Pensions Act (Northern Ireland) 2015: Chapter 5. - iv, 102p.: 30 cm. - Royal Assent, 23 June 2015. An Act to make provision about pensions and about benefits payable in connection with bereavement. Explanatory notes to the Act are available separately (ISBN 9780105961642). - 978-0-10-595158-2 £16.50

Reservoirs Act (Northern Ireland) 2015: Chapter 8. - vi, 79p.: 30 cm. - Royal assent, 24th July 2015. An Act to Make provision about the regulation of the management, construction and alteration of certain reservoirs, in particular in relation to their safety to collect and store water. Explanatory notes to assist in the understanding of the Act are available separately (ISBN 9780105962113). - 978-0-10-595161-2 £16.00

Work and Families Act (Northern Ireland) 2015: Chapter 1. - [70]p.: 30 cm. - Royal assent, 8 January 2015. An Act to make provision about shared rights to leave from work and statutory pay in connection with caring for children; time off work to accompany to ante-natal appointments or to attend adoption appointments; to make provision about the right to request flexible working. - 978-0-10-595154-4 £14.25

Acts of the Northern Ireland Assembly - Explanatory and financial memorandum 2015

Budget Act (Northern Ireland) 2015: Chapter 4; explanatory notes. - [6]p.: 30 cm. - These Notes refer to the Budget Act (Northern Ireland) 2015 (c. 4) (ISBN 9780105951575) which received Royal Assent on 12 March 2015. - 978-0-10-596162-8 £6.00

Budget (No. 2) Act (Northern Ireland) 2015: Chapter 7; explanatory notes. - [8]p.: 30 cm. - These Notes refer to the Budget (No. 2) Act (Northern Ireland) 2015 (c. 7) (ISBN 9780105951605) which received Royal Assent on 24th July 2015. - 978-0-10-596209-0 £4.25

Human Trafficking and Exploitation (Criminal Justice and Support for Victims) Act (Northern Ireland) 2015: Chapter 2; explanatory notes. - 21, [1]p.: 30 cm. - These Notes refer to the Human Trafficking and Exploitation (Criminal Justice and Support for Victims) Act (Northern Ireland) 2015 (c. 2) which received Royal Assent on 13 January 2015. - 978-0-10-596160-4 £6.00

Justice Act (Northern Ireland) 2015: Chapter 9; explanatory notes. - [36]p.: 30 cm. - These Notes refer to the Justice Act (Northern Ireland) 2015 (c. 9) (ISBN 9780105951629) which received Royal Assent on 24th July 2015. - 978-0-10-596210-6 £10.00

Off-street Parking (Functions of District Councils) Act (Northern Ireland) 2015: Chapter 3; explanatory notes. - [2], 3, [3]p.: 30 cm. - These Notes refer to the Off-street Parking (Functions of District Councils) Act (Northern Ireland) 2015 (c. 3) (ISBN 9780105951568) which received Royal Assent on 12 March 2015. - 978-0-10-596163-5 £4.25

Pensions Act (Northern Ireland) 2015: Chapter 5; explanatory notes. - 30p.: 30 cm. - These Notes refer to the Pensions Act (Northern Ireland) 2015 (c. 5) (ISBN 9780105951582) which received Royal Assent on 23 June 2015. - 978-0-10-596164-2 £6.00

Reservoirs Act (Northern Ireland) 2015: Chapter 8; explanatory notes. - 37p.: 30 cm. - These Notes refer to the Reservoirs Act (Northern Ireland) 2015 (c. 8) (ISBN 9780105951612) which received Royal Assent on 24th July 2015. - 978-0-10-596211-3 £10.00

Work and Families Act (Northern Ireland) 2015: Chapter 1; explanatory notes. - 32p.: 30 cm. - These notes refer to the Work and Families Act (Northern Ireland) 2015 (c.1) which received Royal Assent on 8th January 2015. - 978-0-10-596161-1 £10.00

Other statutory publications

Statutory Publications Office.

Chronological table of statutory rules Northern Ireland: covering the legislation to 31 December 2014. - 11th ed. - ca. 982 pages: looseleaf with binder holes: 30 cm. - Supersedes 10th edition (ISBN 9780337099366). - 978-0-337-09985-4 £138.00

Chronological table of the statutes Northern Ireland: covering the legislation to 31 December 2013. - 40th ed. - x, 762p.: looseleaf with binder holes: 30 cm. - 978-0-337-09967-0 £132.00

Chronological table of the statutes Northern Ireland: covering the legislation to 31 December 2014. - 41st ed. - x, 771, [1]p.: looseleaf with binder holes: 30 cm. - 978-0-337-09915-1 £110.00

Northern Ireland statutes 2014: [binder]. - 1 binder: 31 cm. - 978-0-337-09977-9 £25.00 + VAT

The statutes revised: Northern Ireland. - Cumulative supplement vols A-D (1537 - 1920) to 31 December 2014. - 2nd ed. - x, 70p.: looseleaf with binder holes: 30 cm. - The material held in the main updated Statutes revised has been integrated into the UK Statute Law Database, available online at http://www.legislation.gov.uk. However, pre-1921 legislation published in vols A to D and amended since is not currently covered by the Statute Law Database, so printed supplements will continue to be issued for amendments made to that legislation. - 978-0-337-09916-8 £12.00

Title page and index to Northern Ireland statutes volume 2014. - 14p.: looseleaf with binder holes: 30 cm. - A binder for the 2014 statutes is also available (ISBN 9780337099779). - 978-0-337-09978-6 £5.75

Statutory Rules of Northern Ireland

By Subject Heading

Access to justice

The Access to Justice (2003 Order) (Commencement No. 7, Transitional Provisions and Savings) Order (Northern Ireland) 2015 No. 2015/194 (C.13). - Enabling power: S.I. 2003/435 (N.I. 10), arts 1 (2), 48 (1). Bringing into operation various provisions of the 2003 Order on 01.04.2015. - Issued: 13.04.2015. Made: 26.03.2015. Coming into operation: 01.04.2015. Effect: None. Territorial extent & classification: NI. General. - 8p: 30 cm. - 978-0-337-99765-5 £6.00

The Access to Justice (2003 Order) (Commencement No. 8) Order (Northern Ireland) 2015 No. 2015/237 (C.17). - Enabling power: S.I. 2003/435 (N.I. 10), arts 1 (2), 48 (1). Bringing into operation various provisions of the 2003 Order on 01.05.2015. - Issued: 06.05.2015. Made: 30.04.2015. Coming into operation: 01.05.2015. Effect: None. Territorial extent & classification: NI. General. - 8p: 30 cm. - 978-0-337-99789-1 £6.00

The Civil Legal Services (Appeal) Regulations (Northern Ireland) 2015 No. 2015/197. - Enabling power: S.I. 2003/435 (N.I. 10), art. 20A. - Issued: 14.04.2015. Made: 26.03.2015. Coming into operation: 01.04.2015. Effect: None. Territorial extent & classification: NI. General. - Supersedes draft S.R. (ISBN 9780337995774) issued 29/01/15. - 12p.: 30 cm. - 978-0-337-99768-6 £6.00

The Civil Legal Services (Cost Protection) Regulations (Northern Ireland) 2015 No. 2015/199. - Enabling power: S.I. 2003/435 (N.I. 10), arts. 18 (1), 20 (1) (2) (b). - Issued: 14.04.2015. Made: 26.03.2015. Coming into operation: 01.04.2015. Effect: None. Territorial extent & classification: NI. General. - Supersedes draft S.R. 2015/199 (ISBN 9780337995743) issued 29/01/15. - 4p.: 30 cm. - 978-0-337-99770-9 £4.25

The Civil Legal Services (Costs) Regulations (Northern Ireland) 2015 No. 2015/198. - Enabling power: S.I. 2003/435 (N.I. 10), arts. 18 (2), 20 (1) (2) (a) (b) (c) (e) (g), 34 (1) (6) (7). - Issued: 14.04.2015. Made: 26.03.2015. Coming into operation: 01.04.2015. Effect: S.R. 1965/217; 1981/366 partially revoked & S.R. 1965/235 revoked. Territorial extent & classification: NI. General. - 12p.: 30 cm. - 978-0-337-99769-3 £6.00

The Civil Legal Services (Disclosure of Information) Regulations (Northern Ireland) 2015 No. 2015/202. - Enabling power: S.I, 2003/435, arts 32 (1), 34 (1). - Issued: 15.04.2015. Made: 26.03.2015. Coming into operation: 01.04.2015. Effect: None. Territorial extent & classification: NI. General. - Supersedes draft S.R. (ISBN 9780337995767) issued 29/01/15. - 4p.: 30 cm. - 978-0-337-99773-0 £4.25

The Civil Legal Services (Financial) Regulations (Northern Ireland) 2015 No. 2015/196. - Enabling power: S.I. 2003/435 (N.I. 10), arts 13, 17 (1) (2) (b) (5) (6). - Issued: 14.04.2015. Made: 31.03.2015. Coming into operation: 01.04.2015. Effect: S.R. 1965/217; 1981/366 partially revoked & S.R. 1981/189 revoked. Territorial extent & classification: NI. General. - 28p.: 30 cm. - 978-0-337-99767-9 £6.00

The Civil Legal Services (General) Regulations (Northern Ireland) 2015 No. 2015/195. - Enabling power: S.I. 2003/435 (N.I. 10), arts 12 (3), 13, 14 (6), 15, 34 (1). - Issued: 13.04.2015. Made: 31.03.2015. Coming into operation: 01.04.2015. Effect: S.R. 1965/217; 1981/366 partially revoked. Territorial extent & classification: NI. General. - 28p.: 30 cm. - 978-0-337-99766-2 £6.00

The Civil Legal Services (Remuneration) Regulations (Northern Ireland) 2015 No. 2015/201. - Enabling power: S.I. 2003/435 (N.I. 10), arts. 12 (3), 47. - Issued: 15.04.2015. Made: 31.03.2015. Coming into operation: 01.04.2015. Effect: S.R. 1965/217; 1981/366 partially revoked & S.R. 1981/179, 365 revoked. Territorial extent & classification: NI. General. - 38p.: 30 cm. - 978-0-337-99772-3 £10.00

The Civil Legal Services (Statutory Charge) Order (Northern Ireland) 2015 No. 2015/200. - Enabling power: S.I. 2003/435 (N.I. 10), arts. 17 (7) (8). - Issued: 15.04.2015. Made: 26.03.2015. Coming into operation: 01.04.2015. Effect: S.R. 1965/217; 1981/366 partially revoked. Territorial extent & classification: NI. General. - 12p.: 30 cm. - 978-0-337-99771-6 £6.00

Agriculture

The Agriculture (Student fees) (Amendment) Regulations (Northern Ireland) 2015 No. 2015/135. - Enabling power: Agriculture Act (Northern Ireland) 1949, s. 5A (1) (2). - Issued: 11.03.2015. Made: 06.03.2015. Coming into operation: 01.09.2014. Effect: S.R. 2007/54 amended. Territorial extent & classification: NI. General. - 2p: 30 cm. - 978-0-337-99670-2 £4.25

The Common Agricultural Policy Basic Payment and Support Schemes Regulations (Northern Ireland) 2015 No. 2015/191. - Enabling power: European Communities Act 1972, s. 2 (2). - Issued: 01.04.2015. Made: 27.03.2015. Coming into operation: 30.04.2015. Effect: S.R. 2010/161 revoked with saving. Territorial extent & classification: NI. General. - EC note: These Regulations make provision in Northern Ireland for the administration of Regulation (EU) no. 1307/2013 establishing rules for direct payments to farmers under support schemes within the framework of the common agricultural policy. - 8p.: 30 cm. - 978-0-337-99753-2 £6.00

The Common Agricultural Policy (Control and Enforcement) Regulations (Northern Ireland) 2015 No. 2015/192. - Enabling power: European Communities Act 1972, s. 2 (2). - Issued: 01.04.2015. Made: 27.03.2015. Coming into operation: 30.04.2015. Effect: None. Territorial extent & classification: NI. General. - EC note: These Regulations make provision for the implementation in Northern Ireland of the European Regulations (as defined in schedule 1) relating to the administration of the common agricultural policy of the European Union. - With correction slip dated June 2015. - 8p.: 30 cm. - 978-0-337-99756-3 £6.00

The Common Agricultural Policy Direct Payments and Support Schemes (Cross Compliance) (Amendment) Regulations (Northern Ireland) 2015 No. 2015/286. - Enabling power: European Communities Act 1972, s. 2 (2). - Issued: 06.07.2015. Made: 25.06.2015. Coming into operation: 01.08.2015. Effect: S.R. 2014/291 amended. Territorial extent & classification: NI. General. - EC note: In Northern Ireland these Regulations supplement and make provision for the administration and enforcement of Regulation (EU) No. 1306/2013 , Commission Delegated Regulation (EU) No 640/2014 and Commission Implementing Regulation (EU) No 809/2014 in relation to cross compliance under the revised system of direct support schemes under the Common Agricultural Policy which came into force on 1st January 2015. - 4p.: 30 cm. - 978-0-337-99837-9 £4.25

The Common Agricultural Policy (Review of Decisions) Regulations (Northern Ireland) 2015 No. 2015/318. - Enabling power: European Communities Act 1972, s. 2 (2). - Issued: 23.07.2015. Made: 31.07.2015. Coming into operation: 07.08.2015. Effect: None. Territorial extent & classification: NI. General. - With correction slip dated July 2015. - 4p.: 30 cm. - 978-0-337-99853-9 £4.25

The Common Agricultural Policy (Review of SCMO Decisions) Regulations (Northern Ireland) 2015 No. 2015/408. - Enabling power: European Communities Act 1972, s. 2 (2). - Issued: 15.12.2015. Made: 10.12.2015. Coming into operation: 01.01.2016. Effect: None. Territorial extent & classification: NI. General. - EC note: These Regulations enable the Department to establish procedures for the review of relevant determination made by the Department under any of the EU instruments listed in the Schedule to the Regulations, or any statutory provision which implements or supplements those EU instruments in Northern Ireland. - 12p.: 30 cm. - 978-0-337-99927-7 £6.00

The Less Favoured Area Compensatory Allowances (Amendment) Regulations (Northern Ireland) 2015 No. 2015/248. - Enabling power: European Communities Act 1972, s. 2 (2). - Issued: 18.05.2015. Made: 13.05.2015. Coming into operation: 04.06.2015. Effect: S.R. 2015/16 amended. Territorial extent & classification: NI. General. - EC note: These Regulations amend S.R. 2015/16 which provided for the implementation of Articles 13(a), 14(1), 14(2) first and second indent, and 15 of Council Regulation (EC) No. 1257/1999 together with Articles 36(a)(ii) and 51(1) of Council Regulation (EC) No. 1698/2005, in so far as those Council Regulations relate to less favoured areas. - 4p.: 30 cm. - 978-0-337-99797-6 £4.25

The Less Favoured Area Compensatory Allowances Regulations (Northern Ireland) 2015 No. 2015/16. - Enabling power: European Communities Act 1972, s. 2 (2). - Issued: 30.01.2015. Made: 27.01.2015. Coming into operation: 03.02.2015. Effect: None. Territorial extent & classification: NI. General. - EC note: These Regulations provide for the implementation of Articles 13(a), 14(1), 14(2) first and second indent, and 15 of Council Regulation (EC) No. 1257/1999 together with Articles 36(a)(ii) and 51(1) of Council Regulation (EC) No. 1698/2005, in so far as those Council Regulations relate to less favoured areas. - 12p.: 30 cm. - 978-0-337-99581-1 £6.00

The Rural Development Programme Regulations (Northern Ireland) 2015 No. 2015/326. - Enabling power: European Communities Act 1972, s. 2 (2). - Issued: 09.09.2015. Made: 04.09.2015. Coming into operation: 05.10.2015. Effect: S.R. 2007/417, 418; 2008/172, 174, 295, 296, 297, 380; 2010/99 revoked with savings. Territorial extent and classification: NI. General. - 12p.: 30 cm. - 978-0-337-99860-7 £6.00

The Transitional Payment to Disadvantaged Area Scheme (Northern Ireland) 2015 No. 2015/17. - Enabling power: Agriculture (Temporary Assistance) Act (Northern Ireland) 1954, ss 1 (1) (2). - Issued: 30.01.2015. Made: 27.01.2015. Coming into operation: 03.02.2015. Effect: None.Territorial extent & classification: NI. General. - 8p.: 30 cm. - 978-0-337-99582-8 £4.25

Animals

The Brucellosis Control (Amendment) Order (Northern Ireland) 2015 No. 2015/340. - Enabling power: S.I. 1981/1115 (NI.22), arts 10 (6), 19, 60 (1). - Issued: 25.09.2015. Made: 22.09.2015. Coming into operation: 28.09.2015. Effect: S.R. 2004/361 amended & S.R. 2014/266 revoked. Territorial extent & classification: NI. General. - 2p.: 30 cm. - 978-0-337-99870-6 £4.25

The Tuberculosis (Examination and Testing) Scheme (Amendment) Order (Northern Ireland) 2015 No. 2015/322. - Enabling power: S.I. 1981/1115 (NI.22), art. 8. - Issued: 18.08.2015. Made: 13.08.2015. Coming into operation: 04.09.2015. Effect: S.R. 1999/264 amended. Territorial extent & classification: NI. General. - 4p.: 30 cm. - 978-0-337-99857-7 £4.25

The Zoonoses (Fees) (Amendment) Regulations (Northern Ireland) 2015 No. 2015/148. - Enabling power: European Communities Act 1972, s. 2 (2) & Finance Act 1973, s. 56 (1) (2) (5). - Issued: 17.03.2015. Made: 11.03.2015. Coming into operation: 01.04.2015. Effect: S.R. 2011/71 amended. Territorial extent & classification: NI. General. - EC note: They make provision for the Department to charge fees for activities required under Commission Regulation (EC) No. 1003/2005, Commission Regulation (EC) No. 1168/2006, Commission Regulation (EC) No. 646/2007, Commission Regulation (EC) No. 584/2008, Regulation (EC) No. 2160/2003 and Commission Regulation (EC) No. 1237/2007. - 4p.: 30 cm. - 978-0-337-99683-2 £4.25

Animals: Animal health

The Animal By-Products (Enforcement) Regulations (Northern Ireland) 2015 No. 2015/332. - Enabling power: European Communities Act 1972, s. 2 (2). - Issued: 18.09.2015. Made: 15.09.2015. Coming into operation: 14.10.2015. Effect: S.R. 1998/279 amended & S.R. 2011/124, 258; 2014/184 revoked. Territorial extent and classification: NI. General. - 24p.: 30 cm. - 978-0-337-99866-9 £6.00

The Non-Commercial Movement of Pet Animals (Amendment) Order (Northern Ireland) 2015 No. 2015/282. - Enabling power: European Communities Act 1972, s. 2 (2), sch. 2, para. 1A & S.I. 1981/1115 (N.I. 22), arts 5, 19, 24, 60. - Issued: 30.06.2015. Made: 24.06.2015. Coming into operation: 23.07.2015. Effect: S.R. 1977/113; 2011/438, 440; 2014/107 amended. - EC note: This Order amends the Non-Commercial Movement of Pet Animals Order (Northern Ireland) 2011("the 2011 Order") to update the enforcement provisions and import requirements for pet animals entering Northern Ireland as a result of Regulation (EU) No 576/2013 of the European Parliament and of the Council on the non-commercial movement of pet animals and repealing Regulation (EC) no 998/2003. - 8p.: 30 cm. - 978-0-337-99834-8 £6.00

Charities

The Charities (2008 Act) (Commencement No. 6) Order (Northern Ireland) 2015 No. 2015/361 (C.32). - Enabling power: Charities Act (Northern Ireland) 2008, s. 185 (1). Bringing into operation various provisions of the 2008 Act on 26.10.2015, in accord. with art. 2. - Issued: 27.10.2015. Made: 22.10.2015. Effect: None. Territorial extent & classification: NI. General. - 4p.: 30 cm. - 978-0-337-99889-8 £4.25

The Charities (2008 Act) (Commencement No. 7) Order (Northern Ireland) 2015 No. 2015/383 (C.34). - Enabling power: Charities Act (Northern Ireland) 2008, s. 185 (1). Bringing into operation various provisions of the 2008 Act on 28.11.2015, 01.01.2016 in accord. with art. 2. - Issued: 02.12.2015. Made: 27.11.2015. Effect: None. Territorial extent & classification: NI. General. - 4p.: 30 cm. - 978-0-337-99905-5 £4.25

The Charities (2013 Act) (Commencement No. 1) Order (Northern Ireland) 2015 No. 2015/256 (C.19). - Enabling power: Charities Act (Northern Ireland) 2013, s. 10 (2). Bringing into operation various provisions of the 2013 Act on 01.06.2015. - Issued: 27.05.2015. Made: 22.05.2015. Effect: None. Territorial extent & classification: NI. General. - 2p.: 30 cm. - 978-0-337-99814-0 £4.25

The Charities (Accounts and Reports) Regulations (Northern Ireland) 2015 No. 2015/384. - Enabling power: Charities Act (Northern Ireland) 2008, ss. 64 (1) (2), 66 (1), 68 (1) (2), 179 (5), sch. 6, paras 3 (3) to (5), 4 (2) (3), 6 (2), 8 (3), 10 (2) (3), 13. - Issued: 03.12.2015. Made: 30.11.2015. Coming into operation: 01.01.2016. Effect: S.I. 2008/674 (C.26) partially revoked. Territorial extent & classification: NI. General. - 24p.: 30 cm. - 978-0-337-99906-2 £6.00

The Charities Act 2008 (Examination of Accounts) Order (Northern Ireland) 2015 No. 2015/364. - Enabling power: Charities Act (Northern Ireland) 2008, s. 65 (10) (b). - Issued: 05.11.2015. Made: 02.11.2015. Coming into operation: 07.12.2015. Effect: 2008 c.12 (N.I.) amended. Territorial extent & classification: NI. General. - 2p.: 30 cm. - 978-0-337-99893-5 £4.25

The Charities Act 2008 (Substitution of Sums) Order (Northern Ireland) 2015 No. 2015/385. - Enabling power: Charities Act (Northern Ireland) 2008, ss. 64 (6), 65 (10) (a). - Issued: 03.12.2015. Made: 30.11.2015. Coming into operation: 01.01.2016. Effect: 2008 c.12 (N.I.) amended. Territorial extent & classification: NI. General. - 2p.: 30 cm. - 978-0-337-99907-9 £4.25

Clean air

The Smoke Control Areas (Authorised Fuels) (Amendment) Regulations (Northern Ireland) 2015 No. 2015/367. - Enabling power: S.I. 1981/158 (N.I. 4), art. 2 (2). - Issued: 13.11.2015. Made: 10.11.2015. Coming into operation: 10.12.2015. Effect: S.R. 2013/205 amended. Territorial extent & classification: NI. General. - 4p.: 30 cm. - 978-0-337-99898-0 £4.25

The Smoke Control Areas (Exempted Fireplaces) (Amendment No.2) Regulations (Northern Ireland) 2015 No. 2015/406. - Enabling power: S.I. 1981/158 (N.I. 4), art. 17 (7). - Issued: 14.12.2015. Made: 09.12.2015. Coming into operation: 31.01.2016. Effect: S.R. 2013/292 amended. Territorial extent & classification: NI. General. - 34p.: 30 cm. - 978-0-337-99925-3 £10.00

The Smoke Control Areas (Exempted Fireplaces) (Amendment) Regulations (Northern Ireland) 2015 No. 2015/274. - Enabling power: S.I. 1981/158 (N.I. 4), art. 17 (7). - Issued: 17.06.2015. Made: 15.06.2015. Coming into operation: 16.07.2015. Effect: S.R. 2013/292 amended. Territorial extent & classification: NI. General. - 12p.: 30 cm. - 978-0-337-99825-6 £6.00

Court of Judicature, Northern Ireland: Procedure

The Crown Court (Amendment) Rules (Northern Ireland) 2015 No. 2015/241. - Enabling power: Judicature (Northern Ireland) Act 1978, ss. 52 (1), 53A & Proceeds of Crime Act 2002, s. 239. - Issued: 08.05.2015. Made: 01.05.2015. Coming into operation: 01.06.2015. Effect: S.R. 1979/90 amended. Territorial extent & classification: NI. General. - EC note: Amends S.R. 1979/90 which gave effect to Directive 2010/64/EU on the right to interpretation and translation in criminal proceedings. - 4p.: 30 cm. - 978-0-337-99792-1 £4.25

The Rules of the Court of Judicature (Northern Ireland) (Amendment) 2015 No. 2015/235. - Enabling power: Judicature (Northern Ireland) Act 1978, ss. 55, 55A. - Issued: 01.05.2015. Made: 27.04.2015. Coming into operation: 19.05.2015. Effect: S.R. 1980/346 amended. Territorial extent & classification: NI. General. - 8p.: 30 cm. - 978-0-337-99786-0 £6.00

The Rules of the Court of Judicature (Northern Ireland) (Amendment No. 2) 2015 No. 2015/368. - Enabling power: Judicature (Northern Ireland) Act 1978, ss. 55, 55A. - Issued: 17.11.2015. Made: 09.11.2015. Coming into operation: 07.12.2015. Effect: S.R. 1980/346 amended. Territorial extent & classification: NI. General. - 4p.: 30 cm. - 978-0-337-99899-7 £4.25

The Rules of the Court of Judicature (Northern Ireland) (Amendment No. 3) 2015 No. 2015/415. - Enabling power: Judicature (Northern Ireland) Act 1978, ss. 55, 55A. - Issued: 22.12.2015. Made: 16.12.2015. Coming into operation: 06.01.2016. Effect: S.R. 1980/346 amended. Territorial extent & classification: NI. General. - 4p.: 30 cm. - 978-0-337-99931-4 £4.25

Criminal evidence

The Criminal Evidence (Northern Ireland) Order 1999 (Commencement No. 10) Order 2015 No. 2015/157 (C.9). - Enabling power: S.I. 1999/2789 (N.I. 8), art. 1 (2). Bringing various provisions of the 1999 Order into operation on 01.04.2015 in accord. with art. 2. - Issued: 27.03.2015. Made: 12.03.2015. Effect: None. Territorial extent & classification: NI. General. - This Statutory Rule replaces the original S.R. 2015/157 (C.9) (ISBN 9780337996962) issued 18/03/15 and it is being issued free of charge to all known recipients of the original S.R. - 4p.: 30 cm. - 978-0-337-99732-7 £4.25

The Criminal Evidence (Northern Ireland) Order 1999 (Commencement No. 10) Order 2015 No. 2015/157 (C.9). - Enabling power: S.I. 1999/2789 (N.I. 8), art. 1 (2). Bringing various provisions of the 1999 Order into operation on 01.04.2015 in accord. with art. 2. - Issued: 18.03.2015. Made: 12.03.2015. Effect: None. Territorial extent & classification: NI. General. - 4p.: 30 cm. - 978-0-337-99696-2 £4.25

Criminal law

The Criminal Justice (European Protection Order) (Amendment) Regulations (Northern Ireland) 2015 No. 2015/353. - Enabling power: European Communities Act 1972, s. 2 (2). - Issued: 12.10.2015. Made: 08.10.2015. Coming into operation: 02.11.2015. Effect: S.R. 2014/320 amended. Territorial extent & classification: NI. General. - 2p.: 30 cm. - 978-0-337-99882-9 £4.25

The Criminal Justice (Northern Ireland) Order 2008 (Commencement No. 8) Order 2015 No. 2015/255 (C.18). - Enabling power: S.I. 2004/1216 (NI. 1), art. 1 (4). Bringing various provisions of the 2008 Order into operation on 01.06.2015 in accord. with art. 2. - Issued: 27.05.2015. Made: 19.05.2015. Effect: None. Territorial extent & classification: NI. General. - 2p.: 30 cm. - 978-0-337-99813-3 £4.25

The Criminal Justice (Northern Ireland) Order 2008 (Commencement No. 9) Order 2015 No. 2015/290 (C.23). - Enabling power: S.I. 2008/1216 (NI. 1), art. 1 (4). Bringing various provisions of the 2008 Order into operation on 01.07.2015 in accord. with art. 2. - Issued: 06.07.2015. Made: 30.06.2015. Effect: None. Territorial extent & classification: NI. General. - 4p.: 30 cm. - 978-0-337-99842-3 £4.25

The Human Trafficking and Exploitation (2015 Act) (Commencement No. 1) Order (Northern Ireland) 2015 No. 2015/376 (C.33). - Enabling power: Human Trafficking and Exploitation (Criminal Justice and Support for Victims) Act (Northern Ireland) 2015. Bringing into operation various provisions of the 2015 Act on 27.11.2015. - Issued: 27.11.2015. Made: 23.11.2015. Effect: None. Territorial extent & classification: NI. General. - 2p.: 30 cm. - 978-0-337-99904-8 £4.25

The Police Act 1997 (Criminal Records) (Amendment No. 2) Regulations (Northern Ireland) 2015 No. 2015/350. - Enabling power: Police Act 1997, ss. 120ZA, 120AC (7), 125 (1) (5). - Issued: 06.10.2015. Made: 01.10.2015. Coming into operation: 02.11.2015. Effect: S.I. 2007/3283; 2008/542 amended. Territorial extent & classification: NI. General. - 4p.: 30 cm. - 978-0-337-99878-2 £4.25

The Police Act 1997 (Criminal Records) (Disclosure) (Amendment) Regulations (Northern Ireland) 2015 No. 2015/143. - Enabling power: Police Act 1997, ss. 112 (2) (b) (3), 113A (3) (a) 6, 113B (3) (a), 114 (3), 116 (3), 125 (1) (5). - Issued: 12.03.2015. Made: 11.03.2015. Coming into operation: 01.04.2015. Effect: S.I. 2008/542 amended. Territorial extent & classification: NI. General. - 4p.: 30 cm. - 978-0-337-99680-1 £4.25

The Sexual Offences Act 2003 (Prescribed Police Stations) Regulations (Northern Ireland) 2015 No. 2015/345. - Enabling power: Sexual Offences Act 2003, s. 87 (1) (a). - Issued: 30.09.2015. Made: 23.09.2015. Coming into operation: 09.11.2015. Effect: S.R. 2012/325 revoked. Territorial extent & classification: NI. General. - 4p.: 30 cm. - 978-0-337-99873-7 £4.25

Criminal law: Proceeds of crime

The Serious Crime (2015 Act) (Commencement) Regulations (Northern Ireland) 2015 No. 2015/190 (C.11). - Enabling power: Serious Crime Act 2015, ss. 88 (3) (8). Bringing into operation various provisions of the 2015 Act on 03.05.2015; 01.06.2015, in accord. with art. 2, 3. - Issued: 31.03.2015. Made: 26.03.2015. Effect: None. Territorial extent & classification: NI. General- 2p.: 30 cm. - 978-0-337-99752-5 £4.25

Dangerous drugs

The Controlled Drugs (Supervision of Management and Use) (Amendment) Regulations (Northern Ireland) 2015 No. 2015/278. - Enabling power: Health Act 2006, ss. 17, 18, 19 (1) (a), 20 (3) (7), 79 (3). - Issued: 22.06.2015. Made: 18.06.2015. Coming into operation: 16.07.2015. Effect: SR. 2009/225 amended. Territorial extent and classification: NI. General. - 12p.: 30 cm. - 978-0-337-99828-7 £6.00

The Misuse of Drugs (Amendment No. 2) Regulations (Northern Ireland) 2015 No. 2015/227. - Enabling power: Misuse of Drugs Act 1971, ss. 7, 10, 22, 31. - Issued: 24.04.2015. Made: 22.04.2015. Coming into operation: 13.05.2015. Effect: S.R. 2002/1 amended. Territorial extent & classification: NI. General. - 4p.: 30 cm. - 978-0-337-99780-8 £4.25

The Misuse of Drugs (Amendment) Regulations (Northern Ireland) 2015 No. 2015/53. - Enabling power: Misuse of Drugs Act 1971, ss. 7, 10, 22, 31. - Issued: 16.02.2015. Made: 12.02.2015. Coming into operation: 05.03.2015. Effect: S.R. 2011/153 amended. Territorial extent & classification: NI. General. - 4p.: 30 cm. - 978-0-337-99616-0 £4.25

The Misuse of Drugs Designation (Amendment No. 2) Regulations (Northern Ireland) 2015 No. 2015/228. - Enabling power: Misuse of Drugs Act 1971, s. 7 (4). - Issued: 24.04.2015. Made: 22.04.2015. Coming into operation: 13.04.2015. Effect: S.R. 2001/431 amended. Territorial extent & classification: NI. General. - 4p.: 30 cm. - 978-0-337-99781-5 £4.25

The Misuse of Drugs Designation (Amendment) Regulations (Northern Ireland) 2015 No. 2015/54. - Enabling power: Misuse of Drugs Act 1971, s. 7 (4). - Issued: 17.02.2015. Made: 12.02.2015. Coming into operation: 05.03.2015. Effect: S.R. 2001/431 amended. Territorial extent & classification: NI. General. - 4p.: 30 cm. - 978-0-337-99617-7 £4.25

Disabled persons

The Disability Discrimination Act 1995 (Commencement No. 11) Order (Northern Ireland) 2015 No. 2015/333 (C.29). - Enabling power: Disability Discrimination Act 1995, s. 70 (3). Bringing into operation various provisions of the 1995 Act on 18.09.2015, in accord. with art. 2. - Issued: 08.10.2015. Made: 17.09.2015. Effect: None. Territorial extent & classification: NI. General. - 4p: 30 cm. - 978-0-337-99880-5 £4.25

The Taxi Accessibility Regulations (Northern Ireland) 2015 No. 2015/396. - Enabling power: Disability Discrimination Act 1995, s. 32. - Issued: 07.12.2015. Made: 02.12.2015. Coming into operation: 31.05.2016. Effect: None. Territorial extent & classification: NI. General. - 8p.: 30 cm. - 978-0-337-99913-0 £6.00

Education

The Education (1998 Order) (Commencement No. 7) Order (Northern Ireland) 2015 No. 2015/127 (C.8). - Enabling power: S.I. 1998/1759 (N.I. 13), art. 1 (3). Bringing into operation various provisions of the 1998 Order on 06.03.2015, in accord. with art. 2. - Issued: 20.03.2015. Made: 06.03.2015. Effect: None. Territorial extent & classification: NI. General. - 4p: 30 cm. - 978-0-337-99678-8 £4.25

The Education (2014 Act) (Commencement No.1) Order (Northern Ireland) 2015 No. 2015/35 (C.4). - Enabling power: Education Act (Northern Ireland) 2014, s. 7 (2). Bringing into operation various provisions of the 2014 Act on 01.04.2015 in accord. with art. 2. - Issued: 09.02.2015. Made: 04.02.2015. Effect: None. Territorial extent & classification: NI. General. - 2p.: 30 cm. - 978-0-337-99598-9 £4.25

The General Teaching Council for Northern Ireland (Constitution) (Amendment no. 2) Regulations (Northern Ireland) 2015 No. 2015/341. - Enabling power: S.I. 1998/1759 (N.I. 13), art. 34, sch. 1, para. 1. - Issued: 28.09.2015. Made: 23.04.2015. Coming into operation: 15.10.2015. Effect: S.R. 2001/288 amended. Territorial extent & classification: NI. General. - 2p.: 30 cm. - 978-0-337-99871-3 £4.25

The General Teaching Council for Northern Ireland (Constitution) (Amendment) Regulations (Northern Ireland) 2015 No. 2015/224. - Enabling power: S.I. 1998/1759 (N.I. 13), art. 34, sch. 1, para. 1. - Issued: 23.04.2015. Made: 20.04.2015. Coming into operation: 20.05.2015. Effect: S.R. 2001/288 amended. Territorial extent & classification: NI. General. - 2p.: 30 cm. - 978-0-337-99779-2 £4.25

The General Teaching Council for Northern Ireland (Registration of Teachers) (Amendment) Regulations (Northern Ireland) 2015 No. 2015/151. - Enabling power: S.I. 1998/1759 (N.I. 13), arts 36 (1) (3) (f) (5), 40 (3), 90 (3). - Issued: 17.03.2015. Made: 11.03.2015. Coming into operation: 01.04.2015. Effect: S.R. 2004/38 amended. Territorial extent & classification: NI. General. - 4p.: 30 cm. - 978-0-337-99689-4 £4.25

The Student Fees (Amounts) (Amendment) Regulations (Northern Ireland) 2015 No. 2015/243. - Enabling power: S.I. 2005/1116 (NI. 5), arts 4 (8), 14 (4). - Issued: 08.05.2015. Made: 06.05.2015. Coming into operation: 01.09.2016. Effect: S.R. 2014/116 revoked. Territorial extent & classification: NI. General. - 2p.: 30 cm. - 978-0-337-99794-5 £4.25

The Teachers' Pensions (Miscellaneous Amendments) Regulations (Northern Ireland) 2015 No. 2015/126. - Enabling power: S.I. 1972/1073 (N.I. 10), arts. 11 (1) (2) (3) (3A), sch. 3, paras 1, 3, 4, 5, 6, 8, 11, 13. - Issued: 11.03.2015. Made: 06.03.2015. Coming into operation: 01.04.2015. Effect: S.R. 1998/333; 2014/310 amended. - 12p.: 30 cm. - 978-0-337-99666-5 £6.00

The Teachers' Superannuation (Additional Voluntary Contributions) (Amendment) Regulations (Northern Ireland) 2015 No. 2015/294. - Enabling power: S.I. 1972/1073 (N.I. 10), arts. 11 (1) (2) (2A) (3), 14 (1), sch. 3, paras 1, 3, 5, 6, 8, 10, 11, 13 & Public Service Pensions Act (Northern Ireland) 2014, ss. 1 (1) (2) (d), 3 (1) (2) (3) (a) (b) (5), schs 1, 2, para. 4, sch. 3- Issued: 09.07.2015. Made: 06.07.2015. Coming into operation: 26.07.2015. Effect: S.R. 1996/260 amended. - With correction slip dated August 2015. - 12p.: 30 cm. - 978-0-337-99843-0 £6.00

The Teachers' Superannuation (Amendment) Regulations (Northern Ireland) 2015 No. 2015/69. - Enabling power: S.I. 1972/1073 (N.I. 10), art. 11 (1) (2) (3) (3A), sch. 3, paras 1, 3, 4, 5, 6, 8, 11, 13. - Issued: 20.02.2015. Made: 18.02.2015. Coming into operation: 01.04.2015. Effect: S.R. 1998/333 amended & S.R. 2014/70 revoked. Territorial extent & classification: NI. General. - 20p: 30 cm. - 978-0-337-99635-1 £6.00

Electricity

The Electricity and Gas (Ownership Unbundling) Regulations (Northern Ireland) 2015 No. 2015/249. - Enabling power: European Communities Act 1972, s. 2 (2). - Issued: 18.05.2015. Made: 13.05.2015. Coming into operation: 05.06.2015. Effect: S.I. 1992/231 (NI. 1); 1996/275 (NI.2) amended. Territorial extent & classification: NI. General. - 4p.: 30 cm. - 978-0-337-99799-0 £4.25

The Energy (Amendment) Order (Northern Ireland) 2015 No. 2015/247. - Enabling power: S.I. 2003/419 (NI.6), art. 56 (1). - Issued: 18.05.2015. Made: 13.05.2015. Coming into operation: 14.05.2015 in accord. with art. 1 (1). Effect: S.I. 2003/419 (NI.6) amended. Territorial extent and classification: NI. General. - 4p.: 30 cm. - 978-0-337-99798-3 £4.25

The Gas and Electricity Licence Modification and Appeals Regulations (Northern Ireland) 2015 No. 2015/1. - Enabling power: European Communities Act 1972, s. 2 (2). - Issued: 12.01.2015. Made: 05.01.2015. Coming into operation: 06.01.2015. Effect: S.I. 1992/231 (NI. 1); 1996/275 (NI.2); 2003/419 (NI.6) amended. Territorial extent & classification: NI. General. - 30p.: 30 cm. - 978-0-337-99557-6 £6.00

The Renewables Obligation (Amendment) Order (Northern Ireland) 2015 No. 2015/287. - Enabling power: S.I. 2003/419 (N.I. 6), arts. 52 to 55F, 66 (3). - Issued: 03.07.2015. Made: 29.06.2015. Coming into operation: 01.07.2015. Effect: S.R. 2009/154 amended. Territorial extent & classification: NI. General. - 8p.: 30 cm. - 978-0-337-99838-6 £4.25

The Renewables Obligation Closure Order (Northern Ireland) 2015 No. 2015/346. - Enabling power: S.I. 2003/419 (NI. 6), arts 55D, 55EA. - Issued: 01.10.2015. Made: 29.09.2015. Coming into operation: 30.09.2015 in accord. with art. 1. Effect: None. Territorial extent & classification: NI. General. - 8p.: 30 cm. - 978-0-337-99874-4 £6.00

Employer's liability

The Employer's Liability (Compulsory Insurance) (Amendment) Regulations (Northern Ireland) 2015 No. 2015/80. - Enabling power: S.I. 1972/963 (N.I. 6), arts. 7 (c), 10. - Issued: 02.03.2015. Made: 26.02.2015. Coming into operation: 01.04.2015. Effect: S.R. 2013/199 revoked. Territorial extent & classification: NI. General. - 4p.: 30 cm. - 978-0-337-99643-6 £4.25

Employment

The Employment Rights (Increase of Limits) Order (Northern Ireland) 2015 No. 2015/169. - Enabling power: S.I. 1999/2790 (N.I. 9), arts 33 (2) (3), 39 (3). - Issued: 25.03.2015. Made: 19.03.2015. Coming into operation: 22.03.2015. Effect: S.R. 2014/39 revoked. Territorial extent & classification: NI. General. - Revoked by SR 2016/37 (ISBN 9780338003843). - 8p: 30 cm. - 978-0-337-99730-3 £6.00

The Social Security Benefits Up-rating Order (Northern Ireland) 2015 No. 2015/124. - Enabling power: Social Security Administration (Northern Ireland) Act 1992, ss. 132, 132A,165 (1) (4) (5). - Issued: 09.03.2015. Made: 05.03.2015. Coming into operation: In accord. with 1. Effect: 1992 c.7 & S.R. 1987/459; 1996/198; 2006/405, 406; 2008/280 amended & S.R. 2014/78 revoked. Territorial extent & classification: NI. General. - For approval of the Assembly before the expiration of six months from the date of its coming into operation. Superseded by approved version SR 2015/124 (ISBN 9780337997853). - 44p.: 30 cm. - 978-0-337-99663-4 £10.00

The Social Security Benefits Up-rating Order (Northern Ireland) 2015 No. 2015/124. - Enabling power: Social Security Administration (Northern Ireland) Act 1992, ss. 132, 132A, 165 (1) (4) (5). - Issued: 30.04.2015. Made: 05.03.2015. Coming into operation: In accord. with art. 1. Effect: 1966 c.6 (N.I.); 1992 c.7; 1993 c.49; S.R. 1987/30, 460; 1992/32; 1994/461; 1995/35; 1996/198; 2002/380; 2003/28; 2006/405, 406; 2008/280; 2010/407 amended & S.R. 2014/78 revoked (13.04.2015). Territorial extent & classification: NI. General. - Approved by resolution of the Assembly on 27th April 2015. Supersedes pre-approved SR 2015/124 (ISBN 9780337996634). - 48p.: 30 cm. - 978-0-337-99785-3 £10.00

Employment: Work and families

The Employment Rights (Northern Ireland) Order 1996 (Application of Articles 107A, 107B, 107G, 107I, 112A and 112B to Parental Order Cases) Regulations (Northern Ireland) 2015 No. 2015/100. - Enabling power: S.I. 1996/1919 (N.I. 16), arts 107AC, 107BA, 107J (2), 112BAA, 251 (6). - Issued: 18.03.2015. Made: 02.03.2015. Coming into operation: 15.03.2015. Effect: S.I. 1996/1919 (N.I. 16) modified. Territorial extent & classification: NI. General. - For approval of the Assembly before the expiration of six months from the date of their coming into operation. - 8p.: 30 cm. - 978-0-337-99710-5 £6.00

The Employment Rights (Northern Ireland) Order 1996 (Application of Articles 107A, 107B, 107G, 107I, 112A and 112B to Parental Order Cases) Regulations (Northern Ireland) 2015 No. 2015/100. - Enabling power: S.I. 1996/1919 (N.I. 16), arts 107AC, 107BA, 107J (2), 112BAA, 251 (6). - Issued: 22.05.2015. Made: 02.03.2015. Coming into operation: 15.03.2015. Effect: S.I. 1996/1919 (NI. 16) modified. Territorial extent & classification: NI. General. - Approved by resolutions of the Assembly on 12th May 2015. - 8p.: 30 cm. - 978-0-337-99807-2 £6.00

The Employment Rights (Northern Ireland) Order 1996 (Application of Articles 107G and 107I to Adoptions from Overseas) Regulations (Northern Ireland) 2015 No. 2015/97. - Enabling power: S.I. 1996/1919 (N.I. 16), art. 107J (1). - Issued: 18.03.2015. Made: 02.03.2015. Coming into operation: 15.03.2015. Effect: S.I. 1996/1919 (N.I. 16) modified. Territorial extent & classification: NI. General. - For approval of the Assembly before the expiration of six months from the date of their coming into operation. - 4p.: 30 cm. - 978-0-337-99708-2 £4.25

The Employment Rights (Northern Ireland) Order 1996 (Application of Articles 107G and 107I to Adoptions from Overseas) Regulations (Northern Ireland) 2015 No. 2015/97. - Enabling power: S.I. 1996/1919 (N.I. 16), art. 107J (1). - Issued: 22.05.2015. Made: 02.03.2015. Coming into operation: 15.03.2015. Effect: None. Territorial extent & classification: NI. General. - Approved by resolution of the Assembly on 12th May 2015. - 4p.: 30 cm. - 978-0-337-99805-8 £4.25

The Flexible Working Regulations (Northern Ireland) 2015 No. 2015/105. - Enabling power: S.I. 1996/1919 (N.I. 16), arts 112F (1) (b) (5) (8) (a), 112H (3), 112I (3), 251 (6). - Issued: 20.03.2015. Made: 02.03.2015. Coming into operation: 05.04.2015. Effect: None. Territorial extent & classification: NI. General. - 4p: 30 cm. - 978-0-337-99697-9 £4.25

The Maternity and Adoption Leave (Curtailment of Statutory Rights to Leave) Regulations (Northern Ireland) 2015 No. 2015/95. - Enabling power: S.I. 1996/1919 (N.I. 16), arts 103(2) (3) (ba) (bb) (3A), 105 (2) (3) (a) (aa) (3A), 107 (1) (a) (2), 107A (1A) (2) (2A) (2B), 107B (2) (3) (a) (aa) (3A), 107D (1) (a) (2). - Issued: 18.03.2015. Made: 02.03.2015. Coming into operation: 15.03.2015. Effect: None. Territorial extent & classification: NI. General. - For approval of the Assembly before the expiration of six months from the date of their coming into operation. - 8p.: 30 cm. - 978-0-337-99706-8 £6.00

The Maternity and Adoption Leave (Curtailment of Statutory Rights to Leave) Regulations (Northern Ireland) 2015 No. 2015/95. - Enabling power: S.I. 1996/1919 (NI. 16), arts 103 (2) (3) (ba) (bb) (3A), 105 (2) (3) (a) (aa) (3A), 107 (1) (a) (2), 107A (1A) (2) (2A) (2B), 107B (2) (3) (a) (aa) (3A), 107D (1) (a) (2). - Issued: 22.05.2015. Made: 02.03.2015. Coming into operation: 15.03.2015. Effect: None. Territorial extent & classification: NI. General. - Approved by resolution of the Assembly on 12th May 2015. - 8p.: 30 cm. - 978-0-337-99804-1 £6.00

The Maternity and Parental Leave etc. (Amendment) Regulations (Northern Ireland) 2015 No. 2015/104. - Enabling power: S.I. 1996/1919 (N.I. 16), art. 103 (4) (c), 108 (1) (2), 109 (1) (c). - Issued: 20.03.2015. Made: 02.03.2015. Coming into operation: In accord. with reg. 1 (2). Effect: S.R. 1999/471 amended. Territorial extent & classification: NI. General. - For approval of the Assembly before the expiration of six months from the date of their coming into operation. - 4p.: 25 cm. - 978-0-337-99699-3 £4.25

The Maternity and Parental Leave etc. (Amendment) Regulations (Northern Ireland) 2015 No. 2015/104. - Enabling power: S.I. 1996/1919 (NI. 16), art. 103 (4) (c), 108 (1) (2), 109 (1) (c). - Issued: 22.05.2015. Made: 02.03.2015. Coming into operation: In accord. with reg. 1 (2) (3). Effect: S.R. 1999/471 amended. Territorial extent & classification: NI. General. - Approved by resolution of the Assembly on 12th May 2015. - 4p.: 25 cm. - 978-0-337-99810-2 £4.25

The Paternity, Adoption and Shared Parental Leave (Parental Order Cases) Regulations (Northern Ireland) 2015 No. 2015/101. - Enabling power: S.I. 1996/1919 (N.I. 16), arts. 70C (2), 107A (1) (2, (2A) (2B) (3) (6) (7), 107B (1) (2) (3) (3A) (4) (7) (8), 107C (1) (2), 107D, 107G (1) to (6), 107I (1) (4) (7) to (14) (16), 107J (2) (3), 107K (1) (4) (5), 107L, 107M (1), 112A (5) (aa), 112B (1) (2) (4A) (5), 112C (1) (6), 112D (1), 112E, 131. - Issued: 18.03.2015. Made: 02.03.2015. Coming into operation: 15.03.2015. Effect: None. - For approval of the Assembly before the expiration of six months from the date of their coming into operation. - 12p.: 30 cm. - 978-0-337-99714-3 £6.00

The Paternity, Adoption and Shared Parental Leave (Parental Order Cases) Regulations (Northern Ireland) 2015 No. 2015/101. - Enabling power: S.I. 1996/1919 (N.I. 16), arts. 70C (2), 107A (1) (2), (2A) (2B) (3) (6) (7), 107B (1) (2) (3) (3A) (4) (7) (8), 107C (1) (2), 107D, 107G (1) to (6), 107I (1) (4) (7) to (14) (16), 107J (2) (3), 107K (1) (4) (5), 107L, 107M (1), 112A (5) (aa), 112B (1) (2) (4A) (5), 112C (1) (6), 112D (1), 112E, 131. - Issued: 22.05.2015. Made: 02.03.2015. Coming into operation: 15.03.2015. Effect: None. - Approved by resolution of the Assembly on 12th May 2015. - 12p.: 30 cm. - 978-0-337-99808-9 £6.00

The Paternity and Adoption Leave (Amendment) Regulations (Northern Ireland) 2015 No. 2015/87. - Enabling power: S.I. 1996/1919 (N.I. 16), arts 70C (2) (aa) (ab), 107A (1) (1A) (3) (c), 107D (2), 112A (4A), 112B (1) (4A) (5) (aa) (ba), 112BA (1), 112C (1) (c), 112D (1), 131 (1) (2) (3) (aa) (ab). - Issued: 18.03.2015. Made: 02.03.2015. Coming into operation: 15.03.2015, for the purpose of regulations 1, 2, 3 (a) (i) and (ii) (partially), 4, 5 (a), 5 (b) (partially), 6, 9, 10, 12, and 14 (1) (2) (4) and (6); 05.03.2015, for all other purposes. Effect: S.R. 2002/377 amended. - For approval of the Assembly before the expiration of six months from the date of their coming into operation. - 8p.: 30 cm. - 978-0-337-99713-6 £6.00

The Paternity and Adoption Leave (Amendment) Regulations (Northern Ireland) 2015 No. 2015/87. - Enabling power: S.I. 1996/1919 (NI. 16), arts 70C (2) (aa) (ab), 107A (1) (1A) (3) (c), 107D (2), 112A (4A), 112B (1) (4A) (5) (aa) (ba), 112BA (1), 112C (1) (c), 112D (1), 131 (1) (2) (3) (aa) (ab). - Issued: 22.05.2015. Made: 02.03.2015. Coming into operation: 15.03.2015, for the purpose of regulations 1, 2, 3 (a) (i) and (ii) (partially), 4, 5 (a), 5 (b) (partially), 6, 9, 10, 12, and 14 (1) (2) (4) and (6); 05.04.2015, for all other purposes. Effect: S.R. 2002/377 amended. - Approved by resolution of the Assembly on 12th May 2015. - 8p.: 30 cm. - 978-0-337-99801-0 £6.00

The Shared Parental Leave and Paternity and Adoption Leave (Adoptions from Overseas) Regulations (Northern Ireland) 2015 No. 2015/98. - Enabling power: S.I. 1996/1919 (N.I. 16), arts 70C (2), 107A(1) (2A) (2B), 107B (3) (a) (aa) (3A), 107D (1) (a) (2), 107G (1) to (6), 107I (1) (4) (7) to (14) (16), 107J (1), 107K (1) (4) (5), 107L, 107M (1), 112B (2) (4A), 131. - Issued: 18.03.2015. Made: 02.03.2015. Coming into operation: 05.04.2015. Effect: S.R. 2003/222; 2015/93, 95 amended/modified. Territorial extent & classification: NI. General. - For approval of the Assembly before the expiration of six months from the date of their coming into operation. - 8p.: 30 cm. - 978-0-337-99709-9 £6.00

The Shared Parental Leave and Paternity and Adoption Leave (Adoptions from Overseas) Regulations (Northern Ireland) 2015 No. 2015/98. - Enabling power: S.I. 1996/1919 (NI. 16), arts 70C (2), 107A(1) (2A) (2B), 107B (3) (a) (aa) (3A), 107D (1) (a) (2), 107G (1) to (6), 107I (1) (4) (7) to (14) (16), 107J (1), 107K (1) (4) (5), 107L,107M (1), 112B (2) (4A), 131. - Issued: 22.05.2015. Made: 02.03.2015. Coming into operation: 05.04.2015. Effect: S.R. 2003/222; 2015/93, 95 amended/modified. Territorial extent & classification: NI. General. - Approved by resolution of the Assembly on 12th May 2015. - 8p.: 30 cm. - 978-0-337-99806-5 £6.00

The Shared Parental Leave and Statutory Shared Parental Pay (Consequential Amendments to Subordinate Legislation) Order (Northern Ireland) 2015 No. 2015/146. - Enabling power: Work and Families Act (Northern Ireland) 2015, s. 21 (1) (2). - Issued: 20.03.2015. Made: 12.03.2015. Coming into operation: 15.03.2015. Effect: S.I. 2010/832; 2012/1796; 2014/2336; S.R. 1975/113; 1982/263; 1987/30, 459; 1992/341; 1996/198; 1998/333; 2000/104; 2001/18; 2003/28; 2002/382, 2005; 2003/221; 2005/438; 2006/405, 406; 2008/280; 2014/188, 310; amended/modified. Territorial extent & classification: NI. General. - With correction slip dated Agust 2015. - 16p.: 30 cm. - 978-0-337-99717-4 £6.00

The Shared Parental Leave Regulations (Northern Ireland) 2015 No. 2015/93. - Enabling power: S.I. 1996/1919 (N.I. 16), arts 70C (2), 107E, 107F (1) (4) (7) to (14) (16), 107G (1) to (6), 107H (1) (3), 107 (I) (1) (4) (7) to (14) (16), 107K (1) (4) (5), 107L,107M (1). 131. - Issued: 19.03.2015. Made: 02.03.2015. Coming into operation: 15.03.2015. Effect: None. Territorial extent & classification: NI. General. - For approval of the Assembly before the expiration of six months from the date of their coming into operation. - 40p.: 30 cm. - 978-0-337-99704-4 £10.00

The Shared Parental Leave Regulations (Northern Ireland) 2015 No. 2015/93. - Enabling power: S.I. 1996/1919 (NI. 16), arts 70C (2), 107E, 107F (1) (4) (7) to (14) (16), 107G (1) to (6), 107H (1) (3), 107 (I) (1) (4) (7) to (14) (16), 107K (1) (4) (5), 107L,107M (1), 131. - Issued: 22.05.2015. Made: 02.03.2015. Coming into operation: 15.03.2015. Effect: None. Territorial extent & classification: NI. General. - Approved by resolution of the Assembly on 12th May 2015. - 40p.: 30 cm. - 978-0-337-99802-7 £10.00

The Social Security Contributions and Benefits (Northern Ireland) Act 1992 (Application of Parts 12ZA, 12ZB and 12ZC to Parental Order Cases) Regulations (Northern Ireland) 2015 No. 2015/90. - Enabling power: Social Security Contributions and Benefits (Northern Ireland) Act 1992, ss. 167ZK (2), 167ZT (2), 167ZZ8 (2)- Issued: 19.03.2015. Made: 02.03.2015. Coming into operation: 15.03.2015. Effect: 1992 c. 7 modified. Territorial extent & classification: NI. General. - 12p.: 30 cm. - 978-0-337-99701-3 £6.00

The Social Security Contributions and Benefits (Northern Ireland) Act 1992 (Application of Parts 12ZA and 12ZB to Adoptions from Overseas) (Amendment) Regulations (Northern Ireland) 2015 No. 2015/88. - Enabling power: Social Security Contributions and Benefits (Northern Ireland) Act 1992, s. 167ZZ8 (1)- Issued: 20.03.2015. Made: 02.03.2015. Coming into operation: 15.03.2015. Effect: S.R. 2003/221 amended. Territorial extent & classification: NI. General. - 4p.: 30 cm. - 978-0-337-99700-6 £4.25

The Statutory Adoption Pay (Curtailment) Regulations (Northern Ireland) 2015 No. 2015/96. - Enabling power: Social Security Contributions and Benefits (Northern Ireland) Act 1992, ss. 167ZN (2A) (2B) (2C) (2D), 171 (1) (3) (4). - Issued: 18.03.2015. Made: 02.03.2015. Coming into operation: 15.03.2015. Effect: None. Territorial extent & classification: NI. General. - 8p.: 30 cm. - 978-0-337-99707-5 £4.25

The Statutory Paternity Pay and Statutory Adoption Pay (General) (Amendment) Regulations (Northern Ireland) 2015 No. 2015/89. - Enabling power: Social Security Contributions and Benefits (Northern Ireland) Act 1992, s. 167ZC (1A) (3) (c)- Issued: 19.03.2015. Made: 02.03.2015. Coming into operation: 15.03.2015. Effect: S.R. 2002/378 amended. Territorial extent & classification: NI. General. - 4p: 30 cm. - 978-0-337-99702-0 £4.25

The Statutory Paternity Pay and Statutory Adoption Pay (Parental Orders and Prospective Adopters) Regulations (Northern Ireland) 2015 No. 2015/92. - Enabling power: Social Security Contributions and Benefits (Northern Ireland) Act 1992, ss. 167ZB (2) (a), 167ZBA (2) (b), 167ZC (1A) (3) (a) (c) (d) (f) (g), 167ZD (2) (3), 167ZE (2) (3) (7) (8), 167ZG (3), 167ZJ (1) (3) (4) (7) (8), 167ZL (8) (b) to (d) (f) (g), 167ZLA (2) (b), 167ZM (2) (3), 167ZN (2) (5) (6), 167ZP (6), 167ZS (1) (3) (4) (7) (8). 171 (4) & Social Security Administration (Northern Ireland) Act 1992, s. 5 (1) (g) (j) (q) & S.I. 2002/2836 (N.I. 2), arts 9 (1) (2) (c), 16 (1). - Issued: 19.03.2015. Made: 02.03.2015. Coming into operation: 15.03.2015. Effect: S.R. 2002/378, 379 amended. Territorial extent & classification: NI. General. - 12p: 30 cm. - 978-0-337-99703-7 £6.00

The Statutory Shared Parental Pay (Administration) Regulations (Northern Ireland) 2015 No. 2015/91. - Enabling power: S.I. 2002/2836 (N.I.), arts 8, 9, 11, 16 (1) & S.I. 1999/671, arts 7 (1) (fa) (ga), 23 (5) (8). - Issued: 20.03.2015. Made: 02.03.2015. Coming into operation: 15.03.2015. Effect: None. Territorial extent & classification: NI. General. - 8p.: 30 cm. - 978-0-337-99718-1 £6.00

The Statutory Shared Parental Pay (Adoptions from Overseas) Regulations (Northern Ireland) 2015 No. 2015/99. - Enabling power: Social Security Contributions and Benefits (Northern Ireland) Act 1992, ss. 167ZW, 167ZX (1), (8) to (11), 167ZZ (1), 167ZZ1 (2) (3), 167ZZ2 (1), (3) to (5), 167ZZ4 (3), 167ZZ7 (3) (4) (7) (8), 171(3) & Social Security Administration (Northern Ireland) Act 1992, s. 5 (1) (g) (j) (m) (q). - Issued: 18.03.2015. Made: 02.03.2015. Coming into operation: 05.04.2015. Effect: S.R. 2015/94 amended. - For approval of the Assembly before the expiration of six months from the date of their coming into operation. - 8p: 30 cm. - 978-0-337-99711-2 £4.25

The Statutory Shared Parental Pay (Adoptions from Overseas) Regulations (Northern Ireland) 2015 No. 2015/99. - Enabling power: Social Security Contributions and Benefits (Northern Ireland) Act 1992, ss. 167ZW, 167ZX (1), (8) to (11), 167ZZ (1), 167ZZ1 (2) (3), 167ZZ2 (1), (3) to (5), 167ZZ4 (3), 167ZZ7 (3) (4) (7) (8), 171(3) & Social Security Administration (Northern Ireland) Act 1992, s. 5 (1) (g) (j) (m) (q). - Issued: 22.05.2015. Made: 02.03.2015. Coming into operation: 05.04.2015. Effect: S.R. 2015/94 amended. - Approved by resolution of the Assembly on 12th May 2015. - 8p: 30 cm. - 978-0-337-99811-9 £4.25

The Statutory Shared Parental Pay (General) Regulations (Northern Ireland) 2015 No. 2015/94. - Enabling power: Social Security Contributions and Benefits (Northern Ireland) Act 1992, ss. 167ZU (1) (2) (3) (4), 167ZV (1) (9) (10) (11) (12), 167ZW (1) (2) (3) (4), 167ZX (1) (8) (9) (10) (11), 167ZY (1), 167ZZ (1), 167ZZ1 (2) (3), 167ZZ2 (1) (3) (4) (5), 167ZZ4 (3), 167ZZ7 (3) (4) (7) (8), 171(3) & Social Security Administration (Northern Ireland) Act 1992, s. 5 (1) (g) (j) (m) (q). - Issued: 19.03.2015. Made: 02.03.2015. Coming into operation: 15.03.2015. Effect: None. Territorial extent & classification: NI. General. - For approval of the Assembly before the expiration of six months from the date of their coming into operation. - 42p.: 30 cm. - 978-0-337-99705-1 £10.00

The Statutory Shared Parental Pay (General) Regulations (Northern Ireland) 2015 No. 2015/94. - Enabling power: Social Security Contributions and Benefits (Northern Ireland) Act 1992, ss. 167ZU (1) (2) (3) (4), 167ZV (1) (9) (10) (11) (12), 167ZW (1) (2) (3) (4), 167ZX (1) (8) (9) (10) (11), 167ZY (1), 167ZZ (1), 167ZZ1 (2) (3), 167ZZ2 (1) (3) (4) (5), 167ZZ4 (3), 167ZZ7 (3) (4) (7) (8), 171(3) & Social Security Administration (Northern Ireland) Act 1992, s. 5 (1) (g) (j) (m) (q). - Issued: 22.05.2015. Made: 02.03.2015. Coming into operation: 15.03.2015. Effect: None. Territorial extent & classification: NI. General. - Approved by resolution of the Assembly on 12th May 2015. - 42p.: 30 cm. - 978-0-337-99803-4 £10.00

The Statutory Shared Parental Pay (Parental Order Cases) Regulations (Northern Ireland) 2015 No. 2015/102. - Enabling power: Social Security Contributions and Benefits (Northern Ireland) Act 1992, ss. 167ZW (1) (2) (3) (4), 167ZX (1) (8) (9) (10) (11), 167ZZ (1) (2) (3), 167ZZ2 (1) (3) (4) (5), 167ZZ4 (3), 167ZZ7 (3) (4) (7) (8), 171 (3) & Social Security Administration (Northern Ireland) Act 1992, s. 5 (1) (g) (j) (m) (q). - Issued: 20.03.2015. Made: 02.03.2015. Coming into operation: 15.03.2015. Effect: S.R. 2002/382 amended. Territorial extent & classification: NI. General. - For approval of the Assembly before the expiration of six months from the date of their coming into operation. - 8p.: 30 cm. - 978-0-337-99698-6 £6.00

The Statutory Shared Parental Pay (Parental Order Cases) Regulations (Northern Ireland) 2015 No. 2015/102. - Enabling power: Social Security Contributions and Benefits (Northern Ireland) Act 1992, ss. 167ZW (1) (2) (3) (4), 167ZX (1) (8) (9) (10) (11), 167ZZ (1) (2) (3), 167ZZ2 (1) (3) (4) (5), 167ZZ4 (3), 167ZZ7 (3) (4) (7) (8), 171 (3) & Social Security Administration (Northern Ireland) Act 1992, s. 5 (1) (g) (j) (m) (q). - Issued: 22.05.2015. Made: 02.03.2015. Coming into operation: 15.03.2015. Effect: S.R. 2015/94 amended. Territorial extent & classification: NI. General. - Approved by resolution of the Assembly on 12th May 2015. - 8p.: 30 cm. - 978-0-337-99809-6 £6.00

The Statutory Shared Parental Pay (Persons Abroad and Mariners) Regulations (Northern Ireland) 2015 No. 2015/103. - Enabling power: Social Security Contributions and Benefits (Northern Ireland) Act 1992, ss. 167ZZ6 (1), 167ZZ7 (3) (b). - Issued: 18.03.2015. Made: 02.03.2015. Coming into operation: 15.03.2015. Effect: S.R. 2002/382 amended. - 12p.: 30 cm. - 978-0-337-99715-0 £6.00

The Time Off to Attend Adoption Appointments (Prospective Adopters) Regulations (Northern Ireland) 2015 No. 2015/213. - Enabling power: S.I. 1996/1919 (N.I. 16), art. 85ZS (2) (b) (3). - Issued: 13.04.2015. Made: 03.04.2015. Coming into operation: 05.04.2015. Effect: S.I. 1996/1919 (N.I. 16) modified. Territorial extent & classification: NI. General. - 4p.: 30 cm. - 978-0-337-99763-1 £4.25

The Work and Families Act (Northern Ireland) 2015 (Commencement, Transitional Provisions and Savings) Order (Northern Ireland) 2015 No. 2015/86 (C.7). - Enabling power: Work and Families Act (Northern Ireland) 2015, s. 23 (1) (2). Bringing into operation various provisions of the 2015 Act on 15.03.2015; 05.04.2015, in accord. with arts 4 to 7. - Issued: 18.03.2015. Made: 02.03.2015. Effect: None. - 8p.: 30 cm. - 978-0-337-99712-9 £4.25

Energy

The Renewable Heat Incentive Schemes (Amendment) Regulations (Northern Ireland) 2015 No. 2015/371. - Enabling power: Energy Act 2011, s. 113. - Issued: 20.11.2015. Made: 17.11.2015. Coming into operation: In accord. with reg. 1. Effect: S.R. 2012/396 amended. Territorial extent & classification: NI. General. - Supersedes draft S.R. (ISBN 9780337998973) issued 11/11/15. - 8p.: 30 cm. - 978-0-337-99902-4 £6.00

Environmental protection

The Environmental Liability (Prevention and Remediation) (Amendment) Regulations (Northern Ireland) 2015 No. 2015/231. - Enabling power: European Communities Act 1972, s. 2 (2). - Issued: 29.04.2015. Made: 24.04.2015. Coming into operation: 19.07.2015. Effect: S.R. 2009/252 amended. Territorial extent & classification: NI. General. - 4p.: 30 cm. - 978-0-337-99784-6 £4.25

The Fluorinated Greenhouse Gases Regulations (Northern Ireland) 2015 No. 2015/425. - Enabling power: European Communities Act 1972, s. 2 (2), sch. 2, para. 1A. - Issued: 23.12.2015. Made: 21.12.2015. Coming into operation: 31.01.2016. Effect: S.R. 2009/184; 2012/230; 2014/77 revoked. Territorial extent & classification: NI. General. - EC note: These Regulations give effect to Regulation (EU) No 517/2014 of the European Parliament and of the Council on fluorinated greenhouse gases and repealing Regulation (EC) No 842/2006. - 24p.: 30 cm. - 978-0-337-99937-6 £6.00

The Food Waste Regulations (Northern Ireland) 2015 No. 2015/14. - Enabling power: European Communities Act 1972, s. 2 (2) & S.I. 1997/2778 (N.I.19), art. 6 (6) & S.I. 2002/3153 (N.I.7), art. 4 (1) (3). - Issued: 27.01.2015. Made: 22.01.2015. Coming into operation: 14.02.2015. Effect: S.I. 1997/2778 (N.I.19); S.R. 2003/493, 496; 2013/160 amended. Territorial extent & classification: NI. General. - 8p.: 30 cm. - 978-0-337-99571-2 £6.00

The Hazardous Waste (Amendment No. 2) Regulations (Northern Ireland) 2015 No. 2015/288. - Enabling power: European Communities Act 1972, s. 2 (2). - Issued: 03.07.2015. Made: 30.06.2015. Coming into operation: 17.08.2015. Effect: S.I. 1997/2778 (NI.19); S.R. 2002/271; 2003/493; 2005/300 amended & S.R. 2005/301; 2015/238 revoked. Territorial extent & classification: NI. General. - 4p.: 30 cm. - 978-0-337-99840-9 £4.25

The Hazardous Waste (Amendment) Regulations (Northern Ireland) 2015 No. 2015/238. - Enabling power: European Communities Act 1972, s. 2 (2). - Issued: 07.05.2015. Made: 01.05.2015. Coming into operation: 01.06.2015. Effect: S.I. 1997/2778 (NI.19); S.R. 2002/271; 2003/493; 2005/300 amended. Territorial extent & classification: NI. General. - With correction slip dated May 2015. - 4p.: 30 cm. - 978-0-337-99790-7 £4.25

The Nitrates Action Programme (Amendment) Regulations (Northern Ireland) 2015 No. 2015/369. - Enabling power: European Communities Act 1972, s. 2 (2) & S.I. 1997/2778 (N.I. 19), art. 32. - Issued: 18.11.2015. Made: 12.11.2015. Coming into operation: 14.12.2015. Effect: S.R. 2014/307 amended. Territorial extent & classification: NI. General. - 8p.: 30 cm. - 978-0-337-99900-0 £4.25

The Ship Recycling Facilities Regulations (Northern Ireland) 2015 No. 2015/229. - Enabling power: European Communities Act 1972, s. 2 (2) & Waste and Contaminated Land (Northern Ireland) Order 1997, art. 6 (6). - Issued: 24.04.2015. Made: 22.04.2015. Coming into operation: 18.05.2015. Effect: S.R. 2003/493 amended. - 4p.: 30 cm. - 978-0-337-99782-2 £4.25

The Storage of Carbon Dioxide (Access to Infrastructure) Regulations (Northern Ireland) 2015 No. 2015/388. - Enabling power: European Communities Act 1972, s. 2 (2). - Issued: 07.12.2015. Made: 01.12.2015. Coming into operation: 04.01.2016. Effect: None. Territorial extent & classification: NI. General. - EC note: These regs form part of the implementation in Northern Ireland of Directive 2009/31/EC on the geological storage of carbon dioxide. - 16p.: 30 cm. - 978-0-337-99911-6 £6.00

The Storage of Carbon Dioxide (Licensing etc.) Regulations (Northern Ireland) 2015 No. 2015/387. - Enabling power: European Communities Act 1972, s. 2 (2). - Issued: 07.12.2015. Made: 01.12.2015. Coming into operation: 04.01.2016. Effect: None. Territorial extent & classification: NI. General. - EC note: These regs form part of the implementation in Northern Ireland of Directive 2009/31/EC on the geological storage of carbon dioxide. - 24p.: 30 cm. - 978-0-337-99910-9 £6.00

The Waste (Fees and Charges) (Amendment) Regulations (Northern Ireland) 2015 No. 2015/21. - Enabling power: European Communities Act 1972, s. 2 (2) & S.I. 1997/2778 (N.I.19), arts 39 (2) (3). - Issued: 02.02.2015. Made: 27.01.2015. Coming into operation: 27.02.2015. Effect: S.R. 1999/362; 2003/493 amended. Territorial extent & classification: NI. General. - 4p.: 30 cm. - 978-0-337-99583-5 £4.25

The Waste Management Licensing (Amendment No. 2) Regulations (Northern Ireland) 2015 No. 2015/386. - Enabling power: S.I. 1997/2778 (N.I. 19), arts 3 (3) (a), 39 (2) (a). - Issued: 03.12.2015. Made: 30.11.2015. Coming into operation: 31.12.2015. Effect: S.R. 1999/362; 2003/493 amended. Territorial extent and classification: NI. General. - 8p.: 30 cm. - 978-0-337-99908-6 £4.25

The Waste Management Licensing (Amendment) Regulations (Northern Ireland) 2015 No. 2015/301. - Enabling power: S.I. 1997/2778 (NI.19), art. 3 (5). - Issued: 13.07.2015. Made: 08.07.2015. Coming into operation: 17.08.2015. Effect: S.R. 2003/493 amended. Territorial extent and classification: NI. General. - 8p.: 30 cm. - 978-0-337-99845-4 £6.00

The Water Framework Directive (Classification, Priority Substances and Shellfish Waters) Regulations (Northern Ireland) 2015 No. 2015/351. - Enabling power: European Communities Act 1972, s. 2 (2) & S.I. 1999/662 (NI.6), art. 5. - Issued: 07.10.2015. Made: 02.10.2015. Coming into operation: 23.10.2015. Effect: S.R. 2011/10; 2012/442; 2015/45 revoked. Territorial extent & classification: NI. General. - 56p.: 30 cm. - 978-0-337-99879-9 £10.00

The Water Framework Directive (Priority Substances and Classification) (Amendment) Regulations (Northern Ireland) 2015 No. 2015/45. - Enabling power: European Communities Act 1972, s. 2 (2) & S.I. 1999/662 (NI.6), art. 5. - Issued: 13.02.2015. Made: 10.02.2015. Coming into operation: 04.03.2015. Effect: S.R. 2011/10 amended. Territorial extent & classification: NI. General. - Revoked by S.R. 2015/351 (ISBN 9780337998799). - 42p.: 30 cm. - 978-0-337-99608-5 £10.00

Environmental protection: Marine conservation

The Marine Conservation (Fixed Monetary Penalties) Order (Northern Ireland) 2015 No. 2015/279. - Enabling power: Marine Act (Northern Ireland) 2013, ss. 35, 46 (1). - Issued: 23.06.2015. Made: 18.06.2015. Coming into operation: 19.06.2015. Effect: S.I. 2006/3336 (NI. 21) amended. Territorial extent & classification: NI. General. - Laid before the Assembly in draft. - 8p.: 30 cm. - 978-0-337-99830-0 £6.00

European Communities: Nature conservation

The Conservation (Natural Habitats, etc.) (Amendment) Regulations (Northern Ireland) 2015 No. 2015/182. - Enabling power: European Communities Act 1972, s. 2 (2). - Issued: 30.30.2015. Made: 25.03.2015. Coming into operation: 01.04.2015. Effect: S.R. 1995/380 amended. Territorial extent & classification: NI. General. - With correction slip dated April 2015. - 12p.: 30 cm. - 978-0-337-99743-3 £6.00

Fair employment

The Fair Employment and Treatment Order (Amendment) Regulations (Northern Ireland) 2015 No. 2015/144. - Enabling power: European Communities Act 1972, s. 2 (2). - Issued: 23.03.2015. Made: 10.03.2015. Coming into operation: 06.04.2015. Effect: S.I. 1998/3162 (NI.21) amended. Territorial extent & classification: NI. General. - 2p.: 30 cm. - 978-0-337-99719-8 £4.25

The Fair Employment (Specification of Public Authorities) (Amendment) Order (Northern Ireland) 2015 No. 2015/36. - Enabling power: S.I. 1998/3162 (N.I. 21), arts 50, 51. - Issued: 10.02.2015. Made: 04.02.2015. Coming into operation: 01.03.2015. Effect: S.R. 2004/494 amended & S.R. 2013/49 revoked. Territorial extent & classification: NI. General. - 8p.: 30 cm. - With correction slip dated February 2015. - 978-0-337-99600-9 £6.00

Family law: Child support

The Child Maintenance (2008 Act) (Commencement No. 15) Order (Northern Ireland) 2015 No. 2015/57 (C.6). - Enabling power: Child Maintenance Act (Northern Ireland) 2008, s. 41 (1). Bringing into operation various provisions of the 2008 Act on 14.02.2015; 23.03.2015 in accord. with art. 2. - Issued: 18.02.2015. Made: 13.02.2015. Effect: None. Territorial extent & classification: NI. General. - 4p.: 30 cm. - 978-0-337-99620-7 £4.25

The Child Support (Modification, Miscellaneous and Consequential Amendments) Regulations (Northern Ireland) 2015 No. 2015/116. - Enabling power: S.I. 1991/2628 (NI.23), arts 28ZD (1), 34 (1) (b), 38B (3), 45D (2) (c), 47 (1) (2) (i), 48 (4), sch. 1, para. 5 (1). - Issued: 06.03.2015. Made: 03.03.2015. Coming into operation: In accord. with reg. 1. Effect: S.R. 1992/340, 341, 342, 390; 1999/162; 2008/403; 2012/427 amended. Territorial extent & classification: NI. General. - 8p.: 30 cm. - 978-0-337-99658-0 £4.25

Fire and rescue services: Pensions

The Firefighters' Compensation Scheme (Amendment) (No. 2) and the New Firefighters' Pension Scheme (Amendment) (No. 4) Order (Northern Ireland) 2015 No. 2015/422. - Enabling power: S.I. 1984/1821 (N.I. 11), art. 10 (1) (3) (4) (5). - Issued: 22.12.2015. Made: 17.12.2015. Coming into operation: 18.01.2016. Effect: S.R. 2007/143 amended. Territorial extent & classification: NI. General. - 20p.: 30 cm. - 978-0-337-99935-2 £6.00

The Firefighters' Compensation Scheme (Amendment) Order (Northern Ireland) 2015 No. 2015/7. - Enabling power: S.I. 1984/1821 (N.I. 11), art. 10 (1) (3) (4) (5). - Issued: 23.01.2015. Made: 19.01.2015. Coming into operation: 01.04.2015. Effect: S.R. 2007/143 amended. Territorial extent & classification: NI. General. - 8p.: 30 cm. - 978-0-337-99567-5 £6.00

The Firefighters' Pension Scheme (Amendment) (No. 2) Order (Northern Ireland) 2015 No. 2015/11. - Enabling power: S.I. 1984/1821 (N.I. 11), art. 10 (1) (3) (4) (5). - Issued: 22.01.2015. Made: 19.01.2015. Coming into operation: 12.02.2015. Effect: S.R. 2007/144 amended. Territorial extent & classification: NI. General. - 8p.: 30 cm. - 978-0-337-99566-8 £4.25

The Firefighters' Pension Scheme (Amendment) (No. 3) Order (Northern Ireland) 2015 No. 2015/421. - Enabling power: S.I. 1984/1821 (N.I. 11), art. 10 (1) (3) (4) (5). - Issued: 22.12.2015. Made: 17.12.2015. Coming into operation: 18.01.2016. Effect: S.R. 2007/144 amended. Territorial extent & classification: NI. General. - 8p.: 30 cm. - 978-0-337-99934-5 £6.00

The Firefighters' Pension Scheme (Amendment) Order (Northern Ireland) 2015 No. 2015/8. - Enabling power: S.I. 1984/1821 (N.I. 11), art. 10 (1) (3) (4) (5). - Issued: 22.01.2015. Made: 19.01.2015. Coming into operation: 01.04.2015. Effect: S.R. 2007/144 amended. Territorial extent & classification: NI. General. - 8p.: 30 cm. - 978-0-337-99563-7 £4.25

The New Firefighters' Pension Scheme (Amendment) (No. 2) Order (Northern Ireland) 2015 No. 2015/10. - Enabling power: S.I. 1984/1821 (N.I. 11), art. 10 (1) (3) (4) (5). - Issued: 22.01.2015. Made: 19.01.2015. Coming into operation: 12.02.2015. Effect: S.R. 2007/215 amended. Territorial extent & classification: NI. General. - 4p.: 30 cm. - 978-0-337-99565-1 £4.25

The New Firefighters' Pension Scheme (Amendment) (No. 3) Order (Northern Ireland) 2015 No. 2015/355. - Enabling power: S.I. 1984/1821 (NI. 11), art. 10 (1) (3) (4) (5). - Issued: 14.10.2015. Made: 09.10.2015. Coming into operation: 08.12.2015. Effect: S.R. 2007/215 amended. Territorial extent & classification: NI. General. - 4p.: 30 cm. - 978-0-337-99883-6 £4.25

The New Firefighters' Pension Scheme (Amendment) Order (Northern Ireland) 2015 No. 2015/9. - Enabling power: S.I. 1984/1821 (N.I. 11), art. 10 (1) (3) (4) (5). - Issued: 23.01.2015. Made: 19.01.2015. Coming into operation: 01.04.2015. Effect: S.R. 2007/215 amended. Territorial extent & classification: NI. General. - 36p.: 30 cm. - 978-0-337-99564-4 £10.00

Firearms and ammunition

The Firearms (Variation of Fees) Order (Northern Ireland) 2015 No. 2015/405. - Enabling power: S.I. 2004/702 (N.I. 3), art. 75 (3). - Issued: 10.12.2015. Made: 01.12.2015. Coming into operation: 22.02.2016. Effect: S.I. 2004/702 (NI. 3) varied. Territorial extent & classification: NI. General. - 4p.: 30 cm. - 978-0-337-99923-9 £4.25

Fisheries

The European Maritime and Fisheries Fund (Financial Assistance) Regulations (Northern Ireland) 2015 No. 2015/399. - Enabling power: European Communities Act 1972, s. 2 (2), sch. 2, para. 1A. - Issued: 08.12.2015. Made: 03.12.2015. Coming into operation: 14.01.2016. Effect: S.R. 2002/6; 2004/109; 2008/394, 500 revoked with saving. Territorial extent & classification: NI. General. - 8p.: 30 cm. - 978-0-337-99918-5 £6.00

The Fisheries (Amendment) Regulations (Northern Ireland) 2015 No. 2015/239. - Enabling power: Fisheries Act (Northern Ireland) 1966, ss. 26 (1), 89, 95 (1). - Issued: 07.05.2015. Made: 01.05.2015. Coming into operation: 01.06.2015. Effect: S.R. 2014/17 amended. Territorial extent & classification: NI. General. - 4p.: 30 cm. - 978-0-337-99791-4 £4.25

Food

The Country of Origin of Certain Meats Regulations (Northern Ireland) 2015 No. 2015/321. - Enabling power: S.I. 1991/762 (N.I.7), arts 15 (1), 16 (1), 25, 26 (3), 32 (1), 47 (2) & European Communities Act 1972, s. 2 (2), sch. 2, para. 1A. - Issued: 10.08.2015. Made: 04.08.2015. Coming into operation: 11.09.2015. Effect: S.I. 1991/762 (N.I.) modified. Territorial extent & classification: NI. General. - 8p: 30 cm. - 978-0-337-99856-0 £6.00

The Honey Regulations (Northern Ireland) 2015 No. 2015/261. - Enabling power: S.I. 1991/762 (N.I. 7), arts 15 (1) (e), 16 (1), 25 (1) (3), 26 (3), 47 (2). - Issued: 03.06.2015. Made: 29.05.2015. Coming into operation: 24.06.2015. Effect: S.R. 2014/223 amended & S.R. 2003/383; 2005/385; 2008/126 revoked. Territorial extent & classification: NI. General. - EC note: These Regs implement Council Directive 2001/110/EC relating to honey. - 16p.: 30 cm. - 978-0-337-99819-5 £6.00

The Natural Mineral Water, Spring Water and Bottled Drinking Water Regulations (Northern Ireland) 2015 No. 2015/365. - Enabling power: S.I. 1991/762 (N.I. 7), arts 15 (1), 16 (1), 25 (1) (3), 26 (3), 32, 47 (2) & European Communities Act 1972, sch. 2, para. 1A. - Issued: 11.11.2015. Made: 05.11.2015. Coming into operation: 28.11.2015. Effect: S.R. 2009/413; 2013/66; 2014/223 amended & S.R. 2007/420; 2009/260; 2010/68, 127; 2011/ 53 revoked. - These Regulations implement and enforce the following European instruments: (a) Council Directive 98/83/EC relating to the quality of water intended for human consumption; (b) Directive 2009/54/EC of the European Parliament and of the Council on exploitation and marketing of natural mineral waters; (c) Commission Directive 2003/40/EC establishing the list, concentration limits and labelling requirements for the constituents of natural mineral waters; (d) Commission Regulation (EU) no. 115/2010 laying down the conditions for use of activated alumina for the removal of fluoride from natural mineral waters and water bottled and labelled "spring water"; (e) In relation to water bottled and labelled as "spring water" and bottled drinking water, Council Directive 2013/51/Euratom laying down the requirements of the health of the general public with regard to radioactive substances in water. - 44p.: 30 cm. - 978-0-337-99895-9 £10.00

Gas

The Electricity and Gas (Ownership Unbundling) Regulations (Northern Ireland) 2015 No. 2015/249. - Enabling power: European Communities Act 1972, s. 2 (2). - Issued: 18.05.2015. Made: 13.05.2015. Coming into operation: 05.06.2015. Effect: S.I. 1992/231 (NI. 1); 1996/275 (NI.2) amended. Territorial extent & classification: NI. General. - 4p.: 30 cm. - 978-0-337-99799-0 £4.25

The Gas and Electricity Licence Modification and Appeals Regulations (Northern Ireland) 2015 No. 2015/1. - Enabling power: European Communities Act 1972, s. 2 (2). - Issued: 12.01.2015. Made: 05.01.2015. Coming into operation: 06.01.2015. Effect: S.I. 1992/231 (NI. 1); 1996/275 (NI.2); 2003/419 (NI.6) amended. Territorial extent & classification: NI. General. - 30p.: 30 cm. - 978-0-337-99557-6 £6.00

Government resources and accounts

The Whole of Government Accounts (Designation of Bodies) Order (Northern Ireland) 2015 No. 2015/152. - Enabling power: Government Resources and Accounts Act (Northern Ireland) 2001, s. 15 (1). - Issued: 17.03.2015. Made: 12.03.2015. Coming into operation: 14.04.2015. Effect: None. Territorial extent & classification: NI. General. - 8p.: 30 cm. - 978-0-337-99688-7 £6.00

Harbours

The Donaghadee Harbour (Transfer of Harbour Undertaking) Order (Northern Ireland) 2015 No. 2015/22. - Enabling power: Harbours Act (Northern Ireland) 1970, s. 1 (1) (2), sch. 1, 2. - Issued: 02.02.2015. Made: 28.01.2015. Coming into operation: In accord. with art. 1. Effect: Georgii IV Regis Cap CXIII & S.R. 2008/143; 2010/141.Territorial extent & classification: NI. General. - Subject to affirmative resolution of the Assembly. - 6p.: 30 cm. - 978-0-337-99584-2 £4.25

The Donaghadee Harbour (Transfer of Harbour Undertaking) Order (Northern Ireland) 2015 No. 2015/22. - Enabling power: Harbours Act (Northern Ireland) 1970, s. 1 (1) (2), sch. 1, 2. pt. 1. - Issued: 13.03.2015. Made: 28.01.2015. Coming into operation: In accord. with art. 1. Effect: Georgii IV Regis Cap CXIII & S.R. 2008/143; 2010/141 repealed & revoked. Territorial extent & classification: NI. General. - Affirmed by resolution of the Assembly on 2nd March 2015. - 8p., map: 30 cm. - 978-0-337-99677-1 £6.00

The Londonderry Port and Harbour (Variation of Limits) Order (Northern Ireland) 2015 No. 2015/244. - Enabling power: Harbours Act (Northern Ireland) 1970, s. 1, sch. 1. - Issued: 12.05.2015. Made: 07.05.2015. Coming into operation: In accord. with art. 1. Effect: None. - Subject to affirmative resolution procedure of the Assembly. - 2p.: 30 cm. - 978-0-337-99795-2 £4.25

The Londonderry Harbour (Variation of Limits) Order (Northern Ireland) 2015 No. 2015/244. - Enabling power: Harbours Act (Northern Ireland) 1970, s. 1 (1), sch. 1. - Issued: 02.07.2015. Made: 07.05.2015. Coming into operation: 30.06.2015 in accord. with art. 1. Effect: None. - Affirmed by resolution of the Assembly on 29.06.2015. - 2p.: 30 cm. - 978-0-337-99839-3 £4.25

Health and personal social services

The Health and Personal Social Services (General Medical Services Contracts) (Amendment) Regulations (Northern Ireland) 2015 No. 2015/26. - Enabling power: S.I. 1972/1265 (N.I. 14), arts 57A, 57E, 106, 107 (6). - Issued: 04.02.2015 Made: 30.01.2015. Coming into operation: 23.02.2015. Effect: S.R. 2004/140 amended. Territorial extent and classification: NI. General. - 4p.: 30 cm. - 978-0-337-99590-3 £4.25

The Health and Personal Social Services (Superannuation), Health and Social Care (Pension Scheme) (Amendment) Regulations (Northern Ireland) 2015 No. 2015/56. - Enabling power: S.I. 1972/1073 (N.I. 10), arts 12 (1) (2), 14 (1) (2) (3), sch. 3. - Issued: 17.02.2015. Made: 12.02.2015. Coming into operation: 16.03.2015. Effect: S.R. 1995/95; 2008/256 amended. Territorial extent & classification: NI. General. - 8p.: 30 cm. - 978-0-337-99619-1 £6.00

The Health and Personal Social Services (Superannuation Scheme, Additional Voluntary Contributions and Injury Benefits), Health and Social Care (Pensions Scheme) (Amendment) Regulations (Northern Ireland) 2015 No. 2015/121. - Enabling power: S.I. 1972/1073 (N.I. 10), arts 12 (1) (2), 14 (1) (2) (3), sch. 3. - Issued: 11.03.2015. Made: 06.03.2015. Coming into operation: 01.04.2015. Effect: S.R. 1995/95; 1999/294; 2001/367; 2008/256 amended. Territorial extent & classification: NI. General. - 40p.: 30 cm. - 978-0-337-99665-8 £10.00

The Health and Social Care Pension Scheme Regulations (Northern Ireland) 2015 No. 2015/120. - Enabling power: Public Service Pensions Act (Northern Ireland) 2014, ss. 1 (1) (2) (e), 2 to 4, 5 (1) (3) (5), 7 (1) (4), 8 (1) (a) (2) (a), 11 (1), 12 (1), (6) (7), 14, 18 (5) to (8), 25, paragraph (c) of the definition of "employer" in section 34, sch. 2, para. 5, sch. 3. - Issued: 13.03.2015. Made: 06.04.2015. Coming into operation: 01.04.2015. Effect: None. Territorial extent & classification: NI. General. - 148p.: 30 cm. - 978-0-337-99671-9 £23.25

The Health and Social Care Pension Scheme (Transitional and Consequential Provisions) Regulations (Northern Ireland) 2015 No. 2015/122. - Enabling power: S.I. 1972/1073 (N.I. 10), sch. 3, arts 12 (1) (2) & Public Service Pensions Act (Northern Ireland) 2014, ss. 1, 3, 18 (5), sch. 3. - Issued: 11.03.2015. Made: 06.03.2015. Coming into operation: 01.04.2015. Effect: S.R. 1995/95 amended. Territorial extent & classification: NI. General. - 44p.: 30 cm. - 978-0-337-99672-6 £10.00

The Health Service Workers (Consequent Provisions) Regulations (Northern Ireland) 2015 No. 2015/167. - Enabling power: Public Service Pensions Act (Northern Ireland) 2014, ss. 1 (1) (2) (e), 2 (1), 3 (1) (2) (3) (a) (4). - Issued: 24.03.2015. Made: 18.03.2015. Coming into operation: 01.04.2015. Effect: 1993 c.49; S.R. 1996/493 modified. Territorial extent & classification: NI. General. - Laid before the Assembly in draft. - 8p.: 30 cm. - 978-0-337-99728-0 £6.00

The Health Services (Cross-Border Health Care) (Amendment) Regulations (Northern Ireland) 2015 No. 2015/130. - Enabling power: European Communities Act 1972, s. 2 (2). - Issued: 11.03.2015. Made: 06.03.2015. Coming into operation: 27.03.2015. Effect: S.R. 2013/299 amended. Territorial extent and classification: NI. General. - 4p.: 30 cm. - 978-0-337-99669-6 £4.25

Optical Charges and Payments (Amendment) Regulations (Northern Ireland) 2015 No. 2015/266. - Enabling power: S.I 1972/1265 (N.I. 14), arts 62, 98, 106, 107 (6), sch. 15. - Issued: 09.06.2015. Made: 05.06.2015. Coming into operation: 29.06.2015. Effect: S.R. 1997/191 amended. Territorial extent & classification: NI. General. - 8p.: 30 cm. - 978-0-337-99821-8 £4.25

Provision of Health Services to Persons Not Ordinarily Resident Regulations (Northern Ireland) 2015 No. 2015/27. - Enabling power: S.I. 1972/1265 (N.I. 14), arts 42, 106 (b), 107 (6). - Issued: 04.02.2015. Made: 30.01.2015. Coming into force: 23,02,2015. Effect: S.R. 2009/186; partially revoked & S.R. 2005/551; 2008/377; 2013/302 revoked. Territorial extent and classification: NI. General. - 20p.: 30 cm. - 978-0-337-99591-0 £6.00

Health and safety

The Biocidal Products (Fees and Charges) Regulations (Northern Ireland) 2015 No. 2015/254. - Enabling power: European Communities Act 1972, s. 2 (2) & S.I. 1978/1039 (NI. 9), arts. 40 (2) (4), 55 (2). - Issued: 22.05.2015. Made: 20.05.2015. Coming into operation: 01.07.2015. Effect: S.R. 2013/207 revoked with saving. - EC note: The Biocides Regulation replaces Directive 98/8/EC (OJ No. L123, 24.4.98, p.1) of the European Parliament and the Council of 16th February 1998, which laid down harmonised rules for the placing on the market of biocidal products. The Biocides Regulation lays down revised harmonised rules for the approval of active substances and the making available on the market of biocidal products. - 8p.: 30 cm. - 978-0-337-99812-6 £6.00

The Classification, Labelling and Packaging of Chemicals (Amendment) Regulations (Northern Ireland) 2015 No. 2015/265. - Enabling power: European Communities Act 1972, s. 2 (2), sch. 2, para. 1A & S.I. 1978/1039 (N.I. 9), arts. 17 (1) (2) (3), 54 (1), 55 (2). - Issued: 09.06.2015. Made: 04.06.2015. Coming into operation: 01.07.2015. Effect: 1929 c. 13 (NI); S.R. 1991/446; 1996/119; 1997/193, 248; 1999/90; 2000/388; 2003/34, 35, 52, 152; 2010/325; 2012/179; 2013/206 amended. Territorial extent and classification: NI. General. - 12p., col. figs: 30 cm. - 978-0-337-99820-1 £6.00

The Control of Major Accident Hazards Regulations (Northern Ireland) 2015 No. 2015/325. - Enabling power: European Communities Act 1972, s. 2 (2) & S.I. 1978/1039 (N.I. 9), arts 17(1) to (6), 40 (2) to (4), 54 (1), 55 (2), sch. 3, paras 1 (1) (2), 14, 15, 19. - Issued: 28.08.2015. Made: 26.08.2015. Coming into operation: 28.09.2015. Effect: 1929 c. 13 (N.I.) & S.R. & O. 1930 No. 11 & S.R. 1983/43; 2010/412; 2013/160 & S.I. 2005/2042 amended & S.R. 2012/255 amended & partially revoked & S.R. 2013/161 partially revoked & S.R 2000/93; 2005/305; 2014/74 revoked. Territorial extent & classification: NI. General. - EC note: This Statutory Rule implements the Directive 2012/18/EU (Seveso III). - 48p.: 30 cm. - 978-0-337-99859-1 £10.00

The Explosives (Appointment of Authorities and Enforcement) Regulations (Northern Ireland) 2015 No. 2015/236. - Enabling power: European Communities Act 1972, s. 2 (2), sch.2, para. 1A & S.I. 1978/1039 (NI.9), arts 17(1) to (6), 55 (2), sch. 3, paras 1 (1) (4), 5, 12 (1), 14 (1). - Issued: 01.05.2015. Made: 24.04.2015. Coming into operation: in accord with reg. 1(2). Effect: S.R. 2009/273 amended & partially revoked. Territorial extent & classification: NI. General. - EC note: The Explosives (Appointment of Authorities and Enforcement) Regulations (Northern Ireland) 2015 provides for the appointment of competent authorities in relation to Regulation (EC) No 1272/2008 of the European Parliament and of the Council of 16 December 2008 on classification, labelling and packaging of substances and mixtures. - 12p.: 30 cm. - 978-0-337-99787-7 £6.00

The Genetically Modified Organisms (Contained Use) Regulations (Northern Ireland) 2015 No. 2015/339. - Enabling power: European Communities Act 1972, s. 2 (2) & S.I. 1978/1039 (N.I. 9), arts 2 (5), 17 (1) to (5), 40 (2) (4), 54 (1) (2), 55 (2) sch. 3, paras 1 (1) (2) (3) (4) (5), 2, 3 (1), 4, 5, 7 (2), 8, 10, 12 (1) (3), 13, 14 (1), 15, 16, 19. - Issued: 25.09.2015. Made: 18.09.2015. Coming into operation: 23.10.2015. Effect: S.I. 2008/2852 & S.R. 2012/255 amended & S.R. 2001/295; 2006/524; 2010/343 revoked. - With correction slip dated November 2015. - 40p.: 30 cm. - 978-0-337-99868-3 £10.00

The Health and Safety (Miscellaneous Repeals, Revocations and Amendments) Regulations (Northern Ireland) 2015 No. 2015/223. - Enabling power: S.I. 1978/1039 (N.I. 9), arts. 17 (1), 20 (2), 40 (2), 45 (1), 54 (1) (2), 55 (2), paras 1 (1) (2) (3) (4) (8) (9) (10) (11) & S.I. 1978/1039 (N.I. 9), sch. 3, paras. 3, 5, 7, 8, 9, 10, 11, 12 (1), 13, 14, 15, 17, 20 (a) (b). - Issued: 22.04.2015. Made: 17.04.2015. Coming into operation: 01.06.2015. Effect: S.R. 1992/71; 1993/37; 1995/491; 1999/90; 2005/279 & S.I. 2008/2852 amended & 1929 c.13; 1965 c.20 & S.I. 1978/1039 (N.I. 9) partially repealed & 1922 c.35 repealed & 9 SRs partially revoked & 16 SRs revoked. Territorial extent & classification: NI. General. - With correction slip, dated April 2015. - 12p: 30 cm. - 978-0-337-99777-8 £6.00

Health and social care

The Health and Social Care (Disciplinary Procedures) (Amendment) Regulations (Northern Ireland) 2015 No. 2015/205. - Enabling power: S.I. 1972/1265 (N.I. 4), arts 61, 62, 63, 106 & S.I. 1988/2249 (N.I. 24), art. 10. - Issued: 01.04.2015. Made: 30.03.2015. Coming into operation: 23.04.2015. Effect: S.R. 2014/267 amended. Territorial extent & classification: NI. General. - 4p: 30 cm. - 978-0-337-99755-6 £4.25

Health care charges

The Recovery of Health Services Charges (Amounts) (Amendment) Regulations (Northern Ireland) 2015 No. 2015/186. - Enabling power: S.I. 2006/1944 (N.I. 13), arts 5 (2) (5), 19 (3). - Issued: 01.04.2015. Made: 25.03.2015. Coming into operation: 01.04.2015. Effect: S.R. 2006/507 amended. Territorial extent & classification: NI. General. - 4p.: 30 cm. - 978-0-337-99748-8 £4.25

Housing

The Housing Benefit (Executive Determinations) (Amendment) Regulations (Northern Ireland) 2015 No. 2015/2. - Enabling power: Social Security Contributions and Benefits (Northern Ireland) Act 1992, ss 122 (1) (d), 129 (A) (2), 171 (1) (3) to (5). - Issued: 15.01.2015. Made: 13.01.2015. Coming into operation: 20.01.2015. Effect: S.R. 2008/100 amended. Territorial extent and classification: NI. General. - 4p.: 30 cm. - 978-0-337-99558-3 £4.25

The Housing Benefit (Income from earnings) (Amendment) Regulations (Northern Ireland) 2015 No. 2015/19. - Enabling power: Social Security Contributions and Benefits (Northern Ireland) Act 1992, ss. 132 (3) (4), 132A (3). - Issued: 29.01.2015. Made: 26.01.2015. Coming into operation: 18.02.2015. Effect: S.R. 2006/405, 406 amended. Territorial extent and classification: NI. General. - 4p.: 30 cm. - 978-0-337-99579-8 £4.25

The Social Security Benefits Up-rating Order (Northern Ireland) 2015 No. 2015/124. - Enabling power: Social Security Administration (Northern Ireland) Act 1992, ss. 132, 132A,165 (1) (4) (5). - Issued: 09.03.2015. Made: 05.03.2015. Coming into operation: In accord. with 1. Effect: 1992 c.7 & S.R. 1987/459; 1996/198; 2006/405, 406; 2008/280 amended & S.R. 2014/78 revoked. Territorial extent & classification: NI. General. - For approval of the Assembly before the expiration of six months from the date of its coming into operation. Superseded by approved version SR 2015/124 (ISBN 9780337997853). - 44p.: 30 cm. - 978-0-337-99663-4 £10.00

The Social Security Benefits Up-rating Order (Northern Ireland) 2015 No. 2015/124. - Enabling power: Social Security Administration (Northern Ireland) Act 1992, ss. 132, 132A, 165 (1) (4) (5). - Issued: 30.04.2015. Made: 05.03.2015. Coming into operation: In accord. with art. 1. Effect: 1966 c.6 (N.I.); 1992 c.7; 1993 c.49; S.R. 1987/30, 460; 1992/32; 1994/461; 1995/35; 1996/198; 2002/380; 2003/28; 2006/405, 406; 2008/280; 2010/407; amended & S.R. 2014/78 revoked (13.04.2015). Territorial extent & classification: NI. General. - Approved by resolution of the Assembly on 27th April 2015. Supersedes pre-approved SR 2015/124 (ISBN 9780337996634). - 48p.: 30 cm. - 978-0-337-99785-3 £10.00

The Social Security (Miscellaneous Amendments No. 2) Regulations (Northern Ireland) 2015 No. 2015/163. - Enabling power: S.I. 1991/2628 (NI. 23), arts 39 (1), 47 (1) & Social Security Contributions and Benefits (Northern Ireland) Act 1992, ss. 122 (1) (a) (d), 132 (3) (4) (b), 132A (2) (3), 171 (1) (3) (4) & S.I. 1995/2705 (NI.15), arts 6 (5), 14 (1) (4), 36 (1) (2) & S.I. 1998/1506 (NI. 10), arts 11 (6), 74 (1) (5) & Welfare Reform Act (Northern Ireland) 2007, ss. 17 (1) (3), 25 (2). - Issued: 23.03.2015. Made: 16.03.2015. Coming into operation: 06.04.2015. Effect: S.R. 1987/459; 1992/341; 1996/198; 2001/18; 2006/405, 406; 2008/280 amended. Territorial extent & classification: NI. General. - 4p.: 30 cm. - 978-0-337-99724-2 £4.25

The Social Security (Miscellaneous Amendments) Regulations (Northern Ireland) 2015 No. 2015/34. - Enabling power: Social Security Contributions and Benefits (Northern Ireland) Act 1992, ss. 35 (3), 35B (11), 132 (3) (4), 132A, 134 (2) (4), 171 (1) (3) (4) & Social Security Administration (Northern Ireland) Act 1992, ss. 158C, 189 (4) & S.I. 1995/2705, arts 14 (1) (4), 36 (2) & State Pension Credit Act (Northern Ireland) 2002, ss. 15 (3) (6), 19 (1) to (3) & Welfare Reform Act (Northern Ireland) 2007, s. 25 (2) (a). - Issued: 06.02.2015. Made: 03.02.2015. Coming into operation: 23.02.2015. Effect: S.R. 1987/170; 2000/91; 2001/102; 2006/405 amended. Territorial extent & classification: NI. General. - 8p.: 30 cm. - 978-0-337-99595-8 £4.25

Human rights

The Attorney General's Human Rights Guidance (Police Service of Northern Ireland - Protection of Life) Order (Northern Ireland) 2015 No. 2015/356. - Enabling power: Justice (Northern Ireland) Act 2004, s. 8 (3) (c). - Issued: 15.10.2015. Made: 12.10.2015. Coming into operation: 01.12.2015. Effect: None. Territorial extent & classification: NI. General. - 2p: 30 cm. - 978-0-337-99885-0 £4.25

The Attorney General's Human Rights Guidance (Probation Board for Northern Ireland) Order (Northern Ireland) 2015 No. 2015/51. - Enabling power: Justice (Northern Ireland) Act 2004, s. 8 (3) (c). - Issued: 16.02.2015. Made: 12.02.2015. Coming into operation: 23.03.2015. Effect: None. - 2p: 30 cm. - 978-0-337-99614-6 £4.25

The Attorney General's Human Rights Guidance (Youth Justice Agency - Conditions of Detention) Order (Northern Ireland) 2015 No. 2015/50. - Enabling power: Justice (Northern Ireland) Act 2004, s. 8 (3) (c). - Issued: 16.02.2015. Made: 12.02.2015. Coming into operation: 23.02.2015. Effect: None. - 2p: 30 cm. - 978-0-337-99613-9 £4.25

The Attorney General's Human Rights Guidance (Youth Justice Agency - Restorative Justice) Order (Northern Ireland) 2015 No. 2015/362. - Enabling power: Justice (Northern Ireland) Act 2004, s. 8 (3) (c). - Issued: 30.10.2015. Made: 27.10.2015. Coming into operation: 01.01.2016. Effect: None. Territorial extent & classification: NI. General. - 2p: 30 cm. - 978-0-337-99891-1 £4.25

Industrial training

The Industrial Training Levy (Construction Industry) Order (Northern Ireland) 2015 No. 2015/276. - Enabling power: S.I. 1984/1159 (N.I. 9), arts 23 (2) (3), 24 (3) (4). - Issued: 22.06.2015. Made: 03.06.2015. Coming into operation: 31.08.2015. Effect: None. Territorial extent & classification: NI. General. - 8p.: 30 cm. - 978-0-337-99826-3 £4.25

Inquiry into historical institutional abuse

The Inquiry into Historical Institutional Abuse (Amendment of Terms of Reference) Order (Northern Ireland) 2015 No. 2015/55. - Enabling power: Inquiry into Historical Institutional Abuse Act (Northern Ireland) 2013, s. 1 (3). - Issued: 23.02.2015. Made: 10.02.2015. Coming into operation: 11.02.2015. Effect: None. Territorial extent & classification: NI. General. - This Statutory Rule has been printed in substitution of the SR of the same number and ISBN issued 17.02.2015 and is being issued free of charge to all known recipients of that Statutory Rule. - 2p.: 30 cm. - 978-0-337-99618-4 £4.25

Insolvency

The Insolvency (Amendment) Rules (Northern Ireland) 2015 No. 2015/262. - Enabling power: S.I. 1989/2405 (N.I. 19), art. 359. - Issued: 03.06.2015. Made: 28.05.2015. Coming into operation: 03.09.2015. Effect: S.R. 1991/364 amended. Territorial extent & classification: NI. General. - With correction slip dated June 2015. - 16p: 30 cm. - 978-0-337-99818-8 £6.00

The Insolvency (Northern Ireland) Order 2005 (Consequential Amendments) Order (Northern Ireland) 2015 No. 2015/159. - Enabling power: S.I. 2005/1455 (NI. 10), art. 30. - Issued: 23.03.2015. Made: 12.03.2015. Coming into operation: 21.04.2015. Effect: 12 Acts; 9 S.Is & 29 S.Rs amended. Territorial extent & classification: NI. General. - 16p: 30 cm. - 978-0-337-99721-1 £6.00

Justice

The Criminal Justice (2013 Act) (Commencement No.5) Order (Northern Ireland) 2015 No. 2015/296 (C.24). - Enabling power: Criminal Justice Act (Northern Ireland) Act 2013, s. 13 (3). Bringing various provisions of the 2013 Act into operation 10.07.2015, in accord. with art. 2. - Issued: 10.07.2015. Made: 07.07.2015. Effect: None. Territorial extent & classification: NI. General. - 2p.: 30 cm. - 978-0-337-99844-7 £4.25

The Criminal Justice (2015 Act) (Commencement No. 1) Order (Northern Ireland) 2015 No. 2015/320 (C.26). - Enabling power: Justice Act (Northern Ireland) 2015, s. 106 (2). Bringing various provisions of the 2015 Act into operation 01.09.2015, in accord. with art. 2. - Issued: 06.08.2015. Made: 03.08.2015. Effect: None. Territorial extent & classification: NI. General. - 2p.: 30 cm. - 978-0-337-99855-3 £4.25

The Criminal Justice (2015 Act) (Commencement No. 2) Order (Northern Ireland) 2015 No. 2015/324 (C.27). - Enabling power: Justice Act (Northern Ireland) 2015, s. 106 (2). Bringing various provisions of the 2015 Act into operation 01.09.2015; 30.09.2015, in accord. with art. 2 & 3. - Issued: 27.08.2015. Made: 19.08.2015. Effect: None. Territorial extent & classification: NI. General. - 2p.: 30 cm. - 978-0-337-99858-4 £4.25

The Criminal Justice (2015 Act) (Commencement No. 3) Order (Northern Ireland) 2015 No. 2015/358 (C.30). - Enabling power: Justice Act (Northern Ireland) 2015, s. 106 (2). Bringing various provisions of the 2015 Act into operation 02.11.2015 in accord. with art. 2. - Issued: 21.10.2015. Made: 12.10.2015. Effect: None. Territorial extent & classification: NI. General. - 4p.: 30 cm. - 978-0-337-99887-4 £4.25

The Disclosure of Victims' and Witnesses' Information (Prescribed Bodies) Regulations (Northern Ireland) 2015 No. 2015/330. - Enabling power: Justice (Northern Ireland) Act 2015, s. 36, sch. 3, para. 6 (1). - Issued: 18.09.2015. Made: 14.09.2015. Coming into operation: 15.11.2015. Effect: None. Territorial extent and classification: NI. General. - 2p: 30 cm. - 978-0-337-99864-5 £4.25

The Justice (2011 Act) (Commencement No. 8) Order (Northern Ireland) 2015 No. 2015/158 (C.10). - Enabling power: Justice Act (Northern Ireland) 2011, ss. 111 (3). Bringing into operation various provisions of the 2011 Act on 01.04.2015 in accord. with art. 2. - Issued: 18.03.2015. Made: 12.03.2015. Effect: None. Territorial extent & classification: NI. General. - 4p.: 30 cm. - 978-0-337-99690-0 £4.25

The Justice (2015 Act) (Commencement No. 4) Order (Northern Ireland) 2015 No. 2015/418 (C.36). - Enabling power: Justice Act (Northern Ireland) 2015, s. 106 (2). Bringing various provisions of the 2015 Act into operation 29.01.2016; 01.03.2016, in accord. with arts 2 & 3. - Issued: 22.12.2015. Made: 17.12.2015. Effect: None. Territorial extent & classification: NI. General. - 4p.: 30 cm. - 978-0-337-99933-8 £4.25

The Justice (Northern Ireland) Act 2004 (Amendment of section 8(4)) Order (Northern Ireland) 2015 No. 2015/168. - Enabling power: Justice (Northern Ireland) Act 2004, s. 8 (5). - Issued: 24.03.2015. Made: 16.03.2015. Coming into operation: In accord. with art. 1 (2). Effect: 2004 c.4 amended. Territorial extent & classification: NI. General. - Supersedes draft SI (ISBN 9780337995408) issued 12/12/14. Approved. - 2p.: 30 cm. - 978-0-337-99729-7 £4.25

The Victim Charter (Justice Act (Northern Ireland) 2015) Order (Northern Ireland) 2015 No. 2015/370. - Enabling power: Justice Act (Northern Ireland) 2015, s. 31 (3). - Issued: 18.11.2015. Made: 12.11.2015. Coming into operation: 13.11.2015 in accord. with art. 1. Effect: None. Territorial extent & classification: NI. General. - Supersedes draft S.R. (ISBN 9780337998676) issued 25/09/15. - 2p.: 30 cm. - 978-0-337-99901-7 £4.25

Land development values

The Certificates of Alternative Development Value Regulations (Northern Ireland) 2015 No. 2015/174. - Enabling power: S.I. 1982/712 (N.I. 9), art. 17. - Issued: 27.03.2015. Made: 23.03.2015. Coming into operation: 15.04.2015. Effect: S.R.1987/437 revoked. Territorial extent & classification: NI. General. - 4p.: 30 cm. - 978-0-337-99737-2 £4.25

Landlord and tenant

Registered Rents (Increase) Order (Northern Ireland) 2015 No. 2015/204. - Enabling power: S.I. 2006/1459 (N.I. 10), art. 55 (5) (6). - Issued: 01.04.2015. Made: 27.03.2015. Coming into operation: 04.05.2014. Effect: None. Territorial extent & classification: NI. General. - 2p.: 30 cm. - 978-0-337-99754-9 £4.25

Lands Tribunal

The Lands Tribunal (Amendment) Rules (Northern Ireland) 2015 No. 2015/302. - Enabling power: Lands Tribunal and Compensation Act (Northern Ireland) 1964, s. 9 (1). - Issued: 13.07.2015. Made: 08.07.2015. Coming into operation: 10.08.2015. Effect: S.R. 1976/146 amended. Territorial extent & classification: NI. General. - 4p.: 30 cm. - 978-0-337-99846-1 £4.25

Legal aid and advice

The Criminal Legal Aid (Disclosure of Information) Rules (Northern Ireland) 2015 No. 2015/203. - Enabling power: S.I. 1981/228 (N.I.8), arts. 36 (3), 38A. - Issued: 15.04.2015. Made: 26.03.2015. Coming into operation: 01.04.2015. Effect: None. Territorial extent & classification: NI. General. - Supersedes draft S.R. (ISBN 9780337995750) issued 29/01/15. - 4p.: 30 cm. - 978-0-337-99774-7 £4.25

The Legal Aid for Crown Court Proceedings (Costs) (Amendment) Rules (Northern Ireland) 2015 No. 2015/215. - Enabling power: S.I. 1981/228 (N.I. 8), art. 36 (3). - Issued: 22.04.2015. Made: 13.04.2015. Coming into operation: 05.05.2015. Effect: S.R. 2005/112 amended. Territorial extent and classification: NI. General. - 16p.: 30 cm. - 978-0-337-99775-4 £6.00

Legal aid and coroners' courts

The Legal Aid and Coroners' Courts (2014 Act) (Commencement No. 1) Order (Northern Ireland) 2015 No. 2015/193 (C.12). - Enabling power: Legal Aid and Coroners' Courts Act (Northern Ireland) 2014, s. 12 (1). Bringing into operation various provisions of the 2014 Act on 01.04.2015 in accord. with art. 2. - Issued: 13.04.2015. Made: 26.03.2015. Effect: None. Territorial extent & classification: NI. General. - 4p.: 30 cm. - 978-0-337-99764-8 £4.25

The Legal Aid and Coroners' Courts (2014 Act) (Commencement No. 2) Order (Northern Ireland) 2015 No. 2015/359 (C.31). - Enabling power: Legal Aid and Coroners' Courts Act (Northern Ireland) 2014, s. 12 (1). Bringing into operation various provisions of the 2014 Act on 01.11.2015 in accord. with art. 2. - Issued: 22.10.2015. Made: 19.10.2015. Effect: None. Territorial extent & classification: NI. General. - 2p.: 30 cm. - 978-0-337-99888-1 £4.25

Local government

The Local Government (2014 Act) (Commencement No. 3) Order (Northern Ireland) 2015 No. 2015/28 (C.3). - Enabling power: Local Government Act (Northern Ireland) 2014 , s. 129. Bringing into operation various provisions of the 2014 Act on 01.02.2015, in accord. with art. 2. - Issued: 04.02.2015. Made: 30.01.2015. Effect: None. Territorial extent and classification: NI. General. - 4p.: 30 cm. - 978-0-337-99592-7 £4.25

The Local Government (2014 Act) (Commencement No. 4) Order (Northern Ireland) 2015 No. 2015/209 (C.15). - Enabling power: Local Government Act (Northern Ireland) 2014 , s. 129. Bringing into operation various provisions of the 2014 Act on 01.04.2015, 01.04.2016, 01.04.2017, in accord. with arts 2, 3, 4. - Issued: 02.04.2015. Made: 31.03.2015. Effect: None. Territorial extent and classification: NI. General. - 8p.: 30 cm. - 978-0-337-99759-4 £4.25

The Local Government (Accounts and Audit) (Amendment) Regulations (Northern Ireland) 2015 No. 2015/106. - Enabling power: S.I. 2005/1968 (N.I. 18), art. 24. - Issued: 04.03.2015. Made: 27.02.2015. Coming into operation: 01.04.2015. Effect: S.R. 2006/89, 522 revoked with saving. Territorial extent & classification: NI. General. - With correction slip dated March 2015. - 12p: 30 cm. - 978-0-337-99649-8 £6.00

The Local Government (Boundaries) (2008 Act) (Commencement, Transitional Provision and Savings) (Amendment) Order (Northern Ireland) 2015 No. 2015/210. - Enabling power: Local Government (Boundaries) Act (Northern Ireland) 2008, s. 5 (2) (4). - Issued: 02.04.2015. Made: 31.03.2015. Effect: S.R. 2013/238 (C.15) amended. Territorial extent & classification: NI. General. - 4p.: 30 cm. - 978-0-337-99761-7 £4.25

The Local Government (Constituting a Joint Committee a Body Corporate) Order (Northern Ireland) 2015 No. 2015/183. - Enabling power: Local Government Act (Northern Ireland) 1972, s. 19 (9) & Local Government Act (Northern Ireland) 2014, ss. 14 (2), 122 (2). - Issued: 30.03.2015. Made: 25.03.2015. Coming into operation: 01.04.2015. Effect: S.R. 2012/10 revoked. Territorial extent & classification: NI. General. - 8p.: 30 cm. - 978-0-337-99742-6 £4.25

The Local Government (Exclusion of Non-commercial Considerations) Order (Northern Ireland) 2015 No. 2015/289. - Enabling power: S.I. 1992/810 (NI. 6), art. 19 (7) (8). - Issued: 03.07.2015. Made: 30.06.2015. Coming into operation: 30.06.2015. Effect: None. Territorial extent & classification: NI. General. - Laid before the Assembly in draft. Supersedes draft SR (ISBN 9780337998164) issued on 29.05.2015. - 2p.: 30 cm. - 978-0-337-99841-6 £4.25

The Local Government (Executive Arrangements) Regulations (Northern Ireland) 2015 No. 2015/44. - Enabling power: Local Government Act (Northern Ireland) 2014, ss. 22 (3) (5) (6), 23 (5), 25 (1) to (4), 26, 30 (1), 35. - Issued: 13.02.2015. Made: 09.02.2015. Coming into operation: 01.04.2015. Effect: None. Territorial extent & classification: NI. General. - 28p.: 30 cm. - 978-0-337-99607-8 £6.00

The Local Government Pension Scheme (Governance) (Amendment No. 2) Regulations (Northern Ireland) 2015 No. 2015/162. - Enabling power: Public Service Pensions Act (Northern Ireland) 2014, ss. 1 (1), 3, 11, 12, sch. 3. - Issued: 23.03.2015. Made: 16.03.2015. Coming into operation: 06.04.2015. Effect: S.R. 2014/188, 189 amended. Territorial extent & classification: NI. General. - 8p.: 30 cm. - 978-0-337-99723-5 £6.00

The Local Government Pension Scheme (Governance) (Amendment) Regulations (Northern Ireland) 2015 No. 2015/77. - Enabling power: Public Service Pensions Act (Northern Ireland) 2014, ss. 1 (1), 3, 5 (1) (2), 5 (5), 7 (1) (4), sch. 3. - Issued: 26.02.2015. Made: 23.02.2015. Coming into operation: 01.04.2015. Effect: S.R. 2014/188 amended. Territorial extent & classification: NI. General. - 8p.: 30 cm. - 978-0-337-99631-3 £6.00

The Local Government (Performance Indicators and Standards) Order (Northern Ireland) 2015 No. 2015/327. - Enabling power: Local Government Act (Northern Ireland) 2014, s. 89 (1). - Issued: 18.09.2015. Made: 07.09.2015. Coming into operation: 28.09.2015. Effect: None. Territorial extent & classification: NI. General. - 8p.: 30 cm. - 978-0-337-99861-4 £6.00

The Local Government Reorganisation (Compensation for Loss of Employment) (Amendment) Regulations (Northern Ireland) 2015 No. 2015/271. - Enabling power: S.I. 1972/1073 (N.I. 10), art. 19, sch. 3, para. 13. - Issued: 15.06.2015. Made: 10.06.2015. Coming into operation: 02.07.2015. Effect: S.R. 2015/68 amended. Territorial extent & classification: NI. General. - 2p.: 30 cm. - 978-0-337-99822-5 £4.25

The Local Government Reorganisation (Compensation for Loss of Employment) Regulations (Northern Ireland) 2015 No. 2015/68. - Enabling power: S.I.1972/1073 (N.I. 10), art. 19, sch. 3, para. 13. - Issued: 20.02.2015. Made: 17.02.2015. Coming into operation: 01.04.2015. Effect: None. Territorial extent & classification: NI. General. - 8p.: 30 cm. - With correction slip dated March 2015. - 978-0-337-99634-4 £4.25

The Local Government (Transferred Functions Grant) Regulations (Northern Ireland) 2015 No. 2015/160. - Enabling power: Local Government Finance Act (Northern Ireland) 2011, s. 27A. - Issued: 20.03.2015. Made: 12.03.2015. Coming into operation: 02.04.2015. Effect: None. Territorial extent & classification: NI. General. - 4p.: 30 cm. - 978-0-337-99716-7 £4.25

The Local Government (Transitional, Incidental, Consequential and Supplemental Provisions) Regulations (Northern Ireland) 2015 No. 2015/125. - Enabling power: Local Government Act (Northern Ireland) 2014, s. 124. - Issued: 10.03.2015. Made: 05.03.2015. Coming into operation: 09.03.2015. Effect: S.R. & O. (N.I.) 1973/207 revoked. Territorial extent & classification: NI. General. - 8p.: 30 cm. - 978-0-337-99664-1 £4.25

Medicines

The Human Medicines (Amendment) (No. 2) Regulations 2015 No. 2015/259. - Enabling power: European Communities Act 1972, s. 2 (2) (5). - Issued: 01.06.2015. Made: 22.03.2015. Laid: 27.03.2015. Coming into operation: 01.07.2015. Effect: S.I. 2012/1916 amended. Territorial extent & classification: NI. General. - 4p.: 30 cm. - 978-0-337-99817-1 £4.25

The Human Medicines (Amendment) (No.3) Regulations 2015 No. 2015/354. - Enabling power: European Communities Act 1972, s. 2 (2) (5). - Issued: 16.10.2015. Made: 09.07.2015. Laid: 16.07.2015. Coming into operation: 01.10.2015. Effect: S.I. 2012/1916 amended. Territorial extent & classification: NI. General. - 4p.: 30 cm. - 978-0-337-99884-3 £4.25

The Human Medicines (Amendment) Regulations 2015 No. 2015/178. - Enabling power: European Communities Act 1972, s. 2 (2) (5). - Issued: 27.03.2015. Made: 17.02.2015. Laid: 25.03.2015. Coming into operation: 01.04.2015. Effect: S.I. 2012/1916 amended. Territorial extent & classification: NI. General. - 4p.: 30 cm. - 978-0-337-99734-1 £4.25

Official statistics

The Statistics and Registration Service Act 2007 (Disclosure of Patient Registration Information) Regulations (Northern Ireland) 2015 No. 2015/208. - Enabling power: Statistics and Registration Service Act 2007, s. 49 (1) (2) (5) (b) (6) (b). - Issued: 02.04.2015. Made: 16.03.2015. Coming into operation: In accord. with reg. 1. Effect: None. Territorial extent & classification: NI. General. - Subject to affirmative resolution procedure of the Assembly. - 4p.: 30 cm. - 978-0-337-99760-0 £4.25

The Statistics and Registration Service Act 2007 (Disclosure of Patient Registration Information) Regulations (Northern Ireland) 2015 No. 2015/208. - Enabling power: Statistics and Registration Service Act 2007, s. 49 (1) (2) (5) (b) (6) (b). - Issued: 22.05.2015. Made: 16.03.2015. Coming into operation: In accord. with reg. 1. Effect: None. Territorial extent & classification: NI. General. - Affirmed by resolution of the Assembly on 18th May 2015. - 4p.: 30 cm. - 978-0-337-99800-3 £4.25

Pensions

The Automatic Enrolment (Earnings Trigger and Qualifying Earnings Band) Order (Northern Ireland) 2015 No. 2015/119. - Enabling power: Pensions (No. 2) Act (Northern Ireland) 2008, ss. 14, 15A(1). - Issued: 10.03.2015. Made: 4.03.2015. Coming into operation: 06.04.2015. Effect: 2008 c. 13 (N.I.) amended & S.R. 2014/81 partially revoked. Territorial extent & classification: NI. General. - 4p.: 30 cm. - 978-0-337-99661-0 £4.25

The Funded Public Service Pension Schemes (Reduction of Cash Equivalents) Regulations (Northern Ireland) 2015 No. 2015/272. - Enabling power: Pension Schemes (Northern Ireland) Act 1993, ss. 93B, 177 (1) (2) (3) (4), 178 (1). - Issued: 16.06.2015. Made: 11.06.2015. Coming into operation: 07.07.2015. Effect: None. Territorial extent & classification: NI. General. - With correction slip dated July 2015. - 8p.: 30 cm. - 978-0-337-99823-2 £6.00

The Guaranteed Minimum Pensions Increase Order (Northern Ireland) 2015 No. 2015/117. - Enabling power: Pension Schemes (Northern Ireland) Act 1993, s. 105. - Issued: 10.03.2015. Made: 04.03.2015. Coming into operation: 06.04.2015. Effect: None. Territorial extent & classification: NI. General. - 2p.: 30 cm. - 978-0-337-99659-7 £4.25

The Occupational and Personal Pension Schemes (Automatic Enrolment) (Amendment) Regulations (Northern Ireland) 2015 No. 2015/310. - Enabling power: Pensions (No. 2) Act (Northern Ireland) 2008, ss. 3 (5), 4 (1) to (3), 5 (2), 9 (3), 10, 23A (1) (a) (b) (2) (4) (b), 25, 30 (7A), 69A (1) (3) (4), 113 (2). - Issued: 21.07.2015. Made: 16.07.2015. Coming into operation: 06.08.2015. Effect: S.R. 2010/122 amended/partially revoked & S.R. 2010/232 partially revoked. Territorial extent & classification: NI. General. - 12p.: 30 cm. - 978-0-337-99849-2 £6.00

The Occupational and Personal Pension Schemes (Disclosure of Information) (Amendment) Regulations (Northern Ireland) 2015 No. 2015/154. - Enabling power: Pension Schemes (Northern Ireland) Act 1993, ss. 109 (1) (3), 177 (2) to (4), 178 (1). - Issued: 17.03.2015. Made: 12.03.2015. Coming into operation: 06.04.2015. Effect: S.R. 2014/79 amended & S.R. 2014/204 partially revoked. Territorial extent & classification: NI. General. - 12p.: 30 cm. - 978-0-337-99694-8 £6.00

The Occupational and Personal Pension Schemes (Transfer Values) (Amendment and Revocation) Regulations (Northern Ireland) 2015 No. 2015/164. - Enabling power: Pensions Schemes (Northern Ireland) Act 1993, ss. 89 (5) (a) (10) (a) (b), 89A (5), 91 (2) (b) (6A), 93 (1) (2) (a) (b), (3B) (4), 95 (4A) (4B), 97F (6A), 109 (1) (3), 177 (2) to (4), 178 (1) & S.I. 1995/3213, art. 10 (2) (b). - Issued: 23.03.2015. Made: 16.03.2015. Coming into operation: In accord. with reg. 1 (1). Effect: S.R. 2010/121 revoked & 1996/619 partially revoked/amended & 1987/290 amended. Territorial extent & classification: NI. General. - 8p.: 30 cm. - 978-0-337-99725-9 £6.00

The Occupational Pension Schemes (Charges and Governance) Regulations (Northern Ireland) 2015 No. 2015/309. - Enabling power: Pension Schemes (Northern Ireland) Act 1993, ss. 109 (1), 177 (2) to (4) & S.I. 1995/3213 (N.I. 22), arts 35 (1) (3) (4), 36(1), (1A) (a) (9), 47 (6) (a), 68 (2) (e), 166 (1) to (3) & S.I. 1999/3147 (N.I. 11), art. 3 (5) & S.I. 2005/255 (N.I. 1), arts 55 (2) (h), 236 (1), 287 & Pensions Act (Northern Ireland) 2015,s. 42, 51(6), sch. 18, paras 1(1), (2) (a), (3) (5), 2 (1) to (3) (5), 3, 6, 7. - Issued: 21.07.2015. Made: 16.07.2015. Coming into operation: In accord. with reg. 1. Effect: S.R. 2000/262; 2005/93; 2006/48 amended. Territorial extent & classification: NI. - For approval of the Assembly before the expiration of six months from the date of their coming into operation. Superseded by approved S.R. 2015/309 (ISBN 9780337999284) issue 15/12/15. - 32p.: 30 cm. - 978-0-337-99851-5 £6.00

The Occupational Pension Schemes (Charges and Governance) Regulations (Northern Ireland) 2015 No. 2015/309. - Enabling power: Pension Schemes (Northern Ireland) Act 1993, ss. 109 (1), 177 (2) to (4) & S.I. 1995/3213 (N.I. 22), arts 35 (1) (3) (4), 36(1), (1A) (a) (9), 47 (6) (a), 68 (2) (e), 166 (1) to (3) & S.I. 1999/3147 (N.I. 11), art. 3 (5) & S.I. 2005/255 (N.I. 1), arts 55 (2) (h), 236 (1), 287 & Pensions Act (Northern Ireland) 2015,s. 42, 51(6), sch. 18, paras 1(1), (2) (a), (3) (5), 2 (1) to (3) (5), 3, 6, 7. - Issued: 15.12.2015. Made: 16.07.2015. Coming into operation: In accord. with reg. 1. Effect: S.R. 2000/262; 2005/93; 2006/48 amended. Territorial extent & classification: NI. General. - Approved by resolution of the Assembly on 8th December 2015. Supersedes non approved S.R. (ISBN 9780337998515) issued 21/07/15. - 32p.: 30 cm. - 978-0-337-99928-4 £6.00

The Occupational Pension Schemes (Consequential and Miscellaneous Amendments) Regulations (Northern Ireland) 2015 No. 2015/155. - Enabling power: Pension Schemes (Northern Ireland) Act 1993, ss. 8C (1) (c), 67 (6), 177 (2) to (4), 178(1) & S.I. 1995/3213 (N.I. 22), arts 67 (3) (b), 68 (2) (e), 89 (5) (c) (iii), 166 (2) (3)- Issued: 17.03.2015. Made: 12.03.2015. Coming into operation: 06.04.2015. Effect: S.R. 1991/37; 1996/493; 1997/153; 2006/149 amended. - 8p.: 30 cm. - 978-0-337-99693-1 £4.25

The Occupational Pension Schemes (Levies) (Amendment) Regulations (Northern Ireland) 2015 No. 2015/115. - Enabling power: S.I. 2005/255 (N.I. 1), art. 103 (1) (3). - Issued: 06.03.2015. Made: 03.03.2015. Coming into operation: In accord. with reg. 1. Effect: S.R. 2012/98 partially revoked. Territorial extent & classification: NI. General. - 4p: 30 cm. - 978-0-337-99656-6 £4.25

The Occupational Pension Schemes (Power to Amend Schemes to Reflect Abolition of Contracting-out) Regulations (Northern Ireland) 2015 No. 2015/372. - Enabling power: Pensions Act (Northern Ireland) 2015, ss. 24 (5), 51 (6), sch. 14, paras 2 (3) (4), 4, 6, 10 (1), 12, 13, 14 (1) (2). - Issued: 24.11.2015. Made: 19.11.2015. Coming into operation: 14.12.2015. Effect: 2015 c.5 (N.I.) modified. Territorial extent & classification: NI. General. - 12p.: 30 cm. - 978-0-337-99903-1 £6.00

The Occupational Pensions (Revaluation) Order (Northern Ireland) 2015 No. 2015/403. - Enabling power: Pensions Schemes (Northern Ireland) Act 1993, sch. 2, para. 2 (1). - Issued: 10.12.2015. Made: 07.12.2015. Coming into operation: 01.01.2016. Effect: None. Territorial extent & classification: NI. General. - 4p: 30 cm. - 978-0-337-99921-5 £4.25

The Payment of Pension Levies for Past Periods Regulations (Northern Ireland) 2015 No. 2015/402. - Enabling power: Pensions Act (Northern Ireland) 2015, ss. 44 (1) (2) (b), 51 (6). - Issued: 10.12.2015. Made: 07.12.2015. Coming into operation: 31.12.2015. Effect: None. Territorial extent & classification: NI. General. - 4p: 30 cm. - 978-0-337-99920-8 £4.25

The Pension Protection Fund and Occupational Pension Schemes (Levy Ceiling) Order (Northern Ireland) 2015 No. 2015/79. - Enabling power: S.I. 2005/255 (N.I.1), arts 161, 287 (3). - Issued: 02.03.2015. Made: 25.02.2015. Coming into operation: 31.03.2015. Effect: S.R. 2014/61 partially revoked. Territorial extent & classification: NI. General. - Revoked by SR 2016/32 (ISBN 9780337999775). - 2p.: 30 cm. - 978-0-337-99637-5 £4.25

The Pensions (2005 Order) (Code of Practice) (Funding Defined Benefits) (Appointed Day) Order (Northern Ireland) 2015 No. 2015/319. - Enabling power: S.I. 2005/255 (N.I. 1), art. 86 (7). - Issued: 29.07.2015. Made: 24.07.2015. Effect: None. Territorial extent and classification: NI. General. - The appointed day for the coming into operation of the Pensions Regulator Code of practice no. 3 is 29.07.2015. - 2p.: 30 cm. - 978-0-337-99854-6 £4.25

The Pensions (2005 Order) (Code of Practice) (Governance and Administration of Public Service Pension Schemes) (Appointed Day) Order (Northern Ireland) 2015 No. 2015/118. - Enabling power: S.I. 2005/255 (N.I. 1), art. 86 (7). - Issued: 10.03.2015. Made: 04.03.2015. Effect: None. Territorial extent: NI. General. - The appointed day for the coming into operation of the Pensions Regulator Code of practice no. 1 is 01.04.2015. - 2p.: 30 cm. - 978-0-337-99660-3 £4.25

The Pensions (2012 Act) (Commencement No. 5) Order (Northern Ireland) 2015 No. 2015/206 (C.14). - Enabling power: Pensions Act (Northern Ireland) 2012, s. 34 (3). Bringing into operation various provisions of the 2012 Act on 01.04.2015, in accord. with art. 2. - Issued: 02.04.2015. Made: 30.03.2015. Effect: None. Territorial extent & classification: NI. General. - 2p.: 30 cm. - 978-0-337-99757-0 £4.25

The Pensions (2015 Act) (Commencement No. 1) Order (Northern Ireland) 2015 No. 2015/307 (C.25). - Enabling power: Pensions Act (Northern Ireland) 2015, s. 53 (1). Bringing into operation various provisions of the 2015 Act on 16.07.2015, 01.10.2015 in accord. with arts 2, 3. - Issued: 20.07.2015. Made: 15.07.2015. Effect: None. Territorial extent & classification: NI. General. - 4p.: 30 cm. - 978-0-337-99847-8 £4.25

The Pensions (2015 Act) (Commencement No. 2) Order (Northern Ireland) 2015 No. 2015/329 (C.28). - Enabling power: Pensions Act (Northern Ireland) 2015, s. 53 (1). Bringing into operation various provisions of the 2015 Act on 14.09.2015; 12.10.2015; 06.04.2016 in accord. with art. 2. - Issued: 17.09.2015. Made: 11.09.2015. Effect: None. Territorial extent & classification: NI. General. - 4p.: 30 cm. - 978-0-337-99863-8 £4.25

The Pension Schemes Act 2015 (Transitional Provisions and Appropriate Independent Advice) Regulations (Northern Ireland) 2015 No. 2015/165. - Enabling power: Pensions Schemes Act 2015, ss. 51 (2) (3) (a) (4) (8), 52, 86, 89 (6). - Issued: 24.03.2015. Made: 18.03.2015. Coming into operation: 06.04.2015. Effect: None. Territorial extent & classification: NI. General. - 8p: 30 cm. - 978-0-337-99726-6 £6.00

Pensions Increase (Review) Order (Northern Ireland) 2015 No. 2015/180. - Enabling power: S.I. 1975/1503 (N.I. 15), art. 69 (1) (2) (5) (5ZA). - Issued: 30.03.2015. Made: 25.03.2015. Coming into operation: 06.04.2015. Effect: None. Territorial extent and classification: NI. General. - 4p.: 30 cm. - 978-0-337-99744-0 £4.25

The Public Service Pensions (Assembly Ombudsman for Northern Ireland and the Northern Ireland Commissioner for Complaints) Regulations (Northern Ireland) 2015 No. 2015/348. - Enabling power: Public Service Pensions Act (Northern Ireland) 2014, ss. 1 (1) (2) (a), 3 (1) (2), 25 (3). - Issued: 02.10.2015. Made: 30.09.2015. Coming into operation: 21.10.2015. Effect: None. Territorial extent & classification: NI. General. - 2p.: 30 cm. - 978-0-337-99876-8 £4.25

The Public Service Pensions (Employer Cost Cap) Regulations (Northern Ireland) 2015 No. 2015/12. - Enabling power: Public Service Pensions Act (Northern Ireland) 2014, s. 12 (5). - Issued: 24.02.2015. Made: 19.01.2015. Coming into operation: 01.04.2015. Effect: None. Territorial extent & classification: NI. General. - 4p.: 30 cm. - 978-0-337-99629-0 £4.25

The Superannuation (Assembly Ombudsman for Northern Ireland and the Northern Ireland Commissioner for Complaints) Order (Northern Ireland) 2015 No. 2015/347. - Enabling power: S.I. 1972/1073 (NI. 10), art. 3 (4) (7). - Issued: 02.10.2015. Made: 30.09.2015. Coming into force: 21.10.2015. Effect: None. - 2p.: 25 cm. - 978-0-337-99875-1 £4.25

The Superannuation (District Councils) Order (Northern Ireland) 2015 No. 2015/141. - Enabling power: S.I. 1972/1073 (N.I. 10), art. 3 (4). - Issued: 12.03.2015. Made: 10.03.2015. Coming into operation: 01.04.2015. Effect: None. Territorial extent & classification: NI. General. - 2p.: 30 cm. - 978-0-337-99679-5 £4.25

The Unfunded Public Service Defined Benefits Schemes (Transfers) Regulations (Northern Ireland) 2015 No. 2015/328. - Enabling power: Pension Schemes (Northern Ireland) Act 1993, ss. 91 (2A) (d), 91 (5A). - Issued: 16.09.2015. Made: 10.09.2015. Coming into operation: 02.10.2015. Effect: None. Territorial extent & classification: NI. General. - 4p.: 30 cm. - 978-0-337-99862-1 £4.25

Planning

The Planning (2011 Act) (Commencement No.2) Order (Northern Ireland) 2015 No. 2015/25 (C.2). - Enabling power: Planning Act (Northern Ireland) 2011, s. 254 (1). Bringing into operation various provisions of the 2011 Act on 01.02.2015, 01.04.2015, in accord. with arts. 2, 3. - Issued: 02.02.2015. Made: 28.01.2015. Effect: None. Territorial extent & classification: NI. General. - Approved. - 2p: 30 cm. - 978-0-337-99585-9 £4.25

The Planning (2011 Act) (Commencement No.3) and (Transitional Provisions) Order (Northern Ireland) 2015 No. 2015/49 (C.5). - Enabling power: Planning Act (Northern Ireland) 2011, ss. 247 (6), 254 (1). Bringing into operation various provisions of the 2011 Act on 13.02.2015, in accord. with art. 2. - Issued: 16.02.2015. Made: 12.02.2015. Effect: None. - 8p: 30 cm. - 978-0-337-99612-2 £6.00

The Planning (Amount of Fixed Penalty) Regulations (Northern Ireland) 2015 No. 2015/280. - Enabling power: Planning Act (Northern Ireland) 2011, ss. 153 (9), 154 (9), 247 (1). - Issued: 30.06.2015. Made: 23.06.2015. Coming into operation: 06.07.2015. Effect: None. Territorial extent & classification: NI. General. - Laid before the Assembly in draft. Supersedes draft SI (ISBN 9780337997884) issued 05.05.2015. - 2p.: 30 cm. - 978-0-337-99832-4 £4.25

The Planning (Avian Influenza) (Special Development) Order (Northern Ireland) 2015 No. 2015/175. - Enabling power: Planning Act (Northern Ireland) 2011, s. 32. - Issued: 27.03.2015. Made: 23.03.2015. Coming into operation: 15.04.2015. Effect: S.R. 2008/235 revoked. Territorial extent and classification: NI. General. - 4p.: 30 cm. - 978-0-337-99739-6 £4.25

The Planning (Claims for Compensation) Regulations (Northern Ireland) 2015 No. 2015/58. - Enabling power: Planning Act (Northern Ireland) 2011, ss. 186 (2), 247 (1). - Issued: 18.02.2015. Made: 13.02.2015. Coming into operation: 01.04.2015. Effect: S.R. 2006/238 revoked. Territorial extent & classification: NI. General. - 2p.: 30 cm. - 978-0-337-99621-4 £4.25

The Planning (Conservation Area) (Demolition) Regulations (Northern Ireland) 2015 No. 2015/107. - Enabling power: Planning Act (Northern Ireland) 2011, ss. 42 (7), 86 (1) (4) (5), 95 (2), 100 (2), 107 (2), 18 (1), 247 (1) (6). - Issued: 04.03.2015. Made: 26.02.2015. Coming into operation: 01.04.2015. Effect: S.R.1988/5 revoked. Territorial extent & classification: NI. General. - 16p.: 30 cm. - 978-0-337-99650-4 £6.00

The Planning (Conservation Areas) (Consultation) Regulations (Northern Ireland) 2015 No. 2015/177. - Enabling power: Planning Act (Northern Ireland) 2011, ss. 104 (5) (b), 274 (1). - Issued: 27.03.2015. Made: 23.03.2015. Coming into operation: 15.04.2015. Effect: S.R.2006/290 revoked. Territorial extent & classification: NI. General. - 4p.: 30 cm. - 978-0-337-99740-2 £4.25

The Planning (Control of Advertisements) Regulations (Northern Ireland) 2015 No. 2015/66. - Enabling power: Planning Act (Northern Ireland) 2011, ss. 130 (1) (2), 247 (1)- Issued: 20.02.2015. Made: 17.02.2015. Coming into operation: 01.04.2015. Effect: S.R. 1992/448 revoked. Territorial extent & classification: NI. General. - 44p.: 30 cm. - 978-0-337-99627-6 £10.00

The Planning (Development Management) (Amendment) Regulations (Northern Ireland) 2015 No. 2015/273. - Enabling power: Planning Act (Northern Ireland) 2011, ss. 25 (2), 26 (1), 247 (1). - Issued: 17.06.2015. Made: 15.06.2015. Coming into operation: 06.07.2015. Effect: S.R. 2015/71 amended. Territorial extent & classification: NI. General. - 2p.: 30 cm. - 978-0-337-99824-9 £4.25

The Planning (Development Management) Regulations (Northern Ireland) 2015 No. 2015/71. - Enabling power: Planning Act (Northern Ireland) 2011, ss. 25 (2), 26 (1), 27 (4) (5), 30 (1), 31 (1) (3), 50 (2), 247 (1) (6). - Issued: 02.03.2015. Made: 25.02.2015. Coming into operation: 01.04.2015. Effect: None. Territorial extent & classification: NI. General. - 12p.: 30 cm. - 978-0-337-99638-2 £6.00

The Planning (Environmental Impact Assessment) Regulations (Northern Ireland) 2015 No. 2015/74. - Enabling power: European Communities Act 1972, s. 2 (2). - Issued: 03.03.2015. Made: 25.02.2015. Coming into operation: 01.04.2015. Effect: S.R. 1999/73 amended & 2012/59 revoked. Territorial extent & classification: NI. General. - 56p.: 30 cm. - 978-0-337-99642-9 £10.00

The Planning (Fees) (Amendment) Regulations (Northern Ireland) 2015 No. 2015/398. - Enabling power: Planning Act (Northern Ireland) 2011, ss. 223 (1) (9), 247 (1). - Issued: 07.12.2015. Made: 02.12.2015. Coming into operation: 31.12.2015. Effect: S.R. 2015/73 amended. Territorial extent & classification: NI. General. - 4p.: 30 cm. - 978-0-337-99917-8 £4.25

The Planning (Fees) Regulations (Northern Ireland) 2015 No. 2015/73. - Enabling power: 2011 c.25 (N.I.) I, ss. 223 (1) (9), 247 (1). - Issued: 03.03.2015. Made: 25.02.2015. Coming into operation: 01.04.2015. Effect: S.R. 2005/222, 505; 2009/256; 2010/294; 2011/99, 398; 2012/293; 2014/127 revoked. Territorial extent & classification: NI. General. - With correction slip dated March 2015. - 8p.: 30 cm. - 978-0-337-99641-2 £6.00

The Planning General (Amendment)Regulations (Northern Ireland) 2015 No. 2015/176. - Enabling power: Planning Act (Northern Ireland) 2011, ss. 79 (1) (3) (4) (5), 247 (1). - Issued: 27.03.2015. Made: 23.03.2015. Coming into operation: 15.04.2015. Effect: S.R.2015/39 amended. Territorial extent & classification: NI. General. - 2p.: 30 cm. - 978-0-337-99738-9 £4.25

The Planning (General Development Procedure) Order (Northern Ireland) 2015 No. 2015/72. - Enabling power: Planning Act (Northern Ireland) 2011, ss. 32, 40, 41, 42 (7), 45 (2), 54 (2) 56 (1), 60, 67 (5), 171, 185 (3), 187 (5), 191 (4), 229, 242 (1) (2), 247 (6). - Issued: 10.03.2015. Made: 25.02.2015. Coming into operation: 01.04.2015. Effect: S.R.1993/278; 1995/424; 1996/232; 1998/222; 2000/113; 2002/195; 2003/98, 445; 2004/459; 2005/427; 2006/219, 348; 2007/106, 432; 2011/75, 404; 2012/329; 2013/96, 210; 2014/31 revoked. Territorial extent & classification: NI. General. - With correction slip dated March 2015. - 32p.: 30 cm. - 978-0-337-99640-5 £6.00

The Planning (General Permitted Development) (Amendment) Order (Northern Ireland) 2015 No. 2015/70. - Enabling power: Planning Act (Northern Ireland) 2011, ss. 32, 247 (6). - Issued: 02.03.2015. Made: 25.02.2015. Coming into operation: 01.04.2015. Effect: None. Territorial extent & classification: NI. General. - 100p.: 30 cm. - 978-0-337-99639-9 £16.50

The Planning General Regulations (Northern Ireland) 2015 No. 2015/39. - Enabling power: Planning Act (Northern Ireland) 2011, ss. 71 (2), 79 (1) (3) (4) (5), 247 (1). - Issued: 12.02.2015. Made: 09.02.2015. Coming into operation: 01.04.2015. Effect: 2011 c.25 (N.I.) modified. Territorial extent & classification: NI. General. - 8p.: 30 cm. - 978-0-337-99602-3 £4.25

The Planning General (Simplified Planning Zones) Regulations (Northern Ireland) 2015 No. 2015/188. - Enabling power: Planning Act (Northern Ireland) 2011, ss. 34 (4), 247 (1) (6), sch. 1, paras 2 (2), 3 (a) (b) (c), 8. - Issued: 01.04.2015. Made: 26.03.2015. Coming into operation: 22.04.2015. Effect: S.R. 1990/365 revoked. Territorial extent & classification: NI. General. - 16p.: 30 cm. - 978-0-337-99750-1 £6.00

The Planning (Hazardous Substances) (No. 2) Regulations (Northern Ireland) 2015 No. 2015/344. - Enabling power: European Communities Act 1972, s. 2 (2), sch. 2, para. 1A & Planning Act (Northern Ireland) 2011, ss. 8 (5) (c), 9 (6) (c), 108 (4) (5), 109 (1) (2) (4), 111, 115 (7), 116 (3), 162 (4) (10) (12), 223, 247 (1). - Issued: 30.09.2015. Made: 24.09.2015. Coming into operation: 16.10.2015. Effect: S.R. 2015/62, 72 amended & S.R. 2015/61 revoked. Territorial extent & classification: NI. General. - 44p.: 30 cm. - 978-0-337-99872-0 £10.00

The Planning (Hazardous Substances) Regulations (Northern Ireland) 2015 No. 2015/61. - Enabling power: Planning Act (Northern Ireland) 2011, ss. 108 (4), 109 (1) (2) (4), 111, 115 (7), 116 (3), 162 (4) (10) (12), 223, 247 (1). - Issued: 23.01.2015. Made: 16.02.2015. Coming into operation: 01.04.2015. Effect: 2011 c.25 (N.I.) modified & S.R. 1993/275 revoked. Territorial extent & classification: NI. General. - Revoked by S.R. 2015/344 (ISBN 9780337998720). - 44p.: 30 cm. - With correction slip dated March 2015. - 978-0-337-99622-1 £10.00

The Planning (Inquiry Procedure) Rules (Northern Ireland) 2015 No. 2015/189. - Enabling power: Planning Act (Northern Ireland) 2011, s. 231 (3). - Issued: 01.04.2015. Made: 26.03.2015. Coming into operation: 22.04.2015. Effect: S.R. 2006/213 revoked with saving. Territorial extent & classification: NI. General. - 20p.: 30 cm. - 978-0-337-99751-8 £6.00

The Planning (Listed Buildings) Regulations (Northern Ireland) 2015 No. 2015/108. - Enabling power: Planning Act (Northern Ireland) 2011, ss. 42, 80 (5), 86, 95 (2), 100 (2), 107 (2), 181 (1), 247 (1) (6). - Issued: 04.03.2015. Made: 26.02.2015. Coming into operation: 01.04.2015. Effect: S.R. 1992/263 revoked. Territorial extent & classification: NI. General. - 20p.: 30 cm. - 978-0-337-99651-1 £6.00

The Planning (Local Development Plan) Regulations (Northern Ireland) 2015 No. 2015/62. - Enabling power: Planning Act (Northern Ireland) 2011, ss. 7 (5), 8 (2) (3) (5), 9 (2) (3) (6), 10 (3), 11 (1), 12 (3), 13 (1) (3), 17 (7) (9), 21 (2) (3), 22, 247 (1) (6). - Issued: 19.02.2015. Made: 16.02.2015. Coming into operation: 01.04.2015. Effect: None. Territorial extent & classification: NI. General. - 16p.: 30 cm. - 978-0-337-99623-8 £6.00

The Planning (Management of Waste from Extractive Industries) Regulations (Northern Ireland) 2015 No. 2015/85. - Enabling power: European Communities Act 1972, s. 2 (2). - Issued: 10.03.2015. Made: 26.02.2015. Coming into operation: 01.04.2015. Effect: S.R. 2003/496 amended & S.R. 2010/64 revoked with saving. Territorial extent & classification: NI. General. - 28p.: 30 cm. - 978-0-337-99648-1 £6.00

The Planning (Modification and Discharge of Planning Agreements) Regulations (Northern Ireland) 2015 No. 2015/187. - Enabling power: Planning Act (Northern Ireland) 2011, ss. 77 (8) (10), 78 (3), 247 (1) (6). - Issued: 01.04.2015. Made: 26.03.2015. Coming into operation: 22.04.2015. Effect: S.R. 2005/353 revoked. Territorial extent & classification: NI. General. - 8p.: 30 cm. - 978-0-337-99749-5 £6.00

The Planning (Statement of Community Involvement) Regulations (Northern Ireland) 2015 No. 2015/63. - Enabling power: Planning Act (Northern Ireland) 2011, ss. 4 (6), 247 (1) (6). - Issued: 19.02.2015. Made: 16.02.2015. Coming into operation: 01.04.2015. Effect: None. Territorial extent & classification: NI. General. - 4p.: 30 cm. - 978-0-337-99624-5 £4.25

The Planning (Trees) Regulations (Northern Ireland) 2015 No. 2015/84. - Enabling power: Planning Act (Northern Ireland) 2011, ss. 122 (4), 128, 247 (1) (6). - Issued: 05.03.2015. Made: 26.02.2015. Coming into operation: 01.04.2015. Effect: S.R. 2003/444 revoked. Territorial extent & classification: NI. General. - 16p.: 30 cm. - 978-0-337-99647-4 £6.00

The Planning (Use Classes) Order (Northern Ireland) 2015 No. 2015/40. - Enabling power: Planning Act (Northern Ireland) 2011, s. 23 (3) (e). - Issued: 12.02.2015. Made: 09.02.2015. Coming into operation: 01.04.2015. Effect: S.R. 2004/458 revoked. Territorial extent & classification: NI. General. - 8p.: 30 cm. - With correction slip dated March 2015. - 978-0-337-99603-0 £6.00

Planning Appeals Commission procedures

Planning Appeals Commission (Decisions on Appeals and Making of Reports) (Amendment) Rules (Northern Ireland) 2015 No. 2015/137. - Enabling power: Planning Act (Northern Ireland) 2011, s. 204 (5) (6) (7). - Issued: 12.03.2015. Made: 06.03.2015. Coming into operation: 01.04.2015. Effect: S.R. 2006/233 amended. Territorial extent & classification: NI. General. - 2p: 30 cm. - 978-0-337-99675-7 £4.25

Planning fees

The Planning (Fees) (Deemed Planning Applications and Appeals) Regulations (Northern Ireland) 2015 No. 2015/136. - Enabling power: Planning Act (Northern Ireland) 2011, s. 223 (7) (9). - Issued: 12.03.2015. Made: 06.03.2015. Coming into operation: 01.04.2015. Effect: S.R. 1995/78; 2005/222 partially revoked. Territorial extent & classification: NI. General. - With correction slip dated March 2015. - 8p.: 30 cm. - 978-0-337-99673-3 £6.00

Plant health

The Plant Health (Amendment) Order (Northern Ireland) 2015 No. 2015/128. - Enabling power: Plant Health Act (Northern Ireland) 1967, ss. 2, 3 (1) & European Communities Act 1972, sch. 2, para. 1A. - Issued: 12.03.2015. Made: 06.03.2015. Coming into operation: 27.03.2015. Effect: S.R. 2006/82 amended. Territorial extent & classification: NI. General. - 20p.: 30 cm. - 978-0-337-99667-2 £6.00

The Plant Health (Wood and Bark) (Amendment) Order (Northern Ireland) 2015 No. 2015/129. - Enabling power: Plant Health Act (Northern Ireland) 1967, ss. 2, 3 (1) & European Communities Act 1972, sch. 2, para. 1A. - Issued: 11.03.2015. Made: 06.03.2015. Coming into operation: 27.03.2015. Effect: S.R. 2006/66 amended. Territorial extent & classification: NI. General. - EC note: Implements Commission Directive 2014/78/EU on protective measures against the introduction into the Community of organisms harmful to plants or plant products and against their spread within the Community. Also implements Directive 2014/83/EU. - 16p.: 30 cm. - 978-0-337-99668-9 £6.00

Police

The Police and Criminal Evidence (Northern Ireland) Order 1989 (Codes of Practice) Order 2015 No. 2015/225. - Enabling power: S.I. 1989/1341 (NI.12), art. 60, 60A, 65, 66 (6). - Issued: 05.05.2015. Made: 15.04.2015. Coming into operation: 01.06.2015. Effect: None. Territorial extent & classification: NI. General. - 2p.: 30 cm. - 978-0-337-99778-5 £4.25

The Police (Appeals, Conduct and Unsatisfactory Performance and Attendance) (Amendment) Regulations (Northern Ireland) 2015 No. 2015/360. - Enabling power: Police (Northern Ireland) Act 1998, ss. 25, 26. - Issued: 27.10.2015. Made: 20.10.2015. Coming into operation: 30.11.2015. Effect: S.I. 2000/315, 317 amended. Territorial extent & classification: NI. General. - With correction slip dated November 2015. - 2p.: 30 cm. - 978-0-337-99890-4 £4.25

The Police (Northern Ireland) Act 2000 (Designated Places of Detention: Lay Visitors) Order 2015 No. 2015/29. - Enabling power: Police (Northern Ireland) Act 2000, s. 73 (10) (a). - Issued: 05.02.2015. Made: 30.01.2015. Laid: 03.02.2015. Coming into operation: 01.03.2015. Effect: None. Territorial extent and classification: NI. General. - 2p.: 30 cm. - 978-0-337-99593-4 £4.25

The Police Service of Northern Ireland (Amendment) Regulations 2015 No. 2015/419. - Enabling power: Police (Northern Ireland) Act 1998, s. 25. - Issued: 22.12.2015. Made: 17.12.2015. Coming into operation: 05.10.2008. Effect: S.R. 2005/547 amended. Territorial extent & classification: NI. General. - 4p.: 30 cm. - 978-0-337-99936-9 £4.25

Police service pensions

The Police Pensions (Northern Ireland) Regulations 2015 No. 2015/113. - Enabling power: Public Service Pensions Act (Northern Ireland) 2014, ss. 1 (1) (2) (g), 2 (1), 3 (1) (2) (3) (a) (c) (4), 4 (3) (5). - Issued: 15.04.2015. Made: 02.03.2013. Coming into operation: 01.04.2015. Effect: S.R. 1998/374 amended. Territorial extent & classification: NI. General. - 136p.: 30 cm. - 978-0-337-99655-9 £20.75

Public authorities reform

The Public Authorities (Reform) (2009 Act) (Commencement No. 2) Order (Northern Ireland) 2015 No. 2015/230 (C.16). - Enabling power: Public Authorities (Reform) Act (Northern Ireland) 2009, s. 7 (1). Bringing into operation various provisions of the 2009 Act on 01.05.2015. - Issued: 24.04.2015. Made: 21.04.2015. Effect: None. - 2p: 30 cm. - 978-0-337-99783-9 £4.25

Public health

The HIV Testing Kits and Services (Revocation) Regulations (Northern Ireland) 2015 No. 2015/412. - Enabling power: S.I. 1988/2249 (N.I. 24) revoked. - Issued: 18.12.2015. Made: 15.12.2015. Coming into operation: 29.01.2016. Effect: S.R. 1992/293 revoked. Territorial extent & classification: NI. General. - With correction slip dated January 2016. - 2p.: 30 cm. - 978-0-337-99930-7 £4.25

Public passenger transport

The Public Passenger Transport (Service Agreements and Service Permits) Regulations (Northern Ireland) 2015 No. 2015/285. - Enabling power: Transport Act (Northern Ireland) 2011, ss. 1 (9), 2 (1), 2 (3), 4 (2) (3), 5 (1), 8 (2), 13 (1) (6), 14 (2) (3) (4), 15, 45 (1) (2) (7). - Issued: 30.06.2015. Made: 25.06.2015. Coming into operation: 05.10.2015. Effect: None. Territorial extent & classification: NI. General. - EC note: These Regulations lay down the rules for Part 1 of the Transport Act (Northern Ireland) 2011 ("the Act") in relation to the provision of public passenger transport services and do so in accordance with the requirements of Commission Regulation (EC) No. 1370/2007 on public passenger transport services by rail and road. - 16p.: 30 cm. - 978-0-337-99836-2 £6.00

The Transport (2011 Act) (Commencement No. 2) Order (Northern Ireland) 2015 No. 2015/277 (C.21). - Enabling power: Transport Act (Northern Ireland) 2011, s. 48. Bringing into operation various provisions of the 2011 Act on 23.06.2015, in accord. with art. 2. - Issued: 23.06.2015. Made: 18.06.2015. Effect: None. Territorial extent & classification: NI. General. - 4p.: 30 cm. - 978-0-337-99827-0 £4.25

The Transport (2011 Act) (Commencement No. 3) Order (Northern Ireland) 2015 No. 2015/284 (C.22). - Enabling power: Transport Act (Northern Ireland) 2011, s. 48. Bringing into operation various provisions of the 2011 Act on 05.10.2015, in accord. with art. 2. - Issued: 30.06.2015. Made: 25.06.2015. Effect: None. Territorial extent & classification: NI. General. - 4p.: 30 cm. - 978-0-337-99835-5 £4.25

Public service pensions

The Firefighters' Pension Scheme (Consequential Provisions) Regulations (Northern Ireland) 2015 No. 2015/166. - Enabling power: Public Service Pensions Act (Northern Ireland) 2014, ss. 1 (1) (2) (f), 2 (1), 3 (1) (2) (3) (a) (4). - Issued: 24.03.2015. Made: 18.03.2015. Coming into operation: 01.04.2015. Effect: 1993 c.49; S.R. 1996/493, 619 modified. Territorial extent & classification: NI. General. - Supersedes draft SI (ISBN 9780337995996) issued 09/02/15 - 8p.: 30 cm. - 978-0-337-99727-3 £6.00

The Firefighters' Pension Scheme Regulations (Northern Ireland) 2015 No. 2015/78. - Enabling power: Public Service Pensions Act (Northern Ireland) 2014, ss. 1 (1) (2) (f) (3) (4), 2, 3 (1) (2) (3) (a) (c), 4 (1) (2) (5), 5 (1) (3) (c) (5), 7 (1) (4), 8 (1) (a) (2) (a) (4), 11 (1), 12 (1) (6) (7), 14, 18 (1) (2) (4) (5) to (9), schs. 1 & 2, para. 6, sch. 3, sch. 5, para. 6- Issued: 27.02.2015. Made: 24.02.2015. Coming into operation: 01.04.2015. Effect: None. Territorial extent & classification: NI. General. - With correction slip dated March 2015. - 94p.: 30 cm. - 978-0-337-99632-0 £16.00

The Firefighters' Pension Scheme (Transitional and Consequential Provisions) Regulations (Northern Ireland) 2015 No. 2015/420. - Enabling power: Public Service Pensions Act (Northern Ireland) 2014, ss. 1 (1) (2) (f) (3) (4), 2, 3 (a) to (c), 8 (1) (a) (2) (a) (4), 18 (1) (2) (4) (5) to (9), sch. 1 & 2, para. 6, sch. 3 & sch. 7, paras 1 (2) (ii), 2 (2) (ii), 5 (1). - Issued: 22.12.2015. Made: 17.12.2015. Coming into operation: 18.01.2016. Effect: S.R. 2007/144, 215; 2015/78 amended. Territorial extent & classification: NI. General. - 32p.: 30 cm. - 978-0-337-99932-1 £10.00

The Health and Social Care Pension Scheme (Transitional and Consequential Provisions) Regulations (Northern Ireland) 2015 No. 2015/122. - Enabling power: S.I. 1972/1073 (N.I. 10), sch. 3, arts 12 (1) (2) & Public Service Pensions Act (Northern Ireland) 2014, ss. 1, 3, 18 (5), sch. 3. - Issued: 11.03.2015. Made: 06.03.2015. Coming into operation: 01.04.2015. Effect: S.R. 1995/95 amended. Territorial extent & classification: NI. General. - 44p.: 30 cm. - 978-0-337-99672-6 £10.00

The Health Service Workers (Consequential Provisions) Regulations (Northern Ireland) 2015 No. 2015/167. - Enabling power: Public Service Pensions Act (Northern Ireland) 2014, ss. 1 (1) (2) (e), 2 (1), 3 (1) (2) (3) (a) (4). - Issued: 24.03.2015. Made: 18.03.2015. Coming into operation: 01.04.2015. Effect: 1993 c.49; S.R. 1996/493 modified. Territorial extent & classification: NI. General. - Laid before the Assembly in draft. - 8p.: 30 cm. - 978-0-337-99728-0 £6.00

The Judicial Pensions Regulations (Northern Ireland) 2015 No. 2015/76. - Enabling power: Public Service Pensions Act (Northern Ireland) 2014, ss. 1 (1) (2) (b), 2 (1), 3 (1) (2) (3) (a) (3) (c) (4), 4 (3) (6), 5 (3) (c) (4) (5), 7 (1) (4), 8 (1) (a), 12 (6) (7), 14 (1), 18 (5) (6) (7), sch.2, para. 2, sch. 3, sch. 7, paras 1 (2) (ii), 2 (2) (ii), 5 (1). - Issued: 25.02.2015. Made: 18.02.2015. Coming into operation: In accord. with reg. 1 (2) (3). Effect: 1993 c.8, c.49; 2014 c.2 (NI); S.R. 1996/493, 619 modified. Territorial extent and classification: NI. General. - Supersedes draft SI (ISBN 9780337995699) issued 29/01/15 - 104p: 30 cm. - 978-0-337-99630-6 £16.50

The Police Pensions (Consequential Provisions) Regulations (Northern Ireland) 2015 No. 2015/156. - Enabling power: Police Service Pensions Act (Northern Ireland) 2014, ss. 1 (1) (2) (g), 2 (1), 3 (1) (2) (3) (a) (4). - Issued: 18.03.2015. Made: 18.02.2015. Coming into operation: 01.04.2015. Effect: 1993 c.49; S.R. 1996/493, 619 amended. Territorial extent & classification: NI. General. - Laid before the Assembly in draft. - 12p: 30 cm. - 978-0-337-99692-4 £6.00

The Public Service (Civil Servants and Others) Pensions (Amendment) Regulations (Northern Ireland) 2015 No. 2015/181. - Enabling power: Public Service Pensions Act (Northern Ireland) 2014, ss 1 (1) (2) (a), 2 (1), 3 (1) (2) (3) (a) (c), sch. 3. - Issued: 30.03.2015. Made: 25.03.2015. Coming into operation: 15.04.2015. Effect: S.R. 2014/290 amended. Territorial extent & classification: NI. General. - With correction slip dated June 2015. - 16p.: 30 cm. - 978-0-337-99745-7 £6.00

The Public Service (Civil Servants and Others) Pensions (Consequential Provisions) Regulations (Northern Ireland) 2015 No. 2015/81. - Enabling power: Public Service Pensions Act (Northern Ireland) 2014, ss. 1 (1) (2) (a), 2 (1), 3 (1) (2) (3) (a) (4). - Issued: 03.03.2015. Made: 26.02.2015. Coming into operation: 01.04.2015. Effect: S.R. 2015/15 revoked before publishing. Territorial extent & classification: NI. General. - Supersedes draft SI (ISBN 9780337995897) issued 09/02/15. - 8p.: 30 cm. - 978-0-337-99644-3 £6.00

The Public Service Pensions (2014 Act) (Commencement No.2) Order (Northern Ireland) 2015 No. 2015/3 (C.1). - Enabling power: Public Service Pensions Act (Northern Ireland) 2014, s. 37 (2) (3). Bringing into operation various provisions of the 2014 Act on 01.04.2015, in accord. with arts 2 to 5. - Issued: 16.01.2014. Made: 13.01.2015. Effect: None. Territorial extent and classification: NI. General. - 4p.: 30 cm. - 978-0-337-99559-0 £4.25

The Public Service Pensions Act (Northern Ireland) 2014 (Judicial Offices) Order (Northern Ireland) 2015 No. 2015/161. - Enabling power: Public Service Pensions Act (Northern Ireland) 2014, sch. 1, para. 2. - Issued: 23.03.2015. Made: 10.03.2015. Coming into operation: 01.04.2015. Effect: None. Territorial extent & classification: NI. General. - 4p.: 30 cm. - 978-0-337-99722-8 £4.25

The Teachers' Pension Scheme (Consequential Provisions) Regulations (Northern Ireland) 2015 No. 2015/170. - Enabling power: Public Service Pensions Act (Northern Ireland) 2014, ss. 1, 3. - Issued: 25.03.2015. Made: 19.03.2015. Coming into operation: 01.04.2015. Effect: None. Territorial extent and classification: NI. General. - Supersedes draft S.R. (ISBN 9780337995972) issued 09/02/15- 12p.: 30 cm. - 978-0-337-99731-0 £6.00

Rates

The Rates (Exemption for Automatic Telling Machines in Rural Areas) Order (Northern Ireland) 2015 No. 2015/47. - Enabling power: S.I. 1977/2157 (N.I. 28), art. 42 (1G). - Issued: 13.02.2015. Made: 10.02.2015. Coming into operation: 01.04.2015. Effect: None. Territorial extent & classification: NI. General- Subject to affirmative resolution procedure of the Assembly. Superseded by affirmed instrument (ISBN 9780337996863) issued 17.03.2015. - 2p.: 30 cm. - 978-0-337-99610-8 £4.25

The Rates (Exemption for Automatic Telling Machines in Rural Areas) Order (Northern Ireland) 2015 No. 2015/47. - Enabling power: S.I. 1977/2157 (N.I. 28), art. 42 (1G). - Issued: 17.03.2015. Made: 10.02.2015. Coming into operation: 01.04.2015. Effect: None. Territorial extent & classification: NI. General- Affirmed by resolution of the Assembly on 2nd March 2015; Revoked by SR 2016/17 (ISBN 9780337999710). - 2p.: 30 cm. - 978-0-337-99686-3 £4.25

The Rates (Making and Levying of Different Rates) Regulations (Northern Ireland) 2015 No. 2015/20. - Enabling power: S.I. 1977/2157 (N.I. 28), art. 6 (6). - Issued: 30.01.2015. Made: 27.01.2015. Coming into operation: 28.01.2015. Effect: S.R. 2006/498; revoked with savings. Territorial extent & classification: NI. General. - 4p.: 30 cm. - 978-0-337-99580-4 £4.25

The Rates (Owners Allowances) Order (Northern Ireland) 2015 No. 2015/46. - Enabling power: S.I. 1977/2157 (N.I. 28), art. 22 (4) to (4D). - Issued: 13.02.2015. Made: 10.02.2015. Coming into operation: 01.04.2015. Effect: S.I. 1977/2157 (N.I. 28) amended & S.R. 2011/395 partially revoked. Territorial extent & classification: NI. General. - Subject to affirmative resolution procedure of the Assembly. Superseded by affirmed instrument (ISBN 9780337996856) issued 17.03.2015. - 4p.: 30 cm. - 978-0-337-99609-2 £4.25

The Rates (Owners Allowances) Order (Northern Ireland) 2015 No. 2015/46. - Enabling power: S.I. 1977/2157 (N.I. 28), art. 22 (4) to (4D). - Issued: 17.03.2015. Made: 10.02.2015. Coming into operation: 01.04.2015. Effect: S.I. 1977/2157 (N.I. 28) amended & S.R. 2011/395 partially revoked. Territorial extent & classification: NI. General. - Affirmed by resolution of the Assembly on 2nd March 2015. - 4p.: 30 cm. - 978-0-337-99685-6 £4.25

The Rates (Regional Rates) Order (Northern Ireland) 2015 No. 2015/75. - Enabling power: S.I. 1977/2157 (N.I. 28), art. 7 (1) (3). - Issued: 24.02.2015. Made: 19.02.2015. Coming into operation: In accord. with art. 1. Effect: None. Territorial extent and classification: NI. General. - Subject to the affirmative resolution procedure of the Assembly. Superseded by affirmed instrument (ISBN 9780337996870) issued 17.03.2015. - 2p.: 30 cm. - 978-0-337-99628-3 £4.25

The Rates (Regional Rates) Order (Northern Ireland) 2015 No. 2015/75. - Enabling power: S.I. 1977/2157 (N.I. 28), art. 7 (1) (3). - Issued: 17.03.2015. Made: 19.02.2015. Coming into operation: In accord. with art. 1. Effect: None. Territorial extent and classification: NI. General. - Affirmed by resolution of the Assembly on 10th March 2015. - 2p.: 30 cm. - 978-0-337-99687-0 £4.25

The Rates (Small Business Hereditament Relief) (Amendment) Regulations (Northern Ireland) 2015 No. 2015/123. - Enabling power: S.I. 1977/2157 (N.I. 28), art. 31C. - Issued: 10.03.2015. Made: 05.03.2015. Coming into operation: 01.04.2015. Effect: S.R. 2010/4 amended. Territorial extent & classification: NI. General. - 2p: 30 cm. - 978-0-337-99662-7 £4.25

The Rates (Social Sector Value) (Amendment) Regulations (Northern Ireland) 2015 No. 2015/82. - Enabling power: S.I. 1977/2157 (N.I. 28), art. 23A. - Issued: 03.03.2015. Made: 26.02.2015. Coming into operation: 01.04.2015. Effect: S.R. 2007/86 amended & S.R. 2012/79 revoked. Territorial extent & classification: NI. General. - 4p.: 30 cm. - 978-0-337-99645-0 £4.25

The Rates (Temporary Rebate) (Amendment) Order (Northern Ireland) 2015 No. 2015/48. - Enabling power: S.I. 1977/2157 (N.I. 28), art. 31D(15) (16). - Issued: 13.02.2015. Made: 10.02.2015. Coming into operation: 01.04.2015. Effect: S.R. 2013/15 revoked. Territorial extent & classification: NI. General. - Subject to affirmative resolution procedure of the Assembly. - 4p.: 30 cm. - 978-0-337-99611-5 £4.25

The Rates (Temporary Rebate) (Amendment) Order (Northern Ireland) 2015 No. 2015/48. - Enabling power: S.I. 1977/2157 (N.I. 28), art. 31D(15) (16). - Issued: 18.03.2015. Made: 10.02.2015. Coming into operation: 01.04.2015. Effect: S.I. 1977/2157 (N.28) amended & S.R. 2013/15 revoked. Territorial extent & classification: NI. General. - Affirmed by resolution of the Assembly on 02/03/2015. Revoked by SR 2016/18 (ISBN 9780337999727). - 4p.: 30 cm. - 978-0-337-99691-7 £4.25

The Rates (Transitional Relief) Order (Northern Ireland) 2015 No. 2015/83. - Enabling power: S.I. 1977/2157 (N.I. 28), art. 33A (2A). - Issued: 03.03.2015. Made: 26.02.2015. Coming into operation: 01.04.2015. Effect: None. Territorial extent & classification: NI. General. - 8p.: 30 cm. - 978-0-337-99646-7 £6.00

The Social Security Benefits Up-rating Order (Northern Ireland) 2015 No. 2015/124. - Enabling power: Social Security Administration (Northern Ireland) Act 1992, ss. 132, 132A,165 (1) (4) (5)- Issued: 09.03.2015. Made: 05.03.2015. Coming into operation: In accord. with 1. Effect: 1992 c.7 & S.R. 1987/459; 1996/198; 2006/405, 406; 2008/280 amended & S.R. 2014/78 revoked. Territorial extent & classification: NI. General. - For approval of the Assembly before the expiration of six months from the date of its coming into operation. Superseded by approved version SR 2015/124 (ISBN 9780337997853). - 44p.: 30 cm. - 978-0-337-99663-4 £10.00

The Social Security Benefits Up-rating Order (Northern Ireland) 2015 No. 2015/124. - Enabling power: Social Security Administration (Northern Ireland) Act 1992, ss. 132, 132A, 165 (1) (4) (5). - Issued: 30.04.2015. Made: 05.03.2015. Coming into operation: In accord. with art. 1. Effect: 1966 c.6 (N.I.); 1992 c.7; 1993 c.49; S.R. 1987/30, 460; 1992/32; 1994/461; 1995/35; 1996/198; 2002/380; 2003/28; 2006/405, 406; 2008/280; 2010/407; amended & S.R. 2014/78 revoked (13.04.2015). Territorial extent & classification: NI. General. - Approved by resolution of the Assembly on 27th April 2015. Supersedes pre-approved SR 2015/124 (ISBN 9780337996634). - 48p.: 30 cm. - 978-0-337-99785-3 £10.00

The Social Security (Miscellaneous Amendments No. 2) Regulations (Northern Ireland) 2015 No. 2015/163. - Enabling power: S.I. 1991/2628 (NI. 23), arts 39 (1), 47 (1) & Social Security Contributions and Benefits (Northern Ireland) Act 1992, ss. 122 (1) (a) (d), 132 (3) (4) (b), 132A (2) (3), 171 (1) (3) (4) & S.I. 1995/2705 (NI.15), arts 6 (5), 14 (1) (4), 36 (1) (2) & S.I. 1998/1506 (NI. 10), arts 11 (6), 74 (1) (5) & Welfare Reform Act (Northern Ireland) 2007, ss. 17 (1) (3), 25 (2). - Issued: 23.03.2015. Made: 16.03.2015. Coming into operation: 06.04.2015. Effect: S.R. 1987/459; 1992/341; 1996/198; 2001/18; 2006/405, 406; 2008/280 amended. Territorial extent & classification: NI. General. - 4p.: 30 cm. - 978-0-337-99724-2 £4.25

The Social Security (Miscellaneous Amendments) Regulations (Northern Ireland) 2015 No. 2015/34. - Enabling power: Social Security Contributions and Benefits (Northern Ireland) Act 1992, ss. 35 (3), 35B (11), 132 (3) (4), 132A, 134 (2) (4), 171 (1) (3) (4) & Social Security Administration (Northern Ireland) Act 1992, ss. 158C, 189 (4) & S.I. 1995/2705, arts 14 (1) (4), 36 (2) & State Pension Credit Act (Northern Ireland) 2002, ss. 15 (3) (6), 19 (1) to (3) & Welfare Reform Act (Northern Ireland) 2007, s. 25 (2) (a). - Issued: 06.02.2015. Made: 03.02.2015. Coming into operation: 23.02.2015. Effect: S.R. 1987/170; 2000/91; 2001/102; 2006/405 amended. Territorial extent & classification: NI. General. - 8p.: 30 cm. - 978-0-337-99595-8 £4.25

The Valuation for Rating (Decapitalisation Rate) Regulations (Northern Ireland) 2015 No. 2015/32. - Enabling power: S.I. 1977/2157 (NI.28), sch. 12, part 1, paras. 5, 6. - Issued: 05.02.2015. Made: 02.02.2015. Coming into operation: 24.02.2015. Effect: S.R. 2009/241 revoked. Territorial extent and classification: NI. General. - 4p.: 30 cm. - 978-0-337-99594-1 £4.25

The Valuation (Telecommunications, Natural Gas and Water) (Amendment) Regulations (Northern Ireland) 2015 No. 2015/147. - Enabling power: S.I. 1977/2157 (N.I. 28), art. 37 (4) (5), sch. 12, pt. 1, para. 5. - Issued: 17.03.2017. Made: 11.03.2015. Coming into operation: 01.04.2015. Effect: S.R. 2010/431 amended. Territorial extent & classification: NI. General. - 4p.: 30 cm. - 978-0-337-99682-5 £4.25

Road and railway transport

The Level Crossing (Cullybackey South) Order (Northern Ireland) 2015 No. 2015/13. - Enabling power: Transport Act (Northern Ireland) 1967, s. 66 (1) (2). - Issued: 26.01.2015. Made: 21.01.2015. Coming into operation: 16.02.2015. Effect: S.R. 1986/7 revoked. Territorial extent & classification: NI. General. - 8p.: 30 cm. - 978-0-337-99568-2 £6.00

Roads

The A29 Moy Road and U7004 Drumcairn Road, Armagh (Abandonment) Order (Northern Ireland) 2015 No. 2015/306. - Enabling power: S.I. 1993/3160 (N.I. 15), art. 68 (1) (5). - Issued: 17.07.2015. Made: 15.07.2015. Coming into force: 07.10.2015. Effect: None. Territorial extent & classification: NI. Local. - Available at http://www.legislation.gov.uk/nisr/2015/306/contents/made Non-print

The Ballinderry Road/Glenavy Road, Lisburn (Stopping-Up) Order (Northern Ireland) 2015 No. 2015/253. - Enabling power: S.I. 1993/3160 (N.I.15), arts 68 (1) (3) (5). - Issued: 20.05.2015. Made: 18.05.2015. Coming into operation: 01.07.2015. Effect: None. Territorial extent & classification: NI. Local. - Available at http://www.legislation.gov.uk/nisr/2015/253/contents/made Non-print

The Carnbane Road, Newry (Abandonment) Order (Northern Ireland) 2015 No. 2015/392. - Enabling power: S.I. 1993/3160 (N.I. 15), art. 68 (1) (5). - Issued: 04.12.2015. Made: 02.12.2015. Coming into force: 10.02.2016. Effect: None. Territorial extent & classification: NI. Local. - Available at http://www.legislation.gov.uk/nisr/2015/392/contents/made Non-print

The Clifton Street/Carrick Hill, Belfast (Footway) (Abandonment) Order (Northern Ireland) 2015 No. 2015/390. - Enabling power: S.I. 1993/3160 (N.I. 15), art. 68 (1). - Issued: 04.12.2015. Made: 02.12.2015. Coming into force: 10.02.2016. Effect: None. Territorial extent & classification: NI. Local. - Available at http://www.legislation.gov.uk/nisr/2015/390/contents/made Non-print

The Glebe Way, Moira (Abandonment) Order (Northern Ireland) 2015 No. 2015/342. - Enabling power: S.I. 1993/3160 (N.I. 15), art. 68 (1). - Issued: 29.09.2015. Made: 25.09.2015. Coming into force: 11.09.2015. Effect: None. Territorial extent & classification: NI. Local. - Available at http://www.legislation.gov.uk/nisr/2015/342/contents/made Non-print

The Parkside Gardens, Belfast (Abandonment) Order (Northern Ireland) 2015 No. 2015/220. - Enabling power: S.I. 1993/3160 (N.I. 15), art. 68 (1) (5). - Issued: 21.04.2015. Made: 17.04.2015. Coming into force: 03.06.2015. Effect: None. Territorial extent & classification: NI. Local. - Available at http://www.legislation.gov.uk/nisr/2015/220/contents/made Non-print

The Rathdown Walk, Lisburn (Abandonment) Order (Northern Ireland) 2015 No. 2015/30. - Enabling power: S.I. 1993/3160 (N.I. 15), art. 68 (1) (5). - Issued: 04.02.2015. Made: 02.02.2015. Coming into force: 11.03.2015. Effect: None. Territorial extent & classification: NI. Local. - Available at http://www.legislation.gov.uk/nisr/2015/30/contents/made Non-print

The Sliabh Dubh Glen and Sliabh Dubh View, Belfast (Footpath) (Abandonment) Order (Northern Ireland) 2015 No. 2015/221. - Enabling power: S.I. 1993/3160 (N.I. 15), art. 68 (1) (5). - Issued: 21.04.2015. Made: 17.04.2015. Coming into force: 03.06.2015. Effect: None. Territorial extent & classification: NI. Local. - Available at http://www.legislation.gov.uk/nisr/2015/221/contents/made Non-print

The U125 Old Grand Jury Road, Saintfield (Abandonment) Order (Northern Ireland) 2015 No. 2015/373. - Enabling power: S.I. 1993/3160 (N.I. 15), art. 68 (1) (5). - Issued: 26.11.2015. Made: 24.11.2015. Coming into force: 27.01.2016. Effect: None. Territorial extent & classification: NI. Local. - Available at http://www.legislation.gov.uk/nisr/2015/373/contents/made Non-print

The U6076 Cloghanramer Road, Newry (Abandonment) Order (Northern Ireland) 2015 No. 2015/374. - Enabling power: S.I. 1993/3160 (N.I. 15), art. 68 (1) (5). - Issued: 26.11.2015. Made: 24.11.2015. Coming into force: 27.01.2016. Effect: None. Territorial extent & classification: NI. Local. - Available at http://www.legislation.gov.uk/nisr/2015/374/contents/made Non-print

The White Lodge Court, Greenisland (Abandonment) Order (Northern Ireland) 2015 No. 2015/234. - Enabling power: S.I. 1993/3160 (N.I. 15), art. 68 (1) (5). - Issued: 29.04.2015. Made: 27.04.2015. Coming into force: 10.06.2015. Effect: None. Territorial extent & classification: NI. Local. - Available at http://www.legislation.gov.uk/nisr/2015/234/contents/made Non-print

Road traffic and vehicles

The A54 Ballymacombs Road, Portglenone (Abandonment) Order (Northern Ireland) 2015 No. 2015/134. - Enabling power: S.I. 1993/3160 (NI. 15), art. 68 (1) (5). - Issued: 12.03.2015. Made: 06.03.2015. Coming into force: 13.05.2015. Effect: None. Territorial extent & classification: NI. Local. - Available at http://www.legislation.gov.uk/nisr/2015/134/contents/made Non-print

The Bus Lanes (Falls Road, Belfast - between Grosvenor Road and Whiterock Road) Order (Northern Ireland) 2015 No. 2015/336. - Enabling power: S.I. 1997/276 (N.I. 2), arts 4 (1) (2) (3), sch.1, para. 5. - Issued: 23.09.2015. Made: 18.09.2015. Coming into operation: 19.10.2015. Effect: S.R. 2002/103; 2004/279 partially revoked. Territorial extent & classification: NI. Local. - Available at http://www.legislation.gov.uk/nisr/2015/336/contents/made Non-print

The Bus Lanes (Upper Newtownards Road, Belfast - between Sandown Road and Knock Road) (Amendment) Order (Northern Ireland) 2015 No. 2015/382. - Enabling power: S.I. 1997/276 (N.I. 2), art. 4 (1) (2) (3). - Issued: 01.12.2015. Made: 27.11.2015. Coming into operation: 04.01.2015. Effect: S.R. 2015/297 amended. Territorial extent & classification: NI. Local. - Available at http://www.legislation.gov.uk/nisr/2015/382/contents/made Non-print

The Bus Lanes (Upper Newtownards Road, Belfast - between Sandown Road and Knock Road) Order (Northern Ireland) 2015 No. 2015/297. - Enabling power: S.I. 1997/276 (N.I. 2), art. 4 (1) (2) (3). - Issued: 10.07.2015. Made: 08.07.2015. Coming into operation: 27.07.2015. Effect: None. Territorial extent & classification: NI. Local. - Available at http://www.legislation.gov.uk/nisr/2015/297/contents/made Non-print

The Compulsory Right or Left-Hand Turn (Belfast) Order (Northern Ireland) 2015 No. 2015/131. - Enabling power: S.I. 1997/276 (N.I. 2), art. 4 (1), sch. 1, para. 5. - Issued: 12.03.2015. Made: 06.03.2015. Coming into force: 30.03.2015. Effect: S.R. 1987/40; 1990/65; 1991/103; 1994/7; 1998/109; 1999/153; 2012/197 partially revoked & S.R. 1985/21, 200; 1987/237, 386; 1988/33, 78; 1995/326 revoked. Territorial extent & classification: NI. Local. - Available at http://www.legislation.gov.uk/nisr/2015/131/contents/made Non-print

The Concession Road, Route A37, Clonalig (Part-Time 20mph Speed Limit) Order (Northern Ireland) 2015 No. 2015/417. - Enabling power: S.I. 1997/276 (N.I. 2), art. 38 (1) (2). - Issued: 22.12.2015. Made: 18.12.2015. Coming into force: 14.01.2016. Effect: None. Territorial extent & classification: NI. Local. - Available at http://www.legislation.gov.uk/nisr/2015/417/contents/made Non-print

The Control of Traffic (Albert Street / Durham Street / College Square North, Belfast) Order (Northern Ireland) 2015 No. 2015/413. - Enabling power: S.I. 1997/276 (N.I. 2), arts 4 (1) (2) (3), sch. 1, para. 5. - Issued: 21.12.2015. Made: 16.12.2015. Coming into operation: 07.01.2016. Effect: S.R. 2009/49 amended. Territorial extent & classification: NI. Local. - Available at http://www.legislation.gov.uk/nisr/2015/413/contents/made Non-print

The Control of Traffic (Alfred Street / Upper Arthur Street, Belfast) Order (Northern Ireland) 2015 No. 2015/409. - Enabling power: S.I. 1997/276 (N.I. 2), arts 4 (1) (2) (3). - Issued: 15.12.2015. Made: 11.12.2015. Coming into operation: 04.01.2016. Effect: S.R. 2009/49 amended. Territorial extent & classification: NI. Local. - Available at http://www.legislation.gov.uk/nisr/2015/409/contents/made Non-print

The Control of Traffic (Lisburn) Order (Northern Ireland) 2015 No. 2015/305. - Enabling power: S.I. 1997/283 (N.I. 1), art. 4 (1) (2) (3) & S.I. 1991/1220 (N.I. 11), art. 100 (1) (2). - Issued: 17.07.2015. Made: 15.07.2015. Coming into operation: 05.08.2015. Effect: S.R. 1982/158; 2008/43 amended. Territorial extent & classification: NI. Local. - Available at http://www.legislation.gov.uk/nisr/2015/305/contents/made Non-print

The Cycle Routes (Amendment No. 2) Order (Northern Ireland) 2015 No. 2015/268. - Enabling power: S.I. 1997/276 (N.I.2), art. 4 (1) (2) (3). - Issued: 10.06.2015. Made: 08.06.2015. Coming into force: 29.06.2015. Effect: S.R. 2008/317 amended. Territorial extent & classification: NI. Local. - Available at http://www.legislation.gov.uk/nisr/2015/268/contents/made Non-print

The Cycle Routes (Amendment No. 3) Order (Northern Ireland) 2015 No. 2015/377. - Enabling power: S.I. 1997/276 (N.I.2), art. 4 (1) (2) (3). - Issued: 30.11.2015. Made: 26.11.2015. Coming into force: 16.12.2015. Effect: S.R. 2008/317 amended. Territorial extent & classification: NI. Local. - Available at http://www.legislation.gov.uk/nisr/2015/377/contents/made Non-print

ROAD TRAFFIC AND VEHICLES

The Cycle Routes (Amendment) Order (Northern Ireland) 2015 No. 2015/233. - Enabling power: S.I. 1997/276 (N.I.2), art. 4 (1) (2) (3). - Issued: 29.04.2015. Made: 27.04.2015. Coming into force: 18.05.2015. Effect: S.R. 2008/317 amended. Territorial extent & classification: NI. Local. - Available at http://www.legislation.gov.uk/nisr/2015/233/contents/made Non-print

The Disabled Persons (Badges for Motor Vehicles) (Amendment) Regulations (Northern Ireland) 2015 No. 2015/407. - Enabling power: Chronically Sick and Disabled Persons (Northern Ireland) Act 1978, s. 14. - Issued: 15.12.2015. Made: 10.12.2015. Coming into operation: 17.02.2016. Effect: S.R. 1993/202 amended. Territorial extent & classification: NI. General. - 4p.: 30 cm. - 978-0-337-99926-0 £4.25

The Footways (Prohibition of Waiting) Order (Northern Ireland) 2015 No. 2015/252. - Enabling power: S.I. 1997/276 (N.I. 2), art. 4 (1) (2). - Issued: 20.05.2015. Made: 18.05.2015. Coming into force: 08.06.2015. Effect: S.R. 1981/280; 1993/415 revoked. Territorial extent & classification: NI. Local. - Available at http://www.legislation.gov.uk/nisr/2015/252/contents/made Non-print

The Goods Vehicles (Testing) (Amendment) Regulations (Northern Ireland) 2015 No. 2015/43. - Enabling power: S.I. 1995/2994 (N.I. 18), arts 65 (1), 67 (1) (i) (j), 110 (2). - Issued: 13.02.2015. Made: 09.02.2015. Coming into operation: 06.04.2015. Effect: S.R. 2003/304 amended. Territorial extent & classification: NI. General. - 2p.: 30 cm. - 978-0-337-99606-1 £4.25

The Loading Bays on Roads (Amendment No. 2) Order (Northern Ireland) 2015 No. 2015/251. - Enabling power: S.I. 1997/276 (N.I. 2), arts 10 (4), 13 (1), sch. 4, para. 5. - Issued: 20.05.2015. Made: 18.05.2015. Coming into force: 08.06.2015. Effect: S.R. 2007/270 amended. Territorial extent & classification: NI. Local. - Available at http://www.legislation.gov.uk/nisr/2015/251/contents/made Non-print

The Loading Bays on Roads (Amendment No. 3) Order (Northern Ireland) 2015 No. 2015/391. - Enabling power: S.I. 1997/276 (N.I. 2), arts 10 (4), 13 (1), 15 (1) (4). - Issued: 04.12.2015. Made: 02.12.2015. Coming into force: 04.01.2016. Effect: S.R. 2000/383 amended. Territorial extent & classification: NI. Local. - Available at http://www.legislation.gov.uk/nisr/2015/391/contents/made Non-print

The Loading Bays on Roads (Amendment) Order (Northern Ireland) 2015 No. 2015/37. - Enabling power: S.I. 1997/276 (N.I. 2), arts 10 (4), 13 (1). - Issued: 11.02.2015. Made: 06.02.2015. Coming into force: 27.02.2015. Effect: S.R. 2007/270 amended. Territorial extent & classification: NI. Local. - Available at http://www.legislation.gov.uk/nisr/2015/37/contents/made Non-print

The Motor Vehicles (Driving Instruction) (Amendment) Regulations (Northern Ireland) 2015 No. 2015/5. - Enabling power: S.I. 2007/916 (N.I. 10), arts. 48 (4), 50 (1), 52 (2) (4) (6) (7), 61, 62, 70 (1), 76. - Issued: 22.01.2015. Made: 15.01.2015. Coming into operation: 28.02.2015. Effect: S.R. 2010/227 amended. Territorial extent & classification: NI. General. - 4p.: 30 cm. - 978-0-337-99561-3 £4.25

The Motor Vehicles (Driving Instruction) (Trainee Licence) (Amendment) Regulations (Northern Ireland) 2015 No. 2015/4. - Enabling power: S.I. 1981/154 (N.I. 1), arts 132 (2), 135 (1), 218 (1). - Issued: 22.01.2015. Made: 15.01.2015. Coming into operation: 28.02.2015. Effect: S.R. 2010/228 amended. Territorial extent & classification: NI. General. - 4p: 30 cm. - 978-0-337-99560-6 £4.25

The Motor Vehicles (Driving Licences) (Amendment No. 2) Regulations (Northern Ireland) 2015 No. 2015/242. - Enabling power: S.I. 1981/154 (N.I. 1), arts 5 (3) (4), 19C (1) (1A)(c), 218 (1). - Issued: 08.05.2015. Made: 05.05.2015. Coming into operation: 29.05.2015. Effect: S.R. 1996/542 amended. Territorial extent & classification: NI. General. - EC note: In accordance with Article 7(5)(a) of Directive 2006/126/EC on driving licences regulation 2(2) of these regs inserts a new regulation 16B into S.R. 1996/542 to prohibit a person from holding more than one Northern Ireland, Great Britain or Community driving licence. - 4p: 30 cm. - 978-0-337-99793-8 £4.25

The Motor Vehicles (Driving Licences) (Amendment No. 3) Regulations (Northern Ireland) 2015 No. 2015/357. - Enabling power: S.I. 1981/154 (N.I. 1), arts 4 (7) (8), 5 (3) (4) (5), 11 (4), 13 (1) (3) (a), 14 (4), 19C (1) (1A) (a) (f) (2). - Issued: 26.10.2015. Made: 14.10.2015. Coming into operation: 30.11.2015. Effect: S.R. 1996/542 amended. Territorial extent & classification: NI. General. - Corrected reprint of instrument issued 21.10.15 amending the title from Amendment No. 2. to Amendment No. 3. EC note: S.R. 1996/542 amended as a consequence of EU Directive 2014/85 which amends Annex II to EU Directive 2006/126, introducing a requirement for the theory test to include questions on safe driving in road tunnels and by adding more items to the list of specified requirements which may be tested in the practical or unitary test. - 4p: 30 cm. - 978-0-337-99886-7 £4.25

The Motor Vehicles (Driving Licences) (Amendment) Regulations (Northern Ireland) 2015 No. 2015/6. - Enabling power: European Communities Act 1972, s. 2 (2) & S.I. 1981/154 (N.I. 1), arts 5 (3) (4), 19C (1) (1A) (a) (f) (2), 218 (1). - Issued: 22.01.2015. Made: 15.01.2015. Coming into operation: 23.02.2015. Effect: S.I. 1981/154 (N.I. 1) & S.R. 1996/542 amended. Territorial extent & classification: NI. General. - EC note: These Regulations make further provision to implement Directive 2006/126/EC. - 8p; 30 cm. - 978-0-337-99562-0 £6.00

The Motor Vehicles (Wearing of Seat Belts) (Amendment) Regulations (Northern Ireland) 2015 No. 2015/24. - Enabling power: S.I. 1995/2994 (N.I. 18), arts 24 (3) (6). - Issued: 17.03.2015. Made: 27.01.2015. Coming into operation: 20.04.2015. Effect: S.R. 1993/362 amended. Territorial extent & classification: NI. General. - Affirmed by resolution of the Assembly on 10th March 2015. - 4p.: 30 cm. - 978-0-337-99681-8 £4.25

The Motor Vehicles (Wearing of Seat Belts) (Amendment) Regulations (Northern Ireland) 2015 No. 2015/24. - Enabling power: S.I. 1995/2994 (N.I. 18), arts 24 (3) (6). - Issued: 02.02.2015. Made: 27.01.2015. Coming into operation: 20.04.2015. Effect: S.R. 1993/362 amended. Territorial extent & classification: NI. General. - Subject to affirmative resolution of the Assembly. Superseded by affirmed instrument (ISBN 9780337996818) issued 17.03.2015. - 4p: 30 cm. - 978-0-337-99586-6 £4.25

The Motor Vehicles (Wearing of Seat Belts by Children in Front Seats) (Amendment) Regulations (Northern Ireland) 2015 No. 2015/23. - Enabling power: S.I. 1995/2994 (N.I. 18), art 24 (1) (6). - Issued: 30.01.2015. Made: 27.01.2015. Coming into operation: 20.04.2015. Effect: S.R. 1993/363 amended. Territorial extent & classification: NI. General. - EC note: Implements for Northern Ireland, requirements of Council Directive 2014/37/EC. - 4p.: 30 cm. - 978-0-337-99587-3 £4.25

The Motor Vehicle Testing (Amendment) Regulations (Northern Ireland) 2015 No. 2015/41. - Enabling power: S.I. 1995/2994 (N.I. 18), art. 61 (2) (6), 62, 110 (2). - Issued: 13.02.2015. Made: 09.02.2015. Coming into operation: 06.02.2015. Effect: S.R. 2003/303 amended. Territorial extent & classification: NI. General. - 2p.: 30 cm. - 978-0-337-99604-7 £4.25

The Off-Street Parking (Amendment) Order (Northern Ireland) 2015 No. 2015/240. - Enabling power: S.I. 1997/276 (N.I. 2), arts 11 (1) (c), 13 (1) (2) (6) (7) (14) (16), 26 (1), sch. 4, para. 5. - Issued: 07.05.2015. Made: 05.05.2015. Coming into force: 26.05.2015. Effect: S.R. 2000/384 amended. Territorial extent & classification: NI. Local. - Available at http://www.legislation.gov.uk/nisr/2015/240/contents/made Non-print

The One-Way Traffic (Ballymena) (Amendment) Order (Northern Ireland) 2015 No. 2015/303. - Enabling power: S.I. 1997/276 (N.I. 2), art. 4 (1) (2) (3). - Issued: 14.07.2015. Made: 10.07.2015. Coming into force: 27.07.2015. Effect: S.R. 2008/438 amended. Territorial extent & classification: NI. Local. - Available at http://www.legislation.gov.uk/nisr/2015/303/contents/made Non-print

The One-Way Traffic (Belfast) (Amendment No. 2) Order (Northern Ireland) 2015 No. 2015/217. - Enabling power: S.I. 1997/276 (N.I. 2), art. 4 (1) (2) (3). - Issued: 21.04.2015. Made: 17.04.2015. Coming into force: 11.05.2015. Effect: S.R. 2009/49 amended. Territorial extent & classification: NI. Local. - Available at http://www.legislation.gov.uk/nisr/2015/217/contents/made Non-print

The One-Way Traffic (Belfast) (Amendment) Order (Northern Ireland) 2015 No. 2015/59. - Enabling power: S.I. 1997/276 (N.I. 2), art. 4 (1) (2) (3). - Issued: 18.02.2015. Made: 16.02.2015. Coming into force: 09.03.2015. Effect: S.R. 2009/49 amended. Territorial extent & classification: NI. Local. - Available at http://www.legislation.gov.uk/nisr/2015/59/contents/made Non-print

ROAD TRAFFIC AND VEHICLES

The Parking and Waiting Restrictions (Antrim) Order (Northern Ireland) 2015 No. 2015/232. - Enabling power: S.I. 1997/276 (N.I. 2), art. 4 (1) (2) (3), 10 (4), 13 (1) (13) (16). - Issued: 29.04.2015. Made: 27.04.2015. Coming into force: 18.05.2015. Effect: S.R 2008/366; 2009/213; 2014/165 (non-prints) revoked. Territorial extent & classification: NI. Local. - Available at http://www.legislation.gov.uk/nisr/2015/232/contents/made Non-print

The Parking and Waiting Restrictions (Banbridge) (Amendment) Order (Northern Ireland) 2015 No. 2015/343. - Enabling power: S.I. 1997/276 (N.I. 2), art. 4 (1) (2) (3). - Issued: 29.09.2015. Made: 25.09.2015. Coming into force: 19.10.2015. Effect: S.R. 2014/260 amended. Territorial extent & classification: NI. Local. - Available at http://www.legislation.gov.uk/nisr/2015/343/contents/made Non-print

The Parking and Waiting Restrictions (Belfast) (Amendment No. 2) Order (Northern Ireland) 2015 No. 2015/275. - Enabling power: S.I. 1997/276 (N.I. 2), arts 4 (1) (2)(3). - Issued: 19.06.2015. Made: 17.06.2015. Coming into force: 08.07.2015. Effect: S.R. 2008/180 amended. Territorial extent & classification: NI. Local. - Available at http://www.legislation.gov.uk/nisr/2015/275/contents/made Non-print

The Parking and Waiting Restrictions (Belfast) (Amendment No. 3) Order (Northern Ireland) 2015 No. 2015/300. - Enabling power: S.I. 1997/276 (N.I. 2), art. 4 (1) (2) (3), 10 (4), 13 (1). - Issued: 10.07.2015. Made: 08.07.2015. Coming into force: 28.07.2015. Effect: S.R. 2008/180 amended. Territorial extent & classification: NI. Local. - Available at http://www.legislation.gov.uk/nisr/2015/300/contents/made Non-print

The Parking and Waiting Restrictions (Belfast) (Amendment No. 4) Order (Northern Ireland) 2015 No. 2015/381. - Enabling power: S.I. 1997/276 (N.I. 2), sch. 1, para. 5, art. 4 (1) (2) (3). - Issued: 01.12.2015. Made: 27.11.2015. Coming into force: 04.01.2016. Effect: S.R. 2008/180 amended. Territorial extent & classification: NI. Local. - Available at http://www.legislation.gov.uk/nisr/2015/381/contents/made Non-print

The Parking and Waiting Restrictions (Belfast) (Amendment) Order (Northern Ireland) 2015 No. 2015/60. - Enabling power: S.I. 1997/276 (N.I. 2), art. 4 (1) (2) (3), 10 (4), 13 (1), sch. 1, para. 5, sch. 4, para. 5. - Issued: 18.02.2015. Made: 16.02.2015. Coming into force: 09.03.2015. Effect: S.R 2008/180 amended. Territorial extent & classification: NI. Local. - Available at http://www.legislation.gov.uk/nisr/2015/60/contents/made Non-print

The Parking and Waiting Restrictions (Belfast City Centre) Order (Northern Ireland) 2015 No. 2015/378. - Enabling power: S.I. 1997/276 (N.I. 2), arts 4 (1) (2) (3), 10 94), 13 (1) (13) (16), 15 (1) (4). - Issued: 30.11.2015. Made: 26.11.2015. Coming into force: 16.12.2015. Effect: S.R. 2000/383; 2010/268 amended & S.R. 2014/243 partially revoked & S.R. 2012/199; 2014/251 revoked.Territorial extent & classification: NI. Local. - Available at http://www.legislation.gov.uk/nisr/2015/378/contents/made Non-print

The Parking and Waiting Restrictions (Cathedral Quarter, Belfast) (Amendment) Order (Northern Ireland) 2015 No. 2015/335. - Enabling power: S.I. 1997/276 (N.I. 2), art. 4 (1) (2) (3). - Issued: 22.09.2015. Made: 18.09.2015. Coming into force: 12.10.2015. Effect: S.R 2014/161 amended. Territorial extent & classification: NI. Local. - Available at http://www.legislation.gov.uk/nisr/2015/335/contents/made Non-print

The Parking and Waiting Restrictions (Dungannon) Order (Northern Ireland) 2015 No. 2015/337. - Enabling power: S.I. 1997/276 (N.I. 2), art. 4 (1) (2) (3), 10 (4), 13 (1) (13) (16). - Issued: 23.09.2015. Made: 18.09.2015. Coming into force: 12.10.2015. Effect: None. Territorial extent & classification: NI. Local. - Available at http://www.legislation.gov.uk/nisr/2015/337/contents/made Non-print

The Parking and Waiting Restrictions (Fivemiletown) (Amendment) Order (Northern Ireland) 2015 No. 2015/245. - Enabling power: S.I. 1997/276 (N.I. 2), art. 10 (4), 13 (1). - Issued: 12.05.2015. Made: 08.05.2015. Coming into force: 29.05.2015. Effect: S.I. 1999/283 (N.I. 1) amended. Territorial extent & classification: NI. Local. - Available at http://www.legislation.gov.uk/nisr/2015/245/contents/made Non-print

The Parking and Waiting Restrictions (Londonderry) Order (Northern Ireland) 2015 No. 2015/67. - Enabling power: S.I. 1997/276 (N.I. 2), art. 4 (1) (2) (3), 10 (4), 13 (1) (13) (16). - Issued: 23.02.2015. Made: 18.02.2015. Coming into force: 10.03.2015. Effect: S.R 2008/10; 2010/398; 2012/80, 346; 2014/83 partially revoked & S.R. 2010/256; 2011/138, 193; 2012/243, 352; 2013/21, 100, 136; 2014/115 revoked. Territorial extent & classification: NI. Local. - Available at http://www.legislation.gov.uk/nisr/2015/67/contents/made Non-print

The Parking and Waiting Restrictions (Newtownabbey) Order (Northern Ireland) 2015 No. 2015/222. - Enabling power: S.I. 1997/276 (N.I. 2), art. 4 (1) (2) (3), 10 (4), 13 (1) (13) (16). - Issued: 21.04.2015. Made: 17.04.2015. Coming into force: 11.05.2015. Effect: S.R 2008/461; 2011/317, 318 (non-prints) revoked. Territorial extent & classification: NI. Local. - Available at http://www.legislation.gov.uk/nisr/2015/222/contents/made Non-print

The Parking and Waiting Restrictions (Portballintrae) Order (Northern Ireland) 2015 No. 2015/401. - Enabling power: S.I. 1997/276 (N.I. 2), arts 4 (1) (2) (3). - Issued: 09.12.2015. Made: 07.12.2015. Coming into force: 04.01.2016. Effect: None. Territorial extent & classification: NI. Local. - Available at http://www.legislation.gov.uk/nisr/2015/401/contents/made Non-print

The Parking and Waiting Restrictions (Strabane) Order (Northern Ireland) 2015 No. 2015/400. - Enabling power: S.I. 1997/276 (N.I. 2), arts 4 (1) (2) (3), 10 (4), 13 (1) (13) (16). - Issued: 09.12.2015. Made: 07.12.2015. Coming into force: 04.01.2016. Effect: S.R. 2008/335, 398; 2010/265; 2011/196, 400; 2012/102, 224; 2013/133; 2014/90 revoked. Territorial extent & classification: NI. Local. - Available at http://www.legislation.gov.uk/nisr/2015/400/contents/made Non-print

The Parking Places and Waiting Restrictions (Alfred Street / Upper Arthur Street, Belfast) Order (Northern Ireland) 2015 No. 2015/410. - Enabling power: S.I. 1997/276 (NI 2), arts 4 (1) (2) (3), 10 (4), 13 (1) (9) (10) (12) (13) (16), 15 (1). - Issued: 15.12.2015. Made: 11.12.2015. Coming into operation: 04.01.2016. Effect: S.R. 2000/383; 2007/270; 2015/33 amended. Territorial extent & classification: NI. Local. - Available at http://www.legislation.gov.uk/nisr/2015/410/contents/made Non-print

The Parking Places (Disabled Persons' Vehicles) (Amendment No. 3) Order (Northern Ireland) 2015 No. 2015/380. - Enabling power: S.I. 1997/276 (N.I.2), sch. 4, para. 5, arts 10 (4), 13 (1) (16). - Issued: 01.12.2015. Made: 26.11.2015. Coming into force: 16.12.2015. Effect: S.R. 2015/33 amended. Territorial extent & classification: NI. Local. - Available at http://www.legislation.gov.uk/nisr/2015/380/contents/made Non-print

The Parking Places, Loading Bay and Waiting Restrictions (Lisburn City Centre) Order (Northern Ireland) 2015 No. 2015/263. - Enabling power: S.I. 1997/276 (N.I. 2), arts 4 (1) (2) (3), 10 (4), 13 (1), 15 (1) , sch.1, para. 5, sch. 4, para. 5. - Issued: 04.06.2015. Made: 01.06.2015. Coming into force: 18.06.2015. Effect: S.R. 2000/383; 2007/270; 2015/260 amended. Territorial extent & classification: NI. Local. - Available at http://www.legislation.gov.uk/nisr/2015/263/contents/made Non-print

The Parking Places on Roads and Waiting Restrictions (Ballymoney) Order (Northern Ireland) 2015 No. 2015/316. - Enabling power: S.I. 1997/276 (N.I. 2), arts 4 (1) (2) (3), 10 (4), 13 (1) (13) (16). - Issued: 21.07.2015. Made: 17.07.2015. Coming into force: 06.08.2015. Effect: S.R. 2008/5, 482; 2009/193, 371; 2010/266, 389; 2011/140, 149; 2012/4; 2014/241 revoked. Territorial extent & classification: NI. Local. - Available at http://www.legislation.gov.uk/nisr/2015/316/contents/made Non-print

The Parking Places on Roads and Waiting Restrictions (Newry) (Amendment) Order (Northern Ireland) 2015 No. 2015/423. - Enabling power: S.I. 1997/276 (N.I. 2), arts 4 (1) (2) (3). - Issued: 23.12.2015. Made: 21.12.2015. Coming into force: 18.01.2016. Effect: S.R. 2015/270 amended. Territorial extent & classification: NI. Local. - Available at http://www.legislation.gov.uk/nisr/2015/423/contents/made Non-print

The Parking Places on Roads and Waiting Restrictions (Newry) Order (Northern Ireland) 2015 No. 2015/270. - Enabling power: S.I. 1997/276 (N.I. 2), arts 4 (1) (2) (3), 10 (4), 13 (1) (13) (16). - Issued: 11.06.2015. Made: 08.06.2015. Coming into force: 29.06.2015. Effect: S.R.2008/313, 449; 2009/165, 214, 299; 2010/211, 240, 257, 424; 2011/96, 198, 267, 334, 361 revoked. Territorial extent & classification: NI. Local. - Available at http://www.legislation.gov.uk/nisr/2015/270/contents/made Non-print

The Parking Places on Roads (Coaches) (Amendment) Order (Northern Ireland) 2015 No. 2015/142. - Enabling power: S.I. 1997/276 (NI 2), arts 10 (4), 13 (1). - Issued: 12.03.2015. Made: 10.03.2015. Coming into operation: 31.03.2015. Effect: S.R. 2012/201 amended. Territorial extent & classification: NI. Local. - Revoked by SR 2015/414 (Non-print) (ISBN 9786666441890) issued 21/12/15. - Available at http://www.legislation.gov.uk/nisr/2015/142/contents/made Non-print

ROAD TRAFFIC AND VEHICLES

The Parking Places on Roads (Coaches) Order (Northern Ireland) 2015 No. 2015/414. - Enabling power: S.I. 1997/276 (N.I.2), arts 10 (4), 13 (1) (13) (16). - Issued: 21.12.2015. Made: 16.12.2015. Coming into force: 07.01.2016. Effect: S.R.2014/243; 2015/317 partially revoked & S.R. 2012/201; 2015/142 revoked. Territorial extent & classification: NI. Local. - Available at http://www.legislation.gov.uk/nisr/2015/414/contents/made Non-print

The Parking Places on Roads (Disabled Persons' Vehicles) (Amendment No. 2) Order (Northern Ireland) 2015 No. 2015/314. - Enabling power: S.I. 1997/276 (NI 2), arts 10 (4), 13 (1) (16), 15 (1). - Issued: 21.07.2015. Made: 17.07.2015. Coming into operation: 06.008.2015. Effect: S.R. 2015/33 amended. Territorial extent & classification: NI. Local. - Available at http://www.legislation.gov.uk/nisr/2015/314/contents/made Non-print

The Parking Places on Roads (Disabled Persons' Vehicles) (Amendment No. 4) Order (Northern Ireland) 2015 No. 2015/424. - Enabling power: S.I. 1997/276 (N.I.2), arts 10 (4), 13 (1) (16). - Issued: 23.12.2015. Made: 21.12.2015. Coming into force: 14.01.2015. Effect: S.R. 2015/33 amended. Territorial extent & classification: NI. Local. - Available at http://www.legislation.gov.uk/nisr/2015/424/contents/made Non-print

The Parking Places on Roads (Disabled Persons' Vehicles) (Amendment) Order (Northern Ireland) 2015 No. 2015/258. - Enabling power: S.I. 1997/276 (N.I.2), arts 10 (4), 13 (1) (16), sch. 4, para. 5. - Issued: 01.06.2015. Made: 28.05.2015. Coming into force: 17.06.2015. Effect: S.R. 2015/33 amended. Territorial extent & classification: NI. Local. - Available at http://www.legislation.gov.uk/nisr/2015/258/contents/made Non-print

The Parking Places on Roads (Disabled Persons' Vehicles) Order (Northern Ireland) 2015 No. 2015/33. - Enabling power: S.I. 1997/276 (NI 2), arts 10 (4), 13 (1) (16). - Issued: 06.02.2015. Made: 02.02.2015. Coming into operation: 23.02.2015. Effect: 64 SRs revoked & 8 SRs partially revoked. Territorial extent & classification: NI. Local. - Available at http://www.legislation.gov.uk/nisr/2015/33/contents/made Non-print

The Parking Places on Roads (Lisburn City Centre) Order (Northern Ireland) 2015 No. 2015/317. - Enabling power: S.I. 1997/276 (N.I. 2), arts 10 (4), 13 (1) (13) (16), 15 (1), sch. 4, para. 5. - Issued: 21.07.2015. Made: 17.07.2015. Coming into force: 06.08.2015. Effect: S.R. 2000/383; 2007/270; 2012/201 amended. Territorial extent & classification: NI. Local. - Available at http://www.legislation.gov.uk/nisr/2015/317/contents/made. - by SR 2015/414 (Non-print) (ISBN 9786666441890) Non-print

The Parking Places on Roads (Medical Practitioners) (Amendment) Order (Northern Ireland) 2015 No. 2015/299. - Enabling power: S.I. 1997/276 (N.I. 2), arts 10 (4), 13 (1) (16). - Issued: 10.07.2015. Made: 08.07.2015. Coming into force: 28.07.2015. Effect: S.R. 2009/268 amended. Territorial extent & classification: NI. Local. - Available at http://www.legislation.gov.uk/nisr/2015/299/contents/made Non-print

The Prohibition of Right-Hand Turn (Larne) Order (Northern Ireland) 2015 No. 2015/219. - Enabling power: S.I. 1997/276 (N.I. 2), art. 4 (1) (2) (3). - Issued: 21.04.2015. Made: 17.04.2015. Coming into force: 12.05.2015. Effect: None. Territorial extent & classification: NI. Local. - Available at http://www.legislation.gov.uk/nisr/2015/219/contents/made Non-print

The Prohibition of U-Turn (A2 Belfast Road, Carrickfergus) Order (Northern Ireland) 2015 No. 2015/298. - Enabling power: S.I. 1997/276 (N.I. 2), art. 4 (1) (2) (3). - Issued: 10.07.2015. Made: 08.07.2015. Coming into operation: 28.07.2015. Effect: None. Territorial extent & classification: NI. Local. - Available at http://www.legislation.gov.uk/nisr/2015/298/contents/made Non-print

The Prohibition of Waiting (Amendment No. 2) Order (Northern Ireland) 2015 No. 2015/338. - Enabling power: S.I. 1997/276 (N.I. 2), art. 4 (1) (2) (3). - Issued: 23.09.2015. Made: 18.09.2015. Coming into force: 12.10.2015. Effect: S.R. 2001/59 amended. Territorial extent & classification: NI. Local. - Revoked by SR 2015/379 (Non-print) (ISBN 9786666441692). - Available at http://www.legislation.gov.uk/nisr/2015/338/contents/made Non-print

The Prohibition of Waiting (Amendment) Order (Northern Ireland) 2015 No. 2015/264. - Enabling power: S.I. 1997/276 (N.I. 2), art. 4 (1) (2) (3). - Issued: 04.06.2015. Made: 01.06.2015. Coming into force: 22.06.2015. Effect: S.R. 2001/59 amended. Territorial extent & classification: NI. Local. - Revoked by SR 2015/379 (Non-print) (ISBN 9786666441692). - Available at http://www.legislation.gov.uk/nisr/2015/264/contents/made Non-print

The Prohibition of Waiting (Schools) Order (Northern Ireland) 2015 No. 2015/379. - Enabling power: S.I. 1997/276 (N.I. 2), art. 4 (1) (2) (3). - Issued: 30.11.2015. Made: 26.11.2015. Coming into force: 16.12.2015. Effect: S.R. 2001/59; 2005/100; 2007/63; 2010/359; 2011/194; 2012/364; 2014/236; 2015/264, 338 revoked. Territorial extent & classification: NI. Local. - Available at http://www.legislation.gov.uk/nisr/2015/379/contents/made Non-print

The Public Service Vehicles (Amendment) Regulations (Northern Ireland) 2015 No. 2015/42. - Enabling power: S.I. 1981/154 (N.I. 1), arts 61 (1), 66 (1), 218 (1). - Issued: 13.02.2015. Made: 09.02.2015. Coming into operation: 06.04.2015. Effect: S.R. 1985/123 amended. Territorial extent & classification: NI. General. - 2p.: 30 cm. - 978-0-337-99605-4 £4.25

The Road Races (Armoy Motorcycle Race) Order (Northern Ireland) 2015 No. 2015/283. - Enabling power: S.I. 1986/1887 (N.I. 17), art. 3. - Issued: 29.06.2015. Made: 25.06.2015. Coming into force: 23.07.2015. Effect: None. Territorial extent & classification: NI. Local. - Available at http://www.legislation.gov.uk/nisr/2015/283/contents/made Non-print

The Road Races (Bushwhacker Rally) Order (Northern Ireland) 2015 No. 2015/323. - Enabling power: S.I. 1986/1887 (N.I. 17), art. 3. - Issued: 20.08.2015. Made: 18.08.2015. Coming into force: 25.09.2015. Effect: None. Territorial extent & classification: NI. Local. - Available at http://www.legislation.gov.uk/nisr/2015/323/contents/made Non-print

The Road Races (Cairncastle Hill Climb) Order (Northern Ireland) 2015 No. 2015/246. - Enabling power: S.I. 1986/1887 (N.I. 17), art. 3. - Issued: 12.05.2015. Made: 08.05.2015. Coming into force: 25.06.2015. Effect: None. Territorial extent & classification: NI. Local. - Available at http://www.legislation.gov.uk/nisr/2015/246/contents/made Non-print

The Road Races (Circuit of Ireland Rally) Order (Northern Ireland) 2015 No. 2015/133. - Enabling power: S.I. 1986/1887 (N.I. 17), art. 3. - Issued: 12.03.2015. Made: 06.03.2015. Coming into force: 01.04.2015. Effect: None. Territorial extent & classification: NI. Local. - Available at http://www.legislation.gov.uk/nisr/2015/133/contents/made Non-print

The Road Races (Cookstown 100) Order (Northern Ireland) 2015 No. 2015/171. - Enabling power: S.I. 1986/1887 (N.I. 17), art. 3. - Issued: 24.03.2015. Made: 20.03.2015. Coming into force: 23.04.2015. Effect: None. Territorial extent & classification: NI. Local. - Available at http://www.legislation.gov.uk/nisr/2015/171/contents/made Non-print

The Road Races (Craigantlet Hill Climb) Order (Northern Ireland) 2015 No. 2015/173. - Enabling power: S.I. 1986/1887 (N.I. 17), art. 3. - Issued: 24.03.2015. Made: 20.03.2015. Coming into force: 01.05.2015. Effect: None. Territorial extent & classification: NI. Local. - Available at http://www.legislation.gov.uk/nisr/2015/173/contents/made Non-print

The Road Races (Croft Hill Climb) Order (Northern Ireland) 2015 No. 2015/132. - Enabling power: S.I. 1986/1887 (N.I. 17), art. 3. - Issued: 12.03.2015. Made: 06.03.2015. Coming into force: 17.04.2015. Effect: None. Territorial extent & classification: NI. Local. - Available at http://www.legislation.gov.uk/nisr/2015/132/contents/made Non-print

The Road Races (Drumhorc Hill Climb) Order (Northern Ireland) 2015 No. 2015/212. - Enabling power: S.I. 1986/1887 (N.I. 17), art. 3. - Issued: 21.04.2015. Made: 02.04.2015. Coming into force: 15.05.2015. Effect: None. Territorial extent & classification: NI. Local. - Available at http://www.legislation.gov.uk/nisr/2015/212/contents/made Non-print

The Road Races (Garron Point Hill Climb) Order (Northern Ireland) 2015 No. 2015/313. - Enabling power: S.I. 1986/1887 (N.I. 17), art. 3. - Issued: 21.07.2015. Made: 17.07.2015. Coming into force: 21.08.2015. Effect: None. Territorial extent & classification: NI. Local. - Available at http://www.legislation.gov.uk/nisr/2015/313/contents/made Non-print

The Road Races (North West 200) Order (Northern Ireland) 2015 No. 2015/226. - Enabling power: S.I. 1986/1887 (N.I. 17), art. 3. - Issued: 24.04.2015. Made: 22.04.2015. Coming into force: 11.05.2015. Effect: None. Territorial extent & classification: NI. Local. - Available at http://www.legislation.gov.uk/nisr/2015/226/contents/made Non-print

The Road Races (POC NI Oils Stages Rally) Order (Northern Ireland) 2015 No. 2015/291. - Enabling power: S.I. 1986/1887 (N.I. 17), art. 3. - Issued: 07.07.2015. Made: 03.07.2015. Coming into force: 24.07.2015. Effect: None. Territorial extent & classification: NI. Local. - Available at http://www.legislation.gov.uk/nisr/2015/291/contents/made Non-print

The Road Races (Spamount Hill Climb) Order (Northern Ireland) 2015 No. 2015/218. - Enabling power: S.I. 1986/1887 (N.I. 17), art. 3. - Issued: 21.04.2015. Made: 17.04.2015. Coming into force: 29.05.2015. Effect: None. Territorial extent & classification: NI. Local. - Available at http://www.legislation.gov.uk/nisr/2015/218/contents/made Non-print

ROAD TRAFFIC AND VEHICLES

The Road Races (Tandragee 100) Order (Northern Ireland) 2015 No. 2015/172. - Enabling power: S.I. 1986/1887 (N.I. 17), art. 3. - Issued: 24.03.2015. Made: 20.03.2015. Coming into force: 30.04.2015. Effect: None. Territorial extent & classification: NI. Local. - Available at http://www.legislation.gov.uk/nisr/2015/172/contents/made Non-print

The Road Races (Tour of the Sperrins Rally) Order (Northern Ireland) 2015 No. 2015/214. - Enabling power: S.I. 1986/1887 (N.I. 17), art. 3. - Issued: 14.04.2015. Made: 10.04.2015. Coming into force: 08.05.2015. Effect: None. Territorial extent & classification: NI. Local. - Available at http://www.legislation.gov.uk/nisr/2015/214/contents/made Non-print

The Road Races (Ulster Grand Prix Bike Week) Order (Northern Ireland) 2015 No. 2015/292. - Enabling power: S.I. 1986/1887 (N.I. 17), art. 3. - Issued: 07.07.2015. Made: 03.07.2015. Coming into force: 04.08.2015. Effect: None. Territorial extent & classification: NI. Local. - Available at http://www.legislation.gov.uk/nisr/2015/292/contents/made Non-print

The Road Races (Ulster Rally) Order (Northern Ireland) 2015 No. 2015/312. - Enabling power: S.I. 1986/1887 (N.I. 17), art. 3. - Issued: 21.07.2015. Made: 17.07.2015. Coming into force: 13.08.2015. Effect: None. Territorial extent & classification: NI. Local. - Available at http://www.legislation.gov.uk/nisr/2015/312/contents/made Non-print

The Roads (Speed Limit) (No. 2) Order (Northern Ireland) 2015 No. 2015/295. - Enabling power: S.I. 1997/276 (N.I. 2), arts 37 (3) (4), 38 (1) (a). - Issued: 09.07.2015. Made: 07.07.2015. Coming into force: 28.07.2015. Effect: S.R. & O. 1956/124; S.R. 1977/40; 1997/238, 348; 1998/340; 1999/458; 2000/112; 2007/367; 2013/274 revoked with saving & S.R. 2007/253 revoked. Territorial extent & classification: NI. Local. - Available at http://www.legislation.gov.uk/nisr/2015/293/contents/made Non-print

The Roads (Speed Limit) (No. 3) Order (Northern Ireland) 2015 No. 2015/334. - Enabling power: S.I. 1997/276 (NI. 2), arts 37 (3) (4), 38 (1) (a). - Issued: 23.09.2015. Made: 18.09.2015. Coming into force: 12.10.2015. Effect: S.R. 1982/131; 1989/108; 1990/165, 166; 1994/373, 374; 1997/238; 1998/340; 2004/434; 2005/530 partially revoked. Territorial extent & classification: NI. Local. - Available at http://www.legislation.gov.uk/nisr/2015/334/contents/made Non-print

The Roads (Speed Limit) (No. 4) Order (Northern Ireland) 2015 No. 2015/375. - Enabling power: S.I. 1997/276 (NI. 2), arts 37 (3) (4), 38 (1) (a). - Issued: 26.11.2015. Made: 24.11.2015. Coming into force: 14.12.2015. Effect: S.R. & O. 1956/124; 1965/225; S.R. 1979/61; 1997/238, 285, 415; 1998/340, 450; 2004/434; 2006/275; 2010/213; 2013/274 partially revoked. Territorial extent & classification: NI. Local. - Available at http://www.legislation.gov.uk/nisr/2015/375/contents/made Non-print

The Roads (Speed Limit) (No. 5) Order (Northern Ireland) 2015 No. 2015/416. - Enabling power: S.I. 1997/276 (NI. 2), arts 37 (3) (4), 38 (1) (a). - Issued: 22.12.2015. Made: 18.12.2015. Coming into force: 14.01.2016. Effect: S.R. & O 1956/124; S.R. 1996/2; 1997/416; 2001/356; 2003/82; 2007/232; 2010/213 partially revoked. Territorial extent & classification: NI. Local. - Available at http://www.legislation.gov.uk/nisr/2015/416/contents/made Non-print

The Roads (Speed Limit) Order (Northern Ireland) 2015 No. 2015/293. - Enabling power: S.I. 1997/276 (N.I. 2), arts 37 (3) (4), 38 (1) (a). - Issued: 08.07.2015. Made: 06.07.2015. Coming into force: 27.07.2015. Effect: S.R. 1973/231; 1980/205; 1993/408; 1997/85, 206,415, 416; 2000/288; 2004/434; 2010/313; 2012/166 revoked. Territorial extent & classification: NI. Local. - Available at http://www.legislation.gov.uk/nisr/2015/293/contents/made Non-print

The Road Traffic (Fixed Penalty) (Offences) (Amendment) Order (Northern Ireland) 2015 No. 2015/349. - Enabling power: S.I. 1996/1320 (N.I. 10), art. 57 (2). - Issued: 05.10.2015. Made: 30.09.2015. Coming into operation: 16.11.2015. Effect: S.R. 1997/369 amended. Territorial extent & classification: NI. General. - With correction slip dated November 2015. - 2p.: 30 cm. - 978-0-337-99877-5 £4.25

The Road Vehicles Lighting (Amendment) Regulations (Northern Ireland) 2015 No. 2015/397. - Enabling power: S.I. 1995/2994 (N.I. 18), arts. 55 (1) (2) (4), 110 (2). - Issued: 07.12.2015. Made: 02.12.2015. Coming into operation: 31.05.2016. Effect: S.R. 2000/169 amended. Territorial extent & classification: NI. General. - 2p.: 30 cm. - 978-0-337-99912-3 £4.25

The Taxi Licensing Regulations (Northern Ireland) 2015 No. 2015/393. - Enabling power: Taxis Act (Northern Ireland) 2008, ss. 13 (2) (3) (5), 15 (2), 19 (1), 20, 30 (1) (2), 56 (1), 57 (1)- Issued: 07.12.2015. Made: 02.12.2015. Coming into operation: In accord. with reg. 1. Effect: S.R. 2014/302 revoked. Territorial extent & classification: NI. General. - 24p.: 30 cm. - 978-0-337-99915-4 £6.00

The Taxi Operators Licensing (Amendment) Regulations (Northern Ireland) 2015 No. 2015/395. - Enabling power: Taxis Act (Northern Ireland) 2008, ss 1 (4), 2 (5), 3 (2) (3) (7), 56 (1). - Issued: 07.12.2015. Made: 02.12.2015. Coming into operation: 31.05.2016. Effect: S.R. 2012/316 amended & S.R. 2014/303 revoked. Territorial extent & classification: NI. General. - 4p.: 30 cm. - 978-0-337-99914-7 £4.25

The Taxis (2008 Act) (Commencement No. 4) (Amendment) Order (Northern Ireland) 2015 No. 2015/257 (C.20). - Enabling power: Taxis Act (Northern Ireland) 2008, s. 59. - Issued: 28.05.2015. Made: 22.05.2015. Effect: S.R. 2014/300 (C.16) amended. Territorial extent & classification: NI. General. - 2p.: 30 cm. - 978-0-337-99815-7 £4.25

The Taxis (2008 Act) (Commencement No. 5) Order (Northern Ireland) 2015 No. 2015/389 (C.35). - Enabling power: Taxis Act (Northern Ireland) 2008, s. 59. - Issued: 04.12.2015. Made: 01.12.2015. Effect: None. Territorial extent & classification: NI. General. - With correction slip dated January 2015. - 6p.: 30 cm. - 978-0-337-99909-3 £4.25

The Taxis (Antrim) Order (Northern Ireland) 2015 No. 2015/38. - Enabling power: S.I. 1997/276 (N.I. 2), art. 27A (1). - Issued: 11.02.2015. Made: 06.02.2015. Coming into force: 27.02.2015. Effect: S.R. 2008/230 revoked. Territorial extent & classification: NI. Local. - Available at http://www.legislation.gov.uk/nisr/2015/38/contents/made Non-print

The Taxis (Lisburn) Order (Northern Ireland) 2015 No. 2015/250. - Enabling power: S.I. 1997/276 (N.I. 2), art. 27A (1). - Issued: 20.05.2015. Made: 18.05.2015. Coming into operation: 08.06.2015. Effect: Bye-Laws as respects Motor Hackney Carriages used in standing or plying for hire made by Lisburn Borough Council on 2nd June 1970 partially revoked & S.R. 1992/344; 2010/401 revoked. Territorial extent & classification: NI. Local. - Available at http://www.legislation.gov.uk/nisr/2015/250/contents/made Non-print

The Taxis (Taximeters, Devices and Maximum Fares) Regulations (Northern Ireland) 2015 No. 2015/394. - Enabling power: Taxis Act (Northern Ireland) 2008, ss. 16 (1), 17 (1), 18 (1) (4) (5), 30 (1) (e) (2), 44 (3) (f), 56 (2). - Issued: 07.12.2015. Made: 02.12.2015. Coming into operation: In accord. with reg. 1. Effect: None. Territorial extent & classification: NI. General. - 12p.: 30 cm. - 978-0-337-99916-1 £6.00

The Traffic Weight Restrictions (Amendment) Order (Northern Ireland) 2015 No. 2015/269. - Enabling power: S.I. 1997/276 (N.I. 2), art. 4 (1) (2). - Issued: 10.06.2015. Made: 08.06.2015. Coming into force: 29.06.2015. Effect: S.R. 2004/231 amended. Territorial extent & classification: NI. Local. - Available at http://www.legislation.gov.uk/nisr/2015/269/contents/made Non-print

The Urban Clearways (Amendment) Order (Northern Ireland) 2015 No. 2015/31. - Enabling power: S.I. 1997/276 (N.I.2), art. 4 (1) (2) (3). - Issued: 04.02.2015. Made: 02.02.2015. Coming into force: 25.02.2015. Effect: S.R. 1997/197 amended. Territorial extent & classification: NI. Local. - Available at http://www.legislation.gov.uk/nisr/2015/31/contents/made Non-print

The Waiting Restrictions (Castlederg) Order (Northern Ireland) 2015 No. 2015/110. - Enabling power: S.I. 1997/276 (N.I. 2), art. 4 (1) (2) (3). - Issued: 05.03.2015. Made: 02.03.2015. Coming into operation: 23.03.2015. Effect: None. Territorial extent & classification: NI. Local. - Available at http://www.legislation.gov.uk/nisr/2015/110/contents/made Non-print

The Waiting Restrictions (Clogher) Order (Northern Ireland) 2015 No. 2015/267. - Enabling power: S.I. 1997/276 (N.I. 2), art. 4 (1) (2) (3). - Issued: 10.06.2015. Made: 08.06.2015. Coming into force: 29.06.2015. Effect: None. Territorial extent & classification: NI. Local. - Available at http://www.legislation.gov.uk/nisr/2015/267/contents/made Non-print

The Waiting Restrictions (Cookstown) Order (Northern Ireland) 2015 No. 2015/304. - Enabling power: S.I. 1997/276 (N.I. 2), art. 4 (1) (2) (3). - Issued: 17.07.2015. Made: 15.07.2015. Coming into force: 05.08.2015. Effect: S.R. 2007/509; 2008/269; 2013/124; 2014/250 revoked. Territorial extent & classification: NI. Local. - Available at http://www.legislation.gov.uk/nisr/2015/304/contents/made Non-print

The Waiting Restrictions (Lisburn) Order (Northern Ireland) 2015s No. 2015/260. - Enabling power: S.I. 1997/276 (N.I. 2), art. 4 (1) (2) (3). - Issued: 03.06.2015. Made: 29.05.2015. Coming into force: 17.06.2015. Effect: S.R. 2014/34 partially revoked & S.R. 2012/195, 362 revoked Territorial extent & classification: NI. Local. - Available at http://www.legislation.gov.uk/nisr/2015/260/contents/made Non-print

The Waiting Restrictions (Portadown) (Amendment) Order (Northern Ireland) 2015 No. 2015/140. - Enabling power: S.I. 1997/276 (N.I. 2), art. 4 (1) (2) (3). - Issued: 12.03.2015. Made: 09.03.2015. Coming into force: 30.03.2015. Effect: S.R. 2013/14 amended. Territorial extent & classification: NI. Local. - Available at http://www.legislation.gov.uk/nisr/2015/140/contents/made Non-print

Salaries

The Salaries (Assembly Ombudsman and Commissioner for Complaints) Order (Northern Ireland) 2015 No. 2015/18. - Enabling power: S.I. 1996/1298 (N.I.8), art. 5 (1) (2) & S.I. 1996/1297 (N.I.7), art. 4 (1) (2). - Issued: 29.01.2014. Made: 26.01.2015. Coming into operation: 17.02.2015. Effect: S.R. 2014/55 revoked. Territorial extent & classification: NI. General. - Revoked by SR 2016/35 (ISBN 9780338003829). - 2p.: 30 cm. - 978-0-337-99573-6 £4.25

Sex discrimination

The Sex Discrimination Order 1976 (Amendment) Regulations (Northern Ireland) 2015 No. 2015/145. - Enabling power: European Communities Act 1972, s. 2 (2). - Issued: 23.03.2015. Made: 10.03.2015. Coming into operation: 06.04.2015. Effect: S.I. 1976/1042 (N.I. 15) amended. Territorial extent & classification: NI. General. - EC note: These Regulations give full effect in Northern Ireland to a rt. 4 (5) of Council Directive 204/113/EC on the implementation of the principle of equal treatment between men and women in the access to and supply of goods and services. - 2p.: 30 cm. - 978-0-337-99720-4 £4.25

Social security

The Employment and Support Allowance (Repeat Assessments and Pending Appeal Awards) (Amendment) Regulations (Northern Ireland) 2015 No. 2015/185. - Enabling power: Social Security Administration (Northern Ireland) Act 1992, ss. 1 (1), 165 (1) (4) & Welfare Reform Act (Northern Ireland) 2007, ss. 8 (1) (5) (6), 22, 25 (2), 29, sch. 2, para. 1, sch. 4, paras 1, 7, 8. - Issued: 01.04.2015. Made: 26.03.2015. Coming into operation: 30.03.2015. Effect: S.R. 1987/465; 2008/280; 2010/312 amended & S.R. 2010/200; 2013/246 partially revoked. Territorial extent & classification: NI. General. - 8p.: 30 cm. - 978-0-337-99747-1 £4.25

The Jobseeker's Allowance (Extended Period of Sickness) (Amendment) Regulations (Northern Ireland) 2015 No. 2015/138. - Enabling power: Social Security Contributions and Benefits (Northern Ireland) Act 1992, ss. 167D, 171 (3) to (5) & S.I. 1995/2705 (N.I. 15), arts 8 (4), 9 (4), 36 (2) & S.I. 1998/1506 (NI.10), arts. 10 (1), 11 (6), 74 (1). - Issued: 12.03.2015. Made: 06.03.2015. Coming into operation: 30.03.2015. Effect: S.R. 1996/198; 1999/162; 2008/280 amended & S.R. 1996/358; 2004/308 partially revoked. Territorial extent & classification: NI. General. - For approval of the Assembly before the expiration of 6 months from the date of their coming into operation. - 8p.: 30 cm. - 978-0-337-99674-0 £6.00

The Jobseeker's Allowance (Extended Period of Sickness) (Amendment) Regulations (Northern Ireland) 2015 No. 2015/138. - Enabling power: Social Security Contributions and Benefits (Northern Ireland) Act 1992, ss. 167D, 171 (3) to (5) & S.I. 1995/2705 (N.I. 15), arts 8 (4), 9 (4), 36 (2) & S.I. 1998/1506 (NI. 10), arts. 10 (1), 11 (6), 74 (1). - Issued: 23.06.2015. Made: 06.03.2015. Coming into operation: 30.03.2015. Effect: S.R. 1996/198; 1999/162; 2008/280 amended & S.R. 1996/358; 2004/308 partially revoked. Territorial extent & classification: NI. General. - Approved by resolution of the Assembly on 15th June 2015. - 8p.: 30 cm. - 978-0-337-99829-4 £6.00

The Maternity Allowance (Curtailment) Regulations (Northern Ireland) 2015 No. 2015/149. - Enabling power: Social Security Contributions and Benefits (Northern Ireland) Act 1992. ss. 161 (3A) (3B) (3C) (3D), 171 (1) (3) to (5). - Issued: 17.03.2015. Made: 11.03.2015. Coming into operation: 15.03.2015. Effect: None. Territorial extent & classification: NI. General. - 8p.: 30 cm. - 978-0-337-99684-9 £4.25

The Mesothelioma Lump Sum Payments (Conditions and Amounts) (Amendment) Regulations (Northern Ireland) 2015 No. 2015/65. - Enabling power: Mesothelioma, etc., Act (Northern Ireland) 2008, s. 1 (3). - Issued: 19.02.2015. Made: 17.02.2015. Coming into operation: 01.04.2015. Effect: S.R. 2008/354 amended. Territorial extent & classification: NI. General. - For approval of the Assembly before the expiration of six months from the date of their coming into operation. - 8p.: 30 cm. - 978-0-337-99626-9 £4.25

The Mesothelioma Lump Sum Payments (Conditions and Amounts) (Amendment) Regulations (Northern Ireland) 2015 No. 2015/65. - Enabling power: Mesothelioma, etc., Act (Northern Ireland) 2008, s. 1 (3). - Issued: 27.03.2015. Made: 17.02.2015. Coming into operation: 01.04.2015. Effect: S.R. 2008/354 amended. Territorial extent & classification: NI. General. - Approved by resolution of the Assembly on 23 March 2015. - 4p.: 30 cm. - 978-0-337-99736-5 £4.25

The Pensions (2012 Act) (Consequential Amendments) (Units of Additional Pension) Order (Northern Ireland) 2015 No. 2015/308. - Enabling power: Pensions Act (Northern Ireland) 2015, s. 50. - Issued: 21.07.2015. Made: 16.07.2015. Coming into operation: 12.10.2015. Effect: 1992 c.7; 1993 c.49 & S.R. 2001/441 amended. Territorial extent & classification: NI. General. - For approval of the Assembly before the expiration of six months from the day of its coming into operation. - 4p: 30 cm. - 978-0-337-99850-8 £4.25

The Pensions (2012 Act) (Consequential Amendments) (Units of Additional Pension) Order (Northern Ireland) 2015 No. 2015/308. - Enabling power: Pensions Act (Northern Ireland) 2015, s. 50. - Issued: 16.03.2016. Made: 16.07.2015. Coming into operation: 12.10.2015. Effect: 1992 c.7; 1993 c.49 & S.R. 2001/441 amended. Territorial extent & classification: NI. General. - Approved by resolution of the Assembly on 8th March 2016. - 4p: 30 cm. - 978-0-337-99973-4 £4.25

The Pensions (2015 Act) (Consequential, Supplementary and Incidental Amendments) Order (Northern Ireland) 2015 No. 2015/411. - Enabling power: Pensions Act (Northern Ireland) 2015, s. 50, 51 (6). - Issued: 17.12.2015. Made: 14.12.2015. Coming into operation: In accord. with art. 1. Effect: S.R. 1975/113; 1978/114; 1979/193, 242, 243; 1984/92; 1987/459, 465; 1988/21, 142; 1992/341; 1996/198; 1999/162; 2001/18, 213, 420, 441; 2003/28; 2004/8; 2005/120, 506; 2006/405, 406; 2008/280; 2010/62; 2012/427; 2015/315 amended. Territorial extent & classification: NI. General. - 20p: 30 cm. - 978-0-337-99929-1 £6.00

The Pneumoconiosis, etc., (Workers' Compensation) (Payment of Claims) (Amendment) Regulations (Northern Ireland) 2015 No. 2015/64. - Enabling power: S.I. 1979/925 (N.I.9), arts. 3 (3), 4 (3), 11 (1) (4). - Issued: 19.002.2015. Made: 17.02.2015. Coming into operation: In accord. with reg. 1 (1). Effect: S.R. 1988/242 amended. Territorial extent & classification: NI. General. - Subject to affirmative resolution of the Assembly. - 8p.: 30 cm. - 978-0-337-99625-2 £6.00

The Pneumoconiosis, etc., (Workers' Compensation) (Payment of Claims) (Amendment) Regulations (Northern Ireland) 2015 No. 2015/64. - Enabling power: S.I. 1979/925 (N.I.9), arts. 3 (3), 4 (3), 11 (1) (4). - Issued: 27.03.2015. Made: 17.03.2015. Coming into operation: In accord. with reg. 1 (1). Effect: S.R. 1988/242 amended. Territorial extent & classification: NI. General. - Affirmed by resolution of the Assembly on 23 March 2015. - 8p.: 30 cm. - 978-0-337-99735-8 £6.00

The Social Fund Winter Fuel Payment (Amendment) Regulations (Northern Ireland) 2015 No. 2015/216. - Enabling power: Social Security Contributions and Benefits (Northern Ireland) Act 1992, ss. 134 (2), 171 (1) (3). - Issued: 22.04.2015. Made: 16.04.2015. Coming into operation: 21.09.2015. Effect: S.R. 2000/91 amended. Territorial extent & classification: NI. General. - 4p.: 30 cm. - 978-0-337-99776-1 £4.25

The Social Security (Application of Reciprocal Agreements with Australia, Canada and New Zealand) (EEA States and Switzerland) (Northern Ireland) Regulations 2015 No. 2015/207. - Enabling power: European Communities Act 1972, s. 2 (2). - Issued: 02.04.2015. Made: 28.03.2015. Coming into operation: 01.04.2015. Effect: S.R. 1983/432; 1992/269; 1995/405 modified. Territorial extent & classification: NI. General. - Revoked by S.R. 2015/281 (ISBN 9780337998331). - 4p.: 30 cm. - 978-0-337-99758-7 £4.25

The Social Security (Application of Reciprocal Agreements with Australia, Canada and New Zealand) (EEA States and Switzerland) (Northern Ireland) Regulations 2015 No. 2015/281. - Enabling power: European Communities Act 1972, s. 2 (2). - Issued: 30.06.2015. Made: 24.06.2015. Coming into operation: 15.07.2015. Effect: S.R. 2015/207 revoked. Territorial extent & classification: NI. General. - 4p.: 30 cm. - 978-0-337-99833-1 £4.25

The Social Security Benefits Up-rating Order (Northern Ireland) 2015 No. 2015/124. - Enabling power: Social Security Administration (Northern Ireland) Act 1992, ss. 132, 132A,165 (1) (4) (5). - Issued: 09.03.2015. Made: 05.03.2015. Coming into operation: In accord. with 1. Effect: 1992 c.7 & S.R. 1987/459; 1996/198; 2006/405, 406; 2008/280 amended & S.R. 2014/78 revoked. Territorial extent & classification: NI. General. - For approval of the Assembly before the expiration of six months from the date of its coming into operation. Superseded by approved version SR 2015/124 (ISBN 9780337997853). - 44p.: 30 cm. - 978-0-337-99663-4 £10.00

SOCIAL SECURITY

The Social Security Benefits Up-rating Order (Northern Ireland) 2015 No. 2015/124. - Enabling power: Social Security Administration (Northern Ireland) Act 1992, ss. 132, 132A, 165 (1) (4) (5). - Issued: 30.04.2015. Made: 05.03.2015. Coming into operation: In accord. with art. 1. Effect: 1966 c.6 (N.I.); 1992 c.7; 1993 c.49; S.R. 1987/30, 460; 1992/32; 1994/461; 1995/35; 1996/198; 2002/380; 2003/28; 2006/405, 406; 2008/280; 2010/407; amended & S.R. 2014/78 revoked (13.04.2015). Territorial extent & classification: NI. General. - Approved by resolution of the Assembly on 27th April 2015. Supersedes pre-approved SR 2015/124 (ISBN 9780337996634). - 48p.: 30 cm. - 978-0-337-99785-3 £10.00

The Social Security Benefits Up-rating Regulations (Northern Ireland) 2015 No. 2015/139. - Enabling power: Social Security Administration (Northern Ireland) Act 1992, ss. 5 (1) (q), 135 (3), 165 (1) (4) & Social Security Contributions and Benefits (Northern Ireland) Act 1992, ss. 90, 113 (1) (a), 117 (1) (3). - Issued: 12.03.2015. Made: 06.03.2015. Coming into operation: 06.04.2015. Effect: S.R. 1997/74; 1987/465 amended & S.R. 2014/80 revoked. Territorial extent & classification: NI. General. - 4p.: 30 cm. - 978-0-337-99676-4 £4.25

The Social Security (Claims and Payments) (Amendment) Regulations (Northern Ireland) 2015 No. 2015/109. - Enabling power: Social Security Administration (Northern Ireland) Act 1992, ss. 13A (2) (b), 165 (1) (4). - Issued: 05.03.2015. Made: 27.02.2015. Coming into operation: 01.04.2015. Effect: S.R. 1987/465 amended & S.R. 2014/73 revoked. Territorial extent & classification: NI. General. - 2p.: 30 cm. - 978-0-337-99652-8 £4.25

The Social Security (Contributions) (Republic of Chile) Order (Northern Ireland) 2015 No. 2015/179. - Enabling power: Social Security Administration (Northern Ireland) Act 1992, ss. 155 (1) (a) (2). - Issued: 27.03.2015. Made: 23.03.2015. Coming into force: 01.06.2015. Effect: 1992 c. 7, c. 8 modified. Territorial extent and classification: NI. General. - 8p.: 30 cm. - 978-0-337-99733-4 £6.00

The Social Security (Crediting and Treatment of Contributions, and National Insurance Numbers) (Amendment) Regulations (Northern Ireland) 2015 No. 2015/404. - Enabling power: Social Security Administration (Northern Ireland) Act 1992, ss. 158C, 165 (1) (4). - Issued: 10.12.2015. Made: 07.12.2015. Coming into operation: 28.12.2015. Effect: S.R. 2001/102 amended. Territorial extent & classification: NI. General. - 2p.: 30 cm. - 978-0-337-99922-2 £4.25

The Social Security (Industrial Injuries) (Prescribed Diseases) (Amendment) Regulations (Northern Ireland) 2015 No. 2015/52. - Enabling power: Social Security Contributions and Benefits (Northern Ireland) Act 1992, ss. 108 (2), 109 (2), 171 (1) (3) to (5), sch. 6, para. 2. - Issued: 16.02.2015. Made: 12.02.2015. Coming into operation: 16.03.2015. Effect: S.R. 1986/179 amended & S.R. 1993/148, 350; 1996/57; 2003/63; 2006/96 revoked with saving. Territorial extent & classification: NI. General. - 8p.: 30 cm. - 978-0-337-99615-3 £6.00

The Social Security (Invalid Care Allowance) (Amendment) Regulations (Northern Ireland) 2015 No. 2015/153. - Enabling power: Social Security Contributions and Benefits (Northern Ireland) Act 1992, ss. 70 (8), 171 (1). - Issued: 17.03.2015. Made: 12.03.2015. Coming into operation: 06.04.2015. Effect: S.R. 1976/99 amended & S.R. 2014/121 revoked. Territorial extent & classification: NI. General. - 2p.: 30 cm. - 978-0-337-99695-5 £4.25

The Social Security (Maternity Allowance) (Earnings) (Amendment) Regulations (Northern Ireland) 2015 No. 2015/211. - Enabling power: Social Security Contributions and Benefits (Northern Ireland) Act 1992, ss. 35A (4) (5), 171 (1) (3) (4). - Issued: 13.04.2015. Made: 01.04.2015. Coming into operation: 06.04.2015. Effect: S.R. 2000/104 amended. Territorial extent & classification: NI. General. - 4p.: 30 cm. - 978-0-337-99762-4 £4.25

The Social Security (Members of the Reserve Forces) (Amendment) Regulations (Northern Ireland) 2015 No. 2015/184. - Enabling power: Social Security Contributions and Benefits (Northern Ireland) Act 1992, ss. 122 (1) (a), 132 (3) (4) (b), 171 (3) (4) & S.I. 1995/2705 (N.I. 15), arts 8 (4), 9 (4), 14 (1) to (3) (4) (b), 36 (2) & Welfare Reform Act (Northern Ireland) 2007, ss. 17 (1) (2) (3) (b), 25 (2). - Issued: 31.03.2015. Made: 26.03.2015. Coming into operation: 06.04.2015. Effect: S.R. 1987/459; 1996/198; 2008/280 amended & S.R. 2012/377 partially revoked. Territorial extent & classification: NI. General. - For approval of the Assembly before the expiration of 6 months from the date of their coming into operation. - 8p.: 30 cm. - 978-0-337-99746-4 £6.00

The Social Security (Members of the Reserve Forces) (Amendment) Regulations (Northern Ireland) 2015 No. 2015/184. - Enabling power: Social Security Contributions and Benefits (Northern Ireland) Act 1992, ss. 122 (1) (a), 132 (3) (4) (b), 171 (3) (4) & S.I. 1995/2705 (N.I. 15), arts 8 (4), 9 (4), 14 (1) to (3) (4) (b), 36 (2) & Welfare Reform Act (Northern Ireland) 2007, ss. 17 (1) (2) (3) (b), 25 (2). - Issued: 23.06.2015. Made: 26.03.2015. Coming into operation: 06.04.2015. Effect: S.R. 1987/459; 1996/198; 2008/280 amended & S.R. 2012/377 partially revoked. Territorial extent & classification: NI. General. - Approved by resolution of the Assembly on 15th June 2015. - 8p.: 30 cm. - 978-0-337-99831-7 £6.00

The Social Security (Miscellaneous Amendments No. 2) Regulations (Northern Ireland) 2015 No. 2015/163. - Enabling power: S.I. 1991/2628 (NI. 23), arts 39 (1), 47 (1) & Social Security Contributions and Benefits (Northern Ireland) Act 1992, ss. 122 (1) (a) (d), 132 (3) (4) (b), 132A (2) (3), 171 (1) (3) (4) & S.I. 1995/2705 (NI.15), arts 6 (5), 14 (1) (4), 36 (1) (2) & S.I. 1998/1506 (NI. 10), arts 11 (6), 74 (1) (5) & Welfare Reform Act (Northern Ireland) 2007, ss. 17 (1) (3), 25 (2). - Issued: 23.03.2015. Made: 16.03.2015. Coming into operation: 06.04.2015. Effect: S.R. 1987/459; 1992/341; 1996/198; 2001/18; 2006/405, 406; 2008/280 amended. Territorial extent & classification: NI. General. - 4p.: 30 cm. - 978-0-337-99724-2 £4.25

The Social Security (Miscellaneous Amendments) Regulations (Northern Ireland) 2015 No. 2015/34. - Enabling power: Social Security Contributions and Benefits (Northern Ireland) Act 1992, ss. 35 (3), 35B (11), 132 (3) (4), 132A, 134 (2) (4), 171 (1) (3) (4) & Social Security Administration (Northern Ireland) Act 1992, ss. 158C, 189 (4) & S.I. 1995/2705, arts 14 (1) (4), 36 (2) & State Pension Credit Act (Northern Ireland) 2002, ss. 15 (3) (6), 19 (1) to (3) & Welfare Reform Act (Northern Ireland) 2007, s. 25 (2) (a). - Issued: 06.02.2015. Made: 03.02.2015. Coming into operation: 23.02.2015. Effect: S.R. 1987/170; 2000/91; 2001/102; 2006/405 amended. Territorial extent & classification: NI. General. - 8p.: 30 cm. - 978-0-337-99595-8 £4.25

The Social Security Pensions (Flat Rate Accrual Amount) Order (Northern Ireland) 2015 No. 2015/114. - Enabling power: Social Security Administration (Northern Ireland) Act 1992, s. 130AA. - Issued: 06.03.2014. Made: 03.03.2014. Coming into operation: 06.04.2014. Effect: None. Territorial extent & classification: NI. General. - 2p.: 30 cm. - 978-0-337-99657-3 £4.25

The Social Security Pensions (Low Earnings Threshold) Order (Northern Ireland) 2015 No. 2015/112. - Enabling power: Social Security Administration (Northern Ireland) Act 1992, ss. 130A, 165 (1) (4) (5). - Issued: 05.03.2015. Made: 02.03.2015. Coming into operation: 06.04.2015. Effect: None. Territorial extent & classification: NI. General. - 2p.: 30 cm. - 978-0-337-99654-2 £4.25

The Social Security Revaluation of Earnings Factors Order (Northern Ireland) 2015 No. 2015/111. - Enabling power: Social Security Administration (Northern Ireland) Act 1992, ss. 130, 165 (1) (4) (5). - Issued: 05.03.2015. Made: 02.03.2015. Coming into operation: 06.04.2015. Effect: None. Territorial extent & classification: NI. General. - 4p.: 30 cm. - 978-0-337-99653-5 £4.25

The Social Security (Units of Additional Pension) Regulations (Northern Ireland) 2015 No. 2015/311. - Enabling power: Social Security Contributions and Benefits (Northern Ireland) Act 1992, s. 45 (2A). - Issued: 21.07.2015. Made: 16.07.2015. Coming into operation: 12.10.2015. Effect: None. Territorial extent & classification: NI. General. - 2p.: 30 cm. - 978-0-337-99848-5 £4.25

The State Pension Credit (Amendment) Regulations (Northern Ireland) 2015 No. 2015/331. - Enabling power: State Pension Credit Act (Northern Ireland) 2002, ss. 3ZA, 9 (5), 19 (1) to (3) & Pensions Act (Northern Ireland) 2015, s. 27 (3). - Issued: 18.09.2015. Made: 15.09.2015. Coming into force: 06.04.2016. Effect: S.R. 2003/28 amended. Territorial extent and classification: NI. General. - 4p.: 30 cm. - 978-0-337-99865-2 £4.25

The State Pension Regulations (Northern Ireland) 2015 No. 2015/315. - Enabling power: Social Security Contributions and Benefits (Northern Ireland) Act 1992, ss. 55A (6), 171 (4) & S.I. 1999/3147, arts 21 (1) (a) (b) (ii) (c) (i) (2), 46 (4) (4A) & Pensions Act (Northern Ireland) 2015, ss. 2 (3), 4 (2), 8 (3) (7) (8), 16 (1) (6), 17 (4) (5), 18 (1), 19 (1) (3), 51 (6), sch. 8, para. 4, sch. 10, para. 4. - Issued: 21.07.2015. Made: 16.07.2015. Coming into force: 06.04.2016. Effect: S.R. 2000/362 amended. Territorial extent & classification: NI. General. - For approval of the Assembly before the expiration of 6 months from the date of their coming into operation. - 12p.: 30 cm. - 978-0-337-99852-2 £6.00

Statutory maternity pay

The Social Security Benefits Up-rating Order (Northern Ireland) 2015 No. 2015/124. - Enabling power: Social Security Administration (Northern Ireland) Act 1992, ss. 132, 132A,165 (1) (4) (5). - Issued: 09.03.2015. Made: 05.03.2015. Coming into operation: In accord. with 1. Effect: 1992 c.7 & S.R. 1987/459; 1996/198; 2006/405, 406; 2008/280 amended & S.R. 2014/78 revoked. Territorial extent & classification: NI. General. - For approval of the Assembly before the expiration of six months from the date of its coming into operation. Superseded by approved version SR 2015/124 (ISBN 9780337997853). - 44p.: 30 cm. - 978-0-337-99663-4 £10.00

The Social Security Benefits Up-rating Order (Northern Ireland) 2015 No. 2015/124. - Enabling power: Social Security Administration (Northern Ireland) Act 1992, ss. 132, 132A, 165 (1) (4) (5). - Issued: 30.04.2015. Made: 05.03.2015. Coming into operation: In accord. with art. 1. Effect: 1966 c.6 (N.I.); 1992 c.7; 1993 c.49; S.R. 1987/30, 460; 1992/32; 1994/461; 1995/35; 1996/198; 2002/380; 2003/28; 2006/405, 406; 2008/280; 2010/407; amended & S.R. 2014/78 revoked (13.04.2015). Territorial extent & classification: NI. General. - Approved by resolution of the Assembly on 27th April 2015. Supersedes pre-approved SR 2015/124 (ISBN 9780337996634). - 48p.: 30 cm. - 978-0-337-99785-3 £10.00

Statutory maternity pay: Curtailment

The Statutory Maternity Pay (Curtailment) Regulations (Northern Ireland) 2015 No. 2015/150. - Enabling power: Social Contributions and Benefits (Northern Ireland) Act 1992, ss. 161 (3A) (3B) (3C) (3D), 171 (1) (3) (4). - Issued: 26.03.2015. Made: 11.03.2015. Coming into operation: 15.03.2015. Effect: None. - 8p.: 30 cm. - 978-0-337-99741-9 £4.25

Statutory sick pay

The Social Security Benefits Up-rating Order (Northern Ireland) 2015 No. 2015/124. - Enabling power: Social Security Administration (Northern Ireland) Act 1992, ss. 132, 132A,165 (1) (4) (5). - Issued: 09.03.2015. Made: 05.03.2015. Coming into operation: In accord. with 1. Effect: 1992 c.7 & S.R. 1987/459; 1996/198; 2006/405, 406; 2008/280 amended & S.R. 2014/78 revoked. Territorial extent & classification: NI. General. - For approval of the Assembly before the expiration of six months from the date of its coming into operation. Superseded by approved version SR 2015/124 (ISBN 9780337997853). - 44p.: 30 cm. - 978-0-337-99663-4 £10.00

The Social Security Benefits Up-rating Order (Northern Ireland) 2015 No. 2015/124. - Enabling power: Social Security Administration (Northern Ireland) Act 1992, ss. 132, 132A, 165 (1) (4) (5). - Issued: 30.04.2015. Made: 05.03.2015. Coming into operation: In accord. with art. 1. Effect: 1966 c.6 (N.I.); 1992 c.7; 1993 c.49; S.R. 1987/30, 460; 1992/32; 1994/461; 1995/35; 1996/198; 2002/380; 2003/28; 2006/405, 406; 2008/280; 2010/407; amended & S.R. 2014/78 revoked (13.04.2015). Territorial extent & classification: NI. General. - Approved by resolution of the Assembly on 27th April 2015. Supersedes pre-approved SR 2015/124 (ISBN 9780337996634). - 48p.: 30 cm. - 978-0-337-99785-3 £10.00

Water and sewerage

The Private Water Supplies (Amendment) Regulations (Northern Ireland) 2015 No. 2015/366. - Enabling power: S.I. 2006/3336 (N.I. 21), arts. 107 (2) (3), 118 (3) (4) & European Communities Act 1972, s. 2 (2). - Issued: 11.11.2015. Made: 06.11.2015. Coming into operation: 28.11.2015. Effect: S.R. 2009/413 amended. Territorial extent & classification: NI. - EC note: These Regulations amend the Private Water Supplies Regulations (Northern Ireland) 2009 with the aim of further protecting human health from the adverse effects of any contamination of water supplied for human consumption purposes. In particular, they make further provision to implement Council Directive 2013/51/Euratom laying down requirements for the protection of the health of the general public with regard to radioactive substances in water intended for human consumption. - 12p.: 30 cm. - 978-0-337-99896-6 £6.00

The Water Supply (Water Quality) (Amendment) Regulations (Northern Ireland) 2015 No. 2015/363. - Enabling power: S.I. 2006/3336 (N.I. 21), 107 (1) (3), 109, 300 (2) & European Communities Act 1972, s. 2 (2). - Issued: 06.11.2015. Made: 29.10.2015. Coming into operation: 28.11.2015. Effect: S.R. 2007/147; 2009/255 amended. - EC note: The regulation updates references to Directive 89/106/EEC on the approximation of laws, regulations and administrative provisions of the Member States relating to construction products. - 12p.: 30 cm. - 978-0-337-99892-8 £6.00

Wildlife

The Snares Order (Northern Ireland) 2015 No. 2015/352. - Enabling power: S.I. 1985/171 (N.I. 2), art. 12 (2F). - Issued: 09.10.2015. Made: 06.10.2015. Coming into operation: In accord. with art. 1. Effect: None. Territorial extent & classification: NI. General. - Subject to affirmative resolution procedure of the Assembly. - 4p.: 30 cm. - 978-0-337-99881-2 £4.25

Statutory Rules of Northern Ireland

Arranged by Number

Statutory rules 2015

1	Gas
	Electricity
2	Housing
3 (C.1)	Public service pensions
4	Road traffic and vehicles
5	Road traffic and vehicles
6	Road traffic and vehicles
7	Fire and rescue services
8	Fire and rescue services
9	Fire and rescue services
10	Fire and rescue services
11	Fire and rescue services
12	Pensions
13	Road and railway transport
14	Environmental protection
16	Agriculture
17	Agriculture
18	Salaries
19	Housing
20	Rates
21	Environmental protection
22	HarboursHarbours
23	Road traffic and vehicles
24	Road traffic and vehiclesRoad traffic and vehicles
25 (C.2)	Planning
26	Health and personal social services
27	Health and personal social services
28 (C.3)	Local government
29	Police
30	Roads
31	Road traffic and vehicles
32	Rates
33	Road traffic and vehicles
34	Social security
	Housing
	Rates
35 (C.4)	Education
36	Fair employment
37	Road traffic and vehicles
38	Road traffic and vehicles
39	Planning
40	Planning
41	Road traffic and vehicles
42	Road traffic and vehicles
43	Road traffic and vehicles
44	Local government
45	Environmental protection
46	RatesRates
47	RatesRates
48	RatesRates
49 (C.5)	Planning
50	Human rights
51	Human rights
52	Social security
53	Dangerous drugs
54	Dangerous drugs
55	Inquiry into historical institutional abuse
56	Health and personal social services
57 (C.6)	Family law
58	Planning
59	Road traffic and vehicles
60	Road traffic and vehicles
61	Planning
62	Planning
63	Planning
64	Social securitySocial security
65	Social securitySocial security
66	Planning
67	Road traffic and vehicles
68	Local government
69	Education
70	Planning
71	Planning
72	Planning
73	Planning
74	Planning
75	RatesRates
76	Public service pensions
77	Local government
78	Public service pensions
79	Pensions
80	Employer's liability
81	Public service pensions
82	Rates
83	Rates
84	Planning
85	Planning
86 (C.7)	Employment
87	EmploymentEmployment
88	Employment
89	Employment
90	Employment
91	Employment
92	Employment
93	EmploymentEmployment
94	EmploymentEmployment
95	EmploymentEmployment
96	Employment
97	EmploymentEmployment
98	EmploymentEmployment
99	EmploymentEmployment
100	EmploymentEmployment
101	EmploymentEmployment
102	EmploymentEmployment
103	Employment
104	EmploymentEmployment
105	Employment
106	Local government
107	Planning
108	Planning
109	Social security
110	Road traffic and vehicles
111	Social security
112	Social security
113	Police service pensions
114	Social security
115	Pensions

No.	Subject	No.	Subject
116	Family law	167	Health and personal social services
117	Pensions		Public service pensions
118	Pensions	168	Justice
119	Pensions	169	Employment
120	Health and personal social services	170	Public service pensions
121	Health and personal social services	171	Road traffic and vehicles
122	Health and personal social services	172	Road traffic and vehicles
	Public service pensions	173	Road traffic and vehicles
123	Rates	174	Land development values
124	Social security	175	Planning
	Statutory maternity pay	176	Planning
	Statutory sick pay	177	Planning
	Employment	178	Medicines
	Housing	179	Social security
	RatesSocial security	180	Pensions
	Statutory maternity pay	181	Public service pensions
	Statutory sick pay	182	European Communities
	Employment	183	Local government
	Housing	184	Social securitySocial security
	Rates	185	Social security
125	Local government	186	Health care charges
126	Education	187	Planning
127 (C.8)	Education	188	Planning
128	Plant health	189	Planning
129	Plant health	190 (C.11)	Criminal law
130	Health and personal social services	191	Agriculture
131	Road traffic and vehicles	192	Agriculture
132	Road traffic and vehicles	193 (C.12)	Legal aid and coroners' courts
133	Road traffic and vehicles	194 (C.13)	Access to justice
134	Road traffic and vehicles	195	Access to justice
135	Agriculture	196	Access to justice
136	Planning fees	197	Access to justice
137	Planning Appeals Commission procedures	198	Access to justice
138	Social securitySocial security	199	Access to justice
139	Social security	200	Access to justice
140	Road traffic and vehicles	201	Access to justice
141	Pensions	202	Access to justice
142	Road traffic and vehicles	203	Legal aid and advice
143	Criminal law	204	Landlord and tenant
144	Fair employment	205	Health and social care
145	Sex discrimination	206 (C.14)	Pensions
146	Employment	207	Social security
147	Rates	208	Official statisticsOfficial statistics
148	Animals	209 (C.15)	Local government
149	Social security	210	Local government
150	Statutory maternity pay: Curtailment	211	Social security
151	Education	212	Road traffic and vehicles
152	Government resources and accounts	213	Employment
153	Social security	214	Road traffic and vehicles
154	Pensions	215	Legal aid and advice
155	Pensions	216	Social security
156	Public service pensions	217	Road traffic and vehicles
157 (C.9)	Criminal evidenceCriminal evidence	218	Road traffic and vehicles
158 (C.10)	Justice	219	Road traffic and vehicles
159	Insolvency	220	Roads
160	Local government	221	Roads
161	Public service pensions	222	Road traffic and vehicles
162	Local government	223	Health and safety
163	Social security	224	Education
	Housing	225	Police
	Rates	226	Road traffic and vehicles
164	Pensions	227	Dangerous drugs
165	Pensions		
166	Public service pensions		

228	Dangerous drugs	289	Local government
229	Environmental protection	290 (C.23)	Criminal law
230 (C.16)	Public authorities reform	291	Road traffic and vehicles
231	Environmental protection	292	Road traffic and vehicles
232	Road traffic and vehicles	293	Road traffic and vehicles
233	Road traffic and vehicles	294	Education
234	Roads	295	Road traffic and vehicles
235	Court of Judicature, Northern Ireland	296 (C.24)	Justice
236	Health and safety	297	Road traffic and vehicles
237 (C.17)	Access to justice	298	Road traffic and vehicles
238	Environmental protection	299	Road traffic and vehicles
239	Fisheries	300	Road traffic and vehicles
240	Road traffic and vehicles	301	Environmental protection
241	Court of Judicature, Northern Ireland	302	Lands Tribunal
242	Road traffic and vehicles	303	Road traffic and vehicles
243	Education	304	Road traffic and vehicles
244	HarboursHarbours	305	Road traffic and vehicles
245	Road traffic and vehicles	306	Roads
246	Road traffic and vehicles	307 (C.25)	Pensions
247	Electricity	308	Social security
248	Agriculture	309	PensionsPensions
249	Gas	310	Pensions
	Electricity	311	Social security
250	Road traffic and vehicles	312	Road traffic and vehicles
251	Road traffic and vehicles	313	Road traffic and vehicles
252	Road traffic and vehicles	314	Road traffic and vehicles
253	Roads	315	Social security
254	Health and safety	316	Road traffic and vehicles
255 (C.18)	Criminal law	317	Road traffic and vehicles
256 (C.19)	Charities	318	Agriculture
257 (C.20)	Road traffic and vehicles	319	Pensions
258	Road traffic and vehicles	320 (C.26)	Justice
259	Medicines	321	Food
260	Road traffic and vehicles	322	Animals
261	Food	323	Road traffic and vehicles
262	Insolvency	324 (C.27)	Justice
263	Road traffic and vehicles	325	Health and safety
264	Road traffic and vehicles	326	Agriculture
265	Health and safety	327	Local government
266	Health and personal social services	328	Pensions
267	Road traffic and vehicles	329 (C.28)	Pensions
268	Road traffic and vehicles	330	Justice
269	Road traffic and vehicles	331	Social security
270	Road traffic and vehicles	332	Animals
271	Local government	333 (C.29)	Disabled persons
272	Pensions	334	Road traffic and vehicles
273	Planning	335	Road traffic and vehicles
274	Clean air	336	Road traffic and vehicles
275	Road traffic and vehicles	337	Road traffic and vehicles
276	Industrial training	338	Road traffic and vehicles
277 (C.21)	Public passenger transport	339	Health and safety
278	Dangerous drugs	340	Animals
279	Environmental protection	341	Education
280	Planning	342	Roads
281	Social security	343	Road traffic and vehicles
282	Animals	344	Planning
283	Road traffic and vehicles	345	Criminal law
284 (C.22)	Public passenger transport	346	Electricity
285	Public passenger transport	347	Pensions
286	Agriculture	348	Pensions
287	Electricity	349	Road traffic and vehicles
288	Environmental protection	350	Criminal law

351	Environmental protection	408	Agriculture
352	Wildlife	409	Road traffic and vehicles
353	Criminal law	410	Road traffic and vehicles
354	Medicines	411	Social security
355	Fire and rescue services	412	Public health
356	Human rights	413	Road traffic and vehicles
357	Road traffic and vehicles	414	Road traffic and vehicles
358 (C.30)	Justice	415	Court of Judicature, Northern Ireland
359 (C.31)	Legal aid and coroners' courts	416	Road traffic and vehicles
360	Police	417	Road traffic and vehicles
361 (C.32)	Charities	418 (C.36)	Justice
362	Human rights	419	Police
363	Water and sewerage	420	Public service pensions
364	Charities	421	Fire and rescue services
365	Food	422	Fire and rescue services
366	Water and sewerage	423	Road traffic and vehicles
367	Clean air	424	Road traffic and vehicles
368	Court of Judicature, Northern Ireland	425	Environmental protection
369	Environmental protection		
370	Justice		
371	Energy		
372	Pensions		
373	Roads		
374	Roads		
375	Road traffic and vehicles		
376 (C.33)	Criminal law		
377	Road traffic and vehicles		
378	Road traffic and vehicles		
379	Road traffic and vehicles		
380	Road traffic and vehicles		
381	Road traffic and vehicles		
382	Road traffic and vehicles		
383 (C.34)	Charities		
384	Charities		
385	Charities		
386	Environmental protection		
387	Environmental protection		
388	Environmental protection		
389 (C.35)	Road traffic and vehicles		
390	Roads		
391	Road traffic and vehicles		
392	Roads		
393	Road traffic and vehicles		
394	Road traffic and vehicles		
395	Road traffic and vehicles		
396	Disabled persons		
397	Road traffic and vehicles		
398	Planning		
399	Fisheries		
400	Road traffic and vehicles		
401	Road traffic and vehicles		
402	Pensions		
403	Pensions		
404	Social security		
405	Firearms and ammunition		
406	Clean air		
407	Road traffic and vehicles		

List of Commencement Orders 2015

3 (C.1)
25 (C.2)
28 (C.3)
35 (C.4)
49 (C.5)
57 (C.6)
86 (C.7)
127 (C.8)
157 (C.9)
157 (C.9)
158 (C.10)
190 (C.11)
193 (C.12)
194 (C.13)
206 (C.14)
209 (C.15)
230 (C.16)
237 (C.17)
255 (C.18)
256 (C.19)
257 (C.20)
277 (C.21)
284 (C.22)
290 (C.23)
296 (C.24)
307 (C.25)
320 (C.26)
324 (C.27)
329 (C.28)
333 (C.29)
358 (C.30)
359 (C.31)
361 (C.32)
376 (C.33)
383 (C.34)
389 (C.35)
418 (C.36)

WELSH ASSEMBLY LEGISLATION

Acts of the National Assembly for Wales

Acts of the National Assembly for Wales 2013

Local Government Democracy (Wales) Act 2013 (correction slip): 2013 anaw 4. - 1 sheet: 30 cm. - Correction slip (to ISBN 9780348105063) dated March 2015. - Parallel texts in English and Welsh. Welsh title: Deddf Llywodraeth Leol (Democratiaeth) (Cymru) 2013: 2013 dccc 4. - Free

Acts of the National Assembly for Wales 2015

Higher Education (Wales) Act 2015: 2015 anaw 1. - iv, iv, 35, 35p.: 30 cm. - Royal assent, 12 March 2015. An Act of the National Assembly for Wales to make provision about student fees payable to certain institutions providing higher education; to make provision about the quality of education provided by and on behalf of those institutions and about their financial management. Explanatory notes to assist in the understanding of the Act are available separately (ISBN 9780348110807). - Parallel texts in English and Welsh. Welsh title: Deddf Addysg Uwch (Cymru) 2015 2015 dcc 1. - 978-0-348-11079-1 £14.25

Local Government (Wales) Act 2015: 2015 anaw 6. - i - ii, 27; i - ii, 27p.: 30 cm. - Royal assent, 25 November 2015. An Act of the National Assembly for Wales to make provision for and in connection with a reduction in the number of principal local authorities in Wales and to make other amendments of local government law as it applies in relation to Wales Explanatory notes to assist in the understanding of the Act are available separately (ISBN 9780348112092). - Parallel texts in English and Welsh. Welsh title: Deddf Llywodraeth Leol (Cymru) 2015 2015 dccc 6. - 978-0-348-11194-1 £11.00

Planning (Wales) Act 2015: 2015 anaw 4. - i - iv, 96; i - iv, 96p.: 30 cm. - Royal assent, 6 July 2015. An Act of the National Assembly for Wales to make provision about national, strategic and local development planning in Wales; to make provision for certain applications for planning permission and certain other applications to be made to the Welsh Ministers; to make other provision about development management and applications for planning permission; to make other provision about planning enforcement, appeals and certain other proceedings; to amend the Commons Act 2006. Explanatory notes to assist in the understanding of the Act are available separately (ISBN 9780348110869). - Parallel texts in English and Welsh. Welsh title: Deddf Cynllunio (Cymru) 2015 2015 dccc 4. - 978-0-348-11085-2 £27.50

Qualifications Wales Act 2015: 2015 anaw 5. - iv, iv, 55, 55p.: 30 cm. - Royal assent, 5 August 2015. An Act of the National Assembly for Wales to establish a new body to be known as Qualifications Wales; providing for Qualfications Wales to be able to recognise bodies responsible for awarding certain qualifications in Wales and to approve certain qualifications awarded in Wales and to perform certain other functions. Explanatory notes to assist in the understanding of the Act are available separately (ISBN 9780348110883). - Parallel texts in English and Welsh. Welsh title: Deddf Cymwysterau Cymru 2015 2015 dccc 5. - 978-0-348-11087-6 £19.00

Violence against Women, Domestic Abuse and Sexual Violence (Wales) Act 2015: 2015 anaw 3. - ii, ii, 16, 16p.: 30 cm. - Royal assent, 29 April 2015. An Act of the National Assembly for Wales to improve arrangements for the prevention of gender-based violence, domestic abuse and sexual violence; to improve arrangements for the protection of victims of such abuse and violence; to improve support for people affected by such abuse and violence; and to require the appointment of a National Adviser on gender-based violence, domestic abuse and sexual violence. Explanatory notes to assist in the understanding of the Act will are available separately (ISBN 9780348110838). - Parallel texts in English and Welsh. Welsh title: Deddf Trais yn erbyn Menywod, Cam-drin Domestig a Thrais Rhywiol (Cymru) 2015 dccc 3. - 978-0-348-11082-1 £10.00

Well-being of Future Generations (Wales) Act 2015: 2015 anaw 2. - iii, iii, 52, 52p.: 30 cm. - Royal assent, 29 April 2015. An Act of the National Assembly for Wales to make provision requiring public bodies to do things in pursuit of the economic, social, environmental and cultural well-being of Wales in a way that accords with the sustainable development principle; to require public bodies to report on such action; to establish a Commissioner for Future Generations to advise and assist public bodies in doing things in accordance with this Act; to establish public services boards in local authority areas; to make provision requiring those boards to plan and take action in pursuit of economic, social, environmental and cultural well-being in their area. Explanatory notes to assist in the understanding of the Act are available separately (ISBN 9780348110845). - Parallel texts in English and Welsh. Welsh title: Deddf Llesiant Cenedlaethau'r Dyfodol (Cymru) 2015 dccc 2. - 978-0-348-11081-4 £16.50

Acts of the National Assembly for Wales - Explanatory Notes 2015

Higher Education (Wales) Act 2015: 2015 anaw 1: explanatory notes. - 27, 27p.: 30 cm. - These notes refer to the Higher Education (Wales) Act 2015 (anaw 1) which received Royal Assent on 12 March 2015 (ISBN 9780348110791). - Parallel texts in English and Welsh. Welsh title: Deddf Addysg Uwch (Cymru) 2015 2015 dcc 1Nodiadau Esboniadol. - 978-0-348-11080-7 £10.00

Local Government (Wales) Act 2015: 2015 anaw 6: explanatory notes. - 17, 17p.: 30 cm. - These notes refer to the Local Government (Wales) Act 2015 (anaw 6) which received Royal Assent on 25 November 2015 (ISBN 9780348111941). - Parallel texts in English and Welsh. Welsh title: Deddf Llywodraeth Leol (Cymru) 2015 2015 dccc 6 Nodiadau Esboniadol. - 978-0-348-11209-2 £10.00

Planning (Wales) Act 2015: 2015 anaw 4: explanatory notes. - 35p.: 30 cm. - These notes refer to the Planning (Wales) Act 2015 (anaw 4) which received Royal Assent on 6 July 2015 (ISBN 9780348110852). - Parallel texts in English and Welsh. Welsh title: Deddf Cynllunio (Cymru) 2015 dccc 4 Nodiadau Esboniadol. - 978-0-348-11086-9 £14.25

Qualifications Wales Act 2015: 2015 anaw 5: explanatory notes. - 35, 35p.: 30 cm. - These notes refer to the Qualifications Wales Act 2015 (anaw 5) which received Royal Assent on 5 August 2015 (ISBN 9780348110876). - Parallel texts in English and Welsh. Welsh title: Deddf Cymwysterau Cymru 2015 2015 dccc 5 Nodiadau Esboniadol. - 978-0-348-11088-3 £14.25

Violence against Women, Domestic Abuse and Sexual Violence (Wales) Act 2015: 2015 anaw 3: explanatory notes. - 10, 10p.: 30 cm. - These notes refer to the Violence against Women, Domestic Abuse and Sexual Violence (Wales) Act 2015 (anaw 3) which received Royal Assent on 29 April 2015 (ISBN 9780348110821). - Parallel texts in English and Welsh. Welsh title: Deddf Trais yn erbyn Menywod, Cam-drin Domestig a Thrais Rhywiol (Cymru) 2015- 978-0-348-11083-8 £6.00

Well-being of Future Generations (Wales) Act 2015: 2015 anaw 2: explanatory notes. - 25, 25p.: 30 cm. - These notes refer to the Well-being of Future Generations (Wales) Act 2015 (anaw 2) which received Royal Assent on 29 April 2015 (ISBN 9780348110814). - Parallel texts in English and Welsh. Welsh title: Deddf Llesiant Cenedlaethau'r Dyfodol (Cymru) 2015. - 978-0-348-11084-5 £10.00

ALPHABETICAL INDEX

A

ABWR nuclear reactor: Electricity generation: Justification decision	41, 51
Access to Justice Order 2003: Commencements: Northern Ireland	200
Access to justice: Civil legal services: Appeal: Northern Ireland	200
Access to justice: Civil legal services: Cost protection: Northern Ireland	200
Access to justice: Civil legal services: Costs: Northern Ireland	200
Access to justice: Civil legal services: Disclosure of information: Northern Ireland	200
Access to justice: Civil legal services: Financial: Northern Ireland	200
Access to justice: Civil legal services: General: Northern Ireland	200
Access to justice: Civil legal services: Remuneration: Northern Ireland	200
Access to justice: Civil legal services: Statutory charge: Northern Ireland	200
Accident hazards: Major: Control: Health & safety	50
Accounting standards: Prescribed bodies: United States & Japan: Companies	20
Acquisition of land: Home loss payments: Prescribed amounts: England	8, 21
Acquisition of land: Home loss payments: Prescribed amounts: Wales	8, 55
Act of Adjournal: Criminal Procedure Rules 1996: Final decision requests: Scotland	172, 174, 189
Act of Adjournal: Criminal Procedure Rules 1996: Reporting restrictions: Scotland	172, 174, 189
Act of Adjournal: Criminal Procedure Rules 1996: Scotland	172, 173, 174, 188, 189
Act of Adjournal: Justice of the Peace Court: Special measures: Scotland	172, 174, 189
Act of Sederunt: Adoption rules: Sheriff Court: Scotland	189
Act of Sederunt: Court of Session: Rules, Ordinary cause rules: Child welfare reporters: Scotland	167, 189
Act of Sederunt: Court of Session: Rules: Court reform: Scotland	166
Act of Sederunt: Court of Session: Rules: Protective expenses orders: Scotland	166
Act of Sederunt: Court of Session: Rules: Regulatory reform: Scotland	167
Act of Sederunt: Court of Session: Rules: Scotland	167
Act of Sederunt: Court of Session: Sheriff Court: Rules: Bankruptcy and Debt Advice (Scotland) Act 2014: Scotland	167, 189
Act of Sederunt: Court of Session: Sheriff Court: Rules: Personal injury & remits: Scotland	167, 189
Act of Sederunt: Court of Session: Sheriff Court: Rules: Scotland	166, 167, 189
Act of sederunt: Fees of solicitors: Scotland	188
Act of Sederunt: Fitness for judicial office tribunal rules: Scotland	173
Act of Sederunt: Ordinary cause rules 1993: Amendment: Scotland	166, 189
Act of Sederunt: Ordinary cause rules: Proving the tenor & reduction: Scotland	189
Act of Sederunt: Sheriff Appeal Court: Rules: Scotland	188
Act of Sederunt: Sheriff Court: Rules: Scotland	189
Acts: National Assembly for Wales: Annual volumes	7
Additional voluntary contributions: Health & personal social services: Northern Ireland	208
Additional voluntary contributions: Superannuation: Teachers	35
Additional voluntary contributions: Teachers' superannuation: Northern Ireland	203
Administrative forfeiture of cash: Forfeiture notices: England & Wales	84
Adoption & paternity leave: Northern Ireland	204
Adoption leave: Curtailment of statutory rights to leave: Northern Ireland	204
Adoption: Information & intermediary services: Pre-commencement adoptions: England	13, 123
Adoption: Information & intermediary services: Pre-commencement adoptions: Wales	14
Adoption: Paternity: Shared parental leave: Order cases: Northern Ireland	204
Adoption: Statutory paternity pay & statutory adoption pay: Northern Ireland	205
Adoption: Statutory paternity pay & statutory adoption pay: Parental orders & prospective adopters: Northern Ireland	205
Adoptions: Overseas: Employment rights: Northern Ireland	204
Adoptions: Overseas: Shared parental leave & paternity & adoption leave: Northern Ireland	204
Adoptions: Overseas: Statutory shared parental pay: Northern Ireland	205
Adoptions: Time off to attend adoption appointments: Northern Ireland	205
Adult protection & support orders: Authorised officer: Wales	124
Adults with incapacity: Public Guardian: Fees: Scotland	163
Advice & assistance: Representation: Scotland	175
Advisory Committees on Pesticides: Abolition: Public bodies	81, 85
African Development Bank: Further payments to capital stock	63
Aftercare: Eligible needs: Children & young persons: Scotland	165
Aggregates levy: Northern Ireland tax credit	8
Aggregates levy: Registration & miscellaneous provisions	8
Agricultural & forestry tractors: Emission of gaseous & particulate pollutants	40, 92
Agricultural Holdings Act 1986: Variations: Schedule 8	65
Agricultural holdings: Units of production: England	65
Agricultural holdings: Units of production: Wales	65, 66
Agricultural occupancies: Assured tenancies: Forms: England	65
Agricultural Sector (Wales) Act 2014: Consequential modifications: Wales	9
Agricultural: Agricultural Sector (Wales) Act 2014: Consequential modifications: Wales	9
Agriculture: Animal feed: Composition, marketing & use: England	8
Agriculture: Animal feed: Hygiene, sampling & enforcement England	8
Agriculture: Brucellosis: England	8, 9
Agriculture: Common Agricultural Policy	8
Agriculture: Common Agricultural Policy: Basic payment & support: Northern Ireland	200
Agriculture: Common Agricultural Policy: Basic payment & support: Wales	9

Agriculture: Common Agricultural Policy: Control & enforcement: Northern Ireland 200
Agriculture: Common Agricultural Policy: Decisions: Review of SCMO: Northern Ireland 200
Agriculture: Common Agricultural Policy: Decisions: Review: Northern Ireland 200
Agriculture: Common Agricultural Policy: Direct payments & support schemes: Northern Ireland 200
Agriculture: Common Agricultural Policy: Direct payments, etc.: Scotland 163
Agriculture: Common Agricultural Policy: Non-IACS support schemes: Scotland 163
Agriculture: Compensation: Calculation 65
Agriculture: Environmental protection: Environment & rural affairs: England 8, 9, 42, 135
Agriculture: Fixed equipment: Model clauses: England. 65
Agriculture: Less favoured area support schemes: Scotland 163
Agriculture: Less favoured areas: Compensatory allowances: Northern Ireland 201
Agriculture: Milk Marketing Board: Revocations: England & Wales 8
Agriculture: Milk producers: Single Common Market Organisation: Emergency aid 8
Agriculture: Nitrate pollution: Prevention 8, 135
Agriculture: Nitrate pollution: Prevention: Wales 9, 136
Agriculture: Organic products 8
Agriculture: Rural development contracts: Land managers options: Scotland. 163
Agriculture: Rural development programme: Northern Ireland. 201
Agriculture: Rural payments: Appeals: Scotland 163
Agriculture: Scotland Act 1998: Functions exercisable in or as regards Scotland 8, 22, 31
Agriculture: Student fees: Northern Ireland 200
Agriculture: Transitional payments: Disadvantaged area scheme: Northern Ireland 201
Air Force: Disablement & death: Service pensions 79
Air navigation: Dangerous goods 15
Air navigation: Feltwell 16
Air navigation: Flying restrictions: Abingdon Air & Country Show 15
Air navigation: Flying restrictions: Anmer Hall. 15
Air navigation: Flying restrictions: Ascot 15
Air navigation: Flying restrictions: Balado. 15, 16
Air navigation: Flying restrictions: Bermondsey. 16
Air navigation: Flying restrictions: Bethnal Green 16
Air navigation: Flying restrictions: Bournemouth 16
Air navigation: Flying restrictions: Cheltenham Festival 16
Air navigation: Flying restrictions: Clacton-on-Sea 16
Air navigation: Flying restrictions: Donna Nook 16
Air navigation: Flying restrictions: Dunsfold. 16
Air navigation: Flying restrictions: Duxford 16
Air navigation: Flying restrictions: East Fortune. 16
Air navigation: Flying restrictions: Eastbourne 16
Air navigation: Flying restrictions: Glastonbury Festival 16
Air navigation: Flying restrictions: Guildford 16
Air navigation: Flying restrictions: Hylands Park 16
Air navigation: Flying restrictions: Jet Formation Display Teams 16, 17
Air navigation: Flying restrictions: Jet formation display teams 16, 17
Air navigation: Flying restrictions: Kensworth. 17
Air navigation: Flying restrictions: Kensworth: Revocations. 17
Air navigation: Flying restrictions: Manchester 17
Air navigation: Flying restrictions: Newport. 18
Air navigation: Flying restrictions: Northampton Sywell. 17
Air navigation: Flying restrictions: Northern Ireland International Air Show 17
Air navigation: Flying restrictions: Oulton Park 17
Air navigation: Flying restrictions: Overton 17
Air navigation: Flying restrictions: Portsmouth 17
Air navigation: Flying restrictions: Queen's birthday flypast 16
Air navigation: Flying restrictions: Remembrance Sunday 17
Air navigation: Flying restrictions: RNAS Yeovilton 17
Air navigation: Flying restrictions: Royal Air Force Cosford 17
Air navigation: Flying restrictions: Royal International Air Tattoo RAF Fairford 17
Air navigation: Flying restrictions: Royal Naval Air Station Culdrose 17
Air navigation: Flying restrictions: Runnymede 17
Air navigation: Flying restrictions: Sandringham 17
Air navigation: Flying restrictions: Scottish Highlands. 17
Air navigation: Flying restrictions: Shoreham 18
Air navigation: Flying restrictions: Shoreham-by-Sea. 17
Air navigation: Flying restrictions: Silverstone & Turweston 18
Air navigation: Flying restrictions: Solent, Hampshire. 18
Air navigation: Flying restrictions: Southport 18
Air navigation: Flying restrictions: State opening of Parliament 18
Air navigation: Flying restrictions: Stokes Bay 18
Air navigation: Flying restrictions: Stonehenge 18
Air navigation: Flying restrictions: Strathallan Castle 18
Air navigation: Flying restrictions: Sunderland 18
Air navigation: Flying restrictions: Tonbridge 18
Air navigation: Flying restrictions: Tonbridge: Emergency 18
Air navigation: Flying restrictions: Trooping the Colour 18
Air navigation: Flying restrictions: Weston Park. 18
Air navigation: Flying restrictions: Wimbledon 18
Air navigation: Isle of Man 15

Air navigation: Overseas territories	15
Air navigation: Overseas territories: Environmental standards	15
Air navigation: Rules of the air: Civil aviation	19
Air Weapons & Licensing (Scotland) Act 2015: Commencements: Scotland	164, 167, 175
Air weapons & licensing: Acts: Explanatory notes: Scotland	163
Air weapons & licensing: Acts: Scotland	162
Aircraft operators: Accounts & records	43
Alcohol: Abstinence & monitoring requirements: Criminal Justice Act 2003	27
Alcohol: Abstinence & monitoring requirements: Legal Aid, Sentencing & Punishment of Offenders Act 2012: Commencements	27
Alcohol: Liquor: Controlled: Wholesaling	44
Algeria: Double taxation: Relief	12, 24, 58
Amateur sports clubs: Taxation	12, 24, 58
Ancient monuments: First planning period: Scotland	164
Ancient monuments: Historic Environment Scotland Act 2014: Ancillary provision: Scotland	164, 180
Ancient monuments: Historic Environment Scotland Act 2014: Commencements: Scotland	164
Ancient monuments: Historic Environment Scotland Act 2014: Saving, transitional & consequential provisions: Scotland	164, 191
Ancient monuments: Scheduled monument consent: Procedures: Scotland	164
Ancient monuments: Scheduled monuments & listed buildings: Scotland	164, 191, 192
Ancient monuments: Scheduled monuments: Appeals: Appointed persons: Prescribed classes: Scotland	164
Ancient monuments: Scheduled monuments: Appeals: Scotland	164
Ancient monuments: Scheduled monuments: Notification & publication: Scotland	164
Angler's lead weights: England	42
Anglian Water Parks: Byelaws: Extension	135
Animal by-products: Enforcement: England	9, 85
Animal by-products: Enforcement: Northern Ireland	201
Animal by-products: Scotland	164
Animal health: Cattle: Identification	9
Animal health: England & Wales	10
Animal health: Pets: Non-commercial movements: Northern Ireland	201
Animal health: Sheep & goats: Records, identification & movement: Wales	10
Animal health: Specified diseases: Notification:	9
Animal health: Specified diseases: Notification: England	9
Animal welfare: Dogs: Microchipping: England	9
Animals & related products: Trade: Scotland	164, 171
Animals (Scientific Procedures) Act 1986: Fees	9
Animals welfare: Time of killing	9
Animals: Animal feed: Composition, marketing & use: England	8
Animals: Animal feed: Hygiene, sampling & enforcement England	8
Animals: Animals & related products: Trade: Scotland	164, 171
Animals: Bovine viral diarrhoea: Scotland	164
Animals: Brucellosis: England	8, 9
Animals: Brucellosis: Northern Ireland	201
Animals: By-products: Enforcement: England	9, 85
Animals: Destructive animals: Mink & Coypus: England	9
Animals: Dogs: Microchipping: England	9
Animals: Environmental protection: Environment & rural affairs: England	8, 9, 42, 135
Animals: Horses: Public places: Control: Acts	4
Animals: Horses: Public places: Control: Acts: Explanatory notes	6
Animals: Miscellaneous provisions: England	10, 42, 71, 135
Animals: Miscellaneous revocations: England	9, 121, 135
Animals: People's Dispensary for Sick Animals: Charities	13
Animals: Prevention of cruelty: Animals welfare: Time of killing	9
Animals: Prevention of cruelty: Spring traps: Approval: Variations: England	9
Animals: Products of animal origin: Meats: Country of origin: England	48
Animals: Products of animal origin: Meats: Country of origin: Northern Ireland	207
Animals: Tuberculosis: England	9
Animals: Tuberculosis: Examination & testing scheme: Northern Ireland	201
Animals: Tuberculosis: Scotland	164
Animals: Tuberculosis: Wales	10
Animals: Welfare: At time of killing: Scotland	164
Animals: Welfare: Microchipping of dogs: Wales	10
Animals: Zoonoses: Fees: Northern Ireland	201
Animals: Zootechnical standards	10
Antarctic Act 1994: Isle of Man	10
Antarctic Act 1994: Overseas Territories	10
Antarctic: Dogs: Recognised assistance	10
Anti-social Behaviour, Crime & Policing Act 2014: Commencements	26, 42, 44, 54, 82, 83
Anti-social Behaviour, Crime & Policing Act 2014: Consequential amendments: Wales	54
Anti-social behaviour: Authorised persons	42
Anti-social behaviour: City of London Corporation: Designation	42
Anti-social behaviour: Crime & policing: Acts	4
Anti-social behaviour: Injunctions: Magistrates' courts: England & Wales	70
Antrim: Parking & waiting restrictions: Northern Ireland	218
Apprenticeship standards: Modifications: England	39
Apprenticeships: Specification of apprenticeship standards: England	39
Apprenticeships: Welsh certifying authority: Designation	39
Aquaculture & Fisheries (Scotland) Act 2007: Fixed penalty notices: Scotland	169, 171, 175, 187, 188
Aquaculture: Alien & locally absent species: Scotland	164

Aquaculture: Animals & related products: Trade: Scotland 164, 171
Aquaculture: European maritime & fisheries fund: Grants: Scotland 164, 171, 187
Archaeological areas: Scheduled monuments: Appeals: Appointed persons: Prescribed classes: Scotland 164
Archaeological areas: Scheduled monuments: Appeals: Scotland 164
Archaeological areas: Scheduled monuments: Consent: Procedures: Scotland 164
Archaeological areas: Scheduled monuments: Notification & publication: Scotland 164
Armed Forces & Reserve Forces: Compensation schemes 79
Armed Forces (Service Complaints & Financial Assistance) Act 2015: Commencements 30
Armed Forces (Service Complaints & Financial Assistance) Act 2015: Transitional & saving provisions 30
Armed Forces Act: Continuation 29
Armed Forces: Code of practice for victims of crime 26, 30
Armed Forces: Compensation schemes 79
Armed Forces: Enhanced Learning Credit Scheme & Further & Higher Education Commitment Scheme 79
Armed Forces: Pension schemes & early departure schemes 87
Armed Forces: Pensions 87
Armed Forces: Pensions: Compensation schemes 79
Armed Forces: Service complaints 30
Armed Forces: Service complaints & financial assistance: Acts 4
Armed Forces: Service complaints & financial assistance: Acts: Explanatory notes 6
Armed Forces: Service complaints: Miscellaneous provisions 30
Armed Forces: Service complaints: Ombudsman investigations 30
Armed Forces: Service Courts: Rules 30
Armoy Motorcycle Race: Road races: Northern Ireland 220
Arms & ammunition: Air Weapons & Licensing (Scotland) Act 2015: Commencements: Scotland 164, 167, 175
Arms & ammunition: Firearms 10
Arms & ammunition: Firearms: Fees 10
Army: Disablement & death: Service pensions 79
Ash dieback: Wood & bark: Plant health: Northern Ireland 214
Ashfield: Electoral changes 67
Asian infrastructure investment bank: Immunities & privileges 63
Asian Infrastructure Investment Bank: Initial capital contribution 63
Assembly Ombudsman for Northern Ireland: Public service pensions: Northern Ireland 212
Assembly Ombudsman for Northern Ireland: Superannuation: Northern Ireland 213
Assembly Ombudsman: Salaries: Northern Ireland 221
Association agreement: Georgia: European Communities: Definition of treaties 43
Association agreement: Moldova: European Communities: Definition of treaties 43
Association agreement: Ukraine: European Communities: Definition of treaties 43
Assured tenancies: Agricultural occupancies: Forms: England 65
Asylum: Immigration Act 2014 56
Asylum: Immigration: Police: Passenger, crew & service information 56
Asylum: Immigration: Police: Passenger, crew & service information: Civil penalties 57, 82
Asylum: Support 56
Attorney general: Human rights guidance: Police Service: Northern Ireland: Northern Ireland 209
Attorney general: Human rights guidance: Probation Board: Northern Ireland: Northern Ireland 209
Attorney general: Human rights guidance: Youth Justice Agency: Detention conditions: Northern Ireland: Northern Ireland . . . 209
Attorney general: Human rights guidance: Youth Justice Agency: Restorative justice: Northern Ireland: Northern Ireland 209
Authorised Investment Funds: Taxes 24
Automatic enrolment: Pensions: Earnings trigger & qualifying earnings band: Northern Ireland 211
Automatic telling machines: Rates: Rural areas: Exemptions: Northern Ireland 215, 216
Autority to carry scheme: Civil Penalties 56, 83
Avian influenza: Planning: Northern Ireland 213
Aviation Security Act 1982: Civil penalties 19
Aviation: Civil: Air navigation: Isle of Man 15
Aviation: Civil: Rules of the air 19
Awdurdod Gwasanaethau Busnes y GIG: NHS Business Services Authority: Delegation of additional functions 73

B

Backford Church of England School: Educational endowments 33
Badges: Motor vehicles: Disabled persons: Northern Ireland 217
Ballinderry,Glenavy Roads, Lisburn: Stopping-up: Northern Ireland 217
Ballot papers: Representation of the people 90
Ballymena: One-way traffic: Northern Ireland 218
Ballymoney: Parking places on roads & waiting restrictions: Northern Ireland 219
Banbridge: Parking & waiting restrictions: Northern Ireland 218
Bank levy: Double taxation: Arrangements: Netherlands 10
Bank levy: Double taxation: Relief: Netherlands 10
Bank of England Act 1998: Macro-prudential measures 45
Banking Act 2009: Inter-bank payment systems: Disclosure & publication of specified information 10
Banking: Financial Services (Banking Reform) Act 2013 47
Banking: Financial Services (Banking Reform) Act 2013: Transitional & saving provisions 47
Bankruptcy: Bankruptcy & Debt Advice (Scotland) Act 2014: Commencements: Scotland 165, 168, 173
Bankruptcy: Common financial tool: Scotland 165, 168, 173
Bankruptcy: Debt advice: Acts: Explanatory notes: Scotland 163
Bankruptcy: Debt advice: Acts: Scotland 162
Bankruptcy: Insolvency Act 1986 . . . . 10, 63
Bankruptcy: Scotland 165, 173
Banks & banking: Deposit guarantee scheme 11

Banks & banking: Financial Services (Banking Reform) Act 2013: Commencements 11
Batteries & accumulators: Market: Placing: Environmental protection 40
Belarus: Asset-freezing 26
Belfast, Cathedral Quarter: Parking & waiting restrictions: Northern Ireland 219
Belfast: Alfred Street/Upper Arthur Street: Roads: Parking places & waiting restrictions: Northern Ireland 219
Belfast: Alfred Street/Upper Arthur Street: Traffic control: Northern Ireland 217
Belfast: Compulsory Right or left-hand turn: Northern Ireland 217
Belfast: One-way traffic: Northern Ireland 218, 220
Belfast: Parking & waiting restrictions: Northern Ireland 218, 219
Belfast: Traffic control: Northern Ireland 217
Betting, gaming & lotteries: Gaming machine: Circumstances of use 11
Betting, gaming & lotteries: Olympic lotteries: Olympic Lottery Distribution Fund: Winding up 11
Biocidal products: Health & safety: Northern Ireland 208
Biometric registration: Civil penalty: Code of practice: Immigration 57
Biometric registration: Immigration 56, 57
Biometric registration: Immigration: Civil penalty: Objection 57
Bird flu see Avian influenza . . . .
Birds: Captive: Registration, ringing & marking: England 137
Birmingham, City: Scheme of elections 68
Bishops: Lords Spiritual: Women: Consecration: Acts 5
Bishops: Lords Spiritual: Women: Consecration: Acts: Explanatory notes 7
Blackthorn & Piddington: Network Rail: Land acquisition 134
Blood tests: Paternity evidence 43
Blyth Harbour 50
Boats & fishing methods: Fishing boats designation: England 121
Bodmin Moor Commons Council: Establishment 20
Bottled drinking water: Northern Ireland 207
Bottled drinking water: Wales 49
Bournemouth-Swanage Motor Road: Tolls: Revision 53
Bovine viral diarrhoea: Scotland 164
Bradford (City) Metropolitan District: Permit schemes: Traffic management 53
Brazil: International tax: Enforcement 12, 25, 44, 59, 62, 135
Brighton & Hove City Council: Permit schemes: Traffic management 53
Bristol: Electoral changes 67
British nationality 11
British nationality: Gambia 11
British nationality: General 76
British nationality: Proof of paternity 11
British Sign Language: Acts: Explanatory notes: Scotland 163
British Sign Language: Acts: Scotland 162
Broadcasting Act 1996: Local radio multiplex licences: Renewal 11
Broadcasting: Community radio 11
Broadcasting: Legislative reform: Radio licences renewal 11, 89
Brodick: Caledonian Maritime Assets: Harbour revision: Scotland 172
Broxtowe: Electoral changes 67
Brucellosis: England 8, 9
Brucellosis: Northern Ireland 201
Buckinghamshire County Council: Filming on highways: Local acts 7
Buckinghamshire, South: Electoral changes 69
Budget (Scotland) Act 2014: Amendment: Scotland 178
Budget (Scotland) Act 2015: Amendment: Scotland 178
Budget: Acts: Explanatory notes: Northern Ireland 199
Budget: Acts: Northern Ireland 199
Budget: Acts: Scotland 162
Building & buildings: Energy performance: England & Wales 11
Building & buildings: Energy performance: Scotland 165, 169
Building & buildings: England & Wales 11
Building & buildings: Wales 11
Building societies: Income tax: Interest payments 59
Building: Scotland: Scotland 165
Building: Self-build & custom housebuilding: Acts 5
Building: Self-build & custom housebuilding: Acts: Explanatory notes 7
Buildings: Listed: Conservation areas: Planning: England 132
Bulgaria: Double taxation: Relief 12, 24, 58
Burundi: European Communities: Financial sanctions 26
Burundi: Sanctions 77
Bus lanes: Falls Road, Belfast: Northern Ireland 217
Bus lanes: Upper Newtownards Road, Belfast: Northern Ireland 217
Buses: National travel concession schemes: Older & disabled persons: Scotland 192
Bushwhacker Rally: Road races: Northern Ireland 220
Business failure: Care & support: Wales 124
Business Improvement Districts: Community challenge: England 68
Businesses: Names & trading disclosures 11, 20, 67

C

Cairncastle Hill climb: Road races: Northern Ireland 220
Calderdale Borough Council: Permit schemes: Traffic management 53

Caledonian Maritime Assets: Harbour revision: Brodick: Scotland 172
Cambridgeshire County Council: A142 Ely Southern Bypass: Bridge scheme: Confirmation instruments: England 53
Canada: Double taxation: Relief & international tax enforcement 130
Cape Town Convention: International interests: Civil aviation. 19
Capital allowances. 24, 58
Capital allowances: Designed assisted areas 24
Capital allowances: Energy-saving plant & machinery 24, 58
Capital allowances: Environmentally beneficial plant & machinery 24, 58
Capital gains tax: Double taxation: Relief: Algeria 12, 24, 58
Capital gains tax: Double taxation: Relief: Bulgaria 12, 24, 58
Capital gains tax: Double taxation: Relief: Croatia 12, 24, 58
Capital gains tax: Double taxation: Relief: Kosovo 12, 24, 58
Capital gains tax: Double taxation: Relief: Senegal 12, 24, 58
Capital gains tax: Double taxation: Relief: Sweden 12, 24, 58
Capital gains tax: Finance Act 2007: Schedule 26: Shares: Valuation of: Appointed day: Commencements 12, 25, 58
Capital gains tax: Finance Act 2014 . . . . 12, 25, 59
Capital gains tax: Finance Act 2014: High risk promoters: Prescribed information 12, 25, 58
Capital gains tax: Individual savings accounts 12, 59
Capital gains tax: International tax: Enforcement: Brazil 12, 25, 44, 59, 62, 135
Capital gains tax: Offshore asset moves penalty: Specified territories 12, 60, 62
Capital gains tax: Shares, securities & strips: Market value of 12, 25, 59
Capital gains tax: Sports clubs, amateur: Taxation 12, 24, 58
Capital gains tax: Taxation: Chargeable gains: Gilt-edged securities 12, 25
Capital gains tax: Taxation: Regulatory capital securities 12, 25, 60, 129
Capital gains tax: Unit trusts: Unauthorised 13, 25, 60
Capital requirements: Capital buffers: Macro-prudential measures 46
Carbon accounting scheme: Scotland 166
Carbon accounting: Climate change: Budgetary period 2013-2017 19
Carbon dioxide: Storage: Access to infrastructure: Northern Ireland 206
Carbon dioxide: Storage: Licensing: Northern Ireland 206
Carbon monoxide alarms: England 40, 54
Care & support: Amendments 123
Care & support: Assessments: Wales 124
Care & support: Business failure 123
Care & support: Business failure: Wales 124
Care & support: Charging decisions & determinations: Review: Wales 124
Care & support: Charging: Wales 124
Care & support: Children's carers: England 123
Care & support: Choice of accommodation: Wales 124
Care & support: Deferred payment: Wales 124
Care & support: Direct payments: Wales 124
Care & support: Eligibility criteria: England 123
Care & support: Eligibility: Wales 124
Care & support: Financial assessment: Wales 124
Care & support: Market oversight criteria: England 123
Care & support: Ordinary residence: Disputes: Wales 124
Care & support: Ordinary residence: Specified accommodation: Wales 124
Care & support: Partnership arrangements: Wales 125
Care & support: Population assessment: Wales 124
Care & support: Population assessments: Partnership arrangements: Wales 124
Care & support: Provision of health services: Wales 124
Care Act 2014: Amendments 129
Care Act 2014: Commencements 72, 73, 123
Care Act 2014: Consequential amendments: England 123
Care Act 2014: Health Education England & Health Research Authority 52, 75, 124
Care Act 2014: Transitional provisions: England 123
Care of Churches & Ecclesiastical Jurisdiction (Amendment) Measure 2015: Commencements 32
Care planning, placement & case review: Children & young persons: Wales 14
Care planning: Fostering: England 13
Care Quality Commission: Membership 73, 85, 123
Care: Acts 4
Care: Continuing care: Children & young persons: Scotland 165
Caribbean & North Atlantic territories: Virgin Islands: Constitution 13
Carnbane Road: Abandonment: Northern Ireland 217
Carrier bags: Single use: Charges 42
Cars: Motor cars: Driving instruction 92
Cash searches: Constables: Proceeds of Crime Act 2002: Code of practice: Scotland 177
Castlederg: Waiting restrictions: Northern Ireland 221
Cathedral Quarter, Belfast: Parking & waiting restrictions: Northern Ireland 219
Cattle: Identification 9
Central African Republic: Overseas territories: Sanctions 77
Certification of Death (Scotland) Act 2011: Commencements: Scotland 178
Certification of Death (Scotland) Act 2011: Cremation authorisation: Death outwith Scotland 178
Certification of Death (Scotland) Act 2011: Post-Mortem examinations: Death outwith United Kingdom 178
Certification of Death (Scotland) Act 2011: Provisions: Scotland 178
Chancellor: Duchy of Lancaster 72
Channel Tunnel: International arrangements 13
Channel Tunnel: International arrangements: Miscellaneous provisions 56

Charities Act 2008: Commencements: Northern Ireland . . . 201
Charities Act 2008: Examination of accounts: Northern Ireland . . . 201
Charities Act 2008: Substitution of sums: Northern Ireland . . . 201
Charities Act 2011: Accounts & audit . . . 13
Charities Act 2011: Group accounts . . . 13
Charities Act 2013: Commencements: Northern Ireland . . . 201
Charities Exempt . . . 13
Charities: Accounts & reports: Northern Ireland . . . 201
Charities: Charity test: Specified bodies: Charities assets: Scotland . . . 165
Charities: Exempt charities . . . 13
Charities: People's Dispensary for Sick Animals . . . 13
Charities: Small Charitable Donations Act . . . 13
Charity test: Specified bodies: Charities assets: Scotland . . . 165
Chemicals: Classification, labelling & packaging . . . 50
Chemicals: Classification, labelling & packaging: Northern Ireland . . . 208
Cherwell: Electoral changes . . . 67
Chief Inspector of Education, Children's Services & Skills . . . 13, 14, 33, 34
Child benefit: General . . . 125
Child benefit: Tax credits: Up-rating . . . 125, 130
Child Maintenance & Other Payments Act 2008: Commencements . . . 44
Child Maintenance Act 2008 Act: Commencements: Northern Ireland . . . 206
Child Poverty Act 2010: Publication deadline: Extension . . . 13
Child support . . . 45
Child support: Child Maintenance & Other Payments Act 2008: Commencements . . . 44
Child support: Family law: Northern Ireland . . . 206
Child tax credit: Up-rating . . . 130
Child trust funds . . . 15
Childcare . . . 14
Childcare payments . . . 13, 79
Childcare Payments Act 2014 . . . 13, 79
Childcare payments: Eligibility . . . 13, 79
Childcare: Early years register . . . 13
Childcare: Information: Supply & disclosure . . . 14
Childcare: Qualifying: Income tax . . . 59
Childcare: Young children: Information provision: England . . . 14
Children & Families Act 2014 . . . 33
Children & Families Act 2014: Amendments . . . 129
Children & Families Act 2014: Commencements . . . 13, 14
Children & Young People (Scotland) Act 2014: Commencements: Scotland . . . 165, 168
Children & Young People (Scotland) Act 2014: Consequential & saving provisions . . . 13, 21, 31
Children & young persons: Adoption: Information & intermediary services: Pre-commencement adoptions: Wales . . . 14
Children & young persons: Aftercare: Eligible needs: Scotland . . . 165
Children & young persons: Care leavers: Wales . . . 14
Children & young persons: Care planning, placement & case review: Wales . . . 14
Children & young persons: Care planning: Fostering: England . . . 13
Children & young persons: Chief Inspector of Education, Children's Services & Skills . . . 13, 14, 33, 34
Children & young persons: Child Poverty Act 2010: Publication deadline: Extension . . . 13
Children & young persons: Childcare . . . 14
Children & young persons: Childcare: Early years register . . . 13
Children & young persons: Childcare: Young children: Information provision: England . . . 14
Children & young persons: Children & Families Act 2014: Commencements . . . 13, 14
Children & young persons: Children & Young People (Scotland) Act 2014: Commencements: Scotland . . . 165
Children & young persons: Children Act 2004: Joint area reviews . . . 14
Children & young persons: Children in detention: Visits: Wales . . . 15
Children & young persons: Children: Secure accommodation . . . 14
Children & young persons: Children's Hearings (Scotland) Act 2011: Rules of procedure: Children's hearings: Scotland . . . 165
Children & young persons: Children's homes . . . 14, 123
Children & young persons: Continuing care: Scotland . . . 165
Children & young persons: Health & social care . . . 14, 74, 86, 123
Children & young persons: Her Majesty's Inspector of Education, Children's Services & Skills . . . 14, 34
Children & young persons: Her Majesty's Inspector of Education, Children's Services & Skills: Children's homes etc.: Fees & frequency of inspections . . . 14
Children & young persons: Her Majesty's Inspector of Education, Children's Services & Skills: England . . . 14, 34
Children & young persons: Information & intermediary services: Pre-commencement adoptions: England . . . 13, 123
Children & young persons: Information: Supply & disclosure . . . 14
Children & young persons: Inspectors of Education, Children's Services & Skills . . . 14, 34
Children & young persons: Police Act 1997 & Protection of Vulnerable Grops (Scotland) Act 2007: Remedial: Scotland . . . 165, 177, 178
Children & young persons: Police: Police Act 1997 & Protection of Vulnerable Groups (Scotland) Act 2007: Remedial: Scotland . . 165, 177, 178
Children & young persons: Protection of Vulnerable Groups (Scotland) Act 2007: Scheme membership & disclosure requests: Fees: Scotland . . . 165, 178
Children & young persons: Secure accommodation: Scotland . . . 165
Children & young persons: Secure accommodation: Wales . . . 15, 125
Children & young persons: Small Business, Enterprise and Employment Act 2015: Commencements . . . 14, 20, 62, 89, 131
Children & young persons: Young carers: Needs assessments: England . . . 14
Children & young persons: Young people leaving care: Support & assistance Scotland: Scotland . . . 166
Children Act 2004: Joint area reviews . . . 14
Children: Care leavers: Wales . . . 14

Children: Early learning & childcare: Specified children: Scotland	169
Children: Performances & activities: Wales	15
Children: Secure accommodation	14
Children's Hearings (Scotland) Act 2011: Rules of procedure: Children's hearings: Scotland	165
Children's homes: Her Majesty's Inspector of Education, Children's Services & Skills	14, 34
Children's homes: Her Majesty's Inspector of Education, Children's Services & Skills: Fees & frequency of inspections	14
Children's services: Co-operation: Acts: Northern Ireland	199
Chile: Social security: Contributions	127
Chiropractors: Indemnity arrangements	51
Choice of court agreements 2005: Hague convention: Civil jurisdiction & judgments	63
Chronological tables: Statutes	7
Church of England: General Synod: Measures	7
Churches: Conservation Trust: Grants	33
Cinemas & films: British film: Definition	15
Cinemas & films: Films: Co-production agreements	15
Circuit of Ireland Rally: Road races: Northern Ireland	220
City of London Corporation: Designation: Anti-social behaviour	42
Civil & criminal legal aid: England & Wales	66
Civil & criminal legal aid: Remuneration: England & Wales	66
Civil aviation	18
Civil aviation: Air navigation	15
Civil aviation: Air navigation: Dangerous goods	15
Civil aviation: Air navigation: Isle of Man	15
Civil aviation: Air navigation: Overseas territories	15
Civil aviation: Aviation Security Act 1982: Civil penalties	19
Civil aviation: Cape Town Convention: International interests	19
Civil aviation: Flying restrictions	15, 16, 17, 18
Civil aviation: Overseas territories: Environmental standards	15
Civil aviation: Rules of the air	19
Civil enforcement: Parking contraventions: England	109
Civil jurisdiction & judgements & international recovery: Maintenance	64
Civil jurisdiction & judgments: Hague convention: Choice of court agreements 2005	63
Civil jurisdiction & judgments: Scotland	173
Civil legal aid: Merits criteria	66
Civil legal aid: Merits criteria & information about financial resources: England & Wales	66
Civil legal aid: Remuneration: England & Wales	66
Civil legal aid: Scotland	175
Civil legal services: Appeal: Northern Ireland	200
Civil legal services: Cost protection: Northern Ireland	200
Civil legal services: Costs: Northern Ireland	200
Civil legal services: Disclosure of information: Northern Ireland	200
Civil legal services: Financial: Northern Ireland	200
Civil legal services: General: Northern Ireland	200
Civil legal services: Remuneration: Northern Ireland	200
Civil legal services: Statutory charge: Northern Ireland	200
Civil partnership: Marriage & Civil Partnership (Scotland) Act 2014: Commencements	166, 176
Civil partnership: Marriage: Referral	19, 58, 71
Civil partnership: Marriage: Registration: Authorised persons	19, 89
Civil partnership: Marriages: Investigations conduct	19, 57, 71
Civil partnership: Marriages: Proposed: Referral & investigation	19, 57, 71
Civil partnership: Meaning of exempt persons & notice	19, 57, 71
Civil partnership: Modifications: Scotland	166, 176
Civil partnership: Referral & investigation: Provisions	19, 57, 71
Civil partnership: Sham marriage: Civil partnership: Scotland & Northern Ireland	19, 58, 71
Civil partnership: Waiting period	19, 57, 71
Civil procedure	26, 122
Civil procedure: Rules: England & Wales	26, 122
Civil proceedings: Fees	26, 45, 122
Civil Service: Public service pensions	87
Civil Service: Public service pensions: England & Wales	88
Civil Service: Public service pensions: Northern Ireland	215
Clean air: Smoke control areas: Authorised fuels: Northern Ireland	201
Clean air: Smoke control areas: Authorised fuels: Wales	19
Clean air: Smoke control areas: Fireplaces: Exempt: England	19
Clean air: Smoke control areas: Fireplaces: Exempt: Northern Ireland	201
Clean air: Smoke control areas: Fireplaces: Exempt: Wales	19
Clean Neighbourhoods & Environment Act 2005: Commencements	42
Clifton Street/Carrick Hill, Belfast: Footway: Abandonment : Northern Ireland	217
Climate change levy: General	20
Climate change: Carbon accounting scheme: Scotland	166
Climate change: Carbon accounting: Budgetary period 2013-2017	19
Climate change: Greenhouse gas emissions trading scheme	19
Climate change: Greenhouse gas: Additional: Scotland	166
Climate change: Public bodies: Duties: Reporting requirements: Scotland	166
Clinical negligence scheme: National Health Service: England	74
Clinical thermometers: EEC requirements	22, 136
Clogher: Waiting restrictions: Northern Ireland	221
Coaches: Parking places: Northern Ireland	219

Coaches: Parking places: Roads: Northern Ireland . . . 219
Coast protection: Excluded waters: Variation: England. . . . 20
Colchester: Electoral changes . . . 68
Cold weather payments: Social fund . . . 126
Collective investment schemes: Financial Services & Markets Act 2000 . . . 46
Commercial debts: Late payments: England, Wales & Northern Ireland . . . 23
Commercial debts: Late payments: Scotland. . . . 166
Commissioner for Complaints: Salaries: Northern Ireland . . . 221
Common Agricultural Policy. . . . 8
Common Agricultural Policy: Basic Payment & Support Schemes: Wales . . . 9
Common Agricultural Policy: Basic payment & support: Northern Ireland . . . 200
Common Agricultural Policy: Control & enforcement: Northern Ireland . . . 200
Common Agricultural Policy: Decisions: Review of SCMO: Northern Ireland . . . 200
Common Agricultural Policy: Decisions: Review: Northern Ireland . . . 200
Common Agricultural Policy: Direct payments & support schemes: Northern Ireland . . . 200
Common Agricultural Policy: Direct payments, etc.: Scotland . . . 163
Common Agricultural Policy: Non-IACS support schemes: Scotland . . . 163
Common financial tool: Scotland . . . 165, 168, 173
Common land: Registration, management & protection: Acts . . . 4
Commons: Bodmin Moor Commons Council: Establishment . . . 20
Communications data: Acquisition & disclosure: Code of practice . . . 63
Communications data: Regulation of investigatory powers. . . . 63
Communications data: Retention: Code of practice . . . 63
Community Care & Health (Scotland) Act 2002: Commencements . . . 176
Community care: Personal care & nursing care: Scotland . . . 190
Community care: Residential accommodation provision: Outwith Scotland: Scotland . . . 190
Community charge: Debt : Acts: Scotland . . . 162
Community Empowerment (Scotland) Act 2015: Commencements: Scotland . . . 166, 175, 180
Community empowerment: Acts: Explanatory notes: Scotland . . . 163
Community empowerment: Acts: Scotland. . . . 162
Community Health Councils: Constitution, membership & procedures: Wales . . . 76
Community Health Councils: Establishment, transfer of functions & abolition: Wales . . . 76
Community infrastructure levy: Amendments . . . 20
Community radio . . . 11
Community right to buy: Scotland . . . 175
Companies Act 2006: Part 17: Amendments . . . 20
Companies Act 2006: Part 18: Amendments . . . 20
Companies: Accounting standards: Prescribed bodies: United States & Japan . . . 20
Companies: Cross-border mergers . . . 20
Companies: Date of birth: Information disclosure . . . 20
Companies: Disclosure of address. . . . 20
Companies: European grouping of territorial co-operation . . . 43
Companies: Limited liability partnerships: Filing requirements . . . 20, 67
Companies: Names & trading disclosures . . . 11, 20, 67
Companies: Partnership: Accounts & reports . . . 20, 79
Companies: Payments to governments: Reports . . . 20, 79
Companies: Small Business, Enterprise & Employment Act 2015: Commencements. . . . 14, 20, 21, 39, 47, 62, 65, 89, 131
Companies: Small Business, Enterprise & Employment Act 2015: Insolvency & company directors disqualification . . . 21, 62
Compensation & pension scheme: Firefighters: Wales . . . 48, 81
Compensation: Claims management services: England & Wales. . . . 23
Compensation: Home loss payments: Prescribed amounts: England . . . 8, 21
Competition & Markets Authority: Rules . . . 21
Competition Act 1998: Competition & Markets Authority: Rules . . . 21
Competition Act 1998: Redress scheme. . . . 21
Competition appeal tribunal: Rules. . . . 21
Competition: Competition appeal tribunal: Rules. . . . 21
Competition: Consumer Rights Act 2015: Commencements . . . 21
Competition: Groceries Code Adjudicator: Financial penalty . . . 21
Competition: Water mergers . . . 21, 136
Congo (Democratic Republic): Overseas territories. . . . 77
Congo: Sanctions: Export control . . . 28
Consecration: Bishops: Lords Spiritual: Women: Acts. . . . 5
Consecration: Bishops: Lords Spiritual: Women: Acts: Explanatory notes . . . 7
Conservation areas: Listed buildings: Planning: England . . . 132
Conservation areas: Town & country planning: Notification & publication: Scotland. . . . 191
Conservation areas: Wales . . . 132
Conservation of sea fish: Outer Hebrides: Crabs & lobsters: Scotland . . . 187
Conservation of sea fish: Specified crustaceans: fishing, landing, sale & carriage: Prohibition. . . . 121
Conservation: Natural habitats: Northern Ireland . . . 206
Constitutional law: Children & Young People (Scotland) Act 2014: Consequential & saving provisions . . . 13, 21, 31
Constitutional law: Courts Reform (Scotland) Act 2014: Provisions & modifications. . . . 21, 26, 31, 123
Constitutional law: Food (Scotland) Act 2015: Consequential provisions . . . 21, 31, 48
Constitutional law: Government of Wales Act 2006 . . . 21, 32
Constitutional law: Government of Wales Act 2006: Designation of receipts . . . 21, 32
Constitutional law: Higher Education (Wales) Act 2015: Consequential provision . . . 21, 32, 35
Constitutional law: Human Transplantation (Wales) Act 2013: Consequential provision. . . . 21, 32, 55, 56
Constitutional law: National Assembly for Wales: Disqualifications . . . 21
Constitutional law: Regulatory Reform (Scotland) Act 2014: Consequential modifications . . . 21, 31, 38, 41, 67

Constitutional law: Reservoirs (Scotland) Act 2011: National security: Disclosure information: Restrictions 21, 31, 136
Constitutional law: River Tweed 22, 31, 91
Constitutional law: River Tweed: Scotland 166, 168, 181
Constitutional law: Scotland Act 1998: Schedule 4 & 5: Modifications 22, 31
Constitutional law: Scotland Act 1998: Schedule 5: Modifications 22, 31
Constitutional law: Scotland Act 1998: Variation: Borrowing power 22, 31, 85
Constitutional law: Scotland Act 2012: Commencements 22, 31
Constitutional law: Scotland Act 2012: Consequential provisions 22, 31
Constitutional law: Scottish Administration: Offices 22, 31
Constitutional law: Scottish Parliament: Disqualification: Scotland 166, 168
Constitutional law: Scottish Parliament: Elections: Scotland 166, 181
Constitutional law: Scottish Parliament: Regional returning officers 22, 32, 90
Constitutional law: Scottish Parliament: Returning officers charges 22, 32, 90
Construction industry scheme: Income tax: Amendments 25, 59
Construction industry scheme: Income tax: Finance Act 2004: Amendment 25, 59
Construction Industry Training Board: Industrial training levy 39
Construction industry: Industrial training levy: Northern Ireland 209
Construction: Design & management: Health & safety 50
Consultant lobbying: Consultant lobbyists: Registration 22
Consultant lobbying: Registration 22
Consultant lobbying: Transparency of Lobbying, Non-Party Campaigning & Trade Union Administration Act 2014: Commencements 22, 133
Consumer contracts 23
Consumer protection: Acts 4
Consumer protection: Acts: Explanatory notes 6
Consumer protection: Clinical thermometers: EEC requirements 22, 136
Consumer protection: Compensation: Claims management services: England & Wales 23
Consumer protection: Consumer contracts 23
Consumer protection: Consumer Rights Act 2015: Commencements 21, 23, 54
Consumer protection: Consumer Rights Act 2015: Commencements: England 23
Consumer protection: Consumer Rights Act 2015: Consequential amendments 23
Consumer protection: Dispute resolution 22
Consumer protection: Enterprise Act 2002: Part 8: Community infringements & specified UK laws 23
Consumer protection: Enterprise Act 2002: Part 8: Domestic infringements 23
Consumer protection: Letting agents: Duty to publicise fees: Exclusion: England 23
Consumer protection: Pyrotechnics articles: Safety 23, 51
Consumer Rights Act 2015: Commencements 21, 23, 35, 54
Consumer Rights Act 2015: Commencements: England 23
Consumer Rights Act 2015: Consequential amendments 23
Consumer rights: Acts 4
Consumer rights: Acts: Explanatory notes 6
Contracts: Commercial debts: Late payments: England, Wales & Northern Ireland 23
Contracts: Commercial debts: Late payments: Scotland 166
Contracts: Legal Writings (Counterparts & Delivery) (Scotland) Act 2015: Commencements: Scotland 166
Controlled liquor: Wholesaling 44
Cookstown 100: Road races: Northern Ireland 220
Cookstown: Waiting restrictions: Northern Ireland 221
Copyright & performances: Application to other countries 23, 91
Copyright: Cayman Islands 23
Copyright: Enterprise & Regulatory Reform Act 2013: Commencements 23, 24
Coroners & Justice Act 2009: Commencements: England & Wales 27
Coroners & Justice Act 2009: Coroner areas: Alteration 24
Coroners: Criminal Justice and Courts Act 2015: Commencements 24, 27, 28, 30, 64, 67, 70, 83, 122, 130, 137
Corporation tax :Exchange gains & losses: Fair value accounting 25
Corporation tax: Authorised Investment Funds 24
Corporation tax: Capital allowances 24, 58
Corporation tax: Capital allowances: Designed assisted areas 24
Corporation tax: Capital allowances: Energy-saving plant & machinery 24, 58
Corporation tax: Capital allowances: Environmentally beneficial plant & machinery 24, 58
Corporation tax: Cultural test: Television programmes 24
Corporation tax: Double taxation relief: International tax enforcement: Kosovo 12, 24, 58
Corporation tax: Double taxation: Relief: Algeria 12, 24, 58
Corporation tax: Double taxation: Relief: Bulgaria 12, 24, 58
Corporation tax: Double taxation: Relief: Croatia 12, 24, 58
Corporation tax: Double taxation: Relief: Guernsey 24, 58
Corporation tax: Double taxation: Relief: Jersey 24, 58
Corporation tax: Double taxation: Relief: Senegal 12, 24, 58
Corporation tax: Double taxation: Relief: Sweden 12, 24, 58
Corporation tax: Exchange gains & losses 24
Corporation tax: Finance Act 2007: Schedule 26: Shares: Valuation of: Appointed day: Commencements 12, 25, 58
Corporation tax: Finance Act 2012: Section 26 & 30: Relief for equalisation reserves: Abolition: Specified day 25, 58
Corporation tax: Finance Act 2013: Schedule 21: Appointed day 25
Corporation tax: Finance Act 2014 . . . . 12, 25, 59
Corporation tax: Finance Act 2014: High risk promoters: Prescribed information 12, 25, 58
Corporation tax: Finance Act 2015: Section 29: Film tax relief 25
Corporation tax: Financing costs & income: Treatment: Change of accounting standards: Investment entities 25
Corporation tax: Housing & regeneration transfer schemes: Tax consequences 25
Corporation tax: Insurance companies: Finance Act 2012: Amendment 25
Corporation tax: International tax: Enforcement: Brazil 12, 25, 44, 59, 62, 135

Corporation tax: Lloyd's underwriters: Transitional equalisation reserves. 25, 59
Corporation tax: Loan relationships & derivative contracts: Accounting practice: Change 25
Corporation tax: Loan relationships & derivative contracts: Change of accounting practice 25
Corporation tax: Loan relationships & derivative contracts: Profits & losses: Disregard & bringing into account. 25
Corporation tax: Northern Ireland: Acts 4
Corporation tax: Northern Ireland: Acts: Explanatory notes 6
Corporation tax: Shares, securities & strips: Market value of 12, 25, 59
Corporation tax: Sports clubs, amateur: Taxation 12, 24, 58
Corporation tax: Statutory shared parental pay 25, 38, 60
Corporation tax: Taxation: Chargeable gains: Gilt-edged securities 12, 25
Corporation tax: Taxation: Regulatory capital securities. 12, 25, 60, 129
Corporation tax: Unit trusts: Unauthorised 13, 25, 60
Cotswold: Electoral changes. 68
Council tax: Demand notices: England. 88
Council tax: Exceptions to higher amounts: Wales. 89
Council tax: Non-domestic rating: Powers of entry Safeguards: England. 68, 88
Council tax: Reduction schemes: Prescribed requirements & default scheme: Wales 26
Council tax: Reduction schemes: Prescribed requirements: England. 26
Council tax: Reduction: Scotland. 166
Counter-Terrorism & Security Act 2015: Authority to carry scheme 56, 83
Counter-Terrorism & Security Act 2015: Commencements 83, 133
Counter-Terrorism & Security Act 2015: Officers functions: Codes of practice 83
Counter-Terrorism & Security Act 2015: Risk of being drawn into terrorism 83
Counter-terrorism & security: Acts 4
Counter-terrorism & security: Acts: Explanatory notes. 6
Countryside: Birds: Captive: Registration, ringing & marking: England 137
Countryside: National Park Authorities: England 26
Countryside: Wildlife & Countryside Act 1981: Schedule 9: Variation: Wales 137
County court: Civil & family proceedings: Fees 26, 45, 122
County court: Civil procedure. 26, 122
County court: Civil procedure: Rules: England & Wales. 26, 122
County court: Crime & Courts Act 2013: Commencements 26, 122, 129
Court Martial & Service Civilian Court: Youth Justice & Criminal Evidence Act 1999 30
Court martial appeals: Courts 26
Court of Judicature, Northern Ireland: Crown Court: Rules: Amendments: Northern Ireland. 202
Court of Judicature, Northern Ireland: Rules: Northern Ireland 202
Court of Protection: Rules 72
Court of Session: : Rules: Act of Sederunt: Scotland 167, 189
Court of Session: Act of Sederunt: Court of Session: Rules: Protective expenses orders: Scotland. 166
Court of Session: Act of Sederunt: Rules: Regulatory reform: Scotland 167
Court of Session: Act of Sederunt: Rules: Scotland. 167
Court of Session: Courts Reform (Scotland) Act 2014 . . . . 167, 173, 190
Court of Session: Courts Reform (Scotland) Act 2014: Commencements: Scotland. 167, 172, 173, 174, 187, 188, 189, 191
Court of Session: Courts Reform (Scotland) Act 2014: Consequential provisions: Scotland 167, 172, 174, 188, 190, 191
Court of Session: Courts Reform (Scotland) Act 2014: Provisions & modifications 21, 26, 31, 123
Court of Session: Courts Reform (Scotland) Act 2014: Transitional & saving provisions: Commencements: Scotland 167, 188, 190
Court of Session: Fees: Scotland. 167
Court of Session: Ordinary cause rules: Amendment: Act of Sederunt: Scotland 166, 189
Court of Session: Rules: Bankruptcy and Debt Advice (Scotland) Act 2014: Act of Sederunt: Scotland 167, 189
Court of Session: Rules: Child welfare reporters: Act of Sederunt: Scotland. 167, 189
Court of Session: Rules: Court of Session, Sheriff Appeal Court & Sheriff Court: Scotland 167, 188, 189
Court of Session: Rules: Court reform: Scotland 166
Court of Session: Sheriff Court: Rules: Personal injury & remits: Scotland 167, 189
Court of Session: Sheriff Court: Rules: Scotland 166, 189
Courts Reform (Scotland) Act 2014 . . . . 167, 173, 190
Courts Reform (Scotland) Act 2014: Commencements: Scotland 167, 168, 172, 173, 174, 187, 188, 189, 191
Courts Reform (Scotland) Act 2014: Consequential provisions: Scotland 167, 172, 174, 188, 190, 191
Courts Reform (Scotland) Act 2014: Provisions & modifications 21, 26, 31, 123
Courts Reform (Scotland) Act 2014: Transitional & saving provisions: Commencements: Scotland 167, 188, 190
Courts: Criminal justice: Acts 4
Courts: Criminal justice: Acts: Explanatory notes 6
Coypus: England 9
Crabs & lobsters: Outer Hebrides: Scotland 187
Craigantlet Hill Climb: Road races: Northern Ireland 220
Crediting: Contributions: Treatment: National Insurance numbers 127
Crime & Courts Act 2013 . . . . 73, 77, 84, 92
Crime & Courts Act 2013: Commencements 26, 66, 84
Crime & Courts Act 2013: Northern Ireland 77
Crime & policing: Anti-social behaviour: Acts 4
Crime: Police & Crime Commissioners: Elections 82
Crime: Police & Crime Commissioners: Elections: Returning officers: Area designation: England & Wales 82
Crime: Policing & Crime Act 2009: Commencements 84
Crime: Proceeds of Crime Act 2002: Cash Searches: Code of Practice 84
Crime: Proceeds of Crime Act 2002: Code of practice: Investigations: England & Wales 84
Crime: Proceeds of Crime Act 2002: Code of practice: Investigations: Prosecutors power: England & Wales 84
Crime: Proceeds of Crime Act 2002: External investigations: Scotland. 84
Crime: Proceeds of Crime Act 2002: Investigations 84
Crime: Proceeds of Crime Act 2002: Property: Search, seizure & detention: Code of practice: England & Wales. 84

Crime: Proceeds of Crime Act 2002: Restraint orders: Legal aid exception: England & Wales 67, 85
Crime: Serious crime: Acts 6
Crime: Serious crime: Acts: Explanatory notes 7
Crimea, Russia & Sevastopol: Sanctions. 28
Crimea: Sanctions 78
Criminal cases: Costs: England & Wales. 27
Criminal Evidence (Northern Ireland) Order 1999: Commencements: Northern Ireland 202
Criminal Justice & Courts Act 2015: Commencements 24, 27, 28, 30, 64, 67, 70, 83, 122, 130, 137
Criminal Justice & Courts Act 2015: Simple cautions 27
Criminal Justice & Courts Act 2015: Simple cautions: Specification of police ranks 27
Criminal justice & courts: Acts. 4
Criminal justice & courts: Acts: Explanatory notes 6
Criminal Justice & Licensing (Scotland) Act 2010: Commencements: Scotland. 167, 168, 172, 188
Criminal Justice & Licensing (Scotland) Act 2010: Supplementary provisions: Scotland. 187
Criminal justice & support for victims: Human trafficking & exploitation: Acts: Northern Ireland 199
Criminal Justice (Northern Ireland) Order 2008: Commencements: Northern Ireland 202
Criminal Justice Act 2003: Alcohol abstinence & monitoring requirements 27
Criminal Justice Act 2013: Commencements: Northern Ireland 210
Criminal justice: Armed Forces: Code of practice for victims of crime 26, 30
Criminal justice: Class B drugs. 27
Criminal justice: European protection order: Northern Ireland 202
Criminal justice: Sentencing: Licence conditions: England & Wales 27
Criminal law: Air Weapons & Licensing (Scotland) Act 2015: Commencements: Scotland 164, 167, 175
Criminal law: Anti-social Behaviour, Crime & Policing Act 2014: Commencements. 26, 42, 54, 82, 83
Criminal law: Belarus: Asset-freezing 26
Criminal law: Burundi: European Communities: Financial sanctions 26
Criminal law: Coroners & Justice Act 2009: Commencements: England & Wales 27
Criminal law: Courts Reform (Scotland) Act 2014: Commencements: Scotland 168, 172, 188
Criminal law: Crime & Courts Act 2013: Commencements. 26, 66, 84
Criminal law: Criminal cases: Costs: England & Wales. 27
Criminal law: Criminal Justice & Courts Act 2015: Commencements. 24, 27, 28, 30, 64, 67, 70, 83, 122, 130, 137
Criminal law: Criminal Justice & Courts Act 2015: Simple cautions. 27
Criminal law: Criminal Justice & Licensing (Scotland) Act 2010: Commencements: Scotland 168, 172, 188
Criminal law: Criminal Justice (Northern Ireland) Order 2008: Commencements: Northern Ireland 202
Criminal law: Criminal justice: European protection order: Northern Ireland 202
Criminal law: Criminal justice: Sentencing: Licence conditions: England & Wales. 27
Criminal law: Criminal Procedure & Investigations Act 1996: Code of practice 27
Criminal law: Domestic Violence & Victims Act 2004: Victims' Code of Practice: England & Wales 27
Criminal law: Human Trafficking and Exploitation: Commencements: Northern Ireland 202
Criminal law: Justice & Security (Northern Ireland) Act 2007: Non-jury trial provisions: Duration: Extension 28, 64
Criminal law: Legal Aid, Sentencing & Punishment of Offenders Act 2012: Commencements 27
Criminal law: Legal Aid, Sentencing & Punishment of Offenders Act 2012: Fines: Summary conviction. 27
Criminal law: Management of Offenders etc. (Scotland) Act 2005: Commencements: Scotland 168
Criminal law: Management of Offenders etc. (Scotland) Act 2005: Specification of persons: Scotland 168
Criminal law: Offender Rehabilitation Act 2014: Commencements 27, 30
Criminal law: Offender Rehabilitation Act 2014: Incidental provisions. 27
Criminal law: Police Act 1997: Criminal records: Disclosure: Northern Ireland. 202
Criminal law: Police Act 1997: Criminal records: Northern Ireland. 202
Criminal law: Prosecution of Offences Act 1985: Criminal courts charge 27
Criminal law: Serious Crime Act 2015: Commencements. 27, 28, 84, 122
Criminal law: Serious Crime Act 2015: Commencements: England & Wales 28
Criminal law: Serious Crime Act 2015: Consequential amendments 28
Criminal law: Sexual Offences Act 2003: Prescribed police stations 28
Criminal law: Sexual Offences Act 2003: Prescribed police stations: Northern Ireland. 202
Criminal law: Sudan: European Union: Financial sanctions 27
Criminal law: Victims & Witnesses (Scotland) Act 2014: Commencements: Scotland 168
Criminal law: Victims' rights: Scotland 168
Criminal law: Youth detention accommodation: Remand: Recovery of costs. 27
Criminal law: Youth Justice & Criminal Evidence Act 1999: Commencements 28
Criminal law: Youth Justice Board for England & Wales 28
Criminal law: Yugoslavia, Federal Republic: Freezing of funds 27
Criminal legal aid: Contribution orders: England & Wales. 66
Criminal legal aid: Disclosure of information: Northern Ireland. 210
Criminal legal aid: England & Wales 66
Criminal legal aid: Remuneration: England & Wales 66
Criminal Procedure & Investigations Act 1996: Code of practice 27
Criminal procedure: Criminal Justice & Courts Act 2015: Commencements 24, 27, 28, 30, 64, 67, 70, 83, 122, 130, 132, 137
Criminal procedure: European Protection Order: Scotland 168
Criminal procedure: Evidence: Justice of the Peace Courts: Special measures: Scotland. 168
Criminal procedure: Rules: Act of Adjournal: Reporting restrictions: Scotland 172, 174, 189
Criminal procedure: Rules: Act of Adjournal: Scotland. 172, 173, 174, 188, 189
Criminal procedure: Rules: England & Wales 70, 122
Criminal procedure: Vulnerable Witnesses (Scotland) Act 2004: Commencements: Scotland. 168
Criminal proceedings: Criminal Justice and Courts Act 2015: Commencements. 24, 27, 28, 30, 64, 67, 70, 83, 122, 130, 137
Croatia: Double taxation: Relief 12, 24, 58
Croft Hill Climb: Road races: Northern Ireland 220
Crofters, cottars & small landholders: Crofting counties agricultural grants: Scotland 168
Crofting counties agricultural grants: Scotland 168

Cross-border healthcare: National Health Service 75
Crossrail: Plumstead sidings 134
Crossrail: Services: Exemption 134
Crown Court proceedings: Legal aid: Costs: Northern Ireland 210
Crown Court: Rules: Northern Ireland 202
Crown Dependencies: Taxes: International compliance. 130
Cullybackey South: Level crossing: Northern Ireland 216
Cultural objects: Return 28
Cultural test: Television programmes 24
Cultural test: Television programmes: Corporation tax 24
Curriculum: National: England 34
Curriculum: National: Specified purpose: England 34
Customs: Contravention of a relevant rule 28
Customs: Export control. 28, 29
Customs: Export control: Sanctions: Congo 28
Customs: Export control: Sanctions: Iran 28
Customs: Export control: Sanctions: Russia, Crimea & Sevastopol 28
Customs: Export control: Sanctions: Yemen. 29
Customs: Finance Act 2014: Schedule 21: Commencements 29, 44
Cycle racing: Highways: Wales 110
Cycle routes: Amendments: Northern Ireland 217
Cycle track: Fochabers: Scotland 181
Cycles: Pedal cycles: Construction & use 92
Cycles: Pedal: Electrically assisted. 92

D

Dangerous dogs: Exemption schemes. 32
Dangerous drugs: Controlled drugs: Supervision of management & use: Northern Ireland 202
Dangerous drugs: Misuse of drugs 29
Dangerous drugs: Misuse of Drugs Act 1971: Amendments 29
Dangerous drugs: Misuse of drugs: Designation: Northern Ireland 202
Dangerous drugs: Misuse of drugs: Northern Ireland 202
Dangerous goods: Air navigation 15
Data Protection Act 1998: Commencements 29
Data protection: Protection of Freedoms Act 2012: Commencements 29, 49
Data Retention & Investigatory Powers Act 2014: Commencements. 38
Data-gathering powers: Relevant data: Amendments 58
Death & disablement: Navy, Army & Air Force: Service pensions. 79
Deaths: Certification of Death (Scotland) Act 2011: Application for review: Scotland 180
Debt arrangement schemes: Scotland 168
Debt: Bankruptcy & Debt Advice (Scotland) Act 2014: Commencements: Scotland 165, 168, 173
Debt: Common financial tool: Scotland 165, 168, 173
Debtors (Scotland) Act 1987: Diligence against earnings: Variations: Scotland 169
Debts: Commercial debts: Late payments: England, Wales & Northern Ireland. 23
Decapitalisation rate: Valuation for rating: Northern Ireland 216
Deceased persons: Estates: Inheritance & trustees' powers: Acts: Explanatory notes 6
Decisions review: Local Government: Acts: Explanatory notes 7
Deduction from accounts: Prescribed information: Enforcement 40
Deep Sea Mining Act 1981: Isle of Man 29
Defence Reform Act 2014: Commencements 30
Defence Support Group Trading Fund 50
Defence: Armed Forces (Service Complaints & Financial Assistance) Act 2015: Commencements 30
Defence: Armed Forces (Service Complaints & Financial Assistance) Act 2015: Transitional & saving provisions 30
Defence: Armed Forces Act: Continuation 29
Defence: Armed Forces: Code of practice for victims of crime 26, 30
Defence: Armed Forces: Service complaints 30
Defence: Armed Forces: Service complaints: Miscellaneous provisions 30
Defence: Armed Forces: Service complaints: Ombudsman investigations 30
Defence: Armed Forces: Service Courts rules 30
Defence: Court Martial & Service Civilian Court: Youth Justice & Criminal Evidence Act 1999 30
Defence: Criminal Justice and Courts Act 2015: Commencements 24, 27, 28, 30, 64, 67, 70, 83, 122, 130, 137
Defence: Offender Rehabilitation Act 2014: Commencements 27, 30
Defence: RAF Brize Norton: Byelaws 30
Defence: Reserve forces: Call-out & recall: Financial assistance 30
Defence: Sculthorpe training area: Byelaws 30
Defence: Service courts application: Youth Justice & Criminal Evidence Act 1999 30
Defence: Summary appeal courts: Youth Justice & Criminal Evidence Act 1999 30
Defence: Youth Justice & Criminal Evidence Act 1999: Service courts: Applications 30
Dental charges: National Health Service: Wales 76
Dental services: Primary: England 75
Dentists & dental care professionals: General Dental Council: Indemnity arrangements 51
Dentists Act 1984: Medical authorities 51
Dentists: General Dental Council: Overseas registration examination 30, 51
Deposit guarantee scheme: Banks 11
Derbyshire County Council: Permit schemes: Traffic management 53
Deregulation Act 2015 31
Deregulation Act 2015: Commencements 30, 31

Deregulation Act 2015: Commencements: England & Wales	35
Deregulation Act 2015: Insolvency	31
Deregulation Act 2015: Poisons & explosives precursors	31
Deregulation Act 2015: Working conditions: Self-employed persons	50
Deregulation: Acts	4
Deregulation: Acts: Explanatory notes	6
Designs: Appointed person: Rules	31
Destructive animals: Mink & Coypus: England	9
Detention conditions: Youth Justice Agency: Attorney general: Human rights guidance: Northern Ireland: Northern Ireland	209
Determination of appeals: Appointed persons: Prescribed classes: Wales	132
Development corporations: Ebbsfleet Development Corporation: Area & constitution	135
Development: International: Official development assistance: Targets: Acts	5
Development: International: Official development assistance: Targets: Acts: Explanatory notes	7
Devolution, Scotland Children & Young People (Scotland) Act 2014: Consequential & saving provisions	13, 21, 31
Devolution, Scotland: Courts Reform (Scotland) Act 2014: Provisions & modifications	21, 26, 31, 123
Devolution, Scotland: River Tweed	22, 31, 91, 166, 168, 181
Devolution, Scotland: Scotland Act 1998: Schedule 4 & 5: Modifications	22, 31
Devolution, Scotland: Scotland Act 1998: Schedule 5: Modifications	22, 31
Devolution, Scotland: Scotland Act 2012: Commencements	22, 31
Devolution, Scotland: Scotland Act 2012: Consequential provisions	22, 31
Devolution, Scotland: Scottish Parliament: Regional returning officers	22, 32, 90
Devolution, Scotland: Scottish Parliament: Returning officers charges	22, 32, 90
Devolution, Wales: Government of Wales Act 2006	21, 32
Devolution: Food (Scotland) Act 2015: Consequential provisions	21, 31, 48
Devolution: Government of Wales Act 2006: Designation of receipts	21, 32
Devolution: Higher Education (Wales) Act 2015: Consequential provision: Wales	21, 32, 35
Devolution: Human Transplantation (Wales) Act 2013: Consequential provision	21, 32, 55, 56
Devolution: Landfill tax	64
Devolution: Regulatory Reform (Scotland) Act 2014: Consequential modifications	21, 31, 38, 41, 67
Devolution: Reservoirs (Scotland) Act 2011: National security: Disclosure information: Restrictions	21, 31, 136
Devolution: Scotland Act 1998: Functions exercisable in or as regards Scotland	8, 22, 31
Devolution: Scotland Act 1998: Schedules 4 & 5: Modifications	22, 31
Devolution: Scotland Act 1998: Variation: Borrowing power	22, 31, 85
Devolution: Scottish Administration: Offices	22, 31
Devolution: Scottish Parliament: Disqualification: Scotland	166, 168
Devon, West: Electoral changes	69
Diligence against earnings: Variations: Scotland	169
Diocese of Chester: Backford Church of England School: Educational endowments	33
Diocese of Derby: Former Edward Revell Endowed Voluntary Controlled Primary School: Educational endowments	33
Diocese of Durham: Cleadon Village CD Infants' School: Educational endowments	33
Diocese of Ely: Fincham Church of England School: Educational endowments	33
Diocese of Ely: Shouldham Church of England School: Educational endowments	33
Diocese of Guildford: Down Road Church of England School: Educational endowments	33
Diocese of Newcastle: Craster Church of England School: Educational endowments	33
Diocese of Worcester: Evesham Church of England First School: Educational endowments	33
Disability Discrimination Act 1995: Commencements: Northern Ireland	202
Disabled persons: Disability Discrimination Act 1995: Commencements: Northern Ireland	202
Disabled persons: Motor vehicles: Badges: Northern Ireland	217
Disabled persons: Motor vehicles: Badges: Scotland	181
Disabled persons: Rail vehicles: Accessibility: B2007 Vehicles: Exemptions	32, 133
Disabled persons: Rail vehicles: Accessibility: Non-interoperable rail system: London Underground Northern Line 95TS Vehicles	32, 133
Disabled persons: Taxi accessibility: Northern Ireland	202
Disabled Persons' Parking Badges (Scotland) Act 2014: Commencements: Scotland	181
Disabled persons' vehicles: Parking places: Northern Ireland	219, 220
Disabled persons' vehicles: Roads: Parking places: Northern Ireland	219, 220
Disablement & death: Navy, Army & Air Force: Service pensions	79
Disciplinary & grievance procedures: Employment: Code of practice	130
Disclosure of information: Exporter information	32
Discrimination: Disability Discrimination Act 1995: Commencements: Northern Ireland	202
Dispute resolution: Consumer protection	22
District councils: Functions: Off-street parking: Acts: Explanatory notes: Northern Ireland	199
District councils: Functions: Off-street parking: Acts: Northern Ireland	199
District councils: Superannuation: Northern Ireland	213
Diverted profits tax: Finance Act 2009: Commencements	32
Doctors: General Medical Council: General Medical Council: Provisional registration: Maximum period	52
Doctors: General Medical Council: Licence to practise	52
Dogger Bank Creyke Beck	61
Dogger Bank Teeside A & B Offshore Wind Farm	61
Dogs: Dangerous dogs: Exemption schemes	32
Domestic abuse: Acts: Wales	229
Domestic Violence & Victims Act 2004: Victims' Code of Practice: England & Wales	27
Donaghadee Harbour: Northern Ireland	207, 208
Doncaster: Electoral changes	68
Dorset and Wiltshire Fire & Rescue Authority: Combination scheme	47
Dorset: West Dorset: Electoral changes	69
Double taxation: Arrangements: Netherlands	10
Double taxation: Relief	12, 24, 58, 130
Drink: Rehabilitation courses: Relevant drink offences	92

Driver & Vehicle Standards Agency Trading Fund 50
Drivers: Vehicle drivers: Professional competence: Certificates: Amendments 93
Driving instruction: Motor vehicles: Northern Ireland 218
Driving instruction: Trainee licences: Motor vehicles: Northern Ireland 218
Driving licences: Motor vehicles: Amendments: Northern Ireland 218
Driving: Drug driving: Specified limits 109
Drug driving: Specified limits 109
Drugs & appliances: Charges: National Health Service: England 74
Drugs & appliances: Charges: National Health Service: Scotland 176
Drugs: Class B: Specified: Criminal justice 27
Drugs: Controlled drugs: Supervision of management & use: Northern Ireland 202
Drugs: Misuse of drugs 29
Drugs: Misuse of Drugs Act 1971: Amendments 29
Drugs: Misuse of Drugs Act 1971: Temporary class drugs 29
Drugs: Misuse of drugs: Designation: Northern Ireland 202
Drugs: Misuse of drugs: Northern Ireland 202
Drumhorc Hill Climb: Road races: Northern Ireland 220
Ducks & geese: Food protection: Emergency prohibitions: Lead: England 86
Dungannon: Parking & waiting restrictions: Northern Ireland 219
Dwellings: Enveloped dwellings: Annual tax: Avoidance schemes: Prescribed descriptions of arrangements 10

E

Earnings: Computation: Social security: Benefits 126
Earnings: Computation: Social security: Benefits: Northern Ireland 129
East Northamptonshire: Electoral changes 68
Ebbsfleet Development Corporation: Area & constitution 135
Ebbsfleet Development Corporation: Planning functions: England 135
Ecclesbourne Valley Railway: England 134
Ecclesiastical judges, legal officers & others: Fees 32
Ecclesiastical law: Care of Churches & Ecclesiastical Jurisdiction (Amendment) Measure 2015: Commencements 32
Ecclesiastical law: Churches: Conservation Trust: Grants 33
Ecclesiastical law: Ecclesiastical judges, legal officers & others: Fees 32
Ecclesiastical law: Ecclesiastical offices: Terms of service 32
Ecclesiastical law: Ecclesiastical Property Measure 2015: Commencements 32
Ecclesiastical law: Ecclesiastical property: Exceptions: Dealings: Requirement for consent 32
Ecclesiastical law: Faculty jurisdiction: Rules 32
Ecclesiastical law: Legal officers: Annual fees 32
Ecclesiastical offices: Terms of service 32
Ecclesiastical Property Measure 2015: Commencements 32
Ecclesiastical property: Dealings: Requirement for consent 32
Ecodesign: Energy-related products & energy information: Amendments 40
Education & training: Inspectors: Wales 35
Education (Wales) Act 2014: Commencements 36
Education Act 2002: Commencements 35
Education Workforce Council: Main functions: Wales 36
Education Workforce Council: Registration fees: Wales 36
Education: 1998 Order: Commencements: Northern Ireland 203
Education: 2014 Act: Commencements: Northern Ireland 203
Education: Aided places: St Mary's Music School: Scotland 169
Education: Assisted places: Scotland 168
Education: Chief Inspector of Education, Children's Services & Skills 13, 14, 33, 34
Education: Children & Families Act 2014 33
Education: Children & Young People (Scotland) Act 2014: Commencements: Scotland 165, 168
Education: Consumer Rights Act 2015: Commencements 35
Education: Deregulation Act 2015: Commencements: England & Wales 35
Education: Designated institutions 33
Education: Diocese of Bradford: Cleadon Village CD Infants' School: Educational endowments 33
Education: Diocese of Chester: Backford Church of England School: Educational endowments 33
Education: Diocese of Derby: Former Edward Revell Endowed Voluntary Controlled Primary School: Educational endowments 33
Education: Diocese of Ely: Fincham Church of England School: Educational endowments 33
Education: Diocese of Ely: Shouldham Church of England School: Educational endowments 33
Education: Diocese of Guildford: Down Road Church of England School: Educational endowments 33
Education: Diocese of Lichfield: Bicton Church of England school: Educational endowments 33
Education: Diocese of Newcastle: Craster Church of England School: Educational endowments 33
Education: Diocese of Worcester: Evesham Church of England First School: Educational endowments 33
Education: Early learning & childcare: Specified children: Scotland 169
Education: Further education: Destination information: Prescribed activities 34
Education: Further: Loans: England 34
Education: General Teaching Council for Northern Ireland 203
Education: General Teaching Council for Northern Ireland: Teachers: Registration 203
Education: Glasgow Clyde College: Removal & appointment of board members: Scotland 169
Education: Her Majesty's Inspector of Education, Children's Services & Skills 14, 34
Education: Her Majesty's Inspector of Education, Children's Services & Skills: Children's homes etc.: Fees & frequency of inspections . . 14
Education: Her Majesty's Inspector of Education, Children's Services & Skills: England 14, 34
Education: Higher Education (Wales) Act 2015: Commencements 36
Education: Higher Education (Wales) Act 2015: Consequential provision: England & Wales 21, 32, 35
Education: Higher education: Acts: Explanatory notes: Wales 229

Education: Higher education: Acts: Wales 229
Education: Higher Education: Amounts 36
Education: Higher Education: Designation of providers 36
Education: Higher Education: Fee & access plans 36
Education: Higher Education: Fee & access plans: Notices & directions 36
Education: Higher education: Prescribed courses: Information requirements. 34
Education: Higher Education: Qualifying courses, persons & supplementary provision 36
Education: Higher education: Student loans: Living costs liability: Cancellation. 35
Education: Information: England 34
Education: Inspections: Nursery: Wales 35
Education: Inspectors of Education, Children's Services & Skills 14, 34
Education: Merthyr Tydfil College Limited: Designated institution: Further education: Wales 36
Education: National College for High Speed Rail: Government: England 34
Education: National College for High Speed Rail: Incorporation: England 34
Education: National curriculum: Assessment arrangements: Foundation phase: Desirable outcomes, educational programmes & baseline & end of phase: Wales. 37
Education: National curriculum: Assessment arrangements: KS2, KS3: Moderation: Wales 37
Education: National curriculum: England 34
Education: National curriculum: Specified purpose: England 34
Education: National curriculum: Study: Attainment targets & programmes: Wales 36
Education: Post-16 Education (Scotland) Act 2013: Commencements: Scotland. 169
Education: Post-16 Education (Scotland) Act 2013: Scotland 169
Education: Pupil referral units: Application of enactments: Wales 36
Education: Qualifications Wales Act 2015: Commencements 37
Education: Qualifications: Acts: Explanatory notes: Wales 229
Education: Qualifications: Acts: Wales 229
Education: Queen Margaret University, Edinburgh: Order of Council: Scotland 169
Education: Religious schools: Designation: England 33
Education: Rural primary schools: Designations: England 33
Education: School & early years finance: England 34
Education: School governance: England. 34
Education: School governance: Federations: England 34
Education: School lunches: Scotland. 169
Education: School teachers: Pay & conditions: England & Wales 35
Education: Schools: Eastern High School: Session times: Changes: Wales 35
Education: Schools: Independent: Religious character: Designation: England 33
Education: Schools: Inspection: England 34
Education: Schools: Maintained schools: Government: Change of category: Wales 36
Education: Schools: Performance information: England 34
Education: Schools: Religious character: Designation: Independent schools: Revocations: England 33
Education: Schools: Special non-maintained: England. 34
Education: Schools: Staffing: England 34
Education: Special Educational Needs & Disability First-tier Tribunal: Recommendation power: Pilot. 35
Education: Special educational needs & disability: England 35
Education: Special educational needs: Codes of practice: England 35
Education: Special educational needs: Disability: England 35
Education: Specified work & registration: Wales 36
Education: Student fees: Amounts: Northern Ireland 203
Education: Student information: England 34
Education: Student support 34
Education: Student support: Scotland 169
Education: Student support: Wales 36
Education: Teachers: Induction arrangements: Wales 35
Education: Teachers: Pensions: Amendments: Northern Ireland 203
Education: Teachers: Redundancy & premature retirement: Compensation 35
Education: Teachers: Superannuation: Additional voluntary contributions 35
Education: Teachers: Superannuation: Northern Ireland 203
Education: Teachers' pensions scheme: England & Wales. 35, 88
Education: University of the West of Scotland: University of Paisley: Order of Council: Amendments: Scotland 169
Elections: European Parliament: Northern Irish forms 91
Elections: Judges rota: Rules. 90, 122
Elections: Parliament: Forms: Northern Ireland 91
Elections: Parliament: Returning officers' charges 90
Elections: Parliamentary elections: Returning officers' charges: Northern Ireland 91
Elections: Policy development grants scheme 90
Electoral changes: Ashfield 67
Electoral changes: Bristol 67
Electoral changes: Broxtowe 67
Electoral changes: Cherwell 67
Electoral changes: Colchester 68
Electoral changes: Cotswold. 68
Electoral changes: Doncaster 68
Electoral changes: East Northamptonshire. 68
Electoral changes: Erewash 68
Electoral changes: Gloucester 68
Electoral changes: Hertfordshire 68
Electoral changes: High Peak 68
Electoral changes: Knowsley 68

Electoral changes: Lichfield	68
Electoral changes: Lincoln	68
Electoral changes: Peterborogh	69
Electoral changes: Poole	69
Electoral changes: Purbeck	69
Electoral changes: Rochford	69
Electoral changes: Rugby	69
Electoral changes: Sheffield	69
Electoral changes: South Bucks	69
Electoral changes: Stafford	69
Electoral changes: Stroud	69
Electoral changes: Swindon	69
Electoral changes: Warwickshire	69
Electoral changes: West Devon	69
Electoral changes: West Dorset	69
Electoral changes: Woking	69
Electoral changes: Wyre Forest	69
Electoral Registration & Administration Act 2013: Transitional provisions	90
Electrically assisted pedal cycles	92
Electricity generation: ABWR nuclear reactor: Electricity generation: Justification decision	41, 51
Electricity generation: Hinkley Point C: Nuclear generating station	61
Electricity generation: Hydrocarbon oil duties reliefs: Carbon price support	44
Electricity generation: North Killingholme generating station: Correction	61
Electricity: Capacity	37
Electricity: Connection: Performance standards	37
Electricity: Contracts for difference: Allocation	37
Electricity: Contracts for difference: Standard terms	37
Electricity: Electricity supplier obligations	37
Electricity: Emissions performance standard	37
Electricity: Exemption: Requirement for a generation licence: Galawhistle	37
Electricity: Feed-in tariffs: Amendments	38
Electricity: Gas: Market integrity & transparency: Enforcement	37, 49
Electricity: Generation: Licence requirement: Exemption: Ferrybridge MFE: England & Wales	37
Electricity: Generation: Licence requirement: Exemption: Frodsham: England & Wales	38
Electricity: Generation: Licence requirement: Exemption: Moy	37
Electricity: Licence modifications: Northern Ireland	203, 207
Electricity: Market integrity & transparency: Criminal sanctions	37, 49
Electricity: Market reform	37
Electricity: Northern Ireland	203
Electricity: Offshore transmission licences: Competitive tenders	37
Electricity: Ownership unbundling: Northern Ireland	203, 207
Electricity: Performance standards	37
Electricity: Power purchase agreement scheme	38
Electricity: Regulatory Reform (Scotland) Act 2014: Consequential modifications	21, 31, 38, 41, 67
Electricity: Renewables obligation	38
Electricity: Renewables obligation: Closure	38
Electricity: Renewables obligation: Closure: Northern Ireland	203
Electricity: Renewables obligation: Northern Ireland	203
Electricity: Renewables obligation: Scotland	169
Electricity: Standards of performance: Suppliers	37, 49
Electricity: Warm home discount	38, 49
Electronic Commerce Directive: Financial services & markets	38, 46
Electronic communications: 823-832 MHz & 1785-1805 MHz frequency bands: Management	38
Electronic communications: Data Retention & Investigatory Powers Act 2014: Commencements	38
Electronic communications: Electronic Commerce Directive	38, 46
Electronic communications: Local government	68
Electronic communications: Privacy: EC directive	38
Electronic communications: Statutory shared parental pay	25, 38, 60
Electronic communications: Wireless telegraphy: Licence charges	38
Electronic communications: Wireless telegraphy: Licence charges: 900 & 1800 MHz frequency bands	38
Electronic communications: Wireless telegraphy: Licences: Limitation of number	39
Electronic communications: Wireless telegraphy: Register: Amendments	39
Electronic communications: Wireless telegraphy: Spectrum access & licence: Spectrum trading	39
Electronic communications: Wireless telegraphy: Spectrum access: Charges	39
Electronic communications: Wireless telegraphy: Spectrum access: Satellite receive-only Earth stations	39
Electronic communications: Wireless telegraphy: Spectrum access: Satellite receive-only Earth stations: Grants: Limitation	38
Electronic communications: Wireless telegraphy: Spectrum trading	39
Electronic communications: Wireless telegraphy: Spectrum trading: Mobile: Amendments	39
Electronic communications: Wireless telegraphy: Ultra- wideband equipment: Exemptions	39
Electronic communications: Wireless telegraphy: White space devices: Exemption	39
Electronic prescription service: Primary care: Terms of service: National Health Service	74
Embryology: Human fertilisation & embryology: Mitrochondrial donation	55
Emissions performance: Standards	37
Emissions performance: Standards: Enforcement: Wales	38
Employer's liability: Compulsory insurance: Northern Ireland	203
Employment & support allowance: Northern Ireland	222
Employment & support allowance: Report assessments: Pending appeal awards	125
Employment & training: Apprenticeship standards: Modifications: England	39

Employment & training: Apprenticeships: Welsh certifying authority: Designation. 39
Employment & training: English apprenticeships: Primary legislation: Consequential amendments 39
Employment & training: Industrial training levy: Construction Industry Training Board. 39
Employment & training: Industrial training levy: Engineering Construction Industry Training Board 39
Employment Rights (Northern Ireland) Order 1996: Overseas adoptions: Application of articles: Northern Ireland 204
Employment Rights Act 1996: Protected disclosures: Extension of meaning of worker 131
Employment rights: Increase of limits: Northern Ireland. 203
Employment rights: Limits: Increase 130
Employment Tribunals Act 1996: Conciliation provisions: Application of 131
Employment tribunals: Early conciliation: Exemptions & rules of procedure. 39
Employment tribunals: Employment Appeal Tribunal: Fees 134
Employment: Acts 6
Employment: Acts: Explanatory notes. 7
Employment: Adoption leave: Curtailment of statutory rights to leave: Northern Ireland. 204
Employment: Adoptions: Overseas: Employment rights: Northern Ireland. 204
Employment: Adoptions: Time off to attend adoption appointments: Northern Ireland 205
Employment: Allowance: Care & support workers 125
Employment: Companies: Cross-border mergers 20
Employment: Disciplinary & grievance procedures: Code of practice 130
Employment: Flexible working: Northern Ireland 204
Employment: Gangmasters: Licensing authority 39
Employment: Maternity & parental leave: Northern Ireland 204
Employment: Maternity leave: Curtailment of statutory rights to leave: Northern Ireland. 204
Employment: Parental orders: Employment rights: Northern Ireland 203
Employment: Paternity: Adoption leave: Northern Ireland 204
Employment: Paternity: Adoption: Shared parental leave: Order cases: Northern Ireland 204
Employment: Shared parental leave & paternity & adoption leave: Adoptions from overseas: Northern Ireland 204
Employment: Shared parental leave: Northern Ireland 204
Employment: Shared parental leave: Statutory shared parental pay: Northern Ireland. 204
Employment: Small Business, Enterprise & Employment Act 2015: Commencements 21, 39
Employment: Social Security Contributions & Benefits (Northern Ireland) Act 1992: Application of parts: Northern Ireland 204, 205
Employment: Social security: Benefits: Up-rating: Northern Ireland. 203, 209, 216, 222, 223, 224
Employment: Specification of apprenticeship standards: England 39
Employment: Statutory adoption pay: Curtailment: Northern Ireland 205
Employment: Statutory paternity pay & statutory adoption pay: Northern Ireland 205
Employment: Statutory paternity pay & statutory adoption pay: Parental orders & prospective adopters: Northern Ireland 205
Employment: Statutory shared parental pay: Northern Ireland 205
Employment: Statutory shared parental pay: Overseas adoptions: Northern Ireland 205
Employment: Statutory shared parental pay: Parental order cases: Northern Ireland 205
Employment: Statutory shared parental pay: Persons abroad & mariners: Northern Ireland 205
Employment: Terms & conditions: Redundancy payments: Local government: Continuity of employment 131
Employment: Terms & conditions: Social Security Contributions & Benefits Act 1992: Application: Parts 12ZA &12ZB & 12ZC 131
Employment: Terms & conditions: Welfare benefits: Up-rating. 128, 131
Employment: Work & Families Act (Northern Ireland) 2015: Commencements: Northern Ireland 205
Energy Act 2011: Commencements 39
Energy Act 2013: Commencements 40
Energy conservation: Ecodesign: Energy-related products & energy information: Amendments 40
Energy conservation: Energy efficiency: Properties: Domestic & private rented. 40
Energy conservation: Energy efficiency: Properties: Private rented 40
Energy efficiency: Properties: Domestic & private rented. 40
Energy efficiency: Properties: Private rented 40
Energy performance: Building & buildings: England & Wales 11
Energy savings opportunity scheme 40
Energy: Electricity & gas licences: Northern Ireland 203, 207
Energy: Electricity: Northern Ireland. 203
Energy: Electricity: Renewables obligation 38
Energy: Electricity: Renewables obligation: Closure 38
Energy: Electricity: Renewables obligation: Closure: Northern Ireland 203
Energy: Electricity: Renewables obligation: Northern Ireland 203
Energy: Gas & electricity licences: Northern Ireland 203, 207
Energy: Gas & electricity: Ownership unbundling: Northern Ireland 203, 207
Energy: Heat: Network metering & billing 40
Energy: Infrastructure Act 2015: Commencements. 40, 52, 137
Energy: Performance of buildings: Scotland. 165, 169
Energy: Renewable heat incentives 40
Energy: Renewable heat incentives: Domestic 39
Energy: Renewable heat incentives: Schemes 40
Energy: Renewable heat incentives: Schemes: Northern Ireland 205
Energy: Renewable: Dogger Bank Creyke Beck 61
Energy: Renewable: Dogger Bank Teeside A & B Offshore Wind Farm. 61
Energy: Renewable: Galloper Wind Farm 61
Energy: Renewable: Hornsea One Offshore Wind Farm 61
Energy: Renewable: Rampion Wind Farm 62
Energy: Smoke & carbon monoxide: Alarms: England 40, 54
Energy: Transport: Fuels: Renewables obligation. 40, 134
Enforcement: Deduction from accounts: Prescribed information 40
Enforcement: Diligence against earnings: Variations: Scotland 169
Engineering Construction Industry Training Board: Industrial training levy 39

English apprenticeships: Primary legislation: Consequential amendments 39
Enhanced Learning Credit Scheme: Armed forces 79
Enterprise & Regulatory Reform Act 2013: Commencements 23, 24
Enterprise & Regulatory Reform Act 2013: Gas & electricity appeals 38, 49
Enterprise Act 2002: Part 8: Community infringements & specified UK laws 23
Enterprise Act 2002: Part 8: Domestic infringements 23
Enterprise Act 2002: Section 16 134
Enterprise: Acts 6
Enterprise: Acts: Explanatory notes 7
Enveloped dwellings: Annual tax: Avoidance schemes: Prescribed descriptions of arrangements 10
Environment Act 1995: Commencements: Scotland 169
Environment: Taxes: Landfill tax 64, 65
Environment: Water resources: Framework directive: England & Wales 136
Environmental damage: Prevention & remediation: England 42
Environmental damage: Prevention & remediation: Wales 43
Environmental impact assessment: Planning: Northern Ireland 213
Environmental liability: Prevention & remediation: Northern Ireland 205
Environmental liability: Scotland 169
Environmental permitting: England 42
Environmental permitting: England & Wales 42
Environmental permitting: Environmental protection 42
Environmental Protection Act 1990: Commencements: Scotland 169
Environmental protection: ABWR nuclear reactor: Electricity generation: Justification decision 41, 51
Environmental protection: Agricultural & forestry tractors: Emission of gaseous & particulate pollutants 40, 92
Environmental protection: Angler's lead weights: England 42
Environmental protection: Anti-social Behaviour, Crime & Policing Act 2014: Commencements 26, 42, 54, 82, 83
Environmental protection: Anti-social behaviour: Authorised persons 42
Environmental protection: Anti-social behaviour: City of London Corporation: Designation 42
Environmental protection: Aquaculture & Fisheries (Scotland) Act 2007: Fixed penalty notices: Scotland 169, 171, 175, 187, 188
Environmental protection: Batteries & accumulators: Market: Placing 40
Environmental protection: Carbon dioxide: Storage: Access to infrastructure: Northern Ireland 206
Environmental protection: Carbon dioxide: Storage: Licensing: Northern Ireland 206
Environmental protection: Carrier bags: Single use: ; Charges 42
Environmental protection: Clean Neighbourhoods & Environment Act 2005: Commencements 42
Environmental protection: Environment & rural affairs: England 8, 9, 42, 135
Environmental protection: Environment Act 1995: Commencements: Scotland 169
Environmental protection: Environmental damage: Prevention & remediation: England 42
Environmental protection: Environmental damage: Prevention & remediation: Wales 43
Environmental protection: Environmental liability: Prevention & remediation: Northern Ireland 205
Environmental protection: Environmental liability: Scotland 169
Environmental protection: Environmental permitting 42
Environmental protection: Environmental permitting: England 42
Environmental protection: Environmental permitting: England & Wales 42
Environmental protection: Environmental Protection Act 1990: Commencements: Scotland 169
Environmental protection: Environmental regulation: Enforcement measures: Scotland 169, 170
Environmental protection: Financial assistance: England & Wales 42
Environmental protection: Financial assistance: Scotland 170
Environmental protection: Food waste: Northern Ireland 206
Environmental protection: Greenhouse gases: Fluorinated 41
Environmental protection: Greenhouse gases: Fluorinated: Northern Ireland 206
Environmental protection: Hazardous waste 41
Environmental protection: Hazardous waste: European waste catalogue: Scotland 170
Environmental protection: Hazardous waste: Northern Ireland 206
Environmental protection: Hazardous waste: Wales 43
Environmental protection: Household waste: Penalty charges 42, 70
Environmental protection: Large combustion plants: Transitional national plan 41
Environmental protection: Marine conservation: Fixed monetary penalties: Northern Ireland 206
Environmental protection: Marine conservation: South Arran: Urgent continuation: Scotland 170, 176
Environmental protection: Marine conservation: Wester Ross: Scotland 170, 176
Environmental protection: Marine works: Environmental impact assessment 41, 67, 71
Environmental protection: Miscellaneous provisions: England 10, 42, 71, 135
Environmental protection: Nagoya protocol 41
Environmental protection: Nagoya protocol: Compliance 41
Environmental protection: Nitrates Action Programme: Northern Ireland 206
Environmental protection: Noise emissions: Outdoor equipment 41
Environmental protection: Offshore installations: Safety Directive 41, 51
Environmental protection: Ozone depleting substances 41
Environmental protection: Packaging: Essential requirements 41
Environmental protection: Pollution Prevention & Control Act 1999: Commencements: Scotland 170
Environmental protection: Pollution: Prevention & control: Designation of directives: England & Wales 43
Environmental protection: Pollution: Prevention & control: Fees 41
Environmental protection: Regulatory Reform (Scotland) Act 2014: Commencements: Scotland 170, 180
Environmental protection: Regulatory Reform (Scotland) Act 2014: Consequential modifications 21, 31, 38, 41, 67
Environmental protection: Scottish marine regions: Scotland 170
Environmental protection: Ship recycling facilities 41, 51
Environmental protection: Ship recycling facilities: Northern Ireland 206
Environmental protection: Single use carrier bags: Charge: Scotland: Scotland 170
Environmental protection: South Arran Nature Conservation Marine Protected Area: Scotland 170, 176

Environmental protection: Waste batteries & accumulators 41
Environmental protection: Waste electrical & electronic equipment. 41
Environmental protection: Waste management: Licensing: Northern Ireland 206
Environmental protection: Waste: Control: Seized property: England & Wales 42
Environmental protection: Waste: Fees & charges: Northern Ireland 206
Environmental protection: Waste: Meaning of recovery: Scotland. 170
Environmental protection: Waste: Recyclate quality: Scotland 170
Environmental protection: Water Environment & Water Services (Scotland) Act 2003: Part 1: Modification: Scotland 170
Environmental protection: Water environment: Responsible authorities & functions: Relevant enactments & designation: Scotland 170
Environmental protection: Water environment: River basin management planning: Scotland 170, 193
Environmental protection: Water: Classification, priority substances & shellfish waters: EC directive: Northern Ireland. 206
Environmental protection: Water: Priority substances & classification: EC directive: Northern Ireland 206
Environmental regulation: Enforcement measures: Scotland. 169, 170
Environmental standards: Civil aviation: Overseas territories 15
Equality Act 2010: Public authorities: Specification: Scotland. 170
Equality Act 2010: Specific duties: Scotland 170
Erewash: Electoral changes 68
Essential supplies: Protection 62
Essex County Council: Permit schemes: Traffic management 53
Estates: Deceased persons: Inheritance & trustees' powers: Acts: Explanatory notes 6
Estimates & accounts: Government Resources & Accounts Act 2000 49
European Communities: Burundi: Financial sanctions 26
European Communities: Conservation: Natural habitats: Northern Ireland 206
European Communities: Definition of treaties: Association agreement: Georgia 43
European Communities: Definition of treaties: Association agreement: Moldova 43
European Communities: Definition of treaties: Association agreement: Ukraine 43
European Communities: Designation 43
European Communities: Financial transparency: EC directives. 47
European Economic Area: Immigration 57
European investment funds: Long-term investments. 46
European Maritime & Fisheries Fund: Financial assistance: Northern Ireland 207
European maritime & fisheries fund: Grants: Scotland 164, 171, 187
European Parliamentary elections 90
European parliamentary elections: Miscellaneous provisions: United Kingdom & Gibraltar 73, 83, 90
European Parliamentary elections: Northern Irish forms 91
European Union finance: Acts. 4
European Union finance: Acts: Explanatory notes 6
European Union: Approvals: Acts 4
European Union: European communities: Designation 43
European Union: European grouping of territorial co-operation 43
European Union: Membership: Referendums: Acts 4
European Union: Professional qualifications: Recognition 85
Evidence: Blood tests: Paternity 43
Evidence: Paternity: Blood tests: Review: England & Wales 43
Evidence: Police & criminal evidence: Codes of practice: Northern Ireland 214
Excise: Aircraft operators: Accounts & records. 43
Excise: Alcoholic liquor: Duties: Alcoholic ingredients: Relief 44
Excise: Controlled liquor: Wholesaling 44
Excise: Finance Act 2014: Schedule 21: Commencements 29, 44
Excise: Gaming: Duty 44
Excise: Hydrocarbon oil & biofuels: Road fuel: Defined areas: Reliefs 44
Excise: Hydrocarbon oil duties: Electricity generation reliefs: Carbon price support 44
Excise: Hydrocarbon oil: Marking 44
Excise: International tax: Enforcement: Brazil 12, 25, 44, 59, 62, 135
Excise: Revenue traders: Accounts & records 44
Excise: Stores: Aircraft & ship 44
Exclusion orders: Temporary: Notices 83
Exemption: Requirement for a generation licence: Galawhistle. 37
Explosives: Hazard information & packaging for supply: Northern Ireland 208
Export control 28, 29
Export control: Sanctions: Congo 28
Export control: Sanctions: Iran. 28
Export control: Sanctions: Russia, Crimea & Sevastopol 28
Export control: Sanctions: Yemen 29
Exporter information: Disclosure 32
Extractive industries: Waste management: Planning: Northern Ireland 214
Extradition Act 2003: Designations: Amendments 44
Extradition: Anti-social Behaviour, Crime & Policing Act 2014: Commencements 44

F

Faculty jurisdiction: Rules 32
Fair employment : Northern Ireland. 206
Fair employment: Public authorities: Specification: Northern Ireland 206
Family court: Business: Composition & distribution: England & Wales 44, 45
Family court: Family procedure: England & Wales 44, 45, 122
Family court: Family procedure: Rules 44, 45, 122
Family court: Family proceedings: Fees. 44, 45, 122

Family court: Justices' clerks & assistants rules: England & Wales . . . 44
Family law: Child Maintenance & Other Payments Act 2008: Commencements . . . 44
Family law: Child support . . . 45
Family law: Child support: Child Maintenance Act 2008 Act: Commencements: Northern Ireland . . . 206
Family law: Child support: Northern Ireland . . . 206
Family law: Female genital mutilation: Protection orders: Third party: England & Wales . . . 45
Family law: Serious Crime Act 2015: Commencements . . . 45
Family procedure: Rules . . . 44, 45, 122
Family proceedings: Family court: Business: Composition & distribution: England & Wales . . . 44, 45
Family proceedings: Family procedure: England & Wales . . . 44, 45, 122
Family proceedings: Family procedure: Rules . . . 44, 45, 122
Family proceedings: Fees . . . 26, 44, 45, 122
Farriers: Qualifications: European recognition . . . 45
Feed-in tariffs: Amendments . . . 38
Feed: Animal feed: Composition, marketing & use: England . . . 8
Feed: Animal feed: Hygiene, sampling & enforcement England . . . 8
Fees & charges: Global Entry Scheme: Screening process . . . 45
Fees: insolvency practitioners & services account . . . 45, 63
Fees: Insolvency proceedings . . . 45, 63
Female genital mutilation: Protection orders: Third party: England & Wales . . . 45
Ferrybridge MFE: Electricity: Licence requirement: Exemption: England & Wales . . . 37
Films: British film: Definition . . . 15
Films: Co-production agreements . . . 15
Finance (No. 2) Act 2015 . . . 4
Finance Act 2004: Part 7: Application: National insurance: Contributions . . . 126
Finance Act 2004: Pension schemes: Allowance: Charge . . . 58
Finance Act 2007: Schedule 26: Shares: Valuation of: Appointed day: Commencements . . . 12, 25, 58
Finance Act 2009: Diverted profits tax: Commencements . . . 32
Finance Act 2012: Part 4 amendments: Social security: Contributions . . . 126
Finance Act 2012: Sections 26 & 30: Relief for equalisation reserves: Abolition: Specified day . . . 25, 58
Finance Act 2013 . . . 4
Finance Act 2013: Schedule 21: Appointed day . . . 25
Finance Act 2014: Explanatory notes . . . 6
Finance Act 2014: High risk promoters: Prescribed information . . . 12, 25, 58
Finance Act 2014: Schedule 9: Consequential amendments . . . 58
Finance Act 2014: Section 18 (2) to (4): Appointed day . . . 59
Finance Act 2015 . . . 4
Finance Act 2015: Explanatory notes . . . 6
Finance Act 2015: Schedule 6, paragraphs 10 to 12 . . . 59
Finance Act 2015: Section 23: Appointed days . . . 59
Financial assistance: Environmental purposes: England & Wales . . . 42
Financial investigators: References: England & Wales . . . 84
Financial Services & Markets Act 2000: Auditors & actuaries: Regulations . . . 46
Financial Services & Markets Act 2000: Banking reform: Pensions . . . 46
Financial Services & Markets Act 2000: Collective investment schemes . . . 46
Financial Services & Markets Act 2000: Exemptions . . . 46
Financial Services & Markets Act 2000: Miscellaneous provisions . . . 46
Financial Services & Markets Act 2000: Misconduct & appropriate regulator . . . 46
Financial Services & Markets Act 2000: Over the counter derivatives: Central counterparties: Trade repositories . . . 46
Financial Services & Markets Act 2000: Provisions . . . 46
Financial Services & Markets Act 2000: Regulated activities . . . 46
Financial Services & Markets Act 2000: Relevant authorised persons . . . 46
Financial services & markets: Bank of England Act 1998: Macro-prudential measures . . . 45
Financial services & markets: Capital requirements: Capital buffers: Macro-prudential measures . . . 46
Financial services & markets: Electronic Commerce Directive . . . 38, 46
Financial services & markets: European investment funds: Long-term investments . . . 46
Financial services & markets: Financial Services & Markets Act 2000: Misconduct & appropriate regulator . . . 46
Financial services & markets: Financial Services (Banking Reform) Act 2013: Commencements . . . 47
Financial services & markets: Financial transparency: EC directives . . . 47
Financial services & markets: Insolvency: Settlement finality . . . 46
Financial Services & markets: Mortgages . . . 47
Financial services & markets: Payment accounts . . . 47
Financial services & markets: Payment cards: Interchange: Fees . . . 47
Financial services & markets: Payment services . . . 47
Financial services & markets: Small & medium sized businesses: Credit information . . . 47
Financial services & markets: Small & medium sized businesses: Finance platforms . . . 47
Financial services & markets: Small Business, Enterprise & Employment Act 2015: Commencements . . . 20, 47, 62, 65
Financial services & markets: Solvency . . . 47
Financial services & markets: Treasury: Penalty payments: Enforcement costs . . . 47
Financial Services (Banking Reform) Act 2013 . . . 47
Financial Services (Banking Reform) Act 2013: Commencements . . . 47
Financial Services (Banking Reform) Act 2013: Transitional & saving provisions . . . 47
Financial services: Banking reform: Commencements . . . 11
Financial services: Financial markets: Insolvency: Settlement finality . . . 46
Financial services: Money laundering . . . 45
Fire & rescue authorities: Performance indicators: Wales . . . 47
Fire & rescue services: Dorset and Wiltshire Fire & Rescue Authority: Combination scheme . . . 47
Fire & rescue services: Firefighters: Compensation & pension scheme: Wales . . . 48, 81

Fire & rescue services: Firefighters: New: Pension schemes: Northern Ireland	207
Fire & rescue services: Firefighters: Pension schemes: England	47, 81
Fire & rescue services: Firefighters: Pension schemes: Northern Ireland	207
Fire & rescue services: Firefighters: Pension schemes: Wales	48, 81
Fire & rescue services: Firefighters' compensation schemes: England	47, 81
Fire & rescue services: Firefighters' pension scheme: England	87
Fire & rescue services: Firefighters' pension scheme: Northern Ireland	215
Fire & rescue services: Inspectors: Appointment: Wales	47
Fire & rescue services: National framework: Revision	48
Fire & rescue services: Pension schemes: Northern Ireland	207
Fire & rescue services: Pensions: Compensation schemes: Northern Ireland	207
Fire and rescue services: Fire & rescue authorities: Performance indicators: Wales	47
Fire services: Firefighters: Pension schemes: Scotland	179
Fire services: Firefighters' compensation & pension schemes: Scotland	171, 177
Fire services: Firemen: Pension schemes: Scotland	171, 177
Firearms	10
Firearms & ammunition: Variation of fees: Northern Ireland	207
Firearms: Fees	10
Firefighters: Compensation & pension scheme: Wales	48, 81
Firefighters: New: Pension schemes: Northern Ireland	207
Firefighters: Pension schemes: England	47, 81
Firefighters: Pension schemes: Northern Ireland	207, 215
Firefighters: Pension schemes: Scotland	179
Firefighters: Pension schemes: Wales	48, 81, 88
Firefighters: Pensions: Compensation schemes: Northern Ireland	207
Firefighters' compensation & pension schemes: Scotland	171, 177
Firefighters' compensation schemes: England	47, 81
Firefighters' pension scheme: Governance: England	87
Firemen: Pension schemes: Scotland	171, 177
Fireplaces: Exempt: Smoke control areas: England	19
Fireplaces: Exempt: Smoke control areas: Northern Ireland	201
Fireplaces: Exempt: Smoke control areas: Wales	19
Fireworks: Safety	23, 51
Fish farming: Animals & related products: Trade: Scotland	164, 171
Fish farming: Aquaculture & Fisheries (Scotland) Act 2007: Fixed penalty notices: Scotland	169, 171, 175, 187, 188
Fish farming: European maritime & fisheries fund: Grants: Scotland	164, 171, 187
Fish farming: Fishing & aquaculture industries: Grants: England	48, 121
Fish: Keeping & introduction: River Esk	91
Fish: Labelling: Scotland	171
Fisheries: European Maritime & Fisheries Fund: Financial assistance: Northern Ireland	207
Fisheries: Northern Ireland	207
Fisheries: Poole Harbour: England	121
Fishery limits: Fishing boats designation: England	121
Fishing & aquaculture industries: Grants: England	48, 121
Fishing boats designation: England	121
Fishing: Inshore fishing: Fishing & fishing methods: Prohibition: Luce Bay: Scotland	187
Fishing: Inshore fishing: Fishing & fishing methods: Prohibition: Scotland	187
Fivemiletown: Parking & waiting restrictions: Northern Ireland	219
Fixed penalty offences: Road traffic & vehicles: Northern Ireland	221
Flexible working: Northern Ireland	204
Flood reinsurance: Scheme & scheme administrator designation	63
Flood reinsurance: Scheme funding & administration	63
Flood risk management: Reservoirs (Scotland) Act 2011: Commencements: Scotland	171, 193
Flood risk management: Reservoirs: Engineers: Panels: Scotland	171, 193
Flood risk management: Reservoirs: Scotland	171, 193
Fluorinated greenhouse gases	41
Fluorinated greenhouse gases: Northern Ireland	206
Food (Scotland) Act 2015: Commencements: Scotland	171
Food (Scotland) Act 2015: Consequential provisions	21, 31, 48, 171
Food protection: Emergency prohibitions: Ducks & geese: Lead: England	86
Food waste: Northern Ireland	206
Food: Acts: Explanatory notes: Scotland	163
Food: Acts: Scotland	162
Food: Animals & animal products: Examination for residues & maximum residue limits	48
Food: Fish: Labelling: Scotland	171
Food: Honey: England	48
Food: Honey: Northern Ireland	207
Food: Honey: Scotland	171
Food: Honey: Wales	49
Food: Information: Scotland	171
Food: Meat: Country of origin: England	48
Food: Meat: Country of origin: Northern Ireland	207
Food: Meat: Country of origin: Wales	49
Food: Milk: Condensed & dried milk: England	48
Food: Natural mineral water, spring water & bottled drinking water: Northern Ireland	207
Food: Natural mineral water, spring water & bottled drinking water: Scotland	172
Food: Natural mineral water, spring water & bottled drinking water: Wales	49
Food: Welfare food	48

Football spectators: Corresponding offences . . . 129
Forestry: Plant health: Fees: England & Scotland . . . 81, 82
Forestry: Plant health: Miscellaneous revocations: England . . . 82
Forestry: Plant health: Wales . . . 82
Forfeiture notices: England & Wales: England & Wales . . . 84
Forth Road Bridge Act 2013: Commencements: Scotland . . . 181
Foundation phase: National curriculum: Desirable outcomes, educational programmes & baseline & end of phase: Wales . . . 37
Freedom of information: Protection of Freedoms Act 2012: Commencements . . . 29, 49
Freedom of information: Public authorities: Designation . . . 49
Fuels: Authorised fuels: Smoke control areas: Northern Ireland . . . 201
Fuels: Authorised fuels: Smoke control areas: Wales . . . 19
Fuels: Renewables obligations: Transport . . . 40, 134
Further & Higher Education Commitment Scheme: Armed forces . . . 79
Further education loans: England . . . 34
Further education: Destination information: Prescribed activities . . . 34
Further education: Merthyr Tydfil College Limited: Designated institution: Wales . . . 36
Further education: National College for High Speed Rail: Government: England . . . 34
Further education: National College for High Speed Rail: Incorporation: England . . . 34
Future generation: Well-being: Acts: Wales . . . 229
Future generation: Well-being: Acts: Wales: Explanatory notes: Wales . . . 229

G

Galloper Wind Farm . . . 61
Gaming machine: Circumstances of use . . . 11
Gaming: Duty . . . 44
Gangmasters: Licensing authority . . . 39
Garron Point Hill climb: Road races: Northern Ireland . . . 220
Gas & electricity appeals: Enterprise & Regulatory Reform Act 2013 . . . 38, 49
Gas: Electricity: Market integrity & transparency: Enforcement . . . 37, 49
Gas: Licence modifications: Northern Ireland . . . 203, 207
Gas: Market integrity & transparency: Criminal sanctions . . . 37, 49
Gas: Ownership unbundling: Northern Ireland . . . 203, 207
Gas: Standards of performance: Suppliers . . . 37, 49
Gas: Thermal energy: Calculation . . . 49
Gas: Warm home discount . . . 38, 49
Gender recognition: Marriage & civil partnership . . . 89
General Chiropractic Council: Chiropractors: Indemnity arrangements . . . 51
General Dental Council: Overseas registration examination . . . 30, 51
General Medical Council (Fitness to Practise & Over-arching Objective) & the Professional Standards Authority for Health & Social Care (References to Court) Order 2015: Commencements . . . 52
General Medical Council: Constitution of panels, tribunals & investigative committee . . . 52
General Medical Council: Fitness to practice: Professional Standards Authority: References to court . . . 51
General Medical Council: Legal assessors: Legally qualified persons . . . 52
General Medical Council: Licence to practise . . . 52
General Medical Council: Medical Practitioners Tribunal Service: Constitution . . . 52
General Medical Council: Miscellaneous rules & regulations . . . 51
General Medical Council: Provisional registration: Maximum period . . . 52
General medical services: Contracts . . . 75
General medical services: Contracts: England . . . 74
General Osteopathic Council: Constitution . . . 52
General Osteopathic Council: Indemnity arrangements . . . 52
General Synod of the Church of England: Measures . . . 7
General Teaching Council for Northern Ireland . . . 203
General Teaching Council for Northern Ireland: Teachers: Registration . . . 203
Genetically modified organisms: Contained use: Northern Ireland . . . 208
Gibraltar: Taxes: International compliance . . . 130
Glasgow Clyde College: Removal & appointment of board members: Scotland . . . 169
Global Entry Scheme: Screening process: Fees . . . 45
Gloucester: Electoral changes . . . 68
Goats & sheep: Records, identification & movement: Wales . . . 10
Goods vehicles: Recording equipment: Downloading of data . . . 92
Goods vehicles: Testing: Northern Ireland . . . 218
Government of Wales Act 2006 . . . 21, 32
Government of Wales Act 2006: Designation of receipts . . . 21, 32
Government Resources & Accounts Act 2000: Estimates & accounts . . . 49
Government resources & accounts: Whole of government accounts: Bodies: Designation . . . 49
Government resources & accounts: Whole of government accounts: Bodies: Designation: Northern Ireland . . . 207
Government trading funds: Defence Support Group Trading Fund . . . 50
Government trading funds: Driver & Vehicle Standards Agency Trading Fund . . . 50
Government: Whole of government accounts: Bodies: Designation . . . 49
Government: Whole of government accounts: Bodies: Designation: Northern Ireland . . . 207
Great Yarmouth Port Authority: Revision . . . 50
Greater London Authority: Council tax: Requirement procedure . . . 70
Greater Manchester Combined Authority . . . 68, 134
Greater Manchester: Light Rapid Transit System: Exemptions . . . 133
Greenhouse gas emissions trading scheme . . . 19
Greenhouse gas: Climate change: Scotland . . . 166

252 | 22 JULY 2016 | LONDON GAZETTE | SUPPLEMENT NO.1

Greenhouse gases: Fluorinated 41
Greenhouse gases: Fluorinated: Northern Ireland. 206
Groceries Code Adjudicator: Competition: Financial penalty 21
Guardian's allowance: Up-rating 125
Guardian's allowance: Up-rating: Northern Ireland 129
Guernsey: Double taxation: Relief 24, 58
Guernsey: Immigration. 57
Guernsey: Territorial sea: Limits 131

H

H5N1see Avian influenza
Harbour authorities: Designation. 50
Harbours, docks, piers & ferries: Blyth Harbour 50
Harbours, docks, piers & ferries: Caledonian Maritime Assets: Lochaline Ferry Services slipway: Harbour: Empowerment: Scotland . . . 172
Harbours, docks, piers & ferries: Donaghadee Harbour: Northern Ireland 207, 208
Harbours, docks, piers & ferries: Great Yarmouth Port Authority: Harbour revision 50
Harbours, docks, piers & ferries: Harbour directions: Harbour authorities: Designation. 50
Harbours, docks, piers & ferries: Lerwick Harbour: Revisions: Scotland 172
Harbours, docks, piers & ferries: Littlehampton: Harbour revision 50
Harbours, docks, piers & ferries: Londonderry Harbour: Limits: Variation: Northern Ireland 208
Harbours, docks, piers & ferries: Peterhead Port Authority: Harbour revision: Scotland 172
Harbours, docks, piers & ferries: Poole Harbour works revision 50
Harbours, docks, piers & ferries: Port of London Authority: Harbour: Revision 50
Harbours: Acts: Explanatory notes: Scotland 163
Harbours: Acts: Scotland. 162
Hazardous substances: Inquiry session procedure: Planning: Scotland. 192
Hazardous substances: Planning: Northern Ireland 213, 214
Hazardous waste 41
Hazardous waste facility & disposal: Infrastructure planning: White Moss landfill 62
Hazardous waste: Northern Ireland. 206
Hazardous waste: Wales 43, 132
Health & Care Professions Council: Registration & fee 52
Health & personal services: Persons not ordinarily resident: Northern Ireland 208
Health & personal social services: Additional voluntary contributions: Northern Ireland 208
Health & personal social services: General medical services contracts: Northern Ireland 208
Health & personal social services: Health & social care: Pension schemes: Northern Ireland 208
Health & personal social services: Health & social pension scheme: Northern Ireland 208, 215
Health & personal social services: Health service workers: Northern Ireland 208, 215
Health & personal social services: Health services: Cross-border health care: Northern Ireland 208
Health & personal social services: Injury benefits: Northern Ireland 208
Health & personal social services: Optical charges & payments: Northern Ireland 208
Health & personal social services: Superannuation scheme: Northern Ireland 208
Health & Safety at Work etc Act 1974: Self-employed persons: General duties 50
Health & safety: ABWR nuclear reactor: Electricity generation: Justification decision 41, 51
Health & safety: Biocidal products: Northern Ireland 208
Health & safety: Chemicals: Classification, labelling & packaging. 50
Health & safety: Chemicals: Classification, labelling & packaging: Northern Ireland 208
Health & safety: Construction: Design & management 50
Health & safety: Deregulation Act 2015: Working conditions: Self-employed persons 50
Health & safety: Explosives: Hazard information & packaging for supply: Northern Ireland 208
Health & safety: Genetically modified organisms: Contained use: Northern Ireland 208
Health & safety: Local government: Ombudsman: Powers: Acts 5
Health & safety: Major accident hazards: Control 50
Health & safety: Nuclear: Fees. 50
Health & safety: Offshore installations: Safety Directive. 41, 51
Health & safety: Offshore installations: Safety zones 77
Health & safety: Poisons & explosives precursors: Control 50
Health & safety: Pressure equipment. 51
Health & safety: Pyrotechnics articles: Safety 23, 51
Health & safety: Railways & other guided transport systems 51
Health & safety: Repeals, revocations & amendments: Northern Ireland 209
Health & Social Care Act 2008: Regulated activities 73, 85, 123
Health & Social Care Act 2012: Commencements. 51, 73
Health & Social Care Act 2012: Consistent identifier: England 73, 85, 123
Health & Social Care Act 2012: Continuity of information: England 74, 85, 123
Health & social care: Disciplinary procedures: Northern Ireland 209
Health & social care: Pension scheme: Northern Ireland 208
Health & social care: Pension schemes: Northern Ireland. 208
Health & social care: Safety & quality: Acts 4
Health & social care: Safety & quality: Acts: Explanatory notes 6
Health and safety: Ship recycling facilities 41, 51
Health and Social Care (Safety and Quality) Act 2015: Commencements: England 74, 86, 123
Health care & associated professions: Chiropractors: Indemnity arrangements 51
Health care & associated professions: Dentists Act 1984: Medical authorities 51
Health care & associated professions: Doctors 51, 52
Health care & associated professions: Doctors: General Medical Council: Constitution of panels, tribunals & investigative committee . . . 52
Health care & associated professions: Doctors: General Medical Council: Medical Practitioners Tribunal Service: Constitution. 52

Health care & associated professions: General Dental Council: Indemnity arrangements 51
Health care & associated professions: General Dental Council: Overseas registration examination 30, 51
Health care & associated professions: General Medical Council (Fitness to Practise & Over-arching Objective) & the Professional Standards Authority for Health & Social Care (Reference 52
Health care & associated professions: General Medical Council: Fitness to practice: Professional Standards Authority: References to court 51
Health care & associated professions: General Medical Council: Licence to practise 52
Health care & associated professions: General Medical Council: Provisional registration: Maximum period 52
Health care & associated professions: General Osteopathic Council: Indemnity arrangements 52
Health care & associated professions: Health & Care Professions Council: Registration & fees 52
Health care & associated professions: Health & Social Care Act 2012: Commencements 51, 73
Health care & associated professions: Knowledge of English 51
Health care & associated professions: Nursing & Midwifery Council: Fitness to practise: Education, registration & registration appeals . . . 52
Health care & associated professions: Osteopaths: General Osteopathic Council: Constitution 52
Health care & associated professions: Professional Standards Authority for Health & Social Care: Fees 51
Health care: Health services: Charges: Recovery: Amounts: Northern Ireland 209
Health Education England 52, 75, 124
Health education: Acts 4
Health Research Authority 52, 75, 124
Health Service Commissioner for England: Complaint handling: Acts 5
Health Service Commissioner for England: Complaint handling: Acts: Explanatory notes 6
Health Service Commissioner for England: Revocations 74
Health service workers: Northern Ireland 208, 215
Health service: Medicines: Branded medicines: Prices control: Information supply 50, 75, 76
Health Service: National Trusts 74, 75
Health Service: National: Cross-border healthcare 75
Health services: Care & support: Isles of Scilly: England 52, 123
Health services: Care Act 2014: Health Education England & Health Research Authority 52, 75, 124
Health services: Charges: Recovery: Amounts: Northern Ireland 209
Health services: Cross-border health care: Northern Ireland 208
Hearings & inquiries: Procedure: Town & country planning 134
Heat: Network metering & billing 40
Her Majesty's Inspector of Education, Children's Services & Skills 14, 34
Her Majesty's Inspector of Education, Children's Services & Skills: Children's homes etc.: Fees & frequency of inspections 14
Hertfordshire County Council: Filming on highways: Local acts 7
Hertfordshire: Electoral changes 68
High Court of Justiciary: Act of Adjournal: Criminal procedure: Rules: Final decision requests: Scotland 172, 174, 189
High Court of Justiciary: Act of Adjournal: Criminal procedure: Rules: Reporting restrictions: Scotland 172, 174, 189
High Court of Justiciary: Act of Adjournal: Criminal procedure: Rules: Scotland 172, 173, 174, 188, 189
High Court of Justiciary: Act of Adjournal: Justice of the Peace Court: Special measures: Scotland 172, 174, 189
High Court of Justiciary: Courts Reform (Scotland) Act 2014: Commencements: Scotland 167, 168, 172, 174, 187, 188, 189, 191
High Court of Justiciary: Courts Reform (Scotland) Act 2014: Consequential provisions: Scotland 167, 172, 174, 188, 190, 191
High Court of Justiciary: Criminal Justice & Licensing (Scotland) Act 2010: Commencements: Scotland 168, 172, 188
High Court of Justiciary: Fees: Scotland 172
High Peak: Electoral changes 68
High speed rail: HS2: Preparation: Acts: Explanatory notes 6
Higher Education (Wales) Act 2015: Commencements 36
Higher Education (Wales) Act 2015: Consequential provision 21, 32, 35
Higher education: Acts: Explanatory notes: Wales 229
Higher education: Acts: Wales 229
Higher Education: Amounts 36
Higher Education: Designation of providers 36
Higher Education: Fee & access plans 36
Higher Education: Fee & access plans: Notices & directions 36
Higher education: Prescribed courses: Information requirements 34
Higher Education: Qualifying courses, persons & supplementary provision 36
Higher education: Student loans: Living costs liability: Cancellation 35
Highways 53
Highways: Cambridgeshire County Council: A142 Ely Southern Bypass: Bridge scheme: Confirmation instruments: England 53
Highways: England 53
Highways: Hoobrook Bridge scheme 54
Highways: Infrastructure Act 2015: Commencements 40, 52, 137
Highways: Invalid carriages: Use: Wales 110
Highways: Office of Rail Regulation: Change of name: England 53, 86
Highways: Severn Bridges: Tolls 53
Highways: Strategic highways companies: Appointment 53
Highways: Strategic highways companies: Delegation of functions 53
Highways: Strategic highways companies: Infrastructure Act 2015 53
Highways: Street works: Qualifications of supervisors & operatives: England 53
Highways: Sunderland City Council: New Wear Bridge scheme 53
Highways: Traffic Management Act 2004: Commencements 53
Highways: Traffic management: Permit schemes: Bradford (City) Metropolitan District 53
Highways: Traffic management: Permit schemes: Brighton & Hove City Council 53
Highways: Traffic management: Permit schemes: Calderdale Borough Council 53
Highways: Traffic management: Permit schemes: Derbyshire County Council 53
Highways: Traffic management: Permit schemes: England 54
Highways: Traffic management: Permit schemes: Essex County Council 53
Highways: Traffic management: Permit schemes: Knowsley Metropolitan Borough Council 53
Highways: Traffic management: Permit schemes: Lancashire County Council 53

Highways: Traffic management: Permit schemes: Milton Keynes Council	54
Highways: Traffic management: Permit schemes: Nottingham City Council	54
Highways: Traffic management: Permit schemes: Southampton City Council	54
Highways: Traffic management: Permit schemes: Wakefield City Council	53
Highways: Whitchurch Bridge: Tolls revision: England	54
Highways: Whitney-on-Wye Bridge: Tolls: Revisions: England	54
Hinkley Point C: Nuclear generating station: Infrastructure planning	61
Hirwaun generating station: Corrections	61
Hirwaun generating station: Tidal generating station	61
Historic Environment Scotland Act 2014: Ancillary provision	164, 180
Historic Environment Scotland Act 2014: Commencements	164
Historic Environment Scotland: First planning period: Scotland	164
HIV testing kits & services: Revocation: Northern Ireland	215
Home Grown Timber Advisory Committee: Abolition: Public bodies	49, 85
Home loss payments: Prescribed amounts: England	8, 21
Home loss payments: Prescribed amounts: Wales	8, 55
Homelessness: Intentionality: Specified categories: Wales	54
Homelessness: Review procedure: Wales	54
Homelessness: Suitability of accommodation: Wales	55
Homes & Communities Agency: Transfer of property: England	64
Honey: England	48
Honey: Northern Ireland	207
Honey: Scotland	171
Honey: Wales	49
Hoobrook Bridge scheme	54
Hornsea One Offshore Wind Farm	61
Horses: Public places: Control: Acts	4
Horses: Public places: Control: Acts: Explanatory notes	6
House of Commons Commission: Acts	5
House of Commons Commission: Acts: Explanatory notes	6
House of Lords: Members: Expulsion & suspension: Acts	5
Household waste: Penalty charges	42, 70
Household waste: Recycling centres: Prohibition of charges: Local government	68
Housing & regeneration transfer schemes: Tax consequences	25
Housing (Scotland) Act 2006: Repayment charge & discharge: Scotland	172
Housing (Scotland) Act 2014: Commencements: Scotland	172, 173
Housing (Wales) Act 2014: Commencements	55
Housing (Wales) Act 2014: Consequential amendments	55
Housing benefit: Earnings income: Northern Ireland	209
Housing benefit: Executive determinations: Northern Ireland	209
Housing benefit: Family premium: Abolition	125
Housing benefit: Social security:	125
Housing costs: Social security	127
Housing: Acts: Scotland	162
Housing: Allocation: Right to move: Qualification criteria	54
Housing: Anti-social Behaviour, Crime & Policing Act 2014: Commencements.	26, 42, 54, 82, 83
Housing: Anti-social Behaviour, Crime & Policing Act 2014: Consequential amendments: Wales	54
Housing: Areas scheme: Enforcement: Scotland	172
Housing: Consumer Rights Act 2015: Commencements	23, 54
Housing: Home loss payments: Prescribed amounts: Wales	8, 55
Housing: Homelessness: Intentionality: Specified categories: Wales	54
Housing: Homelessness: Review procedure: Wales	54
Housing: Homelessness: Suitability of accommodation: Wales	55
Housing: Housing (Scotland) Act 2014: Commencements: Scotland	173
Housing: Landlords & agents: Code of practice	54
Housing: Private Rented Housing (Scotland) Act 2011: Commencements: Scotland	173
Housing: Private rented housing panel: Landlord applications: Scotland	173
Housing: Private rented housing panel: Tenant & third party: Applications: Scotland	173
Housing: Private rented housing: Information, periods & fees: Registration & licensing	55
Housing: Private rented housing: Training requirements	55
Housing: Private rented sector: Licensing authority	55
Housing: Rent officers: Housing benefit & universal credit functions: Local housing allowance amendments	54
Housing: Residential property tribunal: Procedures & fees: Wales	55
Housing: Right to buy & acquire: Discount limits: Wales	55
Housing: Right to buy: Prescribed forms: England	54
Housing: Right to buy: Prescribed forms: Wales	55
Housing: Selective licensing: Additional conditions: England	54
Housing: Self-build & custom housebuilding: Acts	5
Housing: Self-build & custom housebuilding: Acts: Explanatory notes	7
Housing: Small Business, Enterprise & Employment Act 2015: Commencements	55, 66
Housing: Smoke & carbon monoxide: Alarms: England	40, 54
Housing: Social security: Amendments: Northern Ireland	209, 216, 223
Housing: Social security: Benefits: Up-rating: Northern Ireland	203, 209, 216, 222, 223, 224
Housing: Tenancy deposits: Specified interest rates: England	54
HS2: High speed rail: Preparation: Acts: Explanatory notes	6
Human fertilisation & embryology: Mitochondrial donation	55
Human medicines	71
Human medicines: Northern Ireland	211

Human rights: Attorney general: Guidance: Police Service: Northern Ireland 209
Human rights: Attorney general: Guidance: Probation Board: Northern Ireland 209
Human rights: Attorney general: Guidance: Youth Justice Agency: Detention conditions: Northern Ireland: Northern Ireland 209
Human rights: Attorney general: Guidance: Youth Justice Agency: Restorative justice: Northern Ireland: Northern Ireland 209
Human tissue: Human Transplantation (Wales) Act 2013: Commencements: Wales 56
Human tissue: Human Transplantation (Wales) Act 2013: Consequential provision 21, 32, 55, 56
Human tissue: Human transplantation: Appointed representatives: Wales 56
Human tissue: Human transplantation: Excluded relevant material: Wales 56
Human tissue: Human transplantation: Persons who lack capacity to consent: Wales 56
Human trafficking & exploitation: Acts: Explanatory notes: Scotland 163
Human trafficking & exploitation: Acts: Scotland 162
Human trafficking & exploitation: Criminal justice & support for victims: Acts: Northern Ireland 199
Human Trafficking and Exploitation (Criminal Justice and Support for Victims) Act (Northern Ireland) 2015: Commencements: Northern Ireland 202
Human trafficking: Criminal justice & support for victims: Acts: Explanatory notes: Northern Ireland 199
Human Transplantation (Wales) Act 2013: Commencements: Wales 56
Human Transplantation (Wales) Act 2013: Consequential provision 21, 32, 55, 56
Human transplantation: Appointed representatives: Wales 56
Human transplantation: Excluded relevant material: Wales 56
Human transplantation: Persons who lack capacity to consent: Wales 56
Hydrocarbon oil & biofuels: Road fuel: Defined areas: Reliefs 44
Hydrocarbon oil duties: Electricity generation reliefs: Carbon price support 44
Hydrocarbon oil: Marking 44

I

Immigration Act 2014: Commencements 56
Immigration: Acts 4
Immigration: Appeals: Saving provisions & amendments 56
Immigration: Asylum: Support 56
Immigration: Authority to carry scheme 56, 83
Immigration: Biometric registration 56, 57
Immigration: Biometric registration: Civil penalty: Code of practice 57
Immigration: Biometric registration: Civil penalty: Objection 57
Immigration: Channel Tunnel: International arrangements: Miscellaneous provisions 56
Immigration: Counter-Terrorism Act 2015: Authority to carry scheme 56, 83
Immigration: European Economic Area 57
Immigration: Exemption from control 57
Immigration: Guernsey 57
Immigration: Health charges 57
Immigration: Isle of Man 57
Immigration: Jersey 57
Immigration: Leave to enter & remain 57
Immigration: Leave: Variation 57
Immigration: Marriages & civil partnerships: Investigations conduct 19, 57, 71
Immigration: Marriages & civil partnerships: Meaning of exempt persons & notice 19, 57, 71
Immigration: Marriages & civil partnerships: Proposed: Referral & investigation 19, 57, 71
Immigration: Marriages & civil partnerships: Waiting period 19, 57, 71
Immigration: Nationality: Fees 56, 76
Immigration: Passenger transit: Visas 57
Immigration: Physical data: Provision 57
Immigration: Police: Passenger, crew & service information 56, 57, 82
Immigration: Proposed marriages: Civil partnerships: Referral 19, 58, 71
Immigration: Referral & investigation: Marriages & civil partnerships: Provisions 19, 57, 71
Immigration: Sham marriage: Civil partnership: Scotland & Northern Ireland 19, 58, 71
Immigration: Special Immigration Appeals Commission: Procedure 58
Immigration: Travel bans: Designation 57
Immunities & privileges: International: International organisations: Scotland 173
Incapacity: Adults with incapacity: Public Guardian: Fees: Scotland 163
Income tax: Approved expenses 59
Income tax: Capital allowances 24, 58
Income tax: Capital allowances: Energy-saving plant & machinery 24, 58
Income tax: Capital allowances: Environmentally beneficial plant & machinery 24, 58
Income tax: Childcare: Qualifying 59
Income tax: Construction industry scheme: Amendments 25, 59
Income tax: Construction industry scheme: Finance Act 2004: Amendment 25, 59
Income tax: Deposit-takers & building societies: Interest payments 59
Income tax: Double taxation: Relief: Algeria 12, 24, 58
Income tax: Double taxation: Relief: Bulgaria 12, 24, 58
Income tax: Double taxation: Relief: Croatia 12, 24, 58
Income tax: Double taxation: Relief: Guernsey 24, 58
Income tax: Double taxation: Relief: Jersey 24, 58
Income tax: Double taxation: Relief: Kosovo 12, 24, 58
Income tax: Double taxation: Relief: Senegal 12, 24, 58
Income tax: Double taxation: Relief: Sweden 12, 24, 58
Income tax: Finance Act 2004: Pension schemes: Allowance: Charge 58
Income tax: Finance Act 2007: Schedule 26: Shares: Valuation of: Appointed day: Commencements 12, 25, 58
Income tax: Finance Act 2012: Sections 26 & 30: Relief for equalisation reserves: Abolition: Specified day 25, 58

Income tax: Finance Act 2014 . . . 12, 25, 59
Income tax: Finance Act 2014: High risk promoters: Prescribed information . . . 12, 25, 58
Income tax: Finance Act 2014: Schedule 9: Consequential amendments . . . 58
Income tax: Finance Act 2014: Section 18 (2) to (4): Appointed day . . . 59
Income tax: Finance Act 2015: Schedule 6, paragraphs 10 to 12 . . . 59
Income tax: Finance Act 2015: Section 23: Appointed days . . . 59
Income tax: Individual savings accounts . . . 12, 59
Income tax: Interest rates . . . 60
Income tax: International tax: Enforcement: Brazil . . . 12, 25, 44, 59, 62, 135
Income tax: Life insurance: Qualifying policies: Statement & reporting requirements . . . 59
Income tax: Lloyd's underwriters: Transitional equalisation reserves . . . 25, 59
Income tax: Offshore asset moves penalty: Specified territories . . . 12, 60, 62
Income tax: PAYE . . . 59
Income tax: Pension schemes: Overseas: Amendments . . . 60
Income tax: Pension schemes: Registered: Provision of information . . . 60
Income tax: Pension schemes: Sums & assets: Transfer . . . 60
Income tax: Professional fees . . . 59
Income tax: Qualifying private placement . . . 60
Income tax: Registered pension schemes: Audited accounts: Specified Persons . . . 60
Income tax: Registered pension schemes: Splitting of schemes . . . 60
Income tax: Rent-a-room relief: Limit . . . 59
Income tax: Scotland Act 2012: Section 25: Appointed years . . . 60
Income tax: Scottish rate: Amendments . . . 60
Income tax: Shares, securities & strips: Market value of . . . 12, 25, 59
Income tax: Sports clubs, amateur: Taxation . . . 12, 24, 58
Income tax: Statutory shared parental pay . . . 25, 38, 60
Income tax: Tax relief: Social investments: Accreditation of social impact contractor . . . 60
Income tax: Taxation: Regulatory capital securities . . . 12, 25, 60, 129
Income tax: Unit trusts: Unauthorised . . . 13, 25, 60
Income tax: Van benefit: Car & van fuel benefit . . . 60
Income tax: Venture capital trusts: Winding up & mergers: Tax . . . 60
Income-related benefits: Subsidy to authorities . . . 126
Independent Police Complaints Commission: Complaints & misconduct: England & Wales . . . 82
Independent schools: Religious character: Designation: England . . . 33
Individual savings accounts . . . 12, 59
Industrial injuries: Prescribed diseases . . . 127
Industrial injuries: Prescribed diseases: Northern Ireland . . . 223
Industrial training levy: Construction Industry Training Board . . . 39
Industrial training levy: Construction industry: Northern Ireland . . . 209
Industrial training levy: Engineering Construction Industry Training Board . . . 39
Information & public records: Transfer of functions . . . 72
Infrastructure Act 2015: Commencements . . . 40, 52, 61, 137
Infrastructure Act 2015: Commencements: Wales . . . 137
Infrastructure Act 2015: Provisions: Commencements . . . 61
Infrastructure planning: A160/A180: Port of Immingham: Improvements . . . 60, 61
Infrastructure planning: Development consent orders: Changes & revocation . . . 61
Infrastructure planning: Dogger Bank Creyke Beck: Offshore wind farms . . . 61
Infrastructure planning: Dogger Bank Teeside A & B Offshore Wind Farm . . . 61
Infrastructure planning: Ferrybridge power station . . . 61
Infrastructure planning: Galloper Wind Farm . . . 61
Infrastructure planning: Hazardous substances: England . . . 61, 131
Infrastructure planning: Hinkley Point C: Nuclear generating station . . . 61
Infrastructure planning: Hirwaun generating station: Corrections . . . 61
Infrastructure planning: Hirwaun generating station: Tidal generating station . . . 61
Infrastructure planning: Hornsea One Offshore Wind Farm . . . 61
Infrastructure planning: Lancashire County Council: Torrisholme to the M6 Link . . . 61
Infrastructure planning: Miscellaneous prescribed provisions . . . 61
Infrastructure planning: Norfolk County Council: Norwich Northern Distributor Road (A1067 to A47(T) . . . 61
Infrastructure planning: North Killingholme generating station: Correction . . . 61
Infrastructure planning: Northumberland County Council: A1 - South East Northumberland Link Road: Morpeth Northern Bypass . . . 61
Infrastructure planning: Port of Immingham: A160/A180: Improvements . . . 60, 61
Infrastructure planning: Port Talbot generating station . . . 62
Infrastructure planning: Power plants: Knottingley . . . 61
Infrastructure planning: Preesall Underground Storage Facility . . . 62
Infrastructure planning: Progress power: Gas fired power station . . . 62
Infrastructure planning: Radioactive Waste Geological Disposal Facilities . . . 61
Infrastructure planning: Rampion Wind Farm . . . 62
Infrastructure planning: Swansea Bay: Tidal generating station . . . 62
Infrastructure planning: Thames tideway tunnel: Thames Water Utilities Ltd . . . 62
Infrastructure planning: Thames Water Utilities Ltd: Thames tideway tunnel . . . 62
Infrastructure planning: Walney extension offshore wind farm . . . 62
Infrastructure planning: White Moss landfill: Hazardous waste facility & disposal . . . 62
Infrastructure planning: Willington C Gas Pipeline: Corrections . . . 62
Infrastructure: Acts . . . 5
Infrastructure: Acts: Explanatory notes . . . 6
Inheritance tax: Electronic communications . . . 62
Inheritance tax: International tax: Enforcement: Brazil . . . 12, 25, 44, 59, 62, 135
Inheritance tax: Offshore asset moves penalty: Specified territories . . . 12, 60, 62

Injunctions: Magistrates' courts: Anti-social behaviour: England & Wales 70
Injury benefit: Pensions: Police: England & Wales 81, 82
Injury benefits: Health & personal social services: Northern Ireland 208
Inquiry into Historical Institutional Abuse: Terms of Reference: Amendment: Northern Ireland. 209
Inshore fishing: Fishing & fishing methods: Prohibition: Luce Bay: Scotland. 187
Inshore fishing: Fishing & fishing methods: Prohibition: Scotland 187
Insolvency 63
Insolvency Act 1986: Bankruptcy 10, 63
Insolvency Order 2005: Consequential amendments: Northern Ireland 210
Insolvency practitioners & services account: Fees 45, 63
Insolvency: Bankruptcy & Debt Advice (Scotland) Act 2014: Commencements: Scotland 165, 168, 173
Insolvency: Bankruptcy: Scotland 165, 173
Insolvency: Common financial tool: Scotland 165, 168, 173
Insolvency: Essential supplies: Protection 62
Insolvency: Financial markets: Settlement finality. 46
Insolvency: Insolvency practitioners: Recognised professional bodies: Revocation of recognition 63
Insolvency: Practitioners: Amendment 62
Insolvency: Proceedings: Fees. 45, 63
Insolvency: Proceedings: Monetary limits 63
Insolvency: Rules: Amendments: Northern Ireland 210
Insolvency: Small Business, Enterprise and Employment Act 2015: Commencements 14, 20, 47, 62, 65, 89, 131
Insolvency: Small Business, Enterprise and Employment Act 2015: Insolvency & company directors disqualification 21, 62
Inspectors of Education, Children's Services & Skills. 14, 34
Insurance companies: Finance Act 2012: Amendment. 25
Insurance: Acts 5
Insurance: Employer's liability: Compulsory insurance: Northern Ireland 203
Insurance: Flood reinsurance: Scheme & scheme administrator designation 63
Insurance: Flood reinsurance: Scheme funding & administration 63
Intellectual Property Act 2014: Commencements 63
Internal Drainage Districts: Natural Resources Body for Wales: Lower Wye, Caldicot & Wentlooge. 64
International development: African Development Bank: Further payments to capital stock 63
International development: Asian Infrastructure Investment Bank: Initial capital contribution 63
International development: International Fund for Agricultural Development: Tenth replenishment 63
International development: Official development assistance: Targets: Acts 5
International development: Official development assistance: Targets: Acts: Explanatory notes. 7
International Fund for Agricultural Development: Tenth replenishment 63
International immunities & privileges: Asian infrastructure investment bank: Immunities & privileges 63
International immunities & privileges: International organisations: Scotland 173
Invalid care allowance: Northern Ireland 223
Invalid care allowance: Social security 127
Investigatory powers: Communications data: Acquisition & disclosure: Code of practice 63
Investigatory powers: Communications data: Retention: Code of practice 63
Investigatory powers: Regulation: Communications data 63
Investigatory powers: Regulation: Covert human intelligence sources 63
Investigatory powers: Regulation: Covert human intelligence sources: Code of practice: Scotland 173
Investigatory powers: Regulation: Covert surveillance & property interference: Code of practice: Scotland 173
Investigatory powers: Regulation: Directed surveillance 63
Investigatory powers: Regulation: Modification: Authorisation provisions: Legal consultations: Scotland 173
Investment exchanges & clearing houses: Stamp duty & stamp duty reserve tax 129
Investment: Collective investment schemes: Financial Services & Markets Act 2000 46
Iran: Export control: Sanctions 28
Iran: Restrictive measures: Overseas territories 77
Isle of Wight: Yarmouth: Pilotage: Harbour commissioners: Removal of pilotage functions 81

J

Japan: Accounting standards: Prescribed bodies: Companies. 20
Jersey: Double taxation: Relief & international enforcement 24, 58
Jersey: Immigration 57
Jersey: Merchant shipping: Oil pollution 72
Jobseeker's allowance: Extended period of sickness: Northern Ireland 222
Jobseeker's allowance: Sickness: Extended period 126
Jobseeker's allowance: Traineeships & qualifying young persons 127
Judgements: Maintenance: Civil jurisdiction & judgments & international recovery 64
Judges: Maximum number: Senior courts of England & Wales 122
Judgments: Civil jurisdiction & judgments: Hague convention: Choice of court agreements 2005 63
Judgments: Civil jurisdiction: Scotland 173
Judicature: Justice & Security (Northern Ireland) Act 2007: Non-jury trial provisions: Duration: Extension 28, 64
Judicial appointments & discipline: Act of Sederunt: Fitness for judicial office tribunal rules: Scotland 173
Judicial appointments & discipline: Courts Reform (Scotland) Act 2014: Commencements: Scotland 167, 173, 187, 189
Judicial appointments & discipline: Courts Reform (Scotland) Act 2014: Scotland 167, 173, 190
Judicial office: Fitness for: Tribunal rules: Scotland 173
Judicial offices: Public service pensions: Northern Ireland 215
Judicial pensions 79, 87
Judicial Pensions & Retirement Act 1993: Qualifying judicial offices 79
Judicial pensions: Northern Ireland 215
Juries: Criminal Justice and Courts Act 2015: Commencements 24, 27, 28, 30, 64, 67, 70, 83, 122, 130, 137
Justice (Northern Ireland) Act 2004: Amendments: Northern Ireland 210

Justice 2015 Act: Commencements: Northern Ireland 210
Justice 2015 Act: Victim charter: Northern Ireland 210
Justice Act (Northern Ireland) 2011: Commencements: Northern Ireland 210
Justice and Security (Northern Ireland) Act 2007: Non-jury trial provisions: Duration: Extension 28, 64
Justice of the Peace Court: Act of Adjournal: Criminal Procedure Rules 1996: Final decision requests: Scotland. 172, 174, 189
Justice of the Peace Court: Act of Adjournal: Criminal procedure: Rules: Scotland. 172, 174, 189
Justice of the Peace Court: Act of Adjournal: Justice of the Peace Court: Special measures: Scotland 172, 174, 189
Justice of the Peace Court: Courts Reform (Scotland) Act 2014: Commencements: Scotland 167, 172, 174, 187, 188, 189, 191
Justice of the Peace Court: Courts Reform (Scotland) Act 2014: Consequential provisions: Scotland 167, 172, 174, 188, 190, 191
Justice of the Peace Court: Criminal procedure rules 1996: Act of Adjournal: Amendment: Scotland. 172, 173, 174, 188
Justice of the Peace Court: Criminal procedure: Rules: Reporting restrictions: Scotland 172, 174, 189
Justice of the Peace Court: Fees: Scotland. 174
Justice of the Peace Court: Special measures: Criminal procedure: Scotland. 168
Justice: Access: 2003 Order: Commencements: Northern Ireland 200
Justice: Acts: Explanatory notes: Northern Ireland 199
Justice: Acts: Northern Ireland 199
Justice: Criminal Justice: 2013 Act: Commencements: Northern Ireland 210
Justice: Criminal: Drugs: Class B: Specified 27
Justice: Victims & witnesses: Information: Disclosure: Prescribed bodies: Northern Ireland: Northern Ireland 210
Justices of the peace: Allowances: England & Wales 64
Justices of the peace: Local justice areas: England & Wales 64
Justices' clerks & assistants rules: England & Wales 44

K

Key stage 2: National curriculum: Assessment arrangements: Moderation: Wales 37
Key stage 3: National curriculum: Assessment arrangements: Moderation: Wales 37
Knottingley power plant 61
Knowsley Metropolitan Borough Council: Permit schemes: Traffic management 53
Kosovo: Double taxation relief: International tax enforcement 12, 24, 58

L

Lancashire County Council: Permit schemes: Traffic management 53
Lancashire County Council: Torrisholme to the M6 Link: Infrastructure planning 61
Land & Buildings Transaction Tax (Scotland) Act 2013: Commencements: Scotland 174
Land & Buildings Transaction Tax (Scotland) Act 2013: Open-ended investment companies: Scotland. 174
Land & buildings transaction tax: Acts: Explanatory notes: Scotland 162
Land & buildings transaction tax: Reliefs: Addition & modification: Scotland 174
Land & buildings transaction tax: Reliefs: Sub-sale, development & multiple dwellings: Scotland 174
Land & buildings transaction tax: Tax rates & bands: Scotland 174
Land & buildings transaction tax: Transitional provisions: Scotland 174
Land development values: Certificates: Northern Ireland 210
Land drainage: Internal Drainage Districts: Natural Resources Body for Wales: Lower Wye, Caldicot & Wentlooge 64
Land drainage: Lombards Wall to Gravesend Bridge Internal Drainage District 64
Land drainage: Lower Wye, Caldicot & Wentlooge: Internal Drainage Districts: Abolition 64
Land drainage: Powysland Internal Drainage District 64
Land reform: Community Empowerment (Scotland) Act 2015: Commencements: Scotland. 166, 175
Land reform: Community right to buy: Scotland 175
Land: Acquisition: Home loss payments: Prescribed amounts: England 8, 21
Land: Homes & Communities Agency: Transfer of property: England 64
Landfill tax 64, 65
Landfill Tax (Scotland) Act 2014: Commencements: Scotland 174
Landfill tax, Northern Ireland 64, 65
Landfill tax: Devolution 64
Landfill tax: Qualifying fines 64, 65
Landfill tax: Scotland Act 2012: Section 31: Disapplication: Appointed day Commencements 64
Landfill: Scottish landfill tax: Administration: Scotland 174
Landfill: Scottish landfill tax: Exemption certificates: Scotland 174
Landfill: Scottish landfill tax: Qualifying material: Scotland 175
Landfill: Scottish landfill tax: Standard & lower rates: Scotland 175
Landlord & tenant: Agricultural Holdings Act 1986: Variations: Schedule 8 65
Landlord & tenant: Agricultural holdings: Units of production: England 65
Landlord & tenant: Agricultural holdings: Units of production: Wales 65, 66
Landlord & tenant: Agriculture: Compensation: Calculation 65
Landlord & tenant: Assured shorthold tenancy notices & prescribed requirements: England 65
Landlord & tenant: Assured tenancies: Agricultural occupancies: Forms: England 65
Landlord & tenant: Fixed equipment: Model clauses: England 65
Landlord & Tenant: Notices: Revocations: England 65
Landlord & tenant: Registered rents: Increases: Northern Ireland 210
Landlord & tenant: Small Business, Enterprise & Employment Act 2015: Commencements 20, 47, 55, 62, 65, 66
Landlord & tenant: Tenancy deposits: Specified interest rates: Housing: England 54
Landlords & agents: Code of practice 54
Lands Tribunal for Scotland: Fees 175
Lands Tribunal: Rules: Northern Ireland 210
Large combustion plants: Transitional national plan 41
Late payments: Commercial debts: Scotland 166
Law Society: Modification of functions: Legal Services Act 2007 67

Legal aid & advice: Advice & assistance: Representation: Scotland 175
Legal aid & advice: Civil & criminal legal aid: England & Wales 66
Legal aid & advice: Civil legal aid: England & Wales 66
Legal aid & advice: Civil legal aid: Merits criteria 66
Legal aid & advice: Civil legal aid: Scotland 175
Legal aid & advice: Community legal service: Criminal defence service: England & Wales 66
Legal aid & advice: Crime & Courts Act 2013: Commencements 26, 66, 84
Legal aid & advice: Criminal defence service: Community legal service: England & Wales 66
Legal aid & advice: Criminal legal aid: Contribution orders: England & Wales 66
Legal aid & advice: Criminal legal aid: Disclosure of information: Northern Ireland 210
Legal aid & advice: Criminal legal aid: England & Wales 66
Legal aid & advice: Criminal legal aid: Remuneration: England & Wales 66
Legal aid & advice: Crown Court proceedings: Costs: Northern Ireland 210
Legal aid & advice: Financial resources: Information 66
Legal aid & advice: Merits criteria & information about financial resources: England & Wales 66
Legal Aid & Coroners' Courts Act (Northern Ireland) 2014: Commencements: Northern Ireland 210
Legal aid exception: Restraint orders: England & Wales 67, 85
Legal Aid, Sentencing & Punishment of Offenders Act 2012: Alcohol abstinence & monitoring requirements: Commencements 27
Legal Aid, Sentencing & Punishment of Offenders Act 2012: Commencements 27
Legal Aid, Sentencing & Punishment of Offenders Act 2012: Fines: Summary conviction 27
Legal aid: Miscellaneous amendments: Scotland 175
Legal officers: Annual fees: Ecclesiastical law 32
Legal Services Act 2007: Law Society: Modification of functions 67
Legal Services Act 2007: Warrants 67
Legal Services Act 2007: Warrants: Licensing authority 67
Legal services: Criminal Justice and Courts Act 2015: Commencements 24, 27, 28, 30, 64, 67, 70, 83, 122, 130, 137
Legal Writings (Counterparts & Delivery) (Scotland) Act 2015: Commencements: Scotland 166
Legal writings, counterparts & delivery: Acts: Scotland 162
Legislative reform: Community governance reviews 69, 90
Legislative reform: Duchy of Lancaster 32
Lerwick Harbour: Revisions: Scotland 172
Letting agents: Duty to publicise fees: Exclusion: England 23
Liberia: Sanctions: Overseas territories 78
Libraries: Public Lending Right Scheme 1982: Variation: Commencements 67
Library Advisory Council for England: Abolition 85
Licences & licensing: Air Weapons & Licensing (Scotland) Act 2015: Commencements: Scotland 164, 167, 175
Licences & licensing: Licensing Act 2003: Late night refreshment 67
Licensing (liquor): Air Weapons & Licensing (Scotland) Act 2015: Commencements: Scotland 164, 167, 175
Licensing (marine): Aquaculture & Fisheries (Scotland) Act 2007: Fixed penalty notices: Scotland 169, 171, 175, 187, 188
Licensing Act 2003: Late night refreshment 67
Licensing: Marine licensing : Delegation of functions 67, 71
Licensing: Marine works: Environmental impact assessment 41, 67, 71
Licensing: Marine: Regulatory Reform (Scotland) Act 2014: Consequential modifications 21, 31, 38, 41, 67
Lichfield: Electoral changes 68
Life insurance: Qualifying policies: Statement & reporting requirements 59
Limited liability partnerships: Filing requirements 20, 67
Limited liability partnerships: Names & trading disclosures 11, 20, 67
Lincoln: Electoral changes 68
Liquor: Controlled liquor: Wholesaling 44
Liquor: Controlled: Wholesaling 44
Liquor: Duties: Alcoholic ingredients: Relief 44
Lisburn City Centre: Parking places on road: Northern Ireland 220
Lisburn City: Parking places, loading bays & waiting restrictions: Northern Ireland 219
Lisburn: Traffic control: Northern Ireland 217
Lisburn: Waiting restrictions: Northern Ireland 221
Listed buildings & conservation areas: Consent procedures: Scotland 191
Listed buildings & conservation areas: Planning: England 132
Listed buildings & conservation areas: Urgent works: Crown Land: Scotland 191
Listed buildings: Wales 132
Litigants in person: Costs & expenses: Sheriff Appeal Court: Scotland 188
Little Loch Broom: Scallops: Several fishery: Shellfish: Scotland 187
Littlehampton harbour: Revision 50
Lloyd's underwriters: Transitional equalisation reserves 25, 59
Loading bays on roads: Northern Ireland 218
Loan relationships & derivative contracts: Accounting practice: Change 25
Loan relationships & derivative contracts: Change of accounting practice 25
Loan relationships & derivative contracts: Exchange gains & losses: Fair value accounting 25
Loan relationships & derivative contracts: Profits & losses: Disregard & bringing into account 25
Lobbying: Transparency of Lobbying, Non-Party Campaigning & Trade Union Administration Act 2014: Commencements 22, 133
Local Audit & Accountability Act 2014: Appointing person 70
Local Audit & Accountability Act 2014: Commencements 69, 70
Local Audit & Accountability Act 2014: National Health Service: Independent Trustees 74
Local Audit & Accountability Act 2014: National Health Service: Special trustees 74
Local Audit & Accountability Act 2014: Smaller authorities 70
Local audit: Local audit: Health service bodies auditor panel & independence 74
Local authorities see also Local government
Local authorities: Capital finance & accounting 70
Local authorities: Greater Manchester Combined Authority 68, 134

Local authorities: Partnership: National Health Service bodies 68, 75
Local authorities: Public health functions: Local healthwatch representatives & Public health & wellbeing boards: Entry to premises. . 74, 86, 123
Local authorities: Residents: Charges: Deposit household waste: England. 68
Local authorities: Standing orders: England 68
Local elections: Forms: Northern Ireland 77
Local elections: Parishes & communities: England & Wales 90
Local elections: Principal areas: England & Wales 90
Local Governance (Scotland) Act 2004: Remuneration & severance: Amendments: Scotland 175
Local government see also Local authorities
Local Government (Democracy) (Wales) Act 2013: Commencements 70
Local Government Act (Northern Ireland) 2014: Commencements: Northern Ireland 210, 211
Local Government Byelaws (Wales) Act 2012: Commencements 70
Local Government Finance Act 1988: Non-domestic rating multipliers: England 88
Local Government Finance Act 1992: Commencement: Scotland. 176, 193
Local government: Accounts & audit. 69
Local government: Accounts & audit: Northern Ireland 211
Local government: Acts: Explanatory notes: Wales. 229
Local government: Acts: Wales. 229
Local government: Boundaries: 2008 Act: Commencements: Northern Ireland. 211
Local government: Business Improvement Districts: Community challenge: England. 68
Local government: Colchester: Electoral changes 68
Local government: Community empowerment (Scotland) Act 2015: Commencements: Scotland. 166, 175
Local government: Council tax: Non-domestic rating: Powers of entry Safeguards: England. 68, 88
Local Government: Decisions review: Acts: Explanatory notes 7
Local government: Democracy: Acts: Wales 229
Local government: Electoral changes: Ashfield. 67
Local government: Electoral changes: Bristol 67
Local government: Electoral changes: Broxtowe. 67
Local government: Electoral changes: Cherwell 67
Local government: Electoral changes: Cotswold. 68
Local government: Electoral changes: Doncaster 68
Local government: Electoral changes: East Northamptonshire. 68
Local government: Electoral changes: Erewash 68
Local government: Electoral changes: Hertfordshire 68
Local government: Electoral changes: High Peak 68
Local government: Electoral changes: Knowsley. 68
Local government: Electoral changes: Lichfield 68
Local government: Electoral changes: Lincoln 68
Local government: Electoral changes: Poole. 69
Local government: Electoral changes: Purbeck 69
Local government: Electoral changes: Rugby 69
Local government: Electoral changes: South Bucks 69
Local government: Electoral changes: Stafford 69
Local government: Electoral changes: Stroud 69
Local government: Electoral changes: Swindon 69
Local government: Electoral changes: Warwickshire 69
Local government: Electoral changes: West Devon 69
Local government: Electoral changes: West Dorset 69
Local government: Electoral changes: Woking. 69
Local government: Electoral changes: Wyre Forest 69
Local government: Electronic communications 68
Local government: Exclusion of non-commercial considerations: Northern Ireland 211
Local government: Executive arrangements: Northern Ireland 211
Local government: Finance: Scotland 176
Local government: Gloucester: Electoral changes 68
Local government: Household waste: Penalty charges. 42, 70
Local government: Joint Committees: Constituting as bodies corporate: Northern Ireland 211
Local government: Legislative reform: Community governance reviews 69, 90
Local government: Local Audit & Accountability Act 2014: Appointing person 70
Local government: Local Audit & Accountability Act 2014: Commencements 69, 70
Local government: Local Audit & Accountability Act 2014: Smaller authorities 70
Local government: Local authorities: Capital finance & accounting. 70
Local government: Local authorities: Residents: Charges: Deposit household waste: England. 68
Local government: Local authorities: Standing orders: England 68
Local government: Local Governance (Scotland) Act 2004: Remuneration & severance: Amendments: Scotland. 175
Local government: Ombudsman: Powers: Acts 5
Local government: Pension schemes 87
Local government: Pension schemes: Governance: Scotland 179
Local government: Pension schemes: Northern Ireland. 211
Local government: Pension schemes: Scotland 179
Local government: Performance standards & indicators: Northern Ireland 211
Local government: Peterborough: Electoral changes 69
Local government: Playing fields: Community involvement: Disposal decisions: Wales. 70
Local government: Recycling centres: Household waste: Prohibition of charges 68
Local government: Redundancy payments: Continuity of employment 131
Local government: Religious observances: Acts. 5
Local government: Religious observances: Acts: Explanatory notes 7

Local government: Reorganisation: Compensation for loss of employment: Northern Ireland 211
Local government: Review of decisions: Acts 5
Local government: Rochford: Electoral changes 69
Local government: Scheme of elections: Birmingham, City 68
Local government: Scheme of elections: Borough of Rotherham 67
Local government: Sheffield: Electoral changes 69
Local government: Smaller authorities: Transparency requirements 69
Local government: Transitional functions grant: Northern Ireland 211
Local government: Transitional provisions: Northern Ireland 211
Local government: Transparency requirements 68
Local government: Transparency: Descriptions of information 68
Local government: Transport levying bodies 69
Local government: Violence against Women, Domestic Abuse and Sexual Violence (Wales) Act 2015: Commencements 70
Local justice areas: England & Wales 64
Local pharmaceutical services: National Health Service: England 75
Loch Ewe, Isle of Ewe, Wester Ross, Scallop Several Fishery: Shellfish: Scotland 187
Lombards Wall to Gravesend Bridge Internal Drainage District 64
London government: Greater London Authority: Council tax: Requirement procedure 70
London Legacy Development Corporation: Value added tax: Refunds 135
London Northwest Healthcare: National Health Service Trust 74
London Underground: Bank Station: Capacity upgrade 134
London: Port of London Authority: Harbour: Revision 50
Londonderry Harbour: Limits: Variation: Northern Ireland 208
Londonderry: Parking & waiting restrictions: Northern Ireland 219
Lower Wye, Caldicot & Wentlooge: Internal Drainage Districts: Abolition 64
Luce Bay: Inshore fishing: Prohibited methods of fishing: Scotland 187

M

M4: Junction 23A Magor & junction 29 Castleton: Speed limits: Wales 110
Macao: International tax: Enforcement 130
Magistrates' courts: Criminal Justice & Courts Act 2015: Commencements 24, 27, 28, 30, 64, 67, 70, 83, 122, 130, 137
Magistrates' courts: Criminal procedure: Rules: England & Wales 70, 122
Magistrates' courts: Injunctions: Anti-social behaviour: England & Wales 70
Magistrates' courts: Injunctions: Gang-related violence: England & Wales 71
Magistrates' courts: Rules: Modern Slavery Act 2015: England & Wales 71
Main estimates: Supply & appropriation: Acts 6
Maintenance: Civil jurisdiction & judgements & international recovery 64
Major accident hazards: Control: Northern Ireland 208
Management of Offenders etc. (Scotland) Act 2005: Commencements: Scotland 168
Management of Offenders etc. (Scotland) Act 2005: Specification of persons: Scotland 168
Marine conservation: Fixed monetary penalties: Northern Ireland 206
Marine licensing: Delegation of functions 67, 71
Marine management: Marine conservation: South Arran: Urgent continuation: Scotland 170, 176
Marine management: Marine conservation: Wester Ross: Scotland 170, 176
Marine management: Marine licensing: Delegation of functions 67, 71
Marine management: Marine works: Environmental impact assessment 41, 67, 71
Marine management: South Arran Nature Conservation Marine Protected Area: Scotland 170, 176
Marine pollution: Miscellaneous provisions: England 10, 42, 71, 135
Marine pollution: Oil Pollution Preparedness, Response and Co-operation Convention 71
Marine works: Environmental impact assessment 41, 67, 71
Mariners: Statutory shared parental pay: Persons abroad: Northern Ireland 205
Marriage & Civil Partnership (Scotland) Act 2014: Commencements 166, 176
Marriage: Civil partnership: Modifications: Scotland 166, 176
Marriage: Civil partnerships: Proposed: Referral & investigation 19, 57, 71
Marriage: Forms: Prescription: Scotland 176
Marriage: Meaning of exempt persons & notice 19, 57, 71
Marriage: Referral & investigation: Provisions 19, 57, 71
Marriage: Same sex couples: Acts 4
Marriage: Sham marriage: Civil partnership: Scotland & Northern Ireland 19, 58, 71
Marriage: Waiting period 19, 57, 71
Marriages & civil partnerships: Investigations conduct 19, 57, 71
Marriages: Civil partnership: Referral 19, 58, 71
Marriages: Registration: England & Wales 89
Maternity & parental leave: Northern Ireland 204
Maternity allowance: Curtailment: Northern Ireland 222
Maternity allowance: Earnings 127
Maternity allowance: Earnings: Northern Ireland 223
Maternity leave: Curtailment of statutory rights to leave: Northern Ireland 204
Meat: Country of origin: Northern Ireland 207
Meat: Country of origin: Wales 49
Medical profession: General Medical Council: Fitness to practice: Professional Standards Authority: References to court 51
Medical profession: General Medical Council: Provisional registration: Maximum period 52
Medical services: General & personal: Contracts: England 74
Medical services: General: Contracts: England 74
Medical services: General: Contracts: Northern Ireland 208
Medicines: Branded medicines: Prices control: Information supply: National Health Service 50, 75, 76
Medicines: Human medicines 71

Medicines: Human medicines: Northern Ireland	211
Medicines: Human: Northern Ireland	211
Membership audit certificate: Specified conditions	133
Mental capacity: Court of Protection: Rules	72
Mental capacity: Public Guardian: Powers of attorney: Enduring & lasting: England & Wales	72
Mental health (Scotland) Act 2015: Commencements: Scotland	176
Mental health (Scotland) Act 2015: Transitional & saving provisions: Commencements: Scotland	176
Mental Health Tribunal for Scotland: Practice & procedure: Scotland	176
Mental health: Acts: Explanatory notes: Scotland	163
Mental health: Acts: Scotland	162
Mental health: Care Act 2014: Commencement	72, 73, 123
Mental health: Patients: Detention: Excessive security: Scotland	176
Merchant shipping: Alcohol & drugs	72
Merchant shipping: Boatmasters' qualifications	72
Merchant shipping: Fees	72
Merchant shipping: Light dues	72
Merchant shipping: Oil pollution: Jersey	72
Merchant shipping: Port security: Port of Oban	72
Merchant shipping: Safe working practices: Code	72
Merchant shipping: Safety	72
Merchant shipping: Survey & certification	72
Merchant shipping: Training, certification & watchkeeping: Standards	72
Merchant shipping: United Kingdom: Wreck convention area	72
Merchant shipping: Wreck Removal Convention Act 2011: Commencements	72
Mergers: Companies: Cross-border mergers	20
Merthyr Tydfil College Limited: Designated institution: Further education: Wales	36
Mesothelioma: Diffuse mesothelioma: Payment scheme	79
Mesothelioma: Lump sum payments: Conditions & amounts	126
Mesothelioma: Lump sum payments: Conditions & amounts: Northern Ireland	222
Midwives: Nursing & Midwifery Council: Fitness to practise: Education & registration	52
Milk Marketing Board: Revocations: England & Wales	8
Milk producers: Single Common Market Organisation: Emergency aid	8
Milk: Condensed & dried milk: England	48
Milton Keynes Council: Permit schemes: Traffic management	54
Mining: Deep Sea Mining Act 1981: Isle of Man	29
Ministers of the Crown: Chancellor: Duchy of Lancaster	72
Ministers of the Crown: Functions: Transfer: Police & crime commissioners elections	73
Ministers of the Crown: Transfer of functions: Information & public records	72
Ministers of the Crown: Transfer of functions: Pensions guidance	73
Ministry of Defence: Police: Conduct	82
Mink: England	9
Misuse of drugs	29
Misuse of Drugs Act 1971: Amendments	29
Misuse of Drugs Act 1971: Temporary class drugs	29
Misuse of drugs: Dangerous drugs	29
Modern Slavery Act 2015: Commencements	73
Modern Slavery Act 2015: Consequential amendments: England & Wales	73
Modern Slavery Act 2015: Duty to notify: England & Wales	73
Modern Slavery Act 2015: Magistrates' courts: Rules: England & Wales	71
Modern slavery Act 2015: Transparency in supply chains	73
Monaco: International tax: Enforcement	130
Money laundering	45
Mortgages: Financial Services & markets	47
Motor cars: Driving instruction	92
Motor fuel: Composition & content	85
Motor vehicles: Disabled persons: Badges: Northern Ireland	217
Motor vehicles: Disabled persons: Badges: Scotland	181
Motor vehicles: Driving instruction: Trainee licences: Northern Ireland	218
Motor vehicles: Driving licences	92
Motor vehicles: Driving licences: Northern Ireland	218
Motor vehicles: Immobilisation, removal & disposal: Insurance requirements	92
Motor vehicles: Naval, military & air force: Speed limits: Variation	109
Motor vehicles: Seat belts: Wearing	92
Motor vehicles: Seat belts: Wearing: Children	92
Motor vehicles: Seat belts: Wearing: Children in front seats: Northern Ireland	218
Motor vehicles: Seat belts: Wearing: Northern Ireland	218
Motor vehicles: Testing: Northern Ireland	218
Motorways: A1(M)	93, 94
Motorways: A1(M)/A1	93, 94
Motorways: A1(M)/M1	93
Motorways: A1(M)/M18	105
Motorways: A2/A282/M25	106
Motorways: A20/M20	105
Motorways: A27/M27/A3(M)	96
Motorways: A3(M)/A27/M27	96
Motorways: A40/M25	106
Motorways: A725/M8/M74: Scotland	184
Motorways: M1	102

Motorways: M1/A1(M) 93
Motorways: M1/A52 102
Motorways: M1: Junction 28 to 35a: Variable speed limits 109
Motorways: M1: Junction 39 to 42 109
Motorways: M11 105
Motorways: M18 105
Motorways: M18/A1(M) 105
Motorways: M180 108
Motorways: M181 108
Motorways: M2 102
Motorways: M2/A2 102
Motorways: M20 105
Motorways: M20/A20 105
Motorways: M25 . . . . 105, 106
Motorways: M25/A2/A282 . . . . 105, 106
Motorways: M25/A282 106
Motorways: M25/A40 106
Motorways: M25/M3 103
Motorways: M25/M4/M40 106
Motorways: M27 106
Motorways: M27/A3(M)/A27 96
Motorways: M27/M275 106
Motorways: M27/M3 102
Motorways: M275 & M27: Speed limits 109
Motorways: M275/M27 106
Motorways: M3 . . . . 93, 103
Motorways: M3/M25 103
Motorways: M3/M27 102
Motorways: M32 106
Motorways: M4 . . . . 103, 120
Motorways: M4/#a470 120
Motorways: M4/A465 . . . . 115, 120
Motorways: M4/M40/M25 106
Motorways: M4/M5 103
Motorways: M40 106
Motorways: M40/M25/M4 106
Motorways: M40/M42 106
Motorways: M42 . . . . 106, 107
Motorways: M42/M40 106
Motorways: M42/M5 103
Motorways: M42/M6 . . . . 104, 106, 109
Motorways: M45 107
Motorways: M48 107
Motorways: M5 . . . . 103, 104, 109
Motorways: M5/A4 95
Motorways: M5/M4 103
Motorways: M5/M42 103
Motorways: M5/M6 104
Motorways: M50 107
Motorways: M53 107
Motorways: M54 107
Motorways: M55 107
Motorways: M56 . . . . 107, 109
Motorways: M56/M6 . . . . 105, 107
Motorways: M56/M60 107
Motorways: M57 107
Motorways: M6 . . . . 104, 105, 109
Motorways: M6/A590 101
Motorways: M6/M42 . . . . 104, 106, 109
Motorways: M6/M5 104
Motorways: M6/M56 . . . . 105, 107
Motorways: M6/M69 . . . . 104, 108
Motorways: M6: Junction 10 to 13: Variable speed limits 109
Motorways: M60 107
Motorways: M60/M56 107
Motorways: M60/M61/M62/M66/M602 107
Motorways: M602/M60/M61/M62/M66 107
Motorways: M61 107
Motorways: M61/M62/M66/M602/M60 107
Motorways: M62 . . . . 107, 108, 109
Motorways: M62/M66/M602/M60/M61 107
Motorways: M621 108
Motorways: M65 108
Motorways: M66/M602/M60/M61/M62 107
Motorways: M69/M6 . . . . 104, 108
Motorways: M74/A725/M8: Scotland 184
Motorways: M74: Scotland 184
Motorways: M8/A8: Junction 4: Scotland 184

Motorways: M8/M74/A725: Scotland 184
Motorways: M9/A9: Scotland 184
Motorways: M90/A90: Scotland 182, 184
Motorways: Traffic: England & Wales 110
Moy: Electricity: Licence requirement: Exemption 37
Moy: Electricity: Licence requirement: Exemption: Frodsham: England & Wales 38
Mutuals' deferred shares: Acts 5

N

Nagoya protocol. 41
Nagoya protocol: Compliance 41
National Assembly for Wales: Acts 229
National Assembly for Wales: Acts: Annual volumes. 7
National Assembly for Wales: Acts: Explanatory notes 229
National Assembly for Wales: Disqualifications 21
National assistance services: Personal requirements: Social care charges: Wales 125
National assistance services: Personal requirements: Sums: Scotland 176
National assistance services: Resources: Assessment: Scotland 176
National College for High Speed Rail: Government: England 34
National College for High Speed Rail: Incorporation: England 34
National Crime Agency: Crime & Courts Act 2013 . . . . 73, 77, 84
National curriculum: Assessment arrangements: Foundation phase: Desirable outcomes, educational programmes & baseline & end of phase: Wales 37
National curriculum: Assessment arrangements: KS2, KS3: Moderation: Wales 37
National curriculum: England 34
National curriculum: Specified purpose: England. 34
National curriculum: Study: Attainment targets & programmes: Wales 36
National debt: National savings 73
National election expenditure: National election expenditure: European parliamentary elections: Miscellaneous provisions: United Kingdom & Gibraltar. 73, 83, 90
National Employment Savings Trust: Pension schemes 79
National Galleries: Acts: Scotland: Explanatory notes. 163
National Health Service 75
National Health Service bodies: Partnership: Local authorities 68, 75
National Health Service Foundation Trusts: Trust funds: Trustees appointment: England. 75
National Health Service Litigation Authority: England & Wales 75
National Health Service pension scheme: Provisions: Scotland 179
National Health Service Trust Development Authority 75
National Health Service Trusts: London Northwest Healthcare 74
National Health Service: Care Act 2014: Commencement 72, 73, 123
National Health Service: Care Act 2014: Health Education England & Health Research Authority 52, 75, 124
National Health Service: Care providers & information: England 73, 85
National Health Service: Care Quality Commission: Membership 73, 85, 123
National Health Service: Charges, payments & remission of charges: England 74
National Health Service: Charges, payments & remission of charges: Scotland 177
National Health Service: Charges: Overseas visitors 74
National Health Service: Charges: Personal injuries: Amounts: England & Wales 76
National Health Service: Clinical negligence & other risks: Indemnity scheme: Scotland. 176
National Health Service: Clinical negligence scheme: England 74
National Health Service: Commissioning board & clinical commissioning groups: Responsibilities & standing rules: England 74
National Health Service: Community Care & Health (Scotland) Act 2002: Commencements: Scotland 176
National Health Service: Community Health Councils: Constitution, membership & procedures: Wales 76
National Health Service: Community Health Councils: Establishment, transfer of functions & abolition: Wales 76
National Health Service: Constitution guiding principles: Revision: England 75
National Health Service: Cross-border health care 75
National Health Service: Cross-border health care: Scotland 176
National Health Service: Dental charges: Wales 76
National Health Service: Drugs & appliances: Charges: England 74
National Health Service: Drugs & appliances: Charges: Free prescriptions: Scotland 176
National Health Service: General & personal medical services contracts: England 74
National Health Service: General medical services: Contracts 75
National Health Service: Health & Social Care 14, 74, 75, 86, 123
National Health Service: Health & Social Care Act 2008: Regulated activities 73, 85, 123
National Health Service: Health & Social Care Act 2012: Commencements 51, 73
National Health Service: Health & Social Care Act 2012: Consistent identifier: England 73, 85, 123
National Health Service: Health & Social Care Act 2012: Continuity of information: England 74, 85, 123
National Health Service: Health and Social Care (Safety & Quality) Act 2015: Commencements: England 74, 86, 123
National Health Service: Health Service Commissioner for England: Revocations 74
National Health Service: Injury benefits: England & Wales 76
National Health Service: Licence exemptions: England. 75
National Health Service: Licensing & pricing 75
National Health Service: Local Audit & Accountability Act 2014: Independent Trustees 74
National Health Service: Local Audit & Accountability Act 2014: Special trustees 74
National Health Service: Local audit: Health service bodies auditor panel & independence 74
National Health Service: Local authorities: Public health functions: Local healthwatch representatives & Public health & wellbeing boards: Entry to premises. 74, 86, 123
National Health Service: Medicines: Branded medicines: Prices control: Information supply 50, 75, 76

National Health Service: Optical charges & payments: Ophthalmic services: Scotland 177
National Health Service: Optical charges & payments: Scotland 177
National Health Service: Optical charges & payments: Wales 76
National Health Service: Overseas visitors: Charges 74
National Health Service: Payments & remission charges: Scotland 177
National Health Service: Pension scheme: England & Wales 76, 87, 88
National Health Service: Pension scheme: Scotland 179
National Health Service: Performers lists: England 75
National Health Service: Personal injuries: Charges: Amounts: Scotland 177
National Health Service: Pharmaceutical & local pharmaceutical services: England. 75
National Health Service: Primary care: Terms of service: Electronic prescription service 74
National Health Service: Primary dental services: England 75
National Health Service: Primary dental services: General ophthalmic services: England 75
National Health Service: Retirement: Premature: Compensation: England & Wales. 76
National Health Service: Superannuation schemes: Scotland 177
National Health Service: Welfare reform: Consequential amendments: Wales 76
National Health Service: West Middlesex University Hospital National Health Service Trust: Dissolutions 75
National Independent Safeguarding Board: Wales 125
National insurance contributions: Rate ceilings: Acts 5
National insurance: Contributions: Acts 5
National insurance: Contributions: Acts: Explanatory notes 7
National insurance: Contributions: Application of part 7 of the Finance Act 2004 126
National insurance: Social security: Contributions & national insurance numbers: Crediting & treatment: Northern Ireland. 223
National Park Authorities: England. 26
National savings 73
Nationality, Immigration: Fees 56
Nationality: Immigration Act 2014 56
Nationality: Immigration: Fees 56, 76
Nationality: Immigration: Health charges 57
Nationality: Immigration: Police: Passenger, crew & service information 56
Nationality: Immigration: Police: Passenger, crew & service information: Civil penalties. 57, 82
Natural gas: Valuation: Northern Ireland 216
Natural habitats: Conservation: Northern Ireland 206
Natural mineral water: Northern Ireland 207
Natural mineral water: Wales. 49
Navy: Disablement & death: Service pensions 79
Negligence & statutory duty: Social action: Acts. 6
Negligence & statutory duty: Social action: Acts: Explanatory notes. 7
Negligence: Clinical negligence scheme: National Health Service: England. 74
Neighbourhood planning: General: England 131
Netherlands: Double taxation: Arrangements 10
Netherlands: Double taxation: Relief 10
Network Rail: Blackthorn & Piddington: Land acquisition 134
Network rail: Ordsall Chord. 134
New Wear Bridge scheme: Temporary works 53
Newry: Parking & waiting restrictions: Northern Ireland 219
Newry: Parking places on roads & waiting restrictions: Northern Ireland 219
Newtownabbey: Parking & waiting restrictions: Northern Ireland 219
NHS Business Services Authority (Awdurdod Gwasanaethau Busnes y GIG): Delegation of additional functions 73
NHS payments & remission of charges: Social security: Information sharing 75, 129
Nicotine inhaling products: Age of sale: Proxy purchasing 86
Nitrate pollution: Agriculture: Water: Prevention 8, 135
Nitrate pollution: Prevention: Wales 9, 136
Nitrate: Vulnerable zones designation: Scotland 193
Nitrates Action Programme: Environmental protection: Northern Ireland 206
Noise emissions: Outdoor equipment 41
Noise: Control: Construction & open sites: Code of practice 85
Non-domestic rates: Levying: Scotland. 180
Non-domestic rates: Scotland 180
Non-domestic rates: Utilities: Valuation: Scotland. 180
Non-domestic rating multipliers: England 88
Non-domestic rating: Alteration of lists & appeals: England 88
Non-domestic rating: Contributions: Wales 89
Non-domestic rating: Council tax: Powers of entry Safeguards: England. 68, 88
Non-domestic rating: Demand notices: England 88
Non-domestic rating: Demand notices: Wales 89
Non-domestic rating: Designated area: England 88
Non-domestic rating: Levy & safety net: England 88, 89
Non-domestic rating: Northern line extension: England 89
Non-domestic rating: Small business rate relief: England. 89
Non-domestic rating: Small business rate relief: Wales. 89
Non-domestic rating: Wales 89
Non-domestic rating: Waterways: Wales. 89
Norfolk County Council: Norwich Northern Distributor Road (A1067 to A47(T): Infrastructure planning 61
North Killingholme generating station: Infrastructure planning: Correction 61
North West 200: Road races: Northern Ireland 220
Northern Ireland Assembly: Elections 77, 90
Northern Ireland Assembly: Elections: Forms 77

Northern Ireland Commissioner for Complaints: Public service pensions: Northern Ireland 212
Northern Ireland Commissioner for Complaints: Superannuation: Northern Ireland 213
Northern Ireland: Corporation tax: Acts 4
Northern Ireland: Corporation tax: Acts: Explanatory notes 6
Northern Ireland: Crime & Courts Act 2013 . . . . 73, 77, 84
Northern Ireland: Elections: Forms 77
Northern Ireland: European Parliamentary elections: Northern Irish forms 91
Northern Ireland: Local elections: Forms 77
Northern Ireland: Parliamentary elections: forms 91
Northern Ireland: Representation of the people: Elections 77, 90
Northern Ireland: Statutes 200
Northern Ireland: Statutes: Chronological tables 200
Northern Ireland: Statutory rules: Chronological tables 199
Northern Ireland: Welfare reform: Acts 5
Northern Ireland: Welfare reform: Acts: Explanatory notes 7
Northumberland County Council: A1 - South East Northumberland Link Road: Morpeth Northern Bypass: Infrastructure planning 61
Nottingham City Council: Permit schemes: Traffic management 54
Nuclear generation: Infrastructure planning: Hinkley Point C: Nuclear generating station 61
Nuclear reactor: ABWR nuclear reactor: Electricity generation: Justification decision 41, 51
Nurses & midwives: Nursing & Midwifery Council: Fitness to practise: Education, registration & registration appeals 52
Nurses: Nursing & Midwifery Council: Fitness to practise: Education & registration 52
Nursing & Midwifery Council: Fitness to practise: Education, registration & registration appeals 52
Nursing care & personal care: Community care: Scotland 190

O

Oban: Port security: Merchant shipping 72
Occupational & personal pension schemes 80
Occupational & personal pension schemes: Automatic enrolment 79
Occupational & personal pension schemes: Disclosure of information 79
Occupational & personal pension schemes: Transfer values 79
Occupational & personal pension schemes: Transfer values: Northern Ireland 212
Occupational pension schemes: Amendments: Northern Ireland 212
Occupational pension schemes: Automatic enrolment: Northern Ireland 212
Occupational pension schemes: Charges & governance 80
Occupational pension schemes: Charges & governance: Northern Ireland 212
Occupational pension schemes: Contracted-out schemes 80
Occupational pension schemes: Contracting-out abolition 80
Occupational pension schemes: Contracting-out: Power to amend: Reflect abolition: Northern Ireland 212
Occupational pension schemes: Disclosure of information: Northern Ireland 212
Occupational pension schemes: Levies 80
Occupational pension schemes: Levies: Northern Ireland 212
Occupational pension schemes: Levy ceiling & compensation cap: Northern Ireland 212
Occupational pension schemes: Pension Protection Fund 80
Occupational pensions: Revaluation 80
Occupational pensions: Revaluation: Northern Ireland 212
Off-street parking: Northern Ireland 218
Offender Rehabilitation Act 2014: Commencements 27, 30
Offender Rehabilitation Act 2014: Incidental provisions 27
Offenders: Rehabilitation of Offenders Act 1974: Exceptions: England & Wales 90
Official statistics: Statistics & Registration Service Act 2007: Patient registration information: Disclosure: Northern Ireland 211
Offshore installations: Safety Directive 41, 51
Offshore installations: Safety zones 77
Offshore petroleum: Licensing: Offshore safety directive 81
Offshore transmission licences: Electricity: Competitive tenders 37
Ofsted: Chief Inspector of Education, Children's Services & Skills 13, 14, 33, 34
Ofsted: Children's homes etc.: Fees & frequency of inspections 14
Oil & gas authority: Levy 81
Oil Pollution Preparedness, Response and Co-operation Convention: Merchant shipping 71
Oil pollution: Merchant shipping: Jersey 72
Oil: Hydrocarbon: Marking 44
Old Oak & Park Royal Development Corporation: Establishment: England 135
Old Oak & Park Royal Development Corporation: Planning functions 135
Olympic lotteries: Olympic Lottery Distribution Fund: Winding up 11
Olympic Lottery Distribution Fund: Winding up 11
Ombudsman & Commissioner for Complaints: Acts: Northern Ireland 199
Ombudsman: Local government: Powers: Acts 5
Ophthalmic services: General: England 75
Optical charges & payments: National Health Service: Scotland 177
Optical charges & payments: Northern Ireland 208
Optical charges & payments: Ophthalmic services: National Health Service: Scotland 177
Ordinary cause rules 1993: Amendment: Act of Sederunt: Scotland 166, 189
Ordinary cause rules: Sheriff Court: Proving the tenor & reduction: Act of Sederunt: Scotland 189
Ordinary cause: Rule: Child welfare reporters: Act of Sederunt: Scotland 167, 189
Ordsall Chord: Network Rail 134
Organic products 8
Osteopaths: General Osteopathic Council: Indemnity arrangements 52
Overseas adoptions: Application of articles: Employment Rights (Northern Ireland) Order 1996: Northern Ireland 204

Overseas territories . . . 78
Overseas territories: Burundi: Sanctions . . . 77
Overseas territories: Central African Republic: Sanctions . . . 77
Overseas territories: Civil aviation: Environmental standards . . . 15
Overseas territories: Iran: Restrictive measures . . . 77
Overseas territories: Iraq: Sanctions . . . 78
Overseas territories: Liberia: Sanctions . . . 78
Overseas territories: Russia, Crimea & Sevastopol . . . 78
Overseas territories: South Sudan: Sanctions . . . 78
Overseas territories: Syria: Restrictive measures . . . 78
Overseas territories: Yemen: Sanctions . . . 78
Overseas territories: Zimbabwe: Sanctions . . . 78
Ozone depleting substances: Environmental protection . . . 41

P

PACE: Codes of practice: Revision code . . . 82
Packaging: Essential requirements . . . 41
Parental leave: Shared . . . 131
Parental leave: Shared: Northern Ireland . . . 204
Parental order cases: Social Security Contributions & Benefits Act 1992: Application: Parts 12ZA &12ZB & 12ZC . . . 131
Parental orders: Employment rights: Northern Ireland . . . 203
Parental pay: Shared . . . 25, 38, 60, 131
Parking badges: Disabled Persons' Parking Badges (Scotland) Act 2014: Commencements: Scotland . . . 181
Parking places on roads: Road traffic & vehicles: Northern Ireland . . . 220
Parking: Off-street: District councils: Functions: Acts: Northern Ireland . . . 199
Parking: Off-street: District councils: Functions: Acts: Northern Ireland: Explanatory notes . . . 199
Parkside Gardens, Belfast: Abandonment: Northern Ireland . . . 217
Parliament: Recall of MPs: Acts . . . 5
Parliament: Recall of MPs: Acts: Explanatory notes . . . 7
Parliamentary Commissioner . . . 78
Parliamentary elections: Forms: Northern Ireland . . . 91
Parliamentary elections: Returning officers' charges . . . 90
Parliamentary elections: Returning officers' charges: Northern Ireland . . . 91
Parliamentary elections: Welsh forms . . . 91
Partnership: Accounts & reports . . . 20, 79
Partnership: Payments to governments: Reports . . . 20, 79
Partnerships & groups: Accounts & reports . . . 20
Partnerships: Limited liability partnerships: Names & trading disclosures . . . 11, 20, 67
Passenger vehicles: Recording equipment: Downloading of data . . . 92
Paternity: Adoption leave: Northern Ireland . . . 204
Paternity: Adoption: Shared parental leave: Order cases: Northern Ireland . . . 204
Paternity: Blood tests: Review: England & Wales . . . 43
Patient registration information: Disclosure: Statistics & Registration Service Act 2007: Northern Ireland . . . 211
Patients: Conditions of detention: Security: Scotland . . . 176
Pay as You Earn see PAYE
PAYE: Income tax . . . 59
Payment accounts: Financial services & markets . . . 47
Payment cards: Interchange: Fees . . . 47
Payment Scheme: Childcare payments . . . 13, 79
Payment Scheme: Childcare Payments Act 2014 . . . 13, 79
Payment Scheme: Childcare payments: Eligibility . . . 13, 79
Payment scheme: Diffuse mesothelioma . . . 79
Payment services: Financial services & markets . . . 47
Pedal cycles: Construction & use . . . 92
Pedal cycles: Electrically assisted . . . 92
Pension levies: Payment: Past periods: Northern Ireland . . . 212
Pension Protection Fund: Levy ceiling & compensation cap: Northern Ireland . . . 212
Pension Protection Fund: Occupational pension schemes . . . 80
Pension scheme: Health & social care: Northern Ireland . . . 208
Pension Schemes Act 2015: Commencements . . . 80
Pension Schemes Act 2015: Transitional provisions . . . 80
Pension schemes: Acts . . . 5
Pension schemes: Acts: Explanatory notes . . . 7
Pension schemes: Firefighters: Wales . . . 48, 81
Pension schemes: Health & social care: Northern Ireland . . . 208, 215
Pension schemes: National Employment Savings Trust . . . 79
Pension schemes: Overseas: Amendments . . . 60
Pension schemes: Registered: Provision of information . . . 60
Pension schemes: Registered: Sums & assets: Transfer . . . 60
Pensions Act 2004: Codes of Practice: Governance & administration of public service pension scheme: Appointed Day . . . 80
Pensions Act 2011: Commencements . . . 80
Pensions Act 2012: Commencements: Northern Ireland . . . 212
Pensions Act 2014: Commencements . . . 80
Pensions Act 2014: Consequential, supplementary & incidental amendments . . . 126
Pensions Act 2014: Savings . . . 80
Pensions Act 2015: Additional pension: Units: Northern Ireland . . . 222
Pensions Act 2015: Consequential, supplementary & incidental amendments: Northern Ireland . . . 222

Pensions guidance: Ministers of the Crown: Transfer of functions 73
Pensions Order 2005: Codes of practice: Appointed day: Northern Ireland 212
Pensions Order 2005: Public service pension schemes: Governance & administration: Code of practice: Appointed day: Northern Ireland 212
Pensions Schemes Act 2015: Appropriate independent advice : Northern Ireland 212
Pensions schemes: Reduction of cash equivalents: Northern Ireland 211
Pensions: Acts: Explanatory notes: Northern Ireland 199
Pensions: Acts: Northern Ireland 199
Pensions: Armed Forces & Reserve Forces: Compensation schemes 79
Pensions: Armed forces pension 87
Pensions: Armed Forces: Pension schemes & early departure schemes 87
Pensions: Automatic enrolment: Earnings trigger 79
Pensions: Automatic enrolment: Earnings trigger & qualifying earnings band: Northern Ireland 211
Pensions: Fire & rescue services: Compensation scheme: Northern Ireland 207
Pensions: Firefighters: Compensation scheme: England 47, 81
Pensions: Firefighters: Compensation Scheme: Scotland 171, 177
Pensions: Firefighters: New: Pension schemes: Northern Ireland 207
Pensions: Firefighters: Pension scheme: England 47, 81, 87
Pensions: Firefighters: Pension scheme: Governance: England 87
Pensions: Firefighters: Pension scheme: Northern Ireland 207, 215
Pensions: Firefighters: Pension scheme: Scotland 179
Pensions: Firefighters: Pension scheme: Transitional provisions: Northern Ireland 215
Pensions: Firefighters: Pension schemes: Wales 88
Pensions: Firemen: Pension schemes: Scotland 171, 177
Pensions: Guaranteed minimum increase 79
Pensions: Guaranteed minimum increase: Northern Ireland 211
Pensions: Increase: Review 80
Pensions: Increase: Review: Northern Ireland 212
Pensions: Judicial pensions 79
Pensions: Judicial Pensions & Retirement Act 1993: Qualifying judicial offices 79
Pensions: Judicial pensions: Northern Ireland 215
Pensions: Levies: Payment: Past periods: Northern Ireland 212
Pensions: Local government pension schemes 87
Pensions: Local government pension schemes: Governance: Scotland 179
Pensions: Local government pension schemes: Northern Ireland 211
Pensions: National Health Service: Pension scheme: Contributions: England & Wales 76
Pensions: National Health Service: Pension scheme: England & Wales 76, 87, 88
Pensions: Navy, army & air force: Disablement & death: Service pensions 79
Pensions: Occupational & personal pension schemes 80
Pensions: Occupational & personal pension schemes: Automatic enrolment 79
Pensions: Occupational & personal pension schemes: Automatic enrolment: Northern Ireland 212
Pensions: Occupational & personal pension schemes: Disclosure of information 79
Pensions: Occupational & personal pension schemes: Transfer values 79
Pensions: Occupational pension schemes & Pension Protection Fund 80
Pensions: Occupational pension schemes: Amendments: Northern Ireland 212
Pensions: Occupational pension schemes: Charges & governance 80
Pensions: Occupational pension schemes: Charges & governance: Northern Ireland 212
Pensions: Occupational pension schemes: Contracted-out schemes 80
Pensions: Occupational pension schemes: Contracting-out: Power to amend: Reflect abolition: Northern Ireland . . . 212
Pensions: Occupational pension schemes: Levies 80
Pensions: Occupational pension schemes: Levies: Northern Ireland 212
Pensions: Occupational pensions: Revaluation 80
Pensions: Occupational pensions: Revaluation: Northern Ireland 212
Pensions: Occupational, personal & stakeholder schemes: Disclosure of information: Northern Ireland 212
Pensions: Pension Protection Fund & occupational pension schemes: Northern Ireland 212
Pensions: Pension Schemes Act 2015: Transitional provisions 80
Pensions: Personal injuries: Civilians 80
Pensions: Police 88
Pensions: Police pensions: Northern Ireland 215
Pensions: Police Service: Northern Ireland 214
Pensions: Police: Injury benefit: England & Wales 81, 82
Pensions: Police: Scotland 177
Pensions: Public service pension schemes: Funded: Reduction of cash equivalents 79
Pensions: Public Service Pensions Act 2013: Commencements 87
Pensions: Public Service Pensions Act 2013: Judicial offices 87
Pensions: Public service pensions: Assembly Ombudsman for Northern Ireland: Northern Ireland 212
Pensions: Public service pensions: Civil servants & others 87
Pensions: Public service pensions: Employer cost cap: Northern Ireland 213
Pensions: Public service pensions: Revaluation: England & Wales 88
Pensions: Public Service: Defined benefits schemes: Unfunded: Transfers: Northern Ireland 213
Pensions: Public service: Pension scheme: Provisions: England & Wales 76, 88
Pensions: Public service: Pension scheme: Transfers 81
Pensions: Registered pension schemes: Splitting of schemes 60
Pensions: Schemes: Audited accounts: Specified Persons 60
Pensions: Social security: Flat rate accrual amounts 127
Pensions: Social security: Flat rate accrual amounts: Northern Ireland 223
Pensions: Social security: Low earnings threshold 127
Pensions: Social security: Low earnings threshold: Northern Ireland 223
Pensions: Social security: Pensions: Additional units: Northern Ireland 223

Pensions: State pension: Social security: Northern Ireland 223
Pensions: Superannuation: 1972 Act: Admission to schedule 1 81
Pensions: Superannuation: Assembly Ombudsman for Northern Ireland & Northern Ireland Commissioner for Complaints: Northern Ireland
. . . . 213
Pensions: Superannuation: District councils: Northern Ireland 213
Pensions: Teachers: Schemes: Scotland 180
Pensions: Teachers: Superannuation: Scotland 177
Pensions: Teachers' pensions scheme: England & Wales 35, 88
Pensions: Teachers' pensions scheme: Northern Ireland 215
Pensions: Teachers' pensions: Amendments: Northern Ireland 203
People's Dispensary for Sick Animals: Charities 13
Permit schemes: Traffic management: England 54
Personal care & nursing care: Community care: Scotland 190
Personal injuries: Charges: Amounts: National Health Service: Scotland 177
Personal injuries: Civilians 80
Personal injuries: NHS charges: Amounts: England & Wales 76
Personal medical services: Agreements: National Health Service: England 74
Personal pension schemes: Automatic enrolment: Northern Ireland 212
Personal pension schemes: Contracting-out abolition 80
Personal pension schemes: Disclosure of information: Northern Ireland 212
Personal pension schemes: Transfer values: Northern Ireland 212
Pesticides: Advisory Committees on Pesticides: Abolition: Public bodies 81, 85
Peterborough: Electoral changes 69
Peterhead Port Authority: Harbour revision: Scotland 172
Petroleum: Licensing: Applications 81
Petroleum: Offshore petroleum: Licensing: Offshore safety directive 81
Petroleum: Oil & gas authority: Levy 81
Pets: Non-commercial movements: Animal health: Northern Ireland 201
Pharmaceutical services: National Health Service: England 75
Pilotage: Yarmouth: Harbour commissioners: Removal of pilotage functions 81
Planning & Compulsory Purchase Act 2004: Commencements: Wales 132
Planning (Wales) Act 2015: Commencements 132
Planning Act (Northern Ireland) 2011: Commencements: Northern Ireland 213
Planning Appeals Commission: Procedures: Appeals & making of reports: Decisions: Northern Ireland 214
Planning general: Northern Ireland 213
Planning see also Infrastructure planning
Planning see also Town & country planning
Planning: Acts: Explanatory notes: Wales 229
Planning: Acts: Wales 229
Planning: Agreements: Modification & discharge: Northern Ireland 214
Planning: Avian influenza: Northern Ireland 213
Planning: Compensation claims: Northern Ireland 213
Planning: Conservation areas: Consultation: Northern Ireland 213
Planning: Conservation areas: Demolition: Northern Ireland 213
Planning: Control of advertisements: Northern Ireland 213
Planning: Development management: Northern Ireland 213
Planning: Environmental impact assessment: Northern Ireland 213
Planning: Extractive industries: Waste management: Northern Ireland 214
Planning: Fees: Northern Ireland 213, 214
Planning: Fixed penalty: Northern Ireland 213
Planning: General development procedure: Northern Ireland 213
Planning: General development: Northern Ireland 213
Planning: General: Northern Ireland 213
Planning: Hazardous substances: England 61, 131
Planning: Hazardous substances: Northern Ireland 213, 214
Planning: Hazardous waste: Wales 132
Planning: Infrastructure planning: Development consent orders: Changes & revocation 61
Planning: Infrastructure planning: Dogger Bank Creyke Beck 61
Planning: Infrastructure planning: Hornsea One Offshore Wind Farm 61
Planning: Infrastructure planning: Miscellaneous prescribed provisions 61
Planning: Infrastructure planning: Northumberland County Council: A1 - South East Northumberland Link Road: Morpeth Northern Bypass 61
Planning: Infrastructure planning: Radioactive Waste Geological Disposal Facilities 61
Planning: Infrastructure planning: Rampion Wind Farm 62
Planning: Infrastructure planning: White Moss landfill: Hazardous waste facility & disposal 62
Planning: Inquiry procedure: Rules: Northern Ireland 214
Planning: Listed buildings: Northern Ireland 214
Planning: Local development plan: Northern Ireland 214
Planning: Simplified planning zones: Northern Ireland 213
Planning: Statement of community involvement: Northern Ireland 214
Planning: Town & country planning: Appeals by appointed persons: Determination: Prescribed classes: Scotland 192
Planning: Town & country planning: Appeals: Scotland 191
Planning: Town & country planning: England 132
Planning: Town & country planning: Environmental impact assessment 132
Planning: Town & country planning: General permitted development: England 132
Planning: Town & country planning: General permitted development: Scotland 192
Planning: Trees: Northern Ireland 214
Planning: Use classes: Northern Ireland 214
Plant & machinery: Environmentally beneficial: Capital allowances 24, 58

Plant health: England . . . 81
Plant health: Export certification: England . . . 81
Plant health: Fees: England . . . 81
Plant health: Forestry: Fees: England & Scotland . . . 81, 82
Plant health: Forestry: Miscellaneous revocations: England . . . 82
Plant health: Forestry: Wales . . . 82
Plant health: Import inspection fees: Scotland . . . 177
Plant health: Northern Ireland . . . 214
Plant health: Scotland . . . 177
Plant health: Wales . . . 82
Plant health: Wood & bark: Ash dieback: Northern Ireland . . . 214
Playing fields: Community involvement: Disposal decisions: Wales . . . 70
Plumstead sidings: Crossrail . . . 134
Pneumoconiosis etc.: Workers' compensation: Claims: Payments . . . 126
Pneumoconiosis etc.: Workers' compensation: Claims: Payments: Northern Ireland . . . 222
POC NI Oils Stages Rally: Road races: Northern Ireland . . . 220
Poisons & explosives precursors: Control . . . 50
Police & crime commissioners: Elections . . . 82
Police & crime commissioners: Elections: Functions: Transfer . . . 73
Police & crime commissioners: Elections: Returning officers: Area designation: England & Wales . . . 82
Police & Criminal Evidence Act 1984 . . . 91
Police & Criminal Evidence Act 1984: Application: Proceeds of Crime Act 2002 . . . 84
Police & Criminal Evidence Act 1984: Codes of practice: Revision code A . . . 82
Police & criminal evidence: Codes of practice: Northern Ireland . . . 214
Police (Northern Ireland) Act 2000: Detention: Designated places: Northern Ireland . . . 214
Police Act 1997: Criminal records: Disclosure: Northern Ireland . . . 202
Police Act 1997: Criminal records: Northern Ireland . . . 202
Police Act 1997: Remedial: Scotland . . . 165, 177, 178
Police cells: Legalised: Discontinuance: Scotland . . . 177
Police Federation: Amendments: England & Wales . . . 82
Police pension scheme: Scotland . . . 179
Police pensions: Consequential provisions: Scotland . . . 179
Police pensions: Northern Ireland . . . 215
Police Service of Northern Ireland: Northern Ireland . . . 214
Police Service: Attorney general: Human rights guidance: Northern Ireland: Northern Ireland . . . 209
Police Service: Pensions: Northern Ireland . . . 214
Police stations: Prescribed: Criminal law: Sexual Offences Act 2003 . . . 28
Police, England & Wales . . . 82
Police: Anti-social Behaviour, Crime & Policing Act 2014: Commencements . . . 26, 42, 54, 82, 83
Police: Appeals tribunals . . . 82
Police: Appeals: Conduct & unsatisfactory performance: Northern Ireland . . . 214
Police: Conduct . . . 82
Police: England & Wales . . . 82
Police: Immigration: Passenger, crew & service information . . . 56, 57, 82
Police: Independent Police Complaints Commission: Complaints & misconduct: England & Wales . . . 82
Police: Ministry of Defence: Conduct . . . 82
Police: Pensions . . . 88
Police: Pensions: Injury benefit: England & Wales . . . 81, 82
Police: Pensions: Scotland . . . 177
Police: Prescribed police stations: Sexual Offences Act 2003: Northern Ireland . . . 202
Police: Promotion: England & Wales . . . 82
Police: Protection of Freedoms Act 2012: Destruction, retention & use of biometric data . . . 82
Police: Protection of Freedoms Act 2012: Powers of entry: Code of practice . . . 82, 91
Police: Serious Organised Crime & Police Act 2005: Commencements . . . 82
Police: Special constables . . . 83
Policing & Crime Act 2009: Commencements . . . 84
Political parties: European parliamentary elections: Miscellaneous provisions: United Kingdom & Gibraltar . . . 73, 83, 90
Pollution Prevention & Control Act 1999: Commencements: Scotland . . . 170
Pollution: Nitrate pollution: Prevention: Wales . . . 9, 136
Pollution: Nitrate: Agriculture: Water: Prevention . . . 8, 135
Pollution: Nitrates Action Programme: Northern Ireland . . . 206
Pollution: Oil Pollution Preparedness, Response and Co-operation Convention: Merchant shipping . . . 71
Pollution: Prevention & control: Designation of directives: England & Wales . . . 43
Pollution: Prevention & control: Fees . . . 41
Poole Harbour: Works revision . . . 50
Poole: Electoral changes . . . 69
Port of Oban: Port security: Merchant shipping . . . 72
Port security: Merchant shipping: Port of Oban . . . 72
Port Talbot generating station: Infrastructure planning . . . 62
Portadown: Waiting restrictions: Northern Ireland . . . 221
Portballintrae: Parking & waiting restrictions: Northern Ireland . . . 219
Post-16 Education (Scotland) Act 2013: Commencements: Scotland . . . 169
Post-16 Education (Scotland) Act 2013: Scotland . . . 169
Potatoes: Seed potatoes: Fees: Scotland . . . 188
Potatoes: Seed potatoes: Scotland . . . 188
Power plants: Knottingley . . . 61
Powers of attorney: Enduring & lasting: Public Guardian: England & Wales . . . 72
Powysland: Internal Drainage District . . . 64

Preesall Underground Storage Facility . . . 62
Prescriptions: Free: National Health Service: Scotland . . . 176
Pressure equipment . . . 51
Prevention & suppression of terrorism: Authority to carry scheme: Civil Penalties . . . 56, 83
Prevention & suppression of terrorism: Counter-Terrorism & Security Act 2015: Commencements . . . 83, 133
Prevention & suppression of terrorism: Counter-Terrorism & Security Act 2015: Risk of being drawn into terrorism . . . 83
Prevention & suppression of terrorism: Counter-Terrorism Act 2015: Authority to carry scheme . . . 56, 83
Prevention & suppression of terrorism: Counter-Terrorism Act 2015: Officers functions: Codes of practice . . . 83
Prevention & suppression of terrorism: Exclusion orders: Temporary: Notices . . . 83
Prevention & suppression of terrorism: Terrorism Act 2000: Examining & review Officers: Codes of practice . . . 83
Prevention & suppression of terrorism: Terrorism Act 2000: Proscribed organisations . . . 83
Prevention & suppression of terrorism: Terrorist Asset-Freezing Act 2010: Isle of Man: Revocation . . . 83
Primary care: Terms of service: Electronic prescription service: National Health Service . . . 74
Printing equipment & materials: Specialist: Offences: Acts . . . 6
Printing equipment & materials: Specialist: Offences: Acts: Explanatory notes . . . 7
Prisoners: Control of release: Acts: Explanatory notes: Scotland . . . 163
Prisoners: Control of release: Acts: Scotland . . . 162
Prisoners: Control of release: Commencements: Scotland . . . 177
Prisons: Criminal Justice and Courts Act 2015: Commencements . . . 24, 27, 28, 30, 64, 67, 70, 83, 122, 130, 137
Prisons: Inspection & monitoring: Public services reform: Scotland . . . 180
Prisons: Police cells: Legalised: Discontinuance: Scotland . . . 177
Prisons: Prisoners: Control of release: Commencements: Scotland . . . 177
Prisons: Prisons (Property) Act 2013: Commencements . . . 83
Prisons: Young offender institutions . . . 83, 137
Privacy: Electronic communications: EC directive . . . 38
Private Rented Housing (Scotland) Act 2011: Commencements: Scotland . . . 173
Private rented housing panel: Landlord applications: Scotland . . . 173
Private rented housing panel: Tenant & third party: Applications: Scotland . . . 173
Private rented housing: Information, periods & fees: Registration & licensing . . . 55
Private rented housing: Training requirements . . . 55
Private water supplies: Northern Ireland . . . 224
Probation Board: Attorney general: Human rights guidance: Northern Ireland: Northern Ireland . . . 209
Proceeds of Crime Act 2002: Amendment: Scotland . . . 177
Proceeds of Crime Act 2002: Appeals . . . 84
Proceeds of Crime Act 2002: Cash searches: Code of Practice . . . 84
Proceeds of Crime Act 2002: Cash searches: Constables: Code of practice : Scotland . . . 177
Proceeds of Crime Act 2002: Code of practice: Investigations: England & Wales . . . 84
Proceeds of Crime Act 2002: Code of practice: Investigations: Prosecutors power: England & Wales . . . 84
Proceeds of Crime Act 2002: Enforcement: United Kingdom . . . 84
Proceeds of Crime Act 2002: External investigations . . . 84
Proceeds of Crime Act 2002: External investigations: England & Wales . . . 84, 85
Proceeds of Crime Act 2002: External investigations: Northern Ireland . . . 84, 85
Proceeds of Crime Act 2002: External investigations: Scotland . . . 84
Proceeds of Crime Act 2002: External requests & orders . . . 84
Proceeds of Crime Act 2002: Financial investigators: References: England & Wales . . . 84
Proceeds of Crime Act 2002: Investigations . . . 84
Proceeds of Crime Act 2002: Police & Criminal Evidence Act 1984: Application . . . 84
Proceeds of Crime Act 2002: Property: Search, seizure & detention: Code of practice: England & Wales . . . 84
Proceeds of Crime Act 2002: Restraint orders: Legal aid exception: England & Wales . . . 67, 85
Proceeds of crime: Administrative forfeiture of cash: Forfeiture notices: England & Wales . . . 84
Proceeds of crime: Crime & Courts Act 2013 . . . 73, 77, 84
Proceeds of crime: Crime & Courts Act 2013: Commencements . . . 26, 66, 84
Proceeds of crime: Crime & Courts Act 2013: Northern Ireland . . . 77
Proceeds of Crime: Forfeiture notices: England & Wales . . . 84
Proceeds of crime: Policing & Crime Act 2009: Commencements . . . 84
Proceeds of crime: Proceeds of Crime Act 2002: Enforcement: United Kingdom . . . 84
Proceeds of crime: Proceeds of Crime Act 2002: External investigations . . . 84
Proceeds of crime: Proceeds of Crime Act 2002: External investigations: England & Wales . . . 84, 85
Proceeds of crime: Proceeds of Crime Act 2002: External investigations: Northern Ireland . . . 84, 85
Proceeds of crime: Proceeds of Crime Act 2002: External requests & orders . . . 84
Proceeds of crime: Serious Crime Act 2015: Commencements . . . 27, 84, 122
Procurement Reform (Scotland) Act 2014: Commencements: Scotland . . . 179
Products of animal origin: Meats: Country of origin: England . . . 48
Professional qualifications: Recognition: European Union . . . 85
Professional Standards Authority for Health & Social Care: Fees . . . 51
Progress power: Gas fired power station . . . 62
Prohibition of U-turn: A2, Belfast Road: Northern Ireland . . . 220
Properties: Domestic & private rented: Energy efficiency: Energy conservation . . . 40
Properties: Private rented: Energy efficiency: Energy conservation . . . 40
Property factors: Registration: Scotland . . . 178
Prosecution of Offences Act 1985: Criminal courts charge . . . 27
Protection of Freedoms Act 2012: Commencements . . . 29, 49
Protection of Freedoms Act 2012: Destruction, retention & use of biometric data . . . 82
Protection of Freedoms Act 2012: Powers of entry: Code of practice . . . 82, 91
Protection of vulnerable adults: Police: Police Act 1997 & Protection of Vulnerable Groups (Scotland) Act 2007: Remedial: Scotland . . 165, 177, 178
Protection of Vulnerable Groups (Scotland) Act 2007: Remedial: Scotland . . . 165, 177, 178
Protection of Vulnerable Groups (Scotland) Act 2007: Scheme membership & disclosure requests: Fees: Scotland . . . 165, 178

Provisions: Financial Services & Markets Act 2000 46
Proxy purchasing: Tobacco: Nicotine products: Penalty notice: Wales 86
Public authorities: Fair employment: Specification: Northern Ireland 206
Public authorities: Reform: 2009 Act: Commencements: Northern Ireland 214
Public Bodies (Joint Working) (Scotland) Act 2014: Commencements: Scotland 178, 190
Public Bodies (Joint Working) (Scotland) Act 2014: Modifications: Scotland 179, 190
Public bodies: Advisory Committees on Pesticides: Abolition 81, 85
Public bodies: Home Grown Timber Advisory Committee 49, 85
Public Bodies: Joint working: Integration Joint Board: Establishment: Scotland 178, 190
Public Bodies: Joint working: Integration joint monitoring committees: Scotland 178, 190
Public bodies: Library Advisory Council for England: Abolition 85
Public Bodies: Public health: Joint working: Integration Joint Board: Establishment: Scotland 178, 190
Public Bodies: Social care: Joint working: Integration Joint Board: Establishment: Scotland 178, 190
Public contracts: Public procurement 87
Public finance & accountability: Budget (Scotland) Act 2014: Amendments: Scotland 178
Public finance and accountability: Scotland Act 1998: Variation: Borrowing power 22, 31, 85
Public Guardian: Fees: Scotland 163
Public Guardian: Powers of attorney: Enduring & lasting: England & Wales 72
Public health: Animal health: By-products: Enforcement: England 9, 85
Public health: Care providers & information: England 73, 85
Public health: Care Quality Commission: Membership 73, 85, 123
Public health: Certification of Death (Scotland) Act 2011: Commencements: Scotland 178
Public health: Certification of Death (Scotland) Act 2011: Cremation authorisation: Death outwith Scotland: Scotland 178
Public health: Certification of Death (Scotland) Act 2011: Post-Mortem examinations: Death outwith United Kingdom: Scotland 178
Public health: Certification of Death (Scotland) Act 2011: Provisions: Scotland 178
Public health: Contamination of food 86
Public health: Health & Social Care 14, 74, 75, 86, 123
Public health: Health & Social Care Act 2008: Regulated activities 73, 85, 123
Public Health: Health & Social Care Act 2012: Consistent identifier: England 73, 85, 123
Public Health: Health & Social Care Act 2012: Continuity of information: England 74, 85, 123
Public Health: Health & Social Care (Safety and Quality) Act 2015: Commencements: England 74, 86, 123
Public health: HIV testing kits & services: Revocation: Northern Ireland 215
Public health: Joint working: Integration joint board establishment: Scotland 178, 190
Public health: Local authorities: Public health functions: Local healthwatch representatives & Public health & wellbeing boards: Entry to
premises 74, 86, 123
Public health: Motor fuel: Composition & content 85
Public health: Nicotine inhaling products: Age of sale: Proxy purchasing 86
Public health: Noise: Control: Construction & open sites: Code of practice 85
Public health: Proxy purchasing: Tobacco: Nicotine products: Penalty notice: Wales 86
Public health: Public Bodies (Joint Working) (Scotland) Act 2014: Commencements: Scotland 178, 190
Public health: Public Bodies (Joint Working) (Scotland) Act 2014: Modifications: Scotland 179, 190
Public health: Public Bodies: Joint working: Integration joint boards & integration joint monitoring: Committees: Scotland 178, 190
Public health: Public Bodies: Joint working: Integration joint monitoring committees: Scotland 178, 190
Public health: Smoke-free premises: Wales 86
Public health: Smoke-free: Exemptions & vehicles: England 86
Public health: Smoke-free: Vehicle operators: Penalty notices: England 86
Public health: Tobacco & nicotine products: Proxy purchasing: Penalties 86
Public health: Tobacco products: Standardised packaging 85
Public health: Vaccine damage payments: Specified disease 85
Public interest disclosure: Prescribed persons 131
Public Lending Right Scheme 1982: Variation: Commencements 67
Public passenger transport: Local services: Registration: Scotland 179
Public passenger transport: Office of Rail Regulation: Change of name 53, 86
Public passenger transport: Public service vehicles: Drivers, inspectors, conductors & passengers: Conduct: England & Wales 86
Public passenger transport: Service agreements & permits: Northern Ireland 215
Public passenger transport: Transport 2011 Act: Commencements: Northern Ireland 215
Public Processions: Electronic communication of notices 86
Public procurement: Procurement Reform (Scotland) Act 2014: Commencements: Scotland 179
Public procurement: Public contracts 87
Public procurement: Public contracts: Scotland 179
Public record office: Fees 87
Public Records (Scotland) Act 2011: Authorities: Scotland 179
Public records: Public record office: Fees 87
Public records: Public Records (Scotland) Act 2011: Authorities: Scotland 179
Public sector information: Re-use 87
Public service pension schemes: Funded: Reduction of cash equivalents 79
Public service pension schemes: Governance & administration: Code of practice: Appointed day: Northern Ireland 212
Public Service Pensions Act 2013: Commencements 87
Public service pensions Act 2013: Judicial offices 87
Public service pensions: Armed forces pension 87
Public service pensions: Armed Forces: Pension schemes & early departure schemes 87
Public service pensions: Civil servants & others 87
Public service pensions: Civil servants & others: Northern Ireland 215
Public service pensions: Commencements: Northern Ireland 215
Public service pensions: Employer cost cap: Northern Ireland 213
Public service pensions: Firefighters: Pension scheme: England 87
Public service pensions: Firefighters: Pension scheme: Governance: England 87
Public service pensions: Firefighters: Pension scheme: Northern Ireland 215

Public service pensions: Firefighters: Pension scheme: Scotland 179
Public service pensions: Firefighters: Pension scheme: Transitional provisions: Northern Ireland 215
Public service pensions: Firefighters: Pension scheme: Wales 88
Public service pensions: Judicial offices: Northern Ireland 215
Public service pensions: Judicial pensions 87
Public service pensions: Judicial pensions: Northern Ireland 215
Public service pensions: Local government pension scheme 87
Public service pensions: Local government pension scheme: Governance: Scotland 179
Public service pensions: Local government pension scheme: Scotland 179
Public service pensions: National Health Service: Pension scheme: England & Wales 76, 87, 88
Public service pensions: National Health Service: Pension scheme: Scotland 179
Public service pensions: Pensions schemes: Reduction of cash equivalents: Northern Ireland 211
Public service pensions: Police 88
Public service pensions: Police pension scheme: Scotland 179
Public service pensions: Police pensions: Consequential provisions: Scotland 179
Public service pensions: Police pensions: Northern Ireland 215
Public service pensions: Revaluation: England & Wales 88
Public service pensions: Teachers: Pensions scheme: England & Wales 35, 88
Public service pensions: Teachers: Pensions scheme: Northern Ireland 215
Public service pensions: Teachers: Pension schemes: Scotland 180
Public service vehicles: Drivers, inspectors, conductors & passengers: Conduct: England & Wales 86
Public service vehicles: Northern Ireland 220
Public Service: Defined benefits schemes: Unfunded: Transfers: Northern Ireland 213
Public service: Pension schemes: Transfers 81
Public service: Pensions: Pension scheme: Provisions: England & Wales 76, 88
Public Services Reform (Scotland) Act 2010: Part 2 extension: Scotland 180
Public services reform: Prisons: Inspection & monitoring: Scotland 180
Purbeck: Electoral changes 69
Pyrotechnics articles: Safety 23, 51

Q

Qualifications Wales Act 2015: Commencements 37
Qualifications: Acts: Explanatory notes: Wales 229
Qualifications: Acts: Wales 229
Qualifications: European recognition 45
Qualifications: European recognition & knowledge of language 135
Queen Margaret University, Edinburgh: Order of Council: Scotland 169

R

Radio: 823-832 MHz & 1785-1805 MHz frequency bands: Management 38
Radio: Community radio 11
Radioactive Waste Geological Disposal Facilities: Infrastructure planning 61
RAF Brize Norton: Byelaws 30
Rail vehicles: Accessibility: B2007 Vehicles: Exemptions 32, 133
Rail vehicles: Accessibility: Non-interoperable rail system: London Underground Northern Line 95TS Vehicles 32, 133
Rail: Office of Rail Regulation: Change of name 53, 86
Railways: Channel Tunnel: International arrangements 13
Railways: Crossrail: Services: Exemption 134
Railways: Ecclesbourne Valley Railway: England 134
Railways: Guided transport systems: Health & safety 51
Railways: High speed rail: HS2: Preparation: Acts: Explanatory notes 6
Railways: Infrastructure: Access & management 133
Railways: Interoperability: Transport 88, 133
Railways: Passengers: Rights & obligations: Exemptions 133
Rampion Wind Farm 62
Rates: Making & levying: Different rates: Northern Ireland 216
Rates: Owners allowances: Northern Ireland 216
Rates: Regional rates: Northern Ireland 216
Rates: Rural areas: Automatic telling machines: Exemptions: Northern Ireland 215, 216
Rates: Small business hereditament relief: Northern Ireland 216
Rates: Social sector value: Northern Ireland 216
Rates: Social security: Amendments: Northern Ireland 209, 216, 223
Rates: Social security: Benefits: Up-rating: Northern Ireland 203, 209, 216, 222, 223, 224
Rates: Temporary rebate: Northern Ireland 216
Rates: Transitional relief: Northern Ireland 216
Rates: Valuation for rating: Decapitalisation rate: Northern Ireland 216
Rates: Valuation: Telecommunications, natural gas & water: Northern Ireland 216
Rathdown Walk, Lisburn: Abandonment: Northern Ireland 217
Rating & valuation: Community Empowerment (Scotland) Act 2015: Commencements: Scotland 180
Rating & valuation: Council tax & non-domestic rating: Demand notices: England 88
Rating & valuation: Council tax: Exceptions to higher amounts: Wales 89
Rating & valuation: Council tax: Non-domestic rating: Powers of entry Safeguards: England 68, 88
Rating & valuation: Non-domestic rates: Levying: Scotland 180
Rating & valuation: Non-domestic rates: Scotland 180
Rating & valuation: Non-domestic rates: Utilities: Valuation: Scotland 180
Rating & valuation: Non-domestic rating multipliers: England 88

Rating & valuation: Non-domestic rating: Contributions: Wales . . . 89
Rating & valuation: Non-domestic rating: Designated area: England . . . 88
Rating & valuation: Non-domestic rating: Levy & safety net: England . . . 88, 89
Rating & valuation: Non-domestic rating: Northern line extension: England . . . 89
Rating & valuation: Non-domestic rating: Shale oil & gas . . . 89
Rating & valuation: Non-domestic rating: Small business rate relief: England . . . 89
Rating & valuation: Non-domestic rating: Small business rate relief: Wales . . . 89
Rating & valuation: Non-domestic rating: Wales . . . 89
Rating & valuation: Non-domestic rating: Waterways: Wales . . . 89
Rating & valuation: Valuation timetable: Scotland . . . 180
Rating and valuation: Non-domestic rating: Alteration of lists & appeals: England . . . 88
Rating: Non-domestic: Demand notes: Wales . . . 89
Recycling centres: Household waste: Prohibition of charges: Local government . . . 68
Recycling facilities: Ships: Northern Ireland . . . 206
Reduction schemes: Prescribed requirements: England . . . 26
Redundancy & premature retirement: Compensation: Teachers . . . 35
Redundancy payments: Local government: Continuity of employment . . . 131
Referral & investigation: Provisions . . . 19, 57, 71
Registers & records: Land registers: Fees: Scotland . . . 180
Registers & records: Registers of Scotland: Scotland . . . 180
Registers: Land registers: Fees: Scotland . . . 180
Registration of births, deaths & marriages (Scotland) Act 1965: Body disposal: Prohibition & authorisation: Scotland . . . 180
Registration of births, deaths, marriages, etc.: Certification of Death (Scotland) Act 2011: Application for review: Scotland . . . 180
Registration of births, deaths, marriages, etc.: Forms: Prescription: Scotland . . . 180
Registration of births, deaths, marriages, etc.: Gender recognition: Marriage & civil partnership . . . 89
Registration of births, deaths, marriages, etc.: Civil partnerships: Fees . . . 89
Registration of births, deaths, marriages, etc.: Marriages: England & Wales . . . 89
Registration of births, deaths, marriages, etc.: Marriages: Registration: Authorised persons . . . 19, 89
Regulation of investigatory powers: Communications data . . . 63
Regulation of investigatory powers: Covert human intelligence sources . . . 63
Regulation of investigatory powers: Covert human intelligence sources: Code of practice: Scotland . . . 173
Regulation of investigatory powers: Covert surveillance & property interference: Code of practice: Scotland . . . 173
Regulation of investigatory powers: Directed surveillance . . . 63
Regulation of investigatory powers: Modification: Authorisation provisions: Legal consultations: Scotland . . . 173
Regulatory Reform (Scotland) Act 2014: Commencements . . . 170, 180
Regulatory Reform (Scotland) Act 2014: Consequential modifications . . . 21, 31, 38, 41, 67
Regulatory reform: Historic Environment Scotland Act 2014: Ancillary provision: Scotland . . . 164, 180
Regulatory reform: Legislative reform: Community governance reviews . . . 69, 90
Regulatory reform: Legislative reform: Radio licences renewal . . . 11, 89
Regulatory reform: Small Business, Enterprise and Employment Act 2015: Commencements . . . 14, 20, 62, 89, 131
Rehabilitation courses: Relevant drink offences . . . 92
Rehabilitation of Offenders Act 1974: Exceptions: England & Wales . . . 90
Rehabilitation of Offenders Act 1974: Exclusions & exceptions: Amendments: Scotland . . . 180
Rehabilitation of offenders: Legal Aid, Sentencing & Punishment of Offenders Act 2012: Commencements . . . 27
Religious observances: Local government: Acts . . . 5
Religious observances: Local government: Acts: Explanatory notes . . . 7
Remand: Youth detention accommodation: Recovery of costs . . . 27
Renewable energy: Dogger Bank Creyke Beck . . . 61
Renewable energy: Dogger Bank Teeside A & B Offshore Wind Farm . . . 61
Renewable energy: Galloper Wind Farm . . . 61
Renewable energy: Hornsea One Offshore Wind Farm . . . 61
Renewable energy: Rampion Wind Farm . . . 62
Renewable heat incentive schemes: Northern Ireland . . . 205
Renewable heat incentives . . . 40
Renewable heat incentives: Domestic . . . 39
Renewable heat incentives: Schemes . . . 40
Renewable obligations closure: Electricity . . . 38
Renewables obligation . . . 38
Renewables obligation: Electricity: Closure: Northern Ireland . . . 203
Renewables obligation: Electricity: Northern Ireland . . . 203
Renewables obligation: Scotland . . . 169
Renewables obligation: Transport: Fuels . . . 40, 134
Rent officers: Housing benefit & universal credit functions: Local housing allowance amendments . . . 54
Rents: Registered rents: Increases: Northern Ireland . . . 210
Reporting restrictions: Criminal procedure: Rules: Act of Adjournal: Scotland . . . 172, 174, 189
Representation of the people: Ballot papers . . . 90
Representation of the people: Combination of polls: England & Wales . . . 90
Representation of the people: Elections . . . 77, 90
Representation of the people: Elections: Judges rota: Rules . . . 90, 122
Representation of the people: Elections: Policy development grants scheme . . . 90
Representation of the people: Electoral Registration & Administration Act 2013: Transitional provisions . . . 90
Representation of the people: England & Wales . . . 90
Representation of the people: European Parliamentary elections . . . 90
Representation of the people: European parliamentary elections: Miscellaneous provisions: United Kingdom & Gibraltar . . . 73, 83, 90
Representation of the people: European Parliamentary elections: Northern Irish forms . . . 91
Representation of the people: Local elections: Parishes & communities: England & Wales . . . 90
Representation of the people: Local elections: Principal areas: England & Wales . . . 90
Representation of the people: Parliamentary elections: Northern Ireland forms . . . 91

Representation of the people: Parliamentary elections: Returning officer's charges 90
Representation of the people: Parliamentary elections: Returning officers' charges: Northern Ireland. 91
Representation of the people: Parliamentary elections: Welsh forms 91
Representation of the people: Scotland 91
Representation of the people: Scottish Independence Referendum: Chief counting officer & counting officer charges & expenses: Scotland
. . . . 181
Representation of the people: Scottish Parliament: Elections: Scotland 166, 181
Representation of the people: Scottish Parliament: Regional returning officers 22, 32, 90
Representation of the people: Scottish Parliament: Returning officers charges 22, 32, 90
Reserve Forces members: Northern Ireland 223
Reserve forces: Call-out & recall: Financial assistance 30
Reserve Forces: Compensation schemes 79
Reserve Forces: Pensions: Compensation schemes 79
Reservoirs (Scotland) Act 2011: Commencements: Scotland 171, 193
Reservoirs (Scotland) Act 2011: National security: Disclosure information: Restrictions 21, 31, 136
Reservoirs: Acts: Explanatory notes: Northern Ireland 199
Reservoirs: Acts: Northern Ireland 199
Reservoirs: Engineers: Panels: Scotland 171, 193
Reservoirs: Scotland: Scotland 171, 193
Restorative justice: Youth Justice Agency: Attorney general: Human rights guidance: Northern Ireland 209
Restraint orders: Legal aid exception: England & Wales 67, 85
Retirement: Premature & redundancy: Compensation: Teachers 35
Returning officers' charges: Parliamentary elections 90
Returning officers' charges: Parliamentary elections: Northern Ireland 91
Revenue & customs: Police & Criminal Evidence Act 1984 91
Revenue & customs: Taxes: Payment by internet 91
Revenue Scotland & Tax Powers Act: Interest & unpaid tax: Scotland 191
Revenue Scotland & Tax Powers Act: Record keeping: Scotland. 191
Revenue Scotland & Tax Powers Act: Reimbursement arrangements: Scotland 191
Revenue Scotland & Tax Powers Act: Tax postponement: Scotland 191
Revenue Scotland & tax powers: Acts: Explanatory notes: Scotland 163
Revenue traders: Accounts & records 44
Rights in performances: Copyright & performances: Application to other countries 23, 91
Rights of the subject: Protection of Freedoms Act 2012: Powers of entry: Code of practice 82, 91
River Esk: Fish: Keeping & introduction 91
River Tweed 22, 31, 91
River Tweed: Scotland 166, 168, 181
River: Fish: Keeping or release: Prohibition: Wales 92, 121
Road & railway transport: Level crossing: Cullybackey South: Northern Ireland 216
Road Safety Act 2006: Commencements 92
Road Safety Act 2006: Consequential amendments 93
Road Traffic Offenders Act 1988: Motor vehicles: Driving licences 93
Road Traffic Offenders Act 1988: Traffic regulation: Motor vehicles: Driving licences 93
Road traffic & vehicles: Alfred Street/Upper Arthur Street, Belfast: Traffic control: Northern Ireland 217
Road traffic & vehicles: Antrim: Parking & waiting restrictions: Northern Ireland 218
Road traffic & vehicles: Armoy Motorcycle Race: Road races: Northern Ireland 220
Road traffic & vehicles: Ballymoney: Parking places on roads & waiting restrictions: Northern Ireland 219
Road traffic & vehicles: Banbridge: Parking & waiting restrictions: Northern Ireland 218
Road traffic & vehicles: Belfast city centre: Parking & waiting restrictions: Northern Ireland 219
Road traffic & vehicles: Belfast: Parking & waiting restrictions: Northern Ireland 219
Road traffic & vehicles: Belfast: Parking & waiting restrictions: Northern Ireland 218, 219
Road traffic & vehicles: Belfast: Traffic control: Northern Ireland 217
Road traffic & vehicles: Bus lanes: Falls Road, Belfast: Northern Ireland 217
Road traffic & vehicles: Bus lanes: Upper Newtownards Road, Belfast: Northern Ireland 217
Road traffic & vehicles: Bushwhacker Rally: Road races: Northern Ireland 220
Road traffic & vehicles: Cairncastle Hill climb: Road races: Northern Ireland 220
Road traffic & vehicles: Castlederg: Waiting restrictions: Northern Ireland 221
Road traffic & vehicles: Cathedral Quarter, Belfast: Parking & waiting restrictions: Northern Ireland 219
Road traffic & vehicles: Circuit of Ireland Rally: Road races: Northern Ireland 220
Road traffic & vehicles: Clonalig: A37: Concession Road: Northern Ireland 217
Road traffic & vehicles: Cookstown 100: Road races: Northern Ireland 220
Road traffic & vehicles: Craigantlet Hill Climb: Road races: Northern Ireland 220
Road traffic & vehicles: Croft Hill Climb: Road races: Northern Ireland 220
Road traffic & vehicles: Cycle routes: Amendments: Northern Ireland 217
Road traffic & vehicles: Disabled persons: Motor vehicles: Badges: Northern Ireland 217
Road traffic & vehicles: Drumhorc Hill Climb: Road races: Northern Ireland 220
Road traffic & vehicles: Dungannon: Parking & waiting restrictions: Northern Ireland 219
Road traffic & vehicles: Fivemiletown: Parking & waiting restrictions: Northern Ireland 219
Road traffic & vehicles: Fixed penalty: Offences: Northern Ireland 221
Road traffic & vehicles: Footways: Waiting: Prohibitions: Northern Ireland 218
Road traffic & vehicles: Garron Point Hill climb: Road races: Northern Ireland 220
Road traffic & vehicles: Goods vehicles: Testing: Northern Ireland 218
Road traffic & vehicles: Lisburn City: Parking places, loading bays & waiting restrictions: Northern Ireland 219
Road traffic & vehicles: Lisburn: Traffic control: Northern Ireland 217
Road traffic & vehicles: Lisburn: Waiting restrictions: Northern Ireland 221
Road traffic & vehicles: Loading bays on roads: Northern Ireland 218
Road traffic & vehicles: Londonderry: Parking & waiting restrictions: Northern Ireland 219
Road traffic & vehicles: Motor vehicles: Driving instruction: Northern Ireland 218

Road traffic & vehicles: Motor vehicles: Driving instruction: Trainee licences: Northern Ireland	218
Road traffic & vehicles: Motor vehicles: Driving licences: Amendments: Northern Ireland	218
Road traffic & vehicles: Motor vehicles: Testing: Northern Ireland	218
Road traffic & vehicles: Newry: Parking & waiting restrictions: Northern Ireland	219
Road traffic & vehicles: Newry: Parking places on roads & waiting restrictions: Northern Ireland	219
Road traffic & vehicles: Newtownabbey: Parking & waiting restrictions: Northern Ireland	219
Road traffic & vehicles: North West 200: Road races: Northern Ireland	220
Road traffic & vehicles: Northern Ireland	217
Road traffic & vehicles: Public service vehicles: Northern Ireland	220
Road traffic & vehicles: Road vehicles: Lighting: Northern Ireland	221
Road traffic & vehicles: Roads: Speed limits: Northern Ireland	221
Road traffic & vehicles: Seat belts: Wearing: Children in front seats: Northern Ireland	218
Road traffic & vehicles: Seat belts: Wearing: Northern Ireland	218
Road traffic & vehicles: Taxi operators: Licencing: Northern Ireland	221
Road traffic & vehicles: Taxis Act 2008: Commencements: Northern Ireland	221
Road traffic & vehicles: Taxis: Antrim: Northern Ireland	221
Road traffic & vehicles: Taxis: Lisburn: Northern Ireland	221
Road traffic & vehicles: Taxis: Licencing: Northern Ireland	221
Road traffic & vehicles: Taxis: Taximeters, devices & maximum fares: Northern Ireland	221
Road traffic, Wales: Traffic regulation	118
Road traffic: A85: Scotland	182
Road traffic: Agricultural & forestry tractors: Emission of gaseous & particulate pollutahts	40, 92
Road traffic: Civil enforcement: Parking contraventions: England	109
Road traffic: Crime & Courts Act 2013	92
Road traffic: Cycle racing: Highways: Wales	110
Road traffic: Disabled persons: Motor vehicles: Badges: Scotland	181
Road traffic: Disabled Persons' Parking Badges (Scotland) Act 2014: Commencements: Scotland	181
Road traffic: Drug driving: Specified limits	109
Road traffic: Electrically assisted pedal cycles	92
Road traffic: Highways: Invalid carriages: Use: Wales	110
Road traffic: Highways: Use of invalid carriages	109, 110
Road traffic: M275 & M27: Speed limits	109
Road traffic: M4: Junction 23A Magor & junction 29 Castleton: Speed limits: Wales	110
Road traffic: M56	109
Road traffic: M80: Castlecary interchange: Scotland	181
Road traffic: Motor cars: Driving instruction	92
Road traffic: Motor vehicles: Driving licences	92
Road traffic: Motor vehicles: Insurance requirements	92
Road traffic: Motor vehicles: Naval, military & air force: Speed limits: Variation	109
Road traffic: Motor vehicles: Seat belts: Wearing	92
Road traffic: Motor vehicles: Seat belts: Wearing: Children	92
Road traffic: Motorways traffic: England & Wales	110
Road traffic: Motorways: M1: Junction 39 to 42	109
Road traffic: Passenger & goods vehicles: Recording equipment: Downloading of data	92
Road traffic: Pedal cycles: Construction & use	92
Road traffic: Rehabilitation courses: Relevant drink offences	92
Road traffic: Road Safety Act 2006: Commencements	92
Road traffic: Road Safety Act 2006: Consequential amendments	93
Road traffic: Road vehicles: Construction & use	93
Road traffic: Road vehicles: Registration & licensing	93
Road traffic: Road vehicles: Registration marks: Retention & sale	92
Road traffic: Scotland	182, 183, 184, 185, 186
Road traffic: Special roads	93
Road traffic: Special roads: England	109
Road traffic: Speed limits	93, 110, 118
Road traffic: Speed limits: Scotland	181, 182
Road traffic: Traffic regulation	53, 92, 93, 94, 95, 96, 97, 98, 99, 100, 101, 102, 103, 104, 105, 106, 107, 108, 109, 110, 111, 112, 113, 114, 115, 116, 117, 118, 119, 120
Road traffic: Traffic regulation: Scotland	181, 182, 183, 184, 185, 186, 187
Road traffic: Traffic regulation: Vehicle drivers: Professional competence: Certificates: Amendments	93
Road traffic: Traffic regulation: Wales	120
Road vehicles: Construction & use	93
Road vehicles: Registration & licensing	93
Road vehicles: Registration marks: Retention & sale	92
Roads & bridges: Forth Road Bridge Act 2013: Commencements: Scotland	181
Roads & bridges: M80: Castlecary interchange: Scotland	181
Roads & bridges: Scotland	181, 182
Roads & bridges: Scottish Road Works Register: Prescribed fees: Scotland	181
Roads: A29/U7004 Moy Road & Drumcairn Road: Abandonment : Northern Ireland	216
Roads: Ballinderry, Glenavy Roads, Lisburn: Stopping-up: Northern Ireland	217
Roads: Carnbane Road: Abandonment : Northern Ireland	217
Roads: Clifton Street/Carrick Hill, Belfast: Footway: Abandonment : Northern Ireland	217
Roads: Glebe Way, Moira: Abandonment : Northern Ireland	217
Roads: Parking places & waiting restrictions: Alfred Street/Upper Arthur Street, Belfast: Northern Ireland	219
Roads: Parking places: Coaches: Northern Ireland	219
Roads: Parking places: Disabled persons' vehicles: Northern Ireland	219, 220
Roads: Parkside Gardens, Belfast: Abandonment: Northern Ireland	217
Roads: Rathdown Walk, Lisburn: Abandonment: Northern Ireland	217

Roads: Speed limit: Northern Ireland . . . 221
Roads: U125 Old Grand Jury Road, Saintfield: Abandonment : Northern Ireland . . . 217
Roads: U6076 Cloghanramer Road, Newry: Abandonment : Northern Ireland . . . 217
Roads: White Lodge Court, Greenisland: Abandonment: Northern Ireland . . . 217
Rochford: Electoral changes . . . 69
Rotherham, Borough: Scheme of elections . . . 67
Rugby: Electoral changes . . . 69
Rules of the air: Civil aviation . . . 19
Rural development contracts: Land managers options: Scotland . . . 163
Rural development programme: Northern Ireland . . . 201
Rural payments: Appeals: Scotland . . . 163
Rural primary schools: Designations: England . . . 33
Russia, Crimea & Sevastopol: Sanctions . . . 28
Russia: Sanctions . . . 78

S

Safeguarding Boards: Functions & procedures: Wales . . . 125
Safeguarding Boards: Wales . . . 125
Safety: Merchant shipping . . . 72
Salaries: Assembly Ombudsman & Commissioner for Complaints: Northern Ireland . . . 221
Salmon & freshwater fisheries: Fish: Keeping or release: Prohibition: Wales . . . 92, 121
Salmon & migratory trout: Fishing & landing: Prohibition: England . . . 121
Same sex couples: Marriage: Acts . . . 4
Sanctions: Iraq . . . 78
Scheduled monuments & listed buildings: Scotland . . . 164, 191, 192
School & early years finance: England . . . 34
School governance: England . . . 34
School governance: Federations: Education: England . . . 34
School lunches: Scotland . . . 169
School teachers: Pay & conditions: England & Wales . . . 35
Schools: Eastern High School: Session times: Changes: Wales . . . 35
Schools: Independent schools: Religious character: Designation: England . . . 33
Schools: Independent: Religious character: Designation: England . . . 33
Schools: Inspection: England . . . 34
Schools: Maintained schools: Government: Change of category: Wales . . . 36
Schools: Performance information: England . . . 34
Schools: Special non-maintained: England . . . 34
Schools: Staffing: England . . . 34
Scotland Act 1998: Functions exercisable in or as regards Scotland . . . 8, 22, 31
Scotland Act 1998: River Tweed . . . 22, 31, 91
Scotland Act 1998: Schedule 5: Modifications . . . 22, 31
Scotland Act 1998: Schedules 4 & 5: Modifications . . . 22, 31
Scotland Act 1998: Variation: Borrowing power . . . 22, 31, 85
Scotland Act 2012: Commencements . . . 22, 31
Scotland Act 2012: Consequential provisions . . . 22, 31
Scotland Act 2012: Section 29: UK stamp duty land tax: Disapplication of: Appointed day: Commencements . . . 129
Scotland Act 2012: Section 31: UK landfill tax: Disapplication: Appointed day Commencements . . . 64
Scotland: Elections: Voting age: Reduction: Acts: Scotland . . . 162
Scottish Administration: Offices . . . 22, 31
Scottish Court Service: Courts Reform (Scotland) Act 2014: Commencements: Scotland . . . 167, 173, 187, 189, 191
Scottish Court Service: Procedure: Appointment of members: Scotland . . . 187
Scottish Courts & Tribunals Service: Administrative support: Specified persons: Scotland . . . 187
Scottish Courts & Tribunals Service: Criminal Justice & Licensing (Scotland) Act 2010: Supplementary provisions: Scotland . . . 187
Scottish Courts & Tribunals Service: Scottish Sentencing Council: Appointment of members: Procedures : Scotland . . . 187
Scottish elections: Voting age: Reduction: Acts: Scotland . . . 162
Scottish Independence Referendum: Chief counting officer & counting officer charges & expenses: Scotland . . . 181
Scottish Land Court: Courts Reform (Scotland) Act 2014: Commencements: Scotland . . . 167, 172, 174, 187, 188, 189, 191
Scottish landfill tax: Administration: Scotland . . . 174
Scottish landfill tax: Exemption certificates: Scotland . . . 174
Scottish landfill tax: Qualifying material: Scotland . . . 175
Scottish landfill tax: Standard & lower rates: Scotland . . . 175
Scottish marine regions: Scotland . . . 170
Scottish Parliament: Disqualification: Scotland . . . 166, 168
Scottish Parliament: Elections: Scotland . . . 166, 181
Scottish Parliament: Regional returning officers . . . 22, 32, 90
Scottish Public Services Ombudsman Act 2002: Amendments: Scotland . . . 187
Scottish rate: Income tax: Amendments . . . 60
Scottish Road Works Register: Prescribed fees: Scotland . . . 181
Scottish tax tribunals: Conduct & Fitness Assessment Tribunal: Scotland . . . 192
Scottish tax tribunals: Time limits & procedure rules: Scotland . . . 192
Scottish tax tribunals: Voting & offences: Scotland . . . 192
Scottish tribunals: Administrative support: Listed tribunals: Scotland . . . 192
Scottish tribunals: Listed tribunals: Scotland . . . 192
Sculthorpe training area: Byelaws . . . 30
Sea fish licensing: England . . . 121
Sea fisheries . . . 121
Sea fisheries: Conservation of sea fish: Specified crustaceans: fishing, landing, sale & carriage: Prohibition . . . 121

Sea fisheries: Enforcement & Provisions	121
Sea fisheries: EU control measures: Scotland	187
Sea fisheries: European maritime & fisheries fund: Grants: Scotland	164, 171, 187
Sea fisheries: Fishing & aquaculture industries: Grants: England	48, 121
Sea fisheries: Fishing boats designation: England	121
Sea fisheries: Inshore fishing: Prohibited methods of fishing: Luce Bay: Scotland	187
Sea fisheries: Inshore fishing: Prohibited methods of fishing: Prohibition: Scotland	187
Sea fisheries: Little Loch Broom: Scallop several fishery: Scotland	187
Sea fisheries: Loch Ewe, Isle of Ewe, Wester Ross, Scallop Several Fishery: Scotland	187
Sea fisheries: Miscellaneous revocations: England	9, 121, 135
Sea fisheries: Outer Hebrides: Crabs & lobsters: Scotland	187
Sea fisheries: Poole Harbour: England	121
Sea fisheries: Salmon & migratory trout: Fishing & landing: Prohibition: England	121
Sea fisheries: Sea fish licensing: England	121
Seat belts: Wearing: Children in front seats: Motor vehicles: Northern Ireland	218
Secure accommodation: Children & young persons: Scotland	165
Seed potatoes	122
Seeds: Seed potatoes: Fees: Scotland	188
Seeds: Seed potatoes: Scotland	188
Self-build & custom housebuilding: Acts	5
Self-build & custom housebuilding: Acts: Explanatory notes	7
Self-directed support: Social care: Direct payments: Scotland	190
Senegal: Double taxation: Relief	12, 24, 58
Senior courts of England & Wales: Civil & family proceedings: Fees	26, 44, 45, 122
Senior courts of England & Wales: Civil procedure	26, 122
Senior courts of England & Wales: Civil procedure: Rules	26, 122
Senior courts of England & Wales: Crime & Courts Act 2013: Commencements	26, 122, 129
Senior courts of England & Wales: Criminal Justice & Courts Act 2015: Commencements	24, 27, 28, 30, 64, 67, 70, 83, 122, 130, 137
Senior courts of England & Wales: Criminal procedure: Rules	70, 122
Senior courts of England & Wales: Elections: Judges rota: Rules	90, 122
Senior courts of England & Wales: Family procedure	44, 45, 122
Senior courts of England & Wales: Family procedure: Rules	44, 45, 122
Senior courts of England & Wales: Family procedure: England & Wales	44, 45, 122
Senior courts of England & Wales: Family proceedings: Fees	44, 45, 122
Senior courts of England & Wales: Judges: Maximum number	122
Serious Crime Act 2015: Commencements	28, 45
Serious Crime Act 2015: Commencements: Northern Ireland	202
Serious Crime Act 2015: Consequential amendments	28
Serious crime prevention orders: Serious Crime Act 2015: Commencements	27, 84, 122
Serious crime: Acts	6
Serious crime: Acts: Explanatory notes	7
Serious Organised Crime & Police Act 2005: Commencements	82
Service complaints & financial assistance: Armed Forces: Acts	4
Service complaints & financial assistance: Armed Forces: Acts: Explanatory notes	6
Service courts application: Youth Justice & Criminal Evidence Act 1999	30
Sevastopol, Russia & Crimea: Sanctions	28
Sevastopol: Sanctions	78
Severn Bridges: Tolls	53
Sewerage: Water & sewerage services: Provision: Reasonable costs: Scotland	193
Sex discrimination: 1976 Order: Amendments: Northern Ireland	222
Sexual Offences Act 2003: Prescribed police stations: Northern Ireland	202
Sexual violence: Acts: Wales	229
Shale oil & gas: Non-domestic rating: England	89
Sham marriage: Civil partnership: Scotland & Northern Ireland	19, 58, 71
Shared parental leave & paternity & adoption leave: Adoptions from overseas: Northern Ireland	204
Shared parental leave: Statutory shared parental pay: Northern Ireland	204
Sheep & goats: Records, identification & movement: Wales	10
Sheffield: Electoral changes	69
Shellfish: Aquaculture & Fisheries (Scotland) Act 2007: Fixed penalty notices: Scotland	169, 171, 175, 187, 188
Shellfish: Little Loch Broom: Scallop several fishery: Scotland	187
Shellfish: Loch Ewe, Isle of Ewe, Wester Ross, Scallop Several Fishery: Scotland	187
Shellfish: Poole Harbour: England	121
Sheriff Appeal Court: Act of Sederunt: Fees of solicitors: Scotland	188
Sheriff appeal Court: Act of Sederunt: Sheriff Appeal Court: Rules: Scotland	188
Sheriff Appeal Court: Courts Reform (Scotland) Act 2014: Commencements: Scotland	167, 168, 172, 174, 187, 188, 189, 191
Sheriff Appeal Court: Courts Reform (Scotland) Act 2014: Consequential & supplemental provisions: Scotland	167, 188, 190
Sheriff Appeal Court: Courts Reform (Scotland) Act 2014: Consequential provisions: Scotland	167, 172, 174, 188, 190, 191
Sheriff Appeal Court: Courts Reform (Scotland) Act 2014: Transitional & saving provisions: Commencements: Scotland	167, 188, 190
Sheriff Appeal Court: Criminal Justice & Licensing (Scotland) Act 2010: Commencements: Scotland	168, 172, 188
Sheriff Appeal Court: Criminal procedure rules 1996: Act of Adjournal: Amendment: Scotland	172, 174, 188, 189
Sheriff Appeal Court: Fees: Scotland	188
Sheriff Appeal Court: Litigants in person: Costs & expenses: Scotland	188
Sheriff Appeal Court: Rules: Scotland	167, 188, 189
Sheriff Court: Act of Adjournal: Criminal Procedure Rules 1996: Final decision requests: Scotland	172, 174, 189
Sheriff Court: Act of Adjournal: Criminal procedure rules: Scotland	172, 174, 189
Sheriff Court: Act of Adjournal: Criminal procedure: Rules: Reporting restrictions: Scotland	172, 174, 189
Sheriff Court: Act of Adjournal: Justice of the Peace Court: Special measures: Scotland	172, 174, 189
Sheriff Court: Act of Sederunt: Adoption rules: Scotland	189

Sheriff Court: Act of Sederunt: Child support rules : Scotland . . . 189
Sheriff Court: Act of Sederunt: Rules: Scotland . . . 189
Sheriff Court: Court of Session rules, Ordinary cause rules: Child welfare reporters: Act of Sederunt: Scotland . . . 167, 189
Sheriff Court: Court of Session: Rules: Personal injury & remits: Scotland . . . 167, 189
Sheriff Court: Court of Session: Rules: Scotland . . . 167, 189
Sheriff Court: Court of Session: Rules: Scotland . . . 166, 189
Sheriff Court: Courts Reform (Scotland) Act 2014: Commencements: Scotland . . . 167, 172, 173, 174, 187, 188, 189, 191
Sheriff Court: Courts Reform (Scotland) Act 2014: Consequential & supplemental provisions: Scotland . . . 167, 188, 190
Sheriff Court: Courts Reform (Scotland) Act 2014: Consequential provisions: Scotland . . . 167, 172, 174, 188, 190, 191
Sheriff Court: Courts Reform (Scotland) Act 2014: Provisions & modifications . . . 21, 26, 31, 123
Sheriff Court: Courts Reform (Scotland) Act 2014: Scotland . . . 167, 173, 190
Sheriff Court: Courts Reform (Scotland) Act 2014: Transitional & saving provisions: Commencements: Scotland . . . 167, 188, 190
Sheriff Court: Criminal procedure rules 1996: Act of Adjournal: Amendment: Scotland . . . 172, 173, 174, 188, 189
Sheriff Court: Fees: Scotland . . . 190
Sheriff Court: Ordinary cause rules: Amendment: Act of Sederunt: Scotland . . . 166, 189
Sheriff Court: Ordinary cause rules: Proving the tenor & reduction: Act of Sederunt: Scotland . . . 189
Sheriff Court: Rules: Act of Sederunt: Scotland . . . 167, 189
Sheriff Court: Rules: Bankruptcy and Debt Advice (Scotland) Act 2014: Act of Sederunt: Scotland . . . 167, 189
Sheriff Court: Rules: Scotland . . . 167, 188, 189
Sheriff Court: Sheriff Personal Injury Court: Scotland . . . 189
Ship recycling facilities . . . 41, 51
Ships: Recycling facilities: Northern Ireland . . . 206
Shouldham Church of England School: Educational endowments . . . 33
Single use carrier bags: Charge: Environmental protection: Scotland: Scotland . . . 170
Slavery: Modern: Acts . . . 5
Slavery: Modern: Acts: Explanatory notes . . . 7
Sliabh Dubh Glen and Sliabh Dubh View, Belfast (Footpath): Abandonment: Northern Ireland . . . 217
Small & medium sized businesses: Credit information . . . 47
Small & medium sized businesses: Finance platforms . . . 47
Small business hereditament relief: Northern Ireland . . . 216
Small Business, Enterprise & Employment Act 2015: Commencements . . . 21, 39, 55, 66
Small Business, Enterprise & Employment Act 2015: Insolvency & company directors disqualification . . . 21, 62
Small business, enterprise & employment: Acts . . . 6
Small business, enterprise & employment: Acts: Explanatory notes . . . 7
Small businesses: Acts . . . 6
Small businesses: Acts: Explanatory notes . . . 7
Small Charitable Donations Act . . . 13
Small non-commercial consignments: Relief . . . 135
Smoke alarms: England . . . 40, 54
Smoke control areas: Authorised fuels: Northern Ireland . . . 201
Smoke control areas: Authorised fuels: Wales . . . 19
Smoke control areas: Fireplaces: Exempt: England . . . 19
Smoke control areas: Fireplaces: Exempt: Northern Ireland . . . 201
Smoke-free premises: Wales . . . 86
Smoke-free: Exemptions & vehicles: England . . . 86
Smoke-free: Vehicle operators: Penalty notices: England . . . 86
Snares: Northern Ireland . . . 224
Snares: Training: Scotland . . . 193
Social action: Negligence & statutory duty: Acts . . . 6
Social action: Negligence & statutory duty: Acts: Explanatory notes . . . 7
Social care & health: Safety & quality: Acts: Explanatory notes . . . 6
Social care charges: National assistance services: Personal requirements: Wales . . . 125
Social care: Acts . . . 4
Social care: Adult protection & support orders: Authorised officer: Wales . . . 124
Social care: Care & support: Amendments . . . 123
Social care: Care & support: Assessment: Wales . . . 124
Social care: Care & support: Business failure . . . 123
Social care: Care & support: Business failure: Wales . . . 124
Social care: Care & support: Charging decisions & determinations: Review: Wales . . . 124
Social care: Care & support: Charging: Wales . . . 124
Social care: Care & support: Children's carers: England . . . 123
Social care: Care & support: Choice of accommodation: Wales . . . 124
Social care: Care & support: Deferred payment: Wales . . . 124
Social care: Care & support: Direct payments: Wales . . . 124
Social care: Care & support: Eligibility criteria: England . . . 123
Social care: Care & support: Eligibility: Wales . . . 124
Social care: Care & support: Financial assessment: Wales . . . 124
Social care: Care & support: Isles of Scilly: England . . . 52, 123
Social care: Care & support: Market oversight criteria: England . . . 123
Social care: Care & support: Ordinary residence: Disputes: Wales . . . 124
Social care: Care & support: Ordinary residence: Specified accommodation: Wales . . . 124
Social care: Care & support: Partnership arrangements: Wales . . . 125
Social care: Care & support: Population assessment: Wales . . . 124
Social care: Care & support: Population assessments: Partnership arrangements: Wales . . . 124
Social care: Care & support: Provision of health services: Wales . . . 124
Social care: Care Act 2014: Commencement . . . 72, 73, 123
Social care: Care Act 2014: Consequential amendments: England . . . 123
Social care: Care Act 2014: Health Education England & Health Research Authority . . . 52, 75, 124

Social care: Care Act 2014: Transitional provisions: England 123
Social care: Care planning: Wales 124
Social care: Care Quality Commission: Membership 73, 85, 123
Social care: Children: Secure accommodation: Wales 15, 125
Social care: Children's homes 14, 123
Social care: Community care: Personal care & nursing care: Scotland 190
Social care: Community care: Residential accommodation provision: Outwith Scotland: Scotland 190
Social care: Health & Social Care 14, 74, 86, 123
Social care: Health & Social Care Act 2008: Regulated activities 73, 85, 123
Social care: Health & Social Care Act 2012: Consistent identifier: England 73, 85, 123
Social care: Health & Social Care Act 2012: Continuity of information: England 74, 85, 123
Social care: Health & Social Care (Safety and Quality) Act 2015: Commencements: England 74, 86, 123
Social care: Health: Disciplinary procedures: Northern Ireland 209
Social care: Health: Safety & quality: Acts 4
Social care: Joint working: Integration joint board establishment: Scotland 178, 190
Social care: Local authorities: Public health functions: Local healthwatch representatives & Public health & wellbeing boards: Entry to premises 74, 86, 123
Social care: National Independent Safeguarding Board: Wales 125
Social care: Public Bodies (Joint Working) (Scotland) Act 2014: Commencements: Scotland 178, 190
Social care: Public Bodies (Joint Working) (Scotland) Act 2014: Modifications: Scotland 179, 190
Social care: Public Bodies: Joint working: Integration joint boards & integration joint monitoring: Committees: Scotland 178, 190
Social care: Public Bodies: Joint working: Integration joint monitoring committees: Scotland 178, 190
Social care: Safeguarding Boards: Functions & procedures: Wales 125
Social care: Safeguarding Boards: Wales 125
Social care: Self-directed support: Direct payments: Scotland 190
Social care: Social Services & Well-being (Wales) Act 2014 125
Social care: Social Services & Well-being (Wales) Act 2014: Commencements 125
Social fund: Cold weather payments 126
Social fund: Winter fuel payments: Amendments: Northern Ireland 222
Social security 127
Social Security Contributions & Benefits (Northern Ireland) Act 1992: Application of parts: Northern Ireland 204, 205
Social Security Contributions & Benefits Act 1992: Application: Parts 12ZA &12ZB & 12ZC: Parental order cases 131
Social security: Welfare Reform Act 2012: Transitional & transitory provisions: Commencements 128
Social security: Amendments 126, 130
Social security: Amendments: Northern Ireland 209, 216, 223
Social security: Australia: Reciprocal agreements: Northern Ireland 222
Social security: Benefits: Earnings: Computation 126
Social security: Benefits: Earnings: Computation: Northern Ireland 129
Social security: Benefits: Up-rating 126
Social security: Benefits: Up-rating: Northern Ireland 203, 209, 216, 222, 223, 224
Social security: Budgeting loans: Applications & miscellaneous provisions 126
Social security: Canada: Reciprocal agreements: Northern Ireland 222
Social security: Child benefit: General 125
Social security: Child benefit: Tax credits: Up-rating 125, 130
Social security: Claims & payments: Northern Ireland 223
Social security: Contributions 126
Social security: Contributions & national insurance numbers: Crediting & treatment: Northern Ireland 223
Social security: Contributions: Chile 127
Social security: Contributions: Decisions & appeals 126
Social security: Contributions: Finance Act 2012: Part 4 amendments 126
Social security: Contributions: Limited liability partnership 126
Social security: Contributions: Limits & thresholds 127
Social security: Contributions: Re-rating & national insurance fund payments 127
Social security: Contributions: Republic of Chile: Northern Ireland 223
Social security: Crediting: Contributions: Treatment: National Insurance numbers 127
Social security: Earnings factors: Revaluation 127
Social security: Earnings factors: Revaluations: Northern Ireland 223
Social security: EEA states: Reciprocal agreements: Northern Ireland 222
Social security: Employment & support allowance: Northern Ireland 222
Social security: Employment & support allowance: Report assessments: Pending appeal awards 125
Social security: Employment: Allowance: Care & support workers 125
Social security: Fees payable by qualifying lenders 127
Social security: Guardian's allowance: Up-rating 125
Social security: Guardian's allowance: Up-rating: Northern Ireland 129
Social security: Housing benefit 125
Social security: Housing benefit: Family premium: Abolition 125
Social security: Housing costs 127
Social security: Income-related benefits: Subsidy to authorities 126
Social security: Industrial injuries: Prescribed diseases 127
Social security: Industrial injuries: Prescribed diseases: Northern Ireland 223
Social security: Information sharing: NHS payments & remission of charges 75, 129
Social security: Invalid care allowance 127
Social security: Invalid care allowance: Northern Ireland 223
Social security: Jobseeker's allowance: Extended period of sickness: Northern Ireland 222
Social security: Jobseeker's allowance: Sickness: Extended period 126
Social security: Jobseeker's allowance: Traineeships & qualifying young persons 127
Social security: Maternity allowance: Curtailment: Northern Ireland 222
Social security: Maternity allowance: Earnings 127

Social security: Maternity allowance: Earnings: Northern Ireland 223
Social security: Members of the Reserve Forces 127
Social security: Mesothelioma: Lump sum payments: Conditions & amounts 126
Social security: Mesothelioma: Lump sum payments: Conditions & amounts: Northern Ireland 222
Social security: Miscellaneous amendments 127
Social security: National insurance: Contributions: Application of part 7 of the Finance Act 2004 126
Social security: New Zealand: Reciprocal agreements: Northern Ireland 222
Social security: Overpayments & recovery 127
Social security: Penalty: Alternative to prosecution: Maximum amount 127
Social security: Pensions Act 2014: Consequential, supplementary & incidental amendments 126
Social security: Pensions Act 2015: Additional pension: Units: Northern Ireland 222
Social security: Pensions Act 2015: Consequential, supplementary & incidental amendments: Northern Ireland 222
Social security: Pensions: Additional units: Northern Ireland 223
Social security: Pensions: Flat rate accrual amount 127
Social security: Pensions: Flat rate accrual amounts: Northern Ireland 223
Social security: Pensions: Low earnings threshold 127
Social security: Pensions: Low earnings threshold: Northern Ireland 223
Social security: Pneumoconiosis etc.: Workers' compensation: Claims: Payments 126
Social security: Reciprocal agreements. 126
Social security: Reserve Forces members: Northern Ireland 223
Social security: Social fund: Cold weather payments 126
Social security: Social fund: Winter fuel payments: Amendments: Northern Ireland 222
Social security: State pension 128
Social security: State pension credit 128
Social security: State pension credit: Northern Ireland 223
Social security: State pension: Northern Ireland 223
Social security: Switzerland: Reciprocal agreements: Northern Ireland 222
Social security: Tax credits: Claims & notifications 130
Social security: Universal credit & miscellaneous amendments 128
Social security: Universal credit regulations: Surpluses & self-employed losses: Digital service 128
Social security: Universal credit regulations: Waiting days 128
Social security: Universal credit regulations: Work-related requirements: In Work pilot scheme 128
Social security: Universal credit: EEA jobseekers 128
Social security: Universal credit: Transitional provisions 128
Social security: Universal credit: Work allowance 128
Social security: Welfare benefits: Up-rating 128, 131
Social security: Welfare Funds (Scotland) Act 2015: Commencements: Scotland. 190
Social security: Welfare Reform. 128
Social security: Welfare Reform Act 2012: Commencements 128
Social security: Welfare services: Information sharing 127
Social security: Workers' compensation: Pneumoconiosis etc.: Claims: Payments: Northern Ireland 222
Social Services & Well-being (Wales) Act 2014 125
Social Services & Well-being (Wales) Act 2014: Commencements 125
Social services: Care Act 2014: Amendments 129
Social services: Children & Families Act 2014: Amendments 129
Social services: Young people leaving care: Support & assistance Scotland: Scotland 166
Social, Responsibility and Heroism Act 2015: Commencements 131
Solvency. 47
South Arran Nature Conservation Marine Protected Area: Conservation: Scotland 170, 176
South Bucks: Electoral changes 69
South Sudan: Sanctions: Overseas territories 78
Southampton City Council: Permit schemes: Traffic management 54
Spamount Hill Climb: Road races: Northern Ireland. 220
Special constables: Police 83
Special Educational Needs & Disability First-tier Tribunal: Recommendation power: Pilot 35
Special educational needs & disability: England 35
Special educational needs: Codes of practice: England 35
Special educational needs: Disability: England. 35
Special Immigration Appeals Commission: Procedure 58
Special roads: M80: Castlecary interchange: Scotland 181
Specified crustaceans: fishing, landing, sale & carriage: Prohibition 121
Sperrins Rally: Road races: Northern Ireland 220
Sports clubs, amateur: Taxation 12, 24, 58
Sports grounds & sporting events: Football spectators: Corresponding offences 129
Sports grounds & sporting events: Safety: Designation: England & Wales 129
Sports grounds: Safety: Designation 129
Sports grounds: Safety: Designation: England & Wales 129
Spring traps: Animals: Approval: Variations: Prevention of cruelty: England 9
Spring water: Northern Ireland 207
Spring water: Wales 49
St Mary's Music School: Aided places: Scotland 169
Stafford: Electoral changes 69
Stakeholder pension schemes: Disclosure of information: Northern Ireland 212
Stamp duty land tax: : Scotland Act 2012: Commencements 129
Stamp duty land tax: Acts. 6
Stamp duty land tax: Acts: Explanatory notes 7
Stamp duty reserve tax: Investment exchanges & clearing houses 129
Stamp duty reserve tax: Taxation: Regulatory capital securities. 12, 25, 60, 129

Stamp duty: Investment exchanges & clearing houses 129
Stamp duty: Taxation: Regulatory capital securities. 12, 25, 60, 129
State pension 128
State pension credit 128
State pension credit: Northern Ireland 223
State pension: Social security: Northern Ireland 223
Statistics & Registration Service Act 2007: Patient registration information: Disclosure: Northern Ireland 211
Statistics & Registration Service Act 2007: Revenue information: Disclosures. 129
Statistics Board: Statistics & Registration Service Act 2007: Revenue information: Disclosures 129
Statutes: Chronological tables 7
Statutes: Chronological tables: Northern Ireland 200
Statutes: Northern Ireland 200
Statutes: Title page & index: Northern Ireland. 200
Statutory adoption pay. 131
Statutory adoption pay: Curtailment: Northern Ireland 205
Statutory adoption pay: Northern Ireland 205
Statutory adoption pay: Parental orders & prospective adopters: Northern Ireland 205
Statutory instruments: National Assembly for Wales: Annual volumes 7
Statutory maternity pay: Curtailment: Northern Ireland 224
Statutory maternity pay: Social security: Benefits: Up-rating: Northern Ireland 203, 209, 216, 222, 223, 224
Statutory paternity pay 131
Statutory paternity pay: Northern Ireland 205
Statutory paternity pay: Parental orders & prospective adopters: Northern Ireland 205
Statutory rules (Northern Ireland): Chronological tables: Northern Ireland 199
Statutory shared parental pay 131
Statutory shared parental pay: Northern Ireland 205
Statutory shared parental pay: Overseas adoptions: Northern Ireland. 205
Statutory shared parental pay: Parental order cases: Northern Ireland 205
Statutory shared parental pay: Persons abroad & mariners: Northern Ireland 205
Statutory sick pay: Social security: Benefits: Up-rating: Northern Ireland 203, 209, 216, 222, 223, 224
Strabane: Parking & waiting restrictions: Northern Ireland 219
Strategic highways companies: Appointment 53
Strategic highways companies: Delegation of functions 53
Strategic highways companies: Infrastructure Act 2015 53
Street works: Qualifications of supervisors & operatives: England 53
Student fees: Agriculture: Northern Ireland 200
Student fees: Amounts: Northern Ireland 203
Student loans: Living costs liability: Cancellation 35
Succession to the Crown Act 2013: Commencements. 129
Sudan: European Union: Financial sanctions. 27
Summary appeal courts: Youth Justice & Criminal Evidence Act 1999 30
Sunderland City Council: Sunderland Strategic Transport Corridor: New Wear Bridge scheme 53
Superannuation Act 1972: Admission to schedule 1. 81
Superannuation schemes: Health & personal social services: Northern Ireland 208
Superannuation: Additional voluntary contributions: Teachers 35
Superannuation: District councils: Northern Ireland 213
Superannuation: Northern Ireland Commissioner for Complaints: Northern Ireland 213
Superannuation: Teachers: Northern Ireland 203
Superannuation: Teachers' superannuation: Additional voluntary contributions: Northern Ireland 203
Supply & appropriation: Main estimates: Acts 6
Supreme Court of the United Kingdom: Courts Reform (Scotland) Act 2014: Commencements: Scotland 167, 172, 174, 187, 188, 189, 191
Supreme Court of the United Kingdom: Courts Reform (Scotland) Act 2014: Consequential provisions: Scotland . 167, 172, 174, 188, 190, 191
Supreme Court of the United Kingdom: Crime & Courts Act 2013: Commencements. 26, 122, 129
Supreme Court of the United Kingdom: Criminal Justice and Courts Act 2015: Commencements . 24, 27, 28, 30, 64, 67, 70, 83, 122, 130, 137
Surface waters: Water resources: England & Wales 136
Swansea Bay: Tidal generating station. 62
Sweden: Double taxation: Relief 12, 24, 58
Swindon: Electoral changes 69
Syria: Restrictive measures: Overseas territories 78

T

Tandragee 100: Road races: Northern Ireland 220
Tax credit: Aggregates levy: Northern Ireland tax credit 8
Tax credits: Amendments. 126, 130
Tax credits: Appeals: Northern Ireland 130
Tax credits: Child benefit: Up-rating. 125, 130
Tax credits: Claims & notifications 130
Tax credits: Up-rating 130
Tax credits: Working tax credit: Entitlement & maximum rate 130
Taxation: Chargeable gains: Gilt-edged securities 12, 25
Taxation: Regulatory capital securities 12, 25, 60, 129
Taxes see also Capital gains tax
Taxes see also Corporation tax
Taxes see also Income tax
Taxes see also Inheritance tax

Taxes see also Landfill tax
Taxes see also Value added tax
Taxes: Avoidance schemes: Promoters & prescribed circumstances 130
Taxes: Data-gathering powers: Relevant data: Amendments 58
Taxes: Diverted profits tax: Finance Act 2009: Commencements 32
Taxes: Double taxation: Relief & international tax enforcement: Canada 130
Taxes: Double taxation: Relief: Netherlands 10
Taxes: Enveloped dwellings: Annual tax: Avoidance schemes: Prescribed descriptions of arrangements. 10
Taxes: International tax: Compliance 130
Taxes: International tax: Compliance: Crown Dependencies & Gibraltar 130
Taxes: International tax: Enforcement: Macao 130
Taxes: International tax: Enforcement: Monaco. 130
Taxes: Land & buildings transaction tax: Acts: Explanatory notes: Scotland 162
Taxes: Loan relationships & derivative contracts: Exchange gains & losses: Fair value accounting 25
Taxes: Loan relationships & derivative contracts: Profits & losses: Disregard & bringing into account. 25
Taxes: Regulatory capital securities 12, 25, 60, 129
Taxes: Revenue Scotland & Tax Powers Act 2014: Commencements: Scotland 191
Taxes: Revenue Scotland & Tax Powers Act 2014: Fees for payment: Scotland 191
Taxes: Revenue Scotland & Tax Powers Act 2014: First planning period: Scotland. 191
Taxes: Revenue Scotland & Tax Powers Act: Interest & unpaid tax: Scotland 191
Taxes: Revenue Scotland & Tax Powers Act: Privileged communications: Scotland 191
Taxes: Revenue Scotland & Tax Powers Act: Record keeping: Scotland 191
Taxes: Revenue Scotland & Tax Powers Act: Reimbursement arrangements: Scotland. 191
Taxes: Revenue Scotland & Tax Powers Act: Tax postponement: Scotland 191
Taxes: Revenue Scotland & Tax Powers Act: Third party: Scotland. 191
Taxes: Tax avoidance schemes: Information 130
Taxes: Tax avoidance schemes: Promoters & prescribed circumstances 130
Taxes: Tax credits: Appeals: Northern Ireland 130
Taxes: Tax credits: Claims & notifications. 130
Taxes: Taxation relief: Community amateur sports clubs 12, 24, 58
Taxes: Tonnage tax: Training requirements 130
Taxes: Unit trusts: Unauthorised 13, 25, 60
Taxi accessibility: Disabled persons: Northern Ireland. 202
Taxi operators: Licencing: Northern Ireland 221
Taxis Act 2008: Commencements: Amendments: Northern Ireland. 221
Taxis: Antrim: Road traffic & vehicles: Northern Ireland 221
Taxis: Licencing: Northern Ireland 221
Taxis: Taximeters, devices & maximum fares: Northern Ireland 221
TB see Tuberculosis
Teachers: Induction arrangements: Wales 35
Teachers: Pension schemes: England & Wales 35, 88
Teachers: Pension schemes: Scotland 180
Teachers: Pension schemes: Northern Ireland 215
Teachers: Pensions: Amendments: Northern Ireland. 203
Teachers: Redundancy & premature retirement: Compensation 35
Teachers: Registration: General Teaching Council for Northern Ireland: Northern Ireland 203
Teachers: Superannuation: Additional voluntary contributions 35
Teachers: Superannuation: Additional voluntary contributions: Northern Ireland 203
Teachers: Superannuation: Northern Ireland 203
Teachers: Superannuation: Scotland 177
Telecommunications: Valuation: Northern Ireland 216
Television programmes: Cultural test: Corporation tax 24
Temple: Higher Carblake: Cornwall Council: Improvements 61
Tenancies: Assured: Agricultural occupancies: Forms: England 65
Tenancy deposits: Specified interest rates: Housing: England 54
Terms & conditions of employment: Disciplinary & grievance procedures: Code of practice 130
Terms & conditions of employment: Employment Rights Act 1996: Protected disclosures: Extension of meaning of worker 131
Terms & conditions of employment: Employment rights: Limits: Increase 130
Terms & conditions of employment: Employment Tribunals Act 1996: Conciliation provisions: Application of 131
Terms & conditions of employment: National minimum wage 131
Terms & conditions of employment: Public interest disclosure: Prescribed persons 131
Terms & conditions of employment: Redundancy payments: Local government: Continuity of employment 131
Terms & conditions of employment: Social Security Contributions & Benefits Act 1992: Application: Parts 12ZA &12ZB & 12ZC : Parental order cases 131
Terms & conditions of employment: Shared parental leave & leave curtailment 131
Terms & conditions of employment: Small Business, Enterprise and Employment Act 2015: Commencements 14, 20, 62, 89, 131
Terms & conditions of employment: Statutory paternity pay: Statutory adoption pay: Statutory shared parental pay 131
Terms & conditions of employment: Statutory shared parental pay 131
Terms & conditions of employment: Welfare benefits: Up-rating 128, 131
Terms & conditions of employment: Zero hours contracts: Exclusivity terms: Redress 131
Territorial sea: Limits: Guernsey 131
Terrorism Act 2000: Examining & review Officers: Codes of practice 83
Terrorism Act 2000: Proscribed organisations 83
Terrorism: Counter-Terrorism & Security Act 2015: Authority to carry scheme 56, 83
Terrorism: Counter-Terrorism & Security Act 2015: Commencements 83, 133
Terrorism: Counter-Terrorism & Security Act 2015: Officers functions: Codes of practice 83
Terrorism: Counter-Terrorism & Security Act 2015: Risk of being drawn into terrorism 83
Terrorism: Counter-terrorism & security: Acts 4

Terrorism: Counter-terrorism & security: Acts: Explanatory notes	6
Terrorist Asset-Freezing Act 2010: Isle of Man: Revocation	83
Thermal energy: Gas: Calculation	49
Title conditions: Historic Environment Scotland Act 2014: Saving, transitional & consequential provisions: Scotland	164, 191
Tobacco & nicotine products: Proxy purchasing: Penalties	86
Tobacco products: Standardised packaging	85
Tonnage tax: Training requirements	130
Torts: Social, Responsibility and Heroism Act 2015: Commencements	131
Town & country planning see also Planning	
Town & country planning: Appeals by appointed persons: Determination: Prescribed classes: Scotland	192
Town & country planning: Appeals: Scotland	191
Town & country planning: Applications, deemed applications & site visits: Fees: Wales	133
Town & country planning: Compensation: England	132
Town & country planning: Criminal Justice and Courts Act 2015: Commencements	28, 132
Town & country planning: Determination of appeals: Appointed persons: Prescribed classes: Wales	132
Town & country planning: Development management procedure: England	132
Town & country planning: Development management procedure: Wales	133
Town & country planning: Easements & applications: Power to override: Statutory undertakers: Wales	133
Town & country planning: Environmental impact assessment	132
Town & country planning: General permitted development: England	132
Town & country planning: General permitted development: Scotland	192
Town & country planning: Hazardous substances: England	61, 131
Town & country planning: Hazardous substances: Inquiry session procedure: Scotland	192
Town & country planning: Hazardous substances: Wales	132
Town & country planning: Hearings & inquiries procedure	134
Town & country planning: Historic Environment Scotland Act 2014: Saving, transitional & consequential provisions: Scotland	164, 191
Town & country planning: Historic environment: Scotland	192
Town & country planning: Listed building & conservation area: Consent procedures: Scotland	191
Town & country planning: Listed buildings & conservation areas: England	132
Town & country planning: Listed buildings & conservation areas: Urgent works: Crown Land: Scotland	191
Town & country planning: Listed buildings & conservation areas: Wales	132
Town & country planning: Listed buildings: Notification & publication: Scotland	191
Town & country planning: Local development plan: Wales	133
Town & country planning: Neighbourhood planning: General: England	131
Town & country planning: Operation stack: Special development: England	132
Town & country planning: Referrals & appeals: Written representations procedure: Wales	133
Town & country planning: Scheduled monuments & listed buildings: Scotland	164, 191, 192
Town & country planning: Scotland	192
Town & country planning: Section 62A applications: England	132
Town & country planning: Use classes: England	132
Town & village greens: Common land: Registration, management & protection: Acts	4
Tractors: Agricultural & forestry: Emission of gaseous & particulate pollutants	40, 92
Tractors: EC type-approval	40, 92
Trade unions: Membership audit certificate: Specified conditions	133
Trade unions: Transparency of Lobbying, Non-Party Campaigning & Trade Union Administration Act 2014: Commencements	133
Traffic Management Act 2004: Commencements	53
Traffic management: Permit schemes: Bradford (City) Metropolitan District	53
Traffic management: Permit schemes: Brighton & Hove City Council	53
Traffic management: Permit schemes: Calderdale Borough Council	53
Traffic management: Permit schemes: Derbyshire County Council	53
Traffic management: Permit schemes: England	54
Traffic management: Permit schemes: Essex County Council	53
Traffic management: Permit schemes: Knowsley Metropolitan Borough Council	53
Traffic management: Permit schemes: Lancashire County Council	53
Traffic management: Permit schemes: Milton Keynes Council	54
Traffic management: Permit schemes: Nottingham City Council	54
Traffic management: Permit schemes: Southampton City Council	54
Traffic management: Permit schemes: Wakefield City Council	53
Traffic: Weight restrictions: Northern Ireland	221
Train driving licences & certificates	133
Traineeships & qualifying young persons: Jobseeker's allowance	127
Training: Education: Inspectors: Wales	35
Transitional payments: Disadvantaged area scheme: Northern Ireland	201
Transparency of Lobbying, Non-Party Campaigning & Trade Union Administration Act 2014: Commencements	22, 133
Transport & works: London Underground: Bank Station: Capacity upgrade	134
Transport & works: Network Rail: Blackthorn & Piddington: Land acquisition	134
Transport & works: Network rail: Ordsall Chord	134
Transport & works: Network rail: Tinsley Chord	134
Transport & works: Railways: Ecclesbourne Valley Railway: England	134
Transport & works: Scheduled monuments & listed buildings: Scotland	164, 191, 192
Transport 2011 Act: Commencements: Northern Ireland	215
Transport levying bodies: Local government	69
Transport: Buses: National travel concession schemes: Older & disabled persons: Scotland	192
Transport: Counter-Terrorism & Security Act 2015: Commencements	83, 133
Transport: Crossrail: Plumstead sidings	134
Transport: Crossrail: Services: Exemption	134
Transport: Fuels: Renewables obligation	40, 134
Transport: Greater Manchester Combined Authority	68, 134

Transport: Greater Manchester: Light Rapid Transit System: Exemptions 133
Transport: London Underground: Bank Station: Capacity upgrade 134
Transport: Network rail: Tinsley Chord 134
Transport: Office of Rail Regulation: Change of name 53, 86
Transport: Public passenger: Public service vehicles: Drivers, inspectors, conductors & passengers: Conduct: England & Wales 86
Transport: Rail vehicles: Accessibility: B2007 Vehicles: Exemptions 32, 133
Transport: Rail vehicles: Accessibility: Non-interoperable rail system: London Underground Northern Line 95TS Vehicles 32, 133
Transport: Railways: Infrastructure: Access & management 133
Transport: Railways: Interoperability 88, 133
Transport: Railways: Level crossing: Cullybackey South: Northern Ireland 216
Transport: Railways: Passengers: Rights & obligations: Exemptions 133
Transport: Train driving licences & certificates 133
Treasury: Penalty payments: Enforcement costs 47
Tribunals & inquiries: Courts Reform (Scotland) Act 2014: Commencement: Scotland 187, 192
Tribunals & inquiries: Employment tribunals: Employment Appeal Tribunal: Fees 134
Tribunals & inquiries: Enterprise Act 2002: Section 16 134
Tribunals & inquiries: First-tier & Upper tribunals: Chambers 134
Tribunals & inquiries: Planning: Hazardous substances: Inquiry session procedure: Scotland 192
Tribunals & inquiries: Scottish tax tribunals: Conduct & Fitness Assessment Tribunal: Scotland 192
Tribunals & inquiries: Scottish tax tribunals: Time limits & procedure rules: Scotland 192
Tribunals & inquiries: Scottish tax tribunals: Voting & offences: Scotland 192
Tribunals & inquiries: Scottish tribunals: Administrative support: Listed tribunals: Scotland 192
Tribunals & inquiries: Scottish tribunals: Eligibility for appointment: Scotland 192
Tribunals & inquiries: Scottish tribunals: Listed tribunals: Scotland 192
Tribunals & inquiries: Town & country planning: Hearings & inquiries procedure 134
Tribunals & inquiries: Tribunal procedure: Rules 134
Tribunals & inquiries: Tribunals (Scotland) Act 2014: Commencements: Scotland 193
Tribunals & inquiries: Tribunals: Functions: Transfer. 134
Tribunals (Scotland) Act 2014: Commencements: Scotland. 192, 193
Tribunals: Functions: Transfer 134
Trunk roads: A1 94
Trunk roads: A1/A1(M). 93, 94
Trunk roads: A1/A52 99
Trunk roads: A1: Scotland 182
Trunk roads: A11 . . . . 53, 95, 108
Trunk roads: A11/A14 95
Trunk roads: A12 95
Trunk roads: A13 95
Trunk roads: A14 . . . . 92, 95, 96
Trunk roads: A14/A11 95
Trunk roads: A160 100
Trunk roads: A162 101
Trunk roads: A168 101
Trunk roads: A180 101
Trunk roads: A19. . . . . 96, 108
Trunk roads: A19/A66 96
Trunk roads: A2 94
Trunk roads: A2/A282/M25 105
Trunk roads: A2/M25/A282 106
Trunk roads: A21 96
Trunk roads: A259 101
Trunk roads: A259/A268 101
Trunk roads: A268/A259 101
Trunk roads: A27 96
Trunk roads: A282/M25 106
Trunk roads: A282/M25/A2 105
Trunk roads: A3 94
Trunk roads: A30 96
Trunk roads: A30: Temple: Higher Carblake: Cornwall Council: Improvements. 61
Trunk roads: A303 . . . . 101, 109
Trunk roads: A31 . . . . 96, 97
Trunk roads: A34 97
Trunk roads: A35 97
Trunk roads: A36. . . . . 97, 109
Trunk roads: A37: Concession Road: Clonalig: Northern Ireland 217
Trunk roads: A38 97
Trunk roads: A38/A50 97
Trunk roads: A38/A5148 102
Trunk roads: A4/M5 95
Trunk roads: A40 . . . . 97, 98, 110, 111, 112
Trunk roads: A40/A4076/A477. 117
Trunk roads: A40/A479/A483/A470 115
Trunk roads: A40/A48 . . . . 110, 113
Trunk roads: A40/A483 117
Trunk roads: A4042 119
Trunk roads: A4076 119
Trunk roads: A4076/A477/A40. 117
Trunk roads: A41 98

Trunk roads: A42	98
Trunk roads: A421	101
Trunk roads: A4232	119
Trunk roads: A43	93, 98
Trunk roads: A44	112
Trunk roads: A446	101
Trunk roads: A449	101
Trunk roads: A45	98
Trunk roads: A453/A50	93
Trunk roads: A458	115
Trunk roads: A46	98
Trunk roads: A465	115
Trunk roads: A465/M4	115, 120
Trunk roads: A47	98, 99
Trunk roads: A470	110, 116
Trunk roads: A470/A40/A479/A483	115
Trunk roads: A470/A479	116
Trunk roads: A470/A5	110
Trunk roads: A470/M4	120
Trunk roads: A477	116, 117
Trunk roads: A477/A40/A4076	117
Trunk roads: A479	117
Trunk roads: A479/A470	116
Trunk roads: A479/A483/A470/A40	115
Trunk roads: A48	113
Trunk roads: A48/A40	110, 113
Trunk roads: A4810	120
Trunk roads: A483	117, 118
Trunk roads: A483/A40	117
Trunk roads: A483/A470/A40/A479	115
Trunk roads: A483/A489	53
Trunk roads: A487	111, 118, 119
Trunk roads: A489/A483	53
Trunk roads: A49	93
Trunk roads: A490/A550	113
Trunk roads: A494	119
Trunk roads: A494/A55	113
Trunk roads: A494/A550	119
Trunk roads: A5	95, 110, 111
Trunk roads: A5/A470	110
Trunk roads: A5/A505	95
Trunk roads: A50	99
Trunk roads: A50/A38	97
Trunk roads: A50/A453	93
Trunk roads: A500	101
Trunk roads: A5005	102
Trunk roads: A5036	102
Trunk roads: A505/A5	95
Trunk roads: A5148/A38	102
Trunk roads: A52	99
Trunk roads: A52/A1	99
Trunk roads: A52/M1	102
Trunk roads: A54: Ballymacombs Road, Portglenone: Northern Ireland	217
Trunk roads: A55	110, 113, 114, 115
Trunk roads: A55/A494	113
Trunk roads: A550	101
Trunk roads: A550/A490	113
Trunk roads: A550/A494	119
Trunk roads: A57	93, 99
Trunk roads: A585	109
Trunk roads: A590	101
Trunk roads: A590/M6	101
Trunk roads: A595	101
Trunk roads: A595/A66	100
Trunk roads: A61/A616	99
Trunk roads: A616	101
Trunk roads: A616/A61	99
Trunk roads: A63	99
Trunk roads: A631	102
Trunk roads: A64	100
Trunk roads: A66	100
Trunk roads: A66/A19	96
Trunk roads: A66/A595	100
Trunk roads: A68: Scotland	181, 182
Trunk roads: A69	100
Trunk roads: A696	102
Trunk roads: A701: Scotland	182
Trunk roads: A702: Scotland	184

Trunk roads: A725/M8/M73/M74: Scotland 184
Trunk roads: A725/M8/M74: Scotland 184
Trunk roads: A737/A738: Scotland 181, 184
Trunk roads: A738/A737: Scotland 181, 184
Trunk roads: A75: Scotland 182
Trunk roads: A77: Scotland. 181, 182
Trunk roads: A78: Scotland 182
Trunk roads: A8/M8: Junction 4: Scotland 184
Trunk roads: A82/A830: Scotland 181
Trunk roads: A82: Scotland. 182, 183
Trunk roads: A83: Scotland 183
Trunk roads: A830/A82: Scotland 181
Trunk roads: A830: Scotland 182
Trunk roads: A84: Scotland. 182, 183
Trunk roads: A85: Scotland 183
Trunk roads: A9/M9: Scotland 184
Trunk roads: A9: Scotland 181, 182
Trunk roads: A90/A972: Scotland 184
Trunk roads: A90/M90: Scotland 182, 184
Trunk roads: A90: Scotland 182, 183
Trunk roads: A96: Scotland 181, 183, 184
Trunk roads: A972/A90: Scotland 184
Trunk roads: A985: Scotland 184
Trunk roads: M73/M74/A725/M8: Scotland 184
Trunk roads: M74/A725/M8/M73: Scotland 184
Trunk roads: M74/A725/M8: Scotland 184
Trunk roads: M8/M73/M74/A725: Scotland 184
Trunk roads: M8/M74/A725: Scotland 184
Trunk roads: M9/A9: Scotland 184
Trunk roads: North east trunk roads area: Scotland. 184, 185
Trunk roads: North west trunk roads area: Scotland 185
Trunk roads: Old Great North Road 108
Trunk roads: South east trunk roads area: Scotland 186
Trunk roads: South west trunk roads area: Scotland 186
Trunks: A2/M2 102
Trustees powers: Acts: Explanatory notes 6
Tuberculosis: Animals: England 9
Tuberculosis: Animals: Scotland 164
Tuberculosis: Animals: Wales 10
Tuberculosis: Examination & testing scheme: Animals: Northern Ireland 201

U

Ulster Grand Prix Bike Week: Road races: Northern Ireland 220
Ulster Rally: Road races: Northern Ireland 220
Unit trusts: Unauthorised 60
United Kingdom: Wreck convention area 72
United nations: Sanctions: Miscellaneous amendments 135
United States: Accounting standards: Prescribed bodies: Companies 20
Universal credit & miscellaneous amendments 128
Universal credit regulations: Surpluses & self-employed losses: Digital service 128
Universal credit regulations: Waiting days 128
Universal credit regulations: Work-related requirements: In Work pilot scheme 128
Universal credit: EEA jobseekers 128
Universal credit: Work allowance 128
University of the West of Scotland: University of Paisley: Order of Council: Amendments: Scotland. 169
Urban clearways: Amendments: Northern Ireland 221
Urban development: Ebbsfleet Development Corporation: Planning functions: England 135
Urban development: Old Oak & Park Royal Development Corporation: Planning functions 135

V

Vaccine damage payments: Specified disease 85
Valuation for rating: Decapitalisation rate: Northern Ireland 216
Valuation timetable: Scotland 180
Valuation: Telecommunications, natural gas & water: Northern Ireland 216
Value added tax: Amendments 135
Value added tax: Caravans 135
Value added tax: International tax: Enforcement: Brazil 12, 25, 44, 59, 62, 135
Value added tax: Refunds: London Legacy Development Corporation 135
Value added tax: Registration limits: Increases 135
Value added tax: Small non-commercial consignments: Relief 135
Van benefit: Car & van fuel benefit 60
Vehicle drivers: Professional competence: Certificates: Amendments 93
Vehicles: Goods vehicles: Testing: Northern Ireland 218
Vehicles: Motor vehicles: Driving instruction: Northern Ireland 218
Vehicles: Motor vehicles: Driving instruction: Trainee licences: Northern Ireland 218
Vehicles: Motor vehicles: Driving licences: Amendments: Northern Ireland 218

Vehicles: Motor vehicles: Testing: Northern Ireland 218
Vehicles: Passenger & goods vehicles: Recording equipment: Downloading of data 92
Vehicles: Public service vehicles: Northern Ireland 220
Vehicles: Road vehicles: Lighting: Northern Ireland 221
Vehicles: Road vehicles: Registration marks: Retention & sale 92
Vehicles: Road: Registration & licensing 93
Venture capital trusts: Winding up & mergers: Tax 60
Veterinary surgeons: Exemptions 135
Veterinary surgeons: Qualifications: European recognition & knowledge of language 135
Victims & Witnesses (Scotland) Act 2014: Commencements: Scotland 168
Victims & witnesses: Information: Disclosure: Prescribed bodies: Northern Ireland 210
Victims' rights: Scotland 168
Violence against Women, Domestic Abuse & Sexual Violence (Wales) Act 2015: Commencements 70
Violence against women: Domestic abuse & sexual violence: Acts: Explanatory notes: Wales 229
Violence: Against women, domestic abuse & sexual violence: Acts: Wales 229
Violence: Women: Domestic & sexual abuse: Acts: Explanatory notes: Wales 229
Virgin Islands: Constitution 13
Visas: Passenger transit: Immigration 57
Voting age: Reduction: Scottish elections: Acts: Scotland 162
Vulnerable persons: Protection of Vulnerable Groups (Scotland) Act 2007: Scheme membership & disclosure requests: Fees: Scotland. 165, 178
Vulnerable Witnesses (Scotland) Act 2004: Commencements: Scotland 168
W . . . .
Wakefield City Council: Permit schemes: Traffic management 53
Wakefield City Council: Wakefield Eastern Relief Road: Bridge scheme 53
Wakefield Eastern Relief Road: Bridge scheme 53
Wales: Government of Wales Act 2006: Designation of receipts 21, 32
Walney extension offshore wind farm 62
Warm home discount 38, 49
Warwickshire: Electoral changes 69
Waste batteries & accumulators 41
Waste electrical & electronic equipment 41
Waste management: Extractive industries: Planning: Northern Ireland 214
Waste management: Licensing: Northern Ireland 206
Waste: Control: Seized property: England & Wales 42
Waste: Fees & charges: Northern Ireland 206
Waste: Hazardous waste 41
Waste: Hazardous waste: European waste catalogue: Scotland 170
Waste: Hazardous waste: Northern Ireland 206
Waste: Landfill tax 64, 65
Waste: Meaning of recovery: Scotland 170
Waste: Recycle quality: Scotland 170
Water & sewerage services: Provision: Reasonable costs: Scotland 193
Water & sewerage: Private water supplies: Northern Ireland 224
Water & sewerage: Water supply: Quality: Northern Ireland 224
Water Act 2014: Commencements 136
Water Act 2014: Commencements: England & Wales 136
Water Act 2014: Commencements: Wales 136
Water Environment & Water Services (Scotland) Act 2003: Part 1: Modification: Scotland 170
Water environment: Responsible authorities & functions: Relevant enactments & designation: Scotland 170
Water environment: River basin management planning: Scotland 170, 193
Water industry: Charges: Vulnerable groups: England & Wales 136
Water industry: Specified infrastructure projects: English undertakers 136
Water industry: Water Act 2014: Commencements: England & Wales 136
Water industry: Water Act 2014: Commencements: Scotland 193
Water industry: Water mergers: England & Wales 21, 136
Water resources: Framework directive: England & Wales 136
Water resources: Surface waters: England & Wales 136
Water supply: Local Government Finance Act 1992: Commencement: Scotland 176, 193
Water supply: Public & private supplies: Scotland 193
Water supply: Quality: Northern Ireland 224
Water supply: Reservoirs (Scotland) Act 2011: Commencements: Scotland 171, 193
Water supply: Reservoirs (Scotland) Act 2011: National security: Disclosure information: Restrictions 21, 31, 136
Water supply: Reservoirs: Engineers: Panels: Scotland 171, 193
Water supply: Reservoirs: Scotland: Scotland 171, 193
Water supply: Water & sewerage services: Provision: Reasonable costs: Scotland 193
Water undertakers: Byelaws: Extension 135
Water: Classification, priority substances & shellfish waters: EC directive: Northern Ireland 206
Water: Environmental protection: Environment & rural affairs: England & Wales 8, 9, 42, 135
Water: Miscellaneous provisions: England & Wales 9, 10, 42, 71, 121, 135
Water: Natural mineral water, spring water & bottled drinking water: Northern Ireland 207
Water: Natural mineral water, spring water & bottled drinking water: Scotland 172
Water: Natural mineral water, spring water & bottled drinking water: Wales 49
Water: Nitrate pollution: Prevention 8, 135
Water: Nitrate pollution: Prevention: Wales 9, 136
Water: Nitrate: Vulnerable zones: Designation: Scotland 193
Water: Priority substances & classification: EC directive: Northern Ireland 206
Water: Valuation: Northern Ireland 216

Weapons: Licensing: Acts: Explanatory notes: Scotland	163
Weapons: Licensing: Acts: Scotland	162
Weights & measures	136
Weights & measures: Clinical thermometers: EEC requirements	22, 136
Welfare benefits: Up-rating	128, 131
Welfare food	48
Welfare Funds (Scotland) Act 2015: Commencements: Scotland	190
Welfare funds: Acts: Explanatory notes: Scotland	163
Welfare funds: Acts: Scotland	162
Welfare Reform Act 2012: Commencements	128
Welfare Reform Act 2012: Transitional & transitory provisions: Commencements	128
Welfare reform: Northern Ireland: Acts	5
Welfare reform: Northern Ireland: Acts: Explanatory notes	7
Welfare services: Information sharing	127
Welfare: Microchipping of dogs: Wales	10
Well-being of Future Generations (Wales) Act 2015: Commencements	136
Well-being of Future Generations (Wales) Act 2015: Consequential provisions	136
Well-being of Future Generations (Wales) Act 2015: Registrable interests	137
Well-being: Future generations: Acts: Wales	229
Well-being: Future generations: Acts: Wales: Explanatory notes: Wales	229
Welsh certifying authority: Apprenticeships: Designation	39
Welsh Language (Wales) Measure 2011: Commencements	137
Welsh Language Tribunal: Rules	137
Welsh language: Standards	137
Welsh Statutory instruments: National Assembly for Wales: Annual volumes	7
West Devon: Electoral changes	69
West Dorset: Electoral changes	69
West Middlesex University Hospital National Health Service Trust: Dissolutions	75
Whitchurch Bridge: Tolls revision: Highways: England	54
White Lodge Court, Greenisland: Abandonment: Northern Ireland	217
Whitney-on-Wye Bridge: Tolls: Revisions	54
Wildlife & Countryside Act 1981: Schedule 9: Variation: Wales	137
Wildlife & countryside: Birds: Captive: Registration, ringing & marking: England	137
Wildlife: Infrastructure Act 2015: Commencements	40, 52, 137
Wildlife: Snares: Northern Ireland	224
Wildlife: Snares: Training: Scotland	193
Willington C Gas Pipeline: Corrections	62
Winter fuel payments: Social fund: Amendments: Northern Ireland	222
Wireless telegraphy: Licence charges	38
Wireless telegraphy: Licence charges: 900 & 1800 MHz frequency bands	38
Wireless telegraphy: Licences: Limitation of number	39
Wireless telegraphy: Register: Amendments	39
Wireless telegraphy: Spectrum access & licence: Spectrum trading	39
Wireless telegraphy: Spectrum access: Charges	39
Wireless telegraphy: Spectrum access: Satellite receive-only Earth stations	39
Wireless telegraphy: Spectrum access: Satellite receive-only Earth stations: Grants: Limitation	38
Wireless telegraphy: Spectrum trading	39
Wireless telegraphy: Spectrum trading: Mobile: Amendments	39
Wireless telegraphy: Ultra- wideband equipment: Exemptions	39
Wireless telegraphy: White space devices: Exemption	39
Woking: Electoral changes	69
Women: Consecration: Bishops: Lords Spiritual: Acts	5
Women: Consecration: Bishops: Lords Spiritual: Acts: Explanatory notes	7
Women: Female Genital Mutilation: Protection orders: Third party: England & Wales	45
Wood & bark: Ash dieback: Plant health: Northern Ireland	214
Worcestershire County Council: Hoobrook Bridge scheme	54
Work & Families Act (Northern Ireland) 2015: Commencements: Northern Ireland	205
Work & families: Acts: Northern Ireland	199
Work & families: Acts: Northern Ireland: Explanatory notes	199
Work & families: Adoption leave: Curtailment of statutory rights to leave: Northern Ireland	204
Work & families: Adoptions: Overseas: Employment rights: Northern Ireland	204
Work & families: Adoptions: Time off to attend adoption appointments: Northern Ireland	205
Work & families: Flexible working: Northern Ireland	204
Work & families: Maternity leave: Curtailment of statutory rights to leave: Northern Ireland	204
Work & families: Parental orders: Employment rights: Northern Ireland	203
Work & families: Paternity: Adoption leave: Northern Ireland	204
Work & families: Paternity: Adoption: Shared parental leave: Order cases: Northern Ireland	204
Work & families: Shared parental leave & paternity & adoption leave: Adoptions from overseas: Northern Ireland	204
Work & families: Shared parental leave: Northern Ireland	204
Work & families: Shared parental leave: Statutory shared parental pay: Northern Ireland	204
Work & families: Social Security Contributions & Benefits (Northern Ireland) Act 1992: Application of parts: Northern Ireland	204, 205
Work & families: Statutory adoption pay: Curtailment: Northern Ireland	205
Work & families: Statutory paternity pay & statutory adoption pay: Northern Ireland	205
Work & families: Statutory paternity pay & statutory adoption pay: Parental orders & prospective adopters: Northern Ireland	205
Work & families: Statutory shared parental pay: Northern Ireland	205
Work & families: Statutory shared parental pay: Overseas adoptions: Northern Ireland	205
Work & families: Statutory shared parental pay: Parental order cases: Northern Ireland	205
Work & families: Statutory shared parental pay: Persons abroad & mariners: Northern Ireland	205

Workers' compensation: Claims: Payments: Pneumoconiosis etc. 126
Workers' compensation: Pneumoconiosis etc.: Claims: Payments: Northern Ireland 222
Working tax credit: Entitlement & maximum rate 130
Working tax credit: Up-rating 130
Wreck Removal Convention Act 2011: Commencements 72
Wyre Forest: Electoral changes 69

Y

Yarmouth: Pilotage: Harbour commissioners: Removal of pilotage functions 81
Yemen: Export control: Sanctions 29
Yemen: Sanctions: Overseas territories 78
Young carers: Needs assessments: England 14
Young offender institutions 83, 137
Young people leaving care: Support & assistance Scotland: Scotland 166
Youth detention accommodation: Remand: Recovery of costs 27
Youth Justice & Criminal Evidence Act 1999: Commencements 28
Youth Justice & Criminal Evidence Act 1999: Court Martial & Service Civilian Court 30
Youth Justice & Criminal Evidence Act 1999: Service courts: Applications 30
Youth Justice Board for England & Wales 28
Yugoslavia, Federal Republic: Freezing of funds 27

Z

Zero hours contracts: Exclusivity terms: Redress 131
Zimbabwe: Sanctions: Overseas territories 78
Zoonoses: Fees: Northern Ireland 201
Zootechnical standards 10